CHRONOLOGY OF WORLD HISTORY

VOLUME I

Prehistory – AD 1491

The Ancient and Medieval World

CHRONOLOGY OF WORLD HISTORY

Volume I   Prehistory – AD 1491
The Ancient and Medieval World

Volume II   1492 – 1775
The Expanding World

Volume III   1776 – 1900
The Changing World

Volume IV   1901 – 1998
The Modern World

CHRONOLOGY OF WORLD HISTORY

VOLUME I

Prehistory – AD 1491

The Ancient and Medieval World

H. E. L. Mellersh

ABC-CLIO

Santa Barbara, California
Denver, Colorado
Oxford, England

Photo credits: Back: Engraving of the *Mayflower* after a painting
by Marshall Johnson, © Corbis-Bettmann; hand-colored
photographic portrait of Sitting Bull, © Corbis-Bettmann.

Library of Congress Cataloging-in-Publication Data
Mellersh, H.E.L.
   Chronology of World history/H.E.L. Mellersh.
      p.   cm.
   Vols. 2–4 by Neville Williams.
Contents: 1. The ancient and medieval world, prehistory–AD
1491—2. The expanding world, 1492–1775—3. The changing
world, 1776–1900—4. The modern world, 1901–1998.
   Includes bibliographical references and indexes.
   ISBN 1-57607-155-3 (alk. paper)
   1. Chronology, Historical.   I. Williams, Neville, 1924–   .
II. Title.
D11.M39   1999
902'.02—dc21   99–19300
                                                                      CIP

04 03 02 01 00 99   10 9 8 7 6 5 4 3 2
ISBN 1-57607-155-3

Published in the United Kingdom by

Helicon Publishing Ltd
42 Hythe Bridge Street
Oxford OX1 2EP
England

Published in the United States of America by
ABC-CLIO, Inc.
130 Cremona Drive, P.O. Box 1911
Santa Barbara, California 93116-1911
Reprinted 2000
Printed and bound in Italy

Contents

Special Features

Preface

The *Chronology of World History* has over 70,000 entries. *The Ancient and Medieval World* is therefore the most detailed and comprehensive chronological account of the ancient and medieval world available in one volume. Starting with the year 3000 BC, it traces the growth of civilizations and empires around the world—Sumeria, Mesopotamia, Egypt, China, India, Greece, Italy, the Americas. It begins as the Neolithic and Bronze Age culture of Siyalk comes to an end, and concludes in the year that Christopher Columbus made preparations for his momentous voyage, a year that also saw the births of Henry VIII, the future king of England, and Jacques Cartier, the French explorer of the North American Atlantic coast, and the death of William Caxton, the first English printer.

Order of Entries
The Ancient and Medieval World is arranged in strict chronological sequence by year, and where known, month and day. Individual years have been grouped into time periods to help you place particular events in context and obtain panoramic views of contemporaneous developments. The number of years included in one time period becomes smaller as time moves on. For each time period, the entries have been carefully grouped into four main categories and 25 subcategories: Subcategories are arranged alphabetically within each main category.

Politics, Government, and Economics
  Business and Economics
  Colonization
  Human Rights
  Politics and Government
Science, Technology, and Medicine
  Agriculture
  Computing
  Ecology
  Exploration
  Health and Medicine
  Math
  Science
  Technology
  Transportation

Arts and Ideas
  Architecture
  Arts
  Film
  Literature and Language
  Music
  Theatre and Dance
  Thought and Scholarship
Society
  Education
  Everyday Life
  Media and Communication
  Religion
  Sports

Whether you are looking for a specific fact, tracing events over a period of time, or reading for pure enjoyment, the date coupled with the categories, subcategories, and indexes will help you find your way around.

Special Features
Special mini-chronologies provide at-a-glance information about important people, topics, or events. They have been designed to provide an overview of an event or development in a concise, easy-to-read format. For a more extensive study of the subject, the mini-chronologies provide guidelines to the dates of numerous related entries in the body of the *Chronology*. Birth and death dates of noteworthy people can be found at the end of each year in tinted boxes. Where available, birth announcements include the year of death in parentheses, e.g. (–AD 17), while death entries conclude with the age at death, e.g. (60).

Indexes
An extensive main index includes virtually every name, title, place, event, and subject appearing in the *Chronology*. The volume's vast coverage of works of art, literature, music, dance, theatre, and scholarship can be searched using the titles index.

3000 BC–2001 BC

POLITICS, GOVERNMENT, AND ECONOMICS

Business and Economics

2675 BC
- Trade and prospecting flourish in the Middle East and are considered heroic occupations. Egypt imports cedar wood from Lebanon and, apparently, so does Sumeria.

c. **2575 BC**
- The Egyptian king Khufu (Greek Cheops) sends expeditions into Nubia for slaves and into Sinai for copper and malachite.

c. **2500 BC**
- Among the grave goods at Barkaer in Jutland (modern Denmark) there are both amber beads and copper pendants: evidence of trade, north and south, of these two much-prized substances.

2300 BC
- King Sargon of Sumeria trades for frankincense from Lebanon and prospects for silver in the Taurus Mountains.

c. 2300 BC Mining for flint begins at "Grime's Graves," in Norfolk, England. Picks made of red-deer antler are used to dig nearly 300 12 m/40 ft shafts with radiating tunnels.

Politics and Government

c. **3000 BC**
- The southern Sumerian cities form a federation under the holy city of Nippur but it does not last.

2890 BC
- Egypt's 2nd dynasty is founded by Hetepsekhemui. Little is known of the kings of the 2nd dynasty, although this was a formative period for Egypt in terms of art, technology, architecture, writing, and government.

2800 BC
- Supremacy in Sumeria shifts for a while to the more northerly city of Kish; intercity rivalry becomes endemic and one king after another claims sovereignty. As opposed to the truly Sumerian cities of the south, the northern cities appear to be inhabited by people of a Semitic race.

2700 BC
- King Enmebaragisi of Kish in northern Sumeria campaigns successfully against his eastern neighbors, the Elamites.

c. 2700 BC The Sumerian city of Ur first comes to prominence, under King Meskalam-dug and Queen Shub-ad. Its influence, although evident archeologically, may have been short-lived, since it is not reflected in the traditional lists of Sumerian kings.

2686 BC
- Egypt's 3rd dynasty is founded by Sanakht and is the start of Egypt's Old Kingdom (2686 BC–2180 BC). Under Zoser (Djoser), its second king, Egypt's southern boundary is established at the Nile's first cataract, and the first, step-sided pyramid is built at the necropolis of Saqqara in the city of Memphis (Cairo), by his minister Imhotep, physician, architect, and author. The oldest monument of hewn stone in the world, it consists of six steps and is 62 m/200 ft high.

2675 BC
- Gilgamesh, king of the Sumerian city of Uruk, revolts against another Sumerian city, Kish. He becomes a legendary hero and later has an epic written about him.

2613 BC
- Egypt's 4th dynasty is founded by Snefru, who builds the first true pyramid at Dahshur.

2520 BC
- The Sumerian city of Ur rises to prominence again, under King Mes-anni-pad-da.

c. **2500 BC**
- Troy I is destroyed in a catastrophe. Immediate rebuilding on the site forms the nucleus of the larger and more prosperous Troy II, the first city in the world to show evidence of town planning.

2500 BC–2205 BC China's legendary and most benign and exemplary kings are in power, culminating in the Xia dynasty.

2494 BC
- Egypt's weak 5th dynasty begins with the reign of Userkaf. There are no records regarding the change of dynasty, but the 5th dynasty is characterized by an emphasis on the worship of the sun god Re (Ra).

2470 BC
- King Eanatum of Lagash, one of Sumeria's great kings, becomes head of the southern cities, and possibly (though doubtfully) of Kish and the northern cities.

2370 BC
- The Sumerian city of Kish comes under the rule of a queen described as once having been a barmaid or brothel-keeper.

2345 BC
- With the establishment of Egypt's 6th dynasty by Teti, the decline of central authority continues.

2340 BC
- King Lugal-zaggisi of the Sumerian city of Umma, an ambitious ruler, seeks to revive the old Sumerian League and the holy city of Nippur. He defeats the Sumerian city of Lagash and boasts that he rules from the Persian Gulf to the Mediterranean Sea.

2334 BC
- Sargon of Akkad, a man of humble origin, usurps the throne of the north Sumerian city of Kish and sweeps south, defeating King Lugal-zaggisi of Umma, to make himself master of all Sumeria. He conquers the Elamite city of Susa and may even have conquered Cyprus. He builds a new capital near Kish, which he calls Akkad (the exact site of which is still unknown).

2294 BC
- Pepi II comes to the Egyptian throne as a six-year-old child and is said to rule for 94 years. During his reign, the Old Kingdom lapses into a period of near anarchy and revolution leading to what is known as Egypt's First Intermediate Period (c. 2160 BC–2040 BC).

2279 BC
- King Sargon of Sumeria dies while subduing a revolt.

2250 BC
- King Naram Sin of Sumeria, Sargon's third son, acceding after the short but unsuccessful reigns of his brothers, extends his father's kingdom northward into the city of Mari and the land later to be known as Assyria, and also eastward into Elam and the land later to be known as Persia. He subsequently has to contend with 17 rebel nations, one of which may have been the Hittites, who are emerging on the Anatolian plateau. He installs his daughters, probably as high priestesses, in the conquered town of Mari.

2205 BC
- Chinese civilization traditionally begins with the founding of the Xia dynasty by You the Great, although 1989 BC has been put forward as an alternative date.

2200 BC
- Troy II (now Hissarlik, northwest Turkey) is destroyed, apparently in an invasion, and the inhabitants hide caches of valuables and jewelry.

2190 BC
- The Sumerian Empire of Sargon is swept away by barbarians from the mountains to the north, whom the Sumerians call the Guti or "the Vipers from the Hills." The invasion and the ensuing confusion is described as a time of terror by Sumerian literature.

c. 2160 BC–c. 2040 BC
- Egypt's 1st Intermediate Period begins after the death of King Pepi II. It is a time of warring, near anarchy, and a host of local rulers lasting through the 7th to 10th dynasties.

2150 BC
- King Gudea of Lagash in Sumeria achieves fame as a good ruler, although he seems to have ruled under the sufferance of the Guti (the mountain tribesmen from the north who destroyed King Sargon's Sumerian Empire in 2190 BC). He rebuilds a ziggurat and is later deified.

Gudea's reign is attested by many statues, some with inscriptions.

2133 BC
- Egypt's 11th dynasty, established by Sehertowy Intef, begins a reunification of the country.

2113 BC
- Sumeria revives for the last time under the third and most famous of Ur's dynasties, founded by Ur-nammu. Prosperity lasts for about a century under him and his descendants, Dungi and Ibi-Sin.

2100 BC
- King Ur-nammu of the Sumerian city of Ur's 3rd dynasty collects together local city laws and publishes them in a code designed for general use. He creates a large police force to uphold these laws. He also standardizes Sumerian weights and measures, rebuilds part of the ziggurat of Ur, and builds a canal dedicated to the moon god Nanna, the patron deity of Ur.

2040 BC
- King Mentuhotep (or Nebhapetre) II of the 11th dynasty, who came to power in 2060, achieves the reunion of Egypt, and establishes Egypt's Middle Kingdom (2040 BC–1786 BC).

SCIENCE, TECHNOLOGY, AND MEDICINE

Agriculture

c. 3000 BC
- Camels are domesticated in the Middle East.
- Irrigation canals begin to be built in Mesopotamia and Egypt.
- Rice begins to be cultivated in India.
- Sorghum is domesticated in Ethiopia.
- Systematic three-year crop rotation is introduced in Mesopotamia.
- The soy bean is first cultivated, in China.

c. 2700 BC
- The horse is domesticated, probably by pastoral nomads in the Ukraine.

c. 2650 BC
- The wife of Chinese emperor Huang Di reputedly discovers how to produce silk, and the domestication of the silkworm begins.

c. 2500 BC
- Cabbages are cultivated in the Middle East.
- Elephants are domesticated in India.
- Peanuts are cultivated in South America. The potato is domesticated and is the chief crop there until about 1600 AD.
- Wheat and barley are cultivated at Mohenjo Daro in northwest India. Millet, dates, melons, and other fruits and vegetables are also eaten.

c. 2400 BC
- Irrigation of fields begins in Peru.

c. 2300 BC

- The horse displaces the onager (wild ass) as a draft animal in Mesopotamia, when bridles and bits are introduced.
- The Mesopotamian king Sargon returns from his campaigns in the Indus valley, Mediterranean, and other areas with specimens of foreign trees, vines, figs, and roses for acclimatization in his own land.
- The Nahrawan canal is built between the Tigris and the Euphrates in the Middle East. A year-round navigational channel, it is 120 m/400 ft wide and 335 km/200 mi long, and is used for irrigation.

Ecology

c. 3000 BC

- The Sumerians, Assyrians, and Egyptians use crude oil and asphalt ("pitch") collected from seeps for many purposes, but not as a source of fuel. Liquid oil is used as a wound dressing, liniment, and laxative by the Egyptians.

c. 2900 BC

- The Deluge or Flood commemorated in Sumerian and biblical legend is most likely to have happened at this time. Archeological evidence suggests more than one flood.

Exploration

c. 2300 BC

- The Babylonians portray canals, rivers, and surrounding mountains on clay tablets—the first maps. Egyptian map-making is developing at about the same time.

Health and Medicine

c. 2800 BC

- Chinese emperor Shen Nong describes the therapeutic powers of numerous medicinal plants.

c. 2650 BC

- Chinese emperor Huang Di begins the canon of internal medicine, with the text *Nei Jing/Inner Canon of Medicine*, which balances ideas of yin and yang. Most subsequent Chinese medical literature is founded on it. There is some evidence, however, suggesting that the *Nei Jing* may actually date from only the 3rd century BC.
- The Egyptian physician and architect Imhotep is the first to attempt to find nonreligious causes of disease.

c. 2600 BC

- Egyptian dentist Neferites is the first to make artificial teeth. They are made of ivory and held in place by gold or silver ligaments. He also uses resin as a filling.
- The Egyptians begin the art of mummification; internal organs are removed and preserved in jars containing a salt solution. The body is prepared with bitumen, which is thought to have medicinal properties.

c. 2500 BC

- The practice of acupuncture is developed in China.

c. 2100 BC

- Sumerian physicians prescribe beer for certain ailments.

Math

c. 3000 BC

- The Sumerians of Babylon develop a sexagesimal (based on 60) numbering system. Used for recording financial transactions, the order of the numbers determines their relative, or unit, value (place-value), although no zero value is used. It continues to be used for mathematics and astronomy until the 17th century AD, and is still used for measuring angles and time.

Science

c. 3000 BC

- The cubit, the length of the arm from the elbow to the extended finger tips, is devised in Egypt as the standard unit of linear measure. A royal cubit of black granite serves as the standard for all other cubit sticks.

c. 2800 BC

- The first (premegalithic) Stonehenge is built in England near Salisbury, Wiltshire. It is a Neolithic monument comprising a circular earthwork 97.5 m/320 ft in diameter with 56 small pits around the circumference (later known as the Aubrey holes). A 274-m/900-ft long *cursus*, or race track, is laid out nearby, perhaps for funeral games. The position of the probably natural "heel stone" outside the circle suggests a connection with sun worship and observation. It is probably an astronomical observatory with religious functions; the motions of the sun and moon are followed with the aid of carefully aligned rocks.

c. 2700 BC

- A lunar calendar is developed in Mesopotamia in which new months begin at each new moon. A year is 354 days long and the calendar is used primarily for administrative purposes.

c. 2400 BC

- Sumerian scribes develop a calendar consisting of 12 30-day months (360 days).

2296 BC

- The Chinese record the earliest sighting of a comet.

c. 2100 BC

- An intercalated month is added to the Sumerian calendar to bring the lunar calendar in line with the solar year.

Technology

c. 3000 BC

- An artificial stone is in use in Uruk in Mesopotamia. It is the forerunner of concrete but the secret of its manufacture is lost.
- Bronze is produced in Egypt and Crete.
- Candles made of tallow begin to be used in Egypt and Crete.
- Cotton fabric is first woven in the Indus valley.

Early Astronomy (c. 2800 BC–c. 80 BC)

c. 2800 BC

- Stonehenge is built in England near Salisbury, Wiltshire. It is a Neolithic monument comprising a circular earthwork 97.5 m/320 ft in diameter with 56 small pits around the circumference (later known as the Aubrey holes). It is probably an astronomical observatory with religious functions; the motions of the sun and moon are followed with the aid of carefully aligned rocks.

c. 2700 BC

- A lunar calendar is developed in Mesopotamia in which new months begin at each new moon. A year is 354 days long and the calendar is used primarily for administrative purposes.

2296 BC

- Chinese astronomers record the earliest sighting of a comet.

c. 2100 BC

- An intercalated month is added to the Sumerian calendar to bring the lunar calendar in line with the solar year.

1361 BC

- Chinese astronomers make the first recording of an eclipse of the moon.

c. 1300 BC

- Egyptian astronomers have identified 43 constellations and are familiar with those planets visible to the naked eye: Mercury, Venus, Mars, Jupiter, and Saturn.
- The Shang dynasty in China establishes the solar year at 365 ¼ days. The calendar consists of 12 months of 30 days each, with intercalary months added to adjust the lunar year to the solar.

1217 BC

- Chinese astronomers make the first recording of an eclipse of the sun.

c. 1000 BC

- The Hindu calendar is developed in India. It is based on a solar year of 360 days divided into 12 lunar months of 27 or 28 days with a leap month intercalated every 60 months to bring it into line with the true solar year.

c. 975 BC

- The Gezer Calendar is devised. Based on a lunar cycle of 12 months and 354 days, it is tied into the solar year but it is not known how. It forms the basis of the Hebrew calendar.

763 BC

June 15 Assyrian archivists record an eclipse of the sun. The same event is recorded in the Bible (Amos 8:9).

c. 467 BC

- Greek philosopher Anaxagoras supposes that the sun is a mass of red-hot iron larger than the Peloponnese. He also discovers the true cause of eclipses.

432 BC

- Athenian astronomer Meton accurately calculates the 19-year cycle when lunar phases recur on the same days of the solar year—the Metonic cycle.

c. 366 BC

- Greek mathematician and astronomer Eudoxus of Cnidus builds an observatory and constructs a model of 27 nested spheres to give the first systematic explanation of the motion of the sun, moon, and planets around the earth.

352 BC

- Chinese astronomers make the earliest known record of a supernova.

- Papyrus, derived from reed, is invented in Egypt.
- The abacus, which uses rods and beads for making calculations, is developed in the Middle East and adopted throughout the Mediterranean. A form of the abacus is also used in China at this time.
- The distaff—a wooden spindle onto which fibers are wound after they have been disentangled and twisted between the fingers during spinning—comes into use in Egypt.
- The ox-drawn wooden plow is used in Egypt.
- The Sumerians invent the helmet for protection.
- The use of cuprum (copper) begins to spread throughout the Mediterranean. It is produced extensively on Cyprus which becomes almost the sole source of copper for Rome.

c. 2700 BC

- Stone (limestone) first begins to be quarried; it is used to build the first pyramids in Egypt.

c. 2600 BC

- Iron is first used; it is valued as a precious metal without its superior qualities being recognized. Two iron artifacts are placed in the Great Pyramid at El Gîza.

c. 350 BC

- Aristotle defends the doctrine that the earth is a sphere, in *De caelo/Concerning the Heavens*, and estimates its circumference to be about 400,000 stadia (one stadium varied from 154 m/505 ft to 215 m/705 ft). It is the first scientific attempt to estimate the circumference of the earth.
- Greek astronomer Heracleides is the first to suggest that the earth rotates and that the motion of Mercury and Venus is influenced by their revolution around the sun.

c. 300 BC

- Aristarchus of Samos uses a geometric method to calculate the distance of the sun and the moon from the earth.
- Babylonian astronomer Berosus invents the hemispherical sundial. It consists of a block of stone or wood with a hemispherical opening with arcs inscribed on the inner surface. Time is reckoned by the position of the shadow of a pointer, which is attached to the outer part of the hemisphere, as it crosses the arcs.
- Greek navigator Pytheas observes that the moon affects the tides.

c. 280 BC

- Greek astronomer Aristarchus of Samos writes *On the Size and Distances of the Sun and the Moon*. He is the first to maintain that the earth rotates and revolves around the sun.

240 BC

- Chinese astronomers make the first recorded sighting of Halley's Comet.

235 BC

- Based on knowledge of the length of an arc and the size of the corresponding angle, the Greek scholar Eratosthenes estimates the earth's circumference to be 46,250 km/28,790 mi—about 15% too large.

c. 200 BC

- The Greeks invent the astrolabe—the first scientific instrument. It is used for observing the positions and altitudes of stars.

c. 165 BC

- Chinese astronomers first observe and record sunspots.

c. 150 BC

- Greek scientist Hipparchus of Bithynia builds an observatory on the island of Rhodes, containing instruments to accurately measure the positions of celestial bodies.

129 BC

- Hipparchus creates the first known star catalog. It gives the latitude and longitude and brightness of nearly 850 stars and is later used by Ptolemy.

127 BC

- Hipparchus discovers the precession of the equinoxes and calculates the year to within 6.5 minutes.

c. 100 BC

- Greek philosopher Poseidonius correlates tides with the lunar cycle.

87 BC

- The differential gear is invented by the Greek mathematician Geminus of Rhodes. The gears and axles are used in a device to measure the lunar cycle.

80 BC

- Poseidonius estimates the circumference of the earth by measuring the distance from Rhodes to Alexandria, and by using the difference in the height of the star Canopius above the horizon at each location to estimate the angle of arc. His estimate is 11% too large.

c. 2550 BC
- Soldiers in the city of Ur, Mesopotamia, use shields.

c. 2500 BC
- Bronze is manufactured in Sicily—the first place in Europe to do so.
- Copper ax-heads are being made in Ireland; the technique soon spreads to the mainland of the British Isles.
- Copper is used in China.
- Highly advanced water-supply systems, involving wells, storage reservoirs, aqueducts, and canals, are built along the Tigris, Euphrates, Nile, and Indus rivers.

- Iron smelting on a limited scale begins in the Middle East.
- Lead is first produced by the Greeks at Troy.
- Metal mirrors, made of highly polished silver, gold, and bronze, are used in Egypt.
- Most jewelry-making techniques are known: inlay, stamping, repoussé, raising, soldering, riveting, and granulation.
- Most mason's tools, including the plumbline, level, square, and mallet, have been developed.
- The art of dyeing fabrics begins in Egypt. The practice probably began earlier in India with indigo.

- The Egyptians make glass beads—the earliest glass objects known. The glass is cut and polished after cooling, rather than molded while hot.
- The Harappans at Mohenjo Daro in the Indus river basin build brick-lined wells and drainage systems of burned brick. Most houses have indoor toilets.

c. 2300 BC

- Pottery is made in the Tehuacán valley in Mexico.

Transportation

c. 3000 BC

- Imperial roads begin to be built in China. Radiating from Sianfu, Nanjing, and Cheng-du, the 3,200 km/2,000 mi of roads are wide, well-built, surfaced with stone, and have bridges or ferries at rivers, but they are poorly maintained.
- Roads in the cities of the Indus civilization in Sind, Baluchistan, and Punjab are paved and cemented with bitumen and are properly drained.
- The chariot is invented in Ur and Tutub in Sumeria. It is constructed of solid wheels that rotate on a fixed axle, a wooden platform protected by sidescreens framed with wood and covered with skins, and a draft pole linked to the yoke of a pair of oxen. They are mounted by both spear-carriers and charioteers.
- The Egyptians venture into the Mediterranean in reed boats. Steered by long oars over the stern they are rowed as far as Crete and Lebanon to bring back logs and other materials.

c. 2500 BC

- Wheeled vehicles appear in the Indus valley and the central Asian Steppes.

c. 2400 BC

- The city of Troy (now Hissarlik, northwest Turkey) begins to take advantage of its strategic position to grow rich. It commands a strip of coast where sea currents probably make it necessary to carry cargoes overland by porters for any ship trading with the Black Sea.

ARTS AND IDEAS

Architecture

c. 3000 BC

- The arch, a fundamental architectural structure, is first used in Egypt at a tomb in Helouan, outside Cairo.
- The building of megalithic monuments begins to spread throughout northwestern Europe. Great stones are used to build either chambered barrows (passage graves such as those found at West Kennet in Wiltshire, England, or at New Grange, Ireland) or, later, impressive monuments of upright stones for religious and/or social purposes (such as those at Avebury and Stonehenge in England, or at Carnac in France).

c. 2750 BC

- The first city of Troy in Asia Minor (now Hissarlik, northwest Turkey) is probably founded. It is the small but strongly walled fortress of a petty chieftain.

2686 BC

- The tomb of the Egyptian king Khasekhemui, last king of the 2nd dynasty, is built. It is the earliest stone building that can be accurately dated.

c. 2650 BC

- Silbury Hill, the largest artificial mound in Europe (40 m/130 ft high and 168 m/550 ft in diameter), is built in Wiltshire, England.

c. 2590 BC

- King Snefru has two pyramids built at Dahshur in Egypt; the first, called the "bent" pyramid, has a double slope and is the first attempt to build a true pyramid (one without steps). The second, the North Stone Pyramid, is the first true pyramid.

c. 2575 BC

- The Egyptian king Khufu (Greek Cheops) builds the Great Pyramid at El Gîza. One of the Seven Wonders of the World, it is the largest pyramid ever built, measuring 270 m/776 ft each side and standing 146 m/481 ft high. Consisting of 2.3 million bricks, each weighing 2,500 kg/2.5 metric tons, the pyramid is a marvel of engineering skill. Its base is an almost perfect square with its right angles deviating by only 0.05%. Alongside the pyramid a separate pit contains a dismantled boat. Khufu's nobles are buried in *mustabas*, mud-brick tombs covered with a flat-roofed superstructure of brick.

c. 2550 BC

- The temple of the Great Sphinx is built at El Gîza by the Egyptian king Khafre (Chephren). It is smaller than those built by Khufu (Cheops).

2350 BC

- The Harappan civilization in the Indus valley invent a method of writing that consists of 500 characters. They exhibit skill in building, town planning, and drainage. In the city of Harappa, the great central storehouses, lines of workmen's dwellings, and communal bath-house all indicate a paternal government and a regimented way of life.

c. 2300 BC

- A holy city exists in Sumeria in King Sargon's time called the Gate of God, which in Semitic translates as Babylon.

c. 2200 BC

- Sumerian architects are familiar with the basic architectural forms: the column, arch, vault, and dome.
- The Avebury stone circles are constructed in Wiltshire, England. Consisting of three circles of about one hundred sandstone pillars, some weighing over 50,000 kg/50 metric tons each, it is the largest such stone monument in Europe.

c. 2150 BC

- King Gudea of Lagash engraves the plan of a temple in stone—the earliest engineering graphics. A life-sized statue of him includes a carpenter's rule, which enables archeologists to define the Sumerian unit as 16.5 mm/0.6 in.

Arts

c. 2685 BC

- The *Standard of Ur* is made at Ur, Mesopotamia, the capital of the Sumerian civilization. It is a two-sided mosaic of shell, lapis lazuli, and carnelian, and depicts scenes of peace and war.

c. 2650 BC

- The Egyptians invent the chair, the earliest piece of furniture. It consists of a wooden seat and cushion, with legs often carved in the shapes of animals.

c. 2550 BC

- The Sumerian city of Lagash (or Sirpurla) rises to prominence under a ruler called Ur-nina. He leaves his inscription on the buildings of the city, together with the bas-relief of himself and family. His third successor leaves the famous *Stele of the Vultures*.

c. 2500 BC

- The Minoan civilization of Crete begins to produce true bronze metallurgy. This form of Minoan art is best represented by a division into Pre-Palatial (7000 BC–2000 BC), Palatial (2000 BC–1470 BC), and Post-Palatial (1470 BC–1000 BC) elements.

2470 BC

- King Eanatum of Lagash in Sumeria erects a victory monument commemorating his exploits, the *Stele of the Vultures*, on which is shown the earliest known picture of an ordered formation of armed infantrymen.

c. 2300 BC

- The statue of Egyptian king Pepi I is made using the lost-wax method—the earliest known example of the method. The statue is cast in wax and then covered with a claylike material to form the mold which is then heated to harden it and to melt the wax. The mold is then filled with molten metal.

2250 BC

- The Mesopotamian king Naram Sin, third son of Sargon, king of Akkad, erects a stele *Victory of Naram Sin*, which boasts of his conquests, depicting his military campaigns and the warlike Akkadians, and showing him trampling his enemies. In later legend, however, Naram-sin appears as an unlucky ruler.

Literature and Language

2900 BC

- Egyptian cursive writing develops, using modified forms of hieroglyphic characters, written with a brush-pen on papyrus in vertical columns.

c. 2900 BC The Sumerian people improve the cuneiform script by introducing a phonetic element, by which some signs come to represent distinct words and syllables.

c. 2650 BC

- The Egyptian *Books of Wisdom* are written, using papyrus as a writing material. Written for religious instruction, one of them is credited to the Egyptian physician and architect Imhotep.

2450 BC

- The earliest extant papyrus document is written. It is temple accounts of Abusir, Egypt.

Thought and Scholarship

c. 2500 BC

- A temple in the Babylonian city of Nippur is filled with clay tablets to create the first known library.
- Ptahhotep, governor of Memphis at the time of the 5th dynasty of Egypt, writes the first known book of philosophy, his *Instructions* to his son.

SOCIETY

Everyday Life

c. 3000 BC

- Native Americans make popped corn.
- The Egyptians develop a civil calendar of 365 days divided into 12 30-day months, plus five intercalated days added at the end. It is based on the lunar cycle and regulated by the appearance of Sirius (the Dog Star) above the horizon, and the flooding of the Nile.
- The Neolithic and Bronze Age culture of Siyalk in southwestern Elam (founded in 4400 BC) comes to an end.

c. 2900 BC

- The Indus valley civilization (known as the Harappan) is formed. Considerable Sumerian influence is apparent. Its two chief cities are Mohenjo Daro, in modern Sind, about 400 km/250 mi up the River Indus, and Harappa, 560 km/350 mi further upstream on the River Ravi in the Punjab.

BIRTHS & DEATHS

2613 BC
- Zoser (Djoser), king of Egypt 2686 BC–2613 BC, who was the first to begin building stone pyramids, dies.

2279 BC
- Sargon, ruler of Mesopotamia 2334 BC–2279 BC, who conquered southern Mesopotamia, Syria, Anatolia, and Elam, dies.

2010 BC
- Mentuhotep II (or Nebhapetre), king of Egypt 2060 BC–2010 BC, who reunified the country and thus started the Middle Kingdom period, dies.

c. 2700 BC

- Tea is known in China.

c. 2600 BC

- The Bronze Age begins in Crete (although some authorities set the date three centuries earlier) with the so-called Early Minoan Period, also called its Pre-Palace Period, which lasts until 2000 BC.
- The Egyptians use leavening to make bread.

c. 2500 BC

- At Barkaer in Jutland (modern Denmark) the first farming settlement is established among the Mesolithic hunters. Its pottery is "Danubian."

c. 2400 BC

- A prosperous civilization is growing up on the Anatolian plateau, the future home of the Hittites. The royal tombs of Alaca Hayuk (in the bend of the Halys River) illustrate this prosperity and also a high artistic ability.
- The honeybee is domesticated in Egypt, and viticulture (grape cultivation) is featured in hieroglyphics.

c. 2250 BC

- Models begin to be placed in Egyptian tombs at this time.
- The use of the scarab beetle as an amulet begins to appear in Egypt.

c. 2200 BC

- Round communal tombs are built in the Mesara plain of Crete, resembling to a large extent the later beehive-shaped *tholos* tombs of 1600 BC–1200 BC. Present-day understanding of Minoan civilization depends largely on such burial sites.

Religion

c. 2316 BC

- The legend of Sargon, king of the Mesopotamian kingdom of Akkad, suggests a background similar to that of Moses, in that he is set adrift as a baby, but found and rescued. In Sargon's case, he is reputedly found on the Euphrates River. Sargon establishes a unified kingdom covering all of Mesopotamia.

Sports

c. 2650 BC

- A stone relief in the Step Pyramid at Saqqara, Egypt, depicts the Egyptian king Zoser (Djoser) in a running race. It is the earliest known representation of a runner.

◆

2000 BC–1501 BC

POLITICS, GOVERNMENT, AND ECONOMICS

Business and Economics

c. 2000 BC

- Assyrian merchants write business letters describing convoys of pack asses regularly crossing the Syrian desert and the Taurus Mountains in Turkey.

c. 1900 BC

- The "amber routes," the earliest roads in Europe, are built by the Etruscans and Greeks to transport amber and tin from northern Europe to the Mediterranean and Adriatic. They are used until about 300 BC.
- The city of Ugarit, an ancient city dating from the

5th millennium BC and located on the western Syrian coast, grows in commercial importance.

c. 1800 BC

- The Amorite city of Alalakh (Tel Atchana on the Orontes River in Syria) experiences a period of prosperity.
- The Assyrians enter history in a reference to their merchants' activities at the site of Kanesh (modern Kultepe) at the eastern end of the Anatolian plateau. The city has been excavated showing Assyrian merchants' quarters in one section of the native city.

1750 BC

- The activities of the Assyrian merchants come to an end about this time. Their colonies disappear from towns such as Kanesh in Anatolia.

c. 1600 BC

- Crete's favorable position on trade routes across the eastern Mediterranean extends Minoan influence throughout the Aegean. The new palaces develop into political, economic, administrative, and religious centers, also containing storehouses and craftsmen's workshops, and the Minoan rulers go down in Greek legend as great lawmakers.

Colonization

c. 2000 BC

- Disturbances force Aryan-speaking Indo-Europeans to move southward into Asia Minor and northern Greece and Italy. The disturbances must have begun in the steppe north of the Caspian Sea where Aryan-speaking Indo-Europeans have been leading a nomadic existence, tending horses, for centuries.

c. 1800 BC

- Greece is probably undergoing further infiltrations of Indo-Europeans.

c. 1700 BC

- An Aryan-speaking people of the Ukraine and north Turkey begins to spread westward at about this time. They are called "the battle-ax people" from their choice of weapon. They finally reach Scandinavia where, in a curious reversal of usual practice, the bronze ax of their original culture is imitated in more primitive stone copies.

c. 1600 BC

- Greek-speaking invaders in the Aegean have penetrated the Peloponnese, where they begin to prosper and grow rich. They evolve the Mycenaean culture, named for its chief stronghold. Mycenae is ruled by a dynasty of kings, whose "shaft graves" contain great wealth and fine art and weaponry, indicating that the Mycenaean princes are rapidly accumulating wealth.

Politics and Government

c. 2000 BC

- Sumeria is invaded from the north by the Amorites (Semitic desert tribes), led by the king of Mari, and from the east by the Elamites. The Sumerian city of Ur is besieged. Its great 3rd dynasty comes to an end and King Ibi-Sin is carried away in chains.

1991 BC

- Amenemhet I, the first king of the great 12th dynasty, comes to the throne and consolidates the reunification of Egypt begun by the 11th dynasty. A noble of Thebes, he establishes Itj-towy, a new capital further north, close to the Old Kingdom's Memphis. The 12th dynasty creates a feudal age in Egypt, the king ruling with enhanced economic and religious sanction but through the local nobles, or nomarchs.

1971 BC

- Amenemhet I makes his son Senusret (Sesostris) coregent to ensure continuation of the dynasty. Subsequent rulers continue the practice.

1928 BC

- Amenemhat II succeeds his father Senusret (Sesostris) I as pharaoh of Egypt; he is the least well known of his dynasty and is said to have been murdered by his guard.

c. 1900 BC

- In Sumeria—which has undergone an influx of Semitic peoples and relapsed into its old condition of

warfare between cities—the new city of Babylon begins to acquire importance.

1897 BC

- Senusret (Sesostris) II, a peaceful king, becomes king in Egypt. He initiates the development of the fertile Fayyum depression.

1878 BC

- Senusret (Sesostris) III becomes king in Egypt. He continues military campaigns in Nubia, builds numerous forts and garrisons, seeks for the first time to extend Egypt's power in Syria, and centralizes the government, reducing the power and influence of the feudal nobles.

1842 BC

- King Amenemhet III, the greatest monarch of the Middle Kingdom, comes to the throne in Egypt and reigns for 45 years. He is known as "the good god," who benefits Egypt more than any before him. He restores the outpost garrison at the third cataract of the River Nile.

c. 1800 BC

- The Assyrians and the Hittites, from the Anatolian plateau, begin to make an impact.
- The Babylonians (the inhabitants of northern Sumeria), under Kassite rulers, are lapsing into unimportance but retain commercial prosperity. The Kassites, who may have originated in the Zagros Mountains of modern southern Iran, rule Babylon peacefully for 400 years.

1797 BC

- King Amenemhet IV, the last of the 12th dynasty, succeeds his father, Amenemhet III, to the Egyptian throne, starting the decline of the Middle Kingdom.

1792 BC

- King Hammurabi the Great establishes the first Babylonian Empire and a golden age of peace, prosperity, and law and order. He extends his empire west to the Mediterranean, east to Elam, defeating Rim-Sin, king of Elam, who occupied most of Sumeria, and north to the land of the Assyrians, conquering their city of Eshnunna.

1790 BC

- King Hammurabi of Babylon establishes a great bureaucracy to run his empire and personally attends to details such as correcting the calendar. His *Code of Laws*, although harsh, attempts to fit punishments to crimes; it protects the rights of women and recognizes an upper class, imposing harsher penalties for upper-class transgressors.
- On the death of her half brother Amenemhet IV of Egypt, Queen Sebeknefru becomes "king" of Egypt. She rules for about four years and is the last ruler of the 12th dynasty. It is probable that she then marries the founder of the 13th dynasty.

1786 BC

- Egypt's 13th dynasty reigns in the north but is not recognized in Thebes. It begins Egypt's Second Intermediate Period (1786 BC–1567 BC) and consists of a series of short-lived and unimportant kings who rule until the end of the century. The Second Intermediate Period is characterized by a loss of central political control and social upheaval. Power rests in the hands of the vizier, the king's chief advisor.

1760 BC

- King Hammurabi of Babylon encounters trouble toward the end of his reign and destroys the city of Mari in the north of the Babylonian Empire.

1750 BC

- King Hammurabi of Babylon is succeeded by Samsu-Iluna, whose reign only lasts about a decade before the Kassites, of Indo-European stock or leadership, make their first entrance into Babylonia.
- On the Anatolian plateau, a local prince called Anittas is said to have conquered many other local cities, including Hatti or Hattusas, which in the next few centuries will become famous as the capital of the Hittites.

c. **1750 BC** The Indus valley civilization collapses as some of its cities are destroyed and their populations slaughtered, probably by Aryan peoples moving in from the west. The Aryan tribes move gradually eastward, out of the InduS valley and into the valley of the Ganges.

c. **1720 BC**

- The Hyksos ("the Shepherd Kings" or more correctly "the Hill People"), Bedouin tribesmen, occupy Egypt's eastern Delta and begin the worship of Seth, their local deity. Israelites such as the biblical Jacob and Joseph may have appeared among these Hyksos.

1715 BC

- Under King Shamsi-Adad II, Assyria begins to show military prowess, pressing westward toward Syria. The town of Nineveh is built.

1680 BC

- King Labarnas (or Labernash) unites the hardy people of the Anatolian plateau (whose proper name is unknown) to form the powerful empire of the Hittites.

c. **1674 BC**

- Memphis comes under the control of the Hyksos after about a century in which their power has gradually increased.

1650 BC

- King Hattusilis I, the son of King Labarnas (or Labernash), turns his capital Hattusas, which lies at the conjunction of east–west and north–south trade routes on the Anatolian plateau, into a great Hittite stronghold. He begins a southward and eastward expansion. When work is completed, Hattusas is protected by a 9-m/30-ft-thick wall with a 6.5 km/4 mi circumference.

c. **1650 BC** The 17th dynasty begins in Thebes. Under their rulers Seqenere I, II, and III, they increasingly wage war against the Hyksos kings based in the city of Avaris, Egypt, and gradually gain the upper hand.

1625 BC

- Hittite king Hattusilis I summons his assembly of aristocrats and declares his adoption of Mursilis (or Murshilish) as his successor. Mursilis replaces his unsuitable nephew, whose mother reportedly "bellows like an ox" at the news. The speech is reported in what seems a very natural and spontaneous style.

1620 BC

- The Hittite king Mursilis (or Murshilish) I strikes south. He captures first Yamhad (Aleppo) and then Babylon.

However, his success is short-lived: on his return home (1590 BC) he is murdered and Kassite Babylon resumes its quiet trading prosperity.

c. **1600 BC**

- The civilizations of the Fertile Crescent (from the Nile valley through Palestine and Syria to the Tigris–Euphrates valley) start to become entangled with each other. A new power, the Mitanni, begin to appear in Asia Minor; its people are known as Hurrians but its ruling aristocracy speak an Aryan tongue.

1590 BC

- Hittite king Mursilis (or Murshilish) I is murdered and a period of anarchy begins, with insurrections in the Hittite Empire and loss of territory.
- King Seqenere III, established in folklore as the liberator of Egypt from the Hyksos, is killed in battle.

c. **1580 BC**

- Theban king Kamose mounts a successful surprise attack against the Hyksos, making their expulsion from Egypt inevitable.

c. **1570 BC**

- Amose I becomes king and founds Egypt's great 18th dynasty. He finally destroys the Hyksos in their capital of Avaris and pursues what is left of them into Syria. He thus unites Egypt's new kingdom or New Empire (1567 BC–1085 BC). Ahmose I marries his sister, Ahmose-Nofretari.

1557 BC

- The last ruler of China's Xia dynasty, the tyrant Jie, is deposed by the victorious Tang, who founds the Shang dynasty. (The date is sometimes said to be 1766 BC, but this is less probable.)

c. **1546 BC**

- The Egyptian king Amenhotep I accedes to the throne (1546 BC–1526 BC) and changes to an expansionist foreign policy, in direct contrast to the former policy of restoring or maintaining the country's boundaries. In the south he begins to subdue and colonize Nubia ("Kush"), while in the north he reaches the upper Euphrates and possibly penetrates the lands of the Hittites and the Mitanni in Asia Minor. He also initiates the practice of being buried in a rock-cut tomb rather than a pyramid.

1525 BC

- The Hittite king Telepinus achieves some consolidation in a troubled realm, making a treaty with his southern neighbors. He is the last of the Old Kingdom kings of which anything is known with certainty.

c. **1525 BC** Thutmose I succeeds Amenhotep I as king in Egypt. His is the first tomb to be built in the Valley of the Kings; Egypt's 18th dynasty is now well established, with its capital at Thebes, and experiences a century and a half of greatness.

c. **1523 BC**

- King Thutmose I of Egypt brings back the body of the Nubian king head downward on the prow of his ship, and then sends his armies back to the upper Euphrates to penetrate the land of the Mitanni.

1512 BC

- Thutmose II becomes king of Egypt. Little is known of him except that he puts down a revolt in Nubia and that he has a formidable wife, his half sister Hatshepsut.

c. 1504 BC
- The Egyptian king Thutmose II dies and is succeeded by his son, the warlike Thutmose III, initially controlled by his stepmother Queen Hatshepsut.

c. 1503 BC
- Queen Hatshepsut has herself crowned pharaoh of Egypt. She assumes the double crown of Egypt, dresses as a man, and even wears the king's ritual wooden beard. With the help of her chief favorite, Senenmut, she concentrates on internal progress rather than foreign conquest.

SCIENCE, TECHNOLOGY, AND MEDICINE

Agriculture

c. 2000 BC
- Alfalfa is cultivated in Elam.
- Apples begin to be cultivated in the Middle East.
- Bananas and tea begin to be cultivated in India.
- Fowl are domesticated in the Indus valley, probably from *Gallus gallus*.
- The first seed drills are used in Egypt. Seeds are deposited into the plowed furrow by a funnel attached to the back of the plow.
- The watermelon is cultivated in Africa.

c. 1820 BC
- Egyptian king Amenemhet III widens and deepens the channel from the Nile to lake Moeris in the Fayyum depression, thereby controlling the Nile floods and reclaiming 62,200 hectares/153,600 acres of agricultural land.

c. 1800 BC
- Neolithic farming reaches the Orkney Islands, off the northeast coast of Scotland, in the shape of a settlement at Skara Brae of well-built stone huts skillfully protected from the elements.

Ecology

1800 BC
- The large and prosperous city of Troy VI is destroyed by an earthquake and is rebuilt as Troy VII (modern Hissarlik, northwest Turkey).

c. 1700 BC
- The first series of Minoan palaces on the island of Crete (at Knossos, Phaestus, and Mallia) are destroyed, probably by an earthquake. The Minoan civilization recovers to enter its Middle Minoan III or New Palace Period I (1700 BC–1600 BC).

Health and Medicine

c. 1750 BC
- Hammurabi, king of Babylon, has laws relating to medical practice inscribed on a stone pillar. They detail regulations for fees, and contain harsh penalties for malpractice, such as the amputation of hands for killing a patient.

c. 1600 BC
- The Edwin Smith papyrus is written. The first medical book, it contains clinical descriptions of the examination, diagnosis, and treatment of injuries, and reveals an accurate understanding of the workings of the heart, stomach, bowels, and larger blood vessels. The papyrus is named for U.S. scientist Edwin Smith, a pioneer in the study of Egyptian science who acquired it in Luxor, Egypt, in 1862.

c. 1550 BC
- The Ebers papyrus is written. One of the oldest known medical works, it lists over 700 hundred remedies for various afflictions, accurately describes the circulatory system, and, for the first time, recognizes the brain's central control function. The papyrus is named for German Egyptologist and novelist George Maurice Ebers, who acquires it in 1873.

Math

c. 1900 BC
- The Golenishev papyrus is written. It documents Egyptian knowledge of geometry.

c. 1750 BC
- The Babylonians under Hammurabi use the sexagesimal system to solve linear and quadratic algebraic equations, compile tables of square and cube roots, and to extend Sumerian astronomical knowledge. They are also aware of the property of the right triangle described by Pythagoras 1200 years later.

c. 1700 BC
- The Rhind papyrus is written. It shows that Egyptian mathematics is poorly developed; multiplication is done by repeated duplication, and fractions by successive halvings.

Science

c. 1800 BC
- The Babylonian Empire standardizes the year by adopting the lunar calendar of the Sumerian sacred city of Nippur. Previously, each city inserted intercalated months according to its own needs.

Technology

c. 2000 BC
- Metalworkers in Mesopotamia begin to produce glass.
- The art of making bronze spreads further with the migration of people from the Middle East to Europe, Egypt, India, and possibly China.
- The shadoof, a hand-operated device for lifting water, is invented in Egypt and Mesopotamia. It consists of a long pole on a pivot with a bucket suspended from one end and a counterweight at the other. It is still in use in Egypt and India.

Early Medicine (*c.* 3000 BC–*c.* 90 BC)

c. 3000 BC

- Liquid oil is used as a wound dressing, liniment, and laxative by the Egyptians.

c. 2800 BC

- Chinese emperor Shen Nong describes the therapeutic powers of numerous medicinal plants.

c. 2650 BC

- Chinese emperor Huang Di begins the canon of internal medicine, with the text *Nei Jing/Inner Canon of Medicine*, which balances ideas of yin and yang. Most subsequent Chinese medical literature is founded on it.
- Egyptian physician and architect Imhotep is the first to attempt to find nonreligious causes of disease.

c. 2500 BC

- The practice of acupuncture is developed in China.

c. 2100 BC

- Sumerian physicians prescribe beer for certain ailments.

c. 1750 BC

- Hammurabi, king of Babylon, has laws relating to medical practice inscribed on a stone pillar. They detail regulations for fees, and contain harsh penalties for malpractice, such as the amputation of hands for killing a patient.

c. 1600 BC

- The Edwin Smith papyrus is written. The first medical book, it contains clinical descriptions of the examination, diagnosis, and treatment of injuries, and reveals an accurate understanding of the workings of the heart, stomach, bowels, and larger blood vessels. The papyrus is named for U.S. scientist Edwin Smith, a pioneer in the study of Egyptian science who acquires it in Luxor, Egypt, in 1862.

c. 1550 BC

- The Ebers papyrus is written. One of the oldest known medical works, it lists over 700 hundred remedies for various afflictions, accurately describes the circulatory system, and, for the first time, recognizes the brain's central control function. The papyrus is named for German Egyptologist and novelist George Maurice Ebers, who acquires it in 1873.

c. 650 BC

- Tuberculosis, leprosy, and gonorrhea are first described with accuracy.

c. 550 BC

- A document from Mohenjo Daro, in the Indus valley, describes the use of 960 medicinal plants and includes information on anatomy, physiology, pathology, and obstetrics.

c. 400 BC

- Greek physician Hippocrates of Cos begins the corpus of the Hippocratic Collection of about 70 medical treatises which cover topics such as epidemics and epilepsy. There is no evidence that he wrote any of them himself, but by recognizing that disease has natural causes he begins the science of medicine.

c. 285 BC

- Herophilus, an anatomist working at Alexandria, dissects human bodies and compares them with large mammals. He distinguishes the cerebrum and cerebellum, establishes the brain as the seat of thought, writes treatises on the human eye and on general anatomy, and writes a handbook for midwives.

c. 255 BC

- The doctrine of the pulse, which emphasizes feeling the pulse as the most important aspect of diagnosis, and that a healthy life is achieved by a balance of yin and yang, is introduced in China. It will be compiled into the *Mo Jing* in about 300 AD by Wang Shu-he.

c. 250 BC

- Greek anatomist Erasistratus of Ceos notes the difference between sensory and motor nerves, and correctly describes the functions of the valves of the heart.

c. 90 BC

- The Greek physician Asclepiades of Bithynia teaches that bodily harmony can be achieved through fresh air, exercise, and proper diet; he has mentally ill people freed from confinement and treats them with occupational therapy.
- The Roman scholar Marcus Terentius Varro writes that disease is caused by the entry of imperceptible particles into the body—the first enunciation of germ theory.

1870 BC

- Egyptian king Senusret (Sesostris) III's engineers cut a channel 79 m/260 ft long, and 10 m/34 ft wide, through the cliffs of the Nile's first cataract at Elephantine so that his war galleys may pass.

c. **1842 BC**

- King Amenemhet III of Egypt begins to exploit the copper and turquoise of Sinai.

c. **1800 BC**

- Bellows are used in furnaces in Mesopotamia for smelting metal.
- Bronze is manufactured in Britain and Scandinavia. Skills in making metal tools and weapons improve in the British Isles as trade routes with continental Europe develop.

c. **1766 BC**

- Bronze begins to be produced by the Shang dynasty in China.

c. **1700 BC**

- The doors in the palace of Khorsabad in Nineveh, Assyria, are sealed with a device consisting of a pin-tumbler, a large wooden bolt pierced by several holes, and several wooden pins positioned to drop into these holes and grip the bolt—the first lock.
- The increasing use of bronze in Britain leads to the decline of "Grime's Graves," the large Neolithic flint-mining and flint-working complex 130 km/80 mi northeast of modern London, England. Goldsmiths become skilled in producing gold artifacts, jewelry and warriors' adornments, particularly in Ireland and Wessex.
- Windmills are used in Babylon to pump water for irrigation.

c. **1675 BC**

- The horse-drawn war chariot is introduced into Egypt by the Hyksos, a Semitic nomad people. It becomes the great new fighting weapon and status symbol for the military aristocracy of the Middle East. War chariots are also used by the Mycenaeans, but not the Minoans.

c. **1600 BC**

- Brass, an alloy of copper and zinc, begins to be made in Asia Minor, but its qualities of hardness and malleability are not appreciated, and it is little used until Roman times.

c. **1550 BC**

- Fabric armor consisting of 14 layers of linen is made in Mycenae.

Transportation

c. **2000 BC**

- A two-wheeled chariot with spoked wheels is depicted on a seal from Hissar in northern Elam. The body of the chariot is light, consisting of a high wickerwork dashboard and a floor of leather planks. Domesticated horses are yoked on either side of a pole and controlled by a bit made of two links of metal. This military chariot revolutionizes warfare by providing armies with unprecedented mobility.
- The first skis appear in what is modern Norway.

- The Minoans in Crete develop ships with log keels, ribbing, and planking on the sides from stem and stern to protect the bow against damage from waves.
- The Scythians invent the saddle.

c. 2000 BC–*c.* 1500 BC "Rut" roads are cut into the sandstone of Malta. They consist of two V-shaped ruts 1.35 m/4.5 ft apart in which the wheels of carts are drawn.

c. **1700 BC**

- The domestication of the horse is increasing. It is brought to Babylonia with the Kassites and to Egypt with the Hyksos. It is also enthusiastically used by the Mitanni and Hittites in Asia Minor and revolutionizes both transport and, along with the chariot, war.

ARTS AND IDEAS

Architecture

c. **2000 BC–*c.* 1700 BC**

- Minoan civilization enters its Palatial period with the construction of palaces, built around large open courts, at Knossos, Phaestus, and Mallia on the island of Crete. They show an advanced engineering skill, for the first time incorporating columns into the design. The palaces become a focus for settlement and cult as well as political power.

c. **1800 BC**

- More than 3,000 menhirs, or standing stones, are erected in several parallel rows 4.8–6.4 km/3–4 mi long at Carnac, Brittany, in France.

c. **1600 BC**

- Stonehenge, the megalithic monument in Wiltshire, England, probably reaches its final form at the end of this century.
- The four great Minoan palaces of Crete are built or rebuilt in this century with an architectural and artistic skill and sophistication that causes surprise when they are later discovered. The palaces are at Knossos, Phaestus (with its "summer residence" at nearby Hagia Triada), Mallia, and Zakro. Frescos are now commonplace, and are used on the walls of Knossos palace. The new Minoan palaces use "light wells" to give illumination without heat from the sun, tied to an aqueduct system, and sanitation facilities flushed with water.

Arts

c. **1900 BC**

- The tomb of Chnemhotep, administrator of the Eastern Desert, is built in Egypt, with wall paintings depicting the great man fishing and fowling, and such captions as "how delightful is the day of hunting the hippopotamus."

c. **1840 BC**

- Egyptian sculpture receives a new burst of vigor under the rule of the 12th dynasty, demonstrated by a head of Amenemhet III, monarch of the Middle Kingdom, crafted in diorite, a dark gray granite-like rock.

1780 BC

- Sophisticated inlay is used to decorate faience (glazed earthenware) at Knossos in Crete. The most famous example is the so-called *Town Mosaic* which shows houses of considerable sophistication, some with three stories.

c. 1600 BC

- The shaft graves at Mycenae show great skill in metalwork and weaponry. For at least the next three centuries Mycenaean art shows a strong Minoan influence, for example in the style of dress depicted, though the typical subject matter remains Mycenaean rather than Minoan (hunting and fighting rather than idyllic natural scenes or sport).

Literature and Language

1962 BC

- The Egyptian official Sinuhe travels in Syria. *The Story of Sinuhe* describes his travels abroad and his penitential reappearance before his king, Senusret (Sesostris) I. It provides details about the culture and politics of Egypt's 12th dynasty.

1955 BC

- A "lament" is written for the destruction of Ur, the ancient city of Sumerian civilization, in Babylon, Mesopotamia.

c. 1900 BC

- The Sumerians reduce cuneiform script to about 600 characters.

c. 1700 BC

- The nations of the Near East begin to adopt the cuneiform script, particularly as a means of

international diplomatic communication. While some also use the Semitic Babylonian language, others endeavor to adapt the cuneiform signs to their own language—the Hittites do both.

c. 1600 BC

- The Minoan people begin to abandon their largely pictographic hieroglyphic script, and start to use Linear A, a form of Mycenaean Greek. This new script is not so elaborate or efficient as the later Linear B and remains largely undeciphered.

SOCIETY

Everyday Life

c. 2000 BC

- The "Beaker People," named for their distinctive drinking vessel, the bell beaker, migrate from Spain. They reach areas in modern southern Europe and England. They are agriculturists, their weapon is the bow and arrow, and they introduce the use of bronze.
- The Chalcolithic (Copper) Age begins in Italy. It lasts until about 1800 BC.

c. 1900 BC

- At the site of Yangshao in northwest Henan, evidence has been discovered of a Chinese chalcolithic culture: wheel-made pottery and evidence of the domestication of pigs and dogs.
- The Middle Bronze Age is considered to have begun in the Fertile Crescent (an area stretching from the Tigris and Euphrates rivers to the Nile). It lasts until about 1500 BC.

BIRTHS & DEATHS

1928 BC
- Senusret (Sesostris) I, king of Egypt 1971 BC–1928 BC, who conquered Nubia and built the temple of Amon at Karnak, dies in Egypt.

1908 BC
- Amenemhet I, king of Egypt 1991 BC–1962 BC, who restored unity to Egypt after civil war, is assassinated.

1895 BC
- Amenemhet II, king of Egypt 1929 BC–1895 BC, who furthered Egypt's trade relations and internal development, dies.

1878 BC
- Senusret (Sesostris) II, king of Egypt 1897 BC–1878 BC, who developed the Fayyum depression in Egypt, dies in Egypt.

1843 BC
- Senusret (Sesostris) III, king of Egypt 1878 BC–1842 BC, who centralized the government and

decreased the power of the nobles, dies in Egypt.

1797 BC
- Amenemhet III, king of Egypt 1842 BC–1797 BC, who introduced improvements in land drainage and brought his kingdom to a peak in prosperity, dies.

1750 BC
- Hammurabi, sixth Babylonian king of the Amorite dynasty c. 1792 BC–c. 1750 BC, dies.

1650 BC
- Labarnas (or Labernash), Hittite king c. 1680 BC–c. 1650 BC, traditionally considered the founder of the Hittite Old Kingdom, dies.

1620 BC
- Hattusilis I (or Labarnas II), Hittite king c. 1650 BC–c. 1620 BC, dies.

1590 BC
- Mursilis (or Murshilish) I, Hittite king c. 1620 BC–c. 1590 BC, who raided

Babylon and put an end to the Amorite dynasty, dies.

c. 1546 BC
- Ahmose I, king of Egypt c. 1512 BC–1504 BC, founder of the 18th dynasty who invaded Palestine and restored Egypt's hegemony over Nubia, dies.

c. 1526 BC
- Amenhotep I, king of Egypt 1546 BC–1526 BC, who extended Egypt's territories in Nubia (now Sudan), dies.

1512 BC
- Thutmose I, king of Egypt c. 1525 BC–1512 BC, who expanded Egypt's territory to include Syria and Nubia (modern Sudan), dies.

c. 1504 BC
- Egyptian king Thutmose II dies.

c. 1800 BC

- The Bronze Age begins in China.
- The Early Bronze Age begins in Italy. It lasts until about 1600 BC.
- The Indus valley Harappan civilization, with its magnificently planned cities, is coming to an end due to invaders who, with little doubt, must be the peoples of Indo-European stock who later write the Vedas (Hindu scriptures).
- The typical barrow or tumulus (burial mound) in northwestern Europe becomes the round barrow rather than the Neolithic or megalithic long or chambered barrow. The use of round barrows continues into the Iron Age.
- After four hundred years of relative obscurity (Troys III, IV, V) Troy VI, a more prosperous city, appears on the site (now Hissarlik, Turkey), built on top of the previous ruins. The discovery of horse skeletons implies that the Aryan-speaking Indo-Europeans have arrived from the north.

c. 1600 BC

- The cat is domesticated in Egypt. (Although it has been proclaimed sacred since *c.* 2500 BC it is unlikely to have been domesticated at this time.)
- The Middle Bronze Age begins in Italy. It lasts until about 1300 BC.

c. 1575 BC

- *The Book of the Dead* is increasingly placed in the tombs of the Egyptian nobility from the time of the 18th dynasty. It contains spells and incantations, believed to be necessary for passage to the other world.

Religion

1800 BC

- Abraham, generally recognized as the first historical character in the Bible, leaves the Sumerian city of Ur, where he was born. He and his family may well have sojourned in Egypt, along with other wandering Semites.

c. 1600 BC

- The *snake goddess* and other artifacts found at Knossos and elsewhere in Crete probably indicate that the Minoan people worship a mother earth goddess at this time. The *bull-leap fresco* at Knossos and similar works demonstrate a great Minoan preoccupation with the bull.

1560 BC

- The Kassite king of Babylon Agum III retrieves a captured image of Marduk, the patron deity of the city of Babylon, from the Hittite people.

Sports

c. 1829 BC

- The annual Tailteann Games originate in Ireland at what is now Teltown, County Meath. The games, which survive until the 12th century AD, include running, jumping, throwing, and wrestling events.

c. 1520 BC

- A wall painting on the island of Thera (Santorini), Greece, depicts boxers.

1500 BC–1001 BC

POLITICS, GOVERNMENT, AND ECONOMICS

Business and Economics

c. 1500 BC

- Highly prized gold jewelry is exported from the British Isles to continental Europe.

1460 BC

- The scenes in the tomb of Rekhmire, vizier to the Egyptian king Thutmose III at Thebes, show "tribute"

(trade goods) being brought in; some comes from Crete, carried by slim-waisted Minoans. The duties of the office of vizier are set out in this tomb, including a statement that the vizier sits in court with the 40 rolls of the law open before him. These rolls have never been discovered.

c. 1400 BC

- Contemporary ship sheds excavated at Kommos, near Phaestus on the southern coast of Crete, suggest that there was a commercial shipping fleet, trading with Egypt and the eastern Mediterranean.
- The Phoenician coastal towns of Tyre, Sidon, and Byblos thrive as trading cities. It may be from this time that their inhabitants are known as Phoenicians.

c. 1400 BC–*c.* 1300 BC   The Mycenaeans in Greece increase their wealth and nurse their military strength.

1352 BC

- Egypt's wealth is demonstrated by the magnificent grave goods of Tutankhamen, a youthful and comparatively unimportant king. They include iron daggers, a chariot, a wooden chest, depicting the king in battle behind his prancing chariot horses, the throne-panel showing Ankhesenamen endearingly touching her husband, and the scene on an ivory chest of the young Ankhesenamen and Tutankhamen picking flowers. The tomb, which—exceptionally—was not robbed, was discovered by the English archeologist Howard Carter in 1922, and opened in 1923.

1350 BC

- A shipwreck from this period found at Ulu Burun (near Kas, in southern Turkey) includes metal objects (copper and tin), amphoras, ebony, ivory, bronze weapons and tools, cylinder seals from the Middle East, a gold scarab from Egypt, and pottery from Cyprus. It throws light on the nature of international trade in the late Bronze Age.

c. 1300 BC–c. 1250 BC

- Mycenaean maritime trade is extensive, extending into Syria in the east and probably as far as the British Isles in the west.

1235 BC

- During this century, the medium of exchange throughout the Middle East is silver and the standard unit of weight is the Babylonian *shekel* (8.4 gm/0.3 oz), 60 *shekels* making one *mina*.

c. 1100 BC

- The Phoenicians are beginning to create a colonial empire, certainly trading with Spain, and possibly founding Tarshish and Gades in Spain, although these foundations may have been later. Similarly the Israelites, left alone for a while by their powerful neighbors, are succeeding in their efforts to develop from a collection of tribes into a united people and to dominate Palestine.

1091 BC

- The papyri of Medinet Habu, Egypt, tell of an Egyptian named Wenamun who is sent on a mission to the Phoenician coast to collect timber for his god and his king, but he is badly treated by the Phoenicians because both god and king have suffered a considerable decline in status there.

Colonization

1450 BC

- Cyprus, already influenced by Minoan culture, receives an influx of Mycenaeanized Minoans at about this time.

c. 1400 BC–c. 1300 BC

- Israelites probably begin to infiltrate into Palestine. Jericho, apparently deserted since Hyksos times (Egypt 1700 BC–1575 BC), is rebuilt and prospers.

1340 BC

- The Hittite king Suppiluliumas defeats and ends the power of the Mitanni, capturing Carchemish and making Syria his dependency. The Assyrians, however, absorb the Mitanni's lands.

c. 1200 BC

- The Dorian Greeks, or at least a new group of Greek speakers, probably first arrive in the Peloponnese. Their arrival is followed during the remainder of the century by the destruction of the Mycenaean palaces. The palaces destroyed are Mycenae itself, Tiryns (probably caused by an earthquake), and Pylos.

c. 1100 BC

- The Dorians spread to Crete. The Minoans reach the end of their distinctive civilization after three centuries of Mycenaean domination during which they have still retained their identity; for a few generations they flee before the invaders to live in the hills. The dispossessed Mycenaeans escape, partly to Arcadia, but largely to Attica and Athens itself. They also begin the so-called Ionian migration into the Aegean coastline of Asia Minor. The Dorians themselves migrate to the southern corner of this coastline. Cyprus has an influx of Greek immigrants at about this time, or even earlier.

c. 1100 BC–c. 1000 BC Both Assyria and Babylonia suffer from incursions by a confederacy of tribes, speaking a northern Semitic language called Aramaeans. Even the Assyrians, relapsing into a dark-age period of which little is known, are apparently fighting for their very existence.

Human Rights

c. 1272 BC

- Litigation over land ownership in Egypt, as described on a scribe's tomb, shows the equality of men and women before the law.

Politics and Government

c. 1500 BC

- Hittite law codes from this period put less emphasis on "fitting" and harsh punishment than those of the former king Hammurabi of Babylon. The only offenses incurring capital penalties are rape, unnatural sexual intercourse, defiance of the authority of the state, and disobedience by a slave.
- The laws of the Minoans on the island of Crete date from this time or earlier. Nothing is known of these—except that the mythical king Rhadamanthys becomes a legendary lawgiver. Minoan civilization enters its Late Minoan II Period (1500 BC–1400 BC).
- The Mitanni dominate the scene in Asia Minor and Syria. Telepinus, the Hittite king, dies and for the next 40 years four unimportant kings reign.

c. 1482 BC

- King Thutmose III enlists the help of the Theban priesthood in asserting his power in Egypt; the power of the priesthood grows, culminating in the usurpation of the king by the priest Hrihor in 1095 BC. From this time on, decisions of state are increasingly made by means of oracles directed by priests.

c. 1481 BC

- The Egyptian king Thutmose III advances north to defeat the petty Palestine princes under the prince of

Kadesh at Megiddo. (This battle should not be confused with either of the biblical battles of Megiddo, which occur in 1125 BC and 608 BC.)

c. 1471 BC

- Egyptian king Thutmose III reaches the height of his success in his eighth campaign by crossing the upper reaches of the Euphrates River and temporarily defeating the Mitanni of Asia Minor, possibly with Hittite help. This is the farthest point that Egyptian armies will reach for nearly 800 years.

1469 BC

- Queen Hatshepsut of Egypt dies and her stepson, Thutmose III, comes into his own as king, reigning until 1450 BC.

1460 BC

- A new dynasty appears in the land of the Hittites under King Tudhaliyas II. The "Hittite New Empire" dates from his accession, but for the rest of the century Tudhaliyas and his two successors do little more than struggle against their surrounding enemies under the tutelage of the Mitanni.

1450 BC

- Amenhotep II succeeds to the Egyptian throne. In the early years of his reign he parades his strength in Syria but, having retired with a wealth of booty and prisoners, he leaves the Mitanni influence there undisputed.

1425 BC

- Thutmose IV becomes king in Egypt. He makes peace with the Mitanni by marrying the Mitanni king's daughter and during the later part of his reign erects the tallest known obelisk (32 m/105 ft high), at Thebes, Egypt. It now stands in Rome.

1420 BC

- The Hittite Empire is still suffering invasion from all quarters.

1417 BC

- Amenhotep III becomes king of Egypt, which through trade, conquest, and the exploitation of Nubian gold, has become fabulously rich. The new king does little campaigning but is content to rest on his gilded laurels, sponsoring many building projects.
- The Egyptian king Thutmose IV goes on his sole recorded campaign, to put down revolt in Nubia, to the south of Egypt.

1400 BC

- King Tudhaliyas III comes to the Hittite throne and rules for 20 years; his reign is characterized by difficulty and ineptitude.
- c. 1400 BC Both the Babylonian and the Mitanni kings are allied by royal marriage to King Amenhotep III of Egypt.
- c. 1400 BC Further destruction occurs in Crete, caused either by the final eruption on the island of Thera (Santorini) and local earthquakes; by further Mycenaean invasion; or possibly by revolt against Mycenaean rule.

1395 BC

- The founding of the Chinese city of An Yang is traditionally dated to this year, but 1300 BC appears to be a more accurate date.

1380 BC

- Suppiluliumas, the Hittites' greatest king, comes to the throne. He begins by strengthening his capital Hattusas and prepares for his main task, which is to destroy the power of the Mitanni.
- The Assyrians, currently vassals to the Mitanni, begin to interfere in Mitanni politics.

1379 BC

- Egyptian king Amenhotep III dies and is succeeded by his son under the name of Amenhotep IV.

1370 BC

- King Suppiluliumas of the Hittites crosses the Euphrates River and attacks the kings of the Mitanni and of Kadesh, whom he defeats, though not decisively. He extends his kingdom to the Lebanon and the Syrian town of Alalakh.
- c. 1370 The "El-Amarna" correspondence takes place between the rulers of the civilizations in the Fertile Crescent, the area of fertile land around the River Tigris and the River Euphrates, including Egypt, Babylon, the Hittite kingdom, the Mitanni kingdom, Assyria, and Syria. It is written in Babylonian cuneiform script, the diplomatic language of the age, on tablets subsequently found in 1887 AD at Tell el Amarna, Egypt. The language is polite, as from one brother potentate to another, but the tablets include close bargaining for the diplomatic exchange of daughters in marriage and for gifts, particularly of gold. They also indicate that in his closing years the Egyptian king Amenhotep III failed to protect and support his regents in Syria and Palestine against their enemies, who include the *Habiru*, either "bandits" or possibly the Hebrews.

c. 1367 BC

- Egyptian king Akhenaton totally neglects his empire and continues the later policy of his predecessor in refusing all help to his governors in Syria and Palestine. His religious revolution also has its political aspect, a struggle against the established domination of the priesthood.

1364 BC

- Smenkhkare accedes to the Egyptian throne as coregent with his father-in-law, Akhenaton. He spends his three-year reign at the new capital Akhetaton.

1361 BC

- The boy king Tutankhaton, son-in-law of Akhenaton and younger brother of Smenkhkare, ascends to the Egyptian throne. Two years later he changes his name to Tutankhamen, rejecting the worship of Aton in favor of the worship of Amon-Re, and returns to Thebes. The religious revolution is over and the new capital of Akhetaton is left to crumble.

1352 BC

- The power of the Hittites at this time is demonstrated by the fact that Tutankhamen's widow Ankhesenamen sends two letters to their king, Suppiluliumas, suggesting that one of his sons should become her husband and hence king of Egypt. A Hittite prince is sent but is murdered before he reaches Egypt.
- The priest Ay becomes king of Egypt by marrying Tutankhamen's widow, Ankhesenamen.

1350 BC

- The fortress of Tiryns, second only to Mycenae in strength, is built by the Mycenaeans on the plain of Argolis, Greece.
- *c.* 1350 BC The king of the Mitanni, Tushratta, having sought alliance with Egypt and been let down, is deposed and assassinated by a faction who have sought help from Assyria. Mitanni power is waning, while Assyria is rising.

1348 BC

- The Egyptian army commander Horemheb becomes king of Egypt. He destroys the symbols and monuments of the Aton religion, restores trading relations with foreign lands, and reforms the judicial system.

1339 BC

- The Hittite king Suppiluliumas dies of plague; his son Mursilis (or Murshilish) II consolidates his empire and defeats a western foe called the Arzawa.

1330 BC

- Syria, encouraged by the Egyptian king Horemheb, unsuccessfully revolts against the Hittites.

1320 BC

- King Horemheb, secure on the throne of a revived and orthodox Egypt, spends his last years in sponsoring rebuilding at Thebes. He begins the Hypostyle Hall at Karnak (which Ramses II is to complete), probably being responsible for the avenue of ram-headed sphinxes. He dies without a son and is the last king of the 18th dynasty.
- Ramses I, general and vizier to Horemheb, succeeds to the throne of Egypt and begins the 19th dynasty.
- *c.* 1320 BC King Muwatallis accedes to the Hittite throne, finding it stable but facing a growing threat from a revived Egypt over control of Syria.

1318 BC

- Seti I succeeds Ramses I as king of Egypt. He campaigns against the Hittites in Syria but makes little headway.

c. 1315 BC

- Egyptian king Seti I restores law and order in Syria and advances to Kadesh, where he confronts the Hittites but does not seek battle with them. The young crown prince, later to be Ramses II, appears to have accompanied his father on his campaigns and in the latter's final years to have acted as coregent.

c. 1300 BC

- The great city of the Shang dynasty in China—Anyang on the Huan River, north of the Huang He—is founded. This is the last of seven capitals of the Shang dynasty. Archeological digging has shown that the traditional claim for a great city is justified, and that a brilliant but barbaric culture exists for two and a half centuries.

1299 BC

- The inconclusive Battle of Kadesh on the Orontes River in Syria is fought between Egypt under Ramses the Great and the Hittites under King Muwatallis. Hittite records show that the battle is not the Egyptian victory that Ramses claims but, rather, a draw, as the Hittites are subsequently able to advance further.

1290 BC

- Ramses II the Great becomes king of Egypt. He builds the city of Pi-Ramses, and prepares for a confrontation with the Hittites.

1286 BC

- King Hattusilis III comes to the Hittite throne. The rising might of Assyria draws him closer to the Egyptian king Ramses II.

c. 1283 BC

- A treaty of peace and mutual protection is signed between the Hittites and Egyptians.

1276 BC

- With the accession of Shalmaneser I to the Assyrian throne, Assyria enters the first of its three periods of power. Shalmaneser strikes north and west, taking Carchemish but leaving Babylon to his successor.

1270 BC

- The eldest daughter of the Hittite king Hattusilis III is given in marriage to King Ramses II, thus sealing the Hittite–Egyptian alliance.

1250 BC

- The second half of the century sees the beginning of the disintegration of the Mycenaean culture. It is significant that on their return from Troy, the heroes of Homer's *Iliad* meet with internal trouble and the stories of their dynasties end.
- The territorial war of the Mycenaeans against the Trojans (the Trojan War of Homer's *Iliad*) is most likely to have taken place at this date. Hittite references to the Ahhiyawa (Mycenaean Greeks) lead to the supposition that the Mycenaeans, besides punishing the abduction of Helen, are seeking to gain commercial advantages in the control of the entrance to the Black Sea by war.
- Tudhaliyas IV, a peaceful and religiously minded king, comes to the Hittite throne as the Hittite Empire is declining.
- *c.* 1250 BC Egypt's struggles from now into the next century against the so-called Peoples of the Sea show a general increase of turmoil in the Mediterranean area. The Peoples of the Sea seem to have been essentially displaced persons seeking new homes. Serious famines in Anatolia occur around this time, possibly forcing whole nations to move south in search of new lands.
- 1250 BC–1200 BC The Minoan civilization comes to an end, with the final destruction of Knossos, Crete, playing a significant part in its downfall.

1249 BC

- Babylon falls temporarily to the Assyrians.

c. 1240 BC

- During the latter years of King Ramses II's reign, danger grows for Egypt from the Libyans west of the Nile delta.
- The Exodus of the Israelites from Egypt is most likely to have happened at this date, almost certainly in the reign of King Ramses II, though possibly earlier. The Israelites leave after being used to build the city of Pi-Ramses on the Nile delta; they are led by Moses.

1237 BC

- King Ramses II of Egypt dies and Merneptah, Ramses II's 13th son, succeeds him. Merneptah puts down disorder in Syria and Palestine.

1235 BC

- The Laws of Moses (including the Ten Commandments) show some similarity to the laws established by King Hammurabi of Babylon in the 18th century BC, for example in their harsh insistence on appropriate punishments—"an eye for an eye."

1232 BC

- The Egyptian king Merneptah achieves a victory over the invading Libyans, who are helped by the displaced Peoples of the Sea. Nearly 10,000 Libyans and their allies are killed, with few Egyptian casualties.

1223 BC

- The reign of Merneptah is followed by a 20-year period of five relatively unimportant kings and internal unrest. The last of these, and the last of the 19th dynasty, is a woman, Tausert—the only queen of Egypt, besides Hatshepsut, to be buried in the Valley of the Kings.

1207 BC

- There is renewed fighting between Assyria and Kassite Babylon.

1200 BC

- Egypt's 20th dynasty begins with the brief reign of Setnakhti, whose origins are unknown.
- c. 1200 BC–c. 1100 BC This century sees the end of the Bronze Age in the Middle East and the Aegean and the beginning of a Dark Age, at least in the latter area. The turmoil caused by the displaced Peoples of the Sea may have been prompted by renewed pressure, from the north, of Indo-European tribes; as the century progresses these tribes, in particular the Phrygians and Dorian Greeks, penetrate Asia Minor and Greece.

1198 BC

- Ramses III, the most important king of Egypt's otherwise insignificant 20th dynasty, becomes king.

1195 BC

- The death of Moses and the entrance of the Israelites into Palestine under their military leader Joshua probably occur at this time. The Israelites cross the River Jordan and capture Jericho.

1194 BC

- The destruction by the Peoples of the Sea of the town of Alalakh in Syria, which is under Hittite domination, probably occurs at this date.

1193 BC

- The Egyptian king Ramses III beats off a renewed attack by the Libyans and in 1190 BC spectacularly defeats the Peoples of the Sea. The latter are checked in their substantial advance into the Nile delta and the coastal regions of Palestine and Syria.

1190 BC

- The last recorded Hittite king, Suppiluliumas II, comes to the throne. He can do nothing to revive the failing glory of the Hittites, whose records end with him.

1187 BC

- Egyptian king Ramses III again beats off the Libyans. After this, success seems to leave him: attempts to recreate a Syrian Empire are abortive and he ends his reign with trouble at home and a conspiracy by one of his wives to assassinate him and place her son on the throne.

1183 BC

- According to traditional dating, the Trojan War ends (but 1240 BC is more likely).

1174 BC

- The 12 tribes of Israel, struggling to establish themselves in Palestine against both the Canaanites and later the Philistines, meet at the sanctuary of Shiloh to develop unity. They are ruled by their "Judges," national heroes who also help to keep them on the straight course of their monotheistic religion.
- The Egyptian king Ramses III decorates the walls of his temple and palace at Madinat Habu with a vivid picture of his naval battle against the "Peoples of the Sea." There also exists a boastful account of his victory, which is just as vivid: "As for those who reached my boundary, their seed is not. Their hearts and their souls are finished into all eternity."

1173 BC

- The second Babylonian dynasty, established by the Kassites, comes to an end when the Elamites sack Babylon.

1166 BC

- Ramses III, king of Egypt, dies. His reign is followed by a series of short-lived kings, all called Ramses. During this period the Theban priesthood probably holds the chief power.

1146 BC–1123 BC

- Babylon, under its new "Pashē" dynasty, experiences a short revival of military importance under Nebuchadnezzar I (not to be confused with the biblical "king of the Jews" 605 BC–561 BC). He defeats the Elamites but fails to defeat the Assyrians.

1125 BC

- The second great Battle of Megiddo is fought, in which the Israelites, called to arms by their "Judge," the prophetess Deborah, defeat the Canaanites under their general, Sisera. The later Song of Deborah (*Judges 5*) tells of the defeat of Sisera—"the stars in their courses fought against Sisera"—and his assassination by Jael.

1122 BC

- China's Shang dynasty declines, although some sources state that it lasts until 1027 BC, and the Zhou dynasty begins, said to have been founded by kings Wën and Wu. The Zhou dynasty makes China stable and prosperous for at least three centuries. For the first time China is knit, though loosely, into one feudal kingdom.

1115 BC

- King Tiglath-Pileser I comes to the Assyrian throne and consolidates Assyrian power. He strikes northwest into the Taurus Mountains, relieves the pressure of a combination of petty princes on his province of Kummukh (Roman Commegane), and defeats the remnants of the Hittites. He also reaches the Mediterranean coast and extracts tribute from Lebanon, Byblos, and Sidon.

c. 1100 BC

- In the last third of the century there is a struggle among the Israelites, between those who want to continue as a theocracy and those who want to be like other nations with a king. The latter win.

- With the Egyptian empire much reduced the flow of riches into Egypt diminishes, and the country reverts to a state of near anarchy. The high priest falls and tomb robbery and the depredation of monuments becomes rife. Civil war also rages in Egypt, with Libyans and also Nubians taking part.

1097 BC

- The Assyrian accounts of the victories of Assyrian ruler Tiglath-Pileser I foreshadow the full horror of later accounts. They are as boastful as contemporary Egyptian tales of victory, but revel in ruthlessness and cruelty to a much greater degree.

c. 1095 BC

- In the reign of Ramses XI, Herihor, an Egyptian army officer, usurps the position of the high priest of Amon and finally takes over the power of the kings in Egypt, creating a theocracy at Thebes. He is outlived by Ramses XI.

1085 BC

- The death of the Egyptian king Ramses XI brings Egypt's New Kingdom, or New Empire, to an end. The country suffers confusion and rebellion during its 21st, 22nd, and 23rd dynasties, with occasional upsurges of interference in the Middle East, where its reputation, though lessened, is still considerable. Egypt loses control of Nubia and its Asiatic Empire during the 21st dynasty.

1075 BC

- The Israelites in Palestine suffer at the hands of the Midianites, whose home is to the east of the Gulf of Aqaba, but are given renewed strength of purpose by their "Judge," Gideon.

1050 BC

- The Israelites in Palestine reach the height of their struggle with the Philistines, originally one of the displaced Peoples of the Sea but now settled along the coast of Canaan, as the Ark of the Covenant (the symbolic residence of the Israelite God) is captured and their holy city of Shiloh destroyed.
- The Phrygians, an Indo-European tribe who have migrated into Asia Minor, found their city of Gordion (some 160 km/100 mi west of modern Ankara, Turkey) and establish themselves as the main successors to the Hittites.

c. 1050 BC   Samuel, the last of the "Judges," becomes ruler of the Israelites.

1030 BC

- Samuel, ruler of Israel, the last of the "Judges," achieves a temporary victory over the Philistines.

1027 BC

- The Zhou dynasty, traditionally said to have been founded by kings Wën and Wu in 1122 BC, overruns the failing Shang dynasty, establishing the Zhou people as the ruling force in China.

1025 BC

- Saul is made king of Israel and saves his country from the Amalekites (in the Negeb). Agag, king of the Amalekites, is spared by Saul but is assassinated by Samuel, the last of the "Judges," as a fitting sacrifice in a holy war.

1020 BC

- King Saul of Israel, with the help of David, the future king, is successful against the Philistines for a while.

1016 BC

- David, a heroic figure at King Saul's court in Israel and, by one biblical account, already anointed king by the aged Samuel, so arouses Saul's jealousy that he has to flee. For six years he lives the life of an outlaw, at one time allying himself with the Philistines.

1010 BC

- King Saul of Israel and his son Jonathan are defeated and slain by the Philistines at the Battle of Mt. Gilboa.

1003 BC

- David becomes king of a united Israel and Judah; he defeats the Jebusites and from their city creates his new capital, Jerusalem, the city of David. The Philistines attack him and he wins two battles over them.

SCIENCE, TECHNOLOGY, AND MEDICINE

Agriculture

c. 1500 BC

- The water buffalo is domesticated in China. The horse is introduced.

c. 1500 BC–c. 1000 BC   Sorghum is cultivated in India.

c. 1300 BC

- Wheat and barley are introduced in China.

c. 1250 BC

- Swarms of locusts destroy crops in the Nile valley in Egypt.

c. 1040 BC

- Assyria experiences widespread famine under the rule of Ashurnasirpal I.

Ecology

c. 1500 BC

- A volcanic explosion on the Aegean island of Thera (modern Santorini) covers the town of Thera with pumice. Its houses (including a wealth of wall paintings) remain hidden until AD 1967.

c. 1470 BC

- The island of Thera is destroyed in a volcanic eruption. It causes a tidal wave and subsequent famine in Egypt, and destroys the Minoan civilization on the island of Crete over 120 km/75 mi away. It may be the source of the Atlantis myth.

1450 BC

- Many Minoan and Cycladic sites are destroyed (in part by volcanic activity), leading to a decline in Minoan culture, though Knossos survives and a Mycenaean dynasty begins to establish itself there. Much of the glory is departing from Crete but by no means all its prosperity.

1226 BC

- The first record of Mt. Etna in Italy erupting is made. It has erupted 190 times since.

c. 1115 BC

- King Tiglath-Pileser I does much for the economy of Assyria, repairing all the "water-machines," storing grain, increasing the flocks and herds and improving agriculture and fruit growing. He also experiments with breeding ibex and deer, and collects wild animals, including the Egyptian gift of a crocodile.

Health and Medicine

1141 BC

- Plague kills 50,000 throughout Israel.

c. 1122 BC

- Smallpox is first described, in China. Pharaoh Ramses V, who dies in 1157 BC, is considered the first known victim of the disease.

1080 BC

- Assyria's dark-age period is worsened by famine, flood, and plague in addition to the wandering Semitic peoples known as Aramaeans.

Science

1361 BC

- Chinese astronomers make the first recording of an eclipse of the moon.

c. 1300 BC

- The Egyptians have identified 43 constellations and are familiar with those planets visible to the naked eye: Mercury, Venus, Mars, Jupiter, and Saturn.
- The Shang dynasty in China establishes the solar year at 365 ¼ days. The calendar consists of 12 months of 30 days each, with intercalary months added to adjust the lunar year to the solar.

1217 BC

- Chinese astronomers make the first recording of an eclipse of the sun.

Technology

c. 1500 BC

- The Egyptians use saws to cut planks used in ship construction and manufacture the first files, made of bronze. The Greeks use shark-skin files.
- The liquid metal mercury is known to the Egyptians who place it in a tomb about this date. It is also known to the Chinese and Hindus.

c. 1450 BC

- A balance with a pointer indicating the weight is developed in Egypt.
- The first bronze armor is used in Mycenae.

c. 1400 BC

- The clepsydra (water clock), consisting of a vessel with a hole in the base and lines on the inside to indicate the passage of time, begins to be used in Egypt.

It has the advantage over the sundial in that it can be used to tell the time at night. It may already have been in use in Babylon.

c. 1350 BC

- The Hittites, who live in the mountainous country to the south of the Black Sea, originate the art of iron-making. In 1339 BC an iron dagger, probably a gift of the Hittites, is placed among the grave-goods in Tutankhamen's tomb.

c. 1300 BC

- Iron-smelting furnaces begin to be established in Israel and Palestine.
- The manufacture of silk begins in the Chinese city of Anyang.
- The Orontes River in Syria is dammed by a 6-m/20-ft-high, rock-filled dam. It is still in use.

c. 1300 BC–c. 1200 BC   Important developments in weapons are made in Central Europe and Germany, partly due to technological innovations in bronze casting. The short dagger becomes longer and develops into a true sword, the blade becomes leaf-shaped, and a flange hilt is developed to hold the wooden handle. These swords spread all across Europe, from Britain and Scandinavia to Cyprus and even Mycenaean Greece, and are still in use at the start of the Iron Age.

c. 1200 BC

- The Chinese begin to make bells cast in bronze.
- The Egyptians begin to make linen from flax.
- The Iron Age begins as iron displaces bronze as the most important metal in Egypt and elsewhere.

c. 1100 BC

- Eurasian horseriders develop the mouth bit, made of bone and antler, to control horses.
- Rotary querns (hand mills), in which a handle is used to rotate one stone placed on top of a stationary one, are developed in Greece and replace saddle querns. They are the precursors to water mills.
- The spinning wheel is invented in China, derived from the machines used to draw out silk from the silkworm. It subsequently spreads to India and reaches Europe about the 13th century AD.

1084 BC

- Greek poet Aeschylus records that in this year Queen Clytemnestra, at her palace in Argos, Greece, is informed of the fall of Troy and her husband Agamemnon's return by a system of signal fires—the first recorded telegraph system.

c. 1050 BC

- Chinese warriors wear armor made from rhinoceros skin.

Transportation

c. 1500 BC

- Log roads are built extensively in northern Europe to cross swampy areas.
- Wheeled vehicles appear in China.

c. 1450 BC

- Barges 60 m/200 ft long are built by the Egyptians to transport obelisks; they are the largest ships built to date.

c. 1400 BC

- Chariots are introduced in China as indicated from chariot plaques and horse trappings on Shang dynasty graves.

c. 1300 BC

- The Phoenicians build harbors at Tyre and Sidon in the Middle East.
- Wheeled vehicles are used in Sweden.

c. 1200 BC

- Caballitos, reed boats consisting of bunches of reeds lashed side by side with the pointed end turned up to form a prow are in use in Peru.

c. 1075 BC

- The Midianites bring the camel out of the Arabian desert and use it as a war-steed against the Israelites.

ARTS AND IDEAS

Architecture

c. 1480 BC

- Egyptian queen Hatshepsut builds her magnificent funerary temple, with colonnades of white limestone, and within semicircular cliffs (at modern Deir el-Bahri). Its imagery depicts the divine origins of the queen, but also catalogs great activity in shipping and trade across the Mediterranean Sea, from a port on the Red Sea, and up the River Nile, demonstrating the fact that Egypt is acquiring a reputation for wealth and gold.

1470 BC

- Mallia, Zakro, Phaestus, and other sites in Crete are destroyed by fire, marking the end of the Palatial period of Minoan Crete, and beginning the Post-Palatial period. Knossos survives the destruction.

1390 BC

- The Egyptian king Amenhotep III begins to construct his palaces, and includes two colossi of himself and a large artificial pleasure lake for his wife Tiye (or Tiy). Her barge is named *The Aton Gleams*, indicating that the cult of *Aton* (solar disc) is not entirely new when the later king Akhenaton (or Aknaton, or Ikhnaton) subsequently adopts it. A new fashion of inscribing narratives on scarabs instead of on the walls of tombs appears at this time.

c. 1300 BC

- *Tholoi*, dry-stone beehive-shaped tombs, are built outside the walls of Mycenae, Greece, demonstrating considerable architectural skill in their construction. Grave goods include engraved gems, ivories, and decorated pottery.
- *c.* 1300 BC–*c.* 1200 BC There is evidence of considerable building activity by the Minoans in Crete during this century—for example, additions at Hagia Triada and Tylissos—though all glory has disappeared from their palaces.

c. 1290 BC

- The Hypostyle Hall at Karnak, Egypt, started by Horemheb in 1320 BC but now completed by Ramses II, shows Ramses II in his chariot behind prancing steeds.

Arts

c. 1500 BC–*c.* 1450 BC

- The Egyptians begin to mold glass while it is in a hot, malleable state. It is used for ornamental purposes.

c. 1400 BC

- Stoneware pottery, fired at a high temperatures (1,200°C/2,200°F) that makes it impervious to liquid, originates in China.

c. 1300 BC

- In this final century before the decline of the Hittite people of Anatolia and Syria, Hittite art shows considerable sophistication, from monumental rock carvings to small gold figurines. Artifacts include a rock carving of the Hittite king Tudhaliyas IV in the protective embrace of a god, beautiful belts and head-circlets of pure pale golds, and models of a stag in bronze and electrum (a gold–silver alloy).

c. 1290 BC

- The Egyptian king Ramses II erects enormous statues glorifying himself, including those at Abu Simbel on the banks of the River Nile in southern Egypt. His chief wife, Nefertiri, receives a magnificent tomb in the Valley of the Queens, west of Thebes.

c. 1200 BC

- Gold bowls are in production in Thrace, indicating the influence of the Bronze Age in Greece. The bowls are discovered in Vulchitrun in modern times.

c. 1150 BC–*c.* 900 BC

- At San Lorenzo, Mexico, the Olmecs construct stone monuments—colossal heads—2.7 m/9 ft high, carved from stones weighing up to 44.7 metric tons/44 tons. The stones are transported from a quarry over 80 km/50 mi away.

1050 BC

- Greek pottery is of the angular-patterned "protogeometric" style associated with Cretan pottery at this time.

Literature and Language

1500 BC

- Clay tablets from Cyprus use the Cypro-Minoan script, which remains undeciphered to this day.

c. 1450 BC–1400 BC

- The Linear B script supersedes Linear A at Knossos, Crete. Linear B is an early form of Greek, and its adoption in Crete demonstrates Mycenaean domination there. It is not as flexible as current cuneiform or Egyptian hieroglyphics, and seems to have been used for administration purposes only, for example in accounting, ration issues, lists of personnel, and tallies of tax receipts in kind. These documents (incised on clay but also probably written on papyrus) show signs of agricultural prosperity, particularly in the number of sheep.

c. 1400 BC

- An alphabet is developed in Ugarit, Syria, that consists of 30 characters.

c. 1300 BC

- Tablets inscribed with Linear B script, found at Mycenaean Thebes and at Tiryns (on the Peloponnese peninsula of Greece), are thought to date from this time, bridging the temporal gap between those at Knossos and Pylos on Crete.
- The first Chinese writing appears. About 2,000 characters of three kinds—pictographs, ideograms, and phonograms—are used to make oracular inscriptions on bone and tortoise shell.

1275 BC

- Hittite king Hattusilis III publishes his "autobiography" in which he justifies taking the throne and stresses his links with Ishtar, goddess of love and war.

c. 1200 BC

- At the Mycenaean palace of Pylos in the Peloponnese (legendary home of the Homeric Nestor) the Linear B tablets expand from their traditional function of ration indents and so on to record a series of military and naval dispositions—perhaps made in an effort to halt the invasion of the Dorian Greeks.

1122 BC

- The earliest recorded poems in the Chinese *Shi Jing/ Book of Songs*, one of the five classics of the Confucian canon, date to this period.

1100 BC

- The Babylonian "Creation" epic is probably composed at this time.

c. 1075 BC

- The Phoenicians (among other Semitic peoples) develop a true alphabetical script. The oldest significant Phoenician inscription known in modern times, on the sarcophagus of Ahiram of Byblos, Phoenicia, is dated to about 1000 BC.

Thought and Scholarship

c. 1200 BC

- The *I Ching/Book of Changes*, a Chinese dissertation on divination, may have been written in this century.

SOCIETY

Everyday Life

c. 1500 BC

- Neolithic skills similar to those in Europe—weaving, basketmaking, pottery, the building of houses, and the formation of villages—develop in the Americas, as well as a priest class. The use of iron, the wheel, the plow, and money will not develop until the coming of European colonialists.

BIRTHS & DEATHS

1469 BC
- Queen Hatshepsut of Egypt dies.

c. 1450 BC
- Thutmose III, king of Egypt 1504 BC–1450 BC, who greatly expanded the Egyptian Empire, bringing it to the peak of its power, dies.

1425 BC
- Amenhotep II, king of Egypt c. 1450 BC–1425 BC, who consolidated Egypt's conquests in Syria and Nubia (now Sudan), dies.

1379 BC
- Amenhotep III the Magnificent, king of Egypt 1417 BC–1379 BC, who extended Egypt's diplomatic relations and built works in Egypt and Nubia (now Sudan), dies.

c. 1370 BC
- Tutankhamen, king of Egypt 1361 BC–1352 BC, whose intact tomb was discovered in 1922, born (–1352 BC).

1362 BC
- Akhenaton (or Aknaton, or Ikhnaton), king of Egypt 1379 BC– 1362 BC, who founded the cult of Aton and the new capital city of Akhetaton, dies.

1352 BC
- Tutankhamen, king of Egypt 1361 BC–1352 BC, whose intact tomb was discovered in 1922, dies (c. 18).

1346 BC
- Supilluliumas, Hittite king 1380 BC– 1346 BC, who transformed the Hittite kingdom into an empire, dies.

1320 BC
- Horemheb, king of Egypt 1319 BC– 1292 BC, who restored the traditional religion of Amon to Egypt, dies.
- Mursilis (or Murshilish) II, Hittite king c. 1346 BC–c. 1320 BC, who left detailed written accounts of his military campaigns, dies.

1294 BC
- Muwatallis, Hittite king c. 1320 BC– c. 1294 BC who fought Egypt for supremacy in Syria, dies.

1265 BC
- Hattusilis III, Hittite king c. 1286 BC– c. 1265 BC, dies.

1256 BC
- King Shalmaneser of Assyria dies.

1237 BC
- Ramses II ("Ramses the Great"), king of Egypt 1307 BC–1237 BC, known for his ambitious building program, dies (c. 85 BC).

1204 BC
- Meremptah, king of Egypt 1236 BC– 1223 BC, the son of Ramses II, who defended Egypt against Libyan invasion, dies.

1166 BC
- Ramses III, king of Egypt (1198 BC– 1166 BC), dies in Thebes, Egypt.

1098 BC
- Nebuchadnezzar I, king of Babylonia c. 1119 BC–c. 1098 BC, dies.

1076 BC
- King Tiglath-Pileser I of Assyria dies.

- The dog is domesticated in Central America.
- The Late Bronze Age begins in the Middle East. It lasts until about 1200 BC.
- The Urnfield cultures flourish in this and the following century in England (in Wessex), southern Germany, and Denmark. The Urnfield people are pastoral rather than agricultural, use bronze extensively, and are ruled by a warrior class of aristocracy. They cremate chiefs and their families and place the remains in urns which are then interred in cemeteries. The culture continues into the Iron Age (c. 700 BC).

1380 BC

- During King Suppiluliumas' reign over the Hittite Empire, the first Hittite reference to people of consequence called the Ahhiyawa, thought by some to be the Homeric *Achaioi* or Achaeans (the Mycenaean Greeks), occurs.

c. 1300 BC

- The Late Bronze Age begins in Italy. It lasts until about 900 BC.
- The people of the Chinese Shang dynasty demonstrate skill in architecture (with rammed earth buildings) and ceramics (with near-porcelain) at their capital, Anyang. The dynasty sees the start of the Bronze Age, with the development of bronze-casting techniques which enable the manufacture of a variety of urns or chalices, probably for use in religious services, each type having a different function. A sophisticated range of skills, including writing, chariot construction, and specialized forms of divination are to be found at this time.
- *c.* 1300 BC–*c.* 1200 BC In the area north of the Alps and particularly in the basins of the Rhine and upper Danube rivers, a culture of mixed farming develops. It makes more efficient use of bronze, which is helped by trade with the Mediterranean area. The people use horses, and their chiefs possess fine swords.

c. 1200 BC

- The Hallstatt culture appears in southern Germany, named for a later cemetery found at Hallstatt, Austria. This culture originates in the Late Bronze Age in southern Germany and Austria and later, in the Iron Age, spreads throughout most of Europe. Burial is by inhumation below a tumulus (grave mound or barrow), with bronze (or later iron) swords, brooches, and pottery.
- The Olmec civilization begins at San Lorenzo on the Gulf Coast plain of Mexico, near modern Vera Cruz. This is the first civilization of Mesoamerica (the area of the Mexican and Mayan civilizations). San Lorenzo is the predominant center until 900 BC. Corn is almost certainly the staple crop. The Olmecs are skilled stone workers and also carve small jade objects.

c. 1140 BC

- Chinese emperor Wen Wang establishes the first zoo. It covers 1,500 acres and is named the *Ling-Yo*/Garden of Intelligence.

1111 BC

- The Shang dynasty in China collapses. Its capital city Yin (modern An Yang) is excavated in the twentieth century; finds include ornaments in bronze, marble, jade, and ivory, and thousands of inscribed bones and shells left over from oracle activity.

Religion

c. 1500 BC

- The Hindu Vedic hymns and religious rituals become established in India.

c. 1417 BC

- The popular Egyptian cult of Apis (or Hapis), the sacred bull of Memphis, increases in significance from the time of Amenhotep III, demonstrated by the presence of mummified bulls. The birthday of Apis becomes a great celebration.

c. 1400 BC

- Religious activity in Crete is recorded in Linear B tablets, with rations of grain being given to "Potnia the Lady," the earth mother goddess, as well as to people.

1374 BC

- Egyptian king Amenhotep IV changes his name to Akhenaton (or Aknaton, or Ikhnaton) to conform to a new religion which worships the sun god Aton over the previous cult of Amon. Akhenaton institutes a religious and cultural revolution with the worship of Aton. He builds a large temple to Aton at Karnak and constructs a new capital, Akhetaton ("The Horizon of Aton"), halfway between Thebes and Memphis.

1250 BC

- The legend of Jason and the golden fleece is thought to originate with a Mycenaean sea venture into the Black Sea at about the same time as their greater venture to Troy. It is possible that the legend might indicate a real search for gold, since a sheep's fleece was sometimes used in the process of catching river gold.
- The stone reliefs found at the sanctuary of Hattusas, probably erected by King Tudhaliyas IV, reveal that the official Hittite pantheon of "a thousand gods" was headed by a weather god and a sun goddess. At Alaja Hayuk, a king and queen are depicted worshiping a sacred bull.

1249 BC

- Assyrian looters carry off the effigy of the god Marduk, creator of Earth and humans, from Babylon.

c. 1200 BC

- The *Atharva-Veda* is written in India; a metrical or rhyming text, it is used by priests officiating at rituals.

1150 BC

- The biblical Samson is probably alive at this time.

1124 BC

- In the reign of Ramses IX of Egypt, the high priest is depicted on monuments as the same height as the king. This is taken to indicate that they had equal power, although texts indicate that the king still outranked the high priest.

Sports

c. 1500 BC

- The Chichimeca people of the Mexican plateau play wall handball.

1000 BC–901 BC

POLITICS, GOVERNMENT, AND ECONOMICS

Business and Economics

960 BC
- In order to build his temples and palaces in Jerusalem, King Solomon of Israel and Judah raises a levy of workmen and begins to overtax his people.

950 BC
- King Solomon of Israel and Judah and King Hiram of Tyre equip a fleet to obtain the gold and sandalwood of Ophir (possibly South Arabia or India).

945 BC
- The queen of Sheba's train of camels bearing spices, gold, and precious stones provides evidence of trade between Israel and South Arabia.

Colonization

c. 1000 BC
- The Greeks, presumably proliferating but hardly yet emerging from their Dark Age, continue to migrate across the Aegean Sea to Asia Minor.

Politics and Government

c. 1000 BC
- Assyria is quiet until at least the end of the century. The Israelites are therefore able, with the help of the Phoenicians, to develop their brief period of political significance and economic greatness.
- Mounted cavalry begins to be used in warfare by the Hittites, Assyrians, and Babylonians.

1000 BC–961 BC The reign of David, king of Israel and Judah, faces internal dissent. The chief events of his reign (to which exact dates cannot be given) are: David brings the Ark of the Covenant to his new city, Jerusalem. He becomes prosperous and subdues his enemies, including the Edomites, whom he all but exterminates. During the Ammonite War, David has Uriah the Hittite "put in the forefront of the battle" so that he can take Uriah's wife Bathsheba for his own. She bears David two children, of whom the second is the future king Solomon. David's favorite son, Absalom, murders his half brother for the incestuous rape of his sister and flees the court. He is forgiven by David, but then revolts against him. David in turn has to flee Jerusalem. Absalom is defeated, slain, and ultimately lamented. Further revolts and wars accompanied by pestilence bring David's reign to a close.

c. 1000 BC–*c.* 900 BC The Neo-Hittite civilization develops in Syria, with its center at Carchemish. It pays tribute to Syria but is prosperous in its own right by the time of the biblical Uriah the Hittite.

c. 961 BC
- Solomon comes to the throne of Israel and Judah, and marries the daughter of Siamon, the king of Egypt.

950 BC
- King Solomon of Israel and Judah completes his building work in Jerusalem and he and King Hiram of Tyre exchange gifts. The Egyptian pharaoh, his father-in-law, makes Solomon a present of the town of Gezer, which he has earlier sacked.

c. 950 BC Around this time the title pharaoh, meaning "great house," which earlier referred to the royal household, is first applied to the king of Egypt.

945 BC
- Libyan chieftains, calling themselves chiefs of the Meshwash, take control in Egypt and begin the 22nd dynasty under Sheshonk I. They rule from the Nile delta. Thebes remains a religious center, although considerable power is still exerted by the priesthood, which is increasingly dependent on the oracle.
- Queen of Sheba's visit to King Solomon of Israel and Judah takes place about this time. Solomon begins to collect his vast harem of foreign women and attempts to please them with a proliferation of idolatries.

934 BC
- King Assurdan II of Assyria begins the revival of his country.

931 BC
- King Solomon dies, and the combined kingdom of Israel and Judah begins to disintegrate. He is succeeded by his son Rehoboam.

c. 930 BC
- The Egyptian pharaoh, Sheshonk I (the biblical Shishak), stages a military expedition into Palestine, penetrates Jerusalem, and seizes the treasures of the temple and royal palaces.

925 BC–914 BC
- King Rehoboam of Israel and Judah, Solomon's son, is faced with discontent from his people as well as many external enemies. This dual pressure results in splitting the territory into two separate kingdoms: Israel (or the Ten Tribes) in the north, under King Jeroboam I, and

Judah (hence "the Jews") in the south, under King Rehoboam, with Jerusalem as its capital.

911 BC
- Assyria's revival is continued by King Adad-nirari II, who forcefully pacifies Babylon and defeats both the Aramaeans (a wandering Semitic tribe) and the Urartu (later the Vannic civilization).

SCIENCE, TECHNOLOGY, AND MEDICINE

Agriculture

c. 1000 BC
- Human excrement, manure, and plant waste are used as fertilizer in Mesopotamia and Egypt. The idea of fertilization subsequently spreads throughout the Mediterranean.
- Oats are first cultivated in western Europe.
- The reindeer is domesticated by the Altair people in the Pazyryk valley, Siberia.

Exploration

c. 1000 BC
- A clay tablet is made in Babylon depicting the earth as a disc surrounded by water with Babylon at its center – the first map of the world.

Science

c. 1000 BC
- The Hindu calendar is developed in India. It is based on a solar year of 360 days divided into 12 lunar months of 27 or 28 days with a leap month intercalated every 60 months to bring it into line with the true solar year.

c. 975 BC
- The Gezer Calendar is devised. Based on a lunar cycle of 12 months and 354 days, it is tied into the solar year but it is not known how. It forms the basis of the Hebrew calendar.

Technology

c. 1000 BC
- Coal, for use in smelting copper, is mined at the Fi-shun mine in China.
- Iron is beginning to be used in central Europe.
- The Assyrians use wheeled battering rams.
- The Chinese use a brush and ink for writing.
- The following elements are known by this date: carbon, copper, gold, iron, lead, mercury, silver, sulfur, tin, and zinc.

Transportation

945 BC
- King Solomon of Israel and Judah provides an example of the convention that the horse and chariot is a status symbol. The Bible credits him with stabling for 40,000 horses. Archeological excavation (at Megiddo) has unearthed at least 450 such stables, but recent work dates them to the time of Ahab (after 877 BC).

ARTS AND IDEAS

Architecture

959 BC
- The temple of King Solomon of Israel and Judah in Jerusalem is completed. He proceeds to build palaces for himself and his wives. According to the Old Testament, Solomon's temple is made of ashlar stone and with liberal use of gold. However, at 27m/90 ft by 9 m/30 ft (taking the cubit at 46 cm/18 in) it is still smaller than his palace, which measures some 46 m/150 ft by 23 m/75 ft. Solomon's temple is said to be designed more to Canaanite standards than Jewish.

958 BC
- The Bible states that King Solomon of Israel and Judah rebuilds the cities of Hazor, Megiddo, and Gezer (I Kings 9:15–17). Archeology has proved that these three cities were rebuilt in the 10th century BC.

BIRTHS & DEATHS

c. 990 BC
- Solomon, King of Israel, traditionally regarded as the author of the Old Testament books, the Book of Proverbs and the Song of Solomon, born (–930 BC).

c. 962 BC
- David, second king of Israel, who established Israel as a united kingdom, and features prominently in the holy texts of the Jewish, Christian, and Islamic religions, dies (c. 70).

c. 931 BC
- Solomon, king of Israel, traditionally regarded as the author of the Book of Proverbs and the Song of Solomon of the Old Testament, dies (c. 59).

901 BC
- Jeroboam I, first king of the northern kingdom of Israel 922 BC–901 BC, dies.

c. 950 BC

- King Solomon of Israel and Judah begins to build the temple in Jerusalem. He is helped by the Phoenician king Hiram of Tyre, who supplies Lebanese cedarwood.

Literature and Language

c. 1000 BC

- The "Homeric" poems of Greece and the *Vedas* Hindu hymns of India are recited at this time, and are transmitted orally from one generation to the next.

SOCIETY

Everyday Life

c. 1000 BC

- A Bronze-Age settlement is established at Hallstatt, Austria. The presence of salt is the primary attraction. The salt mines are worked using techniques developed in the Alps for the extraction of copper. At this time the Hallstatt culture is still confined to the area around southern Germany and Austria.
- Finds from the valley of the Forum in Rome suggest that it was occupied from at least the 10th century BC.

- Four techniques for preserving food are in use in China: salting, using spices, fermentation in wine, and drying with smoking.
- Primitive settlements exist on the site of Rome, Italy.

980 BC

- David's census, which takes over nine months to complete, shows there to be of "men that drew the sword, 800,000 in Israel and 500,000 in Judah."

Religion

970 BC

- The biblical story of the Judgment of Solomon (I Kings 3:16–28), states that Solomon, king of Israel and Judah, having been blessed by God with an understanding heart, judges between two harlots, each of whom claims that of two babies (one of which has died and one of which is alive) she is the mother of the living child. Solomon proves his wisdom by stating that the child should be cut in two, with one half given to each woman. One of the woman accedes to this, the other takes back her claim, proving her to be the real mother by her refusal to see her child killed.

962 BC

- King David of Israel acquires a reputation as a great poet, 73 of the biblical Psalms being credited to him.

900 BC–801 BC

POLITICS, GOVERNMENT, AND ECONOMICS

Business and Economics

870 BC

- The Phrygians of Asia Minor seem to have access to a source of gold, judging from the Midas legends.

Colonization

c. 900 BC–*c.* 800 BC

- The Etruscans begin to infiltrate into northern Italy, probably coming from the East.

814 BC

- The city of Carthage in north Africa is traditionally founded. It is developed as a Phoenician colony by the city of Tyre.

Politics and Government

c. 900 BC–*c.* 800 BC

- The Phrygians in Asia Minor reach the height of their prosperity under their Midas dynasty of kings.

889 BC

- Israel emerges from a period of strife with the now separate and stronger kingdom of Judah; Omri is chosen as king of Israel.
- King Ashurnasirpal II, one of Assyria's great conquerors, comes to the throne.

880 BC

- King Omri establishes the Israelite capital at Samaria.

876 BC

- Jehosaphat comes to the throne of Judah and "walks in the ways of the Lord." His daughter marries King Ahab of Israel's son and so repairs relations between Israel and Judah. Jehosaphat brings some peace and prosperity to Judah.
- King Ashurnasirpal II of Assyria marches west to the Mediterranean and conquers Syria, founding the fortress of Harran from which to administer the country. He appears to leave the Jews alone, but extracts tribute from the Phoenicians. On his way he subdues the Neo-Hittite city of Carchemish.

876 BC–851 BC   King Jehosaphat of Judah sends Levites, with the book of the law, to teach in the cities of Judah and appoints Judges in the larger (walled) towns. He builds ships to trade with Ophir (possibly South Arabia or India), but they are wrecked.

c. 874 BC

- King Omri's son Ahab comes to the throne of Israel. He marries Jezebel, a Phoenician, daughter of the king of Tyre and a worshiper of Baal. Ahab carries out much building work, including a palace in Samaria and the rebuilding and refortification of the cities of Megiddo and Hazor, destroyed by the Egyptian pharaoh Sheshonk I; he provides these two cities with complex water systems.

870 BC

870 BC–855 BC   Hebrew prophet Elijah denounces both Jezebel, a worshiper of Baal, and her husband Ahab, king of Israel, and correctly foretells a three-year drought, which also occurs in Phoenicia. He brings rain, so confounding the prophets of Baal who are subsequently massacred. He again denounces Ahab for plotting the death of Naboth in order to take his vineyard.

870 BC–840 BC   The moral and political influence of the prophets Elijah and Elisha in Israel is considerable, including (as with Samuel) the power of kingmaking. Both denounce King Ahab for his marriage to Jezebel (a follower of Baal), and Elisha backs a dashing army captain named Jehu as his successor.

859 BC

- King Shalmaneser III comes to the Assyrian throne. A powerful combination of Canaanite and Syrian states is allied against him under the leadership of the Syrian king Adad-idri (the biblical Ben Hadad) at Damascus.

855 BC

- King Shalmaneser III of Assyria claims a victory over the federation under the Syrian king Adad-idri at the Battle of Karka, probably on the Orontes River in Syria.

853 BC

- King Ahab of Israel dies fighting King Adad-idri of Syria at the siege of Ramoth. Two of Ahab's sons reign briefly in succession, but the real power behind the throne at this time is probably his widow Jezebel.

842 BC

- Jehu, the prophet Elisha's chosen successor to King Ahab of Israel, massacres the royal families of both Israel and Judah (including Ahab's widow Jezebel), though King David's line survives in Judah in the person of Jehoash. Jehu reigns in Israel until 814 BC and pays tribute to Assyria.

841 BC

- The oppressive Chinese king Li is dethroned in favor of the Gong He or Public Harmony regency. Authentic chronology in Chinese history now begins; a feudal age follows, until the arrival of the Han dynasty in 206 BC.

840 BC

- King Sarduris I founds the city of Van (on the southern shores of the lake of that name, south of Mt. Ararat, Turkey). The Vannic kingdom (called Urartu by Assyria and Ararat by the Jews) withstands the might of Assyria for over 100 years.

831 BC

- An Assyrian general claims a victory over the king of Urartu (the kingdom of Van).

827 BC

- The Chinese drive the nomadic Huns out of their domains. This may set in motion a movement of their western neighbors, the Scythians, which becomes apparent in the next two centuries.

824 BC

- Shamshi-Adad V succeeds to the Assyrian throne and spends two years putting down internal revolt, having to ask for help from Babylon. He then extends his boundaries east and south, attacking and humbling Babylon but leaving Palestine largely alone.

811 BC

- Adad-nirari III succeeds to the Assyrian throne, but his mother Sammu-ramat exerts the real power. The legendary founder of Babylon, Semiramis, and her husband Ninus, king of Assyria, are probably based on them.

802 BC

- King Adad-nirari III of Assyria campaigns successfully in Syria before having to face Vannic aggression. He besieges the Syrian capital Damascus.

SCIENCE, TECHNOLOGY, AND MEDICINE

Math

876 BC

- The Hindus in India invent a symbol for zero—one of the greatest inventions in mathematics.

Technology

c. 900 BC

- Natural gas begins to be used in China.
- The Phoenicians develop Tyrian purple dye from mollusks in the eastern Mediterranean belonging to the genera *Murox* and *Purpura*.

c. 900 BC–c. 800 BC   The use of iron spreads into Europe, particularly to Hallstatt (Austria).

Discoveries in Mathematics (*c.* 3000 BC–AD 780)

c. 3000 BC

- The abacus, which uses rods and beads for making calculations, is developed in the Middle East and adopted throughout the Mediterranean. A form of the abacus is also used in China at this time.
- The Sumerians of Babylon develop a sexagesimal (based on 60) numbering system. Used for recording financial transactions, the order of the numbers determines their relative, or unit value (place-value), although no zero value is used. It continues to be used for mathematics and astronomy until the 17th century AD, and is still used for measuring angles and time.

c. 1900 BC

- The Golenishev papyrus is written. It documents Egyptian knowledge of geometry.

876 BC

- The Hindus in India invent a symbol for zero—one of the greatest inventions in mathematics.

530 BC

- Pythagoras of Samos, scientist and philosopher, moves to Croton and starts researching and teaching theories of mathematics, geometry, music, and reincarnation. A mystic as well as a mathematician, he argues that the key to the universe lies in numbers, while preaching immortality and the transmigration of souls. He founds a brotherhood in Croton which is to remain influential for several generations. His work leads to a number of important results, including the Pythagorean theorem of right triangles and the discovery of irrational numbers (those that cannot be represented by fractions).

c. 300 BC

- Alexandrian mathematician Euclid sets out the laws of geometry in his *Stoicheion/Elements*; it remains a standard text for 2,000 years.

287–212 BC

- The prolific Greek mathematician Archimedes of Syracuse produces a number of works on two- and three-dimensional geometry, including circles, spheres, and spirals.

c. 250 BC

- Greek mathematician and inventor Archimedes, in his *On the Sphere and the Cylinder*, provides the formulae for finding the volume of a sphere and a cylinder; in *Measurement of the Circle* he arrives at an approximation of the value of pi; and in *The Sand Reckoner* he creates a place-value system of notation for Greek mathematics.

c. 230 BC

- Alexandrian mathematician Apollonius of Perga, writes *Conics*, a systematic treatise on the principles of conics in which he introduces the terms, parabola, ellipse, and hyperbola.
- Greek scholar Eratosthenes of Cyrene develops a method of finding all prime numbers. Known as the sieve of Eratosthenes it involves striking out the number 1 and every nth number following the number n. Only prime numbers then remain.

c. 190 BC

- Chinese mathematicians use powers of 10 to express magnitudes.

c. 100 BC

- Chinese mathematicians begin using negative numbers.

AD 62

- Greek mathematician and engineer Hero of Alexandria writes *Metrica/Measurements*, containing many formulae for working out areas and volumes.

100

- Greek mathematician and inventor Hero of Alexandria devises a method of representing numbers and performing simple calculating tasks using a train of gears—a primitive computer.

516

- The Indian astronomer and mathematician Aryabhata I produces his *Aryabhatiya*, a treatise on quadratic equations, the value of π, and other scientific problems, in which he adds tilted epicycles to the orbits of the planets to explain their movement.

595

- Decimal notation is used for numbers in India. This is the system on which our current system is based.

780–850

- Arab mathematician Muhammad ibn Musa al-Khwârizma writes *Al-jam' w'al-tafriq ib hisab al-hind/Addition and Subtraction in Indian Arithmetic*, which introduces the Indian system of numbers to the West. His other book, *Hisab al-jabr w'almuqabala/Calculation by Restoration and Reduction* gives us the word "algebra," from "al-jabr."

Transportation

c. 900 BC

- Coracles (roundish hide-covered boats) are commonly used for carrying cargo on the Tigris and Euphrates.

c. 850 BC

- The first arched bridge is built, at Izmir in present-day Turkey.

ARTS AND IDEAS

Architecture

879 BC–824 BC

- The rulers Ashurnasirpal II and Shalmaneser III of Assyria build themselves palaces at Calah, Assyria, (modern Nimrud, Iraq) including outstanding features such as colossal carvings of winged bulls and reliefs showing royal lion hunts and battle scenes. The archeologist Sir Henry Layard unearths the palaces in the 19th century AD.

c. 850 BC

- The Chauvín de Huantar temple in Peru is constructed. Built without using mortar and with cantilevered ceilings, it is the oldest known building in South America.

SOCIETY

Everyday Life

900 BC

- *c.* 900 BC–*c.* 740 BC The Iron Age Villanovan culture is spreading in Italy, named for a typical site at Villanova near Bologna. There is greater skill in metallurgy and a gradual increase in the use of iron. Cremation is practiced, with ashes being placed in an urn in a round hole in the ground. One of the main areas of Villanovan culture is Etruria.
- *c.* 900 BC–*c.* 500 BC La Venta becomes the major center of the second phase of Olmec civilization in Mexico. The site of San Lorenzo is abandoned, possibly in a violent overthrow of the local elite, or possibly for religious reasons. La Venta is a ceremonial or elite center, supported by a large agricultural population. It has a large main pyramid in addition to smaller ones.

834 BC

- The Medes, an Indo-European people, are first mentioned in the Assyrian records.

Religion

870 BC–840 BC

- The stories of the Hebrew prophets Elijah and Elisha are told in I Kings 17 to II Kings 13 of the Old Testament.

BIRTHS & DEATHS

c. 872 BC • Omri, king of Israel who conquered Moab, dies.	853 BC • Ahab, king of the northern kingdom of Israel *c.* 874 BC–853 BC, dies.	824 BC • Shalmaneser III, king of Assyria who expanded the empire through military conquest, dies.
859 BC • Ashurnasirpal II, king of Assyria 883 BC–859 BC, who consolidated the conquests of his father Tukulti-Ninurta II and was notorious for his cruelty, dies.	849 BC • Jehoshaphat (or Josaphat), king of Judah *c.* 873 BC–*c.* 849 BC, dies. 842 BC • Jezebel, wife of King Ahab of Israel, is killed by the new king Jehu.	815 BC • Jehu, king of Israel *c.* 842 BC–815 BC, dies (*c.* 27). 811 BC • Shamshi-Adad V, king of Assyria 823 BC–811 BC, dies.

800 BC–701 BC

POLITICS, GOVERNMENT, AND ECONOMICS

Colonization

c. 800 BC
- The Greeks begin colonization and foundation of new cities along the mid-Mediterranean and Aegean coasts. This movement is caused by increased prosperity and the pressure of expanding populations.

c. 750 BC
- The Greeks found the colony of Pithecusae (Ischia, Italy).

745 BC–735 BC
- Greek colonization continues: the colonies at Cumae in Italy, at Poseideion on the Orontes River, and at Syracuse and Naxos in Sicily are founded.

720 BC–700 BC
- Greek colonization in southern Italy continues with the founding of Sybaris, Croton, and Tarentum on the mainland and Zancle (later Messina), Hyblaea, and Selinus in Sicily. The process is soon so widespread that the area becomes known as Magna Graecia.

Politics and Government

790 BC
- A treaty is made between Assyria and Babylon, establishing Assyria as Babylon's protector.

783 BC
- In Egypt, which is still experiencing internal trouble due to the lack of a strong central government, the pharaoh Sheshonk III dies after a reign of 52 years. He is succeeded by Pemay "the Cat." The 23rd dynasty is now running concurrently with the 22nd.
- King Adad-nirari III of Assyria dies, and is succeeded by three weak kings, leading to a decline in Assyrian power and stability.

771 BC
- The original Zhou dynasty of China (also known as the West Zhou period) ends with the deposing of its king, You, and the shifting of the capital city to Luoyang. The Zhou dynasty continues for another five centuries, but

as a much looser confederacy of often-warring barons under a head who is little more than a religious symbol, "the king of Heaven."

754 BC
- In the Greek city-state of Sparta, the *Ephoroi*, a board of five overseers elected annually by the assembly, is established, according to a later list giving names starting in this year. The *ephors* are in addition to the Spartan kings, and there is often conflict between the two.

753 BC
- Rome is traditionally founded by Romulus and Remus: this is the year from which the Romans date all subsequent events. The date is not completely reliable, though by now Latin-speaking tribes do exist in Italy, probably arriving from further east, with Etruscans to their north and Greek colonial city-states about to be founded to their south.

750 BC
- The city-state, or *polis*, is on the rise in Greece; it is distinguished by common gods and common law administered from a fixed place. With the political change come different military needs, and the hoplite formation, heavily armed infantrymen in close order behind a wall of shields, is developed.

747 BC
- Nabonassar becomes king of Babylon; he is anti-Assyrian.

745 BC
- An Assyrian by the name of Pul comes to the throne and assumes the title of Tiglath-Pileser III. He revives his country and resumes its conquests.

733 BC
- Israel and Syria form a confederacy against Assyria, which King Ahaz of Judah refuses to join. The confederacy invades Judah, laying siege to Jerusalem. The Assyrian king Tiglath-Pileser III comes to the support of King Ahaz and invades Syria and northern Israel. He extinguishes the Syrian monarchy, sets up a puppet king, Hoshea, in Israel, and deports the leading citizens of Galilee.

c. 730 BC
- Piankhi, an Ethiopian king of the Cush, advances north from Jabal Barkal in the Sudan and defeats Tefnakhte, last ruler of the 23rd dynasty, who had attempted to gain control over all of Egypt. Piankhi returns home to Jabal Barkal with the spoils of war and Tefnakhte reasserts his authority in the north.

728 BC
- King Tiglath-Pileser III of Assyria establishes full sovereignty over Babylon and declares himself its king.

c. 727 BC

- King Hoshea of Israel ignores the exhortations of the prophet Isaiah of Judah and revolts against Assyria with Egyptian support. The Assyrian king Shalamanser retaliates and the Israelite capital of Samaria is besieged for three years.

722 BC

- A new king, known as Sargon II, comes to the Assyrian throne, following more dynastic turmoil. Having completed the pacification of Samaria, the Israelite capital, he turns his attention north and east to the Neo-Hittites and the kingdom of Van (or Urartu).
- The Israelite capital of Samaria falls to Assyria after a three-year siege and 27,290 Israelites are deported wholesale into Mesopotamia. This marks the end of Israel as a nation and the start of the so-called Captivity of the Ten Tribes. Judah is left alone. Israel becomes the land of the Samaritans, while Judah, under King Hezekiah, remains inviolate.

721 BC

- Fragments of stele that have survived from this time show that Assyrian law is harsh and owes little to the precepts laid down by Hammurabi, King of Babylon in the 18th century BC. For example, "If a woman has had a miscarriage by her own act, when they have prosecuted and convicted her, they shall impale her on stakes without burial."

720 BC

- The Dorian Greeks in the south and west of the Peloponnese (the Spartans) successfully fight to gain control of the rich Messenian plain, once the property of King Nestor of Pylos.

718 BC

- Bocchoris, son of Tefnakhte, becomes king of Egypt. He is the only king of the 24th dynasty.

717 BC

- The Neo-Hittite city of Carchemish falls to the Assyrians.

715 BC

- Numa Pompilius, Rome's first king after Romulus and Remus, traditionally accedes to the throne, and is the founder of Roman religious customs.

714 BC

- Sargon II of Assyria defeats the Vannic army and seizes its king's treasure. This defeat ends the prosperity and historical significance of the kingdom of Van (or Urartu). The vacuum thus created allows the Scythians and Cimmerians, to the north of the Black Sea, to move south.

712 BC

- Shabaka, the brother of Piankhi, king of Cush, conquers Egypt, burning Egyptian king Bocchoris alive and founding the 25th dynasty of Egypt. He reunites Egypt in preparation for taking on the might of Assyria.

710 BC

- There is a revolt against Assyrian rule in Babylon and King Merodach-Baladan (his biblical name) takes the throne.

709 BC

- The Neo-Hittite kingdom comes to an end following defeat by Assyria.

705 BC

- Sennacherib succeeds to the Assyrian throne. Assyria's vassal states and external enemies take the opportunity to stage a general revolt led by the king of Babylon and supported by the pharaoh of Egypt. King Hezekiah of Israel agrees to join the revolt (against the advice of the prophet Isaiah), hoping for Egyptian support.

703 BC–701 BC

- The Assyrian king Sennacherib reacts energetically to the revolt by vassal states and defeats Babylon, which supported the revolt. He then turns west into Palestine, defeating an Egyptian army and taking Lachish (a city to the south of Jerusalem) as well as "forty-six walled cities." He records in stone the feats of his army at the siege of Lachish.

SCIENCE, TECHNOLOGY, AND MEDICINE

Health and Medicine

c. 767 BC

- Bubonic plague sweeps throughout the known world.

Science

c. 800 BC

- The Greek poet Homer describes the earth as a convex disc surrounded by ocean.

c. 780 BC

- Chinese scholars make the first record of an earthquake.

763 BC

June 15   Assyrian archivists record an eclipse of the sun. The same event is recorded in the Bible (Amos 8:9).

738 BC

- Romulus, traditionally the founder of Rome, devises a lunar calendar with 10 months, 6 of 30 days and 4 of 31 days. The year begins in March and ends in December and is followed by an uncounted winter gap.

Technology

c. 800 BC

- Long underground aqueducts called "qanats" are driven horizontally into hillsides in Persia to tap groundwater. They are still a major source of water in Iran.
- The first sundials appear in Egypt. They consist of a straight calibrated base with six divisions, and a raised

cross piece at one end. The shadow of the cross piece on the base is used to tell the time; in the morning the arm is pointed east, and in the afternoon it is turned to face the west. They are still used in Egypt.

c. 775 BC
- King Uzziah of Judah supervises the making of a catapult device to "shoot arrows and great stones" at enemies.

Transportation

c. 800 BC
- The Chinese develop a steam-propelled cart.
- The Scythians introduce the horse into Greece.

ARTS AND IDEAS

Architecture

c. 750 BC
- The Marib Dam is built in Yemen; a rock-fill dam 14 m/50 ft high and 600 m/1,970 ft long, it provides water for irrigation for nearly 1,000 years.
- The radiating arch, where each wedge-shaped piece radiates away from its support, is developed by Etruscan architects.

Arts

c. 750 BC
- The Greek "geometric" style of pottery gives way to an "orientalizing" style, which introduces new motifs, particularly fantastic animals.

709 BC
- A monument from this time in Cyprus (where pre-Dorian rather than Dorian influence seems to have followed the Minoan) shows a chieftain paying tribute to Assyria.

Literature and Language

c. 800 BC
- The monuments at Neo-Hittite Karatepe, near Adena, Anatolia, in modern Turkestan, include

inscriptions in both Hittite and Phoenician scripts, thus enabling modern scholars to decipher the former. Reliefs also found at the site include figures of lions.

c. 750 BC
- The *Iliad* and the *Odyssey*, the two great epic poems ascribed to the legendary Greek poet Homer, are composed. Though written around this date, they draw on a long tradition of oral poetry dating back to at least 1000 BC.

740 BC
- The people of Etruria, Italy, begin to adopt the Greek alphabet.

Music

c. 730 BC
- A Greek myth credits a Phrygian musician called Olympus with inventing the enharmonic scale of quarter tones.

Thought and Scholarship

705 BC
- The poet and farmer Hesiod of Boeotia, Greece, writes his *Works and Days*, a compilation of practical and ethical advice based on rural life, which is also the first recorded instructional book on agricultural practice, and his *Theogony*, which gives an account of the origin of the world and the birth of the Greek gods. He and Homer are said to have "given the Greeks their gods."

SOCIETY

Everyday Life

750 BC
- The Hallstatt C culture starts among the Celts in western Europe. Aristocratic graves contain buried ceremonial wagons and characteristic iron or bronze longswords.
  750 BC–700 BC Villanovan culture in Italy is in its late stage, and gradually adapts to form the Etruscan civilization.

c. 705 BC
- The Assyrian king Sennacherib rebuilds the city of Nineveh, constructing two encircling walls (both still in

BIRTHS & DEATHS

783 BC
- Adad-nirari III, king of Assyria 810 BC–783 BC, dies.

c. 751 BC
- Piankhi (Pharaoh), ruler of the kingdom of Cush 751 BC–716 BC in the Sudan, born (–*c.* 716 BC).

727 BC
- Tiglath-Pileser III, king of Assyria 728 BC–727 BC, who expanded the Assyrian Empire to include Syria and Babylon, dies.

720 BC
- Ahaz, king of Judah *c.* 735 BC–720 BC and Assyrian vassal, dies.

c. 716 BC
- Piankhi (Pharaoh), ruler of the kingdom of Cush 751 BC–716 BC in the Sudan, dies.

705 BC
- Sargon II, Assyrian ruler 721 BC–705 BC, who expanded the Assyrian Empire, dies in battle.

existence). The inner wall is 13 km/8 mi long. He also establishes plantations of fruit trees and parks of exotic trees and plants. One imported plant is the "wool-bearing tree" (cotton plant).

Religion

c. 800 BC

- The Hindu metaphysical treatises *Upanishads*, sacred texts in Hinduism, are begun. The earlier *Upanishads*, written in archaic Sanskrit, are completed before 500 BC, though they continue to be produced for centuries.

c. 765 BC–735 BC

- According to Jewish tradition, the Hebrew prophets Amos and Hosea are active at this time. They are said to be the first to write down their prophecies and to denounce public immorality and the social injustice of Judah.

733 BC

- According to the Old Testament, the Hebrew prophets Micah and Isaiah warn that the Hebrew people must take action if they wish to avoid disaster. Both regard Assyria as the necessary instrument of God's displeasure if the people will not mend their ways.

733 BC–701 BC   The prophecies of the Hebrew prophet Isaiah are set in this period, in the Old Testament Book of Isaiah, chapters 1 to 39.

721 BC

- Assyrian religion has a militaristic theme at this time. The principal god, Ashur (also Assur), is the god of war, and usually appears within the symbol of a winged disc. This symbol is carried into battle, preferably in the king's own chariot.

Sports

c. 800 BC

- Book XXIII of the Greek epic poem *Iliad* contains the earliest known extensive description of a sporting event,

---

The Olympic Games (776 BC–AD 393)

776 BC
- Coriobis of Elis becomes the first recorded victor in the pan-Hellenic games, the Olympiad, winning the only event—the stade running race (a distance of 192.27 m/630.80 ft). This is the first definite date in Greek history.

724 BC
- A second event, the two-stage race or *dialus*, a running event of approximately 385 m/1263 ft, is added to the 14th Olympic Games. At the previous 13 Olympiads the single-stade race was the only event at the games.

720 BC
- At the 15th Olympiad, the *dolichos*, a long-distance race of 24 stadia, approximately 4.5 km/2.8 mi, is introduced.

708 BC
- The pentathlon is introduced to the 18th Olympic Games. Athletes compete in sprinting, jumping, javelin and discus throwing, and wrestling—all of which, except wrestling, are included in modern track and field pentathlon competitions.

***c.* 688 BC**
- Boxing is introduced to the 23rd Olympic Games. Boxers wear leather coverings on their hands.

680 BC
- Chariot racing with four horses, quadriga racing, is introduced to the 25th Olympic Games.

664–656 BC
- Chionis, a Spartan athlete, wins the stade race at three successive Olympic Games.

632 BC
- Boys' running races and wrestling events are introduced to the 40th Olympic Games.

572 BC
- Control of the Olympian festival passes to the Elians (of the city-state of Elis in the northwestern Peloponnese). The games and festival are assuming great importance in the Greek world.

536 BC–516 BC
- Milon (or Milo) of Croton, the most famous wrestler in the history of the ancient Olympic Games, wins Olympic titles in six successive games.

520 BC
- Running races in armor, called *hoplitodromos*, are introduced to the Olympic Games.

***c.* 450 BC**
- Mechanical starting gates for running and chariot races are introduced at the Olympic Games.

164 BC–152 BC
- Leonidas of Rhodes wins three running events at four consecutive Olympic Games.

AD 393
- The Roman emperor Theodosius I the Great abolishes the Greek Olympic Games by decree because of their association with paganism.

the Funeral Games of Patroclus. It is mostly devoted to chariot racing, but there are briefer descriptions of boxing, wrestling, discus and javelin throwing, and foot races. In another epic poem, *Odyssey*, Homer describes a game resembling team handball, which he says was invented by Angagalla, a Spartan princess.

776 BC
- Coriobis of Elis becomes the first recorded victor in the pan-Hellenic games, the Olympiad, winning the onlyevent—the stade running race (a distance of 192.27 m/630.80 ft). This is the first definite date in Greek history.

724 BC
- A second event, the two-stage race or *dialus*, a running event of approximately 385 m/1263 ft, is added to the

14th Olympic Games in Greece. At the previous 13 Olympiads the single-stade race was the only event at the games.

720 BC
- At the 15th Olympiad in Greece, the *dolichos*, a long-distance race of 24 stadia, approximately 4.5 km/2.8 mi, is introduced.

708 BC
- The pentathlon is introduced to the 18th Olympic Games at Olympia, Greece. Athletes compete in sprinting, jumping, javelin and discus throwing, and wrestling—all of which, except wrestling, are included in modern track and field pentathlon competitions.

◆

700 BC–601 BC

POLITICS, GOVERNMENT, AND ECONOMICS

Business and Economics

660 BC
- The newly founded Ethiopian city of Meroe (in modern Sudan) has the economic advantage of access to iron.

c. 650 BC
- The first stamped coins (as opposed to a mere standard weight of metal) are introduced in Lydia, Anatolia. They are made of gold and silver and manufactured by pouring the molten metal onto an anvil where they solidify and are then punched. Their use is quickly adopted around the Mediterranean.

Colonization

c. 700 BC
- The Celts begin to settle in Spain and a few reach England.
- The city of Tartessus (biblical Tarshish) in Spain throws off the rule of its founder, the Phoenician city of Tyre, and achieves power in its own right under Iberian chiefs. A kingdom is founded under the legendary Arganthonius ("Silver Man") and prospers, with the help of the local mines, for about 150 years.

- The Hallstatt culture spreads west through Switzerland and the Vosges to eastern France, and later to the Atlantic coast and Spain.

688 BC
- The Greek colony of Gela is founded on the south coast of Sicily. It goes on to become one of the most important cities on the island, and the center of its pottery industry.

650 BC
- A second wave of Greek colonization spearheaded by the city-states of Megara and Miletus creates city-states around the Black Sea.
- The Etruscans, having established themselves in northern Italy, seek to infiltrate into the district of Campania during this period. Their way is partially blocked by Rome on the River Tiber.

630 BC
- The Minyae, early inhabitants of the island of Thera (modern Santorini), quarrel with later Dorian settlers. They leave Thera and eventually found the colony of Cyrene in north Africa.

620 BC
- A Greek Phocaean colony is founded near Tartessus in Spain, the most westerly Greek colony so far.

Politics and Government

c. 700 BC
- The Assyrian king Sennacherib continues his campaign in Palestine and besieges Jerusalem. Hezekiah, king of Judah, with the prophet Isaiah's moral support, defies the Assyrians and successfully repulses them. Although he has to pay considerable tribute to Sennacherib, Judah

remains independent. Sennacherib lists the booty stolen from Jerusalem and taken to his capital, Nineveh, on what has become known as the Rassam cylinder, named for the 19th-century archeologist who found it, Hormuzd Rassam.

- The Greeks develop the phalanx tactical formation consisting of eight rows of infantry. Each hoplite (heavily armed infantryman) carries a pike for thrusting and as a barrier to cavalry, a shield, and a two-foot, double-edged sword. The phalanx advances in step to the tune of a flute.
- The rulers of the old civilizations, Egypt, Babylon, and Assyria, spend much of this period warring among themselves and so fail to appreciate the threat presented by new powers of different races, such as the Cimmerians, Scythians, Phrygians, Medes, Lydians, and Ionian Greeks.

c. 700 BC–*c.* 500 BC The vassal states of the Zhou dynasty in China grow in power and weaken the power of the dynasty.

692 BC

- The Chaldeans, with Elamite support, defy Assyria and seize the throne of Babylon.

689 BC

- Babylon has now become a stronghold of the Chaldean party. While Elam is temporarily unable to provide support due to internal dynastic trouble, Babylon is besieged by the Assyrian king Sennacherib, who takes and sacks the city.
- Taharqa (biblical Tirhakah), a son of King Shabaka, becomes pharaoh of Egypt. Although Egypt is prosperous during the initial years of his reign, he later inspires the Phoenician city of Tyre to revolt against Assyria.

683 BC

- The office of archon (Greek "ruler") is restricted to annual terms in Athens. The list of archons begins.

681 BC

January The Assyrian king Sennacherib is assassinated by his sons. Civil war follows but Esarhaddon, one of his sons, gains control.

676 BC

- King Esarhaddon of Assyria continues his policy of expansion and conducts a campaign in Arabia, extracting tribute and then retiring.

675 BC

- King Esarhaddon of Assyria, recognizing Egypt as the real threat to his ambitions, attacks the fortresses of the Nile delta, but with little success.

673 BC

- As a subordinate operation to King Esarhaddon's invasion of Egypt, the Assyrians besiege the Phoenician city of Tyre but fail to take it.

671 BC

- Assyria renews its attack on Egypt, taking the city of Memphis. The pharaoh Taharqa is defeated but escapes to Nubia. King Esarhaddon of Assyria appoints local rulers, including Necho of Saïs, and then retires to deal with home affairs.

670 BC

- Gyges ("Gugu" in Assyrian) comes to the Lydian throne and begins to build up the country's power and wealth. He establishes his reputation for wealth among the Greeks by sending rich gifts to Delphi. In the eyes of later Greeks, Gyges is the typical *tyrannos*, or autocrat.
- The Greek city-state of Argos, under King Pheidon, is at the height of its power, though soon to decline. Mycenae and Tiryns, two client states of Argos, temporarily defeat the city-state of Sparta in the Battle of Hysiai.

669 BC

- Egyptian king Taharqa returns to Egypt and reoccupies Memphis. King Esarhaddon of Assyria, setting out for Egypt to put down the rebellion, dies at the fortress of Harran.

668 BC

- Ashurbanipal succeeds to the Assyrian throne, the last great king of Assyria. He concludes a treaty with the Phoenician city of Tyre, and the Phoenician coastal cities acknowledge Assyrian sovereignty.

667 BC

- In his first Egyptian campaign, King Ashurbanipal of Assyria turns Pharaoh Taharqa out of Memphis, reappoints pro-Assyrian governors throughout the country, and then retires. Taharqa flees south to Nubia, where, in 664 BC, he dies. Assyria's puppet king in Egypt, Necho of Saïs, who had joined the rebels against Assyria, is temporarily taken away to the Assyrian capital of Nineveh as a captive.

664 BC

- Psamtik I is made governor of Egypt by Assyrian king Ashurbanipal.
- Tanutamon succeeds Taharqa as pharaoh of Egypt and reoccupies Memphis.

663 BC

- In his final Egyptian campaign, King Ashurbanipal of Assyria claims to have penetrated to Thebes and to have carried away vast booty. However, the Egyptians also claim a victory. Both the pharaoh Tanutamon and the Assyrians retire, the former to his native Ethiopia (modern Sudan) where he settles in the city of Meroe. The 25th dynasty of Egypt ends with his passing from the Egyptian scene.

660 BC

- Gyges of Lydia is threatened by the Cimmerians and asks for help from Assyria. He succeeds in repelling the threat, with or without Assyrian help, and ceases his pro-Assyrian stance.
- Japan's first emperor, Jimmu, traditionally comes to power. A Mongolian people begin to enter Japan, probably coming through Korea, and oust the indigenous Ainus.
- Nomad barbarians ravage the area of north Henan in China.
- The first recorded Greek naval battle takes place between Corinth, at this time probably the most powerful city-state on the Greek mainland, and its colony Corcyra (Corfu).

658 BC

- Psamtik I, possibly the son of Necho of Saïs (a rebel Assyrian puppet ruler in Egypt), expels Assyria's vassals in the Delta and establishes his capital city at Saïs to found Egypt's 26th (Saïte) dynasty.

655 BC

- The aristocratic Bacchiadae, rulers of the Greek city-state of Corinth, are expelled by Cypselus, tyrant of Corith, for suppressing the kingship.

653 BC

- The Medes, an Indo-European people, fail in an attack on the Assyrian capital of Nineveh.

652 BC

- Babylon's puppet king, in spite of being the brother of King Ashurbanipal of Assyria, is persuaded to join a coalition against Assyria.
- The Cimmerians return to attack Lydia and capture its capital, Sardis, and kill King Gyges. The Assyrians manage to defeat the Cimmerians and to throw them back to the north (where they are absorbed by the Scythians), but this all-out effort strains their resources and contributes to their exhaustion.

651 BC

- Assyria retreats from Egypt for the last time, in order to deal with trouble nearer home. Egyptian pharaoh Psamtik I reforms the Egyptian government and removes the last traces of Cush rule.

650 BC

- Pharaoh Psamtik I of Egypt uses his daughter Nitocris (not to be confused with the Babylonian queen) to gain political power at Thebes, where the 25th dynasty still reigns. He makes her the god's (that is, the pharaoh's) wife and she is received with acclaim by the priesthood.
- The Assyrians manage to defeat a coalition of their enemies at the Battle of Babsame on the River Tigris.

650 BC–630 BC The Scythians carry out a series of raids on horseback toward the south and are a constant source of terror to Assyria, Syria, Lydia, and Palestine, though they also keep the Medes in check.

***c.* 649 BC**

- Egyptian pharaoh Psamtik I continues his rise to power. From now on, Greek influence is more predominant in Egypt than trends from Mesopotamia, and its greatest threat is posed by Assyria's enemies rather than Assyria itself.

648 BC

- Assyrian king Ashurbanipal besieges Babylon, causing famine in the city and driving its citizens to cannibalism. Babylon capitulates to Assyria and is again devastated, but Ashurbanipal orders that the city be rebuilt.

639 BC

- Elam, one of Babylon's main allies in the coalition against Assyria, is quelled. The capital Susa is sacked, its ziggurat destroyed, and the statues of its gods looted.

637 BC

- Josiah comes to the throne of Judah, at the age of eight, with the high priest as his regent. He reissues the Deuteronomic Laws and endeavors to purify the Jews' religion, destroying all local sanctuaries in favor of the pure and centralized worship in the temple at Jerusalem.

632 BC

- Athenian nobleman Cylon, after his victory in the Olympic Games, seizes the Acropolis in Athens, Greece, with the intention of making himself tyrant. He is besieged and takes refuge at the altar of Athena, but is lured away and put to death.

630 BC

- Nabopolasser, a Chaldean, is appointed by the Assyrians as administrator of Babylon and quashes a rebellion, but then rebels against the Assyrians himself.
- The Greek city-state of Sparta wages its second war against Messenia, southwest of the Peleponnese. The revolt and second subjugation of the Messenians may well be the origin of the unique system of government in Sparta, by which a dedicated military aristocracy perennially suppresses a subjugated serf class of Messenians known as the helots. Particularly noted for its peculiar harsh laws and customs, the Spartans themselves credit their laws and constitution to a semimythical figure, Lycurgus.

***c.* 627 BC**

- King Ashurbanipal of Assyria dies, and the disintegration of Assyria's last span of greatness begins as it finds itself overextended and without allies.

626 BC

- The Assyrians endeavor to oust their own administrator, Nabopolasser, from Babylon following his rebellion. They fail and he becomes acknowledged as king of Babylon, founding his Chaldean dynasty and the city's final but most splendid period of greatness.
- The Scythians pour down through Syria and Palestine, helping to weaken Assyria, annihilating the Philistines, and reaching the borders of Egypt.

625 BC

- Periander becomes tyrant of the Greek city-state of Corinth; he has a reputation as a philosopher.

623 BC–616 BC

- There is a prolonged and inconclusive war between Assyria and Babylon, with a small Egyptian force either helping Assyria or seeking to defend its country's own interests in Syria.

621 BC

- According to tradition, the Draconian Laws of Athens are issued at this time. They are said to be written in blood, not ink, because death is the punishment for nearly all crimes.

616 BC

- Tarquinius Priscus traditionally becomes king of Rome, marking the start of the reign of the Etruscan Tarquins, the last line of kings before Rome becomes a republic. The Forum is drained during his reign.

615 BC

- The Medes under their king Cyaxares get the better of the Scythians and advance to the borders of Assyria.

614 BC

- King Nabopolasser of Babylon and King Cyaxares the Mede sign a treaty, probably binding it with the marriage of their children.

613 BC

- The Assyrian army holds its own against the combined Medes and Babylonians in the usual summer campaign.

612 BC

- The Medes persuade the Scythians to join with them and the Babylonians. They besiege the Assyrian capital Nineveh, which falls after three months and the Assyrian king perishes in the burning city. An Assyrian general, Assuruballit, assumes the kingship and takes up a new stand at Harran.

611 BC

- The Medes temporarily retire from the campaign against the Assyrians, but their ally King Nabopolasser of Babylon continues to harry the country around Harran, although he cannot take the fortress itself. The Phoenician coastal cities regain some measure of independence as Assyria becomes weaker.

610 BC

- Necho II succeeds Psamtik I as Egyptian pharaoh.

609 BC

- The Assyrian garrison at Harran, bolstered by a contingent of Egyptians, is threatened by a renewed coalition of Babylonians and Medes who lived in what is now present day Iran. The garrison flees, leaving Harran undefended.

608 BC

- Pharaoh Necho II, seeing the chance to fill the vacuum left by Assyria and to reassert Egypt's traditional sway over Syria, sends his full army north. King Josiah of Judah, who still considers himself Assyria's vassal, meets the Egyptians single-handed at Megiddo and is slain. It is this battle that gives its name to the prophetic world-battle of the biblical book of Revelations: "Har" (the Mountain of) "Megiddo," Armageddon.
- The Assyrians under Assuruballit fail to recapture Harran from the Babylonians and Medes and fade out of the records. The victorious Medes turn upon the Scythians, their temporary allies, who retire to their own lands.

605 BC

- The Egyptians are finally defeated near the Syrian city of Carchemish by a Babylonian army under the command of the Crown Prince Nebuchadnezzar, who succeeds to the Babylonian throne in September.

604 BC

- The people and towns of the old Assyrian Empire acknowledge Nebuchadnezzar, the Chaldean king of Babylon, as their new master. Only the Phoenician town of Askelon, and Jehoiakim, king of Judah, resist. Askelon is destroyed while Jehoiakim relies on the strength of Egypt, against the advice of the prophet Jeremiah.

601 BC

- Egypt, under King Necho II, is for a while able to withstand the might of King Nebuchadnezzar of Babylon's army, repulsing it from its borders.

SCIENCE, TECHNOLOGY, AND MEDICINE

Agriculture

c. **700 BC**

- The Egyptians develop the first egg incubators—"chicken ovens."

Exploration

c. **605 BC**

- Egyptian pharaoh Necho II sponsors an expedition that circumnavigates Africa.

Health and Medicine

c. **650 BC**

- Tuberculosis, leprosy, and gonorrhea are first described with accuracy.

Science

c. **690 BC**

- Numa Pompilius, the second king of Rome, improves Romulus' calendar by adding two months—January and February—thereby increasing the total number of days by 50 to make a year of 354 days.

c. **650 BC**

- The Chinese use chemicals to fumigate their houses.

648 BC

April 6 Greek poet Archilochus records a total eclipse of the sun.

Technology

c. **700 BC**

- Oil lamps appear in Greece, replacing torches. The Greeks also invent the fibula (safety-pin), although the idea is lost after the fall of the Roman Empire.
- The Assyrian king Sennacherib introduces a number of technological advances including easier methods of bronze-casting and raising water from wells.
- To supply Jerusalem with water, Hezekiah, king of Judah, builds a tunnel (still in existence), from Gihon Spring outside Jerusalem's city walls to the Pool of Siloam within. Cut through solid rock, it is 530 m/1,750 ft long, and 2 m/6 ft in high.

c. **650 BC**

- The Romans develop iron saws enabling them to saw stone.

Transportation

c. 700 BC

- The Greeks develop the bireme, a galley about 24 m/80 ft long with two banks of oars staggered on either side of the vessel.
- c. 700 BC–c. 600 BC Paved roads of burned brick, and stone laid with bituminous mortar, connect the temples and palaces of Assur, Babylon, and Tall al-Admar. They may have been the forerunners of the Roman system.

642 BC

- The Roman king Ancus Marcius, who traditionally came to power on this date, builds a bridge over the Tiber and founds the port of Ostia.

c. 625 BC

- The Chaldean king Nabopolasser builds a bridge over the Euphrates. It is 116 m/380 ft long and contains the oldest known drawbridge.

c. 610 BC

- Egyptian pharaoh Necho II begins the construction of a canal between the Nile and the Red Sea, but discontinues it on the counsel of an oracle, and after 120,000 men die building it.

ARTS AND IDEAS

Architecture

691 BC

- The Assyrian king Sennacherib builds the 20-m/66-ft wide Jerwan aqueduct which brings water from a

tributary of the Greater Zab River to Nineveh 80 km/ 50 mi away. Stone-lined, and constructed in 15 months, according to a surviving plaque, the aqueduct uses advanced techniques including sluice gates and a 275 m/900 ft limestone bridge, 9 m/30 ft high and 15 m/30 ft wide. It is the earliest significant public water-works project.

680 BC

- King Esarhaddon of Assyria, who has married a Babylonian wife, rebuilds Babylon despite local opposition (it was destroyed by his father Sennacherib in 689 BC).

c. 675 BC

- At Tell Jemmeh, Palestine, the first semicircular vaults—an arrangement of arches that form a ceiling—are used.

Arts

c. 700 BC

- Tables begin to be made out of wood in Egypt, out of metal in Assyria, and out of bronze in Greece. The legs are often carved in animal shapes.

673 BC

- An Assyrian monument is erected claiming that King Esarhaddon of Assyria deprived Baal (chief god) of the Phoenician city of Tyre of all his possessions. The work clearly shows a degree of wishful thinking.

668 BC

- The scenes of royal lion hunts decorating the palace of Ashurbanipal in Assyria show Assyrian art at its finest, as do other excellent works in bronze and ivory. Military scenes have declined in popularity as the subject of works of art.

BIRTHS & DEATHS

694 BC
- Merodach-Baladan II, king of Babylonia 721 BC–710 BC and 703 BC, who maintained Babylonian independence against superior Assyrian military strength for more than a decade, dies.

c. 690 BC
- Ashurbanipal, last great king of Assyria 668 BC–c. 627 BC, who created, at Nineveh, the first ancient library in the Middle East, born (–c. 627 BC).

681 BC
January Sennacherib, king of Assyria 705 BC–681 BC, who rebuilt the city of Nineveh, dies in Nineveh.

669 BC
- Esarhaddon, king of Assyria 680 BC–669 BC, who conquered Egypt in 671 BC, dies.

652 BC
- Gyges, king of Lydia in Asia Minor 680 BC–c. 652 BC, dies.

c. 630 BC
- Solon, Athenian statesman who replaced the ruling aristocracy with a rule by the wealthy, born (–c. 560 BC).

c. 628 BC
- Zoroaster, Iranian religious leader who founded Zoroastrianism, born in Rhages, Iran.

c. 627 BC
- Ashurbanipal, last great king of Assyria 668 BC–c. 627 BC, dies (c. 63).

624 BC
- Thales of Miletus, Greek philosopher who believed that water was the principal substance of all

matter, and who predicted an eclipse of the sun on May 28, 585 BC, born (–c. 546).

610 BC
- Anaximander, Greek philosopher, cosmologer, astronomer, and geographer, born in Miletus, Asia Minor (–c. 545 BC).
- Psamtik (Psammetichus) I, king of Egypt 664 BC–610 BC, who expelled the Assyrians and began Egypt's 26th dynasty, dies.

609 BC
- Josiah, king of Judah c. 640 BC–609 BC, dies (c. 40).

605 BC
August 16 Nabopolasser, father of Nebuchadnezzar II and founder of the Chaldean Empire, dies.

663 BC

- The stele of Tanutamon, the *Dream Stele*, tells how the Egyptian pharaoh saw two snakes, one on his right and the other on his left. This was interpreted to mean "Upper Egypt belongs to thee; take to thyself Lower Egypt!" This forecast is contradicted by the Assyrian account of the final campaign of the Assyrian king Ashurbanipal in Egypt, which suggests that the Egyptians were defeated.

Literature and Language

648 BC

- Archilochus of Paros, one of the earliest of the Greek lyric poets, is writing at this time. He directs some of his poems at the family who barred him from marrying their daughter, reputedly leading some members of the family to commit suicide.

626 BC

- According to the Old Testament, the Hebrew prophet Jeremiah (credited with writing Lamentations and the Book of Jeremiah) warns his countrymen of a disaster that is about to befall them, in an invective full of phrases that have survived to become part of European literature. His warning refers to the Captivity, in which Jewish deportees are exiled to Babylon. The Hebrew prophets Zephaniah, Nahum, and Habakkuk are also active at this time.

625 BC

- Greek poet and musician Arion reputedly formalizes the *dithyramb*, a song sacred to the Greek god Dionysus, which hitherto has always been improvised. This is thought to be an important step in the development of the tragic chorus.
- Sappho of Lesbos, the famed female Greek lyric poet, is active at this time. Her lyric poems are famous for their depiction of erotic love between women.

c. 625 BC Spartan lyric poet Alcman writes *Partheneia*, choral songs for maidens. Parts of two songs survive to modern times.

Music

676 BC

- Terpander, a Greek lyre-player, wins the prize in the first lyre competition held at Sparta, Greece. He is credited with innovations in lyre design and musical modes, and is said to have written many drinking songs.

Thought and Scholarship

668 BC

- A letter, probably from the Assyrian ruler Ashurbanipal, shows him giving instructions to his agents to send texts to his library.
- At Nineveh, Assyrian king Ashurbanipal begins to assemble the world's first great library. Consisting of thousands of cataloged tablets (over 20,000 still exist) accumulated from temple libraries throughout the Middle East, the collection includes medical treatises (including prescriptions and guides to the diagnosis and treatment of disease), tables of multiplication, lists of plants, astronomical and astrological tables, and a treatise on glassmaking.

SOCIETY

Everyday Life

c. 700 BC

- The Iron Age starts in much of Europe. (In Greece it began much earlier, about 1050 BC, and in Italy about 900 BC. In Britain it is later, about 650 BC.)

650 BC

- The Hallstatt people learn to make use of iron and emerge as the great Iron Age Celtic culture of northern Europe. As trade routes reach them via the Rhône and Danube rivers, so their influence grows. They bury their chiefs in great style, the dead leader lying in his four-wheeled chariot with his weapons around him. They make their swords of iron or from iron models copied in bronze.
- The Late Iron Age is starting in Italy.
- The use of the Roman Forum as a cemetery ceases.

Religion

670 BC

- The oracle of Apollo at Delphi, Greece, has already established a reputation for giving inspiration and the advice of the gods.

608 BC

- Following his victory at the Battle of Megiddo, where he used Ionian mercenaries to overcome King Josiah of Judah, the Egyptian pharaoh Necho II sends a thanks offering to the shrine of Apollo at Miletus, Greece.

Sports

c. 688 BC

- Boxing is introduced to the 23rd Olympic Games in Greece. Boxers wear leather coverings on their hands.

680 BC

- Chariot racing with four horses, quadriga racing, is introduced to the 25th Olympic Games in Greece.

664 BC–656 BC

- Chionis, a Spartan athlete, wins the stade race (192.27 m/630.80 ft long) at three successive Olympic Games in Greece.

648 BC

- Horse races with bareback jockeys are introduced to the 36th Olympic Games in Greece.

632 BC

- Boys' running races and wrestling events are introduced to the 40th Olympic Games in Greece.

600 BC–501 BC

POLITICS, GOVERNMENT, AND ECONOMICS

Business and Economics

595 BC
- Corinth in Greece begins to export its pottery, its skills in manufacturing earthenware having improved greatly.

594 BC
- The Athenian statesman Solon introduces measures to stimulate trade and the economy in Athens, Greece, including encouraging foreign craftsmen to settle there.

560 BC
- Under king Croesus Lydia benefits from being well situated for trade between East and West. The Greek cities on the coast of Asia Minor also benefit so, despite their precarious situation, they find it worthwhile to pay tribute to Croesus.

550 BC
- The Greek city-state of Corinth mints its first coinage.

545 BC
- The Ionian Greek cities of Asia Minor are forced to accept Persian suzerainty, although they retain their freedom to trade so long as they pay tribute. However, the Phocaeans, "pioneer navigators of the Greeks," refuse to submit and flee to Corsica where they reinforce the colony of Alalia (or Aleria).

530 BC
- The Phoenician coastal towns, Sidon now surpassing Tyre, help to provide the Persians with both a merchant fleet and a fighting navy.

510 BC
- The Greek city-state of Athens increases its export trade in pottery at the expense of Corinth.
- *c.* 510 BC   The Persian king Darius I introduces a bimetallic system of coinage to the Persian Empire.

Colonization

***c.* 600 BC**
- Carthage in north Africa, traditionally founded by the Phoenician city of Tyre some 200 years earlier, increases in prosperity and begins to occupy parts of Sicily.

- The colony of Massilia (Marseille in southern France) is founded as a trading post by the Phocaean Greeks.

599 BC
- Syracuse, itself once a colony or city-state founded from the Greek mainland, founds another city in Sicily, Camarina.

580 BC
- Greek colonists found the city of Acragas (Agrigentum) in Sicily. At about the same time Dorian Greeks, under an adventurer called Pentathlus, endeavor to oust the Carthaginians from their northwest corner of the island.

560 BC
- A Phocaean colony is founded at Alalia (or Aleria) in Corsica.

559 BC
- Under the rule of the tyrant Pisistratus, the Athenian aristocrat and general Miltiades the Elder founds an Athenian colony in the Thracian Chersonese, the northern shore of the Hellespont.

550 BC
- Celts from Europe begin to arrive in the British Isles, mainly in Ireland, but also in Scotland and England.

Human Rights

507 BC
- Would-be chief magistrate Cleisthenes' legal constitutional reforms in the Greek city-state of Athens and establishes firmly its particular form of democracy. The four ancient tribes are abolished and replaced by ten new ones, and all citizens are enfranchised with a personal vote in the popular assembly.

Politics and Government

***c.* 600 BC**
- History begins to emerge with some certainty in northern India. Tribes are settling down into either monarchies (primarily in the Ganges plain) or republics (mainly based in the foothills of the Himalayas and the Punjab). The monarchy of Magadha, northwest of modern Calcutta, is gradually coming to the fore.
- The Babylonian king Nebuchadnezzar overreaches himself in Egypt and has to retire to recuperate and reequip his army.
- The future rivals Sparta and Athens in Greece settle into what are to become their defining characteristics: Sparta, the closed military power of the Peloponnese; Athens, the politically free (but no less aggressive) trading and maritime city-state.

- The Athenians undertake their first overseas venture, the capture of Sigeum (a promontory controlling the Hellespont) from their neighbor Megara. The expedition is motivated more by economic than political or military considerations and marks the beginning of Megara's lagging behind in the great rivalry between the various Greek city-states.

599 BC

- King Nebuchadnezzar of Babylon campaigns again and defeats the nomad Arabs of Syria.

598 BC

- King Jehoiakim of Judah, ignoring the warnings of the prophet Jeremiah, allies himself with Egypt. He is removed from the throne by the Babylonian king Nebuchadnezzar and replaced by Jehoichin, who is not much more satisfactory to the Babylonians. In the autumn Nebuchadnezzar advances on Jerusalem, destroying the city of Lachish on the way.

597 BC

- King Nebuchadnezzar of Babylon lays siege to Jerusalem in January and finally captures the city in March. A puppet king, Zedekiah, is installed, while King Jehoiakim and the leading men and artisans of the city are deported into Babylonia. The future prophet Daniel is a child among them. This period (until 538 BC) is known as the "Exile" or "Captivity of the Jews" in Jewish history.

596 BC

- Sparta, by now the most powerful Greek city, arbitrates in the long dispute and war between Athens and Megara over the island of Salamis and decides in Athens' favor.

595 BC

- Pharaoh Necho II of Egypt is succeeded by Psamtik II who continues a defensive policy, except for a foray into Nubia.
- The Amphictyonic League of Anthela, near Thermopylae, intervenes in the first Sacred War to protect pilgrims to the shrine of Apollo at Delphi against the indigenous Phocians. The League is one of the earliest authenticated examples of cooperation among the Greek city-states.
- The Babylonian king Nebuchadnezzar puts down a palace revolt.

594 BC

- In the Greek city-state of Athens, the statesman Solon is appointed archon with unlimited powers. He lays down new laws and a constitution, which end the practice of selling bad debtors into slavery and make a compulsory reduction in all debts. The reforms also include opening the Assembly to the lowest classes, the codification of the law, democratic reforms in the law courts, and a system of appointment to office by the drawing of lots among all citizens.

593 BC–592 BC

- Athenian statesman Solon leaves the Greek city-state of Athens to travel overseas, allowing time for his new laws at home to become accepted. Athens attempts to uphold his laws in his absence, but tends nevertheless toward unrest.

590 BC

- King Cyaxares of the Medes makes war on Lydia.
- Tarquinius Priscus, who traditionally reigns in Rome from 616 BC to 578 BC, has his greatest successes in this decade. He does much to establish Rome as powerful and prosperous, quelling the Sabines and other Latin tribes.

589 BC

- Apries (biblical Hophra) becomes pharaoh of Egypt. He is young and belligerent, attempting to oust the Babylonians from Syria and Palestine and attacking the Greek colony at Cyrene.
- The Greek city-state of Athens has no archon for two years—technically it is in "anarchy," although the state continues to function.

588 BC

- King Zedekiah of Judah rebels against Babylonian domination and the Babylonian army besieges Jerusalem again.
- The Egyptian pharaoh Apries sends a naval expedition up the coast and, for a couple of years, gains control of the Phoenician coastal towns.

587 BC

- The Egyptian pharaoh Apries advances overland into Palestine and King Nebuchadnezzar of Babylon breaks off the siege of Jerusalem to meet the threat. Apries is forced to retire ignominiously, once more proving that Egypt is a hollow threat so far as the Jews are concerned.

586 BC

- King Nebuchadnezzar of Babylon resumes the siege of Jerusalem in response to King Zedekiah's rebellion against Babylonian rule, and the city falls—this time it is completely destroyed. This is the end of Judah as a nation, 136 years after the end of Israel. King Zedekiah of Judah flees but is captured at Jericho, and has to witness the death of his sons before being blinded.
- The Babylonian king Nebuchadnezzar lays siege to the Phoenician city of Tyre, eventually taking the city 13 years later. The Phoenician city of Sidon, however, falls immediately.
- The Temple of Jerusalem is destroyed by the occupying Babylonian forces.

585 BC

- Peace between the Medes and Lydia is sealed by a royal marriage with Babylonian help.

584 BC

- In the Greek city-state of Athens, the archon Damasias attempts to convert his office into a tyranny but fails after two years.

580 BC

- Little is known of the last 20 years of King Nebuchadnezzar of Babylon's reign. The Bible says that he goes mad, but his own inscriptions refer to a four-year suspension of interest in public affairs.
- Regional rivalry exists in the Greek city-state of Athens between the "Men of the Plain" and the "Men of the Coast."

578 BC

- Servius Tullius becomes king of Rome. He reigns for 43 years and organizes Rome as a soldier state, dividing all citizens into "classes" according to their material worth. Taxation is based on these classes as is a citizen's role in the army.

575 BC

- Alyattes, king of Lydia, remains unmolested by the Medes and has a prosperous reign. He also brings a long war with the Ionian cities to an end. In Miletus, a particularly fierce opponent, he builds two temples to the goddess Athena.

573 BC

- The Phoenician city of Tyre submits to King Nebuchadnezzar of Babylon after 13 years under siege.

571 BC

- Athenian statesman Solon returns to the Greek city-state of Athens from his travels and stirs up enthusiasm for a final effort to win the island of Salamis from Megara, the city-state between Athens and Corinth.

570 BC

- The Egyptian pharaoh Apries tries to help the Libyans to destroy the Greek city of Cyrene in north Africa but fails and is deposed by the army, which mutinies. After a short civil war, Ahmose II, an Egyptian army general, is elected king of Egypt. Egypt prospers under his reign, during which he marries a Cyrenean, develops the delta town of Naucratis as a (mainly Greek) port, and acquires a reputation for being philhellenic.
- The Greek city-state of Athens finally succeeds in winning the island of Salamis from Megara, the city-state between Athens and Corinth. The young politician Pisistratus makes his name on the expedition.
- The Sicilian Phalaris becomes tyrant of the Greek city of Acragas in Sicily and is reputed to have gained control, by his ruthless cruelty, of most of the island.
- *c.* 570 BC Athenian statesman Solon introduces a new system of weights and measures along with the first Greek coins. He forbids the export of all produce except olive oil because so much food has been exported that people are starving. He also institutes the first land reform when he abolishes the debt system whereby peasants mortgage their land and work as tenant-laborers for their creditors.

568 BC

- The Egyptian pharaoh Ahmose II has a skirmish with Babylonian forces. However, neither King Nebuchadnezzar nor his successors seem to have seriously contemplated a full-scale conquest of Egypt.

562 BC

- King Nebuchadnezzar of Babylon dies and is succeeded by Amelmarduk, who is said to have ruled without law or restraint. He shows mercy to King Jehoiakim of Judah, however, releasing him from prison and inviting him to dine at the king's own table.

561 BC

- In the Greek city-state of Athens, Pisistratus, hero of the victory over Megara, the city-state between Athens and Corinth, at Salamis, displays self-inflicted wounds, saying he has been attacked by enemies hostile to both him and the people. He is granted a bodyguard for his protection, which he later uses as a personal force in his bid for power.

560 BC

- Croesus becomes king of Lydia and reigns for 14 years. He embarks upon a policy of expansion, and becomes a byword for great wealth, extending his power along the coast of the Black Sea as far as the mouth of the River Halys.
- Pisistratus becomes tyrant of the Greek city-state of Athens.

559 BC

- Cyrus becomes king of Anshan, a southern province of what later will become Persia.
- Neriglissar succeeds to or possibly usurps the Babylonian throne, having won the hand of Nebuchadnezzar's daughter.

557 BC

- King Neriglissar of Babylon campaigns in Cilicia to defend this part of his empire.

556 BC

- King Nabonidus of Babylon makes a pact against the Medes with King Cyrus of Anshan.
- Neriglissar's son is deposed after only three months on the throne of Babylon by the last of the Chaldean or Neo-Babylonian kings, Nabonidus, a Syrian. The Medes take the opportunity to seize and hold northern Syria and the old Assyrian fortress of Harran.
- Pisistratus, the tyrant of the Greek city-state of Athens, is ousted and forced into exile.

555 BC

- The Babylonian king Nabonidus besieges the city of Harran, held by the Medes.

554 BC

- King Nabonidus of Babylon falls ill while advancing into the Lebanon, and Belshazzar is made regent.
- Phalaris, the cruel tyrant of Acragas in Sicily, is overthrown in a popular rising led by Telemachus and is killed.

553 BC

- King Cyrus of Anshan begins his three-year struggle against King Astyages of the Medes. King Nabonidus of Babylon, apparently not realizing the danger Cyrus poses, marches south on an expedition against Teima, and stays there for up to 20 years, apparently trying to form a new capital city in a safe spot. Babylon is left in the care of the regent Belshazzar.

550 BC

- King Cyrus of Anshan wins the Median throne and spends the next two years consolidating his position as king of the Medes, southwest of the Caspian Sea, and Persians.
- Rome's second Etruscan king, Servius Tullius, achieves his greatest political successes in this decade. He begins an alliance with his neighbors in the shape of a Latin League, while at home he is reputed to have given a modicum of power to the assembly of the plebeians, set up in addition to the existing senate of elders which advises the king.
- The Babylonian Empire, having been powerful for little more than half a century, steadily declines during this decade. Prince Belshazzar is in Babylon while King Nabonidus tries to make Teima his new capital.

c. 550 BC The ousted tyrant Pisistratus returns to the Greek city-state of Athens but is forced into exile again almost at once. He improves the city's water supply by building an aqueduct to the main marketplace. He also institutes an agricultural tax, encourages the growth of olive trees and vines as cash crops, and makes loans to farmers for tools and equipment.

547 BC

- King Cyrus of Persia, ready for expansion, crosses the River Tigris and reaches the River Halys in Asia Minor where he fights an inconclusive battle with King Croesus of Lydia.

546 BC

- King Croesus of Lydia retires to his capital, Sardis, for the winter and sends for help against Persia from Egypt, Sparta, and Babylon. However, King Cyrus of Persia follows rapidly and Sardis falls; Croesus is probably spared.

541 BC

- King Cyrus of Persia becomes master of Syria by bribery and propaganda rather than fighting.

540 BC

- During this period King Cyrus of Persia begins to create the most efficient empire to date and brings relative peace to the Middle East which has spent so long embroiled in war.
- King Bimbisara rises to power in the Ganges kingdom of Magadha, India, controlling trade with the delta ports and building roads.
- King Cyrus of Persia defeats the Bedouin sheikhs around Teima. King Nabonidus of Babylon is forced to leave his new capital and to face Cyrus along the protective wall that Nebuchadnezzar built, but is defeated.
- The exiled tyrant Pisistratus returns to the Greek city-state of Athens once more and remains tyrant until his death in 527 BC. His tyranny is remarkable for his respect for law and constitutional procedure, and his encouragement of agriculture and trade.

539 BC

- According to the Bible, the prophet Daniel manages to remain popular and retain high office after Persia takes over from the Chaldeans in Babylon.
- Rebellion has broken out in Babylon. The Greek account speaks of feasting, while the Bible (Daniel 5) tells the tale of the writing on the wall, read by the prophet Daniel. The Euphrates River is partially diverted and King Cyrus of Persia's army achieves an easy victory over Babylon.

October 29   King Cyrus of Persia triumphantly enters Babylon. The Persian Empire takes over from the short-lived Neo-Babylonian Empire and absorbs the kingdom of the Medes.

538 BC

- King Cyrus of Persia occupies Jerusalem and allows all the Jews in Babylon who wish to do so to return to their native land.

535 BC

- The Carthaginians, allied on this occasion with the Etruscans, defeat the Greek Phocaeans in a naval battle off the coast of their Corsican colony Alalia (or Aleria), which is subsequently abandoned. The victory gives Carthage command of the western Mediterranean and the ability to close the Straits of Gibraltar. The merchants of Tartessus in Spain are badly hit and the city now declines in prosperity. At the same time the Greeks leave Spain.

c. 535 BC Polycrates becomes tyrant of Samos, defying Persia, allying himself with Egypt, and building up a fleet of 100 ships. In 525 BC, however, he abandons Egypt and aids the Persians in their invasion of Egypt, sending 40 ships.

534 BC

- The last of Rome's kings, Tarquinius Superbus ("the Proud" or "Arrogant"), traditionally accedes to the throne. He sets the tone of his 24-year reign by putting to death many senators and revoking his predecessor's concessions to the plebeians. Roman territory is extended during his reign.

533 BC

- King Cyrus of Persia crosses the Hindu Kush mountains (in modern Afghanistan) and receives tribute from the Indian cities of the Indus valley. The Greek historian Herodotus says he forms his twentieth satrapy (administrative district) of Gandhara there.

529 BC

- King Cyrus of Persia is killed leading an expedition against the Massagetae, an Asiatic people from around the Sea of Aral. His son Cambyses becomes king of Persia. The Persian Empire has now been firmly established, and this is considered to be its foundation date.

527 BC

- Hippias and Hipparchus, sons of the late Pisistratus, continue his tyranny in the Greek city-state of Athens.
- The Greek cities of Magna Graecia in southern Italy are indulging in a self-destructive rivalry that makes their influence in Italian history minimal. At this time, the cities of Sybaris and Croton combine to suppress Siris, although later they turn on one another.

526 BC

- Dynastic troubles in Persia result in the death of King Cambyses' brother Smerdis (or Bardiya).
- Egyptian pharaoh Ahmose II is succeeded by Psamtik III, last king of Egypt's 26th dynasty, who fails to stop the Persian invasion and is executed for treason the following year.

525 BC

- During his three-year stay in Egypt, King Cambyses of Persia meets successive failures: expeditions into the western desert and into Ethiopia fail, and his Phoenician sailors refuse to fight against their compatriots the Carthaginians. Cambyses' anger is said to have driven him mad.
- King Cambyses II of Persia invades Egypt, wins the stubbornly fought Battle of Pelusium, and besieges Memphis. Egypt passes into the Persian Empire under Persian kings who form the 27th dynasty.
- The tyrant Polycrates of Samos fails to come to Egypt's aid when it is attacked by the Persians. Instead, he sends a fleet to aid the Persians, which he sabotages by manning it with men who hate him. This fleet turns back and attempts a revolution. It receives Spartan and Corinthian aid but fails.

524 BC

- The Etruscans attack the Greek city of Cumae in Campania, which had remained neutral when the Etruscan and Carthaginian forces attacked the Phocaeans off Alalia in Corsica in 535 BC. The Etruscans are defeated by King Aristodemus of Cumae.

522 BC

- King Cambyses of Persia dies in Syria while traveling home to put down a usurper to the throne.
- Polycrates, the tyrant of Samos, is lured to the Greek mainland, captured by the Persians, and crucified.

521 BC

- After dynastic trouble, Darius I becomes king of Persia. There are revolts in Babylon and other parts of the Persian Empire.

520 BC

- King Tarquinius Superbus makes Rome the undisputed head of the Latin League. He uses a combination of guile, military power, and diplomatic marriage.

519 BC

- King Darius of Persia has to put down a second revolt in Babylon and crushes all resistance.

518 BC

- King Darius of Persia visits Egypt, at the time a province of Persia, and orders the priests and wise men to undertake a codification of Egyptian law, a task which takes some 15 years to complete.

517 BC

- King Darius of Persia puts down the revolt in Babylon.

514 BC

- There is a conspiracy against the tyrants Hipparchus and Hippias in the Greek city-state of Athens, led by Harmodius and Aristogeiton. It fails, although Hipparchus is killed, and the tyranny under Hippias becomes even harsher.

512 BC

- To protect his empire from potential enemies beyond the Bosporus, King Darius of Persia invades Thrace with the help of conscripts from the Greek cities of Asia Minor. Thrace and Macedon acknowledge Persian overlordship. He also crosses the River Danube and manages to impress the Scythians.

511 BC

- Aristagoras becomes governor of the Greek city-state of Miletus under the Persians.
- The Alcmaeonidae seek the help of King Cleomenes of Sparta to oust the tyrant Hippias in the Greek city-state of Athens.

510 BC

- In Magna Graecia (the Greek colonies in Italy), the city of Croton finally defeats and destroys Sybaris with the help of Dorieus, a younger half brother of Cleomenes, king of Sparta. Doreius then goes on to fight the Carthaginians in Sicily.
- King Cleomenes of Sparta helps the Athenians oust the tyrant Hippias, the son of Pisistratus, and the period of "tyranny" in Athens ends. In return, Athens is forced to join Sparta's Peloponnesian League.
- The king of Rome Tarquinius Superbus is expelled from Rome, apparently because of the misconduct of his son,

who rapes a Roman noblewoman, Lucretia. She commits suicide, causing her menfolk to swear vengeance. Stories tell of the struggle to prevent his return, including the fight on a bridge into Rome between Lars Porsena, king of Clusium, and Horatius Cocles, who single-handedly holds off the army of Lars Porsena before escaping into the river. Mucius, priest of Rome, fails in his attempt to kill Lars Porsena, and earns his family name of Scaevola (the left-handed) when he holds his right hand in a fire to show his captors that he can endure torture.

509 BC

- After the expulsion of King Tarquinius Superbus, the Romans draw up a republican constitution. The system of an annual twin consulate is established along with the twin office of quaestors as financial and legal officers.

508 BC

- Carthage and Rome make a treaty under which Roman ships undertake not to trade westward of Carthage and the Carthaginians undertake not to interfere on Latin soil.
- The exiled king of Rome, Tarquinius Superbus, fights the indecisive Battle of Silva Arsia against the Romans, with the help of the Etruscan people of Veii, and fails to win back his throne. He allies himself with the Etruscan Lars Porsena, king of Clusium.

507 BC

- Cleisthenes (a member of the noble Alcmaeonidae family and grandson of Cleisthenes of Sicyon) rises to power in the Greek city-state of Athens as a champion of the ideas of the earlier statesman Solon. Cleomenes of Sparta attempts to interfere but is forced off.
- Lars Porsena, the Etruscan king of Clusium, marches on Rome and besieges it. It is probable that he captures the city, but his stay there is brief.

506 BC

- Cleomenes of Sparta organizes a full-scale Peloponnesian invasion of Attica. However, the city-state of Corinth withdraws support and the plan collapses. Athens demonstrates its new-found power by defeating the Boeotians and Chalcidians.
- While Lars Porsena, king of Clusium, is in Rome, the other Latin allies are encouraged to break free from Etruscan domination, and defeat the Etruscan forces at the Battle of Aricia with the help of King Aristodemus of the Greek city of Cumae in Campania.

505 BC

- The ex-king of Rome, Tarquinius Superbus, although by now in exile, issues an edict forbidding Roman citizens to use iron weapons.

501 BC

- The Chinese sage Confucius is made governor of the city of Zhongdu and institutes practical reforms.

SCIENCE, TECHNOLOGY, AND MEDICINE

Agriculture

c. 600 BC
- The Phoenicians introduce the grape into France.

Ecology

c. 538 BC
- Most of the city of Babylon is destroyed by fire.

Exploration

c. 570 BC
- Greek philosopher Anaximander produces the first geographical map of the world. He is also the first thinker to develop a cosmology based on systematic observation and rational principles—he does not believe that the earth is supported on the backs of turtles.

c. 515 BC
- The Persian king Darius I sends Scylax of Caria to sail down the River Indus and explore the ocean from the Indian Ocean to the Red Sea. In so doing he establishes a sea route between India and Persia.

Health and Medicine

c. 600 BC
- The Phoenicians make soap from wood ashes and goats' tallow.

c. 550 BC
- A document from Mohenjo Daro, in the Indus valley, describes the use of 960 medicinal plants and includes information on anatomy, physiology, pathology, and obstetrics.

Math

575 BC
- Greek philosopher Thales is the first to give a purely natural explanation for the origin of the earth. He tries to use Babylonian mathematical knowledge to solve practical problems such as the determination of the distance of ships from the shore.

530 BC
- Pythagoras of Samos, scientist and philosopher, moves to Croton and starts researching and teaching theories of mathematics, geometry, music, and reincarnation. A mystic as well as a mathematician, he argues that the key to the universe lies in numbers, while preaching immortality and the transmigration of souls. He founds a brotherhood in Croton which is to remain influential for several generations. His work leads to a number of important results, including the Pythagorean theorem of right triangles and the discovery of irrational numbers (those that cannot be represented by fractions).

Science

c. 600 BC
- Roman king Tarquinius Priscus introduces the Roman Republican calendar. It consists of 12 months with a total of 355 days. An intercalated month is added between February 23 and 24 every two years in order to keep step with the seasons. Intercalations, however, are made irregularly and it becomes hopelessly confused. The calendar forms the basis of the Gregorian calendar.

587 BC
- The Babylonians introduce their calendar to Jerusalem after their conquest of the city. It provides the Jews with a finite calendar with a New Year's day. The Babylonian names continue to be used.

585 BC
May 28 The Greek philosopher Thales of Miletus, pioneer of Greek rational thinking, correctly predicts the eclipse of the sun.

c. 560 BC
- The Greek philosopher Xenophanes correctly recognizes the nature of fossils when he suggests that fossil seashells are the result of a great flood that buried them in the mud.

c. 530 BC
- Pythagoras of Samos proposes the notion of a spherical earth.

510 BC
- Greek geographers are influenced by the building of the Royal Road by the Persians under Darius; on contemporary Greek maps it is presented with the same importance as the equator on modern maps.

Technology

c. 600 BC
- Bronze begins to be replaced by iron in central Europe because of the growing ability to smelt and work metallic ores at high temperatures.
- Iron is introduced in China, although bronze remains the standard metal for weapons at least until about 200 BC (the early Han period).
- The plow begins to be used in India.

c. 590 BC
- The Greeks discover iron-welding.

c. 535 BC
- Polycrates, the tyrant of Samos, employs Eupalinus of Megara to build the Samos Tunnel, an aqueduct 2 m/ 6 ft in diameter and more than 1,000 m/3,300 ft long. Drilled simultaneously from both ends through solid rock by slaves using hammers and chisels, it brings water from the far side of Mt. Castros to Samos' capital city.

Transportation

600 BC–c. 400 BC

- During this period the Zhou dynasty in China classifies roads into five grades: paths for people on foot and pack animals; roads for narrow-gauge vehicles; roads for larger vehicles; roads where single vehicles can pass each other; and highways that can take three wagons abreast. A highways commissioner with a separate budget is appointed, and the volume of traffic necessitates imposing prohibitions against reckless driving, and traffic regulations for busy intersections. A uniform wheel-size is also instituted.

559 BC–c. 350 BC

- Persian emperors build a network of roads to maintain swift communications with provincial administrators, making them the first empire-builders to see the importance of organizing transport. Tracks are leveled and partly paved and policed by guards at rest houses every 24 km/15 mi. Most significantly, they construct the great Royal Road, running from Sardis in Asia Minor to the capital Susa, north of the Persian Gulf, 2,600 km/1,600 mi away and a journey of three months on foot.

c. 510 BC

- The Persian king Darius I completes the canal from the Nile to the Red Sea begun by Necho II.

ARTS AND IDEAS

Architecture

590 BC

- Roman king Tarquinius Priscus builds a wall around Rome and also lays down its drainage system.
- The kings of Etruria, renowned as great builders, are thought to have introduced the arch into Roman architecture.
- c. 590 BC The *Cloaca Maxima* ("great sewer") is built in Rome by lining an existing stream bed with stone during the reign of Tarquinius Priscus, giving the city a central drainage and sewage system. Originally an open channel, it is vaulted and enclosed in the 3rd century BC.

565 BC

- King Nebuchadnezzar builds a defensive wall north of Babylon, presumably against his one-time ally, the Medes. Shortly afterwards he also constructs the Hanging Gardens of Babylon, one of the Seven Wonders of the World. Babylon at this time contains 53 temples, 55 shrines, and 372 altars.

C. 550 BC

- Lydian king Croesus builds the Temple of Artemis at Ephesus. One of the Seven Wonders of the World, it is known for its great size, being 110 m/350 ft by 55 m/180 ft.

548 BC

- The reconstruction of the sanctuary of Apollo at Delphi, Greece, begins, following its destruction by fire. Most

Greek cities send contributions to support the project, but the main sponsor is the noble Alcmaeonidae family of Athens.

540 BC

- Greek architect Eupalinos constructs an aqueduct on Samos for the tyrant Polycrates, which includes a 1 km/0.6 mi long tunnel, with a cross-section of 1.8 m/6 ft by 1.8 m/6 ft.
- Polycrates, the tyrant of Samos, builds a temple to Hera, Greek goddess of women and marriage, on his island, Samos.

537 BC

- Zerubbabal, governor of Judah, begins the restoration of the Temple of Jerusalem.

529 BC

- Following the death of King Cyrus of Persia, his tomb is erected in white marble at Pasargadae, the new city that Cyrus built in Persia.

521 BC

- The reconstruction of the Temple of Jerusalem is resumed after a temporary halt, and it is completed within five years.

520 BC

- The king of Rome Tarquinius Superbus uses the spoils of war to begin building the famous Capitol of Rome.

c. 518 BC

- Qanats (long underground aqueducts) begin to be built in Egypt.

c. 510 BC

- The temple of the virgin goddess Aphaea is built on the island of Aegina. It is famed for its sculptures, which in modern times are held in Munich, Germany.

Arts

c. 600 BC–c. 480 BC

- The Greek Archaic period of sculpture is evident, a typical form being the *kouros*, a rigid freestanding nude.

595 BC

- Near-Eastern motifs and subjects are influencing Greek art at this time, especially in Corinth.

566 BC

- The Panathenaea festival is depicted on friezes in the Parthenon, Athens.

540 BC

- The production of Athenian black-figure pottery is at its peak. The names of some potters and painters of the period, such as Nearchus, his son Tleson, and Execias, survive to modern times.

c. 530 BC

- The golden age of Athenian vase pottery begins, in which the pottery is distinguished by red figures, left in the natural color of the clay, on black. The Greek vase painters Euphronius and Euthymides are working at this time.

519 BC

- King Darius I the Great of Persia inscribes an account of his early successes on the great rock face of Behistun,

Persia, on the Ecbatana to Babylon road. The monument features a relief and a trilingual inscription in Old Persian, Elamite (a Persian dialect), and Babylonian.

510 BC

- Statues are erected in Athens in honor of the tyrant-slayers Harmodius and Aristogeiton, who conspired to murder Hippias and Hipparchus, the tyrants, in 514 BC.

Literature and Language

c. 600 BC

- Greek lyric poet Alcaeus of Mytilene, Lesbos, is active, writing poetry covering a wide range of subjects, from politics and war to love and wine.

566 BC

- Eusebius of Cyrene reputedly writes *Telegonia*, the final poem in the epic cycle of the Trojan War.

550 BC

- A contemporary belief suggests that Aesop, author of Greek fables, is active, but it is likely that Aesop is a legendary character.
- *c. 550 BC Phocylides*, a gnomic poem often attributed to Phocylides, is written in Miletus.
- 550 BC–540 BC Greek elegaic poet Theognis of Megara is reputedly active, though there is evidence to suggest that he may have worked much earlier. At least 308 genuine verses survive to modern times.

c. 540 BC

- Athenian tyrant Pisistratus has Homer's *Iliad* and *Odyssey* recorded.

522 BC

- Following the murder of Polycrates, tyrant of Samos, Greek poet Anacreon of Teos flees Samos to join the court of the Athenian tyrant Pisistratus. Anacreon's witty, urbane poetry deals with wine and love (heterosexual and homosexual), and continues to attract imitators for centuries.

Music

586 BC

- Greek flute-player Sakadas of Argos performs a solo flute piece unaccompanied by voice at the Pythian festival held at Delphi, Greece. He sets a tend toward virtuoso instrumental performances.

Theater and Dance

511 BC

- Athenian tragedian Phrynichus, reputedly the first poet to introduce female characters into tragedies, wins his first competition at Athens, Greece.

Thought and Scholarship

c. 570 BC

- Greek philosopher Anaximander argues that life evolved from the sea, and that land animals are

descendants of sea animals—the first evolutionary theory.
- Greek astronomer and philosopher Anaximander of Miletus continues the work of the Greek philosopher Thales of Miletus and his speculation on ultimate reality, in *On the Nature of Things*.

540 BC

- Greek astronomer and philosopher Anaximenes of Miletus, who studies cosmogony, the study of the origins of the universe, is active.
- Greek poet and philosopher Xenophanes is active. He opposes anthropomorphism (the attribution of human form to deities), instead formulating the idea of a cosmic god.
- *c. 540 BC* Greek philosopher of nature Anaximenes suggests that air is the origin of all things and that condensation and rarefaction play a part in the making of the world. His thought is part way between mythology and science, and influences the development of scientific thought.

530 BC

- Chinese philosopher Confucius marries, and enters into the service of the Duke of Lu.
- Theano, wife of the Greek philosopher and mathematician Pythagoras, reputedly makes her own contribution to philosophical writing.

517 BC

- Chinese philosophers Confucius and Lao Zi (Lao Tzu) reputedly meet. Lao Zi, who is credited with *Tao Te Ching/The Book of the World Law and its Power*, may be a mythical founder figure, invented to support the philosophy of Taoism.

SOCIETY

Everyday Life

c. 600 BC

- Babylonian king Nebuchadnezzar begins building the Hanging Gardens of Babylon. One of the Seven Wonders of the World, the gardens, located on terraces on a ziggurat, are irrigated by pumps from the River Euphrates.
- *c. 600 BC–c. 500 BC* The Late Hallstatt period unfolds in Europe. Important sites include the Heuneberg, Baden-Württemberg, Germany, a defended hillfort; the Magdalensberg, Baden-Württemberg, the largest prehistoric burial mound in Europe; and Mont Lassois and the associated burial mound of Vix, France, where the Vix Crater was found—a large bronze vessel for mixing wine, imported from the Greek Mediterranean.

550 BC

- The Hallstatt Iron Age culture spreads throughout northwestern Europe, taking with it its distinctive modes of decoration and skill in making weapons.

520 BC

- Great riches are placed in the tomb of a princess at Vix, France, including a massive wine-mixing bowl from

Greece. This illustrates not only the wealth of Celtic chiefs, but also their desire for objects from the classical world, in particular those connected with wine. Heuneberg, an elaborate contemporary Iron Age fort on the River Danube, also imports Greek drinking vessels.

Religion

c. 600 BC
- The commonest sacrifice among the people of the emerging Indian kingdoms at this time is the horse.

595 BC
- The Greek Sacred War to protect pilgrims to the shrine of Apollo at Delphi earns Cleisthenes of Sicyon lasting fame. He marries his daughter into the aristocratic Athenian Alcmaeonidae family, and through that line his grandson is the radical politician Cleisthenes.

592 BC–580 BC
- Hebrew prophet Ezekiel reputedly begins to make prophecies while in Babylonian captivity at the hands of Nebuchadnezzar, king of Babylonia. His later prophecies relate to the Jews' captivity in Babylon, and see Nebuchadnezzar as a divine instrument of chastisement. Nevertheless, he promises that the Jews will be restored to their homeland

586 BC
- The oracle at Delphi, Greece, grows in importance under the management of the Amphictyonic League (of delegates from a number of Greek states).

581 BC
- Greek historian Herodotus recounts the legend which suggests that King Cyrus of Persia is the son of a Persian noble and the daughter of Astyages, king of the Medes. According to the legend, a prophecy causes Astyages to order the death of Cyrus, who is saved and reared by a peasant.

580 BC
- The biblical Book of Daniel (written about 165 BC) tells of Daniel's heroic deeds around this time; no other contemporary account of the Jewish captivity in Babylon has survived.

c. 569 BC
- Indian sage Mahavira takes up the ascetic life, renounces his family, and spends the next 12 years wandering India and developing the doctrine of *ahimsa*, or nonviolence, after which he reorganizes Jaina doctrine, founding Jainism.

554 BC
- Syrian king of Babylon, Nabonidus, restores the temple of the moon god at Harran, Assyria, which was destroyed by the Median people. In doing so, he affronts the priests in Babylon, who disapprove of his unorthodox religious predilections.

c. 550 BC
- Kings I and II of the Old Testament are reputedly completed.

542 BC
- Siddhartha Gautama (later Gautama Buddha) marries. At this time he is living the privileged life of a minor Bengal prince.

540 BC
- Athenian tyrant Pisistratus encourages religious festivals such as the greater Dionysia, the festival of the god Dionysus at the end of March. Under his administration new buildings are constructed in the Agora to develop its role as a civic center.
c. 540 BC Athens, under its tyrant Pisistratus, takes over the Ionian religious festival on the sacred island of Delos.

538 BC
- Hebrew prophet Isaiah sees hope for the Jews in their restoration to their homeland by King Cyrus of Persia.

534 BC
- The king of Rome Tarquinius Superbus reputedly builds a temple for Juno, the Roman principal goddess, in Rome.

530 BC
- Siddhartha Gautama (later Gautama Buddha) leaves his life as a Bengal prince at the age of 30, and becomes an ascetic.

c. 525 BC
- Chronicles I and II of the Old Testament are reputedly written.

524 BC
- Siddhartha Gautama (later Gautama Buddha) is said to abandon his life of strict asceticism when he sits under the famous Bo tree at Benares, India, and has a vision which reveals to him what he must teach. He becomes the Buddha and he and his disciples spend the next 40 years or so teaching by word of mouth.

522 BC
- According to the Greek historian Herodotus, King Cambyses of Persia acquires an evil reputation in Egypt by the time of his death because of his destruction of Egyptian temples and disregard for the religion there. Various Egyptian documents, however, suggest that Cambyses succeeds in conciliating the Egyptian élite.

520 BC
- The Sibyl, one of many prophetic priestesses, offers to sell the Sibylline Books, a collection of prophecies, to the king of Rome Tarquinius Superbus. He initially refuses to pay the price of 300 pieces of gold, and only after the Sibyl has burned most of them does he realize their worth. He purchases the remaining books for the original price. They are consulted by the Roman senate in times of crisis, the last known occasion being in AD 363.

509 BC
- This is the traditional date for the building of the temple of Jupiter Optimus Maximus temple on the Roman Capitol.

Sports

582 BC
- At the Isthmus of Corinth, a local festival is expanded into a Panhellenic festival modeled on the Olympic Games, with athletic and equestrian competitions, and musical and poetry contests. It is held every two years.
- The Pythian Games are inaugurated at Delphi, Greece. In the cycle of the four Panhellenic festivals, the Pythian

Games are eventually held in the third year of each Olympiad.

573 BC

- The Nemean Games, in the valley of Nemea in Argos, are reorganized as a Panhellenic festival with athletic and equestrian competition and musical and poetry contests. They take place every two years, two months after the Isthmian Games.

572 BC

- Control of the Olympian festival passes to the Elians (of the city-state of Elis in the northwestern Peloponnese). The games and festival are assuming great importance in the Greek world.

566 BC

- The Panathenaea, the greatest of the Greek local festivals, is inaugurated at Athens. Held every year in summer with an even grander celebration (the Greater Panathenaea) every four years, it includes athletic and equestrian events, and musical, dancing, and poetry contests.

536 BC–516 BC

- Milon (or Milo) of Croton, the most famous wrestler in the history of the ancient Olympic Games in Greece, wins Olympic titles in six successive games.

520 BC

- Running races in armor, called *hoplitodromos*, are introduced to the Olympic Games in Greece.

BIRTHS & DEATHS

599 BC
- Mahavira (real name Vardhamana), one of the 24 Tirthankaras (founders of Jainism) and Jaina monastic reformer, born in Ksatriyakundagrama, India (–527 BC).

598 BC
- Jehoiakim (or Joakim), king of Judah c. 609 BC–598 BC, son of King Josiah, dies.

595 BC
- Necho II, king of Egypt 610 BC–595 BC who sponsored the first known circumnavigation of Africa, dies.

582 BC
- Anacreon, Greek lyric poet of whose work only fragments survive, born in Teos, Ionia (now Sighajik, Turkey) (–c. 485 BC).

c. 581 BC
- Cyrus the Elder ("Cyrus the Great"), Persian emperor who founded the Achaemenid empire which stretched from the Indus River to the Aegean, born in Media Orpersis (–c. 529 BC).

c. 570 BC
- Cleithenes of Athens, statesman and magistrate of Athens 525 BC–524 BC, who founded Athenian democracy, born (–c. 508 BC).

563 BC
- Gautama Buddha (Siddhartha Gautama), Indian philosopher and founder of Buddhism, born in Kapilavastu, India (–c. 483 BC).

c. 562 BC
- Nebuchadnezzar II, second king of the Chaldean dynasty of Babylonia c. 605 BC–c. 561 BC, dies (c. 69).

c. 560 BC
- Solon, Athenian statesman who replaced the ruling aristocracy with a rule by the wealthy, dies (c. 70).
- Xenophanes, Greek poet and philosopher, born in Colophon, Ionia (–c. 478 BC).

c. 556 BC
- Simonides of Ceos, lyric poet and epigrammatist, probably the originator of the epinicion (ode in honor of victors in the Olympic Games), born in Iulis, Ceos, Greece (–c. 468 BC).

554 BC
- Phalaris, tyrant of Acragas (modern Agrigento), Sicily, notorious for his cruelty, dies.

551 BC
- Zoroaster, Iranian religious leader who founded Zoroastrianism, dies (c. 77).
- Confucius (Chinese: K'ung-fu-tzu, or Pinyin: Kongfuzi), celebrated Chinese philosopher and political theorist, born in Ch'u-fu, Lu, now in Shantung Province, China (–479 BC).

546 BC
- Thales of Miletus, Greek philosopher who believed that water was the principal substance of all matter, and who predicted an eclipse of the sun on 28 May 585 BC, dies

545 BC
- Anaximander, Greek philosopher, cosmologer, astronomer, and geographer, dies (63).

529 BC
- King Cyrus II the Great of Persia, who founded the Persian Achaemenid Empire, dies (c. 52).

527 BC
- Mahavira (real name Vardhamana), one of the 24 Tirthankaras (founders of Jainism) and Jaina monastic reformer, dies in Pavapuri, India (c. 72).
- Peisistratus, tyrant of Athens who unified Attica and helped make Athens the dominant city in ancient Greece, dies.

526 BC
- Ahmose II, king of Egypt 570 BC–526 BC, dies.

c. 525 BC
- Aeschylus, first Athenian tragic dramatist, born (–c. 456).

c. 524 BC
- Themistocles, Greek naval commander who made Athens a sea power and defended Greece from the Persians at the Battle of Salamis, born (–c. 449 BC).

522 BC
- Cambyses II, Achaemenid king of Persia 529 BC–522 BC, conqueror of Egypt (525 BC), eldest son of King Cyrus of Persia, dies in Syria.
- Pindar, ancient Greek poet noted for his odes celebrating victories in various athletic events, born in Cynoscephalae, Boeotia, Greece (–446 BC).
- Polycrates, tyrant (535 BC–522 BC) of Samos, whose navy dominated the Aegean during the 6th century BC, is crucified.

c. 519 BC
- Xerxes I, king of Persia 486 BC–465 BC), who invaded Greece, born in Persia (–465 BC).

c. 515 BC
- Parmenides, Greek philosopher, founder of Eliaticism, born (–c. 440 BC).

c. 510 BC
- Cimon, Athenian statesman who was instrumental in building the Athenian empire after the Greco-Persian Wars, born (–451 BC).

c. 508 BC
- Cleithenes of Athens, statesman and magistrate of Athens 525 BC–52 BC), who founded Athenian democracy, dies (c. 62).

500 BC–451 BC

POLITICS, GOVERNMENT, AND ECONOMICS

Business and Economics

c. **500 BC**
- Salt trading begins in the Midland region of England and the Severn valley.
- *c.* 500 BC–*c.* 400 BC Roman trade—never much of a concern to the landed aristocracy—begins to decline during the 5th century BC, and remains insubstantial for the next 200 years.

459 BC
- Athens launches an expedition to Egypt to help the pharaoh Inaros revolt against the Persians. The prospects of increasing their trade, as much as the desire to attack Persian interests, motivate the Athenians in this venture.

457 BC
- The Peloponnesian city of Aegina, on being forced to join the Delian League, is assessed, with the island of Thasos, for a yearly contribution of some 30 talents (money).

Colonization

495 BC
- A Latin colony is founded at Signia commanding the Trerus valley southeast of Rome, in territory disputed with the tribe of the Volsci. Diminishing Etruscan power in the area of Latium has tempted the Volsci to move into the rich farmland of Latium, while the Romans and Latins are beginning to expand and consolidate their power in this area, mainly by establishing colonies.

494 BC–492 BC
- A Latin colony is founded at Velitrae and, two years later, at Norba, both to the southeast of Rome, guarding the fertile plain below the Alban Hills of Rome against the rival Volsci tribe.

c. **490 BC–*c.* 480 BC**
- The Carthaginian navigator Hanno sets out with 60 ships and 30,000 people intending to found colonies along the coast of Africa. He reaches present-day Gambia, Sierra Leone, and possibly Cameroon, and probably comes to within 12 degrees of the Equator. He establishes colonies along the way.

480 BC
- Celts of the Hallstatt culture of upper Austria begin to arrive in Britain in substantial numbers. This is the main period of Celtic immigration, greatly augmenting and changing the balance of Britain's population, and is known as Britain's "Iron Age" culture.

Politics and Government

c. **500 BC**
- Darius the Great begins building the splendid new capital of the Persian Empire, Parsae (Persepolis to the Greeks). It lies some 240 km/150 mi northwest of Cyrus' capital of Pasargadae.
- The office of strategia (generalship) is established in the Greek city-state of Athens. Each of the ten tribes elects a strategus (general), making up a board of ten which serves as a council of war and takes charge of campaigns.
- The Carthaginians oust the Greeks from Malta.
- 500 BC–490 BC King Darius the Great is enraged by mainland Greek intervention in Asia Minor. He demands earth and water, the symbols of submission, from the Greek city-states. Some, including Aegina, submit but Athens and Sparta disdainfully reject his demand and in 490 BC the Persian Wars begin.
- *c.* 500 BC–*c.* 400 BC Rome and its Latin allies are almost constantly at war with both the Etruscans in the north and the native mountain tribes to the south, in particular the Aequi and the Volscians.

499 BC
- Aristagoras, governor of the Greek city-state of Miletus under the Persians, attacks Naxos in Sicily on Persia's behalf but is terrified of the consequences when he fails.
- Aristagoras, tyrant of Miletus in Asia Minor, induces the Ionian cities of Asia Minor to revolt against Persia. The Spartans fail to respond to a request for help but Athens and Eretria (in Euboea) send troops. During the revolt, the pro-Persian tyrant of Mytilene is stoned to death.

496 BC
- A combined force of Thracians and Scythians drives the tyrant Miltiades the Younger from the Chersonese peninsula. He flees to the Greek city-state of Athens.
- According to Roman tradition, the Romans defeat the Latins at the Battle of Lake Regillus, and a treaty is made between them as equal partners. (This tradition may be doubtful, and may reflect the Latins fighting Etruscan Rome.)
- The island of Cyprus attempts to throw off Persian domination, as does Caria, a mountainous region in Asia Minor. A Persian army with Phoenician help

reconquers Cyprus, and a Phoenician fleet suppresses Caria.

494 BC
- At the end of a military campaign, the plebeian element in the Roman army (those who do not belong to the privileged patrician class) retires to the Sacred Mt. outside Rome—the so-called "Secession of the Plebs"—and threatens to found a new city. The Senate grants concessions, including establishing the Tribunate, an office charged with the protection of plebeian interests.
- Persians burn down the temple of Apollo at Didyma, near Miletus in Ionia.
- The Ionian revolt against Persia ends with the Persian capture of the Greek city of Miletus in Asia Minor and the defeat of the Greek fleet at the Battle of Lade.

493 BC
- Athenian soldier and politician Themistocles becomes archon (chief magistrate) in the Greek city-state of Athens and develops the port at Piraeus.
- Rome and the Latin League recognize commercial contracts binding throughout their cities. Rome abandons its claim to domination over the League.

492 BC
- The Greek cities in Sicily are warring among themselves. Syracuse is only saved from destruction at the hands of neighboring Gela by the intervention of its mother-city, Corinth.
- The Persian general Mardonius, nephew and son-in-law of King Darius I the Great of Persia, subdues Thrace and Macedon, but the Persians lose part of their fleet on the promontory of Mt. Athos (Chalcidice).

491 BC
- In the Ganges kingdom of Magadha in India, King Bimbisara is murdered by his son Ajatashatru, who takes the throne, fortifies his capital city Pataliputra (modern Patna), and expands his kingdom by force of arms.
- Sicilian soldier and politician Gelon becomes tyrant of the Greek city of Gela on the south coast of Sicily.
- The Peloponnesian city of Aegina, afraid of losing its trade with the region of Pontus in northern Asia Minor, submits to Persian demands for earth and water.

490 BC
- King Darius I of Persia launches an expedition to mainland Greece, seeking revenge on the Athenians and Eretrians who backed the Ionian revolt against Persian rule. The city of Eretria is destroyed and Athens is in danger. The Persians land in the Bay of Marathon, north of Athens, where they meet in battle against the Athenians, supported by the Plataeans. The runner Philippides (or Pheidippides) is sent to Sparta to get help, but the Spartans delay sending troops, and the Greeks under Miltiades the Younger defeat the Persians without their help. The decisive role of the city-state of Athens in this anti-Persian coalition and the Spartans' failure to back the venture will have great ramifications for Greek politics in the 5th century BC.

489 BC
- The Athenian general Miltiades the Younger, after his great victory at Marathon, leads a naval expedition to the island of Paros, supposedly to pay off a private score. He is unsuccessful, and on his return to Athens is fined and put in prison where he dies of wounds received at Paros.

488 BC
- Sicilian general Theron becomes tyrant of the Greek city of Acragas in Sicily.

487 BC
- Archons (chief magistrates) are to be appointed by lot from all citizens in the Greek city-state of Athens. This change is partly due to the increasing practice of democracy in Athens, and partly because the office of *strategia* (generalship) has pushed the archonship into the background.
- The Peloponnesian city of Aegina and its long-time rival Athens are still at war over the Athenian refusal to hand back Aeginan hostages given to them by Sparta after Aegina submitted to the Persians in 491 BC.
- King Cleomenes of the Greek city-state of Sparta, having fled in 490 BC after his unpopular action over the Aeginan hostages, commits suicide. His successor is his brother Leonidas.

486 BC
- Encouraged by the news of the Greek victory over the Persians at Marathon in 490 BC, the Egyptians revolt against Persian rule after the death of Darius I.
- King Darius I the Great of Persia dies and his son Xerxes succeeds to the Persian throne, a harsher king than his father. His first act is to quell the Egyptian revolt against Persian rule. He never visits Egypt and uses Persian rather than Egyptian administrators.

c. 486 BC The Romans make a treaty with the tribe of the Hernici, who live in the Trerus valley southeast of Rome, between the powerful tribes of the Volsci on the coast and the Aequi in the mountains between the Trerus and Anio rivers. This treaty prevents the Hernici being crushed between its two powerful neighbors and gives Rome a buffer state between its enemies. The triple alliance of Rome, the Latins, and the Hernici fights intermittent wars with the Aequi and Volsci for the next century.

485 BC
- Gelon, the tyrant of Gela in Sicily, also becomes tyrant of the Greek city of Syracuse in Sicily.

483 BC
- King Xerxes of Persia, having crushed the Egyptian revolt, prepares for his great expedition against the Greeks. The plan is for a land army to cross the Bosporus and to skirt round the Thracian and Macedonian coast, with a fleet always in support. He has a canal cut through the promontory of Mt. Athos and builds a pontoon (floating bridge) over the Hellespont (Dardanelles) for his invading army to cross. According to Herodotus, it is 3 km/2 mi long and consists of 676 ships positioned in two rows.
- Rome is at war with its old enemy the Etruscan town of Veii. Veii is situated 19 km/12 mi north of Rome on the west bank of the River Tiber, and both cities stand in the way of the other's expansion.
- The archon (chief magistrate) Themistocles persuades the Athenians to devote the wealth from the new-found silver mines at Mt. Laurium, in South Attica, to the creation of a fleet.

482 BC

- The Athenian archon (chief magistrate) Themistocles, using the glory he acquired at the Battle of Marathon, establishes himself as the leading politician in Athens by securing the ostracism (expulsion by majority vote) of his opponents, including Aristides the Just.

481 BC

- Central control under the Zhou dynasty in China becomes weaker still: the "period of the Warring States" begins and lasts until 221 BC.
- The Greeks hold a congress on the isthmus of Corinth to plan their defense against the threatened Persian invasion under King Xerxes.

480 BC

- In a shrewd political move, King Xerxes of Persia encourages the Carthaginians to attack the Greek cities in Sicily. The Carthaginians are defeated at the Battle of Himera on the north coast of Sicily.
- In the spring, King Xerxes of Persia watches his huge multinational army cross the Hellespont into Greece.
- The Carthaginian general Hamilcar, having failed to defeat the Syracusans after making a sacrifice to his god Baal to ensure victory is said to have immolated himself.
- August 8 A small force under King Leonidas of Sparta holds the invading Persian land force at the pass of Thermopylae (leading from Thessaly to Phocis in central Greece), inflicting heavy casualties on them. The Spartans are wiped out but their bravery becomes almost legendary.
- September 9 The Greek city of Athens is besieged and burned by the Persians, but the Athenians, under general Themistocles and Aristides, who has recently been recalled from exile, destroy the Persian fleet in a naval battle in the Bay of Salamis. The Persian army retires to winter in Thessaly.

479 BC

- Cimon, the son of Miltiades, victor of the Battle of Marathon in 490 BC, is elected strategus (general) in the Greek city-state of Athens.
- King Xerxes of Persia leaves the conduct of the war in Greece to his general, Mardonius, and the Persians are defeated at the Battle of Plataea. They are also defeated at sea in the Battle of Mycale, off the coast of Asia Minor, and their ships are destroyed. The task of freeing the Ionian cities from Persian domination begins: the Athenians under the command of Xanthippus proceed to the Hellespont and capture the town of Sestos.
- The Romans are defeated by the Etruscan town of Veii in a battle on the River Cremera, and the Etruscans maintain their foothold east of the River Tiber, although their power is on the wane.

478 BC

- Hieron succeeds his brother Gelon as tyrant of the Greek city of Syracuse in Sicily. He defeats the Etruscans in their efforts to win the Greek city of Cumae in Italy: this may be said to mark the end of Etruscan power.
- The Spartan general Pausanias, nephew of King Leonidas of Sparta and commander of the Greeks at the Battle of Plataea, captures Byzantium in operations against the Persians. He begins to foster autocratic ambitions and appears to want to become tyrant of all Greece, with Persian help.

477 BC

- The Delian League, an alliance of Greek states around the Aegean Sea, is formed to continue the fight against the Persians. Although formally all the allies have an equal say, the confederacy is very much under the leadership of Athenian politician Cimon.

476 BC

- Athenian statesman Cimon, son of Miltiades, ousts the Spartan general Pausanias and the Spartans from the area of the Bosporus. The Spartans, hearing that Pausanias is intriguing with the Persians, recall him to Sparta. Under the leadership of Cimon, the Delian League continues to fight the Persians and to release the Ionian cities from Persian domination.

474 BC

- After the defeat of the Romans on the Cremera River in 479 BC, the Etruscan town of Veii is a serious threat to Rome itself. The power of the Etruscans is waning, however, as shown by their defeat by Hieron of Syracuse this year, and Rome makes a 40-year peace with Veii.
- Athenian statesman Cimon clears the Aegean island of Scyros of pirates.

471 BC

- Themistocles, the Greek chief magistrate, is ostracized (expelled by majority vote) by the Athenians who suspect him of corruption.

c. **470 BC**

- Pausanias, the Spartan regent, is convicted of treason and flees to the local temple of Athena, seeking sanctuary. The sanctuary is not violated, but Pausanias is starved to death, his dying body being carried out of the temple so that he does not pollute it by dying there.
- The Greek city-state of Sparta, abandoning dreams of empire, has to deal with trouble nearer home, chiefly from Peloponnesian Arcadia, with the support of the Peloponnesian city of Argos. Argos regains control of the city of Tiryns.
- Athenian statesmen Cimon continues the Greek war against Persia. The Delian League, and with it the power of Athens, continues to grow.

467 BC

- The Greek island of Naxos tries to secede from the Delian League but is blockaded and brought into subjection by the Athenian-dominated fleet, a high-handed action resented by the rest of Greece and widely seen as an early attempt by the Athenians to treat the confederacy as their own personal empire.
- 467 BC–466 BC Athenian statesman Cimon carries the war against Persia into Asia Minor and rallies all the cities of Lycia to the Greek cause by winning the battle of the River Eurymedon. Persia is decisively defeated, though it remains an enemy of the Greeks.

465 BC

- King Xerxes of Persia is murdered by Artabanus, his uncle and the head of his bodyguard. Artaxerxes I (also known as Longimanus) succeeds his father, Xerxes, to the Persian throne. Egypt seizes the opportunity to revolt against Persia in an uprising led by Inaros, a Libyan ruler.
- The Athenians attack and defeat the island of Thasos, a fellow member of the Delian League, in a naval battle.

Greek–Persian War (490 BC–444 BC)

500 BC–490 BC

- King Darius the Great is enraged by mainland Greek intervention in Asia Minor. He demands earth and water, the symbols of submission, from the Greek city-states. Some, including Aegina, submit but Athens and Sparta disdainfully reject his demand and in 490 BC the Persian Wars begin.

499 BC

- Aristagoras, tyrant of Miletus in Asia Minor, induces the Ionian cities of Asia Minor to revolt against Persia. The Spartans fail to respond to a request for help but Athens and Eretria (in Eubea) send troops. During the revolt, the pro-Persian tyrant of Mytilene is stoned to death.

496 BC

- The island of Cyprus attempts to throw off Persian domination, as does Caria, a mountainous region in Asia Minor. A Persian army with Phoenician help reconquers Cyprus, and a Phoenician fleet suppresses Caria.

494 BC

- The Ionian revolt against Persia ends with the Persian capture of the Greek city of Miletus in Asia Minor and the defeat of the Greek fleet at the Battle of Lade.

492 BC

- The Persian general Mardonius, nephew and son-in-law of King Darius I the Great of Persia, subdues Thrace and Macedon, but the Persians lose part of their fleet on the promontory of Mt. Athos (Chalcidice).

491 BC

- The Peloponnesian city of Aegina, afraid of losing its trade with the region of Pontus in northern Asia Minor, submits to Persian demands for earth and water.

490 BC

- King Darius I of Persia launches an expedition to mainland Greece, seeking revenge on the Athenians and Eretrians who backed the Ionian revolt against Persian rule. The city of Eretria is destroyed and Athens is in danger. The Persians land in the Bay of Marathon, north of Athens, where they meet in battle against the Athenians, supported by the Plataeans. The runner Philippides (or Pheidippides) is sent to Sparta to get help, but the Spartans delay sending troops, and the Greeks under Miltiades the Younger defeat the Persians without their help. The decisive role of the city-state of Athens in this anti-Persian coalition and the Spartans' failure to back the venture will have great ramifications for Greek politics in the 5th century BC.

483 BC

- King Xerxes of Persia, having crushed the Egyptian revolt, prepares for his great expedition against the Greeks. The plan is for a land army to cross the Bosporus and to skirt round the Thracian and Macedonian coast, with a fleet always in support. He has a canal cut through the promontory of Mt. Athos and builds a pontoon (floating bridge) over the Hellespont (Dardanelles) for his invading army to cross. According to Herodotus, it is 3 km/2 mi long and consists of 676 ships positioned in two rows.

481 BC

- The Greeks hold a congress on the isthmus of Corinth to plan their defense against the threatened Persian invasion under King Xerxes.

The attack arises from rivalry over trade with the Thracian hinterland, in particular over ownership of a gold mine. Thasos attempts to withdraw from the league.

463 BC

- Athenian democrat Ephialtes and the young statesman Pericles attempt to get Athenian statesman Cimon, a political enemy, ostracized for allegedly receiving bribes.
- The former archon (chief magistrate) Themistocles, now exiled from Athens, approaches King Artaxerxes I of Persia, hoping to receive assistance in regaining his former position in Athens. He fails but is given the satrapy (province) of Magnesia in Asia Minor by the Persians.

463 BC–461 BC   The democratic statesman Ephialtes, with the support of the statesman Pericles, introduces a package of radical democratic reforms in the Greek city-state of Athens. They reduce the powers of the Council of the Areopagus, transferring them to "democratic" popular institutions—the Council of Five Hundred, the Assembly, and the popular law courts. The office of judge becomes paid (so that it is no longer the exclusive preserve of the wealthy) and is recruited by lot from a list open to any citizen.

462 BC

- Cimon of Athens sends troops to Sparta to help them suppress the revolt of the helots (serfs) but suffers a severe setback when Spartan mistrust leads them to tell him that his help is not wanted; the following year he is ostracized (expelled by majority vote).

480 BC

- In a shrewd political move, King Xerxes of Persia encourages the Carthaginians to attack the Greek cities in Sicily. The Carthaginians are defeated at the Battle of Himera on the north coast of Sicily.
- In the spring, King Xerxes of Persia watches his huge multinational army cross the Hellespont into Greece.

August 8 A small force under King Leonidas of Sparta holds the invading Persian land force at the pass of Thermopylae (leading from Thessaly to Phocis in central Greece), inflicting heavy casualties on them. The Spartans are wiped out but their bravery becomes legendary.

September 9 The Greek city of Athens is besieged and burned by the Persians, but the Athenians, under general Themistocles and Aristides, who has recently been recalled from exile, destroy the Persian fleet in a naval battle in the Bay of Salamis. During their siege of Athens the Persians use arrows wrapped in oil-soaked fibers—the first incendiary weapons. The Persian army retires to winter in Thessaly.

479 BC

- King Xerxes of Persia leaves the conduct of the war in Greece to his general, Mardonius, and the Persians are defeated at the Battle of Plataea. They are also defeated at sea in the Battle of Mycale, off the coast of Asia Minor, and their ships are destroyed. The task of freeing the Ionian cities from Persian domination begins: the Athenians under the command of Xanthippus proceed to the Hellespont and capture the town of Sestos.

478 BC

- Delos, a center for the worship of Apollo, god of light, poetry, and music, is considered so holy that it needs no fortification and is chosen as a fitting headquarters for the anti-Persian confederacy of which Athens is the head.
- The Spartan general Pausanias, nephew of King Leonidas of Sparta and commander of the Greeks at the Battle of Plataea, captures Byzantium in operations against the Persians. He begins to foster autocratic ambitions and appears to want to become tyrant of all Greece, with Persian help.

472 BC

- The earliest extant play of the Athenian tragedian Aeschylus, *Persae/Persians*, describing the Persians at the Battle of Salamis, wins the Athenian tragedy prize. Aeschylus gained firsthand experience of the wars, having fought at the Battle of Marathon and, probably, at the Battle of Salamis.

470 BC

- Athenian statesmen Cimon continues the Greek war against Persia. The Delian League, and with it the power of Athens, continues to grow.

467 BC–466 BC

- Athenian statesman Cimon carries the war against Persia into Asia Minor and rallies all the cities of Lycia to the Greek cause by winning the battle of the River Eurymedon. Persia is decisively defeated, though it remains an enemy of the Greeks.

449 BC

- The Greek city-states finally make peace with Persia, the so-called Peace of Callias, which is maintained for most of the next century. There is no longer any formal need for the Delian League and the Athenians now have to force members to pay their contributions. The Peace of Callias traditionally marks the transformation of the Delian League into the Athenian Empire.

c. 444 BC

- Greek historian Herodotus, the "father of history," is reputed to be one of the colonists of the new city of Thurii, Italy. In his *Histories*, Herodotus records the events of the wars between Persia and Greece, and takes a much wider view of history than his contemporaries, such as the Athenian historian Thucydides, going beyond political and military history to include geography and anthropology.

- The Peloponnesian city of Argos, taking advantage of Sparta's preoccupation with its internal problems, finally conquers the city of Mycenae (which seems to have been temporarily independent). The inhabitants are dispersed, some finding their way into Macedon.

461 BC–446 BC

- Athenian foreign policy, now under the control of the nationalistic statesman Pericles, becomes very aggressive and imperialist. This period sees intermittent war, known as the First Peloponnesian War, between the Athenian-led Delian League, edging ever closer to becoming an Athenian Empire, and the Spartan-dominated Peloponnesian League, consisting of the Peloponnesian states of Laconia (Sparta), Messenia, Ellis, and Arcadia, plus Corinth and Megara.

460 BC

- A remarkable native Sicilian leader, Ducetius, makes his mark during this decade and the next. He founds many native cities and for a while threatens the Greek cities in Sicily.

459 BC

- The Athenian politician Pericles' first move in his aggressive foreign policy is to try to isolate central Greece and replace Theban control by Athenian occupation. Athens makes strategic alliances with the city-states Argos and Megara, and the region of Thessaly. Corinth and the island of Aegina feel that these actions threaten their sea trade, and declare war on Athens.

458 BC

- After a great effort, the Greek city-state of Athens is victorious over its Peloponnesian enemies and the Peloponnesian city of Aegina is forced to join the Delian League.
- The Athenian statesman Pericles continues Ephialtes' democratic reforms in the Greek city-state of Athens by making the archonship a paid office and the lower class of citizens eligible for it.
- The Greek city-states of Sparta and Thebes, the capital of Boeotia, declare war on Athens. A Spartan force, going to the help of Boeotia in a local dispute, is nearly cut off by the Athenians on its return.
- The Roman army, blockaded on Mt. Algidus, southeast of Rome, by the Aequi, escapes disaster by calling the Roman general Cincinnatus from his farm to command the army and take on the office of dictator. Cincinnatus defeats the Aequi, then returns to his farm.

457 BC

- On returning from their Boeotian expedition, the Spartans are drawn into fighting with the Athenians, the latter being defeated at the ensuing Battle of Tanagra. The Spartans are unable to follow up their victory, however, and withdraw from the area. Athens then advances into Boeotia, which becomes a member of the Delian League.

456 BC–454 BC

- The Athenian-led expedition to Egypt to assist the pharaoh Inaros in his revolt against Persia ends in disaster: the fleet is defeated with heavy losses and the army retreats in disarray. The army retreats across the Sinai Desert to Byblos before its remnants are rescued; Inaros is crucified.

454 BC

- Athenian statesman Pericles declares that the treasury of the Delian League is not safe from the Persian navy on the island of Delos and has it transferred to Athens.
- The Roman plebeian class, suffering from very much the same economic and financial ills that Solon had earlier lifted from the Athenian *polloi*, force the patricians to begin a reform and codification of the law. A commission is sent to Athens to study the laws of the Greek city-state.

453 BC

- Achaea, on the southern shore of the Corinthian Gulf, is forced to join the Delian League, which is now all but an Athenian Empire.

451 BC

- An Athenian law is passed restricting citizenship to those born of Athenian parents only, not just of an Athenian father as before.
- Athenian politician Pericles introduces pay for men serving on juries, who are drawn by lot from a panel of 600. Pay for public service is a recent principle in Greece, starting with pay for the office of judge, *c.* 462 BC. It is strongly criticized by the oligarchs, but is a great aid to poor citizens. The following year it is extended to soldiers, sailors, officials, and members of the council.
- The next step in the plebeian demands for reforming and codifying the laws in Rome is the establishment of a Board of Ten, the Decemviri, followed by a second

board of which half the members are plebeian. They produce the Twelve Tables of the Law.
- The Persian fleet moves to a rebellious Cyprus to restore order. Athenian military leader Cimon, who has returned to favor though not to power in Athens, plans an expedition to help Cyprus, which is approved by the Athenian statesman Pericles.
- The warring Greek city-states are temporarily exhausted and a five-year truce is arranged between Athens and the Peloponnese.

SCIENCE, TECHNOLOGY, AND MEDICINE

Ecology

465 BC–462 BC

- The Greek city-state of Sparta is unable to help the island of Thasos fight off the Athenians, despite increasing concern at the rise of Athens as an imperial power, as the Spartans have their own troubles at home—they are suffering the effects of a severe earthquake and the ensuing revolt of the helots (serfs) in Messenia.

464 BC

- Tens of thousands of people die in Sparta during an earthquake.

Health and Medicine

c. **500 BC**

- Greek physiologist Alcmaeon is the first person to dissect the human body for research purposes. He discovers the optic nerve, describes the difference between arteries and veins, and recognizes that the brain, which he describes in detail, is the source of intelligence. He also possibly practices vivisection.
- The first cataract operations are performed in India.

Math

c. **500 BC**

- Astronomers in Mesopotamia, Greece, Alexandria, and India use the Babylonian sexagesimal mathematical system to predict the positions of the sun, moon, and planets.

Science

500 BC

- Greek traveler and geographer Hecataeus of Miletus, writes *Ges periodos/Tour Around the World*, a description of the geography and ethnography of

Europe, northern Africa, and Asia—the first book on geography.

c. 475 BC

- The Greek philosopher Parmenides of Elea, Italy, is active. He claims the earth is a sphere, and promulgates the idea of immutability of elements. Large fragments of his philosophical poem survive.

Technology

c. 500 BC

- The Persians develop the composite bow using animal tendons and horn instead of wood.
- The Romans develop the catapult; powered by twisted fibers it can fire a rock weighing 23 kg/50 lb over 350 m/1,148 ft.
- The use of iron is widespread in Greece and the Aegean islands from where it spreads rapidly westward.

c. 480 BC

- During their siege of Athens the Persians use arrows wrapped in oil-soaked fibers—the first incendiary weapons.
- The plowshare appears in China; it is a V-shaped metal point pushed by humans.

Transportation

c. 500 BC

- Chariots are used by the Celts in Britain; they are introduced via the Etruscans.
- The Greeks introduce the trireme, a galley about 45 m/ 150 ft long and 6 m/20 ft wide with three banks of oars. The oars are worked from an outrigger that extends down the length of the hull, and the ship carries about 200 people, mostly oarsmen. It becomes the model warship for both the Greeks and the Romans.

c. 475 BC

- The two-masted sailing ship, with the forward sail being the smaller, is depicted on the wall of an Etruscan tomb.

ARTS AND IDEAS

Architecture

489 BC

- The Athenians build a treasure-house at Delphi from the spoils of the Battle of Marathon. It is still standing in modern times.

478 BC

- The Greek city of Athens and its port Piraeus are refortified as well as rebuilt by Themistocles after the Persian destruction of 480 BC, in spite of Spartan opposition.

475 BC

- Theron, tyrant of Acragas, Sicily (modern Agrigento), begins to build a row of temples along the city's southern wall, a work continued after his death two years later.

460 BC–457 BC

- The temple of Zeus is built at Olympia, Greece. The labors of the Greek hero Heracles are illustrated on friezes in the temple.

458 BC

- The Long Walls of Athens are built; two parallel walls 168 m/550 ft apart, they link Athens to the port of Piraeus 6.4 km/4 mi away permitting supplies to reach the city in safety in case of siege.

Arts

c. 500 BC

- Etruscan art flourishes, especially in the fields of bronze, pottery, and tomb wall paintings.

480 BC–330 BC

- The Greek classical style of sculpture develops more realism than the preceding Archaic period. Its leading exponents are Phidias (in the 5th century BC), and Praxiteles, Scopas, and Lysippus (in the 4th century BC).

477 BC

- A monument is raised in Athens in honor of the tyrant-slayers, Harmodius and Aristogeiton, to replace the statues erected in 510 BC, which were looted by the Persians.

c. 470 BC

- One of the extant bronze statues at Delphi, that of a charioteer, is made.

465 BC

- Scenes of the Battle of Marathon are included in the "Painted Stoa," a covered walk in the agora of Athens which is completed sometime between 475 BC and 450 BC. The stoa is decorated by the Greek painter Polygnotus of Thasos, friend of the Athenian statesman Cimon, with assistance from Micon, an Athenian painter and sculptor.

458 BC–447 BC

- The Greek painter Polygnotus of Thasos paints murals at Delphi. In later times they are described by the historian and traveler Pausanias.

Literature and Language

498 BC–446 BC

- Greek lyric poet Pindar composes odes in honor of athletes, most of them charioteers, at the Olympic, Pythian, Isthmian, and Nemean Games in Greece.

480 BC

- Greek choral poet Simonides composes his poem *The Battle of Plataea*.

476 BC

- Greek poets Pindar and Bacchylides write odes celebrating the chariot team of Hieron I, tyrant of

Syracuse, winning a victory at the Olympics. Four books of Pindar's victory odes survive to modern times, but only fragments of the rest of his work. Some of the works of Bacchylides, written on papyrus, also survive to modern times.

455 BC

- Greek poet and philosopher Ion of Chios, a friend of both the Athenian statesman Cimon and the dramatist Sophocles, is active. Only fragments of his work survive to modern times.

Theater and Dance

499 BC

- Athenian dramatist and tragedian Aeschylus, aged about 25, competes in the Athenian tragedy festival, but is unsuccessful.

494 BC

- Athenian tragic poet Phrynichus is fined 1,000 drachmae for producing his play *Capture of Miletus* because Athenian audiences, still distressed by the crushing of the Ionian revolt, are moved to tears during its performance.

484 BC

- Athenian dramatist and tragedian Aeschylus wins the Athenian tragedy prize for the first time.

480 BC

- The young Athenian dramatist Sophocles reputedly leads the chorus of triumph around the trophy raised at Salamis following the battle there. However, biographical details about Sophocles were often invented in later years.

475 BC–425 BC

- In the 50 years that follow the end of the Persian Wars, the Greek city-state of Athens reaches the zenith of its greatness. In addition to its empire and political power, creative and intellectual culture flourish. The great tragic playwrights Aeschylus, Sophocles, and Euripides are writing, as is the comic playwright Aristophanes. The sculptor Phidias supervises the construction of the frieze on the Parthenon, and the painter Polygnotus decorates the wall of the Stoa (the colonnade in the marketplace) with murals. Athens is now one of the main commercial centers of the eastern Mediterranean.

472 BC

- The earliest extant play of the Athenian tragedian Aeschylus, *Persae/Persians*, describing the Persians at the Battle of Salamis, wins the Athenian tragedy prize. Aeschylus gained firsthand experience of the wars, having fought at the Battle of Marathon and, probably, at the Battle of Salamis.

468 BC

- Athenian tragedian Sophocles defeats Aeschylus in the contest for tragedy at the Dionysia festival in Athens. Of Sophocles's 120 plays, only seven survive, and of those only two can be dated accurately, *Philoctetes*, dated from 409 BC and *Oedipus at Colonos*, produced posthumously in 401 BC, both of which win prizes. The remaining five plays are *Ajax*, probably written in the

period 451 BC–444 BC, *Antigone* and *Trachiniae*, which are dated after 441 BC, and *Electra* and *Oedipus Tyrannus*, probably written in the period 430 BC–415 BC. An eighth play, the satyr-drama *Ichneutai/ Trackers*, survives in fragments.

467 BC

- Athenian dramatist Aeschylus' *Seven Against Thebes*, one of his surviving plays, is produced in Athens.

458 BC

- The trilogy *Oresteia*, by the Athenian dramatist Aeschylus, is performed. It comprises *Agamemnon*, *Choephoroi*, and *Eumenides*.

455 BC

- The first play by the Athenian tragic dramatist Euripides, *Daughters of Pelias*, comes third at the Dionysia, a competition held in honor of Dionysus, the Greek god of wine, in Athens.

Thought and Scholarship

c. **500 BC**

- Greek philosopher Heraclitus of Ephesus centers his philosophy on the proposition that "everything flows," and the belief that the cosmos is in a constant process of change.

497 BC

- Chinese philosopher Confucius sets out on his travels as a wandering teacher, moving from court to court among the many rulers of a divided China.

c. **480 BC**

- Greek cosmologist and philosopher Anaxagoras moves to Athens and becomes a teacher of Pericles (later a politician in Athens).

478 BC

- Greek historian Herodotus begins his *Histories*, which tells of the wars between the Greeks and the Persians, ending with the description of the retreat of the king of Persia, Xerxes, from Greece.

c. **470 BC**

- The disciples of the Chinese philosopher Confucius reputedly collect and record his teachings, which are ethical rather than religious and center on the golden rule of doing to others as one would have done to oneself.

c. **467 BC**

- Greek philosopher Anaxagoras supposes that the sun is a mass of red-hot iron larger than the Peloponnese. He also discovers the true cause of eclipses.

SOCIETY

Everyday Life

c. **500 BC**

- Societies of horse-riding nomads are well established on the Eurasian Steppes. Tombs belonging to these peoples have been found in the frozen ground at Pazyryk in Siberia. Their dwellings are felt-covered tents which can be quickly dismantled and moved on to new pastures. The felts are richly decorated with geometric designs or scenes of horse riders.

- The native Americans in central America start their "formative" period, which lasts for some eight centuries and develops into the distinctive culture of the Mayas, particularly noted for its astronomical skills. Due to the climate of the area, there is little in the way of archeological evidence.

- The population of the region that will become Ecuador increases and their society becomes more complex.

Sophisticated regional ceramic styles are developed, for example at Bahiá, where cast and molded sculptures of human figures are produced, or in the Jama Coaque culture, known for clay figures of humans, with very little use of paint.

- The site of La Venta is abandoned and Tres Zapotes rises to prominence in the final stage of the Olmec civilization in Mexico. As with the site of San Lorenzo, stone statues at La Venta are mutilated and buried, suggesting some kind of religious ritual. The Olmecs use hieroglyphic writing (not yet deciphered) which seems to be in part a much earlier form of the Mayan hieroglyphics.

BIRTHS & DEATHS

500 BC
- Anaxagoras, Greek philosopher of nature who discovered the true cause of eclipses, born in Clazomenae, Anatolia (– 428 BC).

496 BC
- Sophocles, Greek playwright, author of *Oedipus Rex*, born in Colonus, near Athens (–406 BC).

c. 495 BC
- Pericles, Athenian statesman chiefly responsible for making Athens the center of Greece and for Athenian democracy, born in Athens, Greece (–429 BC).
- Zeno of Elea, Greek philosopher who developed dialectic and logical rigor in philosophic thinking, born (–c. 430 BC).

491 BC
- Bimbisara, first great king of Magadha c. 543 BC–c. 491 BC, dies.

c. 490 BC
- Phidias, Athenian architect who directed the construction of the Parthenon, born (–432 BC).
- Hippias, tyrant of Athens c. 528 BC–510 BC, dies.

489 BC
- Miltiades the Younger, Athenian general who won a decisive victory over the Persians in the Battle of Marathon in 490 BC, dies in Athens.

486 BC
- Darius I the Great, Achaemenid king of Persia 522 BC–486 BC, who made several attempts to conquer Greece, dies.

c. 485 BC
- Protagoras, Greek Sophist philosopher known for his dictum "Man is the measure of all things," born in Abdera, Greece (–410 BC).

c. 484 BC
- Euripides, one the great Athenian tragic dramatists, whose best-known plays include *Medea*

(431 BC) and *Electra* (418 BC), born (–406 BC).
- Herodotus, Greek historian, author of an important history of the Greco-Persian wars, born in Halicarnassus, Asia Minor (now Bodrum, Turkey) (–c. 425 BC).

c. 483 BC
- Gautama Buddha (Siddhartha Gautama), Indian philosopher and founder of Buddhism, dies in Kusinagara, Nepal (c. 80).

480 BC
- Antiphon, Athenian orator and statesman, the earliest known professional rhetorician, born (–411 BC).
- Leonidas, king of Sparta c. 490 BC–480 BC, renowned for his defense of the pass of Thermopylae against a vastly superior force under the Persian king Xerxes, falls in battle with his royal guard at Thermopylae, Greece.

479 BC
- Confucius (Chinese: K'ung-fu-tzu, or Pinyin: Kongfuzi), celebrated Chinese philosopher and political theorist, dies in Lu, now in Shantung Province, China (c. 72).
- September Mardonius, Achaemenid Persian general, falls in battle at Plataea, Boeotia.

478 BC
- Gelon, tyrant of Gela and Syracuse in Sicily, chiefly responsible for the Greek victory over the Carthaginians at Himera, dies (c. 62).
- c. 478 BC Xenophanes, Greek poet and philosopher, dies (c. 82).

c. 471 BC
- Thucydides, Greek historian, author of *History of the Peloponnesian War*, which describes the war between Athens and Sparta, born (–c. 401 BC).

c. 470 BC
- Socrates, Athenian philosopher, born in Athens (–399 BC).

468 BC
- Simonides of Ceos, lyric poet and epigrammatist, probably the originator of the epinicion (ode in honor of victors in the Olympic Games), dies in Syracuse, Sicily (c. 88).

465 BC
- Anacreon, Greek lyric poet, of whose work only fragments survive, dies (c. 97).
- Xerxes I, king of Persia (486 BC–465 BC), who invaded Greece, is assassinated in Persepolis, Persia, by Artabanus, his uncle, and the head of his bodyguard (c. 54).

461 BC
- The Athenian democratic statesman Ephialtes, who introduced a package of radical democratic reforms, is assassinated.

460 BC
- Hippocrates, Greek physician, born on Cos, Greece (–c. 357 BC).
- c. 460 BC Democritus, influential Greek philosopher, born (–c. 370 BC).
- c. 460 BC Themistocles, Greek naval commander who made Athens a sea power and defended Greece from the Persians at the Battle of Salamis, dies (c. 64).

c. 456 BC
- Aeschylus, first Athenian tragic dramatist, dies in Gela, Sicily (c. 69).

454 BC
- Inaros of Egypt, a prince who rebelled against Achaemenid Persian rule, is crucified by the Persians.

- The town of Monte Albán is founded in the Oaxaca region of Mexico. It becomes the capital of the Zapotec culture. The town is sited on a steep, high bluff in the center of a valley, and dominates the surrounding area for the next 12 centuries.
- The people of the Paracas culture in southern Peru begin to mummify their dead in hand-spun shrouds. Surviving mummies show that the fine cloth is of outstanding workmanship.
- *c.* 500 BC–*c.* 400 BC Persian influence on its Indus valley province of Gandhara is considerable. This is evident in many aspects of life, such as religion and coinage. The capital city, Takshashila, becomes known to the Greeks as Taxila.
- *c.* 500 BC–*c.* 400 BC The Celts begin to make an impression on European history. They are divided into a number of different tribes, sharing a distinctive decorative style of art, characterized by curving designs and mythical animals. These can be seen on their jewelry (gold and bronze torques), their weapons (decorated shields and sword scabbards), and their pottery and other vessels. The Celts probably originate in northwest and central Europe, France (particularly the area of Champagne), Switzerland, Lower Austria, and western Slovakia. The area of the western Hallstatt, Upper Austria, is also associated with the Celts.

Religion

c. 500 BC
- Phrygian religion influences Greece and, at a later date, Rome, with their mother goddess Cybele and her male attendant-god Attis.

483 BC
- Following the death of Gautama Buddha, an increasing number of monks and nuns are found wandering, preaching, and seeking alms. Their teaching supplements the education provided by the Brahmans.

478 BC
- Delos, a center for the worship of Apollo, god of light, poetry, and music, is considered so holy that it needs no fortification and is chosen as a fitting headquarters for the anti-Persian confederacy of which Athens is the head.

c. **474 BC**
- Athenian statesman Cimon brings back what are believed to be the bones of Theseus, the hero of Attica, from his expedition to the Greek island of Scyros. This act of piety is well-received in Athens.

458 BC
- The Old Testament Book of Ezra tells how the Babylonian priest and scribe Ezra is sent by King Artaxerxes I of Persia to Jerusalem to restore the neglected Jewish laws of the Pentateuch. He is accompanied by a large number of Jewish exiles and carries valuable gifts for the temple, from both Jews and the Persian king himself. After fasting and prayer, he and a chosen committee blacklist those guilty of mixed marriage.

Sports

c. 500 BC–*c.* 450 BC
- Chariot racing is popular among the Etruscans in central Italy.

450 BC–401 BC

POLITICS, GOVERNMENT, AND ECONOMICS

Business and Economics

450 BC
- The Athenians reduce the tribute due from the members of the Delian League and each city is allowed to issue its own coinage.
- The city of Babylon is bearing a considerable burden as part of the Persian Empire at the time of the Greek

historian Herodotus' visit during this decade. An annual levy of about 30 tons of silver is enforced and Babylon has to provide supplies for the Persian army and host the court for four months each year, as well as providing for the needs of the local satrap (provincial governor).

c. 450 BC Trade and industry have to a large extent migrated westward across the Aegean Sea from the Ionian cities. Athenian pottery has reached Etruria and the Po valley in Italy.

448 BC
- The Athenian statesman Pericles tries to persuade the other members of the Delian League to agree to spend the funds collected for combatting Persia on repairing the damage done to Athens by the Persians. He fails, but perseveres with his project to use the funds in decking Athens out in true imperial style.

437 BC

- The Athenian statesman Pericles, concerned for Athens' eastern trade, and attempting to counteract a new and possibly threatening Thracian–Scythian alliance, pays an impressive visit into the Black Sea area.

Colonization

447 BC

- The Athenian statesman Pericles starts a policy of *kleruchoi* or "out-settlements" in the Chersonese (Gallipoli). This is a new form of colonization, by which poor and unemployed people are helped to emigrate. These people keep their Athenian citizenship and provide centers of Athenian loyalty.

443 BC

- Athens attempts but fails to build a new Sybaris in south Italy (the original city having been destroyed in 510 BC). Instead, the Athenian statesman Pericles founds the nearby colony of Thurii.

440 BC

- By 440 BC, the Athenian Empire includes about 300 members, stretching from the coastline of the Aegean to Macedon to southern Asia Minor. Athens extends its empire by diplomacy or by planting Athenian colonies, and keeps control in varying ways, from pro-Athenian factions to garrisons in strategic sites. Any attempt to break away from the empire is dealt with very harshly.

436 BC

- To follow up the Athenian statesman Pericles' visit to the Black Sea area the previous year, an Athenian colony is founded at Amphipolis in Thrace.

435 BC

- The Greek city-state of Corinth attacks its recalcitrant colony Corcyra, an island off the coast of Epirus in western Greece, in a dispute concerning the latter's colony of Epidamnus in Illyria. This is one of the first incidents in the buildup to the Peloponnesian War.

428 BC

- The Greek colony of Cumae in Italy falls to the Samnite people, who begin to take control of the Campanian plain, southern Italy.

Human Rights

445 BC

- The *Lex Canuleia* removes the ban on marriage between the plebeian and patrician orders in Rome. It also introduces the office of military tribune (magistrate) with consular power, which replaces the consulship. This office is set up to exercise high military command and is open to plebeians.

Politics and Government

450 BC

- The Athenian expedition to help Cyprus in its revolt against the Persians is a failure. Cimon, the Athenian military leader, meets his death there and the Cypriots remain under Phoenician (essentially Persian) control.
- The Roman Decemviri ("Board of Ten"), established to codify the laws, refuse to disband themselves and threaten to assume dictatorial powers. Their leader, Appius Claudius, is seriously discredited when Virginia, a girl he is attempting to seduce, is spectacularly killed by her father to save her from a fate which he considers worse than death. Claudius commits suicide, and the attempt at dictatorship collapses. The plebeian element in the army mutinies again.
- *c.* 450 BC   A code of law is incised on the walls of the Cretan town of Gortyn, one of the few pieces of evidence of Doric occupation of the island. It is mainly a civil code, with a mixture of premature and developed regulations.

449 BC

- Athenian statesman Pericles institutes a building program that is as much aimed at relieving unemployment as glorifying Athens. It includes the refortification of the port of Piraeus.
- The Greek city-states finally make peace with Persia, the so-called Peace of Callias, which is maintained for most of the next century. There is no longer any formal need for the Delian League and the Athenians now have to force members to pay their contributions. The Peace of Callias traditionally marks the transformation of the Delian League into the Athenian Empire.
- Under the consulship of Valerius and Horatius in Rome, the Twelve Tables of the Law (produced in 451 BC) are officially adopted and the rights of the tribunes defined, ending the Second Secession of the Plebeians.

447 BC

- Athens loses control of Boeotia after Thebes, the capital, successfully instigates a revolt in the cities taken over by the Athenians. The Athenian general Tolmides, sent to recapture them, is defeated at the Battle of Coronea. This encourages the city of Euboea to revolt and the city of Megara to declare independence. Before Euboea can be recovered, the Athenian truce with Sparta lapses and the Spartan army invades Attica.

446 BC

- The Athenian statesman Pericles rounds off a difficult period in foreign affairs by negotiating a somewhat humiliating peace treaty with Sparta and its Peloponnesian allies, restoring independence to Achaea on the southern shore of the Corinthian Gulf, and extending the 5-year truce for another 30 years. This brings the First Peloponnesian War to an end.

445 BC

- Nehemiah, the Jewish cup-bearer to King Artaxerxes I of Persia at Susa, returns to Jerusalem as governor. He inspires the people of Jerusalem with great enthusiasm and the city's walls are rebuilt in spite of active Gentile opposition. Nehemiah also restores some of the religious observances which the Jews have allowed to lapse.

c. **444 BC**

- Athenian leader Pericles asks the sophist (itinerant teacher of oratory and argument) Protagoras of Abdera to write a constitution for the new colony of Thurii in Italy. Protagoras is famed for his agnosticism, his belief that the existence of God cannot be proved.

443 BC

- The Roman consul's task is lightened by the creation of two censors. They are to be elected every five years to take the census of the people and to carry out the purification ceremony that accompanies it. Another of their jobs is to oversee the morals of senators, and to remove the senators from the senatorial lists if necessary.

442 BC

- The aristocratic Athenian politician Thucydides continues his opposition to the statesman Pericles' abuse of the funds of the Delian League to rebuild the city of Athens and is ostracized (expelled by majority vote) by the people with whom Pericles' policy is very popular. Pericles is now unopposed and governs Athens for a further 15 years.

440 BC

- During the war against the island of Samos the Athenian statesman Pericles puts some restraint on free speech, for example on the license of the comic drama.
- The island of Samos off the coast of Asia Minor, an autonomous member of the Delian League, quarrels with the Greek city of Miletus on the Ionian coast and appeals to Athens. The Athenian statesman Pericles decides in favor of Miletus and installs a democratic government on Samos. Despite help from Persia, Samos surrenders after a nine-month siege.

439 BC

- The distribution of cheap corn is tried for the first time to alleviate famine in Rome.

c. 435 BC

- In the last years of his life the Athenian statesman Pericles has political pressure put on him by attacks on his friends: the sculptor Phidias is accused of corruption in building the statue of Athena in the Parthenon, and Pericles' mistress, Aspasia, is accused of being a procuress. She is exonerated.

433 BC

- Corcyra and Corinth are at war: Athenian ships are deployed in the Battle of Sybota at the request of Corcyra, a Corinthian colony, enraging the Corinthians. The quarrel spreads to Potidaea in Chalcidice, a member of the Athenian Empire but originally a Corinthian colony, which now revolts in sympathy.

432 BC

- The Athenian statesman Pericles punishes the city of Megara for assisting Corinth in the Battle of Sybota against Corcyra, by depriving it of its maritime trade.
- The Athenians besiege the city of Potidaea in Chalcidice; Corinth appeals to Sparta. At an intercity assembly at Sparta, Athens is accused of breaking the 30-year peace treaty agreed in 446 BC.

431 BC

- The Athenian statesman Pericles makes his famous funeral oration for the fallen in the year's campaigns. The Athenian historian Thucydides describes the incident in his *History*, showing that the speech is much more than an oration for the dead and amounts to an assertion of Athenian values and aspirations.
- The Peloponnesian War is precipitated by an incident at Plataea, the only pro-Athenian city in Boeotia. A

Theban raid on the city is a failure and the Plataeans take 180 prisoners and put them to death. Athens supports Plataea and Sparta aligns itself on the other side. Sparta enlists the help of the Greek cities of Italy and Sicily, and both sides appeal unsuccessfully to Persia.
- The Romans finally defeat the Aequi at the Battle of the River Algidus, southeast of Rome.
- The Thebans besiege the pro-Athenian city of Plataea in Boeotia.

May 5   The Spartans invade Attica, marking the start of the 27-year Peloponnesian War. The Athenian army is outclassed by the Spartans and Athens' power lies in its navy, so the Athenian statesman Pericles brings the population of the country districts into the city of Athens while pursuing an active naval war. Athens insures itself against danger from the island of Aegina by supplanting its Doric population with Athenians.

430 BC

- The Spartans make the second of their five invasions of Attica. The Athenians have some successes in sea raids on their enemies and the city of Potidaea in Chalcidice is taken. In Athens itself, full to bursting point with refugees, plague breaks out. Pericles is deposed from his position as strategus (general) and fined, but is soon reappointed.

430 BC–424 BC   The Peloponnesian War, essentially a struggle between a land power and a sea power, is initially dominated by the sea power, Athens. After 424 BC, largely thanks to their more daring general Brasidas, Sparta begins to gain the upper hand.

429 BC

- Athenian statesman Pericles dies. Cleon, the tanner, a more radical opponent and popular demagogue, takes over the premier position in Athenian politics.
- The illegitimate son of the Athenian statesman Pericles and his mistress Aspasia is legitimized by the Athenian Assembly.

428 BC

- The city of Mytilene takes advantage of Athens' weakened state to revolt.

427 BC

- Attica is again invaded by Sparta.
- Civil war breaks out in the Corinthian colony of Corcyra between the oligarchs and the democrats—the Athenians and Spartans interfere ineffectually. The democrats defeat and then massacre the oligarchs.
- In an effort to blockade the Greek city-state of Sparta and deprive it of desperately needed Sicilian corn, Athens responds to a plea for help made by the city of Leontini in Sicily. Little is achieved but some feel this is a preliminary mission to the large-scale Athenian intervention in Sicily of 415 BC–412 BC.
- The Athenian Assembly, influenced by the demagogue Cleon, votes for the destruction of the population of Mytilene, following its revolt and surrender to Athens. However, in response to the pleading of Diodotus, this harsh decision is reversed and only the ringleaders of the Mytilenean revolt are executed.
- The southern Boeotian city of Plataea surrenders to Sparta, and the Aegean city of Mytilene to Athens. The Athenians are more merciful in victory than the

Spartans. Thebes and Sparta show no mercy to the Plataeans following their revolt and subsequent surrender to Sparta. Each prisoner is asked: "Have you in the present war done any service to the Lacedaemonians (Spartans) or their allies?" Some 200 prisoners who cannot say yes are put to death.

426 BC

- The Greek city-state of Athens has some naval successes against Sparta under its new general Demosthenes.

425 BC

- The Athenian general Demosthenes lands at the Peloponnesian city of Pylos, defeats the Spartans, and captures 420 Spartan hoplites (soldiers) on the neighboring island of Sphacteria. He then fortifies Pylos and Sphacteria. Sparta breaks off its invasion of Attica to send troops to Pylos. The Athenian statesman Cleon takes command and wins a victory for Athens. Sparta makes peace overtures which Cleon persuades Athens to reject.

424 BC

- Artaxerxes I, Persian pharaoh of Egypt, who put down an Egyptian revolution, dies and is succeeded by Darius II, who rules Egypt until 404 BC.
- Cleon of Athens captures the Peloponnesian island of Cythera, from which he harries the Spartans. Athens also captures Nisaea and Pegae, the ports of Megara on the isthmus of Corinth.
- The Athenians spread the Second Peloponnesian War into Boeotia, but are defeated at the Battle of Delium. They suffer worse defeats in Thrace at the hands of the Spartan general Brasidas, who captures the city of Amphipolis. The Athenian historian Thucydides, the general in command, is held responsible and banished.

423 BC

- A year's truce in the Second Peloponnesian War is agreed between the Greek city-states of Athens and Sparta.

422 BC

- Athenian politician and general Alcibiades becomes the most prominent figure in the prowar faction in the Greek city-state of Athens.
- Cleon of Athens ends the truce in the Second Peloponnesian War and resolves on the rescue of the Athenian colony of Amphipolis in Thrace, captured by Sparta in 424 BC. In a battle outside the city both the Athenian leader Cleon and the Spartan general Brasidas are killed; the victory goes to the Spartans.

421 BC

- Nicias, leader of the aristocratic propeace faction in the Greek city-state of Athens, arranges a peace treaty with Sparta and its Peloponnesian allies. Some of the allies, most notably the Corinthians, consider the terms unjust and break with Sparta, making an alliance with the Peloponnesian city of Argos.
- The quaestorship (office of financial official) in Rome is increased in number to four and opened to the plebeians.

420 BC

- A new dynasty, the Shishunaga, reigns successfully in the kingdom of Magadha, northeast India, for about half a century.

- The Greek city-state of Athens enters into an alliance with the Peloponnesian city of Argos, which has so far taken no part in the Second Peloponnesian War because of a treaty of neutrality with Sparta, which ran out in 421 BC. Athens also allies itself with the Peloponnesian cities of Mantinea and Elis.

420 BC–385 BC Rome continues to increase its dominance in Italy during this period, defeating the Aequi and clearing the coastal plain of the Volscians.

418 BC

- Political intrigue in the Greek city-state of Athens results in the unexpected alliance of the prowar politician and general Alcibiades and the propeace aristocratic statesman Nicias, and the ostracism of the demagogue Hyperbolus. This is the last use of ostracism (expulsion by majority vote).
- Sparta invades the Peloponnesian city of Argos, and Athens, which allied itself with Argos in 420 BC, breaks the peace and comes to the aid of the Argives, attacking the Peloponnesian city of Epidaurus and advancing on the city-state of Tegea in southeast Arcadia.
- The Argives (inhabitants of the Peloponnesian city of Argos) and the Athenians are defeated at the Battle of Mantinea in the center of the Peloponnese, and Argos switches allegiance from Athens to Sparta, as do its allies. Athens is becoming increasingly isolated.

416 BC

- With the encouragement of the politician and general Alcibiades, the Athenians take the island of Melos, in the Cyclades. Its inhabitants are treated with great cruelty, an action later regretted by the Athenians.

416 BC–415 BC The Sicilian city of Segesta asks for Athenian help against the Dorian city of Selinus, which has the backing of the powerful Greek city of Syracuse. A large Athenian expedition under the joint command of the Athenian leaders Nicias and Alcibiades sets sail for Sicily to aid Segesta, hoping to gain a foothold in Sicily and attain control of the sea. Alcibiades is immediately recalled to meet charges of impiety arising from the mutilation of all the protective statues of Hermes outside the house of Athens, the *Hermae*, on the eve of the Sicilian expedition; the sacrilege is believed to have been committed during drunken pranks by Alcibiades and his friends. He flees to the court of the Spartan king Agis II.

414 BC

- Nicias of Athens lays siege to the powerful Greek city of Syracuse in Sicily and initially gains the upper hand in the fighting outside its walls. However, he fails to follow up on this early success and the Syracusans outflank the Athenians and place them under siege. The Syracusans obtain the assistance of the Spartan general Gylippus.

413 BC

- The Spartans advance almost to the gates of the Greek city-state of Athens, occupying Decelea on the slopes of Mt. Parnes, northwest of Athens. This gives them a stranglehold on the city, causing great hardship in Athens.

September 9 Despite the arrival of a second fleet under the command of the Athenian general Demosthenes, the Athenian expedition in Sicily is heavily defeated in a joint land and sea battle near Syracuse. The Athenian

Peloponnesian Wars (461 BC–404 BC)

First Peloponnesian War

461 BC–446 BC

- Athenian foreign policy, now under the control of the nationalistic statesman Pericles, becomes very aggressive and imperialist. This period sees intermittent war, known as the First Peloponnesian War, between the Athenian-led Delian League, edging ever closer to becoming an Athenian Empire, and the Spartan-dominated Peloponnesian League, consisting of the Peloponnesian states of Laconia (Sparta), Messenia, Ellis, and Arcadia, plus Corinth and Megara.

459 BC

- Athenian politician Pericles' first move in his aggressive foreign policy is to try to isolate central Greece and replace Theban control by Athenian occupation. Athens makes strategic alliances with the city-states Argos and Megara, and the region of Thessaly. Corinth and the island of Aegina feel that these actions threaten their sea trade, and declare war on Athens.

458 BC

- After a great effort, the Greek city-state of Athens is victorious over its Peloponnesian enemies and the Peloponnesian city of Aegina is forced to join the Delian League.
- The Greek city-states of Sparta and Thebes, the capital of Boeotia, declare war on Athens. A Spartan force, going to the help of Boeotia in a local dispute, is nearly cut off by the Athenians on its return.

457 BC

- On returning from their Boeotian expedition, the Spartans are drawn into fighting with the Athenians, the latter being defeated at the ensuing Battle of Tanagra. The Spartans are unable to follow up their victory, however, and withdraw from the area. Athens then advances into Boeotia, which becomes a member of the Delian League.

451 BC

- The warring Greek city-states are temporarily exhausted and a five-year truce is arranged between Athens and the Peloponnese.

447 BC

- Athens loses control of Boeotia after Thebes, the capital, successfully instigates a revolt in the cities taken over by the Athenians. The Athenian general Tolmides, sent to recapture them, is defeated at the Battle of Coronea. This encourages the city of Eubea to revolt and the city of Megara to declare independence. Before Eubea can be recovered, the Athenian truce with Sparta lapses and the Spartan army invades Attica.

446 BC

- The Athenian statesman Pericles rounds off a difficult period in foreign affairs by negotiating a somewhat humiliating peace treaty with Sparta and its Peloponnesian allies, restoring independence to Achaea on the southern shore of the Corinthian Gulf, and extending the 5-year truce for another 30 years. This brings the First Peloponnesian War to an end.

435 BC

- The Greek city-state of Corinth attacks its recalcitrant colony Corcyra, an island off the coast of Epirus in western Greece, in a dispute concerning the latter's colony of Epidamnus in Illyria. This is one of the first incidents in the buildup to the Second Peloponnesian War.

433 BC

- Corcyra and Corinth are at war: Athenian ships are deployed in the Battle of Sybota at the request of Corcyra, a Corinthian colony, enraging the Corinthians. The quarrel spreads to Potidaea in Chalcidice, a member of the Athenian Empire but originally a Corinthian colony, which now revolts in sympathy.

432 BC

- The Athenian statesman Pericles punishes the city of Megara for assisting Corinth in the Battle of Sybota against Corcyra, by depriving it of its maritime trade.
- The Athenians besiege the city of Potidaea in Chalcidice; Corinth appeals to Sparta. At an intercity assembly at Sparta, Athens is accused of breaking the 30-year peace treaty agreed in 446 BC.

431 BC

- The Athenian statesman Pericles makes his famous funeral oration for the fallen in the year's campaigns. The Athenian historian Thucydides describes the incident in his *History*, showing that the speech is much more than an oration for the dead and amounts to an assertion of Athenian values and aspirations.

Second Peloponnesian War

431 BC

- The Second Peloponnesian War is precipitated by an incident at Plataea, the only pro-Athenian city in Boeotia. A Theban raid on the city is a failure and the Plataeans take 180 prisoners and put them to death. Athens supports Plataea and Sparta aligns itself on the other side. Sparta enlists the help of the Greek cities of Italy and Sicily, and both sides appeal unsuccessfully to Persia.
- The Thebans besiege the pro-Athenian city of Plataea in Boeotia.
- May 5 The Spartans invade Attica, marking the start of the 27-year Peloponnesian War. The Athenian army is outclassed by the Spartans and Athens' power lies in its navy, so the Athenian statesman Pericles brings the population of the country districts into the city of Athens while pursuing an active naval war. Athens insures itself against danger from the island of Aegina by supplanting its Doric population with Athenians.

430 BC

- The Spartans make the second of their five invasions of Attica. The Athenians have some successes in sea raids on their enemies and the city of Potidaea in Chalcidice is taken. In Athens itself, full to bursting point with refugees, plague breaks out, killing much of the population, including Pericles.

428 BC

- The city of Mytilene takes advantage of Athens' weakened state to revolt.

427 BC

- Attica is again invaded by Sparta.

- In an effort to blockade Sparta and deprive it of desperately needed Sicilian corn, Athens responds to a plea for help made by the city of Leontini in Sicily. This is a preliminary mission to the large-scale Athenian intervention in Sicily of 415 BC–412 BC.

- The southern Boeotian city of Plataea surrenders to Sparta, and the Aegean city of Mytilene to Athens. The Athenian Assembly, influenced by the demagogue Cleon, votes for the destruction of the population of Mytilene. Thebes and Sparta show no mercy to the Plataeans following their revolt and subsequent surrender to Sparta. Each prisoner is asked: "Have you in the present war done any service to the Lacedaemonians (Spartans) or their allies?" Some 200 prisoners who cannot say yes are put to death.

425 BC

- The Athenian general Demosthenes lands at the Peloponnesian city of Pylos, defeats the Spartans, and captures 420 Spartan hoplites (soldiers) on the neighboring island of Sphacteria. He then fortifies Pylos and Sphacteria. Sparta breaks off its invasion of Attica to send troops to Pylos. The Athenian statesman Cleon takes command and wins a victory for Athens. Sparta makes peace overtures which Cleon persuades Athens to reject.

424 BC

- Cleon of Athens captures the Peloponnesian island of Cythera, from which he harries the Spartans. Athens also captures Nisaea and Pegae, the ports of Megara on the isthmus of Corinth.

- The Athenians spread the Second Peloponnesian War into Boeotia, but are defeated at the Battle of Delium. They suffer worse defeats in Thrace at the hands of the Spartan general Brasidas, who captures the city of Amphipolis. The Athenian historian Thucydides, the general in command, is held responsible and banished.

423 BC

- A year's truce in the Second Peloponnesian War is agreed between the Greek city-states of Athens and Sparta.

422 BC

- Cleon of Athens ends the truce in the Second Peloponnesian War and resolves on the rescue of the Athenian colony of Amphipolis in Thrace, captured by Sparta in 424 BC. In a battle outside the city both the Athenian leader Cleon and the Spartan general Brasidas are killed; the victory goes to the Spartans.

421 BC

- Nicias, leader of the aristocratic propeace faction in the Greek city-state of Athens, arranges a peace treaty with Sparta and its Peloponnesian allies. Some of the allies, most notably the Corinthians, consider the terms unjust and break with Sparta, making an alliance with the Peloponnesian city of Argos.

420 BC

- Athens enters into an alliance with Argos, which has so far taken no part in the Second Peloponnesian War because of a treaty of neutrality with Sparta, which ran out in 421 BC. Athens also allies itself with the Peloponnesian cities of Mantinea and Elis.

418 BC

- Sparta invades Argos, and Athens, which allied itself with Argos in 420 BC, breaks the peace and comes to the aid of the Argives, attacking the Peloponnesian city of Epidaurus and advancing on the city-state of Tegea in southeast Arcadia.

- The Argives (inhabitants of the Peloponnesian city of Argos) and the Athenians are defeated at the Battle of Mantinea in the center of the Peloponnese, and Argos switches allegiance from Athens to Sparta, as do its allies. Athens is becoming increasingly isolated.

416 BC

- With the encouragement of the politician and general Alcibiades, the Athenians take the island of Melos, in the Cyclades, slaughtering many of the inhabitants.

414 BC

- Nicias of Athens lays siege to the powerful Greek city of Syracuse in Sicily and initially gains the upper hand in the fighting outside its walls. However, he fails to follow up on this early success and the Syracusans outflank the Athenians and place them under siege. The Syracusans obtain the assistance of the Spartan general Gylippus.

413 BC

- The Spartans advance almost to the gates of Athens, occupying Decelea on the slopes of Mt. Parnes, northwest of Athens. This gives them a stranglehold on the city, causing great hardship in Athens.

September 9   Despite the arrival of a second fleet under the command of the Athenian general Demosthenes, the Athenian expedition in Sicily is heavily defeated in a joint land and sea battle near Syracuse. The Athenian leaders Nicias and Demosthenes are captured and put to death; most of the surviving soldiers are sent to die in the Sicilian quarries.

412 BC

- Athens' allies in the Aegean begin to desert, led by the island of Chios, which is besieged and punished.

- The Spartans sign a treaty of mutual aid with the Persian satrap (provincial governor) of Lower Asia, Tissaphernes. The treacherous Athenian politician and general Alcibiades, who helped the Spartans gain a stranglehold on Athens, deserts the Spartans in turn, and goes to the court of Tissaphernes whom he dissuades from helping Sparta. The Persians see their opportunity to play off one Greek city-state against another and so regain control of the Greek cities of Asia Minor.

Peloponnesian Wars (461 BC–404 BC) *continued*

411 BC

- An oligarchic Council of 400 seizes power in Athens in an effort to exert more efficient control in the conduct of the Second Peloponnesian War. The orator Antiphon is one of the chief instigators of this oligarchic revolution, and one of the two ringleaders. A fragment of his defense speech, recorded on papyrus, survives to modern times, together with three other complete speeches.

- Thrasybulus, the Athenian naval commander in charge of the fleet at Samos, leads a reaction against the harsh rule of the oligarchs in Athens and recalls the turncoat Alcibiades. The Athenian statesman Theramenes takes control in the city and establishes the Rule of the Five Thousand, a mixture of oligarchy and democracy.

410 BC

- Alcibiades wins naval victories for the Athenians, including the Battle of Cyzicus, gaining control of the Hellespont area. Athens is however badly led at home and these are

its last successes. The Rule of the Five Thousand is displaced and democracy restored, largely under the influence of the demagogue Cleophon.

408 BC

- At the Panhellenic gathering at Olympia the philosopher Gorgias rails against the shame of Greeks (the Spartans) allying with Persia against fellow Greeks for the sake of short-term expediency.

407 BC

- Alcibiades returns to Athens to great acclaim, having gained control of the Hellespont area, and is appointed commander in chief. However, almost immediately he is blamed for the naval defeat of one of his lieutenants at Notium by the Spartan general Lysander, and is relieved of his command. He retires into voluntary exile in Bithynia.

- With the Athenian war chest all but exhausted, the gold and silver statues of the Acropolis are melted down to help pay for a new fleet.

leaders Nicias and Demosthenes are captured and put to death; most of the surviving soldiers are sent to die in the Sicilian quarries.

412 BC

- Athens' allies in the Aegean begin to desert Athens, led by the island of Chios, which is besieged and punished.
- The Spartans sign a treaty of mutual aid with the Persian satrap (provincial governor) of Lower Asia, Tissaphernes. The treacherous Athenian politician and general Alcibiades, who helped the Spartans gain a stranglehold on Athens, deserts the Spartans in turn, and goes to the court of Tissaphernes whom he dissuades from helping Sparta. The Persians see their opportunity to play off one Greek city-state against another and so regain control of the Greek cities of Asia Minor.

411 BC

- An oligarchic Council of 400 seizes power in the Greek city-state of Athens in an effort to exert more efficient control in the conduct of the Second Peloponnesian War. The orator Antiphon is one of the chief instigators of this oligarchic revolution, and one of the two ringleaders to be executed. A fragment of his defense speech, recorded on papyrus, survives to modern times, together with three other complete speeches.
- Thrasybulus, the Athenian naval commander in charge of the fleet at Samos, leads a reaction against the harsh rule of the oligarchs in Athens and recalls the turncoat politician and general Alcibiades. The Athenian statesman Theramenes takes control in the city and establishes the Rule of the Five Thousand, a mixture of oligarchy and democracy. Thrasybulus wins a naval battle over the Spartans at Cynossema in the Hellespont.

410 BC

- The Athenian politician and general Alcibiades wins naval victories for the Athenians, including the Battle of Cyzicus, gaining control of the Hellespont area. Athens is however badly led at home and these are its last successes. The Rule of the Five Thousand is displaced and democracy restored, largely under the influence of the demagogue Cleophon.

409 BC

- The Carthaginian general Hannibal, grandson of Hamilcar, invades Sicily with a strong force, intending to reimpose its influence over the island, and defeats the Sicilian Greeks at a second Battle of Himera. Hannibal avenges his grandfather by the torture and immolation of 3,000 prisoners.

408 BC

- At the Panhellenic gathering at Olympia the philosopher Gorgias rails against the shame of Greeks (the Spartans) allying with Persia against fellow Greeks for the sake of short-term expediency.
- King Darius II of Persia sends his second son Cyrus as satrap (provincial governor) to Sardis in Asia Minor with instructions to increase Persian support for Sparta. Tissaphernes, the Persian satrap of Lower Asia, is sent to watch him. Cyrus begins to collect an army of mercenaries (including Greeks) for his own ends.

407 BC

- The Athenian general Alcibiades returns to Athens to great acclaim, having gained control of the Hellespont area, and is appointed commander in chief. However, almost immediately he is blamed for the naval defeat of one of his lieutenants at Notium by the Spartan general Lysander, and is relieved of his command. He retires into voluntary exile in Bithynia.
- With the Athenian war chest all but exhausted, the gold and silver statues of the Acropolis are melted down to help pay for a new fleet.

406 BC

- The Carthaginians again invade Sicily. Plague kills the Carthaginian general Hannibal, the grandson of Hamilcar; Himilco assumes command and besieges the city of Acragas. The plague is carried back to Carthage by soldiers from the campaign.
- The Greek city-state of Athens wins its last naval battle at Arginusae, near Lesbos. The Athenian generals

406 BC

- Athens wins its last naval battle at Arginusae, near Lesbos. The Athenian generals (including the late Athenian statesman Pericles' son) are put on trial, after allegedly failing to save their damaged vessels and pick up survivors, and are put to death.

405 BC

- Athenian naval supremacy is finally shattered by the Spartans under Lysander at the Battle of Aegospotami in the Sea of Marmara. When the news reaches the Athenians, they remember their harsh treatment of the inhabitants of the island of Melos in 416 BC and are afraid that they too will be enslaved.

404 BC

- Athenian historian Thucydides returns to Athens and dies shortly afterwards. His *History of the Peloponnesian War* appears posthumously.

- The Peloponnesians lay siege to the Greek city of Athens, which falls to the Spartans. The Second Peloponnesian War is over. The long walls between Athens and its port of Piraeus are pulled down to the playing of flutes, and a puppet oligarchic government, the Council of Thirty, is set up, led by the Athenian orator and politician Critias. It rules by a bloody reign of terror.

- The Spartan peace terms to end the Second Peloponnesian War are relatively moderate: Athens has to surrender all its foreign possessions and what remains of its fleet; it has to become an ally of Sparta but retains its independence.

(including the late Athenian statesman Pericles' son) are put on trial, after allegedly failing to save their damaged vessels and pick up survivors, and are put to death.

406 BC–396 BC   The Romans besiege the Etruscan town of Veii, north of Rome.

405 BC

- Athenian naval supremacy is finally shattered by the Spartans under the general Lysander at the Battle of Aegospotami in the Sea of Marmara. When the news reaches the Athenians, they remember their harsh treatment of the inhabitants of the island of Melos in 416 BC and are afraid that they too will be enslaved.
- The wealthy Sicilian Dionysius the Elder, son of Hermocritus, gains power in the Greek city of Syracuse in Sicily. He shows great political acumen as a tyrant: he is cruel and oppressive but never commits outrages to gratify purely personal aims. He makes peace with Carthage and fortifies Syracuse. He later styles himself archon (ruler) of Sicily.

404 BC

- King Darius II of Persia dies and his eldest son, Artaxerxes II, ascends the Persian throne. The Egyptian Amyrtaeus takes the opportunity to mount a successful rebellion against Persian rule, founding Egypt's 28th dynasty 404 BC–399 BC, of which he is the only king.
- The Peloponnesians lay siege to the Greek city of Athens, which falls to the Spartans. The Second Peloponnesian War is over. The long walls between Athens and its port of Piraeus are pulled down to the playing of flutes, and a puppet oligarchic government, the Council of Thirty, is set up, led by the Athenian orator and politician Critias. It rules by a bloody reign of terror.
- The Spartan general Lysander sails to the island of Samos, conquers it, and sets himself up as ruler. He holds court at Samos, where he is accorded divine honors. He is probably the first living Greek to receive such honors.
- The Spartan peace terms to end the Second Peloponnesian War are relatively moderate: Athens has

to surrender all its foreign possessions and what remains of its fleet; it has to become an ally of Sparta but retains its independence.

- The treacherous Athenian general and politician Alcibiades flees to the Persians and is assassinated.

403 BC

- Spartan governors, who are appointed over Athens and its late dependencies and allies, prove highly unpopular; they seem to lose their moral and political sense once they have left their homeland.
- The former Athenian naval commander Thrasybulus deposes the oligarchic Council of Thirty and restores democracy in the Greek city-state of Athens. The Council is dissolved and its leader, Critias, killed.

402 BC–399 BC

- Dionysius the Elder, tyrant of the Greek city of Syracuse, extends his power over the Sicel cities in Sicily (indigenous as opposed to Greek cities).

401 BC

- Cyrus' defeat at Cunaxa, north of Babylon, by his brother, King Artaxerxes II of Persia, has repercussions in Egypt. The Persian governor of Ionia, an Egyptian called Tamos, flees home, where he is said to have been put to death by Amyrteos, the sole pharaoh of the 28th dynasty.
- Cyrus, the second son of the late Persian king Darius II, sets out from Sardis in Asia Minor with his army in an attempt to win the Persian throne, but is defeated by his elder brother, Artaxerxes II, at the Battle of Cunaxa (north of Babylon). The 10,000 Greek mercenaries who accompanied him make their way back home under Xenophon.
- King Artaxerxes II of Persia appoints Tissaphernes, the Persian satrap (provincial governor) of Lower Asia, to take over all the districts in Asia Minor over which Artaxerxes' brother Cyrus had been governor before his rebellion and defeat in the Battle of Cunaxa the previous year.

SCIENCE, TECHNOLOGY, AND MEDICINE

Agriculture

436 BC

- Rome suffers a famine; thousands throw themselves into the Tiber to avoid starvation.

Health and Medicine

437 BC

- The world's first hospital is established in Ceylon.

430 BC–426 BC

- At least one third of the population of Athens succumb to plague, most probably typhus or smallpox.

404 BC

- Weakened by famine, thousands of people in Athens die from the plague, most likely typhus or smallpox.

Math

***c.* 440 BC**

- Greek mathematician Hippocrates of Chios writes *Elements*, the first compilation of the elements of geometry.

***c.* 425 BC**

- Greek mathematician Theodorus of Cyrene demonstrates that certain square roots cannot be written as fractions.

Science

***c.* 450 BC**

- Greek historian Herodotus concludes, correctly, that the Nile delta is caused by the deposition of mud carried by the Nile. He declares the Caspian to be an inland sea and not part of the northern ocean as most scholars of the time believe.

432 BC

- Athenian astronomer Meton accurately calculates the 19-year cycle when lunar phases recur on the same days of the solar year—the Metonic cycle.

***c.* 420 BC**

- Greek philosopher Democritus of Abdera develops Leucippus' atomic theory and states that space is a vacuum and that all things consist of eternal, invisible and indivisible *atomon* (atoms). He also posits necessary laws by which they interact.

Technology

***c.* 450 BC**

- Mail armor is used in Scythia, near modern Kiev, Russia—the earliest known use.

- The Romans begin to make barrels for storing wine.

424 BC

- The Greeks use sulfur gas in their siege of Delium in Boeotia—the first instance of chemical warfare.

***c.* 420 BC**

- The Gauls invent the claymore ("great sword"), a double-edged and double-handed sword.

ARTS AND IDEAS

Architecture

447 BC

- Athenian statesman Pericles commissions the construction of the great temple of Athena, the Parthenon, on the Acropolis in Athens. He intends the Parthenon and other edifices to have a dual religious and patriotic symbolism. Supervised by his friend, the Greek sculptor Phidias, the work is completed in about ten years. Also built on the Acropolis is the Propylaea (or "entrance") and, in later times, the temple of Athene Nike and the temple known as the Erechtheum.

430 BC

- The Hall of a Hundred Pillars, at the Persian royal complex of Persepolis, is completed during the reign of the Persian king Artaxerxes I, joining other monuments built by the previous Persian monarchs Darius I and Xerxes I.

421 BC

- Construction begins on the temple known as the Erechtheum, on the Acropolis in Athens. Completed in 407 BC, the temple is to house several cults and contains many different altars.

***c.* 420 BC**

- The Corinthian column, a column topped by a capital in the shape of an acanthus leaf, becomes a feature of Greek architecture.
- The temple of Athene Nike, the goddess of victory, is built on the Acropolis in Athens.

Arts

450 BC

- At La Tène (in modern Switzerland), Lake Neuchâtel becomes a site for Celtic votive offerings, and the artistic style of the same name also flourishes at this time. It is an art of curved lines and patterns. The votive offerings often include imported objects from classical cultures. These mark definite progress in Celtic art and have given their name to the Iron Age culture of northwestern Europe of this time. The La Tène culture lasts until the time, some three and a half centuries later, of Germanic interference and then Roman conquest.
- *c.* 450 BC   The Athenian sculptor Myron makes his bronze statue of a discus thrower, the original of which is lost in modern times.

438 BC

- The Greek sculptor Phidias erects his chryselephantine (gold and ivory) statue of Athena, which stands 11 m/ 36 ft high, in the Parthenon in the Acropolis at Athens.

c. 431 BC

- The Greek sculptor Phidias moves to Olympia and carves his statue of Zeus, which becomes celebrated as one of the Seven Wonders of the World. It does not survive to modern times, but is described by the 1st century AD Greek historian Strabo and the 2nd century AD historian Pausanias.

c. 430 BC

- The sculptor Polyclitus of Argos is active, and gains a reputation for being unsurpassable in making images of men, as Phidias is in creating images of gods.

Literature and Language

439 BC

- Athenian commander Pericles makes a moving funeral oration for the Athenians who died in the revolt of Samos, famously stating that "the Spring has been taken out of the year."

402 BC

- The city-state of Athens standardizes its alphabet, basing it on the East Ionic model: other Greek states are doing the same.

Music

406 BC

- Musician and dithyrambic poet Timotheus of Miletus acquires a reputation as an innovator, writing a *nome* (a song sung to the accompaniment of the cithara, a stringed musical instrument) called *Persae*, for which the Athenian tragic dramatist Euripides writes the prologue.

Theater and Dance

441 BC

- The Athenian tragic dramatist Euripides wins the first prize in the Festival of Dionysus for an unknown play.
- *c. 441 BC* Athenian dramatist Sophocles' play *Antigone* is thought to be produced after this date. It is significant in the development of political thought, dealing with the problem of divided loyalties, to the state or to one's conscience.

440 BC

- Sophocles, better known as a tragedian, becomes a general under the Athenian commander Pericles during the revolt of Samos.

438 BC

- Athenian tragic dramatist Euripides writes his *Alcestis*.

431 BC

- Athenian tragic dramatist Euripides writes his *Medea*.

430 BC

- Greek comic dramatist Cratinus attacks the Athenian leader Pericles for bringing war on the Athenians in his play *Dionysalexandros*. Cratinus, Eupolis, and Aristophanes are the leading exponents of what becomes

known as Greek Old Comedy; topical, satirical, surreal, and frequently obscene.

428 BC

- Athenian tragic dramatist Euripides writes his *Hippolytus*.

426 BC

- Athenian tragic dramatist Euripides writes his *Andromache*.

425 BC

- Athenian orator and statesman Callistratus produces *Acharnanians*, the first surviving play by the great master of Old Comedy, Aristophanes.

424 BC

- Greek comedy dramatist Aristophanes produces his own play *The Knights* in Athens. It includes an attack on the Athenian politician and general Cleon.

423 BC

- The play *The Clouds*, by the Greek comedy dramatist Aristophanes, is produced. It includes ridicule of the Athenian philosopher Socrates.

422 BC

- The play *The Wasps*, by the Greek comedy dramatist Aristophanes, is produced. It mocks the enthusiasm of old men for taking part in jury service.

421 BC

- The play *Peace*, by the Greek comedy dramatist Aristophanes, is produced. It celebrates Athenian peace with Sparta.

416 BC

- Agathon wins the prize for tragedy at the Lenaea, a drama competition and festival in Athens. The banquet he gives in celebration of this victory is the setting of the Greek philosopher Plato's *Symposium*.

415 BC

- Athenian tragic dramatist Euripides writes his *Troades/ Trojan Women*.

414 BC

- The play *The Birds*, by the Greek comedy dramatist Aristophanes is produced.

412 BC

- Athenian tragic dramatist Euripides writes his play *Helen*, which although technically a tragedy has a happy ending.

411 BC

- The comedy *Lysistrata*, by the Greek comedy dramatist Aristophanes, voices the war-weariness of Athens. Women in the play withdraw sex in order try to force their menfolk to make peace.

409 BC

- Athenian tragic dramatist Euripides produces his play *Phoenissae*.
- Greek dramatist Sophocles wins a prize at Athens with his tragedy *Philoctetes*. This is one of only two plays by Sophocles which can be accurately dated.

408 BC

- *Orestes*, by the Athenian tragic dramatist Euripides, is produced. Euripides spends the final two years of his life (408 BC–406 BC) at the court of the king of Macedon, writing *Bacchae* and *Iphigenia at Aulis* in that period.

405 BC

- *The Frogs*, a comedy by the Greek comedy dramatist Aristophanes, is produced.

401 BC

- Athenian dramatist Sophocles wins a posthumous prize at the Festival of Dionysus with his play *Oedipus at Colonos*, one of only two plays that can be accurately dated.

Thought and Scholarship

450 BC

c. 450 BC Greek philosopher Zeno of Elea, Italy, is active. He becomes famous for his paradoxes, including that of the hare and the tortoise, and a number of paradoxes showing the difficulties with the assertion that a line can be infinitely subdivided. The Greek philosopher Aristotle gives him the name "inventor of dialectic" because of his liking for argument and logic.

450 BC–445 BC According to his own accounts, the Greek historian Herodotus visits Babylon and Egypt in order to collect stories for his *Histories*.

c. 445 BC

- Greek philosopher and scientist Empedocles distinguishes the "four elements"—earth, fire, water, and air—which he claims all substances are made of, and which also explain the development of the Universe by the forces of attraction and repulsion. The doctrine is embodied in Aristotle's works and influences Western thought until the 17th century AD.

c. 444 BC

- Greek historian Herodotus, the "father of history," is reputed to be one of the colonists of the new city of Thurii, Italy. In his *Histories*, Herodotus records the events of the wars between Persia and Greece, and takes a much wider view of history than his contemporaries, such as the Athenian historian Thucydides, going beyond political and military history to include geography and anthropology.

c. 437 BC

- Greek philosopher and astronomer Anaxagoras is accused of impiety, but is saved from the death penalty by the oratory of the Athenian statesman Pericles, and is fined and banished. He settles in Lampsacus, Mysia.

c. 435 BC

- Greek philosopher Leucippus is the first to propose the atomic theory. It is developed later by his pupil Democritus.

c. 430 BC

- Athenian philosopher Socrates is active. He claims to know nothing and to be a "midwife to truth," bringing forth the truth which others already know, but his participation in intellectual debates changes philosophy, focusing it on the inner nature of humanity. He writes no accounts of his work and, in later times, is known mainly through the works of the philosophers and historians Plato, Xenophon, and Aristotle.

427 BC

- The sophist and rhetorician Gorgias of Sicily leads an embassy to Athens from Leontini, Sicily. His *Encomium*

of Helen and *Defence of Palamedes* survive to modern times.

424 BC

- Diagoras of Melos "the Atheist" resides in Athens in the last decades of the century, but after ridiculing the Eleusinian Mysteries, the ceremonies in honor of the Greek deities Demeter and Persephone, is forced to flee from a death sentence.
- Following his banishment after leading an Athenian force to defeat at the hands of the Spartans, the Athenian soldier and historian Thucydides travels widely, researching his *History of the Peloponnesian War*.

420 BC

- Chinese philosopher Mo Tzu leads a sect which aims to create an egalitarian society, through respect for the law, and pacifism.
- The sophist and rhetorician Thrasymachus of Chalcedon is active. He features as a character in the Greek philosopher Plato's *Republic*.

411 BC

- Athenian historian Thucydides finishes writing his *History*. The Greek historian Xenophon continues the work in 383 BC.

410 BC

- Andocides, one of the ten leading canonical Attic orators, delivers his speech "On His Return," one of only three of his speeches which survive to modern times.

404 BC

- Athenian historian Thucydides returns to Athens and dies shortly afterwards. His *History of the Peloponnesian War* appears posthumously.
- The Athenian Council of the Thirty order the Athenian philosopher Socrates to arrest a man whom Socrates considers innocent. Socrates refuses with impunity.

403 BC

- Athenian orator Lysias writes speeches against the oligarchic Council of Thirty in the campaign to oust it from power in Athens.

SOCIETY

Education

c. 450 BC

- The growth of democracy in many of the Greek city-states during this period, especially in Athens, has created a demand for education, particularly in the art of rhetoric.

Everyday Life

449 BC

- The total population of Attica reaches a quarter of a million people, very large for a *polis* (city-state), but nearly half of these may have been slaves.

426 BC

- The Athenians purify the island of Delos by removing all burials and by decreeing that no one can be born or die on the island. The Athenian politician and general Nicias leads a particularly splendid procession to the festival of Delos in 417 BC.

420 BC

- The cult of Asclepius, the god of medicine and son of Apollo, arrives in Athens.

Religion

433 BC

- The governor of Jerusalem, Nehemiah, leaves the city for a while, and the Jews slip back into some of their old sinful ways of living, such as marriage with Gentiles. Nehemiah has to correct these religious abuses on his return.

BIRTHS & DEATHS

450 BC

- Alcibiades, Athenian politician and military commander, born in Athens, Greece (–404 BC).
- Aristophanes, outstanding Greek comic dramatist, 11 of whose plays survive, including *The Clouds*, *The Birds*, and *The Frogs*, born (–c. 388 BC).

447 BC

- Marcus Furius Camillus, Roman soldier and five-time dictator or Rome, born (–365 BC).

446 BC

- c. 446 BC Pindar, ancient Greek poet noted for his odes celebrating victories in various athletic events, dies in Argos, Greece (76)
- Timotheus, celebrated Greek musician of Miletus (now in Turkey), born (–357 BC).

445 BC

- Lysias, Greek orator, a number of whose speeches survive, born (–after 380 BC).

c. 444 BC

- Agesilaus II, King of Sparta 399–360, during Sparta's ascendancy, born (–360 BC).

440 BC

- c. 440 BC Parmenides, Greek philosopher, founder of Eleaticism, dies (c. 65).
- Andocides, Athenian orator and politician, born (–c. 391 BC).

436 BC

- Isocrates, Greek orator and teacher of rhetoric, a number of whose speeches survive, born in Athens, Greece (–338 BC).

c. 432 BC

- Phidias, Athenian architect who directed the construction of the Parthenon, dies (c. 58).

431 BC

- Xenophon, Greek historian, author of *Anabasis*, born (–c. 350 BC).

c. 430 BC

- Dionysius the Elder, tyrant of Syracuse 405 BC–367 BC whose

wars against the Carthaginians saved Sicily for Greece and made Syracuse one of the most powerful cities in ancient Greece, born (–367 BC).
- Zeno of Elea, Greek philosopher who developed dialectic and logical rigor in philosophic thinking, dies (c. 65).

429 BC

- Pericles, Athenian statesman chiefly responsible for making Athens the center of Greece and for Athenian democracy, dies in Athens, Greece (c. 66)

428 BC

- Anaxagoras, Greek philosopher of nature who discovered the true cause of eclipses, dies in Lampsacus, Anatolia, Asia Minor (72).
- Plato, Greek philosopher, often considered one of the greatest in history, born in Athens, or possibly Aegina, Greece (–347 BC).

425 BC

- c. 425 BC Herodotus, Greek historian, author of an important history of the Greco-Persian wars, dies (c. 59).
- Artaxerxes I, Achaemenid king of Persia 464 BC–425 BC, son of Xerxes I, is assassinated in Susa, Elam, Iran.

422 BC

- c. 422 BC Cratinus, a leading Athenian comic playwright, of whose works only fragments survive, dies.
- Brasidas, celebrated Spartan commander during the Archidamian War between Sparta and Athens 431 BC–421 BC, falls in battle against the Athenians at the Athenian colony of Amphipolis in Thrace.
- Cleon, leader of the Athenian democracy (429 BC), falls in battle against the Spartans at Amphipolis.

413 BC

- Demosthenes, Athenian general during the Peloponnesian War between Athens and Sparta 431 BC–404 BC, is captured and

executed during the siege of Syracuse.

411 BC

- Antiphon, Athenian orator and statesman, the earliest known professional rhetorician, is executed for treason (c. 69).

410 BC

- c. 410 BC Epaminondas, Theban military commander, born in Thebes, Egypt (–362 BC).
- Protagoras, Greek Sophist philosopher known for his dictum "Man is the measure of all things," dies (c. 75).

406 BC

- Euripides, one the great Athenian tragic dramatists, whose best-known plays include *Medea* (431 BC) and *Electra* (418 BC), dies in Macedon (c. 78).
- Sophocles, Greek playwright, author of *Oedipus Rex*, dies in Athens (90).

404 BC

- Alcibiades, Athenian politician and military commander, dies in Phrygia (now in Turkey) (c. 46).
- Darius II ("Ochus"), Achaemenid king of Persia 423 BC–404 BC, Persian pharaoh of Egypt 424 BC–404 BC, son of Artaxerxes I, dies in Babylon.
- Darius III ("Codommanus"), last Achaemenid king of Persia 336 BC–330 BC, is killed in Bactria (in present-day Afghanistan) (c. 49).

401 BC

- c. 401 BC Thucydides, Greek historian, author of *History of the Peloponnesian War* which describes the war between Athens and Sparta, dies (c. 70).
- Cyrus the Younger, Achaemenid Persian prince, son of Darius II, and pretender to the Achaemenid throne, falls in battle against his brother Artaxerxes II at Cunaxa, Babylon (c. 22).

c. 425 BC
- The Old Testament Book of Esther is written.

410 BC
- Egyptian priests destroy the Jewish temple of Jehovah on the Elephantine island on the River Nile.

Sports

c. 450 BC
- Mechanical starting gates for running and chariot races are introduced at the Olympic Games in Greece.

c. 430 BC–c. 355 BC
- A treatise on hunting, *Cynegeticus*, is written around this time. It is mostly devoted to the techniques of hunting hares and deer on foot, and also expounds on the moral and physical benefits of the sport.

400 BC–351 BC

POLITICS, GOVERNMENT, AND ECONOMICS

Business and Economics

c. 400 BC
- Coins begin to appear in northern India, the idea having arrived from Greece via Persia.
- The culture of the Scythian region (north of the Black Sea) comes into contact with the Greek world, leading to the founding of the first fortified Scythian city on the River Dnieper. Greek artifacts are placed in Scythian tombs from this time.
- The Greek city-state of Athens is still important as a trade center, and its port, Piraeus, increases in size and importance. Commercial banks spring up, taking over depositing and lending money from the temples and priests.

387 BC
- The Greek city-state of Athens is deprived of its Bosporus trade and tolls by Spartan military action in the area, in spite of initial successes by the Athenian soldier Iphicrates.

377 BC
- Taxation in the Greek city-state of Athens is reorganized: the richer citizens are made responsible for collection of the taxes from the less well off.

362 BC
- The sarcophagi (stone coffins) of the kings of Sidon, Phoenicia, show a Greek influence.

Colonization

c. 400 BC
- Celtic tribes begin to move into northern Italy; the Boii and Senones cross the River Po and settle in the Po valley. The Insubres occupy Lombardy, with their capital at Milan (Roman Mediolanum). These Celtic tribes are collectively called Gauls by the Romans. At the same time, other Celtic groups are colonizing the banks of the Yonne and Seine rivers in France, and yet others are moving into Bohemia and Bavaria.

Human Rights

400 BC
- Mania, widow of a satrap (provincial governor), strikes an early blow for women's rights in the Troad (the area around Troy), by persuading the Persian satrap Pharnabazus to let her govern in place of her deceased husband.

395 BC
- King Agesilaus of Sparta treats his Persian and Greek prisoners taken in Asia Minor with remarkable humanity, though he is not above showing them off to his soldiers as a warning against leading an unathletic life.

387 BC
- Greek philosopher Plato returns to Athens and founds the Academy, a school of philosophy at Academe, which he heads for the remainder of his life. The Academy allows women to study philosophy, unusual at this time.

380 BC
- The women Axiothea, who dresses as a man, and Lastheneia are pupils of the Greek philosopher Plato, unusual at a time when women were generally not allowed to study philosophy.

376 BC
- The Roman tribunes Licinius and Sextius strive to end the traditional class enmity between patricians and plebeians in Rome with liberalizing laws.

Politics and Government

400 BC
- Sparta makes war on Persia in Asia Minor. Most of Xenophon's 10,000 Greek mercenaries, returning from the Battle of Cunaxa in 401 BC, enlist under the Spartans.
- The restoration of democracy in the Greek city-state of Athens after the end of the oligarchy of the Council of Thirty is accomplished with remarkable restraint and success. A small change is effected by making members of the Council preside in the Assembly.
- *c.* 400 BC–*c.* 390 BC The Greek city-states begin to squabble among themselves during this decade and the decades that follow, right up until the Macedonian domination, signally failing to unite against the common threat from the north. For the next 30 years Sparta pursues a policy of aggrandisement until it collapses before Thebes.

399 BC
- The 29th dynasty begins in Egypt. It is virtually free from the domination of Persia, which is preoccupied with the aftermath of Cyrus' attempt to take over the empire and the Spartan attacks in Asia Minor. Egypt gives some help to Sparta.
- The Spartan general Lysander attempts a political revolution in Sparta. He wants kings to be elected and the kingship separated from leadership of the army. He tries to bring religious influence to bear and persuades some priests at Olympia to cooperate in a plot to reveal some alleged hidden documents that tell a tale in his favor, but he is unsuccessful and earns the disfavor of Agesilaus, who becomes king in the usual way.

398 BC
- Dionysius the Elder, tyrant of the Greek city of Syracuse in Sicily, strikes at Carthage while it is still weakened by plague, attacking its cities in the western corner of Sicily. There is a massacre of Carthaginians in many cities and the city of Motya with its fine harbor is taken.

397 BC
- To avenge the massacre of Carthaginians by Dionysius the Elder, the tyrant of the Greek city of Syracuse in Sicily, the Carthaginian general Himilco is sent to Sicily with a fresh army, puts Dionysius on the defensive, and besieges Syracuse. Himilco is defeated, however, and flees back to Carthage, although he succeeds in establishing the town of Lilybaeum to replace Motya, which was taken by Dionysius.

396 BC
- During the siege of the Etruscan town of Veii, Roman citizen-soldiers are paid for the first time.
- King Agesilaus of Sparta campaigns with some success in Asia Minor against the Persian satraps (governors) Pharnabazus and Tissaphernes. After the Peloponnesian War, Persia regained control of the Greek cities of Asia Minor; Sparta is now determined to liberate them.
- Roman statesman Camillus is made dictator by the Romans and finally destroys the Etruscan town of Veii after a siege reputedly lasting ten years. This marks the effective end of Etruscan power in Italy.

- The Persian satrap (provincial governor) Tissaphernes is assassinated on the orders of the Persian queen Parysatis, who cannot forgive the rough treatment handed out to her favorite son, the dead Cyrus.

395 BC
- Before King Agesilaus of Sparta can win any major victories in Asia Minor, the Corinthian War begins, with the Greek cities of Corinth, Thebes, and Argos, soon joined by Athens, all allied against Sparta.
- Conon, an Athenian general who escaped from the Spartan victory at Aegospotami in 405 BC, is hired by the Persians and appointed admiral of a Persian fleet. The Persians aid the Athenians to continue the war with Sparta, in order to keep Sparta out of Asia Minor.
- Himilco returns from Sicily, ashamed at his defeat at the hands of Dionysius I, tyrant of Syracuse. He abases himself, confesses his sins in every temple of Carthage, and starves himself to death.
- *c.* 395 BC Athenian general Iphicrates introduces lightly armored troops *peltastae* into the Athenian army. Equipped with a lighter shield, reduced armor, and a longer sword and spear, they are more maneuverable.

394 BC
- The Athenian general Conon and the Persian satrap (provincial governor) Pharnabazus win a naval victory over the Spartans at Cnidus. The Athenians are avenged, at the expense of receiving help from Persia, and the Spartan bid for empire begins to crumble. Persia is virtually the arbiter of Greece.

392 BC
- Dionysius the Elder, tyrant of the Greek city of Syracuse in Sicily, is attacked by a second Carthaginian expedition and again allies himself with the Sicels (indigenous Sicilians). The Carthaginians are defeated, make peace, and leave.

391 BC
- Dionysius the Elder, tyrant of the Greek city of Syracuse in Sicily, begins an attempt to extend his rule to the Greek cities of southern Italy: he unsuccessfully besieges Rhegium.
- Roman dictator Camillus is accused in Rome of unfairly distributing the spoils of the Etruscan town of Veii; he goes into voluntary exile.

390 BC
- A wandering tribe of Celts (whom the Romans call Gauls) defeats the Romans, deserted by their allies, at the Battle of the Allia and Rome is besieged for six months until only the Capitol is unconquered. The rest of the city is sacked by the Gauls. They are probably bought off with gold, though the legend grows that the former Roman dictator Camillus is recalled from exile and defeats them.
- When the citizens of Rome flee before the Gauls' attack of the Capitol, the senators, according to legend, stay seated majestically in their robes while the barbarian Gauls wonder at them. When a Gaul strokes the beard of Papirius, he strikes the offending Gaul, and the Gauls massacre the entire Senate.
- After the sack of Rome by the Gauls, Rome has to deal with unrest and revolt by all its former enemies and most of its allies, including Etruria, the Aequi, the Volsci, the Latins, and the Hernici.

- King Evagoras of Cyprus is assisted against Persia by the Athenians.

388 BC

- Rome defeats the Aequi at Bola; they are completely vanquished.
- Sparta seeks and gets help from Dionysius the Elder, tyrant of the Greek city of Syracuse, Sicily, in the Corinthian War.

387 BC

- Dionysius the Elder, tyrant of the Greek city of Syracuse in Sicily, captures the Greek city of Rhegium in Italy and then turns his attention to the Adriatic.
- Sparta is unsuccessful in the war against Persia and the attempt at empire and so concludes "the King's Peace" (sometimes known as the Peace of Antalcidas, after the Spartan envoy), which hands back the Greek cities of Asia Minor to Persian rule.

386 BC

- Persia, freed from Spartan attacks, turns to quietening Cyprus and Egypt and is occupied there for the rest of the decade. The wars drag on owing to the skill of King Evagoras of Cyprus (who for a time captures the Phoenician city of Tyre) and Egypt's Greek mercenary general Chabrias.

386 BC–383 BC Dionysius the Elder, tyrant of the Greek city of Syracuse in Sicily, extends the influence and trade of Syracuse to the Adriatic, planting a colony as far north as Hadria on the east coast of northern Italy.

385 BC

- Rome defeats an alliance of the Latins, Volsci, and Hernici. A Latin colony is established in the Volscian town of Satricum and three years later, one at Setia. The Latins and Volsci continue to give trouble, especially the Volscian towns of Satricum, Antium, and Velitrae, which are repeatedly captured and besieged by each side, until Rome is victorious with the defeat of the Latin League in 338 BC.

383 BC

- The Greek city-state of Sparta sends an expedition northward to disrupt the Chalcidian League of petty kings with whom King Amyntas III of Macedon has formed a temporary alliance. On their way north, they gain control of the Theban citadel with help from a pro-Spartan party of Thebans.
- War breaks out again between Dionysius the Elder, tyrant of the Greek city of Syracuse in Sicily, and Carthage.

382 BC

- The Greek city-state of Sparta increases its hold on central Greece still further by refounding the city of Plataea, which it previously destroyed in 427 BC.

381 BC

- Persia makes peace with King Evagoras of Cyprus, accepting his submission on honorable terms.

380 BC

- Egypt's 30th dynasty, the last native house to rule Egypt according to the Egyptian historian Manetho, begins with the pharaoh Nectanebo I, an Egyptian general who usurps the throne and who builds many monuments and restores many temples, including a temple to Thoth, god of wisdom and learning, at Hermopolis, Egypt.

- The Athenian orator Isocrates publishes his speech, the *Panegyricus*, at the Olympian festival, advocating a grand expedition to set the Greek cities of Asia Minor free again under the combined leadership of Athens and Sparta, but it is not a practical proposition.
- The Theban general and politician Epaminondas comes to power in the Greek city of Thebes after an Athenian-backed coup. Thebans in Athens, refugees from the Spartan occupation of their home city in 383 BC, send seven conspirators, dressed as women, to gain access to the Spartan rulers at Thebes and murder them. The Spartans retire from Thebes, the conspirators are crowned with wreaths, and Epaminondas takes command.

379 BC

- A Spartan attempt to seize the Athenian port of Piraeus sends the Greek city-state of Athens into a closer relationship with the city of Thebes in Boeotia.
- Dionysius the Elder, tyrant of the Greek city of Syracuse in Sicily, suffers a severe defeat in Sicily and has to make a disadvantageous peace, surrendering some western towns to the Carthaginians.
- The Greek city-state of Sparta suppresses the Chalcidian League of petty kings with whom King Amyntas III of Macedon has formed a temporary alliance and imposes terms favorable to Amyntas III.

378 BC

- The Thebans form their Sacred Band of warriors, made up of 150 pairs of friends and lovers. All are dedicated and highly trained fighters and their ferocity and loyalty in battle, heightened by their loyalty to each other, become renowned.

378 BC–377 BC The Greek city-state of Athens allies itself with the city of Thebes and forms a second Athenian Confederacy (the first being the Delian League, formed in 477 BC). Most of the other Boeotian cities and some of the Ionian islands join the confederacy. War breaks out between the Thebans and Spartans in Boeotia.

377 BC–373 BC

- The Greek city-state of Sparta and the Boeotian capital, Thebes, are at war in Boeotia, with little success for Sparta.

376 BC

- Chabrias, the Greek mercenary leader who caused the Persians so much trouble in Egypt, returns from there and fights again for Athens, winning a naval victory over the Spartan fleet off the island of Naxos. The Athenians fight the battle to break the Spartans' blockade of their corn ships from the Black Sea.

374 BC

- Jason, ruler of Pherae in Thessaly, the Greek state south of Macedon, allies himself first with Athens and then with Macedon.
- The Greek city-state of Athens wishes to retire from the Theban–Spartan war and makes peace with Sparta, but it is immediately broken.
- The Greek city-state of Sparta attacks the Corinthian colony of Corcyra, enlisting Syracusan help, and Athens comes to the island's aid. Sparta is soon discouraged by a series of earthquakes.

373 BC

- King Artaxerxes II of Persia invades Egypt in an attempt to bring it back under Persian rule. The expedition, led by the Persian satrap (provincial governor) Pharnabazus, has some initial successes but is then forced to retreat when the Greek mercenaries push on toward Memphis too boldly and the River Nile floods.

371 BC

- The Greek city-states of Sparta and Athens make peace, another Peace of Callias (the first being that of 449 BC). The treaty is again named for one of the Athenian envoys.
- Theban statesman Epaminondas introduces a tactical military innovation at the Battle of Leuctra; instead of drawing out a long even line of soldiers he forms a heavy wedge, 50 men deep, on one wing, including the Theban Sacred Band (a special elite unit).

July 7   Theban general Epaminondas wins a decisive victory over the Spartans at the Battle of Leuctra in southern Boetia. The victory shocks Greece, as Spartan soldiers have always been believed to be invincible; Athens does not welcome the victory, fearing the rising aggression of the city of Thebes. The Arcadians decide to reassert their independence from Sparta and form an Arcadian League; they rebuild their city of Mantinea as well as building a new federal city, Megalopolis.

370 BC

- Dionysius the Elder, tyrant of the Greek city of Syracuse in Sicily, takes the initiative against Carthage during this period and acts as the champion of Europe against Asia and the Semites. Towards the end of his reign Syracuse is the most powerful of the Greek cities.
- The new capital city of Megalopolis in the Peleponnese state of Arcadia is completed and a democratic system is established, with an Assembly "of Ten Thousand" and "the Council of Fifty."
- The short-lived low-caste Nanda dynasty is founded in the Magadha kingdom of northeast India.
- The Spartans under King Agesilaus invade Arcadia because the Peleponnese state of Arcadia has revived to an extent that threatens Sparta. Arcadia, having appealed in vain to the Athenians, turns to the Thebans; the Theban leader Epaminondas arrives with an army, finds the Spartans gone home, and follows them, ravaging all in his path.

369 BC

- The Theban leader Epaminondas frees the Peloponnesian state of Messenia from Spartan rule. Not wishing to disturb the balance of power, the Greek city-state of Athens allies itself with Sparta, its traditional enemy.
- Theban general Epaminondas founds Messene (modern Mavrovati) in Messenia, southwest Greece, in order to act as a buffer state against the Spartans.

368 BC

- Dionysius the Elder, tyrant of the Greek city of Syracuse in Sicily, renews his war against Carthaginian Sicily, but with little success. He gives help to Sparta as the Thebans again invade the Peloponnese.

367 BC

- Dionysius the Elder, tyrant of the Greek city of Syracuse in Sicily, dies. After his death he acquires a reputation as the archetypal tyrant: suspicious, bloodthirsty, and with delusions of divinity. He is succeeded by his son, Dionysius the Younger.
- The aged Persian king Artaxerxes II issues peace terms for the Greeks to observe in the form of an edict. He is not obeyed.
- The Licinian laws are promulgated in Rome. The consulship is restored and one of the two consuls must be a plebeian. The offices of praetor (magisterial) and of aedile (a civil office, previously plebeian, with responsibility for temples, buildings, streets, markets, and games) are greatly enlarged in scope and the number of aediles is doubled from two to four, all four open to both patricians and plebeians.

366 BC

- King Perdiccas III, a son of King Amyntas III, comes to the throne of Macedon.
- The Boeotian city of Thebes makes peace with the city-state of Sparta and turns against its other Greek rival, Athens. Athens is trying to revive its maritime empire and is interfering in Macedonian dynastic quarrels.

365 BC

- The pharaoh Tachos, son of Nectanebo I, succeeds to the Egyptian throne. He plans a great attack on Persia and invites the aging Spartan king Agesilaus to help him. Agesilaus arrives with 1,000 hoplites (soldiers) in 363 BC.

364 BC

- Philip of Macedon, brother of the reigning king Perdiccas III, returns to his native land after having spent a few years as a hostage in the Boeotian capital of Thebes.
- The Boeotian city of Thebes builds a fleet of 100 triremes (warships) to combat Athens. The Thebans win no naval battles but the existence of the fleet influences the ever-changing kaleidoscope of Greek city alliances. Thebes shocks the Greek world by destroying its Boeotian rival Orchomenus.

July 13   The Theban general and statesman Pelopidas, friend of the Theban politician Epaminondas, is killed in battle at Cynoscephalae, Thessaly, after setting out under the bad auspices of a solar eclipse.

363 BC

- The Athenian Demosthenes, aged 21, succeeds in a lawsuit against one of his guardians and is encouraged to come forward as a speaker in the Athenian Assembly.

362 BC

- The Peloponnesian state of Arcadia is drifting into an alliance with the city-state of Sparta. The Thebans invade Arcadia and win the Battle of Mantinea, but the Theban leader Epaminondas is killed. His dying wish, for *Koine Eirene* (a general peace), is met and the brief supremacy of the Boeotian city of Thebes comes to an end.

361 BC

- The Egyptians and Spartans, with some Athenian mercenaries under the Greek general Chabrias, set out to attack the Persians' Phoenician cities, but have to return almost at once to meet revolt at home.

- The Nanda dynasty of the kingdom of Magadha in northeast India taxes efficiently, creates a large army, and builds canals.
- The Persian Empire is weakening, despite the failure of a joint Egyptian-Spartan expedition to the Phoenician coast, and many satraps (provincial governors) revolt, including Straton I at Sidon. The city of Sidon (in modern Lebanon) has become rich and prosperous again by this time.

360 BC

- King Agesilaus of Sparta, displeased with his reception in Egypt in 363 BC, supports a revolt against the pharaoh Tachos, who flees to Susa, Persia, and makes peace with the Persians. The new pharaoh, Nectanebo II, a grandson of Nectanebo I, pays the Spartans off. He reigns until 343 BC and carries out considerable building work. With him Egypt's 30th and last native dynasty comes to an end.
- The Gauls again reach the gates of Rome but this time are beaten back.

359 BC

- Philip II of Macedon improves the Greek *phalanx*. He doubles the eight-rank formation, arms his soldiers with the *sarissa*, a pike 1.5 times as long as the Greek spear, and adds units of lightly armored archers, slingers, and javelin throwers to the flanks of the phalanx. He also uses cavalry, making his army the first to effectively combine infantry, cavalry, and artillery.
- The Macedonian king Perdiccas III dies defending his country against an Illyrian attack. He is succeeded by his infant son, Amyntas IV; Amyntas' uncle, Philip, assumes the regency. There are three main factors to help him achieve his ambition to dominate the Greek world: ample troops, a recently discovered gold mine in his country, and his considerable political acumen.

358 BC

- Artaxerxes III ("Ochus") succeeds Artaxerxes II as king of Persia and restores central authority over the Persian Empire's satraps (provincial governors).
- The Gauls are again beaten off from Rome.

357 BC

- Dion, the exiled brother-in-law of the late tyrant Dionysius the Elder of Syracuse, Sicily, makes a spectacular return and temporarily wrests power from the weak Dionysius the Younger.
- Philip II of Macedon, having disposed of an Illyrian threat, occupies the Athenian city of Amphipolis in Thrace, which would otherwise bar his way into Thrace and eventually Greece.

356 BC

- Philip II of Macedon, regent for Amyntas IV, assumes the full title of king and takes Potidaea and other Athenian strongholds in Thessaly and Chalcidice. He forges a unified professional army with a national spirit from the disparate groups of warring Macedonian tribesmen.
- Philip II of Macedon forges a unified professional army with a national spirit from the mishmash of warring Macedonian tribesmen.

- The internecine quarrels of the Greek world continue. Caria and the islands of Chios, Cos, and Rhodes rebel against the city-state of Athens. A second Sacred War breaks out to protect pilgrims to the shrine of Apollo at Delphi following the seizure of the city of Delphi by the Phocians of central Greece.
- The Phocians attain dominance temporarily in Greece, aided by their control of the city of Delphi and their strategic use of mercenary soldiers.

355 BC

- The Athenian Demosthenes, having cured his stammer, begins to come to the fore as a public orator, and becomes a critic of the powerful in Athens.
- Timotheus, son of the Athenian general Conon and one of Athens' most successful generals for 20 years, fails in an attempt to reestablish Athenian control over the island of Chios. He is indicted and heavily fined and leaves Athens a broken man.

354 BC

- Dion, the brother-in-law of the late Dionysius the Elder, who has assumed control in the Greek city of Syracuse in Sicily, is murdered despite his attempt at liberal reform. Syracuse suffers from a number of short-lived tyrants, while Dionysius the Younger, deposed by Dion and in exile in Italy, bides his time.
- Rome allies with the Samnites and defeats the Etruscans at Caere. The inhabitants of Caere have previously helped Rome against the Gauls. Rome and Caere agree a 100-year truce.
- The Greek city-state of Athens recognizes the independence of the islands of Chios, Cos, and Rhodes and makes peace with King Mausolus of Caria in southwest Asia.
- The Phocians of central Greece are defeated in the Sacred War over the protection of pilgrims to the shrine of Apollo in the Phocian-held city of Delphi, but they revive under a new leader.

353 BC

- The Phocians of central Greece threaten Thessaly to their north and Philip II of Macedon sees his opportunity to penetrate south into Greece.

352 BC

- After two initial defeats, Philip II of Macedon drives the Phocians of central Greece south as he begins to execute his plan to dominate the Greek world. The city-states of Athens and Sparta support the Phocians and Philip is checked at Thermopylae but then moves against Thrace. Athens is saved by Philip falling ill.
- The Athenian politician Demosthenes tries to persuade the Athenians to cease depending on paid mercenaries and to return to their old conception of a citizen army.

351 BC

- King Artaxerxes III of Persia makes an abortive attempt to invade Egypt. Encouraged by his failure Phoenicia and Cyprus revolt against Persia.
- The Athenian orator and politician Demosthenes delivers his first *Philippic* against Philip II of Macedon when speaking in favor of the people of Rhodes in the Athenian Assembly.

SCIENCE, TECHNOLOGY, AND MEDICINE

Health and Medicine

c. 400 BC
- Greek physician Hippocrates of Cos begins the corpus of the Hippocratic Collection of about 70 medical treatises which cover topics such as epidemics and epilepsy. There is no evidence that he wrote any of them himself, but by recognizing that disease has natural causes he begins the science of medicine.
- In his *De regimen/On Government* the Greek physician Hippocrates expounds on the therapeutic value of physical exercise.
- The Greek physician Hippocrates recommends milk as a medicine.

Math

c. 360 BC
- Greek mathematician and astronomer Eudoxus of Cnidus develops the theory of proportion (dealing with irrational numbers), and the method of exhaustion (for calculating the area bounded by a curve) in mathematics.

Science

c. 400 BC
- Crude rain gauges 46 cm/18 in wide are used in India.

c. 375 BC
- Greek scientist Archytas of Tarentum develops the science of mechanics. He constructs a model of a pigeon suspended on a pivoted bar which revolves by jets of steam—the first automaton. He also solves the problem of doubling the cube in geometry and applies mathematical principles to music.

c. 366 BC
- Greek mathematician and astronomer Eudoxus of Cnidus builds an observatory and constructs a model of 27 nested spheres to give the first systematic explanation of the motion of the sun, moon, and planets around the earth.

352 BC
- Chinese astronomers make the earliest known record of a supernova.

Technology

c. 400 BC
- The Chinese begin to use bitumen for cooking food and burning in lamps—the first use of oil as a source of energy. In Europe it is used as a lubricant and as a medicinal ointment.

- The iron is invented in China for pressing clothes; it is heated by filling it with glowing embers.
- The round file, made of bronze, is made in Europe.

c. 375 BC
- Greek scientist Archytas of Tarentum invents the screw.

Transportation

c. 400 BC
- The first pilot book or "periplus," a sailing guide to coastal navigation between ports, is developed by the Greeks. It gives wind directions, descriptions of routes, headlands, anchorages, landmarks, and currents around the Mediterranean.
- The Scythians are the first to use saddles with stirrups.

c. 400 BC–*c.* 300 BC A Chinese work describes wheels with 30 spokes, dished wheels for greater strength, and the shaft chariot.

ARTS AND IDEAS

Architecture

393 BC
- The Long Walls of Athens first built in 458 BC to connect the city with its port of Piraeus, are rebuilt with Persian monetary aid and a new navy is built.

370 BC
- The temple of Aesculapius (or Asclepius), the Greco-Roman god of medicine, is built at Epidaurus, Greece.

367 BC–353 BC
- King Mausolus of Caria commissions the architect Pythius of Priene to build a royal tomb, with a colossal statue, at Halicarnassus (now in Budrum).

356 BC
- The temple of Artemis at Ephesus, one of the Seven Wonders of the World, is burned down by Herostratus, who wishes to do something that history will remember him by.

c. 353 BC
- The building of the tomb of Mausolus, tyrant of Caria in Asia Minor, at Halicarnassus, is completed. The tomb becomes celebrated as one of the Seven Wonders of the World, and gives rise to the word "mausoleum." It is a 125 m/411 ft square and has 26 columns on top of which rests a 24-step pyramid surmounted by a four-horse, marble chariot.

Arts

c. 400 BC
- Chavín de Huantar art becomes associated with the culture of the Parracas people on the south coast of Peru.

364 BC

- The Greek sculptor Praxiteles of Athens sculpts his *Hermes* and his masterpiece, the *Aphrodite* of Cnidus. The *Aphrodite* does not survive to modern times, but is known from contemporary references and praise.

Literature and Language

c. **400 BC**

- The epic Indian poem *Mahabharata* and the popular collection of cosmic stories *Puranas* are first composed, though both gradually grow over the next thousand years.

399 BC

- Andocides, one of the ten leading Attic orators, defends himself from accusations of being involved in the mutilation of the Hermae, the protective statues of Hermes outside houses in Athens, with his speech *On the Mysteries*. The work survives to modern times.

c. **394 BC**

- The exiled Athenian historian Xenophon writes his *Anabasis*, the story of the Persian expedition and the retreat of the 10,000 Greek mercenaries.

Music

396 BC

- Contests for heralds and trumpeters are introduced to the Olympic Games in Greece.

Theater and Dance

c. **400 BC–*c.* 323 BC**

- Works in the style known as Middle Comedy are produced in Athens, the writers Antiphanes, Timocles, and Alexis (who continues into the era of New Comedy) being among the leading proponents. Middle Comedy tends to be more naturalistic in its content than Old Comedy and avoids satire of individuals. Only fragments survive to modern times.

388 BC

- The play *Plutus*, by the Greek comedy dramatist Aristophanes, is produced. The play is his last to survive to modern times.

367 BC

- The tyrant of Syracuse Dionysius I the Elder wins the prize at the Lenaea festival in Athens for his play *The Ransom of Hector*.

Thought and Scholarship

399 BC

- Athenian philosopher Socrates is convicted for impiety and for corrupting the young. He is sentenced to death by drinking the poison hemlock, but is also offered the option of exile which, despite entreaties from his friends, he refuses. His last days are described by his pupil, the philosopher Plato, in *Apology* and *Phaedo*.

Plato (428 BC–347 BC)

428 BC

- Plato, Greek philosopher, often considered one of the greatest in history, is born in Greece.

399 BC

- Athenian philosopher Socrates is convicted for impiety and for corrupting the young and is sentenced to death. His last days are described by his pupil Plato, in *Apology* and *Phaedo*.

c. **390 BC**

- Plato explains the origins of streams and rivers as the result of water from a huge underground reservoir escaping through holes in the earth's surface.

387 BC

- In Athens, Plato founds the Academy, a school of philosophy which he heads for the remainder of his life. The Academy allows women to study philosophy, unusual at this time.

c. **380 BC**

- Plato reputedly composes his first group of Socratic dialogues, including *Ion, Laches, Lysis, Apology,*

Euthyphro, Charmides, Menexenus, Hippias Major, Hippias Minor, Protagoras, Crito, and *Cleitophon*.

c. **370 BC**

- Plato works on the "middle" group of his dialogues, including *Phaedo, Republic, Symposium,* and *Phaedrus*.

367 BC

- Dion, the brother-in-law of Dionysius I, the tyrant of Syracuse, asks Plato to visit Syracuse to educate the son of Dionysius I, Dionysius II. Plato's mission is not a success and both he and Dion are forced to leave in 366.

- The philosopher Aristotle arrives in Athens from his native Chalcidice, Macedon, to become a pupil of Plato.

c. **360 BC**

- Plato works on his "later" dialogues, including *Cratylus, Parmenides, Sophist, Statesman, Philetus, Laws,* and possibly *Timaeus* and *Critias*.

347 BC

- Plato dies in Athens.

c. **391** BC

- Andocides, one of the ten leading Attic orators, urges the Athenians to make peace with Sparta in his speech "De pace"/"On Peace," but the Athenians reject his advice. He preempts condemnation by going into exile.

c. **390** BC

- Greek philosopher Antisthenes, an associate of Socrates and founder of the Cynic school of philosophy, is active.
- Greek philosopher Plato explains the origins of streams and rivers as the result of water from a huge

BIRTHS & DEATHS

c. **400** BC

- Agis II, king of Sparta 427 BC–398 BC, who commanded the Spartan army during the Peloponnesian war, dies.

399 BC

- Socrates, Athenian philosopher, commits suicide in Athens (*c.* 70).

395 BC

- Himilco, Carthaginian general, who was defeated by the Syracusans in Sicily, commits suicide in Carthage.

395 BC

- Lysander, Spartan general and political leader, who won the decisive victory for Sparta in the Peloponnesian War, dies in battle at Haliartus, Boeotia.

c. **390** BC

- Conon, Athenian admiral famous for his defeat of the Spartan fleet of Cnidus (394 BC), dies, probably in Cyprus.
- Aeschines, Athenian orator and opponent of Demosthenes, born in Athens (–*c.* 314 BC).

388 BC

- Aristophanes, outstanding Greek comic dramatist, 11 of whose plays survive, including *The Clouds*, *The Birds*, and *The Frogs*, dies (*c.* 62).
- Thrasybulus, Athenian general who persuaded Athens to fight against Sparta and who democratized Byzantium, dies.

384 BC

- Aristotle, celebrated Greek philosopher and scientist, pupil of Plato, and tutor of Alexander the Great, born in Stagira, Chalcidice, Greece (–322 BC).
- Demosthenes, Athenian statesman and celebrated orator, a number of whose speeches survive, born in Athens (–322 BC).

382 BC

- Antigonus I, Macedonian general under Alexander the Great who controlled Asia Minor, born (–301 BC).
- Philip II of Macedon, king of Macedon 359 BC–336 BC, who laid the foundations for Macedonian imperial expansion under his son,

Alexander the Great, born (–336 BC).

c. **380** BC

- Theopompus of Chios, Greek rhetorician and historian, born in Chios, Ionia (–305 BC).

377 BC

- Hippocrates, Greek physician, dies in Larissa, Thessaly, Greece (*c.* 84).

c. **375** BC

- Olympias, mother of Alexander the Great, and who was involved in Macedonian power struggles after the death of her husband Philip II of Macedonia, born (–216 BC).

374 BC

- Evagoras, king of Salamis, Cyprus *c.* 410 BC–374 BC, is assassinated.

c. **372** BC

- Mencius (Chinese: Meng-tzu, or (Pinyin) Mengzi, original name: Meng K'o), important early Chinese Confucianist philosopher, whose work *Mencius* survives, born in China (–*c.* 289 BC).
- Theophrastus, Greek philosopher and student of Aristotle, born in Eresus, Lesbos (–*c.* 287 BC).

c. **370** BC

- Democritus, influential Greek philosopher, dies (*c.* 90).

367 BC

- Dionysius the Elder, tyrant of Syracuse 405 BC–367 BC whose wars against the Carthaginians saved Sicily for Greece and made Syracuse one of the most powerful cities in Ancient Greece, dies (*c.* 67).
- Ptolemy I, Macedonian ruler of Egypt 323 BC–285 BC, and founder of the Ptolemaic dynasty, born in Macedonia (–283 BC).

365 BC

- Marcus Furius Camillus, Roman soldier and statesman, who was honored as the second founder of Rome after it was sacked by the Gauls (*c.* 390 BC), dies (*c.* 82).

362 BC

- Epaminondas, Theban military commander, falls in battle against the Athenians and Spartans at

Mantinea, in the Peloponnese, Greece (*c.* 48).

361 BC

- Agathocles, tyrant of Syracuse in Sicily 317 BC–304 BC, then self-styled king of Sicily 304 BC–289 BC, born in Thermae Himeraeae, Sicily (–289 BC).

360 BC

- Agesilaus II, king of Sparta 399 BC–360 BC, during Sparta's ascendancy, dies in Cyrene, Cyrenaica (84).

358 BC

- Artaxerxes II, Achaemenid king of Persia 404 BC–*c.* 358 BC, who lost control of Egypt in 404 BC, dies.

357 BC

- Seleucus I (Nicator), Macedonian army commander who founded the Seleucid kingdom in 312 BC, born in Europus, Macedonia (–280 BC).

356 BC

- Alexander the Great, king of Macedon who conquered Persia and much of the Near East, born in Pella, Macedon (–323 BC).

354 BC

- Dion, brother-in-law of Dionysius the Elder, tyrant of Syracuse, who ruled Syracuse at various times between 357 BC and 354 BC, is assassinated.
- Timotheus, Athenian statesman and general who attempted to revive Athenian imperial ambitions, thereby provoking the Social War 357 BC–355 BC, dies in Chalcis, Euboea.

353 BC

- Iphicrates, Athenian general noted for his use of lightly armed troops (peltasts), as against the Spartans in the Corinthian War 395 BC–387 BC, dies.
- Mausolus, Persian satrap (provincial governor) of Caria 377 BC/376 BC–353 BC, whose Mausoleum was one of the Seven Wonders of the ancient world, dies.

underground reservoir escaping through holes in the earth's surface.

384 BC

- Athenian orator Lysias rebukes the Greeks at the Olympiad for allowing themselves to be dominated by the Syracusan tyrant Dionysius the Elder and the barbarian Persians.

383 BC

- Greek historian Xenophon writes the first part of his *Hellenica*, beginning in the year 411 BC, which corresponds to the end of the historian Thucydides' history, and ending with the surrender of Samos in 404 BC.

c. 380 BC

- Greek philosopher Plato reputedly composes his first group of Socratic dialogues, including *Ion, Laches, Lysis, Apology, Euthyphro, Charmides, Menexenus, Hippias Major, Hippias Minor, Protagoras, Crito,* and *Cleitophon.*

372 BC

- Greek rhetorician Isocrates writes his *To Nicocles* to advise the Cypriot prince of that name. He follows it in about 368 BC with his *Nicocles.*

370 BC

- Greek philosopher Aristippus of Cyrene, an associate of Socrates, reputedly founds the Cyrenaic school of philosophy, though some believe that the school was founded by his grandson.
- *c.* 370 BC   Greek philosopher Plato works on the "middle" group of his dialogues, including *Phaedo, Republic, Symposium,* and *Phaedrus.*

367 BC

- Dion, the brother-in-law of Dionysius I, the tyrant of Syracuse, asks the Greek philosopher Plato to visit Syracuse to educate the son of Dionysius I, Dionysius II. Plato's mission is not a success and both he and Dion are forced to leave in 366 BC.
- The philosopher Aristotle arrives in Athens from his native Chalcidice, Macedon, to become a pupil of the Greek philosopher Plato.

c. 360 BC

- Greek philosopher Plato works on his "later" dialogues, including *Cratylus, Parmenides, Sophist, Statesman, Philetus, Laws,* and possibly *Timaeus* and *Critias.*

355 BC

- Greek historian Xenophon writes the second part of his *Hellenica,* including accounts from 404 BC to the Battle of Mantinea, Arcadia, in 362 BC.

SOCIETY

Education

393 BC

- Athenian orator Isocrates sets up a school of rhetoric in Chios and writes speeches for the island's very efficient law courts.

Everyday Life

c. 400 BC

- Finely wrought brooches, used as fasteners for cloaks or dresses, become popular in the British Isles. Many are made in the south, in Wiltshire.
- Greek scientist Archytas of Tarentum invents the kite. Kites also appear in China about the same time.
- The Zapotec culture develops in Mexico; it lasts more than 1,100 years, centered on the town of Monte Albán in Oaxaca. The Zapotecs use a basic writing system (possibly borrowed from the Olmecs) and a calendar. Over the course of the next 11 centuries, Monte Albán grows to be an enormous ceremonial center and elite residence.
- *c.* 400 BC–*c.* 250 AD   The Late Formative (or pre-Classic) period of Mayan culture takes place in Mexico. By 400 BC, large structures have been built at several sites in the tropical lowland jungle. In the highlands, people begin to put up large clay platforms, some the basis for temples and others for elite houses, flanking open plazas.

Religion

390 BC

- The sacred geese of the temple of Juno reputedly warn the Romans of the approaching Gauls.

356 BC

- The Phocian people scandalize the Greek world by pillaging the treasures of the Panhellenic religious center at Delphi. Dedicatory offerings are reputedly given to favorites of the Phocian general, including a golden wreath for a dancing girl and a silver beaker for a flute-player.

350 BC–301 BC

POLITICS, GOVERNMENT, AND ECONOMICS

Business and Economics

350 BC
- Coinage is introduced in China, along with the use of the horse as a cavalry charger rather than for drawing chariots. Earthwork walls are built at various places along the northern and western frontiers as protection against the surrounding nomads. (These are later used as a basis for the Great Wall.) In central China, the Han state is being formed, though it is the Qin state that is the most powerful.

347 BC
- Coinage is introduced in Rome for the first time, leading to much borrowing and a financial crisis.

343 BC
- Gold coins are issued to commemorate the liberation of Syracuse from tyranny.

340 BC
- The Athenian statesman Demosthenes alters an archaic law stipulating that groups of richer citizens are responsible for financing the building of ships for the Athenian navy, making the provision more equitable. He also persuades the citizens to devote the Athenian festival funds to military purposes.

338 BC
- The Greek city of Tarentum, Italy, issues golden coins to show its gratitude for Spartan efforts on behalf of the city.
- The stores in the Roman Forum make way for bankers' establishments.

324 BC
- The first-known system of insurance is introduced on the Greek island of Rhodes—against runaway slaves.

310 BC
- During the 4th century BC the Hellenic world is stricken by rampant inflation. Prices rise disproportionately to wages and the Greek drachma loses half its value.

Human Rights

312 BC
- The Roman censor Appius Claudius asserts the right of freed slaves to hold office.

Politics and Government

350 BC
- A plebeian is elected as censor for the first time in Rome.
- By the beginning of this decade the Romans have finally recovered from the setback caused by the sack of their city by the Gauls in 390 BC and have reasserted their ascendancy in Italy. The Gauls, once more threatening Rome, are decisively beaten.
- The Phoenician coastal city of Sidon (in modern Lebanon), the center of the revolt against Persia, is taken and punished with great cruelty by King Artaxerxes III of Persia. Sidon seeks help from both its sister city Tyre, which refuses, and Egypt, which gives very little help.

349 BC
- Philip II of Macedon cements his control over the remaining Greek cities in Macedon, in particular taking the city of Olynthus. The Athenians send help to Olynthus eventually, but are diverted by a revolt in Euboea, stirred up by Philip, which leads to Euboea being declared independent.

348 BC
- Rome and Carthage make a second trade agreement. Carthage agrees not to attack Latin states which are friends of Rome.

347 BC
- The Greek city-state of Athens sends embassies to Philip II of Macedon, and the Peace of Philocrates establishes a *status-quo ante*. Philip refuses to forgo the right to punish the Phocians for their "sacrilege" of looting the temple at Delphi in the Sacred War. Greece and Macedon spend much of the rest of the decade preparing for war in an interval of uneasy peace.

346 BC
- Dionysius the Younger returns as tyrant to the Greek city of Syracuse in Sicily, leaving his family behind in Italy where they are murdered.
- Philip II of Macedon punishes the Phocians for starting the Sacred War over the rights of pilgrims to visit the shrine of Apollo at the Phocian-held city of Delphi. He is elected president of the Pythian games and a member of the Greek religious body, the Amphictyonic League, in place of Phocis. He also opens the pass of Thermopylae (between Thessaly in the north and Phocis in central Greece).
- The Greek rhetorician Isocrates writes his *Philippus*, calling on Philip II of Macedon to lead a Greek crusade against Persia. Isocrates has already written in similar fashion to other Greek rulers. Twenty of his works survive to modern times.

344 BC

- The Corinthians, in response to a plea from the Greek city of Syracuse in Sicily for help against tyranny under Dionysius the Younger, send Timoleon who has already destroyed a would-be tyrant in Corinth—his own brother.

343 BC

- Dionysius the Younger, tyrant of the Greek city of Syracuse in Sicily, surrenders to Timoleon, who has been sent from Corinth at the request of the Syracusans. Timoleon takes over the rule of Syracuse, repopulates the city, and revives the democratic constitution that had existed before the Carthaginian defeat of 409 BC. In the next few years, Timoleon attacks other tyrannies throughout Sicily and prepares against an anticipated Carthaginian invasion.
- King Artaxerxes III of Persia personally leads his invading force into Egypt. The frontier town of Pelusium (biblical Sin) puts up some resistance but the pharaoh Nectanebo II is forced to retreat to Memphis. Pelusium and other strongholds then capitulate on promise of good treatment, and Nectanebo flees to Ethiopia. Artaxerxes and his favorite general, Bagoas, retire loaded with spoil.
- The Greek city-state of Sparta responds to Hellenic calls for help. In southern Italy the native tribes, no longer awed by the might of the Greek city of Syracuse in Sicily, are attacking the Magna Graecia (Greek) cities, in particular Tarentum. King Archidamus of Sparta sets sail for Italy with a band of mercenaries.
- There is another secession of the citizen army in Rome and an attempt is made to make usury illegal.

343 BC–341 BC The Samnites, a group of warlike tribes in eastern central Italy, are at war with Rome in what is known as the First Samnite War. Defeated by Rome, they successfully plead with Rome not to destroy their city of Capua. The war effectively dissolves the Latin League, a confederation of villages and tribes around and including Rome which had banded together for protection. Rome is left in control of Latium after the war.

342 BC–341 BC

- Philip II of Macedon conquers Thrace (modern Bulgaria); this is regarded by the Greek city-state of Athens as a further threat to its safety. Thrace has been governed by native princes since Persia's expulsion from Europe by the Greeks. Philip builds several cities in Thrace, including Philippopolis.

341 BC

- The Athenian orator Demosthenes delivers his third *Philippic* in reaction to Philip II of Macedon's conquest of Thrace, and in order to appeal for a Hellenic league against Macedonian ambitions.
- The Latin League proposes a political amalgamation to Rome that would restrict the Romans' freedom of action. Rome refuses and declares war.

340 BC

- A legend about the Roman defeat of the confederation of Italian cities known as the Latin League tells how a consul's son is put to death by his father for disobeying the order not to indulge in personal combats.

- Philip II of Macedon starts a war against the Greek city-state of Athens in the Bosporus area, and is not successful at first. He then has to attend to trouble from the Scythians near the mouth of the River Danube; he is wounded but soon recovers.

340 BC–338 BC The Romans are at war with the Latin League. The Romans defeat the Latins at a battle on the Campanian coast, near Mt. Vesuvius, according to the Roman historian Livy.

339 BC

- The Carthaginian "Sacred Band" of dedicated warriors is defeated at the Battle of Crimisus, Sicily. The opposing Corinthian general Timoleon overcomes his soldiers' superstitious fears while marching to the battle when, upon meeting mules laden with wild celery for use in decorating graves, he makes a wreath of it for his own head, and his soldiers follow suit.

338 BC

- King Archidamus of Sparta, after five years of campaigning against native tribes in South Italy, fails to achieve any decisive results and is killed in battle.
- Persian general Bagoas murders King Artaxerxes III of Persia and his elder sons; one of the king's younger son, Arses, is installed in his place.
- Philip II of Macedon is invited by the Greek religious council, the Amphictyonic League, to lead a third Sacred War against the people of Amphissa in central Greece for the sacrilege of cultivating the sacred wooded plain of Crisa. Philip advances through the pass of Thermopylae. Athens, fearing a Persian invasion, competes with Macedon for an alliance with the Boeotian city of Thebes, which elects to join with Athens.
- Philip II of Macedon wins the battle for the supremacy of the Greek world against the Athenians and Thebans, at Chaeronea, west of the Boeotian capital of Thebes. He advances into the Peloponnese, subdues the city-state of Sparta, and summons a pan-Hellenic congress at Corinth where he announces that the Greeks will set about reliberating the Greek cities of Asia Minor from Persian rule.
- Rome gives remarkably liberal peace terms to the cities of the defeated Latin League.
- The Corinthian Timoleon, ruler of the Greek city of Syracuse in Sicily, makes advantageous peace terms with Carthage, deposes two more tyrants in Sicily, and gives the island a peace that lasts for the next 20 years.

336 BC

- A form of conscription for young men—the *Epheboi*—is introduced in the Greek city-state of Athens. Their duties are part military, part civic.
- Philip II of Macedon, while sending an advance force to begin the invasion of Asia Minor, attends to his personal affairs. He puts away his wife, Olympias, sister of King Alexander of Epirus, and marries a nobleman's daughter called Cleopatra. Then, to appease Alexander of Epirus, he gives him his own daughter in marriage and attends the wedding feast. At the feast he is murdered, supposedly by Olympias (46).
- After the murder of Philip II of Macedon, his 20-year-old son, Prince Alexander the Great, becomes king of Macedon. He puts down rebellion at home and subdues

the Boeotian city of Thebes. He is elected by the Greeks assembled at Corinth as their commander against Persia.

- Persian general Bagoas murders King Arses of Persia, who came to the throne after Bagoas murdered Arses' father, Artaxerxes III. Bagoas himself is murdered, and Darius III succeeds to the throne.

335 BC

- While Alexander the Great of Macedon is campaigning against the barbarians across the River Danube, a report of his death causes the Thebans to take up arms against Macedon again. Alexander defeats them and punishes them mercilessly.

Roman-Samnite Wars (343 BC–290 BC)

343 BC–341 BC

- The Samnites, a group of warlike tribes in eastern central Italy, are at war with Rome in what is known as the First Samnite War. Defeated by Rome, they successfully plead with Rome not to destroy their city of Capua. The war effectively dissolves the Latin League, a confederation of villages and tribes around and including Rome which had banded together for protection. Rome is left in control of Latium after the war.

327 BC

- The Romans, who have been pushing south while the native Samnites have been occupied with the Greek town of Tarentum in southern Italy, are invited to intervene in a dispute over the city of Neapolis (Naples). They take the opportunity and after a long siege evict the Samnites from Neapolis.

326 BC

- Roman intervention in the dispute over Neapolis (Naples) causes the Samnites to declare war on Rome—the Second Samnite War.

321 BC

- During the Second Samnite War, a Roman army is caught by the Samnites at a mountain pass, the Caudine Forks, and forced to capitulate. It suffers the indignity of "passing under the yoke"—the Roman soldiers are stripped of their weapons and forced to pass under a "yoke" of weapons held by their enemies. Rome surrenders the colony of Fregellae.

316 BC

- The Second Samnite War is renewed. The Romans try to seize the Samnite city of Luceria in southern Italy and are badly beaten at Lautulae near Tarracina; the Samnites reach to within 32 km/20 mi of Rome. The city of Capua revolts and goes over to the Samnites.

314 BC

- The Romans inflict a crushing defeat on the Samnites at the Battle of Tarracina in southern Italy. Samnite losses are said to be over 10,000. The Romans reduce the city of Capua which had defected to the Samnites. A Latin colony is founded at Luceria.

313 BC

- Roman victories against the Samnites continue. Fregellae and Nora are recaptured, Nola and Calatia made allies, and Latin colonies are established at Suessa and Pontia to guard the coast road, at Saticula to watch the Campanian frontier, and at Interamna to cover the middle Liris valley.

310 BC

- Rome has to deal with renewed trouble from the Etruscans, who join the Samnites and march on Sutrium. Rome advances into Etruria and makes treaties with the Etruscan cities of Cortona, Perusia, and Arretium, and takes Volsinii.

310 BC–305 BC

- The tribes of the central Apennines, Italy, rise against the Romans, who, with the Second Samnite War on their hands, have a very difficult time. They are saved by their command of the coastal strip and their growing military efficiency.

307 BC

- Just as Rome is finally winning against the Samnites, the Hernici revolt, with many of their cities going over to the Samnites. The Aequi join them two years later.

304 BC

- The Second Samnite War ends with a peace under which Rome gains no territory but the Samnites renounce their hegemony over Campania in southern Italy.

298 BC

- The Third Samnite War in Italy is started by the Samnites, aided by Gaulish marauders and Etruscan allies. The Samnites seize their chance while Rome is engaged on the Lombard plain. The Romans penetrate into the heart of Samnite country.

296 BC

- A Samnite force in Italy slips northward and, with the Gauls and Umbrians, prepares to advance on Rome. The joint force is held off and defeated by the Romans at the Battle of Sentinum.

290 BC

- The Third Samnite War ends in Italy, with the Samnites subdued but recognized by the Romans as autonomous allies.

Campaigns of Alexander the Great (336 BC–323 BC)

336 BC

- After the murder of Philip II of Macedon, his 20-year-old son, Prince Alexander, becomes king of Macedon. He puts down rebellion at home and subdues the Boeotian city of Thebes. He is elected by the Greeks assembled at Corinth as their commander against Persia.

335 BC

- While Alexander is campaigning against the barbarians across the River Danube, a report of his death causes the Thebans to take up arms against Macedon again. Alexander defeats them and punishes them mercilessly.

334 BC

- Alexander sets out on his conquest of the Persian Empire. He crosses the Hellespont with some 35,000 troops, visits Troy, and then marches east to the River Granicus where he defeats a Persian army commanded by the Greek mercenary Memnon. He subdues the Greek cities of Miletus and Halicarnassus and winters in Gordium, the ancient capital of Phrygia in one-time Hittite territory.
- Alexander shows the influence Homer has over him by offering heroic honors to the dead at Troy. He is said to always carry a copy of the *Iliad*.

333 BC

- Alexander has to pay attention to the Phoenician coastal towns in his rear as he moves south toward Egypt. The city of Tyre takes seven months to subdue.
- Alexander proves to the priests and people of Gordium, the capital of Phrygia, that he is the destined conqueror of Asia by cutting the Gordian knot. According to tradition, the chariot of Gordius, founder of Gordium, was lashed to a pole by an intricate knot which could only be untied by the future conqueror of Asia. By cutting the knot instead of untying it Alexander's actions give rise to the phrase "cutting the Gordian knot," meaning a bold solution to a difficult problem.

October 10   Alexander defeats King Darius III of Persia at Issus in southeast Cilicia and becomes master of Syria. Darius flees; his family are captured but treated well by Alexander. The Greeks send congratulations and a golden crown.

332 BC

- Alexander is depicted at the Battle of Issus (where he is victorious over the Persians) on a funerary sarcophagus of a king from Sidon, the principal town in Phoenicia.
- Alexander pleases the Egyptians by not killing the sacred bull of Apis and by generally respecting their religion. He travels 300 miles into the desert to visit the temple of Amon at the oasis of Siwa, where the priests salute him as son of the god.

November   Alexander enters Egypt, meeting no Persian resistance. He is greeted as a liberator.

331 BC

- The Greek city-state of Sparta makes a last attempt to fight against Macedonian control of Greece, but is defeated at a battle near Megalopolis in Arcadia.

April 7   Alexander takes the first major step in his Hellenizing process by founding the greatest of the cities he names after himself, Alexandria, in the Nile delta, Egypt. Many Greeks emigrate to these new cities.

330 BC

- Alexander regards himself as the new king of Persia. He begins to wear Persian dress and to observe Persian customs and court ritual.
- King Darius III of Persia is made prisoner by Bessus, his satrap (provincial governor) of Bactria (northern Afghanistan), and is assassinated in July, just as Alexander catches up with the Persians, who cease all resistance.
- The king of Macedon Alexander burns the Persian royal palace at Persepolis, possibly as revenge for the burning of Athens.

---

334 BC

- Alexander the Great of Macedon sets out on his conquest of the Persian Empire. He crosses the Hellespont with some 35,000 troops, visits Troy, and then marches east to the River Granicus where he defeats a Persian army commanded by the Greek mercenary Memnon. He subdues the Greek cities of Miletus and Halicarnassus and winters in Gordium, the ancient capital of Phrygia in one-time Hittite territory.
- King Alexander of Epirus responds to an appeal for help from the citizens of Tarentum in southern Italy against the native tribes after the Spartans let them down. He wins victories over the Italian tribes and enters into an agreement with the Romans, who fear he may have designs on Sicily.

333 BC

- Alexander the Great of Macedon has to pay attention to the Phoenician coastal towns in his rear as he moves

south toward Egypt. The city of Tyre takes seven months to subdue.

October 10   Alexander the Great of Macedon defeats King Darius III of Persia at Issus in southeast Cilicia and becomes master of Syria. Darius flees; his family are captured but treated well by Alexander. The Greeks send congratulations and a golden crown.

332 BC

November   Alexander the Great of Macedon enters Egypt, meeting no Persian resistance. He is greeted as a liberator.

331 BC

- The Greek city-state of Sparta makes a last attempt to fight against Macedonian control of Greece, but is defeated at a battle near Megalopolis in Arcadia.

April 7   Alexander the Great of Macedon takes the first major step in his Hellenizing process by founding the greatest of the cities he names after himself, Alexandria,

329 BC

- Alexander penetrates eastward into Bactria and northward into Sogdiana, crossing the River Jaxartes to subdue the Scythians. In Sogdiana he meets resistance and is wounded. Bessus, the Persian satrap (provincial governor) of Bactria, is captured and crucified.

327 BC

- Alexander marries Roxana, the captured princess of a Bactrian chief. He invades India, with the intent of securing trade routes, and defeats the Indian king Porus in a well-contested battle on the River Hydaspes. At Samarkand in the early months of the year, Alexander kills his foster-brother Clitus who dares to criticize him. A plot against him is discovered but suppressed.
- On the death of his horse, Alexander the Great founds a city in its memory, Bucephala.

326 BC

- Alexander reaches his farthest point in the east, the River Hyphasis in India where his Macedonian troops refuse to go any further. He retraces his steps to the River Hydaspes, and, by water and land, retreats down the river and then down the River Indus to the sea. He is seriously wounded at the siege of the capital of a local Indian tribe, the Malli.

325 BC

- Alexander reaches the Indian Ocean. With his army of perhaps 30,000, he makes a difficult retreat westward along the coast and through the desert of Gedrosia (modern Makran, Pakistan). His army reaches the Persian capital of Persepolis in December, while his navy, under the Macedonian general Nearchus, reaches Susa, Persia, in the same month.

324 BC

- Alexander spends the summer and autumn at the Median capital, Ecbatana, where his greatest friend Hephaistion dies. Afterwards he sets out for Babylon, destroying a tribe of brigands on the way, as an offering to the spirit of his friend.
- When Alexander arrives back at Susa in Persia from his campaign in India, he punishes those who have failed in their duties in his absence, particularly those who have plundered tombs and temples. His treasurer, Harpalus, who has appropriated a large sum of money, flees to Athens.

323 BC

- Alexander reaches Babylon, which he intends to develop as the capital of his empire, and plans the conquest of Arabia. On reaching Babylon, he is met by deputations from most of the western Mediterranean peoples, fearful that the great king now intends to conquer Europe.
- Legend tells that Alexander's entire army files past him on his deathbed, and that he bequeaths his kingdom to the strongest.

320 BC

- Alexander's empire begins to disintegrate in the major power struggle to succeed him between his former generals, the Diadochi. This struggle dominates the scene for the next two decades. The main protagonists are Ptolemy (Egypt), Seleucus (Babylon and Syria), Antipater and his son Cassander (Macedon and Greece), Antigonus (Phrygia and other parts of Asia Minor), Lysimachus (Thrace and Pergamum), and Eumenes (the Pontus area).

---

in the Nile delta, Egypt. Many Greeks emigrate to these new cities.

October 1　Alexander the Great of Macedon, having left Egypt earlier in the year, defeats the Persian king Darius III at the Battle of Gaugamela (near present-day Mosul, Iraq). He is now master of the Persian Empire. After Gaugamela he advances to Babylon, which surrenders to him, then into Persia, where he finds vast treasure at Susa.

330 BC

- Alexander the Great of Macedon regards himself as the new king of Persia. He begins to wear Persian dress and to observe Persian customs and court ritual.
- Athenian orator Demosthenes writes his masterpiece *On the Crown*, defending his actions in political life.
- King Alexander of Epirus finds the Tarentines turning against him in southern Italy, thus giving the native Italians the same opportunity. He is defeated and killed

in battle, and the possibility of an Epirot kingdom in Magna Graecia (Greek territory in Italy) ends. The city of Tarentum, however, is able to hold its own against the Italian tribes.

- King Darius III of Persia is made prisoner by Bessus, his satrap (provincial governor) of Bactria (northern Afghanistan), and is assassinated in July, just as Alexander the Great catches up with the Persians, who cease all resistance.

329 BC

- Alexander the Great penetrates eastward into Bactria and northward into Sogdiana, crossing the River Jaxartes to subdue the Scythians. In Sogdiana he meets resistance and is wounded. Bessus, the Persian satrap (provincial governor) of Bactria, is captured and crucified.

327 BC

- Alexander the Great marries Roxana, the captured princess of a Bactrian chief. He invades India, with the intent of securing trade routes, and defeats the Indian king Porus in a well-contested battle on the River Hydaspes. At Samarkand in the early months of the year, Alexander kills his foster-brother Clitus who dares to criticize him. A plot against him is discovered but suppressed.
- On the death of his horse, Alexander the Great founds a city in its memory, Bucephala.
- The Romans, who have been pushing south while the native Samnites have been occupied with the Greek town of Tarentum in southern Italy, are invited to intervene in a dispute over the city of Neapolis (Naples). They take the opportunity and after a long siege evict the Samnites from Neapolis.

326 BC

- Alexander the Great reaches his farthest point in the east, the River Hyphasis in India where his Macedonian troops refuse to go any further. He retraces his steps to the River Hydaspes, and, by water and land, retreats down the river and then down the River Indus to the sea. He is seriously wounded at the siege of the capital of a local Indian tribe, the Malli.
- Roman intervention in the dispute over Neapolis (Naples) causes the Samnites to declare war on Rome— the Second Samnite War.

325 BC

- Agathocles, a rich and ambitious citizen of the Greek city of Syracuse in Sicily, is exiled for attempting to overthrow the oligarchical government of Syracuse.
- Alexander the Great reaches the Indian Ocean. With his army of perhaps 30,000, he makes a difficult retreat westward along the coast and through the desert of Gedrosia (modern Makran, Pakistan). His army reaches the Persian capital of Persepolis in December, while his navy, under the Macedonian general Nearchus, reaches Susa, Persia, in the same month.
- Alexander the Great wants to establish maritime trade routes, with the Indian Ocean as another Mediterranean, and sends the Macedonian general Nearchus, in command of the fleet, back to Persia to explore the sea route up the Persian Gulf.

324 BC

- Alexander the Great spends the summer and autumn at the Median capital, Ecbatana, where his greatest friend Hephaistion dies. Afterwards he sets out for Babylon, destroying a tribe of brigands on the way, as an offering to the spirit of his friend.
- When Alexander the Great arrives back at Susa in Persia from his campaign in India, he punishes those who have failed in their duties in his absence, particularly those who have plundered tombs and temples. His treasurer, Harpalus, who has appropriated a large sum of money, flees to Athens.

323 BC

- Alexander the Great reaches Babylon, which he intends to develop as the capital of his empire, and plans the conquest of Arabia. On reaching Babylon, he is met by deputations from most of the western Mediterranean

peoples, fearful that the great king now intends to conquer Europe.
- Athenian politician Demosthenes is accused of misappropriating some of the funds that Alexander the Great's treasurer, Harpalus, has stolen and brought with him from Susa, Persia. Demosthenes is convicted and imprisoned in the Greek city-state of Athens, but escapes.
- Legend tells that Alexander the Great's entire army files past him on his deathbed, and that he bequeaths his kingdom to the strongest.

323 BC–322 BC Ptolemy, one of Alexander the Great's generals and possibly his half brother, has Alexander's body brought to Memphis in Egypt and buried there in a gold sarcophagus. He marries Alexander's mistress, Thaïs, and claims the position of satrap of Egypt, thereby founding the Ptolemaic dynasty.

323 BC–322 BC Some of the northern Greek cities, including Athens, revolt against the Macedonian regent, Antipater, in what is known as the Lamian War. After some brief successes around Thermopylae, including one at Lamia, the Greeks are defeated at the Battle of Crannon and their resistance peters out due to their traditional disunity.

322 BC

- Agathocles, the rich and ambitious citizen who was exiled in 325 BC, returns to the Greek city of Syracuse in Sicily.
- Athenian politician Demosthenes has returned to favor in Athens, after having been convicted of misappropriating funds stolen from Alexander the Great, but the Macedonians now demand his surrender. He flees but is captured and takes poison.
- On Macedonian orders, the Greek city-state of Athens ceases to be a true democracy when the poorer of its citizens, more than half the total, are disenfranchised.
- The struggle to succeed Alexander the Great develops in Babylon. A compromise is reached whereby Roxana's son, Alexander Aegus, and the dead king's young half brother, Arrhidaeus, are to be considered rulers. Perdiccas, Alexander's head general, is appointed regent of the empire, and tries to keep effective control. Antipater, Alexander's regent in Macedon, is confirmed in his position.

321 BC

- During the Second Samnite War, a Roman army is caught by the Samnites at a mountain pass, the Caudine Forks, and forced to capitulate. It suffers the indignity of "passing under the yoke"—the Roman soldiers are stripped of their weapons and forced to pass under a "yoke" of weapons held by their enemies. Rome surrenders the colony of Fregellae.
- Perdiccas, regent of the late Alexander the Great's empire, invades Egypt but is murdered by his own mutinous army, led by the Macedonian general Seleucus. A truce is arranged, leaving Ptolemy, one of Alexander's generals and possibly his half brother, in power in Egypt and Seleucus in Babylon. Antipater, the regent in Macedon, is made regent of the whole empire.
- The Greek city-state of Athens accepts Macedonian overlordship and experiences a prosperous and peaceful decade under the leadership of the Athenians Phocion and Lycurgus.

- The young adventurer Chandragupta Maurya overthrows the Nanda dynasty in northeast India and begins to create the Mauryan Empire by gaining control of the Ganges valley.

320 BC

- Alexander the Great's empire begins to disintegrate in the major power struggle to succeed him between his former generals, the Diadochi. This struggle dominates the scene for the next two decades. The main protagonists are Ptolemy (Egypt), Seleucus (Babylon and Syria), Antipater and his son Cassander (Macedon and Greece), Antigonus (Phrygia and other parts of Asia Minor), Lysimachus (Thrace and Pergamum), and Eumenes (the Pontus area).
- Judea and Syria are annexed by the Egyptian ruler Ptolemy I and remain part of the Egyptian domains of the Ptolemies until the beginning of the 2nd century BC. Judea is granted a large measure of self-government by Ptolemy I.

319 BC

- Antipater, the regent of Macedon, dies. His son, Cassander (one of the Diadochi, former generals of Alexander the Great), is not appointed his successor and begins to fight for his rights.
- Two of the Diadochi (former generals of Alexander the Great), Eumenes and Antigonus, fight for control of Asia.

318 BC

- Eumenes, one of the contenders for Alexander the Great's empire, captures Babylon.

317 BC

- Cassander, the son of Antipater, regent of Macedon, entrusts the government of the city-state of Athens to the philosopher and orator Demetrius Phalereus.
- In the struggles between Alexander the Great's former generals, Seleucus joins Antigonus against Eumenes and recaptures Babylon from Eumenes. Antigonus then turns Seleucus out.

316 BC

- Cassander, ruler of Macedon, has Philip II of Macedon's widow, Olympias, murdered and Alexander the Great's widow, Roxana, and their son, Alexander Aegus, imprisoned. He puts them to death five years later.
- Eumenes, one of the generals fighting for control of Alexander the Great's empire, is defeated by another general, Antigonus, and executed. Antigonus now has control of Asia Minor.
- The ambitious citizen Agathocles becomes tyrant of the Greek city of Syracuse in Sicily and extends his rule over most of the island of Sicily.
- The Boeotian city of Thebes, which was destroyed by Alexander the Great, is rebuilt by Cassander, son of Antipater, the regent of Macedon, with help from Athens.
- The Second Samnite War is renewed. The Romans try to seize the Samnite city of Luceria in southern Italy and are badly beaten at Lautulae near Tarracina; the Samnites reach to within 32 km/20 mi of Rome. The city of Capua revolts and goes over to the Samnites.

315 BC

- In the struggle for power in Alexander the Great's empire, Antigonus, ruler of Asia Minor, is recognized as the common enemy by the other Diadochi (former generals of Alexander) and they combine against him. Cassander, in control of Macedon, is joined by his brother-in-law Lysimachus of Thrace.

c. 315 BC The Romans abandon the *phalanx* in favor of the *maniple* or "handful" of men. Consisting of 120 men in 12 files and 10 ranks, armed with javelin and short sword, it is a less cumbersome formation.

314 BC

- Antigonus, the ruler of Asia Minor, captures the Phoenician city of Tyre.
- The Romans inflict a crushing defeat on the Samnites at the Battle of Tarracina in southern Italy. Samnite losses are said to be over 10,000. The Romans reduce the city of Capua which had defected to the Samnites. A Latin colony is founded at Luceria.

313 BC

- Cassander, the ruler of Macedon, largely loses his grip on central Greece, and Antigonus, the ruler of Asia Minor, declares the "freedom" of the Greek cities.
- Roman victories against the Samnites continue. Fregellae and Nora are recaptured, Nola and Calatia made allies, and Latin colonies are established at Suessa and Pontia to guard the coast road, at Saticula to watch the Campanian frontier, and at Interamna to cover the middle Liris valley.

312 BC

- The Syracusans ask the Carthaginians for help against their tyrant, Agathocles. After a victory on the Himeras River, the Carthaginian general Hamilcar besieges Agathocles in Syracuse, Sicily.

311 BC

- Antigonus, the ruler of Asia Minor, makes a truce with his rivals for power in Alexander the Great's empire, except Seleucus who now holds Babylon.

310 BC

- Agathocles, the tyrant of the Greek city of Syracuse in Sicily, escapes from captivity in Syracuse and over the next three years nearly succeeds in conquering Carthage, which is in the throes of a civil war against its would-be tyrant Bomilcar. He employs a ruthless method of raising funds for his invasion, helping rich citizens of Syracuse to escape the siege and then having them murdered and robbed of their riches.
- Antigonus, the ruler of Asia Minor, resumes his attacks on Seleucus, the ruler of Babylon, but without success.
- Rome has to deal with renewed trouble from the Etruscans, who join the Samnites and march on Sutrium. Rome advances into Etruria and makes treaties with the Etruscan cities of Cortona, Perusia, and Arretium, and takes Volsinii.

310 BC–305 BC The tribes of the central Apennines, Italy, rise against the Romans, who, with the Second Samnite War on their hands, have a very difficult time. They are saved by their command of the coastal strip and their growing military efficiency.

307 BC

- Antigonus, the ruler of Asia Minor, makes peace with Seleucus, who is thus left free to consolidate his kingdom in Babylon.

- Just as Rome is finally winning against the Samnites, the Hernici revolt, with many of their cities going over to the Samnites. The Aequi join them two years later.
- The Attic orator and writer Demetrius of Phaleron is obliged to flee from Athens on the approach of his namesake and political rival, the son of Antigonus. He settles in Alexandria, where he later becomes librarian.

306 BC

- Antigonus, the ruler of Asia Minor, gives himself the title of king; the other Diadochi (former generals of Alexander the Great) follow suit.
- The Egyptian ruler Ptolemy I, whose authority extends to Cyprus, is defeated in a naval battle near Salamis on Cyprus by the satrap (provincial governor) of Asia Minor Antigones I, and his son Demetrius Poliorcetes.

305 BC

- Seleucus, the ruler of Babylon, consolidates his Asian empire as far as India where he is checked by Indian emperor Chandragupta Maurya who gains control of the Indus valley as well as the Ganges valley, laying the foundations of the Mauryan Empire. Seleucus relinquishes all claims, receiving 500 war-trained elephants as a gift.
- Though Lysimachus of Thrace and King Antigonus I of Asia Minor, former generals of Alexander the Great, both found cities to which they give their own names, it is only the one founded by Seleucus of Babylon at this time, Seleucia on the River Tigris, that grows to historical and economic importance. Its prosperity spells the final end of the dominance of Babylon.

November 7 Ptolemy I openly declares himself king of Egypt.

304 BC

- Agathocles rules with great cruelty in the Greek city of Syracuse in Sicily and follows the example of the Diadochi (former generals of Alexander the Great) by calling himself king.
- Demetrius Poliorcetes, son of King Antigonus I of Asia Minor, tries to besiege the independent Greek island state of Rhodes but fails. The Rhodians are saved by Ptolemy I of Egypt who has built himself a fleet, and they bestow on him the title of Soter ("Savior").
- The Second Samnite War ends with a peace under which Rome gains no territory but the Samnites renounce their hegemony over Campania in southern Italy.

302 BC

- Demetrius Poliorcetes, son of King Antigonus I of Asia Minor, launches a substantial attack on King Cassander of Macedon in Thessaly. This however has to be abandoned when Antigonus finds his enemies closing in on him, and a truce is made. Demetrius goes to Ephesus in his father's support.

301 BC

- King Cassander of Macedon and Lysimachus of Thrace persuade Seleucus of Babylon and Ptolemy I of Egypt to join them in trying to destroy King Antigonus I of Asia Minor. They defeat him at Ipsus in Asia Minor, resulting in the final dissolution of Alexander the Great's empire.
- Pyrrhus, the young king of Epirus, has been turned out of his kingdom at the instigation of King Cassander of Macedon, son of Antipater, and so fights under

Demetrius Poliorcetes, son of King Antigonus I, in the "Battle of the Kings" at Ipsus in Phrygia.

SCIENCE, TECHNOLOGY, AND MEDICINE

Agriculture

c. **350 BC**

- Wheat suitable for making bread is introduced into Egypt.

320 BC

- Egyptian agriculture is encouraged by the Egyptian ruler Ptolemy I, who founds the Ptolemaic dynasty of pharaohs, and his successors, so that it eventually becomes the granary of Rome and indeed much of the Mediterranean world.

Ecology

c. **350 BC**

- Aristotle writes of the weather and climate in *Meteorologica/Meteorology*.

c. **325 BC**

- Greek scholar Theophrastus writes about the relationship between organisms, and between organisms and their environment—the first ecological study.

Exploration

c. **350 BC**

- Aristotle describes the diving bell consisting of metal helmets with hoses to the surface down which air is pumped or sucked.

325 BC

- Macedonian army officer Nearchus, under Alexander the Great's orders, sails down the Indus, across the Persian Gulf and up the Euphrates.

Science

c. **350 BC**

- Aristotle defends the doctrine that the earth is a sphere, in *De caelo/Concerning the Heavens*, and estimates its circumference to be about 400,000 stadia (one stadium varied from 154 m/505 ft to 215 m/705 ft). It is the first scientific attempt to estimate the circumference of the earth.
- Greek astronomer Heracleides is the first to suggest that the earth rotates and that the motion of Mercury and Venus is influenced by their revolution around the sun.

c. **320 BC**

- Greek philosopher Theophrastus begins the science of botany with his books *De causis plantarum/The Causes* of *Plants* and *De historia plantarum/The History of Plants*. In them he classifies 500 plants, develops a scientific terminology for describing biological structures, distinguishes between the internal organs and external tissues of plants, and gives the first clear account of plant sexual reproduction, including how to pollinate the date palm by hand.

c. 306 BC

- The Greek philosopher Epicurus supports the atomic theory of Democritus and Leucippus.

Technology

347 BC

- The Chinese scholar Zhang Zhu writes that bamboo pipes caulked with bitumen are used to transport methane to towns to be used for lighting.

340 BC

- In his Bosporus campaign, Philip II of Macedon introduces new siege machinery, including towers and rams.

c. 310 BC

- The Chinese invent double-acting bellows that produce a continuous stream of air. They are used for smelting metal.

305 BC

- Macedonian king Demetrius I introduces catapults onto ships; they fire heavy darts and stones—the first missile weapons—and result in the building of forecastles and sterncastles—temporary wooden turrets—to provide elevated platforms from which to fire.

Transportation

c. 350 BC

- Athens begins to employ quadriremes, galleys with four banks of rowers.

c. 325 BC–*c.* 275 BC

- There is an arms race in the Mediterranean with larger and larger warships built. Macedon builds a galley requiring a crew of 1,800.

c. 312 BC

- Roman statesman Appius Claudius begins the construction of the first great Roman road, the Via Appia (Appian Way), which links Rome with the military center of Capua. Cambered, flanked with a curb, and with solid foundation layers, its construction serves as the standard for road building for the next 2,000 years. At the height of the Roman Empire (about AD 200) 85,000 km/53,000 mi of road have been built.

ARTS AND IDEAS

Architecture

c. 350 BC

- Work begins on Shan-yang Canal in China; it later forms the Southern Grand Canal.

336 BC

- Philip II of Macedon is buried at Aegae (modern Vergina). In modern times (AD 1977) his tomb is discovered with the burial chamber intact and containing grave goods of a splendor unparalleled in the Greek world.

335 BC

- Corinthian statesman and general Timoleon is buried in the agora at Syracuse, Sicily, to be celebrated by a public monument in his honor.

c. 330 BC

- Athenian architect Philo of Eleusis designs the portico of the temple of Demeter at Eleusis, Attica, and the arsenal at Piraeus, port of Athens.

312 BC

- Roman statesman Appius Claudius builds the Aqua Appia, Rome's first aqueduct. Bringing water from the Sabine Hills, it is 15,947 m/52,320 ft long; only 0.5% is above ground.

Arts

c. 350 BC

- The original of the statue known as the *Apollo Belvedere* is made.
- The terracotta figures of Tanagra, Boeotia, are made over the next 150 years.

332 BC

- Alexander the Great, king of Macedon, is depicted at the Battle of Issus (where he is victorious over the Persians) on a funerary sarcophagus of a king from Sidon, the principal town in Phoenicia.
- Greek painter Apelles of Colophon paints a portrait of Alexander the Great—the only artist ever permitted to do so. Apelles' paintings, done with brushes onto wooden panels, were regarded as the greatest of antiquity: those most likely to deceive an observer into believing he was viewing the real thing.

330 BC

- The Greek sculptor Lysippus of Sicyon is reputedly the favorite of the king of Macedon Alexander the Great, and his portraits of Alexander profoundly influence the iconography of rulers of the time. The colossal statue *Farnese Hercules* is thought to be a Roman copy of an original by Lysippus.

c. 330 BC   A new style of Greek sculpture emerges around this time. Hellenistic sculpture comes closer to realism than the preceding classical style. Its lack of restraint can be seen as a search for melodramatic effects or as energetically innovative.

304 BC

- In admiration of the valor of the people of Rhodes, the king of Macedon Demetrius I Poliorcetes, bequeaths his siege engines to them. The Rhodians sell them to provide money to build the *Colossus* of Rhodes, a giant bronze statue of Apollo.

Literature and Language

334 BC
- Alexander the Great shows the influence Homer has over him by offering heroic honors to the dead at Troy. He is said to always carry a copy of the *Iliad*.

c. **324 BC**
- Theopompus of Chios, possibly a pupil of the Greek rhetorician Isocrates, publishes his *Philippica*, praising the deceased King Philip of Macedon. Only later quotations from his works survive to modern times.

Music

324 BC
- Three thousand Dionysiac artists (professional players) arrive at Ecbatana, Media, from Greece, in order to entertain Alexander the Great, King of Macedon, and his court.

c. **318 BC**
- The philosopher Aristoxenus of Tarentum, a pupil of the Greek philosopher Aristotle, writes a treatise on music, the *Harmonics*, which survives to modern times.

Theater and Dance

c. **330 BC**
- Athenian orator Lycurgus renovates the theater of Dionysus below the Acropolis at Athens. Only one of his mercilessly severe speeches *Against Leocrates* survives to modern times.

327 BC
- Philemon, a writer of New Comedy, wins a prize at the Festival of Dionysia. Of his 97 plays, only fragments preserved in later writers survive.

324 BC
- Greek comic dramatist Menander, the leading exponent of New Comedy, makes his debut, centering his work on contemporary private life. Most of one play (*Old Cantankerous*) and reasonably large fragments of six others, on papyrus, survive to modern times.

Thought and Scholarship

347 BC
- Following the death of the Greek philosopher Plato, his pupil, the philosopher Aristotle, goes to Assos, on the Asiatic coast facing the island of Lesbos, and marries the young Pythias.

335 BC
- Greek philosopher Aristotle returns to Athens and founds the Peripatetic school, named for the *peripatoi* (walks) in the Lyceum, the garden of Athens. He lectures there, mainly to small groups, and begins his work in the fields of philosophy (especially metaphysics, logic, and ethics), biology, and politics.

332 BC
- Chinese philosopher and moralist Mencius (Mengzi) begins his travels from court to court in China, lecturing on ethics, with political applications.

331 BC
- When Alexander the Great destroys Persepolis, soft clay tablets covered with Persian writing are baked hard in the flames, preserving them for archeologists.

330 BC–323 BC
- Greek philosopher Aristotle composes his *History of Animals*, *Rhetoric*, *Physics*, *Metaphysics*, *Nicomachean Ethics*, *Logic*, *Poetics*, *Politics*, and a large number of other works. In politics he shows no sympathy with either his one-time pupil Alexander the Great, king of Macedon, or the democracy of Athens.

325 BC
- The Greeks acquire much knowledge about India as a result of the expedition there by Alexander the Great, king of Macedon. A large part of the information, both real and fantastic, comes from the memoirs of Alexander's Macedonian general Nearchus. The memoirs are used extensively by the later Greek historians and geographers, Arrian and Strabo, though they do not survive to modern times.

323 BC
- The career of Alexander the Great, King of Macedon, encourages Greek political philosophers to create a new genre of works *Peri basileias/On Kingship*, justifying monarchic rule.

322 BC
- Greek philosopher Theophrastus of Lesbos, pupil of the philosopher Aristotle, takes over the Peripatetic school in Athens following the death of his master. Two of his works on botany and his *Characters* survive to modern times.

320 BC
- Chanakya, a Brahman statesman and adviser to the ruler of the north of India, Chandragupta, reputedly writes *Arthashatra*, a work on statecraft.

306 BC
- Greek philosopher Epicurus of Samos takes up permanent residence in Athens and establishes his Epicurean school there, following Plato's example in allowing female pupils. Only fragments of his works survive to modern times, but he teaches that the wise man seeks only personal peace.

302 BC
- Greek historian and geographer Megasthenes serves as an ambassador to Chandragupta, ruler of northern India, and incorporates his experiences into his *History of India*. Although only fragments of this work survive to modern times, it is much used by later writers, including the historians Arrian, Strabo, and Pliny the Elder.

BIRTHS & DEATHS

c. 350 BC
- Xenophon, Greek historian, author of *Anabasis*, dies (*c.* 81).

347 BC
- Plato, Greek philosopher, often considered one of the greatest in history, dies in Athens (*c.* 81).

342 BC
- Menander, influential Athenian dramatist, chief dramatist of Greek New Comedy whose *Dyscolus* survives, born (–*c.* 292 BC).

341 BC
- Epicurus, influential Greek philosopher, born on Samos, Greece (–270 BC).

338 BC
- Artaxerxes III, Achaemenid king of Persia *c.* 359 BC–338 BC, son of Artaxerxes II, who subjugated Egypt in 343 BC, is murdered.
- Isocrates, Greek orator and teacher of rhetoric, a number of whose speeches survive, dies in Athens, Greece (*c.* 98).

337 BC
- Timoleon, Greek general who liberated Sicily from the Carthaginians, dies.

c. 335 BC
- Zeno of Citium, Greek philosopher who founded the Stoic school of philosophy, born in Citium, Cyprus (–*c.* 263 BC).

331 BC
- Agis III, king of Sparta 338 BC–331 BC, who led a rebellion against Alexander the Great, is killed in battle near Megalopolis.
- Alexander the Molossian, king of Epirus, falls in battle against Roman forces in southern Italy.
- Cleanthes, Greek Stoic philosopher, head of the Stoic school 263 BC–232 BC, of whose works only fragments survive, born in Assos in the Troad, Asia Minor (–*c.* 231 BC).

329 BC
- Bessus, Achaemenid satrap (provincial governor) of Bactria and Sogdiana under King Darius III of Persia, who murdered Darius and assumed the throne as Artaxerxes IV, executed by Alexander the Great of Macedon.

327 BC
- Cleitus, Macedonian general under Alexander I the Great, is killed by Alexander in a drunken brawl in Maracanda, now Samarkand.

c. 325 BC
- Cleander, Macedonian general under Alexander I the Great, is executed.

324 BC
- Hephaestion, Macedonian general, closest friend of Alexander the Great, dies in Ecbatana, Iran.
- Lycurgus, Athenian statesman and orator, dies (*c.* 66).
c. 324 BC Antiochus I ("Soter"), Seleucid king of eastern Syria *c.* 292 BC–281 BC and the consolidated kingdom of Syria 281–261 BC, born (–261 BC).

323 BC
- Alexander Aegus, son of Alexander the Great of Macedon, born (–311 BC).
June 13   Alexander the Great, king of Macedon, who conquered Persia and much of the Near East, develops a fever and dies in the palace of Nebuchadnezzar in Babylon (now in Iraq) (*c.* 33).

322 BC
- Aristotle, celebrated Greek philosopher and scientist, pupil of Plato, and tutor of Alexander the Great, dies in Chalcis, Euboea (*c.* 62).
October 12   Demosthenes, Athenian statesman and celebrated orator, a number of whose speeches survive, dies on Calouria, Argolis, Greece (*c.* 62).

c. 320 BC
- Diogenes, Greek Cynic philosopher, dies, probably in Corinth, Greece.

319 BC
- Antipater, Macedonian general under Alexander the Great, regent after Alexander's death 321 BC–319 BC, father of Cassander, who later becomes king of Macedon, dies (*c.* 74).

c. 318 BC
- Pyrrhus, king of Epirus 307 BC–272 BC, who conducted successful but costly military campaigns against Macedon and Rome, born (–272 BC).

316 BC
- Olympias, mother of Alexander the Great who was involved in Macedonian power struggles after the death of her husband Philip II of Macedonia, dies (*c.* 59).

311 BC
- Alexander Aegus, son of Alexander the Great of Macedon, executed with his mother Roxana by order of Cassander of Macedon (*c.* 12).

c. 310 BC
- Theocritus, Greek poet who invented pastoral poetry, born in Syracuse, Sicily (–250 BC).

308 BC
- Ptolemy II, king of Egypt 285 BC–246 BC, who developed Alexandria as a center of learning, born in Cos (–246 BC).

305 BC
- Callimachus, Greek poet of the Alexandrian school, born in Cyrene, North Africa (now Shahhat, Libya) (–*c.* 240 BC).
- Theopompus of Chios, Greek rhetorician and historian, dies (*c.* 75).

301 BC
- Antigonus I ("Cyclops"), Macedonian general under Alexander the Great, later king of Macedon 306 BC–301 BC, falls in battle in Ipsus, Phrygia (now in Turkey) (*c.* 81).

SOCIETY

Education

342 BC

- Greek philosopher Aristotle goes to Macedon as tutor to Alexander, son of Philip II of Macedon. Aristotle already has a connection to the Macedonian court in that his father was a physician there.

305 BC

- Under the Indian emperor Chandragupta Maurya, the city of Taxila in India becomes a center of learning and law.

Everyday Life

c. 350 BC

- Aristotle mentions that pure water can be obtained by the evaporation of sea water. It is likely, however, that the process of distillation to extract alcohol from fermented drinks has been known from about 5000 BC–4000 BC.
- Hot air from underground fires is directed into clay pipes beneath the floors of houses in the Greek city of Lacedaemon, Sparta—the first central heating.

c. 325 BC

- The population of the British Isles is around half a million.

324 BC

- In another effort to bring East and West together, Alexander the Great establishes military schools in conquered territory: by this date he is said to have 30,000 Hellenized barbarians at his disposition for military service.

Religion

343 BC

- Egypt accuses the king of Persia, Artaxerxes III, of destroying many of its religious monuments, comparing his deeds with those of the earlier king Cambyses. Among other impieties, he is accused of destroying the sacred bull of Apis.

336 BC

- The ascetic Greek philosopher Diogenes the Cynic reputedly meets the king of Macedon Alexander the Great at Corinth and, on being offered any favor, asks him to "stand out of the sun."

333 BC

- The king of Macedon Alexander the Great proves to the priests and people of Gordium, the capital of Phrygia, that he is the destined conqueror of Asia by cutting the Gordian knot. According to tradition, the chariot of Gordius, founder of Gordium, was lashed to a pole by an intricate knot which could only be untied by the future conqueror of Asia. By cutting the knot instead of untying it Alexander's actions give rise to the phrase "cutting the Gordian knot," meaning a bold solution to a difficult problem.

332 BC

- The king of Macedon Alexander the Great pleases the Egyptians by not killing the sacred bull of Apis and by generally respecting their religion. He travels 300 miles into the desert to visit the temple of Amon at the oasis of Siwa, where the priests salute him as son of the god.

326 BC

- The king of Macedon Alexander the Great erects 12 towering altars to the Olympian gods on the banks of the River Hyphasis in India, as an offering of thanks for his victories.

325 BC

- The king of Macedon Alexander the Great makes sacrifices to Poseidon, the god of the deep, from a ship in the Indian Ocean, and hurls the cup into the waves before sending his Macedonian general and admiral Nearchus on his voyage.

320 BC

- The Diadochi (former generals of the king of Macedon Alexander the Great) deliberately spread Hellenic culture, founding new cities as part of this process. Conversely, the religions of the East begin to influence Greek thought, and as a consequence, a trend develops by which Hellenic rulers are deified.

310 BC

- Greek philosopher Euhemerus writes his *Sacred Scripture*, a travel novel which ascribes a historical basis to all myths, suggesting that the gods were once human. The term "euhemerism" comes to describe the interpretation of myths as if founded in real, human history.

300 BC–251 BC

POLITICS, GOVERNMENT, AND ECONOMICS

Business and Economics

c. 300 BC
- Athens and Corinth remain the most important of the Greek city-states but even they are suffering from the self-seeking of the rich and a decline in economic prosperity. The only openings for the people seem to be emigration or service as mercenary soldiers abroad.
- Greece, in its trade, culture, and emigration, begins to be concerned much more with the lands to the east than with those to the west. The western Mediterranean becomes the scene of the Roman-Carthaginian struggle, although it is sparked off by the last activity of the Greeks in these parts, on the part of King Pyrrhus of Epirus.
- The Mauryan Empire in India consists of four provinces, ruled by viceroys. There are very heavy taxes to support a standing army, the bureaucracy, irrigation programs, and public works, such as a road from the capital city of Pataliputra (Patna) to Taxila.

289 BC
- Roman king Pomponius establishes a mint in the temple of Juno Moneta, although bronze bars rather than true coins are produced.

280 BC
- Under the Seleucids the cities of Asia Minor regain commercial prosperity and even achieve some specialization, Miletus becoming a textile center. There is some slave-based mass production.

269 BC
- The first true coins appear in Rome. Made of cast bronze in different denominations, the obverses depict the head of a deity and the reverses a ship's prow.

Colonization

270 BC
- Rome, having successfully concluded its lengthy Italian wars, continues with a determined economic policy of colony planting within Italy and road building; the Via Appia is extended southward.

268 BC
- The Romans found a colony at Malventum, for religious reasons changing its name to Beneventum.

Politics and Government

300 BC
- Pyrrhus, the young king of Epirus, is sent to Egypt as a hostage after the "Battle of the Kings" at Ipsus in Phrygia and makes a diplomatic marriage to Princess Antigone, daughter of King Ptolemy I and Berenice.
- With the defeat of King Antigonus I of Asia Minor and his son, Demetrius Poliorcetes, at Ipsus in Phrygia, Seleucus' position in Babylon becomes more secure and he declares himself king at his capital city of Seleucia. He founds the city of Antioch, in Syria, some 32 km/ 20 mi up the River Orontes, naming it after his father. Antioch is designed and constructed on a grid plan; it becomes one of the major cities of the Mediterranean world.
- *c.* 300 BC The early Ptolemies set up an efficient bureaucracy in Egypt, run mostly by Greeks. Trade, mainly conducted by Jews, prospers in the region.

298 BC
- The Third Samnite War in Italy is started by the Samnites, aided by Gaulish marauders and Etruscan allies. The Samnites seize their chance while Rome is engaged on the Lombard plain. The Romans penetrate into the heart of Samnite country.

297 BC
- Cassander, secure as king of Macedon after the Battle of Ipsus in Phrygia, dies a natural death. His sons rule for three years, then Demetrius Poliorcetes, son of the late king Antigonus I of Asia Minor, who has held on to some Greek cities after his defeat at Ipsus, moves back into Macedon.
- Indian emperor Chandragupta Maurya abdicates in favor of his son Bindusara who extends the Mauryan Empire as far south as Mysore in India. Bindusara is known to the Greeks as Amitrochates, perhaps from the Sanskrit for "the Destroyer of Foes," and continues cultural contact with the Seleucids.
- The young king Pyrrhus regains the throne of Epirus, on the Adriatic coast of Greece, with forces supplied by his father-in-law, King Ptolemy I of Egypt.

296 BC
- A Samnite force in Italy slips northward and, with the Gauls and Umbrians, prepares to advance on Rome. The joint force is held off and defeated by the Romans at the Battle of Sentinum.

294 BC

- Demetrius Poliorcetes, son of the late king Antigonus I of Asia Minor, is acknowledged king of Macedon and manages to keep his throne for seven years.

293 BC

- King Seleucus I hands over the government of his lands west of the River Euphrates to his son Antiochus; he also hands over his young wife Stratonice.

290 BC

- The Third Samnite War ends in Italy, with the Samnites subdued but recognized by the Romans as autonomous allies.

289 BC

- Agathocles, the tyrant of the Greek city of Syracuse in Sicily, ends his life amidst dynastic turmoil. His power and prestige have spread to southern Italy, and his death leaves the somewhat weak Greek cities of Magna Graecia in Italy at the mercy of the native Italians again. Some of his disbanded mercenaries seize Messina in northeast Sicily and set up a society, calling themselves Mamertines or Children of Mars.

287 BC

- Demetrius Poliorcetes of Macedon is deserted by his troops, who proclaim King Pyrrhus of Epirus king of Macedon in his place.
- The plebeians in Rome secede again. The Senate appoints Hortensius as dictator to deal with the situation, and the *Lex Hortensia* is passed. This law recognizes the plebiscites (laws passed by the plebeians) of the plebeian tribal assembly as valid and binding on the whole state, without the need for senatorial ratification as previously, so that the will of the people as a whole becomes sovereign.

286 BC

- Demetrius Poliorcetes, driven out of Macedon by Lysimachus of Thrace, flees to the court of King Seleucus I and dies three years later, reputedly of drink.
- King Pyrrhus of Epirus is driven out of Macedon by Lysimachus, governor of Thrace, who for a while becomes king of Macedon.

285 BC

June 26 King Ptolemy I Soter of Egypt appoints his youngest son, Ptolemy II (Philadelphus), coregent and successor.

283 BC

- Antigonus II assumes the title of king of Macedon on the death of his father, Demetrius Poliorcetes.
- At a battle near Lake Vadimo, Rome finally quells the allied Etruscans and Gauls, becoming undisputed master of northern and central Italy.
- King Ptolemy I of Egypt dies during the winter. He has already abdicated in favor of his son, Ptolemy II.

282 BC

- The Greek city of Thurii in Italy appeals to Rome for help against the pressure of native tribes, and is saved. The city of Tarentum, jealous of Rome's interference, attacks and sinks some Roman ships entering its harbor; Rome then declares war on Tarentum, which finds a new champion in King Pyrrhus of Epirus.

281 BC

- King Seleucus I of Nicator invades Macedon and kills Lysimachus of Thrace in the Battle of Corupedion, leaving him master of western Asia Minor. Seleucus and his son Antiochus also extend their territory east into Persia to the borders of India, making the Seleucid dynasty heir to the greater part of Alexander the Great's Persian Empire.
- King Seleucus I is then assassinated by one of the sons of the late king Ptolemy I of Egypt. His son, Antiochus I, succeeds to the throne of the Seleucid or Syrian Empire.

280 BC

- King Pyrrhus of Epirus responds to the Greek city of Tarentum's appeal for help against Roman interference and crosses to Italy. He defeats the Romans at Heraclea but his losses are nearly as great as theirs, giving rise to the phrase "Pyrrhic victory." Pyrrhus' war with Rome lasts until 275 BC.
- The independent Greek island of Rhodes, rising to prosperity after its defiance of Demetrius Poliorcetes in 304 BC, becomes head of an "Island League" and helps to keep the peace and freedom of the Aegean Sea.

279 BC

- A horde of Gauls—a Celtic people from central Europe—sweeps down from the Danube valley through Macedon into Greece, killing and plundering. They are only just halted by the Aetolian League before they reach Delphi, where they intended to plunder the shrine. They turn back north, where King Antigonus II defeats them in Macedon, winning popular support for his kingship.
- In renewed fighting, King Pyrrhus of Epirus wins another "Pyrrhic" victory (in which his losses are almost as great as those of his opponents) against the Romans at Asculum in Italy. Disheartened, he retires to the Greek city of Tarentum in Italy. Later in the year, he marches on Rome but realizes he cannot take the city and suggests peace terms. These are refused, largely at the instigation of the ex-censor, Appius Claudius.
- The Aetolian League, north of the Corinthian Gulf, and the Achaean League in the Peloponnese are refounded in Greece. Within each league a common coinage and foreign policy is adopted and their armed forces are pooled. However, the two leagues are mutually hostile.

278 BC

- Another band of Gauls, having swept through Greece, crosses to Asia Minor where they eventually settle in the district of Galatia in the center of Anatolia, becoming known as the Galatians. They are subsidized by the Seleucids for about 50 years to keep the peace.

278 BC–276 BC The Carthaginians besiege the Greek city of Syracuse in Sicily, which appeals to King Pyrrhus of Epirus for help. He crosses from the Greek town of Tarentum in Italy to Sicily and drives the Carthaginians back to the town of Lilybaeum. After two years the Greeks of Sicily ask him to leave, and he returns to Italy.

277 BC

- King Antigonus II gains firm possession of his Macedonian throne. In addition, he already controls a considerable part of Greece, including the strategic fortresses of the Piraeus at Athens, Corinth, Chalcis in Euboea, and Demetrias in Thessaly, a new town founded by his father, Demetrius Poliorcetes.

c. 277 BC   The Egyptian pharaoh Ptolemy II marries his sister Arsinoe II, an act which causes a scandal among the Greeks, but is lauded by the Egyptians.

275 BC

- From about this time the Near East and Aegean are relatively peaceful with the stabilizing of the three great Hellenistic kingdoms that were formed from Alexander's Persian Empire—Ptolemaic Egypt, Seleucid Asia, and Antigonid Macedon. These kingdoms maintain a balance of power through diplomacy and limited war until about 220 BC, with the accession of ambitious rulers to the thrones of Macedon and Asia and the rise of Rome.
- King Pyrrhus of Epirus, having lost some of his fleet to the Carthaginians on returning from Sicily to Italy, continues the fight against Rome with diminishing success and after a defeat at Malventum (soon to be called Beneventum) returns home with only about a third of his original army.

274 BC

- Antiochus I, son of King Seleucus I and successor to the Seleucid or Syrian Empire, defends his possessions in the First Syrian War.

273 BC

- King Ptolemy II of Egypt, impressed by Rome's defeat of King Pyrrhus of Epirus, sends a friendly embassy, and the visit is reciprocated; Rome has begun to be recognized as a power on the international scene.
- King Pyrrhus of Epirus invades Macedon and turns out King Antigonus II.

272 BC

- King Antigonus II regains his throne in Macedon from King Pyrrhus of Epirus, and settles down to rule with moderation for 33 years. Pyrrhus turns his arms against the Greek city-states of Sparta and Argos. He is eventually killed in Argos by a tile hurled by a woman from an upper window.
- Rome makes peace with the city of Tarentum and the other Greek cities of South Italy; they are left as free allies, and have to supply a quota of ships rather than of soldiers.
- The emperor Asoka succeeds Bindusara on the Mauryan throne in India and continues his predecessor's policy of war and expansion. The empire comprises all of the Indian subcontinent except the extreme southern tip and part of the eastern seaboard.

270 BC

- The city of Rhegium in South Italy, having been seized by the Romans in their war with King Pyrrhus of Epirus, is restored to its Greek inhabitants.
- The emperor Asoka consolidates his Mauryan Empire in India during this period but fails to conquer Kalinga (modern Orissa) on the east coast.
- The north African city of Carthage is ruled by an oligarchy of merchants under two *suffetes* or chief magistrates. It produces good military commanders but relies on mercenary soldiers. By this time, Carthage controls Sardinia as well as southern Spain and its own Numidian neighbors, and has naval control of the western Mediterranean. In Sicily, since the departure of King Pyrrhus of Epirus, it has reoccupied most of the island, excluding, however, the Greek city of Syracuse.

Syrian Wars (274 BC–217 BC)

274 BC
- Antiochus I, son of King Seleucus I and successor to the Seleucid or Syrian Empire, defends his possessions in the First Syrian War.

c. 260–253 BC
- The Seleucids of Syria and Ptolemy II of Egypt are at war again in the Second Syrian War. The war ends when Ptolemy II gives his daughter Berenice to the Seleucid king Antiochus I.

246 BC
- King Ptolemy III of Egypt sets out on a career of conquest in the Seleucid Empire, now under Seleucus II: the Third Syrian War. Ptolemy is partly motivated by a desire for revenge for the murders of the Seleucid king Antiochus II and his wife Berenice (Ptolemy III's sister) by Antiochus's ex-wife Laodice in 249 BC.

245 BC
- King Ptolemy III of Egypt temporarily defeats and permanently weakens most of the Seleucid Empire. He reaches as far as Bactria and the borders of India. However, he is forced to return to Egypt to meet internal trouble and the Seleucid rulers resume control.

231 BC
- Seleucus II, king of the Seleucid kingdom in Syria, following the example of Ptolemy III, campaigns in Bactria, and also in the newly formed Parthia, where King Tiridates, brother of Arsaces, king of Persia, defeats him.

219 BC
- The two post-Alexandrian empires of the Ptolemies (Egypt) and the Seleucids (Syria) go to war over the ownership of Phoenicia and Palestine, beginning the Fourth Syrian War.

217 BC
- Antiochus III the Great of Syria is defeated in his war with Ptolemy III at the Battle of Raphia, near Gaza in Palestine. Native Egyptian forces take part in this battle alongside the Macedonian soldiers. Their success spurs nationalist feelings.

267 BC

- Hieron, the young king of Syracuse in Sicily and a descendant of the tyrant Hieron who came to power in 474 BC, beats back the Mamertines from his territory. (The Mamertines are a society of disbanded mercenaries formed in 289 BC.) .

267 BC–261 BC King Ptolemy II of Egypt encourages the Greek city-states of Athens and Sparta to rise against King Antigonus II of Macedon. The Athenians turn out their Macedonian garrison. They are led by Chremonides, a young disciple of Zeno, founder of the Stoic school of philosophy, and this war, which lasts until 261 BC, comes to be known as the Chremonidean War.

264 BC

- King Hieron of Syracuse, Sicily, threatens to renew his attack on the Mamertines (society of disbanded mercenaries), who appeal to Carthage and receive a Carthaginian garrison; they then appeal to Rome, get rid of the Carthaginian garrison, and welcome two Roman legions under Appius Claudius (a relative of the Roman censor). The Carthaginians, affronted, send a force to Sicily, and they are supported by Hieron. Appius Claudius beats them off, and the First Punic War breaks out.

263 BC

- The Romans attack the city of Syracuse in Sicily and force its king, Hieron, into alliance with them. He continues to rule Syracuse benevolently.

262 BC

- The Carthaginians are defeated by the Romans at Agrigentum in Sicily. They retire to reorganize their fleet, while the Romans sack Agrigentum and enslave its Greek inhabitants.

261 BC

- Antiochus II succeeds King Antiochus I to the Seleucid throne.
- King Antigonus II of Macedon recaptures the Greek city-state of Athens, ending the Chremonidean War. This ends Athens' last attempt to gain some political power. Antigonus regarrisons the city and forbids it to make war, but otherwise leaves it to itself as the seat of philosophy and learning.
- The Romans, now determined to win Sicily from Carthage, realize the need for a navy. They rapidly produce 100 copies of a captured Carthaginian quinquereme (warship) and train the necessary oarsmen.

260 BC

- The Mauryan emperor Asoka completes the conquest of virtually the whole of the Indian subcontinent by the bloody defeat of Kalinga on the east coast. After this he renounces war, and Buddhism prospers throughout India. It is introduced to the island of Ceylon (Sri Lanka), where it has continued to flourish.
- The Romans win a resounding naval victory over the Carthaginians off Mylae in Sicily (the date may be two years earlier).

c. 260 BC–c. 253 BC The Seleucids of Syria and Ptolemy II of Egypt are at war again in the Second Syrian War. The war ends when Ptolemy II gives his daughter Berenice to the Seleucid king Antiochus I.

259 BC

- The state of Qin, climbing rapidly to power in China, defeats the state of Zhao at the Battle of Chang Ping (in the great bend of the Yellow River).

258 BC

- The Romans take the island of Corsica from the Carthaginians.

256 BC

- The Chinese state of Qin makes war upon the last of the Zhou emperors, who abdicates.
- The Romans repeat their naval success against the Carthaginians at the Battle of Mylae by defeating them again at the Battle of Ecnomus. They send a force under the consul Regulus to Africa, who settles down for the winter in the hope of capturing the city of Carthage in the spring.

255 BC

- The Roman consul Regulus, sent to capture Carthage, is defeated and taken prisoner by the Carthaginians. A Roman fleet sent to rescue Regulus is wrecked.

254 BC

- The Romans capture the Carthaginian naval base of Panormus (modern Palermo) in Sicily but find it difficult to make further progress without controlling the sea.

251 BC

- The Achaean League in the Peloponnese is revived by the accession of the young Aratus of Sicyon, who frees the city of Sicyon, near Corinth, from its tyrants.

SCIENCE, TECHNOLOGY, AND MEDICINE

Agriculture

c. **300 BC**

- The noria is invented in Mesopotamia. An irrigation device, it consists of a horizontal, geared wheel that activates a vertical wheel equipped with buckets partially submerged in water. When operated by animals or humans, water is raised into an irrigation channel.
- Wet rice cultivation begins in Japan.

c. **260 BC**

- Egyptian king Ptolemy II lowers lake Moeris in the Fayyum to its present level thus reclaiming valuable agricultural land.

Exploration

c. **300 BC**

- Greek navigator Pytheas, is the first Greek to reach the British Isles and northern Europe. In his book, *On the Ocean,* he describes "Thule," the most northerly point of the world, and also the occupations of various peoples, including tin-mining in Cornwall and amber-collecting by Goths on the shores of the Baltic. He also observes that the moon affects the tides.

Health and Medicine

293 BC

- Rome suffers from the plague.

c. 285 BC

- Herophilus, an anatomist working at Alexandria, dissects human bodies and compares them with large mammals. He distinguishes the cerebrum and cerebellum, establishes the brain as the seat of thought, writes treatises on the human eye and on general anatomy, and writes a handbook for midwives.

272 BC–269 BC

- The Roman censor Manius Curius Dentatus builds the Aqua Anio Vetus aqueduct in Rome. Water is transported (mostly underground) from the Anio River 69 km/43 mi away, and is used for gardens and sanitation.

256 BC

- The first hospitals are founded in India by Mauryan emperor Asoka. He also supplies medicines, and encourages the education of women.

c. 255 BC

- The doctrine of the pulse, which emphasizes feeling the pulse as the most important aspect of diagnosis, and that a healthy life is achieved by a balance of yin and yang, is introduced in China. It will be compiled into the *Mo Jing* in about AD 300 by Wang Shu-he.

Math

c. 300 BC

- Alexandrian mathematician Euclid sets out the laws of geometry in his *Stoicheion/Elements*; it remains a standard text for 2,000 years. He also sets out the laws of reflection in *Catoptrics*.
- Aristarchus of Samos uses a geometric method to calculate the distance of the sun and the moon from the earth.

287 BC–212 BC

- The prolific Greek mathematician Archimedes of Syracuse produces a number of works on two- and three-dimensional geometry, including circles, spheres, and spirals.

Science

c. 300 BC

- Babylonian astronomer Berosus invents the hemispherical sundial. It consists of a block of stone or wood with a hemispherical opening with arcs inscribed on the inner surface. Time is reckoned by the position of the shadow of a pointer, which is attached to the outer part of the hemisphere, as it crosses the arcs.

- Greek scholar Dicaearachus places the first orientation line on a map of the world; it runs through Gibraltar and Rhodes. The idea eventually leads to the system of parallels and meridians, and methods of projecting them.

c. 295 BC

- Greek philosopher Theophrastus writes *De lapidibus/On Stones*, a classification of 70 different minerals. It is the oldest known work on rocks and minerals and is the best treatise on the subject for nearly 2,000 years.

280 BC

- The Egyptian pharaoh Ptolemy II develops Alexandria, Egypt, as a center of art, science, philosophy, and literature, and keeps a large zoological garden.
- c. 280 BC   Greek astronomer Aristarchus of Samos writes *On the Size and Distances of the Sun and the Moon*. He is the first to maintain that the earth revolves around the sun.

Technology

c. 300 BC

- The Egyptians write with pens made of shaped reeds filled with ink—the precursor of the fountain pen.
- The Greeks devise a method of optical telegraphy using an alphabetic signaling system. The 24 letters of the Greek alphabet are signified by placing large vases, visible from a distance, in particular positions in a grid of rows and columns.
- The Parracas people of the Andes of South Peru achieve a high level of sophistication in their textiles, using advanced techniques unknown elsewhere. They use wool and cotton in distinctive color combinations and designs.

290 BC

- The first sundial, captured from the Samnites, is set up in Rome.

c. 270 BC

- Greek physicist and inventor Ctesibius of Alexandria lays the foundations for the development of modern pumps with his invention of a small pipe organ, the hydraulis, which is supplied with air by a piston pump.

c. 260 BC

- The Romans invent the *corvus*, a hinged and hooked plank at the bow of a war galley allowing boarding parties.

Transportation

c. 300 BC

- The Mauryan emperors in India begin constructing a system of roads stretching from the Himalayas to the Indus.

283 BC

- The canal from the River Nile to the Red Sea, built by the pharaoh Necho II and repaired by Darius I of Persia, is again repaired by King Ptolemy II of Egypt.

ARTS AND IDEAS

Architecture

c. 300 BC

- Engineers begin enclosing the *Cloaca Maxima* ("great sewer") in Rome within a barrel vault made of stone.
- The Romans invent the hypocaust. Developed from the Spartan heating system, hot air from underground fires is funnelled through pipes in the walls and under floors to heat public baths and most private houses.

290 BC

- Berenice, the wife of King Ptolemy I of Egypt, is made queen of Egypt and has the city of Berenice built on the Red Sea; it becomes a great emporium for Egyptian trade with the East.
- The lighthouse at Pharus Island, off the coast of Alexandria, Egypt, is built by the Greek architect Sostratus of Cnidos. One of the Seven Wonders of the World, it stands 100 m/328 ft tall.

270 BC

- Egyptian pharaoh Ptolemy II erects the Rotunda at Samothrace, Greece, dedicated to the worship of his sister Arsinoe II, who is also his wife.

Arts

292 BC

- The *Colossus* of Rhodes, one of the Seven Wonders of the World, is begun by Chares of Lindus. Cast in bronze, it is 32m/105 ft high, holds a torch aloft, and guards the entrance to the harbor at Rhodes.

c. 283 BC

- Egyptian ruler Ptolemy II enlarges the museum and library at Alexandria.

280 BC

- The *Colossus* of Rhodes, the greatest of many new statues in this now flourishing city, is finally erected. Celebrated as one of the Seven Wonders of the World, the bronze statue stands 32 m/105 ft high, holds a torch aloft, and guards the entrance to the harbor at the Greek island state of Rhodes. It was completed by the sculptor Laches after the original sculptor, Chares of Lindus, dies. Lindus is said to have committed suicide when the cost exceeded his estimate.

Literature and Language

c. 277 BC

- Cilician didactic poet Aratus of Soli writes a hymn glorifying Antigonus II of Macedon and his victory over the Gauls. Aratus' *Phaenomena*, his best-known poem and still extant, is a treatise on stars and weather.

275 BC

- Greek poet Callimachus of Cyrene (modern Shahat) is active under the reign of the Egyptian pharaoh Ptolemy

II. His most notable work is the *Aetia*, an extended miscellany of poetry notable for its learned, ironic, polished manner.

- Syracusan poet Theocritus, creator of the bucolic (pastoral) genre, writes in praise of the tyrant of Syracuse Hieron II and, later, in praise of the Egyptian pharaoh Ptolemy II.

272 BC

- Latin poet Livius Andronicus, the founder of Roman epic poetry, is reputedly brought to Rome from Tarentum as a captive slave.

270 BC

- Apollonius Rhodius becomes royal tutor and librarian in Alexandria, Egypt, and between now and 245 BC writes his epic *Argonautica* on Jason's quest for the golden fleece. The work survives to modern times.

260 BC

- The poet and scholar Callimachus of Cyrene catalogs the library at Alexandria, Egypt. Many of his works survive to modern times, including 6 hymns and 63 epigrams.

Thought and Scholarship

c. 300 BC

- Egyptian ruler Ptolemy I establishes a museum and library at Alexandria, Egypt. Organized by Demetrius of Phaleron, the library contains hundreds of thousands of vellum and papyrus scrolls, the texts of classical antiquity. Although it is intended to be an international library most scrolls are in Greek. It is destroyed in AD 391.
- Greek philosopher Zeno of Citium, having lived and studied in Athens for about 12 years, opens his Stoic school of philosophy at the *Stoa Poikile* there, which specializes in paradoxes. Legend tells that Zeno lives to the age of 98.
- The Egyptian pharaoh Ptolemy I writes a history of the wars of Alexander the Great. Though the work does not survive to modern times, it is used by the later Greek historian Arrian in his account of the period.

296 BC

- Even as the Chinese Zhou dynasty disintegrates, China's literary output remains immense. The books buried in a king's tomb are said to have filled ten wagons.

289 BC

- Following the death of the Chinese philosopher Mengzi or Meng-tzu (original name Meng K'o, known in the West as Mencius), his disciples publish his teachings as the *Book of Mengzi*.

283 BC

- The Egyptian pharaoh Ptolemy II appoints the critic Zenodotus of Ephesus as the head of the library at Alexandria. Zenodotus classifies the works of Greek lyric and epic poets, and produces editions of some of their works.

c. 280 BC

- Egyptian priest, historian, and chronologist Manetho is active. Only fragments of his work survive to modern times but they have been invaluable in reconstructing Egyptian history.

272 BC

- Antigonus II of Macedon, a liberal and artistic ruler, endeavors to persuade the Greek philosopher Zeno to reside at his court and teach him to be a philosopher-king. Zeno sends two of his pupils in his stead.

263 BC

- Greek philosopher Cleanthes of Assos succeeds Zeno as head of the Stoic school, in Athens, which advocates virtue and the control of passions. Much of his *Hymn to Zeus* survives to modern times.

SOCIETY

Education

275 BC

- Timon of Phlius, a Greek sophist and skeptic philosopher, amasses a fortune from his teaching activities.

Everyday Life

c. 300 BC

- The population of the Mexican Basin has expanded rapidly in the last 300 years, reaching about 75,000. The largest site in the area is Cuicuilco, with a population of 5,000–10,000 people. Large temple platforms are built. All this suggests that a major chiefdom has emerged in the area.
- There is rapid population growth and the development of a two-tiered settlement hierarchy—large ceremonial centers where the elite live, surrounded by smaller villages, in the Mayan jungle lowlands of Mexico. The site of El Mirador in Guatemala is probably the main lowland center of the Mayan Late Formative period.

280 BC

- Ptolemy II introduces the camel to Egypt, and uses it to start a postal service.

275 BC

- Celts of the La Tène culture (known in Britain as the Iron Age B culture) settle in England, particularly in the Yorkshire Wolds. They spread out from Yorkshire and where they meet Iron Age A forts they tend to refortify them in a most elaborate way, with triple fortifications.

BIRTHS & DEATHS

c. 297 BC

- Chandragupta Maurya, first emperor of the Maurya dynasty of India c. 321 BC–c. 297 BC, who unified most of India under his rule, fasts to death.
- Cassander, king of Macedon 305 BC–297 BC, murderer of Alexander the Great's wife Roxana and son Alexander, dies (c. 61).

292 BC

- Menander, influential Athenian dramatist, chief dramatist of Greek New Comedy whose *Dyscolus* survives, dies (c. 50).

289 BC

- Agathocles, tyrant of Syracuse in Sicily 317 BC–304 BC, then self-styled king of Sicily 304 BC–289 BC, dies (c. 72).
- Mengzi or Meng-tzu (original name Meng K'o, known in the West as Mencius), important early Chinese Confucianist philosopher whose work *Mencius* survives, dies in China (c. 83).

c. 287 BC

- Theophrastus, Greek philosopher and student of Aristotle, dies (c. 85).

285 BC

- Archimedes, celebrated Greek mathematician and inventor, born in Syracuse, Sicily (–212 BC).

283 BC

- Ptolemy I, Macedonian ruler of Egypt (323 BC–285 BC), and founder of the Ptolemaic dynasty, dies in Egypt (c. 81).

281 BC

- Lysimachus, king of Macedon, dies in battle at Corupedium, Lydia (c. 79).
- August Seleucus I (Nicator), Macedonian army commander who founded the Seleucid Kingdom in 312 BC, dies near Lysimachia, Thrace (76).

c. 280 BC

- Chrysippus, Greek Stoic philosopher, born (–206 BC).

c. 276 BC

- Eratosthenes of Cyrene, Greek scientist, astronomer, and poet, born in Cyrene, Libya (–196 BC).

272 BC

- Bindusara, King of Maurya, dies.
- Pyrrhus, king of Epirus 307 BC–272 BC, who conducted successful but costly military campaigns against Macedon and Rome, killed in a skirmish in Argos, Argolis, Greece (c. 47).

270 BC

- Epicurus, influential Greek philosopher, dies in Athens (c. 71).

July Arsinoe, wife of Lysimachus, king of Thrace, and later, as Arsinoe II, wife of her brother, King Ptolemy II Philadelphus of Egypt, dies (c. 46).

263 BC

- Zeno of Citium, Greek philosopher who founded the Stoic school of philosophy, dies in Athens, Greece (72).

c. 262 BC

- Apollonius, Greek mathematician known for his book *Conics*, born in Perga, Anatolia (–c. 190 BC).

261 BC

- Antiochus I ("Soter"), Seleucid king of eastern Syria c. 292 BC–281 BC and the consolidated kingdom of Syria 281 BC–261 BC, dies (c. 63).

259 BC

- Shih Huang-ti, Chinese emperor of the Ch'in dynasty 221 BC–c. 209 BC who united China in a short-lived empire, born in Ch'in, China (–c. 209 BC).

254 BC

- Plautus, Roman comic dramatist, born in Sarsina, Umbria (–184 BC).

252 BC
- A census gives the number of Roman citizens as 297,797, although the reliability of the figures is doubtful.

Religion

c. **300 BC**
- Oriental cults and religions spread from Asia Minor and the Near East.
- The Jews of Jerusalem, surrounded and threatened by a sophisticated Hellenism, found a puritan sect called Chasidim.

c. **297 BC**
- Northern Indian ruler Chandragupta Maurya reputedly starves himself to death as prescribed by Jainism, a religion associated with Hinduism.

291 BC
- The worship of Asclepius, Greek god of medicine, is introduced to Rome from Epidaurus, on the Peloponnese, in the hope of averting a plague.

279 BC
- Celtic chieftain Brennus the Gaul is reputedly prevented from desecrating the shrine of Apollo at Delphi by a miraculous storm and, having been defeated in this way, kills himself in shame.

258 BC
- Mauryan emperor of India Asoka is repelled by his conquests and becomes a Buddhist and pacifist, setting out to spread the original teachings of Gautama Buddha.
- The great Buddhist *stupa* (a domed structure for housing Buddhist relics) is founded at Sanchi (in the Madhya Pradesh, India) under the direction of Asoka, the Mauryan emperor of India.

Sports

c. **300 BC**
- A form of polo known as *Sagol Kangjei* is played in the area that is now Manipur state in northeastern India.

250 BC–201 BC

POLITICS, GOVERNMENT, AND ECONOMICS

Business and Economics

240 BC
- Rome takes over full control of Sicily and stations a legion there; it treats Sicily more like a defeated country than it has ever treated any part of Italy. Sicilian peasants are heavily taxed and an increasing amount of corn is imported from the island, Roman farmers now turning more to the olive and the vine.

221 BC
- Chinese emperor Shih Huang-ti issues round coins. They supersede all previous forms of currency in China. He also standardizes the system of weights and measures basing them on a decimal system.

Human Rights

c. **215 BC**
- Chinese emperor Shih Huang-ti abolishes the feudal system of land tenure in China.

Politics and Government

250 BC
- A group of Celts of the tribe of the Volcae Tectosages invades southern France and settles there, mixing with the local population. Another group settles in Bohemia.
- The Greek governor of Bactria, Diodotus, takes advantage of Seleucid family quarrels to break away from the Seleucid Kingdom and establish himself as an ally, rather than a governor, of King Antiochus II of Syria.
- The Romans begin the siege of the Carthaginian city of Lilybaeum in Sicily.

249 BC
- The Roman consul Regulus, captured by the Carthaginians in 255 BC, is sent to Rome with Carthaginian peace terms. They are refused on his advice, but he still honorably returns to captivity in Carthage and is tortured to death. His widow tortures

two Carthaginian prisoners in reprisal. The Romans have previously suffered further naval defeats outside Lilybaeum in Sicily and failed to take the city.

247 BC

- Arsaces, chief of the Parsii, murders the Seleucid governor of Persia and establishes the kingdom of the Parthians. The Parthian Empire grows and will later cause Rome much trouble.
- Rome enters into a treaty, on equal terms, with King Hieron of Syracuse, Sicily, which is to be "forever."
- The Carthaginian general Hamilcar Barca leads a major attempt to recapture Sicily from the occupying Roman forces. While Carthaginian forces attack the Romans in the west of the island, Hamilcar lands a force of regular troops on the north coast, near modern Palermo. The Carthaginian oligarchy shows more interest in carving out large estates in the African interior than carrying on the Roman war over Sicily.

246 BC

- King Ptolemy II of Egypt dies and is succeeded by Ptolemy III, who is more interested in military conquest than his predecessor.
- King Ptolemy III of Egypt sets out on a career of conquest in the Seleucid Empire, now under Seleucus II: the Third Syrian War. Ptolemy is partly motivated by a desire for revenge for the murders of the Seleucid king Antiochus II and his wife Berenice (Ptolemy III's sister) by Antiochus's ex-wife Laodice.
- The emperor Asoka in India (following the Persian practice of erecting rock inscriptions) mentions that he has exchanged diplomatic missions during his reign with kings who have been identified as Antiochus II of the Seleucid Empire, Ptolemy III of Egypt, and Antigonus II of Macedon. For the next hundred years there is considerable Indian contact with the West, in particular with the Seleucid Empire. Asoka also makes diplomatic contacts with Nepal and Ceylon.
- The short-lived Qin dynasty is set up in China with the accession of King Zheng, who changes his name to Shih Huang-ti.
- With the Carthaginian general Hamilcar Barca wearing them down in Sicily, the Romans determine on an effort to regain command of the sea and build yet another fleet.

245 BC

- Aratus of Sicyon is elected general of the Achaean League in the Peloponnese and frees the Greek city-state of Corinth from its Macedonian garrison.
- King Ptolemy III of Egypt temporarily defeats and permanently weakens most of the Seleucid Empire. He reaches as far as Bactria and the borders of India. However, he is forced to return to Egypt to meet internal trouble and the Seleucid rulers resume control.

242 BC

- A second praetor is appointed in Rome to deal with lawsuits involving noncitizens; this official's yearly edict becomes the basis of Rome's code of law for foreigners, the *Ius Gentium* ("Law of Nations").

241 BC

- Attalus I succeeds to the throne of Pergamum in Asia.
- Egyptian pharaoh Ptolemy III returns from his conquests of the Seleucids, a dynasty in Near Asia (312 BC–65 BC),

with much booty, including many statues of Egyptian gods carried off by the earlier king of Persia Cambyses. He restores these to their temples, earning the title *Euergetes/the Benefactor*.

- The Romans win a resounding victory off the Carthaginian city of Lilybaeum in Sicily with their new fleet and the Carthaginians accept severe peace terms; the First Punic War is over. Carthage agrees to abandon all claim to Sicily, to refrain from sailing its warships in Italian waters, and to pay an indemnity of 3,200 talents. The Carthaginian army, however, is allowed to return home with its arms.

240 BC

- China's emperor, Shih Huang-ti, beats back the Huns. He attempts to change China's feudal system into a totalitarian one, with communal land-holding and a standardization of all weights, measures, and tools throughout the land.

240 BC–237 BC   The rulers of Carthage in north Africa refuse to pay the troops returning from the First Punic War in Sicily, provoking a ruthless civil war in which the proletariat join the mercenaries under Spendius and Matho, who are later executed. The Carthaginian general Hamilcar Barca finally puts down the rebellion.

239 BC

- Sardinia revolts against Carthage, and Rome takes the opportunity to annex the island.

237 BC

- Over the last three decades Carthage's hold on Spain has weakened and the Carthaginian general Hamilcar Barca is sent to reestablish it. Hamilcar sees in this command the opportunity to build up a base from which war against Rome can be renewed.
- Roman legend tells how the Carthaginian general Hamilcar Barca, on setting out for his campaign in Spain, makes his young son Hannibal vow eternal hostility to Rome.

235 BC

- Attalus I, the greatest king of the Greek city-state of Pergamum in Asia Minor, begins to build up the city's power and importance.

232 BC

- The emperor Asoka dies and the Mauryan Empire in India declines rapidly, disappearing completely in the next 50 years.

231 BC

- Seleucus II, king of the Seleucid kingdom in Syria, following the example of King Ptolemy III of Egypt, campaigns in Bactria, and also in the newly formed Parthia, where King Tiridates, brother of Arsaces, king of Persia, defeats him.
- The queen mother Teuta comes to power in Illyria as regent. She extends Illyrian influence to Epirus and Acarnania to the south, and increases the sea raiding that Illyria has always practiced further into the Ionian Sea, and even to the coast of Italy.

230 BC

- King Cleomenes III of the Greek city-state of Sparta, having come to the throne in 236 BC, endeavors to restore the ancient Spartan constitution and in the

Punic Wars (264 BC–146 BC)

First Punic War

264 BC

- King Hieron of Syracuse, Sicily, threatens to renew his attack on the Mamertines (society of disbanded mercenaries), who appeal to Carthage and receive a Carthaginian garrison; they then appeal to Rome, get rid of the Carthaginian garrison, and welcome two Roman legions under Appius Claudius (a relative of the Roman censor). The Carthaginians, affronted, send a force to Sicily, and they are supported by Hieron. Appius Claudius beats them off, and the First Punic War breaks out.

263 BC

- The Romans attack the city of Syracuse in Sicily and force its king, Hieron, into alliance with them. He continues to rule Syracuse benevolently.

262 BC

- The Carthaginians are defeated by the Romans at Agrigentum in Sicily. They retire to reorganize their fleet, while the Romans sack Agrigentum and enslave its Greek inhabitants.

261 BC

- The Romans, now determined to win Sicily from Carthage, realize the need for a navy. They rapidly produce 100 copies of a captured Carthaginian quinquereme (warship) and train the necessary oarsmen.

260 BC

- The Romans win a resounding naval victory over the Carthaginians off Mylae in Sicily (the date may be two years earlier).

258 BC

- The Romans take the island of Corsica from the Carthaginians.

256 BC

- The Romans repeat their naval success against the Carthaginians at the Battle of Mylae by defeating them again at the Battle of Ecnomus. They send a force under the consul Regulus to Africa, who settles down for the winter in the hope of capturing the city of Carthage in the spring.

255 BC

- The Roman consul Regulus, sent to capture Carthage, is defeated and taken prisoner by the Carthaginians. A Roman fleet sent to rescue Regulus is wrecked.

254 BC

- The Romans capture the Carthaginian naval base of Panormus (modern Palermo) in Sicily but find it difficult to make further progress without controlling the sea.

250 BC

- The Romans begin the siege of the Carthaginian city of Lilybaeum in Sicily.

249 BC

- The Roman consul Regulus, captured by the Carthaginians in 255 BC, is sent to Rome with Carthaginian peace terms. They are refused on his advice, but he still honorably returns to captivity in Carthage and is tortured to death. His widow tortures two Carthaginian prisoners in reprisal. The Romans have previously suffered further naval defeats outside Lilybaeum in Sicily and failed to take the city.

247 BC

- The Carthaginian general Hamilcar Barca leads a major attempt to recapture Sicily from the occupying Roman forces. While Carthaginian forces attack the Romans in the west of the island, Hamilcar lands a force of regular troops on the north coast, near modern Palermo. The Carthaginian oligarchy shows more interest in carving out large estates in the African interior than carrying on the Roman war over Sicily.

246 BC

- With the Carthaginian general Hamilcar Barca wearing them down in Sicily, the Romans determine on an effort to regain command of the sea and build yet another fleet.

241 BC

- The Romans win a resounding victory off the Carthaginian city of Lilybaeum in Sicily with their new fleet and the Carthaginians accept severe peace terms; the First Punic War is over. Carthage agrees to abandon all claim to Sicily, to refrain from sailing its warships in Italian waters, and to pay an indemnity of 3,200 talents. The Carthaginian army, however, is allowed to return home with its arms.

237 BC

- A Roman legend tells how the Carthaginian general Hamilcar Barca, on setting out for his campaign in Spain, makes his young son Hannibal vow eternal hostility to Rome.

Second Punic War

219 BC

- The Carthaginian general Hannibal attacks the Spanish city of Saguntum, which is allied with Rome. The Romans send the dictator and consul Quintus Fabius to Carthage to negotiate peace or war; he makes a symbolic gesture with the folds of his toga, asking "Shall it be peace or war?" The Carthaginians leave the decision to him and he chooses war. Hannibal presses the siege of Saguntum, and the Second Punic War begins the following year.

218 BC

- In the spring the Carthaginian general Hannibal sets out from New Carthage (Cartagena) in Spain to invade Italy, reputedly with nearly 100,000 men and 50 elephants. The Romans send an army to Spain under Gnaeus Scipio, which arrives too late to stop Hannibal, but it remains in Spain to prevent reinforcements from reaching them. Hannibal crosses the Alps and, after meeting great hardships and dangers, reaches the Po valley in Italy in the late autumn.

December 12 The Roman general Publius Scipio is wounded in a minor engagement with the Carthaginians at Ticinus in Italy. He is saved from death by his 17-year-old son, later to become famous as Scipio Africanus Major. The less skillful general, Sempronius, is defeated at the Battle of the River Trebia.

217 BC

- Quintus Fabius is elected dictator by the Romans and earns the cognomen *Cunctator* (the Delayer) by avoiding a set battle and creating a "scorched earth" area around Hannibal's invading army to deprive the Carthaginians of supplies.

- The Roman consul T. Quinctius Flamininus, instead of remaining at Arretium to guard the western route through the Apennines, decides to pursue the Carthaginian general Hannibal. T. Quinctius Flamininus and his army are ambushed and defeated by Hannibal at Lake Trasimene. Two complete legions are wiped out in a serious defeat for the Romans.

216 BC

- The Roman dictator Quintus Fabius *Cunctator* is relieved of his command by an impatient Senate. The Romans are devastatingly defeated by the Carthaginians at Cannae (modern Canne in Apulia, Italy), after which Quintus Fabius is reinstated. There are revolts in central Italy, and the city of Capua sides with the Carthaginian general Hannibal. However, Hannibal fails to obtain reinforcements from Carthage, and the whole of Latium, Umbria, and Etruria remain loyal to Rome.

215 BC

- The Carthaginian general Hannibal reaches the south of Italy. King Philip V of Macedon and Hannibal enter into a treaty of promised mutual help, although it leads to no immediate action.

- The Carthaginians fail to recapture Sardinia. Their general, Hannibal, captures the city of Tarentum in southern Italy, but is denied any reinforcements from Spain by the activities of the Roman general Publius Scipio senior and his brother Gnaeus. The Greek city of Syracuse in Sicily revolts against Rome and holds out for four years.

212 BC

- The Numidian chiefs Syphax and Masinissa on Carthage's eastern border declare war on Carthage with Roman encouragement. The Carthaginian general Hasdrubal dashes across to Africa from Spain and stamps out this rebellion. He then returns to Spain, where he manages to turn the tide against the Romans; the Roman generals Publius Scipio and his brother, Gnaeus, are killed in battle.

211 BC

- The Romans besiege the city of Capua, in Campania, Italy, which had gone over to the Carthaginians, and the Carthaginian general Hannibal, as a diversion, makes an unsuccessful attempt on Rome. Capua falls, and is punished for its treachery. The following year 12 Latin colonies refuse to send military contingents to Rome.

- The Sicilian city of Syracuse falls to the siege of the Roman commander Marcus Claudius Marcellus, who also suppresses the remaining resistance in Sicily. Syracuse is looted and many citizens killed, including Archimedes, the Greek mathematician and inventor.

210 BC

- Scipio the Younger (later known as Scipio Africanus Major) is chosen to take over the Roman campaign against the Carthaginians in Spain after the death of his father and uncle, Publius and Gnaeus Scipio.

209 BC

- The Roman general Scipio Africanus makes skillful use of the tide to besiege and capture New Carthage (Cartagena) in Spain, encouraging his soldiers by telling them that Neptune, god of the sea, is on their side. He frees the hostages taken from Spanish tribes by the Carthaginians to ensure their loyalty. Several Spanish tribes come over to the Roman side. Scipio recruits the young Numidian prince Masinissa.

208 BC

- The Roman general Scipio the Younger (Scipio Africanus Major) fights the Carthaginian general Hasdrubal at Baecula in an attempt to prevent him escaping from Spain and going to aid his brother Hannibal in Italy. The Roman commander Marcus Claudius Marcellus, fighting under Scipio, is killed in battle.

207 BC

- The Carthaginian general Hasdrubal escapes from defeat in Spain and, crossing the Alps with an army of 25,000 men, tries to come to his brother Hannibal's rescue. On the River Metaurus in northern Italy (at the northern end of the Via Flaminia) Hasdrubal is defeated by the Romans and his head is thrown into Hannibal's camp. Hannibal realizes that he has virtually lost the war in Italy.

206 BC

- Scipio the Younger defeats the remaining Carthaginian forces in Spain at the Battle of Ilipa (near Seville).

- The Roman general Scipio the Younger (Scipio Africanus Major), having successfully driven the Carthaginians out of Spain, is elected consul. He prepares to carry the war into the enemy's country and attack Carthage itself, but is hampered by a jealous Roman Senate.

204 BC

- The Roman general Scipio the Younger (Scipio Africanus Major) invades Carthaginian territory and unsuccessfully besieges the city of Utica.

203 BC

- The Numidian chief Syphax and Carthaginian armies under General Gisco are defeated by the Roman general Scipio the Younger (Scipio Africanus Major) at the Battle of the Great Plains. The Carthaginian general Hannibal is compelled to return home from Italy.

- The Romans defeat Mago, the brother of the Carthaginian general Hannibal, in the Po valley, Italy. Mago captured the city of Genoa in 205 BC, in a last attempt to help Hannibal and prevent Scipio the Younger from invading Africa. The Carthaginian government sent him reinforcements, but the local Gallic and Ligurian tribes were reluctant to join him.

Punic Wars (264 BC–146 BC) *continued*

202 BC

- Numidian queen Sophonisba poisons herself to avoid capture by Roman forces. Her story is widely retold in subsequent literature.
- The Roman general Scipio the Younger (Scipio Africanus Major) advances on Carthage with the Numidian prince Masinissa. Masinissa captures the Numidian chief Syphax, but becomes ensnared by his wife, Sophonisba, until Scipio extricates him.
- The Roman general Scipio the Younger (Scipio Africanus Major) and the Carthaginian general Hannibal meet in front of their armies at Zama (modern Tunisia) and Hannibal makes peace proposals which are rejected.

201 BC

- Rome and Carthage sign a peace treaty to end formally the Second Punic War. The peace terms are harsh: Carthage has to surrender all but 10 ships of its great fleet, pay an indemnity of 10,000 talents, allow the Numidian prince Masinissa independence as king of Numidia, give up Spain to Rome, and refrain from warmongering without Rome's approval. The Romans then oust the Carthaginians from Malta.

c. 200 BC

- The Second Punic War has changed the Romans, as it has changed the whole political situation in the Mediterranean. They begin to treat their Italian allies more harshly, demanding troops but not conceding citizenship. The power of the aristocracy and the Senate is supreme. The yeoman farmer is being superseded by the great landowner.

195 BC

- Rome demands that the Carthaginian general Hannibal surrender but instead he goes into voluntary exile.

191 BC

- Scipio Africanus is now a figure of great authority in Rome and has borne the cognomen "Africanus" since just after his success against the Carthaginian general Hannibal in the Battle of Zama in Africa. He persuades the Senate to continue the war in Greece against King Antiochus III the Great of Syria and to complete his defeat by pursuing him into Asia Minor.
- The Carthaginians have already managed to collect the indemnity due to Rome as part of the peace settlement following the end of the Second Punic War. It was to be paid within 50 years, and the Romans refuse to accept it in advance in order to keep their hold over Carthage.

process becomes something of a proletarian champion in the Peloponnese.

- The city of Pergamum in Asia, under King Attalus I, beats off a fresh wave of invading Gauls.

229 BC

- Antigonus III ("Doson") comes to the Macedonian throne as regent for the future king Philip V of Macedon, now only eight years old.

229 BC–228 BC Rome becomes embroiled for the first time with the affairs of Greece by taking retaliatory action for the murder of Italian merchants and Roman envoys in Illyria, and for Illyrian piracy in the Adriatic Sea; the First Illyrian War takes place. The Greeks congratulate Rome on quelling the pirates; Antigonus III, the new king of Macedon, is not so pleased, however, and pursues a policy of befriending the Illyrians, a policy continued by his successor Philip V.

228 BC

- Following the success of Rome over the Illyrian people, Corinth permits Roman citizens to participate in the Isthmian games.
- The Carthaginian general Hamilcar Barca dies in battle during his successful campaign to resubdue Spain and is succeeded by his son-in-law Hasdrubal. Hasdrubal founds New Carthage (Cartagena) as a Spanish naval base, and penetrates further inland.

227 BC

- Rome makes Sardinia and Corsica a combined province. To deal with this rearrangement of the provinces, it appoints, and in future annually elects, two new praetors (with autocratic consular powers) to govern this province and Sicily.

226 BC

- A formidable host of Gauls, some of them from across the Alps, threaten Rome.
- The Greek merchants of Massilia (modern Marseille, France), frightened by Carthaginian successes in Spain (including their exploitation of the silver mines), appeal to Rome. The Carthaginian general Hasdrubal has to confine his activities in Spain to south of the River Ebro. Rome makes an alliance with an independent city in Spain, Saguntum.

225 BC

- The Romans decisively defeat the Gauls, who have been threatening Rome, at the Battle of Telamon.

223 BC

- King Seleucus III of Syria is assassinated after a reign of only three years and is succeeded by his brother, Antiochus III the Great.

222 BC

- King Cleomenes III of the Greek city-state of Sparta becomes involved in war with King Antigonus III of Macedon and the Achaean League. On being defeated, he flees to Egypt but commits suicide.
- Mediolanum (modern Milan), stronghold of the Gallic tribe of the Insubres, is taken by the Romans—the Roman consul Marcus Claudius Marcellus personally slays the Insubre chief, Britomartus, at the Battle of Clastidium. This means that Rome's northern frontier is secure to the Julian Alps. The threat seemingly posed by the Gauls in the year 226 BC subsides.

221 BC

- Carthaginian general Hasdrubal, still campaigning to increase the Carthaginian hold over Spain, is murdered;

182 BC
- When the Romans demand the extradition of the Carthaginian general Hannibal from Bithynia in Asia Minor, he commits suicide.

153 BC
- The Carthaginians appeal to Rome against the depredations of King Masinissa of Numidia. Rome sends out a commission, of which the Roman censor Marcus Porcius Cato ("the Elder" or "the Censor") is a member, and he is so alarmed by the prosperity he witnesses in Carthage that he begins his campaign for the final destruction of Rome's old enemy. By the treaty between Rome and Carthage that ended the Second Punic War in 201 BC, the Carthaginians are prevented from armed resistance but are guaranteed against loss of territory. When Cato returns to Rome he begins his practice of winding up his speeches to the Roman senate with the phrase, "*Censeo Carthaginem esse delendam*"/"I declare that Carthage must be destroyed."

Third Punic War

149 BC
- Rome regards the action of Carthage in defending itself against Numidian incursions in 150 BC as a *casus belli* (justification for war) and the Third Punic War begins. The oligarchic government of Carthage capitulates unconditionally. The Roman terms, however, are harsh. These state that the city shall be destroyed and that its 700,000 inhabitants shall rebuild their homes elsewhere, "but not within 10 miles of the sea."

146 BC
- After a prolonged and terrible siege Carthage is finally taken by the Roman consul Scipio Aemilianus. The Carthaginians make their final stand in their temple of Eshmoun (equivalent to Aesculapius, god of medicine), reputedly setting fire to the building and dying in the flames. The wife of the Carthaginian commander Hasdrubal shows herself in splendor with her two children before she and they are burned. Carthage is destroyed and the Roman province of "Africa" is established. Scipio Aemilianus is the son of the Roman consul Aemilius Paullus and adopted heir of Scipio Africanus Major whose name he takes, being known as Scipio Africanus the Younger.

he is succeeded by Hannibal, Hamilcar Barca's young son. The city of Saguntum in Spain, allied to Rome, appeals to Rome against Hannibal.
- Having defeated all his enemies, Shih Huang-ti's position as emperor of China is now undisputed.
- Ptolemy IV Philopator comes to the Egyptian throne, murders his mother Berenice II, wife of Ptolemy III, his brother, and uncle, and begins a reign of personal luxury, during which his kingdom deteriorates.

220 BC
- Antigonus III (Doson) is succeeded by the young Philip V as king of Macedon. Philip immediately comes into collision with Rome over the Illyrian pirates, when Rome again tries to drive them from the area and their chief seeks refuge with Philip who is deeply resentful of Roman interference. The Second Illyrian War takes place (220 BC–219 BC).
220 BC–219 BC   There is a period of internal wars in Greece known as the Social War.

219 BC
- The Carthaginian general Hannibal attacks the Spanish city of Saguntum, which is allied with Rome. The Romans send the dictator and consul Quintus Fabius to Carthage to negotiate peace or war; he makes a symbolic gesture with the folds of his toga, asking "Shall it be peace or war?" The Carthaginians leave the decision to him and he chooses war. Hannibal presses the siege of Saguntum, and the Second Punic War begins.
- The two post-Alexandrian empires of the Ptolemies (Egypt) and the Seleucids (Syria) go to war over the ownership of Phoenicia and Palestine, beginning the Fourth Syrian War.

218 BC
- In the spring the Carthaginian general Hannibal sets out from New Carthage (Cartagena) in Spain to invade Italy, reputedly with nearly 100,000 men and 50 elephants. The Romans send an army to Spain under Gnaeus Scipio, which arrives too late to stop Hannibal, but it remains in Spain to prevent reinforcements from reaching them. Hannibal crosses the Alps and, after meeting great hardships and dangers, reaches the Po valley in Italy in the late autumn.
December 12   The Roman general Publius Scipio is wounded in a minor engagement with the Carthaginians at Ticinus in Italy. He is saved from death by his 17-year-old son, later to become famous as Scipio Africanus Major. The less skillful general, Sempronius, is defeated at the Battle of the River Trebia.

217 BC
- Antiochus III the Great of Syria is defeated in his war with Ptolemy III of Egypt at the Battle of Raphia, near Gaza in Palestine. Native Egyptian forces take part in this battle alongside the Macedonian soldiers. Their success spurs nationalist feelings.
- Quintus Fabius is elected dictator by the Romans and earns the cognomen *Cunctator* (the Delayer) by avoiding a set battle and creating a "scorched earth" area around Hannibal's invading army to deprive the Carthaginians of supplies.
- The Roman consul T. Quinctius Flamininus, instead of remaining at Arretium to guard the western route through the Apennines, decides to pursue the Carthaginian general Hannibal. T. Quinctius Flamininus and his army are ambushed and defeated by Hannibal at

Lake Trasimene. Two complete legions are wiped out in a serious defeat for the Romans.

216 BC

- King Ptolemy IV suppresses a revolt of Egyptian peasants. By 205 BC the revolt has spread to Upper Egypt.
- The Roman dictator Quintus Fabius *Cunctator* is relieved of his command by an impatient Senate. The Romans are devastatingly defeated by the Carthaginians at Cannae (modern Canne in Apulia, Italy), after which Quintus Fabius is reinstated. There are revolts in central Italy, and the city of Capua sides with the Carthaginian general Hannibal. However, Hannibal fails to obtain reinforcements from Carthage, and the whole of Latium, Umbria, and Etruria remain loyal to Rome.

216 BC–205 BC King Philip V of Macedon, resenting Rome's interference in Illyria, seizes his opportunity and invades Illyria, starting the First Macedonian War. The war continues in a somewhat desultory fashion for 11 years.

215 BC

- The Carthaginian general Hannibal reaches the south of Italy. King Philip V of Macedon and Hannibal enter into a treaty of promised mutual help, although it leads to no immediate action.
- The Carthaginians fail to recapture Sardinia. Their general, Hannibal, captures the city of Tarentum in southern Italy, but is denied any reinforcements from Spain by the activities of the Roman general Publius Scipio senior and his brother Gnaeus. The Greek city of Syracuse in Sicily revolts against Rome and holds out for four years.

212 BC

- Antiochus III the Great of Syria begins an effort to emulate Alexander the Great in his eastern conquests.
- Scipio the Younger (later known as Scipio Africanus Major), the son of the Roman general Publius Scipio, is elected aedile (magistrate responsible for temples, buildings, streets, markets, and games in Rome) though legally too young for the post.
- The Numidian chiefs Syphax and Masinissa on Carthage's eastern border declare war on Carthage with Roman encouragement. The Carthaginian general Hasdrubal dashes across to Africa from Spain and stamps out this rebellion. He then returns to Spain, where he manages to turn the tide against the Romans; the Roman generals Publius Scipio and his brother, Gnaeus, are killed in battle.
- The Romans have some 25 legions, reputedly a full quarter of Italian manhood, under arms. Their corn supplies are failing.

211 BC

- The Romans besiege the city of Capua, in Campania, Italy, which had gone over to the Carthaginians, and the Carthaginian general Hannibal, as a diversion, makes an unsuccessful attempt on Rome. Capua falls, and is punished for its treachery. The following year 12 Latin colonies refuse to send military contingents to Rome.
- The Sicilian city of Syracuse falls to the siege of the Roman commander Marcus Claudius Marcellus, who also suppresses the remaining resistance in Sicily.

Syracuse is looted and many citizens killed, including Archimedes, the Greek mathematician and inventor.

210 BC

- Chinese emperor Shih Huang-ti dies and leaves a weak successor in his son Ershi Huang-ti.
- Scipio the Younger (later known as Scipio Africanus Major) is chosen to take over the Roman campaign against the Carthaginians in Spain after the deaths of his father and uncle, Publius and Gnaeus Scipio.

c. 210 BC Euthydemus, a Greek soldier from Magnesia in Asia Minor, and his son Demetrius consolidate Bactria and Sogdiana (Tajikistan/Uzbekistan) under their rule, basing themselves in the fortified city of Bactria. Euthydemus fights off nomadic raiders and the Parthians from his kingdom.

209 BC

- The Roman general Scipio Africanus makes skillful use of the tide to besiege and capture New Carthage (Cartagena) in Spain, encouraging his soldiers by telling them that Neptune, god of the sea, is on their side. He frees the hostages taken from Spanish tribes by the Carthaginians to ensure their loyalty. Several Spanish tribes come over to the Roman side. Scipio recruits the young Numidian prince Masinissa.

208 BC

- King Antiochus III of Syria besieges the city of Bactria, capital of the Greek kingdom of Bactria. He is held off by King Euthydemus, and a treaty of mutual support is made.
- The Roman general Scipio the Younger (Scipio Africanus Major) fights the Carthaginian general Hasdrubal at Baecula in an attempt to prevent him escaping from Spain and going to aid his brother Hannibal in Italy. The Roman commander Marcus Claudius Marcellus, fighting under Scipio, is killed in battle.

207 BC

- Nabis, a Syrian slave, comes to power in the Greek city-state of Sparta and brings about a social revolution. He frees the helots (serfs), redistributes land, cancels debts, and destroys the ruling oligarchy.
- The Carthaginian general Hasdrubal escapes from defeat in Spain and, crossing the Alps with an army of 25,000 men, tries to come to his brother Hannibal's rescue. On the River Metaurus in northern Italy (at the northern end of the Via Flaminia) Hasdrubal is defeated by the Romans and his head is thrown into Hannibal's camp. Hannibal realizes that he has virtually lost the war in Italy.

206 BC

- Chinese emperor Ershi Huang-ti is deposed after a reign of only four years, and China's Han dynasty is formed by Liu Bang, a populist monarch.
- Scipio the Younger defeats the remaining Carthaginian forces in Spain at the Battle of Ilipa (near Seville).
- The Roman general Scipio the Younger (Scipio Africanus Major), having successfully driven the Carthaginians out of Spain, is elected consul. He prepares to carry the war into the enemy's country and attack Carthage itself, but is hampered by a jealous Roman Senate.

Macedonian-Roman Wars (216 BC–150 BC)

216 BC–205 BC

- King Philip V of Macedon, resenting Rome's interference in Illyria, seizes his opportunity and invades Illyria, starting the First Macedonian War. The war continues in a somewhat desultory fashion for 11 years.

215 BC

- The Carthaginian general Hannibal reaches the south of Italy. Philip V and Hannibal enter into a treaty of promised mutual help, although it leads to no immediate action.

205 BC

- King Philip, who made an alliance with Carthage in 215 BC, expecting the Carthaginian general Hannibal to rapidly conquer Rome so that he could regain control of the Roman protectorate in western Greece, makes a temporary peace with Rome at Phoenice, ending the First Macedonian War. Rome retains most of its protectorate.

200 BC

- At the start of the Second Macedonian War, the Roman consul Sulpicius Galba lands troops in Greece, sending a naval squadron to protect Athens, the only Greek city to have immediately joined Rome. After Galba has a minor success against King Philip V of Macedon's army, the Aetolian League declares for Rome.
- Following appeals from the Aetolian League and many other Greek city-states, especially Rhodes and Pergamum, the Romans declare war on Philip —the Second Macedonian War begins. Rome is concerned about the changes in the balance of power among the Hellenistic kingdoms to the east that are currently occurring. Athens immediately joins Rome.

198 BC

- The Roman consul T. Quinctius Flamininus crosses to Macedon with an army and pushes King Philip's forces to disaster in the Vale of Tempe. Abortive peace negotiations take place. The Greek cities of Boeotia, Sparta, and the Aetolian League come over to Rome.

197 BC

- Flamininus defeats the Macedonians at Cynoscephalae in Thessaly and dictates peace terms. The Second Macedonian War is over.

196 BC

- Flamininus becomes the hero of the Greek world. At the Isthmian Games, held in July at Corinth, he proclaims the "freedom" of Greece.

172 BC

- King Eumenes II of Pergamum travels to Rome to warn the Senate of the threat posed by King Perseus of Macedon. On his return, rocks fall upon him at Delphi and nearly kill him; Perseus is suspected as the instigator.

171 BC–167 BC

- Rome declares war on King Perseus of Macedon, who is vehemently anti-Roman, and the Third Macedonian War begins. The Romans initially suffer several defeats due to bad leadership. The Greek kingdom of Epirus joins Macedon, but the Greek leagues hold back.

168 BC

- During the Third Macedonian War, Perseus gains the support of Genthius, the Illyrian king who reigns in Scodra. The Roman consul Aemilius Paullus takes charge of the Roman forces fighting Perseus in Thessaly. He defeats Perseus at the Battle of Pydna, and later captures him to adorn his subsequent triumphal parade in Rome. The Roman praetor L. Anicius Gallus campaigns against Genthius in Illyria, defeating him and taking the city of Scodra. The Third Illyrian War is over in less than a month; by the postwar settlement, towns loyal to Rome are granted freedom from taxation and the rest pay to Rome about half the previous royal tax. Rome then withdraws from the area.

167 BC

- Before leaving Greece at the end of the Third Macedonian War, the Roman consul Paullus is goaded into brutal revenge on the Epirots. He destroys 70 of their towns and sells 100,000 citizens into slavery. The Greek mainland remains tranquil, albeit discontented, for 20 years.
- The private papers of King Perseus of Macedon are discovered and incriminate many political leaders of the Achaean League. A thousand distinguished Greeks are deported to Rome, among them the future historian Polybius.
- Under the terms of peace imposed on Macedon by Aemilius Paullus, the monarchy is suppressed, the country is divided into four administrative areas, and an elaborate democratic constitution is invented which lasts for no more than 20 years.

150 BC

- The Greeks exiled to Rome in 167 BC for plotting with Perseus are allowed to return home to Greece.

205 BC

- Antiochus III the Great of Syria returns from his eastern campaigns, having failed to subjugate either the Bactrians or the Parthians.
- King Philip V of Macedon, who made an alliance with Carthage in 215 BC, expecting the Carthaginian general Hannibal to rapidly conquer Rome so that he could regain control of the Roman protectorate in western Greece, makes a temporary peace with Rome at Phoenice, ending the First Macedonian War. Rome retains most of its protectorate.
- The Roman Senate, partly due to caution but mainly jealousy, allots the Roman general Scipio the Younger (Scipio Africanus Major) no legions for his command of Sicily other than the two stationed there. Scipio recruits his own army and boosts their morale by arming 300 of them as cavalry.
- November   King Ptolemy IV of Egypt ends his life in dissipation. His death is kept a secret by his court favorites. He is succeeded by Ptolemy V, aged five. King Philip V of Macedon and Antiochus III the Great of Syria make an agreement to divide the Ptolemaic kingdom between them.

204 BC

- The Roman general Scipio the Younger (Scipio Africanus Major) invades Carthaginian territory and unsuccessfully besieges the city of Utica.

203 BC

- The Numidian chief Syphax and Carthaginian armies under General Gisco are defeated by the Roman general Scipio the Younger (Scipio Africanus Major) at the Battle of the Great Plains. The Carthaginian general Hannibal is compelled to return home from Italy.
- The Romans defeat Mago, the brother of the Carthaginian general Hannibal, in the Po valley, Italy. Mago captured the city of Genoa in 205 BC, in a last attempt to help Hannibal and prevent Scipio the Younger from invading Africa. The Carthaginian government sent him reinforcements, but the local Gallic and Ligurian tribes were reluctant to join him.

202 BC

- The Roman general Scipio the Younger (Scipio Africanus Major) advances on Carthage with the Numidian prince Masinissa. Masinissa captures the Numidian chief Syphax, but becomes ensnared by his wife, Sophonisba, until Scipio extricates him.
- The Roman general Scipio the Younger (Scipio Africanus Major) and the Carthaginian general Hannibal meet in front of their armies at Zama (modern Tunisia) and Hannibal makes peace proposals which are rejected.

201 BC

- Rome and Carthage sign a peace treaty to end formally the Second Punic War. The peace terms are harsh: Carthage has to surrender all but 10 ships of its great fleet, pay an indemnity of 10,000 talents, allow the Numidian prince Masinissa independence as king of Numidia, give up Spain to Rome, and refrain from warmongering without Rome's approval. The Romans then oust the Carthaginians from Malta.

SCIENCE, TECHNOLOGY, AND MEDICINE

Agriculture

c. 250 BC

- The Romans begin systematic crop rotation using a two-year rotation system.

232 BC

- The land just north of Rome, the Ager Gallicus, is parceled out in small tracts to poor citizens. It proves an attraction to the Gauls further north.

Ecology

225 BC

- The Greek island of Rhodes is devastated by an earthquake, and the entire Hellenic world—Seleucid, Ptolemaic, and Macedonian—comes to its aid with both magnificent and practical gifts. The *Colossus* is toppled by the earthquake.

217 BC

- Over 50,000 die in an earthquake in northern Africa.

Exploration

c. 240 BC

- Greek scholar Eratosthenes of Cyrene makes a map of the Nile valley and correctly explains the reasons for the Nile's annual floods as being due to heavy rains in the upper reaches.

Health and Medicine

c. 250 BC

- Greek anatomist Erasistratus of Ceos notes the difference between sensory and motor nerves, and correctly describes the functions of the valves of the heart.

Math

c. 250 BC

- Greek mathematician and inventor Archimedes, in his *On the Sphere and the Cylinder*, provides the formulae for finding the volume of a sphere and a cylinder; in *Measurement of the Circle* he arrives at an approximation of the value of pi; in *The Sand Reckoner* he creates a place-value system of notation for Greek mathematics; and in *Floating Bodies*, the first known work on hydrostatics, he discovers the principle that bears his name—that submerged bodies are acted upon by an upward or buoyant force equal to the weight of the fluid displaced.

235 BC

- Based on knowledge of the length of an arc, and the size of the corresponding angle, the Greek scholar Eratosthenes estimates the earth's circumference to be 46,250 km/28,790 mi—about 15% too large.

***c.* 230 BC**

- Alexandrian mathematician Apollonius of Perga, writes *Conics*, a systematic treatise on the principles of conics in which he introduces the terms parabola, ellipse, and hyperbola.
- Greek scholar Eratosthenes of Cyrene develops a method of finding all prime numbers. Known as the sieve of Eratosthenes it involves striking out the number 1 and every *n*th number following the number *n*. Only prime numbers then remain.

Science

***c.* 250 BC**

- In *Lü-shi Chun Qui/The Spring and Autumn Annals of Mr. Lu*, Chinese scholars explicitly describe the hydrologic cycle. The idea has been known in China for a century.

240 BC

- Chinese astronomers make the first recorded sighting of Halley's Comet.

237 BC

- Egyptian king Ptolemy III improves the Egyptian calendar by introducing an extra day every four years to the basic 356 day calendar.

Technology

***c.* 250 BC**

- Apollonius of Perga develops the hemicyclium, a conical-shaped sundial.
- Greek mathematician and inventor Archimedes invents the Archimedes screw for removing water from the hold of a large ship. A similar device is already in use in Egypt for irrigation.
- Greek physicist and inventor Ctesibius of Alexandria improves the clepsydra, or water clock, by employing a siphon to automatically recycle itself—the first robot.

***c.* 245 BC**

- The Greek engineer Ctesibius builds the first gun. It consists of a bronze tube sealed at one end and contains a piston. When the piston is pulled back the air in the tube is compressed. Pulling the stop catch releases the air violently forcing out projectiles such as arrows.

***c.* 230 BC**

- Copper-lined pottery jars, with asphalt plugs, containing metal rods—the first electric battery—are used in Baghdad to coat objects with thin layers of gold or silver—the first example of electroplating.

211 BC

- The world's first natural gas well is drilled in China. Bamboo poles, and percussion bits made of cast-iron, are used to drill to a depth of about 140 m/460 ft.

Transportation

***c.* 245 BC–*c.* 240 BC**

- Ptolemy III of Egypt builds a warship 122 m/400 ft long that requires 4,000 rowers.

220 BC

- The Via Flaminia that links Rome with the Po valley on the northern Adriatic coast, is completed.

ARTS AND IDEAS

Architecture

240 BC

- Chinese emperor Shih Huang-ti builds a vast number of palaces at his new capital Hsien-yan, one for each prince he defeats. The plan of the city is said to imitate the Milky Way, each house representing a star.

220 BC

- Chinese emperor Shih Huang-ti builds a huge mausoleum for himself, surrounded by burial pits containing thousands of life-sized terracotta warriors guarding the approach.

214 BC–206 BC

- Chinese emperor Shi Huang-ti employs general Meng Dian to connect a number of existing defensive walls in northern China to form a single fortified system with watchtowers to keep out the Xiongnu (Huns). Known as the Great Wall of China, it is 2,400 km/1,500 mi long, 9 m/30 ft high, 8 m/25 ft wide at its base, and 5 m/17 ft wide at its top. It is the largest building project ever undertaken.

Arts

***c.* 245 BC**

- The art of the mosaic, using cube tesserae (small pieces of mosaic material), is introduced into Greece and Egypt.

230 BC

- Statues are erected to celebrate the defeat of the Gauls by the kingdom of Pergamum, including the *Dying Gaul*.

Literature and Language

241 BC

- Berenice, wife of the Egyptian pharaoh Ptolemy III, dedicates a lock of her hair to the gods in thanks for her husband's military successes, giving rise to the naming of a constellation "The Lock of Berenice." The Greek poet Callimachus and the Roman poet Catullus commemorate this in poems in later times.

240 BC

- Latin poet and playwright Livius Andronicus has his first tragedy and first comedy produced in Rome. He subsequently translates Homer's *Odyssey* into Latin.

202 BC

- Numidian queen Sophonisba poisons herself to avoid capture by Roman forces. Her story is widely retold in subsequent literature.

Thought and Scholarship

250 BC

- Egyptian pharaoh Ptolemy II encourages the Jews in Alexandria, Egypt, to have the Old Testament translated into Greek. By tradition 70 translators worked on the translation, hence engendering the name "the Septuagint," though in reality the translation took place over a long period.

c. **245 BC**

- The Greek mathematician and astronomer Eratosthenes of Cyrene succeeds Apollonius Rhodius as librarian of the library at Alexandria, Egypt.

240 BC

- Chinese philosopher Xun-zi is active in developing the ideas of the philosopher Confucius.

BIRTHS & DEATHS

250 BC

- Theocritus, Greek poet who invented pastoral poetry, dies (*c.* 60).

247 BC

- Hannibal the Great, celebrated Carthaginian general who conducted the Second Punic War against Rome 218 BC–201 BC, born in North Africa (–*c.* 182 BC).

246 BC

- Antiochus II (Theos), Seleucid king of Syria 261 BC–246 BC who spent much of his reign at war with Egypt and recovered a large part of Anatolia, dies (*c.* 41).
- Ptolemy II Philadelphus, king of Egypt 285 BC–246 BC, who ruled Egypt with his sister Arisonoe II, whom he married, dies (62).

242 BC

- Antiochus III, Seleucid king of the Hellenistic Syrian Empire 223 BC–187 BC, who rebuilt the empire, born (–187).

c. **240 BC**

- Callimachus, Greek poet of the Alexandrian school, whose *Aetia/Causes* survives, dies (*c.* 65).
- Masinissa, king of Numidia 201 BC–148 BC, born (–148 BC).

239 BC

- Antigonus II, king of Macedon 276 BC–239 BC, who established his kingdom's hegemony over Greece, dies (*c.* 80).
- Quintus Ennius, Roman epic poet, dramatist and satirist, author of the epic poem "Annales"/"Annals," born in Rudiae, Italy (–169 BC).

238 BC

- Asoka, last major emperor in the Mauryan dynasty of India *c.* 265 BC–238 BC, who encouraged the expansion of Buddhism, dies.
- Philip V, king of Macedon 221 BC–179 BC, whose attempts at Macedonian expansion were thwarted by Rome, born (–179 BC).

236 BC

- Scipio Africanus the Elder (Publius Cornelius Scipio), Roman general noted for his victory over Hannibal at Zama ending the Second Punic War (218 BC–201 BC), born (–184 BC).

234 BC

- Marcus Porcius Cato ("the Elder" or "the Censor"), Roman statesman and orator, the first major Latin prose writer, whose *De agri cultura/On Agriculture* survives, born in Tusculum, Latium (–149 BC).

c. **232 BC**

- Cleanthes, Greek Stoic philosopher, head of the Stoic school 263 BC–232 BC, of whose works only fragments survive, dies (*c.* 99).

228 BC

- Hamilcar Barca, Carthaginian general, father of Hannibal, dies in battle (*c.* 42).

221 BC

- Antigonus III, king of Macedon 229 BC–221 BC, conqueror of Sparta, dies (*c.* 42).
- Berenice II, daughter of Magas, king of Cyrene, and wife of Ptolemy III, king of Egypt, whose marriage reunited Cyrene and Egypt, is murdered in Cyrene (*c.* 48).
- Hasdrubal, Carthaginian general, brother-in-law of Hannibal, is assassinated.
- Ptolemy III, Macedonian king of Egypt 246 BC–221 BC, who united Egypt and Cyrenaica, dies.

215 BC

c. 215 BC Antiochus IV, Seleucid king of the Hellenistic Syrian Empire 175 BC–164 BC, who was responsible for the Wars of the Maccabees, born (–164 BC).

- Hieron II, tyrant of Syracuse *c.* 270 BC–*c.* 215 BC, who allied his city with Rome in 263 BC, dies.

c. **214 BC**

- Carneades, Greek Skeptic philosopher, head of the New Academy at Athens, born (–129 BC).

212 BC

- Archimedes, celebrated Greek mathematician and inventor, dies (*c.* 74).
- Gnaeus Cornelius Scipio, Roman general, brother of Publius Cornelius Scipio, falls in battle against the Carthaginians near Cartagena in Spain.
- Publius Cornelius Scipio, Roman general, brother of Gnaeus Cornelius Scipio and father of Scipio Africanus the Elder, falls in battle against the Carthaginians on the Guadalquivir River in Spain.

210 BC

- Shih Huang-ti, Chinese emperor of the Ch'in dynasty 221 BC–210 BC/209 BC, who united China in a short-lived empire, dies in Ch'in, China (*c.* 49).

208 BC

- Marcus Claudius Marcellus, Roman general who captured Syracuse during the Second Punic War (218 BC–201 BC), dies near Venusia, Apulia, Italy (*c.* 60).

207 BC

- Chrysippus, Greek Stoic philosopher, dies (*c.* 74).

205 BC

- Ptolemy IV, Macedonian king of Egypt 238 BC–205 BC, dies.

204 BC

- Lucius Livius Andronicus, a freed Greek slave who wrote some of the earliest epic poetry and drama in Latin, dies, probably in Rome (*c.* 80).

- Greek philosopher Chrysippus teaches Stoic philosophy at Athens and combats academic skepticism: he is also a prolific writer.

223 BC

- Chinese emperor Shih Huang-ti and his premier Li Si order "the burning of the books" and discourage ancient learning as being too conservative and reactionary, although a copy of Confucius' works is officially retained.

SOCIETY

Everyday Life

250 BC

- The Middle La Tène period begins in Celtic Europe; it lasts until 150 BC.

235 BC

- Rome closes the gates of the Temple of Janus as a sign that it is at peace.

Religion

213 BC

- Prophetic verses attributed to a seer called Marcius circulate. They suggest that Rome will only be freed of its foreign enemy (Hannibal) if games honoring Apollo are founded. The Sybilline books are found to agree, and the *Ludi Apollinares* are established.

204 BC

- An image of Cybele, the Phrygian mother goddess, is brought to Rome from Pessinus in Asia Minor.

Sports

216 BC

- A spectacle of 22 combats is staged at the funeral of a member of the Roman Lepidus family—the Greek funeral games are evolving into the Roman gladiatorial combats.

c. **206 BC**

- According to the Chinese poet Li-Yu (*c.* AD 50– *c.* 130), a game of *zuzhu*, an ancient Chinese form of football, is played on the emperor's birthday in 206 BC. The game he describes has some remarkable similarities to modern football, with a stuffed leather ball and two goal areas.

200 BC–151 BC

POLITICS, GOVERNMENT, AND ECONOMICS

Business and Economics

189 BC

- Booty and indemnity settlements from its various recent wars make Rome wealthy on such a scale that it encourages extravagance and financial speculation. At the Roman consul Gaius Flaminius' triumph (ritual victory procession in Rome), besides marble and bronze statues, 8,165 kg/18,000 lb of silver and 1,685 kg/ 3,714 lb of gold are paraded.

175 BC

- Private minting of copper coins is allowed in China and serious inflation ensues.

170 BC

- The north African city and state of Carthage is rebuilding its prosperity during this period. However, King Masinissa is also building up his strength in the neighboring kingdom of Numidia, and is encroaching on Carthaginian territory.

160 BC

- The increase in personal wealth and the desire for still more wealth continues in Rome. Rome is now afraid of Carthage economically as well as militarily, as it has prospered very rapidly since its defeat by Scipio Africanus the Elder in 202 BC, despite having had to make a large indemnity payment to Rome.

Colonization

195 BC

- A Spanish revolt against Roman consolidation of Carthage's former colonies is put down by praetor M. Fulvus Nobilior, under the Roman consul Marcus Porcius Cato ("the Elder" or "the Censor"). Aemilius Paullus succeeds Nobilior as praetor, and Spain continues to be a troublesome area and a most unpopular assignment for the Roman legionaries.

189 BC

- The kingdom of Bactria (in modern Afghanistan) under Euthydemus and his son Demetrius is now strong enough to expand and to take over the Persian satrapies (provinces) that lie between it and India. This consolidates Bactria's hold on the trade routes and eventually leads its kings on to India.

183 BC

- King Demetrius of Bactria crosses the mountains between Bactria and India and proceeds down the Kabul valley to the town of Taxila, which he captures. He advances to the River Indus, capturing the city of Pattala in Arachosia and refounding it as Demetrias. He sends his general, Menander, east through the Punjab, where he occupies Sagala and the Mauryan capital, Paliputra, on the Upper Ganges River. Demetrius takes his Indian allies into the ruling council to form a joint government. Greek craftsmen are brought in, coins minted, and the sea route from the Indus to Arabia is developed.

181 BC

- Rome founds a Latin colony at Aquileia in northeast Italy, at the head of the Adriatic Sea, to control the Veneti and bar the passage of the eastern Alps.

171 BC

- The first Roman colony outside Italy is founded at Carteia near the Pillars of Hercules.

Human Rights

163 BC

- On the news of King Antiochus IV of Syria's death, the Syrian general in Judea offers the Jews full religious freedom if they will lay down their arms. Even though the Chasidim consent, Judas Maccabaeus, the leader of the revolt against Syrian rule, holds out for full political as well as religious freedom.

162 BC

- Judas Maccabaeus, the leader of the revolt against Syrian rule, and his brothers Jonathan and Simon continue their fanatical struggle for Jewish religious and political freedom and persecute the Hellenizing faction in Judea.

Politics and Government

200 BC

- Following appeals from the Aetolian League and many other Greek city-states, especially Rhodes and Pergamum, the Romans declare war on King Philip V of Macedon—the Second Macedonian War begins. Rome is concerned about the changes in the balance of power among the Hellenistic kingdoms to the east that are currently occurring. Athens immediately joins Rome.
- At the start of the Second Macedonian War, the Roman consul Sulpicius Galba lands troops in Greece, sending a naval squadron to protect Athens, the only Greek city to have immediately joined Rome. After Galba has a minor success against King Philip V of Macedon's army, the Aetolian League declares for Rome.

- In accordance with the agreement made with King Philip V of Macedon in 204 BC, Antiochus III the Great of Syria goes to war with the Ptolemies of Egypt and wrests Judea from them. The Jews initially welcome a change of master.
- The Han dynasty, which lasts for four centuries, begins its consolidation of China. It gradually increases its trade with the West, institutes a settled bureaucracy with recruitment by examination basis, and expands its population, even beyond the Great Wall.
- c. 200 BC The Second Punic War has changed the Romans, as it has changed the whole political situation in the Mediterranean. They begin to treat their Italian allies more harshly, demanding troops but not conceding citizenship. The power of the aristocracy and the Senate is supreme. The yeoman farmer is being superseded by the great landowner.

198 BC

- The Roman consul T. Quinctius Flamininus crosses to Macedon with an army and pushes King Philip V of Macedon's forces to disaster in the Vale of Tempe. Abortive peace negotiations take place. The Greek cities of Boeotia, Sparta, and the Aetolian League come over to Rome.

197 BC

- Eumenes II becomes king of the city of Pergamum, center of a large kingdom in northwest Asia Minor.
- Spain is organized as two Roman provinces, Nearer Spain and Further Spain, and the number of praetors is increased from four to six to govern them.
- The Roman consul T. Quinctius Flamininus defeats the Macedonians at Cynoscephalae in Thessaly and dictates peace terms. The Second Macedonian War is over.

196 BC

- The Carthaginian general Hannibal, who has been struggling to rehabilitate Carthage, is elected magistrate. He restores democratic elections and reorganizes public finance and taxation.
- The Gallic tribe of the Insubres of the Po valley in northern Italy are finally defeated by the Roman consul Marcellus near Comum. The Romans believe they were incited to revolt by Carthage. Soon afterwards the district around the Insubres' capital at Mediolanum (modern Milan) is occupied by Italian settlers.
- The Roman consul T. Quinctius Flamininus, the victor of the Second Macedonian War, becomes the hero of the Greek world. At the Isthmian Games, held in July at Corinth, he proclaims the "freedom" of Greece.

195 BC

- Rome demands that the Carthaginian general Hannibal surrender but instead he goes into voluntary exile.
- The Carthaginian general Hannibal, who has fled to the Seleucid court, encourages Antiochus III the Great, Seleucid king of Syria, to challenge Rome's protection of the Greeks.

193 BC

- Antiochus III the Great of Syria concludes his war with Egypt by marrying his daughter Cleopatra to the adolescent Egyptian king Ptolemy V.
- The Spartan king Nabis is defeated by the general of the Achaean League, Philopoemen, and is later assassinated.

The Aetolian League asks for help from Antiochus III the Great of Syria in revolting against Rome.

192 BC–189 BC

- The Romans are at war in Greece with King Antiochus III the Great of Syria, who is trying to extend his empire westward.

191 BC

- King Antiochus III the Great of Syria is defeated by the Romans at Thermopylae in Greece and only just manages to escape. His flank is turned by a Roman contingent under Marcus Porcius Cato ("the Elder" or "the Censor").
- Scipio Africanus is now a figure of great authority in Rome and has borne the cognomen "Africanus" since just after his success against the Carthaginian general Hannibal in the Battle of Zama in Africa. He persuades the Senate to continue the war in Greece against King Antiochus III the Great of Syria and to complete his defeat by pursuing him into Asia Minor.
- The Carthaginians have already managed to collect the indemnity due to Rome as part of the peace settlement following the end of the Second Punic War. It was to be paid within 50 years, and the Romans refuse to accept it in advance in order to keep their hold over Carthage.
- The Roman consul P. Cornelius Scipio Nasica, cousin of Scipio Africanus the Elder, wins a final victory over the Gallic tribe of the Boii in Cisalpine Gaul. The Boii give up half their land to Rome, and gradually leave Italy for Bohemia, or are absorbed by the spread of Roman civilization.

190 BC

- In little more than a decade after the end of the Second Punic War, Rome becomes master of the eastern Mediterranean.
- The Romans under the command of Domitius Ahenobarbus defeat King Antiochus III the Great of Syria at the Battle of Magnesia in Caria, Asia Minor. Ahenobarbus is aided by King Eumenes II of Pergamum, who is rewarded with a great increase of territory. The towns of Asia Minor surrender to the Romans and Antiochus flees.

189 BC

- Following the defeat of King Antiochus III the Great of Syria at Magnesia, an armistice is concluded between the king and the Romans. Antiochus agrees to withdraw from Asia Minor beyond the River Taurus, to pay a large indemnity, and to surrender the Carthaginian general Hannibal. Hannibal is forced to flee from the Seleucid court and seeks refuge first in Crete and then with the king of Bithynia in Asia Minor. Antiochus has now lost all of Asia Minor.
- The Romans force the Galatians in Asia Minor into subjection to their ally King Eumenes II of Pergamum. In mainland Greece, the Aetolian League is punished and made a subject-ally. The Romans then retire with much booty from their recent campaigns.

188 BC

- In the spring a board of ten Roman senatorial commissioners meet at Apamea in Asia Minor and set out the final treaty terms between Rome and King Antiochus III the Great after his defeat at Magnesia the previous year. The Senate imposes harsher restrictions on Antiochus than those provisionally set out in 189 BC. The treaty is signed and honored by Antiochus. Most of the territory ceded by him is shared between King Eumenes II of Pergamum and the island of Rhodes, which also helped Rome during the war. In the autumn Rome withdraws all troops from Asia Minor.
- Philopoemen, the Greek general of the Achaean League, marches into Sparta, restores its oligarchic rulers, and ends the revolution started by King Nabis by selling his remaining followers into slavery. The Greek cities and leagues continue to quarrel among themselves and the conviction grows in Rome that there will be no peace until it takes full control.

187 BC

- King Antiochus III the Great of Syria pillages the temple at Bel Zeus in Elymais (in modern northern Iran) in order to raise funds to pay his indemnity to Rome, but is fatally wounded in the process. He is succeeded by his son, the feeble Seleucus IV Philopator.
- Tiberius Gracchus senior, as Roman tribune (magistrate), vetoes proceedings against Lucius Scipio, brother of Scipio Africanus the Elder, preventing Lucius from being imprisoned. The proceedings were instigated by Marcus Porcius Cato ("the Elder" or "the Censor"), an enemy of the Scipios. Gracchus is rewarded by Scipio Africanus the Elder for this service with the hand of his daughter Cornelia.

185 BC

- In the Ganges area of India, the warlike Shungas follow the Mauryan kings and exist as a dynasty for about 100 years. Buddhism decays and there is a brief period of fanatical Brahmanism. The western part of the Mauryan Empire is largely taken over by the line of kings known as the Indo-Greeks during this period.

184 BC

- Roman general Scipio Africanus the Elder and his brother Lucius are accused of having received bribes from King Antiochus III the Great of Syria. Scipio Africanus defies the law, tears up the evidence against his brother (reminding the Romans of their debt to him), and retires to his country house, where he dies a year later.
- Roman statesman and orator Marcus Porcius Cato ("the Elder" or "the Censor") is elected censor in Rome. He has already become a champion of the ancient, austere, Roman way of life, and he now inaugurates a campaign of puritanical tyranny.

182 BC

- When the Romans demand the extradition of the Carthaginian general Hannibal from Bithynia in Asia Minor, he commits suicide.

181 BC–179 BC

- In Spain, the Lusones, a Celtiberian tribe, try to migrate into Carpetania, and the First Celtiberian War begins. Fulvius Flaccus defeats them at Aebura, captures their capital at Contrebia, and takes the district known as Celtiberia Citerior (Nearer Celtiberia) to the Romans. The following year Tiberius Sempronius Gracchus senior takes over the war, and continues to defeat the Celtiberians. He makes a treaty with the Nearer Celtiberians, by which they provide tribute and auxiliary troops, and an alliance with Further Celtiberia.

180 BC

- Rome rounds off its subjugation of all Italy by defeating the Ligurians who live in the Apennines between the River Arno and Savoy (in the area of modern Genoa) and deporting 40,000 of them to the area around Beneventum in Samnium, southern Italy.
- The descendants of King Arsaces are making Parthia a powerful kingdom in Asia, which is partly Hellenized.

May   King Ptolemy V of Egypt is poisoned after a reign of 25 years in which the Egyptian monarchy has greatly declined. Little is now left of its empire but Cyprus and Cyrenaica. Ptolemy VI Philometor, a child, succeeds him, with his mother as regent.

179 BC

- King Philip V of Macedon dies, remorseful for having put his son Demetrius to death for being pro-Roman, at the instigation of his other son, Perseus, who now becomes the last king of Macedon. King Perseus of Macedon is as anti-Roman as his father. He builds up his army and puts out feelers for alliances with the Greek leagues, with his northern barbarian neighbors, and also with King Seleucus IV of Syria, whose daughter he marries.
- Tiberius Sempronius Gracchus senior goes to Spain as Roman governor of the province and bequeaths a quarter of a century of tranquility.

177 BC

- Tiberius Gracchus senior subdues Sardinia, enslaving some of the population.

175 BC

- King Seleucus IV of Syria is assassinated by his chief minister and succeeded by his brother Antiochus IV ("Epiphanes"). Antiochus regards Judea as a source of revenue and also fit for forcible Hellenization.

173 BC

- For the first time, both consuls in Rome are plebeians (members of the ordinary people rather than the privileged class of patricians).

172 BC

- King Eumenes II of Pergamum travels to Rome to warn the Senate of the threat posed by King Perseus of Macedon. On his return, rocks fall upon him at Delphi and nearly kill him; Perseus is suspected as the instigator.

171 BC

- Under the benevolent government of the Roman governor Tiberius Sempronius Gracchus senior, Spanish claims for redress against official extortion are heard in Rome.

171 BC–167 BC   Rome declares war on King Perseus of Macedon, who is vehemently anti-Roman, and the Third Macedonian War begins. The Romans initially suffer several defeats due to bad leadership. The Greek kingdom of Epirus joins Macedon, but the Greek leagues hold back.

170 BC

- The young Ptolemy VI Philometor of Egypt, along with his brother Ptolemy VIII Euergetes, makes war on King Antiochus IV of Syria but is soundly defeated. Antiochus IV then invades Egypt.

169 BC

- King Antiochus IV of Syria attempts to regain the kingdom of Bactria and India for the Seleucid Empire. Although he does not succeed, he weakens the kingdom sufficiently to lead to its subsequent downfall. With increasing nomadic pressure from the steppes, the kingdom has disappeared by 128 BC.

168 BC

- Antiochus IV, Seleucid king of Syria, invades Egypt but is ordered to withdraw by the Roman ambassador to the Seleucids Popillius Laenus.
- During the Third Macedonian War, King Perseus of Macedon gains the support of Genthius, the Illyrian king who reigns in Scodra. The Roman consul Aemilius Paullus takes charge of the Roman forces fighting Perseus in Thessaly. He defeats Perseus at the Battle of Pydna, and later captures him to adorn his subsequent triumphal parade in Rome. The Roman praetor L. Anicius Gallus campaigns against Genthius in Illyria, defeating him and taking the city of Scodra. The Third Illyrian War is over in less than a month; by the postwar settlement, towns loyal to Rome are granted freedom from taxation and the rest pay to Rome about half the previous royal tax. Rome then withdraws from the area.

167 BC

- Before leaving Greece at the end of the Third Macedonian War, the Roman consul L. Aemilius Paullus is goaded into brutal revenge on the Epirots. He destroys 70 of their towns and sells 100,000 citizens into slavery. The Greek mainland remains tranquil, albeit discontented, for 20 years.
- The private papers of King Perseus of Macedon are discovered and incriminate many political leaders of the Achaean League. A thousand distinguished Greeks are deported to Rome, among them the future historian Polybius.
- Under the terms of peace imposed on Macedon by the Roman consul Aemilius Paullus, the monarchy is suppressed, the country is divided into four administrative areas, and an elaborate democratic constitution is invented which lasts for no more than 20 years.

166 BC

- Judas, called Maccabee or the Hammer, or Judas Maccabaeus, takes up leadership of the rebellion against the rule of King Antiochus IV of Syria.

164 BC

- King Antiochus IV of Syria goes mad, which is taken as a judgment on his sacrileges in Judea (setting up a statue of the Greek god Zeus in the temple in Jerusalem), and he is given the nickname Epimanes ("mad") instead of the more usual Epiphanes ("famous, glorious").

October   King Ptolemy VI of Egypt is deposed by his brother Ptolemy VIII Euergetes. He travels to Rome and is reinstated on the Egyptian throne. Ptolemy VIII is given Cyrenaica.

December 12   Judas Maccabaeus, leader of the rebellion against the rule of King Antiochus IV of Syria, defeats the Seleucid forces by guerrilla tactics and gains control of Jerusalem. He cleanses and rededicates the temple, destroys the idols, and restores Judaism.

163 BC

- King Antiochus IV of Syria dies and his nine-year-old son reigns for a year as Antiochus V.

162 BC

- The child king Antiochus V of Syria is assassinated by his cousin Demetrius who then becomes the next Seleucid king. Demetrius, son of Seleucus IV, has spent his youth as a hostage in Rome.

161 BC

- Judas Maccabaeus, the leader of the revolt against Syria in Judea, strengthens himself by an alliance with Rome but is slain in the Battle of Elasa against the Seleucid forces, leaving his brother Jonathan to continue the struggle.

160 BC

160 BC–150 BC   Seleucid king Demetrius I is struggling in this decade to protect his weakened and reduced kingdom of Syria against the enemies that surround it—Pergamum, Parthia, Egypt, and Rome—all of whom are fomenting internal faction and civil war.

157 BC

- Jonathan Maccabaeus, the leader against Syrian rule in Judea, is recognized by the Seleucids as a minor king within the Syrian dominions.

155 BC

- Menander (or Milinda), the most famous of the Indo-Greek kings, rules for about 25 years (–130BC) and extends his Indian kingdom north and east. .

154 BC

- The Lusitanians (from modern Portugal) raid Roman territory in Spain and defeat two Roman praetors, beginning the Lusitanian War (which continues until 138 BC).
- The thriving Greek commercial port of Massilia (modern Marseille) in southern France asks for help from Rome to combat raids from the Ligurians of Cisalpine Gaul, who are attacking its trading posts at Antipolis (Antibes) and Nicea (Nice). The Roman consul quickly defeats them and gives part of their territory to the Massilians.

153 BC

- Rome supports a pretender to the Syrian throne, Alexander Balas, against the established Seleucid king Demetrius I.
- The Carthaginians appeal to Rome against the depredations of King Masinissa of Numidia. Rome sends out a commission, of which the Roman censor Marcus Porcius Cato ("the Elder" or "the Censor") is a member, and he is so alarmed by the prosperity he witnesses in Carthage that he begins his campaign for the final destruction of Rome's old enemy. By the treaty between Rome and Carthage that ended the Second Punic War in 201 BC, the Carthaginians are prevented from armed resistance but are guaranteed against loss of territory. When Cato returns to Rome he begins his practice of winding up his speeches to the Roman senate with the phrase, "*Censeo Carthaginem esse delendam*"/"I declare that Carthage must be destroyed."
- The start of the civil year in Rome, the date at which civic officials take office, is moved to January 1.

- The tribes in Nearer Celtiberia revolt against Rome again, starting the Second Celtiberian War (153 BC–151 BC). The consul Nobilior is sent to Spain with four legions. The tribes of Further Celtiberia join the revolt, and Nobilior is heavily defeated near the town of Numantia.

152 BC

- Jonathan Maccabaeus continues in his joint religious and political rise to power in Judea by becoming high priest in Jerusalem and being given Samarian territory.

152 BC–151 BC   The Roman consul Marcus Claudius Marcellus takes over the war against the Celtiberians in Spain. He makes peace with the Celtiberians of the town of Numantia by paying them a large sum of money. When the new consul Lucius Licinius Lucullus arrives the following year, he brutally attacks another tribe who were not involved in the war. This stiffens the resistance of other cities and when Lucullus fails to take them he withdraws, ending the Second Celtiberian War.

151 BC

- The Lusitanians (from modern Portugal) in Spain break the treaty they made with Rome in 152 BC and defeat the Roman general Sulpicius Galba. He persuades them to submit to Rome again.
- The people of Carthage expel the supporters of King Masinissa of neighboring Numidia from their city and then defend themselves when the Numidians attack.

SCIENCE, TECHNOLOGY, AND MEDICINE

Agriculture

c. **200 BC**

- The Romans introduce the iron-tipped plowshare used to cultivate harder ground.

Health and Medicine

c. **200 BC**

- The Greek physician Aretaeus of Cappadocia describes manic-depressive psychosis.

187 BC

- Egypt, Syria, and Greece are struck by bubonic plague.

Math

c. **190 BC**

- Chinese mathematicians use powers of 10 to express magnitudes.

Science

c. **200 BC**

- Chinese scholars recognize a relationship between tides and the phases of the moon.

- The Greeks invent the astrolabe—the first scientific instrument. It is used for observing the positions and altitudes of stars.

c. 165 BC

- Chinese astronomers first observe and record sunspots. Continuous records of sunspots are kept by Imperial astronomers from 28 BC to AD 1638.

Technology

c. 200 BC

- Coal is first used in China as fuel.
- Eurasian horseriders invent the horseshoe. It reaches Rome by 100 BC.
- Indians in Peru and Ecuador develop cylindrical clay furnaces to melt gold and silver. They use a blowpipe instead of bellows to increase the temperature.
- The Romans begin to use the ballista, an artillery piece powered by twisted ropes that can hurl javelins weighing 4.5 kg/10 lb up to 420 m/1,378 ft.
- The Romans invent concrete. It is used mainly for public works projects, the largest being the port of Caesarea built by Herod the Great in the early 1st century AD.

c. 200 BC–c. 100 BC The screw press is invented in Greece and is used for pressing clothes.

195 BC

- Parchment is invented at the library of Pergamum after an embargo on papyrus by Egyptian king Ptolemy V hinders copying.

c. 180 BC

- Water is carried by gravity 55 km/35 mi from mountain springs to a reservoir 3 km/2 mi east of the Greek city of Pergamum. From this point the water passes through pipes that cross two valleys and an intervening ridge. To get the water over the ridge pressures up to 21 kg per sq cm/300 lb per sq in are accommodated in the pipes.

Transportation

c. 200 BC

- Roman shipbuilders begin to construct ships with three masts by adding a bowsprit and a small square sail called the artemon.

c. 170 BC

- The first paved streets in the world are created in Rome.

ARTS AND IDEAS

Architecture

c. 200 BC

- Apartment houses in Rome are three stories high.

- In China's Early Han period, the center of government is in the north at Changan (modern Xian). The city is meticulously planned, and built to a grid pattern, with 12 gates and avenues of identical measurements. The southern part of the city contains magnificent palaces and an armory. The city walls stretch 25 km/15 mi, and outside them are burial grounds, temples, and great landscaped parks. The Han dynasty is one of China's most splendid and prosperous periods.
- King Euthydemus and his son Demetrius institute a program of urbanization in the Greek kingdom of Bactria. Villages become walled towns, providing protection from nomad raids. The capital city, Bactria, is at the center of trade routes from India in the east to the Seleucid Empire in the west, bringing great prosperity.

180 BC–170 BC

- The Great Altar to Zeus is erected at Pergamum, Mysia. It depicts, in relief, a battle between the gods and giants, and illustrates the Pergamene school of Greek sculpture at its peak.

179 BC

- The Roman censors commission the building of *basilicae* (halls of justice) in the Roman Forum, selecting the Greek open pillared style of architecture for the buildings. They also begin construction of Rome's first stone bridge, the Pons Aenilius.

Arts

c. 193 BC

- The *Venus de Milo* statue is made, now in the Louvre, Paris, France.

c. 190 BC

- The "First Style" of Italian wall painting is introduced. It is characterized by the use of plaster shaped and painted to imitate marble slabs.

183 BC

- A lifelike bust is made of the Roman general Scipio Africanus. This is one of the earliest Roman examples of this form of sculpture, and it illustrates the realism of Roman portraiture (probably resulting from the practice of making death masks).

Literature and Language

196 BC

- An account of the coronation of the Egyptian pharaoh Ptolemy V and the privileges accorded to Egyptian temples is inscribed on the Rosetta Stone, in Greek, demotic (a cursive writing), and hieroglyphic scripts. Rediscovery pf the parallel texts in 1799 during Napoleon's attempted conquest of Egypt makes possible the decipherment of Egyptian hieroglyphics.

c. 195 BC

- Greek scholar Aristophanes of Byzantium introduces accents in Greek writing.

184 BC

- Latin poet Ennius is given Roman citizenship. Ennius is a writer of tragedies, comedies, and satire, whose greatest work is reputed to be the *Annales/Annals*, an epic poem on Roman history from the earliest times to his own day.

c. **180 BC**

- Greek grammarian and critic Aristarchus of Samothrace becomes the librarian at the library at Alexandria, Egypt. He also publishes an edition of Homer that becomes the basis of the modern text, dividing the *Iliad* and *Odyssey* into 24 books each. Up to now Homer's work has circulated in several different forms.

c. **160 BC**

- Roman statesman and writer Marcus Porcius Cato ("the Elder" or "the Censor") writes his book on agriculture *De agricultura/On Agriculture*, which gives advice to an estate owner.

Theater and Dance

191 BC

- Latin comic poet Plautus produces his play *Pseudolus*. He bases his plays on Greek originals, but adapts them to Roman tastes. Twenty of his plays survive to modern times.

166 BC

- Latin comic poet Terence produces his first play *The Girl from Andros*. Five other plays follow, his last being *The Brothers* in 160 BC.

Thought and Scholarship

c. **200 BC**

- Pergamum, Mysia, reaches its cultural and artistic zenith under King Eumenes II, who founds royal libraries and a palace there. In 133 BC the library is bequeathed to the Roman people and 200,000 volumes are incorporated into the library at Alexandria.

193 BC

- The philosopher Carneades of Cyrene comes to the Greek city-state of Athens, to found the Third or "New" Academy. As an extreme Skeptic, he becomes the antagonist of the Stoic philosopher Chrysippus.

c. **180 BC–***c.* **175 BC**

- Hebrew author Joshua Ben-Sira writes his *Wisdom*, known as the Apocryphal book of Ecclesiasticus.

167 BC

- Greek politician and historian Polybius becomes a friend of the Roman general Scipio Aemilianus and thus part of the intellectual group often called the "Scipionic circle."

155 BC

- A delegation of three Greek philosophers comes to Rome, the Stoic philosopher Diogenes, the Academic philosopher Carneades, and Critolaus the Peripatetic. Their visit inspires the Roman philosophers but the Roman senate is confused when Carneades praises justice on one day and dismisses it as an impractical dream on the next. Carneades disturbs the Roman authorities and the puritanical Roman censor Marcus Porcius Cato ("the Elder" or "the Censor") has him sent home on the third day of his visit.

SOCIETY

Education

c. **200 BC**

- Education in the simple Roman virtues is giving way to education in Greek by Greek slaves in Rome.

Everyday Life

c. **200 BC**

- The Hohokam culture develops around Snaketown, Arizona, in North America. The people live in semiarid desert conditions, but irrigate the area with a complex system of over 500 km/300 mi of canals, plus many more subsidiary drainage ditches. The Hohokam are the ancestors of the modern Papago and Pima Native Americans.
- The Hopewell culture begins in eastern North America, centered on the Ohio valley. The Hopewell people construct large ritual mounds, some forming geometric arrangements, others used for burial. They develop widespread trade contacts, and their cultural influence spreads well outside their centers.
- The population of mainland and Ionian Greece declines as abortion and infanticide become quite common.
- The city of Teotihuacan in modern Mexico starts to grow in importance, with temples and pyramids. It continues as a major urban center until its destruction in AD 750.

c. 200 BC–AD 220 During the Han dynasty in China, polygamy is practiced by the wealthy. A bride often brings several female attendants with her to her new home, where they serve as concubines and are eventually allowed to marry. Upon an emperor's death, his widow chooses the successor, often selecting a weak ruler to ensure her own power as a regent.

159 BC

- Over the previous century the number of Roman citizens has grown by about an eighth to 338,314.

Religion

200 BC

200 BC The Old Testament Book of Ecclesiastes is written.

- The sacred Hindu text the *Bhagavadgītā/Lord's Song* is composed.

200 BC– AD 200 During this period the Nazca Lines are drawn in the desert along the south coast of Peru. These are enormous stylized outlines of animals, including a monkey, whale, spider, and hummingbird, and sets of parallel lines, some as long as 20 km/12 mi. They are

believed to be a development of Chavín de Huantar art; they may have had religious significance, or may have been connected with astronomy.

167 BC

- Hebrew priest Mattathias objects to the Hellenization of the Jews and leads a religious revolt of the people (rather than the priests), making his famous appeal, "Whoever is zealous for Torah and maintains the Covenant, let him come forth after me!"

***c.* 167 BC**

- King Antiochus IV of Syria attempts a policy of religious centralization in the Seleucid Empire to force its people to worship the same gods as do the Greeks. A Syrian god is identified with the Greek god Zeus for this purpose. When Antiochus tries to force the Jews to worship Zeus, putting a statue of Zeus in the temple at Jerusalem, sacrificing swine in the temple, a terrible blasphemy against the Jewish religion, and confiscating the temple treasures, the Jewish priest Mattathias rebels and slays the enforcing official and those Jews who attempt to obey. He leads a rebellion but dies the following year and is succeeded by his son Judas, the Maccabee or the Hammer.

165 BC

- The Old Testament Book of Daniel, the hero of the Jewish captivity in Babylon, is written in an effort to boost Jewish morale.

154 BC

- The last of the Hellenizing high priests, who worship the Greek god Zeus instead of practising the Jewish religion, dies in Jerusalem.

BIRTHS & DEATHS

***c.* 200 BC**

- Polybius, Greek historian who wrote of the rise of the Rome, born in Megalopolis, Arcadia (*–c.* 118 BC).

195 BC

- Kao-tsu, first emperor of the Han dynasty 206 BC–195 BC, husband of Kao-hou, dies in China.

***c.* 194 BC**

- Eratosthenes of Cyrene, Greek scientist, astronomer, and poet, dies in Alexandria, Egypt (*c.* 82).

***c.* 190 BC**

- Apollonius, Greek mathematician known for his book *Conics*, dies in Alexandria, Egypt (*c.* 48).

187 BC

- Antiochus III the Great, Seleucid king of Syria 223 BC–187 BC, who rebuilt the empire in the east but failed to counter Roman ascendancy in Europe and Asia Minor, dies in Susa, Iran (*c.* 55).

186 BC

- Terence, Roman comic dramatist, born in Carthage (–159).

185 BC

- Scipio Aemilianus, Roman general who ended the Third Punic War by destroying Carthage, born (–129 BC).
- Scipio Africanus the Younger (Publius Cornelius Scipio Aemilianus), Roman general famed for his exploits in the Third Punic War 149 BC–146 BC, and for his subjugation of Spain 134 BC–133 BC, born (–129 BC).

184 BC

- Plautus, Roman comic dramatist, dies (70).

183 BC

- Scipio Africanus, Roman general who ended the Second Punic war by defeating the Carthaginian leader Hannibal at the battle of Zama, dies in Liternum, Campania (*c.* 51).

***c.* 182 BC**

- Hannibal the Great, celebrated Carthaginian general who conducted the Second Punic War against Rome 218 BC–201 BC, commits suicide in Libyssa, Bithynia, now in Turkey (*c.* 63).

180 BC

- Aristophanes of Byzantium, Greek literary critic and grammarian, chief librarian of Alexandria, dies in Alexandria (*c.* 63).
- Kao-hou (or Lü-hou, or Lü-shih), the first female ruler of China, wife of Emperor Kao-tsu and regent after his death in 195 BC, dies in China.
- Lucilius, considered the inventor of satirical poetry, born in Aurunca, Campania, Italy (*–c.* 102 BC).
- Ptolemy V, Macedonian King of Egypt 205 BC–180 BC, whose weak rule led to the loss of most of Egypt's possessions, dies.

179 BC

- Philip V, King of Macedon 221 BC–179 BC, whose attempts at Macedonian expansion were thwarted by Rome, is assassinated in Amphipolis, Macedon (58).

169 BC

- Quintus Ennius, Roman epic poet, dramatist and satirist, author of the epic poem "Annales"/"Annals," dies (70).

167 BC

- Tiberius Sempronius Gracchus, Roman tribune (magistrate) who implemented agrarian reforms, born (–133 BC).

166 BC

- Mattathias, Jewish priest and rebel leader, father of the Maccabees (Judas, Simon, and Jonathan Maccabeus), dies.

163 BC

- Antiochus IV ("Epiphanes"), Seleucid king of Syria 175 BC–164 BC, who encouraged Greek culture and institutions, dies in Tabae, Iran (*c.* 51).

161 BC

- Judas Maccabeus, Jewish guerrilla leader who resisted the invasion of Israel by the Seleucid king Antiochus IV ("Epiphanes"), falls in battle.

***c.* 159 BC**

- Terence, Roman comic dramatist, dies (*c.* 27).
- Eumenes II, King of Pergamum 197 BC–160/159 BC, dies.

157 BC

- Gaius Marius, Roman general and consul, born in Cereatae, near Arpino, Italy (–86 BC).

156 BC

- Chinese emperor who made Confucianism the state religion and increased the power of the Han dynasty, born in China (–86 BC).

Sports

186 BC

- *Venationes*, the hunting of wild animals as a public display, is first mentioned in Rome. The activity becomes incorporated into Roman public games.

- The first recorded Greek Games at Rome take place under the patronage of M. Fulvius Nobilior.

164 BC–152 BC

- Leonidas of Rhodes wins three running events at four consecutive Olympic Games in Greece.

150 BC–101 BC

POLITICS, GOVERNMENT, AND ECONOMICS

Business and Economics

c. **150 BC**

- The Silk Road, a trade route from China to India and Europe, begins to be used. By AD 200 it is 12,800 km/8,000 mi long and stretches from the Levant in the eastern Mediterranean to Sian in China. It is the longest road in the world for nearly 2,000 years.

146 BC

- The commerce of the Greek island of Delos benefits from the fall of Corinth, particularly in the sale of slaves.

140 BC

- The Han emperor, Wudi, makes great social reforms in China, curbing speculators and middlemen, creating state monopolies and socialized industries, and regulating prices and incomes. He also enlarges the currency, issuing coins of silver alloyed with tin.

113 BC

- All existing coins in China are declared of no value, and all minting is placed under central control.

Colonization

150 BC

- A fresh wave of Celts, partly Germanic, begins to arrive in Britain—the Belgae, known as the Iron Age C people.
- During this period, the Huns, faced with a strong and expanding China under the Han dynasty, find themselves pushed inward from the east rather than themselves pushing into China. They press on a kindred people, the Yue Ji, who infiltrate westward into Turkestan and around the Sea of Aral. This affects the

Scythians, soon to be known by the Indians as the Shakas.
- Polynesian settlers from the islands of Tonga and Samoa begin to spread and colonize other islands, reaching as far west as Tahiti and the Society Islands.

128 BC

- The Pergamene territory bequeathed to Rome in King Attalus III's will is made into a Roman province, to be called Asia.

121 BC

- The Roman province of Narbonese Gaul is formed out of the coastal strip between the Alps and the Pyrenees (hence France's "Provence"). Rome also absorbs the Balearic Islands at this time.

118 BC

- A Roman colony is founded on the coast of southern France, north of the Pyrenees, called Narbo Martius (modern Narbonne), to protect the road between Italy and Spain and to guard Rome's new province of Narbonese Gaul (Provence, France). The colony develops as a commercial rival to Massilia (modern Marseille).

113 BC

- A Celtic tribe known as the Cimbri to the Romans, having migrated south from Denmark, reach the River Meuse. They then set out on another trek in their covered wagons into Noricum (modern Austria) and threaten northern Italy.

111 BC

- The Chinese emperor, Wudi, conquers and annexes the kingdom of Nan Yue (modern south China and north Vietnam).

108 BC

- The Chinese emperor, Wudi, founds a military colony, Lak Lang, in northern Korea.

Human Rights

125 BC

- Fulvius Flaccus, a follower of the Gracchi brothers and agrarian reformers in Rome, fails in an attempt to obtain Roman enfranchisement for the Italians; the town of Fregellae revolts and is destroyed.

Politics and Government

150 BC

- King Demetrius I of Syria dies fighting the pretender Alexander Balas, who is supported by Rome. Alexander reigns for five years, a puppet of Rome and of his mistress.
- Roman praetor Galba, breaking his promise of 152 BC to the Lusitanian rebels in Spain, institutes a massacre. He is prosecuted by the Roman censor Marcus Porcius Cato ("the Elder" or "the Censor"), but is acquitted.
- The Greeks exiled to Rome in 167 BC for plotting with King Perseus of Macedon, including the historian Polybius, are allowed to return home to Greece.

149 BC

- Rome regards the action of Carthage in defending itself against Numidian incursions in 150 BC as a *casus belli* (justification for war) and the Third Punic War begins. The oligarchic government of Carthage offers to submit but the Roman terms are harsh. They state that the city shall be destroyed and that its 700,000 inhabitants shall rebuild their homes elsewhere, "but not within 10 miles of the sea." The Carthaginians refuse to leave their city.

148 BC

- King Masinissa of Numidia dies, and Rome supervises the division of his north African kingdom between his three sons.
- Popular discontent in Macedonia breaks out into a revolt which is crushed by the Roman praetor Q. Caecilius Metellus. The revolt is led by Andriscus, who claims to be an illegitimate son of the dead king Perseus. Macedonia's period of self-government under the Romans ends and it becomes a Roman province.
- Viriathus, a survivor of the Lusitanian massacre in Spain of 150 BC, persuades the Lusitanians to fight. He defeats and kills a Roman governor and then for eight years withstands the armies of Rome, inflicting several defeats and capturing Roman towns.

147 BC

- A Roman delegation, arriving in Corinth to resolve the dispute between the Spartans and the Achaean League, is snubbed and insulted and the League declares war on Sparta. The Roman praetor Q. Caecilius Metellus hurries south from Macedonia and defeats a Greek force but is recalled to Rome at the end of his term of office.

146 BC

- After a prolonged and terrible siege Carthage is finally taken by the Roman consul Scipio Aemilianus. The Carthaginians make their final stand in their temple of Eshmoun (equivalent to Aesculapius, god of medicine), reputedly setting fire to the building and dying in the flames. The wife of the Carthaginian commander Hasdrubal shows herself in splendor with her two children before she and they are burned. Carthage is destroyed and the Roman province of "Africa" is established. Scipio Aemilianus is the son of the Roman consul Aemilius Paullus and adopted heir of Scipio Africanus Major whose name he takes, being known as Scipio Africanus the Younger.

- After the Greek city-state of Corinth has suffered similar treatment to that meted out to Carthage, all semblance of Greek liberty vanishes. The country, though not yet made a province, is placed under the close surveillance of the Roman governor of Macedonia.
- Q. Caecilius Metellus is replaced by Lucius Mummius as Roman praetor in Greece. Mummius has Corinth destroyed, its treasures shipped to Rome, and its population sold into slavery.

145 BC

- Alexander Balas, king of Syria, is defeated and killed by King Ptolemy VI of Egypt near Antioch, Syria.
- Antiochus IV succeeds his father Alexander Balas as king of Syria following his death in battle.
- Egyptian king Ptolemy VI falls from his horse during a battle with Alexander Balas, King of Syria, near Antioch in Syria. He fractures his skull and dies a few days later.
- Ptolemy VIII Euergetes deposes his nephew Ptolemy VII, who rules Egypt July–August 145 BC, and then marries his predecessor's widow (and his own sister and mother of Ptolemy VII), Cleopatra II. He thus wins the Egyptian throne. The following year he murders Ptolemy VII.

143 BC

c. 143 BC Jonathan Maccabaeus, ruler of Judea, is murdered at Bethshean; he is succeeded by his brother Simon.

- Revolt against the Romans spreads in Spain, encouraged by the success of the Lusitanian rebel Viriathus, and the Celtiberians rebel once more, starting the Third Celtiberian or Numantine War.

142 BC

- Judea gains its independence from Syria under Simon Maccabaeus, who is both ruler and high priest.
- Scipio Aemilianus (Scipio Africanus the Younger) becomes censor in Rome.

141 BC

- During the Third Celtiberian War, the Romans besiege the northern Spanish town of Numantia.

140 BC

- China's greatest Han emperor, Wudi (the "Martial Emperor"), comes to the throne and accelerates the expansion of China.

139 BC

- The Lusitanian rebel Viriathus is murdered in Spain by his friends, who have been bribed by the Romans, and his rebellion against Rome peters out.

138 BC

- The Chinese government official Chang Ch'ien (Zhang Qian) is sent on a mission to the far west and reports upon the fine horses that exist in Sogdiana. By the end of the century the Chinese have acquired some of the breed and are tremendously impressed, calling it the "celestial" or the "blood-sweating" horse.
- The Chinese send an embassy under Zhang Qian to seek alliance with the Yue Ji against the Huns, but without success.

137 BC

- A Roman force of 20,000 soldiers is cut off at the siege of the town of Numantia in Spain and total disaster is only averted by the arrival of Tiberius Gracchus, son of the former governor of the same name. The Romans surrender, and Tiberius Gracchus, who is trusted for his father's sake, guarantees that the peace terms will be fulfilled in Rome. The Senate, however, shamefully refuses to honor them, and the Celtiberian War drags on.
- Antiochus VII comes to the Seleucid (Syrian) throne after his predecessor (his brother Demetrius II) has been defeated and taken prisoner by the Parthians. He continues the fight with the Parthians.

135 BC

- Simon Maccabaeus, his two elder sons, and 300 followers are murdered in Judea by his son-in-law, the governor of Jericho. He is succeeded as ruler and high priest by a younger son, John Hyrcanus, who becomes known as Hyrcanus I.

134 BC

- The conflict over the interpretation of the Jewish Law, the Pentateuchal texts, comes to a head, resulting in the formation of the rival sects of the Pharisees and the Sadducees. The Hasmonaean ruler of Judea John Hyrcanus (Hyrcanus I), virtually a king, begins to extend his kingdom.
- There is an uprising in the Roman province of Sicily by the slaves in the First Servile War. It takes three years to suppress.

133 BC

- King Attalus III of Pergamum dies and bequeaths his treasure and his kingdom to the Romans.
- The Roman siege of the town of Numantia in Spain is finally brought to a successful conclusion by the Roman censor Scipio Aemilianus (Scipio Africanus the Younger), who now adds "Numantinus" to his other title of Africanus.
- Tiberius Gracchus, the elder of the two Gracchi brothers, is elected tribune (magistrate) of the plebeians in Rome. He institutes drastic and highly controversial agrarian reforms and embarks on a radical program aimed at alleviating the worst poverty. When King Attalus III of Pergamum leaves his kingdom to Rome, Tiberius Gracchus attempts to use the legacy to pay for reforms, an unprecedented interference in foreign policy which was previously dictated by the Senate. After much political strife, he is killed in a riot. His brother, Gaius Sempronius Gracchus, completes the agricultural reforms he initiated. Public lands that have fallen into the hands of Roman gentry are redistributed and maximum and minimum land holdings are specified. The unrest during this period may have partly led to the Social War. Clashes between the Senate and the tribunate are a feature of Roman politics until the end of the Republic.

132 BC

- On his return from Spain, the Roman censor Scipio Aemilianus (Scipio Africanus the Younger) finds himself in opposition to the policies put in place by the Roman tribune (magistrate) Tiberius Gracchus, his brother-in-law. He champions Rome's Italian allies (many of whom he has led in battle) against the intended redistribution of land, which, he claims, will be to their disadvantage.

131 BC

- As a result of the Roman tribune (magistrate) Tiberius Gracchus' legislation in 133, more than 80,000 Roman citizens are resettled on the land.
- King Ptolemy VIII of Egypt, having divorced Cleopatra II, his wife and sister, to marry her daughter Cleopatra III, his niece and stepdaughter, is forced to flee to Cyprus by an insurrection in the Egyptian city of Alexandria.

129 BC

- King Antiochus VII of Syria is defeated and slain in battle by the Parthian king Phraates II, who is himself defeated and killed by the Scythians soon afterwards.
- King Ptolemy VIII of Egypt regains his throne, having fled from a rebellion in Alexandria, Egypt, to Cyprus in 131 BC.
- The Roman censor Scipio Aemilianus (Scipio Africanus the Younger), a conservative opponent of the agrarian reformers, the Gracchi brothers, is found dead in Rome, apparently murdered by followers of the Gracchi.

128 BC

- The Satavahana dynasty, also called the Andhra dynasty, comes to prominence in the Deccan area of the Indian peninsula. Its first king, Satakarni, extends his kingdom by conquest—he is an orthodox Brahman.
- The Shakas (Scythians), ousted from China by the Yue Ji, infiltrate into Bactria and Parthia. A Chinese traveler of this date finds the area around the Sea of Aral already clear of the Shakas.

126 BC

- Unrest breaks out in Sardinia, which is under Roman rule.

123 BC

- Gaius Gracchus, the younger of the Gracchi brothers, having served a term as quaestor in Sardinia, is elected tribune (magistrate) in Rome. His popularity is at first immense, partly owing to his brother's actions for agrarian reform and partly to his own policies. He attacks the power of the Senate by seeking to enhance the powers of the Equites (the wealthy nonsenators), transferring control of the jury panels examining cases of praetorial extortion to them. He also extends the corn dole to the Roman populace, under which they receive bread at a cheap rate. When he tries to obtain Roman citizenship for the Italians, the people of Rome turn against him, fearing that an increase in citizenship may mean less corn to go round.
- The Romans again assist the people of Massilia (modern Marseille), France, against the Gallic tribes, founding the town of Aquae Sextiae (Aix-en-Provence) as a military camp. This time, the Romans do not withdraw from the area when they have defeated the tribes in question.

122 BC

- Gaius Gracchus is reelected as Roman tribune (magistrate) and leaves Rome to visit his colonies on the site of Carthage, north Africa. In his absence his popularity wanes, particularly since the Senate supports a tribunician colleague of his, Livius Drusus.

121 BC

- Gaius Gracchus fails to be elected as Roman tribune (magistrate) for a third time in succession. He appears in the Forum to protest against the repeal of some of his enactments and a riot ensues. He is induced to flee, but, on the point of capture, prevails on his slave to kill him; about 3,000 of his followers are killed in the subsequent fighting. His earlier land reforms are reversed; land concentration becomes the norm throughout Europe for centuries.

120 BC

- The kingdom of Pontus (on the eastern half of the southern shores of the Black Sea) crowns its most forceful king, Mithridates VI Eupator the Great, at the age of about 14. Opportunity for expansion is open to

him with the steep decline of the Seleucid (Syrian) Empire.

119 BC

- Gaius Marius is elected a tribune (magistrate) of the plebeians in Rome.

118 BC

- The two grandsons of King Masinissa are bequeathed the throne of the north African kingdom of Numidia, but have to share it with their cousin Jugurtha. Jugurtha kills one grandson and forces the other out, then appeals to Rome to confirm him as king.

116 BC

- King Ptolemy VIII of Egypt is succeeded by his son, Ptolemy IX, who reigns jointly with his mother, Cleopatra III.

Jugurthan War (118 BC–104 BC)

118 BC

- The two grandsons of King Masinissa are bequeathed the throne of the north African kingdom of Numidia, but have to share it with their cousin Jugurtha. Jugurtha kills one grandson and forces the other out, then appeals to Rome to confirm him as king.

116 BC

- While a Roman senatorial commission is examining his claim to the Numidian throne at some length, the claimant Jugurtha, the nephew of King Masinissa, defeats his surviving rival, Masinissa's grandson, at Cirta; he also massacres some of the Italian merchants there.

111 BC

- The Roman Senate finally takes action against King Jugurtha of Numidia, by sending one of the consuls, Calpurnius Bestia, to subjugate him. However, Bestia achieves little and makes peace.

110 BC

- The Equites (the wealthy nonsenators) in Rome press for the continuance of the Jugurthan War, seeing the north African kingdom of Numidia as a potentially lucrative new market.
- The Roman army, under the consul Albinus, pursues Jugurtha into the Numidian desert, in north Africa, but is trapped and made to "pass under the yoke" (divested of its weapons and made to walk under a "yoke" of spears held by the enemy). The consuls Bestia and Albinus are exiled by the Romans.
- The Romans bring Jugurtha to Rome on suspicion that he got peace by bribing Bestia. While in Rome he murders a rival and is sent home in disgrace. War is declared against him once more.

109 BC

- The Roman consul Q. Caecilius Metellus, who has a reputation as both incorruptible and a good soldier, goes

out to Numidia, north Africa, to conduct the Jugurthan War. On his staff is Gaius Marius, who has made his name as a soldier in Spain.

108 BC

- With the Jugurthan War threatening to relapse into stalemate, the legate Gaius Marius presses Metellus to let him return to Rome to seek election as consul, and at the end of a whirlwind demagogic campaign is elected to both the consulship and the African command.

107 BC

- In Numidia, north Africa, Marius penetrates deep into the country with his army and reduces the oasis fortress of Capsa. King Jugurtha however eludes him and is strengthened by support from his father-in-law, King Bocchus of Mauritania.
- Marius provides himself with a new army for his fight against Jugurtha, and appoints the aristocratic Lucius Cornelius Sulla to his staff. Marius recruits from all classes, even slaves, and on a personal basis—loyalty is to him personally rather than the state.

106 BC

- Sulla persuades King Bocchus of Mauritania to turn against Jugurtha, who is lured to a conference and kidnapped. Sulla has the scene of capture carved on his signet ring and makes no secret of his jealousy of Marius.

104 BC

- Marius is elected consul again in Rome and reforms the army to meet the threat of the Cimbri, a Celtic tribe. The captured Jugurtha is displayed at the triumph (victory procession) of Marius and his staff officer Sulla in Rome.

- While a Roman senatorial commission is examining his claim to the Numidian throne at some length, the claimant Jugurtha, the nephew of King Masinissa, defeats his surviving rival, Masinissa's grandson, at Cirta; he also massacres some of the Italian merchants there.

114 BC

- King Mithridates VI the Great of Pontus, in obtaining control of the Crimea, also gains control of the corn and timber trade around the Black Sea and up the River Danube.
- The Greek cities of the Crimea seek help from King Mithridates VI the Great of Pontus against Scythian marauders. Mithridates agrees to help but in return he becomes their ruler.

113 BC

- A Roman army is defeated at Noricum by the Cimbri, a Celtic tribe threatening northern Italy. The Cimbri, however, continue their wanderings in another direction.
- The Roman tribune (magistrate) Gaius Marius marries Julia, aunt of the future Roman statesman and general Julius Caesar.

111 BC

- The Roman Senate finally takes action against King Jugurtha of Numidia, by sending one of the consuls, Calpurnius Bestia, to subjugate him. However, Bestia achieves little and makes peace.

110 BC

- The Equites (the wealthy nonsenators) in Rome press for the continuance of the Jugurthan War, seeing the north African kingdom of Numidia as a potentially lucrative new market. The Roman army, under the consul Albinus, pursues King Jugurtha of Numidia into the Numidian desert, in north Africa, but is trapped and made to "pass under the yoke" (divested of its weapons and made to walk under a "yoke" of spears held by the enemy). The consuls Bestia and Albinus are exiled by the Romans.
- The Romans bring Jugurtha to Rome on suspicion that he got peace by bribing Bestia. While in Rome he murders a rival and is sent home in disgrace. War is declared against him once more.

October   King Ptolemy IX is expelled from Alexandria by his mother and coruler Cleopatra III. He leaves his brother Ptolemy X and his forceful mother Cleopatra III ruling in Egypt.

109 BC

- The Roman consul Q. Caecilius Metellus, who has a reputation as both incorruptible and a good soldier, goes out to Numidia, north Africa, to conduct the Jugurthan War. On his staff is Gaius Marius, who has made his name as a soldier in Spain.
- The wandering Cimbri, a Celtic tribe, inflict another defeat on the Romans.

108 BC

- With the Jugurthan War threatening to relapse into stalemate, the legate Gaius Marius presses the consul Q. Caecilius Metellus to let him return to Rome to seek election as consul, and at the end of a whirlwind demagogic campaign is elected to both the consulship and the African command.

107 BC

- In Numidia, north Africa, the Roman consul Gaius Marius penetrates deep into the country with his army and reduces the oasis fortress of Capsa. King Jugurtha however eludes him and is strengthened by support from his father-in-law, King Bocchus of Mauritania.
- The Cimbri, a Celtic tribe, inflict yet another defeat on the Romans.
- The Roman consul Gaius Marius provides himself with a new army for his fight against King Jugurtha of Numidia, and appoints the aristocratic Lucius Cornelius Sulla to his staff. Marius recruits from all classes, even slaves, and on a personal basis—loyalty is to him personally rather than the state.

106 BC

- Lucius Cornelius Sulla, the Roman commander Gaius Marius' quaestor, persuades King Bocchus of Mauritania to turn against King Jugurtha of Numidia, who is lured to a conference and kidnapped. Sulla has the scene of capture carved on his signet ring and makes no secret of his jealousy of Marius.

105 BC

- The Cimbri, a Celtic tribe, inflict a more serious defeat on the Romans at Arausio (modern Orange) on the River Rhône; the province of Transalpine Gaul in southern France now appears to be at their mercy and Rome itself seems threatened.
- The Equites (the wealthy nonsenators in Rome), in jostling for power with the Senate, nearly lose their control of the law court panels of jurors and in retaliation interfere with the College of Augurs.

104 BC

- Gaius Marius is elected consul again in Rome and reforms the army to meet the threat of the Cimbri, a Celtic tribe. The captured Jugurtha of Numidia is displayed at the triumph (victory procession) of Marius and his staff officer Lucius Cornelius Sulla in Rome. The reforms make the Roman army more professional and democratic. He increases the legion from about 5,000 to 6,000; changes the 120-strong maniple to the 600-strong cohort; abolishes dependence upon class for recruitment to various ranks of the army; and converts the cavalry to an auxiliary arm. He gives the legions names and numbers and introduces the eagle as a standard for each.
- Hyrcanus I of Judea dies after a 30-year reign, and is succeeded by his son Aristobulus I, who completes the conquest of Galilee. Aristobulus dies the following year, and his brother Alexander Jannaeus becomes ruler.
- The Roman Senate faces other difficulties. The first is piracy in the eastern Mediterranean, increased since the decline of Rhodes and Pergamum, although for a while it is subdued. The second is a renewed revolt of the mass of imported slaves in Sicily, another Servile War. This is only subdued at the cost of 100,000 lives.

102 BC

- Roman consul Gaius Marius, preparing to meet the Cimbri, a Celtic tribe, trains his army with great strictness. Homosexuality is punished, with death in the case of one of Marius' own nephews. His soldiers, practicing route-marches, call themselves "Marius' Mules."

- The Cimbri, a Celtic tribe, with Teutonic allies, return to mount a determined and concerted attack on Rome. The Roman consul Gaius Marius defeats the Teutons utterly at Aquae Sextiae (Aix-en-Provence) in the province of Narbonese Gaul, France.

101 BC
- Ptolemy X becomes sole ruler of Egypt after the death of his mother and coruler Cleopatra III.
- The Roman consul Gaius Marius completely defeats the Cimbri, a Celtic tribe, at the Battle of Vercellae in the Po valley, northern Italy, with a reputed slaughter of 120,000 men. Rome has no more threats from the Celtic and Germanic barbarians for another five centuries. Marius returns to Rome a hero.

SCIENCE, TECHNOLOGY, AND MEDICINE

Ecology

150 BC
- The dominant town of Cuicuilco in the southwest of the Mexican Basin is partly destroyed by a massive lava flow which covers most of the town and farmland. Most of its population leaves, although a small group remain.

125 BC
- Parts of Roman Africa are laid waste by locusts.

122 BC
- Mt. Etna in Italy erupts.

Science

c. **150 BC**
- Greek scientist Hipparchus of Bithynia builds an observatory on the island of Rhodes, containing instruments to measure accurately the positions of celestial bodies.

c. **140 BC**
- The Greek Stoic philosopher Crates of Mallus, in Anatolia, makes the first globe.

129 BC
- Greek scientist Hipparchus of Bithynia creates the first known star catalog. It gives the latitude and longitude and brightness of nearly 850 stars and is later used by Ptolemy.

127 BC
- Greek scientist Hipparchus of Bithynia discovers the precession of the equinoxes and calculates the year to within 6.5 minutes. He also makes an early formulation of trigonometry.

105 BC
- Chinese historian Sima Qian reforms the Chinese calendar.

Technology

c. **150 BC**
- Greek scientist Hipparchus of Bithynia builds a diopter, a surveying instrument similar to the theodolite, consisting of a set of two telescopic lenses in line.

Transportation

c. **145 BC**
- Work begins on the Via Egnatia—a continuation of the Via Appia into Greece and Asia Minor where it meets the Persian Royal Road.

142 BC
- The Pons Aemilius, the first stone bridge across the Tiber at Rome, is completed.

c. **140 BC**
- Han emperor Wudi has bridges, canals, and irrigation channels built in China.

109 BC
- The Milvian bridge over the River Tiber at Rome is reconstructed in stone.

ARTS AND IDEAS

Architecture

144 BC
- The Aqua Marcia aqueduct, the first high-level aqueduct, and the longest (91 km/57 mi), is built in Rome, allowing settlement on higher ground. Water is taken from the Anio River.

130 BC
- At about this time the Iron Age forts on the European continent, for example in Gaul and Bohemia, are at their most elaborate. These are the *oppida* ("towns") which the Roman statesman and general Julius Caesar will later talk of having captured during his conquest of Gaul.

c. **125 BC**
- The Aqua Tepula aqueduct is completed in Rome. Built by censors Gnaeus Servilius Caepio and Lucius Cassius Longinus, it draws water from springs in the Alban Hills.

Film

121 BC
- The magic lantern (image projector) is invented in China by Shao Ong.

Literature and Language

c. **130 BC**
- Dionysius Thrax (of Thrace), a pupil of the Greek grammarian Aristarchus, produces a Greek grammar.

c. 120 BC
- Roman poet Lucilius pioneers the literary genre of Latin satire, which features scenes and commentaries on social life. The genre is later developed by the Roman poets Horace and Juvenal.

Thought and Scholarship

c. 150 BC
- Greek historian Polybius publishes the first part of his *History*. Written to explain the rise of Rome, in its final form it covers the period 264 BC–146 BC.

SOCIETY

Everyday Life

150 BC
- The period of Late La Tène culture begins in Europe. It ends at various times in different countries with the coming of the Romans.

115 BC
- The number of Roman citizens registered in the census has gone up to 394,336, although the reliability of this and earlier census figures is not known.

BIRTHS & DEATHS

149 BC
- Marcus Porcius Cato ("the Elder" or "the Censor"), Roman statesman and orator, the first major Latin prose writer, whose *De agri cultura/On Agriculture* survives, dies (*c.* 85).

148 BC
- Masinissa, King of Numidia 201 BC–148 BC, dies (92).

145 BC
- Ptolemy VI, Macedonian king of Egypt 180 BC–145 BC, whose invasion of Syria led to the occupation of Egypt by the Seleucids, dies.

c. 145 BC
- Ssu-ma Chien, Chinese astronomer and historian, author of *Shih-chi/Historical records*, a history of China to the 2nd century BC, born in Lung-men, China (–85 BC).

138 BC
- Lucius Cornelius Sulla (Felix), Roman consul who fought King Mithradates VI of Pontus in Rome's first civil war, and then became Roman dictator 82 BC–79 BC, born (–79 BC).

134 BC
- Mithradates ("the Great"), Eupator, King of Pontus 120 BC–63 BC, who expanded the empire and challenged Rome, born (–63 BC).

133 BC
June Tiberius Sempronius Gracchus, Roman tribune (magistrate) who implemented agrarian reforms, is murdered with about 300 of his friends in the course of Senate elections, in Rome, Italy (*c.* 34).

129 BC
c. 129 BC Carneades, Greek Skeptic philosopher, head of the New Academy at Athens, dies (*c.* 85).
- Antiochus VII ("Sidetes"), Seleucid king of Syria 139 BC–129 BC, who reunited his kingdom, falls in battle against the Parthians (*c.* 30).
- Scipio Aemilianus, Roman general who ended the Third Punic War by destroying Carthage, dies in Rome (56).
- Scipio Africanus the Younger (Publius Cornelius Scipio Aemilianus), Roman general famed for his exploits in the Third Punic War 149 BC–146 BC, and for his subjugation of Spain 134 BC–133 BC, dies in Rome (*c.* 54).

127 BC
- Hipparchus, Greek astronomer and mathematician, dies, probably on Rhodes (*c.* 65).

c. 123 BC
- Quintus Sertorius, Roman military officer who was independent ruler of Spain 80 BC–72 BC, born in Nursia, Sabini (–72 BC).

122 BC
- Polybius, Greek historian who wrote of the rise of the Rome, dies (*c.* 82).

116 BC
- Marcus Terentius Varro, Roman patriotic satirist, author of *Saturae Menippeae/Menippean Satires*, born in Reate, Italy (–27 BC).

114 BC
- Chang Ch'ien, (Zhang Qian), Chinese explorer of central Asia, dies.

109 BC
- Titus Pomponius Atticus, Roman man of letters and friend of Cicero, born (–32 BC).

106 BC
- Marcus Tullius Cicero, Roman statesman, lawyer, scholar, orator, and writer, whose major works include *De republica/On the Republic*, born in Arpino, Italy (–43 BC).
September 29 Pompey, Roman general and statesman, born in Rome (–48 BC).

104 BC
- John Hyrcanus I, King of Judea 135 BC–104 BC and high priest, son of Simon Maccabaeus, dies.
- Jugurtha, King of Numidia 118 BC–105 BC, executed in Rome, Italy (*c.* 54).

102 BC
- Lucilius, considered the inventor of satirical poetry, dies in Naples, Italy (*c.* 78).

101 BC
- Cleopatra III, wife of Ptolemy VIII and effective ruler over Egypt and Cyprus after his death 116 BC, dies.

Religion

150 BC

- Indo-Greek king Milinda (Menander) is celebrated as the hero of the Buddhist text *Milinda-panho*, in which he is converted to Buddhism. On his death 25 years later, many cities compete for possession of his ashes.

142 BC–135 BC

- Hebrew priest Simon Maccabaeus makes the Judean high priesthood hereditary for his family, the Hasmonaean dynasty.

122 BC

- Religious objections are raised against the Carthaginian colonizing project organized by the Roman tribune (magistrate) Gaius Gracchus, on the grounds that the site has been cursed by the Roman general Scipio Aemilianus (Scipio Africanus the Younger).

120 BC

- The temple of Apollo is built at Pompeii, Italy.

104 BC

- As the interpretation of the auguries (signs from the gods) in Rome is by now more an instrument of political obstruction than a religious observance, the Equites (the wealthy nonsenators) seek to take away the right of appointment to the College of Augurs from the Senate. They succeed in imposing election for the office.

102 BC

- The wife of the Roman general Gaius Marius sends him a Syrian prophetess. He puts her to great use, telling the troops that he is waiting for her to announce the propitious moment to attack and thus curbs their impatience. After the Battle of Aquae Sextiae he burns a great sacrifice of captured arms to Mars, Roman god of war. As he watches the sacrifice, news arrives of his reelection as Roman consul.

100 BC–51 BC

POLITICS, GOVERNMENT, AND ECONOMICS

Business and Economics

c. **90 BC**

- The earliest known British coins, found in 1927 in Kent, date from this time.

72 BC

- The Roman general Marcus Crassus, a notoriously rich man, has made his money by clever speculation in the Roman property market. He invests some of his fortune as a political power broker by, for example, making loans to promising young men such as Julius Caesar.

68 BC

- The Roman general Lucius Licinius Lucullus, before leaving Asia, does much for the country financially, curbing the power of the Roman magnates and moneylenders.

southeast and tackle the less well drained and still forested land, farming with a plow that can turn the sod. They are probably responsible for the white horse on the chalk downs at Uffington in Oxfordshire.

- The Shakas (Scythians), having streamed through Parthia, enter the Indus valley through the Bolan Pass and found a dynasty in Gandhara (modern north Pakistan and India).

63 BC

- The Roman general Pompey the Great, in his settlement of his Asian conquests, follows the usual Roman practice of creating client kingdoms and of allowing self-government under Roman tutelage wherever possible.

58 BC

- The tribe of the Helvetii from Switzerland begins to migrate west into Gaul (France) under their leader, Orgetorix, but is checked by the Roman statesman and general Julius Caesar, in alliance with the Gallic tribe of the Aedui, at the Battle of Bibracte (near Autun, France). This victory brings several requests for friendship and help from the tribes of central Gaul against Ariovistus, the leader of the Suevi, a Germanic people who have crossed the River Rhine and settled in northern Gaul, threatening the Gallic tribes in the area.

Colonization

80 BC

- The second wave of Celtic Belgae arrives in Britain from Gaul during this period. They settle mostly in the

Human Rights

82 BC

- One aim of the proscriptions (death and confiscation of property of enemies) announced by the Roman dictator

Lucius Cornelius Sulla, is to accumulate wealth. The young Roman orator and politician Marcus Tullius Cicero boldly defends a victim in the law courts.

Politics and Government

100 BC

c. 100 BC The Roman consul Gaius Marius represents a new phenomenon in Rome, the successful general with an army at his back.

c. 100 BC The two main lines of successors to Alexander the Great's empire, the Ptolemaic in Egypt and the Seleucid in Syria, continue to decline amidst a confusion of petty and complicated intrigue, both to end in Roman absorption (the former by the emperor Augustus, the latter by the soldier Pompey the Great). Parthia, Pontus, and Armenia all gain in strength during this period.

- Gaius Marius is reelected Roman consul for the sixth time. He ousts two unscrupulous demagogic tribunes (magistrates), Lucius Appuleius Saturninus and Gaius Servilius Glaucia, for having created widespread civil disorder and seized the Capitol. Marius shows his usual military efficiency, but fails to prevent the massacre of the two tribunes and leaves Rome in disgust.
- Q. Mucius Scaevola becomes Pontifex Maximus (head of state religion) in Rome and institutes a scientific study of the law. He is considered the founder of Roman jurisprudence.

97 BC

- Roman general and politician Lucius Cornelius Sulla is made praetor (senior magistrate) in Rome.

96 BC

- The Greek colony of Cyrene in north Africa is bequeathed to the Romans by its ruler, Ptolemy Apion of the Egyptian royal house.

95 BC

- Italians anxious to obtain the benefits of Roman citizenship, including prestige, redress against injustice, the privilege of fighting in the regular legions instead of the auxiliaries, and taxation relief, have been seeping into the city and achieving enfranchisement by the back door. An inquiry is established and many are struck off the rolls.

92 BC

- King Mithridates is on the Parthian throne at this time; he remains at peace with Rome. He has forced the king of Cappadocia off the throne, and the Roman propraetor Lucius Cornelius Sulla is sent to restore the *status quo*, which he successfully achieves.

91 BC

- Marcus Drusus becomes tribune (magistrate) of the plebeians in Rome and, in search of popularity, increases the corn dole (allowance of cheap bread) so much as to cause inflation. He debases the currency, issuing copper coins merely coated with silver. He proposes enfranchising the increasingly discontented Italians (sometimes known as confederates or *socii*). The Senate defeats Drusus' reforms by declaring his laws to have infringed the technical requirements, and thus to be invalid; Drusus forms a conspiracy but is murdered. The Italians revolt and the Social War begins.

- Nicomedes Philopator becomes king of Bithynia in Asia Minor. He is a friend of Rome but in great danger from the ambitious King Mithridates VI the Great of Pontus.

90 BC–88 BC

- Rome is seriously threatened during the Social War by the Italians, who establish a federal capital at Corfinium, east of Rome. The Senate, with an apprehensive eye on the threat of King Mithridates VI the Great of Pontus, compromises. While giving command in Campania to the Roman consul for 88 BC Lucius Cornelius Sulla, it offers the Italians, with only a few provisos, what they are fighting for: Roman citizenship.

88 BC

- Greek historians hostile to Rome gather at the court of Mithridates the Great, King of Pontus (in modern Turkey).
- King Mithridates VI the Great of Pontus invades the Roman province of Asia. He captures the city of Pergamum and massacres unpopular Roman and Italian merchants and officials. Mithridates' invasion comes after the king of Bithynia tries to invade Pontus on Roman advice. Mithridates captures the Greek city-state of Delos and seizes the temple treasure.
- King Ptolemy X of Egypt is killed in Asia Minor as he attempts to raid the Lycian coast. His older brother Ptolemy IX, who had been exiled to Cyprus by his mother Cleopatra III, returns to rule Egypt and marries his brother's widow Berenice III, who is also his own daughter.
- Roman praetor Lucius Cornelius Sulla is elected consul and given the much-prized command against King Mithridates VI the Great of Pontus. The Roman general and politician Gaius Marius, however, gets a law pushed through giving himself the command. Sulla enters Rome with his army and, after bitter street fighting, Marius flees and is declared an outlaw.
- The Mithridatic army under its general Archelaus sweeps westward through Asia, taking possession of the land. An Athenian teacher of philosophy turned tyrant, Aristion, persuades his city to throw in its lot with King Mithridates VI the Great of Pontus and openly rebels against Rome.

88 BC–87 BC Rumors abound about the strange adventures of the Roman general Gaius Marius (now nearly 70) following his flight from Rome. One tale relates how he is shipwrecked and imprisoned, and when his executioner enters his cell, Marius roars "Wouldst thou dare slay Gaius Marius!," causing the man to flee in terror.

87 BC–86 BC

- The Roman general Lucius Cornelius Sulla sets sail to take on King Mithridates VI the Great of Pontus with five legions and lands in Epirus, Greece.
- In Rome, Cinna, the consul left behind by Lucius Cornelius Sulla, stirs up trouble and is forced to leave the city. He joins forces with the Roman general and politician Gaius Marius; the two return to Rome, name themselves consuls, and institute a massacre of patricians. After only 18 days of consulship, Marius dies of pleurisy.
- The Roman general Lucius Cornelius Sulla presses Mithridates' general, Archelaus, back onto Athens and besieges the city. In the spring of 86 BC Athens falls and is sacked, though its great reputation saves it from total

Roman-Mithridatic Wars (91–65 BC)

91 BC
- Nicomedes Philopator becomes king of Bithynia in Asia Minor. He is a friend of Rome but in great danger from the ambitious King Mithridates VI the Great of Pontus (in modern Turkey).

88 BC
- Greek historians hostile to Rome gather at the court of Mithridates.
- Mithridates invades the Roman province of Asia. He captures the city of Pergamum and massacres unpopular Roman and Italian merchants and officials. Mithridates' invasion comes after the king of Bithynia tries to invade Pontus on Roman advice.
- Mithridates captures the Greek city-state of Delos and seizes the temple treasure.
- Roman praetor Lucius Cornelius Sulla is elected consul and given the much-prized command against King Mithridates. The Roman general and politician Gaius Marius, however, gets a law pushed through giving himself the command. Sulla enters Rome with his army and, after bitter street fighting, Marius flees and is declared an outlaw.
- The Mithridatic army under its general Archelaus sweeps westward through Asia, taking possession of the land. An Athenian teacher of philosophy turned tyrant, Aristion, persuades his city to throw in its lot with Mithridates and openly rebels against Rome.

87 BC
- In Rome, Cinna, the consul left behind by Sulla, stirs up trouble and is forced to leave the city. He joins forces with the Roman general and politician Gaius Marius; the two return to Rome, name themselves consuls, and institute a massacre of patricians. After only 18 days of consulship, Marius dies of pleurisy.

87 BC–86 BC
- Sulla sets sail to take on King Mithridates with five legions and lands in Epirus, Greece. He presses Mithridates'

general, Archelaus, back onto Athens and besieges the city. In the spring of 86 BC Athens falls and is sacked, though its great reputation saves it from total destruction. The Athenian tyrant and ally of Mithridates, Aristion, is captured and killed. Sulla publishes his losses as only 15 men.

85 BC
- Sulla wins another victory at Orchomenus in Greece in his war with King Mithridates, and then chases him across the Hellespont.

84 BC
- Sulla and Mithridates agree peace terms at a meeting near Troy. Sulla, in granting easy peace terms to Mithridates, leaves a muddled state of affairs in Greece and Asia Minor. Heavy taxation on those who had taken the enemy side, and looting, force people to borrow heavily, swelling the purses of Roman money lenders.

74 BC
- Mithridates invades Bithynia on the northwest coast of Asia Minor, which has just been bequeathed to Rome.
- The Roman rebel general Quintus Sertorius does a deal with Mithridates, exchanging Roman officers for money and ships. He is in the process of losing his struggle against the Roman soldier Pompey the Great in Spain and his popularity is waning.

73 BC
- Mithridates is driven from his kingdom by the Romans under their general Lucius Licinius Lucullus and takes refuge with King Tigranes of Armenia.

65 BC
- Mithridates is decisively defeated by Pompey near Dasteira in Pontus (later renamed Nicopolis, "City of Victory"), and flees to the Crimea. Pompey also defeats King Tigranes, who is allowed to retain his kingdom of Armenia as a vassal prince and a bulwark against Parthia, but loses all his foreign acquisitions.

destruction. The Athenian tyrant and ally of Mithridates, Aristion, is captured and killed. Sulla publishes his losses as only 15 men.

86 BC
- Chinese emperor, Wudi, dies and is succeeded by Zhaodi, who reoccupies Lop Nor and founds a military colony there.

85 BC
- The Egyptian city of Thebes, having revolted against King Ptolemy IX, is reduced to a permanent ruin by him.
- The Roman general Lucius Cornelius Sulla wins another victory at Orchomenus in Greece in his war with King Mithridates VI the Great of Pontus, and then chases Mithridates across the Hellespont.

84 BC
- The Roman general Lucius Cornelius Sulla and King Mithridates VI the Great of Pontus agree peace terms at a meeting near Troy. Sulla sails for Brundisium leaving two legions to police Rome's Asiatic territories. Heavy taxation on those who had taken the enemy side, and looting, force people to borrow heavily, swelling the purses of Roman money lenders.
- Cinna, ruling as a tyrant in Rome, has packed the senate with his followers and declared Sulla an outlaw. There is a financial crisis, which Cinna tries to allay by the remission of debts. He is killed by his own troops.

83 BC
- King Tigranes of Armenia, son-in-law of King Mithridates VI the Great of Pontus, takes over the Seleucid (Syrian) throne by invitation.

- Quintus Sertorius, a Marian general, is sent out to Spain, to secure the country against the Roman general Lucius Cornelius Sulla, who is marching on Rome.
- Returning from his victory over King Mithridates VI the Great of Pontus, the Roman general Lucius Cornelius Sulla lands at Brundisium in southern Italy, recruits many soldiers who had followed the late Gaius Marius to his side, and advances northward toward Rome. He is assisted by the young Roman soldier Pompey the Great (Gnaeus Pompeius Magnus).
- The young Roman statesman and general Julius Caesar, now aged 17, marries Cornelia, the daughter of the Roman politician Cinna.

82 BC

- Roman general Lucius Cornelius Sulla enters Rome as victor and institutes his "Proscription" lists—lists of enemies who are to be murdered and have their property confiscated. He includes Julius Caesar's name in this list after he refuses to divorce his wife, Cornelia, the daughter of the rebel Roman politician Cinna, but is persuaded to delete it. He is appointed dictator under a law of the interrex Lucius Valerius Flaccus.

81 BC

- Lucius Cornelius Sulla has himself made dictator of Rome for an indefinite period of time, using a bodyguard of slaves left over from the victims of his proscription (murder of his enemies and confiscation of their property). He adds 300 new (conservative) members to the Senate and makes the popular Assembly wholly subservient to it.
- Roman orator and politician Marcus Tullius Cicero, acting as an advocate in the Forum in Rome, makes his first extant speech, *Pro Quinctio*.

80 BC

- Berenice III, Queen of Egypt, is murdered by her husband Ptolemy XI after 19 days of joint rule. Ptolemy XI is then killed by the infuriated populace of Alexandria, and succeeded by Ptolemy XII Auletes ("the Piper"). During his reign Egypt becomes a client state of Rome.
- In an effort to restore the Senate's authority in Rome, the Roman dictator Lucius Cornelius Sulla curbs the power of the tribunes (magistrates) and restricts the Assembly to the discussion only of what the Senate allows; he also regulates overseas commands with the *Lex Annalis*.
- The Marian general Quintus Sertorius, who was sent to Spain by the Roman consul and rebel Cinna, is driven into Africa by the dictator Lucius Cornelius Sulla's troops. He returns on the invitation of the Lusitanians and sets up an anti-Sullan regime in Spain with the enthusiastic support of the natives.
- The young Roman nobleman Julius Caesar joins the military campaign in Asia Minor, where mopping-up operations are being undertaken against King Mithridates VI the Great of Pontus. He is entrusted with a political mission to the court of the king of Bithynia. He then takes part in the siege of the Greek city-state of Mytilene and is rewarded with the civic crown for saving the life of a fellow soldier.

79 BC

- Roman dictator Lucius Cornelius Sulla, having put through reactionary reforms, retires to a private life of dissolute ease.

78 BC

- The Roman consul Lepidus quarrels with his coconsul to the point of bloodshed. He assembles an army, advances on Rome, is beaten, and flees the country. The task of rounding up the rebels is entrusted to the Roman soldier Pompey the Great, although some escape to join the rebel Roman general Quintus Sertorius in Spain.

77 BC

- Roman statesman and general Julius Caesar gains some renown as an orator in the law courts in Rome.
- The Roman soldier Pompey the Great, having accomplished his task of rounding up the consul Lepidus and the other rebels, does not disband his troops. The rebel Roman general Quintus Sertorius in Spain is reinforced with the remnants of Lepidus' army, under Marcus Veiento Perperna.

76 BC

- Roman soldier Pompey the Great obtains the Spanish command against the Roman rebel leaders Quintus Sertorius and Marcus Veiento Perperna, but finds it difficult to come to grips with Sertorius and his men.
- The Roman aristocrat Julius Caesar journeys to Rhodes to study philosophy and to improve his oratory. He is captured by pirates but raises his own ransom, and captures and crucifies his kidnappers.

75 BC

- Roman rebel general Quintus Sertorius sets out on a deliberate policy to Romanize the provincials in Spain: he encourages his Spanish officials to wear the toga and starts a school where Latin and Greek are taught.

74 BC

- King Mithridates VI the Great of Pontus invades Bithynia on the northwest coast of Asia Minor, which has just been bequeathed to Rome.
- The Roman rebel general Quintus Sertorius does a deal with King Mithridates VI the Great of Pontus, exchanging Roman officers for money and ships. He is in the process of losing his struggle against the Roman soldier Pompey the Great in Spain and his popularity is waning.

73 BC

- Chinese emperor, Zhaodi, dies and is succeeded by Xuandi, who enlarges the Han Empire to an extent never known before. He makes alliances with all the enemies of the Huns, then penetrates into their territory, conquering parts of it. This causes a civil war among the Huns, and one claimant asks for Xuandi's aid. Xuandi helps him to become ruler of Mongolia, and he marries a Chinese princess.
- King Mithridates VI the Great of Pontus is driven from his kingdom by the Romans under their general Lucius Licinius Lucullus and takes refuge with King Tigranes of Armenia.
- Spartacus, a gladiatorial slave, takes up the cause of the badly treated agricultural slaves in Italy, and sets up bandit headquarters on the slopes of Mt. Vesuvius. Spartacus' followers increase rapidly and he tries to curb

their worst excesses, hoping to march north to the Alps, from where his soldiers can return to their homes.

72 BC

- The rebel Roman general Quintus Sertorius is murdered in Spain by his lieutenant Marcus Veiento Perperna, and his regime crumbles.
- The Roman general Marcus Crassus is given the task, with six legions, of suppressing the revolt of the Italian agricultural slaves led by the gladiatorial slave Spartacus.

71 BC

- As a result of the rebel Roman general Quintus Sertorius's efforts at Romanization in Spain, Roman citizenship is granted to some Spaniards including a certain Balbus, who returns to Rome with the soldier Pompey the Great to become an engineering expert and friend of the statesman and general Julius Caesar.
- The Roman general Marcus Crassus drives the Spartacists (slave rebels led by the gladiatorial slave Spartacus) into the tip of the Italian peninsula, defeats them, and has 6,000 of them crucified along the Appian Way. The Roman soldier Pompey the Great defeats some remnants and the two argue over who has stamped out the rebellion. They are persuaded to settle their differences and stand for the consulate.

70 BC

- Roman commanders Pompey the Great and Marcus Crassus become consuls in Rome and repeal part of the reactionary legislation of the former dictator Lucius Cornelius Sulla.
- Roman orator Marcus Tullius Cicero makes his name by his prosecution of the corrupt Roman governor Gaius Verres for misgovernment of Sicily. Gaius is also prosecuted for the theft of works of art (both publicly and privately owned).

69 BC

- The Roman general Lucius Licinius Lucullus is forced to extend his military campaign eastward due to the belligerence of King Tigranes of Armenia. He captures the king's new capital city of Tigranocerta and restores Syria to the Seleucid (Syrian) line of rulers in the person of Antiochus XIII.

68 BC

- Roman soldier and orator Julius Caesar, seeking both popularity and high office in Rome, takes his first considerable step in being appointed quaestor, a financial magistracy, serving in Further Spain.
- The Roman general Lucius Licinius Lucullus, pushing enthusiastically eastward, faces a mutiny by his troops, many of whom have been away from home for nearly 20 years.

67 BC

- Hasmonaean rule in Judea degenerates, and a dispute develops between the ruler Hyrcanus II (the legitimate holder of the office of high priest, who is supported by the Pharasaic priests), an Idumean prince Antipater, and his brother Aristobulus (who is backed by the more Hellenized Sadducees).
- Roman general Lucius Licinius Lucullus is recalled from Asia. He retires into private life and acquires a reputation as a man of luxury.

- Roman general Pompey the Great rapidly and efficiently clears the Mediterranean of pirates, based on the island of Crete, who have again become a menace. Crete is taken over by Rome. Pompey is comparatively lenient and settles many of the defeated pirates in various parts of the Roman provinces.
- The Roman quaestor Julius Caesar marries Pompeia (cousin of the Roman general Pompey) following the death of his first wife, Cornelia.

66 BC

- A bill is passed in Rome, with the support of the orator and statesman Marcus Tullius Cicero and the quaestor Julius Caesar, giving the Roman general Pompey the Great proconsular command in the East, with powers of declaring war. Pompey sets out on a four-year career of conquest and settlement in the East.
- Roman governor of Africa Catiline (Lucius Sergius Catilina), earlier a supporter of the dictator Lucius Cornelius Sulla, is prevented from becoming consul in Rome for two years because he is charged with bribery, a charge of which he is acquitted by 64 BC.

65 BC

- King Mithridates VI the Great of Pontus is decisively defeated by the Roman general Pompey the Great near Dasteira in Pontus (later renamed Nicopolis, "City of Victory"), and flees to the Crimea. Pompey also defeats King Tigranes of Armenia, who is allowed to retain his kingdom of Armenia as a vassal prince and a bulwark against Parthia, but loses all his foreign acquisitions.
- The situation in Rome is deteriorating into a struggle for power between individuals, with the support of the common people felt to be a necessary asset. The Roman politician Julius Caesar becomes aedile (with responsibility for temples, buildings, streets, markets, and public games), and he spends vast sums on pleasing the public. The Roman politician Catiline conspires to gain power in Rome by force. His plans are betrayed to the orator and statesman Marcus Tullius Cicero, however, by representatives of the Gallic tribe of the Allobroges, who are in Rome to attempt to settle grievances concerning the governing of the province of Gallia Narbonensis in France.

64 BC

- The Roman general Pompey the Great arrives at Antioch in Syria and dictates terms: King Antiochus XIII of Syria is deposed and the Seleucid dynasty ends. Syria becomes part of the Roman provinces. Hyrcanus II and his brother Aristobulus II, rival claimants for the Hasmonaean throne of Judea, bring their claims before Pompey. Pompey supports the claim of Hyrcanus, but makes Palestine into a Roman province, appointing Hyrcanus as high priest of the Jews but the Idumean Antipater as governor of Roman Judea.

63 BC

- Following the collapse of Aristobulus II, the Roman general Pompey inspects the temple of Jerusalem and removes temple treasures. The Jews later see this as the reason for his ensuing turn in fortune.
- Marcus Tullius Cicero uses his denunciation of and campaign against Catiline in Rome to rise to the height of his fame as orator and statesman, particularly as he outshines the more florid orator Hortensius.

- Roman aedile Julius Caesar becomes Pontifex Maximus or High Priest of Rome.
- The Roman general Pompey the Great marches on Jerusalem, where followers of the rival claimant Aristobulus II have refused to submit to Hyrcanus II as high priest and are resisting him on the temple hill. After a three-month siege by Pompey they capitulate. Hyrcanus is recognized as high priest and ruler but not as king of Judea.

December 63 BC–January 61 BC   Roman conspirator Catiline is finally discredited by the Roman consul Marcus Tullius Cicero and his supporters are rounded up and brought before the Senate. The praetor Julius Caesar proposes that they should be spread out in Italian towns for safe-keeping, but the tribune (magistrate) Marcus Procius Cato the Younger and others want them executed; Cicero agrees with this. Catiline flees Rome but is defeated by the other consul, Antonius, and dies in battle.

62 BC

- Julius Caesar continues to advance through the senatorial career offices in Rome and is made praetor (senior magistrate).

December   The Roman general Pompey the Great makes a triumphal return to Italy after his successful campaigns and administrative activities in the East. He brings back a huge amount of booty for the Roman treasury and for his army (which he disbands), plus the revenues of the newly acquired lands in the East.

61 BC

- Roman general Pompey the Great, having returned from the East and demobilized his army, is snubbed by the Senate in Rome, which refuses to ratify his political settlements in the East or his land settlements in favor of his disbanded soldiers.
- Roman praetor (senior magistrate) Julius Caesar is made propraetor for Further Spain. He conducts small successful campaigns against the Lusitanians (from modern Portugal) and improves the commercial position of Gades.

60 BC

- Roman politician Julius Caesar returns from a successful campaign in Further Spain but is refused dispensation by the Senate either to hold a triumph (victory procession) or to run for consulship. Caesar and the Roman military commanders Pompey the Great and Marcus Crassus form the First Triumvirate, a political alliance to acquire and divide power by mutual cooperation.

59 BC

- Julius Caesar is consul in Rome for the year, on behalf of the First Triumvirate (the power-sharing alliance of Caesar, Pompey the Great, and Marcus Crassus). He introduces agrarian laws to resettle the Roman general Pompey's veterans at the expense of aristocratic landowners, and passes various legal reforms, clamping down on bribery, corruption, and immorality by his *Leges Juliae* (Julian Laws). In return for forcing the Senate to sanction Pompey's Eastern settlement, Caesar receives help from Pompey in assuming command in Gaul. Caesar gives his daughter, Julia, in marriage

to Pompey, and himself marries Calpurnia, his third wife.
- The triumvirs Julius Caesar, Pompey the Great, and Marcus Crassus make arrangements to ensure their legislation remains valid. They send the tribune (magistrate) Marcus Porcius Cato the Younger, perhaps their biggest enemy, to govern Cyprus, and they make sure of the election of the unscrupulous Publius Clodius Pulcher, an enemy of the orator and politician Marcus Tullius Cicero, to the tribunate.

58 BC

- King Ptolemy XII Auletes ("the Piper") of Egypt is driven off his throne by the Egyptian people and appeals to Rome to reinstate him.
- Roman tribune (magistrate) Publius Clodius Pulcher has the orator and statesman Marcus Tullius Cicero banished for illegally putting Roman citizens to death without trial when he was consul dealing with the Catiline conspiracy. Cicero's property is confiscated and he goes to Macedonia, although he is reprieved and recalled the following year.
- The Roman statesman and general Julius Caesar begins his campaign to subdue Ariovistus, leader of the Germanic Suevi in northern Gaul, advancing through the Belfort Gap. Ariovistus, with a Teutonic army said to be 120,000 strong and stationed between the Vosges mountain range and the River Rhine, is defeated in a battle near modern Colmar. The Germans move back to the Rhine, and Ariovistus dies soon afterwards.

57 BC

- Roman orator and statesman Marcus Tullius Cicero returns to Rome from Greece in August, with the Roman general Pompey the Great's help.
- The Roman statesman and general Julius Caesar advances to the River Aisne in Gaul and defeats the Belgae, and to the River Sambre and defeats the Nervii, fighting in person. All resistance from Gaulish and Belgian tribes is for the moment ended. Some of the Belgae, having received help from Britain, retire there.

56 BC

- The Breton tribe of the Veneti revolt in Gaul during the absence of the Roman proconsul Julius Caesar, and several other tribes are restless. Caesar sends lieutenants to deal with the Aquitani in the southwest, to watch the Belgae and Germans in the north, and to Normandy, while he moves against the Veneti, defeating them in a naval battle in Quiberon Bay. He takes savage deterrent action against them, executing their councillors and selling the population into slavery.
- The First Triumvirate (Roman power-sharing alliance) is starting to fall apart. A conference is arranged between the triumvirs, Julius Caesar, Pompey the Great, and Marcus Crassus, at Luca in northern Italy, where they agree to continue their cooperation and provide for their own wishes. Caesar's Gallic command is extended for another five years, Pompey and Crassus are to be consuls in 55 BC, and at the end of their year in office, Pompey is to get Spain and Libya as his proconsular area and Crassus is to receive Syria.
- The Teutons, forced by the Germanic Suebi to move west, cross the River Rhine.

Gallic War (58 BC–44 BC)

58 BC

- The tribe of the Helvetii from Switzerland begin to migrate west into Gaul (France) under their leader, Orgetorix, but are checked by Roman statesman and general Julius Caesar in alliance with the Gallic tribe of the Aedui, at the Battle of Bibracte (near Autun, France). This victory brings several requests for friendship and help from the tribes of central Gaul against Ariovistus, leader of the Suevi, a Germanic people who have crossed the River Rhine and settled in northern Gaul, threatening the Gallic tribes in the area.
- Julius Caesar begins his campaign to subdue Ariovistus, advancing through the Belfort Gap. Ariovistus, with a Teutonic army said to be 120,000 strong and stationed between the Vosges mountain range and the River Rhine, is defeated in a battle near modern Colmar. The Germans move back to the Rhine, and Ariovistus dies soon afterwards.

57 BC

- Julius Caesar advances to the River Aisne in Gaul and defeats the Belgae, and to the River Sambre and defeats the Nervii, fighting in person. All resistance from Gaulish and Belgian tribes is for the moment ended. Some of the Belgae, having received help from Britain, retire there.

56 BC

- The Breton tribe of the Veneti revolt in Gaul during the absence of Caesar, and several other tribes are restless. Caesar sends lieutenants to deal with the Aquitani in the southwest, to watch the Belgae and Germans in the north, and to Normandy, while he moves against the Veneti, defeating them in a naval battle in Quiberon Bay. He takes savage deterrent action against them, executing their councillors and selling the population into slavery.
- The Teutons, forced by the Germanic Suebi to move west, cross the River Rhine.

55 BC

- Caesar defeats the Teutons on the River Meuse in Gaul with a terrific massacre, killing all the women and children also, for which he is criticized in the Roman Senate. He follows up his success by crossing the River Rhine and making a punitive raid into Germany.

54 BC

- Caesar invades Britain with five legions and Gallic cavalry. He marches inland and receives the submission of the Trinovantes in Essex. He then defeats the Belgic chiefs under Cassivellaunus, chieftain of the Catuvellauni, in his stronghold near modern Wheathampstead in Hertfordshire. Cassivellaunus sues for peace and Caesar, having shown his strength, returns to Gaul where, in his absence, the Gauls have revolted and the Roman army has suffered a reverse near Liège.

52 BC

- The Gauls unite in revolt under a young Celtic prince, Vercingetorix, of the tribe of the Arverni. Caesar defeats Vercingetorix and forces him into the hill town of Alesia, which he besieges. Caesar then defeats the Gallic relief force, perhaps a quarter of a million strong, and Vercingetorix surrenders and is taken captive. The battle and siege of Alesia are Caesar's greatest military success in Gaul.
- Mark Antony, a friend of Caesar, is elected quaestor. He conducts mopping-up operations in Gaul—King Commius of the Gallic tribe known as the Atrebates makes peace with him on condition that he will never have to look upon the face of a Roman again.

51 BC

- Caesar remains in Gaul to pacify and reconstruct a defeated country. He shows a great deal of clemency to the defeated people, turning the Gauls into his loyal supporters. The area is placed under the governor of the Roman province of Gallia Narbonensis in southern France and is required to pay tribute and supply troops.

50 BC

- Caesar publishes his *De bello gallico/The Gallic War*, written in 52 BC, which is written in a very straightforward style and has instant appeal to Romans. It increases Caesar's popularity in Rome.

44 BC

- Roman soldier and historian Aulus Hirtius writes the eighth and last book of *De bello gallico/The Gallic War* following the death of Julius Caesar. Hirtius is killed the following year fighting against Mark Antony.

55 BC

- King Commius of the Gallic tribe known as the Atrebates is sent to Britain as an ambassador by the Roman statesman and general Julius Caesar, but is put in chains by the Britons as soon as he arrives.
- Ptolemy XII Auletes ("the Piper") is restored to the Egyptian throne by Rome and institutes a proscription of his enemies, including his daughter.
- Roman generals Pompey the Great and Marcus Crassus are consuls for the year in Rome. They carry out the plans made at the conference in Luca in 56 BC. At the end of their year of office, Crassus goes off to the East to his proconsular region of Parthia, while Pompey remains in Rome, governing his province of Spain through legates.
- The Roman proconsul Julius Caesar defeats the Teutons on the River Meuse in Gaul with a terrific massacre, killing all the women and children also, for which he is criticized in the Roman Senate. He follows up his success by crossing the River Rhine and making a punitive raid into Germany.

September 9   The Roman statesman and general Julius

Caesar sails for Britain with two legions. He is content to do no more than show his superiority in arms, but it is received with popular acclaim in Rome. He lands, despite opposition, probably near modern Walmer, Kent. The Britons return the Roman ambassador Commius but sue for peace. However, when a high tide destroys some of Caesar's ships, they renew the fighting and Caesar, having made his point, recrosses the English Channel.

54 BC

- The Roman general Pompey the Great's wife, Julia, daughter of the statesman and general Julius Caesar, dies in childbirth, weakening the ties between Pompey and Caesar.
- The Roman governor of Syria Marcus Crassus plunders the temple in Jerusalem before proceeding on his spectacular bid to make his military name in the East.
- The Roman proconsul Julius Caesar returns to Britain with five legions and Gallic cavalry. He marches inland and receives the submission of the Trinovantes in Essex. He then defeats the Belgic chiefs under Cassivellaunus, chieftain of the Catuvellauni, in his stronghold near modern Wheathampstead in Hertfordshire. Cassivellaunus sues for peace and Caesar, having shown his strength, returns to Gaul where, in his absence, the Gauls have revolted and the Roman army has suffered a reverse near Liège.
- The Roman soldier Mark Antony comes to serve under the Roman proconsul Julius Caesar in Gaul.

53 BC

June 6 The Roman general Marcus Crassus rashly penetrates into the Mesopotamian desert. He is killed and his army utterly defeated at the Battle of Carrhae by the Parthians under their Arsacian king, Orodes II.

52 BC

- In a rapidly deteriorating situation of mob warfare in Rome, Publius Clodius Pulcher is killed by the tribune (magistrate) Milo, leading a rival gang, and Pompey the Great is made sole consul by the Senate in an effort to restore order.
- The Gauls unite in revolt under a young Celtic prince, Vercingetorix, of the tribe of the Arverni. The Roman statesman and general Julius Caesar defeats Vercingetorix and forces him into the hill town of Alesia, which he besieges. Caesar then defeats the Gallic relief force, perhaps a quarter of a million strong, and Vercingetorix surrenders and is taken captive. The battle and siege of Alesia are Caesar's greatest military success in Gaul.
- Roman soldier Mark Antony is elected quaestor. He conducts mopping-up operations in Gaul—King Commius of the Gallic tribe known as the Atrebates makes peace with him on condition that he will never have to look upon the face of a Roman again.

51 BC

- Cleopatra VII and her brother Ptolemy XIII succeed to the Egyptian throne. On her accession, Cleopatra travels to upper Egypt to escort the sacred bull, the manifestation of Apis, to its home.
- The Parthians are defeated in Syria by the Roman soldier Gaius Cassius Longinus, who has taken over the

Eastern command on the defeat and death of the Roman general Marcus Crassus.

- The Roman proconsul Julius Caesar remains in Gaul to pacify and reconstruct a defeated country. He shows a great deal of clemency to the defeated people, turning the Gauls into his loyal supporters. The area is placed under the governor of the Roman province of Gallia Narbonensis in southern France and is required to pay tribute and supply troops.

SCIENCE, TECHNOLOGY, AND MEDICINE

Agriculture

c. **100 BC**

- Sugar cane is cultivated in the Far East.
- The cocoa plant is cultivated in South America.
- The duck is domesticated in China from the mallard (*Anas platyrhyncos*).

79 BC

- The Roman general Lucius Licinius Lucullus imports cherry trees from Persia into Rome.

Health and Medicine

c. **90 BC**

- The Greek physician Asclepiades of Bithynia teaches that bodily harmony can be achieved through fresh air, exercise, and proper diet; he has mentally ill people freed from confinement and treats them with occupational therapy.
- The Roman scholar Marcus Terentius Varro writes that disease is caused by the entry of imperceptible particles into the body—the first enunciation of germ theory.

63 BC

- Mithridates VI the Great, King of Pontus, experiments with poisons and their antidotes in a search for a universal antidote now known as mithridate. He customarily takes small doses of poison as an antidote against assassination and tries, unsuccessfully, to kill himself by poison. He eventually gets a Gaulish servant to kill him.

Math

c. **100 BC**

- Chinese mathematicians begin using negative numbers.

Science

c. **100 BC**

- The Greek philosopher Poseidonius correlates tides with the lunar cycle.

- The Greeks are the first to measure wind direction. They install a wind vane on the Acropolis.
- The Romans produce mercury by heating the sulfide mineral cinnabar and condensing the vapors.

80 BC

- The Greek philosopher Poseidonius estimates the circumference of the earth by measuring the distance from Rhodes to Alexandria, and by using the difference in the height of the star Canopius above the horizon at each location to estimate the angle of arc. His estimate is 11% too large.

Technology

***c.* 100 BC**

- Glass windowpanes begin to be used in Roman houses.
- Syrian glassmakers develop the art of glass blowing.
- The Chinese begin to use ice for refrigeration.

87 BC

- The differential gear is invented by the Greek mathematician Geminus of Rhodes. The gears and axles are used in a device to measure the lunar cycle.

***c.* 85 BC**

- The Greek poet Antipater makes the first mention of a water mill.

Transportation

***c.* 100 BC**

- The Danish Dejbjerg wagon (named for the site at which it was found) has pivoted front axle wheels.

***c.* 90 BC**

- The Chinese historian Sima Qian describes the use of the parachute.

81 BC

- Japanese emperor Sujin, the first known historical Japanese emperor, decrees that each province must build a ship. Previously, only dugouts and small ships had been built, but after this date Japan rapidly develops shipping. The following year Sujin begins to build a fishing fleet to provide more seafood for his growing population.

ARTS AND IDEAS

Architecture

***c.* 100 BC**

- Androcinus of Cyrrhus builds the octagonal Tower of the Winds in Athens; a navigational aid, it contains eight sundials each facing a different cardinal point.
- Apartment houses in Rome are five stories high, built flimsily of cob (a clay and straw mix) and wattle.
- Celts, probably of the Iron Age B culture of Britain, build their most remarkable stone forts in Scotland. The forts, known as *brochs*, are dry-stone towers surrounding a circular internal area of about 8.5 m/28 ft in diameter with walls as thick as 4 m/13 ft, in which rooms and staircases are sometimes inset.

69 BC

- King Tigranes II of Armenia builds his new capital city Tigranocerta in a Hellenic style, and in imitation of all the eponymous city founders of the post-Alexandrian period.

Arts

90 BC

- The "Second Style" of Italian wall painting, in which architectural forms are reproduced on the flat surfaces of walls, becomes popular.

***c.* 85 BC–*c.* AD 52**

c. The earliest known Chinese lacquer (found at Lak Lang in North Korea in modern times) is produced.

Film

***c.* 60 BC**

- The Roman poet Lucretius describes how the sequential display of images can produce the illusion of motion.

Literature and Language

67 BC

- Roman orator and writer Marcus Tullius Cicero begins a series of correspondences, which are intended for publication. The letters, which survive to modern times, are edited by Cicero's freedman Marcus Tullius Tiro after Cicero's death.

63 BC

December 5   Cicero's freedman, Marcus Tullius Tiro, uses his new shorthand system, the first developed in Latin, to record a speech of Marcus Porcius Cato the Younger demanding the death penalty for Catiline.

***c.* 60 BC**

- Latin poet Gaius (Valerius Maximianus) Catullus writes his *Love Poems to Lesbia*, possibly to Clodia, sister of the Roman politician Publius Clodius Pulcher.

58 BC

- Latin poet Lucretius publishes *De rerum natura/On the Nature of Things*, a Latin epic based on the doctrines of the Greek philosopher Epicurus.

52 BC

- The Roman general Julius Caesar writes his *De bello gallico/The Gallic War* with the intention of winning popular support for himself by publicizing his actions in Gaul.

Theater and Dance

57 BC

- Roman politician Pompey builds a theater in the Campus Martius, outside the city walls of Rome.

Thought and Scholarship

84 BC

- Roman general Lucius Cornelius Sulla, returning home via Athens, shows his love of learning by making off with the library of Apellicon of Teos, including most of the works of the Greek philosophers Aristotle and Theophrastus.

BIRTHS & DEATHS

100 BC
- Cornelius Nepos, Roman historian, friend of Cicero and Catullus, born (–*c.* 25 BC).
- Lucius Appuleius Saturninus, tribune (magistrate), who opposed the Roman Senate 104 BC–100 BC, is stoned to death in Rome with his fellow tribune Gaius Servilius Glaucia.

c. July 12 (Gaius) Julius Caesar, Roman general, dictator, and statesman, conqueror of Transalpine Gaul, born (–44 BC).

91 BC
- Marcus Livius Drusus the Younger, Roman tribune (magistrate), who attempted to reform the government of Rome, is murdered (*c.* 33).

87 BC
c. March 29 Wudi (original name Liu Ch'e), Chinese emperor of the Han dynasty 141/140 BC–87/86 BC, who greatly increased Chinese influence abroad and made Confucianism the state religion of China, dies (*c.* 70).

86 BC
c. 86 BC Sallust, Roman historian noted for his narrative style, born in Amiternum, Samnium (–34 BC).

January 13 Gaius Marius, Roman general and consul, dies in Rome (*c.* 71).

85 BC
c. 85 BC Ssu-ma Chien, Chinese astronomer and historian, author of *Shih-chi/Historical records*, a history of China to the 2nd century BC, dies in China (*c.* 60).
- Marcus Junius Brutus, governor of Cisalpine Gaul, a leader of the conspirators who assassinated Julius Caesar (March 44 BC), born (–42 BC).

84 BC
- Cinna, opponent of Lucius Cornelius Sulla, and leader of the Marian party in Rome, killed in a mutiny of his followers.
- Gaius (Valerius Maximianus) Catullus, outstanding Roman lyric poet, born in Verona, Cisalpine Gaul (modern Italy) (–*c.* 54).

82 BC
c. 82 BC Mark Antony, Roman general who influenced the end of the Roman Republic, and who is known for his association with Cleopatra of Egypt, born (–30 BC).

80 BC
- Berenice III, Queen of Egypt, daughter and wife of Ptolemy IX, wife of Ptolemy X and Ptolemy XI, sole ruler after Ptolemy IX's death in 80 BC, is murdered.

78 BC
- Lucius Cornelius Sulla (Felix), Roman consul who fought King Mithridates VI of Pontus in Rome's first civil war, and then became Roman dictator 82 BC–79 BC, dies in Puteoli, near Naples (60).

73 BC
- Herod the Great, King of Judea under the Romans 37 BC–4 BC, born (–4 BC).

72 BC
- Quintus Sertorius, Roman military officer who was independent ruler of Spain 80 BC–72 BC, murdered in Spain (*c.* 51).

71 BC
- Spartacus, Thracian slave and gladiator, leader of the Gladiatorial War against Rome, dies in battle.

70 BC
October 15 Virgil, Roman poet, author of the *Aeneid*, born in Andes, near Mantua, Italy (–19 BC).

69 BC
- Cleopatra VII, Queen of Egypt 51 BC–30 BC, lover and ally of Mark Antony, born (–30 BC).

67 BC
- L. Cornelius Sisenna, Roman historian and legate of Pompey, dies in Crete.

65 BC
December Horace (Quintus Horatius Flaccus), celebrated Roman lyric poet and satirist, born in Venusia, Italy (–8 BC).

c. **64 BC**
- Strabo, Greek geographer, author of *Geography*, which describes the peoples and countries known to the Greeks and Romans at the time, born in Amaseia, Pontus (–*c.* AD 24).

63 BC
- Mithridates ("the Great"), Eupator, King of Pontus 120 BC–63 BC, who expanded the Pontus empire and challenged Rome, dies in Panticapaeum, Asia Minor (71).
- Vipsanius Agrippa, deputy to Roman emperor Augustus who was responsible for defeating Mark Antony and for completing the Pantheon, born (–12 BC).

September 23 Augustus, first emperor of the Roman Empire 27 BC–AD 14, born as Gaius Octavius (Octavian) (–AD 14).

62 BC
- Catiline (full name Lucius Sergius Catilina), a Roman aristocrat who attempted to overthrow the Roman Republic, falls in battle against republican forces at Pistoia, Etruria (*c.* 46).

59 BC
- Livy (Titus Livius), great Roman historian best known for his history of Rome, born in Patavium, Venetia, Italy (–AD 17).

58 BC
January 30 Livia Drusilla (or Julia Augusta from AD 14), wife of Augustus (Octavian), and mother of Tiberius, a highly influential figure in the government of Rome, born (–AD 29).

55 BC
- Albius Tibullus, Roman poet, born (–*c.* 19 BC).
- Tigranes II the Great, King of Armenia 93 BC–55 BC, under whom Armenia briefly became the strongest state in the Roman east, Roman client king from 66 BC after surrendering to Pompey, dies (*c.* 85).

54 BC
c. 54 BC Gaius (Valerius Maximianus) Catullus, outstanding Roman lyric poet, dies in Rome (*c.* 30).
- Julia, Julius Caesar's daughter and only child, wife of Pompey (59 BC–54 BC), dies.

53 BC
- Marcus Crassus, Roman statesman, who formed the First Triumvirate with Pompey and Julius Caesar, falls at the Battle of Carrhae (now Harran, Turkey) fighting the Parthians (*c.* 62).

52 BC
January Publius Clodius Pulcher, opponent of Cicero, leader of a violent political faction, killed in a street battle in Bovillae, Latium, Italy.

51 BC
c. 51 BC Poseidonus, Greek Stoic philosopher, dies (*c.* 84).
- Propertius Sextus, Roman elegiac poet, author of "Cynthia," born.
- Ptolemy XI, Macedonian king of Egypt 76 BC–51 BC who turned Egypt into a client state of Rome, dies.

79 BC

- Roman orator and politician Marcus Tullius Cicero goes to the Greek city of Athens and the island of Rhodes to study philosophy and oratory for two years.

75 BC

- Syrian writer Philodemus of Gadara arrives in Rome. His works include Greek prose treatises on philosophy, aesthetics, and psychology. Many are only coming to light in the twentieth century, in papyrus rolls recovered from the ruins of Herculaneum.

58 BC

c. 58 BC Roman mystic and Pythagorean philosopher Nigidius Figulus is praetor (magistrate).

- Syrian writer Philodemus of Gadara composes *On the Good King According to Homer*, which adapts Greek political philosophy on the subject of monarchy to the world of a Roman senator.

55 BC

- Roman orator and writer Marcus Tullius Cicero wishes to retire from public life to concentrate on literary pursuits, publishing his *De oratore/The Orator* this year and finishing *De republica/On the Republic* in the following year. However, in 51 BC he is appointed governor of Cilicia, in Asia Minor, and goes reluctantly.

51 BC

- Syrian Greek philosopher Poseidonius, who had taught the Roman orator Marcus Tullius Cicero, moves from Rhodes to Rome, but probably dies soon afterwards.

SOCIETY

Everyday Life

100 BC

c. 100 BC The Mochica culture develops on the northern half of the Peruvian coast, approximately contemporary with the Nazca civilization in the south of the country. The Mochica use bronze for tools and weapons, and build great pyramid temples out of mud brick.

c. 100 BC–*c.* 100 AD The population of the Mexican Basin decreases except for the city of Teotihuacán, which grows to three times its previous size. It grows to cover 20 sq km/8 sq mi, and reaches a population figure of over 60,000. The majority of these are farmers, who live in the city, but tend their crops outside it.

Religion

c. **100 BC**

- The popularity of the Roman general Gaius Marius is such that the people make offerings and libations, linking his name with the gods.

c. **90 BC**

- The distinctive curvilinear decorative art of the Celtic La Tène culture is introduced into Britain. The Celts of this culture also introduce the practice of

throwing votive offerings into sacred waters, as at Llyn Cerrig Bach on the island of Anglesey, which is probably used as a holy place until the Roman destruction of AD 78–79. The enameled bronze shield found in modern times in the River Thames at Battersea dates from this period.

87 BC

- Roman politician Lucius Cornelius Cinna makes Julius Caesar *flamen Dialis*, the sacrificial priest of Jupiter, chief of the Greek gods. Caesar resigns this post following the victory of the Roman consul L. Cornelius Sulla over Mithridates VI of Pontus.

75 BC

- Roman general Quintus Sertorius, almost worshiped by the Spanish people, spreads a rumor that his pet doe is an intermediary between himself and Diana, goddess of chastity and hunting, who instils him with prophetic vision.

62 BC

- The profligate Roman politician Publius Clodius Pulcher profanes the mystic female rites of Bona Dea, the good goddess, by sneaking into the ceremonies dressed as a woman. This religious scandal has far-reaching political repercussions. It causes the Roman general Julius Caesar to divorce his second wife Pompeia, allegedly the lover of Clodius because, as Caesar's wife, she must be 'above suspicion'. Clodius becomes the lifelong enemy of the Roman orator and writer Marcus Tullius Cicero, who destroys his alibi.

60 BC

- Druidism, the religion of the Celtic people, flourishes in Britain and Gaul, while Mithraism, the mystery religion based on the worship of the Persian god of light Mithras, begins to permeate the Roman legions, spreading from Persia via Asia Minor.
- The Jewish Essenes sect begins to flourish.

59 BC

- Roman consuls destroy altars to Isis, the principal Egyptian goddess, on the Capitol Hill in Rome.

Sports

100 BC

c. 100 BC–*c.* 1 BC *Ti Jian Zi*, or 'shuttlecock kicking', in which a shuttlecock is hit with hands and feet, is played in China. It is similar to the medieval English game of battledore shuttlecock, the precursor of badminton.

- Swimming contests are held in Japan.

c. **90 BC**

- The earliest reference to the Roman war game *Ludus Latrunculorum*, a board game with similarities to chess and checkers, is made in Volume VII of the Roman scholar Marcus Terentius Varro's *De lingua Latina/On the Latin Language*.

50 BC–1 BC

POLITICS, GOVERNMENT, AND ECONOMICS

Business and Economics

30 BC
- King Herod the Great does much for Judea on a material level, developing its economy, re-fortifying Jerusalem, and beginning the rebuilding of the temple there. By behaving as a Hellenistic monarch, however, he gains the hatred of the Jews and despite restricting his taste for grandeur he has to keep control by force.
- Trade, and hence contact, between Rome and northwest India increases during this period.

19 BC
- After the Roman pacification of Spain its tin mines are opened up, thus decreasing the Cornish tin trade which has been in the hands of the Veneti.

***c.* 15 BC**
- The Roman emperor Augustus, instituting a strict control of the issue of coinage, establishes a mint at Lugdunum (Lyon), the capital of Gaul.

Colonization

50 BC
- After the departure of the Roman proconsul Julius Caesar, Gaul begins its upward path to become a prosperous Roman colony.

46 BC
- The Roman colony at Carthage, north Africa, begins to be developed.

40 BC
- Following the Veneti, a further wave of Belgae arrives in Britain. They meet opposition from the Catuvellauni and so extend through Hampshire into Dorset. This expedition is almost certainly led by King Commius of the Gallic tribe known as the Atrebates.

33 BC
- The northwest African kingdom of Mauritania is bequeathed by King Bocchus to Rome.

26 BC
- Roman emperor Augustus sends the Roman governor in Egypt Aelius Gallus on a military expedition into Arabia

Felix (the southwest corner of the Arabian peninsula, the area of ancient Sheba and modern Yemen) to win new territory. The expedition is forced to return the following year through lack of water.

14 BC
- The Roman co-regent, Marcus Vipsanius Agrippa, sets up a colony of veterans in Syria.

9 BC
- Maroboduus rises to power over the Germanic tribe of the Marcomanni in the valley of the Main and persuades his people to migrate to Bohemia, involving the Romans in fighting again on the River Danube.

5 BC
- The settlement at Qumran (where the Dead Sea Scrolls are produced in the last centuries BC and 1st century AD), in modern Jordan, is reoccupied and rebuilt.

Human Rights

14 BC
- Nicolaus of Damascus, the historian and minister of King Herod the Great of Judea, pleads with the Roman co-regent, Marcus Vipsanius Agrippa, for the rights of the Jews, which are being ignored by the Greeks.

Politics and Government

50 BC
- The Kalingas of India throw up a militant king, Kharavela, who lays claim to land from the Deccan to Burma. Indian culture also penetrates into Cambodia about this time.
- There is much manoeuvring for power in Rome between the Senate, with Pompey the Great as consul, and the supporters of the proconsul Julius Caesar. Mark Antony as tribune (magistrate) acts on Caesar's behalf, but there are arguments over the consulship Caesar was promised at the end of his Gallic command and the demand that he should disband his army. Caesar is declared an enemy of the people by the Senate.

49 BC
- Roman statesman and general Julius Caesar marches through Italy to confront Pompey the Great. However, Pompey crosses to Greece where he has armies and great support. In Numidia, north Africa, King Juba I gains a victory over Caesar's forces on Pompey's behalf. Caesar's general, Labienus, defects to Pompey. Caesar crosses to Spain and defeats Pompey's forces there.

January 1 The Roman proconsul Julius Caesar, accompanied by Mark Antony who has fled from Rome, crosses the River Rubicon from Gaul onto Roman soil without giving up his army – an act of war. The civil war has begun.

48 BC

- Julius Caesar follows Pompey the Great to Greece. He loses the Battle of Dyrrhachium there, but defeats Pompey at Pharsalus in August. Pompey flees to Egypt. Caesar pardons the generals Marcus Junius Brutus and Gaius Cassius along with the orator and statesman Marcus Tullius Cicero who fought on Pompey's side.
- The Roman consul Julius Caesar, in pursuit of his rival Pompey the Great, becomes embroiled in Egypt's dynastic quarrel between Ptolemy XIII and his sister Cleopatra VII, ousted by Ptolemy in 49 BC, and espouses Cleopatra's cause. Her opponents blockade Caesar and Cleopatra in her palace in Alexandria over the winter.
- The Roman province of Asia Minor is attacked by King Pharnaces of Pontus, son of King Mithridates VI the Great of Pontus.

September 28   The Roman general Pompey the Great is assassinated in Egypt by King Ptolemy XIII of Egypt's troops at Pelusium as soon as he lands.

47 BC

- Idumean prince Antipater is appointed procurator of Judea by the Roman dictator Julius Caesar.
- Roman dictator Julius Caesar settles affairs in Egypt, restoring Cleopatra VII to her throne and defeating her brother, Ptolemy XIII.
- Roman dictator Julius Caesar returns briefly to Rome, where there is disquiet over the debt situation. Caesar carries out some administrative reforms, including protecting the rights of property but reducing the rate of interest. He reforms the law courts and reduces bribery. The *Leges Juliae* (Julian Laws) of 59 BC become a practical reality. Caesar then passes on into Africa to meet the threat from Pompey the Great's supporters there.
- Roman dictator Julius Caesar marches rapidly through Syria and Asia Minor and defeats King Pharnaces of Pontus at the Battle of Zela, where he boasts: *Veni, vidi, vici!* ('I came, I saw, I conquered').

46 BC

- After Julius Caesar is made dictator, Roman historian and statesman Gaius Sallustius Crispus remains governor of Africa Nova (modern Algeria). He enriches himself there and upon his return to Rome he is charged with extortion, but through Caesar's intervention the charges against him are dropped. Crispus then retires into private life.
- The Roman statesman and general Julius Caesar overwhelmingly defeats the Pompeian forces at the Battle of Thapsus in Carthaginia, north Africa. Titus Labienus, the only officer of the Gallic Wars to have deserted Caesar for Pompey the Great, and Pompey's son Sextus Pompeius flee to Spain, where Gnaeus Pompeius, another of Pompey's sons, is established. The Roman tribune (magistrate) Marcus Porcius Cato the Younger and King Juba I of Numidia commit suicide, and Numidia becomes a Roman province.
- Roman statesman and general Julius Caesar returns to Rome and is made consul and dictator for ten years. He is also given a new office, Prefect of Morals, equivalent to the office of Censo but with vastly extended powers.

He declares an amnesty for those who have borne arms against him. The defeated Celtic prince Vercingetorix graces Caesar's four-day triumph (victory procession) and is then put to death. Caesar gives cash bounties to his troops and money to all the poorest citizens of Rome. Marcus Lepidus is consul with Caesar.

45 BC

- Roman dictator and consul Julius Caesar increases the Senate to 900 and widens its recruitment. He reduces the free corn ration but encourages colonization for Roman citizens, especially in Africa, Spain, and the East. He also settles many of his veterans in colonies, mainly in Gallia Narbonensis, Sicily, and Africa. He begins the rebuilding and repopulation of both Carthage and Corinth. He issues sumptuary laws against luxury, appoints a commission to simplify the laws, and begins the task of putting Rome's finances in order. On January 1 he also introduces the Julian calendar, which has become the calendar of the Western world.
- The Roman consul and dictator Julius Caesar is forced to fight one last battle against the Pompeians to end the civil war. He returns to Spain, where he finally defeats Pompey the Great's sons and the turncoat general Titus Labienus at the hard-fought Battle of Munda (between Seville and Málaga), although Sextus Pompeius escapes. Caesar severely punishes the Spanish districts that supported the Pompeians, and makes some preliminary plans for the colonies he intends to establish there, then returns to Rome.

44 BC

- Queen Cleopatra VII of Egypt kills her younger brother, who has been reigning with her as Ptolemy XIV.
- Roman dictator Julius Caesar's great-nephew, Octavian, returns to Rome from Illyria, learns of his adoption into the *Gens Julia*, and claims the right to succeed his adoptive father, Julius Caesar, because of their common ancestry. Rivalry over the succession breaks out between him and the triumvir Mark Antony, as well as other minor contenders.
- Roman triumvir Mark Antony attempts to make a compromise with the Senate; all Caesar's legislation is ratified and his funeral is allowed to go ahead. In exchange, the conspirators are not punished.
- The conspirators who murdered the Roman dictator Julius Caesar expect his death to restore freedom to the political life of the Roman Republic, without considering that all the factors that had led to civil war and Caesar's rise to power still exist. Armies are massed in Spain, the Gallic provinces, and Macedonia, and all prove loyal to Caesar's name.
- The Roman orator and writer Marcus Tullius Cicero delivers his first philippic denouncing the Roman politician and soldier Mark Antony.
- The Roman triumvir Mark Antony's compromise with the Senate does not prevent civil war from breaking out. The immediate spark is the reading of the Roman dictator Julius Caesar's will at his funeral. He leaves his private gardens on the River Tiber as a public park, and the sum of 300 sesterces to each Roman citizen. His main heir is his great-nephew Octavian, which bitterly disappoints Mark Antony. On hearing the will, the mob in the Forum take over the funeral and go in search of Caesar's killers, burning the Senate down.

February At the carnival of the Lupercalia in Rome, the Roman dictator Julius Caesar refuses the kingly crown offered by the consul Mark Antony in what may be a carefully staged stunt, either to test the water with regard to his assuming the monarchy or to prove that he is not seeking it.

15 March A conspiracy of 60 Roman senators, led by Gaius Cassius Longinus and Marcus Junius Brutus, reaches fruition and the Roman dictator Julius Caesar is assassinated in the Senate House on the Ides of March.

43 BC

- Roman consul Mark Antony gets a law passed allotting him the provinces of Cisalpine and Transalpine Gaul for five years instead of Macedonia, when his consulship ends. He moves to take up command, but the senator to whom they had originally been allotted, Decimus Junius Brutus, refuses to evacuate the area, and Mark Antony besieges him in Mutina, northern Italy.
- With the support of the Senate (persuaded by the orator and politician Marcus Tullius Cicero that Mark Antony is aiming at dictatorship), Octavian and the consuls march to defeat Mark Antony, and lift the siege of Mutina in northern Italy. A reconciliation is achieved, and Octavian, Mark Antony, and Marcus Aemilius Lepidus meet at Bononia (modern Bologna). Between the three of them they have more than 33 legions at their command. They form the Second Triumvirate and agree to divide power between them. Octavian becomes consul for 42 BC.
- The newly-appointed Triumvirate (power-sharing alliance between the Roman leaders Octavian, Mark Antony, and Marcus Aemilius Lepidus) divide the Roman world between them: Africa, Sicily, and Sardinia to Octavian; the East and Cisalpine and Transalpine Gaul go to Mark Antony; and Spain and the remainder of Gaul go to Lepidus. Lepidus is to be consul in 42 BC while Antony and Octavian go east to attack the armies led by Marcus Junius Brutus and Gaius Cassius Longinus.

December 7 Roman orator and statesman Marcus Tullius Cicero, who has inflamed the Senate against the Roman consul Mark Antony by his brilliant series of speeches *The Philippics*, in which he accuses Antony of aiming at dictatorship, is executed at the order of the Second Triumvirate.

42 BC

- At the Battle of Philippi in Macedonia, the Roman consul and heir to Julius Caesar, Octavian, and Mark Antony defeat Gaius Cassius Longinus and Marcus Junius Brutus, who have gone to the East to raise armies against Antony and the supporters of the former dictator Julius Caesar. Cassius and Brutus both kill themselves.

41 BC

- The Roman triumvir Mark Antony crosses to his provinces in the East. At Tarsus in Cilicia he meets the Egyptian Queen Cleopatra and succumbs to her carefully staged charms. He spends the winter of 40 BC in Egypt with her.
- The Second Triumvirate (power-sharing alliance between Octavian, Mark Antony, and Marcus Aemilius Lepidus) makes some adjustments in the division of Roman provinces: Spain, Sardinia, and Africa go to Octavian; the East and all of Gaul except Cisalpine Gaul, which becomes part of Italy, go to Mark Antony; and Lepidus receives nothing now, as he is suspected of intriguing with Sextus Pompeius, the son of Pompey the Great. Octavian gives Africa to Lepidus in 40 BC. War breaks out sporadically in Italy between Octavian and forces supporting the absent Mark Antony and his wife Fulvia.

40 BC

- Octavian captures Perusia in Italy, Mark Antony's wife Fulvia dies, and the forces of Mark Antony in Italy collapse. Antony returns to Italy.
- The last of the Indo-Greek kings, Hermaeus, is dethroned by the Yue Ji people, in spite of support from China.
- The Parthians invade Syria and take Jerusalem, where Hyrcanus II is overthrown. Herod, his minister, escapes to Rome, where the Senate proclaims him king of Judea.

10 October The Pact of Brundisium is arranged by the Roman triumvir Octavian's friend Maecenas, reconciling the three members of the Second Triumvirate and slightly rearranging their territories and commands of troops. Transalpine Gaul is removed from Mark Antony and given to Octavian. Marcus Aemilius Lepidus remains with Africa. Octavian gives his sister Octavia in marriage to Mark Antony to help cement the alliance again.

39 BC

- After the reaffirmation of the Second Triumvirate at Brundisium, the Roman triumvir Mark Antony returns to the East with his wife, Octavia, where he makes Athens his headquarters.
- The Treaty of Misenum is signed between the Roman triumvirs Mark Antony and Octavian and Sextus Pompeius, the son of the soldier and politician Pompey the Great. Pompeius has held possession of Sicily and Sardinia since the death of the Roman dictator Julius Caesar, constantly interrupting Rome's vital corn supply. It is agreed that Pompeius will be given a proconsular command for five years in Sicily, Corsica, Sardinia, and Achaea. Octavian soon breaks the treaty, accepting Sardinia from a treacherous governor.

38 BC

- Publius Ventidius, the Roman triumvir Mark Antony's lieutenant, defeats the Parthians in Syria. The Parthians are under the joint command of both Pacorus, son of King Orodes II, and the Roman Quintus Labienus, son of Julius Caesar's disloyal general Titus Labienus. Grief-stricken at the death of his son and heir Pacorus, Orodes surrenders the Parthian crown to his son Phraates IV, who immediately kills his father and most of his remaining brothers.
- The Roman triumvir Octavian divorces his wife Scribonia, on the day she bears him a daughter, in order to marry the 19-year-old Livia, forcing her husband Tiberius Claudius Nero, by whom she has two sons (Tiberius and Drusus) to divorce her. Octavian and Livia remain happily married for 50 years.

37 BC

- The Roman triumvir Mark Antony marries Queen Cleopatra of Egypt. His wife Octavia returns to her brother, the triumvir Octavian, who sends her back to Rome. Mark Antony divorces Octavia in 32 BC.

- The Roman triumvir Mark Antony sends two legions under C. Sosius to install Herod, son of Antipater, the former governor of Judea, on the throne of Jerusalem in Judea. After the city is captured the reign of Herod the Great begins. He had previously married a member of the Hasmonaean royal family to support his claim to the throne, but had had her grandfather and brother put to death. With Herod's accession to the throne, Judea is no longer a Roman province, but a client kingdom of Rome.

36 BC

- The Roman triumvir Mark Antony unsuccessfully invades Parthia. Some of his forces are betrayed to the Parthians by King Artavasdes of Armenia.
- The Roman triumvir Marcus Aemilius Lepidus tries to claim Sicily after the former ruler Sextus Pompeius is driven out, but is forced into retirement and banished by his fellow triumvir Octavian.
- The Roman triumvir Octavian prepares to attack Sextus Pompeius in Sicily. Two Roman fleets approach from different directions, and the triumvir Marcus Aemilius Lepidus attacks by land from Africa. Despite initial problems, Sextus is defeated by Octavian's friend and very able aide, the general Marcus Vipsanius Agrippa, at the naval battle of Naulochus.

36 BC–31 BC

- Roman triumvir Octavian cements his power: in 36 BC he is granted the traditional tribunician rights of sacrosanctity as a mark of honour; in 32 BC he makes his adherents and troops swear an oath of personal loyalty; and in 31 BC he is granted the first of nine successive consulships.

35 BC

- Roman soldier Sextus Pompeius, son of Pompey the Great and enemy of the Roman triumvir Octavian, faces capture and execution. He escapes from Sicily and flees to Asia Minor. He thinks of joining the Parthians but is captured and executed on the orders of Octavian.

34 BC

- Roman emperor Octavian wins praise for rebuilding edifices such as the theatre of Pompey in the Campus Martius and the Basilica Aemilia, and not renaming them after himself. He repairs many of Rome's ancient temples and, in 29 BC, creates new patrician families to recruit to the priesthood.
- The Roman triumvir Mark Antony invades Armenia and carries its king Artavasdes, whom he blames for his defeat by the Parthians in 36 BC, captive to Alexandria, Egypt.
- Roman triumvir Mark Antony lapses into the life of an Eastern potentate with Queen Cleopatra of Egypt, his wife since 37 BC, when he celebrates his triumph over the Armenian king Artavasdes in the style of Alexandria. In an episode known as the Donations of Alexandria, Mark Antony stages a pageant at which he and Cleopatra, dressed as the Egyptian gods Osiris and Isis, sit on golden thrones together with their children and Cleopatra's son Caesarion whom they declare to be the legitimate son of the Roman dictator Julius Caesar. They proclaim him king of kings, joint ruler of Egypt and Cyprus along with Cleopatra. Antony and

Cleopatra's children are also named as future rulers of parts of the empire yet to be conquered. The declaration enrages the Roman triumvir Octavian, for he sees it as transferring Roman property into Greek hands.

32 BC

- Chengdi becomes emperor of China, but is in the hands of a court clique, the fate of many of his successors: the slow decline of the Han dynasty is beginning.
- Events in Rome move rapidly towards open war as stories begin to circulate about the Roman general Mark Antony's actions in Egypt. The Roman statesman and leader Octavian institutes the oath of personal loyalty from the Senate and from the Italian towns and provinces of the West, a growing instrument of power for the future emperors of Rome.
- Roman triumvir Mark Antony and Queen Cleopatra of Egypt winter in Greece, making preparations for war against the triumvir Octavian. Cleopatra finances an army of 90,000 men and 500 ships. The fleet moves to Actium in western Greece in preparation to attack Italy in the spring of 31 BC.
- The two Roman consuls and some senators defect to the Roman triumvir Mark Antony, and the triumvir Octavian formally terminates Antony's command in the East and declares war on him.

31 BC

September 2 The Roman leader Octavian's fleet of 400 ships under the general Marcus Vipsanius Agrippa blockade the Roman general Mark Antony's Egyptian fleet at Actium in western Greece. In the ensuing Battle of Actium Agrippa defeats Antony and his wife Queen Cleopatra of Egypt and they flee back to Alexandria, Egypt. Octavian follows them and Antony's troops desert him.

31 BC–23 BC

- Roman leader Octavian is re-elected consul every year for nine years in succession.

30 BC

- Cornelius Gallus, a soldier and poet (although none of his work is extant), is made Roman governor of Egypt.
- Having defeated Cleopatra, Queen of Egypt, and the Roman politician Mark Anthony at the Battle of Actium in 31 BC, Octavian (later Augustus) becomes sole ruler of Rome and its possessions. He executes Cleopatra's son Caesarion (Ptolemy XV Caesar) and Antyllus, Antony's eldest son by his first wife Fulvia, to dispose of possible claimants to the Egyptian throne.

August 30 After their defeat by the triumvir Octavian at the Battle of Actium in 31 BC, Roman triumvir Mark Antony and his wife, Cleopatra VII of Egypt, commit suicide in Alexandria, Egypt. With Cleopatra's death the Ptolemaic dynasty in Egypt comes to an end and the country is annexed by Rome.

29 BC

- Juba II (son of King Juba I of the kingdom of Numidia in north Africa), having been brought up in Rome since Julius Caesar's triumph in 46 BC, is made king of Numidia by the consul Octavian and married to Cleopatra Selene, daughter of the Roman general Mark Antony and Queen Cleopatra of Egypt.
- Roman governor of Egypt, Cornelius Gallus, puts down a revolt and boasts of his feat in a trilingual inscription.

Cleopatra (69 BC–30 BC)

69 BC
- Cleopatra VII, queen of Egypt 51 BC–30 BC, is born.

51 BC
- Cleopatra and her brother Ptolemy XIII succeed to the Egyptian throne. On her accession Cleopatra travels to upper Egypt to escort the sacred bull, the manifestation of Apis, to its home.

48 BC
- Roman consul Julius Caesar, in pursuit of his rival Pompey the Great, becomes embroiled in Egypt's dynastic quarrel between Ptolemy XIII and his sister Cleopatra VII and espouses Cleopatra's cause. Her opponents blockade Caesar and Cleopatra in her palace in Alexandria over the winter.

47 BC
- Julius Caesar settles affairs in Egypt, restoring Cleopatra VII to her throne and defeating Ptolemy XIII.

41 BC
- The Roman triumvir Mark Antony crosses to his provinces in the East. At Tarsus in Cilicia he meets Cleopatra and succumbs to her carefully staged charms. He spends the winter of 40 BC in Egypt with her.

37 BC
- Cleopatra marries Mark Antony, who divorces his wife Octavia in 32 BC.

34 BC
- Mark Antony lapses into the life of an Eastern potentate with Cleopatra when he celebrates his triumph over the Armenian king Artavasdes in the style of Alexandria. In an episode known as the Donations of Alexandria, Mark Antony stages a pageant at which he and Cleopatra, dressed as the Egyptian gods Osiris and Isis, sit on golden thrones together with their children and Cleopatra's son Caesarion whom they declare to be the legitimate son of the Roman dictator Julius Caesar. They proclaim him king of kings, joint ruler of Egypt and Cyprus along with Cleopatra. Antony and Cleopatra's children are also named as future rulers of parts of the empire yet to be conquered. The declaration enrages the Roman triumvir Octavian, for he sees it as transferring Roman property into Greek hands.

32 BC
- Mark Antony and Cleopatra winter in Greece, making preparations for war against Octavian. Cleopatra finances an army of 90,000 men and 500 ships. The fleet moves to Actium in western Greece in preparation to attack Italy in the spring of 31 BC.

31 BC
- Cleopatra orders the execution of Artavasdes II, King of Armenia 53 BC–34 BC, who is captured by Mark Antony in 34 BC.
- September 2   Octavian's fleet of 400 ships under the general Marcus Vipsanius Agrippa blockades Mark Antony's Egyptian fleet at Actium in western Greece. In the ensuing Battle of Actium, Agrippa defeats Antony and Cleopatra and they flee back to Alexandria. Octavian follows them and Antony's troops desert him.

30 BC
- August 30   After their defeat by Octavian at the Battle of Actium, Mark Antony and Cleopatra commit suicide in Alexandria. With Cleopatra's death the Ptolemaic dynasty in Egypt comes to an end and the country is annexed by Rome. Octavian orders the execution of Caesarion (Ptolemy XV Caesar), the 17-year-old son of Julius Caesar and Cleopatra, to wipe out any dynastic claim to the throne.

- Roman triumvir Octavian returns to Rome after the Battle of Actium of 31 BC and his annexation of Egypt, and begins his period of political reform. He receives a triple triumph (victory procession) for his Dalmation campaign, Actium, and Egypt, and is hailed by the Senate and people as their saviour. He initiates a massive refurbishment of Rome. The public spaces of the city are rebuilt, and architecture and art are used to support the ideology of the new monarchy.

28 BC
- Roman consul Octavian purges the Senate, brings its numbers back to 600, and in theory, though not in practice, restores it to its republican power. He also orders a full census.

27 BC
- Augustus, effectively the first Roman emperor, begins to create a civil service for both domestic and foreign affairs and to regularize the taxation of the provinces. Each new province is subjected to a census to assess its tax potential. He visits Gaul and then Spain, leaving his general Marcus Vipsanius Agrippa in charge at Rome.
- Roman emperor Augustus begins reducing the army from 60 legions to no more than 28 legions, a process completed around 13 BC, settling over 100,000 veterans in 28 new colonies in Italy or such ancient and dilapidated cities as Carthage, north Africa. He also resumes control of the issue of coinage and contributes large sums from his private fortune to the public treasury.
- January 16   The Roman Senate, in gratitude, bestows on the Roman consul Octavian the name of *Augustus*. Augustus remains *Imperator* ('emperor', or head of the army), and invents for himself the new title of *Princeps* ('first citizen'). His authority as an elder statesman gradually hardens into imperial power. The Senate also gives him provincial *imperium* for ten years over a large province consisting of Spain, Gaul, Syria, and Egypt. The other provinces are given back to the Senate for administration.

26 BC

- Roman governor Cornelius Gallus is removed from the prefecture of Egypt after erecting statues to himself rather than to the Roman emperor Augustus. He commits suicide, and is succeeded by Aelius Gallus.

26 BC–19 BC

- Spain suffers a period of bitter warfare as the Cantabrians prove themselves brave and fierce enemies of Rome. The Roman emperor Augustus travels to Spain from Gaul and begins the difficult task of pacification, which is later finished by his general Marcus Agrippa.

25 BC

- An embassy sails to Rome from Broach in northwest India, starting in 25 BC but not arriving until about 21 BC. Presents include snakes, tortoises, pheasants, tigers, and a monk, and an armless boy who can shoot arrows with his toes.
- King Juba II of Numidia, North Africa, is transferred to the throne of the client Roman kingdom Mauritania.
- Roman emperor Augustus continues a firm policy against Parthia without becoming involved, holding on to Armenia and annexing Galatia.
- The Roman emperor Augustus arranges the marriage of his daughter Julia, aged 14, to his nephew and adopted son, Marcus Claudius Marcellus.

23 BC

- King Herod the Great of Judea sends two of his sons, Alexander and Aristobulus, to Rome to be educated in the household of the historian C. Asinius Pollio.
- Marcus Claudius Marcellus, the nephew and adopted son of the Roman emperor, Augustus, dies. His widow, Julia, Augustus' daughter, is married to the general Marcus Agrippa.
- Roman emperor Augustus gives up the consulship, which he has held annually since 31 BC. Instead, the Senate gives him a special power over all provincial governors, and the powers of the tribunate, which together give him effective power over all aspects of government.

22 BC–19 BC

- Roman emperor Augustus travels in Greece and Asia Minor. His general Marcus Vipsanius Agrippa visits Gaul and Spain and undertakes to complete the pacification of Spain.

20 BC

- Tasciovanus, King of the Catuvellauni in Britain, moves his capital from the fortress of Cassivellaunus (probably his grandfather) at modern Wheathampstead, Hertfordshire, to unfortified Verulamium, near modern St. Albans, Hertfordshire. His people are now thriving.
- The Roman emperor Augustus orders his stepson Tiberius to advance through Armenia and to meet him on the borders of Parthia. King Phraates IV of Parthia decides not to fight the Romans and negotiates instead. Augustus secures the recovery from the Parthians of the Roman standards lost at the Battle of Carrhae in 53 BC and those prisoners still alive. In Armenia, King Artaxes is murdered and Tiberius crowns Tigranes as a Roman client king.

19 BC

- Roman emperor Augustus returns to Rome and the day is made an annual holiday. The Roman general Marcus Agrippa completes the war of pacification in Spain.

18 BC

- A *Lex Julia* (Roman law) uses financial rewards for large families to encourage procreation within the family in an attempt to reinvigorate the Roman aristocracy, which has been decreasing in numbers.
- King Herod the Great of Judea, styling himself 'Friend of the Romans', pays a state visit to the Roman emperor Augustus.
- The *imperium* of the Roman emperor Augustus is renewed for five years, as is that of his general Marcus Vipsanius Agrippa, who is also made a tribune (magistrate), a position he shares with Augustus only.

17 BC

c. 17 BC King Herod the Great of Judea's sons, Alexander and Aristobulus, return to their father's court after receiving an education in Rome in the home of the historian C. Asinius Pollio.

- A second son, Lucius, is born to Julia (daughter of the Roman emperor, Augustus) and the co-regent Marcus Vipsanius Agrippa, three years after Gaius; Augustus, with an eye on the succession, adopts his two grandsons, giving them the title Caesar.

16 BC

- The Roman co-regent, Marcus Vipsanius Agrippa, is sent to the East with powers to prevent Parthian domination on the Bosporan shores of the Euxine (Black Sea). He settles affairs there to Roman advantage, receiving some slight help from King Herod the Great of Judea.
- Tiberius, the son of Livia and stepson of the Roman emperor Augustus, is made praetor, and his brother Drusus, quaestor, and their period of responsible and successful military command begins. Augustus leaves Rome again to quell trouble on the northern frontiers of the empire.

15 BC

- The Roman co-regent, Marcus Vipsanius Agrippa, shows appreciation of King Herod the Great of Judea's pro-Roman policy by visiting Jerusalem and sacrificing in the temple.

13 BC

- Marcus Vipsanius Agrippa, co-ruler of the Roman Empire (with Augustus) conducts war on the Balkan and Danubian boundaries, in Pannonia. He returns to Rome and dies there.
- Roman emperor Augustus returns to Rome after three years of campaigning in the northern parts of the Empire. He refuses to accept any other honour than the building of an Altar of Peace from the Senate, although they press him to allow them to grant him further honours. His *imperium* is again extended for five years.

12 BC

- Roman emperor Augustus is made Pontifex Maximus (head of the state religion), a title held by subsequent emperors until the Christian emperor Gratian refuses it in the 4th century AD.
- Tiberius, the stepson of the Roman emperor Augustus, successfully continues the Danubian War after the death of the co-regent, Marcus Vipsanius Agrippa. Tiberius'

brother, Drusus, warring against the German tribes, advances to the River Elbe.

11 BC

- On the death of the co-ruler of the Roman Empire (with Augustus) Marcus Vipsanius Agrippa, his widow Julia (daughter of the Roman emperor Augustus) is married to an unwilling Tiberius (Augustus' stepson), who has been made to divorce his beloved wife, Vipsania (Agrippa's daughter). Augustus is hereby positioning Tiberius to protect the Roman Empire for his grandsons, Gaius and Lucius, in case Augustus dies before they come of age.

10 BC

- King Phraates IV of Parthia, at peace with Rome, sends over his four legitimate sons to be brought up in Rome as a token of peace, and to stabilize his position as ruler.

9 BC

- Drusus, the younger stepson of the Roman emperor Augustus, successfully draws his German campaigns towards completion. He and his brother Tiberius are at last allowed the military title of *Imperator* by Augustus, but in the same year Drusus dies of a fall from his horse.
- Under its king Aretas IV, who comes to the throne this year, the kingdom of Nabataean Arabia reaches a peak of wealth and culture and prospers until the Roman emperor Trajan makes it a Roman province in the 2nd century AD. Its capital, Petra, on the caravan route from Aqaba to Gaza, is a Hellenistic city though its written language is a form of Aramaic.

8 BC

- The *imperium* of the Roman emperor Augustus is renewed for another ten year period and another census is taken.
- Tiberius, the stepson of the Roman emperor Augustus, is sent to finish his dead brother Drusus' German conquests.

7 BC

- King Herod the Great of Judea's sons Alexander and Aristobulus are murdered at the command of their father.
- Rome's local administration is put on a sound basis by its division into 14 regions.
- Tiberius, the stepson of the Roman emperor Augustus, is made consul in Rome for the second time.

6 BC

- Tiberius, the stepson of the Roman emperor Augustus, having successfully continued the German campaign started by his brother, Drusus, and twice held the consulship the previous year, is finally made a colleague of the aging Augustus with the grant of tribunician powers. However, he feels that Augustus' grandsons (and adopted sons), Gaius and Lucius Caesar, are being favored over him, and retires to Rhodes where he is to remain for seven years.

5 BC

- Roman emperor Augustus holds the consulship for the first time since 23 BC to introduce his grandson and adopted son Gaius Caesar to public life. Gaius is marked down for the consulship in five years' time.

4 BC

- A Roman legion keeps order in Jerusalem in Judea, and the policy of the Roman emperor Augustus of

weakening the kingdom of Herod the Great is continued. The kingdom is divided between Herod's three surviving sons: Herod Antipas succeeds to the tetrarchy of Galilee and Peraea, which he holds until AD 39; Archelaus gets Judea and Idumaea; and Philip receives the outlying parts in the northeast, which he rules for 37 years.

- King Herod the Great of Judea massacres Pharisees who have attempted to pull down the Roman eagle from the temple in Jerusalem and may also have instituted the biblical 'massacre of the innocents'. He dies in March.

2 BC

- *c.* 2 BC   King Phraates IV of Parthia is murdered by his wife Musa and their son, who takes the throne as Phraates V and marries his mother, ruling jointly with her.
- Julia, the daughter of the Roman emperor Augustus, left behind by Augustus' stepson Tiberius soon after his enforced marriage to her on his retirement to Rhodes, is accused of misconduct with many men (including the Roman triumvir Mark Antony's son), and is banished. Augustus introduces her younger son, Lucius Caesar, into man's estate and public responsibility, as he did for Lucius' brother Gaius in 5 BC.
- Roman emperor Augustus forms the Praetorian Guard, the imperial bodyguard within the city of Rome; minimum service is for 12 years.
- Under the law known as the *Lex Fufia Caninia*, the Roman emperor Augustus limits the rapid liberation of slaves by restricting the number that can be freed at a master's death.

1 BC

- Roman emperor Augustus refuses to let his stepson Tiberius return to Rome from Rhodes, where he retired in 6 BC. He sends his grandson Gaius Caesar to combat the influence of the Parthian king Phraates V in Armenia, which is in revolt against Roman rule. At the meeting of Gaius Caesar and the king, Rome recognizes Parthia as a power of some standing, and the Parthians recognize Armenia as being in the Roman sphere.

SCIENCE, TECHNOLOGY, AND MEDICINE

Agriculture

25 BC

- King Herod the Great provides corn for his people in Judea during a famine.

c. 1 BC

- The wheelbarrow is invented in China.

Ecology

31 BC

- A violent earthquake in the Jericho area probably causes the temporary abandonment of Qumran.

Early Tools (c. 2500 BC–1 BC)

c. 2500 BC
- Most mason's tools, including the plumbline, level, square, and mallet, have been developed.

c. 2000 BC
- The first seed drills are used in Egypt. Seeds are deposited into the plowed furrow by a funnel attached to the back of the plow.
- The shadoof, a hand-operated device for lifting water, is invented in Egypt and Mesopotamia. It consists of a long pole on a pivot with a bucket suspended from one end and a counterweight at the other. It is still in use in Egypt and India.

c. 1700 BC
- The doors in the palace of Khorsabad in Nineveh, Assyria, are sealed with a device consisting of a pin-tumbler, a large wooden bolt pierced by several holes, and several wooden pins positioned to drop into these holes and grip the bolt—the first lock.
- Windmills are used in Babylon to pump water for irrigation.

c. 1500 BC
- The Egyptians use saws to cut planks used in ship construction and manufacture the first files, made of bronze.

c. 1450 BC
- A balance with a pointer indicating the weight is developed in Egypt.

c. 1400 BC
- The clepsydra (water clock), consisting of a vessel with a hole in the base and lines on the inside to indicate the passage of time, begins to be used in Egypt. It has the advantage over the sundial in that it can be used to tell the time at night. It may already have been in use in Babylon.

c. 1100 BC
- Rotary querns (hand mills), in which a handle is used to rotate one stone placed on top of a stationary one, are developed in Greece and replace saddle querns. They are the precursors to water mills.
- The spinning wheel is invented in China, derived from the machines used to draw out silk from the silkworm. It subsequently spreads to India and reaches Europe in about the 13th century AD.

c. 700 BC
- The Greeks invent the fibula (safety-pin), although the idea is lost after the fall of the Roman Empire.

c. 650 BC
- The Romans develop iron saws, enabling them to saw stone.

c. 400 BC
- The iron is invented in China for pressing clothes; it is heated by filling it with glowing embers.

c. 375 BC
- Greek scientist Archytas of Tarentum invents the screw.

c. 310 BC
- The Chinese invent double-acting bellows that produce a continuous stream of air. They are used for smelting metal.

c. 300 BC
- The Romans invent the hypocaust. Developed from the Spartan heating system, hot air from underground fires is funnelled through pipes in the walls and under floors to heat public baths and most private houses.

c. 270 BC
- Greek physicist and inventor Ctesibius of Alexandria lays the foundations for the development of modern pumps with his invention of a small pipe organ, the hydraulis, which is supplied with air by a piston pump.

c. 250 BC
- Greek mathematician and inventor Archimedes invents the Archimedes screw for removing water from the hold of a large ship.

c. 200 BC
- Indians in Peru and Ecuador develop cylindrical clay furnaces to melt gold and silver. They use a blowpipe instead of bellows to increase the temperature.
- The Romans introduce the iron-tipped plowshare used to cultivate harder ground.

c. 200 BC–c. 100 BC
- The screw press is invented in Greece and is used for pressing clothes.

25 BC
- The Roman architect Vitruvius describes a platform that uses pulleys and windlasses, operated by human, animal, or water power, to lift loads—the first elevator.

c. 1 BC
- The wheelbarrow is invented in China.

Health and Medicine

c. 50 BC
- The Indian physician Susruta writes *Susruta-samhita/Suśruta's Compendium*, a treatise on Indian medical practice.

49 BC
- The Indian physician Susruta treats intestinal perforations and obstructions by cutting into the abdomen and joining the damaged part of the intestine using the heads of giant black ants as sutures.

c. 45 BC
- Caesar encourages physicians and men of science to settle in Rome, and starts large engineering projects, including the draining of the Pontine Marshes, an essential public health project.

Science

46 BC
- The Roman consul and dictator Julius Caesar instructs Alexandrian astronomer Sosigenes to bring the Roman

Republican calendar into line with the solar year. He creates the Julian calendar in which the year is 365 ¼ days long and begins on January 1. An extra day is inserted between February 23 and February 24 every four years. The year 46 BC is 445 days long to bring it into line with the solar year.

c. 12 BC

- A geographical commentary written by the Roman co-ruler (with Augustus) Marcus Vipsanius Agrippa, based on surveys of Rome's military roads, is used to produce a map of the world. After his death it is engraved on marble and displayed in Rome at Augustus' command. The map, and the commentary it is based on, later influences the work of the geographers Strabo and Pliny the Elder.

9 BC

- The first calliper rule for measuring the thickness of objects is made by an anonymous Chinese inventor who inscribes the date of manufacture on it.

Technology

36 BC

- The Roman engineer Marcus Vipsanius Agrippa invents the *harpago*, a grapnel shot by catapult; it proves invaluable in the naval defeat of Sextus Pompeius.

31 BC

- The liburnium, a light fast warship, is used by Marcus Vipsanius Agrippa in the Battle of Actium; it becomes the dominant Roman warship.

25 BC

- The Roman architect Marcus Vitruvius Pollio describes a platform that uses pulleys and windlasses, operated by human, animal, or water power, to lift loads—the first lift.

c. 15 BC

- The Chinese develop the belt drive.

Transportation

45 BC

- Traffic congestion in Rome forces Julius Caesar to prohibit the use of wagons in the built-up area of Rome during the day.

36 BC

- The Via Flaminia is tunneled through the Furlo Pass.

c. 35 BC

- The Posilipo bridge between Naples and Puteoli is built; the longest road bridge in the ancient world, it is 6 km/3.7 mi long.

c. 25 BC

- The first suspension bridge is built across the San-Ch'ih-pan Gorge in the Himalayas; made of bamboo it spans 15 m/49 ft.

18 BC

- The Roman general Marcus Vipsanius Agrippa has roads built radiating from Lugdunum (Lyon), the capital of Gaul, and roads are built in all the newly acquired Roman

provinces. The system of *cursus publicus*, using posting stations for official couriers, begins.

12 BC–9 BC

- The Roman commander Drusus Germanicus builds the Fossa Drusiana canal which links the Rhine to the North Sea.

ARTS AND IDEAS

Architecture

50 BC

- Lake villages are built in Britain, such as those at Meare and Glastonbury in Somerset. They are made with elaborate sunken foundations, and the risk of fire is diminished by the use of clay fireplaces. These lake dwellings are sometimes called crannochs, after their Irish equivalents which are used into medieval times.

42 BC

- During the Battle of Philippi in Macedonia, the Roman triumvir Octavian vows to build a temple in Rome to Mars Ultor (the 'avenger') in honour of the assassinated dictator Julius Caesar. It is finally built in 2 BC.

c. 36 BC

- Roman engineer Marcus Vipsanius Agrippa constructs a harbour at Puteoli.

33 BC

- Roman engineer Marcus Vispanius Agrippa builds the Julia aqueduct for Rome; he also repairs Rome's four other aqueducts.

29 BC

- The temple of Divus Julius (the deified Julius Caesar) is completed in the Roman Forum.

28 BC

- A large park adjacent to Octavian's mausoleum is opened to the public. The huge mausoleum, built in 29 BC in the Campus Martius in Rome, symbolizes the place of the ruler's family within the Roman Empire.
- Roman emperor Octavian dedicates the temple of Apollo on the Palatine Hill in Rome.

27 BC

- Roman architect Marcus Vitruvius Pollio writes *De architectura/On Architecture*, a treatise on architecture divided into 10 books dealing with city planning, building materials, and architecture in general. He also emphasizes that architects should have a good knowledge of drawing and discusses the procedures and practices to be followed in making drawings, thus writing the first textbook on engineering drafting.
- Roman general and engineer Marcus Vipsanius Agrippa builds the Pantheon (temple dedicated to all the gods) in Rome to commemorate the victory over the Roman general Mark Antony at Actium by the Roman emperor Octavian (now Augustus).

22 BC–10 BC

- King Herod the Great of Judea rebuilds the ancient Phoenician city of Caesarea, Syria, constructing an artificial harbour there. Both are named after Augustus, who responds with a donation of 500 talents.

19 BC

- King Herod the Great of Judea begins the restoration of the temple in Jerusalem. To preserve religious purity the rebuilding is overseen by priests. However, Herod has a Roman eagle placed over the door, which causes a riot.
- Roman engineer Marcus Vipsanius Agrippa begins construction of the aqueduct known today as the Pont du Gard, near Remoulins, Gaul. He also completes the Aqua Virgo aqueduct, built in Rome to supply the great public baths. It is still in operation and feeds the Trevi Fountain.

13 BC

- Work begins on the Altar of Peace on the Campus Martius, outside the city walls of Rome. Its surrounding walls are covered with reliefs carrying religious and political images linked to the regime of the Roman emperor Augustus.

12 BC

- A temple is dedicated to Vesta, goddess of the hearth, on the Palatine Hill in Rome.

9 BC

- The Altar of Peace in the Campus Martius of Rome is dedicated.

8 BC

- An aqueduct (today known as the Pont du Gard) near Remoulins, Gaul, begun in 19 BC by Roman engineer Marcus Vipsanius Agrippa, is completed. It consists of three tiers of arches, rises 49 m/160 ft above the valley and supplies water to the city of Nemausus (Nîmes).

7 BC

- Roman consul Tiberius and his mother Livia erect a public building in Rome, the *Porticus Liviae*, on the site of the luxurious mansion of Vedius Pollio, a wealthy equestrian (member of an aristocratic order second only to senators).

2 BC

- Roman emperor Augustus builds the Aqua Alsietina aqueduct to bring water from the Alsietinian Lake,

32 km/20 mi away, to the Naumachia – a huge (366 m/1,200 ft by 549 m/1,800 ft) basin across the Tiber designed to stage mock sea battles.

- The temple of Mars Ultor (the "avenger") and the Forum Augustum in which it stands are dedicated in Rome.

Arts

c. **50 BC**

- The *Laocoön* group is created by three sculptors in Rhodes. It depicts the Trojan priest Laocoön and his sons being devoured by serpents. Rediscovered in 1516, it is now in the Vatican, Rome, Italy.
- The "Italian black-and-white" style of mosaic begins to dominate Roman floor decoration.
- A seated figure of Buddha, showing a Hellenistic influence, is sculpted in the Gandhara region (in modern Pakistan).

45 BC

- The Roman dictator and consul Julius Caesar rededicates the fallen statue of the Roman politician Pompey in Rome.

c. **15 BC**

- The "Third Style" of Italian wall painting, in which walls are divided into large blocks of color, which emphasizes their flatness, incorporating fine, elaborate, and slightly surreal painting, becomes popular. The style continues until around AD 50 when it is replaced by the "Fourth Style".

2 BC

- A statue of a *quadriga* (four-horse chariot) is erected in Rome in honor of the Roman emperor Augustus, to mark the completion of his Forum in Rome.

Literature and Language

50 BC

- The Roman proconsul Julius Caesar publishes his *De bello gallico/The Gallic War*, written in 52 BC, which is

BIRTHS & DEATHS

50 BC

- Hortensius, Roman orator and politician, dies (*c.* 64).
- Juba II, King of Numidia 29 BC–25 BC and of Mauritania 25 BC–AD 24, born (–*c.* AD 24).

48 BC

September 28 Pompey, Roman general and statesman, is killed in Pelusium, Egypt (57).

47 BC

June Caesarion (Ptolemy XV Caesar), King of Egypt 44 BC–30 BC, son of Julius Caesar and Cleopatra VII of Egypt, born (–30).

46 BC

- Juba (or Iuba) I, King of Numidia, ally of Pompey against Julius Caesar, commits suicide (*c.* 39).
- Marcius Porcius Cato the Younger, Roman tribune (magistrate), great-grandson of Cato the Elder, who tried to defend the Roman Republic against Julius Caesar, commits suicide in Utica, North Africa (*c.* 49).

45 BC

- Wang Mang, "Usurper," emperor of China AD 6–AD 25, founder of the Hsin dynasty, born in China (–AD 25).

44 BC

March 15 (Gaius) Julius Caesar, Roman general, dictator, and statesman, conqueror of Transalpine Gaul, is assassinated in Rome (*c.* 56).

43 BC

March 20 Ovid, Roman poet known for his poem "Ars amatoria"/"Art of Love," born in Sulmo, Roman Empire (–AD 18).

December 7 Marcus Tullius Cicero, Roman statesman, lawyer, scholar, orator, and writer, whose major works include *De republica/On the Republic*, is executed in Formia, Italy (*c.* 63).

42 BC

- Gaius Cassius Longinus, initiator of the conspiracy to assassinate Julius Caesar (44 BC), dies near Philippi, Macedonia.
- Marcus Claudius Marcellus, nephew of the emperor Augustus, born (–23 BC).
- Marcus Junius Brutus, governor of Cisalpine Gaul, a leader of the conspirators who assassinated Julius Caesar (March 44 BC), commits suicide after losing the Battle of Philippi to Antony and Octavian (later Augustus) (c. 43).

November 16 Tiberius, second Roman emperor AD 14–AD 37, born (–AD 37).

40 BC

- Fulvia, wife of Mark Antony, who participated in the struggle for power in Rome after Julius Caesar's death, dies in Sicyon, Greece.

39 BC

- Quintus Labienus, Roman commander who supported the assassins of Julius Caesar and later joined the Parthians against Rome, is killed in Asia Minor.

38 BC

- Nero Claudius Drusus Germanicus, younger brother of the emperor Tiberius, Roman general who led successful campaigns against the German tribes, born (–9 BC).

c. 34 BC

- Sallust, Roman historian noted for his narrative style, dies (c. 52).

32 BC

- Titus Pomponius Atticus, Roman man of letters and friend of Cicero, dies (c. 77).

31 BC

- Artavasdes II, King of Armenia 53 BC–34 BC, captured by Mark Antony in 34 BC, is executed in Alexandria by Queen Cleopatra VII of Egypt.

30 BC

- Caesarion (Ptolemy XV Caesar), King of Egypt 44 BC–30 BC, son of Julius Caesar and Cleopatra VII of Egypt, executed on the orders of Octavian in Alexandria, Egypt (17).
- John Hyrcanus II, high priest and co-ruler of Judea 76 BC–40 BC with his brother Aristobulus II, in whose reign Judea became a Roman vassal state, dies in Jerusalem.

August 30 Cleopatra VII, Queen of Egypt 51 BC–30 BC, lover and ally of Mark Antony, commits suicide in Alexandria, Egypt (c. 39).

August 30 Mark Antony, Roman general under Julius Caesar and later triumvir 43 BC–32 BC, ally and husband of Cleopatra, Queen of Egypt, commits suicide in Alexandria, Egypt (53).

27 BC

- Marcus Terentius Varro, Roman patriotic satirist, author of *Saturae Menippeae/Menippean Satires*, dies (c. 89).

23 BC

- Marcus Claudius Marcellus, nephew of the emperor Augustus, dies in Baia, Italy (c. 19).

21 BC

- Herod Antipas, son of Herod I the Great, Tetrarch of Galilee 4 BC–AD 39, who executed John the Baptist, born (–AD 39).

c. 20 BC

- Gaius Caesar, Roman proconsul, grandson of the Roman emperor Augustus, born (–AD 4).

19 BC

- Albius Tibullus, Roman poet, dies (c. 36).

September 21 Virgil, Roman poet, author of the *Aeneid*, dies in Brundisium (50).

18 BC

c. 18 BC Hermann ("Arminius" to the Romans), tribal leader of the Teutonic Cherusci, who defeated Publius Quinctilius Varus in the Teutoburg Forest (AD 9), born (–AD 19).

- Agrippina the Elder, granddaughter of Augustus and mother of Caligula, born in Rome (–AD 33).

17 BC

- Lucius Caesar, grandson and adopted heir of the Roman emperor Augustus, born (–AD 2).

c. 16 BC

- Propertius Sextus, Roman elegiac poet, author of "Cynthia," dies in Rome (?).

15 BC

c. 15 BC Marcus Vitruvius Pollio, Roman architect and engineer, author of *De architectura/On Architecture*, a handbook dealing with city planning, construction materials, and architecture in general, dies.

c. 15 BC Philo of Alexandria, Greek-speaking Jewish philosopher who wrote about the development of Judaism and the diaspora, born in Alexandria (c. AD 45).

- Germanicus Caesar, nephew and adopted son of the Roman emperor Tiberius, a successful and popular general and father of the Roman emperor Caligula, born (–AD 19).

13 BC

- Marcus Aemilius Lepidus, Roman statesman, one of the triumvirs who ruled Rome after 43 BC, dies.

12 BC

- Marcus Vipsanius Agrippa, co-ruler of the Roman Empire with Augustus, dies in Campania, Italy (c. 51).

11 BC

- Octavia, sister of Augustus (Octavian) and wife of Mark Antony, dies in Rome (c. 58).

10 BC

- Herod Agrippa I (original name Marcus Julius Agrippa), King of Judea AD 37–AD 44, grandson of Herod the Great, born (–AD 44).

August 1 Claudius (Tiberius Claudius Caesar Augustus Germanicus), Roman emperor AD 41–AD 54, born in Lugdunum, Gaul (now Lyon, France) (–AD 54).

9 BC

- Nero Claudius Drusus Germanicus, younger brother of the emperor Tiberius, Roman general who led successful campaigns against the German tribes, dies (c. 29).

8 BC

- Gaius Maecenas, Roman diplomat, adviser to Augustus, and patron of Virgil and Horace, dies (c. 62).

November 27 Horace (Quintus Horatius Flaccus), celebrated Roman lyric poet and satirist, dies (56).

6 BC

- Jesus Christ, Jewish religious teacher, may have been born, although 4 BC is the more probable date (–AD 30).

4 BC

- Jesus Christ, Jewish religious teacher, probably born this year, although 6 BC is another possible date (–AD 30).
- Seneca, Roman philosopher, orator, tragedian, and virtual ruler of Rome AD 54–AD 62, born in Córdoba, Spain (–AD 65).

March Herod the Great, King of Judea under the Romans 37 BC–4 BC, dies in Jericho, Judea (c. 69).

3 BC

December 24 (Servius) Galba, Roman emperor AD 68–AD 69, born (–AD 69).

written in a very straightforward style and has instant appeal to Romans. It increases Caesar's popularity in Rome.

49 BC–44 BC

- Roman ruler Julius Caesar writes his *Bellum civile/The Civil War*, justifying his actions in the civil war. The work survives to modern times, together with three continuations, *Bellum Alexandrium/Alexandrian War*, *Bellum Africanum/African War*, and *Bellum Hispaniense/Spanish War*.

44 BC

- Roman soldier and historian Aulus Hirtius writes the eighth and last book of *De bello gallico/The Gallic War* following the death of the Roman ruler Julius Caesar. Hirtius is killed the following year fighting against Mark Antony.

c. 39 BC

- Roman poet Virgil writes his pastoral poems, the *Eclogues*.

37 BC

c. 37 BC   Roman poet Horace writes his *Satires* and *Epodes* over the next few years.

- Roman scholar Marcus Terentius Varro publishes *De re rustica/On Rural Matters*, a treatise on farming. Of his huge literary output the only other work of which any substantial part remains is *De lingua Latina/On the Latin Language*.

34 BC

- Latin biographer Cornelius Nepos publishes the first edition of his *De viris illustribus/On Famous Men*. Some of his work survives to modern times, including biographies of the Roman statesman Cato and the Roman literary patron Atticus.

30 BC

- The period following the Battle of Actium (in which the Roman leader Octavian defeats the fleets of Queen Cleopatra of Egypt and the Roman general Mark Antony) sees an upsurge of Latin literature. Much of this work, especially poetry, is enmeshed in the politics of the new Octavian regime. Octavian's friend, the Roman statesman Gaius Maecenas, is patron to many writers, for example Horace, Virgil, and Propertius.

29 BC

- Roman poet Virgil writes his *Georgics*, four books of poetry on farming.

27 BC

- Roman poet Virgil begins composition of the *Aeneid*, a Latin epic poem that describes Aeneas' escape from Troy, his wanderings in the Mediterranean, and his arrival in Italy. The Aeneid reflects the culture and aspirations of Augustus' Rome.

23 BC

- Roman poet Horace publishes the first three books of his *Odes*.

19 BC

- Latin poet Tibullus dies. Those of his elegies which survive to modern times were probably written in the period 27 BC–25 BC.
- Roman poet Virgil and the Roman emperor Augustus meet in Athens, Greece. Virgil, who is on his way to the East to revise his epic poem the *Aeneid*, changes his mind and decides to return to Rome with Augustus.
- September 20   Roman poet Virgil dies at Brundisium, Italy, leaving his *Aeneid* unfinished. When published posthumously, the poem elevates Virgil to the status of a Latin Homer.

17 BC

- *Carmen saeculare/Song of the Age*, by the Roman poet Horace, is sung at the Secular Games (considered to mark the beginning of an era or *saeculum*) by a choir of traditional size (27 boys and 27 girls). It celebrates Augustus' reign as a second Golden Age.

16 BC

- Roman poet Ovid publishes the second edition of his *Amores/Loves*, following it with his *Heroides/Heroines*.

13 BC

- Roman poet Horace completes book IV of his *Odes*, a eulogy of the Augustan epoch which celebrates the military fame of the Roman general Tiberius and his associate the quaestor Drusus.

c. 10 BC

- Sulpicia, the daughter of a Roman consul, writes six poems recording her affair with a young man. They are preserved with the poems of Tibullus.

1 BC

- Latin poet Ovid writes his *Ars amatoria/Art of Love*, a poetic manual of seduction, and *Remedies for Love*, a guide to ending an affair.

Theater and Dance

11 BC

- Roman emperor Augustus dedicates the theatre of Marcellus in Rome.

Thought and Scholarship

48 BC

- Latin scholar Marcus Terentius Varro is pardoned by the Roman ruler Julius Caesar for having fought against him at Pharsalus, Greece, and is employed as a librarian.

48 BC–44 BC

- Roman orator and writer Marcus Tullius Cicero writes philosophical works, including *Tusculan Disputations*, *De natura deorum/On the Nature of Deities*, and *De divinatione/On Divination*.

47 BC

- The library at Alexandria, Egypt, is partially destroyed.

42 BC

- Roman historian and statesman Gaius Sallustius Crispus begins his history, *The Catilinarian War*, which he follows with his *Jugurthine War*. Both these monographs survive to modern times, but only fragments of his last and longest work, *Histories*, survive.

30 BC

- Greek critic and historian Dionysius of Halicarnassus arrives in Rome and begins his *Roman Antiquities*, a history of Rome from mythical times to the start of the

First Punic War, of which only the first 11 books survive to modern times. He also writes literary criticism.

- Sicilian historian Diodorus Siculus completes his *Library of Universal History*, a Greek prose history. Of the original 40 books, 15 survive to modern times.

29 BC

- Roman historian Livy begins his huge history of Rome *Ab urbe condita/From the Founding of the City*. He continues to work on this throughout the reign of the emperor Augustus. Of an original 142 books only 35 survive to modern times.

20 BC

- Greek geographer Strabo writes his *Historical Sketches*. Though they do not survive to modern times, they are believed to be a continuation of the work of the Greek historian Polybius.

14 BC

- The versatile Greek author Nicolaus of Damascus becomes an adviser of King Herod the Great of Judea. Parts of his *Life of Augustus* survive to modern times.

7 BC

- Greek critic and historian Dionysius of Halicarnassus publishes the first part of his *Roman Antiquities*.

6 BC

- The future Roman emperor Tiberius attends intellectual lectures in Rhodes, possibly including those given by his old tutor Theodorus of Gadara.

SOCIETY

Everyday Life

31 BC

- Magnificent gold torques (typical Celtic ornaments) are buried at Snettisham in Norfolk, England, together with coins of the Atrebates tribe, a Belgic tribe of southeastern England. This demonstrates the increased use of coins in Britain at the time.

25 BC

c. 25 BC In Book V of the Latin epic poem the *Aeneid*, Virgil (Publius Vergilius Maro) describes a ship race in his account of the funeral games in Latium organized by Aeneas in honour of his father.

- The doors of the Temple of Janus in Rome are closed for the first time since 235 BC, signifying that peace reigns.

21 BC

- Roman emperor Augustus organizes a fire brigade, the *vigiles*, consisting of 600 slaves, after a fire, inspired by a fire service organized by the aedile Marcus Egnatius Rufus in *c.* 26 BC.

15 BC

- Vedius Pollio, a wealthy equestrian (member of an aristocratic order second only to senators) leaves much of his vast property to the Roman emperor Augustus. He achieved notoriety by feeding his pet fish on human flesh, throwing slaves to them as a punishment.

7 BC

- The population of the world is around 250 million.

Religion

50 BC

- A frieze is painted in what becomes known as the 'Villa of Mysteries' in Pompeii, depicting the Dionysiac Mysteries, the rites associated with the worship of Dionysus, Greek god of wine.

44 BC

July A comet coincides with games held in honor of the Roman ruler Julius Caesar, murdered in March, and its appearance is taken as proof of his divinity.

43 BC

- During a time of great religious and superstitious emotion among the plebeians of Rome, a civic temple to Isis, the Egyptian goddess of fertility, is commissioned. It is probably never built.

23 BC

- The practice of deifying living emperors (the 'imperial cult') begins with the worship of *Augustus et Roma* (Augustus and Rome).

Sports

27 BC

- Roman emperor Augustus inaugurates the Actian Games in Greece to celebrate his victory over Mark Antony and Cleopatra in the Battle of Actium of 31 BC.

17 BC

- The Secular Games (considered to mark the beginning of a new era or *saeculum*) are celebrated in Rome. The Sibylline Books are recopied and old religious customs are revived.

AD **1**–AD **49**

POLITICS, GOVERNMENT, AND ECONOMICS

Colonization

2
- Rome puts a Median king on the Armenian throne. The Roman commander Gaius Caesar, grandson and heir of the emperor Augustus, is seriously wounded while attempting to suppress an uprising.

6
- Judea is made a Roman province under Quirinius, governor of Syria, and a Roman census is taken.

17
- Cappadocia and Commagene (north Syria) are annexed to the Roman Empire.

42
- Mauritania is made a Roman province.

47
- The new Roman governor in Britain, Ostorius Scapula, establishes a frontier from the Severn to the Humber, and disarms the tribes in the Roman area. The Iceni of East Anglia revolt and are allowed to remain independent.

48
- Chinese emperor Guang Wudi reconquers Inner Mongolia, which revolted during the civil wars of 18–25.

Human Rights

39
- Sisters Trung Trac (who was raped by Chinese soldiers) and Trung Nhi lead the Vietnamese kingdom of Rinan in revolt against Chinese domination.

42
- The Vietnamese sisters Trung Trac and Trung Nhi drown themselves to prevent their capture after the Chinese defeat of the rebellion they have led.

Politics and Government

3
- Tiberius, stepson and son-in-law of the emperor Augustus, in self-imposed exile on the island of Rhodes, is called back to Rome by Augustus.

4
- The Roman general Tiberius, stepson, son-in-law, and heir to the emperor Augustus, resumes his military career, winning victories in Germany.
- The Roman law *Lex Aelia Sentia* is passed, further restricting the manumission (emancipation) of slaves. It also establishes the registration of births.

5
- Cunobelinus (Cymbeline) becomes chief of the Catuvellauni in Britain. He conquers the territory of the Trinovantes and moves his capital to Camulodunum (Colchester).
- Roman forces under Tiberius, adopted son and heir of Augustus, reach the River Elbe and prepare to surround the army of Maroboduus, leader of the German Marcomanni tribe, in Bohemia.

6
- Maroboduus, the German leader of the Marcomanni, escapes Roman domination because of a revolt in Pannonia and Dalmatia. After a period of hostility the Romans recognize his kingdom.

6–9 The Parthian empire is affected by internal political and social upheavals.

7–12
- Germanicus, nephew and adopted son of Tiberius, heir to the Roman Empire, conducts campaigns under his uncle in Illyricum and Germany.

9
- German forces under Arminius, chief of the Cherusci people, ambush three Roman legions (17th, 18th, and 19th) under Quintilius Varus in the Teutoburger Forest. The legions are wiped out and Varus commits suicide.
- The Roman law *Lex Papia Poppaea* completes the *Leges Juliae/Julian Laws*, imposing penalties for celibacy and childlessness in an effort to increase the Roman population.

January 10 The chief minister Wang Mang usurps the throne in China and undertakes social and economic reforms.

10
- A Roman military expedition under Germanicus, nephew and adopted son of Tiberius, heir to the Roman Empire, is sent against the German chief Arminius; a series of inconclusive battles follows.

11
- The accession of Artabanus III as king of Parthia prompts widespread unrest; several rival candidates emerge for the throne of the neighboring kingdom of Armenia.
- The Bosporan kingdom (modern Crimea and southern Ukraine) is taken over by a Sarmatian king who is loyal to Rome.

12

- Tiberius, heir to the Roman Empire, returns in triumph to Rome, leaving his nephew Germanicus to continue the protracted war against the Germans.

13

- Tiberius, adopted son and heir to the emperor Augustus, is granted equal powers to Augustus.

14

- Germanicus, heir to the Roman emperor Tiberius, wages successful wars against the Germans but fails to subdue the German chief Arminius.
- Herod Antipas, Tetrarch of Galilee, marries his half brother's wife, Herodias.
- Sejanus is appointed prefect (head) of the Roman Praetorian Guard by the emperor Tiberius. The emperor, continuing Augustus' policy of cooperation with the Senate, makes the Senate the sole electoral body, leaving the people without any direct voice.
- The Roman legions on the Rhine revolt when they learn of the emperor Augustus' death, but are pacified by Germanicus, adopted son and heir of the new emperor Tiberius. Those in Pannonia do likewise and are pacified by Drusus the Younger, Tiberius' son.

September 14   When Emperor Augustus dies, his widow Livia becomes priestess of his cult. Her political machinations enable her first son, not the son of Augustus, to succeed him as the emperor Tiberius.

September 17   Tiberius formally succeeds his adoptive father Augustus as Roman emperor.

15

- A consulship is given to Drusus the Younger, son of the Roman emperor Tiberius.

17

- Germanicus, adopted son and heir of the Roman emperor Tiberius, is given special powers over all the governors of the eastern Roman provinces and installs Artaxias as sovereign of Armenia. Tiberius appoints Gnaeus Piso governor of Syria as a counterbalance to Germanicus.
- Tacfarinas, a Numidian chieftain serving as a Roman auxiliary, deserts and stirs up a serious insurrection in the Roman province of Africa.
- The Roman emperor Tiberius recalls his nephew and heir Germanicus from the wars in Germany. There is no serious trouble from Germany for the next 50 years.

18

- Herod Antipas, the son of Herod the Great, founds the city of Tiberias on the Sea of Galilee, in Roman Palestine.

18–27   Peasant revolts break out in China and civil war begins. The usurping emperor Wang Mang is defeated in 22, but the civil wars continue.

19

- After the German hero Arminius is killed by his own people, the German leader Maroboduus is expelled. He seeks refuge in Italy and is interned in Ravenna.
- The Roman emperor Tiberius expels all Jews from Italy. Many of the strongest are sent to Sardinia as a police force.

c. 19–c. 45   Gondopharnes becomes king of the Sakas in India. Under him, the Sakas reach the height of their power.

20

- Gnaeus Piso, governor of Syria, returns to Rome where his alleged poisoning of Germanicus, adopted son and heir of the Roman emperor Tiberius, is investigated by the Senate; he commits suicide before a verdict is reached. Germanicus' widow, Agrippina, suspects Tiberius of having engineered her husband's death.

21

- A revolt breaks out against Roman rule in Gaul, and is suppressed.
- The prefect Sejanus concentrates the strength of the Roman Praetorian Guard by billeting them in one large barracks just outside Rome.
- The Roman emperor Tiberius begins to groom his son Drusus the Younger for office, making him joint consul.
- The Roman emperor Tiberius interprets the Roman laws known as the *Leges Juliae/Julian Laws* with restraint, ruling that accusations against him as a private person will not count as treason.

22

- Drusus the Younger, son of the Roman emperor Tiberius, is given the power of a tribune (magistrate).

23

- Drusus the Younger, son and heir of the Roman emperor Tiberius, and an effective military commander, dies. Sejanus, commander of the Praetorian Guard, is suspected of poisoning him.

25

- In China's civil war, one of the Han claimants to the throne is proclaimed Emperor Guang Wudi, founding the later Han Dynasty. He finally brings an end to the peasant revolts in 27.
- Sejanus, commander of the Roman Praetorian Guard, urges the Roman emperor Tiberius to retire.

26

- Pontius Pilate is appointed Roman prefect (governor) of Judea, Palestine, by the Roman emperor Tiberius.

27

- The Roman emperor Tiberius retires to Capri, where he spends the last decade of his life. He is saved from a landslide by Sejanus, commander of the Praetorian Guard. Sejanus becomes all-powerful.

29

- At the instigation of Sejanus, commander of the Praetorian Guard, the Roman emperor Tiberius banishes Agrippina the Elder, Germanicus' widow, to the Italian island of Pandateria. Her son Gaius (Caligula) is allowed to remain in Rome with his grandmother Livia, Augustus' widow.

30

- This is the most probable year of the death of the Jewish religious teacher Jesus Christ. On the 14th day of the Jewish month of Nisan, almost certainly in this year, Christ eats the Passover meal with his disciples in Jerusalem, Judea, where he is betrayed by Judas Iscariot and taken to the house of Caiaphas, the High Priest. The next day he is taken before the Roman procurator of Judea, Pontius Pilate, and is crucified for sedition, at Golgotha.

c. 30–c. 50   The Kushans in India are united under King Kadphasis I, and begin to challenge the power of the

Sakas, gaining control of the region around modern Kabul, Afghanistan.

31

- Sejanus, commander of the Roman Praetorian Guard, is brought before the Senate, accused of plotting to overthrow the emperor Tiberius, and executed.

32

- The Roman emperor Tiberius reverses his earlier liberal interpretation of Rome's treason laws and has many people executed as traitors.

35

- Two factions emerge at the court of the aging British king Cunobelinus (Cymbeline): the pro-Roman faction, under his son Adminius, and the anti-Roman faction, under his sons Togodumnus and Caractacus (Caradog).

36

- The Samaritan people of Roman Palestine complain to Rome about Pontius Pilate, governor of Judea, Palestine, when he attacks them on Mt. Gerizim, and he is ordered to return to Rome.

37

- The Roman emperor Tiberius dies and is succeeded by Gaius Caesar, the son of Tiberius' nephew Germanicus; he is popularly known as Caligula.

39

- The Roman emperor Caligula advances with an army to the northern shores of Gaul with the intention of invading Britain, but then orders his troops to collect seashells.
- The Roman emperor Caligula deprives Herod Antipas of his tetrarchy of Galilee and appoints Marcus Julius Agrippa (also known as Herod Agrippa), grandson of Herod the Great, in his place.

40

c. 40   The settlement that the Romans call Londinium (modern London, England) is founded in Britain.
- The emperor Caligula exhausts the Roman treasury by his personal extravagance.
- The Roman emperor Caligula brings the son of the Roman client king Juba II of Mauritania to Rome and starves him to death.

41

- The Roman emperor Claudius makes Herod Agrippa I the Roman client king of Judea and Samaria.
- The Roman philosopher Seneca is exiled to Corsica on a charge of adultery with Julia, daughter of Germanicus and great-niece of the late emperor Tiberius.
January 25   Claudius is proclaimed Roman emperor by the soldiers of the Praetorian Guard who murdered his nephew, the emperor Caligula, the previous day.

43

- Four Roman legions (2nd, 9th, 14th, and 20th) invade Britain under Aulus Plautius, winning a decisive victory over the British chieftain Caractacus on the River Medway. The Roman emperor Claudius receives the surrender of many tribes at Camulodunum (Colchester).
43–47   Aulus Plautius, leader of the Roman invasion of Britain, sends one legion northward to the Midlands and the other westward, where the Isle of Wight and the Wessex hill forts are taken. The Roman hold in the south and east is consolidated.

44

- The British chieftain Caractacus makes his way to the west of Britain (modern Wales) and begins to muster a force to fight against the Roman invaders.

47–50

- The British chieftain Caractacus leads raids against the Roman province of Britain from the unconquered area that is now Wales.

48

- The Roman emperor Claudius has his third wife, Messalina, executed for infidelity and marries his niece Agrippina (Caligula's sister). She persuades him to adopt her son Nero as heir instead of his own son Britannicus.

SCIENCE, TECHNOLOGY, AND MEDICINE

Agriculture

21–30
- China suffers drought and famine.

41–56
- Serious famine ravages Judea, in Roman Palestine.

Ecology

5
- Famine and floods strike Rome.

17
- The city of Ephesus in Asia Minor is severely damaged by an earthquake.

19
- Over 100,000 people die in an earthquake in Syria.

c. **40**
- Roman mining operations begin to exploit Spanish resources of tin, with mines opening up along the western seaboard.

Health and Medicine

c. **1**
- The Roman physician Scribonius Largus describes how the electric shock from a torpedo fish can be used to treat chronic diseases.

17
- Physicians found a meeting place in Rome, a Schola Medicorum (Medical School).

19
- An epidemic illness rages throughout Italy; 10,000 die in one day in Rome.

21–30
- Roman medical author Celsus' treatise on medicine, *De medicina/On Medicine*, describes the surgical

instruments of the time and depicts a remarkably advanced state of medical practice.

Science

c. 20

- The Greek geographer Strabo's *Geography* is finished. A multivolume geography of the world, it is the only extant work covering the history and geography of peoples and countries known to the Greeks and Romans.

Technology

c. 1

- Drilling towers 18 m/60 ft tall and designed to extract salt from underground brine pools appear in China.

c. 30

- Chinese writings describe a waterwheel consisting of belts and pulleys; it operates the bellows of an iron furnace for casting agricultural implements.

c. 40

- The importing of the potter's wheel from Gaul makes it possible for fine pottery to be produced in Britain and leads to a rise in the number of commercial potteries.

Transportation

c. 40

- The Greek merchant Hippalus discovers that the monsoon winds reverse direction twice each year; the knowledge halves the time it takes to sail from Egypt to India and back.

ARTS AND IDEAS

Architecture

10

- The Temple of Jupiter is the first of the magnificent Roman buildings to be constructed at Heliopolis (Baalbek), in Roman Syria (modern Lebanon).

c. 25

- Roman builders complete the Arch of Tiberius at Orange, Gaul (modern France).

33

- Roman prefect Pontius Pilate builds an aqueduct in Jerusalem, Roman Palestine, in spite of bitter opposition on the grounds that he is using sacred funds.

37

- The Villa Jovis at Capri, Italy, built for Roman emperor Tiberius, is completed. It is typical of the country villas built for wealthy Romans.

Arts

c. 1

- The people of the region around the modern town of San Agostín in the highlands of what is now southern Colombia begin to build earth mounds and to develop a distinctive style of stone sculpture.

c. 13

- The Portland Vase (probably made in Greece for a Roman and now in the British Museum, London, England) dates from this time. Made of opaque glass, it is a small amphora on which there are carved cameos depicting mythological scenes. It is one of the very finest pieces of Roman glass.

c. 30

- The art of glass blowing—probably brought to Rome from Sidon or Alexandria at the end of the 1st century BC—reaches great artistic excellence. The technique brings about both cheaper glassware and also a greater range of styles and forms.

Literature and Language

2

- Books of the *Metamorphoses* by the Latin poet Ovid begin to appear. An epic-style poem in 15 books, it retells Greek and Roman legends that involve transformations (metamorphoses). His most important work, it will become one of the best-loved and most influential works of antiquity in the Middle Ages.

8

- Latin poet Ovid is banished from Rome to Tomis on the Black Sea. The anger of the emperor Augustus at the seeming immorality of Ovid's poem "Ars amatoria"/ "Art of Love" is the stated reason, though it is probably because of Ovid's scandalous relationship with the emperor's granddaughter, Julia.

9

- Latin poet Ovid publishes his *Tristia/Songs of Sadness*, an autobiography in verse lamenting his exile in Tomis on the Black Sea.

13

- Latin poet Ovid publishes his *Epistulae ex Ponto/Letters From the Black Sea*, letters in verse to his wife and friends describing his exile in Tomis on the Black Sea and asking them to work for his return.

30

- Roman writers active at this time include Phaedrus, a writer of fables, and Valerius Maximus, a compiler of historical anecdotes.

Theater and Dance

49

- Agrippina, fourth wife of the emperor Claudius, has the Latin philosopher, statesman, and dramatist Lucius Annaeus Seneca returned to Rome from exile in Corsica; he is appointed tutor to her son, Nero. During his exile

BIRTHS & DEATHS

2

August 2 Lucius Caesar, grandson and adopted heir of the Roman emperor Augustus, dies in Massilia, Gaul (now Marseille, France) (19), while en route to take up a command in Spain.

3

- Paul the Apostle, who spread Christianity through his journeys and letters, born in Tarsus, Cilicia, Roman Asia Minor (–c. AD 65).

4

- Asinius Pollio, Roman historian, statesman, orator, and literary patron of Virgil and Horace, dies (80).
- Phraates V, King of Parthia and a traditional enemy of Rome, who ruled c. 2 BC–AD 4, dies.

February 21 Gaius Caesar, grandson and adopted heir of Augustus, dies in Lycia, Turkey (24). Augustus subsequently adopts his stepson Tiberius as his heir, making him in turn adopt his nephew Germanicus, elder son of Tiberius' brother Drusus the Elder.

9

November 17 Vespasian, Roman emperor AD 69–AD 79, born near Reate, Italy (–AD 79).

12

- Gaius Caesar (Caligula), Roman emperor AD 37–AD 40, nephew and adopted son of Tiberius, born in Antium (modern Anzio), Italy (–AD 41).
- Vipsanius Agrippa, deputy to Roman emperor Augustus, and who was responsible for defeating Mark Antony and for completing the Pantheon, dies in Campania (51).

14

August 19 Augustus, first emperor of the Roman Empire 27 BC–AD 14, dies in Nola, near Naples, Italy (75).

15

- Agrippina the Younger, sister of the emperor Caligula, mother of the emperor Nero, and wife of the emperor Claudius, born (–AD 59).

17

- Livy, historian of the Roman Republic, dies in Padua, Italy (76).
- Ovid, Roman poet known for his poem "Ars amatoria"/"Art of Love," dies in Tomis, Moesia (60).

19

- Arminius, leader of the German Cherusci people, who defeated three Roman legions in the Teutoburger Forest, Germany, in AD 9, dies (38).

- Juba II, King of Mauritania in north Africa, an important client ruler under the Roman emperor Augustus, dies.

October 10 Germanicus, Roman military commander, nephew of the emperor Tiberius and father of the emperor Caligula, dies in Antioch, Syria (34). Gnaeus Piso, governor of Syria, had ordered Germanicus to leave his province, and Germanicus dies convinced that Piso has poisoned him.

c. 21

- Strabo, Greek geographer and historian, dies in Amaseia, Pontus, in Roman Asia Minor (c. 88).

23

- Pliny the Elder, prolific Roman writer, author of Naturalis historia/Natural History, born in Como, Italy (–AD 79).

24

- Tacfarinas, Numidian chieftain who stirred up a revolt in Roman Africa, is killed by the Romans.

25

- Wang Mang, "Usurper," emperor of China AD 6–AD 25, founder of the Hsin dynasty, is killed in battle in China (70).

29

- Livia, wife of the Roman emperor Augustus and mother of the emperor Tiberius by her first husband, dies (83).

30

March 17 Jesus Christ, Jewish religious teacher, crucified for sedition probably at this time, at Golgotha, Judea (c. 35).

32

- Ban Chao, Chinese general and administrator under the Later Han Dynasty, born in Xiangyang, Shensi province, China (–AD 102).

33

October 13 Agrippina the Elder, granddaughter of the Roman emperor Augustus and mother of the emperor Caligula, dies on the island of Pandataria, in the Tyrrhenian Sea.

c. 35

- Quintilian, Roman rhetorician, teacher, and writer on education, born in Calahorra, Roman Spain (–c. AD 118).

37

- Josephus, Jewish historian and Roman citizen, born in Jerusalem, Palestine (–c. AD 100).

March 16 Tiberius, second Roman emperor AD 14–AD 37, dies in Capri, Italy (78).

December 15 Nero, Roman emperor AD 54–AD 68, born in Antium (modern Anzio), in Latium, Italy (–AD 68).

39

- Lucan, Roman epic poet, author of the Bellum Civile/Civil War, (also known as the Pharsalia), born in Corduba (modern Córdoba), Roman Spain (–AD 65).

40

- Martial, Roman poet known for his epigrams, born in Bilbilis, Spain (–c. AD 104).
- Octavia, daughter of Claudius (Roman emperor from AD 41) and his third wife Messalina, born (–AD 63).

June 13 Agricola, Roman general known for his conquests in Britain, born in Forum Julii (modern Fréjus), Gaul (now France) (–AD 93).

41

January 24 Gaius (Caligula), Roman emperor AD 37–AD 41 and nephew and adopted son of the emperor Tiberius, is murdered by soldiers of the Praetorian Guard in Rome (29).

February 12 Britannicus, son of the Roman emperor Claudius and his third wife Messalina, born (–AD 55).

December 30 Titus, Roman emperor AD 79–AD 81, son of Vespasian, born in Rome (–AD 81).

c. 42

- Cunobelinus, Roman client king of the British tribe of the Catuvellauni, dies in Verulamium (modern St. Albans, England).

44

- Herod Agrippa I, the client king of Judea and Samaria in Roman Palestine AD 37–44 and grandson of Herod the Great, dies (54). Judea becomes a Roman province again.

c. 45

- Philo of Alexandria, Greek-speaking Jewish philosopher who wrote about the development of Judaism and the diaspora, dies in Alexandria (c. 60).
- Publius Papinus Statius, Roman poet, whose epic Thebaid, dealing with political power and madness, remained popular in Europe until the end of the Renaissance, born in Naples, Italy (–AD 96).

46

- Plutarch, Latin essayist and biographer whose work had a major influence on the development of the essay, biography, and historical writing in Europe between the 16th and 19th centuries, born in Chaeronea, Boeotia, in Roman Greece (–c. AD 120).

he wrote tragedies based on Greek originals. Nine have survived, among them *Medea* and *Phaedrus*. His plays will have a profound effect on the development of European Renaissance drama.

Thought and Scholarship

c. 1

- Roman historian Trogus Pompeius writes *Historiae Philippicae/History of Philip*. Largely concerned with the history of the Macedonian Empire, it is later lost, though parts are preserved in the work of the historian Justin, written in the 2nd century AD.

c. 18

- Greek historian Nicolas of Damascus, the secretary of Herod the Great, completes his *Universal History*. The Jewish historian Josephus will later use it as a source.

c. 37

- Latin writer and statesman Lucius Annaeus Seneca begins work on a series of essays expounding stoic philosophy. Among the better known are "De otio"/"On Leisure" and "Ad Marciam de consolatione"/ "The Consolation of Marcia."

SOCIETY

Education

c. 40

- Corduba (modern Córdoba) in Spain, the birthplace of the Latin poet Lucan, becomes recognized as a school of rhetoric.

Everyday Life

c. 5

- The legionary's term of service is lengthened from 16 to 20 years and that of a Praetorian guardsman from 12 to 16. A legionary receives 10 asses (⅝ths of a denarius) a day and a gratuity of 3,000 denarii; a praetorian guard receives 2 denarii a day and a gratuity of 5,000 denarii.

8

- The Julian calendar is settled.

Religion

14

- After his death, the Roman emperor Augustus (Caesar Octavius) is deified and granted a temple and priests.

19

- As part of the campaign in support of traditional Roman religious practices, the emperor Tiberius has an image of Isis, an Egyptian deity with a growing cult in the Roman world, thrown into the River Tiber. The cult's priests are crucified.

27

- The Jewish prophet John the Baptist is put to death by Herod Antipas, tetrarch of Galilee and son of Herod the

Great. The Jewish historian Josephus attributes his death to Herod's fear of a political rebellion.

- The Jewish religious teacher Jesus Christ begins his mission, in Roman Palestine.

33

- On the road to "Damascus" (almost certainly not Damascus, Syria) to persecute the followers of Jesus Christ, Saul of Tarsus has an intense religious experience and is converted to Christianity. He is later known as the apostle Paul.
- The apostle Stephen becomes the first Christian martyr. Brought before the Sanhedrin (a Jewish legal and religious assembly) in Jerusalem, Roman Palestine, he is convicted of blasphemy and subversive teaching and stoned to death.

39

- The Roman emperor Caligula sets himself up as a god. Various excesses are attributed to him: some are probably true, some the exaggerations of opponents.

c. 40

- The philosopher Philo Judaeus of Alexandria writes works that seek to reconcile the Jewish scriptures and Greek philosophy. His arguments—for example, that the *Logos* (the word) of Greek thought is identical with divine reason—have a profound influence on the development of Christian theology.

41

- A burial mound is raised, either for King Cunobelinus or for one of his nobles, at Lexden, near modern Colchester in Britain. The dead man is buried with his war chariot and many other grave goods, although the decorative style of his grave goods is more Roman than Celtic.

44

- Herod Agrippa I, Roman client king of Judea and Samaria, executes James the Apostle, leader of the Christian community in Judea, and imprisons the apostle Peter.

c. 47

- The Christian apostle Paul undertakes his first missionary journeys, accompanied by Barnabas and Mark. He visits Cyprus and Asia Minor. Their followers begin to be called "Christians."

Sports

c. 1–*c.* 35

- Two new chariot-racing factions, the Veneta (Blue) and the Prasina (Green), emerge in Rome, to rival the established Albata (White) and Russata (Red) factions. They reflect political divisions.

37

- Roman emperor Caligula enlarges the Circus Maximus in Rome upon his accession to his position and holds all-day chariot races there. He also promotes games and gladiatorial shows.

41–54

- Roman emperor Claudius inaugurates new chariot races, promoting race meetings in the Vatican Circus in Rome with animal fights after every five races. He also improves the Circus Maximus.

50–99

POLITICS, GOVERNMENT, AND ECONOMICS

Business and Economics

c. 60
- Roman trade with India flourishes. Indian textiles, as well as turquoise from modern Afghanistan, silk from China (via the Silk Road), and spices from southeast Asia are traded for Roman gold and silver.

71
- Roman emperor Vespasian increases taxation, restores discipline in the army, and maintains friendly relations with the Senate.

Colonization

c. 80
- Drought and disease in east Asia cause the interior tribes, consisting of tens of thousands of people, to begin to move west. They form a cultural group who become known as the Huns.

Human Rights

c. 60
- Boudicca (Boadicea), Queen of the Celtic Iceni tribe in Britain, is beaten by Roman troops. Her daughters are raped and she gathers Celtic forces to take revenge on the Romans.

64
July 18 A great fire destroys half the city of Rome. The emperor Nero blames the Christian community and has many Christians tortured and killed; other observers blame the emperor himself, because the fire allows him to undertake an unpopular redevelopment program for the imperial palace.

c. 66
- Captive Ethiopian women in Rome train as gladiators.

c. 80
- The position of Celtic women in British society changes with Roman occupation. Although they were

previously accustomed to legal, religious, and military prominence, Rome allows them no political or legal status.

Politics and Government

50
c. 50 The town of Colonia Agrippinensis (modern Cologne, Germany) is founded in the part of Germany occupied by Rome to help control the Rhine frontier. The town is named for Nero's mother who was born there.
c. 50–*c.* 78 Kadphises II becomes king of the Kushans. In the west, he siezes the modern Punjab area from the Sakas, and in the east the Kushans occupy the area of Magadha as far as the city of Benares.

51
- Sextus Afranius Burrus is appointed prefect of the Praetorian Guards in Rome by the Roman emperor Claudius.
- The British chieftain Caractacus is finally defeated by Roman forces in the northwest of what is now Wales, and is handed over to the Roman authorities.
51–54 The Roman client-kingdom of Armenia is overrun by Parthian forces under Artabanus and his successors, Gortazes and Vologeses I.

53
- Nero, aged 16, marries his stepsister Octavia, aged 13. She is the daughter of the Roman emperor Claudius.

54
October 13 The Roman emperor Claudius dies in Rome, supposedly by eating a dish of poisoned mushrooms given him by his wife Agrippina the Younger.
October 14 Nero, 16-year-old stepson and heir of the emperor Claudius, is proclaimed Roman emperor by the Praetorian Guard, at the instigation of his mother Agrippina the Younger, Claudius's widow.

55
- Agrippina the Younger, widow of the Roman emperor Claudius, begins to favor her stepson Britannicus over her own son, the emperor Nero, after he refuses to allow her to rule through him. Britannicus dies, perhaps poisoned by order of Nero.

58
- Britain receives a new Roman governor, Suetonius Paulinus. He prepares to conquer the area of modern Wales.
58–60 The Roman general Gnaeus Domitius Corbulo drives the Parthians out of Armenia, burning the Armenian capital Artaxata and establishing the former Cappadocian prince Tigranes as Rome's client ruler.

59

- Agrippina the Younger, wife of the Roman emperor Claudius and mother of the emperor Nero, is killed on Nero's orders in Antium (modern Anzio), Italy, allegedly for conspiring against him, but in fact because she opposes his marriage to Poppaea Sabina.
- The Roman Senate displays its servility by submitting an address congratulating Nero on the death of his mother, Agrippina the Younger, after Nero himself had ordered her death.

61

- Boudicca (Boadicea), Queen of the Iceni of East Anglia, leads a major rebellion against Roman rule. Her people destroy the Roman settlements at Camulodunum (Colchester), Verulamium (St. Albans), and Londinium (London). Boudicca commits suicide after her forces are defeated by Suetonius Paulinus, the governor of Britain. His forces defeat and massacre the British tribes of what is now Wales at Mona (modern Anglesey).

62

- Nero, the Roman emperor, dismisses his advisers Seneca and Burrus, divorces and banishes his wife Octavia, and marries his mistress Poppaea Sabina.

64

- The Cottian Alps, between Gaul and Roman Italy, become a Roman province, and Pontus in Asia Minor is incorporated into the province of Galatia.

65

- Cassius Longinus, a prominent jurist, is banished from Rome by the Roman emperor Nero.

66

- A major revolt breaks out in Judea, Palestine, against the Roman procurator Gessius Florus. A vicious war between Jews and Gentiles follows. Jewish extremists seize the Masada, the strongest of Herod the Great's fortresses.
- Parthia makes a peace treaty with Rome, under which the pro-Parthian Tiridates becomes king of Armenia.

67

- The Roman soldier Vespasian is sent to restore order to Judea, Palestine. The siege and fall of Jotopata in Galilee follows, at which the Jewish general Joseph ben Matthias (later the historian Josephus) surrenders to Vespasian.

68

- The Roman soldier and future emperor Vespasian spends the year forcibly restoring order in Judea, Palestine.

68–69 Anarchy breaks out in Rome after the death of the emperor Nero, with Galba, Otho, Vitellius, and Vespasian each claiming the throne during the so-called "year of four emperors."

69

- Otho, Roman emperor, is defeated in battle by his rival Vitellius, and commits suicide near Cremona, Italy.
- Vitellius, Roman emperor, is put to death by Vespasian's troops after fighting in Rome.
- With the coming to power of the Flavian dynasty, luxury goes out of fashion in Rome as Roman emperor Vespasian embraces old-fashioned standards.

December 21 Vespasian, supported by legions from Egypt, Syria, and Palestine, is proclaimed Roman emperor by the Senate after a campaign by the Danube legions under his ally Antonius Primus defeats the emperor Vitellius in Italy.

70

- Jerusalem is captured and sacked by Titus, elder son of the Roman emperor Vespasian, after a siege lasting 139 days. The Temple is burned down.

71

- Petillius Cerialis, nephew of the Roman emperor Vespasian, becomes governor of Britain. He establishes the 9th legion at Eboracum (modern York, North Yorkshire).
- Roman emperor Vespasian appoints Quintilian as the first state-salaried teacher (of rhetoric).
- Titus, son of the Roman emperor Vespasian, returns to Rome from the Jewish war.

73

- The Chinese general Ban Chao subdues the native princes of Central Asia and gains command of the vital Silk Road to Rome.

April 15 Herod the Great's fortress of Masada in Judea, Palestine, occupied by Jewish extremists, is taken by the Romans under Flavius Silva after a two-year siege.

74

- Agricola, commander of the 20th Roman legion in Britain, is made governor of Aquitania, Gaul (modern France).
- Frontinus is appointed Roman governor of Britain; he subdues the Silures in the southeast of what is now Wales and establishes a fortress at Isca (Caerleon).

75

- Helvidius Priscus, a stoic philosopher and outspoken republican, violently opposes the Roman emperor Vespasian; he is first exiled, then put to death.

77

- Iulius Agricola is made Roman governor of Britain. He completes the conquest of what is now Wales and consolidates the subjugation of the Brigantes.

78

- Kanishka, the greatest king of the Kushan dynasty, founds the kingdom of Kashmir in the north of the Indian subcontinent. He is a keen patron of Buddhism.

79

- The governor Agricola extends Roman occupation of Britain northward to the lowlands of Hibernia (modern Scotland). He builds a naval base for a projected invasion of Caledonia (modern Ireland), but this never materializes.

June 23 Titus becomes Roman emperor on the death of his father, Vespasian.

c. **80**

- Han-dynasty China wages a fierce war against the Xiongnu (Hsiung-Nu), a nomadic pastoral people who have long dominated much of Central Asia. The Silk Road to the west is threatened, as is the Tarim Basin (in modern Sinkiang).

81

81–88 The Roman emperor Domitian enforces the Julian moral laws, forbids the creation of eunuchs, stops speculation, issues fine coinage, and cancels tax arrears over five years old.

81–91 The Chinese general Ban Chao drives the Xiongnu nomads, who have been attacking China, out of the entire Tarim Basin (modern Sinkiang) in Central Asia. He is made protector general of the western regions.

September 13 Domitian becomes Roman emperor on the death of his brother, Titus.

82

- Julius Agricola, the Roman governor of Britain, advances into central Hibernia (modern Scotland), setting up camps on navigable rivers and using his fleet for supplies.

83

- The Roman emperor Domitian crosses the Rhine to subdue a German tribe, the Chatti, and then retreats to construct the *limes* (a fortified frontier) along the river's southern bank.

84

- Julius Agricola, the Roman governor of Britain, wins the battle of Mons Graupius (probably modern Bennachie) against the Picts and considers that he has conquered Hibernia (modern Scotland).

85

- Julius Agricola, the Roman governor of Britain, is recalled. The Roman occupation of Hibernia (modern Scotland), at least as far north as modern Perthshire, endures for about 15 years.

86

- The Dacians, from the area of modern Romania, cross the River Danube into the Roman province of Moesia under their king, Decebalus, defeating the Roman legate there.

- Roman forces invading Dacia under Cornelius Fuscus are defeated by the Dacians under Decebalus. Decebalus is later forced back across the Danube to defend his country against a counterinvasion by the Roman middle Danube legions under Cornelius Fuscus.

88

- Roman forces under Tettius Julianus invade Dacia and defeat Decebalus at Tapae.

89

- The Roman governor of Upper Germany, Antonius Saturninus, persuades two legions in Mainz to declare him emperor. Emperor Domitian patches up a peace with the Dacian king Decebalus to save Rome from invasion.

Dacian Wars (86–106)

86

- Roman forces invading Dacia (roughly equivalent to modern Romania) under Cornelius Fuscus are defeated by the Dacians under their king, Decebalus.
- King Decebalus is forced back across the Danube to defend his country against a counterinvasion by the Roman middle Danube legions under Cornelius Fuscus.
- The Dacians cross the River Danube into the Roman province of Moesia under Decebalus, defeating the Roman legate there.

88

- After the defeat of Cornelius Fuscus in Dacia, Roman forces under Tettius Julianus invade Dacia again and defeat Decebalus at Tapae.

89

- The Roman governor of Upper Germany, Antonius Saturninus, persuades two legions in Mainz to declare him emperor. Emperor Domitian patches up a peace with Decebalus to save Rome from invasion.

101–102

- King Decebalus of Dacia has strengthened his standing and is implacably anti-Roman. The Roman emperor Trajan invades Dacia with ten legions and, after a difficult campaign, forces Decebalus to surrender. The defeated chieftain is allowed to remain on the throne as a client king.

- Trajan's second cousin, the future emperor Hadrian, serves under Trajan during the Dacian campaign. Not to be outdone by the Dacians, he swims his horse and himself across the icy River Danube.

104–106

- King Decebalus revolts again, overwhelming the Roman garrisons left north of the River Danube and raiding the Roman province of Moesia across the Danube.

105

- Trajan invades Dacia with 13 legions. During this war, he wins the confidence of his legionaries—one story tells how during the battle he tears up his own cloak to help bandage the wounded.

106

- At the end of a hard-fought campaign against the Romans, Decebalus and his chiefs commit mass suicide after a final feast. Hadrian discovers the gruesome aftermath of this act.
- Dacia becomes a Roman province. Thousands of Dacians are transported to the southern side of the River Danube, while Dacia is colonized and developed by the Romans after the Roman emperor Trajan has carried off much booty. Trajan recognizes the strategic value of Dacia in any further clash with the German tribes.
- The Roman emperor Trajan returns to Rome to a triumph (ritual processsion) for his Dacian victory and gives the populace a great show of games, said to last for 123 days: Dacian prisoners are used as gladiators.

- Those suspected of being involved in the revolt against Rome led by Antonius Saturninus, the Roman governor of Upper Germany, are hunted down and executed.

91

- Trajan, a professional Roman soldier, is made consul.

92

- The Roman emperor Domitian campaigns against the Sarmations and Suebi in Sarmatia, along the River Danube.

92–102 The Chinese general Ban Chao extends his conquests in Central Asia across the Pamir Mountains to the Caspian Sea.

96

September 18 Domitian, Roman emperor 81–96 and son of the emperor Vespasian, dies in Rome. He is murdered in a conspiracy led by his wife Domitia and one of the Praetorian prefects, Petronius Secundus. The Senate appoints Marcus Cocceius Nerva, a senior senator, as emperor; he restores tranquility.

97

- The Roman emperor Nerva survives a revolt of the Praetorian Guard, who are angered that they are no longer able to create emperors. Realizing that he needs the support of the army, he adopts Trajan, the commander of the Roman legions in Upper Germany, as his son and heir.
- The Roman historian Tacitus is appointed consul.

98

- Trajan arrives in Rome to take up his emperorship, entering the city humbly on foot.

January 25 Nerva, Roman emperor 96–98, selected by the Senate, dies in Rome. He is succeeded by his adopted son, Trajan, who is campaigning on the Rhine frontier.

SCIENCE, TECHNOLOGY, AND MEDICINE

Agriculture

c. **90**

- Many of Rome's neighbors use iron plows with wheels to cut and turn the soil. Plowing deep, long furrows, they cultivate long strips of land; Roman farmers cultivate square blocks using a cross-plowing technique.

Ecology

65

- The Phrygian city of Laodicea is destroyed by an earthquake.

79

August 24 Mt. Vesuvius, in southern Italy, erupts, accompanied by violent earthquakes; Herculaneum, Pompeii, and Stabiae are buried in ash and their citizens are overcome by poisonous gases.

80

- A fire destroys much of Rome; it is followed by an epidemic disease.

Exploration

85

- The Roman governor Julius Agricola's fleet, supporting his land campaign in Hibernia (modern Scotland), circumnavigates the British Isles.

Health and Medicine

71–80

- Pedanios Dioscorides, a Greek physician, writes *Materia medica/The Ingredients of Medicaments*, a description of the medicinal properties of over 600 plants.

c. **80**

- An anthrax epidemic ravages the Roman Empire, killing thousands of animals and people, and strikes the western border regions of China.
- An epigram of the Roman poet Martial shows that false teeth are used in Rome.

c. **85**

- The former Roman governor of Britain, Frontinus, returns to Rome to undertake a major reorganization of the city's water supply, involving the construction of several new aqueducts.

c. **95**

- Malaria appears in the market-garden areas outside Rome which supply the city with fresh produce. The farmers flee to Rome, bringing the disease with them and lowering the birth rate. Fertile land is taken out of cultivation for nearly 500 years.

Math

62

- Greek mathematician and engineer Hero of Alexandria writes *Metrica/Measurements*, containing many formulae for working out areas and volumes.

Science

77

- Pliny the Elder's *Historia naturalis/Natural History* is completed. Divided into 37 books, it covers such topics as cosmology, astronomy, zoology, botany, agricultural techniques, medicine, drugs, minerals, and metals. The book brings together the scattered material of earlier writers and also makes original contributions, combining keen observation with absurd hearsay.

Technology

c. **60**

- Greek engineer Hero of Alexandria, in his *Pneumatica/Pneumatics*, describes a primitive steam turbine that he calls an aeolipile; it is the first known device to use steam to produce rotary motion.

c. 70

- A public lavatory with flush toilets and urinals opens in Rome.

83

- The first compass is described in a Chinese book, the *Louen Heng/Discourses Weighed in the Balance*. It consists of a spoon-shaped piece of magnetite which spins on a bronze plate, the handle of the spoon pointing north. It is derived from a divining board—where objects are scattered on a platter and the direction of their pointing is found significant—and is not likely to have been used for navigation.

Transportation

64–67

- The Roman emperor Nero has a canal built from Ostia to Lake Avernus in Italy, and makes an abortive attempt at organizing the construction of a Corinthian canal in Greece.

ARTS AND IDEAS

Architecture

65

- After the great fire of Rome in 64, the emperor Nero starts to build a less congested, nobler, and more handsome city. He also starts to build his extravagant "Golden House," a vast palace complex.

75

- King Cogidubnus of the British Regni tribe publicly demonstrates his Romanization by building a temple to Neptune and Minerva. He is probably also responsible for the magnificent Romano-British palace at Fishbourne near Chichester, Britain. It has at least sixty rooms with tessellated floors, and artists from Italy must have been imported to do the work.

80

c. 80 Roman governor Agricola begins to encourage the building of towns and urban living among the Britons, a process that continues, with some opposition, throughout the rest of the century.

- The Baths of Titus in Rome are dedicated.

81

- The Triumphal Arch of Titus is completed at the eastern end of the Forum in Rome. It has been built to celebrate the victory of Titus—who later became emperor—over the Jews in AD 70. Its reliefs show the looting from the temple at Jerusalem of the Jews' menorah (sacred seven-branched candlestick).

82–90

- After the fires of AD 82, Rome's temple of Jupiter, Juno, and Minerva is restored at great expense, along with the Pantheon and the city's public libraries.

90

- The Romans establish the city of Lindum Colonia (modern Lincoln, England) in Britain.

92

- The Domus Augustana, an imperial palace built on the Palatine hill in Rome, is completed. Its architect is Rabirius, one of the few Roman architects known by name.

c. 97

- The Forum of Emperor Nerva (Forum Transitorium) is completed in Rome.

Arts

c. 67

- The arrival of Buddhist missionaries in China begins to have a lasting effect upon Chinese art.

77

- A statue of the ruler Kanishka is erected in the Kushan territory of northern India (modern Kashmir), showing his typical Tatar quilted boots. It still survives. In Kanishka's reign, Greco-Buddhist sculpture develops and fine buildings are erected in Taxila and elsewhere.

Literature and Language

64

- Latin poet Martial (Marcus Valerius Martialis), born in Spain, comes to Rome to secure patronage. His links with Seneca end abruptly a year later when Seneca is implicated in a conspiracy to assassinate the emperor Nero. Little is known of Martial's life in Rome, though according to his own accounts he lived in great poverty.

80

- Latin poet Martial publishes *Liber spectaculorum/Book of Spectacles* to mark the dedication of the Colosseum by Emperor Titus. It gives a vivid depiction of the gladiatorial games.

81

c. 81 Roman emperor Domitian, according to Suetonius, writes a book *On the Care of the Hair*, but then goes bald.

- The young poet Publius Papinius Statius, a favorite of Domitian and his court, becomes famous in Rome. The poet Martial, jealous of him, and referring no doubt to Statius' long epic *Thebaid*, observes that a live epigram is worth more than a dead epic.

86

- Latin poet Martial begins publishing his books of epigrams: witty, satirical observations on Roman life and society. The last book will be published around AD 100. He survives in Rome by flattering his patrons and friends and vilifying their enemies.
- Roman emperor Domitian, in imitation of ancient Greece, institutes the Capitoline "Games," for contests in literature and music.

Music

59

- Roman emperor Nero boasts of his skill on the lyre—probably quite genuine—a clear indication that by now the Romans have overcome their earlier rugged disapproval of Greek music and dancing.

Thought and Scholarship

51

- Roman statesman and philosopher Lucius Annaeus Seneca begins a further series of essays on stoic morality, including "De clementia"/"On Clemency," which advises rulers to govern with clemency. (It is written during the reign of the emperor Nero, noted for his cruelty.)

c. 54–c. 68

- Pamphila, a female historian who writes in Greek, writes *Miscellaneous History*.

68

- Latin rhetorician Quintilian, a Spaniard, comes to Rome with Roman emperor Galba and makes his name as an advocate in the Law Courts.

75

- Jewish historian Flavius Josephus publishes his *Bello Judaico/History of the Jewish War*, in Rome. Originally written in Aramaic for a Jewish readership, it gives vivid accounts of the sieges of Jotopata (where he was captured), Jerusalem, and the Masada. Spared by the Roman commander Vespasian, he settles in Rome, where he is given a house and a pension.

80

- The historians Ban Gu and his sister Ban Zhao complete their *Qianhan shu*, a comprehensive history of the Han Dynasty, in China. The work was begun by their father Ban Biao.

c. 90

- Greek writer Plutarch, a native of Chaeronea in Boeotia, Greece, lectures on philosophy in Rome.

93

- Jewish historian Flavius Josephus publishes his *Antiquitates Judaicae/The Antiquities of the Jews*.

95

- Roman emperor Domitian has philosophers banished from the whole of Italy. One of them is the Greek freed slave and stoic philosopher Epictetus, who retires to teach at Epirus, where his ideas are written down by a disciple.

98

- Greek philosopher Dion Chrysostom ("the golden-mouthed") is among the most eminent of Rome's sophists in this period and is highly regarded by emperors Nerva and Trajan. Some 80 of his "Orations" have survived.
- Roman historian Publius Cornelius Tacitus publishes two of his finest works. *Germania* describes the Germanic tribes on the Roman frontier on the River Rhine, and records that the social customs revere

women and encourage them to participate in politics and warfare. *De vita et moribus Julii Agricolae/The Life and Death of Agricola* (usually known simply as *Agricola*) is a biography of the statesman Julius Agricola, his father-in-law.

SOCIETY

Religion

50

- The Christian apostle Paul begins his second missionary journey, this time through Asia Minor into Thrace, visiting Philippi, Thessaloniki, Athens, and Corinth. Another apostle, Thomas, travels to the court of the Shaka king, Gondophernes, at Gandhara in northwest India, and is martyred there.

c. 53

- The Christian apostle Paul begins his third missionary journey, starting from Jerusalem. He visits Ephesus in Asia Minor and Corinth in Greece, and breaks completely with the Judaizing Christians who wish to tie Christianity to the Mosaic Law. His teachings on women spread to Greece. His message praises virginity and chastity, and Christians accept Hebrew laws forbidding women from organized worship until 33 days after bearing a boy-child and twice that for a girl-child.

c. 58

- Emperor Ming-Ti introduces Buddhism to China.
- The Christian apostle Paul is arrested by the Roman authorities in Jerusalem, Roman Palestine, after being accused of preaching against Jewish religious law.

61

c. 61 While in Rome, St. Paul continues to dictate his letters to converts around the Middle East. These epistles become rapidly and widely known and have a profound influence on the early Christian faith. The authenticity of St. Paul as author of all the letters under his name in the New Testament is a matter of dispute.

- The Roman conquest of Anglesey, an island off north Wales, brings an end to Druidism in Britain. According to Roman writers, on crossing the Menai Straits, the legionaries are faced with women in ceremonial dress, warriors, and druid priests standing by fires of human sacrifice.

65–67

- The Chinese emperor sends envoys to India to study Buddhism, and Buddhist missionaries begin to visit China.

70

c. 70 The early Christian text *The Revelation of St. John the Divine* is completed. Its author is almost certainly not John the Apostle. The Christian Gospel of the apostle Luke is also written. It is thought that both the apostles Luke and Matthew drew on the Gospel of the apostle Mark, and that all four Gospels are written between AD 65 and 100.

- During the siege of Jerusalem, the Romans allow the Jewish religious leader Johanan ben Zakkai to leave and later to establish a school at Jamnia (Jabneh). His teaching there will be profoundly important in securing the continuity of Judaism.

73

- The Romans destroy the community at Qumran near the Dead Sea. The inhabitants leave behind the Dead Sea Scrolls hidden in nearby caves. The inhabitants of Qumran are either the Essenes or a similar ascetic sect. This Roman destruction, at about the same time as the destruction of Masada, sees the end of all the Jewish ascetic sects that had flourished since the time of the Maccabees in the 2nd century BC.

92

- The Roman emperor Domitian has Christians executed for refusing to offer sacrifices before his image.

Sports

67

- Roman emperor Nero creates a spectacle by taking part in the Greek games. He is allowed to win 1,808 prizes, but his antics and dubious victories are not officially recorded.

81–92

- Roman emperor Domitian holds up to 100 chariot races a day in the Circus Maximus in Rome. He introduces two new racing teams, the Aureata (Gold) and the Purpurea (Purple), but they are soon disbanded.

90

- The popular Roman board game *Ludus Duodecim Scriptorum* ("the game of 12 lines") is gradually replaced by *Tabula*, a possible precursor of backgammon.

BIRTHS & DEATHS

51
October 24 Domitian, Roman emperor 81–96, son of the emperor Vespasian and brother of the emperor Titus, born in Rome, Italy (–96).

53
September 15 Trajan, Roman emperor 97–117, adopted as the emperor Nerva's heir, born in Italica, Baetica, in Roman Spain (–117).

54
October 13 Tiberius Claudius Caesar, Roman emperor 41–54, who expanded Roman rule to include north Africa and Britain, dies (64).

55
- Epictetus, stoic philosopher whose works were collected by his pupil Arrian, born in Hierapolis, Phrygia, in Roman Asia Minor (–c. 135).
- Tacitus, Roman historian of the 1st century AD, born, probably in southern Gaul (–c. 120).

59
- Agrippina the Younger, wife of the Roman emperor Claudius and mother of the emperor Nero, dies in Antium (44).

60
c. 60 Juvenal (Decimus Junius Juvenalis), Roman satirical poet, author of 16 "Satires," born in Aquinum, Roman Italy (–c. 140).

61
- Pliny the Younger, Roman letter writer and administrator, born in Como, Italy (–c. 113).

62
- Sextus Afranius Burrus, Roman Prefect of the Praetorian Guard 51–62 and, with Seneca, chief advisor of Nero, dies.

63
June 6 Octavia, wife of the Roman emperor Nero and the daughter of the late emperor Claudius and his wife Messalina, divorced and exiled by Nero to the island of Pandateria, is killed on Nero's orders (23).

65
c. 65 Paul the Apostle, who spread Christianity through his journeys and letters, is executed in Rome (c. 62).
- Poppaea, the wife of the Roman emperor Nero, dies in pregnancy, allegedly kicked in the stomach by him in a fit of temper.
- The Latin poet Lucan (Marcus Annaeus Lucanus) and his uncle Seneca the Younger, Roman orator, philosopher, poet, dramatist, and political advisor to Nero, die (26 and 68). They were implicated in a plot against Nero and were forced to commit suicide. Lucan leaves an epic poem, *De Bello Civili/Civil War*, sometimes known as the *Pharsalia*. Seneca leaves his *Letters*, a collection of tragedies, and many works on stoic philosophy and ethics.

68
June 9 Nero, Roman emperor 54–68, hearing that provincial governors have risen against him, commits suicide just outside Rome (31).

69
- Galba, Roman emperor 68–69, is murdered in Rome.

70
- Suetonius, Roman biographer and historian, whose *Lives of the Twelve Caesars* has survived, born in Hippo Regius, Roman Africa (–c. 140).

76
- Hadrian, Roman emperor 117–138, adopted as his heir by the emperor Trajan, born in Rome (–138).

79
June 23 Vespasian, Roman emperor 69–79, dies near Reate, Italy (69).

August 24 Pliny the Elder, Roman writer on natural history and other subjects, is killed in the eruption of Mt. Vesuvius, near Stabiae, in Italy (56).

81
September 13 Titus, Roman emperor 79–81, son of the emperor Vespasian, dies near Reate, Italy (40). His younger brother Domitian is suspected of hastening his death.

86
September 19 Antoninus Pius, Roman emperor 138–161, born in Lanuvium, Latium, Italy (–161).

92
- Ban Gu, Chinese scholar and historian of the Later Han Dynasty, dies in China (c. 60).

93
August 23 Julius Agricola, Roman commander and governor in Britain, the father-in-law of the historian Cornelius Tacitus, dies (56).

96
- Publius Papinius Statius, Roman poet, whose epic *Thebaid*, dealing with political power and madness, remained popular in Europe until the end of the Renaissance, dies in Naples (51).

100–149

POLITICS, GOVERNMENT, AND ECONOMICS

Business and Economics

118
- The Roman emperor Hadrian spends money on games and gifts to the Roman people; he also cancels tax arrears and has the tax records publicly burned in Rome to prove his sincerity.

123
- Roman emperor Hadrian increases the self-respect of the cities of Asia Minor along with their sense of belonging to the Roman Empire by allowing them to issue their own coinage.

137
- A road is built linking the Nile with the Red Sea, opening up the trade routes from Egypt to the East, and ending the control of the Bedouin nomads over trade passing through their region.

Colonization

106
- On the death of King Dabel of Arabia Petraea, the last buffer state between Syria and Parthia, comprising the Sinai Peninsula and the Negev Desert and commanding the trade routes to the East, the area is added to the Roman Empire in a campaign led by A. Cornelius Palma, the Roman governor of Syria.

116
- As a result of the Roman emperor Trajan's campaign, Armenia, Assyria, Mesopotamia, and Parthia are for a little while made Roman provinces, although this is reversed by his successor, Hadrian.

120
- The Roman historian Tacitus refers to the Goths as having moved south from their original home around the Baltic Sea. They are a Germanic people who migrate to Scythia (modern southern Russia) about this time.

122–123
- On his return from Britain, the Roman emperor Hadrian visits the province of Narbonese Gaul (modern Languedoc and Provence, France), where he refounds

the colony of Avignon, and builds a temple at Nîmes. He then goes on to Spain, where he builds many new roads and bridges.

Human Rights

135
- The Roman emperor Hadrian orders Jerusalem to be leveled and a new Roman town, Aelia Capitolina, to be built on the site. All Jews will be barred from the new town.

Politics and Government

100
- Hadrian, the second cousin and nearest male relative of the Roman emperor Trajan, marries Vibia Sabina, Trajan's grandniece and nearest female relative.

101
- As Roman emperor, Trajan proves himself a careful and hardworking administrator. He realizes, like the first emperor, Augustus, that he can rule personally so long as he gives the Senate the appearance of power. There is no reign of terror, and Trajan is credited with the dictum: "It is better that the guilty should remain unpunished than that the innocent should be condemned." Trajan's wife, Plotina, and sister, Marciana, set an example to women and endeavor to improve court morals.
- Britain is peaceful during the next 15 years. Stone-built Roman forts begin to replace temporary wooden fortifications as the Romans consolidate their rule.

101–102 King Decebalus of Dacia has revived and is implacably anti-Roman. The Roman emperor Trajan invades Dacia with ten legions and, after a difficult campaign, forces Decebalus to surrender. The defeated chieftain is allowed to remain on the throne as a client king.

101–102 The Roman emperor Trajan's second cousin, the future emperor Hadrian, serves under Trajan during the Dacian campaign. Not to be outdone by the Dacians, Hadrian swims his horse and himself across the icy River Danube.

103
- The Roman emperor Trajan divides the Roman province of Pannonia into two, Upper and Lower Pannonia, and increases the garrison from four legions to five.

104
104–106 King Decebalus of Dacia revolts again, overwhelming the Roman garrisons left north of the

River Danube and raiding the Roman province of Moesia across the Danube.

105

- The Roman emperor Trajan invades Dacia again, with 13 legions. During this war, he wins the confidence of his legionaries—one story tells how during the battle he tears up his own cloak to help bandage the wounded.

106

- At the end of a hard-fought campaign against the Romans, King Decebalus of Dacia and his chiefs commit mass suicide after a final feast; Hadrian, the second cousin of the Roman emperor Trajan, discovers the gruesome aftermath of this act.
- Dacia becomes a Roman province. Thousands of Dacians are transported to the southern side of the River Danube, while Dacia is colonized and developed by the Romans after the Roman emperor Trajan has carried off much booty. Trajan recognizes the strategic value of Dacia in any further clash with the German tribes.
- The Roman emperor Trajan returns to Rome to a triumph (ritual processsion) for his Dacian victory and gives the populace a great show of games, said to last for 123 days: Dacian prisoners are used as gladiators.

107

- The Roman emperor Trajan is said to have sent ambassadors to India, presumably to the Kushan dynasty.

107–110 The Roman emperor Trajan undertakes many major building and improvement projects in Italy. The Pontine Marshes, southeast of Rome, are drained, and harbors are built at Ostia and Centumcellae, the ports of Rome, and at Ancona and Brundisium on the Adriatic Sea.

107–112 The Roman emperor Trajan passes measures designed to increase the birth rate and population of Italy. Children become eligible for the monthly corn dole and occasional cash hand-outs in Rome; family allowances are instituted; agriculture is encouraged with five percent state mortgages given for buying farm land; and senators, many of whom are non-Italian, have to invest at least a third of their capital in Italian land.

109

- The Roman emperor Trajan sends Maximus to Achaia in the Peloponnese, Greece, to regulate the affairs of the free cities of Athens, Sparta, and Delphi.

109–114 The Roman emperor Trajan appoints officials known as *curatores* to oversee local finances in some of the cities of Italy, in the senatorial provinces, and in some free cities.

111

- The Roman administrator Pliny the Younger is sent to govern the Roman province of Bithynia in Asia Minor (modern Turkey), which is temporarily transferred from the Senate to the emperor. The correspondence between Pliny and Trajan has been preserved and sheds much light on provincial affairs and the character of Trajan.

112

- The Parthians under King Chosroes (or Osroes), though not directly threatening Rome, have invaded Armenia. The Roman emperor Trajan, always happier in the field than at his desk, decides that their power should be broken once and for all, and prepares for a major campaign.

114–116

- The Roman emperor Trajan mounts a campaign of spectacular conquest. He takes Ctesiphon, the Parthian capital, gaining much booty, and reaches the Persian Gulf. Looking toward India, he regrets that he is too old to emulate Alexander the Great and make further conquests there.

115

- The Jews of the Diaspora revolt in Egypt and the Roman provinces of north Africa.

116

- The Parthians regroup under Sanatruces, the brother of King Chosroes (or Osroes), and his son Parthamanpates. The Roman emperor Trajan is forced to concede the throne of Parthia to Parthamanpates in exchange for his moving against his father, Sanatruces.
- The revolt of the Jews spreads to the new Roman province of Mesopotamia, and to the island of Cyprus and the North African province of Cyrenaica (modern Libya). Revolt also breaks out in the Roman province of Assyria. The strategic cities of Nisibis, Edessa, and Seleucia fall, but are retaken by the Romans.

117

- As soon as the Romans withdraw from Parthia, their client king Parthamanpates is overthrown by King Chosroes (or Osroes).
- Hadrian, the second cousin of the Roman emperor Trajan, completes the pacification of Palestine, Egypt, and Cyrenaica. He sends his trusted general Quintus Marcius Turbo to pacify Mauritania.
- Revolts break out against Roman rule among the Moors on the north African coast, and also in northern Britain.
- The Roman emperor Trajan, unable to advance into India, builds a Red Sea fleet to control the passage to, and commerce with, India. He dies in Selinus, Celicia.
- Hadrian, the new Roman emperor, halts the expansionist policy of his predecessor, Trajan: like the former emperor Augustus, he accepts the River Euphrates as the Roman frontier. This policy is not popular with his generals, nor does he achieve popularity at home, in spite of liberal gestures. Hadrian withdraws the legions from Armenia, Assyria, Mesopotamia, and Parthia, and makes Armenia a client kingdom instead of a province.

118

- A plot is hatched in Rome against the new emperor Hadrian led by four ex-consuls and close friends of the late emperor Trajan—C. Avidius Nigranus, Trajan's governor of Dacia; A. Cornelius Palma, conqueror of Arabia Petraea; Lusius Quietus; and L. Publius Celsus. They all opposed Trajan's adoption of Hadrian during his lifetime, and are strongly against Hadrian's policy of retreat on the frontiers of the Roman Empire.
- Hadrian, the new Roman emperor, goes back to Rome via the Danubian provinces and, in a personal interview, persuades the king of the Roxolani, Rasparaganus, to keep the peace.
- The Roman emperor Hadrian reaches Rome in July, hastened there by news of the plot against him. By the time he returns, Acilius Attiacus, the Praetorian prefect,

and Hadrian's supporters in the Senate have executed the four ringleaders. Despite Hadrian's claims that he knew nothing of this, the Senate never forgives or trusts Hadrian. Hadrian replaces Acilius Attiacus as Praetorian prefect with his general Quintus Marcius Turbo. He bestows the great honor of consular insignia and membership in the Senate on Attiacus.

- The Roman general Marcius Turbo divides the province of Dacia (roughly equivalent to modern Romania) into an upper and a lower province, separated by the River Aluta.

118–120   There are serious revolts against the Romans in Britain, with the 9th (Hispana) Roman Legion, stationed at Lindum (modern Lincoln, England), totally disappearing from the records.

120

- The young Antoninus Pius, future emperor, is made one of the consuls in Rome for the year.

121

- The Roman emperor Hadrian builds a more efficient machine of government in Rome, with a *concilium* of businessmen, jurists, and senators to consider policy and advise him. He reforms the Imperial Civil Service, appointing knights instead of freedmen to the secretaryships and administrative posts.

121–131   The Roman emperor Hadrian, having improved government administration at home, spends the decade in a series of businesslike and beneficial tours of the Roman Empire. He visits the western provinces of the Roman Empire, beginning with Gaul, then moving on to the Rhine and Danube frontiers, which he orders to be strengthened. He improves the lot, and the discipline, of the legionaries.

123

- After leading a small punitive expedition to the Roman province of Mauritania in northwest Africa, where the Moors had revolted the previous year, the Roman emperor Hadrian visits Asia Minor where he provides relief after a recent earthquake and generally boosts morale. He recruits Antinous, the handsome Bithynian boy who becomes his favorite, to his staff.

124–126

- The Roman emperor Hadrian arrives in Athens, Greece, and winters there, returning to Rome in the spring of 126, visiting the island of Sicily and climbing Mt. Etna on the way home.

125

- The Chinese general Ban Yong, son of Ban Zhao, temporarily reconquers the Tarim Basin in the northwest from the Huns.

126

- The Roman emperor Hadrian orders a codification of the Roman law which has grown enormously overcomplicated, with a vast amount of judgment law having been added to the original Twelve Tables of the ancient city of Rome. The codification is undertaken from 126 to 129 by the African jurist Salvius Julianus, grandfather of the future emperor Didius Julianus. Its publication gives a great impetus to legal studies in Rome.

127

- The Roman emperor Hadrian tours Italy.

128

- The Roman emperor Hadrian begins his second tour in north Africa, visiting Carthage and reviewing his troops at the new base at Lambaesis.
- The Roman emperor Hadrian makes his second visit to Athens, Greece, and gives full rein to his admiration for all things Greek and his passion to improve them. He initiates a major building program which includes the completion of the great temple of Zeus, the *Olympieum*, begun five centuries earlier.

129

- The Roman emperor Hadrian tours Asia Minor again, fostering building and public works. He then visits Palmyra (in modern Syria), a city which is now prospering at the expense of Petra in Arabia Petraea.

130

- Roman emperor Hadrian visits Alexandria in Egypt, enriching the museum and rebuilding the Roman general Pompey (the Great)'s tomb there. He sails up the River Nile and asks questions of the Sphinx. His favorite, the Bithynian youth Antinous, is drowned, an event which affects the childless emperor profoundly. A shrine, temple, and city, Antinoöpolis, are built in his honor on the banks of the Nile.
- The Roman emperor Hadrian reaches the city Jerusalem in Judea, still in ruins after its destruction by the Roman general Titus in AD 70, and provides resources for its rebuilding.

132–135

- The fanatical Jewish nationalist Simeon Bar-Kokhba, who has declared himself Messiah, leads the Jews in a revolt against the Romans in Judea. They have some success initially, and the Roman emperor Hadrian has to summon the governor Sextus Julius Severus with 35,000 men of the Xth Legion from Britain to deal with the revolt, while he himself crosses to Antioch in Syria to remain in close touch. The Jewish rebels are gradually confined into the fortress of Bethar, southwest of Jerusalem.

135

- The Jews under their leader Simeon Bar-Kokhba are finally defeated by the Romans in Judea, after a rebellion lasting three and a half years and costing over half a million lives. Many Jews are sold into slavery. This is the final destruction of the Jews as a nation in Judea; they are forbidden to enter Jerusalem, which is renamed Aelia Capitolina. From now on, the Jews of the "Diaspora," or "Dispersion," are to take on most significance. Judea is changed into the new consular province of Syria Palaestrina.

136

- Arrian of Bithynia (the historian Flavius Arrianus) is made prefect of the Roman province of Cappadocia in Asia Minor (modern Turkey). He defeats an invasion by the Alans, an Asiatic people probably allied in blood to the Scythians, who are being pushed south by the Huns from central Asia.
- The Roman emperor Hadrian adopts Aelius Verus as his son and heir, and appoints him governor of the province of Pannonia.

138

- Aelius Verus, the adopted heir of the Roman emperor Hadrian, dies and Hadrian adopts the senator Titus Aurelius Antoninus (aged 52) as his son and heir, at the same time instructing Antoninus to adopt two young men, Marcus Aurelius, Antoninus' nephew, and Lucius Verus, the seven-year-old son of Aelius Verus.
- The Roman emperor Antoninus uses his personal fortune to augment the national exchequer and to promulgate charitable works. He is scrupulous in consulting the Senate on all matters of legislation.
- The Roman emperor Hadrian moves into his villa at Tibur while his mausoleum, equally vast, is built on the banks of the River Tiber in Rome. He then retires to see the sea for the last time at Baiae, where he dies in July. Antoninus, of a rich family from Nîmes in the province of Narbonese Gaul (southern France), succeeds him as emperor.

138–139 The northern British tribe of the Brigantes is defeated by the Roman general Quintus Lollius Urbicus.

139

- The Roman emperor Antoninus persuades a reluctant Senate to deify his predecessor, Hadrian, and earns himself the title of "Pius." Unlike Hadrian, he rules from Rome and does not travel about in his empire.

140

- The Roman governor in Britain, Lollius Urbicus, campaigns against the Picts of modern Lowland Scotland, who have recently built many hill forts. He advances toward the Forth–Clyde isthmus.
- The two consuls for the year in Rome are the emperor Antoninus Pius and the young Marcus Aurelius, his adopted son and heir. Antoninus has a wide-ranging experience of administration and law.

141

- During the reign of Antoninus Pius the Roman Empire enters upon what is generally recognized as its most prosperous, settled, and peaceful period.

143

- The Roman rhetorician Marcus Cornelius Fronto and the Greek rhetorician Herodes Atticus, tutors of Marcus Aurelius, the adopted son and heir of the emperor Antoninus Pius, are made consuls in Rome. Herodes acquires great wealth, much of which he spends on the embellishment of the Greek city of Athens—hence the honorary name "Atticus."

145

- The Roman emperor Antoninus Pius has his adopted son and heir, Marcus Aurelius, married to his daughter by his late wife, Faustina. His daughter, also called Faustina, is Aurelius' cousin.

145–152 The Roman army is engaged in suppressing uprisings by the Moors of Mauritania, northwest Africa.

146

- Marcus Aurelius is named by the Roman emperor Antoninus Pius as his partner in the government of the empire, but his other adopted son and heir, Lucius Verus, is neglected.

147

- Rome celebrates the 900th anniversary of the traditional founding of the city in 753 BC.

149

- Vologeses III succeeds Vologeses II as king of Parthia.

SCIENCE, TECHNOLOGY, AND MEDICINE

Agriculture

c. 100

- Chinese agriculturalists use powdered chrysanthemum flowers as an insecticide—the flowers contain the natural insecticide pyrethrum.

Computing

100

- Greek mathematician and inventor Hero of Alexandria devises a method of representing numbers and performing simple calculating tasks using a train of gears—a primitive computer.

Ecology

106

- The Romans begin to exploit the Dacian gold mines.

Health and Medicine

100

- *c.* 100 Greek physician Aspasia's method of moving a breech baby into position before birth by reaching in and repositioning the child rather than grabbing hold of an appendage and dragging, is mentioned in the writings of the Greek physician Aetius. This is one of the earliest known references to an obstetric technique addressing preternatural positions of the fetus.
- *c.* 100 Greek physician Soranus of Ephesus, practicing at Alexandria, publishes his work on gynecology, *On Midwifery and the Diseases of Women*. Although generally opposed to the practice, he recommends abortion induced by exercise, diuretics, spicy foods, herbal baths, or bleeding where delivery would endanger the mother's life. Roman women use primitive contraceptive methods, including squatting and sneezing immediately after the man's ejaculation, and concoctions of olive oil, honey, cedar resin, white lead, myrtle oil, dried figs, and ground pomegranate.
- The Syrian physician Archigenese invents a miniature drill for penetrating decayed teeth and removing diseased tissue from within them.

c. 108

- Public baths are built by the Romans in the city of Lindum (modern Lincoln, England).

147

- Greek physician Galen, whose father chose medicine as his profession as the result of a dream, receives education in his native Pergamum, and later in Smyrna, Corinth, and Alexandria.

Math

100–150

- The classical Chinese mathematics text *Jiuzhang Suanshu/Nine Chapters on the Mathematical Art* is assembled.

Science

c. **100**

- Mary the Jewess, an alchemist, succeeds in her laboratory inventions with metals and lays the foundation for later work in chemistry. She creates the world's first distillation device, a double boiler, a way to capture vapors of metals, and a metal alloy called Mary's Black.
- The geographer Marinus of Tyre develops a system of equal spacing for lines of latitude and longitude. Maps by Marinus are the first in the Roman Empire to show China.

128

- The Greek mathematician and astronomer Theon of Smyrna observes a transit of Venus across the face of the sun. Since this is incompatible with the earth-centered model of the universe, he suggests Venus and Mercury orbit the sun.

132

- Chinese engineer Zhang Heng develops the first seismograph for determining the position of an earthquake's epicentre. It uses a series of balls suspended in the mouths of eight carved dragons. The balls that are dislodged indicate the direction of the earthquake center.

139–151

- The Egyptian astronomer Claudius Ptolemy is making observations in Alexandria, formulating his geocentric (earth-centered) model of the universe.

c. **140**

- Egyptian astronomers at Alexandria devise an armillary sphere with nine circles as a complete representation of the universe and a calculating aid for astronomy.

Technology

c. **100**

- Parchment scrolls begin to be replaced by notebooks (collections of pages, written on both sides and sewn together down the middle), in the Roman Empire.
- The Greek inventor and mathematician Hero of Alexandria first describes a crankshaft for transmitting power in an engine.
- The inventor Dionysius of Alexandria, Egypt, devises a rapid-firing catapult that fires a series of bolts from a magazine, with a range of up to 180 m/600 ft.

- Indian metallurgists invent cast steel. The proportion of carbon within the steel is tightly controlled at less than 1.7% of the total.
- The Romans begin the mining of coal in Britain.

105

- Chinese eunuch Tsai Lun invents a new method of manufacturing paper from tree bark, hemp, and rags, making it a viable alternative to bamboo and wood.

114

- A Chinese sculpture of this date shows an early form of compass—a polished magnetite spoon that spins to align with the earth's magnetic field when placed on a smooth surface.

Transportation

105

- The Alcantara Bridge over the River Tagus in Roman Spain is the first to be completed with a straight floor for crossing over.
- The Roman emperor Trajan builds a stone bridge over the Danube with the help of his Greek engineer and architect Apollodorus of Damascus, in order to supply his legions in Dacia.

106

- An anonymous Greek sea captain produces a *Periplus*, a sort of pilot's guide, to the Red Sea and ports in the Indian Ocean.

107–110

- The Roman emperor Trajan improves the road network in Italy and has several aqueducts built, one of which, the modern Acqua Paola, still supplies Rome today.

c. **120**

- The Romans begin an extensive program of road building in England.

ARTS AND IDEAS

Architecture

c. **100**

- Roman emperor Trajan founds the city of Thamugadi in Numidia, North Africa. Around this time, he also completes the 823 m/2,700 ft long, 36 m/119 ft high, aqueduct at Segovia, Spain. Consisting of two tiers of arches built on piers and without cement, the structure, which is still in use, dominates the city.
- *c.* 100–*c.* 200   Great building projects are carried out in the pre-Toltec city of Teotihuacán in the Mexican Basin. A great central avenue is laid out, now known as the Street of the Dead. The Temple of the Sun is also completed, dominating the Street of the Dead; at 65 m/216 ft, it is the highest pyramid in Mexico. Another slightly smaller pyramid, to the moon, is also constructed. Twenty further temples line the avenue.

112

- A larger and more magnificent forum is built in Rome on the orders of the Emperor Trajan to designs by Apollodorus of Athens. Inside the forum is Trajan's column made of 18 cubes of marble each weighing about 50 tons. It is flanked by two libraries and shows the Emperor's victorious campaigns in Dacia. The transport and construction of Trajan's column is a major engineering feat.

117

- In the Roman province of Africa (encompassing Carthaginia and Numidia), the city of Thamugadi (founded by the Roman emperor Trajan as a military colony in 100) is developing. Its extensive ruins still remain, under the name of Timgad.

118

- The Pantheon, a temple dedicated to all the gods, is rebuilt in Rome. A domed structure, probably designed by the emperor Hadrian himself, it is one of the few classical buildings to have survived virtually intact.

122

- Roman emperor Hadrian crosses to Britain and orders a wall to be built "to divide the barbarians from the Romans," running from the Solway Firth in the northwest to the mouth of the River Tyne in the northeast.
- Roman emperor Hadrian, who in his own words "sets everything right in Britain," revives the town-building program there. In Viroconium (modern Wroxeter, Shropshire), he scraps the half-finished baths and has a new forum built, and Verulamium (modern St. Albans, Hertfordshire) receives its magnificent gateway.

123

- Roman emperor Hadrian orders the building of a great temple in the town of Cyzicus on the Sea of Marmara (in modern Turkey). Completed by Marcus Aurelius about 167, it becomes one of the wonders of the world.

127

- Hadrian's Wall, marking the northern boundary of Roman colonization in Britain, is virtually completed. It is 117 km/73 mi long and interspersed with forts: if well manned, it will be almost impregnable.

131

- Roman emperor Hadrian returns to Rome, where he spends much money on public buildings, beautifying the capital of the Roman Empire.

135

- c. 135 A magnificent villa is completed at Tibur (Tivoli) near Rome. Built for the emperor Hadrian, it is based on his own architectural ideas gathered during his travels throughout the Empire.
- An aqueduct is built in Athens using Roman technology such as concrete and cross-vaulting, to allow the spanning of wide areas without support.

143

- c. 143 Roman emperor Antoninus orders the construction of a second, turf wall across Britain some 160 km/100 mi to the north of Hadrian's Wall. The Antonine Wall, running from the Firth of Forth to the River Clyde in modern Scotland is rapidly overrun, and abandoned before 196.

Arts

100

- c. 100 A new style of Buddhist sculpture is developing in the region of Gandhara (now in northwest Pakistan): deeply influenced by Roman art, especially in the handling of drapery, it produces the first great Buddhist imagery. It is contemporary with an independent school of Buddhist sculptors at Mathura in Uttar Pradesh, where highly sensuous figures carved in red sandstone are produced and traded throughout India.

147

- Shrines erected to members of the Wu family near Jia-Xing in Shandong, China, show typical Han bas reliefs in which traditional scenes are incised in crisp silhouette.

Literature and Language

100

- c. 100 Greek writer Plutarch returns to his native Chaeronea, in Boeotia. There he holds various magisterial offices and concentrates on writing his Lives of famous Greeks and Romans.
- Latin poet Martial (Marcus Valerius Martialis), with the financial help of the writer Pliny the Younger, retires to his native Spain.

109

- Roman satirist Juvenal's first of five books of Satires appears about this time. Each "Satire" attacks a different aspect of what Juvenal saw as the moral degeneracy of Roman society under Domitian.

c. 118

- Suetonius becomes one of the emperor Hadrian's private secretaries. Due to the enmity of the emperor's wife he loses his job and retires to write his De vita Caesarum/Lives of the Caesars, 12 biographies beginning with Julius Caesar and ending with Domitian.

c. 125

- The Chu Elegies, an anthology of Chinese poetry, some dating back to the 3rd century BC, is collected and edited by Wang I. Many of the poems were originally written to be set to music.

c. 135

- Indian poet Asvagosha writes Buddhacarita, an epic poem in classical Sanskrit on the life of the Buddha.

138

- Roman emperor Hadrian, on his deathbed, writes a poem of farewell to his soul, his only surviving literary work.

149

- The writer Lucius Apuleius lectures on philosophy, in Rome. His fame rests on his comic "novel" The Golden Ass, which recounts the adventures of a sorcerer's apprentice accidentally turned into an ass.

Thought and Scholarship

100

- Latin writer Pliny the Younger is chosen to write the "Panegyric" for the Roman emperor Trajan.

124

- Greek historian Arrian of Bithynia receives Roman citizenship from Hadrian and assumes the name of Flavius Arrianus. His most important work is *Anabasis*, an account of the campaigns of Alexander the Great.

133

- The young future Roman emperor Marcus Aurelius studies with the rhetorician Fronto but is more attracted by the Stoic philosophy of Epictetus.

140

- Greek historian Appian writes his *Histories* of Rome and its wars.

SOCIETY

Education

c. 100

- Girls are educated in Rome from age seven to fourteen, studying grammar, Greek and Latin, music, astronomy, history, mythology, philosophy, and dancing.

Everyday Life

c. 100

- Boy-children in Rome are preferred over girl-children, who are often exposed or abandoned. Some orphaned girls are raised by brothel owners to be prostitutes.
- Chocolate is first used as a drink by the Maya people of Central America. It becomes so popular that it is soon adopted as a form of currency.
- Roman women show concern for their health and figures by lifting weights and swimming to stay in shape.
- The Nok culture of what is now Nigeria reaches its high point, producing iron tools and terracotta sculpture.
- Women in Greece are allowed to participate in public athletic contests such as foot and chariot races.

101

- Christians begin to bury their dead in underground burial chambers, the catacombs, outside Rome. The frescoes on the walls mark the beginning of a distinctive

BIRTHS & DEATHS

c. 100

- Flavius Josephus (Joseph ben Matthias), Jewish historian who later moved to Rome from Jerusalem, Palestine, dies in Rome (63).

103

- Martial (Marcus Valerius Martialis), Roman poet, dies (*c.* 64).

106

- Decebalus, King of Dacia (now Romania), who unified the Dacian tribes into one nation, commits suicide.

c. 113

- Pliny the Younger, Roman author whose letters provide a picture of Roman life, dies in Bithynia (*c.* 54).

115

- Ban Zhao, female Chinese historian and moralist, dies (*c.* 80).

117

- Trajan, Roman emperor 98–117, who expanded the Roman Empire eastward to include Dacia, Armenia, Arabia, and Mesopotamia, and who undertook major public works projects, dies in Selinus, Celicia (65).

118

- Quintilian, Latin writer known for his work on rhetoric *Institutio oratoria/ Education of an Orator*, dies in Rome (78).

c. 120

- Plutarch, Latin essayist and biographer whose work had a major influence on the development of the essay, biography, and historical writing in Europe between the 16th and 19th centuries, dies (*c.* 75)
- The Greek biographer and philosopher Plutarch dies at his home in Chaeronea.
- The Roman historian Tacitus dies (64). He leaves behind his two chief works—the *Historiae/Histories*, covering the period 68–96; and his *Annales/Annals*, covering the period from the deaths of Roman emperors Augustus to Nero.

121

April 26 Marcus Aurelius (original name Marcus Annius Verus), Roman emperor 161–180 and joint emperor with his son Commodus from 177, who wrote the book *Meditations* on Stoic philosophy, born in Rome (–180).

c. 122

- Suetonius, Roman biographer who wrote biographies of 12 Roman Emperors, dies (53).

124

- Lucius Apuleius, Platonic philosopher, rhetorician, and author of the prose narrative *The Golden Ass*, born in Madauros, Numidia (now Mdaourouch, Algeria) (date of death unknown).

129

- Galen, celebrated Greek physician, born in Pergamum, Asia Minor (now Burgama, Turkey) (–*c.* 199).

135

c. 135 Akiba ben Joseph, Jewish scholar who founded rabbinic Judaism, dies (*c.* 95).

- Epictetus, Stoic philosopher whose works were collected by his pupil Arrian, dies in Nicopolis, Epirus, Greece (*c.* 80).

138

July 10 Hadrian, Roman emperor 117–138, dies in Baiae, near Naples (62).

c. 140

- Juvenal (Decimus Junius Juvenalis), Roman satirical poet, author of 16 "Satires," dies, probably in Rome (*c.* 73).

c. 143

- Pausanias, Greek traveler whose *Description of Greece* provides a guide to ancient ruins, born in Lydia (–*c.* 176).

146

- Septimius Severus, Roman emperor 193–211, who turned the Roman government into a military monarchy, born in Leptis Magna, Tripolitania (–211).

Christian art. The burials continue until the end of the 4th century AD.

118

- Hadrian returns to Rome wearing a beard, setting a new fashion for Roman emperors.

120

- Rome is the largest city in the world, with an estimated population of more than 1 million.

Religion

108

- Ignatius, bishop of Antioch since AD 69, is summoned to Rome and martyred in the Colosseum for refusing to renounce his faith. His seven *Ignatian Epistles*, written on the journey to Rome, are an important source of information about the early church.

c. **117**

- The Gnostic theologian Basilides founds a sect at Alexandria. His beliefs combine aspects of Christianity, Zoroastrianism, and magic.

135

- The Jewish revolt against the Romans causes even more dislike between Jews and their Gentile neighbors. After 135 Christianity begins to spread more rapidly, and Jerusalem later becomes the home of the Christian church.

140

- Marcion of Sinope comes to Rome and teaches beliefs that are heretical to Christians. He denies the incarnation of Jesus and claims that God of the New Testament is not the same one as of the Old Testament.

141

- In the first of his *Apologies* the Christian philosopher Justin of Samaria defends the church against charges of atheism and immorality.

146

- The worship of Serapis, an ancient Greco-Egyptian sun god, is permitted in Rome.

150–199

POLITICS, GOVERNMENT, AND ECONOMICS

Business and Economics

171

- The Roman emperor Marcus Aurelius conducts the Second Marcomannian War with remarkable economy and Rome is enjoying a degree of commercial prosperity. He settles captive Germans on imperial estates as *coloni* or tenant cultivators.

Colonization

167

- The movements of the northern Germanic tribes set in motion the Iazyges, a nomadic tribe who now overrun the Roman province of Dacia (modern Romania).
- The second wave of northern European peoples moves south in the shape of the Germanic Marcomanni, Quadi, and Vandals. They pose a serious threat to the

borders of the Roman Empire, and the emperor Marcus Aurelius has to recruit from all classes of the population and bring in help from other Germanic tribes to resist them. He leads the army himself. The Germans cross the River Danube, destroy a Roman garrison of 20,000 troops, and pour south until they besiege the town of Aquileia in northern Italy.

181

- Pictish and Scottish tribes cross the Antonine Wall and invade the Roman-ruled area between it and Hadrian's Wall, in the north of Roman Britain.

195

- Continuing his campaigning in the East, the Roman emperor Septimius Severus crosses the River Euphrates, defeating the decaying kingdom of the Parthians. The city of Nisibis in Mesopotamia becomes a Roman colony.

Human Rights

160

- The Roman emperor Antoninus Pius has established an outstandingly humanitarian rule, both at home and in the provinces. He punishes the harsh masters of slaves and instructs his governors and client kings similarly to punish any resort to violence.

185

- Marcia, a Christian concubine of Roman emperor Commodus, is able to win protection for the Christians of Rome.

Politics and Government

152–153

- The Egyptian peasants revolt but are put down by the Romans. Rome's corn supply is cut and widespread unrest breaks out. The Roman emperor Antoninus Pius makes a distribution from his own funds—as he does on eight other occasions during his reign.
- The Roman campaign in Mauritania, northwest Africa, is successfully ended and peace is imposed on the Moors.

154

- The Brigantes in the north of England revolt against Roman rule. Reinforcements have to be brought in from Germany to quell the uprising. Most of the Roman troops in Britain are busy manning the walls to their north.

156

- The Sien-Pei, a Mongol horde who have conquered Mongolia, attack the Liaodong Peninsula in China and continue to make frequent raids over the frontier.

157–159

- A minor disturbance in Roman Dacia is put down and the province is divided administratively into three parts.

160

- A minor rising is put down in the Roman province of Africa.
- Marcus Aurelius and Lucius Verus, the adopted sons and heirs of the Roman emperor Antoninus Pius, are made consuls-designate in Rome. There is no need for promulgation, for the emperor is approaching the end of his life.
- The Roman government creates an agricultural crisis by confiscating peasant lands as gifts for retired legionaries, most of whom are very poor farmers.

161

161–169 The Roman Empire's boundary in the north of Britain remains turbulent, and there are reports of revolts in the years 161 and 169.

March 3 The Roman emperor Antoninus Pius calls his adopted son and heir Marcus Aurelius to his bedside in Lorium, Etruria, Italy, has his golden statue of Fortune transferred to his adopted son's room, and dies. Marcus Aurelius succeeds Antoninus Pius and, remembering Antoninus' wish, has his fellow adopted son and heir, Lucius Verus, made his full colleague. This sets a precedent for later divisions of the imperial *maiestas*.

162

- Lucius Verus, coruler with the Roman emperor Marcus Aurelius, is sent to fight the Parthians who have invaded Armenia, but gets no farther than Antioch in Roman Syria.
- The Britons and the German Chatti revolt against Roman rule; at the same time, the Parthian king Vologeses III declares war on Rome and invades Armenia.

162–166 The Parthian War is successfully continued by the Roman general Avidius Cassius, a Syrian by birth. The city of Seleucia and the capital Ctesiphon are taken and despoiled. Cassius is given a triumph (victory procession in Rome), which he shares with the emperor Marcus Aurelius and is made governor of Rome's eastern provinces.

164

- The Roman emperor Marcus Aurelius marries his daughter Lucilla to his coemperor, Lucius Verus.

166

- Chinese sources record the arrival in Han China of an embassy from the Roman emperor Marcus Aurelius, although it may have been more of a trading expedition.

168–169

- With help (duly paid for) from other German tribes and from the Scythians, the Romans eventually beat back the Marcomanni-led German invaders from the town of Aquileia in northern Italy.

169

- Germanic tribes again break through northern frontiers of the Roman Empire and invade the provinces from Raetia (modern Switzerland) to Moesia (modern Bulgaria)—the Second Marcomannian War. At the same time, the Moors of north Africa invade Spain, and the Lombards appear on the River Rhine.
- The Roman coemperor Lucius Verus dies on the way back from the campaign against the barbarians in northern Italy, and the emperor Marcus Aurelius returns ill and exhausted.

170

- The Roman emperor Marcus Aurelius reluctantly takes up again the burden of military commander against the northern barbarians.
- While campaigning in the Roman province of Pannonia, the Roman emperor Marcus Aurelius appoints the Greek sophist Alexander of Cotyaeum as his secretary.

171–173

- The Roman emperor Marcus Aurelius continues the Second Marcomannian War in Rome's Danubian provinces (Thrace, Moesia, and Dacia) from his base in Upper Pannonia, defeating the Marcomanni in 172.

173

- The Roman general Avidius Cassius, who defeated the Parthians in 166, is sent to quell a revolt in Egypt.

174

- The Roman emperor Marcus Aurelius comes back to Rome from fighting the Marcomannian War but then returns to the war front. He successfully subdues the barbarians, conclusively defeating the Quadi, and makes preparations to extend the boundaries of the Roman Empire to the Carpathian Mountains.

175

- A rebellion in Egypt is suppressed by the Roman general Avidius Cassius, who then declares himself emperor. The Roman emperor Marcus Aurelius, asserting that he will gladly yield to Cassius if the soldiers wish it, advances eastward to meet him but Cassius is killed by one of his own centurions. During Aurelius' progress eastward, his beloved wife Faustina, who is with him, dies. A city, Faustinopolis, near Mt. Taurus in the Roman province of Cappadocia, Asia Minor (modern Turkey), is raised in her honor. Marcus Aurelius returns to Rome via Smyrna in Asia and Athens in Greece. The chief result of the revolt by Cassius is that Aurelius abandons all thoughts of extending the Roman Empire to include the German tribes and makes peace with them, annexing only a 16-km/10-mi-wide strip across the River Danube.

- The Roman emperor Marcus Aurelius' son, Commodus, assumes the *toga virilis*, which denotes that he has reached manhood.
- The Roman emperor Marcus Aurelius sends reinforcements of 5,400 auxiliary cavalry to quell trouble in Britain. He then campaigns in the province of Dacia, which was overrun by the Iazyges in 167. He defeats them and drives them out.

176

- The Roman emperor Marcus Aurelius is given a triumph (victory procession) in Rome. Commodus is included in the honor, and is made partner with his father on the throne.

178–180

- The Roman emperor Marcus Aurelius, believing that Rome will only be safe with its frontiers extended to the Carpathian Mountains, renews the Marcomannian Wars along the River Danube. By 180 he has cleared the Roman provinces of Germanic invaders and is preparing to advance the frontier.

181

- Commodus, the new Roman emperor, returns to Rome and gives himself up to dissipation. He is a skilled huntsman, swordsman, and bowman, and takes part in the gladiatorial shows. He reputedly keeps a harem of some 300 women and an equal number of boys. In the ensuing decade of his reign there is virtually no trouble from the barbarians of the north whom his father, Marcus Aurelius, had fought. Rome is at the apex of its power, but the marks of decay are apparent and in future the initiative will largely be taken by the barbarians.
- The Roman emperor Commodus increases his extravagance and gifts to the people of Rome.

183

- Lucilla, the sister of the Roman emperor Commodus, plots his assassination. She is executed, along with most of the important men of the day. Informers reappear in Rome.
- Perennis is made head of the Praetorian Guard in Rome and given great powers. The Roman emperor Commodus continues with his sporting entertainments and his gladiatorial prowess.

184

- The Han dynasty in China, continuously weakened by the misrule of eunuch ministers, suffers from a popular rising known as the rebellion of the Yellow Turbans. Han China is now sinking into division and anarchy. The rebellion is suppressed by the Chinese general Cao Cao.
- The severely disciplinarian Roman general Ulpius Marcellus is sent as governor to Britain to drive the

Highland tribes back over the Antonine Wall. He is successful, but he is recalled by the emperor Commodus, possibly because his severe rule increases rebellious tendencies in the army in Britain.

185

- The Praetorian prefect, Perennis, is suspected of conspiracy on evidence from legionaries from Dalmatia and Britain and executed in Rome. He is followed as Praetorian prefect and favorite of the Roman emperor Commodus by a one-time slave, Cleander, who spreads corruption.
- The Roman general Helvius Pertinax is sent to restore order among the legionaries in Britain; they cease to be mutinous but hint that Pertinax should usurp the Roman emperor Commodus. The Antonine Wall is dismantled.

186

- Crispina, wife of the Roman emperor Commodus, is banished to the island of Capri for adultery and subsequently put to death.

188

- A revolt against Roman rule in Germany is suppressed.

190

- A Roman mob rises up against the corrupt Praetorian prefect Cleander, who is sentenced to death by the Roman emperor Commodus. Plague breaks out again in Rome, accompanied by famine.
- The Roman general Helvius Pertinax deals with trouble in Africa.
- Xiandi, the last of the Han emperors, ascends the Chinese throne though still a young boy; he is little more than a puppet.

192

- The Chinese general Cao Cao assumes power in China, imprisoning the boy-emperor Xiandi. The court eunuchs are destroyed and the 400-year rule of the Han dynasty is now virtually at an end.
- The Roman emperor Commodus is becoming more paranoid and, as a result, more murderous. To save their own lives, Marcia, one of his concubines who has protected Christians in Rome, and the new head of the Praetorian Guard, Quintus Aemilius Laetus, poison Commodus on the last day of the year. He clings to life but is finished off by his former wrestling companion.

193

- Helvius Pertinax, the Roman general, returns to Rome at the start of the year and is chosen emperor. However, he earns the displeasure of the soldiers for instituting much-needed economies and reforms and is murdered by members of the Praetorian Guard. The Praetorian Guard puts the throne up to the highest bidder. The rich Didius Julianus wins but survives only two months. The people of Rome, angered at the death of Pertinax, appeal to the legions in Britain, Syria, and Pannonia.
- Pescennius Niger, the commander of the Roman army in Syria, is proclaimed emperor by his troops. He rapidly gains control of Egypt and Asia Minor, and occupies Byzantium on the Bosporus as a crossing point to Europe.
- The Roman commander Septimius Severus arrives in Rome, by which time the Praetorian Guard has put the emperor Didius Julianus to death and the Senate has

deified the former emperor Helvius Pertinax. Septimius Severus is declared Roman emperor. One of his first acts is to reorganize and subdue the Praetorian Guard. The Guard is demobilized and replaced with 15,000 legionary soldiers, to give Severus command in Italy while he deals with his rivals. Military service is made compulsory but forbidden to citizens of Italy, thus giving more power to the provincial legionaries. A large part of the Senate are executed for having declared for Clodius Albinus, the Roman governor in Britain, instead of Severus. Once more, all power is taken from the Senate. The imperial throne becomes virtually a hereditary military monarchy. A Phoenician by birth, Severus has been well educated and has practiced law as well as soldiering. Ulpian, a rising jurist, and the emperor's chief adviser, obligingly argues in defense of absolute power.

194

- Clodius Albinus in Britain, one of the two rivals to the Roman emperor Septimius Severus, is placated with the title of Caesar and promises of the succession.
- The Roman emperor Septimius Severus marches against his second rival, Pescennius Niger, and defeats him at Issus in Cilicia, Asia Minor. Severus confiscates vast estates from Niger's supporters and punishes rebellious cities. Antioch is deprived of its position as capital of Syria, and Byzantium is destroyed after a siege of two years.

196

- After campaigning in the East, the Roman emperor Septimius Severus returns to Rome. His son Caracalla, aged eight, is declared Caesar.
- The Roman Governor in Britain, Clodius Albinus, on the discovery of treasonable correspondence, is named a public enemy. He declares himself emperor, leaves Britain with all the troops he can muster, and sets up court at Lyons in Gaul. Outside the city he meets the army of the Roman emperor Septimius Severus, is defeated, and commits suicide. The city of Lyon is looted and partially destroyed.

197

- Sections of Hadrian's Wall in Britain, denuded of Roman troops and with the Antonine Wall already abandoned, are destroyed by the Lowlanders, the Maeatae, who reach southward as far as Roman Eboracum (modern York, North Yorkshire). A new governor, Virius Lupus, is sent to Britain and restores order. He begins the considerable task of rebuilding Hadrian's Wall.
- The Roman emperor Septimius Severus renews his war against the Parthians. Their capital city, Ctesiphon, is again captured and is destroyed. Severus leaves the small state of Osrhoene in Mesopotamia in the hands of a client king, Abgar IX, but he makes the rest of Mesopotamia into a Roman province, with its capital at Nisibis.

198

- The Roman emperor Septimius Severus' son Caracalla is made Augustus, and his other son, Geta, is made Caesar.

199

- The Roman emperor Septimius Severus visits Egypt by way of Palestine and the Roman province of Arabia, and relieves the Egyptians of burdensome taxation.

SCIENCE, TECHNOLOGY, AND MEDICINE

Ecology

151

- A huge earthquake in Asia Minor demolishes a great temple at Cyzicus, and ruins other towns in the region.

152–153

- There are floods in Rome and an earthquake on the Greek island of Rhodes.

178

- The city of Smyrna in the Roman province of Asia suffers an earthquake.

191

- A serious fire in Rome destroys many libraries, and much valuable work is lost to posterity, including some recent works of the physician Galen, primarily on philosophical subjects.

Health and Medicine

c. **160**

- The Romans build public baths and an aqueduct in modern Leicester, England.

161

- The Greek physician Galen travels to Rome and cures the philosopher Eudemus, who introduces him to many powerful people. He becomes court physician to the co-emperors Marcus Aurelius and Lucius Verus.

164–180

- The Roman Empire is swept by a smallpox plague brought back from the East by legions under the coemperor Lucius Verus.

167–170

- Plague—probably bubonic—is brought back from the East by Roman troops. Asia Minor, Greece, Gaul, and Egypt are affected as well as Italy.

170

- Greek physician Claudius Galen develops methods for extracting plant juices, to be used for medicinal purposes.

173–184

- China suffers from the plague, as Rome did earlier.

180

- The Greek physician Claudius Galen, practicing at Rome, writes *Methodus medendi/Method of Physicians*, a medical textbook that will become the ultimate authority for medieval medicine.

Science

150

c. 150 *Physiologus/Naturalist*, a Greek work by an anonymous author, is written in Alexandria. All the medieval "bestiaries" evolve from this work, which is an encyclopedia of real and imagined natural history.

- Egyptian astronomer Claudius Ptolemy publishes the work known as the *Almagest*, a highly influential astronomical textbook that outlines a theory of a geocentric (earth-centered) universe based on years of observations.

151

- The Egyptian cosmographer Claudius Ptolemy's *Geographica/Geography* charts the world as the Roman Empire knew it at this time—stretching from modern Iceland to Ceylon, with unknown lands to the south and east.

157

- The Greek physician Claudius Galen becomes physician to the gladiators in his native Pergamum, offering him a unique insight into anatomy and the treatment of wounds.

Technology

150

- At the order of the Chinese Han Emperor, state documents written on paper and concerning events dating to about 137, are stored within a section of the Great Wall of China itself.

180

- The Chinese inventor Ting Huan invents a human-powered mechanical fan for air conditioning the palace of the Han dynasty emperors.

ARTS AND IDEAS

Architecture

c. 150

- A great building complex known as the Ciudadela is constructed in Teotihuacán in the Mexican Basin, about 1.2 km/ 0.75 mi from the great Pyramid of the Sun. This building is now known as the "Temple of Quetzalcoatl" after the temple in its midst, and may have been the residence of the rulers of Teotihuacán.
- The great temple of Jupiter at Baalbek, Roman Syria (now in Lebanon), is built.

161

- Roman emperor Marcus Aurelius completes the temple in the Forum that his predecessor Antoninus has raised

to his wife and rededicates it to Antoninus as well as Faustina.

193

- The column of Marcus Aurelius, sometimes called the Antonine column, is completed. Its reliefs are bolder and clearer than those of Trajan's column on which it is based.

Literature and Language

165

- The satirist and wit Lucian settles in Athens, Greece, and writes his *Dialogues*.

173

- Greek traveler Pausanias writes his famous guide book of Greece, *Periegesis/Guided Tour*. In the 19th century German archeologist Heinrich Schliemann's intelligent interpretation of this work helps him to make his discoveries at Mycenae.

197

- The writings of Tertullian mark the turning point at which Christian literature becomes written mainly in Latin rather than Greek. His *Apologeticum* seeks to assure the Romans that Christians are good citizens while *De spectaculis/Concerning Theater* attacks the Roman theater and games.

Music

c. 150

- Bellows-powered organs replace the earlier Greek hydraulis or water-regulated organs.

Theater and Dance

162

- The Odeum, a large, roofed theater, is built at Athens for oratory and music by the consul and orator Herodes Atticus.

Thought and Scholarship

174

- While on various military campaigns, Roman emperor Marcus Aurelius composes his *Meditations*: philosophical thoughts, influenced by Stoicism, which reflect his disillusionment with the aspirations of mankind and his own sense of duty.

175

- On his way back to Rome, the Roman emperor Marcus Aurelius attends lectures by the Greek rhetorician Aelius Aristides at Smyrna in the Roman province of Asia, and himself lectures in Athens, Greece, in the Greek language. He also endows professorships in Athens in the four main philosophical doctrines: Platonic, Aristotelian, Stoic, and Epicurean.

SOCIETY

Everyday Life

175

- Roman emperor Marcus Aurelius creates an endowment for the aid of young women in memory of his wife. A bas relief is made showing a younger Faustina pouring money into the laps of girls.

Religion

151

- In a generally peaceful Roman Empire the Christians, disappointed in their expectation of a Second Coming, struggle for unity of belief and suffer from a multitude of splits and heresies.

155

- Polycarp, bishop of Smyrna, visits Rome, where he defends traditional Christianity against the heresies of Marcion. He is martyred on his return to Smyrna.

156

- The Phrygian mystic Montanus prophesies the imminence of the Kingdom of Heaven upon Earth. His followers, the Montanists, practice a strict asceticism and speak in ecstatic utterances.

158

- Artemidorus of Lydia writes *Oneirocritica/The Interpretation of Dreams*, an important source of ancient myths and superstitions.

162

- Mithraism, a secret cult centered on the sacrifice of a bull to the Persian sun god Mithras, becomes increasingly popular, especially in the Roman army.

BIRTHS & DEATHS

c. 150
- Dio Cassius (full name Cassius Dio Cocceianus), Roman administrator and historian, whose major work is *Romaika*, an important history of Rome in Greek, born in Nicaea, in Bithynia, Asia Minor (now Iznik, Turkey) (–235).

c. 156
- St. Polycarp, Greek bishop of Smyrna, author of *Letter to the Philippians*, dies.

157
- Gordian I, briefly Roman emperor March–April 238, coruling with his son Gordian II, born (–238).

c. 160
- Tertullian, Christian theologian who originated ecclesiastical Latin, born in Carthage (–c. 220).

161
August 31 Commodus, Roman emperor notorious for his brutality, born in Lanuvium, Italy (–192).

164
- Macrinus, Roman emperor 217–218, born in Caesarea, Mauritania (now Cherchell, Algeria) (–218).

c. 170
- Claudius Ptolemy, Egyptian scientist, creator of the Ptolemaic astronomical system which dominated Western science for over 1,000 years, dies, probably in Alexandria, Egypt (c. 78).

175
- Annia Galeria Faustina, cousin and wife of the Roman emperor Marcus Aurelius, who accompanied him on several campaigns, dies (c. 50).

July (Gaius) Avidius Cassius, who usurped the title of Roman Emperor for three months in 175, is assassinated.

c. 176
- Pausanias, Greek traveler whose book *Description of Greece* provides a guide to ancient ruins, dies (c. 33).

177
- Herodes Atticus, outstanding orator of the Second Sophistic, a movement that sought to revitalize Greek rhetoric, dies in Rome (c. 76).

180
March 17 Marcus Aurelius (original name Marcus Annius Verus), Roman emperor 161–80 and joint emperor with his son Commodus from 177, who wrote the book *Meditations* on Stoic philosophy, dies, either in Vindobona (Vienna, Austria) or Sirmium, Pannonia (59).

c. 185
- Origen, theologian and biblical scholar of the early Greek Church, author of *Hexalpa*, a synopsis of various versions of the Old Testament, born in Alexandria (–c. 254).

188
April 4 Caracalla (Marcus Aurelius Severus Antoninus Augustus), Roman emperor 198–211 jointly with his father Septimius Severus; 209–212 also with his brother Geta; 212–217 alone, notorious for his tyranny, born in Lugdunum (Lyon), Gaul (–217).

189
- Geta (Publius Septimius Geta), Roman emperor 209–212 with his father Septimius Severus and brother Caracalla, born in Mediolanum (now Milan, Italy) (–212).

192
December 31 Commodus, Roman emperor notorious for his brutality 177–180 with his father, Marcus Aurelius; 180–192 alone, killed in combat in the arena (31).

193
June 1 Marcus Didius Julianus, Roman senator who became emperor March–June 193, effectively by buying the loyalty of the Praetorian Guard, killed by the Danube legions (c. 58).

197
- Decimus Clodius Septimius Albinus, Roman general, who laid claim to the imperial throne 193–197, falls in battle against his rival Lucius Septimius Severus, near Lugdunum, Gaul (modern Lyon, France).

c. 199
- Claudius Galen, celebrated Greek physician, dies, possibly in Rome (c. 70).

166

- Justin of Samaria offends other philosophers in Rome and is put to death as a Christian along with six of his followers.

180

- The Roman emperor Commodus makes Mithraism an imperial cult.

186

- Irenaeus, bishop of Lyons, refutes Gnosticism and stresses the continuity of the New and Old Testaments in his *Adversus haereses/Against Heresies*.

c. **195**

- The theologian Clement of Alexandria is active. He applies Platonism to Christian doctrine and believes Christ to be the source of all human reason as well as the incarnation of the Word.

Sports

c. **150**

- The Greek historian Arrian of Nicomedia writes his *Cynegeticus*, a treatise on coursing (hunting with hounds).

c. **190–*c.* 200**

- Septimius Severus, the Roman commander and emperor from 193, builds the first hippodrome for horse and chariot races in Byzantium (modern Istanbul, Turkey), a smaller version of Rome's Circus Maximus.

200–249

POLITICS, GOVERNMENT, AND ECONOMICS

Business and Economics

202

- Roman emperor Septimius Severus extends the planting of *coloni* (tenant farmers, either poor Romans or conquered Germans) on imperial estates, a practice that is copied by many Roman landowners during the coming century, partly because of the scarcity of slaves. There is a general economic decline during this century, with trade falling off, high taxation, and the currency being debased after Septimius increases the alloy in the denarius to 50%.

Colonization

201

- By the time of the reign of the Roman emperor Septimius Severus, the Goths, a Germanic tribe who moved from their original homeland around the Baltic Sea in the reign of the emperor Hadrian, have founded an empire on the northern shores of the Black Sea (known as the Cernjachov culture) and around the Danube delta (known as Wielbark cultures).

214

- The Roman client kingdom of Osrhoene is incorporated into the Roman province of Mesopotamia. Its capital, Edessa, becomes a Roman colony.

Human Rights

222

- During the reign of the Roman emperor Alexander Severus all persecution of Christians ceases.

Politics and Government

200

- The Japanese state of Yamato is founded, based around the port of Osaka. It soon takes in much of the island of Honshu. The tombs of the first emperors are protected by terracotta figures, as in China. On the other islands indigenous groups remain independent and follow a traditional way of life, such as the Ainu of Hokkaido.
- The Japanese warrior empress, Jingu, invades and subdues part of Korea.

201

- The Roman emperor Septimius Severus reaches Antioch in Syria where he celebrates the attainment of the *toga virilis* by his son Caracalla, signifying that he has reached manhood.

202

- The Roman emperor Septimius Severus returns from the East in triumph to Rome after his defeat of the Parthians.

203

- Fulvius Plautianus, head of the Roman Praetorian Guard, is made one of the consuls in Rome for the year. He has great influence over the emperor Septimius Severus.
- The Roman emperor Septimius Severus visits his African provinces and strengthens their boundaries against the desert tribes.

205

- Caracalla and Geta, the sons of the Roman emperor Septimius Severus, are made consuls in Rome for the year. Caracalla accuses his father-in-law, Fulvius Plautianus, the Praetorian prefect, of a plot against the emperor and Plautianus is murdered by a court attendant. Plautilla, his daughter and the wife of Caracalla, is banished.
- The Roman emperor Septimius Severus replaces the Praetorian prefect Fulvius Plautianus with two prefects, one of whom is the jurist Aemilius Papinian. The Praetorian prefects become the emperor's second in command, in charge of military forces in Italy. Their primary duties, however, are legal. They hear appeals from the provinces, and are expected to develop the principles and administration of law. Severan legislation in general tends to favor the poorer classes.

206–208

- A brigand by the name of Bulla Felix makes himself famous by waylaying travelers on the roads of Italy. Banditry is growing throughout the Roman Empire, from Egypt to the River Rhine.
- The Roman emperor Septimius Severus moves away from Rome and its demoralizing influence on his sons to Campania, southwest Italy, during these years. With the help of the jurist Domitius Ulpian and others of his council he revises the law, making it more equitable and more humanitarian.

208

- Ardashir becomes king of Persis, a vassal kingdom of the Parthians with its capital near Persepolis.
- In order to strengthen the northern boundaries of Britain and to prevent another episode like that of Clodius Albinus (who declared himself emperor and set up a rival court in Lugdunum, Gaul, in 196), the Roman emperor Septimius Severus decides to visit Britain himself with his two sons. He is now 62 years old.

208–210 The Roman emperor Septimius Severus campaigns in northern Britain. Hadrian's Wall has now been repaired, and he plans to subdue the land to the north of it, ravaging it so severely that a second wall will not be necessary. Road-building and forest-clearing as he goes, Severus reaches beyond modern Aberdeen. The Scottish tribes conduct skillful guerrilla warfare against him.

211

- The Roman emperor Septimius Severus' final advice to his sons, Caracalla and Geta, "Enrich the army!," embodies his philosophy of rule, that the need for a strong army is paramount.

212

- The new Roman coemperor Caracalla inherits the oriental cruelty of his late father, Septimius Severus, but none of his statesmanship, and has his brother and coemperor, Geta, and many of his supporters murdered. Caracalla prefers hunting and the company of gladiators to imperial business. He is reputed to have had 20,000 of his brother's supporters put to death.
- The Roman jurist Aemilius Papinian, one of three famous jurists who flourished during the reign of the late emperor Septimius Severus (the other two being Domitius Ulpian and Julius Paulus), refuses to write a legal defense of the coemperor Caracalla's murder of his brother, Geta, and is beheaded in Rome, in Caracalla's presence. Caracalla quietens the objections of the army to Geta's murder by huge donations. Then, to obtain more tax revenue, he extends Roman citizenship to all free male adults throughout the empire: the *Constitutio Antoniniana* ("Antonine Constitution").

213–214

- The Roman emperor Caracalla expels some German marauders from Gaul, then meets the Alemanni, an increasingly powerful collection of German tribes between the upper Danube and the upper Rhine. Caracalla wins a victory over the Alemanni on the banks of the River Main, and gives himself the title "Germanicus." It is probably while campaigning in Germany that he takes a liking to the *caracalla*, a Celtic or German tunic from which he acquires the name by which he is known.

215

- The Roman emperor Caracalla, fearing revolt in Egypt and annoyed at the Alexandrians referring to himself and his mother as Oedipus and Jocasta, visits the city of Alexandria in Egypt and reputedly orders the massacre of all its able-bodied citizens. This may indicate that there had in fact been a serious outbreak of sedition, and that Caracalla wished to ensure Egypt's obedience during his projected Parthian campaign.

216

- The Roman emperor Caracalla, in admiration of Alexander the Great, forms a 16,000-strong troop that he calls "Alexander's Phalanx" and has it equipped with arms of the ancient Macedonian type.
- Wishing to emulate Alexander the Great's conquest of Persia, the Roman emperor Caracalla invades Parthia and attempts to assassinate the Parthian king, Artabanus IV, by a ruse. Artabanus escapes and invades Syria.

217

- While campaigning in Parthia, the Roman emperor Caracalla is assassinated by his legionaries near Edessa. Macrinus, head of the Praetorian Guard, declares himself emperor and makes peace with Parthia.

218

- Julia Maesa, the aunt of the assassinated emperor Caracalla, banished to her home in Syria by the head of the Praetorian Guard and self-proclaimed emperor, Macrinus, declares her grandson Elagabalus emperor. Macrinus advances westward to meet Julia, who fights in person, defeats him, and has him executed. The Syrian legionaries support Elagabalus, a priest of Elagabal (Baal), aged about 14.

219

- Following the defeat and execution of the self-proclaimed emperor Macrinus, the new Roman emperor, the young Syrian priest Elagabalus, enters

Rome rouged, bejeweled, and dressed in gold and purple.

220

- The Roman emperor Elagabalus is made consul in Rome. He makes it clear that he wishes to enjoy the pleasures rather than face the responsibilities of power.

221

- Julia Maesa, the grandmother of the Roman emperor Elagabalus, is unable to control his excesses and so begins training her other grandson, Alexander Severus, to become emperor. She persuades Elagabalus to adopt him and to make him Caesar. Elagabalus then realizes how popular Alexander Severus is with the people, and he and his mother, Julia Soaemias, try unsuccessfully to enlist the Praetorian Guard against him; they are themselves killed by the Praetorians early the following year.
- The puppet Chinese emperor Xiandi is finally deposed, marking the end of the Han dynasty. The Chinese general Cao Cao's son has power in the north, Souen Kiuan secedes from the empire in the area to the south of the River Chang Jiang, while Liu Bei proclaims himself emperor in Sichuan in the west. Three kingdoms thus arise—the Wei in the north, the Wu in the south, and the Shu Han in the west. These kingdoms fight each other for more than half a century.

222

- After the murder of the Roman emperor Elagabalus and his mother by the Praetorian Guard, Elagabalus' cousin Alexander Severus becomes emperor, having successfully undergone a philosophic and severe training. He curbs the power of the army and endeavors to restore the power of the Senate and the aristocracy in Rome. He reduces taxes, lends money at 4%, encourages traders' and workers' associations, and censors public morals. He is advised by the Roman jurist Domitius Ulpian, who is appointed one of the Praetorian prefects.

223

- Julia Mamaea, the mother and guide of the Roman emperor Alexander Severus, is made Augusta (title given to the emperor's wife or, exceptionally, to other female relatives).

224

- The kingdom of Parthia comes to an end. King Ardashir of Persia, having made himself increasingly powerful in the area, defeats King Artabanus IV, the last of the Parthian Arsacid dynasty, in three great battles.

225

- The Roman emperor Alexander Severus continues his benevolent and wise rule with the help of the jurist Domitius Ulpian. He marries Orbiana, and her father, Sallustius, becomes Caesar.

226

- King Ardashir of Persia has himself crowned "king of kings" and founds a new Persian dynasty. Ardashir claims descent from Darius I the Great and the Achaemenid kings of Persia; his new Sassanid dynasty is named for his grandfather, Sassan. With the accession of Ardashir, Rome exchanges one enemy for another, the rising Sassanid Persian enemy taking the place of the long declining Parthian enemy.

227

- The Roman Caesar Sallustius is executed for attempted revolution and his daughter Orbiana is forced into exile in Africa. Both had incurred the enmity of the Roman emperor's mother, Julia Mamaea, who felt that they threatened her power over Alexander Severus.

228

- The Roman jurist Domitius Ulpian who, as Praetorian prefect, tries to restrain the power and licentiousness of the Praetorian Guard, is murdered by members of the Guard in Rome. The ringleader of the plot is later executed.

229

- The Roman historian Dio Cassius is consul in Rome for the second time, along with the emperor Alexander Severus. Dio has gained the dislike of the Pannonian troops, where he was governor, for enforcing discipline, and Alexander Severus suggests that Dio spend his consulship outside Rome, as this dislike may have spread to the Praetorian Guard (revealing the emperor's lack of control over the Praetorian Guard and the army).

231–233

- The Roman emperor Alexander Severus, accompanied by his mother, campaigns against the Persian king Ardashir. Ardashir defeats part of the Roman army, and the Romans win some minor victories, then both sides retire. The Roman–Persian frontier remains the same as it was previously. Roman coinage of the time depicts a Roman victory.

233

- The Germanic tribes of the Alemanni and Marcomanni have noted Roman preoccupation in the East and taken the opportunity to break through the Rhine and Danube frontiers. The Roman emperor Alexander Severus gathers a large army and proceeds to the area, but can only achieve peace by buying off the barbarians.

235

- Alexander Severus' troops condemn his weakness in buying off the Alemanni and Marcomanni, and mutiny. The Pannonian troops murder him and his mother, Julia Mamaea, near Mainz, and declare their Thracian commander, Maximinus, Roman emperor in his place. Rome enters another anarchic period, sometimes known as the 3rd Century Crisis, during which power rests with the legionaries and no fewer than 37 men are declared emperor within 35 years.

235–238   The new Roman emperor, Maximinus, campaigns on the rivers Danube and Rhine in Germany, defeating the Alemanni, and never visits Rome. He is accepted by the Senate, but taxes the rich aristocracy heavily and engenders such hostility among them that they plot against him.

238

- The Roman proconsul of Africa Gordian I accepts the Roman emperorship jointly with his son, Gordian II, when his troops proclaim him. They are defeated by supporters of the Roman emperor, Maximinus. After defeating the first two Gordians, Maximinus takes his revenge with a brutal proscription in Rome.
- The Roman Senate outlaws the Roman emperor Maximinus for his bloodthirsty proscriptions in Rome

and nominates two of its members, Pupienus and Balbinus, to the throne. Maximinus advances upon the Senate's nominees at Aquileia in northern Italy, but is killed by his soldiers. Pupienus and Balbinus return to Rome, only to be killed by the Praetorian Guard who then make Gordian III, son of Gordian II and grandson of the former Roman emperor Gordian I, their emperor.

- Under the new emperor Gordian III, the administration of the Roman Empire is for a while efficient and liberal. Informers are again suppressed and provincial governors are instructed to see that nothing happens which "is not in accordance with the spirit of the age."

239

- Timesithius (sometimes called Misetheus) helps the young Roman emperor Gordian III avoid the influence of the eunuchs of the court, and advises him in his rule.

240

- This year sees the start of the worst danger that Rome has so far experienced, with enemies active on several fronts at the same time. Africa revolts, and tribes in northwest Germany, under the name of the Franks, combine into a warlike federation. In Persia, King Ardashir is assassinated.

241

- In this decade the southern state of China, Wu, sends envoys to Funan (modern Cambodia) and the northern state, Wei, receives envoys from Japan.
- The Roman emperor Gordian III appoints Timesithius head of the Praetorian Guard in Rome and marries his daughter.

241–272   On the assassination of King Ardashir of Persia, his son Shapur I ascends the throne and continues his father's policy of expansion.

243

- The Roman general Timesithius defeats the Persians and drives them back across the River Tigris but then falls ill and dies. His place is taken by Philip the Arab, an ambitious general.

244

- While campaigning in Persia, the Roman emperor Gordian III is murdered by his army commander Philip the Arab who replaces him. Gordian is murdered near Carchemish, where a mound is raised in his memory. Philip makes peace with Persia and returns to Rome as its first Arab emperor.

245

- The new Roman emperor Philip the Arab defeats a German tribe called the Carpi on the River Danube. They are being pressed from behind by the Goths.

247

- Rome celebrates 1,000 years of existence from its traditional foundation in 753 BC.
- The Senate in Rome confirms Philip the Arab's appointment as emperor and his seven-year-old son as Augustus, the heir to the throne. Philip hopes to found a new dynasty. He endeavors to rule well in Rome, declaring an amnesty for those who have been exiled, building roads in the provinces which are much needed for military purposes in these times of danger on all fronts, endeavoring to put down brigandage, and receiving complaints in person.

Gothic War (249–269)

249

- The Goths cross the River Danube and ravage the Roman provinces of Thrace, Moesia, and Dacia. Civil war in Gaul is suppressed.

250

- The Roman emperor Decius sends his son Herennius to counter the Goths, who are attacking the Roman province of Moesia. He then follows in person.

251

- Decius and Herennius are defeated and killed by the Goths in a battle in Moesia (north of Thrace). Vibius Trebonianus Gaius Gallus, senatorial governor of Moesia, is elected emperor by the troops, but Gothic attacks on the Roman Empire's Danubian provinces continue for some 20 years, causing enormous damage.

252

- The Roman emperor Trebonianus Gallus buys off the Goths, who retire from the Danubian provinces of Thrace and Moesia with much booty. Gallus then returns to Rome.

257–259

- The Goths cross the Black Sea and sack the Greek cities on the southern shore.

263

- The Goths sail down the Ionian coast and sack the Greek city of Ephesus and its great Temple of Artemisium.

267

- The Goths, originally from Scandinavia, with the Sarmatians (from modern Iran), pour down into the Balkans and Greece and sail through the Hellespont into the Aegean Sea. The Greek cities of Athens, Argos, Sparta, Corinth, and Thebes are all sacked.

268

- The Roman emperor Publius Gallienus wins a costly victory over the Goths in Thrace.

269

- The new Roman emperor Claudius II saves the empire from the Goths, his great victory being at Naissus, Moesia (modern Nish, Yugoslavia), south of the River Danube. This is a full-scale battle in which 50,000 Goths are reputed to have been slain and in which Claudius shows great personal bravery, earning the title "Gothicus."

249

- Discontented at having an Arab as emperor, the legionaries in several Roman provinces revolt. Philip offers to abdicate, then sends his general Messius Quintus Gaius Decius to pacify the legionaries in Pannonia, who seem to consider themselves the guardians of true Roman virtues. They force Decius to assume the throne and to lead them into Italy. At a battle at Verona, northern Italy, Philip is defeated and slain and Decius becomes emperor.
- The Goths cross the River Danube and ravage the Roman provinces of Thrace, Moesia, and Dacia. Civil war in Gaul is suppressed.

SCIENCE, TECHNOLOGY, AND MEDICINE

Math

200

- Greek astronomer and mathematician Claudius Ptolemy produces many important geometrical results with applications in astronomy.

Technology

200

- *c.* 200 Bronze has been replaced by iron in Chinese metalwork for practical uses such as weapons and utensils, although it continues to be used for decorative sculpture.
- Silkworms from China are introduced into Korea and Japan, and textile industries then rapidly develop in these countries.

222

- A renewed public works program, including the construction of roads, bridges, and aqueducts, is initiated across the Roman Empire by the new emperor, Alexander Severus.

Transportation

200

- Chinese shipbuilders devise hulls separated into individual watertight compartments. This prevents the ship from sinking if the hull is punctured at one point.

ARTS AND IDEAS

Architecture

200

- Roman emperor Septimius Severus begins to build the last of the imperial palaces on the Palatine Hill. His wife Julia Domna provides funds for the Temple of Vesta in the Forum.
- 200–400 In the city of Teotihuacán in the Mexican Basin, the earlier, less substantial dwellings are replaced by stone-walled compounds, housing kinship groups of up to 100 people. Different occupations are established in separate areas of the city.

203

- The arch of Septimius Severus overlooking the Forum of Rome is erected on the tenth anniversary of his accession.

217

- The vast and magnificent baths of Caracalla are completed in Rome.

Literature and Language

214

- Under the patronage of Julia Domna, widow of Roman emperor Septimius Severus, historian Flavius Philostratus of Lemnos writes his *Life of Apollonius*, a biography of the occultist of the early 1st century AD.

220

- The earliest known Chinese encyclopedia, the *Huang-lan/Emperor's Mirror*, is prepared for the Chinese Imperial court.

239

- Flavius Philostratus writes his *Lives of the Sophists*.

Thought and Scholarship

c. **200**

- Alexander of Aphrodisias becomes the head of the Lyceum in Athens. His writings include commentaries on Aristotle and a defense of free will, *On Fate*.

229

- Dio Cassius retires to finish his *History of Rome*. Made up of 80 books, it runs from the arrival of Aeneas in Italy to the author's own times. Less than half the work is still extant.

238

- Herodian, a Greek historian, completes his *History of Rome* from the time of Marcus Aurelius to Gordian III.

244

- Egyptian-born philosopher Plotinus arrives in Rome and for the next ten years teaches his Neoplatonist philosophy of hunger for reabsorption into the "One," the source of all being. This is achieved by intense moral and intellectual discipline.

SOCIETY

Education

220

- Alexander Severus, cousin of the Roman emperor Elagabalus and similarly a protégé of their grandmother Julia Maesa, is educated by the best philosophers in Rome.

Everyday Life

200

c. 200 The Nok culture of west Africa (modern Nigeria) disappears. From c. 900 BC, the Nok had created a remarkable range of terracotta heads and figures, the earliest surviving sculptures of sub-Saharan Africa.

200–700 The Zapotec site of Monte Albán in Central America is at its peak in this period. It may have had 30,000 or more inhabitants. It is the center of a complex of public buildings, temples, and dwellings that covers 40 sq km/15 sq mi.

BIRTHS & DEATHS

201

- Postumus, Roman general who set himself up as emperor of Gaul 258–268 to rival Roman emperor Gallienus, born (–268).

204

- Elagabalus (Caesar Marcus Aurelius Antonius Augustus), Roman emperor 218–222, born in Emesa, Syria (–222).

205

- Plotinus, Roman philosopher, founder of the Neoplatonic school of philosophy, born in Lyco, Egypt (–270).

208

- Alexander Severus, Roman emperor 222–235, whose ineffectual rule resulted in 50 years of civil unrest, born in Phoenicia (–235).

211

February Septimius Severus, Roman emperor 193–211, who turned the Roman government into a military monarchy, dies in Eboracum, Britain (c. 55).

212

February (Publius Septimius) Geta, Roman emperor 209–212 with father Septimius Severus and brother Caracalla, murdered in Rome (c. 23).

214

May Claudius Gothicus, Roman emperor 268–270, who stemmed the Gothic invasion of the Balkans (269), born in Dardania, Moesia Superior (c. 56).

c. 215

- Aurelian, Roman emperor 270–275 who restored the Empire, born (–275).

216

April 14 Mani, founder of Manichaeism, born in southern Mesopotamia (–276).

217

- Julia Domna, second wife of the Roman emperor Septimius Severus, and an important administrator during the reign of the emperor Caracalla, starves to death.

April 8 Caracalla (Marcus Aurelius Severus Antoninus Augustus), Roman emperor 198–211 jointly with his father Septimius Severus and 211–217 alone, notorious for his tyranny, assassinated near Carrhae, Mesopotamia (29).

218

June Macrinus, Roman emperor 217–218, executed in Bithynia, Persia (c. 54).

219

- (Publius Licinius Egnatius) Gallienus, Roman emperor 253–260 with his father Valerian, sole emperor 260–68, born (–268).

220

- Tertullian, Christian theologian who originated ecclesiastical Latin, dies in Carthage (c. 60).

222

- Elagabalus (Caesar Marcus Aurelius Antonius Augustus), Roman emperor 218–222, is murdered during a mutiny of the Praetorian Guard (c. 18).

225

- Gordian III, Roman emperor 238–244, grandson of Gordian I, born (–244).

234

c. 234 Porphyrius, Neoplatonist Greek philosopher, born in Tyre or Batanaea, Palestine (–c. 305).

235

- Alexander Severus, Roman emperor 222–235, whose ineffectual rule resulted in 50 years of civil unrest, is murdered by his army in Gaul (27).
- Dio Cassius (full name Cassius Dio Cocceianus), Roman administrator and historian, whose major work is Romaika, an important history of Rome in Greek, dies (c. 85).

236

- Wu-ti (Wudi), founder and first emperor of the Western China dynasty 265–290, born in China (–290).

238

- (Gaius Julius Verus) Maximinus, Roman emperor 235–238, killed by his own troops near Aquileia, Italy.
- Tiridates II of Armenia (also known as Khosrow the Great), King of Armenia 217–238, assassinated.

April Gordian I, briefly Roman emperor March–April 238, coruling with his son Gordian II, commits suicide (c. 81).

240

- Lactantius, a theologian and early Christian teacher, born in North Africa (–c. 320).

244

- Gordian III, Roman emperor 238–244, grandson of Gordian I, is murdered in Zaitha, Mesopotamia (18).

245

- Diocletian, Roman emperor 284–305, noted for restoring efficient government to the empire, born, possibly in Salonae, Dalmatia, now Split, Croatia (–316).

247

- Himiko, Queen of Japan, first known Japanese ruler, dies.

248

- St. Helena, Roman empress, mother of Constantine I, born in Bithynia, Asia Minor (now Turkey) (–c. 328).

249

- Wang Pi, the most brilliant Chinese philosopher of his time, writer of commentaries on the Taoist classic Dao-de Ching and on the Confucian classic the I Ching, dies (23).

Religion

c. 200

- The Indian Buddhist monk Nagarjuna expounds the *Madhayamika* (Middle Path) of Buddhism. Arguing that all worldly thought is empty (*sunya*), he advocates a middle way which will lead to a realization of the *Buddha* nature beyond being and nonbeing.

203

- The Egyptian-born Christian writer Origen, aged 18, lectures at Alexandria in Egypt.

217

- Callistus is elected as the 16th pope but is opposed by the theologian Hippolytus who accuses him of laxity and of being a Modalist, one who denies any distinction between the three persons of the Trinity. Hippolytus sets up a breakaway church and becomes the first antipope.

218

- Carthaginian theologian Tertullian leaves the Catholic Church and embraces Montanism, a heretical movement.
- Roman emperor Elagabalus enforces the worship of Baal, a middle-eastern fertility god. In Rome he orders the building of a temple to house the black stone, brought from Syria, which is the god's symbol.

219

- A Jewish academy is set up at Sura in Persia. The Jews of the Diaspora (dispersion following the defeat by the Romans in 135), who have spread all round the Mediterranean and the Middle East, thrive in Persia (in spite of sporadic persecution) where they are allowed to practice polygamy.

226

- King Ardashir makes Zoroastrianism the Persian state religion and begins the standardization of its sacred book, the *Avesta*.

c. 230

- The theologian and biblical scholar Origen writes *De principiis*/*On Principles*, a comprehensive outline of Christian doctrine.

231

- Origen moves from Alexandria, Egypt, to Caesarea in Judea and attracts many pupils there.

241

- At the court of Shapur I, Mani, a young mystic of Ctesiphon, proclaims himself a prophet and preaches a new doctrine throughout Persia. His teaching, known as Manichaeism, borrows from Zoroastrianism, Judaism, Mithraism, and Gnosticism, and divides the world into the rival realms of Light and Darkness.

247

- According to some Christian writers, Roman emperor Philip the Arab embraces Christianity.

248

- Cyprian, a recent convert to Christianity, becomes bishop of Carthage. His belief that baptism is not valid if bestowed by heretics or apostates leads to conflict with Pope Stephen II.
- Greek Christian philosopher Origen answers Celsus' attack on Christianity, *True Word*, with his *Contra Celsum*/*Against Celsus*.

Sports

c. 200

- Greek poet Oppian of Apamea composes his *Cynegetica*, a treatise on hunting in four books of hexameters.

250–299

POLITICS, GOVERNMENT, AND ECONOMICS

Business and Economics

261

- Archeological evidence indicates that Britain's towns are suffering economic decline in the last half of the 3rd century. There are slum conditions in Silchester (near Basingstoke in modern Hampshire), and the theater at Verulamium (modern St. Albans, Hertfordshire) falls into ruin. The Cornish tin mines, however, seem to experience a revival as a result of decreased competition from Spain.

293

- Diocletian introduces economic reforms. A vast bureaucracy and a system of what is essentially state socialism and managed economy is set up. The coinage is successfully tied to gold, most production is nationalized, and the freedom of the individual to change his job is further restricted.

Colonization

252

- The Persians under King Shapur I take Armenia.

296

- Constantius Chlorus, Caesar of the Western Empire, establishes his capital at Trier in Germany. The huge fortified gate of the city, the *Porta Nigra*, still stands.

Human Rights

250

- The Roman emperor Decius' persecution of the Christians has political motives behind it: he wishes to encourage national unity in a time of danger.

261

- The Roman emperor Gallienus issues the first edict of toleration for Christians and restores confiscated churches and cemeteries.

297

- The Roman emperor Diocletian issues a repressive edict against the Manichaeans.

Politics and Government

250

- The Late Formative (or Pre-Classic) period in Mayan history comes to an end, and the Classic period (250–c. 800) begins, when the civilization is at its height.
- The Parthian era of settlement in Mesopotamia comes to an end. A fragile device found in a Baghdad tomb of this period appears to be a chemical battery, probably used for electroplating gold onto base metal objects.
- The Roman emperor Decius sends his son, Herennius, to counter the Goths, who are attacking the Roman province of Moesia, and then follows in person.

251

- The prosperity of Roman Britain declines during this period as the Germanic tribes of the Franks and Saxons, whose homelands are in Friesland and the Low Countries, make raids around the southeast coast.
- The Roman emperor Decius and his son, Herennius, are defeated and killed by the Goths in a battle in Moesia (north of Thrace). Vibius Trebonianus Gaius Gallus, senatorial governor of Moesia, is elected emperor by the troops, but Gothic attacks on the Roman Empire's Danubian provinces continue for some 20 years, causing enormous damage.

252

- The Roman emperor Trebonianus Gallus buys off the Goths, who retire from the Danubian provinces of Thrace and Moesia with much booty. Gallus then returns to Rome.

253

- Marcus Aemilius Aemilianus, the Roman general left in charge in Moesia, achieves some successes against the Goths, and is proclaimed emperor by the troops. He advances on Rome and is met by the emperor Trebonianus Gallus and his son. However, Gallus' troops are so few and so disloyal that they assassinate him and his son rather than fight. Aemilianus rules for four months and then meets the same fate as Gallus, being replaced by Publius Valerian of the Rhine legions.

254

- The Roman Empire is threatened simultaneously by the Franks, Alemanni, and Marcomanni in Germany, by the Goths in the Danubian provinces (Thrace and Moesia) and Asia Minor, and by the Persians in the East. The emperor Publius Valerian makes his son, Publius Gallienus, ruler of the Western half of the empire and himself ruler of the Eastern half.

255

- Publius Gallienus, ruler of the Western Roman Empire, seeks to protect the Roman province of Gaul from advancing Franks.

255–265 Peace and unity are finally restored in China with the victories of the Wei Kingdom in the north. The ruling dynasty is worn out by war, and the kingdom is ruled by ministers on their behalf—the Ssu-mas. During the next decade, Ssu-ma Chao conquers the western kingdom of Shu Han.

256

- In simultaneous attacks on the Roman Empire, the Franks penetrate into Spain by sea, the Goths ravage Macedonia, and the Persians invade Mesopotamia and Syria.

257–259

- The Goths cross the Black Sea and sack the Greek cities on the southern shore.

258

- Publius Gallienus is given more power (almost complete power, in fact) in the West by his father, the emperor Publius Valerian. He reinforces both the Senate and the army with new blood and demonstrates his ability to choose men well. He makes the army more flexible and mobile. In particular, he improves and increases the formerly weak cavalry arm, and even creates a corps of *catafractarii*, or heavily armored horsemen, in imitation of the Persians. He also improves the catapult and ballista.

259

- The Alemanni break into Italy but are repulsed by the ruler of the western Roman Empire, Publius Gallienus, at Milan in the north. The eastern emperor of the Roman Empire, Publius Valerian, simultaneously leads an army of 70,000 men to relieve the city of Edessa in Syria, besieged by the forces of King Shapur I of Sassanian Persia.

260

- The Roman emperor Publius Valerian decides to attack the Persians, who have reached Edessa (modern Urfa). He changes his mind, however, and offers to negotiate. King Shapur of Persia demands a personal interview on the field and Valerian consents, and is either treacherously captured by Shapur, or is captured in battle while campaigning, and ends his days a captive.
- The son of the captured Roman emperor Publius Valerian, the Western ruler Publius Gallienus, meets and overcomes rival claimants to the imperial throne in Dalmatia, and becomes emperor of the entire Roman Empire.

261–263

- King Shapur of Persia advances west after his defeat of the Roman emperor Publius Valerian, but is unexpectedly halted and driven back by Odenathus, Rome's vassal king of Palmyra. Shapur has, however, built a vast Persian kingdom stretching from the River Indus in the east to the River Euphrates, and from Oman to Armenia.
- Revolts break out throughout the Roman Empire, and the emperor Publius Gallienus has difficulty retaining his throne.

263

- After his defeat of King Shapur of Persia, King Odenathus of Palmyra declares himself king of the area west of the River Euphrates and is declared "Dux Orientalis" by the Roman emperor Publius Gallienus, who needs his help to suppress rival claimants to the empire.
- The Goths sail down the Ionian coast and sack the Greek city of Ephesus and its great Temple of Artemis.

265

- The Roman emperor Publius Gallienus fails to oust the usurper Postumus, who proclaimed himself ruler of Gaul and emperor in 258.
- The ruling minister of the northern Chinese kingdom of Wei, Ssu-ma Chao, dies, and his son Ssu-ma Yen usurps the throne from the royal family, becoming known as the emperor Wudi, and founding the Western Chin dynasty. For the next 50 years the northern kingdom exerts some suzerainty over the other kingdoms.

266

- King Odenathus of Palmyra is assassinated. His young sons succeed to the throne but real power lies with his widow, Zenobia, a forceful and beautiful woman who claims descent from Queen Cleopatra of Egypt.

267

- The Goths, originally from Scandinavia, with the Sarmatians (from modern Iran), pour down into the Balkans and Greece and sail through the Hellespont into the Aegean Sea. The Greek cities of Athens, Argos, Sparta, Corinth, and Thebes are all sacked.

268

- Roman emperor Publius Gallienus wins a costly victory over the Goths in Thrace.
- Roman usurper Postumus' "emperorship" in Gaul ends when he is killed by his soldiers for refusing to allow them to plunder Mainz in Germania Superior.
- The Roman emperor Publius Gallienus is killed by his soldiers. Claudius II, a Dalmatian of obscure origin, becomes emperor.

269

- The new Roman emperor Claudius II saves the empire from the Goths, his great victory being at Naissus, Moesia (modern Niš, Serbia), south of the River Danube. This is a full-scale battle in which 50,000 Goths are reputed to have been slain and in which Claudius shows great personal bravery, earning the title "Gothicus."

270

- *c. 270* A group of Xiongnu who have crossed the Gobi Desert and settled near the Great Wall of China are threatened by the Mongol Sien-Pei, and ask the Western Chinese emperor Wudi for help. He settles them inside the Great Wall, relying on them to keep other Huns or Mongols off.
- The Roman emperor Claudius II succumbs to the plague and Aurelian (Lucius Domitus Aurelianus), another Dalmatian, becomes emperor. He wins a further battle over the Goths and then makes peace with them. He relinquishes the province of Dacia to the Goths and transfers the name and the civilian population to a province south of the River Danube.

271

- The Roman emperor Aurelian pushes the Vandals back from Pannonia over the River Danube and the Alemanni and Iuthungi out of Italy again, where they had returned after defeat by the former emperor Claudius II, defeating them near Milan in the north with one of the earliest large-scale cavalry actions.

- The Roman emperor Aurelian moves toward a regimented state, beginning the regulation of the trade corporations and the direction of labor. He also acts to stabilize the currency which is suffering from inflation.
- Zenobia, the widow of King Odenathus of Palmyra, declares herself queen of the East and sends her eldest son, Septimus Vaballathus, to invade Egypt. She reputedly acts on the advice of the Greek philosopher Cassius Longinus in throwing off all pretence of allegiance to Rome.

272

- The Roman emperor Aurelian sends his commander Marcus Probus to restore Roman rule in Egypt, and himself advances on Queen Zenobia's capital, Palmyra, which he takes after a difficult campaign. Zenobia is captured; her life is spared but her advisor, the Greek philosopher Longinus, is put to death. Having retraced his steps across the Bosporus, Aurelian receives the news that Palmyra has revolted. He returns and suppresses the revolt, this time dealing more harshly with the city.

274

- The Roman usurper Postumus has been succeeded as "Emperor of Gaul" by Tetricus, whom the Roman emperor Aurelian easily defeats. Rome greets Aurelian as *Restitutor Orbis* ("Restorer of the World") and accords him a magnificent triumph (victory procession), which is graced by his captives Gaius Pius Esuvius Tetricus and Queen Zenobia of Palmyra, the latter loaded with golden chains. Zenobia is allowed to live out her life with her children at Hadrian's palace, Tivoli.

275

- On his way to attack Persia, the Roman emperor Aurelian is murdered by a group of officers who mistakenly believe their lives are in danger. The Roman army passes the appointment of the next emperor to the Senate, which chooses the 75-year old Cornelius Tacitus, a descendant of the historian of the same name.

276

- The Roman emperor Tacitus dies leading an expedition against the Goths, and is succeeded by Marcus Probus, one of the former emperor Aurelian's commanders. Probus is another Dalmatian, a soldier and disciplinarian.

277–279

- The Roman emperor Marcus Probus continues the former emperor Aurelian's forcible pacification of the empire, pushing the Franks back across the River Rhine, expelling the Goths and Vandals from Raetia and Pannonia (modern Switzerland and Hungary)—which he resettles with groups displaced by the Goths— quelling trouble in Britain and Dalmatia, and forcing Moorish invaders of Spain back to North Africa.

280

- Marcus Probus, the Roman emperor, faces widespread unrest and rebellion. He disciplines his armies and sets his troops to clear wasteland, drain marshes, and plant vines in Gaul and the Danubian provinces to restore agriculture. He promises Rome the rule of law again and that one day armies will not be necessary.
- Wudi, the emperor of the northern Chinese kingdom of Wei, occupies most of the southern kingdom of Wu, uniting China once more under one rule. Wudi's capital is the old and prosperous city of Luoyang. It is a thriving center of commerce, and ambassadors from throughout the world arrive there.

281

- At the end of this year the emperor Marcus Probus returns to Rome from his campaigns against the barbarians and earns a triumph (victory procession), which is remarkable for the variety of the prisoners displayed. Probus is named *Pacator Orbis* ("Pacifier of the World") by the Roman people.

282

- The Roman army grows more and more discontented with the emperor Marcus Probus as a result of his crackdown on discipline. His soldiers mutiny and kill him while he is superintending viticulture at Sirmium, his birthplace, a city on the Sava in Pannonia Inferior. Marcus Aurelius Carus, said to be a scholar as well as a soldier, is elected his successor.

283

- The new Roman emperor Marcus Aurelius Carus actively pursues war against Persia, which his predecessor Marcus Probus had intended. He crosses the River Euphrates and takes the city of Seleucia and then Ctesiphon.
- 283–285 The Roman emperor Marcus Aurelius Carus dies in mysterious circumstances near Ctesiphon in Persia, reputedly after being hit by a stroke of lightning. Of his two sons who have been declared his heirs, one, Numerianus, is murdered in the East and the other, Carinus, fights for the throne with the Roman commander Diocletian, the army's choice, who defeats and kills him.

284

- The Roman emperor Diocletian and his successor Constantine, both military men, will introduce major changes and restructure the Roman army, increasing cavalry power and general mobility, and scaling down the importance of garrisons.

285

- Having defeated and killed the late emperor Carus' son, Carinus, the Roman commander Diocletian is now unchallenged as Roman emperor. He makes Maximian, a fellow soldier from the Danubian provinces (Thrace and Moesia), his second in command as Caesar, and sends him to pacify Gaul. Here the Bagaudae, bands of peasants, have revolted and set up two emperors of their own. Maximian deals with Gaul rapidly and mercifully.
- The Roman emperor Diocletian transfers his capital from Rome, Italy, to Nicomedia in Bithynia, near Byzantium, as a more strategic base from which to defend the Empire. Similarly, his second in command, Maximian, chooses Milan in northern Italy as his base.

286

- Following Maximian's successful campaign in Gaul, the Roman emperor Diocletian raises him from Caesar to Augustus, making him his joint ruler with responsibility for the West, reviving the practice of splitting the command of the Empire between East and West.

286–291 Maximian, the Roman emperor of the West, has to deal with intermittent attacks across the Upper Rhine by the Alemanni and Burgundians.

287

- The Roman Caesar, Maximian, places a soldier named Carausius in charge of the Roman fleet at Boulogne, the *Classis Britannica*, to clear the English Channel of Frankish and Saxon pirates. Carausius catches many pirates, but keeps the spoils for himself. When Maximian orders his execution, he revolts, keeping control of the north coasts of Gaul and using his naval power to cross to Britain, where he declares an independent empire on the model of Postumus in Gaul.

288

- The Roman Caesar Maximian's Praetorian Prefect, Constantius Chlorus, achieves a victory against the Franks, who sue for peace in Gaul. Their king, Gennoboudes, is restored as king of the Franks.
- The Roman emperor of the East, Diocletian, makes a treaty with King Vahram of Persia, persuading him to surrender all claims to Mesopotamia and perhaps to Armenia, where Diocletian nominates another, Tiridates (the third), as king of Armenia.

289

- From his base in Nicomedia in Bithynia, the Roman emperor of the East, Diocletian, campaigns against the Sarmatians in the area north of the River Danube.
- The Roman Augustus (emperor) of the West, Maximian, is defeated by Carausius, the self-proclaimed emperor of Britain, in a naval battle.

290

- The Roman emperor of the East, Diocletian, goes to Syria to defend the province against an Arab invasion.
- The soldier and naval commander Carausius, a self-proclaimed Roman emperor who has established himself in Britain, is reluctantly acknowledged by Maximian and Diocletian as a third emperor. He rules in Britain for the next three years, efficiently defeating Saxon and Frankish raids.
- The two Roman emperors Diocletian and Maximian meet in Milan, northern Italy. Envoys come from Rome, southern Italy, to congratulate them on their triumphs and their successful joint rule.

291

- The Roman emperor of the East, Diocletian, puts down a revolt led by Coptos and Busiris in the province of Egypt.

293

- Diocletian, the Roman emperor of the East, further develops his plan for ruling the Empire: it is to be ruled jointly by two Augusti (Diocletian for the East and Maximian for the West), each of whom is to have a Caesar to help him. Diocletian chooses the soldier Galerius as his Caesar and Maximian appoints his Praetorian prefect Constantius Chlorus. The Tetrarchy, known as the *Quattuor Principes Mundi* ("Four Rulers of the World"), has genuine power: all laws and edicts are to be issued in the names of all four rulers and are to be equally valid; no sanction from the Roman Senate is required. Each Caesar will marry into the Augustus'

family and then succeed him after 20 years. So Galerius gives up his wife to marry Diocletian's daughter Valeria, and Constantius gives up his wife Helena, mother of the future emperor Constantine I the Great, to marry Maximian's daughter Theodora.

- The Persian Sassanian Empire suffers from dynastic troubles on the death of its king, Vahram III.
- The Western Roman Caesar, Constantius Chlorus, besieges and captures Boulogne, Gaul, in preparation for regaining Britain for the Roman Empire. The usurping emperor in Britain, Carausius, is murdered by his financial minister Allectus, who seizes power.

294–297

- Galerius, Roman Caesar in the East, proves his worth in campaigning in the Danubian provinces, fighting the Goths, Marcomanni, Sarmatians, Bastarnians, and Carpi, but becomes embittered when he has to follow up with the unspectacular job of land reclamation and repopulation, moving the entire tribe of the Carpi to settlements within the Roman Empire.

296

- After two years of preparation, Constantius Chlorus, Roman Caesar of the West, invades Britain. One squadron of his fleet, led by his Praetorian prefect Asclepiodotus, lands near the Isle of Wight and defeats Allectus in Hampshire. The other Roman squadron, under Constantius, sails up the River Thames to London just in time to prevent the sack of the city by the remains of Allectus' army. He rebuilds at Eboracum (York), Londinium (London), and Verulamium (St. Albans), fortifies the "Saxon Shore" (the coastline from the Wash to the Isle of Wight), and does much to restore prosperity to Britain.
- Narses, the first strong king in Persia since Shapur I, comes to the throne. He attacks Rome's puppet king Tiridates III of Armenia.

296–297 Rebellion again breaks out in Egypt and the Eastern Roman emperor Diocletian goes there in person with the young Constantine I the Great (later the first Christian emperor of Rome) on his staff. He besieges Alexandria and deposes the city's "emperor," Achilleus.

297

- Galerius, the Roman emperor Diocletian's Caesar in the East, is given the job of combating the Sassanian King Narses of Persia. After initial success he suffers a serious defeat near Carrhae; Diocletian deliberately inflames his pride by making him walk behind his chariot as a punishment.

297–298 The Roman emperor of the West, Maximian, crosses from Spain to Africa to quell a rising of Moorish tribes (Quinquegentanei) in Carthage.

298

- Galerius, the Roman emperor Diocletian's Caesar in the East, redeems his humiliation of the previous year by winning a complete victory over King Narses of Sassanian Persia, capturing his wives and children and taking a huge booty, then pressing on to capture Ctesiphon itself, the capital of the Sassanian Empire. King Narses cedes Mesopotamia and five small provinces beyond the River Tigris to Rome. The city of Nisibis is designated a center for commercial relations between the two empires. In return for this, Narses' wives and children are restored.

299
- The 3rd century ends in peace, with the Roman Empire recovered in power and prestige and the emperor Diocletian's innovations in government apparently vindicated.

SCIENCE, TECHNOLOGY, AND MEDICINE

Health and Medicine

255
- Cyprianus, bishop of Carthage, writes *De mortalitate/ Concerning Mortality*, the first treatise on the nature and spread of epidemics.

256
- A terrible epidemic devastates Alexandria, causing many survivors to turn to Christianity.

265
- Rome and many other parts of the Roman Empire have suffered a five-year epidemic of plague.

275
- Another great plague devastates the Roman Empire, causing thousands of deaths as far apart as Mesopotamia and Gaul (modern France).

Math

250
- Greek mathematician Diophantus of Alexandria writes *Arithmetica*, a study of problems in which only whole numbers are allowed as solutions.

Science

265
- Chinese geographer Pei Hsin prepares a large and detailed map in 18 sections of China during the period of the Three Kingdoms.

297
- The tomb of a Chinese military commander of this date contains metal belt ornaments made of aluminum, not isolated by Western scientists until 1827.

Technology

250
- The new Roman emperor Decius orders the building of a huge public baths in Rome, consisting of a domed roof placed on a ten-sided structure, a considerable engineering feat.

251
- At around this time, the earliest records appear of the Chinese using the easily-cleaved silicate mineral mica for glazing windows.

c. 270
- The Chinese invent gunpowder, a mixture of saltpeter, sulfur and charcoal. At first, it appears to have been used only for fireworks.

272
- The Roman emperor Aurelian describes the Syrian queen Zenobia's defenses at Palmyra thus: "Every part of the wall is provided with two or three *ballistae*, and artificial fires are thrown from her military engines." *Ballistae* are a type of mechanical catapult.

285
- Pappus of Alexandria describes several basic mechanical devices in a treatise, including the cogwheel, lever, pulley, screw, and wedge.

Transportation

250
- The earliest Chinese references to a device known as "the emperor's south-pointing carriage" date to this period. An ingenious and complex system of gearing was used so that, whichever way the carriage turned, a statue on the top always pointed in the same direction.

274
- A great oared ship 30 m/100 ft long is built for the Japanese emperor Ojin—the Japanese have not yet developed sail power.

ARTS AND IDEAS

Architecture

262
- The arch of Gallienus is dedicated in Rome.

271–275
- Roman emperor Aurelian persuades the Senate to finance the building of new walls round Rome. These walls are 19 km/12 mi long and 3.6 m/12 ft thick. Fortifying walls are being built around cities throughout the empire during this period, reflecting the upheavals of the time.

292
- Roman emperor Carausius improves the defenses of the south and east coasts of Britain against the Saxons by building some of the so-called Saxon shore forts, such as Portchester, Richborough, and Lympne.

298
- The baths of Diocletian are begun.

Arts

260

- Shapur I of Persia celebrates his victories over the Roman armies by having a rock relief carved at Naqsh-i Rustam showing the Roman emperor Valerian kneeling before his mounted captor.

Literature and Language

250

- Greek writer Heliodorus of Emesa writes *Aethiopica*. One of the earliest surviving novels, it concerns the adventures of an Ethiopian princess and her lover.

Thought and Scholarship

263

- The philosopher Porphyrius comes to Rome from Athens and enrols as a pupil of the Neoplatonist philosopher Plotinus. Cassius Longinus, the Neoplatonist philosopher who taught Porphyrius in Athens, becomes the adviser and teacher of Queen Zenobia, wife of King Odenathus of Palmyra.

291

- The *Historia augusta/Venerable History* is possibly begun about this time. Apparently written by six different authors, it covers the reigns of the Roman emperors from Hadrian to Carus. Several scholars now attribute it to a single author writing in the 4th century AD.

SOCIETY

Everyday Life

250

- Bishop Dionysius of Alexandria in Egypt bemoans the fact that the population of his city is half of its size in former times.

BIRTHS & DEATHS

250
- Arius, Christian priest of Alexandria, Egypt, whose teachings gave rise to the doctrine of Arianism, born in Cyrenaica (modern Libya) (–c. 336).

251
- Decius, Roman emperor 249–51, in whose reign the first systematic persecution of Christians throughout the empire took place, falls in battle against the Goths in the Dobrudja region of Dacia (modern Romania) (c. 50).
- St. Antony of Egypt, religious hermit and founder of Christian monasticism, born in Koma, Egypt (–356).

253
- (Gaius Vibius Trebonianus) Gallus, Roman emperor 251–53, is killed by his own troops near Interamna, Latium, Italy.
- Aemilian (full name Marcus Aemilius Aemilianus), Roman emperor for three months in 253, dies near Spoletium (Spoleto), Umbria, Italy.

254
- Origen, theologian and biblical scholar of the early Greek Church, author of *Hexalpa*, a synopsis of various versions of the Old Testament, dies in Tyre, Phoenicia (c. 69).

258
September 14 Thascius Caecilius Cyprianus (later known as St. Cyprian), theologian, bishop of Carthage, and leader of the Christians of Roman Africa, is martyred in Carthage (c. 58).

268
- (Publius Licinius Egnatius) Gallienus, Roman emperor 253–260 with his father Valerian, sole emperor 260–268, murdered in Milan, Italy (c. 49).

270
- Claudius Gothicus, Roman emperor 268–270, who stemmed the Gothic invasion of the Balkans (269), dies in Sirmium, Pannonia Inferior, (modern Sremska Mitrovica, Serbia) (c. 56).
- Plotinus, Roman philosopher, founder of the Neoplatonic school of philosophy, dies in Campania (65).

272
- Shapur I, King of the Sassanian Empire of Persia, who extended the empire at the expense of the Roman empire, dies.

275
- Aurelian (full name Lucius Domitius Aurelianus), Roman emperor 270–275 who reunited the empire, dies in Byzantium, Thrace (now Istanbul, Turkey).

276
- Mani, founder of Manichaeism, dies in Gundeshapur (61).

283
- (Marcus Aurelius) Carus, Roman emperor, dies during an expedition against the Sasanians.

285
- (Marcus Aurelius) Carinus, emperor of the Western Roman Empire, killed by his own troops in battle against Diocletian on the Morava River in Moesia Superior, now Serbia.

286
c. 286 St. Crispin and St. Crispinian, the patron saints of shoemakers, are executed on the orders of the Roman emperor Maximian.

287
c. 287 Constantine I the Great, first Christian Roman emperor 312–324 of western empire; 324–337 and of whole empire; born at Naissus in Roman Moesia Superior (modern Niš, Serbia) (–337).

290
- Wu-ti (Wudi), founder and first emperor of the Western Chin dynasty 265–290, dies in Lo-yang, China (c. 54).

293
- Carausius, a Roman military commander who created a short-lived independent British state, is assassinated in Britain.
- St. Athanasius, theologian and statesman, chief opponent of Arianism, born in Alexandria, Egypt (–373).

Religion

250

- At the Roman garrison town of Dura Europos in Syria there are places of worship for sixteen different cults including Christianity and Judaism. Religious wall paintings show a stylistic unity, rejecting Hellenic naturalism for a more schematic and symbolic approach.

269

- The Indian scholar Sphujidhvaja writes an influential manual of astrology, based on translations from Greek sources, and rendered in verse.

275

- St. Denis, the first bishop of Paris and later the patron saint of France, converts Paris to Christianity and establishes a religious center on an island in the Seine.

286

- Christian ascetic monk St. Anthony of Egypt retires to a life of solitude at Pispir near the Nile. During this time he experiences hallucinatory temptations to return to a world of sensual pleasures.

288

- Roman shoemaker Crispin and his brother Crispinian, who sought to spread Christianity, are martyred in Gaul.

Sports

c. **250**

- Chariot races are held during the annual Aenach fairs at the Curragh in Kildare, Ireland, which today is the center of Irish horse racing.
- The first known references are made to polo in China and Tibet.

300–349

POLITICS, GOVERNMENT, AND ECONOMICS

Business and Economics

312

- Western Roman emperor Constantine I the Great introduces the gold *solidus* to stabilize the Roman gold coinage; the *solidus* is set at a value of 72 to 0.45 kg/1 lb of gold.

317

- The coins produced under the Western Roman emperor Constantine I the Great begin to lose their pagan effigies.

c. **320**

- The manufacture of textiles for rugs and coats is established in Roman Britain, with exports to the rest of the Empire.

321

- Rising labor costs and the soaring price of food force the Western Roman emperor Constantine to introduce water-powered mills in Rome. Fears of unemployment have prevented their adoption in the past.

Human Rights

303

- The most severe period of Roman persecution of the Christians begins.

310

- Pamphilus, bishop of Caesarea, is martyred. His large library survives until it is destroyed by Arabs in the 7th century.

311

- The Eastern Roman emperor Galerius puts a stop to the persecution of the Christians and asks them to pray for the Roman Empire and himself, but dies soon afterwards of his fatal disease.

313

- In the Edict of Milan, Roman emperors Constantine and Licinius confirm the official toleration of Christianity and extend it to all religions. Helena, Constantine's mother, becomes a Christian about this time or possibly earlier.

321

- The Western Roman emperor Constantine reluctantly grants the Donatists (followers of Bishop Donatus) toleration.

Politics and Government

301

- Legislation passed since the emperor Trajan's reign is codified in the *Codex Gregorianus* and the Roman emperor Diocletian finances law schools.

302

- Diocletian visits Rome as emperor for the first time.
- King Narses of Persia abdicates in favor of his son.

303

- The Roman emperors Diocletian and Maximian are in Rome to celebrate Diocletian's *vicennalia* (his 20th year as emperor). Diocletian is disgusted with the manners of the Roman plebs (the common people) during the celebrations and retires to Ravenna, Italy, before the year is out.

304

- The Eastern Roman emperor Diocletian falls ill with some form of mental breakdown on the way back to Nicomedia, his capital in Bithynia. He recovers, but decides it is time to retire. He extracts a promise from Maximian, the Roman emperor of the West, that both men will retire when Maximian has celebrated his 20th year as emperor the following year.
- The Huns under the Chinese-educated Liu Yuan decide to connect themselves with China's past and form a "Hun Han" dynasty in northern China.

305

- Diocletian, the Roman emperor of the East, abdicates in Nicomedia, Bithynia, and Maximian, the emperor of the West, does the same in Milan, Italy. They are succeeded as Augusti by the former Caesars, Constantius Chlorus in the West and Galerius in the East. The posts of Caesar now go to Severus in the West and Maximinus Daia in the East, both protégés of Galerius. The obvious choices of Maxentius, son of Maximian, and Constantine I the Great, son of Constantius, are passed over.

306

- Constantius Chlorus, the Western Roman emperor, returns to Britain and undertakes a punitive expedition against the Picts beyond the repaired Hadrian's Wall. His son Constantine I the Great, having managed to reach his father safely from the Eastern emperor Galerius' court, is with him, and together father and son win a brilliant victory. However, on his return to Eboracum (York) in July, Constantius dies. Constantine is declared Augustus (emperor) by his troops, and awaits recognition by Galerius. Despite his anger at this development, Galerius compromises and recognizes Constantine as Caesar in order to avert civil war. He makes Caesar Flavius Valerius Severus the new Augustus in the West. Constantine accepts this decision for the moment, also to avoid civil war.
- Goaded by Constantine I the Great's success in being recognized as Caesar, Maxentius, son of the former Western emperor Maximian, joins a revolt by the Praetorian Guard in Rome, angry at its suppression by the current Western emperor Severus. Rome and the south of Italy, bitter over their subjection to taxation and loss of privilege, support Maxentius, as does Africa.

Northern Italy supports Severus, who has his seat in Milan.

307

- Maxentius calls on his father, the former Western Roman emperor Maximian, to come out of retirement to help him. The emperor of the East, Galerius, orders Severus, Emperor of the West, to march on Rome against Maxentius. Many of Severus' soldiers have previously served under Maximian, however, and Severus is forced to retire to Ravenna, where Maximian, who has resumed his position as Augustus (emperor), persuades him to become his hostage against Galerius. Maximian travels to Gaul to gain the support of Constantine against the Eastern emperor, who acknowledges Maxentius as Augustus in the West. Constantine accepts promotion to the rank of Augustus and marries Maximian's daughter Fausta.
- The Roman emperor of the East, Galerius, attempts to invade Italy, leaving his comrade Licinius in charge of Dalmatia, but fails. Severus, former emperor of the West and hostage of the new emperor of the West, Maxentius, is killed.

308

- In a confused situation, there is a conference of Roman Augusti and Caesars at Carnuntum, the seat of government in Upper Pannonia, including the retired Eastern emperor Diocletian. Diocletian declines to return to rule, and refuses to allow his fellow retired Western emperor Maximian to rule either.

309

- Shapur II, sometimes called "the Great" and grandson of King Shapur I, ascends the Sassanid throne in Persia as an infant following internal wars.
- The Western Roman emperor Constantine I the Great saves Gaul from a fresh attack of Franks and Alemanni on the River Rhine. He sends captive Germans as gladiators to the arena.
- There are now six Augusti (emperors) ruling the Roman Empire: Galerius, Licinius, and Maximinus Daia in the East, and Constantine I the Great, Maxentius, and Maximian in the West.

311

- The Western Roman emperor Constantine I the Great marches on Rome, Italy, to meet the army of the Western emperor Maxentius.

312

- The Western Roman emperor Constantine I the Great defeats and kills his rival Western emperor Maxentius at the Battle of the Milvian (or Mulvian) Bridge (sometimes called the Battle of Saxa Rubra) on the River Tiber, about 14 km/9 mi from Rome, Italy. This may be described as Rome's first battle of the Christian religion—Constantine's troops go into battle with the Chi-Rho monogram on their shields after Constantine is reported to have been told in a dream to put the heavenly sign of God on his soldiers' shields.
- The Western Roman emperor Constantine I the Great disbands the Praetorian Guard. The Praetorian prefects become civilian officials with judicial and financial responsibilities. They remain judges of appeal, and their sentences are made final, with no appeal to the emperor. They also supervise provincial governors. Each member

of the Tetrarchy (the two Augusti and two Caesars ruling the Roman Empire) has a Praetorian prefect.

313

- The Eastern Roman emperor Maximinus Daia, who holds Asia and Egypt, attacks his rival emperor Licinius on his return to the East, driving him back into Thrace and capturing Byzantium. Licinius calls up reinforcements and completely defeats Maximinus at Tzurulum, near Adrianople (modern Edirne, Turkey), pursuing him across Asia Minor to Tarsus, where he dies.
- The Western Roman emperor Constantine I the Great meets the Eastern emperor Licinius in Milan, Italy. They issue a joint edict and agree to cooperate. Complete religious tolerance for Christians is agreed. Licinius marries Constantine's sister Constantia. Constantine moves to the defense of Gaul and Licinius to consolidate his Eastern possessions against his rival Maximinus Daia.
- The Western Roman emperor Constantine I the Great defeats the Eastern emperor Licinius in Pannonia and exacts surrender of the provinces of Pannonia and Moesia, thus gaining control of all of Roman Europe except Thrace. Licinius retires to his Eastern capital Nicomedia in Bithynia, Asia Minor.

316

- The Chinese Jin dynasty abandons all northern China to the competing Hunnish kings.

317

- The Hun Han dynasty founded by the Huns in 304 is now fully established in northern China.
- The Western Roman emperor Constantine I the Great's two sons Crispus and Constantine are made Caesars, as is the Eastern emperor Licinius' son, also called Licinius. Another son, Constantius, is born to Constantine. Crispus has the Christian apologist Lucius Lactantius as his tutor.

319

- Unrest occurs again on the northern frontiers of the Roman Empire. The Western emperor Constantine I the Great himself campaigns on the River Danube and his son Crispus does so on the Rhine.

320

- Crispus, son of the Western Roman emperor Constantine I the Great, wins a victory against the invading Germans on the River Rhine.
- The first of the Indian Gupta dynasty, Chandra Gupta, establishes a powerful kingdom in the Magadha area of India (the Ganges plain). He has no connection with his Mauryan predecessor, Chandragupta.

321

- The Western Roman emperor Constantine I the Great expels the barbarians from Roman Dacia, repairs the former emperor Trajan's bridge over the River Danube, penetrates the old province of Dacia, and makes peace with the barbarians.

322

- The Western Roman emperor Constantine I the Great defeats Sarmatian raiders and drives them out of the Roman province of Pannonia.

323

- Goths invade the Roman province of Thrace but the Eastern Roman emperor Licinius takes no action, forcing the Western emperor Constantine I the Great to cross into Thrace and expel the barbarians himself.

324

- Negotiations between the Western Roman emperor Constantine I the Great and the Eastern emperor Licinius fail, and war breaks out. In two battles, near Adrianople (modern Edirne, Turkey) and Chrysopolis (Usküdar, Turkey), Constantine defeats Licinius.

325

- The Eastern Roman emperor Licinius, having been pardoned after his defeat in 324 by the Western emperor Constantine I the Great on the supplication of his wife (who is Constantine's sister) and banished to Thessaloníki (Salonika), is executed on the charge of indulging in renewed intrigue. The Roman Empire once again has a single ruler.

326

- The Roman emperor Constantine I the Great begins to build a new city, Constantinople (modern Istanbul, Turkey), to which he also gives the title "Nova Roma" (New Rome), on the site of Byzantium, which has still not recovered from its desolation by the Goths.
- The Roman emperor Constantine I the Great's son, Crispus, and wife, Fausta, are said to have been put to death, together with the son of the former Eastern emperor Licinius, presumably for plotting against the throne. The evidence for these assassinations is not considered conclusive.

328

- The severe laws against the Arians, supporters of the heretical view in the Christian argument which led to the Council of Nicaea being called in 325, are relaxed.

330

- The culture of the Mayas comes to the end of its Formative Period and enters its Classic Period, which lasts about 600 years. Around this time stone begins to be used in place of wood for buildings, and hieroglyphic inscriptions appear on them—a Mayan stele (inscription) at Uaxactun in Guatemala displays this date.
- The Roman emperor Constantine I the Great dedicates the city of Constantinople, or Nova Roma (modern Istanbul, Turkey), and makes it his new, Christian, base. Although he does not intend to move the capital of the Empire from Rome, his establishment, together with that of the imperial court, in Constantinople effectively brings the long history of Rome as the center of the world to an end.

332

- The Sarmatians ask Rome for protection from the Goths. Emperor Constantine I the Great's eldest son, Constantine II, defeats the Goths and brings the chieftain's son to Rome as a hostage.

333

- The Roman emperor Constantine I the Great passes laws exempting men in the literary and medical professions from military service or compulsory call to public office.

334

- Vandal refugees from the Goths are allowed across the River Danube to settle within the Roman Empire.

335

- Samudra Gupta, the second and greatest ruler of the Gupta dynasty, comes to the throne in the Magadha kingdom (in the Ganges plain) of India.
- The Roman emperor Constantine I the Great, hoping to effect a peaceful transition of power at his death, apportions responsibilities among his sons and nephews: there are five young Caesars –Constantine II, Constantius I, Constans, Dalmatius, and Hanniballianus.

336

- The Roman emperor Constantine I the Great's son, Constantius, marries his cousin, the sister of the future emperor Julian.

337–338

- The Roman army rejects the authority of all the late emperor Constantine I the Great's intended heirs except his sons. All his nephews, except Gallus who is ill and Julian who is not yet six years old, are put to death. Constantine's three sons, Constantius, Constantine II, and Constans, each assume the title of Augustus as joint emperors.

338

- The late Roman emperor Constantine I the Great's three surviving sons—Constantius, Constantine II, and Constans—meet in Pannonia and try to resolve their differences. They divide the Empire up, possibly according to their father's plans: Constantius gets the East; Constantine II receives Spain, Britain, and Gaul; and Constans becomes ruler of northern and southern Italy, Africa, Dalmatia, and Thrace.

339

- The Roman emperor Constantine II, desiring more power in the West, demands Italy and Africa from his younger brother the emperor Constans. Constans seeks the support of his other brother the emperor Constantius in the East, surrendering Thrace and Constantinople (modern Istanbul, Turkey) to him.
- The Roman emperor of the East, Constantius, dynastically minded, issues a decree making the marriage of uncle and niece a capital offense.

339–350 The Roman emperor Constantius hastens to his territory in the East, where a revived Persia under King Shapur II is attacking the Roman province of Mesopotamia. For the next 11 years Rome and Persia engage in a war of border skirmishing with no real victor.

340

- The Roman emperor Constantine II crosses the Alps and attacks his brother Emperor Constans' army at Aquileia in northern Italy. He is ambushed and killed. After defeating Constantine II, Constans is left master of the West, with his other brother, the emperor Constantius, master of the East.

341

341–342 The Franks invade Gaul, but are driven out and forced to conclude peace by the Western Roman emperor Constans.

341–351 During this decade Samudra Gupta, ruler of the Gupta dynasty, extends his kingdom or his influence over most of India. A pillar found at Allahabad, northeast India, sings his praises.

342

- An imperial edict forbids the destruction of pagan temples in the Roman Empire.
- The Picts and Scots from northern Britain and Hibernia (Ireland) combine for the first time to threaten the western half of Roman Britain. The Western Roman emperor Constans crosses the Channel and makes peace with them, probably allowing them to settle in Roman Britain.

345

- The young Julian and his brother Gallus, cousins to the Roman emperors Constantius and Constans and potential rivals for the emperorship, are kept prisoners in the province of Cappadocia in Asia Minor (modern Turkey), with only an aged slave to educate them.

346

- King Shapur II of Persia renews his pressure on the Eastern Roman Empire but fails to take the town of Nisibis (near ancient Sumerian Akkad) in Mesopotamia.

348

- War is renewed between the Eastern Roman emperor Constantius and the Sassanian King Shapur II of Persia. A battle is fought at Singara in northern Mesopotamia during which the Romans take the Persian camp and kill the heir to the Persian throne.

349–350

- Constans, the Western Roman emperor, has made himself extremely unpopular. A Gaulish army commander, Magnus Magnentius, usurps the throne with the support of the military leaders in Rome and Constans flees to Spain, where he is assassinated. Magnus Magnentius is welcomed in Britain, Spain, Africa, and the rest of Italy as well as in Gaul.
- The Eastern Roman emperor Constantius has to abandon dealing with King Shapur II of Sassanian Persia to sort out trouble in the West. Shapur, having once more failed to take the heroically defended town of Nisibis (near ancient Sumerian Akkad) in Mesopotamia, and himself threatened by pressure from the Huns, retires for a while from the Mesopotamian war.

SCIENCE, TECHNOLOGY, AND MEDICINE

Agriculture

340

- The Chinese scholar Hsi Han writes *Records of Plants and Trees of the Southern Regions*, in which he describes the use of the yellow citrus killer-ant to control fruit-eating pests.

Ecology

300

- The city of Cuicuilco in the southwest of the Mexican Basin is completely buried by a second lava flow, following the damage done by the first flow 450 years previously.

341

- Over the next four years, a series of major earthquakes shake the Middle East. Syria, Pontus on the Black Sea, and Epirus in Northwest Greece are badly hit.

Health and Medicine

309

- A plague that may be related to anthrax spreads across the Roman Empire, causing a drastic decline in the population.

315

- There are 144 public lavatories in the city of Rome. Citizens pay a small admission charge and the lavatories are large, single-sex rooms with stalls around the edge.

331

- The Christian Roman emperor Constantine I the Great abolishes pagan hospitals throughout the Empire and the church begins to take responsibility for the care of the sick.

333

- Pestilence and famine break out in Roman Syria.

Math

320

- Pappus of Alexandria writes *Synagoge/Collections*, an invaluable guide to ancient mathematics and astronomy.

Science

300

- Lucius Lactantius, who is later tutor to the son of the Roman emperor Constantius, preaches against Aristotle, and in favor of a "flat earth."

c. **330**

- Chinese scholar Ko Hung writes *Pao-p'u-tzu/He Who Holds to Simplicity*, a manual of alchemy including recipes for mercury and arsenic-based elixirs of life.

346

June 6　During a total eclipse of the sun, astronomers record that the stars become visible in daylight—the first time they have recorded this phenomenon.

Technology

347

- Chinese geographer Ch'ang ch'ü writes *Records of the Country South of Mt. Kua*, in which he describes how the populace use piped natural gas to light and heat their homes.

ARTS AND IDEAS

Architecture

304

- At Spalato (Split) in Dalmatia the palace planned for the Roman emperor Diocletian's retirement is begun in oriental style.

305

- There are 14 aqueducts supplying water to the city of Rome.

306

- Roman emperor Maxentius starts to build an immense basilica in Rome; it marks the climax of classical architecture in the West. It is eventually finished by Constantine.

313

- The oldest extant bridge over the River Rhine is built, at Cologne, in Germany.

315

- The Arch of Constantine is constructed from earlier pagan monuments to celebrate the Roman emperor Constantine's victory over Maxentius.

330

- Work begins on converting the ancient city of Byzantium (modern Istanbul, Turkey) into Roman emperor Constantine's new capital, which is at first called New Rome and later renamed Constantinople. Triple the size of the old city, Constantinople soon becomes the greatest commercial, cultural, and religious center in the Eastern part of the Empire.

Arts

305

- The first tetrach statues are carved; the group built into the corner of San Marco cathedral in Venice, Italy, is an example.

336

- Roman emperor Constantine I the Great patronizes the arts in his last years. The treasures of the empire are used to beautify the new capital, and the *basilica* style of church architecture is established with the construction of the Roman churches of St. Peter and St. Paul Without the Walls.

341

- Indian Guptan king Samudra spends on the arts the treasure brought to him by vassal states.

Literature and Language

337

- Palestinian theologian Eusebius of Caesarea writes his *Life of Constantine*.

Thought and Scholarship

c. 300

- Methodius, bishop of Olympus in Lycia, Asia Minor (modern Turkey), writes *Symposium of the Ten Virgins* in praise of virginity and *Aglaophon* which combats the views of Greek Christian philosopher Origen on the resurrection of the body.

c. 324

- Palestinian theologian Eusebius publishes *Ecclesiastical History*, covering the period from the foundation of the church to the defeat of the Eastern Roman emperor Licinius.

SOCIETY

Everyday Life

c. 300

- The *Kama Sutra*, an Indian handbook on the art of sexual love, is probably produced around this time by the sage Vatsyayana.

315

- The Jewish community in the African kingdom of Axum (modern Ethiopia) reaches half the total population of the kingdom.

330

- One reason for the decline of Rome and the Roman Empire is the decrease in population. Limiting the size of families and infanticide have both been common practice for at least 200 years and the widespread use of eunuchs has been a contributing factor.

Religion

300

c. 300　The influence of Buddhism grows and spreads in China.
- Gregory the Illuminator baptizes King Tiridates III of Armenia, who adopts Christianity as the state religion.

301

- Galerius, Caesar in the East, tries to persuade Roman emperor Diocletian that religious conformity should be insisted upon for the safety of the state.
- Neoplatonist Iamblichus, a Semite, writes on astrology and mysticism and leaves behind his *Life of Pythagoras*.

303

February 23　At the Eastern capital of Nicomedia the Christian cathedral is burned down. The next day the tetrarchs issue a decree which begins a comprehensive attack on Christianity known as the great persecution.

304

- Pope Marcellinus dies after denying his faith during the great persecution.

c. 305

- St. Anthony of Egypt ends his solitary life of study and prayer to instruct those who follow and imitate him.

307

- Lucius Lactantius, a former teacher of rhetoric in Nicomedia, writes *Divinae institutiones/Divine Institutions*, an attempt to summarize Christianity and to show the falsity of pagan beliefs.

311

- The appointment of Bishop Caecilian of Carthage is rejected by some members of his church on the grounds that he was consecrated by a traditor, one who surrendered the scriptures during the great persecution.

314

- A council of bishops at Arles upholds the claims of Caecilian against his critics who are now known as "Donatists" after their own rival Bishop Donatus.
- In his *De mortibus persecutorum/On the Deaths of Persecutors*, Christian apologist Lucius Lactantius gloats over the final agonies of the anti-Christian emperors, Galerius in particular.

315

- Eusebius, known as the "Father of Church History," is made bishop of Caesarea. He is a great admirer of Roman emperor Constantine I the Great.

c. 320

- St. Pachomius, feeling that solitude is selfishness, carries the monastic movement forward by founding a large and strictly organized monastery at Tabennisi in Egypt.

321

- Arius, a Libyan priest, expounds his belief that Christ is not divine, but rather a finite being created by God. He is opposed by his bishop, Alexander of Alexandria, but supported by others including Eusebius of Caeseria and Eusebius of Nicomedia.

c. 323

- Arianism, based on Arius' beliefs, begins to spread among the people, largely through the medium of popular songs.

325

- A schism arises within the Eastern Christian church over the nature of Christ's divinity. The Roman emperor Constantine I the Great, feeling it his religious and imperial duty to ensure unity within the church, summons an ecumenical council of bishops in Nicaea, Asia Minor (now Iznik, Turkey), over which he presides. The ecumenical council confirms the "consubstantiality" of Christ with God the Father. The Nicene Creed, which is adopted as the fundamental statement of Christian belief, contains the anti-Arian statement that the Son "is of one substance with the Father."
- The Mayans in Central America develop a fertility religion based on the cultivation of corn and the passage of the seasons.

c. 326

- Roman emperor Constantine's mother Helena visits Palestine. In Jerusalem she allegedly discovers the wood of the true cross and founds the Church of the Holy Sepulchre on the apparent site of the tomb of Christ.

BIRTHS & DEATHS

c. 305
- Poseidonus, Greek Stoic philosopher, born (–c. 351).

306
- Constantius I ("Chlorus"), Roman emperor 293–306 ruling in a tetrarchy with Maximian, Diocletian, and Galerius, and father of Constantine I the Great, dies in Eboracum, now York, England.

309
- Shapur II, King of the Sassanian Empire of Persia 325–379, who maintained his kingdom against the Romans, born (–379).

310
c. 310   St. Eusebius, pope April 309–August 310, dies in Sicily.
- Ausonius (full name Decimus Magnus Ausonius), Latin poet and rhetorician, born in Burdigala, Gaul (now Bordeaux, France) (–c. 395).
- Marcus Aurelius Valerius Maximianus, Roman emperor 286–305 with Diocletian, dies.

312
- (Marcus Aurelius Valerius) Maxentius, Roman emperor 306–312, son of Maximian, falls at the Battle of the Milvian Bridge.

313
- (Galerius Valerius) Maximinus, Roman emperor 310–313 and a notable persecutor of Christians, dies in Tarsus, in Cilicia, Asia Minor (modern Turkey).

314
- Libanius, Sophist and rhetorician, a number of whose speeches and letters survive, born in Antioch, Syria (–c. 395).

316
- Diocletian, Roman emperor 284–305, noted for restoring efficient government to the empire, dies in Salonae, Dalmatia, now Split, Croatia (68).
- St. Martin of Tours, missionary and monastic founder, born in Sabaria, Pannonia (now Szombathely, Hungary) (–397).

317
August 7   Constantius II, Roman emperor 337–361, at first with his brothers Constantine II, d. 340, and Constans I, d. 350, son of

Constantine I, born in Sirmium, Savia, now Sremska Mitrovica, Serbia (–361).

321
- Valentinian, Roman emperor 364–375, who defended the Western empire from German invaders, born (–375).

325
- Gallus (Flavius Claudius Constantius), ruler of the eastern Roman Empire 351–354, born in Etruria, Italy (–354).
- Lactantius, Christian Father, dies in Augusta Treverorum, Belgica (now Trier, Germany) (c. 80).

326
- Crispus Caesar, eldest son of Roman emperor Constantine I, is executed at Pola, Venetia, Italy on his father's orders.

328
c. 328   Valens, Eastern Roman Emperor 364–378, born (–378).
- St. Helena, Roman empress, mother of Constantine I, dies in Nicomedia, (now Izmit, Turkey) (c. 80).

329
- St. Basil the Great, early Church Father who defended Christian orthodoxy against Arianism, born in Caesarea Mazaca, Cappadocia, in Asia Minor (modern Turkey) (–379).
- St. Gregory of Nazianzus, noted for his defense of Christian orthodoxy against Arianism, born in Arianzus, Cappadocia, Asia Minor (modern Turkey) (–c. 389).

330
- Ammianus Marcellinus, the last major historian of ancient Rome, born in Antioch, Syria (now Antakya, Turkey) (–c. 391).
- Chandra Gupta I, Indian regional king 320–c. 330 who laid the foundations of the Gupta empire in northern India, dies.

331
- Flavius Claudius Julianus (Julian the Apostate), Roman emperor 361–363, a noted scholar and military commander, born in Constantinople (modern Istanbul, Turkey) (–363).
- Jovian (Flavius Jovianus), Christian Roman emperor 363–364, born in

Singidunum, Moesia Superior (now Belgrade, Serbia) (–364).

336
- Arius, Christian priest of Alexandria, Egypt, whose teachings gave rise to the doctrine of Arianism, dies (c. 86).

337
May 22   Constantine I the Great, first Christian Roman emperor of western Europe 312–324 and of whole empire 324–337, dies in Ancyrona, near Nicomedia, in Bithynia, Asia Minor (now Izmir, Turkey) (c. 57).

339
- St. Ambrose, bishop of Milan, biblical critic, and ecclesiastic administrator, born in Augusta Treverorum, Gaul (–397).

340
- Constantine II, Roman emperor 337–340 with his brothers Constans I and Constantius II, son of Constantine I, falls in battle against his brother Constans I at Aquileia, Italy (c. 23).

c. 342
- Eusebius of Nicomedia, bishop, a major proponent of Arianism, dies.

345
- Quintas Aurelias Symmachus, Roman senator opposed to Christianity, born (–402).

347
c. 347   St. John Chrysostom, early father of the Christian church, archbishop of Constantinople, born in Antioch, Roman Syria (–407).
- St. Jerome (Eusebius Hieronymus), biblical translator and monastic founder, born in Stridon, Dalmatia (–c. 419).
January 1   Theodosius I, Roman emperor of the East 379–392, Roman Emperor of the East and West 392–395, who established the Nicene creed in the Christian church, born in Cauca (Coca), Galacia (–395).

348
- Prudentius, Latin allegorical poet, author of "Psychomachia"/"The Contest of the Soul," born in Caesaraugusta, Spain (–after 405).

328
- Athanasius, a staunch opponent of Arianism, becomes bishop of Alexandria.

c. **330**
- St. Nicholas, bishop of Myra in Lycia, Asia Minor (modern Turkey), and one of the most universally venerated of Christian saints, is active at this time.

335
- Greek patriarch of Alexandria, Athanasius, a staunch opponent of Arianism, is excommunicated and exiled to Trier following an attack on him at the Council of Tyre by a pro-Arian bishop, Eusebius of Nicomedia.

336
- Greek Christian theologian Arius, founder of Arianism, dies at Constantinople (modern Istanbul, Turkey) shortly before his planned reconciliation with the church.

337
- Shortly before his death, Roman emperor Constantine is baptized by Eusebius of Nicomedia.

341
- An imperial edict prohibits pagan sacrifice in the Roman Empire.
- The Goth Ulfila is made a missionary bishop. He subsequently establishes Arian Christianity among the Goths and later creates a Gothic alphabet in order to translate the Bible. This translation is the only extant example of this Gothic language.

346
- Bishops at a meeting in Milan declare their adherence to the Nicene creed, which defends Christian orthodoxy from Arianism: the split between the Eastern and Western churches begins to develop.

349
- Greek patriarch of Alexandria, Athanasius, returns from Rome to Alexandria.

350–399

POLITICS, GOVERNMENT, AND ECONOMICS

Business and Economics

388
- The Indian Gupta ruler Chandra Gupta II's war with the Shaka dynasty gives him control of trade with the West, but also destroy any buffer state between him and the Huns.

Colonization

351
- The Franks, spreading generally by peaceful penetration, have by now occupied northwest Gaul.

380
- Easter Island, in the south Pacific Ocean, has been occupied by Neolithic seafarers who about this time begin to fortify the island. They also build platforms of cut and polished stone on which they set statues, although not the gigantic statues for which the island is famous—these do not appear until later.

Human Rights

359
- Anti-Jewish legislation forces the Patriarch of Palestine, Hillel II, to disclose the method for calculating the Jewish calendar.

364
- The new Roman emperor Jovian restores Christianity as the state religion, but issues an edict of toleration for all other religions.

Politics and Government

351
- The Eastern Roman emperor Constantius aims to ensure the loyalty of the East to the dynasty of Constantine I the Great while he is away in the West. His cousin Gallus is married to Constantius' sister, Constantia, and made a Caesar and governor at Antioch, Syria; Gallus's younger brother Julian is allowed to wander in search of teachers of philosophy.
- The Irish "Scots" raid Roman Britain and even Gaul under their most famous king, Niall, reigning at Tara, Ireland.

352
- Eastern Roman emperor Constantius defeats the pretender to the Empire in the West, Magnus Magnentius, at the hard-fought Battle of Mursa in

Mesopotamia. Magnentius flees to Aquileia in northern Italy and fortifies the Alpine passes. Both sides suffer huge losses in the battle. Cavalry armored with chain mail help Constantius win the battle, and this new style of cavalry, or *catafractarii*, will become a major element in the later Roman Empire. Constantius declares an amnesty for Magnentius' men, many of whom desert to him. By the end of the year Constantius is in Milan, Italy, repealing all Magnentius' measures. Magnentius flees to Gaul.

- The Palestinian Jews rebel against Roman rule; their city of Tiberius suffers.

353

- Magnus Magnentius, the usurper of the Western Roman throne, commits suicide in Gaul, but his British follower Martinus holds out. An official named Paulus is sent to control him and proves so harsh in his rule that Martinus kills him and then kills himself. Savage vengeance is taken on the followers of Martinus.

354

- As a result of the armies of the West having been withdrawn by the usurper Magnus Magnentius to fight the Roman emperor Constantius, hoards of barbarians now sweep across the River Rhine into Gaul, ravaging the whole country.
- The brothers Gallus and Julian are summoned before the Roman emperor Constantius, their cousin. Gallus, Caesar and governor of Antioch in Syria since 351, is tried on a charge of cruel and despotic rule, and executed; Julian is held prisoner for some months but he is released on making it clear that his sole interest is philosophy and is banished to Athens.
- The Roman emperor Constantius crosses the Jura Mountains and marches toward Basel to drive the Alemanni out of Roman territory. The Alemanni withdraw, however, and peace is concluded.

355

- The Franks capture Cologne and lay waste to 45 towns, taking the entire valley of the Rhine from the Romans and penetrating deeply into Gaul.
- The Huns of Central Asia begin their great drive westward with an advance into Scythia (modern Russia). They overcome and absorb the Alans, the nomadic and warlike horse-breeding people from the steppes northeast of the Black Sea.
- The Roman emperor Constantius, concerned about the power of army commanders sent to deal with the Germanic incursions into Gaul, decides that only a member of the royal house of Constantine I the Great can command the loyalty of the West, and so banishes any suspicions he may have of his cousin Julian and appoints him Caesar and governor of Gaul. Julian is also given Constantius' sister Helena in marriage.

356–359

- The newly appointed Roman Caesar, Julian, is sent to Gaul to take part in a joint operation with the emperor Constantius against the Alemanni. Julian retakes Cologne from the Franks and makes peace with them. He then retires to winter in Sens, where he is besieged by the Alemanni. He heroically defends the town, winning great respect as a commander, until the Alemanni withdraw.

357

- The Roman emperor Constantius visits Rome for the first time to celebrate the 20th year of his reign after the death of his father, Constantine I the Great. From Rome he proceeds to the Danube where there is renewed pressure on the Empire's frontiers.

357–359 The Roman emperor Constantius appoints Julian, the governor of Gaul, supreme commander over the troops in Gaul. The following year Julian wins an important victory at Strasbourg, and then in a series of brilliant campaigns he drives the barbarians out of Gaul, regaining first the Upper Rhine and then the Lower Rhine for Rome. He goes on to free the Roman hostages taken by the barbarians, and refortifies the frontier. He also builds a fleet to secure the corn supply from Britain for the garrisons of the Rhine and passes several measures which help to restore Gaul's prosperity.

358

- The Persian king Shapur II has dealt with the Huns who were attacking Persia, and once more advances into the Roman province of Mesopotamia. He besieges the city of Amida, which heroically resists the Persians for 73 days before being captured, winning the Romans the time they need to defend their Eastern provinces. The emperor Constantius calls for troops from Gaul to help fight the Persians.

360

- Julian, the Roman Caesar, is declared emperor by his troops in Paris, Gaul; they refuse to go East to the aid of the emperor Constantius struggling against King Shapur II of Persia. Julian and Constantius exchange several letters, both hoping to avoid civil war, although both prepare for it. Julian finally takes the first step toward war by setting out with his army toward the East.
- The Roman Caesar Julian sends a mobile force to Britain to repel an invasion of Picts and Scots; the size of the force and the high rank of its commander, Lupicinus, indicates a severe crisis in a province hitherto secure as a supply base for Julian's campaigns in Gaul.

361

- On the way to confront his cousin Julian, the Roman emperor Constantius dies of a fever in Cilicia, Asia Minor (modern Turkey). Julian takes over the combined emperorship of East and West and rules from Constantinople (modern Istanbul, Turkey). He declares himself a pagan and makes a final attempt at hellenizing the Empire.

361–363 The Roman emperor Julian, ruling from Constantinople (modern Istanbul, Turkey), follows the example of the first Roman emperor, Augustus, in showing great respect for his Senate and for the process of justice. He improves administration and removes many of the abuses of the system.

362

- The Roman emperor Julian sets up headquarters in Antioch, Syria, and prepares for a full-scale invasion of the Sassanian Persian Empire, even though King Shapur II of Persia has ceased to attack Roman possessions and this action is against the advice of Julian's counselors.

363

- The Roman emperor Julian invades Sassanian Persia and reaches the capital Ctesiphon, but his army is enticed into the desert by a ruse. King Shapur II of Persia avoids battle and adopts a scorched earth policy, leaving the Romans desperately short of supplies. As the Romans retreat, Julian is mortally wounded in a skirmish. Jovian, Captain of the Guard and a Christian, succeeds him and makes peace, surrendering four of the five provinces gained by the Caesar Galerius in 298, and the cities of Nisibis and Singara.

364

- The soldier Valentinian is elected Roman emperor. He retains the West and makes his younger brother Valens emperor of the East.

364–375   The Western Roman emperor Valentinian I rules wisely from Milan, Italy, checking political corruption and forbidding infanticide.

365–366

- The Alemanni pour across the frontier into Gaul. The Western Roman emperor Valentinian I moves to Paris to command the war, appointing Jovinus, his master of horse, general of the army. Jovinus defeats the Alemanni in three successive battles.
- The Roman emperor of the East, Valens, faces a challenge to his power by Procopius, a favorite of the late emperor Julian, who declares himself emperor in Constantinople (modern Istanbul, Turkey). Procopius gains much support, but is betrayed to Valens the following year and put to death.

367

- The Western Roman emperor Valentinian I becomes seriously ill, and his advisors discuss possible successors. On his recovery, Valentinian makes his son Gratian, aged nine, his partner and Augustus.

367–369   The Eastern Roman emperor Valens campaigns against the Goths on the River Danube, winning a decisive victory in 369. He strengthens the frontier with garrisons and forts.

368–370

- King Shapur II of Sassanian Persia attempts to make Armenia a vassal, contending that the treaty with the Romans agreed by the emperor Jovian in 363 forbids Roman interference in Armenia.
- Roman Britain suffers a concerted attack by Picts, Scots, Saxons, and Franks. The Roman military commander Count Flavius Theodosius is sent to restore order, which he does. His son, later to become Theodosius I the Great, campaigns with him.

369

- The Japanese invade Korea and establish a small colony and base there.

370

- On his return from Britain, the Roman soldier Theodosius the elder is appointed master of the horse, succeeding Jovinus. He defeats the Alemanni in Raetia and Gaul, and settles many as farmers in the Po Valley, Italy.

371–373

- A Roman army under the Eastern Roman emperor Valens advances from Constantinople (modern Istanbul, Turkey) to Antioch, Syria. In a battle over Armenia between Persians and Romans, Rome is

victorious. A truce is concluded, and King Shapur II of Sassanian Persia retires to his capital, Ctesiphon.

372

- The Huns, under Balamir, cross the River Volga and defeat the Ostrogoths in the area of modern Ukraine. Some Ostrogoths join the Huns while others penetrate into the land of the Visigoths, north of the River Danube.

372–374   The Roman general Flavius Theodosius the elder puts down an insurrection in Roman Africa, which has been suffering from invasion by the Berbers of the North African interior since 363 and from the plots and maladministration of the Roman commander Romanus.

374

- The Quadi and Sarmatians pour across the River Danube and devastate the Roman provinces of Pannonia and Moesia. The Roman soldier Theodosius the younger repels the Sarmatians in Dalmatia.

375

- Chandra Gupta II of the Gupta dynasty begins his reign in India.
- The Western Roman emperor Valentinian I concludes an enduring peace with the Alemanni in Germany, then marches to help defend the Danube frontier. He dies suddenly, while negotiating with the Quadi. His son Gratian succeeds him as emperor of the West. His other son, the four-year-old Valentinian II, is appointed coemperor of the West, to which Gratian agrees.

376

- The Roman general Theodosius the elder falls victim to the plots of his enemies in Carthage, Africa, and is executed. The Western Roman emperor Gratian recalls the military commander Theodosius, son of the executed general Theodosius the elder, from retirement in Spain and puts him in charge of the Roman troops in Thrace. Theodosius defeats the Sarmatians, and in 379 is appointed coemperor by Gratian to replace Valens.

376–378   The Visigoths north of the River Danube, defeated by the Huns, are allowed to settle in Roman territory but revolt and overrun Thrace. The Eastern Roman emperor Valens meets them near Hadrianople and is defeated and killed, leaving Constantinople (modern Istanbul, Turkey) itself in danger from the Goths. The Gothic heavy cavalry proves decisive in the battle.

379

- King Shapur II dies, leaving the Sassanian Empire at the height of its power and at peace with Rome. He is succeeded by Ardashir.
- The Eastern Roman emperor Theodosius I the Great occupies Thessaloníki in Thrace as a base for operations against the Goths. After winning several victories he falls seriously ill and the Goths rise again. The Western emperor Gratian hastens to his aid. The chief leader of the Goths dies, reducing the threat.

381

- Athanarich, one of the chiefs of the Goths and a lifelong enemy of Rome, seeks refuge with the Eastern Roman emperor Theodosius I the Great in Constantinople (modern Istanbul, Turkey). The emperor welcomes him, and when he dies soon after, gives him a royal funeral.

382

- The Eastern Roman emperor Theodosius I the Great, recognizing the impossibility of expelling the Goths from Thrace, concludes a treaty of alliance with the Visigoths and assigns them territory within the province in exchange for military service.

383

- The Western Roman emperor Gratian has relapsed into a weak and inefficient ruler and Magnus Maximus, the Spanish commander left behind by the Roman soldier Theodosius the elder in Britain, claims the throne of the Western Empire. He defeats Gratian near Paris, Gaul, and becomes master of Gaul and Spain. Gratian flees after his defeat and is killed by his own troops. Valentinian II succeeds his half brother Gratian as the rightful emperor of the West. Magnus Maximus crosses from Britain to Gaul in a bid to make himself Roman emperor. He withdraws many of the troops from Britain; Hadrian's Wall, the northern Roman frontier in Britain, is overrun and falls into ruin.

384

- The situation in the East is uncertain after the death of the Persian king Ardashir the previous year, and the accession of Shapur III. The Eastern Roman emperor Theodosius I the Great feels he cannot leave the East at this time, so he acknowledges the self-proclaimed Magnus Maximus as emperor in the West.

387

- After three years of negotiation, with the Roman general Flavius Stilicho representing Rome at the Persian court, the Eastern Roman emperor Theodosius I the Great renews peace with the Sassanian Empire: Armenia, so long a cause of friction, is partitioned between the Roman and Sassanian empires.
- Magnus Maximus, the usurping emperor of the West, invades Italy. The rightful emperor Valentinian II flees with his mother and sister to Thessaloníki, Thrace, where the Eastern emperor Theodosius I the Great meets him and marries Valentinian's sister, Galla.
- Southern China is saved at the Battle of Fei Shui from Hunnish invasion but the weakened north suffers another wave of invading Hunnish or Tatar tribes.

388

- Chandra Gupta II, the ruler of the Indian Gupta dynasty, begins a war against the Shaka dynasty, which finally gives him control of northwest India. He calls himself *Vickramaditya* ("Sun of Prowess").
- The usurping Western Roman emperor Magnus Maximus is defeated in three battles by the Eastern emperor Theodosius I the Great, in command of an army including Goths, Huns, and Alans. Maximus is killed near Aquileia, Italy, and the rightful emperor Valentinian II is restored to power. With the death of his mother Justina, his most influential advisor is the early Christian leader and theologian Bishop Ambrose of Milan.

389

- Resentment among the citizens of Thessaloníki, Thrace, at the billeting of Germanic troops on them, breaks out into violence, in which the captain of the garrison is killed. The Eastern Roman emperor Theodosius I the Great orders vengeance, despite the pleas of Ambrose,

bishop of Milan, for mercy, and more than 7,000 citizens are killed by the troops.

390

- Bishop Ambrose retires to Milan, Italy, refusing to meet the Eastern Roman emperor Theodosius I the Great until he repents for ordering the massacre of over 7,000 citizens in Thessaloníki the previous year. Theodosius is by now filled with remorse at his action, and kneels in humility, stripped of his royal purple, before the altar of the cathedral in Milan, thus humbling himself before the power of the church.

390–392 The Visigoths and Huns invade Thrace, led by Alaric, a Visigoth prince. Command of the Roman defensive campaign goes to Flavius Stilicho, a commander of Vandal origin, who defeats the invaders. The Eastern Roman emperor Theodosius I the Great permits them to go free on condition they provide military services to the Empire.

391

- The Eastern Roman emperor Theodosius I the Great returns to his capital, Constantinople (modern Istanbul, Turkey).

392

- The Western Roman emperor Valentinian II is assassinated while advancing into Gaul against a Frankish usurper, Arbogast, after being sent to restore order in Gaul by the Eastern emperor Theodosius I the Great. Arbogast appoints a weakling, Eugenius, as emperor of the West, and is thus the first of the Germanic kingmakers of the Roman Empire.

393

- The Frankish usurper Arbogast and his appointed emperor of the West, Eugenius, march into Italy with a large army and await the arrival of the Eastern Roman emperor Theodosius I the Great. In Constantinople (modern Istanbul, Turkey), Theodosius appoints his younger son, Honorius, Augustus (emperor). His elder son, Arcadius, has already been created Augustus.

394

- The Eastern Roman emperor Theodosius I the Great defeats the Frankish usurper Arbogast and Arbogast's appointed emperor of the West, Eugenius, near Aquileia, Italy, at the Battle of the River Frigidus. The Gothic contingent of Theodosius' army is commanded by the Visigoth leader Alaric. Theodosius' victory is aided by a storm, which hampers Arbogast's forces, and by desertions to his side.

395

- Shortly before his death, the Roman emperor Theodosius I the Great appoints his 11-year-old son Honorius emperor of the West, with the Roman commander Flavius Stilicho as his guardian and regent, and his 18-year-old son Arcadius emperor of the East.

396

- The Roman general Flavius Stilicho controls the young emperor Honorius as his regent and becomes virtual ruler of the West. The Goths under Alaric rampage through Greece when Stilicho ceases to employ or subsidize them, creating a kingdom for themselves. Alaric destroys the temple of Eleusis, and harries the

Peloponnese. Stilicho advances, makes peace with the Goths, and allows them to settle in Epirus.

397

- The Moorish prince Gildo revolts against Roman rule in Africa, taking much of North Africa and cutting off the corn supply to Rome. The Roman general Flavius Stilicho concludes a hasty treaty with the Goths in the Balkans and returns to Italy to raise troops against the rebel Moorish prince in Africa. Stilicho supervises the war, and Gildo is defeated.

SCIENCE, TECHNOLOGY, AND MEDICINE

Health and Medicine

356

- The heretical Syrian Christian bishop Aëtius the Atheist courts theological controversy, while offering his services as a physician free to the poor.

361

- Under new regulations passed at Constantinople (modern Istanbul, Turkey), eastern capital of the Roman Empire, all physicians must obtain a license in order to practice.

362

- Oribasius of Pergamum, physician to the Roman emperor Julian the Apostate, writes *Synagogue Medicine*, a medical encyclopedia in 70 volumes.

370

- St. Basil of Caesarea establishes a hospital in Cappadocia, Asia Minor (modern Turkey), which includes the first isolation unit for the treatment of leprosy.

Math

370

- Greek mathematician Hypatia writes commentaries on Diophantus and Apollonius. She is the first recorded female mathematician.

Technology

370

- An anonymous Roman author writes *De rebus bellicum/On Military Matters*, a book of designs for military engines and vehicles, including a huge boat powered by six ox-driven paddle wheels.

ARTS AND IDEAS

Architecture

361

- As a provocative gesture toward the Christians, Roman emperor Julian encourages the rebuilding of the Temple at Jerusalem. Work stops when he dies.

c. 370

- Many villas in the Roman style, with estate lands and featuring ornate mosaic work, are built in Roman Britain, especially in the area of the Cotswolds.

380

- Eastern Roman emperor Theodosius I the Great constructs the Golden Gate on the western road into the city of Constantinople (modern Istanbul, Turkey) and enters through it in triumph, drawn by elephants.

391

- The Temple of Serapis, Alexandria, is destroyed by a Christian mob. Among the wonders it contained was said to be a statue of the sun god that floated in mid-air, trapped by the forces of surrounding magnets.

392

- Roman emperor Theodosius I celebrates his victory in the recent civil wars with a triumphal redecoration of Constantinople (modern Istanbul, Turkey), for which he has the obelisk of Egyptian pharaoh Tuthmosis III brought from Karnak. Reinstalling it in the city proves a major engineering feat.

399

- A Chinese account mentions the longest suspension bridge of the time—stretching 120 m/400 ft across the Sanchipan gorge in the Himalayas.

Arts

353

- Chinese calligrapher Wang Xi-zhi produces "Preface to the Poems Composed at the Orchid Pavilion" in running script style. It becomes a model for future calligraphers.

359

- On a classical sarcophagus from St. Peter's in Rome, Christ is represented as young and unbearded and supported on a canopy by the sky god Coleus.

c. 375

- In this period north India rises to its cultural height under King Chandra Gupta II.

392

- Roman emperor Theodosius I the Great, in imitation of Trajan, sets up a column in Constantinople (modern Istanbul, Turkey) to commemorate his victories over the Goths.

Literature and Language

c. 376

- The Latin pastoral romance *Daphnis and Chloe* is written by the sophist Longus.

BIRTHS & DEATHS

350
- Constans I, Christian Roman emperor 337–350, son of Constantine I the Great, is killed in Gaul (30).

353
- St. Paulinus of Nola, bishop of Nola, early Christian Latin poet, born in Burdigala, Gaul (–431).

August 11 Magnentius, usurping Roman emperor, commits suicide in Gaul.

354
- Gallus (Flavius Claudius Constantius), ruler of the eastern Roman Empire 351–354, dies near Pola, Italy (c. 29).

November 13 St. Augustine of Hippo (original name Aurelius Augustinus), the leading theologian of the early Western church, whose best-known works are the *Confessiones/Confessions* and *De civitate Dei/City of God*, born in Tagaste, Numidia (–430).

356
January 17 St. Anthony of Egypt, religious ascetic who founded Christian monasticism, dies in Dayr Mari Antonios hermitage near the Red Sea (c. 105).

359
- Gratian (Flavius Gratianus Augustus), Roman emperor 367–383, sharing power with his father Valentinian I 364–375 and his uncle Valens 364–378, born in Sirmium, Lesser Pannonia (now Sremska Mitrovica, Serbia) (–383).

361
November 3 Constantius II, Roman emperor 337–361, at first with his brothers Constantine II, d. 340, and Constans I, d. 350, son of Constantine I, dies at Mopsucrenae, Asia Minor (now Turkey) (44).

363
- Flavius Claudius Julianus (Julian the Apostate), Roman emperor 361–363, a noted scholar and military commander, dies from wounds received in battle at Ctesiphon, near Baghdad, Persia (c. 32).

364
- Jovian (Flavius Jovianus), Christian Roman emperor 363–364, dies in Dadastana, Bithynia (c. 33).

c. **365**
- Flavius Stilicho, Roman military commander who repelled the

Visigoths and Ostrogoths from Italy, and also acted as regent 394–408 for Emperor Honorius, born (–408).

370
c. 370 Alaric, Visigoth chief who sacked Rome in 410 signaling the decline of the Roman Empire, born in Peuce Island (–410).
- Hypatia, Egyptian Neoplatonist philosopher, the first famous female mathematician, born in Alexandria, Egypt (–415).
- Maximus of Ephesus, Neoplatonist philosopher and magician, is executed.

373
May 2 St. Athanasius, theologian and statesman, chief opponent of Arianism, dies in Alexandria, Egypt (c. 80).

375
November 17 Valentinian, Roman emperor 364–375, who defended the Western empire from German invaders, dies in Sirmium in modern Yugoslavia (c. 54).

377
- Arcadius, Eastern Roman emperor jointly with his father, Theodosius I, 383–395, and on his own 395–402, born (–408).

378
August 9 Valens, Eastern Roman Emperor 364–378, is killed at the Battle of Adrianople, Turkey (c. 50).

379
- Shapur II, king of the Sassanian Empire of Persia 325–79, who maintained his kingdom against the Romans, dies.

January 1 St. Basil the Great, early Church Father who defended Christian orthodoxy against Arianism, dies in Caesarea Mazaca, Cappadocia, Asia Minor (modern Turkey) (c. 50).

380
- Samudra Gupta, emperor of the Gupta empire in northern India c. 330–c. 380, considered the epitome of the ideal Hindu ruler, son of Chandra Gupta I, dies.

383
August 25 Gratian (Flavius Gratianus Augustus), Roman emperor 367–383, sharing power with his father Valentinian I 364–375 and his uncle Valens 364–378, is murdered in Lugdunum, Gaul (now Lyon, France) (25).

384
September 9 (Flavius) Honorius, Roman emperor in the West 393–423, son of Theodosius I and brother of the Eastern Roman emperor Arcadius, born (–423).

c. **385**
- St. Patrick, patron saint of Ireland who brought Christianity to the island, born in Britain (–c. 461).

388
August 28 Magnus Maximus, usurping Roman emperor of Britain, Gaul, and Spain 383–388, is executed.

389
- St. Gregory of Nazianzus, Church Father noted for his defense of Christian orthodoxy against Arianism, dies in Arianzus, Cappadocia (modern Turkey) (c. 60).

c. **390**
- St. Simeon Stylites, Syrian ascetic, first stylite or pillar hermit, who spent much of his life living on a column, born in Sisan, Cilicia (–459).

391
- Ammianus Marcellinus, the last major historian of ancient Rome, dies in Rome (65).

393
- Libanius, Sophist and rhetorician, a number of whose speeches and letters survive, dies (c. 79).

395
- Ausonius (full name Decimus Magnus Ausonius), Latin poet and rhetorician, dies (c. 85).

January 17 Theodosius I the Great, emperor of the eastern Roman empire 379–392, then of the whole empire 392–395, who suppressed paganism and Arianism and established the Nicene creed in the Christian church, dies in Milan (48).

397
- St. Ambrose, bishop of Milan, biblical critic, and ecclesiastic administrator, dies in Milan, Italy (c. 58).

November 8 St. Martin of Tours, missionary and monastic founder, dies in Candas, Gaul (c. 81).

399
- St. Fabiola, Roman Christian matron, founder of the first public hospital in Europe at Ostia, Italy, in 390, dies.

395

- Claudian, the last of the Latin classic poets, moves to Rome. He is patronized by Roman general Stilicho, for whom he writes a panegyric, a form of eulogy in which he specializes.

397

- Bishop Augustine begins his *Confessions*, an autobiography that recounts his intellectual and spiritual development.

Thought and Scholarship

378

- The former soldier Ammianus Marcellinus writes a *History* of Rome which describes Valens' defeat at Hadrianople as the worst since Cannae.

SOCIETY

Education

375

- The earliest extant books—a school textbook and an account book—with bound wooden leaves, are lost at the Dakhla Oasis in western Egypt. The desert sands preserve them for modern archeologists.

Religion

355

- On being banished to Athens future Roman emperor Julian is intiated into the Eleusinian mysteries (the religious rites celebrated at Eleusis in honor of Demeter, the Greek goddess of the harvest). Among his fellow students are Gregory Nazienzen and Basil the Great.

356

- Greek patriarch and leading defender of Christian orthodoxy Athanasius is expelled from Alexandria once more. In exile in the desert he writes *Four Orations Against the Arians*.

362

- St. Martin founds the monastery of Ligugé, the first in Gaul.

374

- St. Ambrose, the governor of Aemilia-Liguria, is the popular choice to become bishop of Milan even though he is unbaptized. He introduces the singing of eastern melodies into the liturgy.

379

- Buddhism is declared the state religion of China.
- St. Basil the Great dies, having encouraged the growth of self-supporting monasteries in Cappadocia in Asia Minor (modern Turkey) and elsewhere. His rule, which emphasized the communal aspect of ascetic life, forms the basis of monasticism in the Greek Orthodox Church.

380

- Pelagius, a British theologian possibly from Verulamium (St. Albans, England), leaves for Rome with his Irish companion Caelestius.

381

- The second ecumenical council of Constantinople (modern Istanbul, Turkey) reasserts the position adopted at the council of Nicea, marking the virtual end of Arianism within the Roman Empire.

382

- St. Jerome goes to Rome as secretary to Pope Damasus and begins work on producing a standardized Latin version of the Bible which later becomes known as the *Vulgate* version.

384

- St. Augustine, a Manichaean and a sensualist, leaves his native North Africa. At Milan he comes under the influence of Bishop Ambrose and, after a prolonged study of Neoplatonism, is baptized two years later.

385

- A Spanish bishop, Priscillian, accused of preaching the Persian doctrine of Manichaeism, is burned at the stake despite protests from bishops Ambrose and Martin.

386

- Pope Siricius decrees that priests should not marry; he is supported by St. Ambrose, St. Jerome, and St. Augustine.

391

- The great temple and library of Serapis, the Egyptian god of the lower world, at Alexandria are destroyed on the orders of Archbishop Theophilus.

395

- Aurelius Augustinus (later known as St. Augustine of Hippo) becomes bishop of Hippo Regius in Mauritania (now Annaba, Algeria).

c. 396

- St. Paulinus and his wife give up their considerable wealth and form a small Christian community at Nola in Italy.

c. 397

- The Christian evangelist Ninian (later St. Ninian) establishes a church at Whithorn in Galloway and begins to make converts among the southern Pictish tribes to the north of Roman Britain.

c. 399–c. 404

- Chinese Buddhist monk Faxian sets out for India where he visits Buddhist holy sites and studies religious texts. On his return to China, he translates several Buddhist scriptures into Chinese.

Sports

393

- The Roman emperor Theodosius I the Great abolishes the Greek Olympic Games by decree because of their association with paganism.

400–449

POLITICS, GOVERNMENT, AND ECONOMICS

Colonization

401

- The Vandals, who had settled in the region between the Danube and the Theiss, together with the Alani from Pannonia, migrate into Roman Noricum and Raetia (modern Austria and Switzerland). The Roman general Stilicho is forced to grant them land in exchange for military service.

438

- Spain is overrun by the Suevi, a group of German migratory tribes.

Human Rights

401

- Patrick, son of a Roman official living on the Severn Estuary and the future patron saint of Ireland, is captured by pirates and sold in Ireland as a slave.

Politics and Government

401

- The Eastern Roman emperor Arcadius is presented with a son in Constantinople (modern Istanbul, Turkey), whom he christens Theodosius after his father, the late emperor Theodosius I the Great.
- Under Alaric, the Visigoths invade Italy. They besiege Milan, where the emperor Honorius is based. The Roman general Stilicho gathers an army, including Vandals and Alani, denuding garrisons as far afield as Britain, and marches to the defense of Milan.

402

- The Roman general Stilicho drives the Visigoth Alaric from Milan, then fights an inconclusive battle at Pollentia (in modern Piedmont), taking Alaric's wife and children prisoner. He bribes Alaric to leave Italy.

403

- Alaric and the Visigoths invade Italy again, but are defeated by the Roman general Stilicho near Verona. A treaty is made, and the emperor Honorius and Stilicho celebrate their victory.

- The Western Roman emperor Honorius deserts Milan for Ravenna, which he makes the Western capital.

405

- The German king Radagaisus gathers an army of Ostrogoths, Vandals, and others, with which he invades Italy. The Roman general Stilicho saves Florence and brings Radagaisus in chains to the emperor Honorius.

December 31 The River Rhine in central Europe freezes over, allowing hordes of Vandals, Alans, and Scieri to invade the Roman Empire, ultimately leading to its collapse.

406

- Vandals under King Gunderic and other Germanic peoples overrun much of Gaul, devastating the province and conquering cities. They are prevented from entering Spain by the Pyrenees.
- As the Roman government has ceased to send out governors or organize troops in the wake of the Vandal conquest of Gaul, the Romano-British elect their own emperors. The first is Marcus, who is succeeded by Gratian.

407

- A third usurper, Constantine, appears in Britain. He crosses the Channel in an effort to create a realm for himself in both Gaul and Spain.
- The Alamanni capture much of Roman Upper Germany.

408

- Arcadius dies in Constantinople (modern Istanbul, Turkey), and his son, Theodosius II, aged seven, becomes emperor of the East. The real power, however, lies in the hands of Theodosius's sister, Pulcheria.
- In Rome, the chancellor Olympius, jealous of the general Stilicho and believing him to be at heart pro-German, persuades the emperor Honorius to have him assassinated, together with many of his Vandal soldiers. Alaric seizes his opportunity and uses the pretext of an unpaid bribe (promised him by Stilicho in 402) to invade Italy once again. Following Stilicho's death, Roman troops are allowed to rob and murder the families of Teutonic troops in Italy, causing many to desert to the Visigoth king Alaric.

409

- The Vandals, under King Gunderic and their allies the Alani and Suevi, invade Spain and plunder the rich cities there. Constans, the son of the usurping emperor Constantine in Gaul, despite having installed Gerontius as prefect in Spain, does nothing to stop the Vandal invasion.
- The Visigoth king Alaric besieges Rome, bringing the inhabitants close to starvation. Twice he is bought off but twice returns. Many Germanic slaves escape to his side. The emperor Honorius in Ravenna refuses to

Barbarian Invasions of Rome (403–476)

403

- Alaric and the Visigoths invade Italy, but are defeated by the Roman general Stilicho near Verona. A treaty is made, and the emperor Honorius and Stilicho celebrate their victory.

405

- German king Radagaisus gathers an army of Ostrogoths, Vandals, and others, with which he invades Italy. Stilicho saves Florence and brings Radagaisus in chains to Honorius.

December 31   The River Rhine in central Europe freezes over, allowing hordes of Vandals, Alans, and Scieri to invade the Roman Empire, ultimately leading to its collapse.

406

- Vandals under King Gunderic and other Germanic peoples overrun much of Gaul, devastating the province and conquering cities. They are prevented from entering Spain by the Pyrenees.

409

- The Visigoth king Alaric besieges Rome, bringing the inhabitants close to starvation. Twice he is bought off but twice returns. Many Germanic slaves escape to his side. Honorius refuses to negotiate for peace, despite repeated offers from Alaric. After his second siege of Rome, Alaric comes to terms with the Senate and sets up the prefect of the city, Attalus, as a rival emperor to Honorius. Attalus proves incapable, however, losing the vital province of Africa (the granary of Rome) to Honorius. Alaric deposes him and reopens negotiations with Honorius. Hindered by the machinations of his Gothic enemy, Sarus, Alaric begins his third siege of Rome.

410

- Having reached Consentia, in the toe of Italy, with the intention of capturing the province of Africa, which is responsible for the supply of Rome's grain, Alaric dies of a fever and is buried with an immolation of slaves.

August   The city of Rome is captured by King Alaric when a slave opens the gates and the Visigoths enter. The city is taken 800 years after its previous fall to the Gauls. The Visigoths spare the churches of St. Peter and St. Paul.

424

- The Roman soldier Aëtius, who spent part of his early years as a hostage among the Goths and Huns, invades Italy at the head of a large force of barbarians in support of the usurper John.

425

- The Vandals capture Cartagena and Seville, the last Roman strongholds in southern Spain, then move on to conquer the Balearic Islands and the coast of Mauritania.

455

c. 455   Much of northern Italy is devastated by this time: towns are walled, farms are abandoned, and the population has shrunk; it is estimated Rome has shrunk from about a million and a half citizens to a third of a million.

- Prior to the arrival of the Vandals in Rome, the emperor Maximus is murdered, and a puppet Avitus put on the throne. The Vandals, who now rule the western Mediterranean, cut off supplies from Italy, causing famine.

472

- The Visigoth Ricimer captures Rome, kills the Western emperor Anthemius, and appoints Olybrius his successor. When Ricimer dies shortly thereafter, Gundobad, King of the Burgundians, takes control of the western armies. Olybrius then dies, leaving the Western Roman Empire without an emperor.

476

- More Germanic tribes invade Italy, and in Rome the emperor Romulus Augustulus resigns his throne to their general, Odoacer. Odoacer agrees to become king of Italy while Zeno of Constantinople becomes emperor of the nominally recombined Eastern and Western Roman empires.

negotiate for peace, despite repeated offers from Alaric. After his second siege of Rome, Alaric comes to terms with the Senate and sets up the prefect of the city, Attalus, as a rival emperor to Honorius. Attalus proves incapable, however, losing the vital province of Africa (the granary of Rome) to Honorius. Alaric deposes him and reopens negotiations with Honorius. Hindered by the machinations of his Gothic enemy Sarus, Alaric begins his third siege of Rome.

- The Western Roman emperor Honorius recognizes the usurper Constantine in Gaul as coemperor in exchange for his help against Alaric and the Visigoths.

410

- Having reached Consentia, in the toe of Italy, with the intention of capturing the province of Africa, responsible for the supply of Rome's grain, the Visigoth

king Alaric dies of a fever and is buried with an immolation of slaves.

August   The city of Rome is captured by the Visigoth king Alaric when a slave opens the gates and the Visigoths enter. The city is taken 800 years after its previous fall to the Gauls. The Visigoths spare the churches of St. Peter and St. Paul.

411

- The Western Roman emperor Honorius tells the Britons that they must look to their own defenses, finally abandoning the Romans' claims to the island. He sends two generals to deal with the usurper Constantine in Gaul. They kill Gerontius, Constantine's rebellious prefect of Spain, then besiege Arles and defeat Constantine. The Teutonic tribes in Spain join the empire as *foederati* (allies with military commitments).

412–414

- On the death of Alaric, his brother-in-law Ataulf (Adolphus) becomes king of the Visigoths. He marches north through Italy and sets up a Visigoth kingdom in Gaul, theoretically subject to the Empire.

414

- King Ataulf of the Visigoths marries the Roman emperor Honorius' half sister Placidia, who is a prisoner of the Visigoths. It is Ataulf's aim to combine the Gothic and Roman nations into one.

415

- King Ataulf is assassinated and Wallia becomes ruler of the Visigoth kingdom in Gaul.
- Kumara Gupta succeeds to the Indian throne as the Huns begin to threaten his kingdom from the northwest. He is successful in keeping his kingdom intact.

417

- Placidia, half sister of the Western Roman emperor Honorius and widow of the Visigoth Ataulf, marries the Roman Constantius, brother-in-law of Honorius.

418

- The western Roman emperor Honorius bribes Wallia, King of the Visigoths, into regaining Spain for the Empire. His victory over the Vandals, who overran Spain in 409, forces them to retire to Vandalusia (Andalusia). The Visigoth land in Gaul now extends from the River Garonne to the Loire, and becomes known as the Visigoth kingdom of Toulouse.

419

- Wallia dies and Theodoric I is chosen by the people as the next king of the Visigoth kingdom in Toulouse.

421

- The Vandals in Spain defeat a Roman force in Baetica, after Visigoth troops in the Roman army change sides.
- The Western Roman emperor Honorius makes his brother-in-law Constantius coemperor, but Constantius dies a few months later.

423–425

- Emperor Honorius, of the Western Roman empire, dies. A struggle for the throne ensues.

424

- The Roman soldier Aëtius, who spent part of his early years as a hostage among the Goths and Huns, invades Italy at the head of a large force of barbarians in support of the usurper John.

425

- The Huns, advancing into Europe from the East, are halted by an outbreak of plague in their ranks, and prevented from reaching the city of Constantinople (modern Istanbul, Turkey).
- The usurper John is defeated and the young Valentinian III, son of the Roman Constantius and Placidia, the daughter of the emperor Theodosius I the Great, becomes Emperor of the West. Real power is in the hands of his mother Placidia, the widow of the Visigoth Ataulf. The Roman soldier Aëtius enters her service.
- The Vandals capture Cartagena and Seville, the last Roman strongholds in southern Spain, then move on to conquer the Balearic Islands and the coast of Mauritania.

426–428

- The Roman commander Aëtius campaigns in Gaul against the Goths and Franks on behalf of the western Roman emperor Valentinian III.

428

- Gunderic, King of the Vandals in Spain, dies and is succeeded by his brother Genseric (or Gaiseric).

429

- Under King Genseric, the Vandals invade the Roman province of Africa, the source of most of Rome's grain supply.

430

- The Vandals in Spain, under King Genseric (or Gaiseric), are invited to come to Africa by the Roman governor Boniface, who has quarreled with the imperial government. The Vandals conquer Roman Africa, helped by a revolt of the Moors and of Donatist Christians. They besiege and take the city of Hippo Regius, killing its bishop, Augustine (later St. Augustine).

431

- Chlodio, the first known king of the Franks, makes Tournai his capital and occupies the region of Cambrai as far as the Somme. He is prevented by the Roman commander Aëtius from taking Cologne.
- The emperor Valentinian III makes peace with the victorious Vandals in Africa, and Governor Boniface retires to Ravenna where he defeats the Roman general Aëtius but dies soon after.

c. 433

- Attila, King of the Huns, consolidates his power in his Hungarian capital, probably on the site of Buda. Both emperors, Theodosius II in the East and Valentinian III in the West, bribe him to keep the peace. Attila initially inherits the Hunnish kingdom with his brother Bleda, but reputedly murders him in 444.

435

- The Burgundians make peace with the Roman commander Aëtius but are attacked by the Huns.

438

- The *Codex Theodosianus* divides the Eastern and Western Empires administratively and provides the Germanic inheritors of Rome with a code of laws.

439

- The Egyptian poet and philosopher Cyrus becomes city and praetorian prefect at Constantinople (modern Istanbul, Turkey). He repairs the city's buildings and protective sea wall.

439–450 The Vandal king Genseric breaks the peace with the Romans in Africa and seizes Carthage. He uses the city as a base for efficient piracy and coastal ravaging by sea-borne cavalry.

440

- St. Leo I, known as Leo the Great, becomes pope.
- Under King Genseric, the Vandals invade Sicily (the main provider of grain to Italy), where they ravage the land before returning to Africa on hearing of the arrival of Roman reinforcements.

441

- The Huns' invasions across the Danube ruin the Balkans and damage the reputation of the river itself as a carrier of commerce.
- The Huns, under Attila, cross the Danube and make their way through the Balkans, taking Belgrade and Sofia. The Eastern emperor, Theodosius II, trebles his tribute money.

442

- The Western Roman emperor Valentinian III makes peace with Genseric, the king of the Vandals, recognizing his rule in Africa as independent. This marks the end of the Vandal migrations; they settle in Africa with Carthage as their capital.

c. 446

- The Britons, suffering attacks from the Picts, Scots, and Saxons, send an appeal for help to the Roman commander Aëtius. The Saxons begin to arrive in numbers to settle. Britain has been left virtually without Roman protection since AD 407.

447

- The Huns, under Attila, enter Thrace, Thessaly, and Scythia. They are bought off by the Eastern Roman emperor Theodosius II and subsequently turn their attentions to the Western empire.

449

- Vortigern, a Welsh king whose authority extends as far east as Kent, invites the Saxons, under their leaders Hengist and Horsa, to settle in Kent, Britain, in order to help him in his struggle with the Picts and Scots.

SCIENCE, TECHNOLOGY, AND MEDICINE

Agriculture

407

- Germanic tribes settling across northwest Europe introduce the cultivation of new crops, such as rye, oats, and hops, and the manufacture of butter.

Ecology

c. 400

- Copper is being mined and smelted by local peoples in the Katanga copper belt (on the borders of Zaire and Zambia).

440

- The Gaulish town of Ys, in Armorica (modern Brittany), is overwhelmed by a great flood, and submerged beneath the sea—the foundation of many such legends of lost cities.

447

December 23 A massive earthquake coinciding with an eclipse of the sun causes panic in Constantinople (modern Istanbul, Turkey).

Health and Medicine

400

- c. 400 The Greco-Roman physician Caelius Aurelianus is practicing. His *De morbis acutis et chronicis/Concerning Acute and Chronic Illness*, a guide to acute and chronic diseases, becomes a highly respected text in the Middle Ages.
- Chinese Buddhist monk Faxian describes the Indian hospital system, which offers free treatment to all, regardless of wealth or rank.

c. 425

- The great Roman military thinker Flavius Vegetius Renatus writes a book on the medical treatment of mules, making him a pioneer in veterinary science.

431

- Persecuted Nestorians fleeing the Roman emperor Zeno introduce Greek texts on medicine and astronomy to Persia and India, where they are eagerly received.

Science

400

- c. 400 Zosimos of Panopolis is the first authenticated alchemist. The first use of the still (Greek *ambix*, Arabic *alembic*) probably occurs about this time, although it is only fully developed by the Arabs some 500 years later.
- Egyptian astronomer and mathematician Hypatia distinguishes herself as one of the first women scientists, becoming head of the Neoplatonist school at Alexandria, and a widely consulted authority on matters of physics and mathematics.

Technology

410

- Byzantine scholar Synosius of Cyrene devises a simple form of astrolabe that he gives to a friend in Constantinople (modern Istanbul, Turkey), with a letter explaining its operation.

ARTS AND IDEAS

Architecture

c. 425

- The mausoleum of Galla Placidia, the sister of Roman emperor Honorius, is constructed in Ravenna on a cruciform plan and is richly decorated with mosaics.

Literature and Language

c. 400

- A runic inscription is made on the Tune Stone at Ostfold (in modern Norway). It is one of the oldest known, though the origin of the script may go back to the 1st century BC.

- Sanskrit becomes established as the literary language of India, and is used for the Hindu epics. India's greatest Sanskrit poet and dramatist Kalidasa is probably active around this time, though little is known about his life. His greatest work, *Abhijnana Shakauntula/The Recognition of Shakula*, tells of the seduction of a nymph by King Duysanta.

401

- Latin lyric poet Prudentius retires in order to devote more time to writing on simple Christian themes. His works include *Peristephanon*, poems in praise of martyrs.

405

- Chinese poet Dao Jian retires from his minor government post for a life cultivating the land. His poetry, written in straightforward language, reflects his love of nature and frustration with the world of officialdom.

Thought and Scholarship

412

- Egyptian mathematician and scientist Hypatia is murdered by a Christian mob at Alexandria. Many other leading scientists and philosophers leave the city, and its importance as an academic center declines.

SOCIETY

Education

425

- A university is founded at Constantinople (modern Istanbul, Turkey).

BIRTHS & DEATHS

401
April 10   Theodosius II, Roman Emperor of the East 408–450, who founded the University of Constantinople and compiled the Theodosian Code of laws, born in Constantinople (–450).
September 10   St. Anastasius, pope 399–401, dies in Rome.

c. 402
- Quintas Aurelias Symmachus, Roman senator opposed to Christianity, dies (*c.* 57).

405
c. 405   Gu Kai-Zhi, Chinese painter whose silk scroll painting *Admonitions of the Instructresses to the Court Ladies* is the earliest to survive, dies.
- Prudentius, Latin allegorical poet, author of "Psychomachia"/"The Contest of the Soul," dies (*c.* 57).

406
- Attila, King of the Huns jointly with his brother Bleda 434–445 and on his own 445–453, who invaded the southern Balkan provinces of the Roman Empire, Greece, Gaul, and Italy, born (–453).

407
September 14   St. John Chrysostom, early father of the Christian church, archbishop of Constantinople, dies in Comana, Helenopontus (*c.* 60).

408
- Arcadius, Eastern Roman emperor jointly with his father, Theodosius I, 383–395, and on his own 395–402, dies in Constantinople (*c.* 31).

August 22   Flavius Stilicho, Roman military commander who repelled the Visigoths and Ostrogoths from Italy, and also acted as regent 394–408 for Emperor Honorius, is beheaded by Honorius (*c.* 43).

410
- Alaric, King of the Visigoths 395–410, dies in Cosentia, Bruttium (now Cosenza, Italy) (*c.* 40).

415
- Ataulf (also Atawulf or Ataulphus), King of the Visigoths 410–415, successor to his brother-in-law Alaric, who led the Visigoths from Italy to Southern Gaul and thence to Spain, is assassinated in Barcelona.
- Chandra Gupta II, a powerful emperor of northern India *c.* 380–*c.* 415 and a patron of learning and the arts, son of Samudra Gupta, dies.
March   Hypatia, Egyptian Neoplatonist philosopher, the first famous female mathematician, dies in Alexandria, Egypt (*c.* 45).

418
- Wallia, King of the Visigoths in southern Gaul 415–418, dies.

420
- St. Jerome (Eusebius Hieronymus), biblical translator and monastic founder, dies in Bethlehem, Palestine (*c. 72).

423
August 15   (Flavius) Honorius, Roman emperor in the West 393–423, son of Theodosius I and brother of the

Eastern Roman emperor Arcadius, dies in Ravenna, Italy (38).

430
c. 430   St. Nilus of Ancyra, Byzantine abbot whose writings influenced European monasticism, dies in Ancyra, Galatia.
- Anastasius I, Eastern Roman emperor 491–518 and perfector of the empire's monetary system, born in Dyrrachium in Dalmatia (now Durrës, Albania) (–518).
August 28   St. Augustine of Hippo (original name Aurelius Augustinus), the leading theologian of the early Western church, whose best-known works are the *Confessiones/ Confessions* and *De civitate Dei/ City of God*, dies in Hippo Regius, in Roman Mauritania (now Annaba, Algeria) (76).

431
June 22   St. Paulinus of Nola, bishop of Nola, early Christian Latin poet, dies in Nola, Italy (*c.* 78).

c. 433
- Odoacer, first barbarian king of Italy 476–495, whose assumption of power marked the end of the Western Roman Empire, born (–493).

434
- Dao Sheng, a Chinese Buddhist monk who taught that actions committed without preconceived thought or will leave no karmic energy behind, dies.

Everyday Life

401

- The Slavs first appear in European history as a confederation of tribes living between the Dnieper and Dniester rivers, known as the Antae.

405

- The Chinese traveler Faxian reports on the prosperity and social liberty that India is enjoying under the Guptas.

Religion

403

- Archbishop of Constantinople St. John Chrysostom offends the Empress Eudoxia by his attack on the morals of the court. He is exiled but recalled after an earthquake before being exiled permanently in 404.

c. **410**

- Kumarajiva, Buddhist scholar and seer, begins translating Buddhist scriptures from Sanskrit into Chinese. When completed, they are highly instrumental in spreading Buddhism throughout China.
- Theodore of Mopsuestia makes a series of biblical commentaries employing an historical and philological approach: he concludes that the Bible should be treated literally rather than as an allegory.

411

- A council called by Roman emperor Honorius meets at Carthage to suppress the Donatists, whose violent activities against their Catholic opponents have been assisted by a Berber sect called the *Circumcelliones* ("Prowlers").

413–426

- Bishop Augustine begins to writes his *De civitate dei/City of God* as a reply to the charge that Christianity was responsible for the decline of the Roman Empire. According to Augustine, obedience to the state is important, although man's ultimate end is the City of God beyond this world.

418

- The British monk Pelagius is excommunicated for expounding the belief that man's nature is essentially good and that through free will he can choose or reject sin. Pelagianism is seen as an attack on the doctrine of Original Sin and on redemption through divine grace alone. Bishop Augustine of Hippo is its leading opponent.

428

- Nestorius, bishop of Constantinople (modern Istanbul, Turkey), preaches against the title Theotokos ("God-Bearer") being applied to the Virgin Mary, on the grounds that it denies Christ's human nature.

429

- St. Simeon Stylites pursues an extreme form of asceticism by living for 37 years on a platform on top of a high pillar at the monastery of Telanissus in Syria.

431

- Nestorius, the Syrian-born patriarch of Constantinople, is excommunicated by the Council of Ephesus. His followers, the Nestorians, believe in the independence of Christ's divine and human natures; their persecution leads them into Persia and finally as far as China.
- Pope Celestine sends Palladius to evangelize the Irish.

c. **432**

- St. Patrick travels to Ireland as a missionary bishop. He later sets up his see at Armagh.

447

- The Christian theologian Germanus of Auxerre visits Britain for the second time in order to counter Pelagianism.

449

- The second Council of Ephesus finds in favor of the "Monophysite" heresy which states that Christ's nature remained divine even when he possessed human attributes.

Sports

c. **400–500**

- *Shaturanga* (or *chaturanga*), "the army game," an ancestor of chess through the Persian game of *shatranj* (or *chatrang*), evolves in the Indus Valley on the Indian subcontinent.

450–499

POLITICS, GOVERNMENT, AND ECONOMICS

Business and Economics

c. 493
- The Ostrogoth king Theodoric restores Italy's economy; at the same time, Anastasius, emperor at Constantinople, improves the Eastern empire's finances and economy.

Colonization

c. 450
- The Polynesian leader Hawaii-Loa discovers the Hawaiian Island after a journey across more than 2,000 miles of open sea from near Tahiti.

454
- The Ostrogoths settle in Pannonia, south and west of the Danube in the valleys of the Drava and Sava.

c. 476
- Many of the Celtic inhabitants of Britain begin to migrate to Armorica (modern Brittany, France) to escape the Saxon invasions.

c. 493
- The Ostrogoth Theodoric the Great, now king of Italy, observes Roman laws and institutions and is respectful to the Senate at Rome. He allots two thirds of the land to the Romans and one third to the Goths. He redrains the Pontine Marshes, issues an edict controlling prices, and brings down the cost of food.

Politics and Government

450
- Emperor Theodosius II dies and is succeeded as head of the Eastern Roman empire by Marcian, who refuses to continue the tribute to Attila and the Huns. Valentinian III of the West follows his example.
- Honoria, the sister of the western Roman emperor Valentinian III who has been banished for misconduct, sends a ring and a plea for help to Attila the Hun. He pretends to take the ring as a proposal of marriage and demands half the kingdom.

451
- Attila, King of the Huns, makes his grand attack on the Western Roman empire. His army is reputedly half a million strong, including the Franks and Ostrogoths. The Roman commander Aëtius, realizing that he cannot defeat the Huns alone, makes an alliance with the Visigoths under Theodoric in southwest Gaul. Although the outcome of the battle of the Catalaunian Fields (Chalons, sometimes called the battle of Troyes) is inconclusive, it proves to be a moral victory for the Romans and the Huns return home. Wallia, the Visigoth king, is killed.

452
- Under Attila, the Huns advance into Italy. The emperor Valentinian III flees from Ravenna to Rome and sends Pope Leo I to persuade Attila to return to his capital. Aquileia falls to Attila and Milan has to buy him off before Pope Leo, his hand strengthened by news of reinforcements from the Eastern Roman Empire and the plague breaking out among the Huns, is able to persuade Attila to withdraw.

453
- After a wedding feast, on his marriage to the German Ildica, King Attila is found dead in bed with a burst blood vessel. His empire is divided between his sons and the Hunnish threat to the Western Roman empire is ended.
- Thorismund, King of the Visigoths in southwest Gaul, is assassinated. His brother Theodoric II becomes king, and fosters a closer relationship with Rome in order to extend Visigoth power in Gaul and Spain.

454
- In Rome, the emperor Valentinian III, who has no heir, becomes jealous of the successful general Aëtius for wanting to marry into his family and has him murdered.

455
- *c. 455* Much of northern Italy is devastated by this time: towns are walled, farms are abandoned, and the population has shrunk; it is estimated Rome has shrunk from about a million and a half citizens to a third of a million.
- Followers of the murdered general Aëtius murder the Western Roman emperor Valentinian III and Maximus comes to the throne. Maximus sends an embassy to the Eastern Roman emperor Marcian suggesting a joint attack on the Vandal empire. Marcian, probably influenced by his powerful general Aspar the Alan, refuses. The Vandals seize the rest of the Roman African provinces and their fleet lays waste to Sicily and the coastal territory of southern Italy.
- Prior to the arrival of the Vandals in Rome, the emperor Maximus is murdered, and a puppet Avitus put on the

throne. The Vandals, who now rule the western Mediterranean, cut off supplies from Italy, causing famine.

- Genseric the Vandal takes advantage of the death of Emperor Valentinian III and crosses from Africa to attack and loot Rome. Along with his booty Genseric abducts the Empress Eudoxia and her two daughters.
- The Saxons rebel against the Welsh king Vortigern and fight the Britons in Britain. The Saxon leader Horsa, brother of Hengist, is said to have been slain at Aylesford.

456–457

- The Western Roman emperor Avitus is forced to flee Rome due to famine caused by Vandal possession of Africa and Vandal control of the western Mediterranean. Rome goes through a period of chaos and changing rulers, with the Visigoth Ricimer the power behind the throne. The new emperor is Majorian.

457

- Leo the Thracian succeeds to the Eastern Roman Empire as Leo I, with the support of by Aspar, king of the Alans, another king-maker like the Visigoth Ricimer in the west. However, the new emperor proves to be strong enough to withstand Alan political influence.

460

- The Western Roman emperor Majorian gathers a large force to attack the Vandals in Africa. The failure of the attack forces him to make peace and leads to his dismissal as emperor the following year by the Visigoth Ricimer. He is replaced by Libius Severus.

460–468 The Vandals continue their attacks along the Mediterranean coasts of Italy.

462

- The Vandals, under King Genseric, capture Sardinia.
- Theodoric the Great, aged seven, future king of the Ostrogoths, becomes a hostage at Constantinople (modern Istanbul, Turkey).

466–470

- Theodoric II, King of the Visigoths, is killed by his brother Euric who succeeds him on the throne. He conquers Spain and Massilia (modern Marseille), adding them to the existing Visigoth kingdom of Toulouse, which includes all Gaul south of the Loire and west of the Rhône.

467

- The Eastern emperor Leo I has Anthemius, a successful general and son-in-law of the former Eastern emperor Marcian, made emperor of the Western Empire.

468

- The Western Roman Empire, under Anthemius, supports the Eastern Empire, under Leo I, in an abortive attempt to invade North Africa and defeat Genseric the Vandal.

471

- Ricimer the Visigoth withdraws to Milan.
- The Alan king Aspar is murdered in Constantinople (modern Istanbul, Turkey) by Basiliscus, brother-in-law of the emperor Leo I, to cover up for Basiliscus's own defeat at the hands of the Vandals.

472

- The Visigoth Ricimer captures Rome, kills the Western emperor Anthemius, and appoints Olybrius his successor. When Ricimer dies shortly thereafter, Gundobad, King of the Burgundians, takes control of the western armies. Olybrius then dies, leaving the Western Roman Empire without an emperor.

474

- Gundobad, King of the Burgundians, names Glycerinus as the Western Roman emperor. Julius Nepos is appointed emperor in Rome by the Eastern Roman emperor Leo I, and marches on Rome, deposing Glycerinus. Leo I dies and is succeeded by his grandson Leo II who in turn, in the same year, is followed by his son-in-law Zeno.

475

- Julius Nepos, the Western Roman emperor, is deposed by the Pannonian general Orestes, who puts his young son Romulus, nicknamed Little Augustus, on the throne.
- Theodoric the Great succeeds to the throne of the Ostrogoths.

476

- More Germanic tribes invade Italy, and in Rome the emperor Romulus Augustulus resigns his throne to their general, Odoacer. Odoacer agrees to become king of Italy while Zeno of Constantinople becomes emperor of the nominally recombined Eastern and Western Roman empires.
- The Roman emperor Zeno makes an agreement with the Vandal king Genseric, formally recognizing the Vandal kingdom as including the Roman province of Africa, the Balearic Isles, Pithecusae, Corsica, Sardinia, and Sicily. Genseric gives Sicily, with the exception of the city of Lilybaeum, to Odoacer, the Germanic king of Italy, in return for tribute.

477

- The Vandal king Genseric dies and is succeeded by his son Huneric, a cruel and vicious ruler who persecutes all non-Arian Christians.

479

- A revolt in Constantinople (modern Istanbul, Turkey) against the Eastern Roman emperor Zeno is quashed.

483

- The Eastern Roman emperor Zeno invites Theodoric the Great of the Ostrogoths to his capital Constantinople and treats him in great style.

484

- Huneric, Vandal king of Africa, dies and is succeeded by his cousin Gunthamund, who puts an end to Huneric's persecution of orthodox Catholic Christians. Gunthamund has to deal with a serious rebellion of the Moors during his reign, which he manages to contain.
- King Balas of Sassanian Persia is forced to pay tribute to the Ephthalites (or White Huns) who have formed a kingdom between the Caspian and the Indus with its capital at Gurgan.

485

- King Euric of the Visigoths in Gaul and Spain dies and is succeeded by his son Alaric II. Although the Visigoths are Arian Christians, they are lenient toward their Catholic subjects. Alaric produces an abstract of Roman law for his Roman subjects known as the "Breviary of Alaric."

486

- Clovis, King of the Franks, defeats a Roman army at Soissons and begins to extend his Frankish kingdom, which is centered on modern-day Belgium.

488

- Hengist, the Saxon leader in Britain, dies, having founded a Saxon kingdom in Kent.
- Theodoric the Great, King of the Ostrogoths, with the emperor Zeno's blessing, advances over the Alps to win back Italy from the Germanic king Odoacer.

489

- The Ostrogoth king Theodoric defeats the Germanic king of Italy, Odoacer, and takes Milan.

490

- The defeated German king of Italy, Odoacer, retires to Ravenna.

491

- The Roman emperor Zeno dies after a troubled reign, and is succeeded by the 61-year-old Anastasius.

c. **493**

- The Ostrogoth king Theodoric invites Odoacer, King of Italy (whom he defeated in 489), and his son to a peace treaty and feast at Ravenna, where he assassinates them. Theodoric extends his realm to the western Balkans and to Sicily and settles down as a king with nominal subordination to the Eastern Roman emperor at Constantinople. Cassiodorus, the historian, becomes his secretary (probably at a fairly early age, although his date of birth is unknown).

495

- The Saxon chief Cerdic lands in Dorset, England.

496

- Gunthamund, King of the Vandals in Roman Africa, dies and is succeeded by his brother Thrasamund. Although Thrasamund does not persecute orthodox Catholic Christians, he actively encourages Arian Christianity.

SCIENCE, TECHNOLOGY, AND MEDICINE

Ecology

472

- The 1,200-m/3,940-ft volcano Mt. Vesuvius in the Bay of Naples, southern Italy, undergoes a violent eruption—ash is said to have fallen as far afield as Constantinople (modern Istanbul, Turkey).

480

- The Eastern Roman capital of Constantinople (modern Istanbul, Turkey) suffers from an earthquake reputedly lasting over 40 days, prompting many citizens to fear the end of the world.

Health and Medicine

491

- The Ch'i dynasty Chinese prince Hsaio Tzu-Liang sets up the earliest private hospital in China, possibly copying the idea from India.

Math

450

- Proclus, a mathematician and Neoplatonist, is one of the last notable philosophers at Plato's Academy at Athens.

Technology

c. **450**

- Nailed horseshoes, similar to those of today, are introduced into Europe by eastern invaders.

490

- Theodoric, King of the Visigoths, presents a water clock, or *clepsydra*, to King Gundebald of Burgundy.

Transportation

494

- Chinese engineer and mathematician Zu Cheng Zhi devises a boat powered by a paddle wheel, driven by a man on a treadmill. This design of boat could apparently travel 1,000 *li* (500 km/310 mi) in a day.

ARTS AND IDEAS

Architecture

455

- The city of Chichén Itzá is founded by the Mayans in the Yucatán Peninsula of Central America. It covers six square miles, and contains many temples, pyramids, and houses.

c. **460**–*c.* **497**

- At Yun-Gang, near the Great Wall of China, the sandstone cliffs are transformed into a temple complex with large sculptures including a seated Buddha 13.7 m/44 ft high.

c. **475**

- The Hindu Dashavatara temple at Deogarh in Uttar Pradesh, India, is built around this time. Sacred to Vishnu, it contains the finest Gupta-period sculpture in India.

c. **490**

- King of the Ostrogoths Theodoric builds the basilica of San Apollinare Nuovo as his palace church at Ravenna.

Arts

c. 479–c. 497

- At Sigiriya in Ceylon, richly colored depictions of full-breasted women are painted onto the rock-face. Thought to be of religious significance, their precise purpose is unknown.

Literature and Language

450

- Greek poet Musaeus writes his epic love poem *Hero and Leander*.

455–461

- Christian missionary St. Patrick writes his *Confessions*, telling of his perils and difficulties in Ireland.

Thought and Scholarship

c. 450

- A large Buddhist monastery complex is founded at Nalanda near Bihar in India. It becomes a great center of Mahayana Buddhist scholarship.

BIRTHS & DEATHS

450
- Placidia, mother of the western Roman emperor Valentinian III, dies.
- July 28 Theodosius II, Roman Emperor of the East 408–450, who founded the University of Constantinople and compiled the Theodosian Code of laws, dies (49).

451
- c. 451 Nestorius, bishop of Constantinople whose radical views on the nature of Christ led to the creation of Nestorian churches, dies in Panopolis, Egypt.
- The Visigoth king Theoderic I is killed during the battle of the Catalaunian Fields against the Huns, and is succeeded by his son Thorismund.

453
- Attila, King of the Huns jointly with his brother Bleda 434–445 and on his own 445–453, who invaded the southern Balkan provinces of the Roman Empire, Greece, Gaul, and Italy, dies (c. 47).

454
- c. 454 Theodoric the Great, King of the Ostrogoths 471–526 who became King of Italy 493–526 by conquering the entire peninsula and Sicily, born (–526).
- September 21 Flavius Aëtius, Roman general and statesman, dies.

457
- Marcian, Eastern Roman emperor 450–457, dies in Constantinople (modern Istanbul, Turkey) (c. 61).
- Merovech, King of the Franks, dies and is succeeded by his son Childeric.

459
- St. Simeon Stylites, Syrian ascetic, first stylite or pillar hermit, who spent much of his life living on a column, dies in Telanissus, Syria (c. 69).

c. 461
- St. Patrick, patron saint of Ireland who brought Christianity to the island, dies (c. 76).

c. 465
- Severus of Antioch, Greek monk, theologian, and patriarch of Antioch, born in Sozopolis, Pisidia, Asia Minor (–538).

c. 466
- Clovis I, Merovingian founder of the Frankish kingdom, born (–511).

471
- Flavius Ardaburius Aspar, Roman general of Alani descent, influential in the eastern Roman empire under Marcian 450–457 and Leo I 457–474, is assassinated.

472
- August 18 Flavius Ricimer, Roman general of Germanic (Suebian/Visigothic) birth, who effectively ruled the western Roman empire through a series of puppet emperors 456–472, dies.

475
- Ancius Manlius Severinus Boethius, Roman scholar, statesman, and philosopher, author of the largely Neoplatonic *De consolatione philosophiae/On the Consolation of Philosophy*, born, possibly in Rome (–524).

477
- Gaiseric (or Genseric), King of the Vandals and Alani 428–477, who sacked Rome (455) and conquered much of Roman Africa, dies.

480
- St. Benedict of Nursia, father of Western monasticism, founder of the Benedictine monastery at Monte Cassino, born in Nursia, Kingdom of the Lombards (now in Italy) (–547).
- May 9 Julius Nepos, last legitimate Western Roman emperor 474–475, is murdered.

481
- Clovis, son of Childeric, becomes king of the Franks at the age of 15.

482
- Justinian I (Flavius Justinianus), Eastern Roman emperor 527–565, nephew of Justin I, born in Tauresium, Moesia (near the modern Niš, Serbia) (–565).

c. 485
- St. Brendan, Irish Celtic abbot who made a legendary voyage across the Atlantic, born in Tralee, Ireland (–578).

c. 490
- (Flavius Magnus Aurelius) Cassiodorus, historian, statesman, and monk, born in Scylletium, Bruttium, kingdom of the Ostrogoths, now Squillace, Italy (–c. 585).
- Procopius, Byzantine historian, born in Caesarea, Palestine (–c. 570).

491
- April Zeno, Eastern Roman emperor 474–491, dies.

493
- March 15 Odoacer, first barbarian king of Italy 476–495, whose assumption of power marked the end of the Western Roman Empire, is killed in Ravenna, Italy (c. 60).

SOCIETY

Religion

451

- The fourth Ecumenical Council held at Chalcedon condemns the Monophysite heresy and declares that Christ has two distinct natures, human and divine, that are nevertheless united with the Godhead. Monophysitism was absorbed into the Armenian, Coptic, Ethiopian, and Syrian churches. The Council also asserted the primacy of the see of Constantinople (modern Istanbul, Turkey) over that of Alexandria.

c. 460–c. 477

- Most of the 30 caves at Ajanta in Central India are completed during this time. Cut into the volcanic rock and elaborately carved and painted, they form the richest surviving Buddhist complex in India.

469

- Sidonius Appolinaris, author and prefect of Rome, returns to his native Clermont, Gaul, and is made bishop there. In 475 he is imprisoned for two years by the Visigoths who besiege and take the city.

482

- The Eastern Roman Emperor Zeno causes a rift between the churches of Rome and Constantinople with his *Henoticon* ("Union Scheme"), an attempt to reconcile Monophysitism with Orthodoxy.

483

- The Nestorian Christians, persecuted by Emperor Zeno, move into Persia where they are tolerated and flourish.

490

- A new religion, Mazdakism (named for its leading proponent Mazdak), enjoys a brief popularity and the support of King Kavadh I in Sassanian Persia. Seemingly an optimistic and gentler version of Manichaeism, it advocates vegetarianism and the common ownership of property and women.

493

- Clovis, King of the Franks, is baptized on the instigation of his Christian wife St. Clothilde.

c. 499

- The Babylonian version of the Talmud, a collection of rabbinical literature, is completed. Consisting of the *Mishnah* (the codified Jewish laws) and the *Gemara* (discussions of those laws), it is completed approximately a hundred years later than the Palestinian version and is more comprehensive.

500–549

POLITICS, GOVERNMENT, AND ECONOMICS

Business and Economics

501

- Eastern Roman emperor Anastasius builds further fortifications around his capital Constantinople (modern Istanbul, Turkey), restores the empire's finances, and puts a stop to shows of wild beasts fighting humans.

Human Rights

523

- Manichaeans are banished from the Roman empire and pagans and heretics denied civil or military office.

Politics and Government

500

c. 500   "Arturus, Dux Bellorum," the legendary King Arthur, takes up the struggle against the Saxons. In 12 battles he subdues the Saxons, the last battle being at Mons Badonicus (site unknown). Arthur is a "war leader," a Christian Romano-Briton, who defeats the Saxons with a mobile field army of armored cavalrymen, the typical army of the British chieftains. The authenticity and provenance of Arthur are ever in dispute, but not his date.

c. 500   By the end of the 5th century AD, the Japanese have coalesced into one nation and culture.

c. 500   The Salic laws of the Franks are formulated. One of the most significant laws prohibits the inheritance of land by women.

- Clovis, King of the Franks, wins a battle over the Burgundians.

- Thrasamund, King of the Vandals in Roman Africa, marries Amalafrida, the widowed sister of Theodoric the Great, King of the Ostrogoths in Italy. The marriage

helps form a strong alliance between the two Arian
Christian Germanic princes.

501

- There is widespread violence in Constantinople (modern
  Istanbul, Turkey), the capital of the Eastern Roman
  Empire, caused by the enmity of the circus factions, the
  "Greens" and the "Blues," each backing their favorite
  chariot drivers. Three thousand supporters are said to
  have died.

502–506

- The Eastern Roman emperor Anastasius, having met
  trouble in both Egypt and Thrace, fights a war in
  Armenia against a revived Sasanian Persia; after an
  inconclusive struggle a seven-year peace is signed.

507–510

- Clovis, King of the Franks, defeats the Visigoth Alaric II
  at the battle of Vouglé, near Poitiers. Clovis ends the
  division between the Riparian and Salic Franks, thus
  uniting under his rule all the Franks on the left bank of
  the Rhine, and moves his capital to Paris.
- The Visigoth king Alaric II dies in battle with the
  Franks. Theodoric the Great, an Ostrogoth and Alaric's
  father-in-law, appoints himself guardian of Alaric's son
  Amalaric, preserving the Spanish kingdom for him.
  Control of Toulouse is passed to the Franks.

508

- The Ostrogoths under Theodoric take southern Gaul
  from the Franks. Clovis, King of the Franks, establishes
  his capital at Lutetia (present-day Paris).

510

- Clovis, King of the Franks, is made a Roman consul and
  patrician by the Emperor Anastasius.

511

- Clovis, King of the Franks, dies and leaves his kingdom
  (in modern France and Germany) to his four sons who
  expand it, imposing their rule over the Franks on the
  right bank of the Rhine.

515

- The Huns break through the Caspian Gate into
  Cappadocia, Asia Minor.

516

- Gundobad, King of Burgundy, dies and is succeeded by
  his son Sigismund, who converts his people from Arian
  Christianity to Catholic Christianity.

518

- The Eastern Roman emperor Anastasius dies at
  Constantinople (modern Istanbul, Turkey) and is
  succeeded by an already old senator, Justin, who leaves
  the management of affairs to his nephew Justinian. Both
  uncle and nephew are of Illyrian stock.

522

- The Roman philosopher Boethius becomes chief
  minister to the Ostrogoth king of Italy, Theodoric the
  Great.

523

523–524 The Ostrogoth king of Italy Theodoric, aging and
suspicious, hears of a senatorial conspiracy to depose
him. The Roman philosopher Boethius, his chief
minister, is among three suspected ringleaders and is
imprisoned and executed the following year.

523–526 Thrasamund, Vandal king of Roman Africa, dies
and is succeeded by the aged and weak Hilderic, son of
the former king Huneric. Hilderic breaks the alliance
with the Ostrogoth kingdom of Italy and enters an
agreement with the Eastern Roman Empire. He
imprisons the Ostrogoth princess Amalafrida, widow of
Thrasamund and sister of Theodoric the Great, and kills
her Ostrogoth followers. Theodoric dies before he can
avenge his loss.

524

- Saxons in Britain cease their aggression and turn instead
  to peaceful settlement after Arthur's successes against
  them.

526

- The Eastern Roman emperor Justin gives the soldier
  Belisarius, a native of Germania in Thrace, his first
  task—combating the renewed aggression of Sasanian
  Persia.
- Theodoric the Great, King of the Ostrogoths in Italy,
  dies and is succeeded by his 10-year old grandson
  Athalaric, although the boy's mother Amalasuntha,
  daughter of Theodoric, is the real ruler.

527

- The Eastern Roman emperor Justin dies and his nephew
  Justinian succeeds as emperor. Justinian declares his
  wife, the actress Theodora, empress.

528

- The Eastern Roman emperor Justinian sets out to codify
  and rationalize the legal system of the Empire. He
  appoints a panel of ten jurists to systematize, reform,
  and clarify the law.
- The White Hun king Mihirakula (sometimes called the
  Attila of India) is deposed and the Hunnish invasion of
  India, which never produces a kingdom, begins to lose
  its force.

529

- The first *Codex Constitutionum* of the Eastern Roman
  emperor Justinian is issued. It is a list of all the
  enactments of the emperors and their answers to still
  valid legal questions. It is known later as *Codex
  Iustinianus*.

530

- The Roman general Belisarius wins a victory over the
  Sasanian Persians at Dara (or Darasin) in northern
  Mesopotamia.
- The Vandal king of Roman Africa, Hilderic, is deposed
  after a serious defeat by the Moors, and Gelimar, a
  great-grandson of Genseric, comes to the throne. This
  gives the Eastern Roman emperor Justinian an excuse to
  attack Gelimar, by claiming to be upholding the rights
  of Hilderic.

531

- The greatest of the Sassanid kings, Chosroes or
  Khosru I, comes to the Persian throne. The Roman
  soldier Belisarius is recalled to Constantinople by the
  emperor Justinian.
- King Chosroes I of Persia reorganizes his government
  and laws and taxes, much as the Roman emperor
  Justinian has done before him. He creates a standing
  army and improves his roads.

532

- The Eastern Roman emperor Justinian faces a serious revolt in Constantinople in the form of the Nika rebellion, which originates among the supporters of different factions in the chariot racing circus.
- The Eastern Roman emperor Justinian patches up an expensive peace with Sasanian Persia and plans to send his general Belisarius on the first campaign to fulfill his own great ambition of reunifying the Roman Empire by taking Africa back from the Vandals. Belisarius is accompanied by the historian Procopius of Caesarea.

533

- The emperor Justinian's *Digesta* (or *Pandecta*) is issued together with a handbook or guide to the Codex, the *Institutionis/Of Education*. The *Digesta* consists of extracts of Roman law from the writings of jurists, compiled by a commission under the jurist Tribonian.

533–534　The Eastern Roman general Belisarius sets sail to win back Vandal Africa for the Empire. He takes Carthage and decisively defeats the Vandal king Gelimar at Tricamarum, effectively destroying the Vandals as a political power. North Africa remains part of the Eastern Roman (Byzantine) empire until its conquest by the Arabs in the following century.

534

- Athalaric, the young Ostrogoth king, dies and his kingdom of Italy and part of southern Gaul falls into decline. It is ruled for a further year by his mother Amalasuntha and her second husband.

535

- The Eastern Roman emperor Justinian, having secured an alliance with the Franks, sets out to recover Italy from the Ostrogoths. The general Belisarius captures Sicily.

536–540

- The Roman general Belisarius captures Naples and enters Rome unopposed. Witigis, new king of the Ostrogoths, besieges Belisarius in Rome but gives up after a year. Belisarius in turn besieges Ravenna, which finally capitulates.

537

- The Eastern Roman general Belisarius, besieged at Rome by the Ostrogoths, and with the city's aqueducts cut off, strips the city's mills, mounts the machinery on floating platforms, and uses the River Tiber to grind corn and keep the city supplied with food.

539

- King Chosroes of Persia declares war on the Roman emperor Justinian.

539–543　King Chosroes of Persia raids Asia and declares war on the Roman emperor Justinian. Justinian buys him off and negotiates a five-year peace settlement, extended for another five years.

540

- The Eastern Roman general Belisarius returns in triumph to Constantinople after his conquest of Italy, but earns the jealousy of Emperor Justinian.

c. 540–*c.* 590　Large numbers of Slavs migrate from northern Europe into the Balkans.

541

- King Chosroes of Persia withdraws to his own territories according to his peace with the Eastern Roman emperor Justinian, having sacked Antioch in Syria and bathed in the Mediterranean.

542–543

- The Roman Empire is scourged by plague, a cause of one of the emperor Justinian's economic difficulties, shortage of man-power. Another difficulty is shortage of cash, leading to tax exactions, directed by his hated finance minister, John of Cappadocia. Wage and price regulations are attempted; trade with India is encouraged; and new harbors are built on the Black Sea.

543–546

- Another Ostrogothic king, Totila, captures Rome but moves to Ravenna and the Roman general Belisarius recaptures Rome.

548–549

- The Roman general Belisarius is recalled to Constantinople and the Ostrogoth king Totila recaptures most of Italy.

SCIENCE, TECHNOLOGY, AND MEDICINE

Ecology

512

- The 1,200-m/3,940-ft volcano Mt. Vesuvius in Italy undergoes a series of eruptions. Theodoric, ruler of the area, exempts people living in the area from payment of taxes.

526

- A massive earthquake in Asia Minor destroys the city of Antioch, and kills over 200,000 people.

536

- Dust from volcanic eruptions in Southeast Asia is flung high in the atmosphere, blocking out sunlight and cooling the climate, causing a severe winter as far away as Europe, where the Mediterranean is covered by a "dry fog."

Exploration

530

- St. Brendan explores the Atlantic in an Irish *curragh*, or coracle, and is said to have reached America. Early Irish monks certainly reached the Shetland Islands and Iceland.

Health and Medicine

c. **501**

- The Indian medical manual *Susruta* is compiled. It becomes a standard text for Indian physicians.

529

- St. Benedict of Nurcia establishes the first Benedictine monastery and hospital at Monte Cassino, near Naples, Italy. The monastery will become a center of medical knowledge throughout the Middle Ages.

542

- Huge numbers of invading rats from Egypt bring bubonic plague to Constantinople. In the following years, it will spread across the whole of Europe.

547

- The great plague reaches Britain, where Welsh monk Gildas records it in his *Liber querulus de excidio Britanniae/Concerning the Ruin of Britain*.

Science

516

- The Indian astronomer and mathematician Aryabhata I produces his *Aryabhatiya*, a treatise on quadratic equations, the value of π, and other scientific problems, in which he adds tilted epicycles to the orbits of the planets to explain their movement.

545

- The Indian astronomer Varahamihira writes *The Complete System of Natural Astrology*. It is based on Greek astronomical texts from the period before Ptolemy, and provides a valuable record of these lost works.

Technology

500

c. 500 The Chinese begin to experiment with printing using carved wooden blocks and vegetable inks.
- The Saxon legend of Volundr, or Wayland the Smith, originating around this time, indicates a knowledge of powder metallurgy among the Saxon people— techniques by which breaking apart and resmelting of metals improve their properties.

530

- A bellows activated by a hydraulic piston motor is invented in China.

Transportation

500

- Chinese flying toys of this date use horizontal propellers in order to slow their descent—an early application of the principle of the helicopter.

ARTS AND IDEAS

Architecture

500

- A large wooden hall is built on the reoccupied hill fort at South Cadbury in Somerset. It is owned by a man rich and important enough to be able to import wine jars from the continent, possibly the war leader "Arturus, Dux Bellorum," the legendary King Arthur.

532

- The building of the great Church of Holy Wisdom, Hagia Sophia, is begun in Constantinople (modern Istanbul, Turkey) at the command of the emperor Justinian. It is designed by two mathematicians, Anthemius of Tralles and Isidorus of Miletus.

537

- The huge cathedral of Hagia Sophia at the Eastern Roman capital of Constantinople (modern Istanbul, Turkey) is completed for the emperor Justinian after just five years. It is the world's largest enclosed building. Justinian boasts that he has outdone the biblical king Solomon in architectural achievements.

547

- After Belisarius's capture of Ravenna the city is rebuilt and beautified. The Church of San Vitale is completed. It is encrusted with opulent mosaics, including images of Justinian and Theodora.

Literature and Language

500

- The philosopher Boethius studies the Greek classics in Athens prior to making Latin translations of them.

523

- While imprisoned in Rome for suspected treason, the philosopher Boethius writes his *De consolatione philosophiae/On the Consolation of Philosophy*, a prose dialogue in which the lady, Philosophy, responds to Boethius's misfortunes with Stoic, Platonic, and Christian advice.

526

- Priscian, a professor at the University of Constantinople (modern Istanbul, Turkey), compiles a Latin and Greek grammar which becomes the standard text during the Middle Ages.

Music

c. 500

- Native Americans in the region of modern Peru are using flutes, horns, tubas, and drums to make music.

c. 505

- Roman philosopher Boethius writes his *De institutione musica/The Fundamentals of Music*, a treatise summarizing classical theories about music. Its underlying belief, that music was a science of numerical ratios, was profoundly influential during the Middle Ages.

Thought and Scholarship

527

- Scythian abbot and scholar Dionysius Exiguus (Dennis the Little) first uses the system of the Christian Era (AD, *anno domini* or "year of our lord") in his *Cyclus Paschalis/The Easter Cycle.*

530

- Alexandrian philosopher John Philoponos, after converting to Christianity, argues against all forms of paganism thus gaining the nickname "trouble-lover." He denies Aristotle's theory of motion but believes stars and planets have the same physical qualities as the earth.

c. 540

- The Roman statesman and historian Cassiodorus retires from public service to the Ostrogoths. He founds a monastery at his estate in Calabria which becomes a center of learning for both classical and Christian studies. His *History of the Goths* survives only as a fragment.

546

- Gildas, a Welsh monk, writes *On the Destruction of Britain*, which criticizes the evils of contemporary British society and mentions Arthur's battle of Mons Badonicus in 500.

SOCIETY

Everyday Life

c. 500

- The habit of tea drinking becomes popular in southern China, a custom that has probably been imported from Tibet.

c. 501

- By the beginning of the 6th century Constantinople (modern Istanbul, Turkey), center of the Eastern Roman empire, is using Egypt as a granary to the extent of some 175,000 tons of wheat a year.

BIRTHS & DEATHS

c. 500

- Theodora, Byzantine empress, influential wife of Justinian I 527–565, born (548).

505

- Belisarius, leading Eastern Roman general during the reign of Emperor Justinian I 527–565, born in Illyria, now part of the Ostrogothic Kingdom (–565).

511

November 27   Clovis I, Merovingian founder of the Frankish kingdom, dies (*c.* 45).

518

- Anastasius I, Eastern Roman emperor 491–518 and perfector of the empire's monetary system, dies in Constantinople.

c. 521

- St. Columba, Irish abbot and missionary, traditionally considered chiefly responsible for converting Scotland to the Christian faith, born in Tyrconnell, in modern County Donegal, Ireland (–597).

524

- Ancius Manlius Severinus Boethius, Roman scholar, statesman, and philosopher, author of the largely Neoplatonic *De consolatione philosophiae/On the Consolation of Philosophy*, executed in Pavia, Italy (*c.* 49).

525

c. 525   Alexander of Tralles, Byzantine physician whose 12-volume treatise

on pathology and therapy was used until the 16th century, born (–*c.* 605).

- St. Brigit, Abbess of Kildare, one of the patron saints of Ireland, who founded the first Irish nunnery at Kildare, dies in Kildare, Ireland.

526

August 30   Theodoric the Great, King of the Ostrogoths 471–526 who became King of Italy 493–526 by conquering the entire peninsula and Sicily, dies in Ravenna, Italy (*c.* 70).

527

August 1   Justin I, Eastern Roman emperor 518–527 and a champion of Christian orthodoxy against the Monophysites and Arians, dies in Constantinople (*c.* 77).

535

- Sigebert, Merovingian king of Austrasia 561–575, son of Chlotar I, born (–575).

538

- Severus of Antioch, Greek monk, theologian, and patriarch of Antioch, dies in Xois, Egypt (*c.* 73).

November 30   St. Gregory of Tours, French bishop, author of *History of the Franks*, which describes the 6th century Franco-Roman kingdom, and also *Lives of the Father*, a book of miracles, born in Augustonemetum, Aquitaine (–594).

539

- Maurice (Mauricius Flavius Tiberius), Eastern Roman emperor

582–602 and an outstanding general, born in Cappadocia, Asia Minor (–602).

540

c. 540   Imru'ul-Qais, the greatest Arab poet of pre-Islamic times, a prolific worker who specialized in the qasida (ode), usually in praise of the poet or his tribe, dies.

- St. Gregory, Pope Gregory I the Great 590–604, theologian and reformer of church organization and liturgy, born in Rome, Italy (–604).

541

- Wen Ti, Chinese emperor 581–604, who reunified and reorganized China and founded the Sui dynasty, born in China (–604).

c. 543

- St. Columban, Irish abbot, writer, and important missionary, born in Leinster, Ireland (–615).

c. 547

- St. Benedict of Nursia, founder of Benedictine monasticism, dies (*c.* 67).

548

June   Theodora, Byzantine empress, influential wife of Justinian I 527–565, dies (48).

Religion

500

c. 500 Italian monk St. Benedict, disapproving of the licentiousness of Rome, retires to a cave at nearby Subiaco.

c. 500–c. 510 A Monophysite, influenced by the Neoplatonism of Proclus, produces four books, including *On the Celestial Hierarchy*, which were supposedly written by a convert of St. Paul, "Dionysius the Areopagite." These forgeries are accepted as genuine and have a profound influence on medieval theology and cosmology.

523

- The Arian Ostrogoth king Theodoric makes a gift of silver chandeliers to the Pope in Rome. More tolerant than Justinian, he protects the Jews against the destruction of their synagogues.

529

- The Eastern Roman emperor Justinian closes the Athenian Academy founded by Plato in 387 BC, because of its adherence to paganism. Some of the teachers later move to a Persian university founded by Chosroes I in 531.

531

- On his accession, King Chosroes I of Persia reestablishes Zoroastrianism and gathers around him scholars from India and Greece.

534

- The Justinian *Codex of Laws* is greatly influenced by orthodox Christianity. It begins by declaring for the

Trinity and establishes the Emperor's dominion over the church.

540

- Christian scholar John Philoponos of the School of Alexandria, Egypt, writes *On the Construction of the World*, in which he argues against the use of the Bible as a scientific text.
- In her later years, the empress Theodora attempts to challenge her husband's religious orthodoxy in favor of the Monophysites and the Eastern church.

542–548

- The empress Theodora becomes an upholder of public morals in her last years, building a Convent of Repentance for fallen women.

547

- Cosmas Indicopleustes, an Alexandrian traveler who has settled as a monk in Ceylon, produces *Topographia Christiana/Christian Topography*, a flat-earth cosmography intended to demonstrate the truth of the biblical account of creation.
- Justinian, in an unsuccessful attempt to reunite the Eastern and Western churches, issues an edict, known as the *Three Chapters*, against three bishops associated with Nestorianism, a form of Orthodox Christianity in which Jesus Christ is seen as both a divine and a separate human individual.

549

- The Emperor of South China, Wu Ti, creates a center of Buddhist culture at Nanjing.

550–599

POLITICS, GOVERNMENT, AND ECONOMICS

Business and Economics

552

- Eastern Roman emperor Justinian begins the silk industry in the West by sending traders to China and Ceylon to smuggle out silkworms. A silk industry begins to flourish in Syria and the Peloponnese, known as Morea after the mulberry tree.

594

- The Eastern Roman emperor Maurice attempts to reduce his soldiers' pay, but a mutiny prompts him to change his mind.

Politics and Government

550

- The Roman eunuch general Narses is sent, in place of Belisarius, to combat the Ostrogoth Totila, who has taken Italy.
- The Toltecs conquer the city of Teotihuacán in the Yucatán Peninsula in Mexico, overcoming its ancient civilization.

551

- The Avars, a central Asian nomadic people, begin to migrate into eastern Europe via the south of modern

Russia. They ultimately drive the Lombards into Italy, and settle in the Balkans.

551–553 The Roman general Narses, successor to Belisarius, defeats the Ostrogoth Totila and expels the Goths from Italy. Narses uses Lombard mercenaries.

553

- By the end of the Gothic war, Italy is economically ruined. Rome's population has dwindled to about 40,000, with its aristocracy so depleted that the Senate peters out.

556–558

- Famine and plague break out in Constantinople. The emperor Justinian relaxes his hold on government and turns to theology.

559

- The Bulgars cross the Danube into the Byzantine province of Paristrion (modern Bulgaria) and advance toward Constantinople. The city is saved by the aged Roman general Belisarius.

c. 561

- Chlotar I, King of the Franks and son of Clovis, amasses a large Frankish kingdom, which includes Burgundy, Provence, and Swabia. He divides it into Austrasia (the Rhineland), Neustria (western France), and Burgundy, and bequeaths a part to each of his three sons, Sigebert, Chilperic I, and Guntram.

562

- King Chosroes of Sasanian Persia and the Eastern Roman emperor Justinian sign a 50-year peace agreement. For 30,000 pieces of gold a year, King Chosroes renounces territorial claims around the Black Sea and the Caucasus.

563

- The Eastern Roman general Belisarius is imprisoned by the aging and suspicious emperor Justinian on a charge of conspiracy, but is released after six months.

c. 564

- King Athanagild establishes a strong Visigothic kingdom in Spain with its capital at Toledo.

565

March The Eastern Roman general Belisarius dies and the emperor Justinian confiscates half his property. Justinian dies himself eight months later (in November) and is succeeded by Justin II, his nephew.

566

- Sigebert, the Frankish king of Austrasia (the Rhineland), marries the Visigoth princess Brunhild, daughter of Athanagild, Visigoth king of Spain.

567

- Chilperic I, the Frankish king of Neustria, follows his brother Sigebert's example and marries the Visigoth princess Galswintha, sister of Brunhild, but he has his Gothic wife strangled. Sigebert declares war on Chilperic but is murdered. His wife Brunhild rules Austrasia in her young son Childebert II's name.

568

- In the Visigoth kingdom of Spain, Leovigild, son of Athanagild, comes to the throne. He reunites the Gaulish and Spanish parts of the kingdom and expands his realm in the northwest and south of Spain.

- Up to 130,000 Lombards, led by King Alboin, pressed from behind by Avars, cross the Alps into the plains of the River Po and overrun northern Italy. With the emperor Justinian and his general Belisarius dead and the general Narses deposed and disgraced, the Eastern Roman Empire is unable to halt their advance.

570

- King Chosroes I of Persia expels the Abyssinians from Arabia.
- The Eastern Roman emperor Justin II endeavors to keep the laws of Justinian up to date by issuing more "novellae" (additions to the law code).

572

- The Eastern Roman emperor Justin II renews the Empire's war with Sasanian Persia.

573

- The Germanic Lombard people take Verona, Milan, and Florence, ending the Eastern Roman rule of Italy achieved by the emperor Justinian.

574

- The Eastern Roman emperor Justin II, who is lapsing into insanity, appoints Tiberius, head of the Palace Guard, as "Caesar."

c. 577

- The Saxons, under Cuthwin and Ceawlin, King of Wessex, win the battle of Deorham and become virtual masters of England. During this period, they form a heptarchy of kingdoms in southern and eastern England: the Jutes in Kent; the Angles in Mercia, Northumbria, and East Anglia; and the Saxons in Essex, Sussex, and Wessex.

578

- Shortly before he dies, the Eastern Roman emperor Justin II appoints Tiberius as his successor. Tiberius' policy as emperor is to concentrate on the East and against Persia. He leaves the West to take its own chances against the German successor kingdoms to the Western Empire.
- The Eastern Roman imperial forces under their general, Maurice, inflict a defeat upon the aging Chosroes I of Sasanian Persia, who retires to his capital Ctesiphon.

579–581

- The Eastern Roman general Maurice continues his successful campaign against Sasanian Persia, which has now lost its great king, Chosroes I.

582

- The Eastern Roman emperor Tiberius dies, having appointed the successful general Maurice as his heir.

584

- Chilperic, the Frankish king of Neustria, is murdered. Brunhild, Sigebert's widow, remains in power in Austrasia.

586

- The Visigoth king of Spain, Leovigild, dies, leaving a greatly enlarged kingdom for his son Recarred. At the end of Leovigild's reign, Visigoth Spain remains Arian Christian by creed, but is surrounded by recently converted Catholic Christians in the Frankish, Suevic, and African kingdoms.

589

- China approaches unity again under the warlike Yang Chien of the short-lived Sui dynasty.

- Sasanian dynastic trouble relieves the pressure on the Eastern Roman Empire. A usurping general, Bahram, declares himself regent for the infant Persian king, Chosroes II.

590

- The usurping general Bahram seizes the Sasanian Persian throne, forcing the young King Chosroes II to flee to Syria where he seeks Roman protection. The emperor Maurice reestablishes him firmly on the Sasanian throne and makes a favorable peace with him.

591

- Ceawlin, the Saxon king of Wessex, is deposed by Ceol at the Battle of Adam's Grave (near modern Alton Priors, England).

592

- Shotoku Taishi (or kotoku, sometimes called the Asoka of Japan) becomes ruler of Buddhist Japan and gives his country a written constitution and decrees based on Buddhist ethics.

592–593 The Eastern Roman emperor Maurice turns against the Avars who are spreading over the Balkans under their king Baian. They are driven back across the Danube.

594

- Peter, the brother of the Eastern Roman emperor Maurice, renews war with the Avars in the Balkan provinces. The conflict will continue for the rest of the century.

597

- The Eastern Roman emperor Maurice draws up a will appointing one son to rule in Rome and the other in Constantinople.

598

- The Roman emperor Maurice has difficulty in recruiting enough troops to fight the Avars, who are by now making inroads into the Balkan provinces.

SCIENCE, TECHNOLOGY, AND MEDICINE

Agriculture

550

- Chinese scholars produce a treatise on animal husbandry (which survives into the 11th century) and begin to use insects to control crops.

Ecology

557

- A major earthquake in Constantinople (modern Istanbul, Turkey) damages the Church of Hagia Sophia. Restoration of the huge church, only 20 years old, takes five years to complete.

Health and Medicine

575

- Byzantine physician Alexander of Tralles writes *De re medica/On Medical Matters*, a highly respected medical textbook noted for the first studies of parasitic worms.

590

- A smallpox plague once again devastates Rome, but subsides rapidly. Divine intervention is credited with the salvation of the city.

594

- Influential French writer and bishop (later St.) Gregory of Tours asserts that he has little faith in medicine and prefers to rely on the power of religion and miracles.
- The long epidemic of plague comes to an end in Rome.

Math

595

- Decimal notation is used for numbers in India. This is the system on which our current system is based.

598–665

- Indian mathematician and astronomer Brahmagupta uses negative numbers in mathematics.

Technology

c. 550

- Egyptian textile workers develop draw looms to weave elaborately patterned silk.

Transportation

559

- The Ch'i dynasty Chinese emperor Kao Yang executes prisoners by lashing wings to them and making them fly from the top of a high tower. He also uses prisoners as test pilots on person-carrying kites.

ARTS AND IDEAS

Architecture

c. 550

- The Mayans build magnificent buildings at Tikal, the largest Mayan city in the southern lowlands, some 190 miles north of modern-day Guatemala City.
- The Palace of Chosroes is built at Ctesiphon near Baghdad. Its great arch and decorative panels influence Islamic architecture after the Muslim invasion of Mesopotamia in 640.

564

- The Visigoth kings build fine churches and palaces in Toledo. All are later destroyed by the Muslim invaders apart from sections of the city walls.

583

- Work begins on a new capital city at Chang-an for the first Sui Emperor of China. When complete it will be the largest walled city ever built.

Literature and Language

565

- Latin poet Venantius Fortunatus settles in Poitiers, France, where he later becomes bishop. He is the author of a biography of St. Martin, in addition to several Christian hymns.

Thought and Scholarship

c. 551

- Gothic historian Joruandes, or Jordanes, writes his history of the Goths, *Getica*, which is largely based on the work of the Roman, Cassiodorus.

c. 591

- Pope Gregory writes *Liber regulae pastoralis/The Book of Pastoral Rule*, a highly influential book of instruction for bishops. It is later translated by King Alfred of Wessex.

SOCIETY

Religion

552

- The king of Paichke (in Korea) sends a bronze Buddha and Buddhist texts to the emperor of Japan. Buddhism gradually becomes the favored religion of the court.

553

- Justinian calls an ecumenical council at Constantinople at which the *Three Chapters* are condemned. Few Western bishops attend and the schism between Eastern and Western churches deepens.

563

- St. Columba flees from Ireland and founds a monastery on the Hebridean island of Iona, from where he sends out missionaries to mainland Britain. Iona becomes a great center of book copying and illustration.

573

- St. Gregory the Great, the wealthy son of a Roman senator, sells his property and founds six monasteries in Sicily and one in Rome.

BIRTHS & DEATHS

553

- Totila (original name Baduila), Ostrogothic king, who recaptured central and southern Italy from the Eastern Roman empire, falls in battle against Eastern Roman forces under Narses at Fabriano, Italy.

555

June 7 Vigilius, Italian pope 537–555, involved in theological debates between the Eastern and Western churches, dies in Syracuse, Sicily.

561

- Chlotar I, Merovingian king of the Franks 558–561, noted for his ruthlessness, dies in Compiègne, France (c. 61).

565

- Justinian I (Flavius Justinianus), Eastern Roman emperor 527–565, nephew of Justin I, dies in Constantinople (c. 83).

March Belisarius, leading general during the reign of Emperor Justinian I 527–565, dies (c. 60).

570

c. 570 Procopius, Byzantine historian, dies (c. 80).

- Gildas (or Gildus), British monk and historian, an important authority on British post-Roman history, dies (54).
- Muhammad, founder of Islam, born in Mecca, Arabia (–632).

575

- Heraclius, Byzantine emperor 610–641, born in Cappadocia, Asia Minor (–641).
- Sigebert, Merovingian king of Austrasia 561–575, son of Chlotar I, is assassinated in Vitry, near Arras, France (c. 40).

578

- St. Brendan, Irish Celtic abbot who made a legendary voyage across the Atlantic, dies in Annaghdow, Ireland (c. 93).

October 4 Justin II, Eastern Roman emperor 565–578, dies.

584

c. 584 St. Paulinus, Italian missionary, first bishop of York, and later archbishop of Rochester, who converted Northumbria to Christianity, born in Rome (–644).

- Chilperic I, Merovingian king of Soissons 561–584, son of Chlotar I, is assassinated in Chelles, France.
- Chlotar II, Merovingian king of Neustria, who seized both Austrasia and Burgundy, reuniting the Frankish lands under his rule 613–629, born (–629).

585

c. 585 (Flavius Magnus Aurelius) Cassiodorus, historian, statesman, and monk, dies near Scylletium, Bruttium, kingdom of the Ostrogoths, now Squillace, Italy (c. 95).

- Edwin, King of Northumbria 616–632, born (–632).

c. 586

- Umar I, Muslim caliph 634–644, who conquered Mesopotamia and Syria and began the conquest of Iran and Egypt, born in Mecca (–644).

594

- St. Gregory of Tours, French bishop, author of *Historia Francorum/History of the Franks*, which describes the 6th century Franco-Roman kingdom, and also *Lives of the Father*, a book of miracles, dies in Tours, Neustria (56).

597

June 8 St. Columba, Irish abbot and important missionary, traditionally considered chiefly responsible for converting Scotland to the Christian faith, dies on the island of Iona, in modern Scotland (c. 76).

598

- Brahmagupta, leading ancient Indian astronomer, born (–c. 665).
- Fredegund, Queen Consort of Chilperic I, King of Soissons, and regent after his death 584–596, notorious for her ruthless persecution of Brunhild of Austrasia, dies.

580

- St. Columba is the first recorded witness to sight the famous Loch Ness monster of Scotland—although the beast he sights is actually in the River Ness, rather than the Loch.

586–601

- During Recarred's reign, Visigoth Spain converts from Arian to orthodox Catholic Christianity.

590

- St. Gregory, now abbot of St. Andrew's monastery in Rome, is elected pope. He sets about reforming the administration of the church and establishing its temporal authority.

593

- The Prince Regent Shotoku Taishi makes Buddhism the state religion of Japan. The Buddhist cultures of China and Korea begin to exert a profound influence on Japan.

594

- Muhammad enters the service of the rich widow Khadija.

595

- The 25-year-old Muhammad marries Khadija, fifteen years his senior.

597

- Pope Gregory sends his former monastic companion Augustine (later St. Augustine of Canterbury) on a mission to convert the Anglo-Saxons to Christianity. Landing in Kent, he is well received by King Ethelbert. Ethelbert and his daughter are later baptized and a cathedral is founded at Canterbury.

600–649

POLITICS, GOVERNMENT, AND ECONOMICS

Business and Economics

646

- A palace revolution in Japan leads to the "Taika" reforms, bringing all land into imperial ownership and introducing a taxation system.

Colonization

633

- The Chalukyas of the Deccan defeat an attempt by King Harsha of Kanauj, northern India, to expand his kingdom into central India.

640

- Slav tribes, later known as the Serbs and Croats, settle in the old Roman provinces of Pannonia (modern Hungary) and Illyria (Dalmatia, modern Croatia). They adopt the Greek and Roman forms of Christianity respectively.

645

- The Chinese emperor Taizong establishes a protectorate over the Ferghana Valley of central Asia.

Politics and Government

602

- Determined to break the power of the nomadic Avars, the Eastern Roman emperor Maurice orders his army to winter in their territory on the River Danube. His decision is unpopular and a rebellion breaks out, led by Phocas, an uneducated centurion. Maurice is killed attempting to escape from Constantinople and seek help from his ally King Chosroes II of Sasanian Persia. Phocas becomes emperor in Maurice's place.

603

- The Sasanian Persian king Chosroes II seeks revenge upon the new Eastern Roman emperor Phocas for the murder of his friend and ally the emperor Maurice and declares war on him.

604

- The Japanese regent, Prince Shotoku Taishi, introduces a Chinese-influenced constitution to increase the power of the Japanese emperors.

605

605–647 During his reign of over 40 years, King Harsha of Kanauj, on the River Ganges, brings most of northern India under his control. He is the last Indian king to rule a more than purely regional state until the 13th century.

605–649 During his 44-year reign, King Srong-btsan-Gyam-po unites the Tibetans in a powerful kingdom, annexes the area of modern Nepal, and builds himself a capital at Lhasa. For the next 200 years Tibet is the major power of central Asia.

606

- The nomadic Avars seize much of the agricultural hinterland of Constantinople, the capital of the Eastern Roman Empire.
- The Sasanian Persians conquer northern Mesopotamia from the Eastern Roman Empire and advance west across the River Euphrates. Phocas, the Eastern Roman emperor, fails to organize an effective defense.

609

- Appalled by the Eastern Roman emperor Phocas's misrule, Heraclius, the military governor of Roman Africa, sends his son, also called Heraclius, with an army to Constantinople to depose Phocas.

610

- The young Heraclius, son of the military governor of Roman Africa, deposes the usurper Phocas and becomes Eastern Roman emperor himself. Phocas, an incompetent and despotical ruler, has allowed the administrative structure of the Empire to decay and Heraclius is forced to undertake far-reaching reforms in the following years: these are so fundamental that the Eastern Roman Empire is subsequently known to historians as the Byzantine Empire after the old Greek name for Constantinople, Byzantion.

612

- The Irish abbot Columban reproves the Frankish court for its bloody dynastic quarrels and is forced to flee for his life.

614

- After dominating Frankish politics for 20 years, the ruthless queen Brunhild is executed by the young Chlotar II who reunites the (Merovingian) Frankish kingdom under a single ruler after 50 years of civil wars.
- King Chosroes II of Sasanian Persia declares holy war on the Christian Byzantine Empire and sacks Jerusalem, capturing the True Cross. His victories over the Byzantines earn Chosroes the nickname Parvez ("the Victorious").

616–619

- King Chosroes II of Persia conquers Byzantine Egypt and Asia Minor. He occupies both Alexandria in Egypt and Chalcedon, across the Bosporus from Constantinople. Byzantine control of the sea prevents Chosroes from attacking Constantinople but the loss of corn supplies from Egypt causes hardship in the city.

618

- Li Yuan, the military governor of Taiyuan, overthrows Yangdi, the despotical last emperor of the Chinese Sui dynasty. Adopting the name of Gaozu, he becomes the first emperor of the highly successful Tang dynasty.
- The nomadic Avars march up to the gates of Constantinople, taking many prisoners as slaves; in the face of the Avar advance and a simultaneous attack by the Sasanian Persians, the Byzantine emperor Heraclius considers transferring his capital to Carthage, Roman Africa.

620

- The Byzantine emperor Heraclius buys peace with the Avars to release troops for a counterattack against the Persians.

621

- The Chinese emperor Kao-tsu orders the establishment of a bureau to regulate and control the manufacture of porcelain.

622–627

- Using the Byzantine fleet to bypass the Persian army occupying Asia Minor, the Byzantine emperor Heraclius sets out on a brilliant campaign against the Persians, penetrating as far as Hamadan. The warlike Persian king Chosroes II has retired from active campaigning and his generals are much less successful against the Byzantines.

625

- The Christian Ethelburga, sister of King Ethelbert of Kent, marries King Edwin of Northumbria. She is accompanied to Northumbria by Paulinus, one of Augustine's priests.

626

- Gaozu, the first emperor of the Chinese Tang dynasty, is overthrown by his son Taizong, one of the ablest rulers in Chinese history. Under his rule trade and agriculture prosper and Chinese control is extended far into central Asia.

627

- The Byzantine emperor Heraclius inflicts a decisive defeat on the Persians under King Chosroes II at Nineveh in Mesopotamia.

628

- Chinese emperor Taizong codifies the law, reintroduces the examination system, and reissues the Chinese classics.
- Following his defeat by the Byzantines at Nineveh, Mesopotamia, in 627, King Chosroes II of Persia is murdered by his son, and the Byzantine emperor Heraclius makes an advantageous peace with the Sassanian Empire. Both the Byzantine and Sasanian Persian empires have been severely weakened by their 24-year long war.

630

c. 630 The East Anglian king, Raedwald, bretwalda or overlord of Britain, is buried at Sutton Hoo in a 30 m/90 ft ship burial, with high-status treasures indicating advanced trade links with the rest of Europe.

630–668 During the reign of Narasimhavarman I, the Pallava dynasty is the dominant power of southern India. After his death, the Pallava kingdom comes under pressure from the Chalukyas and goes into decline, disappearing about 900.

632

- Abu Bakr, the successor to the founder of Islam Muhammad, suppresses an anti-Islamic Arab revolt with the aid of his general Khalid and launches raids on Byzantine Syria.

633

- King Edwin of Northumbria, who has called himself bretwalda or overlord of Britain, is defeated and killed (at the modern Hatfield Chase, near Doncaster, England) by the pagan king of Mercia, Penda, in alliance with the Welsh king Cadwallon.

634

- Oswald, the new king of Northumbria, defeats the Welsh king Cadwallon near Hexham, Northumbria.

July   The Arab caliph Abu Bakr's general Khalid defeats the Byzantine general Theodore at Ajnadain, between Jerusalem and Gaza, beginning almost a century of dramatic Muslim Arab conquests.

August   Umar succeeds Abu Bakr as the second caliph (civic and religious leader of Islam) and adopts the title "commander of the faithful." A stern but just ruler, Umar sees the Arab caliphate become the dominant power of the Middle East during his ten-year reign.

635

September   The Arabs occupy Damascus, Syria, following a six-month siege.

636

August   The Arab general Khalid defeats the Byzantine emperor Heraclius at a decisive engagement on the Yarmuk River near Damascus, Syria, opening the way for the Arab conquest of Syria and Palestine.

637

June–September   The Persian general Rustam, with an army of 50,000 men, is defeated by a much smaller Arab army under Sa'd in a three-day battle at Qadisiya in Persia (modern Iraq). The Persian capital at Ctesiphon falls to the Arab army three months later.

638

January   The Byzantine patriarch Sophronios surrenders Jerusalem to the Arab caliph Umar after a long siege. The city is subsequently regarded as a holy place by Muslims as well as Christians and Jews.

639

- The last effective ruler of the Frankish Merovingian dynasty, Dagobert I, dies. His successors are all short-lived and ineffective characters, the so-called *rois fainéants* (the "do-nothing kings"), who are unable to prevent real power passing into the hands of royal officials, the mayors of the palace.

December   The Arab army invades Egypt, meeting little resistance.

642

c. 642   The decisive Arab victory at Nehavend in Persia (modern Iran) leads to the collapse of organized Persian resistance to Arab aggression.

- Oswald, the Christian king of Northumbria, is defeated and killed by Penda, the pagan king of Mercia, at the Battle of Maserfelth, probably near modern Oswestry, Shropshire, England. This battle marks the rise of Mercia at the expense of Northumbria.

September   Alexandria, the last Byzantine stronghold in Egypt, surrenders to the Arabs. Local resistance to the Arabs is weak because the Orthodox Christian Byzantines have persecuted the Monophysite Christian majority population there: the Arabs offer them freedom from persecution.

643

- Rothari, King of the Lombards in Italy, codifies the traditional Lombard laws in the hope of ending the protracted blood feuds that characterize Lombard justice.

644

- The Arab caliph Umar is murdered by a Persian slave. He is succeeded by Uthman, who centralizes the administration of the Arab caliphate and promulgates an official version of the Koran, the written record of the Islamic prophet Muhammad's teachings.

648

- The Chinese emperor Taizong sends a diplomatic mission to Tibet, accompanied by a Chinese princess.

649

- The Chinese emperor Taizong dies and is succeeded by his indolent and sickly son Gaozong, who soon leaves his able and ruthless consort, the empress Wu Hou, to direct affairs.

SCIENCE, TECHNOLOGY, AND MEDICINE

Agriculture

c. 600

- New techniques in European agriculture, including the introduction of lightweight, deep-cutting plows by the Slavic peoples, vastly increase efficiency, allowing the European population to boom.

628

- Cane sugar is introduced from India into the Byzantine Empire by soldiers.

Ecology

c. 600

- Climate change in Peru accelerates the decline of the South American Moche civilization, silting up the canals that irrigate their principal city.

602

- The Yellow River floods in China, with catastrophic results. In order to prevent a repetition of the disaster, the emperor orders a massive project to recut the riverbed channel.

Exploration

645

- The Chinese Buddhist monk Yuan Chwang returns to China after 16 years of travel, mostly in India. He spends much of the rest of his life translating Sanskrit manuscripts into Chinese.

Health and Medicine

601

- The *Vagbhata*, an Indian medicinal herbal, is compiled around this time.

608

- Young Japanese physicians begin to travel to China for part of their training, leading to a growing convergence between the two countries' traditional medicines.

Science

619

- Chinese scholar Suan Ching compiles a series of scientific textbooks for use in examinations for public office in China.

628

- Indian astronomer and mathematician Brahmagupta writes *Brahmasphutasiddanta/The Opening of the Universe*, a work which takes the calculation of planetary motions to a new degree of accuracy.

c. **633**

- The Spanish scholar Bishop Isidore of Seville is active around this time. His works include *On the Order of Creatures* on natural history, and *De natura rerum/ Concerning the Nature of Things*, on astronomy and cosmography.

c. **640**

- Chinese alchemist Sun Ssu-miao is working around this time. He is author of *Tan chin yao chüeh/Great Secrets of Alchemy*, a famous manual giving many recipes for elixirs of life, mostly based on highly dangerous mercury, sulfur, and arsenic compounds.

Technology

600

- Paper-making begins in Korea.

610

- Paper is made in Japan.

615

- An early record from Japan records the ritual use of "burning water" – the earliest record of petroleum in Japan.

644

- The earliest references to the Arab use of windpower dates to Persia at this time. Persian windmills have towers with horizontal sails inside. The wind enters and exits through carefully-positioned inlets.

Transportation

610

- A land yacht, with horse teams to assist the sail propulsion, is built for the Sui dynasty Chinese emperor Yang. Exaggerated reports claim it carries several thousand people.
- The first stretch of the Chinese Grand Canal, which will ultimately stretch 1,000 km/620 mi and link Beijing with the Chang Jiang River, is opened.

ARTS AND IDEAS

Architecture

600

- Native American settlers in the modern Illinois region of North America found the city of Cahokia, built on a series of flat-topped mounds, and aligned with the cardinal directions and the sun's rising and setting points at the equinoxes.

604

- The first church bell is installed in Rome, Italy.

627

- T'ai Tsung, emperor of China, spends great wealth in beautifying his capital Chang-an. It becomes the site of many grand tombs.

648

- The first church is built at Westminster, London, England.

649

- Instead of the usual sculptured lion guardians, the emperor T'ai Tsung has six narrative panels in bas relief executed on his tomb. They illustrate an incident when one of his generals exchanged his horse for the emperor's wounded horse.

Literature and Language

c. **600**

- By the last quarter of the 6th century the Visigoth rulers of Spain and the Frankish rulers of France have each developed their own distinctive variation of the Latin language.
- Indian author Dandin writes his *Dasakumaracarita/ History of the Ten Princes*, a series of bizarre adventure stories involving a wide range of characters from the whole of Indian society.

622

- Isidore, the scholarly bishop of Seville, compiles his *Originum sive etymologiarum/Etymologies*, an encyclopedia of the arts and sciences, which also founds the study of etymology – the origin of words. Despite its unreliability, it remains influential throughout the Middle Ages.

c. **630**

- Sanskrit poet Bhartrhari writes three collections of short verses. His collection of 100 love poems is his best-known work.

SOCIETY

Everyday Life

c. **600**

- The first spirits are distilled, in Persia.

The Rise of Islam (610–756)

610

- While sleeping in a cave near Mecca (in modern Saudi Arabia), the Arab prophet and founder of Islam, Muhammad, has a vision of the angel Gabriel who announces that he is "the messenger of God." Muhammad subsequently experiences revelations that he believes to come directly from God.

c. 612

- Muhammad begins his mission and calls on the people of Mecca to renounce their old gods in favor of Allah, the one true god. During this period he experiences a vision of a visit to Jerusalem and a meeting with Abraham, Moses, and Jesus, whom he leads in prayer.

622

- Faced with the opposition of the city authorities, Muhammad flees from Mecca to Yathrib (Medina) where he establishes himself as a religious and political leader. His faith becomes known as Islam, the "submission" to Allah, and his followers are called Muslims, "those who submit." Muhammad's flight, known as the Hegira, marks the beginning of the Muslim era.

630

- Muhammad captures the city of Mecca and declares its ancient pagan shrine, the "Kaaba," to be the holy place of Islam. Medina remains his capital, however.

632

- At the time of Muhammad's death most of the Arab peninsula is Muslim. Religious leadership falls to Abu Bakr, one of Muhammad's earliest disciples, who adopts the title of "caliph," or "successor," and who begins supervising the prophetic revelations into a holy book, the Koran.
- Abu Bakr suppresses an anti-Islamic Arab revolt with the aid of his general Khalid and launches raids on Byzantine Syria.

634

July Khalid defeats the Byzantine general Theodore at Ajnadain, between Jerusalem and Gaza, beginning almost a century of dramatic Muslim Arab conquests.

August Umar succeeds Abu Bakr as the second caliph and adopts the title "commander of the faithful." A stern but just ruler, Umar sees the Arab caliphate become the dominant power of the Middle East during his ten-year reign.

638

January The Byzantine patriarch Sophronios surrenders Jerusalem to Umar after a long siege. The city is subsequently regarded as a holy place by Muslims as well as Christians and Jews.

644

- Umar is murdered by a Persian slave. He is succeeded by Uthman, who centralizes the administration of the Arab caliphate and promulgates an official version of the Koran.

656

June 17 The rapid growth of the Arab caliphate causes social and political tensions, culminating in the murder of the caliph Uthman in his own home in Medina by rebel soldiers. The Islamic prophet Muhammad's son-in-law, Ali, becomes the fourth caliph, though many suspect him of complicity in Uthman's murder.

December Muawiya of the Umayyad clan revolts but is defeated by Ali at the Battle of the Camel at Khoraiba in South Iraq. Muawiya is supported by the Islamic prophet Muhammad's widow, Aisha, who commands her contingent of troops from the back of a camel, from which the battle gets its name.

661

January 20 A radical sect, the *Khariji* or "Seceders," breaks away from Ali and murders him.

July Muawiya becomes the fifth caliph of Islam, founding the Umayyad dynasty and establishing his court and capital at Damascus.

680

- Muawiya dies and a war of succession breaks out among the Arabs again. Husein, a son of the murdered fourth caliph Ali, responds to an appeal to him to seize the leadership but is defeated and killed at Karbala in Iraq by supporters of Muawiya's son Yazid, who becomes caliph. Husein is regarded as a martyr by those who believe that the caliphate can only rightly be held by a descendant of the Islamic prophet Muhammad, and they break away to form the minority Shiite movement of Islam.

724

- Hishām becomes caliph. His reign sees the decline of the Arab Umayyad dynasty and the end of the period of runaway Muslim Arab conquests.

749

- Abu-al-Abbas, a descendant of the Islamic prophet Muhammad, becomes the leader of the revolt against the caliph Merwan II, the last of the Umayyad dynasty, after being proclaimed caliph by the rebels at Kufa (Iraq).

750

- Abu-al-Abbas defeats Merwan II at the Battle of the River Zab. Merwan flees to Egypt but is caught and killed and his head is sent to Abu. Abu-al-Abbas's victory is followed by a general massacre of the Umayyad family and of members of his own family whose popularity he fears, for which he earns the nickname *as-Saffah*, "the bloodshedder."

756

- The Moors in Spain break away from the Abbasid caliphate to form an independent emirate under Abd-ar-Rahman I, one of the few survivors of the Abbasid caliph Abu-al-Abbas's massacre of the Umayyad family in 750. He makes the southern Spanish city of Córdoba his capital. This marks the beginning of the breakup of the political unity of the Muslim world.

- The Mayan civilization reaches its peak in this century, with complex temples and sophisticated architecture and sculpture.

629

- A Chinese Buddhist pilgrim, Hsuien-tsang, arrives at the Indian court of King Harsha and reports on its prosperity and on the open-handedness of the king.

Religion

604

- After his death, Pope Gregory I is canonized and becomes known as St. Gregory the Great.

607

- Prince Shotoku Taishi of Japan founds the Buddhist Horyuji temple complex near Nara. It is the earliest surviving example of Sino-Japanese architecture and the oldest existing wooden structure.

610

- While sleeping in a cave near Mecca (in modern Saudi Arabia), the Arab prophet and founder of Islam, Muhammad, has a vision of the angel Gabriel who announces that he is "the messenger of God." Muhammad subsequently experiences revelations that he believes to come directly from God. He confides his vision to his wife Khadija and his immediate family.

c. **612**

- Muhammad receives divine instructions to begin his mission. He calls on the people of Mecca to renounce their old gods in favor of Allah, the one true god. During this period he experiences a vision of a visit to Jerusalem and a meeting with Abraham, Moses, and Jesus, whom he leads in prayer.

613

- St. Columban, having been expelled from the kingdom of the Franks for refusing to bless the illegitimate sons of Theuderic II, founds a new monastery at Bobbio in Lombardy.

622

- Faced with the opposition of the city authorities, Muhammad flees from Mecca to Yathrib (Medina) where he establishes himself as a religious and political leader. His faith becomes known as Islam, the "submission" to Allah, and his followers are called Muslims, "those who submit." Muhammad's flight, known as the Hegira, marks the beginning of the Muslim era.

626

- Raids by the Islamic prophet Muhammad's followers on their caravans provoke the Meccans into an unsuccessful retaliatory attack on the city of Medina (in modern Saudi Arabia), Muhammad's base. A truce is arranged between the two sides.

627

- King Edwin of Northumbria and many of his followers are converted to Christianity by the Roman missionary Paulinus.

630

c. 630   The building of the Buddhist Mahabodhi temple complex at Bodhgaya in eastern India begins. The temple is built largely from brick.

- The Arab prophet and founder of Islam, Muhammad, captures the city of Mecca (in modern Saudi Arabia) and declares its ancient pagan shrine, the "Kaaba," to be the holy place of Islam. Medina (also in modern Saudi Arabia) remains his capital, however.
- The Byzantine emperor Heraclius recaptures the "true cross" of Christ from Persia and restores it to Jerusalem.

632

- At the time of Muhammad's death most of the Arab peninsula is Muslim. Religious leadership falls to Abu Bakr, one of Muhammad's earliest disciples, who adopts the title of "caliph," or "successor," and who begins supervising the prophetic revelations into a holy book, the Koran.

633

c. 633   There is a brief return to paganism in northern England after the defeat of Northumbria's Christian king Edwin in 633 by the pagan kings of Mercia and Wales.

- The Council of Toledo, in Visigoth Spain, rules that relapsed Christians shall be separated from their children and sold into slavery.

635

- Aidan, a monk from Iona, is invited by King Oswald of Northumbria to help restore Christianity to his kingdom. He founds a monastery on the island of Lindisfarne and Celtic Christianity replaces the Roman variant brought from Kent.

638

- The second Muslim caliph, Umar, fixes a site in Jerusalem for a mosque.

c. **639**

- Srong-btsan-Gyam-po of Tibet invites Buddhist monks from India to his capital Llasa. Buddhism is eventually synthesized with the old polytheistic Bon religion. The result is a specifically Tibetan form of Buddhism, sometimes called Lamaism.

648

- In an attempt to unite the Eastern and Western churches, the emperor Constans II issues an edict, the *Typos*, which forbids argument about Christ's divine and human natures. It is opposed by Pope Martin I who is arrested and exiled.

Sports

c. **600**

- The Persian romance *Kārnāmak-i-Artakhshatr-i-Papa kān* contains the earliest reference to the Persian board game of *shatranj* (or *chantrang*), from which chess is directly descended.

BIRTHS & DEATHS

600
- Ali (ibn Abi Talib), son-in-law of the prophet Muhammad and fourth caliph, born in Mecca (–661).
- T'ai Tsung, Emperor of China 626–649 and founder of the T'ang dynasty, born in China (–649).

602
- Maurice (Mauricius Flavius Tiberius), Eastern Roman Emperor 582–602 and an outstanding general, dies in Constantinople (c. 63).
- Mu'awiyah I (also Moawiyah), caliph 661–680, founder of the Umayyad dynasty, who assumed the caliphate after the assassination of Ali, reunified the Arab empire, and transferred the capital to Damascus, born in Mecca (–680).

604
- c. 604 St. Oswald, King of Northumbria (633–641), who introduced Celtic Christian missionaries to England, born (–641).
- St. Gregory, Pope Gregory I the Great 590–604, theologian and reformer of church organization and liturgy, dies in Rome, Italy (c. 64).
- Wen Ti, Chinese emperor 581–604, who reunified and reorganized China and founded the Sui dynasty, dies in China (65).

605
- c. 605 Alexander of Tralles, Byzantine physician whose 12-volume treatise on pathology and therapy was used until the 16th century, dies (c. 80).
- King Dagobert, the last Merovingian king to rule the entire Frankish realm 629–639, son of Chlotar II, born (–639).
- c. March 26 St. Augustine of Canterbury, first archbishop of Canterbury who founded the Christian church in England, dies in Canterbury, Kent.

612
May 3 Constantine IV, Byzantine emperor 668–685, son of Constans II, born in Constantinople (–685).

614
- Brunhild, Queen of the Frankish kingdom of Austrasia, a major political figure of the Merovingian age, is tortured to death in Renève, Burgundy, on the orders of Chlotar II of Neustria (c. 79).
- Aisha (bint Abi Bakr), third wife of the prophet Muhammad, and an important political figure after his death, born in Mecca, Arabia (–678).
- St. Hilda of Whitby, one of the leading abbesses of Anglo-Saxon England, founder of Whitby Abbey, born in Northumbria, England (–680).

615
November 23 St. Columban, Irish abbot, writer, and important missionary, dies in Bobbio, Italy (73).

616
- Agilulf, King of the Lombards 590–616, dies.
February 24 Aethelbert I, King of Kent 560–616, who issued the first code of Anglo-Saxon laws, dies.

619
- Abd Allah ibn al-Abbas (also known as ibn Abbas), companion of the prophet Muhammad and Islamic scholar, born in Arabia (–c. 688).

625
- Wu Hou, Chinese concubine who became empress of China 655–705, and unified the Chinese empire, born in China (–705).

626
January Husein (al-Husayn ibn Ali), grandson of the prophet Muhammad, and Shiite Muslim hero, born in Medina, Arabia (–680).

628
- c. 628 St. Benedict Biscop, English ascetic who founded Benedictine monasticism in England, born in Northumbria, England (–689).
- Chosroes II ("the Victorious"), Sasanian king of Persia 590–628, in whose reign the Sassanian Empire achieved its greatest extent, is deposed and murdered.
- Kao Tsung, Chinese emperor who expanded the T'ang dynasty into Korea, born in Ch'ang-an, China (–683).

629
October 18 Chlotar II, Merovingian king of Neustria, who seized both Austrasia and Burgundy, reuniting the Frankish lands under his rule 613–629, dies (35).

630
- Constans II, son of Constantine III, and Byzantine emperor 641–668, in whose reign the southern and eastern provinces were lost to the Arabs, born in Constantinople (–668).

632
June 8 Muhammad, founder of Islam, dies in Medina, Arabia (62).
October 12 Edwin, King of Northumbria 616–632, is killed in battle at Hatfield Chase, England (47).

633
- Fatimah, youngest daughter of the prophet Muhammad, and wife of the fourth caliph, Ali, dies (c. 28).

634
- St. Wilfrid, English bishop who established close links between the papacy and the Anglo-Saxon church, born in Northumbria, England (–709).

- St. Cuthbert, bishop of Lindisfarne who evangelized Northumbria, born, probably in Northumbria, England (–687).
August 23 Abu Bakr, companion of the prophet Muhammad and first caliph 632–634, who brought central Arabia under Muslim control, and began Arab expansion into Persia and Syria, dies.

639
- King Dagobert, the last Merovingian king to rule the entire Frankish realm 629–39, son of Chlotar II, dies in Saint-Denis, France (c. 34).

640
- Pepin the Elder, councilor of the Merovingian king Chlotar II and founder of the Carolingian dynasty, dies.

641
February 11 Heraclius, Roman emperor of the East 610–641, dies in Constantinople (c. 66).
August 5 St. Oswald, King of Northumbria 633–641, who introduced Celtic Christian missionaries to England, is killed in battle in Maserfield, England (c. 37).

642
- al-Hasan al-Basri, Muslim ascetic who founded two schools of Sunni Islam: the Mutazilah (Philosophical theologians), and Ashari-yah (followers of the theologian al-Ashari), born in Medina, Arabia (–728).

644
- St. Paulinus, Italian missionary, first bishop of York, and later archbishop of Rochester, who converted Northumbria to Christianity, dies in Rochester, Kent (c. 60).
November 3 Umar I, Muslim caliph 634–644, who conquered Mesopotamia and Syria and began the conquest of Iran and Egypt, is assassinated by a Persian slave (58).

646
- Abd-al-Malik (ibn Marwan), fifth caliph 685–705 of the Umayyad dynasty, who made Arabic the language of administration throughout the Arab empire, born in Medina, Arabia (–705).

647
- Bana, Sanskrit writer, court poet of King Harsadeva of Thanesvar, dies.

649
- T'ai Tsung, Emperor of China 626–649, and founder of the T'ang dynasty, dies in China (49).

650–699

POLITICS, GOVERNMENT, AND ECONOMICS

Business and Economics

682

- The trading city of Srivijaya (modern Palembang) on the island of Sumatra begins a period of imperial expansion which makes it the dominant power in Indonesia and Malaysia for the next 400 years.

Colonization

678

- The Bulgars, a nomadic people of the Eurasian steppes, establish themselves in North Thrace and soon become a serious threat to their Slav and Byzantine neighbors.

Politics and Government

652

- An Arab attempt to conquer the Christian Nubian kingdom of Makkura, in northeast Africa, is defeated.

653

- Yezdegird III, the last king of the Sasanian dynasty of Persia, is murdered at Merv (in modern Turkmenistan), bringing Persian resistance to the Arabs to a complete end.

654

- A movement supporting the Islamic prophet Muhammad's son-in-law, Ali, as the only legitimate heir to the Arab caliphate arises in Persia.

655

- Penda, the last pagan ruler of the Anglo-Saxon kingdom of Mercia, is defeated and killed by King Oswy of Northumbria, near modern Leeds, England.

656

June 17 The rapid growth of the Arab caliphate causes social and political tensions, culminating in the murder of the caliph Uthman in his own home in Medina (in modern Saudi Arabia) by rebel soldiers. The Islamic prophet Muhammad's son-in-law, Ali, becomes the fourth caliph, though many suspect him of complicity in Uthman's murder.

December Muawiya of the Umayyad clan revolts but is defeated by Ali, the caliph of Islam, at the Battle of the Camel at Khoraiba in South Iraq. Muawiya is supported by the Islamic prophet Muhammad's widow, Aisha, who commands her contingent of troops from the back of a camel, from which the battle gets its name.

657

- Muawiya renews the struggle for the caliphate of Islam. The caliph Ali is prevented from winning a battle by his enemy's appeal, on the Koran, for arbitration.

661

January 20 A radical sect, the *Khariji* or "Seceders," breaks away from Ali, the caliph of Islam, and murders him.

July On the death of caliph Ali, Muawiya becomes the fifth caliph of Islam, founding the Umayyad dynasty. He realizes that Medina (in modern Saudi Arabia) is too remote from the new centers of Arab power in Syria, Iraq, and Egypt, and moves the capital of the Arab caliphate to Damascus, Syria.

663

- The Byzantine emperor Constans II visits Rome, the first Byzantine emperor to do so for 190 years.

667

- The Arabs overrun Numidia and Mauritania (modern Algeria and Morocco), though Berber resistance remains fierce until 702.

668

- The Byzantine emperor Constans II tries to expel the Lombards from South Italy in an attempt to make this country and Sicily a bastion against the Arabs. However, he is then murdered in Sicily. His son, Constantine IV, succeeds him.

670

- In an attempt to complete the conquest of the Byzantine Empire by capturing its capital at Constantinople, the Arab army begins a seven-year siege of the city.

675

- Muawiya, the fifth caliph (civic and religious leader of Islam), makes the Arab caliphate hereditary by appointing his son Yazid as his successor.

677

- Having suffered heavy losses in their seven-year siege of the city, the Arab army retreats from the Byzantine capital Constantinople. The Byzantine emperor, Constantine IV, who has led the defense, makes an advantageous peace with them.

680

- The caliph Muawiya dies and a war of succession breaks out among the Arabs again. Husein, a son of the murdered fourth caliph Ali, responds to an appeal to him to seize the leadership but is defeated and killed at Karbala in Iraq by supporters of Muawiya's son Yazid, who becomes caliph. Husein is regarded as a martyr by those who believe that the caliphate can only rightly be held by a descendant of the Islamic prophet Muhammad, and they break away to form the minority Shiite movement of Islam.

683

- On the death of her husband, the Chinese emperor Gaozong, the empress Wu Hou exiles his successor, her elder son Zhongzong, and appoints her weak younger son Ruizong emperor while retaining real power for herself.
- The death of the Umayyad caliph Yazid results in two years' anarchy in the Arab caliphate, ending in the comparatively mild and efficient reign of Abd-al-Malik as seventh caliph of Islam.

684

- The powerful Northumbrian king Ecgfrith despatches the ealdorman Beorht from the British mainland with a fleet to plunder Ireland.

685

- The Northumbrian king Ecgfrith is defeated and killed by the Picts at Nechtansmere, near Forfar (in modern Scotland). Following this disaster the power of Northumbria, the dominant Anglo-Saxon kingdom for most of the 7th century, goes into decline.

687

- Pepin the Stout, mayor of the palace (administrator of the royal court of the Merovingian Frankish dynasty), defeats his rivals at the Battle of Tertry and becomes the effective ruler of all the Frankish kingdom (except Aquitaine). He gives himself the title *Dux et Princeps Francorum* ("Duke and Prince of the Franks") but does not depose the Merovingian king, Theuderic III, who is maintained as a powerless figurehead.

688

- The Byzantine emperor, Justinian II, recovers Macedonia and Thrace from the Slavs. Many Slavs are drafted into the Byzantine army while thousands of others are deported and resettled as farmers in northwest Anatolia under the title of "the Abundant People."

691

- The Byzantine emperor, Justinian II, is defeated at the Battle of Sebastopolis in Anatolia, partly owing to the defection of the Slav conscripts in his army, on whom he takes vengeance in a massacre. As a result of the defeat, Byzantine territory in Armenia is lost to the Arabs.

695

- King Jaguar Paw of the Maya city-state of Calakmul in Mesoamerica (the area of the Mexican and Mayan civilizations) is captured and sacrificed to the gods at the rival city-state of Tikal.
- The Byzantine emperor Justinian II provokes a rebellion by his ruthless taxation policies. He is captured by Leontius, a malcontent general, who banishes him to the Crimea before assuming the throne himself.

697

- The Arabs recapture Carthage, the capital of Byzantine Africa, and the Byzantines are never able to recover it.

Following this defeat the Byzantine navy rebels against the emperor, Leontius, who has his nose cut off and is banished. The general Apsimar becomes emperor under the name Tiberius II.

SCIENCE, TECHNOLOGY, AND MEDICINE

Health and Medicine

c. **650**

- Physicians in India have developed operations for bladder problems and digestive disorders.

660

- The Hôtel Dieu is opened in Paris, France. Although it is a hospital, more care is taken for the well-being of the patient's soul than is used in treating the physical ailment.

664

- Plague sweeps through the Saxon settlers in southeastern England.

Science

657

- Pacal, the new Lord of Pallenque, a Mayan religious center in southern Mexico, founds an observatory and builds astronomical monuments, including his own tomb, aligned to the winter solstice.

671

- The Syrian-born Byzantine scholar Kallinikos invents "Greek fire," a highly inflammable mixture of sulfur, petroleum, rock salt, and resin.

678

- A brilliant comet is recorded at Constantinople as visible from August to October. It is taken as a good omen after the Arab forces raise their siege and conclude a treaty.

Technology

c. **650**

- The Chinese invent the horse collar, which enables the animal to pull from the shoulders without restricting its wind-pipe, leading to great improvements in transport and agriculture.

673

- The Byzantine defenders use "Greek fire," a highly inflammable mixture of sulfur, petroleum, rock salt, and resin, against the Arab forces besieging Constantinople.

ARTS AND IDEAS

Architecture

650

- When the Arab invaders pass through Cappadocia, Asia Minor (modern Turkey), the Christian inhabitants build underground cities. Some, such as the site at Kaymakli, southeast of Ankara in modern Turkey, are rediscovered late in the 20th century.

680

- The three-story wooden pagoda of the Yakushiji temple, at Nura, Japan, is built with specific features to prevent its destruction or damage by earthquakes.

Arts

653

- Arab raiders break up and remove the remains of the Colossus of Rhodes, one of the Seven Wonders of the ancient world.

Literature and Language

699

c. 699 An epic poem in Old English describing the exploits of the dragon-slaying hero Beowulf is completed. The finest surviving achievement of Anglo-Saxon poetry, it was probably written in England though set in Scandinavia.

- Arabic replaces Greek as the language of administration in Damascus.

SOCIETY

Religion

c. 650

- A dualistic Christian sect, the Paulicians, emerges in Armenia. Taking many of their ideas from Manichaeism, they believe that a bad God ruled this world and a good God the world to come.
- A Hindu devotional movement emerges called "bhakti" whose followers express a deep emotional attachment to an individual god by visiting pilgrimage sites, reciting the god's name and singing hymns.

651

- A standardized edition of the Koran is produced on the orders of the third caliph, Uthman.

652

- The lamasery of Jokang at Lhasa is built by King Srong-btsan-Gyam-po to house Buddhist images brought from China by his wife.

c. 660

- Caedmon becomes a monk at Whitby Abbey in Northumbria, England, where he produces vernacular verse paraphrases of biblical stories. His only surviving work can be found in translated format in Bede's *Historia ecclesiastica gentis Anglorus/Ecclesiastical History of the English People.*

664

- King Oswy of Northumbria calls the Synod of Whitby, ostensibly to decide on the date for observing Easter. The result establishes the supremacy in England of the Roman church over the Celtic church.

665

c. 665 St. Cuthbert, who accepts the decision of the Synod of Whitby in favor of the Roman church, becomes prior of Lindisfarne but relinquishes the position after about a year in order to live as a hermit on a nearby island.

- St. Wilfrid, champion of the Roman cause at Whitby, is consecrated bishop of York but is replaced by St. Chad when he fails to return from France.

669

- The Greek scholar Theodore of Tarsus is appointed archbishop of Canterbury and begins to organize a diocesan system in England.

673

- Archbishop Theodore of Canterbury imposes stricter discipline on Anglo-Saxon monasteries. A church hierarchy begins to appear in England.

674

- Northumbria becomes the greatest center of learning in England after Benedict Biscop founds a monastery at Wearmouth. He later founds a monastery at Jarrow and endows both establishments with a large collection of books gathered on his several visits to Rome.

678

- Archbishop Theodore quarrels with Wilfrid, bishop of York, after dividing his diocese. Wilfrid leaves England and travels in Europe where he assists in the conversion of the Frisians and makes a successful appeal to the Pope to be restored to his bishopric in York.

680

- The future scholar and historian Bede, aged seven, comes under the tutelage of Benedict Biscop at Wearmouth, Northumbria. He later attends the newly founded monastery at Jarrow.
- The Shia Muslims build a shrine at Kerbela, southwest of Baghdad, at the site where their leader Husein was killed.
- The Sixth Ecumenical Council of the Christian Church meets in Constantinople, the capital of the Byzantine Empire. In addition to considering current theological controversies, the Council also considers the loss of the patriarchial sees of Antioch, Jerusalem, and Alexandria to the Muslim Arabs. The Council condemns Monotheletism, a version of Monophysitism, which argues that Christ had only one will.

683

- In the Arab civil wars the Kaaba, the small temple in Mecca commandeered by Muhammad and his followers, is destroyed. It is later rebuilt.

688

- King Caedwalla of Wessex, the kingdom of the West Saxons in England, makes a pilgrimage to Rome where he dies the following year. His example is followed by his successor Ine (in 726) and many other West Saxon kings including Alfred the Great.

690

- Willibrord, an English monk, travels to Utrecht with twelve disciples to convert the Frisians. He is supported by Pepin II of the Franks.

691

- On the orders of Caliph Abd-al-Malik, work begins on a Muslim shrine in Jerusalem. Built on the rock from which Muhammad is supposed to have ascended into heaven, the shrine later becomes a mosque and is known as the "Dome of the Rock" or the Mosque of Omar. It is the first major monument in Islamic history.

BIRTHS & DEATHS

651
August 31 St. Aidan, founder and first bishop of Lindisfarne, dies at Bamburgh, Northumberland, England.

654
November 15 Penda, Anglo-Saxon king of Mercia c. 632–654, dies.

c. 659
- Caedwalla, King of Wessex 685–689, born (–689).

661
- Ali (ibn Abi Talib), son-in-law of the prophet Muhammad and fourth caliph, dies in Kufa, Persia (65).

668
September 15 Constans II, Byzantine emperor 641–668, son of Constantine III, in whose reign the southern and eastern provinces were lost to the Arabs, is assassinated in Syracuse, Sicily.

671
- Grimoald, Lombard Duke of Benevento 662–671, dies.

672
March 2 St. Chad (or Ceadda), monastic founder, who christianized the English kingdom of Mercia, dies in Lichfield, Mercia.

673
- St. Bede (Baeda or Beda; "the Venerable Bede"), Anglo-Saxon theologian, historian, and chronologist, known chiefly for his *Historia ecclesiastica gentis Anglorum/Ecclesiastical History of the English People*, born, possibly in Monkton in Jarrow, Northumbria, England (–735).

678
- Aisha (bint Abi Bakr), third wife of the prophet Muhammad, and an important political figure after his death, dies in Medina (c. 64).

680
c. 680 Caedmon, first Old English Christian poet, dies (c. 30).
- Leo III, Byzantine emperor 717–741, successful military commander, iconoclast, born in Germanicia, Commagene, Syria (–741).
- Muawiyah I (also Moawiyah), caliph 661–680, founder of the Umayyad dynasty, who assumed the caliphate after the assassination of Ali, reunified the Arab empire, and transferred the capital to Damascus, dies in Damascus (c. 78).
- St. Boniface (original name Wynfrid or Wynfrith), English missionary and ecclesiastic reformer, who played an important part in the christianization of Germany, born in Wessex, England (–754).
October 10 Husein (al-Husayn ibn Ali), grandson of the prophet Muhammad, and Shiite Muslim hero, is murdered in Karbalā, Persia (54).
November 17 St. Hilda of Whitby, one of the leading abbesses of Anglo-Saxon England, founder of Whitby Abbey, dies in Whitby, Northumbria, England (c. 66).

683
- Kao Tsung, Chinese emperor who expanded the T'ang dynasty into Korea, dies in Ch'ang-an, China (c. 55).

685
- Constantine IV, Byzantine emperor 668–685, son of Constans II, dies (c. 73).

687
March 20 St. Cuthbert, bishop of Lindisfarne, who evangelized Northumbria, dies on Inner Farne, off Northumbria, England (c. 52).

688
- Abd Allah ibn al-Abbas (also known as ibn Abbas), companion of the prophet Muhammad and Islamic scholar, dies in at-Taif, Arabia (c. 88).
- Charles Martel, ruler of the Franks 719–741, who defeated the Saracens at the Battle of Poitiers (732), born (–741).

689
January 12 St. Benedict Biscop, English ascetic who founded Benedictine monasticism in England, dies in Wearmouth, Northumbria, England (c. 61).
April 20 Caedwalla, King of Wessex 685–689, dies in Rome (c. 30).

700–749

POLITICS, GOVERNMENT, AND ECONOMICS

Business and Economics

749
- King Aethelbald of the Anglo-Saxon kingdom of Mercia, England, frees his clergy from "burdens," allowing the revenue from church lands to go to the church and not the king.

Colonization

712
- Musa, the Arab caliphate's governor of the former Roman Africa, arrives in Spain to consolidate the Muslim hold on the country. He captures Seville, but dies a year later. The Arabs deal leniently with all those who submit voluntarily to their rule.

720
- Arab and Moorish forces of the Umayyad Caliphate in Spain cross the Pyrenees and occupy Provence in the south of the Frankish kingdom.

725
- The Khazars, nomads of Turkic origin who have spread northwest over the Caucasus into the south of modern Russia, form a prosperous kingdom with its capital at Itil, at the mouth of the River Volga. Merchants of various faiths gather at Itil and suffer no religious persecution.

728–729
- King Liutprand of the Lombards approaches the city of Rome in the extension of his kingdom, and is rebuked and checked by Pope Gregory II despite their political alliance against the interference of the Byzantine emperor in Italy. Liutprand's forces temporarily capture the Byzantine city of Ravenna.

738
- Allah bin al-Habbab, the Umayyad governor of the Maghreb, sends an expedition across the Sahara "to the land of the blacks": it returns laden with slaves and gold.

739
- The Frankish victory over the Arabs at Tours in the Frankish kingdom in 732 gives the Christian king of Asturias in northwest Spain a chance to extend his frontiers into Lusitania (modern Portugal).

Human Rights

748
- Merchants in Venice, Italy, are commanded by Pope Zacharias to stop selling Christian slaves to the Muslim Arabs.

Politics and Government

c. **700**
- King Ine of Wessex, England, issues one of the earliest written Anglo-Saxon law codes. The fact that the area, which includes the modern counties of Dorset and Somerset, still contains many Celts, is shown by a reference to a separate class called Welshmen. Most crimes are punishable by payments of compensation to the victims or their families.
- Teotihuacán in the Valley of Mexico, for over 500 years the dominant power of Mesoamerica (the area of the Mexican and Mayan civilizations), is sacked and burned by unknown attackers and abandoned.
- The gold- and cattle-rich kingdom of Ghana is founded on the west African Sahel: it is probably the first state to develop in sub-Saharan Africa.
- The wealthy state of Moche on the coast of Peru is conquered by the militaristic Andean empire of Huari, which is now reaching the height of its power.

701
- The Taiho laws are issued in Japan, the earliest systematic civil and penal code in that country.

702
- The Arab governor in Byzantine Africa, Musa, completes the pacification of the Berbers (also known as Moors) and they soon become enthusiastic converts to Islam.

705
- Aided by Tervel, Khan (ruler) of the Bulgars, the exiled Byzantine emperor Justinian II returns to Constantinople and the deposed emperor Leontius, his successor, Tiberius II, and most of their followers are massacred.
- Arab caliph Walid builds schools, roads, and houses for the poor and diseased, especially lepers. His governor in Mesopotamia, Hajjaj, restores irrigation.

February   Popular discontent with her depraved courtiers leads to a rebellion against the empress Wu Hou of China. She is compelled to abdicate in favor of her son

Zhongzong, and she retires to her palace where she dies in December.

709

- Bukhara, on the central Asian Silk Road, is taken by the Arabs.

710

- The Japanese empress Gemmyo establishes Nara as the first permanent center for the court and the government. The design for the city is based on that of the Chinese capital Chang-an.

711

- The Byzantine emperor Justinian II's ruthless pursuit of his political opponents causes discontent and fear. When he sends an expedition to punish the people of Cherson who ill-treated him while in exile in the Crimea, the army and navy rebel. Bardanes, an Armenian general, is proclaimed emperor (under the name Philipicus). He sails to Constantinople and captures and executes Justinian and his family.

July 7   At the invitation of the rebel governor of Ceuta, the Arabs and their Moorish allies invade the Visigoth kingdom of Spain. Led by the Moorish chief Tariq, the Muslim army lands at Gibraltar (*Jebel el-Tariq*, "the mountain of Tariq"). At the battles of Guadelete and Ecija the smaller Arab army decisively defeats Roderick, the last Visigoth king of Spain, and before the end of the year the Visigoth capital of Toledo falls without resistance. Except for the mountainous northwest, all of Spain comes under Muslim control within two years.

712

- The accession of Liutprand to the Lombard throne in northern Italy, after a period of dynastic instability, begins a period of territorial expansion and increased prosperity.

713

- The Byzantine emperor Philippicus is deposed in favor of the chief imperial secretary, who becomes a capable but short-lived emperor as Anastasius II.
- Xuanzong becomes the sixth emperor of the Chinese Tang dynasty. During his long and prosperous reign (43 years), the Tang dynasty achieves its greatest power and prestige.

714–717

- The Frankish mayor of the palace, Pepin II the Stout, dies. After three years of civil war, his illegitimate son Charles Martel the Hammer makes himself undisputed ruler of the Frankish kingdom, uniting Neustria and Austrasia. Like his father before him, Charles rules in the capacity of mayor of the palace, maintaining the Merovingian king, Chilperic III, as a powerless figurehead.

716

- Aethelbald becomes king of Mercia, England. During his 41-year reign he makes Mercia the leading Anglo-Saxon kingdom.

716–717   The Byzantine emperor Anastasius II is deposed while attempting to discipline his army. He is followed, unwillingly, by Theodosius III, who abdicates the following year in favor of the general of the army in Asia Minor and a savior of the Empire, Leo III the Isaurian.

717

- The Arabs make their last and greatest effort to take Constantinople, the capital of the Byzantine Empire. The city's walls and defenders both hold out through a winter siege and the Arabs retreat with heavy losses.

718

- Resistance to the Arabs has continued in northwest Spain, and following a convincing victory at Covadonga, the Visigoth Pelaya makes himself king of Asturias. In Spanish tradition this victory marks the beginning of the Christian *Reconquista* ("Reconquest").

719

- Duke Eudo (or Eudas) of Aquitaine acknowledges the sovereignty of the Frankish mayor of the palace, Charles Martel.

721

- Duke Eudo of Aquitaine checks the invading Arabs and Moors near Toulouse, in the south of modern France.

724

- Hishām becomes caliph (civic and religious leader of Islam). His reign sees the decline of the Arab Umayyad dynasty and the end of the period of runaway Muslim Arab conquests.

725

- Charles Martel, the Frankish mayor of the palace, defeats an invasion of the Frankish kingdom by the Alemanni and Saxons. The invading Arabs, moving northward, take the town of Autun (now in central France), but Duke Eudo of Aquitaine stops their further advance.

729

- Pi-lo-ko founds the Thai kingdom of Nanchao (in what is now Yunnan, southern China) by uniting six rival Thai chiefdoms.

730–760

- Under Naghabata I, the first king of the Pratihara dynasty, the Gurjaras become the dominant power of northwest India, stemming Arab advances beyond the Indus River.

731

- Duke Eudo of Aquitaine suffers a defeat by Arab and Moorish forces at Arles, in the south of the Frankish Kingdom.

732

- The Arab general Abd-ar-Rahman resumes the offensive against Duke Eudo of Aquitaine. Eudo is forced to appeal for help to the Frankish mayor of the palace, Charles Martel, who defeats Abd-ar-Rahman at the Battle of Tours (sometimes called the Battle of Poitiers) in the Frankish kingdom, decisively halting the advance of the Arabs into Europe. As a result of this victory Charles Martel earns his title of Martel the Hammer.

733

- The Byzantine emperor Leo III the Isaurian sends a fleet to Italy to force Pope Gregory II to accept his iconoclastic decree of 730, but the fleet is wrecked.

734

- The Frankish mayor of the palace, Charles Martel, sends a fleet against the pagan Frisians who are forced to pay tribute after their pagan shrines are destroyed.

735

- Duke Eudo of Aquitaine dies after inflicting, in alliance with the Frankish mayor of the palace, Charles Martel, further defeats on the Arabs. Charles Martel takes over Aquitaine, allowing Eudo's son to take the title of duke.

737

- The Frankish mayor of the palace, Charles Martel, retakes the city of Avignon in Provence from the Arabs.

739

- The Frankish mayor of the palace, Charles Martel, supported by King Liutprand of the Lombards of northern Italy, finally succeeds in driving the Arabs and Moors out of Provence, southern France, having laid waste to much of the countryside and burned the amphitheater at Nîmes.

740

- The Byzantine emperor Leo III the Isaurian defeats the Arabs at Acroinon in Anatolia.

741

- Pepin the Short and Carloman jointly succeed their father, Charles Martel, as Frankish mayors of the palace—Carloman is to rule the west (Neustria) and Pepin the east (Austrasia). Zacharias succeeds Gregory III as pope; Walid II succeeds Hishām as caliph (ruler of the Islamic world); and Constantine V, a militant iconoclast, succeeds Leo III the Isaurian as Byzantine emperor.

743

- Pope Zacharias prevails upon the Lombard king, Liutprand, to halt the southward expansion of his kingdom in Italy.

744

- The Umayyad caliphate slides into political anarchy following the assassination of the caliph (ruler of the Islamic world) Walid II.

747

- Carloman, the Frankish mayor of the palace of Neustria, retires to a monastery. His brother, Pepin the Short, mayor of the palace of Austrasia, becomes the ruler of the whole Frankish kingdom.
- Discontent among new converts to Islam over the tax and political privileges of the Arabs leads to the outbreak of a rebellion in Khorasan (Persia) against the Umayyad caliph Merwan II.

749

- Abu-al-Abbas, a descendant of the Islamic prophet Muhammad, becomes the leader of the revolt against the caliph Merwan II, the last of the Umayyad dynasty, after being proclaimed caliph (civic and religious leader of Islam) by the rebels at Kufa (Iraq).

SCIENCE, TECHNOLOGY, AND MEDICINE

Agriculture

710

- Cane sugar is cultivated in Egypt for the first time.

Health and Medicine

706

- The first Islamic hospital, the Bimāristān or "Asylum of the Sick," is founded in Damascus. Initially for the treatment of leprosy only, it soon attracts leading Arab physicians, and becomes a medical school.

745

- Bubonic plague arrives in the Byzantine capital of Constantinople, and spreads from there into Europe.

Math

703

- The English monk and historian Bede compiles *De temporibus/On Times*, a brief treatise on chronology and the calculation of Easter.

729

- Chinese astronomer and monk I Hsing, Director of the Imperial Astronomical Bureau, introduces a new calendar, the *Dayan Li* into China, correcting many errors in the earlier version.

Science

700

- Persian scientists make measurements of windspeed using the rotation of windmills.

712

- The English monk Bede, writing his *Historia ecclesiastica gentis Anglorus/Ecclesiastical History of the English People* in the monastery of Jarrow around this time, covers scientific subjects—mathematics, chronology, and grammar—as well as history.

725

- *c. 725* The Arab alchemist Abu Masa Dshaffar is working. According to some sources, he discovers methods for the manufacture of mineral acids and silver nitrate.
- The Chinese astronomer and monk I Hsing, using instruments made by engineer Liang Ling-Tsan, measures the deviation of star coordinates from their expected values, taking precession from the earth's orbit into account. In this way, he discovers the "proper motion" of the stars.

732

- The Indian astronomer Qutan Zhuan accuses the Chinese monk I Hsing of copying the Indian Navagraha

Reconquista of Spain (718–1492)

718
- Resistance to the Arabs has continued in northwest Spain, and following a convincing victory at Covadonga, the Visigoth Pelaya makes himself king of Asturias. In Spanish tradition this victory marks the beginning of the Christian *Reconquista* ("Reconquest").

862
- King Ordoño I of Asturias captures the Spanish city of Salamanca from the Moors.

866
- Alfonso III becomes king of Asturias, Spain. He becomes known as "the Great" for his successful wars against the Moors.

868
- King Alfonso III recaptures Oporto from the Moors.

874
- Alfonso the Great defeats the Moors of Toledo at the Orbedo.

893
- Alfonso the Great defeats and kills Ahmad ibn-Mu'awiyah, who claims to be the Mahdi (messiah), at Zamora, Spain.

939
July 22 King Ramiro II of León, Spain, defeats Abd-ar-Rahman III, the Umayyad caliph (Islamic ruler) of Córdoba at Simancas, near Valladolid in northwestern Spain.

981
- Al-Mansur, regent of the Umayyad caliphate of Córdoba, takes the city of Zamora and subjugates the kingdom of León.

985
July 1 Almanzor, regent of the Umayyad caliphate of Córdoba, sacks the northeastern Spanish city of Barcelona.

988
- Abu Amir al-Mansur (Almanzor), the Umayyad regent of Córdoba, razes the Spanish city of León and makes its king a tributary to the caliphate of Córdoba.

996
- Almanzor, leading the army of the caliph (Islamic ruler) of Córdoba, sacks León.

997
- Almanzor sacks the Church of Santiago de Compostela in a raid into Galicia in northwestern Spain.

1000–1300

1002
August 10 Almanzor dies after his defeat at Calatañazor by the kings of León and Navarre. He is succeeded by his son, al-Muzaffar.

1003
- Moorish forces from the Umayyad caliphate of southern Spain devastate the kingdom of León.

1027
May 5 Alfonso V of León is killed at the siege of Viseu, Spain, which was lost earlier in the century to the caliphate of Córdoba. He is succeeded by his son, Vermudo III.

1108
May 29 Alfonso I is defeated by 'Ali, the Almoravid emir of Morocco and Muslim Spain, at Uclés, near Tarancón.

1113
- Raymond Berengar III, Count of Barcelona, and the Pisans begin their conquest of the Balearic Islands from the Moors.

1115
- The Christian conquest of the Balearic Islands from the Moors is completed; Raymond Berengar III takes possession of the islands of Majorca and Ibiza.

1118
December 19 King Alfonso I of Aragon and Navarre captures the city of Zaragoza in northeast Spain from the Muslim ruler of the Almoravids.

1120
- Alfonso I defeats the Muslims at Cutanda and Daroca.

1125
- Alfonso I leads a spectacular raid deep into Moorish Spain, liberating the Mozarabs (Spanish Christians living under Muslim rule) of Granada and resettling them in the north of Iberia. Few Christians now remain under Muslim rule in Spain.

1126
- Alfonso I defeats the Muslims at Arinsol, near Lucena.

1134
July 17 Alfonso I is defeated by the Muslims at Fraga.

1144
- Alfonso VII of Castile and León, Emperor of Spain, briefly takes Córdoba from the Almoravid Emirate.

1147
- Alfonso VII besieges Almería.

April 4 The Almohad Mahdi (Muslim leader) Abd-al-Mumin completes his conquest of the Almoravid possessions in Morocco with the capture of the capital city of Marrakesh; he then crosses into Spain, where the Almoravid emirate has disintegrated into several kingdoms established in Córdoba, Valencia, Murcia, and other areas.

October 25 English and Flemish crusaders, interrupting their voyage to the Holy Land to join the Second Crusade, assist in the capture of the city of Lisbon from the Moors by King Alfonso of Portugal.

1148
- Raymond Berengar III, Count of Barcelona, takes the city of Tortosa from the Moors.

1149
- Abd-al-Mumin completes his conquest of the Muslim emirates in Spain.

1158
- The Order of Knights of Santiago, a Christian military order, is founded in Castile, Spain, to counteract the Moors. Its members adhere to the Augustinian rule but are allowed to marry and own personal possessions, which is most unusual for military orders.

1177
- Alfonso VIII takes the city of Cuenca from the Muslims.

1179
- King Alfonso VIII of Castile and King Alfonso II of Aragon conclude a treaty defining the boundary between their future conquests within Spain from the Muslims.

1212
July 16   The Spanish kings Alfonso VIII of Castile, Sancho VII of Navarre, and Pedro II of Aragon, and a few crusaders win a decisive victory over the Almohads at Las Navas de Tolosa. Muslim power in Spain is permanently broken.

1213
- Alfonso VIII defeats an invasion by the Muslim Almohads at Febragaen.

1217
September 25   King Afonso II of Portugal defeats the Muslims at Alcazar do Sal.

1225
- King Ferdinand III of Castile takes the town of Andújar in his first campaign against the Muslims.

1228
- King James I of Aragon begins the conquest of the Balearic Islands.

1229
- King Alfonso IX of León takes the Spanish city of Badajoz from the Muslims.

December 31   James I takes Palma, the capital of the Balearic island of Majorca.

1232
- The Muslims of the Balearic island of Minorca surrender to James I.

1235
- With the capture of Ibiza, James I completes his conquest of the Balearic Islands.

1236
June 29   King Ferdinand III takes Córdoba.

1237
- James I conquers the Spanish kingdom of Murcia from the Muslims.

1238
September 9   James I takes Valencia from the Moors.

1241
- The Muslim king of Murcia becomes the vassal of King Ferdinand III of Castile and León.

1244
- Ferdinand III and James I ratify, at Almizra, the treaty of 1179 defining their frontier in newly conquered Muslim lands.

1246
- Mohammad, the Muslim king of Granada, cedes the town of Jaén to Ferdinand II Castile and becomes his vassal.

1247
August 20   Ferdinand III begins his siege of the Muslim city of Seville in southern Spain.

1248
December 22   Seville surrenders to Ferdinand III.

1257
- King Alfonso X of Castile and León and King Mohammad ibn Nasr of Granada expel the last Almohads (members of a Muslim dynasty of Berbers) from Spain.

1262
September 14   Alfonso X takes the city of Cadiz.

1263
- Alfonso X takes Cartagena, southeast Spain. He also cedes the Algarve to Dinis, son of King Afonso III of Portugal.

1266
- Alfonso X, aided by James I, conquers the kingdom of Murcia, taking it from the Muslims and leaving King Mohammad I of Granada as the last Muslim vassal of Castile.

1300–1492

1309
- Guzmán el Bueno takes Gibraltar from the Moors. Valencia is permanently annexed to Aragon.

1340
October 30   Alfonso XI of Castile and his ally Alfonso IV of Portugal defeat a Moslem army from Morocco at Rio Sadade.

1344
- Alfonso IV captures Algeciras.

1481
December 26   Murley Abul Hassan, King of Granada, captures Zahora in Cadiz.

1485
- King Ferdinand of Castile destroys Grenada, the last Moorish outpost in Spain.

1487
August   A Christian Spanish army captures Milagu.

1492
January 2   Granada surrenders to overwhelming Spanish force, bringing to an end nearly 800 years of warfare.

calendar for his *Dayan Li* system, introduced in 729. However, a competition proves Hsing's calendar is far more accurate.

742

- The most famous alchemist of the period, Jābir ibn-Hayyān of Kufa (Geber in Iraq), practices as a physician at Kufa, Persia. He becomes court physician to the caliph Harun ar-Rashid. He is said to have been the first person to manufacture mineral acids (nitric acid, etc.)

748

- A missionary in Bavaria called Vergilius (possibly the Irishman Ferghil, later bishop of Salzburg) is censured by the Pope for believing in the existence of the Antipodes.

Technology

c. 700

- Native Americans abandon the hunting spear in favor of the bow and arrow.

725

- Chinese inventor Yi Xing devises an early form of hydraulically powered escapement, a devise for slowing and regulating the mechanism of clocks.

ARTS AND IDEAS

Architecture

725

- The Native American settlement at Casa Grande, Arizona, incorporates a fortress and extensive irrigation works for the surrounding lands.

c. 730

- The Umayyad palace is built at Khirbat al-Mafjar near Jericho (now in Jordan).

Arts

c. 700

- Wu Tao-tzu, the most famous painter of the T'ang period, known as the "Sage of Painting," is active around this time. None of his works survive.

706

- The tomb of the Princess Yong Tai is built at Chang-an, China. The many wall paintings include the near life-sized depiction of her waiting women in the burial chamber.

713

- Chinese emperor Hsuan Tsung inaugurates a "second blossoming" of Tang culture. He encourages poets, artists, and scholars, and establishes colleges of music.

c. 740

- Wang Wei, Chinese painter, poet, and calligrapher, is active around this time. None of his paintings survive

but he is credited with developing a contemplative style of monochrome landscape painting which was highly influential.

Literature and Language

c. 700

- Japanese poet Kakinomoto Hitomaro is active in this period. As well as producing hundreds of short poems (*tanka*), he raises the art of writing long poems (*choka*) to new heights.

704

- The earliest known printed book, the Buddhist text *Dharani Sutra*, is written; it is discovered in modern South Korea on October 14, 1966.

c. 740

- Under the patronage of Hsuan Tsung, Chinese poetry breaks with the formal conventions of the past and takes on a greater fluency and realism. Two of China's greatest poets, Li Po and Tu Fu, are active at this time.

Music

c. 700

- The Schola Cantorum (Choir School), a school in Rome for the training of church musicians, exists by the beginning of the 8th century.

Theater and Dance

c. 745

- Indian dramatist Bhavabhuti is active during this period. Regarded as the greatest Sanskrit playwright after Kalidasa, his two best known plays are versions of stories from the *Ramayana*.

Thought and Scholarship

720

- The oldest official history of Japan, the *Nihongi/Record of Nippon*, is compiled by order of the imperial court.

725

- English Benedictine scholar Bede, working at the monastery of Jarrow in Northumbria, writes *De temporum ratione/On the Reckoning of Time*, a combination of chronology and astronomy devised to calculate the accurate date of Easter.

c. 731

- The English Benedictine scholar Bede completes his greatest surviving work, *Historia ecclesiastica gentis Anglorum/Ecclesiastical History of the English People*.

SOCIETY

Media and Communication

748
- Printed newspapers are circulated for the first time in China.

Religion

703
- Bede is ordained a priest and devotes his life to scholarship, in particular the study of the Bible.

705
- *c.* 705 Zoroastrians, escaping from the Muslim occupation of their Persian homeland, arrive in India where they form a community and become known as Parsees.
- Under the Caliph Walid, several major Islamic monuments are built, including the great mosque of Damascus which is completed in 715.

712
- The *Kojiki/Record of Ancient Things* is compiled in Japan. More legend than history, it contains information about court ceremonial, religious practices, and mythology.

719
- The English Benedictine monk St. Boniface, known as "the Apostle of Germany," converts many of the Hessians in Bavaria and Thuringia.

c. **720**
- The Benedictine monastery of St. Gall in the north of modern Switzerland is founded. It becomes the most important center of learning north of the Alps and its scriptorium forms the basis of an outstanding library.

721
- The book of the Lindisfarne Gospels is produced, in memory of St. Cuthbert, by the hermit Eadfrith. Its richly decorated pages are one of the best examples of Hiberno-Saxon art.

725
- Influenced by the Muslims' rejection of religious icons, the Byzantine emperor Leo III the Isaurian speaks out against the use of religious images in preparation for a campaign of iconoclasm (destruction of religious images).

BIRTHS & DEATHS

701
- Li Po, one of China's greatest poets, born in Szechwan province, China (–762).

September 8 Sergius I, Italian pope 687–701, dies.

705
October Abd-al-Malik (ibn Marwan), fifth caliph of the Umayyad dynasty 685–705, who made Arabic the language of administration throughout the Arab empire, dies in Damascus, Syria (*c.* 58).

December 16 Wu Hou, Chinese concubine who became Empress of China 655–705, and unified the Chinese empire, dies in China (80).

709
April 24 St. Wilfrid, English bishop who established close links between the papacy and the Anglo-Saxon church, dies in the monastery of Oundle, Mercia (–75).

711
December Justinian II, Byzantine emperor 685–711, killed in Asia Minor.

712
- Tu Fu, great Chinese poet, born in Hsiang-yang, Honan province, China (–770).

c. **714**
- Pepin III ("the Short"), de facto ruler of the Franks from 747, King of the Franks 751–768 and first in the Frankish Carolingian dynasty, born (–768).

715
- al-Walid I, sixth caliph 705–715 of the Umayyad dynasty, famous for the mosques constructed during his reign, dies in Damascus, Syria (*c.* 47).

718
- Constantine V, Byzantine emperor 741–775, born in Constantinople (–775).

722
- Abu al-Abbas as-Saffah, first caliph of the Abbasid dynasty 749–754, born (–754).

728
- al-Hasan al-Basri, Muslim ascetic who founded two schools of Sunni Islam: the Mutazilah (Philosophical theologians), and Ashari-yah (followers of the theologian al-Ashari), dies in Basra, Iraq (*c.* 86).

731
February 11 St. Gregory, Pope Gregory II 715–731, dies in Rome (*c.* 64).

735
- Alcuin, Anglo-Latin poet, educator, and cleric, born in York, England (–804).
- Duke Eudes of Aquitaine, who called the Saracens to his aid against Charles Martel of France (732), dies.

May 25 St. Bede (Baeda or Beda; "the Venerable Bede"), Anglo-Saxon theologian, historian, and chronologist, known chiefly for his *Historia ecclesiastica gentis Anglorum/Ecclesiastical History of the English People* (731), dies in Jarrow, England (*c.* 63).

741
- Hishām ibn Abd-al-Malik, tenth caliph 724–743, dies in Damascus, Syria.

June 18 Leo III, Byzantine emperor 717–741, successful military commander, iconoclast, dies in Constantinople (*c.* 61).

October 22 Charles Martel, ruler of the Franks 719–741, who defeated the Saracens at the Battle of Poitiers (732), dies in Quierzy-sur-Oise, France (*c.* 53).

November St. Gregory, Pope Gregory III 731–741, dies.

742
April 2 Charlemagne (Carolus Magnus), King of the Franks 768–814 and Frankish emperor 800–814, who united much of western Europe under his rule, born (–814).

744
- Liutprand of Lombardy, Lombard king of Italy 712–744, dies.

749
January 25 Leo IV, Byzantine emperor 775–780, born (–780).

- The Danish king Angantyr receives the Anglo-Saxon missionary Willibrord on the first Christian mission to Scandinavia. Willibrord is listened to politely but makes no converts.

726

- Byzantine emperor Leo III the Isaurian issues an edict ordering the destruction of any image representing Christ, the Virgin Mary, or the saints in human form. Pope Gregory II summons the western bishops to oppose the edict, but the dispute between the Iconoclasts (image-breakers) and those who sanction the use of images for religious purposes continues for over 100 years.
- Pope Gregory II resists the Byzantine emperor Leo III the Isaurian not only for his iconoclastic views but also on account of excessive taxation. He begins a process, continued by his successor, Gregory III, of emancipating the papacy from the control of the Byzantine emperor.

730

- Byzantine emperor Leo III's iconoclasm arouses much opposition in the Empire and a rival emperor is proclaimed in Greece but he and his fleet are defeated while attempting to capture the Byzantine capital, Constantinople. Of more lasting consequence, it also arouses great hostility in the Latin West where religious images have great importance as teaching aids in missionary activity, thus beginning the gradual alienation of the Greek Orthodox and Roman Catholic churches. Pope Gregory II refuses to implement the decree. The monk John of Damascus attacks the Iconoclasts in a series of pamphlets. He remains safe from persecution by Leo III because he resides in Muslim territory.

c. 740

- The Khazars, who live between the Sea of Azov and the Lower Volga, are converted to Judaism by traveling Jewish merchants.

742

c. 742 The English Benedictine monk St. Boniface begins reforming the church in France, imposing the Rule of St. Benedict on all Carolingian monasteries.
- Buddhism combines with the ancient indigenous cult of Shinto to form the syncretistic Ryobu Shinto in Japan. Shinto deities are regarded as manifestations of Buddhist deities.

743

c. 743 Buddhism thrives in Japan under the sponsorship of Emperor Shomu. A bronze *daibutsu* or Great Buddha, 16 m/53 ft in height, is made for the Todaiji temple at Nara.
- Caliph Walid II builds a winter palace at Mshatta in the Syrian desert. Its façade contains an ornately carved frieze of repeated triangles, an early example of a distinctly Islamic style.

744

- A Benedictine abbey is founded by a pupil of St. Boniface at Fulda in Germany.

Sports

c. 700

- A swimming race is described in the Anglo-Saxon epic poem *Beowulf*.

750–799

POLITICS, GOVERNMENT, AND ECONOMICS

Business and Economics

751

- Islamic craftsmen in the Middle East learn the secret of paper manufacture from Chinese captured during the Muslim conquest of Samarkand. The Arab paper industry rapidly develops.

778

- King Offa of Mercia introduces the English silver penny. Its manufacture is strictly controlled at mints in London, Kent, and East Anglia.

Colonization

c. 750

- Taking advantage of the power vacuum caused by the fall of Teotihuacán in about 700, the Toltecs, a coalition of tribal farming peoples, migrate into the Valley of Mexico.

Politics and Government

750

- Abu-al-Abbas, founder of the Abbasid dynasty of Arab Islamic rulers, defeats the Umayyad caliph Merwan II at the Battle of the River Zab. Merwan flees to Egypt but is caught and killed and his head is sent to Abu. Abu-al-Abbas's victory is followed by a general massacre of the Umayyad family and of members of his own family whose popularity he fears, for which he earns the nickname *as-Saffah*, "the blood-shedder."
- King Aistulf of the Lombards, Liutprand's successor, takes the city of Ravenna, the last major Byzantine stronghold in northern Italy, and demands suzerainty over Rome as part of his enlarged dominion. Pope Zacharias appeals unsuccessfully for help from the exarch (governor) Eutyehius .

751

- Following an appeal from the ruler of Tashkent for military assistance, the Arabs defeat the Chinese at the Battle of the Talas River near Samarkand, causing the collapse of the Chinese Empire in central Asia. Chinese craftsmen captured after the battle introduce papermaking into the Middle East.
- With Pope Zacharias's support, the Frankish mayor of the palace Pepin the Short deposes Childeric III, the last king of the Merovingian dynasty, and is crowned king of the Franks by St. Boniface at Soissons in the Frankish kingdom, founding the Carolingian dynasty. Childeric, who has been a mere figurehead under Pepin's control, is allowed to retire to a monastery.

753

- Pope Stephen III travels to the Frankish kingdom to ask for King Pepin the Short's help against Aistulf, the Lombard king who is threatening Rome.

754

- The Abbasid caliph Abu-al-Abbas dies of smallpox and is followed as caliph (ruler of the Islamic world) by his half brother Mansur.

755

- Answering Pope Stephen III's appeal for help against the Lombard king, Aistulf, the Frankish king Pepin the Short invades Italy. Besieged by Pepin in Pavia, Lombardy, Aistulf promises to respect the papal lands in Italy.
- The threat of frequent invasions by the Tibetans and steppe nomads leads to a buildup of the Chinese army and an increase in the power of the military governors, culminating in the rebellion of An Lushan, a general of Turkish origin. He seizes the capital Siking (modern Xian), forcing Emperor Xuanzong to flee. Shortly after he is forced to abdicate in favor of his son, Suzong.

756

- The Moors in Spain break away from the Abbasid caliphate to form an independent emirate under Abd-ar-Rahman I, one of the few survivors of the Abbasid caliph Abu-al-Abbas's massacre of the Umayyad family in 750. He makes the southern Spanish city of Córdoba his capital. This marks the beginning of the breakup of the political unity of the Muslim world which has endured since the time of Muhammad, the prophet and founder of Islam.

757

- A short civil war following the death of King Aethelbald results in his cousin Offa becoming king of Mercia, England. Offa reigns for 39 years and brings about the height of Mercian power, making it the leading Anglo-Saxon kingdom. He is addressed by the Popes as "king of England" without qualification. During his reign he builds a 272-km/69-mi-long rampart ("Offa's Dyke") to define the border between his kingdom and the Welsh, one of the most ambitious engineering works of early medieval Europe.
- The Chinese rebel general An Lushan is murdered by one of his officers but the revolt against the Tang dynasty in China continues under another general, Shi Ssu-ming.
- When King Aistulf of Lombardy again threatens Rome, the Frankish king Pepin the Short again invades Italy in support of Pope Stephen III. Pepin takes the city of Ravenna from the Lombards and gives it to the Pope—the so-called "Donation of Pepin." Aistulf dies following a riding accident soon afterwards and is succeeded by Desiderius.

759

- The Frankish king Pepin the Short finally expels the Arab and Moorish invaders from Septimania (modern Languedoc, southern France).

762

- The Abbasid caliph Mansur founds a new capital for himself at Baghdad in Mesopotamia (modern Iraq). The effect of the foundation of Baghdad is profound: the Muslim Arabs change from being military conquerors to become liberal administrators of the Arab caliphate. Mansur discourages speculation, and is financially efficient. His parsimony earns him the name "Father of Farthings."

763

- The rebellion against the Chinese Tang dynasty, begun by An Lushan in 755, is finally put down, but the authority of the dynasty has been permanently weakened. Tibetans sack the Chinese capital, Changan (modern Xian), which has only just been recaptured from the rebels.

768

- Pepin the Short, King of the Franks, dies and his kingdom is divided between his two sons, Charles (known to history as Charlemagne) and Carloman.

769

- The Frankish kings Charlemagne and Carloman quarrel over the division of the Frankish kingdom after the death of their father, Pepin III the Short. The Byzantine emperor Constantine V's son, Leo IV, marries Irene, an orphan from Athens, later to become empress and regent.

770

- The quarreling Frankish kings Charlemagne and Carloman are reconciled by their mother, Bertha, who tries to arrange marriages for them with the daughters of King Desiderius of the Lombards of northern Italy. Only Charlemagne's marriage takes place and he divorces the girl the following year, causing a rift in Frankish relations with the Lombards.

771

- The Frankish king Carloman dies, leaving his brother, Charlemagne, aged 29, sole ruler of the Frankish kingdom.

772

- Charlemagne, King of the Franks, begins his long war against the pagan Saxons to the north by attacking and destroying the sacred shrine of an idol called the Irminsul.

773

- The Lombard king Desiderius threatens Rome and Pope Hadrian (Adrian) I appeals to the Franks for help. Charlemagne, King of the Franks, crosses the Alps and besieges Desiderius in Pavia, Lombardy.

774

- The Lombard city of Pavia is taken by the Franks and Charlemagne, King of the Franks, banishes the Lombard king, Desiderius, to a monastery. Charlemagne promptly assumes the crown of Lombardy in northern Italy, confirms his father's "donation" to the papacy of 757, and accepts the role of protector of the church. Charlemagne and Pope Hadrian I become close friends and allies.

775

- Charlemagne, King of the Franks and Lombards, resolves to complete the conquest of the pagan Saxons to the north and convert them to Christianity or exterminate them in the process.
- The Abbasid caliph Mansur dies on a pilgrimage to Mecca and is succeeded as caliph (ruler of the Islamic world) by his son, Al Mahdi, a generous patron of the arts.
- The Byzantine emperor, Constantine V, dies and is succeeded by his son, Leo IV, with his empress, Irene.

777

- Charlemagne, King of the Franks and Lombards, holds an assembly at Paderborn in Saxony. With the exception of Widukind, who takes refuge with the Danes, the Saxon leaders submit to Charlemagne and accept Christianity.

778

- Asked to interfere in the quarrels of the Muslim Arabs in Spain, Charlemagne, King of the Franks and Lombards, crosses the Pyrenees and advances as far as Zaragoza, before turning back on hearing news that the Saxons have rebelled. Passing through a narrow pass of the mountains at Roncesvalles, his rearguard is cut to pieces by Basques, and many high officials, including Roland, the Count of the Breton March, are killed. The battle is immortalized in the 11th-century *chanson de geste* ("song of exploits"), the *Chanson de Roland/Song of Roland*.

780

- The Buddhist Sailendra family in Java becomes the dominant political force.

September 28   The Byzantine emperor, Leo IV, dies and his widow, the empress Irene, rules in the name of her ten-year old son, Constantine VI.

781

- Under the terms of an agreement made with Charlemagne, King of the Franks and Lombards, and

Pope Hadrian I, the Byzantine regent Irene abandons all claim to sovereignty over the Papal State.

782

- The Abbasid caliph Al Mahdi's son Harun leads an Arab invasion of Byzantine Anatolia and advances as far as the Bosporus, gaining the title *al-Rashid* ("the Upright") for his conduct. The Byzantine empress Irene is forced to pay an indemnity.
- The Frankish king Charlemagne's *Capitulatio de partibus Saxoniae/Capitulary Concerning the Regions of Saxony* punishes by death a number of pagan and anti-Christian practices, including eating meat in Lent, human sacrifice, ritual cannibalism, and burning the dead on a pagan pyre. In the same year Charlemagne orders the execution of 4,500 Saxon rebels at Verdun on the River Aller in Saxony.

785

- With the intention of strengthening his authority, King Offa of Mercia creates a third English archbishopric at Lichfield. It is officially abolished in 803.
- Yahya the Barmakid (of a Persian priestly family) tries to persuade the Abbasid caliph Al Mahdi to appoint his younger son, Harun ar-Rashid, as his heir, at the expense of his elder son, Al Hadi. When Al Mahdi dies without officially changing the succession, Harun is persuaded by Yahya to agree to his elder brother's accession.

786

- The Abbasid caliph Al Hadi dies and is succeeded as caliph (ruler of the Islamic world) by his younger brother, Harun ar-Rashid. Al Hadi is said to have been murdered by his mother, who favors Harun. Harun makes Yahya the Barmakid his vizier and gives him and his four sons great powers. Harun reigns until 809, presiding over a golden age of Arab civilization.

788–791

- Charlemagne, King of the Franks and Lombards, successfully campaigns against the Slavs and Avars from the middle-Danube basin.

789

- Dragowit, King of the Slavic Wiltzite tribe, submits to Charlemagne, King of the Franks and Lombards, in the face of an overwhelming Frankish invasion.
- The first recorded Viking raid in England occurs at Portland in the kingdom of Wessex. The king's reeve Beaduheard is murdered when he mistakes the Norsemen for merchants.

790

- A dispute between King Offa of Mercia, England, and Charlemagne, King of the Franks and Lombards, over a diplomatic marriage disrupts cross-Channel trade.
- Charlemagne, King of the Franks and Lombards, orders no military campaign this year, the only year of peace in his 45-year reign.
- Her support for the use of religious icons makes the Byzantine empress Irene unpopular with the army, which favors iconoclasm. When her son, Constantine VI, comes of age, the army arrests her and forces her to retire from the regency.

791

- Charlemagne, King of the Franks and Lombards, launches a meticulously planned attack on the Avars, a Hunnish nomad people settled in Pannonia (modern Hungary). Avar resistance collapses almost immediately and Charlemagne's armies spend 52 days plundering the Avar lands, taking many prisoners and much treasure. The death of thousands of horses in an epidemic at the end of the expedition prevents major campaigning the following year.
- Following a crushing defeat by the Tibetans at Tingzhou, the Chinese lose control of the strategic Gansu Corridor, shutting them out of central Asia for nearly a thousand years.
- The caliph Harun ar-Rashid of Baghdad has his political rival the Imam Idris of the newly-independent Idrisid Caliphate (modern Morocco) assassinated by means of a poisoned toothpick.
- The deposed Byzantine empress, Irene, is restored to power by her son, Constantine VI, who makes her coruler.

792

- King Offa of Mercia annexes the minor Anglo-Saxon kingdom of East Anglia to Mercia. Of the Anglo-Saxon kingdoms, only Wessex and Northumbria retain their independence of Mercia.
- Pepin, the illegitimate son of Charlemagne, King of the Franks and Lombards, conspires against his father and is sent to a monastery.

793

- The Vikings sack the monastery of St. Cuthbert at Lindisfarne (Holy Island) off the coast of Northumbria, England; many monks are killed or taken prisoner. The destruction of one of the holiest sites in Britain by pagans causes shock throughout western Europe.

794

- The founding of Heian (modern Kyoto) as a new imperial capital for Japan ushers in a golden age of Japanese courtly culture.

June At the general assembly in Frankfurt, Charlemagne, King of the Franks and Lombards, legislates to reform the Frankish church and monasteries and introduces price controls to limit profiteering during times of famine.

795

- On the death of Hadrian I, Leo III becomes pope. He immediately recognizes Charlemagne, King of the Franks, as "patrician of the Romans."
- The Vikings begin to raid the Irish coast, sacking a church on Lambey Island near Dublin, Ireland.

796

- A commercial treaty is signed between King Offa of Mercia, England, and Charlemagne, King of the Franks and Lombards, ending a six-year dispute that began over a diplomatic marriage and disrupted trade between them.
- Pepin, the illegitimate son of Charlemagne, King of the Franks, completes the conquest of the Avar people, capturing their royal residence, the "ring," in Pannonia (modern Hungary). A huge amount of treasure, the accumulated plunder of centuries of Avar raids on their neighbors, is discovered by the Franks.

797

- The Byzantine empress Irene deposes and blinds her son, the emperor Constantine VI, and reigns as emperor (not empress).

799

- Empress Irene's usurpation of the Byzantine throne leads the Anglo-Saxon scholar Alcuin to argue that there is now no Roman emperor, hinting that Charlemagne, King of the Franks and Lombards, could legitimately claim the title.
- Pope Leo III is accused of misconduct and imprisoned by a Roman aristocratic faction but escapes to Charlemagne, King of the Franks and Lombards, who returns him to Rome under escort and demands that both Leo and his accusers appear before him in Rome the following year. This sets in motion the series of events that lead to the crowning of Charlemagne as Roman emperor in 800.

SCIENCE, TECHNOLOGY, AND MEDICINE

Agriculture

765

- The rotation of crops on a threefold system is first mentioned in Europe at this time. Rotation of a winter crop, a summer crop, and a fallow year rapidly improves agricultural yields.

Ecology

764

- A severe winter freezes the Bosporus linking Europe and Asia Minor and allows the channel to be crossed on foot.

Math

780–850

- Arab mathematician Muhammad ibn Musa al-Khwârizma writes *Al-jam' w'al-tafriq ib hisab al-hind/ Addition and Subtraction in Indian Arithmetic*, which introduces the Indian system of numbers to the West. His other book, *Hisab al-jabr w'almuqabala/Calculation by Restoration and Reduction* gives us the word "algebra," from "al-jabr."

Science

762

- Persian, Greek, and Jewish scholars flock to Caliph Mansur's newly established capital at Baghdad, in modern Iraq. The books of classical Greek science begin to be translated into Arabic.

765

- Mayan scientists hold a meeting to discuss astronomy and to adjust their calendar.

772

- Muslim astronomer Al-Fazāri translates the Indian astronomical compendium *Mahāsiddhānta/Treatise on Astronomy*, and begins the establishment of a uniquely Arabic astronomy.

786

- The new Abbasid caliph Harun ar-Rashid and the powerful Barmakid family increase their patronage of the sciences, particularly medicine, astronomy, and chemistry, but also astrology and alchemy. This spurs a great revival of the sciences.

Technology

764

- The earliest known printed work, a series of Buddhist chants prepared for the Japanese empress Shotoku, dates to around this time.

c. 765

- The technique of printing with carved wooden blocks has spread from China to Japan.

785

- The English king Offa of Mercia builds a dyke, a massive earthwork 240km/150 miles long, between the rivers Severn and Dee. It is intended as a defense against raiders from neighboring Wales.

793

- Charlemagne, King of the Franks and Lombards, begins construction of a canal linking tributaries of the great rivers Main and Danube. The project is abandoned when heavy rains cause the canal banks to collapse.

Transportation

783

- A boat built for the Chinese official Li Kao, governor of Hungchao, is propelled by two paddle wheels powered with animal-driven treadmills.

797

- Waystations are established for royal messengers to rest and change their horses on all the main routes through France.

ARTS AND IDEAS

Architecture

760

- At Ellora, in the Deccan province of India, the monolithic Kailasa cave temple represents the high point of Indian rock-cut architecture. Kailasa is a Hindu temple, but Ellora also contains fine Buddhist and Jain temples.

786

- The earliest part of the Great Mosque at Córdoba, Spain, introduces a unique system of double arches.

Arts

c. 786

- The Abbasid caliph Harun ar-Rashid encourages artistic activity at his court. Stories, founded on an earlier Persian collection of tales, are recorded in the archives and give rise to the legend of Scheherezade and the *Alf Laylah wa-Laylah/A Thousand and One Nights—The Arabian Nights*. Some of the tales involve Harun and his friend the great lyric poet Abu Nuwas.

Literature and Language

c. 759

- *Manyoshu*, an anthology of four centuries of Japanese poetry, appears. The most represented poet, Otomo Yakamochi, is probably one of the compilers.

c. 795

- *Hildesbrandslied/Song of Hildebrand*, the only extant example of heroic verse written in Old High German, is written. The surviving fragment tells of the personal combat between Hildebrand and his son.

Music

757

- The first wind organs are introduced into Europe from Byzantium—before this time, only water organs were known.

Thought and Scholarship

773

- The historian Paul the Deacon enters the monastery of Monte Cassino, Italy, where he writes his unfinished *History of the Lombards*.

787

- Abu Abd Allah ash-Shāfii, founder of the major Shafiite school of Islamic law, begins his legal studies under the jurist Abu Abdallah Malik ibn Anas in Medina (in modern Saudi Arabia).
- Charlemagne, King of the Franks and Lombards, issues a directive to his bishops encouraging the study of Latin literature and language in monasteries and bishop's houses. The palace school at Aachen, in the Frankish kingdom, becomes one of Europe's greatest centers of scholarship and learning.

799

c. 799 Shankara, the Brahman philosopher and theologian, is active in this period. An exponent of the Advaita

Vedanta school, he writes commentaries on the *Upanishads*, Hindu philosophical writings, which affirm his belief in an everlasting and unchanging reality.

- Han Yu, the Chinese essayist, returns to the Chinese capital Changan. A vehement anti-Buddhist, his neo-Confucian ideals of public service are exemplified by his essay "On the True Way."

SOCIETY

Education

750

- Chinese emperor Xuanzong founds the Hanlin academy, a center which attracts many of the country's finest scholars.

781

- Charlemagne, King of the Franks and Lombards, meets the scholars Alcuin of York, an Anglo-Saxon, and Paul the Deacon, a Lombard, in Italy and persuades them to come and teach at his palace school in Aachen in the Frankish kingdom. Both become leading figures in the revival of learning fostered by Charlemagne and known as the Carolingian Renaissance.

795

- Theodulph, bishop of Orléans in the Frankish kingdom, organizes free schools in the parishes of his diocese.

796

- Alcuin retires from the Aachen palace school in the Frankish kingdom to become abbot at Tours where he encourages work on the Carolingian miniscule script, the forerunner of lower case Roman type.

Everyday Life

750

- With a population now exceeding one million, Siking (modern Xian), the imperial capital of the Chinese Tang dynasty, is the largest city in the world.

768

- The accession of Charlemagne as king of the Franks marks the beginnings of medieval civilization as the king gathers to his court artists and scholars from across the world. Contemporaries call the period a *renovatio*, the renewal of a surviving tradition of Christian art and learning.

774

- The Chinese handbook of tea, the *Ch'a Ching/Tea Classic*, is written by Lu Yü. It introduces the idea of tea as a refreshment rather than a medicine.

799

- The last monuments are erected at the Mayan city of Palenque in Mesoamerica (the area of the Mexican and Mayan civilizations): it is abandoned soon afterwards, marking the beginning of the decline of the Classic Maya civilization. The causes of the decline are unknown but the most likely explanation is that soil exhaustion caused by overcultivation leads to the collapse of agriculture.

Religion

753

- The Byzantine emperor Constantine V calls the "Synod of Hieria" which intensifies the attack on icon-worshipers.

755

- Arab mercenaries stay in China where they form the nucleus of a Muslim population.
- The English Benedictine monk St. Boniface is murdered by pagans in northeastern Frisia.

757

- An Arabic philosophic school called the Mutazilites ("those who keep themselves apart") is founded. Its followers believe that man has free will, that the unity and transcendence of God can be proved through reason, and that the Koran was "created" rather than constituting the direct word of God.

758

- Abd-ar-Rahman I issues a letter giving protection to Christians in Spain.

760

- *c. 760* The building of a vast pyramidal Buddhist stupa at Borobudur in Java, Indonesia, the largest Buddhist monument in the world, is begun.
- On the death of the sixth Imam, his eldest son, Ismail, is only recognized as his successor by a minority of Shia Muslims. His followers call themselves Ismailis.

c. 763

- The *Life* of Muhammad is produced by ibn Hishām. It revises and expands the edition originally written by ibn Ishaq.

775

- The Byzantine empress Irene uses her influence to lessen the persecution of icon-worshipers.

776

- The abbey church of Saint-Denis in Paris, France, is consecrated in the presence of Emperor Charlemagne. It is designed with a three-aisled Roman basilica with two towers at the west end.

777

- At Paderborn, Saxony is divided into missionary districts and bishoprics. Monasteries are built, under Frankish supervision.

780

- Ceylon's city of Anuradhapura, with its great Buddhist stupas, is abandoned to the Tamils.

787

- The Byzantine empress Irene calls the Seventh Ecumenical Council of the Christian Church at Nicaea (modern Iznik, Turkey) to revoke the iconoclastic decree issued by the emperor Leo III the Isaurian in 730.

788

- The Umayyad dynasty, rulers of Muslim Spain, introduce a post of official astrologer at their court in Córdoba.

791

- Buddhism becomes the official state religion of Tibet.

c. 799

- The illuminated manuscript of the four Gospels known as the *Book of Kells* is produced. It is the last great work of the monastery of Iona in the Inner Hebrides, modern Scotland.

Sports

c. 754

- The Chinese board game *Wei'ch'i* is introduced to Japan where it becomes known as *go*.

BIRTHS & DEATHS

750
- Marwan II, last Umayyad caliph 744–750, is killed in Egypt by the forces of Abu al-Abbas as-Saffah, first Abbasid caliph (*c.* 66).
- Sankara (or Shankara, or Sankaracarya), Hindu philosopher and theologian, founder of the Advaita Vedanta school of philosophy, dies in Kedarnath, India (*c.* 50).

c. 751
- Carloman II, younger brother of Charlemagne, joint king of the Franks 754–771, born (–771).

752
- Irene, Byzantine empress jointly with her son Constantine VI 780–797 and then alone 797–802, a saint of the Greek Orthodox Church, born in Athens, Greece (–803).

754
- Abu al-Abbas as-Saffah, first caliph of the Abbasid dynasty 749–754, dies in Al-Anbar, Persia (*c.* 32).

755
June St. Boniface (original name Wynfrid or Wynfrith), English missionary and ecclesiastic reformer who played an important part in the christianization of Germany, dies in northeast Frisia (*c.* 75).

757
- Aethelbald, King of the Mercians 716–757, chief king of a confederation of Anglo-Saxon kingdoms in southern England, is murdered in Seckington, England.

762
- Li Po, one of China's greatest poets, dies in Tang-t'ui Anhwei province, China (*c.* 61).

766
February Harun arl-Rashid, fifth caliph of the Islamic Abbasid dynasty 786–809, who made Baghdad wealthy and whose court was immortalized in *Alf Laylah wa-Laylah/A Thousand and One Nights—The Arabian Nights*, born in Rayy, Persia (–809).

767
- Abu Abd Allah ash-Shāfii, great Muslim legal scholar who founds the Shafiiyah school of law, born in Arabia (–820).

768
- Han Yü (Han Yu, also known as Han Wen-kung), Chinese poet and first Neo-Confucianist philosopher, born in Teng-chou, Hunan Province, China (–824).
September 24 Pepin III ("Pepin the Short"), de facto ruler of the Franks from 747, King of the Franks 751–768, and first in the Frankish Carolingian dynasty, dies in St.-Denis, Neustria (54).

770
- Einhard (or Eginhard), Frankish historian, born in Maingau, Franconia (–840).
- Tu Fu, Chinese poet known for his poems dealing with war, dies in Hunan, China (*c.* 58).

771
December 4 Carloman II, younger brother of Charlemagne, joint king of the Franks 754–771, dies in Samoussy, France (*c.* 20).

774
July 27 Kobo Daishi (original name Kukai), one of Japan's most popular Buddhist saints, founder of the Shingon school of Buddhism, and an important poet, artist, and calligrapher, born in Byobugaura, Sanuki Province, Japan (–835).

775
- Constantine V, Byzantine emperor 741–775, dies in modern Bulgaria (*c.* 57).

October 7 al-Mansur, second caliph of the Abbasid dynasty 754–775, who established the capital city at Baghdad, dies near Mecca, Arabia (*c.* 64).

780
- Ahmad ibn Hanbal, Muslim theologian, who founded a school of Islamic law called the Hanbali and adopted a traditionalist approach in interpreting and codifying the legal aspects of the Koran (the *sharia*), born in Baghdad, Persia (–855).
- Rabanus Maurus (or Hrabanus Magnentius), archbishop of Mainz, influential Benedictine theologian and scholar, whose major work is *De rerum naturis/On the Nature of Things*, born in Mainz, Germany (–856).
September 28 Leo IV, Byzantine emperor 775–780, dies (31).

785
c. 785 Paschasius Radbertus, French abbot and theologian whose *De corpore et sanguine Christi/Concerning Christ's Body and Blood* has become the main Eucharistic interpretation, born in Soissons, France (–*c.* 860).
- Al Mahdi, Abbasid caliph 775–785, son of Mansur, dies.

786
- Al Hadi, fourth caliph of the Abbasid dynasty 785–786, dies.

787
August 10 Abu Mashar of Balkh ("Albumazar"), leading Muslim astrologer, born in Balkh, Khorasan (–886).

796
July Offa, King of Mercia 757–796, a powerful Anglo-Saxon ruler whose kingdom covered much of southern and central England, dies.

800–849

POLITICS, GOVERNMENT, AND ECONOMICS

Business and Economics

811

- The Chinese Tang emperor, Xianzong, issues "flying-cash" (money-drafts repayable in the capital, Changan) to meet a shortage of money in coin form—despite large-scale production of a copper coinage. These drafts are exchanged by merchants and thus form a precursor to paper currency.

812

- The Chinese government allows private banks to produce official banknotes. Initially, the notes are only valid for three years.

Colonization

841

- Norwegian Vikings found a permanent raiding base at the mouth of the River Liffey in Ireland. It becomes an important trading center and develops into the first city in Ireland (Dublin), until this time a country entirely without urban development.

Human Rights

845

- The anti-Buddhist campaign in China reaches its peak, caused by loss of government revenue as temple and monastic estates have tax-exempt status. Property is confiscated and ritual objects are destroyed. Many monasteries are closed and 250,000 monks are forced back into secular life.

Politics and Government

800

- Charlemagne, King of the Franks and Lombards, arranges for the defense of the Channel coast against the Vikings, ordering the construction of fleets and coastguard stations.

- Ibrahim ibn-al-Aghlab, Emir of Mzab (modern Algeria), establishes the Aghlabid dynasty of Kairouan (in modern Tunisia), ruling northwest Africa in only nominal subjection to the Abbasid caliph of Baghdad.

November 24 Charlemagne, King of the Franks and Lombards, arrives in Rome to receive Pope Leo III's declaration of innocence from accusations made by his enemies in Rome.

December 25 Charlemagne, King of the Franks and Lombards, is crowned Emperor of the Romans by Pope Leo III in Rome on Christmas Day. The coronation ceremony consciously recalls those of the Western Roman Empire, which fell in 476, but the Byzantines refuse to recognize his title as a successor.

801

- The Spanish city of Barcelona is taken by the Franks from the Moors after a two-year siege. The Abbasid caliph Harun ar-Rashid sends the Frankish emperor, Charlemagne, an elephant as a present.

802

- Jayavarman II, a minor king in the Angkor district of southeast Asia (modern Cambodia), declares himself *devaraja* ("god king"); he unites the Khmer peoples and founds the Khmer empire.

- Rumors in Constantinople that the Byzantine empress, Irene, is negotiating with Charlemagne, King of the Franks and Christian Emperor of the West, for their betrothal leads to her deposition by her minister of finance, who succeeds as Nicephorus I.

- The Frankish emperor Charlemagne issues the "Programmatic Capitulary" at Aachen (modern Germany) setting out the rights and responsibilities of rulers, clergy, and people in the Carolingian Empire. Monks are ordered to live according to the "Rule of St. Benedict." The laws are read out and revised where necessary. All men in the empire are ordered to swear allegiance to the emperor and to strive to live a Christian life.

- The monastery of Iona, on the island of Iona in the Inner Hebrides, modern Scotland, is sacked by Vikings for the second time. It is soon sacked a further three times after which its monks retreat to a safer location at Kells in Ireland.

803

- Alarmed by their increasing power and influence, the Abbasid caliph Harun ar-Rashid destroys the Barmakids, the Persian family responsible for the administration of the Arab caliphate.

- Charlemagne, King of the Franks and Christian Emperor of the West, reforms the law codes of the Ripuarian (Rhineland) Franks, Saxons, Frisians, and Thuringians.

804

- Charlemagne, King of the Franks and Christian Emperor of the West, orders the deportation of the Saxons living east of the River Elbe, finally ending Saxon resistance to Frankish rule. The extension of the Frankish Empire to the borders of Denmark causes the Danish king, Godfred, to abandon a planned meeting with Charlemagne.

805

- A capitulary issued by the Frankish emperor Charlemagne orders the setting up of customs posts on the eastern frontier of the Frankish Empire, including one at Magdeburg (in modern Germany), where merchants may cross to trade with Slavs and Avars.
- After the Byzantine emperor, Nicephorus I, withholds payments of tributes, war breaks out with the Abbasid caliphate. It goes badly for the Byzantines from the beginning when Nicephorus is defeated by the Arabs at Crasus in Anatolia.
- The Venetian doges (from Latin *duces*, "dukes") Obelerius and Beatus transfer their allegiance from the Byzantine emperor to the Frankish emperor Charlemagne.

806

- Al-Hakam I, the Umayyad emir of Spain, massacres rebel Arab nobles in the Spanish cities of Córdoba and Toledo.
- Charles, the eldest son of Charlemagne, King of the Franks and Christian Emperor of the West, defeats the Sorbs (Slavs of the Elbe–Saale area), enforcing their submission, but Hadumar, Count of Genoa, is killed in a naval battle against a Moorish pirate fleet off Corsica.
- The Abbasid caliph (ruler of the Islamic world) Harun ar-Rashid invades Anatolia with a force of 135,000 men and takes Heraclea and other places in Cappadocia, Asia Minor, forcing the Byzantine emperor Nicephorus I to resume payment of tribute. In addition, Harun ar-Rashid appoints Ashot Bagratuni the Carnivorous, founder of the Bagratid dynasty, as prince of Armenia.
- The Byzantine emperor, Nicephorus I, sends a fleet to blockade Venice, Italy, which has defected to the Frankish emperor Charlemagne.
- With the death of the emperor Kammu, the power of the Japanese emperors goes into decline as the ideals of the Taika reforms of 646 are abandoned.

February 6 Following Frankish custom, Charlemagne, King of the Franks and Christian Emperor of the West, makes provision for the division of the Frankish Empire between his three sons, Charles, Louis, and Pepin, after his death.

807

- A blockade of Venice, ordered by the Byzantine emperor Nicephorus I in 806, forces the Venetians to return their allegiance to the Byzantine Empire.

809

- The Byzantine emperor, Nicephorus I, raids Pliska, the Bulgar capital, in retaliation for the sack of Sofia by Krum, khan of the Bulgars.

March 24 The Abbasid caliph Harun ar-Rashid falls ill and dies after suppressing a revolt in Samarkand; his Muslim Arab empire is divided between his sons al-Ma'mun and al-Amin.

810

- The Bureau of Archives is established in Japan to draft imperial decrees and transmit petitions to the emperor.
- The Danish king, Godfred, ravages Frisia with a large fleet, exacting a large tribute, and threatens to attack the Frankish emperor Charlemagne's capital, Aachen. Shortly afterwards, Godfred is murdered and is succeeded by his nephew Hemming who makes peace with Charlemagne.

July 8 The Frankish emperor Charlemagne's son Pepin dies shortly after a failed attempt to recover Venice from the Byzantine Empire. The Venetians begin to build a city on the Rialto island.

811

- The formation of the Spanish March (the Carolingian military zone south of the Pyrenees) is completed with the surrender of the Spanish town of Tortosa to Louis, son of the Frankish emperor Charlemagne. With the death of Charlemagne's eldest son, Charles, later in the year, Louis becomes the emperor's sole heir.
- The Frankish emperor Charlemagne sends an army into Pannonia (modern Hungary) to arbitrate in a territorial dispute between the Slavs and Avars.

July 26 The Byzantine emperor, Nicephorus I, is killed when his army is ambushed in a mountain pass by the Bulgars. The Bulgar khan, Krum, has Nicephorus's skull lined with silver for use as a drinking cup.

812

April 4 Ambassadors of the Byzantine emperor Michael I recognize Charlemagne as Frankish emperor, while he renounces his claim to dominion over Venice.

813

June 22 The Byzantine emperor Michael I is defeated by the Bulgars at Versinicia, near Adrianople (modern Edirne, Turkey). He is consequently deposed in favor of Leo (V) the Armenian while the Bulgars take Adrianople and attack Constantinople.

September 11 In an assembly of magnates at his capital, Aachen, the Frankish emperor Charlemagne gives the imperial crown to Louis, his only surviving son.

September 25 Al-Ma'mun reunites the Abbasid Arab caliphate by capturing the Abbasid capital, Baghdad (in modern Iraq), and murdering his brother, al-Amin.

814

January 28 The Frankish emperor Charlemagne dies and is succeeded by his only surviving son, Louis I (known posthumously as "the Pious").

May 5 Al-Hakam I, the Umayyad emir of Spain, crushes a new revolt of Arab nobles in the Spanish city of Córdoba and increases recruitment of Berber (Moorish) mercenaries. Some refugees from the revolt seize control of Alexandria in Egypt.

815

- King Egbert of the Anglo-Saxon kingdom of Wessex, England, conquers the Britons (Welsh) of Cornwall.

816

- Pope Stephen IV crowns Louis I the Pious as King of the Franks and Emperor of the West at Reims, in the Frankish Empire (now France). In the *Pactum Hlodovicianum*, Louis confirms the territories around Rome as papal possessions in Italy.

817

July 7   At a council at Aachen in the northern Frankish Empire (modern Germany), Lothair I is created emperor as the colleague of his father, Louis I the Pious. Louis's other sons, Pepin and Louis the German, respectively receive Aquitaine and Bavaria as sovereign yet dependent kingdoms.

July 7   In an attempt to end the factional rivalry of the Sunni Muslims and breakaway minority Shiite Muslims, the Abbasid caliph al-Ma'mun appoints Ali al-Rida, leader of the Shiites, as his heir. This proves unacceptable to the Sunnite majority, however, and a revolt breaks out in Baghdad (in modern Iraq).

818

- The Shiite Muslim leader Ali al-Rida, the Abbasid caliph al-Ma'mun's appointed heir, dies in mysterious circumstances, possibly murdered on the orders of al-Ma'mun himself.

April 17   After rebelling against Louis I the Pious, King of the Franks and Emperor of the West, Bernard, the dependent king of Italy, is blinded and dies soon afterwards in prison.

August 8   Louis I the Pious, King of the Franks and Emperor of the West, enforces temporary submission by the Bretons, whose leader, Morvan, is killed in a skirmish.

819

- Shortly after the death of his first wife, Irmengardis, the Frankish emperor, Louis I the Pious, marries Judith, daughter of the Count of Bavaria. She is a strong-minded woman whose determination to secure a share of the empire for her own son by Louis, Charles the Bald (born in 823), leads to a series of civil wars.
- The Abbasid caliph al-Ma'mun abandons his attempt at reconciliation with the Shiite Muslims, bringing the rebellion against him at Baghdad (in modern Iraq) to an end.

820

- Frankish coastguards repulse attempts by a Viking fleet to land in Flanders and at the mouth of the River Seine. However, the fleet eventually finds a gap in the Frankish defenses and sacks a village in Aquitaine.
- The Examiners of Misdeeds are instituted in Japan; they soon develop into a police force (as the Police Commissioners).

December 25   The Byzantine emperor, Leo V, is murdered during a Christmas Day service by supporters of Michael the Amorian, who is under sentence of death for treason. He becomes emperor as Michael II.

821

- Following the death of King Coenwulf of Mercia, England, the leading Anglo-Saxon kingdom goes into decline.
- The Abbasid caliph al-Ma'mun appoints his general Tahir governor of Khorasan (eastern Persia); he is allowed considerable local autonomy and founds the Tahirid dynasty which rules Persia in semi-independence until 873.

822

- Al-Hakam I, the Umayyad emir of Spain, is succeeded by his son, Abd ar-Rahman II, who remodels the administrative structure of his emirate on that of the Abbasid caliphate at Baghdad (in modern Iraq).
- Louis I the Pious, King of the Franks and Emperor of the West, does public penance for causing the death of his nephew, King Bernard of Italy.

824

- The Frankish emperor, Louis I the Pious, sends his son, the coemperor Lothair I, to Rome to order the affairs of the papacy. The *Constitutio Romana* ("Roman Constitution") defines an imperial role in papal elections and requires popes to swear allegiance to the Frankish emperors.

825

- In one of the most important battles in English history, King Egbert of Wessex defeats King Beornwulf of Mercia at Ellandun (now Nether Wroughton, Wiltshire). Later the same year, Beornwulf is killed when the East Anglians rebel against Mercian control and Egbert conquers Kent, Sussex, and Essex, making Wessex the strongest Anglo-Saxon kingdom.
- The Byzantine emperor, Michael II, defeats Thomas the Slav, a pretender (as "Constantine VI") to the Byzantine throne supported by the Abbasid caliph, al-Ma'mun, and an army of anti-iconoclast rebels.

826

- Louis I the Pious, King of the Franks and Emperor of the West, recognizes Nomenoë as chief of the Bretons and receives his homage.
- St. Ansegisus, abbot of the monastery of Fontanelle on the River Seine (France), makes a collection of the capitularies of the Frankish emperors Charlemagne and Louis I the Pious, preserving them for future generations.

827

- Muslim fugitives from Córdoba, Spain, are expelled from Alexandria in Egypt and then take Crete from the Byzantines and make it a center for piracy in the Aegean Sea.

June 6   Ziyadat Allah I, emir of Kairouan (in modern Tunisia), exploits a revolt against Byzantine rule to begin the Muslim conquest of Sicily.

828

- On a mission to suppress Muslim pirates, Count Boniface, the Frankish "prefect" of Corsica, takes a fleet to North Africa. Landing near Carthage (in modern Tunisia), he defeats the Arabs in five battles before withdrawing after a defeat at Sousse.
- The Frankish emperor Louis I the Pious's son, Louis the German, repels a Bulgar invasion of Pannonia (modern Hungary).

829

- At the urging of his second wife, Judith of Bavaria, the Frankish emperor, Louis I the Pious, grants Alsace and other territories to their youngest son, Charles the Bald, thus antagonizing the coemperor, Lothair I, Louis's eldest son by his first marriage, to whom they had previously been assigned.
- King Egbert of Wessex, England, conquers Mercia and is declared bretwalda or overlord of Britain.
- The Thai kingdom of Nanchao (in modern Yunnan, south China) invades Sichuan, winning territory from the Chinese Tang dynasty empire.

830

April 4 Backed by his brothers Pepin and Louis the German, Lothair I rebels against his father, the Frankish emperor Louis I the Pious, deposes him, and disinherits his half brother Charles the Bald. Lothair's poor government causes a reaction in Louis's favor and in the autumn Louis is returned to power, but his authority has been permanently weakened.

831

- Following the death of their khan, Omortag, the Bulgars resume their attacks on the Byzantine Empire (which had ceased during his reign).
February 2 The Frankish emperor, Louis I the Pious, punishes his son Lothair I for his rebellion in 830 by depriving him of the imperial title and most of his lands.
September 9 Palermo in Sicily is taken from its Byzantine defenders by the Muslim forces of Ziyadat Allah I, emir of Kairouan (in modern Tunisia).

832

- The Frankish emperor, Louis I the Pious, grants Aquitaine to his youngest son, Charles the Bald, causing Pepin, to whom it had previously been assigned, to rebel with the support of his brothers, Lothair I and Louis the German.
- The Thai kingdom of Nanchao (in modern Yunnan, south China) destroys the kingdom of the Pyu people, the earliest known inhabitants of Burma.
- The Uigur, a Turkish confederation in Manchuria, begins to break up, relieving Tang China of a dangerous enemy.

833

- The Chinese Tang dynasty emperor, Wenzong, attempts to reduce the influence of the palace eunuchs. His plot misfires and the eunuchs massacre his chief ministers in "the Sweet Dew Incident," greatly enhancing their power as a result.
833–836 During his short reign, the weak king Ramabhadra of the Pratihara dynasty loses most of the territory of the Gurjara kingdom in northern India.
June 24 At "the Field of Lies" (near Sigolsheim, Alsace, in the northern Frankish Empire), following Pope Gregory IV's attempt to mediate between the Frankish emperor, Louis I the Pious, and his again rebellious sons, Lothair I, Louis the German, and Pepin, Louis senior is deserted by his followers and surrenders. He is deposed and imprisoned with his youngest son, Charles the Bald.
August 7 The Abbasid caliph al-Ma'mun dies while preparing an expedition to Constantinople. He is succeeded by his brother, al-Mu'tasim, who begins to recruit Turkish mercenaries into the Arab army.

834

- Al-Mu'tasim, the Abbasid caliph (ruler of the Muslim world), expels the Jalt (gypsies) from Persia (modern Iran).
- Taking advantage of the political problems of the Frankish Empire, the Vikings sail down the River Rhine and sack Dorestadt (near Utrecht, in the modern Netherlands), the empire's richest and largest port.
- The city of Hamburg, founded about ten years previously as a Frankish border fortress, becomes the seat of Archbishop Ansgar, under whom it becomes a base for Christian missionary activity in Scandinavia.
March 1 Louis I the Pious is restored as Frankish emperor by his eldest son, Lothair I, after he quarrels with his brothers, Louis the German and Pepin.

836

- A fleet of 35 Viking ships defeats King Egbert of Wessex, England, at Carhampton (in the modern county of Somerset).
- Amran succeeds his father as governor of Sind, an eastern province of the Abbasid Arab caliphate. The tendency for governorships to become hereditary is an indication of the decline of the authority of the Abbasid caliphs.
- Public resentment against his Turkish mercenaries forces the Abbasid caliph (ruler of the Muslim world) al-Mu'tasim to transfer his capital from Baghdad to Samarra (also in Iraq).
- Vikings sail up the River Shannon into the heart of Ireland and sack the rich monastery of Clonmacnoise.
836–890 After the disasters of Ramabhadra's reign, his son, King Bhoja I, restores the Gurjara kingdom as the leading power of northern India.

837

- At the request of its duke, Andreas, the Arabs of Sicily relieve the siege of Naples by Sikard, the Lombard Duke of Benevento.
- Louis I the Pious, King of the Franks and Emperor of the West, despatches *missi* (itinerant officers) to restore order in Frisia in the north of the Frankish Empire, which has been badly hit by Viking raids. Vikings attack a coastguard fort on the island of Walcheren at the mouth of the River Rhine and many senior officers are killed or captured.
- The Magyars, a Turkish nomad people recently established in the Don–Danube area, assist the Bulgars against rebel Slavs.
- The Muslim Arab Umayyad emir of Spain, Abd ar-Rahman II, crushes a revolt of Christians and Jews in the Spanish city of Toledo.
June 29 Giovanni I Particiaco, Doge of Venice, is deposed in the family faction fighting typical of this period of Venetian history and is succeeded by Pietro Tradonico.

838

- Arab pirates sack Marseille.
June 13 In retaliation for a Byzantine invasion, the Abbasid caliph al-Mu'tasim sacks Ankara, the fortress city of Amorium in Anatolia, after defeating the Byzantine emperor, Theophilus, on the River Halys (Kizil Irmak).
December 13 On the death of his son Pepin, the Frankish emperor, Louis I the Pious, assigns his lands in Aquitaine to his youngest son, Charles the Bald, who is faced with opposition from Pepin's son, Pepin II, who believes he has the right to inherit.

839

- The death of Sikard, the Lombard Duke of Benevento, Italy, leads to the division of the duchy into principalities centered on Benevento and Salerno; Amalfi becomes independent under Byzantine suzerainty.
May 30 After putting down a rebellion by his son Louis the

German, the Frankish emperor, Louis I the Pious, holds a meeting at Worms (in modern Germany) with him and his other surviving sons, Lothair I and Charles the Bald, to agree a new division of the empire. When Louis tries to force the Aquitainians to accept Charles (they prefer his nephew Pepin II), Louis the German rebels once again.

840

- Arab pirates from Sicily take the southeastern Italian ports of Taranto and Bari, then plunder the Adriatic coast of Italy as far as Venice.
- Once again benefiting from the Frankish Empire's political problems, the Vikings sail up the River Seine, for the first time, and sack the city of Rouen, France.
- The Uigur, a Turkish nomadic people, are driven from their empire on the Orkhan River in central Asia by the Khirgiz, another Turkish nomadic people, and settle in the Tarim Basin (in modern Xinjiang Uygur province, China).

June 20   The Frankish emperor, Louis I the Pious, dies shortly after an expedition to put down a rebellion by his son Louis the German. He is succeeded as emperor by his eldest son, Lothair I, who is immediately embroiled in territorial disputes with his brothers, Louis the German and Charles the Bald, over their share of the empire.

841

June 25   The Frankish emperor, Lothair I, supported by his nephew Pepin II of Aquitaine, is defeated at Fontenoy (in modern France) by his brothers, Louis the German and Charles the Bald, who oppose his claims to authority over the whole empire. Following his defeat, Lothair is forced to concede the principle of partition.

842

- Radelchis, the Lombard prince of Benevento, Italy, is expelled by Arab mercenaries whom he had engaged against his rival Sikonolf of Salerno.
- Siemowit (Ziemowit), son of the plowman Piast, is (traditionally) elected Duke of Poland, so founding the first Polish ruling house, known from the 17th century as the Piast dynasty.
- The cities of London in Mercia and Quentovic in the Frankish Empire (near modern Etaples, France) are sacked by the Vikings.

January 5   The Abbasid caliph al-Mu'tasim dies and is succeeded by his son, al-Wathiq, who takes little interest in the government of the Muslim world during his six-year reign.

January 20   On the death of the Byzantine emperor, Theophilus, his young son Michael III becomes emperor under the regency of his mother, the empress Theodora. During Michael's long reign the decline of the Byzantine Empire is arrested.

February 14   Louis the German and Charles the Bald, at Strasbourg (in present-day Alsace, France), reaffirm their alliance against their brother, the Frankish emperor, Lothair I. Faced with overwhelming forces, Lothair's supporters defect and within a few weeks he is forced to seek peace.

September 30   A 120-strong commission is appointed to work out a fair partition of the Frankish Empire between the emperor, Lothair I, and his brothers, Louis the German and Charles the Bald.

843

- Kenneth I (called MacAlpin), King of the Scots of Argyll, conquers the Picts of Caledonia to create the kingdom of Alba or "Scotland."
- The Arab conquest of Sicily is almost completed with the capture of Messina in the northeast of the island.
- The Byzantine emperor, Michael III, restores the veneration of religious icons in the Byzantine Empire. Prominent supporters of iconoclasm such as the patriarch Ignatius are soon eased out of power, ending the diplomatically damaging and socially divisive iconoclastic dispute.
- The Vikings sack the city of Nantes and establish a permanent base for year-round raiding at Noirmoutier to the southwest of Nantes, at the mouth of the River Loire.

August 8   The Treaty of Verdun settles the quarrels of the heirs of the late Frankish emperor Louis I the Pious over their inheritance. Lothair I retains the title of emperor and receives "the Middle Kingdom" (Italy, lands between the Rhine and Rhône–Saône–Scheldt, and Frisia, including the imperial capitals Rome and Aachen), while Louis the German receives the East Frankish Kingdom (Saxony, Franconia, Swabia, Bavaria, and Carinthia) and Charles II the Bald receives the West Frankish Kingdom (Neustria, Aquitaine, Gascony, and the Spanish March).

844

- An expedition sent to Aquitaine by the West Frankish king Charles II the Bald fails to defeat Pepin II, who continues to rule there with popular support in defiance of the Treaty of Verdun of 843.
- Vikings from their base of Noirmoutier on the west coast of the Frankish Empire raid the Garonne and go on to sack Lisbon, Cadiz, Algeciras, and Seville in Spain before they are defeated by the Moors. 1,000 Vikings are killed and 400 taken prisoner.

October 10   In a meeting at Yütz, near Thionville in the Middle Kingdom of the Frankish Empire (modern France), the Frankish emperor, Lothair I, and the Frankish kings Charles II the Bald and Louis the German establish principles of fraternal cooperation.

845

- After they sack Paris, the West Frankish king, Charles II the Bald, pays the Vikings "Danegeld" (protection money) to persuade them to leave.
- Arab pirates from Sicily take the islands of Ponza and Ischia as naval bases for raids on the western Italian coast.
- Hamburg is sacked by Danes under King Horik but the town quickly recovers.
- Mael Seachlainn, King of Meath, Ireland, captures Turgeis, the Viking would-be conqueror of Ireland, and drowns him in Lough Owel.

June 6   By the Treaty of St. Benoît-sur-Loire, the West Frankish king, Charles II the Bald, recognizes Pepin II as king of Aquitaine in return for Pepin performing homage to him as overlord.

November 22   The Bretons, led by Duke Nomenoë, defeat an army sent by the West Frankish king, Charles II the Bald, to enforce their subjection, at Ballon, Brittany.

846

- Following his defeat the previous year, the West Frankish king, Charles II the Bald, agrees a treaty with Duke Nomenoë of Brittany, recognizing the independence of Brittany.
- The East Frankish king, Louis the German, defeats Mojmír, the expansionist Slav ruler of Moravia, and appoints Rostislav as his successor.
- With the help of his overlords, the Chalukyas of central India, Vijayalaya captures the city of Tanjore in the Pandya kingdom of South India, marking the birth of the Chola Empire which remains a major power until 1279.

August 26   The basilica of St. Peter and other places outside the walls of Rome are plundered by Arab raiders from the Aghlabid Emirate of Ifriqiya (modern Tunisia).

847

- Louis, son of the Frankish emperor, Lothair I, defeats Arab forces and expels them from Benevento, Italy.
- The Frankish emperor, Lothair I, and his brothers, the Frankish kings Charles II the Bald and Louis the German, meet at Meerssen, near Maastricht (in the present-day Netherlands), and agree to guarantee the inheritances of their children. Charles II the Bald's Capitulary of Meerssen orders every free man to choose himself a lord in order to facilitate the levy of an army.

April 10   Leo IV is crowned as pope. To prevent a repeat of the Arab raid of the previous year, he builds a defensive wall around St. Peter's, Rome, so forming the "Leonine City."

August 10   On the death of the Abbasid caliph al-Wathiq, his brother, al-Mutawakkil, becomes caliph (ruler of the Islamic world). A sternly orthodox Muslim, al-Mutawakkil immediately begins the persecution of the Shiite Muslim minority and introduces restrictions on the activities of Christians and Jews.

848

- According to traditional dating, the city of Pagan, on the Irrawaddy River, is founded as the capital of an emerging Burmese kingdom.

June 6   The West Frankish king, Charles II the Bald, is crowned as king of Aquitaine after Pepin II, discredited by his failure to prevent Viking raids, is deserted by his subjects.

SCIENCE, TECHNOLOGY, AND MEDICINE

Agriculture

800

- Water mills for use in irrigating agricultural land are introduced to Japan from China, where they have been used for hundreds of years.

809

- A severe famine sweeps through Europe, despite the Frankish emperor Charlemagne's best efforts to organize relief.

814

- An unsuccessful attempt is made to grow tea in Japan.

Ecology

800

- Frankish miners exploit copper deposits in Saxony, southern Germany.

848

- An Arab pirate fleet from Sicily is destroyed by a storm on its way to attack Rome.

Health and Medicine

800

- A French manuscript of this date has the first mention of soap in medieval Europe.
- Muslim scholar Al-Batrīq produces Arabic translations of major works by the Greek physicians Galen and Hippocrates; they will have a lasting effect on Arab medicine.

809

- The Abbasid caliph Harun ar-Rashid founds a hospital in Baghdad. He establishes a postal service in his empire and is said to have contemplated making a canal through the Suez Isthmus, linking the Red Sea and Mediterranean Sea.

Math

816

- The Council of Chelsea, a church council convened at King Offa's palace, introduces the *anno Domini* system of dating into England.

Science

800

c. 800   The Abbasid caliph Harun ar-Rashid presents an elaborate astronomical water-clock, built by the Arab engineer al-Jazari, to the Frankish emperor Charlemagne. The mechanism is driven by falling water, and the clock sounds the time by dropping bronze balls.

- The Peruvian city of Machu Picchu, built at this time, contains an astronomical altar, "the hitching post of the sun," which can be used to measure solar and lunar movements with great accuracy.

802

- Rose trees from Asia are introduced to Europe and cultivated there for the first time.

810

- The Arab alchemist Jābir ibn-Hayyān of Kufa (Geber in Iraq) is credited with *The Book of the Composition of Alchemy*. He believes that elements are formed within the earth by the combination of sulfur and mercury.

813

- The brothers Ben Shaku, Hebrew astronomers, attempt to measure the length of a degree of meridian on the earth's surface, and so determine the size of the world, at the order of Caliph al-Ma'mun.

815

- The Arab alchemist Jābir ibn-Hayyān of Kufa (Geber in Iraq) dies in Persia. Vast numbers of stories accumulate around him, and over 2,000 works, mostly written by other Arab and European alchemists, are attributed to him.
- The Muslim scholar Māshā'allah writes on astrology, the astrolabe, and meteorology. As court astrologer, he was responsible for choosing a propitious date for the founding of the new capital at Baghdad.

822

- The Abbasid caliph al-Ma'mun founds the *Bayt al Hikmah* ("House of Wisdom") at Baghdad (in modern Iraq), a center for the translation of philosophical and scientific works from Greek to Arabic.

825

- Irish monk and scholar Dicuil writes *De mensura orbis terrae/Measurement of the World*, which contains descriptions of Iceland and the pyramids of El Gîza.

827

- Muslim scholar Al-Hajjāj translates the 2nd-century Egyptian astronomer Ptolemy's *Great Mathematical Compilation* into Arabic, as *al-Majisti*. It is later known as simply the *Almagest*.

833

- The Abbasid caliph al-Ma'mun founds an observatory at Baghdad and encourages geographical exploration in order to verify the knowledge currently being translated from classical texts.

846

- Muslim geographer ibn-Khurdādhbih compiles the first edition of his *Book of Routes and Kingdoms*, a guide to Asia based on the itinerary of the Arab postal services, which are running regularly by this time.

Technology

800

- Huge reservoirs are built in the Arab province of Ifriqiya (modern Tunisia) on the orders of its newly autonomous governor Ibrahim ibn-al Agrab.
- The Chinese governor Hsü Shang of Shensi province maintains a 1,000-strong standing army, who use pleated paper armor, which is far superior to iron.
- The Muslim engineer Al-Jazarī writes his *Book of Knowledge of Ingenious Mechanical Devices*, which describes water clocks, automata, and other sophisticated inventions.

c. **825**

- The *Utrecht Psalter* has the first illustration of a grinding wheel with a millstone for sharpening swords.

c. **840**

- The gold altar of Sant'Ambrogio Basilica, in Milan, Italy, the decoration on which includes the earliest pictorial representation of a stirrup, dates from this period.

Transportation

837

- A carrier pigeon service is in operation in the Arab Caliphate.

ARTS AND IDEAS

Architecture

800

- The abbey church of Centula (or St. Riquier) near Abbeville, France, is completed. Its innovative design, which includes towers over the crossings and an apse separated from the transepts by a crossing, proves to be highly influential.

802

- Oviedo Cathedral, of which the Cámara Santa survives, is founded, in Spain.

805

- The palace chapel of Charlemagne at Aachen (in modern Germany) is consecrated. Modeled on the octagonal Church of San Vitale in Ravenna, Italy, the Aachen chapel is a more forceful and less mystical building.

806

- The domed church built for Theodulf, bishop of Orléans, at Germigny-des-Prés near Orléans, France, displays a strong Visigothic influence.

808

- Danish king Godfred begins to construct defensive earthworks (the *Danevirke*) across the neck of the Jutland peninsula to protect Denmark against Frankish invasion.

811

- Frankish emperor Charlemagne restores a Roman lighthouse at Boulogne to act as a guide for seafarers in the English Channel.

812

- A circular church, dedicated to St. Donat, is built at Zadar (in modern Croatia) during the Frankish occupation of Dalmatia. It is completed in 876.

819

- The second abbey church of Fulda, Germany, the designs for which were based on St. Peter's basilica in Rome, is consecrated.

c. **820**

- A manuscript plan for a monastery at St. Gall in modern Switzerland shows the innovations of Centula plus the orderly planning of the monastic buildings around the church.
- Small domed hermitages are built on the remote Irish island of Skellig Michael.

825

- Hamsavati (now Pegu) is founded as the capital of the Mon kingdom of south Burma (now Myanmar).

827

- The rebuilding of the mosque at 'Amr employs the earliest pointed arches in Egypt.

c. **836**

- The Great Mosque at Kairouan in Ifriqiya (modern Tunisia) is rebuilt and enlarged for the second time.

c. **847**

- Building begins on the Great Mosque of al-Mutawakkil at the second Abbasid capital of Samarra (in modern Iraq). The largest mosque in the world, its most distinctive feature is its huge spiral minaret built of brick.

848

- The vaulted church of Sta Maria de Naranco, near Oviedo in Asturias, Spain, is consecrated.

Literature and Language

829

- St. Nicephorus writes his *Breviarium Nicephori*, a Byzantine history of the years 602–769.

830

c. **830** Arab writer al-Jahiz is active during this period. His works, including *The Book of Eloquence and Exposition*, are examples of *adab* or culture literature, encyclopedic surveys of useful and entertaining knowledge.

- Einhard, an adviser to the Frankish emperors Charlemagne and Louis I the Pious, retires to Seligenstadt, Franconia, and begins his *Vita Caroli Magni/Life of Charlemagne*. Modeled on Suetonius' *Lives of the Caesars*, it presents a lively picture of the emperor's character and achievements.

842

c. **842** Georgios Monachos (George the Monk) writes his *Chronicle*, a history of the world from its creation to AD 842.

- The "Serment de Strasbourg," an oath of loyalty between two of the Frankish emperor Charlemagne's grandsons, is the earliest extant document in the French language.

847

- Rabanus Maurus completes his *De rerum naturis/On the Nature of Things*, an encyclopedia based on the Etymologiae of St. Isidore of Seville, Spain.
- Zhan Yanyuan writes *Li-tai Ming-hua chi/A Record of the Famous Painters of All Periods*. It deals with every aspect of Chinese painting and seems to have been inspired by the destruction of Buddhist works of art at this time.

Music

c. **845**

- Aurelian of Rome produces the earliest treatise on Gregorian chant, the system of plainsong prevalent in the Middle Ages in which the liturgy is set to music, a single sung line without instrumentation or harmonization.

Thought and Scholarship

803

- Rabanus Maurus, a pupil of the scholar Alcuin at Tours, becomes the head of the monastic school at Fulda. Under his direction Fulda becomes a great center of learning and accumulates many manuscripts and works of art. Rabanus becomes known as the "Teacher of Germany."

810

c. **810** Welsh chronicler Nennius compiles his *Historia Britonum/History of the Britons*. It contains the earliest direct reference to Arthur as a Celtic battle-leader.

- Byzantine chronicler Georgios Syncellos compiles his *Chronicle*, a history of the world from its creation to AD 284. It is arranged in chronological tables.

817

- Byzantine historian Theophanes the Confessor writes his *Chronography*, a continuation of Syncellos' *Chronicle* up to the year 813.

SOCIETY

Education

822

- At the assembly at Attigny, near Reims in the Frankish Empire, the Frankish emperor, Louis I the Pious, gives cathedral schools the responsibility for general education. The emperor had earlier decreed that only those intending to become monks should be educated at monastic schools.

830

- Al-Ma'mun founds the Bayt al-Hikmah, or "House of Wisdom," in Baghdad. It houses a library and is an important center for the translation of Hellenic classic texts into Arabic.

Everyday Life

c. **800**

- Tea is introduced to Japan from China as a medicine.

801

- The Frankish emperor Charlemagne passes laws prohibiting prostitution, principally for moral and religious reasons.

Religion

800

- The Cha'an (or Meditation) Sect become the strongest movement in Chinese Buddhism. Better known by the Japanese name of Zen, its followers believe that enlightenment is best achieved through sudden flashes of insight into the nature of reality.

805

- Returning from China, Saichō introduces the T'ien T'ai school of Buddhism to Japan where it is known as

Tendai. Tendai teaches that the Buddha-nature within everyone can be realized through ethical behavior and discipline.

806

- The esoteric Shingon sect of Buddhism is introduced into Japan from China. It emphasizes the gradual path to enlightenment through meditation and reflection.

813

- The tomb of St. James the Greater is identified at Santiago de Compostela in northwestern Spain. It attracts pilgrims from throughout western Europe.

814

- On his accession, Louis I the Pious orders all monasteries within the empire to observe the Rule of St. Benedict. The reforms are administered by Benedict of Aniane.

815

March 3   The Byzantine emperor Leo V deposes the patriarch Nicephorus and holds a synod of the Greek church that reaffirms the iconoclastic decrees of the council of 754.

c. 820

- The illuminated *Ebbo Gospels*, produced in Reims, France, for Archbishop Ebbo, are painted in an illusionistic style based on Hellenistic art.

826

- Heriold, an exiled Danish king, is baptized at Mainz (in modern Germany) with many of his followers. The Frankish emperor, Louis I the Pious, grants him the county of Rüstringen (Germany) on the North Sea coast.

831

- French theologian St. Paschasius Radbertus writes *De sacramento Corporis et Sanguinis Domini nostri/On the*

BIRTHS & DEATHS

801
September 8   St. Anskar, missionary, first archbishop of Hamburg, and patron saint of Scandinavia, born in Corbie, Austrasia (now in France) (–865).

803
August 9   Irene, Byzantine empress jointly with her son Constantine VI 780–797 and then alone 798–802, a saint of the Greek Orthodox Church, dies on Lesbos, Greece (c. 51).

804
May 19   Alcuin of York, Anglo-Latin poet who introduced Anglo-Saxon humanism to western Europe, dies in Tours, France (c. 72).

809
March 24   Harun arl-Rashid, fifth caliph of the Islamic Abbasid dynasty 786–809, who made Baghdad wealthy and whose court was immortalized in *Alf Laylah wa-Laylah/A Thousand and One Nights—The Arabian Nights*, dies in Tus, Persia (43).

810
- John Scotus Erigena (also known as Johannes Scotus Eriugena), Irish theologian, translator, and commentator, born in Ireland (–c. 877).

814
January 28   Charlemagne (Carolus Magnus), King of the Franks 768–814 and Frankish emperor 800–814, who united much of western Europe under his rule, dies in Aachen, in modern Germany (71).

820
c. 820   Photius, patriarch of Constantinople 858–867 and 877–878, who was largely

responsible for the Byzantine resurgence in the 9th century, born in Constantinople (–c. 891).

c. 820   St. Nicholas I, Italian pope 858–867, who laid the theoretical foundations for the papal theocracy, born in Rome (–867).

January 20   Abu Abd Allah ash-Shāfi'i, great Muslim legal scholar who founded the Shafi'iyah school of law, dies in al-Fustat, Egypt.

823
- The Arab historian Al-Wāqidi, writer of *Kitāb al-Maghāzi/History of the Wars*, an account of Muhammad's military campaigns, dies.

824
- Han Yü (Pinyin: Han Yu, also called Han Wen-kung) Chinese poet and first Neo-Confucianist philosopher, dies in Ch'ang-an, China (c. 56).

827
- St. Cyril (Constantine), scholar, theologian, and missionary, who, together with his brother St. Methodius converted the Danubian Slavs to Christianity, born in Thessaloníki, Greece (–869).

828
- The Arab scholar al-Asma'ī, writer of several works of natural history including *Kitāb al-Khail/On the Horse* and *Kitāb al-Ibil/On the Camel*, dies.

c. 830
- Basil the Macedonian, Byzantine emperor 867–886, who founded the Macedonian dynasty and formulated the *Basilica*, the Byzantine legal code, born in Thrace (–886).

835
April 22   Kobo Daishi (original name Kukai), one of Japan's most popular Buddhist saints, founder of the Shingon school of Buddhism, also an important poet, artist, and calligrapher, dies on Mt. Koya, Japan (60).

840
March 14   Einhard (or Eginhard), Frankish historian, dies in Seligenstadt, Franconia (c. 70).

842
January 20   Theophilus I, Eastern Roman emperor 829–842, who stimulated a cultural revival in the Byzantine empire, rebuilt the University of Constantinople, and was an advocate of Iconoclasm (the destruction of religious images), dies in Constantinople.

846
- Po-Chü-i, Chinese poet, famed for both the formal discipline and the lucidity of his poetry, especially in his greatest work "Ch'ang-hen ko"/"The Song of Everlasting Remorse," dies.

847
- al-Wathiq, 'Abbasid caliph 842–847 and musician (lutenist and composer), dies.

849
- Alfred the Great, King of Wessex 871–899, who defended Saxon England against the Danes, born, probably in Wantage, Oxfordshire, England (–899).

Sacrament of Christ's Body and Blood, a text on the Eucharist which asserts the doctrine of transubstantiation, the belief that the bread and wine become Christ's body and blood.

c. 834

- The illuminated Moutier-Grandval Bible is begun at the Abbey of Tours, in France. From this period Tours becomes an important center of artistic activity.

840

- The accession of Emperor T'ang Wu Tsang, a follower of Taoism, marks the start of a period of anti-Buddhist persecution in China.

c. 841

- Agobard, archbishop of Lyons (in modern France), writes *Liber contra insulsam vulgi opinionem de grandine et tonitruis/Book Against the Foolish Opinion of the Public Concerning Hail and Thunderstorms*, an attack on popular superstitions and the belief in magic.

842

- With the collapse of the Uighurs in 840–843, the religion Manichaeism loses its main adherents in China. Monasteries are closed and the religion is banned.

843

March 3 Theodora, widow of the iconclastic Byzantine emperor Theophilus, brings the iconoclastic controversy to an end. A great festival in honor of the icons takes place on the second Sunday in Lent.

845

January 1 Fourteen Bohemian nobles are baptized at the court of Louis the German, ruler of the East Frankish Kingdom (modern Germany).

847

- The Japanese Buddhist monk Ennin publishes a diary of his 838–847 stay in China. It contains detailed accounts of the country, in particular the anti-Buddhist persecution.

849

- Gottschalk is condemned as a heretic at the Synod of Quierzy for advocating the predestinarian view that the elect are destined for heaven as the damned are to hell, and that Christ's power of redemption is limited.

850–899

POLITICS, GOVERNMENT, AND ECONOMICS

Business and Economics

893

- A hospice for pilgrims to the shrine of St. James at Santiago de Compostela, Spain, is recorded.

Colonization

853

- Mufarrij-ibn-Salim establishes an independent Muslim Arab dynasty at Bari, southeastern Italy, which becomes a base for plundering central Italy.
- Olaf the White, son of the king of Norway, receives the submission of the Vikings in Ireland and makes Dublin his capital.

860

- Rurik, a semilegendary Viking chief, founds a state in northwest Asia with its capital at Novgorod. Taking its name from *Rus*, the Finnish name for the Swedish Vikings, the state becomes known as Russia.

870

- Foster brothers Ingolf and Hjorleif become the first Viking colonists of Iceland. Hjorleif is murdered by his Irish slaves, but Ingolf founds a successful settlement at Reykjavik.

Human Rights

883

- The Abbasid caliph's forces finally suppress the Zenj (African slave) rebellion that started in 869, after immense slaughter has been caused.

Politics and Government

850

c. 850 The city of Chichén Itzá is founded in the northern Yucatán, Mesoamerica, by the Putún Maya: by the end of the century it has become the leading center of Maya civilization.

April 4 Louis II, son of the Frankish emperor Lothair I, is crowned in Rome as emperor and king of Italy.

851

- Aethelwulf of Wessex defeats the Danes at Oakley, England, and King Athelstan of Kent defeats a Danish fleet at Sandwich, but another Danish fleet enters the River Thames, defeats the Mercians, and sacks the cities of London and Canterbury. The Danes then winter in England for the first time, in Thanet, Kent.
- The Danes led by King Oskar ravage Aquitaine, then sail to Rouen and plunder in the Beauvaisis, in the West Frankish Kingdom.

852

May 28   Louis II, King of the Franks, captures and executes Masar, an Arab pirate leader, at Benevento, Italy. The Sicilian Arabs respond with the devastation and occupation of Calabria.

September 9   Pepin II, the former king of Aquitaine, is captured by the Count of Gascony and delivered to the West Frankish king, Charles II the Bald, who forces him to become a monk.

853

- The nobles of Aquitaine rebel against their king, Charles II the Bald, and offer the crown to his brother Louis the German, who immediately invades Charles's kingdom.
- The West Frankish city of Tours is burned by Vikings; however, the inhabitants have warning of the attack and escape with their valuables.

May 22   A Byzantine naval expedition captures and burns the city of Damietta in Egypt.

854

- The former king of Aquitaine, Pepin II, escapes from the monastery where he was placed by the West Frankish king, Charles II the Bald, and reassumes the crown.
- The leading Danish king, Horik, is killed in a civil war following a rebellion within his own family. His kingdom disintegrates and little is known of Denmark for the next century.
- The Vikings sail up the River Loire to attack Orléans but the bishops of Orléans and Chartres gather an army and fleet and force them to retreat. Other Viking pirates successfully raid Frisia.

855

- On the death of Pope Leo IV a succession dispute breaks out. The clergy and people of Rome elect Benedict III, but the Frankish emperor, Louis II, installs Anastasius as pope, by force. When the popular antipathy to Anastasius becomes apparent, Louis gives way and allows Benedict's appointment; his authority suffers a setback as a consequence.

June 6   Charles, son of the West Frankish king, Charles II the Bald, is crowned as king of Aquitaine, but the Aquitainians soon drive him out in favor of their former king, Pepin II.

September 22   Worn out by illness, the Frankish emperor Lothair I retires to the monastery of Prüm (in present-day Germany) and partitions his lands among his three sons. The emperor Louis II receives Italy, Lothair II receives the area from Frisia to the Alps, called *Lotharii regnum* ("Reign of Lothair," Lotharingia or Lorraine), and Charles receives the kingdom of Provence. Lothair I dies six days later (September 28).

November 20   The Byzantine emperor, Michael III, begins his personal rule after arranging the murder of Theoctistus the Logothete, the principal minister of his mother, the empress and regent Theodora. Michael banishes Theodora to a convent.

856

February 10   By the Treaty of Louviers, the West Frankish king, Charles II the Bald, recognizes Erispoë as king of Brittany and grants him the county of Nantes.

August 8   Vikings led by Sidroc establish a camp on the island of Oissel in the River Seine and ravage as far as the River Loire in the West Frankish kingdom; they burn Paris in December.

857

- García Iñiguez, ruler of the Basque city of Pamplona, Spain, adopts the title king of Navarre.

858

- Desperate to acquire a legitimate heir for his kingdom, the Frankish king Lothair II of Lorraine divorces his childless wife Theutberga and marries his mistress Waldrada, by whom he has a son, Hugh.
- Fujiwara Yorifusa, a member of a leading aristocratic family, becomes regent for the young Japanese emperor, Seiwa. Yorifusa uses his position to consolidate the Fujiwara family's hold on power and reduce the emperors to mere figureheads under a perpetual regency. However, the Fujiwara are unable to maintain a strong central government and their rise marks the beginning of Japan's development into a decentralized feudal state.
- Kenneth I MacAlpin, the first king of Scotland, dies. He is succeeded by his brother, Donald I, who establishes a code of ancient laws, the "Laws of Aedh."

September 9   The West Frankish king, Charles II the Bald, is abandoned by his magnates, and his brother Louis the German takes possession of his kingdom.

859

- Making an unexpected counterattack from his last stronghold in Burgundy, the West Frankish king, Charles II the Bald, drives his brother, Louis the German, back into his own East Frankish kingdom.
- Vikings under Björn Ironside and Hastein raid the Moorish port of Algeciras in southern Spain.

860

- Kiev, a Khazar settlement on the Dnieper River in northwest Asia (modern Ukraine) is captured by Askold and Dir, two Viking chieftains.
- Vikings under Björn Ironside and Hastein penetrate the Mediterranean Sea, raiding Majorca, Narbonne, and sailing up the River Rhône as far as Valence. They sack Luna in Italy, mistaking it for Rome, and Pisa before returning home.

June 1   The Frankish kings Charles II the Bald, Louis the German, and Lothair II make peace at Coblenz, in the East Frankish kingdom, but soon afterwards Louis and Lothair ally against Charles.

June 18   Askold and Dir, the Viking rulers of Kiev (in modern Ukraine), are repulsed in an attack on Constantinople, the capital of the Byzantine Empire.

861

- The Moors of Spain defeat the Vikings under Hastein and Björn Ironside as they pass through the Straits of Gibraltar on their way home after raiding in the Mediterranean Sea.

- The West Frankish king, Charles II the Bald, besieges the Vikings based on the island of Oissel in the River Seine. He allows them to withdraw down the Seine after they pay him 2,720 kg/6,000 lbs of gold and silver.

December 11   When the Abbasid caliph (ruler of the Islamic world) al-Mutawakkil appoints al-Mu'tazz, his younger son by a concubine, as his heir, his legitimate son al-Muntasir conspires with the caliph's Turkish bodyguard, who murders him. Al-Muntasir becomes caliph but remains virtually the prisoner of the bodyguard.

862

- King Ordoño I of Asturias captures the Spanish city of Salamanca from the Moors.

May 29   The Abbasid caliph (ruler of the Islamic world) al-Muntasir is murdered by his Turkish bodyguards who place his brother, al-Musta'in, on the throne. The commanders of the bodyguard monopolize power, however.

863

- King Pyinbya of the Thai kingdom of Nanchao (in modern Yunnan, south China) takes Hanoi (in modern Vietnam).
- The Frankish king Lothair II of Lorraine bribes papal legates at a council in Metz to confirm his divorce from his childless wife Theutberga, and ratify his marriage to his mistress, Waldrada. The legates are excommunicated by Pope Nicholas II and Lothair's marriage is declared bigamous.
- The growing strength of Christian Armenia under the Bagratid dynasty is recognized when the Abbasid caliph, al-Musta'in, appoints King Ashot I the Great as "Prince of Princes."
- The West Frankish king, Charles II the Bald, invests his son-in-law, Count Baldwin I, in a march on the Channel coast to organize defenses against the Vikings; this develops into the county of Flanders.

January 25   Charles, King of Provence, dies without issue. His brothers, Louis II and Lothair II, share his lands.

September 3   Petronas, the uncle of the Byzantine emperor, Michael III, annihilates an Abbasid army which has invaded Anatolia. The Abbasid general Omar is killed in the battle, which ends the Arab threat to the Byzantine Empire.

864

- The former king of Aquitaine, Pepin II, having joined the Vikings, is handed over to the West Frankish king, Charles II the Bald, by the Aquitainians and sentenced to death.

865

- Prince Boris of the Bulgar Khanate converts to Christianity. After a short delay he accepts the jurisdiction of Constantinople rather than Rome.
- The conquest of Sicily by the Arabs is completed.
- Under its leaders Halfdan, Guthrum, and Ivar, the "Great Heathen Host," the largest Danish army yet seen, arrives in England bent on conquering lands for settlement.

January 1   Pope Nicholas I asserts papal authority in the Frankish kingdoms by ordering Archbishop Hincmar of Reims to reinstate Rothad as bishop of Soissons, whom he had earlier uncanonically deposed.

February 2   The West Frankish king, Charles II the Bald, and his brother, Louis the German of the East Frankish kingdom, meet at Douzy and agree to share their nephew Lothair II's lands between them if he dies without legitimate issue.

June 6   Threatened with excommunication by Pope Nicholas I, the Frankish king Lothair II obeys the Pope's order to take back his wife, Theutberga.

866

- Alfonso III becomes king of Asturias, Spain. He becomes known as "the Great" for his successful wars against the Moors.
- The Chinese repel invaders from the Thai kingdom of Nanchao in the Song Hong river delta (in modern Vietnam).
- The Frankish emperor, Louis II, makes his third expedition against the Arabs in southern Italy.
- The West Frankish king, Charles II the Bald, pays 1,815 kg/4,000 lb of silver in "Danegeld" to the Vikings who have taken the town of Melun. He uses this as an excuse to raise extraordinary taxes on the population, making a large surplus, which he keeps. Robert the Strong, Count of Angers, is killed in battle with the Vikings at Brissarthe.

January 24   The Abbasid caliph al-Musta'in is deposed and murdered by his Turkish guard and succeeded by his brother, al-Mu'tazz.

April 21   The Byzantine emperor Michael III's protégé Basil the Macedonian murders the logothete (chief minister), Caesar Bardas.

August 8   Khan Boris I of the Bulgars, in revolt against the Byzantine emperor, Michael III, who has refused to allow an independent Bulgarian ecclesiastical establishment, sends an offer of allegiance to Pope Nicholas I. Earlier in the year Boris put down an anti-Christian rebellion among his own people.

November 1   The "Great Heathen Host," the large Danish army which arrived in England in 865, takes the city of York by storm. The Northumbrian king, Aelle, is killed and the Danes place a puppet king on the throne.

867

- Ya'cub ibn-al-Laith al-Saffar ("the coppersmith"), a craftsman turned bandit leader, seizes control of Seistan (in eastern Persia) and establishes the Saffarid dynasty in independence from the Abbasid caliphate. Under Ya'cub the Persian language enjoys a revival after two centuries of strong Arabic influence.

September 24   The Byzantine emperor, Michael III, is murdered by his ruthless protégé, Basil the Macedonian, who succeeds him as Basil I, founding the Macedonian dynasty (867–1059) which brings the Byzantine Empire to the peak of its power.

December 14   Adrian II is crowned as pope.

868

- Ahmad-ibn-Tulun, the Turkish governor of Egypt, makes himself independent of the Abbasid Arab caliphate, founding the Tulunid dynasty.
- By raising the siege of Ragusa (modern Dubrovnik, Croatia) by Muslim forces, the Byzantine Empire restores its control over the Balkans, lost since the 6th century.
- King Alfonso III of Asturias, Spain, recaptures Oporto from the Moors.

869

- Pope Adrian II appoints Methodius as archbishop of Pannonia (modern Hungary). On his return to Moravia, Methodius is opposed by German bishops and imprisoned.

June 16   When the Abbasid caliph al-Mu'tazz attempts to curb the power of his Turkish bodyguard he is murdered and replaced with his brother, al-Muhtadi.

September 9   The West Frankish king, Charles II the Bald, ignoring the rights of the Frankish emperor Louis II and his own agreement with Louis the German of February 2, 865, is crowned as king of Lorraine following the death of Lothair II without legitimate issue.

November 20   King Edmund of East Anglia (later St. Edmund) is defeated and captured by the Danes at Hoxne (in Suffolk). He is used for archery practice and killed.

870

- Following the death of Ermentrude, his first wife, the West Frankish king, Charles II the Bald, marries Richildis, sister of Boso, Count of Vienne. Fearing disinheritance, Carloman, Charles's youngest surviving son by Ermentrude, rebels against his father.
- Prince Rostislav of Moravia is captured and deposed by his nephew, Svátopulk, who has plotted to murder him. Rostislav is handed over to Carloman, the son of the East Frankish king, Louis the German, who then conquers Moravia.
- The Arabs of Kairouan (in modern Tunisia) conquer the Byzantine-held island of Malta.

February 2   Boris I, Khan of the Bulgars, accepts the ecclesiastical authority of the Byzantine patriarch of Constantinople.

June 21   The Abbasid caliph (ruler of the Islamic world) al-Muhtadi is murdered by his Turkish guard when he tries to limit their powers; he is succeeded by his cousin, al-Mu'tamid. Thanks to his brother al-Muwaffak, who brings the Turkish bodyguards under control, he survives to die of natural causes in 892.

August 8   After invading Lorraine, the East Frankish king Louis the German meets the West Frankish king, Charles II the Bald, at Meerssen and forces him to agree to partition Lorraine according to their agreement of February 2, 865.

871

- London, in the Anglo-Saxon kingdom of Mercia, is occupied by the Danes.
- Svátopulk, the de facto ruler of Moravia, expels the Germans from Moravia.
- The West Frankish king, Charles II the Bald, suppresses a revolt by his son, Carloman, whom he has blinded.

January 1   The West Saxons under King Aethelred of Wessex, England, and his younger brother Alfred defeat the Danes at Ashdown (Berkshire) and drive them back into their camp at Reading in Wessex.

February 2   The Frankish emperor, Louis II, with Byzantine naval assistance, takes the Italian port of Bari from the Arabs; he later defeats Arabs from Salerno at Capua, Italy.

April 4   Alfred the Great becomes king of Wessex, England, on the death of his brother, King Aethelred.

872

- The Byzantine emperor, Basil I, defeats the Paulicians, a dualist heretic movement, destroying their fortress at Tephrice, and affecting their conversion to the Orthodox Church.
- The West Frankish king, Charles II the Bald, expels the Vikings from the town of Angers.
- Ya'cub ibn-al-Laith a-Saffar, the emir of Seistan (in eastern Persia), destroys the Tahirid dynasty of Hrasan.

873–874

- The Danes capture Repton, the royal center of the Anglo-Saxon kingdom of Mercia, England. Disheartened by his failure to resist the Danes, the Mercian king, Burgred, flees into exile in Rome. The Danish army winters at Repton and in the spring it splits up, Halfdan returning to York, Guthrum and the other leaders going to Cambridge.

874

- Alfonso III the Great, King of León, Asturias, and Galicia, Spain, defeats the Moors of Toledo at the Orbedo.
- By the Treaty of Forchheim, peace is made between the East Frankish king Louis the German and Svátopulk of Moravia who, for a time, becomes a tributary to the German king.
- Following a terrible drought, a peasant rising led by Huang Chao and Wang Xianzhi takes control of Henan in eastern China.
- Nasr ibn-Ahmad founds the Samanid dynasty of Transoxiana. Its capital at Bukhara becomes the center for a Persian cultural revival.

875

- Catalonia, formerly the Spanish March of the Carolingian Empire, is now being ruled by the counts of Barcelona in only nominal subjection to the Frankish kings.

August 12   Louis II, the Frankish emperor and king of Italy, dies. The Byzantine emperor, Basil I, subsequently takes possession of the Italian port of Bari.

December 12   The East Frankish king, Louis the German, invades Lorraine but withdraws on his failure to win local support.

December 25   The West Frankish king, Charles II the Bald, is crowned as emperor by Pope John VIII in Rome.

876

- Halfdan founds the Danish kingdom of York (which survives until 954). The Danes are now beginning to settle on the lands they have won in eastern England.

January 31   The Frankish emperor, Charles II the Bald, is accepted as king of Italy at Pavia, following the death of Louis II without legitimate issue. Charles promotes Boso, Count of Vienne, to duke and leaves him in charge of Italy when he returns to his West Frankish kingdom.

August 28   The East Frankish king Louis the German dies. His lands are divided between his sons Carloman (Bavaria and the East March), Louis the Younger (Saxony and Franconia), and Charles the Fat (Alemannia).

October 8   The Frankish emperor, Charles II the Bald, attempts to seize the kingdom of his nephew, Louis of

Saxony, but is defeated by Louis at Andernach, on the River Rhine.

877

- Ahmad-ibn-Tulun, Emir of Egypt, seizes Syria from the declining Abbasid caliphate.
- Constantine I, King of Scotland, is killed in battle with the Vikings of Dublin under Halfdan, the Danish king of York. Halfdan is then killed in the Battle of Strangford Lough, Ireland, against Baraidh, a Norse leader in Ireland.
- Photius is restored as patriarch of Constantinople on the death of Ignatius. His restoration is supported by Pope John VIII.

877–889 Indravarman I, ruler of the Khmer Empire (modern Cambodia) conquers the Thai and Mon people to the north and west.

May 7 The Frankish emperor, Charles II the Bald, orders the payment of a tax (*Tributum Normannicum* or "Norman Tribute") to pay the Danes to leave the Seine area of the West Frankish kingdom.

June 14 A capitulary issued by the Frankish emperor, Charles II the Bald, during an assembly at Quierzy seemingly recognizes the heritability of fiefs, in effect weakening the emperor's control over his vassals.

October 6 The Frankish emperor, Charles II the Bald, falls ill after a meeting with Pope John VIII at Vercelli, Italy, and dies at Briançon while returning to Francia to face a rebellion of his magnates. He is succeeded by his son Louis II the Stammerer.

878

- Rhodri Mawr the Great, King of Gwynedd, Powys, and Seisyllwg in Wales, dies. His kingdom disintegrates, leaving the Welsh more vulnerable to English pressure.

January 1 A surprise attack by the Danes in midwinter forces King Alfred the Great of Wessex, England, to take refuge in the marshlands of Athelney (in Somerset).

May 5 King Alfred the Great of Wessex, England, defeats the Danes at Edington (in Wiltshire). By the Peace of Wedmore which follows, the Danish leader, Guthrum, is baptized as a Christian.

May 21 Emir Ibrahim II of Kairouan (in modern Tunisia) captures the Byzantine city of Syracuse in Sicily. The Byzantines are reduced to an enclave around Taormina.

September 7 King Louis II the Stammerer is crowned as King of the Franks for a second time by Pope John VIII, at a synod at Troyes.

879

- Chinese peasant rebels under Huang Chao take the Chinese port of Guangzhou (Canton). About 120,000 "foreigners" (Muslims, Zoroastrians, Christians, and Jews) are said to have been massacred by the rebels. Though probably an exaggeration, this figure indicates the size of foreign trading communities who at this time dominate China's export trade, particularly with Korea and Japan.
- Nepal makes itself independent of Tibet.
- The Byzantine emperor Basil I publishes a revised compilation of Roman law.

April 10 Louis II the Stammerer, King of the Franks, dies. He is succeeded by his sons, Louis III and Carloman, after an abortive invasion by Louis of Saxony who tries to seize the kingdom.

October 15 Boso, Duke of Vienne, is crowned as king of Provence.

November 30 The Frankish kings Louis III and Carloman defeat the Vikings on the River Loire.

880

- Carloman of Bavaria, King of the Franks, dies and is succeeded by his brother, Louis of Saxony.
- Pope John VIII pays tributes to buy off Arab and Moorish attacks from the Aghlabid Emirate of North Africa on Rome.
- The Chinese peasant rebel leader Huang Chao declares himself emperor of China after his rebel forces take the Tang capital of Changan. Later in the year, he is defeated and executed by the Shatuo, the Turkish allies of the Chinese Tang emperor.
- The Greek church makes peace with the Pope after giving up any administrative claims over Bulgaria.
- The Vikings inflict a severe defeat on the forces of the Frankish king Louis the Younger in Saxony, killing 2 bishops, 12 counts, 18 other royal vassals, and a large number of their followers.
- Varagunavarman II of Pandya in southern India, attempting to crush the rising power of the Chola dynasty, is defeated at Sri Parambiyan by King Aditya I and his overlord, Nriputungavarman of Pallava.

March 3 By the Treaty of Ribemont the kingdom of Louis II the Stammerer is divided between his sons Louis III (Francia and Neustria) and Carloman (Burgundy and Aquitaine).

881

881–882 In the worst year of raiding ever experienced by the Low Countries and the Rhineland, the Vikings sack the cities of Liège, Tongres, Maastricht, Deventer, Neuss, Cologne, Bonn, Coblenz, Malmedy, Stavelot, Prüm, Aachen, and Trier.

February 12 Charles III the Fat of Germany is crowned as emperor by Pope John VIII in Rome.

August 3 Louis III, the Frankish king of Francia and Neustria, defeats the Vikings at Saucourt (on the River Somme).

882

- The Russian prince Oleg captures Kiev from the rival Viking leaders Askold and Dir, whom he kills, and makes it the capital of the Rus state (Russia) in place of Novgorod.

January 20 King Louis of Saxony and Bavaria dies and is succeeded by the Frankish emperor, Charles III the Fat of Alemannia, who thus reunites Germany.

August 5 Louis III, the Frankish king of Francia and Neustria, dies. He is succeeded by his brother and coruler, Carloman.

September 9 Richard the Justiciar, on behalf of the Frankish emperor, Charles III the Fat, takes Vienne and expels his brother Boso, the king of Provence.

September 9 The Viking army, having been paid by the Frankish emperor, Charles III the Fat, to leave the Rhineland, invades eastern France, sacking the city of Reims.

883

- The Chinese Tang emperor, Xizong, calls in the Shatuo Turks against the usurper Huang Chao and they quickly drive him out of Changan, the imperial capital.

884

- Count Diego de Porcelos founds Burgos as an outpost of the Spanish kingdom of Asturias; it later becomes the capital of the county and later of the kingdom of Castile.
- The usurping Chinese emperor, Huang Chao, is driven into Henan and finally into Shandong by the Tang emperor's Shatuo Turkish allies. Abandoned by most of his followers, Huang Chao commits suicide. Despite defeating the rebellion, the authority of the Tang dynasty has been permanently broken and power now devolves on provincial warlords.
- June 6   The Frankish king Carloman pays the Viking army 5,445 kg/12,000 lb of silver to leave Amiens; the main part of the army goes to England, the rest to Louvain.
- December 12   The Frankish King Carloman dies. He is succeeded, on the invitation of Carloman's nobles, by the Frankish emperor Charles III the Fat, who thus reunites the empire of Charlemagne under a single ruler.

885

- Ashot I the Great is recognized as king of Armenia by both the Abbasid caliphate and the Byzantine Empire. His reign marks the beginning of a century-long golden age of Armenian Christian culture.
- Godfrid, a Viking king ruling on the Lower Rhine by the grant of the Frankish emperor, Charles III the Fat, is killed in battle, thus ending Viking rule in Frisia.
- 885–900   King Harold Fairhair brings most of Norway under his direct control following his victory in Hafrsfjord (off Stavanger). Only the powerful jarls (earls) of Lade in the Trøndelag retain local autonomy.
- November 24   A Viking army under King Sigfrid lays siege to Paris, where the defense is led by Odo, son of Robert the Strong, Count of Neustria.

886

- A new Byzantine version of the Justinianic Roman law code, the 60-volume *Basilica*, is prepared by order of the Byzantine emperor, Basil I, and published by his son, Leo VI.
- King Alfred the Great of Wessex, England, expels the Danes from London and, in a treaty with the Danish king Guthrum, defines the frontier of the "Danelaw," the area of eastern England which is to be ruled by the Danes.
- August 29   The Byzantine emperor, Basil I, dies in a hunting accident and is succeeded by his son, Leo VI.
- October   After almost a year under siege by the Vikings, Paris is finally relieved by the Frankish emperor Charles III the Fat, but instead of fighting the Vikings he pays them 318 kg/700 lb of silver and allows them to sail further up the River Seine to raid in Burgundy.

887

- Amid dismay at his unwillingness to fight the Vikings, an assembly of German magnates at Tribur, near Darmstadt, deposes the Frankish emperor, Charles III the Fat, leading to the final breakup of Charlemagne's empire (the "Carolingian Empire").
- January 11   King Boso of Provence dies and is succeeded by his son, Louis.
- April 17   A popular rising in Venice compels the doge Giovanni II Particiaco to abdicate in favor of Pietro Candiano. On September 9, Candiano is killed in battle against the Slavs, and Particiaco resumes office as doge.

888

- Arab pirates establish a camp at Garde-Freinet, Provence, from which they prey on travelers crossing the Alpine passes.
- January 13   The deposed Frankish emperor, Charles III the Fat, dies and his empire is dismembered. German vassals declare his successor to be Arnulf of Carinthia, illegitimate son of Carloman of Bavaria; in Italy, Berengar, Margrave of Friuli, and Guy, Duke of Spoleto, contend for the crown; King Boso's son, Louis, holds Provence; Rudolph of Auxerre, Duke of Jurane Burgundy, establishes a kingdom of Burgundy; while in West Francia (which develops into the kingdom of France), surviving royal authority disintegrates.
- February 29   Odo, Count of Neustria and the hero of the siege of Paris in 885, is crowned as king of West Francia (hereafter known as France).
- April 4   Giovanni II Particiaco, the doge of Venice, dies. His successor, Pietro Tribuno, is chosen by the newly introduced system of popular election.
- June 24   King Odo of France defeats the Vikings at Montfaucon (on the Argonne plateau), restoring the prestige of the monarchy.
- October 24   King Arnulf of Germany, the former East Frankish kingdom (hereafter known as Germany), recognizes Rudolph I as king of Jurane Burgundy on the latter's cession of claims to Alsace and Lorraine.

889

- The Tibetan empire has broken up into a loose collection of petty kingdoms and chiefdoms.
- February 2   Guido, Duke of Spoleto, defeats Berengar, Margrave of Friuli, on the River Trebbia and is crowned at Pavia, Lombardy, as king of Italy.

890

- King Ashot I the Great of Armenia dies and is succeeded by Smbat I.
- The late King Boso's son, Louis, is recognized as king of Provence by King Arnulf of Germany and Pope Stephen V.

891

- Benevento, Italy, is briefly occupied by the Byzantines.
- February 11   King Guido of Italy is crowned as Roman emperor by Pope Stephen V.
- April 16   By his victory at Polei (now Aguilar), the Umayyad emir of Spain, Abdallah, defeats the revolt of ibn-Hafsun. In the same year he also suppresses a rebellion in Seville, Spain.
- June 26   A Viking army defeats and kills Count Arnulf and Archbishop Sunderolt of Mainz at Geule near Maastricht.
- October   King Arnulf of Germany wins an impressive victory over the Vikings at the Battle of the Dyle near Louvain and the Vikings withdraw to Boulogne. Arnulf's victory marks the end of the worst period of Viking raiding on the European mainland.

892

- Prince Svátopulk defeats King Arnulf of Germany's expedition into Moravia.
- The Danish army leaves France for England where King Alfred the Great of Wessex has used the respite from

Viking raids following his earlier victories to reform his army and build a fleet and a network of forts ("burhs") to resist them.

October 15 The Abbasid caliph al-Mu'tamid dies and is succeeded by his son, al-Mu'tadid, who returns the capital of the Arab caliphate to Baghdad from Samarra.

893

- King Alfonso III of Asturias defeats and kills Ahmad ibn-Mu'awiyah, who claims to be the Mahdi (messiah), at Zamora, Spain.

January 28 Following a revolt against King Odo of France organized by Archbishop Fulk of Reims, Charles the Simple, the posthumous son of Louis II the Stammerer, King of the Franks, is crowned king of France in his place.

894

- As part of a reaction against Chinese influence, the Japanese court stops sending official embassies to China.
- In an expedition to Italy, King Arnulf of Germany takes the town of Bergamo; Milan, Pavia, and other northern cities subsequently surrender to him.
- Prince Svátopulk of Moravia dies. His sons, Mojmír and Svátopulk II, succeed, recognize the German king Arnulf's supremacy, and engage in civil war.

December 12 The emperor Guido of Spoleto dies and is succeeded by his son and co-Roman emperor, Lambert of Spoleto.

895

- By blocking the River Lea, King Alfred the Great of Wessex, England, traps the Danes led by King Haesten in their camp near London. The Danes escape overland to Bridgnorth in Mercia, but lose their entire fleet to Alfred's West Saxons.
- King Arnulf of Germany appoints his son, Zwentibold, King of Burgundy, but without effect because Rodolph I remains in possession.
- Prince Spytihněv, son of Bořivoj I, regains Bohemia's independence from Moravia and accepts the supremacy of King Arnulf of Germany.
- The Byzantine emperor, Leo VI, prompts the Magyars (a nomadic people settled between the Dnieper and the Danube rivers) to attack the Bulgar Khanate. The Bulgar khan Symeon retaliates by inciting the Pechenegs, recent arrivals on the Dnieper, to invade Magyar territory. Consequently the Magyars, after their expulsion from Bulgaria, are forced to seek lands elsewhere and settle in central Europe, on the River Theiss.

896

- Frustrated by the effectiveness of King Alfred the Great's defenses in England, the Danish army disperses and settles in Northumbria and East Anglia, with a few going to join the Viking army on the River Seine in France.
- Seeking to escape the dominance of the Roman emperor Lambert of Spoleto, Pope Formosus calls on King Arnulf of Germany for help. Arnulf storms Rome and is crowned emperor by Formosus. However, Arnulf falls ill and is forced to leave Italy, Formosus dies soon afterwards, and Lambert recovers his position.
- The Bulgarian khan Symeon defeats a Byzantine army at Bulgarophygon and forces the Byzantine emperor Leo VI to pay tribute.

May 5 Pope Boniface VI is chosen by the Roman mob to succeed Pope Formosus, but dies a few days later. He is succeeded by Stephen VI, an ally of the emperor Lambert of Spoleto, who conducts a trial and condemnation of Formosus's corpse.

897

- King Aditya I defeats and kills Aparajita, the last Pallava king, whose lands in southern India are annexed by the Cholas.
- Odo recovers the French crown and pardons Charles the Simple, who was crowned king of France in opposition to Odo in 893.

July 7 Pope Stephen VI's treatment of the late Pope Formosus's corpse causes a popular rebellion in Rome: Stephen is deposed, jailed, and shortly afterwards strangled. The papacy now falls prey to bitter faction fighting—six Popes rule in the next six years.

898

- Richard the Justiciar, Count of Autun, Burgundy, defeats Vikings at Argenteuil, near Tonnerre.
- The Magyars, a Turkic nomadic people recently arrived in central Europe, raid into the Veneto, around Venice, northeast Italy.

January 1 King Odo of France dies; he is succeeded by Charles the Simple, the posthumous son of Louis II the Stammerer.

October 15 Lambert of Spoleto, Roman emperor and King of Italy, dies without issue; he is succeeded, unopposed, by his old rival Berengar, Margrave of Friuli.

899

- Duke Atenolf I of Capua, Italy, conquers the southern Italian region of Benevento from the Byzantines.
- The Shiite Qarmatian sect of Ismailites establish an independent state in Bahrain, on the Persian Gulf, from where they raid their neighbors.

September 24 After being routed by King Berengar of Italy on the River Brenta, Magyar raiders defeat Italian forces and ravage Lombardy in the north.

October 26 King Alfred the Great of Wessex, England, dies. He is succeeded by his son, Edward the Elder.

November 11 King Arnulf of Germany dies and is succeeded by his son, Louis the Child.

SCIENCE, TECHNOLOGY, AND MEDICINE

Agriculture

850

- According to legend, Kaidi, an Arab goatherd, is the first person to eat the coffee bean.

855

- Avantivarman, King of Kashmīr and founder of the Utpala dynasty, promotes irrigation programs to improve agriculture throughout his reign.

857

- Poisoned grain causes an outbreak of ergotism across western Europe.

Ecology

851

- Rome and central Italy are shaken by a severe earthquake.

Exploration

860

- Gardar the Swede, blown off course on a voyage to the Hebrides, Scotland, becomes the first Viking to visit Iceland.

Health and Medicine

857

- Arab physician Yuhannā ibn-Māsawayh writes *Daghal al-'Ain/Disorder of the Eye*, the oldest Islamic treatise on ophthalmology.

860

- A Chinese bronze of this date indicates hundreds of acupuncture points for use in traditional therapy, proving that treatment by this method is highly sophisticated by this period.

865

- Spanish physician Leon the Iastrosophist writes a medical encyclopedia recommending chemical treatments for illnesses.

869

- Jewish physician Sābūr ben Sahl prepares a pharmacopeia listing various ailments and the traditional remedies prescribed to cure them.

Science

850

- Persian mathematician and astronomer Al-Khwārizmī dies, having written *The Calculation of Integration and Equation – Image of the World*, with a map of the world and heavens, and his *zīj*, a collection of influential astronomical tables.

860

- Muhammad, Ahmad, and Hasan, sons of Musa ibn-Shakīr, spend a fortune on collecting classical scientific works and translating them into Arabic. They also write the *Book of Artifices*, the earliest extant Arabic treatise on mechanical engineering.

869

- Islamic theologian and *adab* writer al-Jahiz writes his *Kitāb al-Hayāwan/Book of Animals*, a description of many different species.

877

- Arab astronomer al-Battānī begins his observations at al-Raqqah observatory in Syria. He refines the calendar and demonstrates the possibility of annular eclipses, in which the moon obscures most of the sun, but leaves a bright ring around the edge.

886

- Islamic astronomer Abu Ma'shār writes a treatise on tides, among various attempts to synthesize Greek, Persian, and Indian astronomy. Other Arab scholars attack him for his belief in astrology, however.

Technology

851

- The crossbow is first used in France. Although it takes longer to load than traditional bows, the bolts it fires travel much further and faster.

868

May 11   A printed paper roll, dated May 11 and containing part of a Chinese translation of the Buddhist text *Dharani Sutra*, is the earliest surviving evidence for a printed book.

870

- The English at this time use slow-burning candles marked with calibrations to measure the time. The invention is attributed to King Alfred the Great, who also devised a lantern to shield them from the draft.

ARTS AND IDEAS

Architecture

c. **850**

- Chan Chan, the vast ceremonial capital of the Chimú state of coastal Peru, is founded.

862

- West Frankish king, Charles II the Bald, orders the construction of a fortified bridge at Pîtres on the River Seine to block the river to Viking raiders.

869

- The last-dated stele appears at the great Mayan city of Tikal. Mayan civilization begins to decline rapidly.

876

- Building begins on the great Mosque of Ahmad ibn Tūlūn at Cairo, Egypt. Built of brick and plaster, it is modeled on the mosque of Al-Mutawakkil at Samarra, Iraq.

885

- The abbey church of Corvey on Weser, Germany, is dedicated. The building contains a good example of the ground level porch called a "westwork," an innovation of Carolingian architecture.

889–910

- King Yasovarman I founds a new capital for the Khmer Empire in southeast Asia at Angkor (now in Cambodia).

Arts

894

- Native themes begin to appear in Japanese painting following the suspension of relations with China.

Literature and Language

c. 850

- Japanese poetess, Ono Komachi, is active around this time. Many of her short passionate love poems are in the *Kokinshu*.
- Jewish immigrants in central Europe form a distinct cultural identity, the Ashkenazim. Their language, Yiddish, is a fusion of various middle-eastern languages and Germanic dialects.
- The *Evangelienbuch/Harmony of the Gospels*, a verse rendition of Christ's life and teaching written in Old High German by a Weissenberg monk named Otfrid, first appears.

860

- The Hiragana phonetic alphabet is introduced in Japan.

c. 885

- The first extant French poem, the *Cantilène de Sainte Eulalie/Song of St. Eulalie*, which tells of a 4th-century Spanish martyr, appears.

890

- *Taketori Monogatari/The Story of the Bamboo Gatherer*, the earliest Japanese prose narrative, is published.

891

- Photius compiles *Myriobiblon/Library*, an enormous collection of notebooks on works read, with learned commentaries and judgments about Greek authors whose writings would otherwise have disappeared.

Thought and Scholarship

c. 851

- John Scotus Erigena, an Irish philosopher at the court of the West Frankish King Charles II the Bald, writes *De praedestinatione/On Predestination*, refuting the German theologian Gottschalk and arguing that sin bears its punishment within itself because evil is unknown to God.

c. 865

- In an attempt to reconcile Christianity with Neoplatonism, the Irish philosopher John Scotus Erigena writes *De divisione naturae/On the Division of Nature*. He divides nature into four categories: that which creates and is not created, that which creates and is created, that which does not create and is created, and that which does not create and is not created.

c. 883

- Notker Balbulus, a monk at the monastery of St. Gall, may have written *Gesta Karoli Magni/Early Tales of Charlemagne* at this time.

887

- *Rikkokushi/Six National Histories*, official court histories, are written in Chinese, based on the model of Chinese court records, and covering Japanese affairs (791–887).

890

- The court of Alfred the Great becomes a center of learning. Alfred translates works by St. Gregory the Great, *Orosius* (a 5th century work of history and geography), Bede, and Boethius. He may also have initiated the *Anglo-Saxon Chronicle*, an annalistic history of England continued to 1154.

894

- Asser, bishop of Sherborne, Wessex, and former tutor to Alfred, writes *Annales rerum gestarum Aelfredi Magni/ Life of King Alfred*.

SOCIETY

Education

850

- A university is founded at Salerno, Italy. It is the first such institution in medieval Europe.

863

- Caesar Bardas founds a secular university in Constantinople under Leo the Mathematician.

Everyday Life

869

September 9   The Zenj, African slaves employed in the saltpeter mines near Basra, Persia, rebel against their dreadful working conditions. Occupying southern Persia, they cut off the city of Baghdad from the lucrative Indian Ocean trade route to the east.

Religion

850

- A collection of documents, both genuine and forged, known as "the False Decretals," is produced in order to strengthen the legal rights of diocesan bishops against metropolitan bishops. The documents are attributed to St. Isidore of Seville.

858

- Pope Nicholas I strengthens papal authority by declaring that bishops are his delegates and not subject to secular authorities.

860

- Hincmar, archbishop of Reims, writes *De divortio Lotharii/On Lothair's Divorce*, a treatise opposing the Frankish king Lothair II's desire to divorce his childless wife and marry his mistress; it is the fullest defense to date of the Christian law of divorce.

861

- A major rift opens between the Roman Catholic and Greek Orthodox churches (the "Photian Schism") when Pope Nicholas I objects to the Byzantine emperor, Michael III, appointing Photius, a lay theologian, as patriarch of Constantinople.

862

- Byzantine emperor Michael III sends the Christian missionaries and brothers, Constantine (later called

Cyril) and Methodius, to convert Moravia, an area of central Europe. Cyril devises "Glagolitic" script (which is later developed into Cyrillic script) in order to translate the Bible and Liturgy into Slavonic.

863

- The schism between the Roman Catholic and Greek Orthodox churches deepens when Pope Nicholas I

excommunicates Photius, the patriarch of Constantinople (capital of the Byzantine Empire), for refusing to recognize his authority.

October 10   Pope Nicholas I deposes the archbishops of Cologne and Trier for their support of the bigamous marriage of Lothair II.

BIRTHS & DEATHS

855

- Ahmad ibn Hanbal, Muslim theologian, who founded a school of Islamic law called the Hanbali and adopted a traditionalist approach in interpreting and codifying the legal aspects of the Koran (the *sharia*), dies in Baghdad, Persia (*c.* 75).

856

February 4   Rabanus Maurus (or Hrabanus Magnentius), archbishop of Mainz, influential Benedictine theologian and scholar whose major work is *De rerum naturis/On the Nature of Things*, dies in Winkel, Franconia (*c.* 76).

858

- Al-Battānī, Arab astronomer and mathematician, born in Haran, Syria (–929).

c. 860

- Paschasius Radbertus, French abbot and theologian whose *De Corpore et Sanguine Christi/ Concerning Christ's Body and Blood*, has become the main Eucharistic interpretation, dies (*c.* 75).

862

- Servatus Lupus, Abbot of Ferrières, classical scholar and collector and copier of manuscripts, dies (*c.* 57).

865

February 3   St. Anskar, missionary, first archbishop of Hamburg, and patron saint of Scandinavia, dies in Bremen, Germany (64).

867

November 13   St. Nicholas I, Italian pope 858–867, who laid the theoretical foundations for the papal theocracy, dies in Rome (*c.* 47).

868

- Gottschalk of Orbais, monk, poet, and theologian, whose teachings on predestination aroused controversy in the medieval church, dies in Hautvilliers near Reims, France (*c.* 65).

869

February 14   St. Cyril (original name Constantine), scholar, theologian, and missionary, who together with his brother St. Methodius converted

the Danubian Slavs to Christianity, dies in Rome (*c.* 42).

870

- Al-Tabarī, Muslim physician, writer of *Firdaws al-Hikmat/Paradise of Wisdom*, the first medical encyclopedia to combine knowledge from all branches of medicine, dies.
- Muslim theologian al-Bukhārī, whose collection of traditional sayings of the prophet (*hadith*), *al-Sahīh/The Genuine Collection* achieves canonical status, dies.

873

c. 873   Al-Kindī, Arab Neoplatonic philosopher, alchemist, astrologer, optician and musical theorist, dies.

- Hunayn ibn Ishaq, Islamic scholar of Baghdad, who wrote *Ten Treatises on the Eye* and produced Arabic translations of works by Aristotle, Euclid, Galen, and Hippocrates, dies.

876

- Henry I the Fowler, German king 919–936, founder of the Saxon dynasty, born (–936).

c. 877

- John Scotus Erigena (or Johannes Scotus Eriugena) Irish theologian, translator, and commentator, dies (*c.* 64).

882

- Saadia ben Joseph, Jewish philosopher known for his Arabic translation and commentary on the Old Testament, and for *The Book of Beliefs and Opinions*, born in Dilaz, Egypt (–942).

December 21   Hincmar of Reims, archbishop of Reims, theologian and scholar of canon law, dies in Epernay, near Reims, France (*c.* 76).

885

April 6   St. Methodius, scholar, theologian, and missionary who, together with his brother St. Cyril, converted the Danubian Slavs to Christianity, dies (*c.* 59).

886

March 9   Abu Ma'shar of Balkh ("Albumazar"), leading Muslim

astrologer, dies in al-Wāsit, Iraq (98).

August 29   Basil the Macedonian, Byzantine emperor 867–886, who founded the Macedonian dynasty and formulated the *Basilica*, the Byzantine legal code, dies (*c.* 56).

887

- Ibn-Firnās, Spanish Muslim scholar and engineer, dies.

889

- Ibn Qutaybah, an *adab* writer, whose *Kitāb al-Ma'ārif/Book of Knowledge* is a manual of Arab history, dies.

891

January   'Abd ar-Rahman III, first caliph 929–961 and greatest ruler of the Umayyad Arab Muslim dynasty of Spain, born (–961).

c. February 6, 891   Photius, patriarch of Constantinople 858–867 and 877–866, who was largely responsible for the Byzantine resurgence in the 9th century, dies in Bordi, Armenia (*c.* 71).

c. 892

- Arab historian Al-Balādhuri, writer of *Futūh al-Buldān/Conquest of the Lands*, a history of Muslim conquests since the time of Muhammad, dies.

897

- Al-Isfahānī (Abu al-Faraj al-Isbahāni), Muslim literary scholar, author of the encyclopedic work on Arabic music *Kitab al-aghani/Book of Songs*, born in Isfahan, Persia (–967).
- Anastasius Bibliothecarus, scholar and papal adviser, who argued in favor of adding the words "from the son" to the Nicene creed against Photius, dies.

899

- Alfred the Great, King of Wessex 871–899, who defended Saxon England against the Danes, dies (*c.* 50).

864

- The Byzantine emperor, Michael III, compels Boris I, Khan of the Bulgars, to receive baptism as a Christian.

867

- Photius, the patriarch of Constantinople (capital of the Byzantine Empire) excommunicates and deposes Pope Nicholas I, declaring him a heretic, in retaliation for being excommunicated by the Pope in 863. Nicholas dies before hearing the patriarch's decree and Photius is himself deposed before the year is out, opening the way to a resolution of the crisis.

November 3 The Byzantine emperor Basil I deposes Photius and restores Ignatius as patriarch of Constantinople, ending the schism between Greek and Roman churches.

c. 873

- Prince Bořivoj of Bohemia converts to Christianity.
- The cult of the Buddha Amida, the "the Buddha of Immeasurable Light" begins to spread in Japan. Followers believe that when they die, Amida will take them to paradise in the western heavens. Many artists are inspired by the cult and the bodhisattva Kwannon (Kuan-yin in China) becomes extremely popular.

875

- Prince Bořivoj I of Bohemia is baptized by Methodius, a Byzantine missionary.

878

- The Serbian zupan Mutimir converts to Orthodox Christianity.

880

- Pope John VIII sanctions the use of Slavonic in the liturgy at the request of Methodius, the archbishop of Pannonia (modern Hungary).

882

December 15 Pope John VIII becomes the first pope to be assassinated when he is clubbed to death in obscure circumstances, probably as the result of a conspiracy by his many political enemies in the Roman aristocracy.

890

- Hamdan Qarmat establishes the headquarters of the (future) Shiite Qarmatian sect of Ismailites at the Dar al-Hirjah, near Kufa, Persia.

900–949

POLITICS, GOVERNMENT, AND ECONOMICS

Business and Economics

c. 942

- The wool and linen industries of Flanders are well established by this time.

948

- Qudama ibn-Ja'far writes the *Kitāb al- Kharāj*, an account of the Islamic taxation system.

Colonization

932

- With the capture of the city of Toledo, the Umayyad caliph Abd-ar-Rahman III completes his reunification of Muslim Spain (begun in 912).

936

- The Khitan nomads of Liao settle in northern China, making Beijing their southern capital.

Politics and Government

900

c. 900 Naymlap founds the Sicán state of coastal Peru.

c. 900 Silla, the leading Korean kingdom, collapses after a century of struggles between the monarchy and the aristocracy.

- Archbishop Fulk of Reims is murdered by Count Baldwin II of Flanders.
- King Donald II of Scotland dies. According to one version, he is killed by the Vikings at Dunottar, Scotland. Another version says that he dies of illness contracted while fighting the Highland clans. He is succeeded by his cousin, Constantine II.
- The Magyars from the Danube Basin raid Italy and Bavaria.
- The Samanid ruler, Ismail, seizes Khorasan (eastern Persia) from the Saffarid dynasty.

901

- Carinthia, a part of the German kingdom, is ravaged by the Magyars from the Danube Basin.

February 2 Louis III, King of Italy and Provence, is crowned Holy Roman emperor by Pope Benedict IV.

902

- The Irish expel the Vikings from Dublin, Ireland; many of the refugees settle in northwest England.

March 6   The Abbasid caliph al-Mu'tadid dies. He is the last caliph (ruler of the Islamic world) to rule in his own right; his successors are, generally, controlled by their Turkish bodyguards.

August 1   Emir Ibrahim II of Kairouan (in modern Tunisia) destroys Taormina, the last Byzantine fortress in Sicily. He is subsequently killed attacking Cosenza in southwestern Italy.

903

- Pope Benedict IV excommunicates Count Baldwin II of Flanders for murdering Archbishop Fulk of Reims in 900.
- The city of Tours is burned by the Vikings.

September   After a reign of only 30 days, Pope Leo V is deposed and jailed by one of his priests, Christopher, who makes himself pope as Sergius II.

904

- The Chinese warlord Zhuwen murders the Chinese Tang emperor, Zhaozong, and all his sons except for Aidi, a 13-year-old boy, whom he sets up as puppet emperor.

July 31   An Arab fleet under Leo of Tripoli, a Greek renegade, sacks the Byzantine port of Thessaloníki (Salonika).

905

- With the extinction of the Tulunid dynasty, the Abbasid caliphate recovers control of Syria and Egypt.

July 21   Berengar of Friuli, the deposed king of Italy, captures the emperor, Louis III, at Verona, blinds him, and expels him from Italy back to his kingdom of Provence.

906

- After defeating a German and Slav army at Pressburg, the Magyars overrun and destroy the Moravian kingdom and also raid Saxony.
- Regino of Prüm publishes *Two Books Concerning Synodical Causes and Church Discipline*, a handbook for bishops on the judicial interrogation of jurymen.

907

- Prince Oleg, the Rus (Swedish Viking) ruler of the principality of Kiev (in modern Ukraine), attacks Constantinople, the capital of the Byzantine Empire, with a large fleet of Rus and their Slav allies, but is driven off by the Byzantines.
- The Chinese warlord Zhuwen deposes Aidi, the last Tang dynasty emperor, and declares himself Chinese emperor. The Tang empire collapses and China fragments into 11 warring states, beginning the "Period of the Five Dynasties and the Ten Kingdoms" (907–960). Zhuwen and his successors, styled the Later Liang dynasty, establish control over the Chang Jiang Basin, the richest region of China.

908

- The "tribal dukes" have their origin in Germany. Faced with weak royal leadership, the Bavarians elect Arnulf as their duke to organize defense against the Magyars and, almost simultaneously, Burchard is elected in Swabia, Conrad in Franconia, and Reginar in Lorraine.
- The Magyars from the Danube Basin defeat the Bavarians, killing the margrave Liutpold, and raid Saxony and Thuringia.

- The Samanid dynasty of Transoxiana extinguishes the Saffarids of Seistan (eastern Persia).

December 17   Al-Mustada is caliph for one day before being deposed and murdered.

909

December 7   After overthrowing the Sunni Aghlabid dynasty of Kairouan (in modern Tunisia), Sa'id ibn-Husayn is proclaimed as Ubaydullah al-Mahdi ("the divinely guided one") in Tunis and sets up an Ismailite (Shiite) caliphate in opposition to the Sunni caliphate of Baghdad (in modern Iraq). Al-Mahdi founds the Fatimid dynasty (named for the Islamic prophet Muhammad's daughter Fatima, from whom Sa'id claims descent).

910

- The Magyars defeat King Louis the Child of Germany near Augsburg.
- Vikings pillage in Berri and kill the archbishop of Bourges.

August 5   King Edward the Elder of Wessex, England, defeats Northumbrian Danes raiding Mercia at Tettenhall, Staffordshire, killing two Danish kings, Halfdan and Eowils, and several jarls (earls).

December 12   King Alfonso III of Asturias, Spain, abdicates in favor of his son, García I, who moves the capital from Oviedo to León, from which the kingdom now takes its name.

911

- Ethelred, ealdorman of Mercia, England, dies and is succeeded by his wife, Aethelflaed (daughter of King Alfred the Great), known as "the Lady of the Mercians." Her brother, King Edward the Elder of Wessex, occupies London, formerly a Mercian city.
- King Charles III the Simple of France receives the homage of Rollo (Hrolf), the Norse leader established on the River Seine, at St. Clair-sur-Epte. Rollo agrees to prevent other Vikings entering the Seine and is baptized as a Christian. In return, Charles grants him the county of Rouen. Rollo's lands become known as Normandy after the *Nordmanni* ("Northmen").
- Prince Oleg of the Rus principality of Kiev agrees a trade treaty with the Byzantine Empire. The treaty gives the Rus (Swedish Vikings of Kiev) the right to serve in the imperial army and navy.

November 11   Duke Conrad of Franconia is elected king of the Germans as Conrad I.

912

- Ubaydullah al-Mahdi, the Fatimid caliph (Islamic ruler) of Kairouan (in modern Tunisia) founds a new capital at Al-Mahdiyah on the east coast of Tunisia.
- With the River Seine closed to them by the Norse leader Rollo (Hrolf) in 911, the Vikings in France turn their full fury on the Bretons to the northwest.
- Zhuwen, the first emperor of the Later Liang dynasty of northern China, is murdered by his son Yingwang, who succeeds him.

April 4   Arabs under the Greek renegades Leo of Tripoli and Damian destroy a Byzantine fleet off the island of Chios in the Aegean Sea.

May 12   The Byzantine emperor Leo VI dies and is succeeded by his brother, Alexander, who withholds payment of tribute from the Bulgars, causing their khan, Symeon, to declare war.

October 15 Abdallah, the Umayyad emir of Córdoba, Spain, dies and is succeeded by his grandson, Abd-ar-Rahman III, whose control in Spain, as a result of a Berber (Moorish) rebellion, is almost confined to Córdoba.

913

June 6 Shortly after provoking a war with the Bulgars, the Byzantine emperor, Alexander, dies leaving the empire in the hands of his seven-year-old nephew Constantine VII (the son of the former emperor Leo VI).

August 8 An invasion by Symeon, Khan of the Bulgars, reaches the walls of Constantinople, the capital of the Byzantine Empire.

December 20 Muslim rebels holding the Spanish town of Seville surrender to Abd-ar-Rahman III, the emir of Córdoba, Spain.

914

- King Smbat I of Armenia is executed by the Sajid emir Yūsuf of Azerbaijan; he is succeeded by Ashot II the Iron.
- Ubaydullah al-Mahdi, the Fatimid caliph (Islamic leader) of Kairouan (in modern Tunisia), takes the city of Alexandria in Egypt from the Abbasid caliphate.
- Vikings from Brittany under Hroald and Ottar raid the Severn estuary in southwestern England but are defeated by the levies of Hereford and Gloucester and are killed.

915

- Duke Henry of Saxony, the most powerful of the German "tribal dukes," successfully defends his independence in a revolt against King Conrad I of Germany.
- Hugh the Black, son of Richard the Justiciar, Duke of (French) Burgundy, becomes the first Count of the Franche-Comté of Burgundy.
- On the initiative of Pope John X, the Arab base on the River Garigliano in Italy is destroyed by Byzantine and Italian forces, thus ending the Arab presence in central Italy.
- The Chola king Parantaka I conquers the Pandya kingdom in southern India.

December 12 Berengar of Friuli, King of Italy, is crowned by Pope John X as emperor of the Romans.

916

- Apaochi, chief of the Qitan (or Khitan Mongol) nomads, proclaims himself emperor of the Qitan and establishes the state of Liao in imitation of Chinese methods of government. Liao survives until 1125. The Qitan are also known as Kitai from which the medieval European name for China, "Cathay," is derived.
- King Indra III of the central Indian Rashtrakuta dynasty takes Kanauj, capital of the Pratihara dynasty of northern India. Although the Pratiharas soon recover their capital, their power does not fully recover.

917

- Duke Arnulf of Bavaria forcibly recovers his duchy after being dispossessed for rebellion against King Conrad I of Germany.
- King Edward the Elder of Wessex, England, conquers the Danes of East Anglia while his sister Aethelflaed, "the Lady of the Mercians," captures Derby from the Danes.

- Magyars raid southern Germany, Alsace, and Burgundy, sacking Basel. The French nobles refuse to join King Charles III the Simple of France in resisting them.
- The Fatimid caliph (Islamic leader) of Kairouan (in modern Tunisia), Ubaydullah al-Mahdi, conquers Arab Sicily.
- The Umayyad emir of Córdoba, Abd-ar-Rahman III, comes closer to establishing control over his Spanish emirate with the death of the rebel leader Umar ibn-Hafsun.
- Vikings under Sihtric recapture Dublin, Ireland, from the Irish.

January 21 King Conrad I of Germany executes the rebel Count Palatine Erchanger.

August 20 The Bulgar khan, Symeon, demands that he should be recognized as Byzantine emperor, after defeating the imperial forces near Anchialus on the River Achelous, invading Thrace, and making himself master of the Balkans.

918

January 2 Count Baldwin II of Flanders is murdered. He is succeeded by his son, Arnold I.

June 12 On the death of his sister Aethelflaed, the "Lady of the Mercians," King Edward the Elder annexes Mercia to his kingdom of Wessex. He also completes the conquest of the Danish Midlands.

December 23 King Conrad I of Germany dies. Shortly before his death he recognizes his failure to establish royal authority and recommends to the magnates that they choose Duke Henry the Fowler of Saxony as his heir.

919

- King Rudolph II of Burgundy is prevented, by his defeat at Winterthür, from extending his domains to the east of the River Rhine.
- Ragnald, a Norwegian Viking from Ireland, seizes the kingdom of York, England, from the Danes and becomes king of Northumbria.
- The Vikings under Rognvald conquer Brittany (northwest France), making Nantes their capital. Those Bretons who are able to escape seek refuge with King Athelstan in England.

May 5 Henry the Fowler, Duke of Saxony, is elected King Henry I of the Germans, the first king of the Saxon dynasty.

September 15 Niall Glúndub ("Black-knee"), High King of Tara, five subkings, and many nobles are killed in battle against the Norsemen near Dublin, Ireland.

920

- Abd-ar-Rahman III, the Umayyad emir of Córdoba, Spain, defeats Ordoño II of León and Sancho of Navarre at Val de Junqueras.

December 17 The young Byzantine emperor, Constantine VII, makes his father-in-law, Romanus Lecapanus, coemperor; he soon becomes effective master of the Empire.

921

- Richard the Justiciar, Duke of French Burgundy, dies. He is succeeded by his son, Raoul.
- Robert, Duke of Neustria, besieges the Vikings on the River Loire for five months but allows them to withdraw after surrendering hostages.

- St. Ludmilla, the widow of King Bořivoj I of Bohemia, is murdered by her daughter-in-law, Drahomira of Stodor, the widow of Vratislav I and guardian of their sons, Wenceslas and Bolesław.

November 7   King Charles III the Simple of France meets King Henry I the Fowler of Germany in Bonn and is recognized by him as king of Lorraine.

922

- King Ashot II of Armenia assumes the title "king of kings" in his attempt to assert supremacy in Caucasia.
- The ecstatic Sufi mystic, al-Hallāj, is executed by the Abbasid authorities in Baghdad for alleged offenses including blasphemy and rebellion.

February 2   King Rudolph II of Burgundia is crowned king of Italy.

June 6   Robert, Duke of Neustria, is crowned as king of France in a revolt against King Charles III the Simple.

923

- Taking advantage of Robert of Neustria's rebellion against King Charles III the Simple of France, the Vikings raid Aquitaine and the Auvergne in southern France.
- The Byzantine city of Adrianople (modern Edirne, Turkey) is taken by Symeon, Khan of the Bulgars.
- The Later Liang dynasty, the first of the "Five Dynasties" of northern China, is overthrown by the Shatuo Turks, who establish the Later Tang dynasty.

June 15   The usurping king of France, Robert of Neustria, defeats King Charles III the Simple of France at Soissons, but is himself killed in the battle. Charles is captured and imprisoned by Count Herbert of Vermandois.

July 13   Duke Raoul of Burgundia is crowned as king of France in succession to Robert of Neustria. He cedes the duchy to Giselbert, who is challenged by Robert's brother, Count Hugh the Black, and by Duke Hugh the Great of the Franks.

July 17   King Rudolph II of Burgundia, who was crowned king of Italy in 922, defeats Berengar of Friuli, the ex-king of Italy, at Fiorenzuola, near Piacenza, northern Italy.

September 9   Ordoño II of León, Spain, dies; he is succeeded by his brother, Froila II, who is immediately faced with a civil war.

924

- Abd-ar-Rahman III, the Umayyad emir of Córdoba, Spain, sacks Pampeluna (modern Pamplona), the capital of the Spanish kingdom of Navarre.
- Alfonso IV succeeds his uncle, Froila II, as king of León, Spain.
- King Raoul of France cedes Bayeux to the Norse Count Rollo of Normandy to buy peace.
- Symeon, Khan of the Bulgars, fails in his attempt to take the Byzantine capital, Constantinople. In negotiations afterwards, the Byzantines recognize Symeon's right to call himself "emperor of the Bulgars" but not his claim to the Byzantine throne.
- The Magyars resume their raids. In Italy they burn the northern city of Pavia, but King Rudolph of Italy and Hugh of Arles, the effective ruler of Provence, drive them off into southern France. They also invade Germany, where King Henry I the Fowler obtains a

truce for Saxony, which he uses to strengthen his duchy by building fortified towns.

- Vikings raiding on the River Loire in France demand that King Raoul of France grant them a fief, like the Norse Count Rollo of Normandy, but are repulsed.

July 17   King Edward the Elder of England dies; he is succeeded by his capable son, Athelstan.

925

- Count Herbert of Vermandois has his son, Hugh (aged five), elected as archbishop of Reims, France.
- Despite King Raoul of France's concessions to the Norse Count Rollo of Normandy in 924, Vikings from Rouen sack the northern French towns of Amiens and Arras.
- King Henry I the Fowler of Germany takes possession of the kingdom of Lorraine and subjects it, as a duchy, to the German crown.

926

- Eastern France is raided by the Magyars.
- Symeon, Khan of the Bulgars, is defeated by Tomislav, the first king of Croatia.
- The Khitan people of Liao, northeastern China, obtain the cession of northeastern Hebei province.

May 2   Duke Burchard of Swabia is killed on his way to assist King Rudolph of Burgundy and Italy against Hugh of Arles, Count of Provence, who has been elected king by the Italians. Rudolph is forced to abandon Lombardy, northern Italy.

July 7   Hugh of Arles, Count of Provence, is crowned as king of Italy.

927

- Athelstan, King of Wessex and Mercia, drives the Norse king Guthfrith out of York and receives the submission of the Northumbrians, so becoming the first king to rule all of England. In a meeting near Penrith, Cumberland, the kings of Scotland and Strathclyde recognize Athelstan as their overlord.
- King Alfonso IV of León, Spain, abdicates in favor of his brother, Ramiro II, and joins a monastery.
- St. Odo becomes abbot of Cluny where he gains papal recognition of the abbey's independence and reasserts the vows of the Rule of Benedict.
- The *Engi Shiki*, an elaboration of older Japanese law codes, is produced in a vain attempt to check the collapse of the imperial fiscal system in Japan.

May 27   Symeon, Khan of the Bulgars, dies; he is succeeded by his son, Peter, who makes peace with the Byzantine emperor. The emperor recovers authority over Serbia, where Caslav, its prince, had previously been subject to the khan.

928

- Abas I succeeds his brother, Ashot II, as king of Armenia.
- King Henry I the Fowler of Germany takes the town of Brandenburg in his war against the pagan Wends (Slavs).
- Mardaviz ebn Zeyar takes advantage of a rebellion in the Samanid emirate's army to found the independent Zeyarid dynasty in Jurjan (Persia).

928–929   King Henry I the Fowler of Germany compels Duke Wenceslas of Bohemia to acknowledge his supremacy.

May 5 Pope John X is deposed and murdered. He is succeeded by Leo VI, who dies before the year is out and is replaced by another puppet pope, Stephen VII, who is completely dominated by the aristocracy of Rome.

929

- Otto, the son of the German king Henry I the Fowler, marries Edith, daughter of King Athelstan of England.

January 16 Abd-ar-Rahman III, the Umayyad emir of Córdoba, Spain, adopts the title caliph (ruler of the Islamic world), thus ending his purely nominal dependence on the Abbasid caliphate of Baghdad.

September 4 A German army defeats the pagan Wends at Lenzen, on the River Elbe, and they are compelled to submit and accept Christianity.

September 28 Duke Wenceslas of Bohemia (later St. Wenceslas) is murdered by his brother, Bolesław I, who succeeds him and asserts his independence of the German king, Henry I the Fowler.

October 7 Charles III the Simple, the deposed king of France, dies, still the prisoner of Count Herbert of Vermandois.

930

- On the death of Emperor Daigo of Japan, members of the Fujiwara family acquire full powers as regents.
- The Althing (parliament) is established in Iceland; it meets annually until it is abolished by the Danes in 1800.
- The Qarmatians (an Ismailite Muslim sect) sack the Islamic holy city of Mecca (in modern Saudi Arabia) and remove the Black Stone revered by Muslims from the Kaaba. It is restored in 951.

931

- Abd-ar-Rahman III, the Umayyad caliph (Islamic ruler) of Córdoba, Spain, takes the port of Ceuta (in modern Morocco) from the Berber Idrisid emirate.
- King Raoul of France removes the 11-year-old Hugh of Vermandois from the archbishopric of Reims and appoints Artaud.
- The Norse Count Rollo of Normandy (northern France) dies; he is succeeded by his son, William Longsword.

932

- Hugh of Arles, King of Italy, marries the Roman senatrix Marozia, Pope John XI's mother. In an ensuing Roman revolt, Hugh is expelled from Rome, the Pope is imprisoned, and Marozia disappears. Alberic, another of her sons, who led the revolt, now rules Rome and becomes its duke.
- The Annamese (ancestors of the Vietnamese) rebel against Chinese rule.

933

- Hugh of Arles, King of Italy, cedes his claims to Provence to King Rudolph II of Burgundy, on the latter promising not to enter Italy; Provence is thus united with the kingdom of Burgundy.
- King Harold I Haarfager of Norway dies; he is succeeded by his son Erik Bloodaxe who kills two of his brothers in order to secure the throne.
- King Raoul of France grants Avranches and Coutances to the Norse Count William Longsword of Normandy in order to gain his allegiance.

March 15 King Henry I the Fowler of Germany defeats the Magyars of the Danube Basin at Riade, near Merseburg.

934

- King Athelstan of England makes a punitive expedition into Scotland to subdue the rebellion of Constantine II, King of Scotland, reaching Kincardineshire.
- King Henry I the Fowler of Germany forces King Gorm the Old of Denmark to make peace and establishes the March of Schleswig. He also completes his subjection of the Wends of the Lower Oder.
- Magyar raiders from Hungary reach Constantinople, the capital of the Byzantine Empire, but fail to take the city.
- The Byzantine general John Curcuas takes Melitene (modern Malatya in Turkey), near the upper Euphrates River.
- The Fatimid caliph (Islamic leader), Ubaydullah al-Mahdi of Kairouan (in modern Tunisia), plunders Genoa, Corsica, and Sardinia. He dies and is succeeded by his son, Mohammad al-Qa'im.

935

c. 935 Topiltzin-Quetzalcoatl, a Toltec ruler whose opposition to human sacrifice ultimately causes the Toltecs to expel him, is born in Central America. He later becomes identified with the god Quetzalcoatl ("feathered serpent").

- King Raoul of France repulses Magyars raiding in Burgundy.
- The Venetian doge, Pietro Candiano, captures and burns the rival Italian port of Comacchio.
- Wang Kon reunites Korea, founding the Koryŏ dynasty (which gives the name "Korea"), with the capital at Kaesong.

February 2 The Turk Mohammad ibn Tughj al-Ikhshid, governor of Egypt, founds the Ikshidid dynasty of Egypt.

936

- Alain Barbetorte, a Breton chief exiled in England, returns to Brittany with King Athelstan of England's help to begin a campaign to liberate the country from the Vikings. He surprises a party of Vikings at Dol and executes them. Later in the same year he destroys a Viking fort at Péran near St. Brieuc.
- Harald Bluetooth succeeds his father, Gorm the Old, as king of Denmark.
- The Later Tang dynasty, the second of the "Five Dynasties" of northern China is overthrown, with help from the Qitan nomads, by the Shatuo Turkish general Shi Jingtang, who founds the Later Jin dynasty.

June 19 Louis IV d'Outremer, son of Charles III the Simple, is recalled from exile in England by Count Hugh the Great, the Capetian Duke of the Franks, and crowned king of France following the death of King Raoul.

July 2 King Henry I the Fowler of Germany dies. He is succeeded by his son, Otto I.

937

- A Magyar force raids France as far west as Reims, and then moves through Berri and Burgundy to Italy.
- Abd-ar-Rahman III, the Umayyad caliph (Islamic ruler) of Córdoba, Spain, takes Zaragoza in a campaign against the Spanish kingdoms of León and Navarre; King García I of Navarre recognizes his suzerainty.

- King Athelstan of England wins a victory against a coalition of Scots, Strathclyde Welsh, and Norsemen at "Brunanburgh" (location unknown), confirming his position as the dominant ruler in the British Isles.
- The Breton chief Alain Barbetorte expels the Vikings from Nantes in Brittany (northwestern France).
- The Turk Mohammad ibn Tughj al-Ikhshid, governor of Egypt, seizes Palestine and Syria from the Abbasid caliphate of Baghdad.

July 12   King Rudolph II of Burgundy dies. He is succeeded by his son, Conrad, a minor.

938

- Erik Bloodaxe, King of Norway, is overthrown by his brother Haakon I.
- King Louis IV of France invades Lorraine at the request of its duke, Gilbert, who is in rebellion against his overlord, King Otto I of Germany.
- King Otto I of Germany seizes King Conrad of Burgundy and his kingdom, enforces recognition of his authority in Bavaria, and repulses a Magyar force in Saxony.
- The French duchy of Burgundy is partitioned by a treaty between Giselbert and his rivals, Hugh the Great and Hugh the Black.

939

- Hugh the Great, Duke of the Franks, and Count Herbert of Vermandois, rebelling against King Louis IV of France, expel Archbishop Artaud from Reims and replace him with the young Hugh of Vermandois, who previously occupied the archbishopric.
- King Otto I of Germany suppresses a rebellion in Saxony and Thuringia.
- Olaf Guthfrithson, the Norse king of Dublin, Ireland, takes the Danish kingdom of York in England.
- The Annamese rebel leader Ngo Quyen defeats the Chinese and founds the kingdom of Dai Viet (or Annam, modern northern Vietnam), with his capital at Co-loa.
- The Breton chief Alain Barbetorte completes the liberation of Brittany (northwestern France) from the Vikings when he takes their stronghold at Trans near Dol.

July 22   King Ramiro II of León, Spain, defeats Abd-ar-Rahman III, the Umayyad caliph (Islamic ruler) of Córdoba, Spain, at Simancas, near Valladolid in northwestern Spain.

September 9   King Otto I of Germany repels an invasion by King Louis IV of France in support of a German rebellion. This collapses after the deaths of its leaders, the dukes Everard of Franconia and Gilbert of Lorraine, in a skirmish at Andernach. Otto takes possession of Franconia.

October 27   King Athelstan of England dies and is succeeded by his brother, Edmund.

940

- Arab pirates raid deep into the Alps, in the kingdom of Burgundy.
- King Edmund of England cedes Northumbria and the Danelaw to Olaf Guthfrithson, the Norse king of Dublin and York, after he occupies the "Five Boroughs" of Lincoln, Stamford, Nottingham, Derby, and Leicester.
- King Otto I of Germany enters France at the request of Duke of the Franks Hugh the Great and Count Herbert

of Vermandois, who are rebelling against King Louis IV of France, and receives their homage.
- The declining authority of the French monarchy is demonstrated when King Louis IV grants the county of Reims to its archbishop (the king hopes he will have more influence over the election of bishops than over counts, whose positions have become hereditary).
- The Mixtecs sack the ancient Zapotec capital of Monte Albán, Mexico.

941

- An attack on the Byzantine capital, Constantinople, by Prince Igor of the Rus principality of Kiev, is repelled.
- Muirchertach, King of the northern Uí Néill, ravages the Viking settlements in the Hebrides, off the west coast of Scotland, in reprisal for pirate raids on Ireland.
- The Byzantine general John Curcuas resumes his conquests in Mesopotamia.

942

- King Edmund of England recaptures the "Five Boroughs" (Lincoln, Stamford, Nottingham, Derby, and Leicester) from Olaf Guthfrithson, the Norse king of York and Dublin.
- King Otto I of Germany releases King Conrad of Burgundy as his vassal.

November 11   King Otto I of Germany and King Louis IV of France meet at Visé (on the River Meuse) and are reconciled. Deprived of his ally, the rebel Hugh the Great, Duke of the Franks, submits to Louis.

December 17   William Longsword, the Norse Count of Normandy in northern France, is murdered by Arnold I, Count of Flanders. He is succeeded by his son Richard I.

943

- Count Herbert II of Vermandois, France, dies. His sons divide his lands.
- King Constantine II of Scotland retires to the monastery of St. Andrews (where he dies in 952) and is succeeded by his nephew, Malcolm I.
- King Louis IV of France grants the duchy of Burgundy to Hugh the Great, Duke of the Franks.
- Viking pirates, possibly from the Rus principality of Kiev, make raids in the Caspian Sea and sack the Caucasian city of Barda.

944

- King Edmund of England expels the Norse kings from York.
- King Louis IV of France is captured by the Vikings of Rouen, Normandy, who deliver him to Hugh the Great, Duke of the Franks.

October 10   Sayf ad-Dawlah establishes himself in Aleppo, Syria, and extends his authority over northern Syria, founding the Hamdanid dynasty.

December 16   The Byzantine emperor, Romanus I Lecapanus, is deposed and exiled by his sons. The coemperor, Constantine VII, assumes sole rule and crushes the rebellion of Romanus's sons.

945

- Berengar, Marquess of Ivrea, leads a revolt against King Hugh of Italy and seizes control of Lombardy.
- King Edmund of England conquers the British (Welsh) kingdom of Strathclyde (including Cumberland and Westmorland) and gives it to his ally, King Malcolm I of Scotland.

- King Louis IV of France surrenders his capital, Laon, to Hugh the Great, Duke of the Franks, to obtain his release from imprisonment.
- Prince Igor, Grand Prince of Kiev, makes peace with the Byzantine Empire. He is killed by rebels soon afterwards, and is succeeded by his son, Svjatoslav, whose mother, Olga, acts as regent.

946

- King Louis IV of France, assisted by King Otto I of Germany, takes the French city of Reims, expels Archbishop Hugh of Vermandois, and restores Artaud in his place.
- Mohammad al-Qa'im, the Fatimid caliph (Islamic leader) of Kairouan (in modern Tunisia), dies. He is succeeded by his son, al-Mansur.

January 17 Ahmad ibn-Buwayh Adud ad-Dawlah, the Shiite Muslim ruler of western Persia, expels the Turks from Baghdad, the capital of the Abbasid caliphate. His Buwayhid dynasty now rules the Arab caliphate from its capital of Shīrāz and has the title of sultan. The Abbasid caliph is reduced to a religious figurehead without political power.

May 26 King Edmund of England is murdered at a feast in Pucklechurch, England, by a common criminal. He is succeeded by his brother, Eadred.

947

- King Otto I of Germany grants the duchy of Bavaria to his brother, Henry, on the death of Duke Berthold.
- Weakened by devastating Khitan nomad invasions, the Later Jin dynasty, the third of the "Five Dynasties" of northern China, is overthrown by Gaozu, a Shatuo Turk general, who establishes the Later Han dynasty.

948

- Al-Mansur, the Fatimid caliph (Islamic ruler) of Kairouan (in modern Tunisia), appoints Hasan ibn-Ali as governor of Sicily. The office continues in his family (the Kalbite dynasty) and it establishes an ordered state in Sicily.
- Erik Bloodaxe, the deposed king of Norway, captures York, England, and makes himself king.

April 10 On the death of King Hugh of Arles (and Italy), the kingdom of Provence becomes, by agreement of the nobles, part of the kingdom of Burgundy.

June 6 A council meets at Ingelheim under a papal legate to resolve the dispute between King Louis IV of France and Duke Hugh the Great over the archbishopric of Reims, France. It pronounces in favor of Louis's candidate, Artaud, and the legate threatens Hugh with excommunication for his rebellion against Louis.

949

- c. 949 *Cyfraith Hywel/The Laws of Hywel*, the earliest Welsh law code, attributed to the Welsh king Hywel Dda, is compiled.
- Erik Bloodaxe, the deposed king of Norway, is expelled from York by Olaf Cuarán, the Norse king of Dublin, Ireland.
- Following the death of Hywel Dda the Good, "king of all Wales," the Welsh reject his policy of subservience to England.
- Krishna III, the Rashtrakuta king, defeats and kills the Chola king Parantaka I's son, Rajaditya, at Takkolam.

He then takes Tanjore, the Chola capital, and much other territory in southern India.

December 10 On the death of Duke Hermann, the duchy of Swabia is granted by King Otto I of Germany to his son, Liudolf, as part of his policy of using family connections to bind the German tribal duchies to the crown.

SCIENCE, TECHNOLOGY, AND MEDICINE

Agriculture

900

- Muslim agriculturalist ibn-Wahshiyya writes his treatise *Nabataean Agriculture*, describing cultivation methods used in Nabataea to the south of the Dead Sea, and applying scientific methods to agriculture.

Ecology

938

- According to tradition, the silver deposits at Rammelsburg, Germany, are discovered when a horse called Rammelius strikes his shoe on an outcrop, revealing a surface vein.

Health and Medicine

900

c. 900 Spices from the East Indies are introduced to Europe around this time. They are used principally for medicinal purposes.
- A medical school is established at the University of Salerno, in Byzantine Sicily. It will come to dominate medieval medicine over the next centuries.
- The Muslim physician al-Razi describes diseases such as plague, consumption, smallpox, and rabies.

930

- Around this time, the *Leech Book of Bald* is written. It is the oldest extant book in English to recommend the medicinal use of leeches for letting blood and restoring balance to the body's internal "humors."

931

- Following the mistreatment and death of a patient in Baghdad, the caliph institutes the regular testing of all general physicians practicing in the city. Over 860 doctors are examined.

932

- The Jewish physician al-Isrāīli, author of *Kitāb al-Hummayāt*, a treatise on fever, and *Kitāb al-Baul*, a treatise on the analysis of urine to diagnose disease, dies.

Science

900

- Al-Battānī writes his *Zīj*, a collection of astronomical tables for calculation of celestial motions. He is one of the first astronomers to recognize the need for observation to confirm calculation.

901

- Turkish Muslim scholar Thābit ibn Qurra dies—he completed many Arabic translations of Greek mathematical works, and wrote *Concerning the Motion of the Eighth Sphere*, an astronomical treatise.

922

- Arabic traveler ibn-Fadlān writes an account of his embassy to the Bulgars in Russia and his travels among the Vikings. He describes their conflicts with a primitive race. It has been suggested that they could have been surviving Neanderthals.

Technology

920

- The earliest European reference is made to the use of a simple collar in harnessing horses, easing pressure on the horse's neck and allowing the drawing of heavier loads and plows.

932

- Chinese prime minister Fêng Tao orders the collection and printing of 132 volumes of Chinese classics including the Confucian, Buddhist, and Taoist canons. Wooden block printing is used for the project.

941

- A Russian fleet besieging Constantinople is destroyed by the use of "Greek Fire," a highly inflammable mixture of sulfur, petroleum, rock salt, and resin.

ARTS AND IDEAS

Architecture

c. 900

- The Lara Jonggrang temple complex at Prambanan in modern Indonesia is built. Probably built by King Dhaksa, the temple is dedicated to Shiva and contains outstanding reliefs illustrating sections of the *Ramayana*.
- Tula is founded in the valley of Mexico as a capital for the Toltec state.

903

- The rebuilding of the Church of St. Martin at Tours, France, includes one of the first ambulatories (aisles behind the sanctuaries) with radiating chapels.

909

September 11 Duke William of Aquitaine founds the Abbey of Cluny. Its almost total independence from any secular authority enables it to become the hub of a monastic empire that dominates Europe for the next 200 years.

c. 912

- "Mozarabic " architecture, a Muslim-influenced Christian style, is introduced into northern Spain by monks fleeing from Córdoba as a result of a new era of

persecution. The Church of San Miguel de la Escalada is the largest extant Mozarabic building.

c. 935

- A Muslim mausoleum is built at Bukhara, Uzbekistan, for one of the Samanid emirs. Domed and with decorative columns at each corner, its surface decoration seems to be modeled on basket weaving.

936

- Abd-ar-Rahman III, the caliph of Córdoba, Spain, builds Madinat az-Zahrā, a complex of administrative and palace buildings just outside Córdoba.

Arts

c. 945

- Buddhist monk and landscape painter Chu-jan is active around this time. Though none of his works survive, his style is known to have been soft-edged and atmospheric.

Literature and Language

905

- *Kokinshu*, an anthology of about 1,100 old and new poems, commissioned by the Japanese emperor, is published. The preface, written by one of the compilers, Ki Tsurayuki, is the earliest example of Japanese literary criticism.

920

- Arab philologist and poet ibn Duraid settles in Baghdad (in modern Iraq) where he writes a substantial Arabic dictionary, *Jamharat al-Lugha/The Collection of a Language*.

936

- Ki Tsurayuki, now governor of Tosa, writes *Tosa nikki*, the earliest extant diary of travels in Japanese. Ki Tsurayuki is a man but the diary is written from the perspective of a woman in his entourage.

937

c. 937 A Latin epic, *Waltharius*, telling of three hostages held by Attila the Hun, is written. Originally ascribed to Ekkehard of St. Gall, it is thought to be by Geraldus, bishop of Eichstatt.

- Rūdakīis dismissed as an official poet from the court of Nasr II of Persia. Known as the father of Persian poetry, he wrote 100,000 couplets of which fewer than 1,000 survive.

938

- Hero of Byzantium writes a treatise on surveying.

c. 940

- *Ecbasis captivi*, an allegorical poetic narrative about a calf captured by a wolf, is written by an unknown monk at Lorraine, France.
- *The Exeter Book*, a manuscript containing many of the best surviving Old English poems, is copied.
- Japanese writer Minamoto Shitagau compiles *Wamyōshō*, a Sino-Japanese dictionary.

945

- The historian Al-Mas'ūdi, known as "the Herodotus of the Arabs," settles in Damascus after years of travel.

Among his many works, the most important to survive is *Murūj al-Dhahab wa-M'ādin al Jawhar/Meadows of Gold and Mines of Gems*, a historico-geographical encyclopedia.

948

- Arab poet al-Mutannabī joins the brilliant court of Sayf ad-Dawlah. His panegyrics to his patron are regarded as among the greatest of all Arab poetry.

Thought and Scholarship

900

- Byzantine emperor Leo VI writes a handbook of military tactics, the *Tacticon/Tactics*.

c. 902

- Byzantine scholar and theologian Arethas becomes metropolitan of Caesarea around this time. During his life he collected and had copied many classical and early

BIRTHS & DEATHS

911
January 21 King Louis the Child, the last Carolingian ruler of Germany, dies.

912
- Nicephorus II, Byzantium emperor 963–969, who mobilized the Byzantine empire against the Muslim Arabs leading to a resurgence of the Empire's power, born in Cappadocia (–969).
- Notker Balbulus, who introduced the "sequence" (sung prose texts written in Latin) into the Liturgy, dies.
May 12 The Byzantine emperor Leo VI, known as "Leo the Wise," writer of many works including *Tacticon*, a military treatise on warfare, dies.
November 23 Otto I, Duke of Saxony 936–961 (as Otto II), German king 936–973, and emperor 962–973, born (–973).

921
- Edmund I the Deed Doer, Anglo-Saxon king of England 939–946, half brother of Athelstan, who recaptures northern England from Norse invaders and established a secure and peaceful border with Scotland, born in England (–946).

923
- Al-Tabari, Muslim scholar whose major works include a commentary on the Koran, which gathered together all previous interpretations, dies.

924
- St. Dunstan, archbishop of Canterbury, monastic reformer, and adviser to the kings of Wessex, born near Glastonbury, Wessex, England (–988).
April 7 Berengar of Friuli, the deposed king of Italy, is murdered.

925
c. 925 St. Oswald of York, Anglo-Saxon archbishop of York who was instrumental in formulating monastic and feudal reforms, born in Britain (–992).

- Al-Rāzi (Rhazes), Arab physician whose works include *Kitāb al-Judari w-al-Hasbah/On Smallpox and Measles* and *Kitāb al-Asrār/The Book of Secrets*, an alchemical treatise, dies.

927
- T'ai Tsu, Chinese emperor 960–976 who reunited China and founded the Sung dynasty, born in Lo-yang, China (–976).

929
- Al-Battānī, Arab astronomer and mathematician, dies near Samarra, Persia (c. 71).

931
- Ibn Masarrah, Andalusian Sufi (Muslim mystic) philosopher, dies.

932
- Roswitha von Gandersheim, German Benedictine nun, poet, and playwright, author of the first known plays by a woman, born in Gandersheim, near Göttingen, Germany (–c. 1002).

935
- Al-Ashari, Muslim theologian and philosopher who attempted to reconcile the opposing strands of reason and mysticism in Muslim thought, dies.

936
c. 936 Abu al-Qasim, medieval Islamic surgeon whose *The Method* is the first illustrated work on surgery, born near Córdoba, Spain (–c. 1013).
- Henry I the Fowler, German king 919–936, founder of the Saxon dynasty, dies in Memleben, Saxony (c. 60).

938
- Abu Amir al-Mansur (Almanzor), chief minister (vizier) and virtual ruler of the Umayyad caliphate of Córdoba, Spain 978–1002, born (–1002).

939
October 27 Athelstan (or Aethelstan or Ethelstan), Anglo-Saxon king of Wessex and Mercia 924–925 and

first king of England 925–939, dies in England (c. 44).

940
- Ibn Muqlah, Arab calligrapher, probable inventor of the cursive *nashki* script which replaced the previous more angular style, dies.

941
- Brian Bórumha, high king of Ireland 1002–14, born near Killaloe, Ireland (–1014).

942
- Al-Jahshyari, compiler of a collection of 480 popular Middle Eastern stories from a planned total of 1,000, which constitute the first version of *Alf Laylah wa-Laylah/A Thousand and One Nights—The Arabian Nights*, dies.
- Saadia ben Joseph, Jewish philosopher known for his Arabic translation and commentary on the Old Testament, and for *The Book of Beliefs and Opinions*, dies in Sura, Babylonia (c. 54).
November 18 St. Odo, abbot of Cluny, monastic reformer, dies in Tours, France (c. 63).

944
- Al-Maturīdī of Samarkand, founder of the Maturidiyah school of Islamic theology, which employs the logical methods of Greek philosophy to reinforce orthodox theological positions, dies.

c. 945
- Sylvester II (Gerbert of Aurillac), French head of the Roman Catholic Church 999–1003, born near Aurillac, Auvergne, France (–1003).

946
May 26 Edmund I the Deed Doer, Anglo-Saxon king of England 939–946, half brother of Athelstan, who recaptured northern England from Norse invaders and established a secure and peaceful border with Scotland, is murdered in Pucklechurch, England (c. 25).

Christian writings which would otherwise have been lost.

SOCIETY

Education

945

• A further endowment is made for the college for Brahmans at Salatgi in southern India.

Religion

937

• King Otto I of Germany founds the monastery of St. Maurice at Magdeburg, Germany, in order to consolidate victories over the Slavs.

939

• St. Dunstan is appointed abbot of Glastonbury where he begins the revival of English monasticism, all but wiped out by Danish invaders.

948

• Bulscu, the Magyar leader, is baptized in Constantinople.
• King Otto I of Germany establishes bishoprics at Brandenburg and Havelberg, Germany, for the conversion of the Wends (a pagan Slavonic people), and at Ribe, Aarhus, and Schleswig, Germany, for missions to the north.

950–999

POLITICS, GOVERNMENT, AND ECONOMICS

Colonization

956

• The Ghuzz (or Oghuz) Turks, led by Seljuk, migrate from Turkestan in Central Asia into Transoxiana.

968

• Jews first settle in Bohemia.

982

• Eric the Red begins the Viking colonization of Greenland.

Politics and Government

950

c. 950 Invading Toltecs from Mexico make the Mayan city of Chichén Itzá their capital. The ensuing improvements to the city are in a hybrid style called Mayan-Toltec.
• By the mediation of King Otto I of Germany, Duke Hugh the Great submits to King Louis IV of France and restores his capital, Laon, to Louis.

• King Otto I of Germany compels Bolesław I, Duke of Bohemia, to recognize his suzerainty and pay tribute.
• The Later Han dynasty, the fourth of the "Five Dynasties" of northern China, is overthrown by Guowei, a Chinese general who establishes the Later Zhou dynasty.

December 15 Following the death of King Lothair II of Italy, Berengar II, Marquess of Ivrea, and his son, Adalbert, are elected kings of Italy.

951

• In their most westerly raid, the Magyars from the Danube Basin devastate the duchy of Aquitaine (western France).

September 9 Adelaide, the widow of King Lothair II of Italy, appeals to the German king Otto I for help against Berengar of Ivrea, who has imprisoned her. Otto invades Italy, takes the northern city of Pavia, marries Adelaide, and assumes the Italian crown. Berengar takes refuge in the Alps.

952

• A long civil war about the accession to the throne breaks out on the death of King Ramiro II of León, Spain, between his son Ordoño and his half brother Sancho. Ordoño III is not able to win control of the kingdom until 957.
• Al-Mansur, the Fatimid caliph (Islamic ruler) of Kairouan (in modern Tunisia), dies. He is succeeded by his son, al-Mu'izz.
• Ashot III succeeds his father, Abas I, as king of Armenia.

- Erik Bloodaxe, the deposed king of Norway, recovers the kingdom of York, England, from Olaf Cuarán, the Norse king of Dublin, Ireland.

August 7 King Otto I of Germany agrees that Berengar II of Ivrea and his son, Adalbert, may hold the kingdom of Italy as his vassals.

953

- Liudolf, Duke of Swabia, leads a revolt, supported by the dukes of Franconia and Bavaria, against his father, King Otto I of Germany.
- Sayf ad-Dawlah, the Hamdanid ruler of Aleppo, Syria, defeats a Byzantine army under Bardas Phocas near Germanicia (Mar'-ash).

954

- Erik Bloodaxe, the last Scandinavian king of York, England, is murdered by a rival at York. King Eadred takes possession of the kingdom and, as a consequence, holds all of England.
- King Malcolm I of Scotland is killed in a border skirmish, probably in Moray. He is succeeded by his cousin, Indulf.
- The Magyars raid through Bavaria, Lorraine, Burgundy, Flanders, and as far as Utrecht.

June 16 The followers of Liudolf, the rebel Duke of Swabia, submit to his father, King Otto I of Germany.

August 8 Alberic, Duke of Rome, dies. On his deathbed, Alberic forces the clergy and nobles of Rome to swear to make his illegitimate son, Octavian, pope on the death of the current incumbent, Agapitus II.

September 10 King Louis IV of France dies. He is succeeded by his son, Lothair IV, the last Carolingian king of France.

December 7 In the redistribution of territories forfeited in the recent rebellion led by his son, Liudolf, King Otto I of Germany grants Liudolf's former duchy of Swabia to Burchard, and Lorraine to Archbishop Bruno of Cologne, Otto's brother.

955

August 10 King Otto I of Germany defeats the Magyars on the Lechfeld, near Augsburg. Their raids on western Europe now cease and they begin a settled life in Hungary. On October 16, he defeats the pagan Wends (a slavonic people) in Mecklenburg.

November 23 King Eadred of England dies. He is succeeded by his nephew Eadwig, the son of the former king Edmund.

December 12 On the death of Pope Agapitus II, the late Roman duke Alberic's 18-year-old illegitimate son, Octavian, is appointed pope, adopting the name John XII.

956

- King Otto I of Germany punishes a revolt by the pagan Wends by ravaging their lands.

April 8 Hugh the Great, Duke of the Franks, inherits the duchy of Burgundy on the death of its ruler, Giselbert. Hugh's lands are now far more extensive than those of his theoretical overlord, King Lothair IV of France. On June 17, Hugh dies at Dourdan and his sons share his lands.

957

- King Eadwig of England exiles Dunstan, abbot of Glastonbury, from England. The Mercians and Northumbrians renounce Eadwig in favor of his brother, Edgar.

June 6 The Byzantine general Nicephorus Phocas takes the city of Hadath, continuing the Byzantine advance in Syria.

August Ordoño III of León dies. He is succeeded by his brother, Sancho I, who is deposed, in civil war, by Ordoño the Bad.

958

- An examination system based on the Chinese (Confucian) model is established for the civil service in Korea.
- Fulk II, Count of Anjou, France, dies. He is succeeded by his son, Geoffrey I.
- The Byzantine general John Tzimisces takes the city of Samosata and defeats Sayf ad-Dawlah, the ruler of Aleppo, Syria, at Raban in Syria.

959

- King Edgar of England recognizes the special laws of the Danes settled in England.
- King Krishna III of the central Indian Rashtrakuta dynasty imposes tribute on the Cholas of southern India and the Simhalese of Ceylon.

October 1 King Eadwig of England dies. He is succeeded by his brother, Edgar, who recalls Abbot Dunstan of Glastonbury from exile.

November 9 The Byzantine emperor Constantine VII dies and is succeeded by his son, Romanus II.

960

c. 960 The baptism takes place of Harald Bluetooth, who establishes Christianity as the official religion in Denmark.

c. 960 The Koryŏ dynasty pushes the border of Koryŏ (Korea) north to the Yalu River, which remains the northern border of Koryŏ.

- A guard commander, Zhao Kuangyin (known posthumously as Taizu), overthrows the Later Zhou dynasty, the last of the "Five Dynasties" of northern China, and founds the Northern Song dynasty.
- Abd-ar-Rahman III, caliph (Islamic ruler) of Córdoba, Spain, exploiting the civil war in the Spanish kingdom of León, takes the city of Oviedo, and with García I of Navarre, restores Sancho I as king of León.
- In the partition of Duke Hugh the Great's lands, King Lothair IV of France invests Hugh's oldest son, Hugh Capet, with Neustria and his younger son, Otto, with the duchy of Burgundy.

960–988 Nine embassies are sent from the Srivijaya empire (in modern Indonesia) to the court of the new Song dynasty of China.

961

- The Umayyad caliph (Islamic ruler) of Córdoba, Spain, Abd-ar-Rahman III, dies. He is succeeded by al-Hakam II, also known as Mustansir Hakam II.

March 3 The Byzantine general Nicephorus Phocas recovers Crete from the Arabs.

May 26 Otto, son of King Otto I of Germany, is crowned as dependent king of Lorraine.

September 9 In answer to an appeal from Pope John XII for protection against King Berengar II of Ivrea, King Otto I of Germany invades Italy and, with his son Otto, is acknowledged as king of Italy on his capture of the northern city of Pavia.

962

- Alptigin founds the Turkish dynasty of the Ghaznavids with the seizure of Ghazni (in modern Afghanistan) from the Samanid emirate.
- King Indulf of Scotland is killed by the Danes. He is succeeded by Dub, son of the former king Malcolm I.
- Prince Svjatoslav I of the Rus principality of Kiev begins his personal rule. A committed pagan, he forces the Christian missionary sent by King Otto I of Germany to his mother and regent, Princess Olga, to return home.

February 2   King Otto I of Germany is crowned Roman emperor by Pope John XII, an event which marks the foundation of the Holy Roman Empire.

December 12   The Byzantine general Nicephorus Phocas (briefly) occupies Aleppo in Syria.

963

- Following his defeats by Count Wichman of Saxony, Mieszko I, Prince of Poland, becomes the "friend" and tributary of the Holy Roman Emperor, Otto I of Germany.
- Zhao Kuangyin (known posthumously as Taizu), the ruler of northern China and first emperor of the Song dynasty, begins a series of military and diplomatic campaigns against the independent "Ten Kingdoms" of southern China.

August 16   Following the death of the Byzantine emperor Romanus II, the Byzantine general Nicephorus Phocas is crowned Byzantine emperor (Nicephorus II), and shortly after marries Romanus's widow.

December 4   The Holy Roman Emperor, Otto I of Germany, deposes Pope John XII for corruption and appoints Leo VIII as his successor. On December 26, Otto captures former king Berengar II of Italy and exiles him to Germany.

964

February 26   The deposed pope John XII organizes a rebellion in Rome and forces Pope Leo VIII to flee into exile with the Holy Roman Emperor, Otto I, in Germany. At a synod, John declares Leo deposed and excommunicated.

May 14   The deposed pope John XII dies after a stroke, allegedly suffered while in bed with a married woman. He was still only in his mid-twenties. The Romans elect Benedict V the Grammarian as John's successor.

June 23   The Holy Roman Emperor, Otto I of Germany, marches on Rome, exiles Pope Benedict V the Grammarian to Hamburg, Germany, and restores Pope Leo VIII.

965

- A Byzantine expedition to Sicily takes the city of Syracuse briefly, but its fleet is destroyed shortly afterwards by the Arabs, off Messina.
- Henry the Great succeeds his brother, Otto, as Duke of Burgundy.
- Prince Svjatoslav I of the Rus principality of Kiev sacks the Khazar cities of Sarkel (on the River Don) and Itil (on the River Volga) and destroys the power of their state.
- The English invade Gwynedd in north Wales.

March 27   On the death of Arnold I, Count of Flanders, King Lothair IV of France occupies Arras and other southern parts of the county, but the Flemings prevent full confiscation and proclaim Arnold's grandson, Arnold II, as their count.

August 8   The Byzantine emperor Nicephorus II regains Cyprus from the Arabs. On August 16, he takes the city of Tarsus in the conquest of Cilicia in Asia Minor (modern Turkey).

October 1   Following the death of Pope Leo VIII, the Holy Roman Emperor, Otto I of Germany, refuses the request of the Romans for the restoration of the deposed pope Benedict V and secures the appointment of John XIII.

966

- King Dub of Scotland is killed in battle. He is succeeded by Culen, the son of his predecessor, Indulf.
- The Byzantine emperor Nicephorus II campaigns on the middle Euphrates River.

967

- Bolesław I, Duke of Bohemia, dies. He is succeeded by his son Bolesław II the Pious.
- King Sancho I the Fat of León, Spain, is murdered. He is succeeded by his son, Ramiro III.
- Prince Mieszko of Poland defeats an invasion by Duke Wichman of Saxony, who is killed.
- Prince Svjatoslav I of the Rus principality of Kiev, urged by the Byzantine emperor Nicephorus II to attack the Bulgarians, occupies the Dobrudja, between the River Danube and the Black Sea.
- The earliest known charter of privileges for a French town is granted to Morville-sur-Seille.

January 1   Pandolf I Ironhead, Duke of Capua-Benevento, Italy, is invested with the March of Spoleto by the Holy Roman Emperor, Otto I of Germany, who thus extends his authority into southern Italy.

December 22   Otto, son of the Holy Roman Emperor, Otto I of Germany, is crowned as Roman emperor by Pope John XIII and so becomes coemperor with his father and heir designate.

968

- Bishop Liutprand of Cremona's embassy to the Byzantine capital, Constantinople, sent by the Holy Roman Emperor Otto I of Germany, is rebuffed by the Byzantine emperor, Nicephorus II. Liutprand writes *Relatio de legatione Constantinopolitana/Account of the Embassy of Constantinople*.
- Dinh Bo Linh, after succeeding as ruler of Dai Viet (Annam) and suppressing all opposition, declares himself emperor (adopting the name Dinh-Tien-hoang), with his capital at Hoa-lu. The Song emperors of China recognize him as a vassal.
- Mathghamain, King of Dal Cais, Ireland, plunders Limerick and briefly expels the Vikings.
- The archbishopric of Magdeburg in Germany is created, which Pope John XIII limits to the land between the River Elbe and the River Oder in order to control the influence of Holy Roman Emperor Otto I over the Slavs. Adalbert is made first archbishop.

969

July 6   The fourth Fatimid caliph (Islamic ruler), al-Mu'izz, already ruling Kairouan, the Maghreb, and Libya in

Byzantine Reconquests (965–1022)

965–999

965

- A Byzantine expedition to Sicily takes the city of Syracuse briefly, but its fleet is destroyed shortly afterwards by the Arabs, off Messina.

August 8   Byzantine emperor Nicephorus II regains Cyprus from the Arabs.

August 16   Nicephorus takes the city of Tarsus in the conquest of Cilicia in Asia Minor (modern Turkey).

966

- Nicephorus campaigns on the middle Euphrates River.

969

October 28   Antioch and Aleppo in Syria are taken by Nicephorus II.

971

- The Fatimid caliphs (Islamic rulers) attempt to take the city of Antioch in Syria from the Byzantines.

April 23   Byzantine emperor John Tzimisces defeats Prince Svjatoslav I of the Rus principality of Kiev at Dorystolum (modern Silistra, Bulgaria) in the Bulgar Khanate.

July 21   Tzimisces again defeats Prince Svjatoslav I of Kiev and compels him to evacuate the Balkans and the Crimea.

972

- Bulgarian czar Boris II abdicates, and the Bulgar Khanate is annexed by the Byzantine Empire.

October 12   Tzimisces sacks Nisibis. He leaves Mesopotamia when Abu Taghlib, Emir of Mosul, promises to pay tribute.

973

July 4   Abu Taghlib defeats a Byzantine army near Amida, on the River Tigris.

974

- In his second Mesopotamian campaign, Tzimisces, supported by King Ashot III of Armenia, advances almost as far south as Baghdad before withdrawing.

975

April 29   Tzimisces enters Baalbek (Heliopolis), Egypt, in the course of his third campaign, when he conquers northern Palestine, taking the cities of Caesarea and Damascus.

976

January 10   Tzimisces dies of typhoid contracted on his triumphant campaign in Syria and Palestine in 975. He is succeeded by Basil II and Constantine VIII, the sons of Romanus II. The Bulgarians, led by Samuel, begin a war for independence.

986

August 17   Byzantine emperor Basil II is routed by the Bulgarians in "Trajan's Gate," Bulgaria.

991

- Basil subjugates the area of modern Albania and begins his pacification of the Bulgar Khanate.

994

September 14   A Byzantine army is defeated near Antioch, Syria, by the forces of al-Aziz, the Fatimid caliph (Islamic ruler) of Egypt.

995

- Basil completes his first subjugation of the Bulgarians.

April 4   Basil raises the siege of Aleppo, Syria, by the Fatimids, and campaigns as far south as Tripoli.

999

- Basil's Syrian campaign restores imperial control in the autumn, after a military revolt.

1000–1022

1000

- Basil extends his empire to the Lower Danube with the occupation of the Dobrudja.

1002

- A Venetian fleet is defeated besieging the Byzantines in Bari, Italy.

1003

- Basil defeats Samuel, the Bulgarian emperor, near Skopje in Macedonia. .

1014

July 29   Basil surrounds and captures a Bulgarian army in the pass of Kleidon, Bulgaria. 15,000 Bulgar prisoners are blinded before being sent home.

October 6   Samuel, the Bulgarian emperor, dies two days after seeing the 15,000 survivors of the defeat at the pass of Kleidon who had been blinded by Basil.

1018

October 10   A Byzantine army defeats southern Italian rebels at Cannae.

1019

- The Byzantine emperor Basil II completes his conquest of Bulgaria and its former empire in the Balkans. The western frontier of his empire now extends to the Adriatic Sea and in the north along the River Danube.

1021

December 12   Emperor Henry II begins a military expedition to Italy in response to further Byzantine successes in Benevento which endanger Rome.

1022

- Henry II's Italian expedition checks the Byzantine advance. He takes Capua and Troia before malaria compels the German army to retire.

northern Africa, conquers Egypt and extinguishes the Ikshidid dynasty. He founds a new capital at Cairo, Egypt, which becomes the center of a Shiite empire.

October 28   Antioch and Aleppo in Syria are taken by the forces of the Byzantine emperor, Nicephorus II.

December 10   Prince Svjatoslav I of the Rus principality of Kiev defeats the Pechenegs besieging his capital, Kiev. He also conquers the eastern part of the Bulgar Khanate.

December 10   The Byzantine emperor Nicephorus II is murdered in a conspiracy between his wife, Theophano, and her lover, the genaral John Tzimisces, who then becomes emperor.

970

- Prince Svjatoslav I of the Rus principality of Kiev invades Thrace, but is defeated at Arcadiopolis by the Byzantine general Bardas Sclerus.
- Sancho II succeeds his father, García I, as king of Navarre, Spain who has died.

971

- King Culen of Scotland is killed in battle with the Britons. He is succeeded by Kenneth II, the brother of the previous king, Dub.
- The Fatimid caliphs (Islamic rulers) attempt to take the city of Antioch in Syria from the Byzantines.
- The southern Chinese port of Guangzhou (Canton) submits to the Song emperor, Taizu.

April 23 The Byzantine emperor John Tzimisces defeats Prince Svjatoslav I of the Rus principality of Kiev at Dorystolum (modern Silistra, Bulgaria) in the Bulgar Khanate. On July 21, he again defeats Prince Svjatoslav I of Kiev and compels him to evacuate the Balkans and the Crimea.

972

- Prince Mieszko I of Poland defeats an invasion by Hodo, Margrave of the Eastern Mark, at Cedynia (or Zehden).
- The Bulgarian czar Boris II abdicates, and the Bulgar Khanate is annexed by the Byzantine Empire.
- The Pechenegs, under Kurya, defeat and kill Prince Svjatoslav I of the Rus principality of Kiev in an ambush on the cataracts of the River Dnieper. Svjatoslav I is succeeded by his son, Jaropolk I.
- Yūsuf Bulukkin, a Berber who was appointed governor of northwestern Africa by the Fatimid caliph (Islamic ruler), establishes the dynasty of Zirids as independent rulers in eastern Algeria.

April 14 An alliance of the Byzantine and Holy Roman Empires is formed by the marriage of the Holy Roman Emperor Otto I's son, Otto, to Theophano, a niece of the Byzantine emperor, John Tzimisces.

July 7 The Arabs of Garde-Freinet in Provence capture Mayeul, abbot of Cluny, in France while he is crossing the Great St. Bernard Pass through the Alps.

October 12 The Byzantine emperor, John Tzimisces, sacks Nisibis. He leaves Mesopotamia when Abu Taghlib, Emir of Mosul, promises to pay tribute.

973

- At the request of Prince Bolesław II of Bohemia, the Holy Roman Emperor, Otto I of Germany, detaches Bohemia from the diocese of Regensburg and establishes the bishopric of Prague under the archbishop of Mainz.
- Taila, a provincial governor, overthrows the Rashtrakuta dynasty of central India, establishing his own Chalukya dynasty.

January 19 Benedict VI is crowned as pope.

March 3 Prince Mieszko I of Poland and Margrave Hodo of the Eastern Mark submit their quarrel over territory to the judgment of the Holy Roman Emperor, Otto I. Mieszko also succeeds in keeping the Polish Christian church away from German authority.

May 7 The Holy Roman Emperor and German king, Otto I the Great, dies. He is succeeded in both positions by his son, Otto II.

May 11 Edgar is crowned as king of all England at Bath. He then goes to Chester, where eight Scottish and Welsh kings row him in a boat on the River Dee in demonstration of their submission.

July 4 Abu Taghlib, Emir of Mosul, Mesopotamia, defeats a Byzantine army near Amida, on the River Tigris.

974

- An army of Mustansir Hakam II, the caliph (Islamic ruler) of Córdoba, Spain, extinguishes the Idrisid dynasty of Fez in Morocco.
- In his second Mesopotamian campaign, the Byzantine emperor, John Tzimisces, supported by King Ashot III of Armenia, advances almost as far south as Baghdad before withdrawing.
- The Holy Roman Emperor, Otto II of Germany, defeats King Harald Bluetooth of Denmark.

June 6 Pope Benedict VI is deposed by a rebellion led by the powerful Crescentius family. The deacon Franco is appointed as Pope Boniface VII, but he is driven out of Rome a month later by a popular rising after he murders Benedict VI.

October 10 Benedict VII is crowned as pope in Rome, Italy.

975

- The Christian kingdom of Axum (in the north of modern Ethiopia) is destroyed by pagan invaders from Damot.
- The rebel Chinese admiral Chu Ling-Pin uses "fire lances," a form of flame-thrower, against the Song emperor's ships in a battle on the Chang Jiang River. However, a change of wind causes the flames to devastate the admiral's own fleet.
- William, Count of Arles, expels the Arabs from Garde-Freinet in Burgundy.

April 29 The Byzantine emperor John Tzimisces enters Baalbek (Heliopolis), Egypt, in the course of his third campaign, when he conquers northern Palestine, taking the cities of Caesarea and Damascus.

July 8 King Edgar of England dies and is succeeded by his son, Edward.

November 24 Caliph al-Mu'izz of Egypt, dies. He is succeeded by his son, al-'Aziz.

976

- Sicilian Arabs ravage Calabria in southern Italy.
- The Byzantine general Bardas Sclerus, claiming the Byzantine throne, leads a military revolt in the spring against the new Byzantine emperors, Basil II and Constantine VIII.
- The Chinese (Song) regular army totals 378,000 men.

January 10 The Byzantine emperor John Tzimisces dies of typhoid contracted on his triumphant campaign in Syria and Palestine in 975. He is succeeded by Basil II and Constantine VIII, the sons of Romanus II. The Bulgarians, led by Samuel, begin a war for independence.

July 7 Henry the Wrangler is deprived of the duchy of Bavaria because of his rebellion against the Holy Roman Emperor and German king Otto II.

October 1 Mustansir Hakam II, the Umayyad caliph (Islamic ruler) of Córdoba, Spain, dies. He is succeeded by his son, Hishām II, whose vizier, Abu Amir al-Mansur (Almanzor), holds effective power as regent.

November 14 Zhao Kuangyin (known posthumously as Taizu), the first Song emperor of China, dies. He is succeeded by his brother, Taizong, who continues his campaigns to reunite China under a single dynasty.

977

- Prince Jaropolk I of the Rus principality of Kiev is defeated in battle in Scandinavia by his exiled brother, Vladimir I, who succeeds him.
- Smbat II succeeds Ashot III as king of Armenia.
- The Holy Roman Emperor, Otto II of Germany, gives the duchy of Lower Lorraine to Charles, who has quarreled with his brother, King Lothair IV of France.

978

- King Harald II Greycloak (also called Graypelt) of Norway is defeated and killed in battle by Haakon Sugurdsson of Lade who succeeds him.

March 3   Prince Bolesław II of Bohemia pays homage to the Holy Roman Emperor and German king Otto II.

March 18   King Edward of England is murdered by servants whilst visiting his stepbrother, Aethelred II the Unready, who succeeds him. Edward is subsequently regarded as a martyr and Aethelred, probably unfairly, is suspected of complicity in the murder.

March 31   The duchy of Bavaria is deprived of its privileged status in the sentences following the Holy Roman Emperor Otto II's defeat of the rebellion known as "the War of the Three Henries."

June 19   The rebel Byzantine general Bardas Sclerus defeats loyal imperial forces on the Plain of Pancalia in Anatolia, and again, in the autumn, at Basilica Therma.

October 10   The Holy Roman Emperor, Otto II of Germany, invades France, harrying as far as Paris, in retaliation for an attempt by King Lothair IV of France to seize Lorraine.

979

- An expedition by the Holy Roman Emperor, Otto II of Germany, fails to defeat Prince Mieszko I of Poland. They come to terms and Mieszko pays homage.
- King Lothair IV of France has his son Louis V crowned as joint king of France and revives the kingdom of Aquitaine for him, but fails to recover direct royal authority there. France proper does not extend south of the River Loire at this time.
- The Chinese Song emperor, Taizong, conquers the independent Chinese kingdoms of Jin and Yen, completing the reunification of China begun by his brother Taizu. Taizong attempts to destroy the Qitan (or Khitan) empire of Liao but is badly defeated near Xijin (modern Beijing).

March 24   The rebel Byzantine general Bardas Sclerus is finally defeated at Pancalia, near the Halys, in Anatolia, by loyal imperial forces assisted by Prince David of Tao, the most powerful ruler in Caucasia.

980

- King Malachy II of Tara, Ireland, defeats Olaf Sihtricson, the Norse king of Dublin, near Tara Hill. Olaf then retires to the island of Iona, in northwestern Scotland.
- Le Dai Hanh usurps the imperial throne of Dai Viet (Annam).
- Mahipala I, King of Bihar, recovers the ancestral lands of his dynasty (the Pala) in Bengal, India, by expelling the Kambojas, a hill tribe.
- The Vikings renew their raids on England.

July 7   The Holy Roman Emperor, Otto II of Germany, and King Lothair IV of France meet at Margut, on the River

Chiers, and swear to their friendship. Lothair abandons his claim on Lorraine.

November 11   The Holy Roman Emperor, Otto II of Germany, begins his expedition to extend his authority in southern Italy.

981

- Al-Mansur, regent of the Umayyad caliphate of Córdoba, Spain, takes the city of Zamora and subjugates the kingdom of León.
- Prince Vladimir I of the Rus principality of Kiev takes Przemyśl, Czerwień, and other areas in Red Russia from Poland.
- The Annamese emperor, Le Dai Hanh, defeats a Chinese invasion of Dai Viet (Annam).

March 3   Duke Pandolf I Ironhead dies and his Italian dominions are divided by his sons, Landolf IV (Capua-Benevento) and Paldolf (Salerno).

982

- Le Dai Hanh, the emperor of Dai Viet (Annam), destroys Indrapura, capital of the Champa kingdom (modern southern Vietnam).

July 13   The Holy Roman Emperor, Otto II of Germany, is defeated at Basientello, in Apulia, Italy, by the Arabs.

December 12   King Ramiro III of León, Spain, dies in Astorga after being exiled as the result of a revolt by nobles favoring his uncle, Vermudo II, who succeeds him.

983

- Ahmad ibn-Buwayh Adud ad-Dawlah, the founder of the Shiite Muslim Buwayhid dynasty, which controls the Abbasid caliphate, dies, having consolidated his control in Persia and assumed the title Shahanshah ("king of kings").
- Following the defeat of the Holy Roman Emperor, Otto II of Germany, in Italy, the Wends revolt against German rule and restore their pagan religion.
- Harald Bluetooth, King of Denmark, is deposed by his son, Sven I Forkbeard.
- The Fatimid caliph (Islamic ruler) of Egypt, Al-Aziz Bi'llah Nizar Abu Mansur, now rules over Palestine and southern Syria.

July 10   Pope Benedict VII dies. John XIV (Peter, bishop of Pavia) is appointed as his successor by the Holy Roman Emperor, Otto II.

December 7   The Holy Roman Emperor and German king Otto II dies in Rome, Italy, of malaria contracted on his expedition to southern Italy. He is succeeded by his three-year-old son, Otto III, under the guardianship of his mother, Theophano.

984

January 1   The infant Holy Roman Emperor and German king Otto III is seized by Henry the Wrangler, the former Duke of Bavaria.

March 3   King Lothair IV of France takes Verdun, his only success in a campaign to seize Lorraine.

March 23   Henry the Wrangler, the former Duke of Bavaria, proclaims himself king of Germany, but the Saxons and many others oppose him.

April 4   Pope John XIV is deposed by the former pope Boniface VII. He dies of starvation in prison in Rome a few months later.

June 29   A diet of German princes recognizes Otto III, the

young son of the late Holy Roman Emperor Otto II, as king of Germany. Henry the Wrangler surrenders Otto to his mother, Theophano, and grandmother, Adelaide, and is restored to the duchy of Bavaria in compensation.

985

- Basil II defeats a palace conspiracy and begins his personal rule as Byzantine emperor.
- Dietrich II is appointed hereditary Count of Holland, part of the East Frankish (German) kingdom.

May 5   King Lothair IV of France calls an assembly to condemn Archbishop Adalbero of Reims, who has organized a rebellion in the interests of the Holy Roman Emperor, Otto III, but it is dispersed by Hugh Capet, Duke of the Franks.

July 1   Almanzor, regent of the Umayyad caliphate of Córdoba, Spain, sacks the northeastern Spanish city of Barcelona.

986

- A second campaign by the Chinese Song emperor, Taizong, against the Khitan empire of Liao ends in failure.
- Sabuktagin of Ghazni (in modern Afghanistan) invades the Punjab, India.

March 2   King Lothair IV of France dies. He is succeeded by his son and joint king, Louis V le Fainéant (the Indolent).

August 17   The Byzantine emperor Basil II is routed by the Bulgarians in "Trajan's Gate," Bulgaria.

987

- Kukulcan ("feathered serpent"), who is probably the exiled Toltec king Topiltzin-Quetzalcoatl, captures Chichén Itzá from the Maya and establishes an empire in the northern Yucatán, Central America.
- Samuel, King of the Bulgars, son of Count Nicholas of Macedonia, is now established as ruler of the revived Bulgar Khanate.
- The Byzantine Empire and the Fatimid caliphate of Egypt conclude a treaty of peace for seven years.

July 3   Hugh Capet, Duke of the Franks, is elected to succeed Louis V and is crowned king of France, so founding the Capetian dynasty. King Hugh's authority is weak and his own duchy of Neustria disintegrates as his vassals make themselves effectively independent.

July 21   Geoffrey I, Count of Anjou, France, dies. He is succeeded by his son, Fulk III Nerra.

November 14   The Byzantine general Bardas Phocas proclaims himself emperor.

December 30   Hugh Capet, King of France, has his son, Robert, crowned as joint king and heir. This method of associating the heir with his father, the king, will remain Capetian practice until Philip II abandons it.

988

- Abu Amir al-Mansur (Almanzor), the Umayyad regent of Córdoba, Spain, razes the Spanish city of León and makes its king a tributary to the caliphate of Córdoba.
- Dietrich II, Count of Holland, dies. He is succeeded by his son, Arnulf the Great.
- King Hugh of France fails in attempts over the summer to recover Laon from Charles, Duke of Lower Lorraine, who, as the brother of the former king Lothair IV, is claiming the French crown.

- Sabuktagin of Ghazni (in modern Afghanistan) takes the city of Kabul from Jaipal I, King of the Punjab, India.
- The Khitan emperors of Liao adopt the Chinese examination system for their civil service.
- The rebel Byzantine general Bardas Phocas is defeated in the summer at Chrysopolis by loyal imperial forces assisted by an army of "Varangians" (Russian Vikings) sent by Prince Vladimir of the Rus principality of Kiev. This is the origin of the Byzantine emperors' Varangian Guard.

February 2   Prince Vladimir of the Rus principality of Kiev is baptized as a condition of a proposed marriage with Anna, the sister of the Byzantine emperor, Basil II. The marriage is a reward for Vladimir's help against the rebel Byzantine general Bardas Phocas.

989

- After the Byzantine emperor Basil II goes back on his agreement to allow Prince Vladimir of the Rus principality of Kiev to marry his sister Anna, Vladimir temporarily seizes Cherson (modern Sevastopol) to force Basil to honor his agreement.
- Smbat II the Conqueror, King of Armenia, dies. He is succeeded by his brother, Gagik I.
- The Japanese Buddhist monastery of Enryakuji sends an army of warrior-monks to destroy a rival monastery at Nara.

January 23   On the death of Archbishop Adalbero of Reims, King Hugh of France appoints as his successor Arnulf, an illegitimate son of the former king Lothair IV.

April 13   The rebel Byzantine general Bardas Phocas is defeated by imperial forces at Abydos.

September 9   Archbishop Arnulf of Reims admits Duke Charles of Lower Lorraine, a claimant to the French throne, to Reims, France.

October 11   The rebel Byzantine general Bardas Phocas surrenders to the Byzantine emperor, Basil II, and renounces his imperial pretensions. He dies soon afterwards, possibly poisoned.

991

- The Byzantine emperor Basil II subjugates the area of modern Albania and begins his pacification of the Bulgar Khanate.

March 29   Bishop Asselin of Laon captures Duke Charles of Lower Lorraine, the pretender to the French throne, and Archbishop Arnulf of Reims on King Hugh of France's behalf, so ending Charles's attempt to win the throne of France.

June 15   The Holy Roman Empress Theophano, who has been ruling the empire on her young son Otto III's behalf, dies. Adelaide, Otto I's widow, takes her place as regent.

June 18   King Hugh of France deprives Arnulf of the archbishopric of Reims for supporting the pretender Charles of Lorraine and appoints Gerbert of Aurillac in his place on June 21.

August 8   The Norwegian Viking leader Olaf Tryggvesson defeats and kills Byrhtnoth, ealdorman of East Anglia, England, in the Battle of Maldon. The Vikings are paid Danegeld to leave.

992

- Prince Mieszko I of Poland dies at Gniezno. His lands (Poland as far west as the River Oder, plus Pomerania and Moravia) are divided among his sons, one of whom,

Bolesław Chrobry (the Brave), subsequently reunites them.

- The Ilek khans of Turkestan in Central Asia take Bukhara.
- The independence of Venice is recognized in treaties with the Byzantine and Holy Roman Empires.

June 27 Count Fulk III of Anjou defeats and kills Duke Conan I of Brittany at Nantes, France.

993

- King Conrad of Burgundy dies. He is succeeded by his son, Rudolph III.
- The Germans recover Brandenburg, which has been held by the Lusatians (a Slav tribe), in their revolt against the Holy Roman Empire, for approximately three years.
- The Indian city of Delhi is founded by Anangapala, chief of the Tomara ethnic group.

994

- Count Fulk III of Anjou, France, builds one of the earliest known castles, at Langeais, as a means of strengthening his authority, but he is unable to control the vassal he appoints to guard it and it becomes a semi-independent stronghold.
- King Sancho II Garcés of Navarre, Spain, dies. He is succeeded by his son, García II.
- King Svein of Denmark and Viking leader Olaf Tryggvesson besiege the city of London in England. They retire upon the payment of Danegeld.
- Nuh II, the Samanid emir, cedes Khorasan (eastern Persia) to Sabuktagin of Ghazni (in modern Afghanistan).

May 10 Vikings devastate the island of Anglesey in north Wales.

September 14 A Byzantine army is defeated near Antioch, Syria, by the forces of al-'Aziz, the Fatimid caliph (Islamic ruler) of Egypt.

995

- King Kenneth II of Scotland is murdered by a group of vengeful Scottish nobles. He is succeeded by Constantine III, son of the former king Culen.
- Now aged 15, the emperor and German king Otto III assumes personal rule.
- Olaf Tryggvesson becomes king of Norway.
- Olof Skötkonung ("the tax-king") becomes king of Sweden.
- The Byzantine emperor Basil II completes his first subjugation of the Bulgarians.

April 4 The Byzantine emperor Basil II raises the siege of Aleppo, Syria, by the Fatimids, and campaigns as far south as Tripoli.

August 8 Henry the Wrangler, Duke of Bavaria and Carinthia, dies. He is succeeded (in Bavaria only) by his son, Henry.

996

- Gerbert of Aurillac, archbishop of Reims, flees to the Emperor Otto III after Pope John XV refuses to accept the legality of the deposition of his predecessor, Arnulf.
- Richard I, Count of Normandy dies. He is succeeded by his son, Richard II the Good.
- The Umayyad regent Abu Amir al-Mansur (Almanzor), leading the army of the caliph (Islamic ruler) of Córdoba, Spain, sacks León.

May 3 Bruno of Carinthia becomes the first German pope when he is crowned as Gregory V.

May 21 Otto III of Germany is crowned as emperor by Pope Gregory V in Rome, Italy.

September 9 Pope Gregory V is expelled by the Roman patrician (secular ruler) Crescentius II.

October 14 Al-Aziz Bi'llah Nizar Abu Mansur, the Fatimid caliph (Islamic ruler) of Egypt, dies. He is succeeded by his son, Mustansir Hākim.

October 24 King Hugh of France, the founder of the Capetian dynasty, dies and is buried at Saint-Denis. He is succeeded by his son, Hugh Cape, Robert II the Pious.

997

- Ardoin, Marquess of Ivrea, leading an Italian revolt, murders Peter, bishop of Vercelli. Emperor Otto III is forced to restore order.
- King Constantine III of Scotland is killed in battle, and is succeeded by Kenneth III, the son of the earlier king Dub.
- Stephen succeeds his father, Geza, as Duke of Hungary.
- The Bulgarian leader Samuel proclaims himself "caesar"; he aspires to create a Balkan empire.
- The Chinese Song emperor, Taizong, dies. Though he has reunited the Chinese under a single dynasty, he has been unable to recover all the territories ruled by the Tang dynasty. Thus the Song empire is the smallest of the Chinese empires, confined only to areas inhabited by ethnic Chinese.
- The Ilek khans extinguish the Samanid dynasty of Transoxiana.
- The Umayyad regent Abu Amir al-Mansur (Almanzor), leading the army of the caliph (Islamic ruler) of Córdoba, Spain, sacks the Church of Santiago de Compostela in a raid into Galicia in northwestern Spain.

April 4 John Philagathus, archbishop of Piacenza, is crowned as Pope John XVI in place of the exiled Gregory V.

998

- Emperor Otto III unites his chanceries for Germany and Italy, thus restoring the Carolingian system of a single secretariat.
- Mahmud III, son of Sabuktagin, deposes his brother, Ismail, and becomes emir of Ghazni (in modern Afghanistan).
- Unable to defend Dalmatia against the Bulgar King Samuel, the Byzantine emperor, Basil II, grants it to Venice.

February 2 Emperor Otto III removes the usurping Pope John XVI and restores Gregory V as pope.

April 4 Emperor Otto III executes the Roman patrician (secular ruler) Crescentius II who had earlier overthrown Popes John XV and Gregory V.

999

- Bolesław II, Duke of Bohemia, dies. Like his father, Bolesław I, he has ruled through ducally appointed officials instead of the nobility. He is succeeded by Bolesław III.
- King Vermudo II of León, Spain, dies. He is succeeded by his son, Alfonso V.
- Malachy II, King of Ireland, and Brian Bórumha, King of Munster, defeat the Danes at Glenmana and sack the Norse kingdom of Dublin, Ireland.

- The Byzantine emperor Basil II's Syrian campaign restores imperial control in the autumn, after a military revolt.
- Following the death of Gregory V, Gerbert of Aurillac is elected as Pope Sylvester II. He is the first French pope.

SCIENCE, TECHNOLOGY, AND MEDICINE

Health and Medicine

975
- Abu Mansur Muwaffaq of Herat writes *The Foundations of the True Properties of Remedies*, in Persian. It describes 585 drugs.

978
- Adud-ad-Dawlah's teaching hospital, al-Bimāristān al-'Adudi, is completed in Baghdad. Its 24 physicians form a medical faculty.

980
- Chinese scholar Lu Tsan-ning writes his *Discourse on the Investigation of Things*, in which he recommends the sterilization by steam of the belongings of sufferers from epidemic fevers.

982
- Yasuyori Tamba writes *Ishino*, the oldest extant Japanese treatise on medicine.

986
- Spanish Muslim surgeon Abul Kasim writes his *al-Tasrif*, a manual of surgery, introducing and illustrating many new techniques and operations.

Math

986
- French monk Abbo of Fleury writes *De numero mensura et pondere/On Weights and Measures*, a mathematical commentary.

997
- The Muslim astronomer Abu'l-Wafā writes translations and commentaries (subsequently lost) on Euclid, among others. He also makes contributions to the development of trigonometry and geometry.

Science

c. 970
- The Muslim astronomer Abu'l-Wafā invents the wall quadrant for the accurate measurement of the declination of stars in the sky. He also discovers, and plots tables for, several new trigonometrical functions.

c. 975
- Ibn Hauqal, Islamic geographer and cartographer, writes *Book of Ways and Provinces*, which is illustrated with maps.

986
- Al-Sufi writes *Kitāb al-Kawākib al-Thābitah/Book of the Fixed Stars*, on his astronomical observations.

987
- Toltec conquerors of the Central American Mayan city of Chichén Itzá construct monuments with ritual astronomical alignments to the rising and setting of the sun and the sacred planet Venus.

Technology

968
- Silver-bearing ore is discovered at Goslav; the production of copper, zinc, and lead also developed here later.

976
- Chang Ssu-Hsün, a Chinese inventor, develops the chain drive for use in a mechanical clock.

984
- Ahmad and Mahmud, sons of Ibrahim the astrolabist, of Isfahan, make the earliest dated astrolabe (now at Oxford, England).

Transportation

984
- Ch'iao Wei-Yo, a Chinese government transport inspector, builds the first canal lock, opening the way for a considerable expansion of the Chinese canal system.

ARTS AND IDEAS

Architecture

954
- The Hindu Lakshmana temple is built at Khajurāho in central India. Its sculptural decoration, much of it depicting sexual acts, is one of the great masterpieces of Indian art.

958
- Chartres Cathedral in France, built in 743, is destroyed by fire. Rebuilding is completed in 1022.

961
- A monastery of St. Cyriakus is founded at Gernrode. Its church, much of which still survives, is significant for elements like the thick walls and piers, which anticipate Romanesque architecture.

970
- The Al-Azhar Mosque is founded in Cairo, Egypt. The university attached to the mosque becomes a highly important center of Islamic learning.

973
- The church at Bradford-on-Avon is founded in England. Its tower displays decorative strip work made of stone.

975

- The Great Mosque at Córdoba, Spain, begun in 786, is extended, and lavish decoration is applied to the new *mihrab* (prayer niche indicating the direction of Mecca).

976

- The first basilica of San Marco in Venice, Italy, is burned down in a rebellion against the doge.

Arts

c. 975

- The life-sized Gero crucifix in Cologne cathedral, Germany, inaugurates a new epoch of Christian art in the West, in which the physical suffering of Christ is explicitly represented.

c. 980

- At Conques in France the relics of St. Foy are preserved in a three-foot statue of the saint which is made of beaten gold and encrusted with gems.
- At Jelling in Denmark, a large rune stone is carved with the figure of Christ surrounded by decorative strip work. It was made on the orders of King Harald Bluetooth of Denmark.

981

- A colossal monolithic statue, the largest in India, of Bahubali is carved at the great Jain religious site of Vindhyagiri at Shravana Belgola in southern India.

Literature and Language

950

c. 950 Arab scholar Al-Isfahānī writes *Kitāb al-Aghāni/ Great Book of Songs*, an encyclopedic survey of Arab song which includes biographical material.

- *Anthologia Palatina/Greek Anthology* is collected by Constantine Cephalas. It consists of poems and brief inscriptions by some 300 writers from the 5th century BC to the 6th century AD.

c. 962

- Hrotswith (or Roswitha), a German nun, writes six comedies in prose in imitation of Terence, the Roman comedy writer. They were intended to provide both moral guidance and entertainment for her fellow nuns.

976

- After being deposed, Li Yu, ruler of the southern Tang dynasty in China, spends his last years writing poetry in which he laments his loss of power.

c. 977

- The *T'ai-ping yü-lan*, a Chinese encyclopedia with extracts from 1,690 works, is produced around this time by Chinese scholar Wu Shu.

985

- Al-Maqdisī writes *Ahsan al-Taqāsim fi Ma'rifat al-Aqālim/The Best of Classification for the Knowledge of Regions*, a description of his travels in Islamic countries of the Middle East.

c. 995

- "The Battle of Maldon," an Old English poem by a now-unknown poet, is written at about this time, dealing with a historically attested skirmish between Saxon forces and Danish raiders at Maldon in Essex, England, in 991.

Music

c. 985

- One of the earliest examples of polyphony, music in more than one voice, appears in the anonymous musical treatise *Musica enchiriadis/Manual of Music*.

Thought and Scholarship

959

- Byzantine emperor Constantine VII dies. As devoted to study as he was to politics, his many writings include *De administrando imperio/On Imperial Administration*, on foreign policy, and *De cerimoniis aulae Byzantina/On the Ceremónies of the Byzantine Court*, which describes the elaborate ceremonial of the Byzantine court.

c. 965

- Liutprand, diplomat and bishop of Cremona, writes *Antapodosis/Revenge*, a history of Europe from 888 to 958, and *De rebus gestis Ottonis I/On Matters Relating to the Deeds of Otto I*, in praise of Otto I.

966

- Flodoard of Reims completes his *Annales/Annals*, a chronicle of the period 919 to 966.

c. 973

- Widukind, a monk of Corvey, writes his *Res gestae Saxonicae/Matters Concerning the Deeds of the Saxons*, a history of the Saxons.

981

- Hsieh Chü-chêng writes *Chiu Wu-tai-shih*, the official Chinese history of the Five Dynasties in the period 907–959.

988

- Ibn-al-Nadīm writes *Index of Sciences*, a catalog of Arabic works.

SOCIETY

Education

961

- Abd-ar-Rahman III, the caliph (Islamic ruler) of Córdoba, Spain, founds the University of Córdoba.

976

- Mustansir Hakam II, the caliph (Islamic ruler) of Córdoba, Spain, enlarges Córdoba University, now preeminent in Europe and the Muslim world. He also founds free schools in the city.

Everyday Life

996

- Cane sugar is introduced into Europe through Venice, having been brought back by traders from Egypt.

BIRTHS & DEATHS

950

c. 950   St. Romuald, Christian ascetic who established the Camaldolese Benedictines (hermits), born in Ravenna (–1027).

- Muslim philosopher Al-Fārābī, writer of a vision of Utopia called *The Model City* and a treatise on music theory, dies.

955

- Otto II, German king 961–983, Holy Roman Emperor 961–983, sole ruler after 973, born (–983).

November 23   Eadred (or Edred), Anglo-Saxon king of England 946–955, brother of Edmund I, who brought Northumbria under permanent English rule, dies in Frome, Somerset, England.

c. 956

- Vladimir I, Grand Prince of Kiev who united Kiev and Novgorod into a single state, and who determined the course of Christianity in Russia, born in Kiev (–1015).

c. 957

- Basil II, Byzantine emperor 976–1025, who enlarged the empire, born (–1025).

959

- Constantine VII, Byzantine emperor 913–959, dies.

961

October 15   Abd ar-Rahman III, first caliph 929–961 and greatest ruler of the Umayyad dynasty of Spain, dies in Córdoba, Spain (70).

c. 964

- Olaf I Tryggvason, Viking king of Norway 995–1000, who was the first to attempt to Christianize Norway, born (–1000).

966

- Berengar of Ivrea, the former King Berengar II of Italy, dies in exile.

967

- Bolesław I Chrobry (the Brave), first king of Poland 1024–25, who made Poland a major European state, is born in Gniezno, Poland (–1025).

February 2   Sayf ad-Dawlah, the emir of Aleppo, Syria, and one of the most prominent rulers of the Hamdanid dynasty, dies.

November 20   Al-Isfahānī (Abu al-Faraj al-Isbahāni), Muslim literary scholar and author of the encyclopedic work on Arabic music *Kitab al-aghani/ Book of Songs*, dies in Baghdad, Persia (c. 70).

969

December 11   Nicephorus II, Byzantium emperor 963–969, who mobilized the Byzantine empire against the Muslim Arabs leading to a resurgence of the Empire's power, is murdered in Constantinople (c. 57).

971

- Mahmud III, Emir of Ghazni 998–1030, an area covering modern Afghanistan and northeastern Persia, who conquered Kashmir, the Punjab, and much of Persia, also noted as a patron of the arts, born (–1030).

973

May 6   Henry II (St. Henry), German king 1002–24 and emperor 1014–24, last of the Saxon dynasty of emperors, born, probably in Albach, Bavaria (–1024).

May 7   Otto I, Duke of Saxony 936–961 (as Otto II), German king 936–973, and emperor 962–973, dies in Memleben, Thuringia (60).

September   Al-Bīrunī, outstanding Muslim scholar and scientist, whose fields of study included astronomy, mathematics, physics, medicine, and history, born in Khwarizm, Ghazni (–1048).

975

July 8   Edgar, Anglo-Saxon king of Mercia and Northumbria 957–959 and king of England 959–975, son of Edmund I, a major patron of the English monastic revival, dies in England (c. 31).

976

June 11   The doge Peter Candiano IV, who has attempted to make himself the feudal lord of Venice, Italy, is murdered in a revolt.

November 14   T'ai Tsu, Chinese emperor 960–976 who reunited China and founded the Sung dynasty, dies in K'ai-feng, China (49).

977

- Stephen I, first king of Hungary (1000–38), founder of the Hungarian state, born (–1038).

978

- Murasaki Shikibu, court lady and author of *Genji Monogatari/The Tale of Genji*, born in Kyoto, Japan (–c. 1014).

980

- Avicenna (ibn Sīnā), celebrated Islamic physician, philosopher, and scientist whose best known work is the *Canon of Medicine*, born in Bukhara, Persia (–1037).

July   Otto III, German king and Holy Roman Emperor 994–1002, born (–1002).

983

December 7   Otto II, German king 961–983, Holy Roman Emperor 961–983, sole ruler after 973, dies in Rome (28).

984

August 1   St. Aethelwold, bishop of Winchester and monastic reformer, dies.

986

April 25   Al-Sufi of Ray (Alsoufi), Muslim astronomer who wrote the *Book of the Fixed Stars*, dies (c. 83).

987

- Louis V, the last Carolingian king of France, dies without issue.

988

May 19   St. Dunstan, archbishop of Canterbury, monastic reformer, and adviser to the kings of Wessex, dies in Canterbury, England (c. 64).

c. 990

- Toghrïl Beg, Iranian leader c. 1040–63, who conquered Iran, Iraq, Syria, and Anatolia and founded the Seljuq dynasty, born (–1063).

992

- Duke Charles of Lower Lorraine, the last Carolingian, dies.

February 29   St. Oswald of York, Anglo-Saxon archbishop of York who was instrumental in formulating monastic and feudal reforms, dies in Worcester (c. 67).

c. 995

- Olaf II Haraldsson, Viking king 1015–30, and patron saint of Norway, who was the first to rule the entire country and who also introduced a religious code which became the country's first national legislation, born (–1030).

997

- King Stephen Držvislav of Croatia, a Byzantine vassal, dies.
- St. Adalbert, first Czech bishop of Prague, dies in the Baltic (c. 41).

c. 999

- Berengar of Tours, leading theologian during the Eucharistic controversy of the 11th century, born in Tours, Touraine (–1088).

Religion

c. 950

- A heretical Christian sect called the Bogomils emerges in the Bulgar Khanate. Bogomilism has links with Manichaeism and the Paulicians: they believed that the world and the body are of Satan and only the spirit is created by God.

951

- The Qarmatians (an Ismailite Muslim sect) restore the Black Stone they took from the Islamic holy city of Mecca in 930.

955

- The baptism in the Byzantine capital, Constantinople, of Princess Olga, regent of the Rus principality of Kiev, stimulates Byzantine missionary activity in Russia.

959

- King Otto I of Germany sends a Christian missionary to Russia at the request of Princess Olga, regent of the Rus principality of Kiev.

960

- The Karakhanids of central Asia become the first Turkic tribe to be converted en masse to Islam.

961

- St. Athanasius the Athonite establishes the first organized monastic foundation on Mt. Athos, Greece.

964

- The Byzantine emperor Nicephorus II ineffectively prohibits the founding of new monasteries and the provision of further endowments to existing monasteries.

c. 965

- King Harald Bluetooth of Denmark becomes the first Christian king in Scandinavia. Subsequently, Christianity spreads rapidly in Scandinavia.

966

- Mieszko I of Poland is converted to Christianity following his marriage to Dobrava, daughter of Duke Bolesław I of Bohemia. The first Christian missionary bishop subsequently arrives in Poland.

c. 970

- Ethelwold of Winchester, England, a friend of Dunstan, writes *Regularis concordia/A Guide to Concord*, rules for English monastic life.

975

- Geza, Duke of the Magyars in Hungary, and his family are baptized into the Roman Catholic Church.

990

- The Orthodox Church is founded in Russia.

992

- The first Benedictine monastery in Bohemia is founded at Břvevnov, near Prague.

993

- Pope John XV canonizes Ulric, bishop of Augsburg, the first formal canonization by a pope.

994

- St. Adalbert, the first Czech bishop of Prague, sets out to evangelize the Baltic coast. He is martyred three years later.

999

- As the millennium approaches, Christians across Europe are gripped with terror at the expected end of the world.

Sports

969

- The Chinese introduce playing cards. The earliest known pack consists of 56 cards divided into 4 suits of 14 cards each. The cards are printed in several inks, using separate wood blocks for each part of the pattern. They are used as paper money as well as for gaming.

c. 995

- The Arab traveler al-Bīrunī rediscovers chess in India, where it has evolved into the modern form of the game. He is responsible for reintroducing it to the Islamic world, and thence to medieval Europe.

1000–1009

POLITICS, GOVERNMENT, AND ECONOMICS

Business and Economics

c. 1000
- Through the influence of Arab merchants, Islam begins to find converts in west and east Africa.

Colonization

c. 1000
- A small settlement is founded at L'Anse aux Meadows in Newfoundland by Norse Greenlanders. It survives only for about 20 years.
- Polynesian migrants reach New Zealand, where they settle and become the Maori people. The Polynesian migration across the Pacific Ocean, using the stars for navigation, has taken centuries to complete.

Politics and Government

1000
c. 1000 The rival Andean empires of Tiahuanaco and Huari collapse within a few years of each other.
c. 1000 Traders and fishermen from Macassar in Sulawesi in southeast Asia (modern Indonesia), make contact with the Aborigines of northern Australia.
- As a result of invasions from Dai Viet (Annam), Yang Po Ku Vijaya, King of Champa (modern southern Vietnam), transfers his capital from Indrapura to Vijaya.
- By a majority decision of the Althing (parliament), Iceland adopts Christianity. Pagan worship is permitted in private.
- Emperor Otto III makes his permanent residence in Rome, Italy.
- King Aethelred II the Unready of England ravages Norse-settled areas in Cumberland and the Isle of Man in retaliation for Viking raids.
- King García II Sanchez of Navarre dies. He is succeeded by his son, Sancho III the Great.
- King Svein of Denmark defeats and kills King Olaf I Tryggvesson of Norway at Svöld and thus conquers Norway.
- The Byzantine emperor Basil II extends his empire to the Lower Danube with the occupation of the Dobrudja.
March 31 Bolesław Chrobry (the Brave) of Poland convinces the Emperor Otto III to create the archbishopric of Gniezno for Poland, with Silesia and Pomerania subject to it. Poland is consequently recognized as independent both politically and ecclesiastically.
March 31 Following the murder of Prince David of Tao (Georgia), the Byzantine emperor Basil II annexes his lands.
December 25 Duke Stephen is crowned as king of Hungary. He has placed his country under the protection of the Pope, from whom he receives the crown and the establishment of a Hungarian ecclesiastical hierarchy under the archbishopric of Gran.

1001
February 2 The Romans revolt, and besiege the Emperor Otto III in his palace on the Aventine hill. He is relieved by Duke Henry of Bavaria, but although peace is restored, he leaves Rome.
November 27 Mahmud of Ghazni defeats Jaipal, Raja of the Punjab at Peshawar. Jaipāl commits suicide and Mahmud occupies his kingdom.

1002
- A Venetian fleet is defeated besieging the Byzantines in Bari, Italy.
- Duke Bolesław III of Bohemia is expelled from Bohemia and succeeded by Vladivoj, the brother of King Bolesław of Poland. In order to win German support against his subjects, Vladivoj becomes the vassal of King Henry II of Germany, who appoints him Duke of Bohemia.
February 15 Ardoin, Marquess of Ivrea, the leader of an Italian revolt against German and ecclesiastical domination, is crowned as king of Italy.
June 7 With the support of the archbishop of Mainz, Duke Henry of Bavaria is crowned as king of the Romans (king of Germany).
July 7 Bolesław Chrobry (the Brave) of Poland recognizes King Henry II of Germany as overlord and cedes his recent conquests, retaining Lusatia and Milsko. As Bolesław leaves their meeting, an attempt is made to murder him, for which he blames Henry, so beginning a war.
August 10 The Umayyad regent Abu Amir al-Mansur (Almanzor), Vizier of Córdoba, dies after his defeat at Calatañazor by the kings of León and Navarre. He is succeeded by his son, al-Muzaffar.
October 15 Henry, Duke of Burgundy, dies without issue. The succession is disputed.
November 13 The "St. Brice's day massacre" takes place in England. Danes resident in southern England are massacred at the instigation of King Aethelred of England.

1003
- Brian Bórumha, King of Munster, becomes high king of Ireland.

- King Svein of Denmark invades England to gain revenge for the "St. Brice's day massacre," in which Danes resident in the south of England were murdered on the orders of of King Aethelred of England.
- Moorish forces from the Umayyad Caliphate of southern Spain devastate the kingdom of León.
- The Byzantine emperor Basil II defeats Samuel, the Bulgarian emperor, near Skopje in Macedonia.
- Vladivoj, Duke of Bohemia dies and is succeeded by his son, Jaromir. Shortly afterwards, Bolesław Chrobry (the Brave) of Poland expels him and restores Duke Bolesław III, who proceeds to murder his former opponents. The Bohemians then call back Bolesław of Poland, who deposes and blinds Bolesław III, and rules Bohemia himself.

June 6   John XVII, a protégé of John II Crescentius, the patrician of Rome, is crowned as pope.

October 1   The acceptance of Henry II as king of the Germans is completed with the homage of Duke Hermann of Swabia, a former rival for the title.

December 25   John XVIII is crowned as pope.

1004

- Following a Qitan (Khitan) attack on their capital Kaifeng, the Chinese Song emperor signs the Treaty of Shan-yüan, recognizing the independence of the Qitan Liao state in northern China and beginning the regular payment of tributes of tea and silk.
- King Kenneth III of Scotland is killed in battle against Malcolm II, the son of Kenneth II, who succeeds him.
- Prince Stephen of Hungary conquers Transylvania.
- The Italian city of Pisa is sacked by Arab pirates.

May 14   King Henry II of Germany invades Italy, forces King Ardoin of Italy to flee, and is crowned as king of Italy at Pavia. An anti-German riot in Pavia on the day of the coronation is followed by the sack of the city.

September 9   King Henry II of Germany restores Jaromir as Duke of Bohemia in a war which follows Bolesław Chrobry (the Brave) of Poland's refusal to pay homage.

1005

- Wang Ch'in-jo becomes the principal editor of *T'sé-fu yüan-kuei*, a 1,000 book encyclopedia of Chinese government, completed in 1013.

March 28   King Henry II of Germany makes an alliance with the Wends (a Slav tribe) against Bolesław Chrobry (the Brave) of Poland, who has seized territory between the River Oder and the River Elbe. Henry later invades Poland as far as Poznań but is defeated by Bolesław.

1006

- An Arab fleet is defeated near Reggio, Italy, by the Pisans.
- Count Richard II of Normandy adopts the title duke.

September 9   A joint expedition by King Henry II of Germany and King Robert II of France fails to recover Valenciennes from the expansionist Count Baldwin IV of Flanders, who has also seized the castle of Ghent.

1007

- Bolesław Chrobry (the Brave) of Poland raids into Germany as far as Magdeburg and recovers territories west of the Oder, including Lausitz (Łużyce).

- King Henry II of Germany finally compels Count Baldwin IV of Flanders to surrender Valenciennes.

1008

- Al-Muzaffar, Umayyad Vizier of Córdoba in Spain, is poisoned, and succeeded by his brother, Abd-ar-Rahman, who is soon afterwards killed in a riot. The military now effectively rule in Córdoba.
- Anandpal, son of Jaipal, raja of the Punjab, is defeated with heavy loss by Mahmud III, Emir of Ghazni, ending his attempt to recover the Punjab.
- Georgia is united under King Bagrat III.
- The English king Aethelred II the Unready constructs the first English fleet as a response to the threat of Danish invaders.

1009

- Al-Hākim, the sixth caliph of the Egyptian Fatimid dynasty, orders the destruction of the Holy Sepulchre in Jerusalem.
- Hishām II, Caliph of Córdoba in Spain, is deposed and succeeded by Mohammad II, a distant relative, who in turn is deposed and succeeded by Suleiman.
- King Henry II of Germany grants Valenciennes back to Count Baldwin IV of Flanders as a royal fief.
- Mahmud III, Emir of Ghazni, conquers the principality of Ghur (in modern Afghanistan). Muslims are now settling in northwest India.

July 7   Pope John XVIII dies and is succeeded by Sergius IV, another candidate of the patrician of Rome, John II Crescentius.

August 1   A large Danish army under Thorkell the Tall lands at Sandwich, England, and attacks Canterbury.

SCIENCE, TECHNOLOGY, AND MEDICINE

Agriculture

1000

c. 1000   The farmers and villagers of Frisia begin to build dykes and sea defenses, in order to reclaim land in northwest Europe.

- The Cochise culture of southern Arizona and New Mexico, the earliest known farmers in North America, are raising a very primitive form of corn at this time.

1006

- The Chinese government sets up granaries throughout the country in order to provide emergency relief in times of famine.

Health and Medicine

c. 1000

- German rulers welcome Arab and Jewish physicians to be doctors at their courts.

Math

1003

- Pope Sylvester II, formerly known as Gerbert of Aurillac, dies. A pioneering scientist, his works include treatises on the abacus, the astrolabe (an astronomical instrument for measuring the altitude of stars and planets), and Spanish-Arabic numerals.

Science

1007

- The Muslim astronomer ibn-Yūnus compiles *The Hakemite Tables*, a collection of astronomical observations compiled in the period 990–1007 in his observatory at Cairo, Egypt, including valuable timings of eclipses.

Technology

1000

- An author known only as Theophilus describes for the first time the manufacture of sheet glass in Europe. The technique used is to open out a cylinder of glass that has been blown in the traditional manner.

Transportation

1000

- The construction of Scandinavian warships is improved with the addition of armor plate, including iron sheets and prows.

ARTS AND IDEAS

Architecture

1000

- A wooden palace is built at Lojsta, Gotland.
- The "Bridge of Ten Thousand Ages" is completed at the Chinese port of Foochow (Fuzhou).

1001

- Building begins on the Church of St. Michael in Hildesheim, Germany. Possibly designed by its bishop, St. Bernward, it is the first example of a church in which the different areas of the interior are clearly articulated.

c. **1006**

- A tall circular tower is built as a mausoleum for the Seljuk prince Qabus at Gurgan, Persia. The austerity of the architecture reflects pre-Islamic traditions.

1007

- Bamberg Cathedral is founded in Bamberg (now in Germany) by King Henry II of Germany in order to ensure the "Germanization" of the Wends (a pagan Slavonic people).

c. **1009**

- The Brihadishvara temple at Thanjavur, India, is completed. Dedicated to the Hindu divinity Siva (or Shiva), it was built by Rajaraja I and is the greatest architectural achievement of the Chola era.

Arts

c. **1000**

- The richly bejeweled cross of Lothair II, containing in its center a cameo of the Roman emperor Augustus, is made. It is one of the masterpieces of Ottoman art.

Literature and Language

1000

- *Makura no Soshi/The Pillow Book* of Sei Shonagon is written around this time. A Japanese lady's commonplace book with often mischievous reflections and anecdotes about court life, it is one of the masterpieces of Japanese literature.

1007

- In the charter of Count Fulk Nerra of Anjou, which establishes the "free borough" of Beaulieu, the first known use of the words "burgess" and "bourgeois" (originally *burgensis*) occurs.

1009

- Byzantine monk and mystic St. Symeon retires to Chrysopolis where he writes *Hymns of the Divine Loves* in Greek, in which he describes his method of achieving a "vision of light."

SOCIETY

Education

1000

- A school of Lombard law is founded in Pavia, a city in Lombardy, Italy.
- French cathedral schools develop in Tours, Orléans, Utrecht, Reims, Chartres, Liège, and Paris.

Everyday Life

1000

c. 1000   Coffee is being drunk in Arabia and Persia. References in the work of the Persian philosopher and physician Avicenna (ibn Sīnā) testify to its use being largely medicinal.

1000–1519   Aztec culture flourishes, producing expert engineers and craftsmen. They use a system of writing with pictures, and develop a religious system. Their rituals include human sacrifice to their tribal leader-deity, Huitzilopotchtli, a god of war.

Religion

c. 1000

- Christianity is fully established in Iceland, having arrived from Norway in the preceding decades.

1005

- Caliph al-Hākim founds the *Dār al-Hikmah* (Hall of Wisdom), a college of Muslim theology, in Cairo, Egypt.

1007

November 1   King Henry II of Germany founds the bishopric of Bamberg, partly for the conversion of the Wends (a pagan Slavonic people), but also as part of furthering the policy (initiated by Otto I) of founding royal authority on the church as a counter to feudal particularism.

1009

March 14   St. Bruno of Querfurt is martyred on a mission to convert the Baltic Jadźwingas tribe.

Sports

1000

c. 1000   Chess is widely known throughout Europe.

1000–1100   "Tables," or backgammon, is introduced to Europe by the Arabs (or reintroduced, as it is similar in name and appearance to the Roman game *Tabula*). It becomes extremely popular over the next few centuries. The name "backgammon" is first used in the mid-17th century.

1000–1100   During this century the tournament (knightly contest) evolves in France as a formal event.

BIRTHS & DEATHS

c. 1000

- Olaf I Tryggvason, Viking king of Norway 995–1000, who was the first to attempt to Christianize Norway, dies (*c.* 36).

1002

- Wu Shu, Chinese encyclopedist, writer of *Shih lei fu*, a scientific encyclopedia, and *T'ai-ping yü-lan*, an anthology of Chinese knowledge in 100 volumes, dies.

January 23   Otto III, king of Germany 984–1002 and emperor 996–1002, dies in Rome (22).

April 30   Eckhard, Margrave of Meissen, an aspirant to the German crown, is murdered.

August 10   Abu Amir al-Mansur (Almanzor), chief minister (vizier) and virtual ruler of the Umayyad caliphate of Córdoba, Spain, dies in Spain (*c.* 64).

1003

- Edward (St. Edward the Confessor), Anglo-Norman king of England 1042–66, son of Aethelred, an ineffectual but pious ruler, born in Islip, England (–1066).

May 12   Sylvester II (Gerbert of Aurillac), French head of the Roman Catholic Church 999–1003, dies in Rome (*c.* 58).

1005

- Abe-no-Seimei, Japanese astronomer, famous astrologer, scholar, and magician, dies.

- Lanfranc, Italian Benedictine monk, archbishop of Canterbury 1070–89 and counselor of William the Conqueror, born in Pavia, Lombardy, Italy (–1089).

1007

- Al-Hamadhāni, Arabic writer of short stories in *Maqāmāt* about a disreputable vagabond called Abu'l-Fath, dies.

- Al-Majrīti, Muslim astronomer, who revised the tables of the 9th-century Baghdad astronomer al-Khwarizmi, adjusting them for Córdoba, Spain, and adapting them for the Muslim calendar, dies.

- Ou-yang Hsiu, Chinese statesman, poet, and historian, born in Mien-yang, Szechwan, China (–1072).

- St. Peter Damian (Pier Damiani), cardinal and church reformer, born in Ravenna, Italy (–1072).

1010–1019

POLITICS, GOVERNMENT, AND ECONOMICS

Politics and Government

1010

- King Robert II of France proclaims a "Peace of God" in France in an attempt to curb endemic private warfare.
- The caliph Suleiman of Córdoba, in Spain, is deposed and Mohammad II is restored. The latter is then murdered and Hishām II restored. The Umayyad Caliphate now slides into political anarchy.
- The Qitans (Khitans) of Liao give the Koreans an ultimatum to hand over disputed territory. When no reply is received the Khitans capture Kaesong, the capital of Koryǒ (Korea) and ravage the north of the country before withdrawing.

1010–1225 Ly Thai-to, founder of the Ly dynasty, usurps the imperial throne of Dai Viet (or Annam, modern northern Vietnam), and founds a new capital at Thang-long.

1011

- After ravaging widely in the English East Midlands, the Danes attack Canterbury and capture Archbishop Aelfeah of Canterbury.
- Arab pirates sack Pisa in Italy.
- Bernard I Billung, Duke of Saxony, dies. He is succeeded by his son, Bernard II.

1012

- Duke Jaromir of Bohemia is deposed and succeeded by his brother Oldřvich.
- Following the death without issue of Duke Hermann III of Swabia (a descendant of Charlemagne), King Henry II of Germany grants the duchy to Ernest of Babenberg.

May 12 The death of Pope Sergius IV within a few weeks of that of his patron John II Crescentius leads to suspicions that they have both been murdered. The election of Sergius IV's successor is disputed: the Crescentius family nominate Gregory, but he is soon expelled by the counts of Tusculum, who put Theophylact of Tusculum, as Benedict VIII, in possession of the papacy.

1013

- King Svein of Denmark, having been accepted in England as king in Northumbria and the Danelaw, now conquers Wessex. King Aethelred II of England flees to Normandy.

April 20 Hishām II, Caliph of Córdoba in Spain, disappears following the capture of the city by Suleiman, who resumes his rule. Civil war between Moors and Arabs is now endemic in the Umayyad Caliphate.

May 24 The Peace of Merseberg is signed. Bolesław Chrobry (the Brave) of Poland pays homage to King Henry II of Germany and is permitted to retain all his conquests with the exception of Bohemia. He is now free to make war in Russia.

1014

January 1 King Henry II of Germany holds a synod at Ravenna, Italy, which makes decrees for ecclesiastical reform.

February 3 Sven Forkbeard, King of Denmark, Norway, and England, dies and is succeeded by his sons, Harold, in Denmark, and Cnut, in England. However, when the English king Aethelred II is restored, Cnut is forced to return to Denmark.

February 14 King Henry II of Germany and Italy is crowned emperor by Pope Benedict VIII in Rome, to the accompaniment of anti-German rioting.

April 18 At the Battle of Clontarf, Ireland, Brian Bórumha, high king of Ireland, defeats a coalition of Vikings and the kingdom of Leinster but is himself killed.

June 6 The newly-crowned Emperor Henry II returns to Germany. In Lombardy, Italy, there follows an anti-German outburst directed against the bishops.

July 29 Byzantine emperor Basil II surrounds and captures a Bulgarian army in the pass of Kleidon, Bulgaria. 15,000 Bulgar prisoners are blinded before being sent home.

October 6 Samuel, the Bulgarian emperor, dies two days after seeing the 15,000 survivors of the defeat at the pass of Kleidon who had been blinded by the Byzantine emperor Basil II.

1015

- Moorish forces from Spain conquer Sardinia (–1016).
- St. Vladimir I, Great Prince of Kiev and first Christian ruler of Russia, dies. He is succeeded by his son Sviatopolk I, after he murders his brothers, Boris and Gleb; another brother, Jaroslav, holds out in Novgorod against him.
- The duchy of Benevento, Italy, establishes a commune for urban self-government.
- The duchy of Burgundy is divided by a treaty by which Henry, son of King Robert II of France, becomes duke and Otto-William, the adopted son of Duke Henry the Great, receives the county of Dijon.

July 7 Bolesław Chrobry (the Brave) of Poland repulses an invasion by Emperor Henry II.

September Cnut, returning from Denmark with a large fleet and army to claim the English throne, lands at Sandwich in Kent.

1016

- King Malcolm II of Scotland defeats Uhtred, Earl of Northumbria, at Carham, on the River Tweed, thus securing Scottish possession of Lothian.
- Mahmud III, Emir of Ghazni, captures Samarkand (modern Uzbekistan).
- Olaf II regains Norwegian independence from Denmark by his naval victory off Nesjar.
- Suleiman, the Umayyad caliph of Córdoba in Spain, is deposed by the general Ali ibn-Hammūd, who founds the Hammūdid dynasty.
- The first Normans arrive in southern Italy as military adventurers, serving the armies of both the Lombard duchies and the Byzantine Empire.

April 4   King Cnut, the Danish claimant to the English throne, attempts to seize London, England, but is repulsed by the inhabitants.

April 23   King Aethelred II the Unready of England dies in London, England. He is succeeded by his son, Edmund Ironside, who revitalizes English resistance to Cnut, the Danish claimant to the English throne.

June 6   King Rudolph III of Burgundy recognizes Emperor Henry II as his heir and receives his (ineffective) assistance against a rebellion by Otto-William, Count of Dijon.

June 6   The Pisans and Genoese expel the Moors, under Mujāhid of Denia, from Sardinia.

July 6   Count Fulk Nerra of Anjou, France, in the process of extending his territories, defeats Count Odo II of Blois at Pontlevoi.

October   After the Danish victory at Ashingdon, Essex, Cnut and King Edmund Ironside of England make a treaty at Alney in Gloucestershire partitioning England: Edmund is to rule south of the River Thames and Cnut to the north.

November 30   On the death of King Edmund Ironside, Cnut, King of Denmark, is accepted as sole king of England.

1017

- The Cholas of southern India begin pirate raids in southeast Asia.

August 1017–September 1018   Emperor Henry II, following an unsuccessful invasion of Poland, retires through Bohemia where Bolesław Chrobry (the Brave) of Poland is campaigning, but fails to defeat him.

November 11   Emperor Henry II restores the duchy of Bavaria to Henry of Luxembourg.

1018

- On the death of the caliph Ali ibn Hammūd, Abd-ar-Rahman IV of the Umayyad dynasty succeeds as caliph of Córdoba in Spain, but is overthrown by Ali's brother al-Qasim within the year.
- The Qitans (Khitans) of Liao, in northern China, again invade Koryŏ (Korea) in pursuit of their territorial claims, but their army is surrounded and defeated with heavy loss near Kaesong. A lasting peace settlement is agreed shortly afterwards.

January 30   The Treaty of Bautzen is signed, making peace between Emperor Henry II and Bolesław Chrobry (the Brave) of Poland on terms favorable to Poland.

March 3   In an assembly at Nijmegen (modern Netherlands), Emperor Henry II establishes peace in Lorraine. He fails, however, to enforce his authority over the rebellious nobles of Burgundy.

July 21   Prince Sviatopolk, having been driven out of Kiev by his brother Jaroslav, appeals to his father-in-law, Bolesław Chrobry (the Brave) of Poland. Bolesław invades Russia and defeats Jaroslav on the River Bug.

August 14   Bolesław Chrobry (the Brave) of Poland enters Kiev, Russia, and restores his son-in-law Sviatopolk I to the throne, but is then forced to retire when Sviatopolk organizes an anti-Polish rising. Bolesław, however, retains Czerwień and Przemyśl for Poland.

October 10   A Byzantine army defeats southern Italian rebels at Cannae.

December 20   Mahmud of Ghazni takes Kanauj, the capital of the Pratihara dynasty of the Gurjara Kingdom.

1019

- Emperor Henry II pronounces, in a synod at Goslar, that the children of marriages of priests of servile birth are unfree.
- Jaroslav expels his brother Sviatopolk and becomes great prince of Kiev.
- King Cnut of England takes possession of the Danish throne in succession to his brother, Harold.
- The Byzantine emperor Basil II completes his conquest of Bulgaria and its former empire in the Balkans. The western frontier of his empire now extends to the Adriatic Sea and in the north along the River Danube.

SCIENCE, TECHNOLOGY, AND MEDICINE

Agriculture

1012

- Rice is introduced into China from Champa (modern southern Vietnam) and becomes the staple diet.

Science

1010

- The Saxon scholar Bridferth of Ramsey writes his *Handboc/Handbook*. This is an astronomical and astrological work written in Latin and, unusually, also in Old English.

1015

- The Muslim physician Māsawayh al-Mārdini writes a pharmacopeia of useful drugs, and treatises on the use of laxatives and emetics.

ARTS AND IDEAS

Architecture

1015

- Decorated bronze doors are made for the Church of St. Michael in Hildesheim, Germany.

1018

- Building begins on the Church of San Miniato in Florence, Italy. Romanesque in design, it has strong classical proportions in its external elevations.

Arts

c. **1015**

- Fan K'uan, whose atmospheric ink landscapes of Chinese mountain scenery epitomize the Northern Song School of painting, is active around this time.

Literature and Language

c. **1010**

- Murasaki Shikibu ("Lady Murasaki") writes *Genji Monogatari/The Tale of Genji* about the love affairs of Prince Genji. The first psychological novel, it is regarded as one of the greatest works of Japanese literature.

Thought and Scholarship

c. **1010**

- Persian poet Firdausī completes his Persian national epic, *Shāh-nāma/The Book of Kings*. Its 50 chapters relate the history of the Persian kings up to the fall of the Sassanian dynasty.

1014

- Wulfstan, archbishop of York, writes his *Sermo lupi ad Anglos/Address to the English Nation*, which attacks the immorality of the English and describes the devastation caused by the Viking raiders.

SOCIETY

Religion

c. **1010**

- The Toltecs introduce the cult of Quetzalcoatl, "the feathered serpent," to the Central American cities that they have recently invaded.

1012

- St. Romuald founds the strict Order of Camaldoli in Tuscany. The order emphasizes the solitary element of monastic life and is to influence the later Carthusian Order.
- The first prosecutions for heresy take place in Germany.

April 19 Archbishop Aelfeah of Canterbury, England, (later known as St. Alphege) is murdered by his Danish captors despite the payment of a ransom.

BIRTHS & DEATHS

1013

c. 1013 Abu al-Qasim, Medieval Islamic surgeon whose *The Method* is the first illustrated work on surgery, dies (*c.* 77).

- Al-Zahrāwi (Abulcasis), writer of *al-Tasrīf li-Man 'an al-Ta'alif*, a 30-volume medical encyclopedia, dies.
- Isaac al-Fez (Alfasi), Jewish Talmudic scholar and founder of a rabbinic academy in Lucena, Spain, born near Fez, in modern Morocco (–1103).

July 18 Hermann von Reichenau ("Hermannus Contractus" or "Hermann the Lame"), German chronicler, composer, astronomer, and mathematician, born in Saulgau, Swabia, Germany (–1054).

1014

- Murasaki Shikibu, court lady and author of *Genji Monogatari/The Tale of Genji*, dies in Kyoto, Japan (*c.* 36).

February 3 Sewyn I, King of Denmark *c.* 987–1014, who gained control of Norway in 1000, and became king

of England in 1013 after conquering the island, dies in Gainsborough, Lincolnshire, England.

April 23 Brian Bórumha, high king of Ireland 1002–14, killed at the Battle of Clontarf, near Dublin, Ireland (*c.* 73).

1015

c. 1015 Robert of Aplua, Norman traveler who settled in Apulia, southern Italy and expanded Norman rule into Calabria, Naples, and Sicily, born in Normandy (–1085).

July 15 Vladimir I, Grand Prince of Kiev who united Kiev and Novgorod into a single state, and who determined the course of Christianity in Russia, dies in Berestova, near Kiev (59).

1016

- Rājarāja the Great, King of the Cholas, who has made himself the supreme ruler in southern India and Ceylon, dies.

April 23 Aethelred II the Unready, Anglo-Saxon king of England 978–1013 and 1014–16, noted for his ineffectual rule and irresolution in

the face of Danish invasion, dies in London, England (*c.* 48).

November 30 Edmund II Ironside, Anglo-Saxon king of England April–November 1016, son of Aethelred II, noted for his spirited resistance to the invasion of the Danish king Cnut, dies (*c.* 23).

1017

c. 1017 Ramanuja, Indian Braham and theologican, whose ideas had a major influence on Hinduism, born in Sriperumbudur, India (–1137).

- Genshin, Buddhist monk whose *Ōjō yōshū/Essentials of Salvation* popularized the cult of Amida in Japan, dies.

October 28 Henry III, German king 1039–56 and emperor 1046–56, son of Conrad II, born (–1056).

1019

- Ssu-ma Kuang, Chinese statesman, poet, and historian, author of *Tzu-chih tung-chien/Comprehensive Mirror for Aid in Government*, a history of China from 403 BC to AD 959, born in Hsia, Hunan, China (–1086).

1020–1029

POLITICS, GOVERNMENT, AND ECONOMICS

Business and Economics

1020

- The earliest known merchant guild is founded at Tiel in Gelderland (modern Netherlands) to win trading and political privileges for its members.

1024

- The Song dynasty government in China takes over the banks of Chengtu, in Szechwan. Their certificates of deposit then become official and thus become the first paper currency in the world.

Politics and Government

1020

- Duke Bernard II of Saxony revolts against the emperor Henry II.
- On the death of Gagik I of Armenia his kingdom is divided among his sons who seek the protection of the Byzantine Empire against the Ottoman Turks.

August 8   Emperor Henry II recaptures Ghent from Count Baldwin of Flanders.

1021

- Arab pirates sack Narbonne in southern France.

February 13   Caliph Al-Hākim of the Egyptian Fatimid dynasty is murdered. He is succeeded by his son, al-Zāhir.

December 12   Emperor Henry II begins a military expedition to Italy in response to further Byzantine successes in Benevento which endanger Rome.

1022

- Anund Jacob succeeds as king of Sweden.
- Emperor Henry II's Italian expedition checks the Byzantine advance. He takes Capua and Troia before malaria compels the German army to retire.

August 11   Emperor Henry II meets King Robert II of France at Ivois where they discuss the reform of the church.

1023

- Al-Qasim, the Hammūdid caliph of Córdoba in Spain is deposed by Abd-ar-Rahman V, an Umayyad.
- Aleppo in Syria is lost to the Byzantine Empire with the establishment there of the independent Mirdasid emirate.
- The marriage of Alfonso V of León to Urracca, the daughter of Sancho III of Navarre, briefly ends the rivalry of the two kingdoms.

1024

- Caliph Abd ar-Rahman V of Córdoba in Spain is deposed and murdered by Mohammad III, a distant relative.
- Prince Jaroslav of Kiev divides Russia with his brother Mstislav, after being defeated by him during a rebellion.

April 4   On the death of Pope Benedict VIII, the powerful Tusculan family enthrones his brother, Romanus, senator of Rome, Italy, as Pope John XIX.

July 13   Emperor Henry II dies without heirs. He is the last of the Saxon dynasty of emperors.

September 8   Duke Conrad II of Franconia, the first of the Salian dynasty, is crowned king of the Germans at Mainz.

December 25   Bolesław Chrobry (the Brave) is crowned as king of Poland with the approval of Pope John XIX.

1025

- Ernest, Duke of Swabia (in modern Germany), revolts against King Conrad II of Germany. Conrad makes an alliance with King Cnut of England and Denmark.
- King Rajendra leads the Cholas of southern India on a devastating naval expedition against the empire of Srivijaya in Sumatra and the Pegu kingdom (in modern Myanmar) to protect Indian trade with China.
- Mohammad III, the Umayyad caliph of Córdoba in Spain, is murdered. He is succeeded by Yahya, a Hammūdid.

January 1   Mahmud III, Emir of Ghazni, sacks the temple of Siva at Somnāth (now Dwārka), the great center of Hinduism.

June 17   Bolesław I Chrobry (the Brave), first king of Poland, dies at Gniezno, Poland. He is succeeded by his son, Mieszko II.

December 15   The Byzantine emperor Basil II the Bulgarslayer dies without an heir. His brother, Constantine VIII, already coemperor, becomes sole emperor.

December 25   The dukes of Lorraine submit to King Conrad II of Germany on the collapse of their revolt.

1026

- Duke Paldolf IV recovers Capua, Italy, from the Holy Roman Empire with Byzantine assistance.

- King Cnut of England and Denmark is defeated in the sea battle of the Holy River by King Anund of Sweden, King Olaf II of Norway, and Ulf, his own regent of Denmark.
- King Conrad II of Germany is crowned as king of Italy.
- On his last campaign in India, Mahmud III, Emir of Ghazni, ravages Gujarat.
- Richard II, Duke of Normandy, dies. He is succeeded by his son, Richard III.

1027

- King Malcolm II of Scotland pays homage to King Cnut of Denmark and England.
- Richard III, Duke of Normandy, dies. He is succeeded by his brother, Robert I.
- Yahya, the Hammūdid caliph of Córdoba in Spain is deposed and Hishām III, an Umayyad, is proclaimed caliph.

March 26   King Conrad II of Germany and Italy is crowned emperor by Pope John XIX in Rome.

May 5   Alfonso V of León is killed at the siege of Viseu, Spain, which was lost earlier in the century to the caliphate of Córdoba. He is succeeded by his son, Vermudo III.

May 14   In accordance with the custom of the Capetian dynasty, Henry, Duke of Burgundy and eldest son of King Robert II, is crowned as king of France during his father's lifetime.

July 7   Emperor Conrad II grants Bavaria to his son Henry and deprives Ernest of Babenberg of the duchy of Swabia (in modern Germany) when he submits after his rebellion.

1028

- By defeating the Hungarians, Břatislav, the son of Duke Oldřvich, unites Moravia with Bohemia.
- Duke Paldolf IV of Capua, Italy, takes Naples from Duke Sergius IV.
- Emperor Conrad II campaigns unsuccessfully in Poland.

- Having made himself unpopular for his brutal imposition of Christianity, Olaf II, King of Norway, is expelled from his kingdom by King Cnut of Denmark and England. The chiefs of the Faroes, Orkneys, and Shetlands also recognize Cnut's rule.
- Sancho III of Navarre unites the Spanish realm of Castile with his kingdom following the murder of its young Count Garcia.
- The Byzantine emperor Constantine VIII dies. He is succeeded by his son-in-law, Romanus III.

April 14   Emperor Conrad II's son Henry is crowned as king of the Romans (king of Germany).

SCIENCE, TECHNOLOGY, AND MEDICINE

Health and Medicine

1021

- An epidemic of St. Vitus's dance sweeps Europe. St. Vitus's dance is a chorea associated with rheumatic fever which causes uncontrollable muscle spasms.

1027

- An epidemic devastates the Central American empire of the Maya, triggering the collapse of their civilization.

Transportation

1020

- The earliest definite reference to the use of a floating magnet in navigation is recorded in a Chinese treatise of this date.

BIRTHS & DEATHS

1021

- Wang An-shih, Chinese poet and administrator who reformed the Chinese government by stimulating growth through loans, and by redesigning the tax and civil service systems, born in Kiangsi Province, China (–1086).

1022

- St. Bernward, influential bishop of Hildesheim and tutor to Emperor Otto III, who was also noted for his patronage of the arts and building of fine churches, dies (c. 62).

June 29   Notker Labeo, monk and scholar of St. Gall (in modern Switzerland) who translated Boethius' De consolatione philosophiae/On the Consolation of

Philosophy into German, dies in St. Gall (c. 72).

1024

- St. Hugh of Cluny (Hugues de Semur), Abbot of Cluny, born in Semur-en-Brionnais, Burgundy (–1109).

July 13   Henry II (St. Henry), German king 1002–24 and emperor 1014–24, last of the Saxon dynasty of emperors, dies near Göttingen, Germany (50).

1025

June 17   Bolesław I Chrobry (the Brave), first king of Poland 1024–25 who made Poland a major European state, dies (c. 58).

December 15   Basil II the Bulgarslayer, Byzantine emperor 976–1025, dies in Bulgaroctonus (c. 67).

1026

- Richard II, Duke of Normandy, dies.

1027

- Richard III, Duke of Normandy, dies.

1028

- Bishop Fulbert (St. Fulbert) of Chartres, France, under whose direction the cathedral school of Chartres has become one of the leading cultural centers in western Europe, dies.
- Constantine VIII, Byzantine emperor 976–1028, dies.
- William I the Conqueror, Duke of Normandy 1035–87, King of England 1066–87, born in Falaise, Normandy (–1087).

ARTS AND IDEAS

Architecture

1020
- Fire destroys the Carolingian cathedral at Chartres, France.

Music

***c.* 1025**
- Italian writer Guido d'Arezzo publishes his musical treatise *Micrologus de disciplina artis musicae/Short Discourse on the Discipline of the Art of Music*. He establishes a system of precise pitch notation through the introduction of a four-line stave and the ut-re-mi-fa-so-la names for notes.

Thought and Scholarship

***c.* 1022**
- Notker Labeo, a monk at St. Gall (in modern Switzerland), translates *De consolatione philosophiae/On the Consolation of Philosophy* of Boethius into German.

1029
c. 1029   Adhemar of Chabannes, France, completes his *Chronicon Aquitanicum et Francicum/Chronicle of Aquitaine and France*. Its third volume is a fairly accurate history of France 814–1028.
- Al-Musabbihi writes *Akhbār misr wa-Fadā'ilhā*, a monumental history of Egypt of which only a fragment survives.

SOCIETY

Everyday Life

1025
- The presence of a Norwegian poet at the court of the Duke of Normandy, France, is the last evidence of Scandinavian cultural influence in Normandy. By now the Viking settlers have been largely assimilated with the native population.

Religion

1022
- A group of French heretics is condemned by a council at Orléans, France. Their dualistic beliefs, which may have derived from Bogomilism, later develop into the widespread Cathar heresy.
August 1   A synod held at Pavia, Italy, by Emperor Henry II denounces the marriage of clergy in Lombardy.

1030–1039

POLITICS, GOVERNMENT, AND ECONOMICS

Colonization

1035
- The Norman adventurer William d'Hauteville and his brothers Drogo and Humphrey arrive in Italy in answer to a request for help from the Norman settler Rainulf of Aversa.

Politics and Government

1030
- Duke Paldolf IV of Capua, Italy, is expelled from Naples by its duke, Sergius IV, who gives Aversa as a fiefdom to the Norman adventurer Rainulf, in reward for his services.
- Emperor Conrad II leads an unsuccessful expedition against King Stephen of Hungary, who in retaliation takes Vienna but is then defeated by Břatislav of Bohemia.
April 21   Mahmud III, Emir of Ghazni and founder of the Muslim Empire in northwest India, dies in Ghazni. He is succeeded by his son, Masūd I.
July 29   King Olaf II of Norway is killed in the Battle of Stiklestad, Norway, while attempting to recover the kingdom of Norway from the Danes. He is succeeded by Cnut the Great and Svein.

August 8   Ernest of Babenberg, who had been restored to the duchy of Swabia (in modern Germany), is killed in a fresh revolt against the Emperor Conrad II.

1031

- King Mieszko II of Poland is attacked by a coalition; the Russians take Red Russia and he has to cede Lusatia to Emperor Conrad II. He is then expelled in a popular rising which establishes his brother, Bezprym, as ruler of Poland.
- King Stephen of Hungary makes peace with Emperor Conrad II, to whom he restores Vienna, and with Oldřich of Bohemia, to whom he cedes Moravia.

July 20   Robert II the Pious, King of France, dies. He is succeeded by his son, Henry I.

November 30   The caliphate of Córdoba comes to an end with the deposing of Hishām III, the last of the Umayyad dynasty. Dozens of independent Moorish and Arab kingdoms arise in Andalusia.

1032

- Domenico Flabanico becomes doge of Venice and restores the right, lost during several decades of aristocratic domination, of the popular assembly to elect the doge.
- King Henry I of France grants the duchy of Burgundy to his brother, Robert, in order to end a war of succession.
- King Mieszko II returns to Poland following the murder of his brother, Bezprym.
- The city of Edessa in Syria is taken by the Byzantine commander George Maniaces.

September 5   Rodolph III, King of Burgundy, dies without legitimate issue. The reversion to the crown had been granted to the Emperor Henry II in 1016, hence Emperor Conrad II is the legitimate heir. However, Rodolph's nephew, Odo II, Count of Blois and Champagne in France, attempts to seize it by invading the kingdom.

1033

- King Sancho III of Navarre creates the kingdom of Castile for his son, Ferdinand I (in modern Spain).
- The Pechenegs, a Turkic tribe settled in the area of modern Ukraine, raid the Balkan provinces of the Byzantine Empire.

February 2   Emperor Conrad II is crowned as king of Burgundy, which now becomes known as the kingdom of Arles and is attached to the German crown. This marks the end of the independent kingdom of Burgundy.

May 5   King Henry of France meets Emperor Conrad II at Deville, on the River Meuse, and they make an alliance against the expansionist Count Odo II of Blois and Champagne, whose lands straddle the border of France and the Holy Roman Empire.

1034

- Oldřich, Duke of Bohemia, dies. He is succeeded by his son, Břatislav I.
- Sancho III of Navarre defeats Vermudo III of León and captures his capital León, where he is crowned emperor of Spain.
- The Pisans and Genoese sack Bône (modern Annaba) in North Africa.

March 15   King Mieszko II of Poland dies. He is succeeded by his son Casimir (Kazimierz) I, a minor, with Queen Richsa (Ryksa) as regent. Several years of political chaos ensue.

April 11   The Byzantine emperor Romanus III dies. He is succeeded by Michael IV the Paphlagonian, who marries Romanus's widow, Zoe, daughter of Constantine VIII.

November 25   King Malcolm II of Scotland dies. He is succeeded by his grandson, Duncan I.

1035

- Following his victory at the Battle of Tarbet Ness, Earl Thorfinn of Orkney establishes Norse rule over most of northern Scotland.
- Prince Jaroslav of Kiev becomes the sole ruler of Russia on the death of his brother, Mstislav of Tmutarakan.
- Sancho III Garcés, King of Navarre, dies. He is succeeded in Navarre by his son García III, while another son Ramiro I is established in the newly-created kingdom of Aragon. Vermudo III of León is able to recover his capital León.

July 2   Robert I ("the Devil" or "the Magnificent"), Duke of Normandy, dies. He is succeeded by his illegitimate son, William I, later known as William the Conqueror.

November 12   Cnut, King of England, Denmark, and, nominally, Norway, dies. He is succeeded by his son Harthacnut in Denmark, with Harold Harefoot, another son, his regent in England. In Norway, Magnus I, the son of St. Olaf, is established as king in a revolt against Cnut.

1036

- A law code (no longer extant) of the Qitan (Khitan) Liao state, in northern China, said to contain 547 items, is published.
- Emperor Conrad II crushes a revolt by the Lyutitzi, a pagan Wendish people living to the east of the River Elbe.
- Prince Jaroslav the Wise of Kiev revises the book *Pravda Russkaia/Russian Law*.
- The caliph of Egypt, al-Zāhir, is murdered. He is succeeded by his seven-year old son al-Mustansir, under the regency of the vizier.
- The Pechenegs, a Turkic tribe settled in the area of modern Ukraine, raid the Balkan provinces of the Byzantine Empire for a second time.

June 12   On the marriage of Emperor Conrad II's son Henry to Cnut's daughter, Gunnhild, Denmark cedes the Kiel district of Schleswig to the empire (as part of the kingdom of Germany).

1037

- Duke Casimir I is driven out of Poland by an anti-Christian uprising.
- Emperor Conrad II's *Constitutio de feudis* secures Lombard subvassals against unjust eviction from their fiefs by their lords.
- Ferdinand I of Castile defeats and kills Vermudo III of León at Tamaron (in modern-day Spain), and takes possession of his kingdom.
- The Seljuk Turks, who migrated from central Asia late in the 10th century, are now, by conquest, established in Khorasan in Persia.

March 3   Emperor Conrad II holds a diet at Pavia, in Italy, to determine Lombard disputes, and arrests Archbishop Aribert of Milan for rebellion. When Aribert escapes Conrad besieges but fails to take Milan.

November 15   Odo II, Count of Blois and Champagne in France, is killed in battle at Bar in an expedition to seize the German crown. Champagne is inherited by his son

Stephen and the remainder of his lands by another son Theobald III of Blois.

December 25 Emperor Conrad II sacks Parma, Italy, to punish its rebellion.

1038

- Emperor Conrad II grants the duchy of Swabia (in modern-day Germany) to his son, Henry, on the death of Duke Hermann.
- Emperor Conrad II takes Capua, Italy, after Duke Paldolf IV refuses to submit: Capua is then granted by Conrad to Duke Guaimar IV of Salerno.
- King Henry I of France defeats a plot by Count Stephen of Champagne and Count Theobald III of Blois to depose him in favor of his brother, Odo. Henry obtains the support of Geoffrey Martel, son of Count Fulk of Anjou, granting him the city of Tours.
- Li Hüang-hao declares himself emperor of the Tanguts (a Tibetan people) of Xixia (in modern Gansu, Ningxia, and Inner Mongolia) and ceases paying tribute to the Chinese Song dynasty.
- Meeting little resistance, Prince Břatislav of Bohemia sacks Kraków and Gniezno in the course of a plundering raid into Poland, and takes possession of Silesia.

August 15 Stephen I, first king of Hungary, dies. His son Imre having predeceased him, Peter the German, a distant relation by marriage, is elected as his successor.

1039

- Count Guy-Geoffrey of Aquitaine seizes the duchy of Gascony (in modern France).
- Gruffydd ap Llywelyn, King of Gwynedd and Powys (in Wales), defeats an English invasion at Rhyd-y-gors on the River Severn.

- In a civil war in Sicily, Emir Ahmad is assisted by the Byzantine general, George Maniaces, who engages Norman soldiers for the campaign.

March 10 While invading Anjou, France, Count Eudes of Poitiers is defeated and killed near Mauzé by Geoffrey Martel.

June 4 Emperor Conrad II dies. He is succeeded by his son Henry III, King of Germany.

SCIENCE, TECHNOLOGY, AND MEDICINE

Science

1039

- The Muslim scientist Abu'Ali al-Hasan (Alhazen) writes *Kitab al-Manāzir*, a treatise on optics explaining the function of lenses, curved mirrors, refraction, and other phenomena.

Technology

1039

- Emperor Henry III builds the Pfalz (palace) at Goslar, Germany. He is later buried in the chapel of St. Ulrich.

BIRTHS & DEATHS

1030

c. 1030 St. Stanislaus (Stanisław) of Kraków, patron saint of Poland, born in Szczepanów, Poland (–1079).

- Ibn-Maskauayh, Persian philosopher and historian, writer of a universal history, *The Eclipse of the Abbasid Caliphate*, notable for its wide range of sources, dies.

April 21 Mahmud III, Emir of Ghazni 998–1030, an area covering modern Afghanistan and northeastern Persia, who conquered Kashmir, the Punjab, and much of Persia, also noted as a patron of the arts, dies in Ghazni (*c.* 59).

July 29 Olaf II Haraldsson, Viking king 1015–30, and patron saint of Norway, who was the first to rule the entire country and who also introduced a religious code which became the country's first national legislation, dies in Stiklestad, Norway (*c.* 35).

1031

- Roger I Guiscard, Count of Sicily 1072–1101, who instituted a centralized and efficient

government, born in Normandy (–1101).

July 20 Robert II the Pious, King of France 996–1031, dies.

1032

September 5 Rodolph III, King of Burgundy 1016–32, dies.

1033

- St. Anselm of Canterbury, founder of scholasticism, born in Aosta, Lombardy, Italy (–1109).

1034

April 11 Romanus III, Byzantine emperor 1028–34, dies.

November 25 Malcolm II, King of Scotland 1005–34, the first Scottish sovereign to rule over approximately the area of modern Scotland, dies (*c.* 80).

1035

c. 1035 Urban II, French pope 1088–99, who started the First Crusade and politicized the papacy, born in Châtillon-sur-Marne or Lagery, Champagne, France (–1099).

- Rājendra-Choladeva I, King of the Cholas, conqueror of the Pegu

kingdom (in modern Myanmar) and the Nīcobar and Andaman Islands, dies.

- Sancho III, King of Navarre, dies.

July 2 Robert I ("the Devil" or "the Magnificent"), Duke of Normandy, dies.

November 12 Cnut I the Great, powerful Danish king of England 1016–35, of Denmark (as Cnut II) 1019–35, and of Norway 1028–35, dies (*c.* 40).

1037

- Avicenna (ibn Sīnā), celebrated Islamic physician, philosopher, and scientist, whose best known work is the *Qanun/Canon of Medicine*, dies in Hamadan, Persia (*c.* 57).

1038

August 15 Stephen I, first king of Hungary 1000–38, founder of the Hungarian state, dies in Esztergom, Hungary (*c.* 61).

1039

June 4 Conrad II, King of Germany 1024–28, King of Italy 1026–39, and Emperor 1027–39, dies in Utrecht, Germany (*c.* 49).

ARTS AND IDEAS

Architecture

1030

- Mahmud III builds a victory tower at Ghazni (in modern Afghanistan).
- Speyer Cathedral is founded in Speyer, Germany, by Emperor Conrad II and is to be one of the largest cathedrals in western Europe. The first building has a flat timber ceiling.

1036

- The priory church of Abdinghof in Paderborn, Germany, is dedicated and becomes the first Cluniac monastery in Germany.

Arts

1035

- A collection of approximately 10,000 religious paintings, books, and manuscripts in Chinese, Tibetan, Uighur, and other languages, are walled up for safety at Tun-huang in the Xixia Kingdom. They are not discovered until 1900.

Literature and Language

1036

- Ekkehard of St. Gall (in modern Switzerland), the fourth of that name, writes his *Casus Sancti Galli/Memoirs of the Monastery of St. Gall*, a mainly fictitious history of the monastery.

1039

- Ting Tu, Song Ch'i, among others, helps produce the *Chi-yün*, a Chinese phonetic dictionary.

Thought and Scholarship

1030

- After accompanying Mahmud III of Ghazni on his campaigns to India, the great Muslim scholar and natural scientist al-Bīrunī completes his highly detailed and objective *Tarikh al-Hind/History of India*.

SOCIETY

Religion

1033

- Just 33 years after the millennium, the thousandth anniversary of the death of Christ approaches, and fears that the world will end grip Christian Europe.

◆

1040–1049

POLITICS, GOVERNMENT, AND ECONOMICS

Politics and Government

1040

- A "Truce of God" is proclaimed in Aquitaine, France, as a measure to limit private warfare.
- Melfi, in Apulia, Italy, is seized from the Byzantines by the Norman d'Hauteville brothers, William, Drogo, and Henry.
- Stephen Vojuslav gains independence for Zeta (roughly modern Montenegro) from the Byzantine Empire.

February 2 Masūd I of Ghazni is deposed following his defeat at Tāliqān by the Seljuk Turks under Tughril Beg and Chagi Beg, who go on to conquer the Ghaznavid territories in Persia.

March 17 Harold I Harefoot, King of England, dies. He is succeeded by his brother, Harthacnut, King of Denmark.

June 21 Count Fulk III Nerra of Anjou, France, dies. He is succeeded by his son, Geoffrey II Martel.

August 1 King Duncan I of Scotland is killed in battle near Elgin by Macbeth, Lord of Moray, who succeeds him as king.

August 8 Emperor Henry III invades Bohemia in response to an appeal for help from Queen Richsa, regent of Poland, but the Bohemians defeat him at Sumava.

1041

- Siward, Earl of Deira, murders Eardwulf, Earl of Bernicia, and now rules all of Northumbria, England.

- The Byzantine emperor Michael IV suppresses a Slav revolt led by Peter Deljan.
- The Chinese army totals 1,259,000 during a war against Tibetan tribes.

May 4   In the Battle of Monte Maggiore, Italy, Lombard rebels employing Norman mercenaries defeat Byzantine forces.

May 5   After a second, this time successful, campaign in Bohemia, Emperor Henry III compels Prince Břatislav to acknowledge his supremacy and surrender all his Polish conquests except Silesia.

December 10   The Byzantine emperor Michael IV dies. He is succeeded by his nephew, Michael V.

1042

- A "Truce of God" is proclaimed in Normandy as a measure against private warfare.
- Emperor Henry III grants the duchy of Bavaria to Henry, Count of Luxembourg.
- The *popolani* of Milan, Italy, a bourgeois movement for urban self-government, temporarily expel the nobles.
- The Ghaznavids extinguish the Persian Ziyarid emirate of Gurgan (roughly modern Turkmenistan).

April 11   Obo is crowned as king of Hungary following King Peter the German's rejection and expulsion.

April 14   The Byzantine emperor Michael V is deposed, blinded, and succeeded by Theodora and Zoe, the popular but incompetent daughters of Constantine VIII. Their rule is marked by intrigue and corruption and weakens the Byzantine empire.

June 8   Harthacnut, King of England and Denmark, dies. He is succeeded in England by his adopted heir, Edward the Confessor, son of Aethelred II the Unready, and in Denmark by Magnus I, King of Norway.

June 12   The Byzantine empresses Zoe and Theodora prove incapable of governing effectively. Zoe therefore remarries, and her husband Constantine IX Monomachus succeeds as emperor.

August 8   Emperor Henry III makes an expedition into Hungary. Its king, Obo, flees, but returns when Henry withdraws.

1043

- Emperor Henry III marries Agnes of Aquitaine, a descendant of the kings of Burgundy and Italy, cementing relations with France.

February 2   The Byzantine general George Maniaces claims the Byzantine Empire, usurping Constantine IX, and defeats imperial forces at Ostrovo, in Macedonia, but is himself killed.

April 3   Edward the Confessor is crowned as king of England.

August 8   On a "Day of Indulgence" Emperor Henry III announces a pardon of all his enemies and urges all his subjects to forget their private enmities.

1044

- Aniruddha becomes the first historical king of Pagan (in modern Myanmar).
- Emperor Henry III deprives Godfrey of Lorraine and Verdun because of a conspiracy. Godfrey now openly rebels.
- Gruffydd ap Llywelyn, King of Gwynedd (in modern Wales) defeats a Viking army from Ireland. The Viking leader Hywel ab Edwin, a rebel prince from south Wales, is killed.

- Ly Thai-tong of Dai Viet defeats and kills Jaya Simhavarman II, King of Champa, and sacks Vijaya, his capital.
- The city of Pagan becomes the capital of Burma and a center of Hinayana Buddhism.
- The Song emperor Jen Tsung defeats an invasion by the Xixia kingdom, but nevertheless undertakes to pay tribute.

July 7   Emperor Henry III defeats King Obo of Hungary on the Raab and restores Peter the German, as king and as his vassal.

August 21   Count Geoffrey II Martel of Anjou, France, defeats and captures Theobald III of Blois at Nouy, and compels him to cede Tours and Touraine.

September   Pope Benedict IX is driven from Rome, Italy, by a revolt caused by his dissolute and immoral lifestyle.

1045

- Emperor Henry III grants the march of Antwerp to Baldwin, son of Count Baldwin V of Flanders.
- The Byzantine emperor Constantine IX Monomachus incorporates Ani, in Armenia, into the Byzantine Empire.
- The English king Edward the Confessor makes Harold Godwinson, son of Godwin, Earl of Wessex, the Earl of East Anglia.
- The Seljuk Turks launch their first raid into Armenia.

January 10   After several months of faction fighting between the great families of Rome, Italy, following the deposition of Benedict IX, Sylvester III, a nominee of the Crescentii, is elected as pope.

March 10   Pope Benedict IX returns from exile to Rome, Italy, and deposes Sylvester III.

April 7   Emperor Henry III grants the duchy of Swabia (in modern-day Germany) to Otto, Count Palatine of Lower Lorraine.

May 1   Pope Benedict IX resigns, after selling the papal office to John Gratian, who is elected as Gregory VI.

1046

- Earl Siward of Northumbria fails in an attempt to overthrow King Macbeth of Scotland and replace him with Malcolm III Canmore, the son of Duncan I.
- Following the death of his brother William, Drogo d'Hauteville is recognized as Count of Apulia, Italy, by Emperor Henry III. Drogo now assumes leadership of Norman campaigns against the Byzantines in southern Italy.

April 4   Emperor Henry III recovers Flushing from Count Dietrich of Holland.

May 8   The Norman adventurer William d'Hauteville defeats Byzantine forces at Trani in southern Italy.

May 18   Emperor Henry III restores the duchy of Upper Lorraine to Godfrey, but grants his former county of Verdun to its bishop. He also invests Adalbert with the archbishopric of Bremen, which Adalbert moves to Hamburg.

August 8   Peter the German, King of Hungary, is deposed for the second time and succeeded by Andrew I.

December 20   In the synod of Sutri held by Emperor Henry III, Sylvester III and Gregory VI are formally deposed from the papacy for simony and other uncanonical practices. Benedict IX is also summoned to appear but he fails to turn up.

December 24   Benedict IX is formally deposed from the papacy by Emperor Henry III and Bishop Suidger of Bamberg is elected as Pope Clement II. Together Henry and Clement begin the reform of the papacy.

December 25   Pope Clement II officially crowns Henry III as emperor.

1047

- Duke William I assumes personal rule of the duchy of Normandy and, assisted by King Henry I of France, defeats Norman rebels at Val-ès-Dunes, near Caen.
- Emperor Henry III again deprives Duke Godfrey of the duchy of Upper Lorraine, as punishment for a fresh rebellion.
- The Byzantines defeat a Seljuk raiding force near Erzerum in Anatolia (modern Turkey).
- With Russian assistance, Duke Casimir I of Poland recovers control of Masovia and Pomerania from the Bohemians.

1047–1080   The earliest known code of laws and customs of any French town, the *Etablissements de St.-Quentin*, is drawn up. (The original code is lost but is known from a copy of 1151.)

October 25   Magnus the Good, King of Denmark and Norway, dies. He is succeeded in Denmark by Svein II Estrithson and in Norway by Harald Hardrada.

November 8   Benedict IX returns to Rome, Italy, and reassumes the papacy.

December 25   Bishop Poppo of Brixen is nominated to succeed Pope Clement II by Emperor Henry III but he cannot be consecrated because the deposed pope Benedict IX has occupied Rome, Italy.

1048

- King Henry I of France and Duke William I of Normandy form an alliance to make war against Count Geoffrey II Martel of Anjou. William I takes Alençon and Maine.
- The French term *bourgeois* (burgher) is used for the first time at St.-Omer, France, signifying the beginning of organized local government in towns.
- The Pechenegs, a Turkish tribe settled in the area of modern Ukraine, begin almost continuous plundering raids in the Byzantine Balkan provinces.
- The Seljuk Turks sack Erzerum in Anatolia (modern Turkey).

July 17   On the orders of Emperor Henry III, Boniface, Count of Tuscany, expels Benedict IX from Rome, after

which Bishop Poppo of Brixen is consecrated as Pope Damasus II.

August 9   Pope Damasus II dies of malaria after a reign of only 23 days.

SCIENCE, TECHNOLOGY, AND MEDICINE

Health and Medicine

1040

- The physician Petrocellus of the medical school at Salerno, Italy, writes his *Practica/Practice*, a manual of applied medicine.

Math

1040

- Ahmad al-Nasawi writes *al-Muqni'fi al-Hisāb al-Hindi/ The Convincer on Hindu Calculation* on fractions, square and cubic roots, and other mathematical phenomena using Hindu (or Arabic) numerals.

Science

1048

- The Muslim astronomer al-Bīrunī ("the master") writes his *Description of India*, which contains much astronomical data. He attacks the idea of astrology as an influence over historical events.

Technology

1040

- Water power is employed in hemp mills at Graisivaudan, France.

1044

- The Chinese text *Wu Ching Tsung Yao* is written, including a recipe for black powder which uses a mix of

---

BIRTHS & DEATHS

1040
- Rashi, French commentator on the Bible and the Talmud, born in Troyes, Champagne (–1105).

August 1   Duncan I, King of Scotland 1034–40, grandson of Malcolm II, killed in battle by Macbeth near Elgin, Moray, Scotland (*c.* 30).

1041
December 10   Michael IV, Byzantine emperor 1034–41, dies.

1042
- Abu-Qasim Mohammad, vizier of the emir of Seville, who established the emir as the paramount Muslim ruler in Spain following the collapse of the caliphate of Córdoba, dies.

1043
- Rodrigo Díaz de Vivar ("El Cid"), Spanish military leader and national hero, conqueror of Valencia, born in Vivar, near Burgos, in Castile, Spain (–1099).

1047
October 9   Pope Clement II dies, in Rome, Italy.

1048
- Alexius I, Byzantine emperor 1081–1118, who was emperor during the First Crusade and who united the empire, born in Constantinople (–1118).

May 18   'Omar Khayyām, Persian poet, mathematician, and astronomer, famous for his *Rubaiyat*, born in Nishapur, Persia (–1131).

saltpeter (potassium nitrate), charcoal, and sulfur to produce an early form of gunpowder.

1045

- The Chinese alchemist Pi Sheng invents a method of printing using movable earthenware type attached to an iron plate.

SOCIETY

Education

1044

- Song dynasty emperor Jen Tsung accepts a proposal by his chief minister Fan Chung-yen for the establishment of a national school system.

1045

- Byzantine emperor Constantine IX refounds the University of Constantinople, establishing faculties of law and philosophy; the notable jurist John Xiphilin is the first head of the new law school.

Religion

1044

- Archbishop Aaron, monk of Brauweiler, begins the reconversion of the Polish people, and establishes a see at Kraków instead of Gniezno, Poland.

1046

October 25 In a council held by Emperor Henry III at Pavia, in Italy, the corrupt ecclesiastical practice of simony (selling clerical offices) is denounced.

1050–1059

POLITICS, GOVERNMENT, AND ECONOMICS

Politics and Government

1050

- Duke Casimir I of Poland recovers Silesia from Bohemia.
- Emperor Henry III makes a treaty of peace with King Andrew I of Hungary after a campaign in Hungary.
- Tughril Beg, the Seljuk leader, takes Isfahan (in modern Iran), which becomes the capital of his empire in Persia and Khorasan.

1051

- The people of Benevento accept Pope Leo IX as their ruler in order to protect themselves from the Normans. A plot to murder all the Normans in southern Italy fails.
- 1051–62 In the Nine Years' War, Minamoto Yoiyoshi, aided by his son Yoshiie, defeats the powerful Abe clan of northern Japan, so securing the Minamoto clan's dominance in Honshu.
- September 9 Godwin, Earl of Wessex, is exiled to Flanders after the failure of his rebellion against the English king Edward the Confessor.

1052

- Duke William I of Normandy visits the English king Edward the Confessor. It is possible that Edward, who is childless, promises to make William his heir.
- Emperor Henry III makes his last expedition into Hungary, where he suppresses a rebellion.
- September 15 Godwin returns to England with a strong force and compels King Edward the Confessor of England to restore to him the earldom of Wessex to avoid civil war.

1053

- A rebellion against Duke William I of Normandy by his vassal William of Arques only ends when the latter is starved out, the duke already having defeated an attempt by his own lord, King Henry I of France, to relieve the rebel.
- Emperor Henry III grants lands in Benevento to the papacy. He also (perhaps in this year) grants the duchy of Bavaria to his young son, Henry, after the rebellion of Duke Conrad.
- April 15 Godwin, Earl of Wessex, dies. He is succeeded by his son, Harold Godwinson.
- June 18 In the Battle of Civitate in Italy the Normans led by Humphrey d'Hauteville, Count of Apulia, capture Pope Leo IX, who has proclaimed a holy war against them. He renounces it to obtain his release.

1054

- Břatislav I of Bohemia (supposedly) decrees that the succession of his duchy should be limited to the eldest member of the house of Přemysl.

- In a diet at Quedlinburg Emperor Henry III awards Silesia to Poland in its dispute with Bohemia.
- The papal legate Cardinal Humbert excommunicates the patriarch of Constantinople, Michael Cerularius, for obstructing an alliance between the Byzantine emperor and the Pope. Cerularius retaliates by excommunicating the cardinal and thus causes the final schism between the Eastern (Orthodox) church and the Western (Roman Catholic) church.
- The Seljuk Turks under Tughril Beg raid Byzantine Anatolia (modern Turkey) but are repulsed from Manzikert.

February 2   King Henry I of France, now the ally of Count Geoffrey II Martel of Anjou, invades Normandy but is defeated by Duke William I at Mortemer.

July 17   Henry IV, son of Emperor Henry III, is elected "King of the Romans" (king of Germany) in Italy, at the age of four.

July 27   Earl Siward of Northumbria defeats King Macbeth of Scotland and compels him to grant Malcolm III Canmore, son of Duncan I, lands in southern Scotland.

September 3   Ferdinand I of Castile defeats and kills his brother García III of Navarre at Atapuerca, near Burgos, Spain. Garcia's son Sancho IV succeeds as king of Navarre.

1055

- Duke Břatislav I of Bohemia dies. He is succeeded by his son Spytihněv II.
- Earl Siward of Northumbria dies. He is succeeded by Tostig, the brother of Harold Godwinson, Earl of Essex.
- Gruffydd ap Llywelyn, King of Gwynedd and Powys, completes the conquest of southern Wales to become the king of all Wales.

January 11   The Byzantine emperor Constantine IX dies. His sister-in-law, the empress Theodora, becomes sole ruler.

February 7   Jaroslav I, Great Prince of Kiev, dies. In his will, Jaroslav divides his lands among his five sons who immediately fall out over their inheritance and civil war follows. Kiev and Novgorod are inherited by Jaroslav's eldest son Iziaslav, who is theoretically superior in status to his brother princes.

April 13   After hesitating for almost a year before accepting the office, Gebhard of Eichstatt is elected as Pope Victor II.

December 18   The city of Baghdad surrenders to the Seljuk Turks, who thus end Buwayhid rule. Tughril Beg is proclaimed sultan, and the Abbasid caliph remains the spiritual leader of Sunni Muslims, under Seljuk control.

1056

- The Lyutitzi, from Lausitz, defeat forces sent by Emperor Henry III to suppress their revolt.
- The Patarines, a popular and apostolic but not heretical movement aspiring to reform the Milanese church, aim to secure control of their government by the establishment of a commune in Milan, Italy.

June 17   Gruffydd ap Llywelyn, King of Wales, defeats and kills Bishop Leofgar of Hereford at Cleobury. Later in the year he is defeated by Earl Harold of Wessex and Earl Leofric of Mercia, and so compelled to recognize the lordship of King Edward the Confessor, who cedes to him English lands west of the River Dee.

August 21   The Byzantine empress Theodora dies. She is the last of the Macedonian dynasty. She is succeeded by her designated heir Michael VI the Aged, a retired civil servant.

October 5   Emperor Henry III dies at Bodfeld. He is succeeded by his six-year-old son Henry IV, with his widow Agnes as regent.

1057

- Aniruddha of Pagan defeats Makuta, King of the Mons of Thaton, and annexes the Irrawaddy Delta.
- Ou-yang Hsiu reforms the civil service examinations in China, encouraging a classical and less florid style of writing.
- The Seljuk Turks sack Malatya, on the Asian frontier of the Byzantine Empire.

August 2   Following the death earlier in the year of Pope Victor II, Frederick of Lorraine, the abbot of Monte Cassino, is elected as Pope Stephen IX. The weak regency of the infant Henry IV of Germany is unable to interfere with the election, which begins the process of freeing the papacy from secular control.

August 8   Robert Guiscard succeeds his brother Humphrey d'Hauteville as Count of Apulia, Italy.

August 15   King Macbeth of Scotland is defeated and killed at Lumphanan, in March, by Macduff and Malcolm III Canmore. He is succeeded by his stepson, Lulach.

August 31   The Byzantine emperor Michael VI the Aged abdicates in favor of the general Isaac Comnenus, whose troops have already proclaimed him as emperor.

1058

March 17   Malcolm III Canmore, son of Duncan I, succeeds as king of Scotland after killing Lulach, Macbeth's stepson.

April 5   Following the death of Pope Stephen IX (March 29), Cardinal John Mincius is elected as Pope Benedict X by Roman nobles who had seized control of Rome, Italy.

August 8   Duke William I of Normandy defeats the invading forces of King Henry I of France and Count Geoffrey II Martel of Anjou at Varaville.

December 12   Bishop Gerard of Florence is elected as Pope Nicholas II at Siena, Italy, by the reforming party of cardinals under the protection of Godfrey, Duke of Lorraine.

1059

- Peter Damian persuades the patarenes of Milan, Italy, to resume their ecclesiastical subjection to Rome.
- The Seljuk Turks raid into the Byzantine Empire as far as Sebastea in Asia Minor (in the west of modern Turkey).

January 24   Supported by the troops of Duke Godfrey of Lorraine, Nicholas II is enthroned as pope in Rome and the usurping Pope Benedict X is deposed.

May 23   Philip, son of King Henry I of France, is crowned as joint king.

August 8   In the Treaty of Melfi, Pope Nicholas II invests Robert Guiscard as his vassal, proclaiming him Duke of Apulia and Calabria and Count of Sicily. These territories are still largely occupied by the Byzantines and the Arabs but the Pope's grant legitimizes Guiscard's campaigns to conquer them.

December 25   Faced with constant opposition from the church and the aristocracy, the Byzantine emperor Isaac Comnenus abdicates in favor of Constantine X Ducas.

SCIENCE, TECHNOLOGY, AND MEDICINE

Exploration

1050

- The German scholar Adam of Bremen expounds his belief that the Baltic Sea opens at its eastern end into an uncharted ocean.

Health and Medicine

1050

- Gariopontus of Lombardy, while working at the medical school of Salerno, Italy, writes his *Passionarius*, a medical encyclopedia based on the work of Galen and Hippocrates.

Science

1050

- The astrolabe, a new device for making astronomical measurements and calculations, arrives in Europe from the East, where Muslim scientists developed it two centuries ago.

1054

- The Austrian monk Hermann Contractus the Lame of the monastery of Reichenau writes treatises on the abacus and the astrolabe (an instrument for measuring the altitude of stars and planets). His work is based on Latin translations of earlier Muslim texts.

July 4 A bright new star, visible in daylight, appears in the constellation Taurus. The supernova (which forms the Crab Nebula) is observed in China and Korea, and is recorded in rock paintings in southwestern America.

1059

- Chinese scholar Fu Kung writes a treatise on crabs entitled *Hsieh-p'u.*

Technology

1050

- Water wheels are used to power mills in the Dauphiné region of France, where machinery is used to beat and press shrunken cloth.

ARTS AND IDEAS

Architecture

1050

- King Edward the Confessor of England orders the rebuilding of Westminster Abbey in England, with Norman architects and masons.

1053

- The Hoodo (Phoenix Hall) is built in Byodoin Temple near Kyoto, Japan. The shape of the hall represents a phoenix with its wings outstretched.

BIRTHS & DEATHS

1050

November 11 Henry IV, German king 1054–1106 and emperor 1084–1106, son of Henry III, born, possibly in Goslar, Saxony (–1106).

1053

July 8 Shirakawa, 72nd emperor of Japan 1072–86 who abdicated the throne to form an *insei*, or cloister government, through which he could rule without the encumbrances of ceremony, born in Kyoto, Japan (–1129).

1054

April 19 Leo IX, pope 1048–54, whose reforming reign did much to restore the prestige of the papacy after more than a century of weak and corrupt popes, dies.

September 24 Hermann von Reichenau ("Hermannus Contractus" or "Hermann the Lame"), German chronicler, composer, astronomer, and mathematician, dies in Reichenau monastery, Germany (41).

1055

January 11 Constantine IX, Byzantine emperor 1042–55, dies.

1056

c. 1056 William II, King of England 1087–1100, born (–1100).

October 5 Henry III, German king 1039–56 and emperor 1046–56, son of Conrad II, dies near Goslar, Saxony (38).

1057

- Al-Ma'arrī, Arab poet, writer of *Risālat al-Ghufrān/Treatise on Forgiveness*, his description of an imaginary journey to paradise, dies.

August 15 Macbeth, King of Scotland 1040–57, probably a grandson of Kenneth II, killed in battle by Malcolm III Canmore, near Lumphanan, Aberdeen, Scotland (*c.* 52).

1058

- Al-Ghazālī (Algazel), Muslim theologian and mystic whose *Ihyā'Ulum al-Dīn/The Revival of the Religious Sciences* helped make Sufism an acceptable part of orthodox Islam, born in Tūs, Persia (–1111).

- Al-Māwardi, author of the *Kitabadāh al-Dunyā wa-l-Dīn/Principles of Government*, dies.

March 17 Lulach, King of Scotland 1057–58, stepson of Macbeth, is killed.

November 28 Duke Casimir (Kazimierz) I the Restorer of Poland who restored the unity of the Polish tribes, recovered lost territories, and rebuilt the ecclesiastical organization of his country after the pagan reaction of his youth, dies in Kraków, Poland.

1059

- The Nan Paya and Manuha temples are built in Pagan, Burma.

Arts

c. 1050

- The art of the Ife culture of Nigeria reaches its high point. Perhaps drawing on the achievements of the earlier Nok culture, the Ife create sculptures in terracotta and in bronze, as well as fine metalwork jewelry.

Literature and Language

c. 1050

- A substantial collection of Japanese folk tales and religious stories known as *Konjaku Monogatari/Tales of Now and Then* is recorded.

SOCIETY

Religion

1050

- Berengar of Tours, France, is excommunicated for his controversial teaching on transubstantiation, in which he denies that the consecrated bread and wine of the Eucharist is the real body and blood of Christ.

1059

April 14   A decree governing the election of popes is made in a council held at the Lateran palace by Pope Nicholas II. In future the choice is to be made by the cardinal bishops; secular authorities, including the people of Rome and the emperor, are allowed only a marginal role.

1060–1069

POLITICS, GOVERNMENT, AND ECONOMICS

Colonization

1061

- The Cumans, a Turkish nomadic people, migrate onto the southern Russian steppes from Kazakhstan.

Politics and Government

1060

- Bhoja, the Rajput king of Malwa (now southeast Rajastan, India), is defeated and killed by the kings of Gujarat and Chedi.
- With the assistance of Duke Bolesław II of Poland, Béla I gains the Hungarian crown by defeating and killing his brother, Andrew I.

August 4   Henry I, King of France, dies. He is succeeded by his eight-year-old son Philip I, already crowned as joint king, with Baldwin V, Count of Flanders, as his guardian.

November 14   Geoffrey II Martel, Count of Anjou, dies. He is succeeded jointly by his nephews Geoffrey III the Bearded and Fulk IV Rechin who share the title until 1068.

1061

- Otto of Nordheim is appointed Duke of Bavaria.
- Roger Guiscard, brother of Robert Guiscard, begins the Norman conquest of Sicily with the capture of Messina, having been invited onto the island by ibn ath-Thimna, one of the Arab leaders in a civil war.
- Spytihněv II, Duke of Bohemia, dies. He is succeeded by his brother, Vratislav II.
- The Scottish king Malcolm III Canmore invades Northumberland.

March 20   The counts of Anjou Geoffrey III the Bearded and Fulk IV Rechin defeat Duke William VIII of Aquitaine at Chef-Boutonne, France.

September 30   Following the death of Pope Nicholas II (July 22), Anselm of Baggio, bishop of Lucca, is elected as Pope Alexander II, the first pope elected according to the election decree of Nicholas II.

October 28   Cadalus, bishop of Parma, Italy, an opponent of the papal reform movement, is crowned as Pope Honorius II in Basel, in the presence of King Henry IV of Germany.

1062

- Duke William I of Normandy seizes Le Mans, France, and declares himself Count of Maine.

March 25   Pope Honorius II defeats Pope Alexander II's troops and forces his way into Rome, but Duke Godfrey of Lorraine arrives with a superior army and persuades both papal contestants to withdraw from the city and await arbitration.

April 4 Anno, archbishop of Cologne, abducts King Henry IV of Germany, taking charge of his government, with Adalbert, archbishop of Bremen, as coregent.

October 27 Alexander II is declared to be the true pope in a synod held at Augsburg, defeating his challenger Honorius II.

1063

- German troops expel King Béla from Hungary and enthrone Salamon, the son of Andrew I.
- The Hashimid sharifs (Muslim leaders) are established in Mecca: they rule the city until the 1920s.

May 5 Harold Godwinson, Earl of Wessex, begins a campaign against King Gruffydd ap Llywelyn of Wales.

August 5 Gruffydd ap Llywelyn, King of Wales, is murdered by his followers after being defeated by Earl Harold Godwinson of Wessex. Wales is again divided among the native princes.

September 20 Sultan Tughril Beg of the Seljuk Turks dies and is succeeded by his nephew, Alp Arslan.

1064

- Either in this year or 1069, Raymond Berengar I, Count of Barcelona, issues the *Usatges de Barcelona/Customs of Barcelona*, a collection of Roman and feudal laws.
- Ferdinand I of Castile captures Coimbra. Under his control it becomes a base for the reconquest of Portugal from the Moors.
- Harold Godwinson, Earl of Wessex, is said to pay homage to Duke William of Normandy while in captivity following a shipwreck on the French coast.
- The Pechenegs, a Turkic people settles in the area of modern Ukraine, raid extensively in Byzantine Greece.
- The Seljuk sultan Alp Arslan conquers Ani, in central Armenia, and the kingdom of Kars.

1065

- Examinations for the Chinese civil service, previously sporadic, are now held every three years.
- In a rebellion in Northumbria, Tostig is expelled and Morcar elected as earl in his place. Tostig goes into exile in Flanders.
- Sultan Alp Arslan of the Seljuk Turks makes conquests in Transoxiana; other Seljuk Turks invade Syria.

March 4 King Henry IV of Germany comes of age, but real power is still in the hands of his regent, Adalbert, archbishop of Hamburg.

May 8 Ramiro I of Aragon is killed attacking the Moors in Graus. He is succeeded by his son, Sancho Ramirez. His death attracts volunteers from western Europe to serve in the campaigns against the Moors.

December 27 Ferdinand I of Castile and León dies. He is succeeded by his sons, Sancho II in Castile and Alfonso VI in León.

1066

January 1 King Henry IV takes personal control of government in Germany after dismissing his regent, Archbishop Adalbert of Hamburg.

January 5 King Edward the Confessor of England dies; on the next day Harold Godwinson, Earl of Wessex, is elected as his successor.

June 28 Ariald, leader of the Patarenes in Milan, is murdered by agents of Guy, archibishop of Vienne.

September 25 Harald Hardrada, King of Norway and Earl Tostig are defeated and killed by King Harold Godwinson of England at Stamford Bridge, England. Harald of Norway is succeeded by his sons Magnus II and Olaf III.

September 28 Duke William I of Normandy begins his invasion of England by landing at Pevensey.

October 14 King Harold Godwinson of England is defeated and killed by Duke William I of Normandy at Hastings, England.

December 25 Duke William I of Normandy is crowned king of England.

1067

- Seljuk Turks sack Caesarea and defeat Byzantine armies at Malatya and Sebastea.

April 5 Count Fulk IV Rechin of Anjou imprisons his brother and cocount Geoffrey III the Bearded.

May 21 The Byzantine emperor Constantine X dies. He is succeeded by his widow Eudocia Macrembolitissa.

1068

- King Philip I of France recognizes Fulk IV Rechin as sole Count of Anjou following Fulk's imprisonment of his brother and cocount Geoffrey III the Bearded.
- King William the Conqueror I of England suppresses a revolt in Yorkshire by Earl Edwin and Earl Morcar.
- Ly Thanh-tong of Dai-co-viet (which he renames Dai Viet) defeats and captures Rudravarman III of Champa, and annexes its northern provinces.
- The Cholas of southern India again raid the empire of Srivijaya on Sumatra.
- The Cumans, a nomadic people of Turkish origin, defeat the Russian princes near Pereyaslavl.
- Wang An-shih becomes chief minister of the Sung dynasty empire in China. In order to solve the problems of the peasantry he introduces a land reform program, which proves unpopular with the land-owning classes.
- Yūsuf-ibn-Tāshfīn, a founder of the Almoravid (or Murābit) Berber Emirate, founds Marrakesh (modern Morocco) as his capital.

January 1 Romanus IV Diogenes, who has married the empress Eudocia Macrembolitissa, is crowned as Byzantine emperor.

1069

- Abbād Mutadid, King of Seville, dies. He is succeeded by his son Mutamid who, by taking Córdoba, makes his kingdom paramount in Muslim Spain.
- Duke Bolesław II of Poland captures Kiev and restores his uncle, Iziaslav, as its prince; Bolesław abandons Kiev within a year but recovers Red Russia for Poland.

January 28 Robert de Comines, the Norman Earl of Northumbria, is killed in Durham by English rebels, who subsequently win control of Yorkshire.

February 2 William I the Conqueror, King of England and Duke of Normandy, sacks York and restores order in the north of England after a time of rebellion.

April 28 Magnus II, King of Norway, dies. He is succeeded by his brother Olaf III, who has been joint king since 1067.

August 15–September 8 A Danish fleet under Cnut, the son of King Svein Estrithson, arrives in the River Humber to support the English rebellion against King William I the

Conqueror. The Anglo-Danish force takes York in October.

December   William I the Conqueror, King of England and Duke of Normandy, retakes York from the English rebels and their Danish allies, and spends the winter in a brutal ravaging campaign, "the Harrying of the North," to force northern England into submission.

SCIENCE, TECHNOLOGY, AND MEDICINE

Agriculture

1064
- The Chinese government develops a system of granaries, and stores excess food in years of plenty for release in times of famine.

1068
- An-Shih, prime minister to the Chinese emperor Shen Tsung, oversees the nationalization of agriculture and introduces state control of all food production and distribution.

Health and Medicine

1067
- The Spanish military leader Rodrigo Díaz de Vivar ("El Cid") founds the world's first leper hospital in Castile.

Science

1066
- The comet later known as Halley's Comet appears in the sky, and is taken as an omen by both the Norman and English sides before the Battle of Hastings. The

victorious Normans record its appearance in the Bayeux Tapestry.

Technology

1066
- A tidal mill (a water mill that draws energy from the rising and falling sea tides) is operating in Dover harbor, England.

1067
- The emperor of China issues an edict prohibiting the export of saltpeter and sulfur, in an effort to stop the secret of gunpowder falling into the wrong hands.

Transportation

1066
- The first floating buoys are used. They are used for marking the deep water channels in the estuary of the River Weser in Lower Saxony.

ARTS AND IDEAS

Architecture

1063
- Construction begins on the cathedral at Pisa, Italy. Designed by Buscheto, it displays a wide range of stylistic influences including Byzantine and Islamic.
- The building of San Marco begins in Venice, Italy. Designed by a Greek architect, its domed structure is based on the Church of the Holy Apostles in Constantinople.

1065
- Stained glass is used for the first time, to decorate a window in the clerestory of Augsburg Cathedral, Germany.

BIRTHS & DEATHS

1060
- St. Stephen Harding, abbot of Cîteaux, a founder of the Cistercian Order, born in Sherborne, Dorset, England (–1134).

August 4   Henry I, King of France 1031–60, dies (c. 52).

1061
- Godfrey of Bouillon, a leader of the First Crusade 1095–99, first Latin ruler ("Defender of the Holy Sepulchre") in Palestine 1099–1100, born (–1100).

May 5   Cardinal Humbert of Silva Candida, theologian and papal legate, dies (c. 61).

1063
September 4   Toghrïl Beg, Iranian leader c. 1040–63, who conquered Iran, Iraq, Syria, and Anatolia and founded the Seljuq dynasty, dies in Ravy, Iran (c. 73).

1064
- Ali ibn-Hazm, Arab writer, best known for his book *Tawq al-Hamāmah/The Dove's Necklace* on chivalric love, and a study of comparative religion, dies.

1066
January 5   Edward (St. Edward the Confessor), Anglo-Norman king of

England 1042–66, son of Aethelred II, an ineffectual but pious ruler, dies in London, England (c. 63).

October 14   Harold II Godwinson, last Anglo-Saxon king of England January–October 1066, falls in battle against William I's Norman forces at Hastings, Sussex, England (c. 46).

1069
- Henry I, King of England 1100–35, son of William I the Conqueror, born in Selby, Yorkshire, England (–1135).

December 25   Duke Godfrey of Lorraine dies.

- The abbey of St. Etienne at Caen, in Normandy, France, is founded by Duke William of Normandy and his wife Matilda. The abbey is a typical example of Norman Romanesque architecture.

Literature and Language

c. 1060
- Ezzo of Bamberg writes his *Ezzolied*, a long rhyming poem on religious themes from the Genesis to the Resurrection.

1066
- With the Norman Conquest, Norman French becomes the language of the English court. Latin continues to be the language of the church and the law.

SOCIETY

Education

1065
- The Nizāmīyah, a Muslim theological college, is founded at Baghdad; others soon follow at Nishapur, Damascus, Jerusalem, Cairo, and Alexandria.

Everyday Life

1065
- A new Chinese calendar is introduced, shown in Chou-Ts'ung's work *Ming-t'ien-li*.

Religion

c. 1060
- Cardinal Humbert writes his "Liber adversus Symoniacos"/"Book Against the Simoniacs" attacking those who buy positions in the church.

1063
- The Rule for Augustinian Canons receives official approval at a synod in the Lateran palace in Rome.

1070–1079

POLITICS, GOVERNMENT, AND ECONOMICS

Politics and Government

1070
- A code of municipal customs is issued in Cambrai.
- Vijayabahu I expels the Cholas from Ceylon and becomes king, founding a capital at Polonnaruwa.
- June The Danish king Svein Estrithson joins his son Cnut in England and, with the English rebels under Hereward the Wake, sacks Peterborough. Realizing that there is little chance of defeating King William I the Conqueror, Svein withdraws soon after and English morale begins to crumble.
- July 14 Alfonso VI of León defeats and captures his brother, Sancho II of Castile, at Valpellage.

- August 8 King Henry IV of Germany deprives Otto of Nordheim of his estates in Saxony and of the duchy of Bavaria on grounds of treason.

1071
- King Henry IV of Germany suppresses a Saxon revolt in favor of the deposed Duke Otto of Nordheim.
- King Salamon of Hungary takes Belgrade after its Byzantine governor instigates an invasion by the Pechenegs, a Turkish people settled in the area of modern Ukraine.
- William I the Conqueror, King of England and Duke of Normandy, expels Hereward the Wake, the last significant English rebel, from his stronghold on the Isle of Ely.
- February 22 Arnold III the Unfortunate, Count of Flanders, defeats King Philip I of France at Cassel but is himself killed.
- April 4 With the capture of Bari, Count Robert Guiscard of Apulia completes the expulsion of the Byzantines from Italy.
- August 19 The Seljuk sultan Alp Arslan destroys a Byzantine army at Manzikert, Armenia, and captures Emperor Romanus IV, whom he frees for a ransom and

the payment of tribute. The Seljuk Turks now complete their conquest of Armenia and overrun most of Anatolia (modern Turkey). In the same year, the Seljuks also conquer Syria and, under the general Atsiz ibn-Abaq, take Jerusalem from the Fatimid caliphate.

October 24   Michael VII, the son of Constantine X, is proclaimed Byzantine emperor, and Romanus IV is deposed, imprisoned, and murdered. Michael unsuccessfully appeals to western Europe for assistance against the Seljuk Turks.

1072

- Chinese poet and retired statesman Ou-yang Hsiu formulates the first censorship rules in China.
- The Russian princes collectively issue a new collection of laws, called *Pravda/Truth*.
- William the Conqueror campaigns in Scotland and compels King Malcolm III Canmore to offer him homage.

January 10   Duke Robert Guiscard of Apulia captures Palermo in Sicily from the Arabs.

October 10   Sancho II of Castile is murdered and succeeded by his brother Alfonso VI of León.

November 25   The Seljuk sultan, Alp Arslan, is murdered while campaigning in Transoxiana. He is succeeded by his son, Malik Shah.

1073

- Suleiman ibn-Qutlamish, the cousin of the Selijuk sultan Alp Arslan, begins the systematic conquest of Byzantine Anatolia (modern Turkey).
- William I the Conqueror, King of England and Duke of Normandy, recovers Le Mans from Count Fulk IV Rechin of Anjou.

April 22   Following the death of Alexander II, Deacon Hildebrand, a radical church reformer, is elected by popular acclaim as Pope Gregory VII.

August 8   King Henry IV of Germany is expelled from Saxony in a new rising under Duke Otto of Nordheim.

1074

- King Henry IV of Germany unsuccessfully campaigns in Hungary in an attempt to restore King Salamon, who has been expelled by Géza I.
- King Henry IV of Germany grants a charter of privileges to the city of Worms, the first such imperial charter conceded to citizens rather than their lord. At Cologne, there is the first known revolt of citizens against their episcopal overlord.
- The duchy of Normandy revolts against William I the Conqueror, King of England and Duke of Normandy.
- The Seljuk sultan Malik Shah conquers the Mirdasid emirate of Aleppo.

February 2   King Henry IV of Germany makes peace with the Saxons at Gerstungen.

March 3   Fearing Norman expansion into the Papal States, Pope Gregory VII excommunicates Duke Robert Guiscard of Apulia.

April 28   Svein Estrithson, King of Denmark, dies; his son Harald III succeeds him after a short war of succession.

1075

- During his absence in Normandy, the regents of William I the Conqueror, King of England and Duke of Normandy, defeat a revolt in England by Earl Waltheof

of Northumbria, Earl Ralf of East Anglia, and Earl Roger FitzOsbern of Hereford.

- Géza I is crowned king of Hungary, with a crown sent by the Byzantine emperor Michael VII.
- The Seljuk general Atsiz takes Damascus from the Fatimids.

March   In an unpublished document, the *Dictatus papae/ Pronouncement of the Pope*, Pope Gregory VII sets out a radical vision of a papal monarchy as the highest power in Christendom, in which the pope would have the right to depose secular rulers and possess supreme legislative and judicial power.

March 3   In a riot in Milan, Italy, Holy Roman Empire, the Patarene leader Erlembald is murdered, and members of the sect are expelled from the city.

June   In defiance of Pope Gregory VII's decree against lay investiture, King Henry IV of Germany appoints his court chaplain to the archbishopric of Milan, so beginning the dispute between the papacy and the German monarchy known as the "Investiture Contest."

June 9   King Henry IV of Germany defeats Saxon rebels at Homburg-on-Unstrut.

November 11   The rebel Saxon nobles surrender to King Henry IV of Germany, who punishes them with imprisonment and confiscation of their lands.

December 25   King Henry IV of Germany's son, Conrad, is named as his successor, in an attempt by Henry to establish hereditary succession. The German monarchy remains theoretically elective.

1076

- The Berbers under the Almoravid Abu Bakr briefly occupy Koumbi, the capital of the west African kingdom of Ghana (roughly equivalent to modern Mali).
- The Fatimids recover Jerusalem from the Seljuks, but after a siege the Seljuk general Atsiz again expels them.
- The Saxons again rebel against King Henry IV of Germany.
- Wang An-shih, chief minister of the Sung Empire of China, is dismissed due to opposition to his extensive government reforms.
- Zvonimir is crowned as king of Croatia by a papal legate and recognizes the Pope's overlordship.

January 24   King Henry IV of Germany responds to a letter from Pope Gregory VII threatening excommunication by holding a council at Worms where the German bishops renounce their allegiance to Gregory and declare him deposed. Gregory shortly afterwards excommunicates Henry and absolves his subjects of their oaths of loyalty.

May 31   Earl Waltheof of Northumbria is executed because of his rebellion against William I the Conqueror, King of England and Duke of Normandy.

June 4   Sancho IV of Navarre is murdered and his kingdom is seized by Sancho V Ramirez of Aragon and Alfonso of Castile and León.

October 16   A diet of German princes at Tribur threatens to depose King Henry IV of Germany unless he resolves his dispute with the papacy within a year.

December 25   Bolesław II is crowned as king of Poland with a crown sent by Pope Gregory VII to reward his zeal in restoring the church in Poland, under the direction of papal legates, and for supporting the Pope against King Henry IV of Germany. Also in this year, Bolesław campaigns against Bohemia with Russian assistance, and moves the Polish capital from Gniezno to Kraków.

1077

- Duke Robert Guiscard of Apulia occupies the Lombard principality of Salerno.
- Robert Curthose leads a Norman rebellion against his father, William I the Conqueror, King of England and Duke of Normandy.
- The conquest of Byzantine Anatolia (modern Turkey) completed, Suleiman ibn-Qutlamish establishes the Seljuk Sultanate of Rūm ("Rome" in Turkish spelling), with his capital at Nicaea.

January 1   King Henry IV of Germany submits to Pope Gregory VII at Canossa and is absolved from excommunication.

March 13   In a diet at Forchheim, King Henry IV of Germany's enemies affirm that the German crown is elective and choose Rudolf, Duke of Swabia, as king.

April 25   King Géza I of Hungary dies. He is succeeded by his brother, Ladislas I.

1078

- King Philip I of France is defeated by Hugh, lord of Le Puiset, one of the vassals in his domain lands.
- Prince Iziaslav of Kiev is killed while defeating his nephews. He is succeeded by his brother, Vsevolod I.
- Roupen establishes himself as the ruler of the exiles from Armenia who are settling in Cilicia (Lesser Armenia) to escape Seljuk rule.

March 31   After a revolt in Constantinople (modern Istanbul, Turkey), the Byzantine emperor Michael VII abdicates and is succeeded by the general Nicephorus III Botaneiates, who has already been proclaimed emperor by the rebels.

August 7   Duke Rudolf of Swabia, the "antiking," is obliged to withdraw after an otherwise indecisive battle with King Henry IV of Germany at Mellrichstadt.

November 11   Pope Gregory VII publishes a decree confirming the abolition of lay investiture of spiritual offices.

1079

- Atsiz, the Seljuk conqueror of Syria and Palestine, is murdered on the order of Tutush, the Seljuk sultan Malik Shah's brother, who takes over his semi-independent principality.
- King Henry IV of Germany grants the duchy of Swabia to Frederick, Count of Staufen, who marries his daughter.

January 1   William I the Conqueror, King of England and Duke of Normandy, and King Philip I of France are routed at Gerberoy by William's son, Robert Curthose, who is leading a Norman rebellion.

August 15–September 8   King Malcolm III Canmore of Scotland devastates Northumberland, plundering as far as the River Tyne.

September   Hugh I resigns the duchy of Burgundy in order to enter a monastery. He is succeeded by his brother Eudes.

SCIENCE, TECHNOLOGY, AND MEDICINE

Health and Medicine

1075

- The Hindu physician Sureśara writes *Sabdapradīpa*, a herbal (catalog of medicinal plants) in Sanskrit.

Science

1070

- The Chinese scholar and horticulturist Wang Kuan writes *Yang-chou shao-yo-p'u* about the peony. The treatise describes 39 different varieties of the plant.

1072

- The Chinese poet and retired statesman Ou-yang Hsiu writes a treatise on the variety and cultivation of the peony.

1074

- The Seljuk sultan Malik Shah of Baghdad builds a new observatory (at Isfahan, Persia), where the astronomer and poet Omar al-Khayyām is appointed to reform the old Persian calendar.

1079

March 15   The Persian Islamic sultan Malik Shah introduces the improved calendar of the Jalālī era. The calendar was computed by the astronomer and poet Omar al-Khayyām at Isfahan, Persia, and is detailed in his *Astronomical Calendar*.

Technology

1070

- Elmer, an English monk and astrologer from Malmesbury Abbey, England, builds a pair of wings and tries to fly off the abbey tower. He succeeds in gliding for 200 meters, but is seriously injured when he crashes, and is forbidden by the abbot from repeating the experiment.

ARTS AND IDEAS

Architecture

1073

- The abbey of St. Augustine is founded in Canterbury, England.

1078–1124

- Work begins on the Romanesque cathedral of Santiago de Compostela, Spain, using French masons. Built on a huge scale to accommodate the large number of pilgrims, it is largely completed by 1124.

Literature and Language

c. **1075**

- Somadeva, a Brahman poet at the court of King Ananta of Kashmir, produces a collection of tales called *Katha-saritsagara/Ocean of the Streams of Story*, which preserves many traditional Indian folk legends.

Thought and Scholarship

c. **1076**

- Adam of Bremen, Germany, writes his *Historia Hammaburgensis Ecclesiae/History of the Bishopric of Hamburg*, which describes the geography and ethnography of northern Europe and makes the first mention of Vinland (an area of the east coast of North America visited by the Vikings).

c. **1077**

- Lambert of Hersfeld writes his *Annales Hersveldenses*, a history from the story of the Creation to 1077. His account of the years 1040–77 describes the dealings of the German emperors with the papacy.

1078

- Byzantine philosopher and historian Michael Psellus writes *Chronography*, a historical narrative of events in the Byzantine Empire from 976 onward. The later sections contain many personal observations.

SOCIETY

Education

1076

- Emperor Ly Thanh-tong of Dai Viet sets up an academy to train a Chinese-style civil service for a centralized government.

Everyday Life

1070

- Roquefort cheese is developed in France.

Religion

1070

August 15   William I the Conqueror, King of England and Duke of Normandy, deposes Archbishop Stigand of Canterbury for pluralism (holding more than one see at a time) and appoints the Italian reformer Lanfranc in his place.

1075

February 24–27   At the Lent synod, Pope Gregory VII suspends seven German bishops for opposing his renewal of decrees against clerical marriage and issues a decree forbidding lay investiture of bishops, whereby secular leaders grant church officials the symbols of their authority. His ruling is strongly opposed, in particular by King Henry IV of Germany.

BIRTHS & DEATHS

1072

- Ou-yang Hsiu, Chinese statesman, poet, and historian, dies in Honan, China (*c.* 65).

February 22   St. Peter Damian (Pier Damiani), cardinal and church reformer, dies in Faenza, Italy (*c.* 65).

March 16   Adalbert, archbishop of Bremen, dies in Goslar, Saxony (*c.* 72).

1073

- Chou Tun-i, Chinese philosopher and government official, founder of a Confucian revival in China, dies.

April 21   Pope Alexander II dies.

1075

February 16   Orderic Vitalis, English monk, author of *Historia ecclesiastica*, which provides a graphic description of Anglo-Norman life in England between 1082 and 1141, born near Shrewsbury, Shropshire (–*c.* 1142).

June   Lothair II (or III), King of Germany 1125–37 and emperor 1133–37, born (–1137).

December 4   St. Anno (or Hanno), archbishop of Cologne, a prominent political figure in the Holy Roman Empire, dies (*c.* 65).

1077

- Aniruddha, first king of united Burma and founder of the Pagan dynasty, dies.
- Shao Yung, Confucian philosopher, who believed that there was a fundamental unity to the universe based on divisions of the number four, dies.

1079

- Peter Abelard (Pierre Abélard), French theologian, philosopher, and poet, also known for his love affair with Héloïse, born near Nantes, Brittany, France (–1142).

April 11   St. Stanislaus (Stanisław) of Kraków, patron saint of Poland, dies in Kraków, Poland (*c.* 49).

1078

- Pope Gregory VII orders all bishops to found cathedral schools.

1079

April 11 St. Stanislaus (Stanisław), bishop of Kraków, dies following his mutilation for suspected treason against King Bolesław II of Poland.

1078

- William I the Conqueror, King of England and Duke of Normandy, clears ancient woodland in England, destroying some Saxon villages and churches in the process, to create the New Forest as a royal hunting ground.

1080–1089

POLITICS, GOVERNMENT, AND ECONOMICS

Business and Economics

1082

- Emperor Alexius I Comnenus grants Venice extensive rights to trade in the Byzantine Empire.

Politics and Government

1080

January 27 King Henry IV of Germany is defeated at Flarchheim and compelled to abandon Saxony.

March 7 Pope Gregory VII again prohibits lay investiture, declares Henry IV to be deposed as king of Germany, and recognizes the "antiking" Rudolf of Swabia in his place.

May 14 Walcher, bishop of Durham and Earl of Northumberland is murdered by the Northumbrians; William I the Conqueror, King of England and Duke of Normandy, consequently ravages the area and builds a castle at Newcastle upon Tyne.

June 25 King Henry IV of Germany holds a council of bishops at Brixen which declares Pope Gregory VII to be deposed and elects Guibert, archbishop of Ravenna, as Pope Clement III. Four days later, on June 29, in the Treaty of Ceprano, Pope Gregory makes an alliance against King Henry with Robert Guiscard, the Norman duke of Apulia, and recognizes his conquests in southern Italy and Sicily.

October 15 In a battle near Hohen-Mölsen, Rudolf of Swabia defeats King Henry IV of Germany, but is mortally wounded.

1081

- Alfonso VI of Castile exiles Rodrigo Díaz de Vivar, also known as the Cid, for making an unauthorized attack on the Moorish emirate of Toledo, then under Alfonso's protection. El Cid enters the service of the Moorish emir of Saragossa.
- William I the Conqueror, King of England and Duke of Normandy, makes an expedition into southern Wales, where Norman marcher lords are now established.

March 3 The Byzantine emperor Nicephorus III Botaneiates is deposed in favor of Alexius I Comnenus, founder of the Comnenian dynasty.

April 4 A rebellion in Poland forces King Bolesław II into exile. He is succeeded by his brother, Władysław I Herman, under whom the Polish territories disintegrate in civil war, and the crown falls into abeyance until 1300.

April 17 King Harald III Whetstone of Denmark, a law reformer, dies. He is succeeded by his brother, Cnut II.

May 5 King Henry IV of Germany unsuccessfully attempts to enter Rome and expel Pope Gregory VII.

June 6 The conquests east of the Dracon by Suleiman, Sultan of Rūm, are recognized in a treaty with the Byzantine emperor Alexius I Comnenus.

June 17 The Norman Duke Robert Guiscard of Apulia invades the Byzantine Empire, occupying Corfu and laying siege to Durazzo (in modern Albania).

August 9 King Henry IV's enemies in Germany elect Hermann of Salm as king in succession to Rudolf of Swabia.

October 18 The Norman Duke Robert Guiscard of Apulia defeats the Byzantine emperor Alexius I Comnenus near Durazzo (in modern Albania).

1082

- William I the Conqueror, King of England and Duke of Normandy, imprisons his brother Odo, bishop of Bayeux and Earl of Kent, for treason.

February 21 The Norman Duke Robert Guiscard of Apulia takes Durazzo in the Byzantine Empire after a siege.

1083

- Byzantine forces defeat the Norman Duke Robert Guiscard of Apulia's son, Bohemond, at Larissa, and recover Durazzo (in modern Albania).
- The county of Maine in Normandy revolts against William I the Conqueror, King of England and Duke of Normandy.

1083–1087 The Kiyowara clan, formerly allies of the Minamoto in the Nine Years' War, challenge Minamoto rule in northern Honshu, Japan. The Minamoto, led by Yoshiie, destroy the Kiyowara and impose absolute rule on the north.

1084

March 21 King Henry IV of Germany captures Rome and besieges Pope Gregory VII in the Castel Sant' Angelo. On March 24, Henry's antipope Clement III assumes the papacy in Rome and on March 31, Clement crowns King Henry IV of Germany as emperor in Rome.

May 5 Answering a call for help from Pope Gregory VII, Robert Guiscard, the Norman Duke of Apulia, expels the Germans from Rome; however, the Norman soldiers do so much damage that Gregory is forced to go into exile with them to escape popular anger.

1085

- Disorder in Denmark prevents King Cnut II from invading England, for which he had allied with King Olaf of Norway and Count Robert of Flanders.
- Emperor Henry IV extends a "Peace of God" over the empire as part of an attempt to restore order after recent civil wars.
- The Seljuk Turks capture the city of Antioch in Syria from the Byzantine Empire.

May 25 Alfonso VI of Castile and León takes the strategic city of Toledo from the Moors, then exacts tribute from the emirs of Valencia.

June 15 Emperor Henry IV grants Vratislav II the title king of Bohemia (for his lifetime only) and excuses him payment of tribute to reward his services in Italy.

July 17 The Norman Duke Robert Guiscard of Apulia is killed at the siege of Cephalonia, Greece. He is succeeded, as Duke of Apulia, by his son, Roger Borsa, who withdraws the Normans from Greece. Robert's brother, Roger, succeeds as Count in Sicily and Calabria.

December 25 William I the Conqueror, King of England and Duke of Normandy, orders a survey of the resources of England subsequently recorded in the *Domesday Book*, possibly because of the threat of invasion from King Cnut IV of Denmark.

1086

c. 1086 Exploiting the confusion following the death of the Seljuk Turkish sultan Suleiman ibn-Qutlamish, Danishmend, a *gazi* (holy warrior for Islam), founds an independent dynasty in eastern Anatolia.

- Suleiman, Sultan of Rūm, is defeated and killed by Tutush, the semi-independent Seljuk governor of Syria and Palestine, while attempting to take Aleppo. He is succeeded by his son, Kilij Arslan.

May 24 Abbot Desiderius of Monte Cassino is elected, against his will, as Pope Victor III to succeed Gregory VII. Rioting forces him to leave Rome before he can be consecrated and he resumes his duties as abbot.

July 10 King Cnut II of Denmark is murdered at Odense. He is succeeded by his brother Olaf IV.

August 1 William I the Conqueror, King of England and Duke of Normandy, receives oaths of loyalty from all who hold land in England, at Salisbury.

August 11 Emperor Henry IV is defeated at Pleichfeld by Duke Welf of Bavaria.

October 23 Yūsuf ibn-Tāshfin, the Almoravid emir of Morocco, who has been called into Spain by al-Mutamid of Seville to stem the Christian advance, defeats Alfonso VI of Castile and León at Azagal, near Badajoz.

1087

- A combined fleet from Genoa and Pisa takes Madhīyah, in modern Tunisia, emphasizing European control of the western Mediterranean.
- The Pechenegs, a Turkish people settled in the area of modern Ukraine, attempt to storm Constantinople. Salamon, the deposed king of Hungary, is thought to have been killed fighting in their ranks.
- The vizier Nizam-al-Mulk regularizes the system of military fiefs in the Seljuk sultanate; these become hereditary, which assists its disintegration.

May 30 In an attempt to confirm the principle of hereditary succession, Emperor Henry IV has his son Conrad, already named as his successor December 25, 1075, crowned as "King of the Romans" (king of Germany), a post which is theoretically elective.

September 9 William I the Conqueror, King of England and Duke of Normandy, dies in Rouen, Normandy, after a fall from his horse. William is succeeded in Normandy by his eldest son, Robert Curthose, who immediately faces a baronial rebellion he is never able to suppress completely: in England William is succeeded by a younger son, William II Rufus.

1088

- Emperor Henry IV makes peace with the Saxons.

March 12 Cardinal Otto of Chatillon is elected as Pope Urban II at Terracina, near Gaeta, Naples, Rome being under the control of the Emperor Henry IV's antipope, Clement III.

June 6 King William II Rufus of England suppresses a revolt led by his uncle Odo of Bayeux, bishop of Rochester, who was supporting his brother Duke Robert Curthose of Normandy.

1089

- David III the Builder becomes joint king of Georgia with his father, George II.
- Sancho Ramirez of Aragon and Navarre pays homage to the Pope as a papal vassal.
- The Fatimids recover Ascalon, Tyre, and Acre from the Seljuk Turks.
- Welf, son of the Duke of Bavaria, marries Matilda, Countess of Tuscany.

September 9 At the council of Melfi, Pope Urban II considers an appeal for military assistance against the Seljuk Turks from the Byzantine emperor Alexius I Comnenus.

September 28 Emperor Henry IV marries Praxedis Adelaide of Kiev.

SCIENCE, TECHNOLOGY, AND MEDICINE

Science

1083

- Mathematical and other scientific textbooks are printed for the first time, in China.

1087

- Al-Zarqellu and other Muslim Andalusian astronomers compile the *Toledan Tables*, which become known for their accuracy, and are translated more widely than any other Arab astronomical tables.

ARTS AND IDEAS

Architecture

c. **1080**

- The Romanesque abbey of St. Sernin in Toulouse, France, is founded. Its church is vaulted and contains several chapels within small apses.

1085

- The tomb-mosque of al-Juyūshī is founded in Cairo, Egypt.

c. **1087**

- Work begins on the San Nicola Church in Bari, Italy, in a Romanesque style new to Italy.

c. **1088**

- Work begins in France on Cluny "III," the largest of all abbey churches, and continues until 1130. Sponsored by King Alfonso VI of Spain, it is to rival Speyer Cathedral in Germany, and will contain five aisles, two transepts, and a barrel-vaulted roof in the nave.

Literature and Language

1088

- Ismaili Muslim philosopher and poet Nasir-i-Khusraw writes *Safar-nāma*, which forms a valuable record of his travels in Syria, Egypt, Arabia, and Asia.

Thought and Scholarship

1083

- Irish monk Marianus Scotus completes his *Chronicon/ Chronicle*, a world history from the Creation to 1082, which is important for its account of the Irish monastic movement in Germany.

1086

- Ssu-ma Kuang compiles *Tzu-chih tung-chien/ Comprehensive Mirror for Aid in Government*, a history of China from 403 BC to AD 959 with a pronounced Confucian bias.

BIRTHS & DEATHS

1080

- Symeon Seth, English scholar who wrote a dictionary on the medical properties of foodstuffs and a botanical dictionary, and translated many Arabic scientific works into Greek, dies.

1081

- Abbot Suger of St.-Denis, adviser to King Louis VI and King Louis VII of France, who contributed to the development of the Gothic style of architecture, born near Paris, France (–1151).

1083

- Anna Comnena, a leading Byzantine historian, daughter of the Byzantine emperor Alexius I Comnenus, born (–*c.* 1153).
- Bolesław II Śmiały (the Bold), the former king of Poland, dies in exile.

January 11   Otto of Nordheim, leader of the Saxon rebellion against King Henry IV of Germany, dies.

1085

- Robert of Apulia, Norman traveler who settled in Apulia, southern Italy,

and expanded Norman rule into Calabria, Naples, and Sicily, dies near Cephalonia, Greece, Byzantine Empire (*c.* 60).

May 25   Pope Gregory VII dies at Salerno, Italy (*c.* 65).

1086

- Ssu-ma Kuang, Chinese statesman, poet, and historian, author of *Tzu-chih tung-chien/Comprehensive Mirror for Aid in Government*, a history of China from 403 BC to AD 959, dies in Pien Lian, Hunan, China (67).
- Wang An-shih, Chinese poet and administrator who reformed the Chinese government by stimulating growth through loans, and by redesigning the tax and civil service systems, dies (65).

August 11   Henry V, German king 1099–1125 and emperor 1111–25, the last emperor of the Salian dynasty, born (–1125).

1087

- Constantinus Africanus, Italian monk and medical scholar who

initiated the translation of Arabic medical texts into Latin, dies in the monastery of Monte Cassino, near Cassino, Italy.

September 9   William I the Conqueror, Duke of Normandy 1035–87, King of England 1066–87, dies in Rouen, Normandy (59).

September 16   Pope Victor III dies.

1088

January 10   Berengar of Tours, leading theologian during the Eucharistic controversy of the 11th century, dies in the priory of St.-Cosme, near Tours (*c.* 88).

September 28   The German "antiking" Hermann of Salm dies.

1089

May 28   Lanfranc, Italian Benedictine, archbishop of Canterbury 1070–89 and counselor of William the Conqueror, dies in Canterbury, Kent, England (*c.* 84).

SOCIETY

Education

1088

- Irnerius begins teaching Roman law at the University of Bologna in Italy, leading to the revival of the study and practice of Roman law in western Europe.

Everyday Life

1087

- The *Domesday Book*, compiled for William I the Conqueror, King of England and Duke of Normandy, records 5,624 water-mills for corn south of the rivers Trent and Severn, roughly one mill for every 400 people,

some stamping-mills for crushing iron-ore, and hammer-mills. It estimates the population of England at between 1 and 1.5 million, with East Anglia the most populous region.

Religion

1084

- St. Bruno founds a hermitage at Chartreuse near Grenoble, France, the origin of the Carthusian Order.

Sports

1080

- The first known publicly announced *corrida* (bullfight) in Christian Spain is held at Avila as part of the wedding celebrations of the Infante Sancho de Estrada. It becomes a convention to hold a bullfight at similar celebrations.

1090–1099

POLITICS, GOVERNMENT, AND ECONOMICS

Politics and Government

1090

- Al-Hasan ibn-al-Sabbāh, founder of the Assassins, a fanatical Ismailite sect, establishes himself in the castle of Alamūt, Persia.
- Count Raymond Berengar II of Barcelona becomes a papal vassal: the willingness of secular rulers to become papal vassals is a sign of the increasing prestige of the papacy.
- Count Roger Guiscard of Sicily and Calabria takes Malta from the Arabs.
- In the course of a pilgrimage to the Holy Land, Count Robert of Flanders fights for the Byzantine emperor Alexius I Comnenus against the Seljuk Turks.

April 29 Aided by the Cumans, a nomadic people of Turkish origin, Byzantine emperor Alexius I Comnenus defeats the Pechenegs, a Turkish people settled in the area of modern Ukraine, who are blockading Constantinople, at Mt. Levunium.

July 7 Alarmed by the marriage alliance between his enemies Duke Welf of Bavaria and Countess Matilda of

Tuscany, Emperor Henry IV invades Italy and lays siege to Mantua.

November 11 The Almoravid emir of Morocco, Yūsuf ibn-Tāshfin, takes Granada in Spain.

1091

- Count Raymond Berengar of Barcelona takes Tarragona from the Moors.
- Duke Roger Guiscard takes Butera, so completing the conquest of Sicily from the Arabs.
- King Ladislas I of Hungary conquers Croatia from the Byzantine Empire.
- King Malcolm III Canmore of Scotland invades England, but after an English counterattack he is forced to pay homage to King William II Rufus.
- King William II Rufus of England helps his elder brother Duke Robert Curthose to expel their youngest brother, Henry, from Normandy.
- The Seljuk sultan Malik Shah makes Baghdad the Seljuk capital.
- Yūsuf ibn-Tashfin, the Almoravid emir of Morocco, conquers and unites the petty Muslim emirates of Andalusia.

April 11 Emperor Henry IV takes Mantua, and subsequently defeats the forces of Countess Matilda of Tuscany at Tricontai.

1092

- Kilij Arslan, sultan of Rūm, seizes Nicaea and Smyrna from their independent Turkish rulers.

- King Vratislav II of Bohemia dies. He is succeeded, as duke only, by his brother Conrad, who dies this year and is succeeded by Vratislav's son, Břatislav II.
- King William II Rufus of England seizes northern Cumberland and Westmorland from the Scots.
- Nizām al-Mulk, vizier to the Seljuk sultan Malik Shah, is murdered shortly after writing the *Siyāsat-nāmah/ Rules for Kings*, a treatise on government for the sultan.

November 11 The Seljuk sultan Malik Shah dies. He is succeeded by his son Mahmud I, who is immediately attacked by his brothers. Torn by civil war, the Seljuk sultanate disintegrates as its provinces and cities become independent under local dynasties.

1093

- Alfonso VI of Castile and León takes Santarem, Cintra, and, briefly, Lisbon.
- King Conrad II of Germany rebels against his father, Emperor Henry IV, and is crowned as king of Italy.

April 4 The last independent native prince in southern Wales, Rhys ap Tewdwr, King of Deheubarth, is killed in battle with the Norman marcher barons near Brecon.

November 13 King Malcolm III Canmore of Scotland is killed at Alnwick while invading England. He is succeeded by his brother, Donald Bane.

1094

- Barkiyāruq succeeds Mahmud I as Seljuk sultan.
- Pope Urban II regains possession of the Lateran Palace in Rome, so completing his recovery of Rome from the antipope Clement III. Although Emperor Henry IV's cause in Italy is now ruined, he is prevented from returning to Germany because of his son King Conrad II of Germany's rebellion, and the empress Adelaide deserts him.
- Rodrigo Díaz de Vivar, El Cid, captures Valencia from the Moors and rules it nominally as a vassal of Alfonso VI of Castile and León.
- The Welsh expel the Normans from Gwynedd and destroy all the Norman castles in Ceredigion and Dyfed except Pembroke and Rhyd-y-gors.

February 26 Umar al-Mutawakkil, the last emir of Badajoz, is killed after the city surrenders to Yūsuf, the Almoravid emir of Morocco.

May–November King Donald Bane of Scotland is overthrown because of his pro-Norman policies. Duncan II, the son of Malcolm III Canmore, briefly holds the Scottish throne with Anglo-Norman aid, but he is killed and Donald Bane regains control.

June 6 Sancho V Ramirez of Aragon and Navarre dies. He is succeeded by his son, Pedro I.

November King Philip I of France thwarts King William II Rufus of England's attempt to conquer the duchy of Normandy, held by his brother Robert Curthose.

December 29 With the death of Caliph al-Munstansir the Fatimid caliphate goes into rapid decline, as the caliphate is held by a succession of powerless nonentities, several of whom are murdered.

1095

- Alfonso VI of Castile and León invests Henry of Burgundy with territories in the county of Portugal.
- King William II Rufus of England suppresses a rebellion led by Robert de Mowbray, Earl of Northumberland.

- The Byzantine emperor Alexius I Comnenus repulses the Cumans, a Turkish people, at Adrianople and appeals to Pope Urban II for western aid against the Turks.
- Tutush, the semi-independent Seljuk governor of Syria and Palestine, dies. He is succeeded by his son Ridwān in Aleppo and Duqāq in Damascus, but other independent Turkish princes establish themselves in Jerusalem and parts of his dominions.
- Welf, son of the Duke of Bavaria, divorces Countess Matilda of Tuscany.

March 3 In a council at Piacenza, Pope Urban II appeals to western Europe to rescue Constantinople from the Turks.

July 29 King Ladislas I of Hungary dies. He is succeeded by his son, Coloman.

November 27 At the council of Clermont, France, Pope Urban II proclaims the First Crusade, calling for the Holy Land to be freed from the Seljuk Turks and for there to be free access to Jerusalem for pilgrims. Participants are granted an indulgence (remission of penances due for sin).

December 1 Count Raymond IV of Toulouse becomes the first major figure to join the First Crusade.

1096

- King William II Rufus of England gains possession of Normandy as pledge for a loan to his brother Duke Robert Curthose who is joining the First Crusade.
- Pedro I of Aragon defeats the Moors at Alcazar and takes Huesca.

May 5 Crusaders in the Rhineland provoke attacks on the Jews there.

August 1 The "People's Crusade," a poorly armed and ill-disciplined peasant army led by Peter the Hermit, arrives in Constantinople.

October 21 Kilij Arslan, Seljuk sultan of Rūm, destroys the army of the "People's Crusade" at Civetot, shortly after it has crossed into Anatolia.

December 23 Godfrey of Bouillon arrives in Constantinople with the first militarily significant contingent of crusaders.

1097

- A reconciliation with Duke Welf of Bavaria enables the Emperor Henry IV to return to Germany from Italy.
- King William II Rufus of England campaigns against the Welsh, but is unable to meet them in battle.
- The Russian princes descended from Jaroslav meet at Liubech, near Kiev, and agree to unite against the Cumans, who now occupy the southern Russian steppes down to the Dnieper. They also agree to a system of strict father-to-son hereditary succession in order to prevent civil war.

January 1 The crusaders in Constantinople riot after the Byzantine emperor Alexius I Comnenus cuts off their food supplies for refusing swear allegiance to him.

May 21 The crusaders defeat Kilij Arslan, sultan of Rūm, outside Nicaea.

June 19 The crusaders take Nicaea, which is returned to Byzantine control.

July 1 The crusaders defeat Kilij Arslan, Seljuk sultan of Rūm, at Dorylaeum, opening the way for their army to cross into Anatolia.

August 8 The crusaders take Iconium, the capital of Kilij Arslan, sultan of Rūm.

October 10   Edgar, the son of Malcolm III Canmore by his second marriage, with Margaret, the grand-daughter of King Aethelred the Unready, with Anglo-Norman assistance, deposes and succeeds Donald Bane, the last Celtic king of Scotland.

October 21   The crusaders begin their siege of the Syrian city of Antioch, held by the Seljuk Turks.

1098

- King Magnus Barelegs of Norway ravages the Orkneys, Shetlands, and the Isle of Man, forcing the Norse settlers there to accept his authority, and plunders and takes tribute from Dublin, Galloway, and Anglesey, where he defeats two Norman earls.
- The Fatimids take advantage of the crusaders' victories over the Seljuk Turks to recover Jerusalem from Seljuk control.

March 10   The crusader Baldwin of Flanders becomes Count of Edessa (modern Urfa), a Christian Armenian city in northern Mesopotamia.

June 3   The crusaders take Antioch after a traitor admits a party of knights led by the Norman prince Bohemond of Taranto under cover of night.

June 28   At Antioch, the crusaders defeat Kerboghā, the atabeg of Mosul, whose relief army had arrived too late to prevent the fall of the city.

1099

- King William II Rufus of England recovers control of the county of Maine in Normandy.

January 5   Henry, son of Emperor Henry IV, is elected as "king of the Romans" (king of Germany) in place of the disloyal son Conrad II.

January 13   The crusaders leave Antioch in the charge of the Norman prince Bohemond of Taranto and continue their march to Jerusalem.

June 6   The crusaders occupy Bethlehem.

July 15   The crusaders take Jerusalem by storm after a short siege.

July 22   Godfrey of Bouillon is elected as "Defender of the Holy Sepulchre," refusing the title king, and so founds the Latin Kingdom of Jerusalem.

August 12   The crusaders defeat a Fatimid army, sent from Egypt to relieve Jerusalem, at Ascalon.

August 13   Cardinal Rainer is elected as Pope Paschal II.

SCIENCE, TECHNOLOGY, AND MEDICINE

Health and Medicine

1092

- Chinese astronomer and statesman Su Sung collates and republishes ancient medical texts.

1098

- The French physician Nicholas Provost of Tours writes his *Antidotarum/Book of Antidotes*, which is a collection of more than 2,500 prescriptions for the treatment of disease, gathered from the medical school at Salerno, Italy.

Science

1091

- The Benedictine abbot and monastic reformer Wilhelm of Hirsau writes his astronomical treatise *De astronomia/On Astronomy*.
- The French-born Prior Walcher of Malvern Abbey, England, records his observations in Italy of an eclipse of the moon. This is one of the earliest accurate western European observations of the phenomenon.

1093

- The Chinese scholar Shên Kua writes *Dream Pool Essays*, which contains sections on mathematics, music, archeology, and other sciences. It includes the earliest literary mention of a magnetic needle, and a description of printing with movable type.

1094

- The Abu U'bayd Al-Bakri dies, having written *The Book of Roads and Kingdoms*. This is the earliest surviving geographical work by a Spanish Muslim, and contains a description of the kingdom of Ghana.

Technology

1090

- The Chinese diplomat and monk Su Sung writes *Hsian I Hsiang Fa Yao/New Design for an Armillary and Globe*, which describes his design for an accurate water clock that improves time and calendar measurements.
- The earliest reference to the Chinese use of a flier to improve weaving in silk-working machinery is recorded.

1092

- Chinese astronomer and statesman Su Sung builds a 9 m/30 ft-high water clock and mechanical armillary sphere. It includes numerous chimes and features to assist astronomical measurements, and is considered the finest mechanical achievement of its time. Twenty years later it is destroyed by barbarians.

1094

- The Chinese engineer, diplomat, and monk Su Sung invents the "Celestial Ladder," an endless, looped chain for transmitting power from a drive shaft to machinery.

1095

- Water power is used to drive the wheels and lifting machinery irrigating the farmland at St. Bertin, France.

Transportation

c. 1094

- Gondolas are recorded in use on the canals of Venice, Italy.

The Crusades (1095–1291)

First Crusade (1095–1124)

1095

November 27 At the council of Clermont, France, Pope Urban II proclaims the First Crusade, calling for the Holy Land to be freed from the Seljuk Turks and for free access to Jerusalem for pilgrims. Participants are granted an indulgence (remission of penances due for sin).

December 1 Count Raymond IV of Toulouse becomes the first major figure to join the First Crusade.

1096

• King William II Rufus of England gains possession of Normandy as pledge for a loan to his brother Duke Robert Curthose who is joining the First Crusade.

May 5 Crusaders in the Rhineland provoke attacks on the Jews there.

August 1 The "People's Crusade," a poorly armed and ill-disciplined peasant army led by Peter the Hermit, arrives in Constantinople.

October 21 Kilij Arslan, Seljuk sultan of Rūm, destroys the army of the "People's Crusade" at Civetot, shortly after it has crossed into Anatolia.

1097

January 1 The crusaders in Constantinople riot after the Byzantine emperor Alexius I Comnenus cuts off their food supplies for refusing to swear allegiance to him.

October 21 The crusaders begin their siege of the Syrian city of Antioch, held by the Seljuk Turks.

1098

March 10 The crusader Baldwin of Flanders becomes Count of Edessa (modern Urfa), a Christian Armenian city in northern Mesopotamia.

June 3 The crusaders take Antioch after a traitor admits a party of knights led by the Norman prince Bohemond of Taranto under cover of night.

June 28 At Antioch, the crusaders defeat Kerboghā, the atabeg of Mosul, whose relief army had arrived too late to prevent the fall of the city.

1099

June 6 The crusaders occupy Bethlehem.

July 15 The crusaders take Jerusalem by storm after a short siege.

July 22 Godfrey of Bouillon is elected as "Defender of the Holy Sepulchre," refusing the title king, and so founds the Latin Kingdom of Jerusalem.

August 12 The crusaders defeat a Fatimid army, sent from Egypt to relieve Jerusalem, at Ascalon.

1104

May 5 King Baldwin I of Jerusalem takes the port of Acre (present-day Akko, Israel) from the Fatimids (Shiite Muslims).

1105

August 27 Baldwin defeats the Fatimids in the third battle of Ramleh, ending their attempts to reconquer Palestine.

1109

July 12 The Fatimid stronghold of Tripoli surrenders to Baldwin.

1110

December 4 The port of Sidon (present-day Saida) surrenders to Baldwin and Norwegian crusaders under King Sigurd I.

1124

July 7 The Fatimids surrender the city of Tyre to King Baldwin II of Jerusalem.

Second Crusade (1144–48)

1144

December 24 Imad ad-Din Zangi, the Muslim governor of Mosul, takes Edessa after a four-week siege; though he massacres the Frankish inhabitants the native Armenian Christians are spared. The fall of the city calls for a new crusade.

1146

March 1 Pope Eugenius III proclaims the Second Crusade on God's behalf. The response is disappointing until the French Cistercian abbot Bernard of Clairvaux begins preaching the crusade.

1147

October 25 English and Flemish crusaders, interrupting their voyage to the Holy Land to join the Second Crusade, assist in the capture of the city of Lisbon from the Moors by King Alfonso of Portugal.

1148

March 19 The Second Crusade reaches Antioch. Its one army, consisting of mostly Frankish and German nobles, is much reduced as a result of defeats by the Seljuk Turks of Rūm while crossing Anatolia.

April 24 King Louis VII of France and Conrad III Hohenstaufen, king of the Germans (who has rejoined the crusade after recovering from his illness) hold a council at Acre (modern Akko, Israel) and decide to attack the city of Damascus rather than try to recover Edessa from the Muslims.

July 24–28 The Second Crusade lays siege to the city of Damascus in Syria but is forced to retreat because of lack of water, so bringing the disastrous crusade to an ignominious end.

Third Crusade (1153–92)

1153

August 19 The Fatimid (Shiite Muslim) garrison of Ascalon, a city on the Mediterranean coast in Palestine, surrenders to King Baldwin III of Jerusalem: the Christians now control the entire coast of the Holy Land.

1177

November 25 The invasion by Saladin, Sultan of Egypt and Syria, of the kingdom of Jerusalem is defeated by King Baldwin IV at Montgisard.

1179

June 10 Saladin defeats King Baldwin V of Jerusalem on the River Litani.

1187

July 3 The Jerusalem army, advancing to raise the siege of Tiberias, is trapped and destroyed by Saladin at the Horns of Hattin; King Guy of Jerusalem is captured and Reynald of Châtillon beheaded. The kingdom of Jerusalem is left virtually defenseless as Saladin takes the Franks' castles one by one.

October 3 Saladin takes Jerusalem after a short siege.

December 17 Pope Gregory VIII dies, shortly after proclaiming the Third Crusade to liberate Jerusalem from the Muslims.

1189

December 12   Having raised money by the sale of offices and privileges, King Richard I the Lion-Hearted leaves England to join the Third Crusade, leaving William de Mandeville, Earl of Essex and Hugh Puiset, bishop of Durham, in charge of England as justiciars (vice regents in the king's absence).

1190

- The Christian military order of the Knights of the Cross (later known as the Teutonic Knights) is founded at the Palestinian port of Acre (present-day Akko, Israel) to crusade against the pagan Slavs and Balts.

1191

April 20   King Philip II of France arrives at Acre.

August 3   Claiming to be in ill health, King Philip II of France sails for home from Palestine.

September 7   Richard the Lion-Hearted leads the crusaders to victory over Saladin at Arsuf, Palestine.

1192

January 1   Richard the Lion-Hearted camps at Beit-Nuba, 19 km/12 mi from Jerusalem, but realizing that the crusaders lack the resources to hold the city, even if they can capture it, he retires to Ascalon which he refortifies.

May 23   Richard the Lion-Hearted takes Daron, thus completing the recovery of the Palestinian coast from Saladin.

June 6   Richard the Lion-Hearted camps within sight of the city of Jerusalem, but again withdraws.

July 30   Saladin takes the Palestinian town of Jaffa but is expelled by Richard the Lion-Hearted the next day.

August 5   Richard the Lion-Hearted defeats Saladin, outside the Palestinian town of Jaffa.

September 2   King Richard I the Lion-Hearted of England negotiates a three-year truce and access to Jerusalem for Christian pilgrims with Saladin , thereby ending the Third Crusade.

Fourth Crusade (1198–1204)

1198

August 15   Pope Innocent III proclaims the Fourth Crusade to recover Jerusalem from the Muslims and offers an indulgence to those who fight the Albigensians (Cathars; members of a heretical Christian sect) in southern France.

1201

April 4   By a treaty negotiated by the doge Enrico Dandolo, Venice agrees to transport the Fourth Crusade to Egypt for 85,000 marks. In addition, the Venetians offer 50 war galleys to support the crusade in return for half of its conquests.

1202

November 15   The crusaders take the Adriatic port of Zadar from the king of Hungary for Venice in lieu of payment for their transport to Egypt, which Venice cannot pay. Here the crusaders meet Alexius IV Angelus, son of the deposed Byzantine emperor Isaac II Angelus, who promises them troops and money for the Fourth Crusade if they will help his father regain the Byzantine throne.

1203

July 17   Carrying out their part of the arrangement made the previous November with Alexius IV, the crusaders force an entry into Constantinople; Alexius flees and Isaac II is restored.

1204

- Pope Innocent III grants a charter to the Sword Brothers, a military order founded by Bishop Albert of Livonia to assist in the conversion of the Livs.

April 12   Realizing that the Byzantine promise of help for their crusade is not going to be kept, the crusaders take the Byzantine capital Constantinople by storm and sack it for three days. The emperor Alexius V Ducas Murtzuphlus flees, as does Constantine XI Lascaris after being offered the throne by Byzantine nobles during the attack.

Albigensian Crusades (1208–29)

1208

January 14   A papal legate sent to convert the Albigensian (Cathar) heretics of Languedoc, southern France, is murdered by a vassal of Raymond V, the Count of Toulouse. Pope Innocent III declares a crusade against the heretics, the "Albigensian Crusade."

1209

July 22   The southern French town of Béziers is sacked by the Albigensian crusaders, as they take up arms against the Albigensian heresy.

August 15   The southern French town of Carcassonne is taken by the Albigensian crusaders; the Norman crusader Simon IV de Montfort is then elected leader and expropriates land from the Albigensian heretics and their supporters, becoming lord of Béziers and Carcassonne.

1210

- The grand master Hermann of Salza obtains papal privileges for the Teutonic Order (a German Christian military order) of crusading knights.

1213

April 19–29   Pope Innocent III proclaims the Fifth Crusade and stops granting indulgences for the Albigensian Crusade against the Albigensian heretics of southern France.

1217

November 12   The first contingents of the Fifth Crusade (among them, briefly, King Andrew II of Hungary) take and sack Baisan in Palestine.

1218

- Pope Honorius III announces a new Albigensian crusade (against the Cathar heretics of southern France).

August 25   The crusaders of the Fifth Crusade capture a defensive tower on the River Nile outside Damietta, Egypt.

1219

- Raymond, the son of Raymond VI, Count of Toulouse, defeats the Albigensian crusaders led by Amauri de Montfort at Basiège, in the spring.

November 5   The Fifth Crusade takes Damietta; the Egyptian garrison, ravaged by disease and starvation, offers little resistance.

1221

August 8   The army of the Fifth Crusade, advancing into Egypt from Damietta, is trapped by the Nile floods and the Egyptian army; the leader of the crusade, Cardinal Pelagius, is forced to accept Sultan al-Kamil of Egypt's terms for withdrawal, including the surrender of Damietta.

1226

- The Polish prince Konrad of Masovia grants the town of Chełmno to the German Order of the Teutonic Knights as a base for their conquest and conversion of the Prussians.

The Crusades (1095–1291) *continued*

1227

September 29   Pope Gregory IX excommunicates the Holy Roman Emperor Frederick II for his failure to fulfill his promise to go on crusade (Frederick has claimed to be too ill).

1228

June 28   The Holy Roman Emperor Frederick II sails for Palestine on the Sixth Crusade. Pope Gregory IX renews his sentence of excommunication, this time because excommunicates cannot go on crusade.

1229

February 18   Frederick II negotiates the return of Jerusalem to Christian control with al-Kamil, the sultan of Egypt; the Albigensian Crusade thus ends without any fighting.

April 11   The Treaty of Paris ends the Albigensian Crusade against the Albigensian (Cathar) heretics of Languedoc, southern France; Count Raymond VII of Toulouse submits to King Louis IX of France, ceding the duchy of Narbonne.

Sixth Crusade (1234–40)

1234

- Pope Gregory IX proclaims a crusade against the city of Rome after a revolt there has forced him into flight.

1237

- Pope Gregory IX confirms the union of the Sword Brothers of Livonia to the Teutonic Knights.

1239

September 1   A crusade led by King Theobald of Navarre and Richard, Earl of Cornwall, King Henry III of England's brother, arrives at the Palestinian port of Acre.

November 13   Theobald's crusading army is defeated by the Egyptians at Gaza; subsequent negotiations, however, result in modest territorial gains for the kingdom of Jerusalem.

December 7   An-Nasir, Prince of Kerak, expels the Latin garrison from their citadel in Jerusalem and destroys the city's fortifications before withdrawing.

1240

September 9   King Leobald of Navarre leaves Palestine, ending his crusade.

Seventh Crusade (1244–50)

1244

August 23   Jerusalem is captured and sacked by Khwarizmian exiles employed by the sultan Ayyub of Egypt in his war against Damascus, Syria; the Christians are expelled, this time for good.

1247

October 15   The Ayyubid (Muslim) Egyptians take the city of Ascalon in the kingdom of Jerusalem.

1248

August 26   King Louis IX of France sails on the Seventh Crusade.

1249

June 5   Having wintered in Cyprus, King Louis IX of France continues on the Seventh Crusade, lands in Egypt, and enters Damietta without opposition.

1250

February 8   Louis IX defeats the Egyptians barring the route to the capital Cairo at Mansurah.

April 6   Louis IX is defeated and captured by the Egyptians at the Battle of Fariskur, while withdrawing from Mansurah.

May 6   Louis IX surrenders the Egyptian town of Damietta as part of the price for his release; he leaves Egypt for the Palestinian port of Acre, where he is accepted as ruler in practice of Outremer, the Crusader kingdoms in the Middle East.

Eighth Crusade (1270–91)

1270

November 1   Charles of Anjou, King of Sicily, leader of the Eighth Crusade to the Holy Land, makes a peace treaty with the emir of Tunis, intending to direct the crusade fleet toward Constantinople. The emir resumes payment of the tribute formerly paid to the Hohenstaufen kings of Sicily.

November 23   The Eighth Crusade fleet is destroyed by a storm at Trapani, Sicily, preventing Charles from directing it toward Constantinople.

1271

May 9   Edward Plantagenet, the son of King Henry III of England, arrives at Acre in the Kingdom of Jerusalem on crusade.

1291

- Acre falls, the last Christian stronghold in Palestine.

ARTS AND IDEAS

Architecture

c. **1090**

- The ancient city of Iconium becomes the capital of the Seljuk sultanate of Rūm. Renamed Konya (now in Turkey), it becomes one of the great cities of the world, with the construction of many new and ornate buildings.

1093

- Work begins on Durham Cathedral in Durham, England, continuing until 1133 and including the first example of decorative rib vaulting.

1096

- Work begins on the abbey church of St. Madeleine in Vézelay, France, continuing until 1104.

1097

- The construction of Westminster Hall, part of the Palace of Westminster, begins in London, England.

1098

- Raymond Gayrard is employed as architect for the building of Conques abbey church in France, the construction of which continues until 1118.

Arts

c. **1090**

- The Bayeux tapestry, a pictorial record of the Norman conquest of England, is embroidered. It may have been commissioned by Odo of Bayeux, half brother of William the Conqueror.

Literature and Language

c. **1095**

- *Eiga Monogatari/A Tale of Glory*, a romanticized chronicle of the Fujiwara family and the earliest known Japanese historical novel, is published.
- *Chanson de Roland/Song of Roland* is recorded. It is the earliest extant example of the chivalric epics known as *chanson de geste* ("song of exploits") which were sung and possibly composed by French *trouvères* (poets with a narrative style).

Thought and Scholarship

c. **1091**

- Nizām-al-Mulk, vizier to the Seljuk sultanate, writes *Siyāsat-nāmah/Rules for Kings*, a treatise on the art of government which criticizes Shiite Muslims, in particular the Ismailis.

SOCIETY

Education

c. **1095**

- Bologna University is founded in Italy, and becomes a major center of canon and civil law.

Religion

c. **1090**

- The Muslim Assassin Sect emerges in Persia. Its members believe that the murder of their opponents is a religious duty. Their name derives from hashish, which they reputedly smoke to make themselves fearless.

1092

- King Philip I of France abducts and "marries" Bertrada, the wife of Count Fulk le Réchin of Anjou: for this Philip is excommunicated by Pope Urban II.
- The council of Soissons in France accuses the philosopher Roscelin of denying the unity of the three persons of the Trinity.

1094

- Anselm, archbishop of Canterbury, completes his *Cur Deus homo/Why did God become Man?*, in which he sees the death of Christ as necessary for the redemption of man from sin and as evidence of God's mercy.

1095

February 25 In a council at Rockingham, Archbishop Anselm of Canterbury quarrels with King William II Rufus of England over the issue of episcopal obedience to the king and pope.

1096

- Robert d'Arbrissel founds the monastic order of Fontevrault.

BIRTHS & DEATHS

1090

- St. Bernard of Clairvaux, influential Cistercian abbot and mystic, founder of the abbey of Clairvaux, born, probably in Fontaine-les-Dijon, near Dijon, France (–1153).

1092

- Peter the Venerable, abbot of Cluny, who commissioned the first Latin translation of the Koran, born in Montboissier, Auvergne, France (–1156).

1093

November 13 Malcolm III Canmore, King of Scotland 1058–93, son of Duncan I, falls in battle near Alnwick, Northumberland, England (*c.* 62).

1094

November Duncan II, King of Scotland May–November 1094, son of Malcolm III Canmore and grandson of Duncan I, is killed.

1096

- Werner, Count of Habsburg, dies.

1097

c. 1097 Stephen of Blois, King of England 1135–54, who usurped the throne, born (–1154).

December 22 Roger II, first king of the Norman Kingdom of Sicily 1130–54, born (–1154).

1098

- Donald Bane (or Donaldbane), King of Scotland 1093–94 and 1094–97, son of Duncan I, dies.

- Hildegard von Bingen, German Benedictine abbess, philosopher, mystic, and musician, born in Bermersheim, Germany (–1179).

August 1 Adhemar, bishop of Le Puy and papal legate, the official leader of the First Crusade, dies.

1099

July 10 Rodrigo Díaz de Vivar ("El Cid"), Spanish military leader and national hero, conqueror of Valencia, dies in Valencia (*c.* 56).

July 29 Urban II, French pope 1088–99, who started the First Crusade and politicized the papacy, dies in Rome (*c.* 64).

1097

October 10 Unable to resolve his disputes with King William II Rufus, Anselm, the archbishop of Canterbury, begins his first exile from England.

1098

March 21 St. Robert of Molesme founds a monastery at Cîteaux Abbey, near Dijon, France, forming the origins of the Cistercian Order.

October 10 Representatives of the Roman and Greek churches debate the Procession of the Holy Ghost in a council at Bari, Italy.

1099

- The Order of the Knights of St. John of Jerusalem is founded.

1100–1109

POLITICS, GOVERNMENT, AND ECONOMICS

Politics and Government

1100

- Duke Břatislav II of Bohemia is murdered. He is succeeded by his brother Bořivoj, who faces a civil war.
- King Constantine Bodin of Zeta, who had formed a Serbian state by the conquest of Rascia and Bosnia, dies; the kingdom now breaks up.
- 1100–1532 The Inca empire dominates the Andes region of South America. Its population numbers as many as 12 million. Incan society is based on a strict hierarchy, with an emperor who rules with absolute power. Their religion is based on sun-worship, and they are skilled builders who create a system of roads and irrigation.
- April 4 The emirs of Ascalon, Caesarea, and Acre submit to Godfrey of Bouillon, Defender of the Holy Sepulchre, as tributaries.
- July 18 Godfrey of Bouillon, Defender of the Holy Sepulchre, dies. He is succeeded by his brother, Baldwin I, who takes the title king of Jerusalem.
- August 5 William II Rufus' brother Henry is crowned king of England; he issues a charter of liberties and recalls Anselm as archbishop of Canterbury.
- September 9 The antipope Clement III dies; a Roman faction takes advantage of the absence of the legitimate pope Paschal II, currently in southern Italy, to crown Theodoric as Clement's successor, but he is expelled later in the year.

1101

- In a meeting at Konungahella, Norway, King Erik I the Good of Denmark, King Inge I of Sweden, and King Magnus III Barelegs of Norway swear to maintain perpetual peace.

- King Philip I of France purchases Bourges from its viscount, who is going to the Holy Land.
- March 3 Tancred, Norman leader of the First Crusade, named Prince of Galilee after the fall of Jerusalem in 1099, assumes the regency of the principality of Antioch following the capture of its Norman prince, Bohemond I (Tancred's uncle), by the Turkish emir of Sebastea.
- May 5 King Baldwin I of Jerusalem takes the cities of Arsuf and Caesarea from the Fatimids (Shiite Muslims).
- June 22 Roger I, Count of Sicily dies; he is succeeded by his son Simon.
- June 23 A new crusading army, led from Constantinople by Raymond IV, Count of Toulouse, takes the city of Ankara from the Seljuk Turkish sultanate of Rūm.
- July 17 By the Treaty of Alton, Robert Curthose, Duke of Normandy, abandons his claim to the English throne against his younger brother King Henry I of England.
- August 8 The crusading army of Raymond IV, Count of Toulouse, is destroyed by the Danishmend Turks at Mersivan in Anatolia.
- September 4 King Baldwin I of Jerusalem defeats the Fatimids (Shiite Muslims) at Ramleh.
- September 9 A crusading army of Aquitainians and Bavarians is destroyed by Seljuk Turkish forces at Heraclea in Asia Minor (modern Turkey).

1102

- Matilda, Countess of Tuscany, wills her lands to the papacy. (When she dies in 1115 she bequeaths her lands to Emperor Henry V of Germany.)
- February 2 Albert is elected as pope by the supporters of the former antipope Clement III. However, he is deposed in a matter of days following popular rioting.
- May 17 The Fatimids (Shiite Muslims) defeat King Baldwin I of Jerusalem at Ramleh. On May 28, Baldwin defeats the Fatimids (Shiite Muslims) at Jaffa.
- July 26 Władysław I Herman, Duke of Poland, dies; he is succeeded by his sons, Zbigniew and Bolesław III, jointly. The latter begins to reconquer Pomerania.

1103

- Simon, Count of Sicily dies; he is succeeded by his brother, Roger II.

- The Norman prince Bohemond I is ransomed from the Turkish emir of Sebastea in the spring and resumes his rule at Antioch.

April 27   Anselm, archbishop of Canterbury, begins his second exile from England after quarreling with King Henry I.

July 11   Following the death of King Erik I the Good of Denmark there is an interregnum until 1105.

August 24   King Magnus III Barelegs of Norway is defeated and killed at Moycoba while invading Ulster, Ireland; he is succeeded by his sons, Eysten I, Olaf IV, and Sigurd I.

1104

- Danishmend, the founder of the Danishmend Turkish dynasty of eastern Anatolia, dies; he is succeeded by his son Ghazi.

- King Philip I of France is absolved from excommunication on promising to part from his mistress Bertrada and take back his legitimate wife Bertha. He also accepts the papacy's ban on the investiture of bishops by lay rulers.

January 1   A civil war ends with the Seljuk sultan Barkiyaruq ceding Mesopotamia and Syria to his brother Mohammad I; a third brother, Sanjar, already holds Khorasan.

May 5   King Baldwin I of Jerusalem takes the port of Acre (present-day Akko, Israel) from the Fatimids (Shiite Muslims).

May 5   Prince Bohemond I of Antioch and Count Baldwin II of Edessa are defeated by the Danishmend Turks when attempting to take the fortress of Harran in Syria.

September 28   King Pedro I of Aragon and Navarre dies; he is succeeded by his brother, Alfonso I.

December 12   Fearful that the continuing conflict with the papacy is undermining royal authority, King Henry V of Germany revolts against his father, Emperor Henry IV.

1105

- A military arsenal is established at Venice.
- After an interregnum, Niels succeeds his brother, the late Erik I the Good, as king of Denmark.

August 27   King Baldwin I of Jerusalem defeats the Fatimids (Shiite Muslims) in the third battle of Ramleh, ending their attempts to reconquer Palestine.

November 18   Imperial sympathizers among the Roman aristocracy elect Sylvester IV as pope in opposition to Paschal II.

December 12   Emperor Henry IV is captured and imprisoned in Mainz, capital of the Rhineland palatinate, Germany, by his son King Henry V of Germany who is in rebellion against him, fearing that the conflict with the papacy is undermining royal authority.

December 28   Raymond IV, Count of Toulouse, dies while besieging Tripoli, one of the few major Muslim strongholds remaining on the Syrian coast.

December 31   Emperor Henry IV abdicates in favor of his son, King Henry V of Germany.

1106

- Count Lothair of Supplinburg becomes Duke of Saxony.

September 9   Yūsuf ibn-Tashfin, the Almoravid emir of Morocco and Muslim Spain, dies; he is succeeded by his son Ali.

September 28   King Henry I of England defeats and captures his brother Robert Curthose, Duke of Normandy, at the Battle of Tinchebrai in Normandy. Robert is imprisoned and Henry becomes Duke of Normandy as well as king of England.

1107

- A civil war in Poland ends with Duke Zbigniew recognizing the supremacy of his brother and coruler Duke Bolesław III.
- Borivoj II, Duke of Bohemia, is deposed and succeeded by Svátopulk, Lord of Olmütz.

January 8   King Edgar of Scotland dies in Edinburgh, Scotland; he is succeeded by his brother, Alexander I.

July 7   Kilij Arslan I, Sultan of Rūm, is drowned in the River Khabur during a battle with the Seljuk Turks, from whom he has recently taken the city of Mosul; he is succeeded by his brother, Malik Shah.

October 9   Prince Bohemond I of Antioch invades the Byzantine Empire, at Avlona, and unsuccessfully attempts to take the port of Durazzo (in modern Albania).

1108

- King Coloman of Hungary grants his newly acquired kingdom of Croatia constitutional independence from Hungary.

May 29   King Alfonso I of Aragon and Navarre is defeated by Ali, the Almoravid emir of Morocco and Muslim Spain, at Uclés, near Tarancón.

July 29   King Philip I of France dies. He is succeeded by his son, Louis VI, who has, in practice, been ruling the country on behalf of his father for several years already.

September 9   Following his defeat by the Byzantines at Durazzo (in modern Albania), Prince Bohemond I of Antioch agrees the Treaty of Devol with the Byzantine emperor Alexius I Comnenus; Bohemond becomes a vassal of the emperor and recognizes Byzantine sovereignty over his principality of Antioch.

1109

March 3   After King Henry I of England refuses to perform homage as Duke of Normandy, King Louis VI of France challenges him to individual combat; Henry refuses.

April 14   Fulk Rechin, Count of Anjou, dies; he is succeeded by his son, Fulk V le Jeune.

June 30   King Alfonso VI of Castile and León dies; he is succeeded by his daughter Urracca, the wife of King Alfonso I of Aragon and Navarre, who begins to style himself "Emperor of the Spains."

July 12   The Fatimid stronghold of Tripoli surrenders to King Baldwin I of Jerusalem.

SCIENCE, TECHNOLOGY, AND MEDICINE

Agriculture

1106

- The bishop of Bremen, Germany, grants Dutch farmers the rights to any land around Bremen, provided that they are able to reclaim it from the waters.

1108

- The first embankments are built on the Red River of Dai Viet in order to protect the rice fields from being flooded. The Red River delta is one of the few regions outside South China and Japan where rice cultivation will be developed intensively.

Ecology

1104

- The Mt. Hekla volcano in Iceland erupts violently, devastating farmland as far as 70 kilometers away. Its continued eruptions over the coming centuries lead to a belief that it is the gateway to hell itself.

Health and Medicine

c. **1100**

- A method is discovered for the distillation of medicinal alcohol, probably at the great medical school of Salerno in southern Italy.

1102

- The new Sung dynasty emperor Hai-tsung introduces a public medical service in China.

1108

- The *Chêng lei pên ts'ao*, an illustrated Chinese encyclopedia of *materia medica* (plants and substances for the preparation of medicines), is produced by an unknown author.

Math

1100

- English scholar Robert of Chester translates the 9th-century *Astronomical Tables* by the Muslim astronomer al-Khwârizmi into Latin.

Science

1100

- The poet and physician Odo of Meung writes *De viribus herbarum/On the Power of Herbs*, a herbal derived from classical sources. Written in verse as an *aide mémoire*, it becomes extremely popular.

1108

- The French-born Prior Walcher of Malvern Abbey, England, compiles tables mapping the movements of the moon in the period 1036–1112. This is the earliest European attempt at such a difficult astronomical feat.

Technology

1100

- Theophilus of Essen (a pseudonym) writes his encyclopedia of arts and crafts *Schedula diversarum artium/List of Diverse Arts*, which describes various metallurgical and chemical techniques such as bell-founding and the making of stained glass.

1103

- The first recorded use of fireworks occurs, in China.

1105

- The Chinese build a cast iron pagoda 28 m/78 ft high, with each level cast from a single piece. It is the largest cast iron structure built so far.

1107

- The Chinese government manufactures banknotes printed in six different colors, using a series of printing blocks for different elements of the design.

Transportation

1100

- The canoe is being used regularly by Native Americans.

ARTS AND IDEAS

Architecture

c. **1105**

- Construction begins on the domed cathedral of Angoulême in France.
- Kyanzittha builds the temple of Anantapanna (or Ananda) at Pagan, Burma (modern Myanmar). The temple is considered the greatest work of Burmese architecture.

1107

- The central tower of Winchester Cathedral, England, collapses. Rib vaults are introduced in its replacement building.

Arts

c. **1100**

- Chang-Tse-tuan paints his great scroll painting *Life on the River on the Eve of the Qingming Festival*, showing daily life in the Chinese city of Suzhou.

1104

- Mi Fei becomes a professor of painting and calligraphy. One of the outstanding figures in Chinese art, he pioneers an atmospheric landscape style using washes.

Literature and Language

1100

c. 1100 Old English, the common language of England, with strong roots in the Germanic languages of the early invaders, begins to be replaced by Middle English. Middle English embodies the Northern European origins of English, but is also starting to reflect the influence of Latin and Norman French.

- French scholar Hugues de St. Victor writes his *Didascalion*, an encyclopedia including chapters on weaving, armaments, navigation, hunting, and theater, as well as more abstract philosophical subjects.

SOCIETY

c. 1106

- Pedro Alfonsi of Spain writes his *Disciplina clericalis/ Clerical Discipline*, a popular collection of tales which are derived principally from Arab sources.

1107

- Daniel of Kiev, the earliest Russian travel writer, writes an account of his pilgrimage to Jerusalem in the period 1106–07.

Music

c. 1100

- The often noble *troubadours* (lyric poets) of northern France and *trouvères* (poets with a narrative style) of southern France emerge, the subject of their songs usually being courtly love. Guillaume IX, Duke of Aquitaine, is the earliest *troubadour* whose works have survived.

Thought and Scholarship

1100

- *Gesta Francorum et aliorum Hierosolimitanorum/The Deeds of the French and other Pilgrims to Jerusalem*, an anonymous chronicle of the First Crusade, is written.

1109

- Aelnoth dedicates his *Historia sancti Canuti/History of St. Canute* to Niels of Denmark.

Education

1108

- French theologian and philosopher William of Champeaux founds a theological school in the abbey of St. Victor, Paris, France.

Everyday Life

1102

- Anselm, the archbishop of Canterbury, criticizes the fashions of the court. Men are wearing beards and long curled hair, and are adopting an "effeminate" style in their dress. Women's dresses have voluminous wide sleeves. Shoes are pointed, often curling up at the toes.

Religion

1103

- Pope Paschal II sends a legate to reform the Polish church.

1104

- The archbishopric of Lund is created in Denmark, the first in Scandinavia.

BIRTHS & DEATHS

1100

c. 1100 Peter Lombard, bishop of Paris, author of *Four Books of Sentences*, one of the main theological works during the Middle Ages, born in Novara, Lombardy (–*c.* 1160).

- Adrian IV (original name Nicholas Breakspear), the only English pope 1154–59, born in Abbot's Langley, near St. Albans, Hertfordshire, England (–1159).

August 2 William II, King of England 1087–1100, is killed, possibly by accident, while hunting near Lyndhurst, Hampshire.

1101

- Su Tung-p'o, Chinese writer, painter, and calligraphist, who tried to break with the conventions of classical Chinese poetry, dies (66).

June 22 Roger I Guiscard, Count of Sicily 1072–1101, who instituted a centralized and efficient government, dies in Mileto, Italy (*c.* 70).

July 27 King Conrad II of Germany, the rebel son of Emperor Henry IV, dies in Florence, Italy (*c.* 49).

October 6 St. Bruno the Carthusian, founder of the Carthusian order,

dies in La Torre monastery, Calabria, Italy (*c.* 71).

1102

- Empress Matilda (or Maud), daughter of King Henry I of England, consort of Emperor Henry V, thereafter claimant to the English throne, born in London, England (–1167).

1103

- Isaac al-Fez (Alphesi), Jewish Talmudic scholar and founder of a rabbinic academy in Lucena, Spain, dies in Lucena, Spain (*c.* 90).

- Joannes Afflacius the Saracen of Salerno, Italian physician and writer of various medical treatises and translations from classical sources, including *De febris et urinis* on the subject of fevers, dies.

1105

- Alexander III (original name Rolando Bandinelli), pope 1159–81, a vigorous defender of papal authority against the Holy Roman Emperor Frederick I Barbarossa and Henry II of England, born in Siena, Italy (–1181).

- Solomon ben Isaac (Rashi), an influential commentator on the Bible

and the Talmud, dies at Troyes, France.

1106

August 7 Henry IV, German king 1054–1106 and emperor 1084–1106, son of Henry III, dies in Liège, Lorraine, France (55).

1107

January 8 Edgar, King of Scotland 1097–1107, son of Malcolm III Canmore and Queen Margaret (granddaughter of Edmund II of England), the first Anglo-Celtic Scottish sovereign, dies in Edinburgh, Scotland (*c.* 32).

1109

April 21 St. Anselm of Canterbury, founder of scholasticism, dies, probably in Canterbury, England (*c.* 73).

April 29 St. Hugh of Cluny (original name Hugues de Semur), Abbot of Cluny, dies in Cluny, France (*c.* 85).

1107

August 8 King Henry I of England and Anselm, archbishop of Canterbury, settle their disagreement over the investiture of bishops at the synod of Westminster: Henry agrees to end lay investiture (investiture by a lay ruler).

Sports

c. **1100**

- *Jeu de paume*, a handball game and the forerunner of real tennis, is first played in France by monks in monastery cloisters; it is later taken up and played on courts by the French monarchy and aristocracy but it is not played with rackets until around 1500.
- The board game drafts evolves in Europe, possibly in southern France.

1110–1119

POLITICS, GOVERNMENT, AND ECONOMICS

Politics and Government

1110

- Basil, leader of the Bulgarian heretics, the Bogomils, is burned at the stake in Constantinople by order of the Byzantine emperor Alexius.
- Civil war breaks out in Bohemia after its duke, Svátopulk, is murdered.
- Emperor Henry V of Germany invades Poland on behalf of the exiled Polish Duke Zbigniew and is defeated near Wrocław by Duke Bolesław III of Poland. Zbigniew is subsequently permitted to return from exile and Bolesław has him killed.
- Rebels in the Spanish kingdom of León declare Alfonso I of Aragon and Navarre to be their king; he imprisons his wife Urracca, the legitimate ruler, but she is rescued.

August 8 Emperor Henry V of Germany begins his first military expedition to Italy in connection with the "Investiture Contest" (conflict between the papacy and the Empire over lay investiture of senior churchmen).

December 4 The port of Sidon (present-day Saida) surrenders to King Baldwin I of Jerusalem and Norwegian crusaders under King Sigurd I.

1111

- According to tradition, the Aztecs under their tribal leader-deity Huitzilopotchtli leave their homeland in northwest Mexico and begin their migration toward the Valley of Mexico.
- Amadeus III, marquis of Maurienne, is made Count of Savoy by Emperor Henry V of Germany.

- The Russian princes led by Vladimir II Monomakh win a decisive victory over the Cuman nomads at Salnitsa.
- Vladislav, the brother of the deposed Duke Borivoj II, is recognized as Duke of Bohemia in the settlement following his defeat by Bolesław III, Duke of Poland, who invaded in support of Vladislav's brother, Soběslav.

February 2 Prince Bohemond I of Antioch dies in Apulia, Italy; his nephew, Tancred, continues to rule in Antioch.

February 4 In a meeting in Sutri, Italy, Pope Paschal II tries to settle the "Investiture Contest" by offering to surrender all church lands in Germany to Emperor Henry V of Germany if he will renounce the practice of lay investiture (investiture by lay rulers). Henry accepts Paschal's offer, knowing that it is unworkable, and opposition by the German bishops, who will lose their wealth and status, ensures that it is never enforced.

February 21 Roger, the Norman Duke of Apulia, dies; he is succeeded by his son, William I.

April 12 Emperor Henry V of Germany forces Pope Paschal II to concede to him the right to invest bishops by threatening to recognize the antipope Sylvester IV. Henry then orders Sylvester to abdicate. The next day, Paschal formally crowns Henry as emperor in Rome. He has held the title unofficially since 1106.

October 26 King Alfonso I of Aragon and Navarre defeats the supporters of his repudiated wife Urracca, Queen of León, at Campo de Espina.

1112

- During Lent, Pope Paschal II withdraws his concession of April 1111 to Emperor Henry V of Germany, by which he allowed Henry to invest bishops.
- King Henry I of England suppresses a Norman rebellion and imprisons Robert of Bellême, its leader.
- Queen Urracca of León has her son, Alfonso, proclaimed as king of Galicia.
- Raymond Berengar III (also known as Ramon Berenguer), Count of Barcelona, gains possession of the county of Provence.

- Tancred, Prince of Antioch, dies; he is succeeded by another Norman, Roger of Salerno.
- **1112–67** During the reign of King Alaungsithu, the Burmese kingdom of Pagan reaches the peak of its political and cultural influence.
- **May 5** Henry of Burgundy, the first Count of Portugal, dies; he is succeeded by his son Alfonso Henriques.
- **September 9** A French synod under Archbishop Guido of Vienne declares lay investiture (investiture of senior churchmen by lay rulers) to be heretical and excommunicates Emperor Henry V of Germany.

1113

- A Saxon rebellion against Emperor Henry V of Germany is defeated at the Battle of Warmstadt.
- Raymond Berengar III, Count of Barcelona, and the Pisans begin their conquest of the Balearic Islands from the Moors.
- **March 3** By the Treaty of Gisors, King Louis VI of France recognizes King Henry I of England's overlordship of Brittany and Maine.
- **April 16** Sviatopolk II of Kiev dies; riots ensue in the city and Vladimir II Monomakh, the victor of Salnitsa in 1111, succeeds by general invitation.

1114

- King Coloman of Hungary, who has made his kingdom the dominant power in the Balkans by conquering Dalmatia, Croatia, and Herzegovina, dies. He is succeeded by his son, Stephen II.
- The Duke of Bohemia is recorded, for the first known time, as hereditary cupbearer to the emperor and thus one of the empire's foremost princes.
- **January 7** Emperor Henry V of Germany marries Matilda, the daughter of King Henry I of England.
- **October 1** Emperor Henry V of Germany is defeated by rebel Rhinelanders at Andernach.
- **October 25** After Pope Paschal II declares their marriage uncanonical, King Alfonso I of Aragon and Navarre and Queen Urracca of Castile and León are separated at the council of Palencia. However, Alfonso keeps Aragonese garrisons in some cities in Castile and León for several years afterwards.

1115

- A-ku-ta, leader of the Juchen (or Jurchen, a Tungusic pastoralist people in Manchuria), rebels against his overlords, the Khitans (Qitans) of Liao, and declares himself emperor, with the Chinese dynastic name of "Jin."
- The Christian conquest of the Balearic Islands from the Moors is completed; Raymond Berengar III, Count of Barcelona, takes possession of the islands of Majorca and Ibiza.
- The Venetians partially suppress a revolt against their rule in Dalmatia.
- **February 11** Duke Lothair of Saxony rebels against Emperor Henry V and defeats him at Welfesholz.
- **July 24** Matilda, Countess of Tuscany, dies. She bequeaths her lands to Emperor Henry V of Germany, setting aside a previous bequest to the papacy.
- **November 11** A popular uprising in Mainz, Germany, forces Emperor Henry V to release its archbishop, Adalbert, a supporter of the Saxon rebellion against the emperor, from three years of imprisonment.

1117

- King Henry I of England fights in Normandy to suppress a rebellion led by his nephew William Clito, son of the imprisoned Robert Curthose, his elder brother and former Duke of Normandy, who is supported by King Louis VI of France.
- Malik Shah, Sultan of Rūm, dies; he is succeeded by his nephew Ma'sud I, son of the former sultan Kilij Arslan.
- Ordelafo Falieri, Doge of Venice, is killed in battle; he is succeeded by Domenico Micheli.
- **March 3** Pope Paschal II flees from Rome as Emperor Henry V of Germany approaches and enters the city.

1118

- Inge II succeeds as king of Sweden.
- Prince Sanjar of Khorasan becomes supreme Seljuk sultan on the death of Mohammad I.
- Roger II, Count of Sicily, makes his first attempt to capture the city of Tunis in North Africa.
- The Byzantine emperor Alexius I Comnenus establishes a form of feudalism in the Byzantine Empire by granting estates conditional upon military service (known as *pronoia*).
- **January 18** Emperor Henry V of Germany leaves Rome, enabling Pope Paschal II to return.
- **January 24** John of Gaeta is elected as Pope Gelasius II following the death of Pope Paschal II.
- **April 2** King Baldwin I of Jerusalem dies; he is succeeded by Baldwin II, Count of Edessa.
- **April 7** Pope Gelasius II, in exile in Capua, Italy, excommunicates Emperor Henry V of Germany.
- **August 8** Threatened with deposition by the nobles, Emperor Henry V returns to Germany from Italy.
- **August 15** The Byzantine emperor Alexius I Comnenus dies; he is succeeded by his son, John II.
- **December 19** King Alfonso I of Aragon and Navarre captures the city of Zaragoza in northeast Spain from the Muslim ruler of the Almoravids.

1119

- Ballal Sen, King of East Bengal, is said to have reorganized the Indian caste system.
- **February 2** Guy, archbishop of Vienne, is elected as Pope Calixtus II following the death of Pope Gelasius II.
- **June 28** On the "Field of Blood" near Aleppo, Syria, the Norman army of Antioch is destroyed by Ghazi, the Danishmend emir. Though Roger of Salerno, Prince of Antioch, is killed in the battle, Ghazi does not follow up his victory.
- **August 20** King Louis VI of France, fighting in support of William Clito's claim to the duchy of Normandy, is defeated by King Henry I of England, Clito's uncle, at Brémule.
- **October 29** Pope Calixtus II renews the excommunication of Emperor Henry V of Germany, at Reims, France.
- **November 20** Mediation by Pope Calixtus II results in King Louis VI of France recognizing King Henry I of England's claim to the duchy of Normandy and ending his support for William Clito, Henry's nephew.

SCIENCE, TECHNOLOGY, AND MEDICINE

Math

1114–85

- Indian mathematician Bhaskara produces *Lilavati/The Beautiful*, about arithmetic, and *Bijaganita/Seed Arithmetic*, about algebra.

Science

1110

- The Spanish astronomer Pedro Alfonsi visits the court of King Henry I of England, bringing Islamic astronomical knowledge to Christian scholars such as Walcher, prior of Malvern Abbey.
- The text *Anatomia porci/The Anatomy of the Pig* describes the dissection of a pig in the medical school at Salerno, Italy. With human dissection still forbidden by the church, it becomes a valuable reference.
- The text *Mappae clavicula/Small Key to Maps* contains the earliest known account of the preparation of alcohol, and various metallurgical, alchemical, and engineering techniques.

1111

- The Persian ascetic theologian and Sufi mystic Al-Ghazzāli inspires Muslim intolerance to science, despite being a former academic himself. This leads to the decline of science in Islamic lands.

1119

- Guido the Geographer writes his *Geographica*, an encyclopedia including maps of Italy and the world.

Transportation

1117

- The Chinese scholar Chu Yü writes *Pingchow Table Talk*, which contains the earliest Chinese reference to the use of a compass for navigation at sea.

ARTS AND IDEAS

Architecture

1115

- A fourth Cistercian house is founded at Clairvaux, France, by St. Bernard, who becomes its abbot.

1117

- Following its destruction in an earthquake, Parma Cathedral, Italy, is rebuilt with a huge crypt similar to the one at Speyer Cathedral in Germany.

Arts

1115

- The richly carved tympanum above the doorway of the abbey church of Moissac, France, signals the revival of sculpture in western Europe.

Literature and Language

1115

- Guibert of Nogent writes his autobiography *De vita sua/On His Life*, which contains many details of contemporary customs.

BIRTHS & DEATHS

1111
December 18   Al-Ghazālī (Algazel), Muslim theologian and mystic, whose *Ihyā'Ulum al-Dīn/The Revival of the Religious Sciences* helped make Sufism an acceptable part of orthodox Islam, dies in Tūs, Persia (*c.* 53).

1113
August 24   Geoffrey Plantagenet, Count of Anjou, initiator of the Royal House of Plantagenet which produced 14 kings of England, born (–1151).

c. **1114**
- Gerard of Cremona, scholar and translator of classical Greek and Arabic texts into Latin, born in Cremona, Lombardy, Italy (–1187).

1115
- St. Ivo, bishop of Chartres, writer of the "Panormia," an important contribution to the development of canon law, dies in Chartres, France.
July 8   Peter the Hermit, religious leader, ascetic, and monastic founder, one of the main initiators of the First Crusade, dies in Neufmoustier, near Huy, Flanders (*c.* 65).

1117
July 15   Anselm of Laon, influential scholastic theologian chiefly known for his biblical commentary, dies in Laon, France.

1118
c. 1118   St. Thomas Becket, chancellor of England 1155–62 and archbishop of Canterbury 1162–70, born in Cheapside, London (–1170).
January 21   Pope Paschal II dies in Rome (*c.* 58).
August 15   Alexius I, Byzantine emperor 1081–1118, who was emperor during the First Crusade and who united the empire, dies in Constantinople (*c.* 70).

1119
January 29   Pope Gelasius II dies at the monastery of Cluny in Burgundy.

Thought and Scholarship

c. 1111
- Guibert of Nogent writes his history of the First Crusade, *Gesta dei per Francos/The Deeds of God through the Franks*.

1112
- The final version of the earliest Russian chronicle, *The Tale of Bygone Years* by Nestor of Kiev, is recorded.

1115
- Hugh of St. Victor enters the abbey of St. Victor in Paris, France. One of the great scholars of the age, he makes the school of St. Victor a great center of learning.

SOCIETY

Education

1110
- Theobald of Etampes is the earliest known teacher at Oxford, England.

1113
- French scholastic philosopher Peter Abelard opens a school for the study of rhetoric, philosophy, and theology in Paris, France.

1115
- Bernard, Chancellor of Chartres cathedral, France, reorganizes its school.

Everyday Life

c. 1110
- The great international fairs of Champagne in France, at Bar-sur-Aube and Troyes, date from this time. They are intended to promote trade in goods.

c. 1115
- King Henry I of England establishes a menagerie at Woodstock; it features lions, camels, and leopards.

Religion

1112
- The monastic order of Savigny is founded. This is later integrated into the Cistercian order.

1113
- St. Bernard enters the monastery of Cîteaux, near Dijon, France.

1114
- Many Paulicians (members of a Christian sect who profess a dualist nature) convert to orthodoxy following disputations with Alexius, the Byzantine emperor, at Philippopolis (in modern Bulgaria).

1118

March 8   Emperor Henry V of Germany has Maurice Bourdin, archbishop of Braga, elected as Pope Gregory VIII and installs him in Rome, forcing the recently elected Pope Gelasius II to flee.

1119
- Hugh de Payens founds the Knights Templar for the purpose of protecting pilgrims in the Holy Land.

December 23   Pope Calixtus II confirms the Cistercian rule *Carta Caritatis*.

1120–1129

POLITICS, GOVERNMENT, AND ECONOMICS

Politics and Government

1120
- King Alfonso I of Aragon and Navarre defeats the Muslims at Cutanda and Daroca.

- The Song Empire of China allies with the Juchen (or Jurchen, a Tungusic pastoralist people in Manchuria) against the Khitans (Qitans) of Liao.

November 25   William, the son and heir of King Henry I of England, is drowned when the *White Ship* is wrecked in the English Channel, on its way to England from Normandy.

1121

April 4   Pope Calixtus II captures the antipope Gregory VIII and imprisons him in a monastery.

September 29   In a diet (legislative assembly) at Würzburg, the Emperor Henry V of Germany makes peace with his German enemies.

November 27   Mohammad ibn-Tumart, the Berber prophet and leader of the Almohads of the Atlas Mountains, northwest Africa, is hailed as Mahdi (Muslim leader) by his followers and begins the conquest of the Almoravid territories in northwest Africa.

November 27 With the capture of the city of Stettin (modern Szczecin), Bolesław III, Duke of Poland, completes his conquest of Pomerania.

1122

- King David III of Georgia takes the city of Tbilisi (modern Tbilisi), the last surviving Muslim stronghold in Caucasia, and makes it his capital.
- The Byzantines exterminate the Pechenegs, a Turkish people settled in the area of modern Ukraine.

September 23 The "Investiture Contest" (conflict between the papacy and the empire over lay investiture of senior churchmen) finally ends with the Concordat at Worms, Germany, between Pope Calixtus II and Emperor Henry V of Germany. Henry agrees to end the practice of lay investiture but in practice is allowed to retain some influence over the election of bishops.

1123

- The Byzantine emperor John II Comnenus defeats the Serbians.
- William Clito, the nephew of King Henry I of England, leads another Norman rebellion against Henry.

April 18 King Baldwin II of Jerusalem is captured and his army destroyed in a surprise attack on his camp near Gargar, on the River Euphrates, by Balak of Khanzit, the nephew of the Danishmend emir Ghazi.

May 29 An invading Fatimid (Shiite Muslim) army flees back to Egypt when faced by the Frankish army of Jerusalem at Ibelin; the Venetians destroy the Fatimid fleet off Ascalon.

June 6 Balak of Khanzit, the nephew of the Danishmend emir Ghazi, takes the city of Aleppo, Syria, from the Seljuk Turks and becomes its independent ruler.

1124

- The Byzantine emperor John II Comnenus defeats the Hungarians.

1124–25 Lothair, Duke of Saxony, penetrates the lands of the pagan Wends as far as the lower River Oder and destroys their great temple at Retra.

April 22 King Alexander I of Scotland dies; he is succeeded by his brother, David I.

May 6 Balak, Emir of Aleppo, Syria, is killed while besieging a rebel governor in the castle of Menbij.

June 6 Following the death of his captor Balak of Khanzit, Emir of Aleppo, in May, King Baldwin II of Jerusalem is released for ransom.

July 7 The Fatimids (Shiite Muslims) surrender the city of Tyre to King Baldwin II of Jerusalem.

August 8 Emperor Henry V of Germany attempts to invade France as the ally of King Henry I of England, but retires as the French vassals respond to King Louis VI of France's summons to military service. Louis's success in exercising his feudal rights marks a major advance in the authority of the French monarchy.

December 15 Cardinal Teobaldo is elected Pope Celestine II, but before he can be ordained armed members of the Frangipani family storm the assembly and proclaim Cardinal Lamberto of Ostia as Pope Honorius II. Celestine is injured in the affray and resigns.

1125

- King Alfonso I of Aragon leads a spectacular raid deep into Moorish Spain, liberating the Mozarabs (Spanish Christians living under Muslim rule) of Granada and resettling them in the north of Iberia. Few Christians now remain under Muslim rule in Spain.
- King David III of Georgia dies, having established his kingdom as the major power in Caucasia and Armenia and ended its theoretical subjection to the Byzantine Empire. He is succeeded by his son, Demetrius I.
- The Khitan (Qitan) state of Liao collapses following the fall of its capital at Beijing, and the Juchen emperor A-ku-ta establishes the Jin dynasty in its place.
- Vladimir II Monomakh, Prince of Kiev, dies and is succeeded by his son, Mstislav I.
- Vladislav I, Duke of Bohemia, dies; he is succeeded by his brother Soběslav.

May 5 King Baldwin II of Jerusalem defeats il-Bursuqi, Emir of Mosul, at Azaz.

August 30 Lothair of Supplinburg, Duke of Saxony, is elected "king of the Romans" (king of Germany) as Lothair III by the German nobles.

1126

- King Alfonso I of Aragon and Navarre defeats the Muslims at Arinsol, near Lucena.
- The Juchen (or Jurchen, a Tungusic pastoralist people from Manchuria) besiege Kaifeng, the capital of the Chinese Song Empire, and are bought off with massive tribute, only to return a few months later when they capture the city along with Emperor Huizong and his son Qinzong, 3,000 courtiers, and the imperial treasury. Gaozong, a younger son of the emperor, escapes to reestablish the Song dynasty in southern China.
- Queen Urracca of Castile and León dies; she is succeeded by her son, Alfonso VII.

February 2 King Lothair III of Germany invades Bohemia on behalf of Otto of Kolmutz, who claims the duchy of Bohemia; Lothair is defeated at Kulm by Soběslav, whom he then recognizes as duke.

1127

- Imad ad-Din Zangi is appointed *atabeg* (governor) of Mosul in succession to il-Bursuqi; he becomes the Muslim champion against the Franks and founds the Zangid dynasty.
- King Louis VI of France dismisses his over-mighty vassal Etienne de Garlande, who holds the offices of seneschal and chancellor by hereditary right, so restoring royal control of appointments to the key offices of state.
- King Stephen II of Hungary invades Byzantine territory, taking the cities of Belgrade and Sofia.
- The Danishmend emir Ghazi captures Kayseri, Kastamonu, Malatya, and Ankara from the sultanate of Rūm.
- The oldest surviving charter of liberties is granted to a Flemish city, St.-Omer. However, it is probable that some other Flemish towns already have communes with powers of jurisdiction.

March 23 William Clito, the nephew of King Henry I of England, is appointed Count of Flanders by King Louis VI of France, but his claim is opposed by Thierry of Alsace.

July 20   William I, Duke of Apulia, dies without issue; his
   cousin Roger II, Count of Sicily, takes possession of the
   duchy.

December 18   King Lothair III of Germany's enemies in
   Germany elect Conrad III Hohenstaufen as a rival king.

1128

- Alfonso Henriques, Count of Portugal, gains control of
   his government by defeating the forces of his mother
   Teresa at St. Mamede, Portugal.

June 17   King Henry I of England's daughter Matilda,
   widow of the late emperor Henry V of Germany,
   marries Geoffrey Plantagenet, heir to the county of
   Anjou; she is recognized in England as her father's heir.

June 29   Conrad III Hohenstaufen, in rebellion against King
   Lothair III of Germany, is crowned king of Italy by his
   supporters.

July 27   William Clito, the nephew of King Henry I of
   England, is killed besieging Flemish rebels at Alost; King
   Louis VI of France then recognizes Thierry of Alsace,
   whom the Flemings, in revolt, have elected as their
   count.

August 22   Pope Honorius II invests Roger II, Count of
   Sicily, as Duke of Apulia.

1129

May 5   Fulk V le Jeune, Count of Anjou, joins King
   Baldwin II of Jerusalem and marries his daughter,
   Melisande; Fulk's son, Geoffrey Plantagenet, succeeds as
   Count of Anjou.

November 11   King Baldwin II of Jerusalem takes
   possession of the fortress of Banyas by arrangement
   with the Assassins (a militant offshoot of the Islamic
   Ismaili sect), but his attempt to seize the city of
   Damascus is repulsed.

December 17   Mohammad, the Almohad Mahdi (Muslim
   leader), dies; he is succeeded by Abd-al-Mu'min.

SCIENCE, TECHNOLOGY, AND MEDICINE

Ecology

1126

- A well drilled at the town of Lillers, in the Artois region
   of France, reaches water trapped under impermeable
   rock. Pressure causes the water to rise naturally, creating
   the first artesian well.

Health and Medicine

1127

- Stephen of Pisa writes *Liber regius/Royal Book*, which
   translates the work of the 10th-century Persian
   physician Ali ibn al-'Abbas (Haly Abbas), and
   introduces Arab and Greek medicine into the West.

Science

1120

- The Chinese scholar Chui-chung writes the treatise
   Pei-shan Chiu ching on the distillation of alcoholic
   spirits.
- The French-born Prior Walcher of Malvern Abbey,
   England, introduces the measurement of latitude and
   longitude in degrees, minutes, and seconds.

1121

- The Islamic scholar Al-Khāzinī writes his *Book of the
   Balance of Wisdom* on mechanics, hydrostatics, and
   physics, in which he develops a theory that gravity acts
   toward the center of the earth.

1126

- The English monk Adelard of Bath translates and adapts
   the 9th-century *Astronomical Tables* by the Muslim
   astronomer al-Khwarizmi. Inconsistencies in the original
   work will cause many problems for later European
   astronomers.

Technology

c. **1125**

- Tidal mills are built near the mouth of the River Adour,
   France, to take advantage of the flow of water
   constantly changing with the tides.

1126

- Gunpowder is first recorded in military use during the
   siege of Kaifeng, China, capital of the Chinese Sung
   dynasty. It is used by troops of the rival Jin dynasty.

ARTS AND IDEAS

Architecture

1120

- The construction of Périgueux Cathedral begins in
   Périgueux, France, modeled on San Marco in Venice.

c. 1120–30   Sculptor Master Gislebertus begins working at
   Autun Cathedral in Autun, France. His finest
   achievement is the tympanum over the west doorway.

1120–32   The abbey church of St. Madeleine in Vézelay,
   France, burns down. Its reconstruction commences and
   includes magnificent stone carvings.

1123

- The priory and hospital of St. Bartholomew is founded
   in Smithfield, London, England.

1125–30

- The nave of the abbey church at Cluny, France,
   collapses and is reconstructed with flying buttresses.

Literature and Language

1120

- The French canon Lambert of St.-Omer writes his *Liber
   floridus/Book of Flowers*, an encyclopedia dealing with
   metaphysical matters. This is to set the trend for

excluding references to astrology and magic from such books.

1123

- The accomplished poet Bishop Marbode of Rennes, France writes his *Liber lapidum/Book of Stones* on precious stones, written in hexameters.

c. 1125

- An Irish monk writes *Navigatio sancti Brandani/The Voyage of St. Brandon*, an account of the voyage of St. Brandon written in Anglo-Norman.

Thought and Scholarship

c. 1120

- Joannes Zonaras completes his *Historical Epitome*. One of the best of the Byzantine world chronicles, it covers the period from the creation to 1118.

c. 1122

- The theologian and philosopher Peter Abelard writes his *Sic et non/Yes and No*, a collection of seemingly contradictory statements from the Bible and the Christian Fathers, compiled in order to promote rational discussion.

1125

c. 1125   Ari Thorgilsson's chronicle *Islendingabók/Book of the Icelanders* is recorded.

1125–49   Raymond, archbishop of Toledo, Spain, organizes the translation into Latin of Arabic versions of the works of Aristotle.

1127

- Fulcher of Chartres completes his *Gesta Francorum Jherusalem peregrinantium/The Deeds of the French Pilgrims to Jerusalem*, a chronicle of the First Crusade and account of Jerusalem.

1128

- Al-Shahrastānī writes *Kitāb al-Milal w-al-Nihal/Book of Religions and Sects*, a comprehensive history of religions.
- James of Venice translates the Greek philosopher Aristotle's *Organon*.

SOCIETY

Education

1121

- French theologian and philosopher William of Champeaux, a founder of realist philosophy, becomes the first master of the cathedral school of Paris, France, to achieve wide fame.

Everyday Life

c. 1120

- The wimple, a fine veil worn by women over the head and wound round the shoulders, becomes fashionable in England.

Religion

1120

- St. Norbert of Xanten, Germany, a friend of St. Bernard of Clairvaux, France, founds the Premonstratensian Order of Conventual Canons.

June 3   Pope Calixtus II returns to Rome from France.

BIRTHS & DEATHS

1122
- Al-Harīri, author of 50 *maqāmāt* (picaresque stories) about the vagabond Abu Zaid, dies.

c. 1123
- Frederick I Barbarossa, German king and Holy Roman Emperor 1152–90, born (–1190).

1124
c. 1124   Eadmer, a monk and author from Canterbury, England, writer of *Historia novorum/History of New Things* (an English history) and *Vita sancti Anselmi/Life of St. Anselm* (a life of his friend St. Anselm), dies.
- Al-Hasan ibn-al-Sabbah, founder of the Assassins (a militant offshoot of the Islamic Ismaili sect), dies.

April   Alexander I, King of Scotland 1107–24, brother of Edgar, son of Malcolm III Canmore and Queen

Margaret (granddaughter of Edmund II of England), dies, probably in Stirling, Scotland (c. 44).
December 13   Pope Calixtus II (Guy of Burgundy) dies in Rome.

1125
- Vladimir II Monomakh, Prince of Kiev 1113–25, writer of *Testament*, a brief autobiography in Russian containing prayers, quotations, and advice on good government, dies in Kiev (c. 72).
May 23   Henry V, German king 1099–1125 and emperor 1111–25, the last emperor of the Salian dynasty, dies in Utrecht, in the modern Netherlands (38).

1126
- Abu'l-Walīd ibn-Rushd (Averroës) of Córdoba, influential Muslim philosopher who wrote important

commentaries on the works of Aristotle and Plato, born in Córdoba, Spain (–1198).

1127
c. 1127   Frau Ava, the first woman to write in Old High German and the author of didactic and religious poems, dies.
March 2   Charles the Good, Count of Flanders, is murdered; he has no heirs.

1129
- Shirakawa, 72nd emperor of Japan (1072–1086) who abdicated the throne to form an *insei*, or cloister government, through which he could rule without the encumbrances of ceremony, dies in Kyoto, Japan (76).

1121

- The philosopher and theologian Peter Abelard is condemned at the council of Soissons, France, for promoting erroneous opinions on the subject of the Trinity.

1123

March 18–April 5   Pope Calixtus II holds the first general council of the church in Western Europe (the first Lateran council), which condemns simony (the buying and selling of church benefits) and the marriage of

priests. He also sends a legate to complete the organization of the Polish church.

1124

- Otto, bishop of Bamberg, Germany, begins his mission to convert western Pomerania to the Catholic faith.

1126

- St. Bernard of Clairvaux, France, writes the sermon "On the Love of God."

1127

- The conversion to Christianity of the Wends (a Slavonic people) is resumed.

◆

1130–1139

POLITICS, GOVERNMENT, AND ECONOMICS

Politics and Government

1130

- King Alfonso I of Aragon and Navarre briefly takes the city of Bordeaux, France.
- Sverker I is elected king of Sweden on the death of Inge II.
- The pipe roll of the English Exchequer for 1129–30 is the earliest surviving example of an administrative record kept annually.
- Yeh-lü Ta-shih, a surviving member of the ruling Khitan (Qitan) dynasty of Liao, founds the Kara-Khitai (or western Liao) Empire in east Turkestan.

February 2   Prince Bohemond II of Antioch and his army, en route to attack the Armenians, are massacred by the Danishmend Turks on the Jihan.

February 13   Following the death of Pope Honorius II, both Gregory Papareschi (as Innocent II) and Peter Pierleoni (as Anacletus II) are elected pope by different factions among the cardinals; Innocent is forced to leave Rome.

March 26   King Sigurd I of Norway dies; he is succeeded jointly by his son Magnus IV the Blind and Harold IV Gille, the grandson of Magnus III Barelegs.

September 27   Roger II, Count of Sicily and Duke of Apulia, undertakes to recognize Anacletus II as pope in return for Anacletus making him king of Sicily and Apulia.

December 25   Roger II, Count of Sicily and Duke of Apulia, is crowned as king of Sicily.

1131

- Dai Viet repulses an invasion by the Khmer emperor Suryavarman II.
- Magnus the Strong, the son of King Niels of Denmark, murders the popular duke Knud Lavard; civil war breaks out when Knud's son Erik Emune seeks revenge against Magnus.
- Stephen II, reputedly Hungary's worst king, abdicates (dying shortly afterwards) in favor of his cousin Béla II.

March 22   King Lothair II of Germany meets Pope Innocent II at Liège and recognizes him as pope.

August 21   King Baldwin II of Jerusalem dies; he is succeeded by his son-in-law Fulk V le Jeune of Anjou.

September 8   The English barons confirm their allegiance to Matilda, the daughter of King Henry I of England, as Henry's heir.

October 25   Louis, the son of King Louis VI of France, is crowned as king by Pope Innocent II at Reims, France; he rules with his father as joint king.

1132

- King Roger II of Sicily withdraws from Rome in the summer to suppress a rebellion in Apulia, so allowing the supporters of Pope Innocent II to gain control and expel Pope Anacletus II.
- Prince Mstislav I of Kiev dies; he is succeeded by his brother, Jaropolk II.

September 9   King Lothair II of Germany begins an expedition into Italy to restore Pope Innocent II to Rome.

1133

- Despite an initial defeat on the Sabbato, King Roger II of Sicily suppresses the revolt in Apulia.
- Pope Innocent II partitions the island of Corsica between Genoa and Pisa.
- The Danishmend emir Ghazi is awarded the title "malik" (king) by al-Mustarshid, the Abbasid caliph, and Sanjar, the Seljuk great sultan, as a reward for his victories over the Christians.

June 4   King Lothair II of Germany is crowned emperor by Pope Innocent II in Rome. As the supporters of the antipope Anacletus II hold St. Peter's, the coronation takes place in the Lateran palace.

June 4   Pope Innocent II grants metropolitan authority in Poland and Pomerania to Archbishop Norbert of Magdeburg.

August 8   Emperor Lothair II returns from Italy to Germany.

1134

- Emperor Lothair II grants the Margravate of Brandenburg to Albert I the Bear, known as the first margrave of Brandenburg.
- King Niels of Denmark is murdered at Schleswig by supporters of the popular duke Knud Lavard, who was murdered in 1131; he is succeeded by Erik II Emune.
- The Danishmend malik (king) Ghazi dies; he is succeeded by his son Mehmed.

July 17   King Alfonso I of Aragon and Navarre is defeated by the Muslims at Fraga.

September 7   King Alfonso I of Aragon and Navarre dies. He is succeeded in Aragon by his brother, Ramiro II, while Navarre recovers its independence under García

IV Ramirez, and Alfonso VII of Castile and León takes possession of Zaragoza.

1135

- The Chinese emperor Gaozong establishes Hangzhou as the capital of the Southern Song dynasty. His father Huizong, captured by the Juchen in 1127, dies in exile in Manchuria.

January 1   King Harold IV of Norway defeats and imprisons his joint king, Magnus IV.

March 3   In a diet (legislative assembly) at Bamberg, the "antiking" Conrad III Hohenstaufen and his son Frederick submit to Emperor Lothair II.

May 26   King Alfonso VII of Castile and León is acclaimed as emperor of Spain.

August 8   Emperor Lothair II makes peace between Poland and Bohemia, receiving homage from Bolesław III, Duke of Poland; he also settles a dispute over the succession to the Hungarian crown.

December 14   King Harold IV of Norway is murdered by his brother Sigurd; he is succeeded by his sons, Sigurd II and Inge I.

Anglo–Scottish Wars (1138–1357)

1138–1318

1138

August 22   In the Battle of the Standard, near Northallerton (in present-day North Yorkshire), English forces rout the invading army of King David I of Scotland.

1296

March 30   King Edward I of England takes the town of Berwick as he begins his campaign to subdue Scotland.

April 27   Edward I defeats the Scots at Dunbar, Scotland, in his campaign to subdue the country.

July 10   John de Balliol, King of Scotland, surrenders to King Edward I of England and abdicates.

August 8   Edward I returns from Scotland, bringing "the Stone of Destiny," on which Scottish kings are crowned, as a symbol of his conquest of Scotland, from Scone to Westminster Abbey, London, England.

1297

May 5   The Scottish nationalist William Wallace leads a Scottish rising against Edward I, burning an English castle and attacking one of the king's justiciars.

September 11   Wallace defeats the English forces, under Earl Warrene, at Stirling Bridge, Scotland.

1298

July 22   Edward I defeats the Scots under Wallace, at Falkirk, Scotland, but is unable to subdue the country.

1303

May 5   Edward I begins his seventh campaign in Scotland. The feudal levy is summoned to Berwick, where a military progress to Elgin commences.

1304

March 3   The Scots submit to King Edward I of England in a parliament at St. Andrews, Scotland.

1305

August 23   William Wallace is executed in London, England, as a traitor against Edward I, after having been betrayed and captured in Glasgow, Scotland. He is tried in Westminster Hall, London, and promptly hanged and quartered. His head is displayed on London Bridge.

1307

May 5   Robert I the Bruce, King of Scotland, returns from Ireland and defeats English forces in Ayrshire, Scotland.

July 7   Edward I dies whilst leading an army to Scotland. He is succeeded by his son, Edward II.

1314

June 24   Robert the Bruce inflicts a disastrous defeat on Edward II in the Battle of Bannockburn and so completes his expulsion of the English from Scotland.

1315

September 10   Edward Bruce, brother of Robert I the Bruce, King of Scotland, defeats English forces under the Earl of Ulster near Connor in Antrim, Ireland.

1317

February–May   Robert the Bruce joins his brother Edward Bruce, King of Ireland, to campaign in Ireland.

1318

October 14   Edward Bruce is defeated and killed by an Anglo-Irish force under John de Bermingham at Faughard, near Dundalk, Ireland.

1320–57

1320

April 26   The Declaration of Arbroath is signed, in which the earls and barons of Scotland announce to Pope John XXII their rejection of English rule and their loyalty to Robert I the Bruce, King of Scotland, stating that "it is not for glory, riches nor honors that we fight, but for freedom alone."

December 26   Stephen of Blois, nephew of the late king Henry I of England and grandson of William the Conqueror, is crowned as king of England.

1136

1136–37   Emperor Lothair II overruns Apulia and Calabria, meeting little opposition because the inhabitants simultaneously revolt against King Roger II of Sicily. Before leaving, Lothair and Pope Innocent II invest Rainulf of Alife as Duke of Apulia.

January 1   Gruffydd ap Cynan, King of Gwynedd, leads a rising against the Anglo-Normans in south Wales.

February 2   King Stephen of England cedes Cumberland to King David I of Scotland, who in return recognizes Stephen as king of England.

May 5   King Louis VI of France invests King Stephen of England as Duke of Normandy.

August 15   While assembling his army for his Italian expedition, Emperor Lothair II (probably) invests Henry the Proud, Duke of Bavaria, as Duke of Saxony, making him the most powerful prince in Germany.

1137

- King Gruffydd ap Cynan of Gwynedd, Wales, dies; he is succeeded by his son, Owain the Great.

- King Stephen of England successfully campaigns in Normandy against Geoffrey of Anjou, who claims the duchy.

- Ramiro II the Monk, King of Aragon, abdicates to become a monk and is succeeded by his daughter Petronilla. She marries Raymond Berengar III, Count of Barcelona, who becomes the effective ruler of the kingdom (though he never takes the title king).

July 4   By the Treaty of Tuy, Alfonso Henriques, Count of Portugal, recognizes the suzerainty of King Alfonso VII of Castile and León, Emperor of Spain.

July 22   Louis, the son of King Louis VI the Fat of France, marries the heiress Eleanor of Aquitaine.

August 1   King Louis VI the Fat of France dies; he is succeeded by his son, Louis VII.

August 8   King Fulk of Jerusalem surrenders the fortress of Montferrand to Imad ad-Din Zangi, the Muslim governor of Mosul, after a siege, but is allowed to go free.

August 8   King Louis VII of France is invested as Duke of Aquitaine.

August 29   The Byzantine emperor John II Comnenus conquers Lesser Armenia (Cilicia). He also besieges Antioch because he is keen to win the recognition of his

---

1322

October 14   King Robert I of Scotland (Robert the Bruce) defeats the English at Byland. Edward II narrowly avoids capture.

1328

March 17   Under the Treaty of Edinburgh, King Edward III of England makes peace with Scotland, recognizing Robert the Bruce as king of Scotland.

May 4   The Treaty of Edinburgh is ratified by King Edward III of England in the Treaty of Northampton.

1332

August 12   Edward, son of John Balliol, and other "disinherited" Scottish nobles make use of English support to defeat and kill the Earl of Mar, regent of Scotland, at Dupplin Moor.

September 24   Edward Balliol is crowned king of Scotland at Scone, Scotland.

December 12   Edward Balliol is defeated by the Earl of Moray at Annan, Scotland, and flees to England.

1333

May 5   Edward III joins Edward Balliol at the siege of the Scottish border town of Berwick.

June 8   Edward III orders the seizure of the Isle of Man from Scotland. The island is henceforth attached to England.

July 19   Edward III defeats the Scots at Halidon Hill when they attempt to relieve the siege of Berwick, Scotland.

July 20   The border town of Berwick surrenders to Edward III.

1334

June 12   By the Treaty of Newcastle upon Tyne, Edward Balliol recognizes Edward III as his overlord and cedes Berwick and eight shires of southern Scotland to England.

September 9   A fresh rising in Scotland forces Edward Balliol to flee to England.

1336

July 7   Edward III campaigns in the Highlands of Scotland.

November 11   Edward III makes his last visit to Scotland for the purpose of strengthening Edward Balliol's position.

1341

June 6   King David II returns to Scotland from France when his supporters succeed in expelling the English from Edinburgh, Scotland.

1342

March 31   On capturing Roxburgh, Scotland, the Scots complete their expulsion of the English from Scotland.

1346

October 17   David II invades England and is defeated and captured at Neville's Cross, outside Durham, England. His action helps to relieve the pressure placed on France by Edward III.

1356

January 20   Edward Balliol abdicates as king of Scotland, selling his claim to King Edward III of England who now invades as far as Edinburgh, Scotland.

1357

October 3   Under the Treaty of Berwick, King Edward III of England releases King David II of Scotland for a ransom and makes a truce for ten years. However, his time in England has set David at odds with the Scottish magnates.

suzerainty, but withdraws when its prince, Raymond of Poitiers, pays homage.

September 18   King Erik II Emude of Denmark is murdered; he is succeeded by Erik III, grandson of Erik I, who faces renewed civil war.

1138

- Bolesław III, Duke of Poland, dies following a defeat in Russia, ending a period of Polish expansion. His lands are partitioned by his sons, civil war follows, and Poland ceases to be a unified state for two centuries. The eldest son, Władysław II, becomes the first grand prince of Poland, with Kraków as his capital; he possesses Silesia and Pomerania and is, in theory, hereditary suzerain in all Polish lands.

January 25   The antipope Anacletus II dies. At the instigation of King Roger II of Sicily, Victor IV is elected to succeed him.

March 3   Conrad III Hohenstaufen is elected "king of the Romans" (king of Germany) by the German nobles as Conrad III. He is opposed by Henry the Proud, Duke of Bavaria and Saxony.

April 20   An attempt by the Byzantine emperor John II Comnenus to take the Syrian city of Aleppo is repulsed.

May 5   Robert, Earl of Gloucester, begins a civil war in England by declaring himself for the late King Henry I's daughter Matilda against King Stephen.

May 21   The Byzantine emperor John II Comnenus raises his siege at Shaizar when its emir promises to pay tribute; he then enters Antioch but leaves for Lesser Armenia (Cilicia) on the outbreak of anti-Byzantine riots.

May 29   The antipope Victor IV resigns and submits to Innocent II following the mediation of the French Cistercian abbot Bernard of Clairvaux.

June 6   'Imad ad-Din Zangi, the Muslim governor of Mosul, takes the city of Homs from the Turkish ruler of Damascus.

July 7   Conrad III Hohenstaufen, king of the Germans, divests Henry the Proud of the duchy of Saxony, but fails to expel him.

August 22   In the Battle of the Standard, near Northallerton (in present-day North Yorkshire), English forces rout the invading army of King David I of Scotland.

1139

- On the death of Prince Jaropolk II of Kiev, Vsevolod II seizes power. The surviving political unity of the Russian federation now finally collapses with the rivalry of princes for leadership and the provincial separatism of their subjects.

April 9   To buy peace with Scotland, King Stephen of England grants the earldom of Northumberland to King David I's son Henry at Durham, England.

June 6   King Stephen of England affronts English churchmen by his arrest of the bishops of Salisbury and Lincoln for supporting Matilda, the daughter of the late King Henry I.

July 22   Pope Innocent II is defeated and captured by King Roger II of Sicily on the River Garigliano.

July 25   Alfonso Henriques, Count of Portugal, defeats the Muslims at Ourique and is hailed as king of Portugal by his troops.

July 25   By the Treaty of Mignano, Pope Innocent II gains his liberty when he recognizes Roger II as king of Sicily.

September 30   The empress Matilda, widow of the late Holy Roman Emperor Henry V and daughter of the late King Henry I of England, comes to England to lead her partisans against King Stephen.

October 20   Henry the Proud, former Duke of Bavaria and Saxony, dies; his son Henry the Lion claims to succeed, but the king of the Germans, Conrad III Hohenstaufen, has granted Bavaria to Leopold IV of Austria and Saxony to Albert I the Bear of Brandenburg.

SCIENCE, TECHNOLOGY, AND MEDICINE

Agriculture

1130

- The earliest European reference to a breast strap harness for horses is recorded. This harness, an improvement on the earlier simple collar, further eases pressure on the horse's neck, allowing it to draw heavier loads.
- Wilster Marsh, east of the River Elbe, Germany, is reclaimed by Dutch farming settlers.

Health and Medicine

1130

- The physician Benevenutus Grassus writes his highly influential treatise *Practica oculorum/Practice of the Eyes*, on eye diseases.

1135

- The Persian Muslim physician Al-Jurjāni writes *The Treasure of the King of Khwarizm*, an immense medical encyclopedia.

Science

1130

- The English monk Adelard of Bath writes *Quaestiones naturales/Inquiries into Nature*, comprising a series of 76 dialogues discussing scientific topics such as botany, meteorology, zoology, and astronomy.

1136

- Silver-bearing ore is discovered at Freiburg in Saxony, southern Germany, triggering a "silver rush" in which Freiburg becomes a center for metallurgy.

1138

- The Muslim philosopher and astronomer al-Kharaqī writes *The Highest Understanding on the Division of Spheres*.

ARTS AND IDEAS

Architecture

1130

October 25 Pope Innocent II dedicates the abbey church at Cluny, France.

1131

- Construction work begins on Cefalù Cathedral in Sicily.

1132–43

- The Palatine Chapel in Palermo, Sicily, is constructed for King Roger II of Sicily. It combines Byzantine, Islamic, and Norman styles of architecture in a dazzling hybrid.

1134

- Construction begins on the north tower of Chartres Cathedral, Chartres, France. This is the first Gothic tower to be built.
- Construction work begins on Uppsala Cathedral in Sweden.

1135

1135–50 The Cistercian Fountains Abbey, near Ripon in Yorkshire, England, is constructed.

1135–1205 The Ulu Cami, a congregational mosque at Kayseri in central Persia, is constructed.

1137–40

- The new west front of St.-Denis in Paris, France, is built. The design and sculpture of its façade mark the beginning of Gothic architecture. Abbot Suger now begins a new east end, with Gothic vaulting and stained glass windows.

1139–47

- The abbey church at Fontenay, France, a good example of the simplicity of Cistercian architecture, is constructed.

Literature and Language

1130

- Norman poet Baudry de Bourgueil writes *Itinerarium/ Journey*, which records his travels in northern France and in England. He is also known for his verse letters written to Adela, daughter of William the Conqueror.

1136

- Spanish Muslim traveler al-Māzinī of Granada writes *Tuhfat al-Albāb*, which describes his recent visit to the Volga area of Russia.

Thought and Scholarship

1131

- While in prison awaiting execution, the great Sufi mystic philosopher 'Ain al-Qudāt al-Hamadhānī writes *Apologia*, a spiritual autobiography.

BIRTHS & DEATHS

1130

c. 1130 Richard de Clare, Earl of Pembroke (and Striguil), who initiated the conquest of Ireland with his invasion of the island in 1170, born (–1176).

- Henry III the Lion, Duke of Saxony 1142–80 and Bavaria (as Henry XII) 1156–80, vigorous supporter of the Holy Roman Emperor Frederick I Barbarossa, founder of the city of Munich, born (–1195).

February 13 Pope Honorius II (Lamberto dei Fagnani) dies in Rome.

1131

January 14 Valdemar I, King of Denmark 1157–82, who defeated the Wends (Slavs) and established the Valdemar dynasty, born in Denmark (–1182).

December 4 Omar Khayyām, Persian poet, mathematician, and astronomer, famous for his *Rubaiyat*, dies in Nishapur, Persia (83).

1133

- Henry II, King of England 1154–89, father of Richard I and John, born in Le Mans, France (–1189).

February 10 Robert II Curthose, Duke of Normandy 1087–1106, son of William I the Conqueror of England, dies in Cardiff, Wales (c. 80).

1134

March 28 St. Stephen Harding, Abbot of Cîteaux, a founder of the Cistercian Order, dies in Cîteaux, Burgundy (c. 74).

June 6 St. Norbert of Xanten, archbishop of Magdeburg, dies in Magdeburg, Saxony.

1135

- The former emperor of China, Huizong, a painter, calligrapher, and great patron of the arts, dies in Manchuria.

March 30 Moses ben Maimōn (or Maimonides), celebrated Jewish philosopher, jurist, and physician, born in Córdoba, Spain (–1204).

December 1 Henry I, King of England and Duke of Normandy 1100–35, son of William I the Conqueror, dies in Lyons-la-Forêt, Normandy, France (c. 66).

1137

- Ramanuja, Indian Braham and theologian, whose ideas had a major influence on Hinduism, dies in

Sriperumbudur, India (traditionally 120).

December 4 Lothair II, King of Germany 1125–37 and emperor 1133–37, dies in Breitenwang, Austria (62).

1138

- Abu-Bakribn-Bājjah (Avempace), Arab philosopher who was part of the Arabic Aristotelian–Neoplatonic tradition, dies.
- Saladin, Sultan of Egypt, Syria, Yemen, and Palestine 1171–1193, who successfully captured Jerusalem from the Franks during the Third Crusade, born in Takrit, Mesopotamia (–1193).
- The Greek historian Nicephorus Bryennius, joint writer of a history of the Byzantine Empire from 1070, dies.

1139

- Moses ben Ezra, Jewish poet, writer of a cycle of Hebrew poems, *Tarshīsh*, and a work in Arabic on Spanish-Hebrew poetry, *Kitāb al Muhādarah*, dies.

April 30 Rainulf of Alife, Duke of Apulia, dies.

c. 1137

- Geoffrey of Monmouth completes his *Historia Regum Britanniae/History of the Kings of Britain*, a largely apocryphal British history containing the stories of King Arthur, King Lear, and other mythical figures.

SOCIETY

Religion

1131

- St. Gilbert founds the Order of Sempringham, the only purely English order.

1139

1139–41 Gratian of Bologna compiles *Concordia discordantium canonum/Reconciliation of Opposing Canons* (known as the *Decretum*), a collection of around 4,000 texts which forms the first systematic codification of canonical law.

April 4 Pope Innocent II excommunicates King Roger II of Sicily for his support of the antipopes Anacletus II and Victor IV.

April 20 The church reformer Arnold of Brescia is condemned at the second Lateran council, in Rome, for his strict views on the priesthood.

1140–1149

POLITICS, GOVERNMENT, AND ECONOMICS

Human Rights

1144

- The murder of a young boy called William in Norwich, England, supposedly at the hands of Jews, leads to anti-Semitic persecution. The dead boy is later canonized by the church.

Politics and Government

1140

- Soběslav, Duke of Bohemia, dies; his nephew Vladislav II, son of Vladislav I, is elected as his successor.

April 4 The Saxons reject Albert I the Bear as their duke and refuse to surrender to Conrad III Hohenstaufen, king of the Germans.

December 12 Conrad III Hohenstaufen, king of the Germans, defeats Welf, duke of Saxony, Henry the Lion's uncle, in battle at Weinsberg; Welf is the leader of the opposition to Conrad's grant of Bavaria to Leopold IV of Austria. According to later tradition, the appellations of "Guelph" (Welf) and "Ghibelline" (Weibling, from the Hohenstaufen castle of Waiblingen) are derived from the battle cries of the opposing sides.

1141

- Qingui, chancellor of the Chinese Southern Song Empire and an exponent of peace with the Jin (Juchen) Empire, arranges the arrest and murder of the general Yuefei, the leader of the war party. The Southern Song then declare themselves vassals of the Jin and pay tribute.

February 2 Robert, Earl of Gloucester, defeats and captures King Stephen of England at Lincoln, England.

February 16 King Béla II of Hungary dies; he is succeeded by Géza II.

March 3 The empress Matilda, widow of the late emperor Henry V and daughter of the late king Henry I of England, is proclaimed queen of England, in Winchester, by her supporters.

September 9 The Seljuk sultan Sanjar is defeated on the Qatwan Steppe, at Samarkand, by the Kara-Khitai Turks who are establishing an empire stretching from China to the River Oxus (present-day Amu Darya) in central Asia.

November 1 King Stephen of England is released in exchange for Robert, Earl of Gloucester, the leader of the rival claimant Matilda's party, whom his partisans have captured; the civil war continues with neither party able to establish ascendancy.

1142

- On the death of the emir Mehmed, the Danishmend emirate is divided between his brothers Yagibasan and 'Ayn ad-Dawlah and his son Dhu an-Nun; Danishmend power goes into decline.

1142–43 France is placed under an interdict by Pope Innocent II because King Louis VII refuses to admit his candidate to the archbishopric of Bourges, France.

May 5 The civil war in Germany is brought to an end by a

diet (legislative assembly) in Frankfurt; Conrad III Hohenstaufen, king of the Germans, grants Saxony to Henry the Lion and Bavaria to Henry Jasomirgott, brother of Leopold IV of Austria.

September 25   The Byzantine emperor John II Comnenus reaches Baghras, after campaigning against the Seljuk Turks in Asia Minor; he sends Prince Raymond of Poitiers orders to surrender Antioch to him and when the latter refuses John plans a campaign against him.

1143

- Henry the Lion, Duke of Saxony, founds the German port of Lübeck as an outpost against the pagan Wends.
- King Alfonso VII of Castile and León, Emperor of Spain, recognizes Alfonso I as king of Portugal; Alfonso does homage to Pope Innocent II's legate, thus making Portugal a papal fief.
- Venice begins the formation of its communal institutions with the establishment of the *Consilium sapientium* ("Council of Wisdom"), an executive council to limit the powers of the doge.
- Vladislav II, Duke of Bohemia, defeats a rebellion with the help of his brother-in-law Conrad III Hohenstaufen, king of the Germans.

April 4   A republic is proclaimed by the Romans in rebellion against Pope Innocent II.

April 8   The Byzantine emperor John II Comnenus dies following a hunting accident. His planned attack on Antioch is abandoned as his son and successor Manuel I Comnenus faces a war of independence by the Armenians of Lesser Armenia (Cilicia) under Theodore II.

September 26   Pope Celestine II is elected following the death of Pope Innocent II.

November 10   King Fulk of Jerusalem dies; his widow, Melisande, assumes the government, with their young son, Baldwin III, as her colleague.

1144

- King Alfonso VII of Castile and León, Emperor of Spain, briefly takes Córdoba from the Almoravid Emirate.

March 12   Pope Lucius II is elected following the death of Pope Celestine II.

April 23   The conquest of Normandy by Geoffrey, Count of Anjou, is completed with the surrender of the capital Rouen.

October 10   Pope Lucius II negotiates a seven-year truce with King Roger II of Sicily, ending his encroachment on papal lands.

December 24   Imad ad-Din Zangi, the Muslim governor of Mosul, takes Edessa (Urfa) (in eastern Turkey) after a four-week siege; though he massacres the Frankish-inhabitants the native Armenian Christians are spared. The fall of the city calls for a new crusade.

1145

- The Khmer emperor Suryavarman II conquers the kingdom of Champa.

February 15   Bernard of Pisa is elected as Pope Eugenius III following the death of Pope Lucius II.

July 7   Abd-al-Mu'min, the Almohad Mahdi (Muslim leader), takes the port of Oran (in present-day Algeria) from the Almoravids.

1146

- George of Antioch, admiral of King Roger II of Sicily, takes Tripoli in North Africa; the Normans of Sicily hold it until 1152.
- Grand Prince Władysław II, attempting to reunite Poland under his rule, is defeated by his brothers Bolesław and Mieczysław and flees to Germany; Bolesław IV replaces him as grand prince.
- Prince Vsevolod II of Kiev dies; he is succeeded briefly by his brother Igor II, who is deposed by Isiaslav II, a distant relative.

March 1   Pope Eugenius III proclaims the Second Crusade on God's behalf. The response is disappointing until the French Cistercian abbot Bernard of Clairvaux begins preaching the crusade.

September 14   Imad ad-Din Zangi, the Muslim governor of Mosul (modern Iraq), is murdered; one son, Sayf-ad-Din Ghazi, succeeds in Mosul, while a second, Nur-ad-Din Mahmud, takes control of Aleppo, Syria.

1147

- King Alfonso VII of Castile and León, Emperor of Spain, besieges Almería.
- King Erik III the Lamb of Denmark abdicates and dies; the succession is disputed by Svein III and Cnut III, descendants of the former kings Erik II and Niels respectively.
- King Roger II of Sicily occupies the island of Corfu and plunders Corinth and Thebes, both important centers of silk manufacturing in the Byzantine Empire. He settles the silk weavers in Palermo, beginning silk manufacturing in Sicily.
- The Knights of Calatrava (the forerunners of the Knights of Alcántara) are founded, by Abbot Ramón Sierra, as a Spanish Christian military order in Castile.

April 4   Prince Yury Vladimirovich Dolgoruky of Suzdal holds a banquet for his ally the prince of Novgorod–Seversk at Moscow. Though traditionally regarded as marking the foundation of Moscow, archeological excavations indicate that there was a settlement here already.

April 4   The Almohad Mahdi (Muslim leader) Abd-al-Mu'min completes his conquest of the Almoravid possessions in Morocco with the capture of the capital city of Marrakesh; he then crosses into Spain, where the Almoravid emirate has disintegrated into several kingdoms established in Córdoba, Valencia, Murcia, and other areas.

May 5   Conrad III Hohenstaufen, king of the Germans, and the German contingent of the Second Crusade depart from Regensburg, Bavaria, for Constantinople in the Byzantine Empire.

June 8   King Louis VII and the French contingent of the Second Crusade set off from St.-Denis, France, to meet the Germans at Constantinople.

June 26–July 31   The pagan Wends sack the German port of Lübeck, and, the following month, defeat the Danes.

June 29   An assembly of Saxon nobles plans a crusade against the pagan Wends of the Baltic.

September 9   The Saxons abandon their crusade against the pagan Wends after failing to take Dobin.

October 25   Conrad III Hohenstaufen, king of the Germans' crusading army, is heavily defeated by the Seljuk Turks on the River Bathys, near Dorylaeum in Anatolia (modern Turkey).

October 25 English and Flemish crusaders, interrupting their voyage to the Holy Land to join the Second Crusade, assist in the capture of the city of Lisbon from the Moors by King Alfonso of Portugal.

November 3 Nur-ad-Din, the Zangid (Muslim) emir of Aleppo, Syria, defeats Joscelin II, Count of Edessa, as he retires after an attempt to recover Edessa (modern Ufar); the city is then depopulated by Nur-ad-Din to discourage further attempts by the Christians to recover it.

November 31 Conrad III Hohenstaufen, king of the Germans, retiring with the remains of his army, meets King Louis VII of France and the French crusaders in Nicaea; they advance to Ephesus, where Conrad falls ill and returns to Constantinople.

1148

- Geoffrey, Count of Anjou, assumes the title of Duke of Normandy.
- Raymond Berengar III, Count of Barcelona, takes the city of Tortosa from the Moors.
- The empress Matilda, daughter of the late king Henry I of England, leaves the country early in the year, having abandoned hope of defeating King Stephen and ascending the English throne.
- With Venetian assistance, the Byzantines expel King Roger II of Sicily from the island of Corfu.

January 8 The Seljuk Turks of Rūm inflict a heavy defeat on the French crusaders at Mt. Cadmus in Anatolia (modern Turkey).

March 19 The Second Crusade, one army consisting mostly Frankish and German nobles and much reduced as a result of defeats by the Seljuk Turks of Rūm while crossing Anatolia, reaches Antioch.

April 24 King Louis VII of France and Conrad III Hohenstaufen, king of the Germans (who has rejoined the crusade after recovering from his illness), hold a council at Acre (modern Akko, Israel) and decide to attack the city of Damascus rather than try to recover Edessa from the Muslims.

July 24–28 The Second Crusade lays siege to the city of Damascus in Syria but is forced to retreat because of lack of water, so bringing the disastrous crusade to an ignominious end.

September 8 Conrad III Hohenstaufen, king of the Germans, leaves Palestine for Constantinople, where he and the Byzantine emperor Manuel I Comnenus make an alliance against King Roger II of Sicily.

November 11 Prince Raymond of Antioch defeats Nur-ad-Din, the Zangid ruler of Syria, at Famiya.

1149

- *Lo codi/Legal Codes*, a summary of Roman law, is the earliest legal document written in Provençal.
- Abd-al-Mu'min, the Almohad Mahdi (Muslim leader), completes his conquest of the Muslim emirates in Spain.
- King Jaya Harivarman I of Champa recaptures Vijaya, his capital, from the Khmer emperor Suryavarman II.
- King Stephen of England attempts to prevent the Lombard jurist Vacarius from teaching Roman civil law in England.

June 29 Prince Raymond of Antioch is defeated and killed by Shirkuh, the general of Nur-ad-Din, the Zengid ruler of Syria, at the Fountain of Murad.

July 7 King Louis VII of France lands in Calabria, Italy, on his return from Palestine; he meets King Roger II of Sicily, who persuades him to take part in an attack on the Byzantine capital Constantinople; however, the move is abortive.

November 11 Henry the Lion, Duke of Saxony, resumes his claim to the duchy of Bavaria.

SCIENCE, TECHNOLOGY, AND MEDICINE

Ecology

c. 1140

- Salt mining becomes established at Berchtesgaden, in the Bavarian Alps of southeastern Germany.

Health and Medicine

1143

- The system of state hospitals in China is reorganized.

1145

- The first known autopsy in China is conducted. Religious taboos forbid the mutilation of the dead body, so autopsies and anatomical investigations can only involve corpses that have been mutilated through the manner of their deaths.

1149

- The Arab physician ibn-Zuh (Avenzoar) writes his *Book of Simplification Concerning Therapeutics and Diet*, with descriptions and treatments for disorders including otitis media (inflammation of the middle ear) and pericarditis (inflammation of the membrane surrounding the heart).

Math

1142

- English monk and scholar Adelard of Bath translates Euclid's *Elements* from Arabic.

Science

1140

- The French astronomer Raymond of Marseille compiles his astronomical treatise *Liber cursuum planetarum/ Book of the Courses of the Planets*, which includes tables adapted from the Muslim *Toledan Tables*.

1141

- Thierry, new chancellor of Chartres School, France, introduces scientific studies.

1143

- Hermann of Dalmatia writes numerous Latin translations of Arabic scientific works on subjects including astronomy.

1144

- The English scholar Robert of Chester makes a Latin translation of the Arabic *Book of the Composition of Alchemy* attributed to the 9th-century Muslim alchemist Jābir (Geber). This is the first such translation of a writing on chemistry.

1145

- A carving near a sacred lake at the Toltec sacred city of Chichén Itzá records a transit of Venus across the face of the sun, an event of great religious significance.
- The Spanish Muslim astronomer Jābir ibn-Aflah writes *Kitāb al-Hay'ah/Book of Astronomy*, which questions the earth-centered Ptolemaic view of the universe.

1149

- The English astronomer Robert of Chester produces astronomical tables for London, England, for the period 1149–50. These are based on the work of the 9th-century Baghdad astronomer al-Khwarizmi.

Technology

c. **1140**

- The Igbo people of West Africa develop elaborate craftsmanship and metalworking techniques, working principally in bronze.

Transportation

1145

- The bridge over the River Danube at the Bavarian town of Ratisbon (Regensburg), Germany, is completed.

ARTS AND IDEAS

Architecture

1140

- The Romanesque Church of San Ambrogio in Milan, Italy, is given a ribbed vault.

1145

- A mosaic of the *Coronation of the Virgin* is introduced into the apse of Sta Maria in Trastavere, Rome.
- Construction begins on the royal portal at the west end of Chartres Cathedral in Chartres, France. Its sculpture shows the transition from the Romanesque to the Gothic style of architecture.
- Construction begins on the "Friday Mosque" at Isfahan, Persia, capital of the Seljuk Turks.

1145–91   The great mosque at Mosul in Mesopotamia is constructed.

1146

- The mausoleum of Halifet Gazi, a member of the Danishmend dynasty, is constructed at Amasya in northern Turkey.

- The Romanesque cathedral at Lund, Sweden, is consecrated.

1149

July 15   The Church of the Holy Sepulchre in Jerusalem is dedicated.

Arts

1143

- Mosaics are included in the apse of the Palatine Chapel in Palermo, Sicily.

1147

- Woodcuts, wooden blocks incised with a design and used as a printing template, are first used to illustrate manuscripts at Engelberg in what is now Switzerland.

1148

- A Byzantine mosaic of Christ Pantocrator is included in the apse of Cefalù Cathedral in Sicily.

Literature and Language

1140

- *Poema di mío Cid/Poem of the Cid* is written. It is the most complete Spanish epic *chanson de geste* ("song of exploits") and tells of the fantastic deeds of the military commander Rodrigo or Ruy Díaz de Vivar (El Cid), who died in 1099.
- Bernard de Morlaix writes his *De contemptu mundi/On the Despisers of the World*, which contains a famous description of the heavenly Jerusalem.

1145

- Abbot Suger writes his *Liber de rebus in administratione sua gestis/Book of Matters and Deeds in His Administration*, an account of his administration of the abbey of St.-Denis in Paris, France.

1148

- The Brahman Kalhana writes his *Rājatarangini/Stream of Kings*, a verse history of the kings of Kashmir written in Sanskrit.

Thought and Scholarship

c. **1140**

- *Le Jeu d'Adam/Play of Adam*, an Anglo-Norman religious drama on the Fall and the story of Cain and Abel, is written.

1141

- Spanish scholar John of Seville translates Arab astrological works and writes a valuable summary of Islamic astrology, *The Epitome of the Whole of Astrology*.

1142

- The philosopher and theologian Peter Abelard writes his "Letters" to his former lover Héloïse, including the celebrated autobiography *Historia calamitatum mearum/Story of My Misfortunes*.
- William of Malmesbury writes his *Historia regum Anglorum/History of the Kings of England* and *Historia novella/New History*, a history of England to 1142.

1144

- Matthew of Edessa (modern Urfa) writes his chronicle of Armenia for the period 953–1136.

1145

- Kim Pu-sik compiles his *Samguk sagi/History of the Three Kingdoms*, a history of Korea written in Chinese.

1146

- Otto, bishop of Freising, writes his *Chronica sive historia de duabus civitatibus/Chronicle or History of Two Cities*, a philosophical history of the spiritual and material worlds inspired by St. Augustine.

1148

- *Landnámabók/Book of Settlements*, an Icelandic family saga based on the work of Ari Thorgilsson, is created.
- Anna Comnena completes the *Alexiad*, an adulatory chronicle of the life and reign of her father Alexius I Comnenus, ruler of the Byzantine Empire. The chronicle was started by her husband Nicephorus Bryennius.

SOCIETY

Education

1145

- Vacarius, a Lombard jurist, introduces the study of Roman civil law to England.

1149

- The first British university is founded at Oxford, England. Robert Grosseteste is appointed its first chancellor, and it attracts scholars including Friar Roger Bacon, making it a center for scientific study.

Religion

1140

- The first Polish Cistercian and Premonstratensian houses are founded.
- The philosopher and theologian Peter Abelard is condemned for heresy at the council of Sens, France, at the instance of St. Bernard.

1141

- Peter of Toledo translates *Risalah/The Apology of Al-Kindi*, an account of Islam, written in Arabic, by an oriental Christian.

1143

- A papal legate begins to enforce clerical celibacy in Bohemia.
- Robert of Chester and Hermann the Dalmatian make the first translation of the Koran into Latin.

1147

- Hildegard, a Benedictine nun, founds a monastery near Bingen in the Rhine valley of Germany. A woman of great learning and piety, she writes fervent religious poetry set to her own music.

1148

- The theologian Gilbert de la Porrée is called to appear before Pope Eugenius III at Reims, France, because of his unorthodox views on the Trinity.

1149

- The first Cathari bishopric is established in northern France.

BIRTHS & DEATHS

1140

- Judah ha-Levi, Jewish poet and philosopher, writer of many poems, such as *Zion ha-lo tish'ali/Ode to Zion*, dies.

1141

- Visnuvardhana, ruler of Halebid and founder of the Hoysala kingdom of Mysore, dies.

1142

c. 1142 Orderic Vitalis, English monk, author of *Historia ecclesiastica*, which provides a graphic description of Anglo-Norman life in England between 1082 and 1141, dies (*c.* 67).

April 21 Peter Abelard (Pierre Abélard), French theologian, philosopher, and poet, also known for his love affair with Héloïse, dies in the priory of Saint-Marcel, near Chalon-sur-Saône, Burgundy, France (*c.* 63).

1143

- William I, King of Scotland (1165–1214) who succeeded in obtaining independence from England, born (–1214).

September 24 Pope Innocent II (Gregory Parareschi) dies in Rome.

1144

March 8 Pope Celestine II dies in Rome.

1145

February 15 Pope Lucius II dies in Rome.

1147

October 31 Robert, Earl of Gloucester, chief supporter of the empress Matilda, daughter of the late king Henry I of England, against king Stephen of England, dies.

1148

November 2 St. Malachy, archbishop of Armagh and church reformer, the first Irish Catholic to be canonized, dies in Clairvaux, France.

1150–1159

POLITICS, GOVERNMENT, AND ECONOMICS

Business and Economics

1157

- The Bank of Venice is founded.

Colonization

1155

- By the papal bull *Laudabiliter*, Pope Adrian IV grants Ireland to King Henry II of England on condition that he reforms its church.

Politics and Government

1150

- Conrad III Hohenstaufen, king of the Germans, appoints Albert the Bear as Elector of Brandenburg.
- Henry Plantagenet, son of Geoffrey, Count of Anjou, and the Empress Matilda, is invested as Duke of Normandy.
- The Khmer emperor Suryavarman II dies while campaigning to recover his control over the kingdom of Champa.

February 2   Henry, son of Conrad III Hohenstaufen, king of the Germans, defeats a rebellion by Welf VI of Swabia incited by King Roger II of Sicily.

April 4   Nur-ad-Din, the Zengid ruler of Syria, captures, blinds, and imprisons Joscelin II, Count of Edessa.

November 21   King García IV Ramirez of Navarre dies; he is succeeded by his son, Sancho VI.

1151

- Ala-ad-Din Husayn, Sultan of Ghur (modern Afghanistan) earns his title "the World-Burner" by sacking the town of Ghazni after the Ghaznavids murder a Ghurid chieftain.
- King Baldwin III of Jerusalem frustrates an attempt by Nur-ad-Din, the Zengid ruler of Syria, to take the Syrian city of Damascus, with which, although it is Muslim, Baldwin is allied.
- The Byzantine emperor Manuel I Comnenus makes his first attack on Hungary in a war which lasts, intermittently, until 1167.

August 8   By a treaty made in Paris, France, Henry Plantagenet, Duke of Normandy, cedes the Vexin area of Normandy to King Louis VII of France.

September 7   Geoffrey Plantagenet, Count of Anjou and Maine, dies; he is succeeded by his son, Henry Plantagenet, Duke of Normandy.

1152

- King Frederick I Barbarossa of Germany appoints Welf of Swabia as Marquis of Tuscany and Duke of Spoleto.
- The Almohad Mahdi (Muslim leader) Abd-al-Mu'min conquers the North African region of modern Algeria from the Almoravid Emirate.

March 4   Frederick I Barbarossa of Hohenstaufen, nephew of the late King Conrad III of Germany, is elected "king of the Romans" (king of Germany).

March 21   The marriage of King Louis VII and Eleanor of Aquitaine is dissolved after Louis accuses Eleanor of adultery.

May 16   Henry Plantagenet, Count of Anjou and Maine and Duke of Normandy, marries Eleanor of Aquitaine, gaining her lands in southern France—he now controls more of France than King Louis VII of France.

May 18   In a diet (legislative assembly) at Merseburg, King Frederick I Barbarossa of Germany adjudges Svein III to be the legitimate king of Denmark (against his rival Cnut III).

1153

- King Frederick I Barbarossa of Germany holds court at Besançon and receives the homage of the Burgundians.
- King Roger II of Sicily takes the city of Bona from the Fatimids, in North Africa; his empire there now extends from Tripoli to Tunis.
- The Jin (emperors of the Juchen people) move their capital from Manchuria to Beijing.

January 1   Henry Plantagenet, Count of Anjou and Maine and Duke of Normandy, lands in England to pursue his claim to the throne inherited from his mother, the Empress Matilda, daughter of the former king Henry I of England.

March 23   Pope Eugenius III and King Frederick I Barbarossa of Germany meet in Constance, Germany, to seal an alliance.

May 24   King David I of Scotland dies, having established an administration on Anglo-Norman lines and created feudal tenures. He is succeeded by his grandson, Malcolm IV.

July 12   Anastasius IV is elected pope following the death of Eugenius III.

August 19   The Fatimid (Shiite Muslim) garrison of Ascalon, a city on the Mediterranean coast in Palestine, surrenders to King Baldwin III of Jerusalem: the Christians now control the entire coast of the Holy Land.

November 7   By the Treaty of Wallingford, Henry Plantagenet, Count of Anjou and Maine and Duke of Normandy, recognizes Stephen as king of England while Stephen accepts Henry as his heir.

1154

● King Svein III flees from Denmark.

February 26   King Roger II of Sicily dies; he is succeeded by his son, William I.

February 26   The Byzantines foment a rebellion against King William I of Sicily.

April 25   Nur-ad-Din, the Zengid ruler of Syria, takes the city of Damascus, thus completing his mastery of Muslim Syria.

October 10   King Frederick I Barbarossa of Germany begins an expedition to Italy to restore royal authority there after the disorders of the "Investiture Contest" (conflict between the papacy and the Empire over lay investiture of senior churchmen) and its aftermath.

December 4   Cardinal Nicholas Breakspear is elected as Pope Adrian IV (the first and only English pope) following the death of Pope Anastasius IV.

December 19   Henry II Plantagenet is crowned as king of England, founding the Plantagenet dynasty.

1155

● King Demetrius I of Georgia abdicates; he is succeeded, successively in this year, by his sons, David IV and George III.

● Prince Isiaslav II of Kiev dies; he is succeeded by Prince Yury (Juri) Vladimirovich Dolgoruki of Suzdal.

January 1   King Henry II of England appoints the archdeacon of Canterbury, Thomas à Becket, as his chancellor.

March 3   After a siege of two months, King Frederick I Barbarossa of Germany takes Tortona (a Milanese dependency) and razes it to the ground.

March 3   Pope Adrian IV places an interdict on Rome, forcing the Romans to banish Arnold of Brescia, the antipapal leader of their commune, and make peace with the Pope.

April 17   King Frederick I Barbarossa of Germany is crowned king of Italy, in Pavia, Lombardy.

June 18   King Frederick I Barbarossa of Germany and Italy captures and executes as a heretic Arnold of Brescia, the antipapal leader of the Roman commune, and is crowned as Holy Roman Emperor (*sacrum Romanum imperator*) by Pope Adrian IV, the first emperor to use the full title.

November 11   Pope Adrian IV makes an alliance with barons in revolt against King William I of Sicily. He also makes an alliance with the Byzantine emperor Manuel I Comnenus, who captures the Adriatic port of Bari from William.

1156

● Erik Jedvardsson becomes king of Sweden following the murder of Sverker I. A resulting feud sees the throne alternating between descendants of Sverker and Erik IX the Saint for the next century.

● King Henry II of England defeats his brother Geoffrey's revolt in Anjou.

● King Vikramanka of Rashtrakuta (in the Deccan) dies; his kingdom, which has been the most powerful in India for three centuries, collapses.

● Mas'ud I, Sultan of Rūm, dies; he is succeeded by his son Kilij Arslan II.

● Reynald of Châtillon, Prince of Antioch, and Prince Thoros II of Lesser Armenia (Cilicia) ravage the Byzantine island of Cyprus in the spring.

● Svein III is restored as king of Denmark with Saxon aid.

● The Holy Roman Emperor Frederick I Barbarossa confers the title "Count Palatine" on his half brother Conrad who controls much territory in the Rhineland. The Rhine Palatinate develops into one of the leading German principalities.

May 28   King William I of Sicily defeats Byzantine forces outside Brindisi on the Adriatic coast then recovers the port of Bari.

June 6   By the Treaty of Benevento, Pope Adrian IV recognizes William I as king of Sicily and receives his homage.

June 6   The Holy Roman Emperor Frederick I Barbarossa marries Beatrice, heiress of Upper Burgundy.

September 9   Hungary recognizes Byzantine overlordship.

September 17   In a diet (legislative assembly) at Regensburg, Bavaria, the Holy Roman Emperor Frederick I Barbarossa grants the duchy of Bavaria to Henry the Lion, Duke of Saxony, and compensates Henry Jasomirgott for his loss by creating the duchy of Austria for him.

1157

● After invading Poland, the Holy Roman Emperor Frederick I Barbarossa compels Grand Prince Bolesław IV of Poland to admit, in the Peace of Krzyszkowo, the imperial overlordship of Poland (for the last time).

● Grand Prince Yury (Juri) of Kiev dies; he is succeeded by his son Andrew (Andrey).

● King Erik IX the St. of Sweden begins the conquest of the area of modern Finland.

● King Henry II of England compels King Malcolm IV of Scotland to surrender the counties of Northumberland, Cumberland, and Westmorland.

● King Henry II of England grants protection to the guilds of merchants of Cologne, Germany, and associated towns settled in London, England.

● King William I of Sicily sacks Byzantine ports in the Aegean.

● Sanjar, the Seljuk sultan, dies; the disintegration of his empire, centered on Persia, now accelerates.

May 4   By the Treaty of Roskilde, Denmark is divided between King Svein III and his rivals Cnut III and Valdemar I.

May 7   King Svein III of Denmark holds a banquet where his rival Cnut III is murdered but Valdemar I escapes.

August 21   King Alfonso VII of Castile and León, Emperor of Spain, dies; by his will his sons, Sancho III and Ferdinand II, become kings of Castile and León respectively.

October 10   The Holy Roman Emperor Frederick I Barbarossa takes formal possession of the kingdom of Burgundy. He rejects claims of papal supremacy implied in a letter from Pope Adrian IV.

October 23   Valdemar I becomes king of Denmark by defeating and killing King Svein III at Viborg on the Jutland peninsula.

1158

- King Henry II of England campaigns against the Welsh and gains the overlordship of Gwynedd and Deheubarth. He also becomes overlord of Brittany on the death of his brother, Geoffrey of Anjou.
- Muslim rebellions break out in King William I of Sicily's North African territories.
- Pope Adrian IV arranges a peace between King William I of Sicily and the Byzantine emperor Manuel I Comnenus, who ends his military intervention in Italy.
- The Order of Knights of Santiago, a Christian military order, is founded in Castile, Spain, to counteract the Moors. Its members adhere to the Augustinian rule but are allowed to marry and own personal possessions, which is most unusual for military orders.

January 11 In a diet (legislative assembly) at Regensburg, Bavaria, the Holy Roman Emperor Frederick I Barbarossa concedes the hereditary title of king of Bohemia to Duke Władysław II.

April 4 King Baldwin III of Jerusalem defeats Nur-ad-Din, the Zengid ruler of Syria, at Butaiha.

July 7 The Holy Roman Emperor Frederick I Barbarossa begins his second Italian expedition with the capture of the northern city of Brescia.

August 31 King Sancho III of Castile dies; he is succeeded by his infant son, Alfonso VIII. Civil war breaks out.

September 8 The Italian city of Milan surrenders to the Holy Roman Emperor Frederick I Barbarossa after a siege.

October 10 The Byzantine emperor Manuel I Comnenus makes an expedition into Lesser Armenia (Cilicia); Prince Thoros II evades capture but his ally Prince Reynald of Antioch submits and receives pardon.

November 11 In a diet (legislative assembly) at Roncaglia, Italy, the Holy Roman Emperor Frederick I Barbarossa promulgates his peace constitution for the empire.

1159

- The Kievans expel Grand Prince Andrew (Andrey) and elect Rostislav I of Smolensk in his place.

April 12 The Byzantine emperor Manuel I Comnenus makes a ceremonial entry into Antioch, then withdraws to the west.

July 4 Władysław II, the former grand prince of Poland, dies; the Holy Roman Emperor Frederick I Barbarossa has his sons restored to Silesia, so attaching it to German interests.

July 7 The Holy Roman Emperor Frederick I Barbarossa begins the siege of Crema, near Cremona, Italy. King William I of Sicily engineers a league of the papacy and the towns of Brescia, Milan, and Piacenza against Frederick.

September 7 Rolando Bandinelli is elected as Pope Alexander III by a majority of the cardinals, but a party favoring the interests of the Holy Roman Emperor Frederick I Barbarossa elects Cardinal Octavian as Pope Victor IV; neither is able to control Rome.

September 9 King Henry II of England abandons his siege of the southern French city of Toulouse when King Louis VII of France enters the city. Henry holds his French lands as the vassal of Louis and cannot be seen to attack his feudal overlord for fear of setting a bad example to his own vassals.

SCIENCE, TECHNOLOGY, AND MEDICINE

Health and Medicine

1151

- Twenty physicians of the medical school at Salerno, Italy, found the Civitas Hippocratica, the first medical society, named for the classical Greek physician Hippocrates.

Science

1150

- Hebrew scholar Solomon Jarchus produces the first almanac, a table for the calculation of celestial movements, and a calendar.
- The Indian astronomer Bhāskara writes *Siddhāntaśiromani/The Head Jewel of Accuracy*, which records his observations of planetary conjunctions, eclipses, and other astronomical events.

1154

- The Egyptian Muslim scholar al-Tīfāshī writes his pioneering work on mineralogy *Flowers of Knowledge of Precious Stones*.

1156

- Henchün Seiken writes his treatise on perfumery, *Kō yō shō*.

Technology

1151

- The first European paper mill is established in Muslim Spain. It has little effect on the culture of Christian Europe.

Transportation

1157

- The first European lighthouse since classical times is erected at Meloria on the Italian coast.

ARTS AND IDEAS

Architecture

1150

- A vast temple complex is built at Angkor Wat (in modern Cambodia) by the Khmer emperor Suryavarman II. The building is to be his mausoleum.

- The Hermitage of San Baudelio in Berlanga, near Burgos, Spain, is completed. It is the last Mozarabic church to be built.

1151

- Mosaics are included in the dome of La Martorana (Santa Maria dell' Amiraglio) in Palermo, Sicily.

1152

- The Romanesque cathedral at Amiens, France, is consecrated.

1153

- Construction begins on the baptistry of Pisa Cathedral in Italy, to a design by Diotisalvi.

1154

- Buono constructs the campanile of San Marco in Venice.

1156

- Prince Yury Vladimirovich Dolgoruky of Suzdal begins the construction of the Kremlin citadel in Moscow.

1157

- Henry the Lion, Duke of Saxony and Bavaria, founds the city of Munich in Bavaria.

1158–1223

- The Cistercian abbey of Alcobaça in Portugal is constructed. The style of architecture is Romanesque.

Literature and Language

c. 1150

- *König Rother/King Rother*, a Middle High German poem of about 5,000 lines concerning the romantic adventures of King Rother, is written.

1158

- Icelandic traveler Nikulas Saemundarson writes an account of his pilgrimage to Rome, Constantinople, and Jerusalem between 1151 and 1154.

Thought and Scholarship

c. 1150

- *Le Pèlerinage de Charlemagne à Jérusalem/The Pilgrimage of Charlemagne to Jerusalem*, a *chanson de geste* ("song of exploits"), is written. It is notable for its comedy as well as its heroic element.

1152

- John of Salisbury writes his *Historia pontificalis/History of the Papacy*, a vivid history of western Europe during the period 1148–52.

1154

- *The Anglo-Saxon Chronicles* are completed. They have been written since 880 and record events in England from 449–1154.
- Al-Idrisi, geographer to Roger II of Sicily, produces a planisphere and writes *al-Kitāb al-Rujarī/Roger's Book*,

BIRTHS & DEATHS

c. 1150

- Suryavarman II, Cambodian king who built the temple at Angkor Wat, the largest temple in the world, dies.
- William of Auxerre, French philosopher and theologian who was the first European author to write about free will, born in Auxerre, France (–1231).

1151

- Geoffrey Plantagenet, Count of Anjou, initiator of the Royal House of Plantagenet which produced 14 kings of England, dies (c. 38).
- Li Ch'ing-chao, Chinese female poet whose poetry about women is written to the meters of popular songs, dies.

January 13 Suger, abbot of St. Denis, adviser to King Louis VI and King Louis VII of France, who contributed to the development of the Gothic style of architecture, dies (c. 70).

1152

February 15 Conrad III, King of Germany 1137–52, dies (59).

1153

May 24 David I, King of Scotland 1125–53, son of Malcolm III Canmore and Queen Margaret (granddaughter of Edmund II of England), a powerful king and a notable religious reformer, dies in Carlisle, Cumberland, England (c. 71).

July 8 Pope Eugenius III (Bernardo Paganelli) dies.

August 20 St. Bernard of Clairvaux, influential Cistercian abbot and mystic, founder of the abbey of Clairvaux, dies in Clairvaux, France (c. 63).

1154

- William II, last Norman king of Sicily, born (–1189).
- William of Conches, writer of commentaries on Plato and Boethius and an original work, *De philosophia mundi/On the Philosophy of the World*, dies.

February 26 Roger II, first king of the Norman kingdom of Sicily (1130–54), dies in Palermo, Sicily (56).

October 25 Stephen of Blois, King of England 1135–1154, who usurped the throne, dies in Dover, Kent (c. 57).

December 3 Pope Anastasius IV (Corrado della Subarra) dies.

1155

- Thierry of Chartres, French theologian and scholar of the classics and of Arab science, dies.

1156

December 25 Peter the Venerable, abbot of Cluny, who commissioned the first Latin translation of the Koran, dies in Cluny, France (c. 64).

1157

September 8 Richard I ("Richard the Lion-Hearted"), King of England 1189–99, who gained popularity through his bravery during the Third Crusade, born in Oxford, England (–1199).

1158

September 22 Otto, German bishop of Freising, author of an influential history of the world, dies in Morimond, Champagne, France (c. 47).

1159

September 1 Adrian IV (original name Nicholas Breakspear), the only English pope 1154–59, dies in Anagni, near Rome, Italy (c. 59).

the most thorough description of the world in medieval times.

1155

- Norman monk Wace completes his *Le Roman de Brut/ The Romance of Brut*, a British chronicle based on Geoffrey of Monmouth's chronicle of *c.* 1137, which includes Arthurian traditions and a reference to the Round Table.

1158

- Otto of Freising completes his *Gesta Frederici imperatoris/The Deeds of Emperor Frederick*, a life of the Holy Roman Emperor Frederick I Barbarossa to 1156.

SOCIETY

Education

1158

- Holy Roman Emperor Frederick I Barbarossa grants his charter, "the Authentic," to the University of Bologna, Italy.

Everyday Life

1155

- The queen of England, Eleanor of Aquitaine, introduces French wines into England, leading to the decline of the English wine industry.

Religion

1152

- A synod at Kells, Ireland, acknowledges the supremacy of the pope in Ireland, where the church is organized under four archbishoprics.

1153

- The Cistercian Order now has 343 monasteries.

1155

- The Carmelite Order (of friars) is founded with the establishment of a community of hermits on Mt. Carmel by St. Berthold.

c. **1158**

- Peter the Lombard writes *Sententiarum libri quator/Four Books of Opinions*, which after initial opposition becomes one of the most popular theological textbooks of the Middle Ages.

1160–1169

POLITICS, GOVERNMENT, AND ECONOMICS

Politics and Government

1160

- Henry the Lion, Duke of Saxony and Bavaria, begins the systematic conquest of Wendish territory east of the River Elbe in the summer.
- King Malcolm IV of Scotland subdues the Irish, Welsh, and Norse inhabitants of Galloway, Scotland.
- Taira Kiyomori, the leader of the Taira samurai clan in Japan, wins control of the imperial government after defeating his rivals in the Hogen and Heijii insurrections of 1156–59.

January 1 The fall of Mahdiyah (in modern Tunisia) to local rebels completes the loss of all the conquests of the kings of Sicily in North Africa.

January 27 The Holy Roman Emperor Frederick I

Barbarossa takes and destroys the Italian town of Crema, near Cremona.

February 11 A synod held in Pavia, Italy, by the Holy Roman Emperor Frederick I Barbarossa declares Victor IV to be the legitimate pope.

March 24 Pope Alexander III excommunicates the Holy Roman Emperor Frederick I Barbarossa for recognizing his rival Victor IV as pope.

May 18 King Erik IX the St. of Sweden is killed in civil warfare.

November 10 King William I of Sicily's unpopular grand emir of Naples, Maione of Bari, is assassinated.

November 11 Nur-ad-Din, the Zengid ruler of Syria, captures Reynald of Châtillon, Prince of Antioch: he is imprisoned for 15 years and does not regain his principality.

December 12 King Henry II of England reoccupies the Vexin area of Normandy, which was ceded by him to King Louis VII of France in 1151.

1161

- An attempt by the Jin (emperors of the Juchen people) to conquer the Chinese Southern Song Empire is defeated at the Battle of Zaishi, near Yangzhou, China.

- King Géza II of Hungary admits German colonists (usually but inaccurately described as Saxons), granting them self-government.
- The Almohad Mahdi (Muslim leader) Abd-al-Mu'min conquers Tripoli in North Africa from the Normans of Sicily.

February 3   King Inge I of Norway is murdered; he is succeeded by Haakon II, a 14-year-old boy.

March 9   King William I of Sicily is captured by rebel barons but escapes, foiling an attempt to depose him.

April 16   King William I of Sicily crushes baronial rebellions in Sicily, Apulia, and Calabria.

May 31   King Géza II of Hungary dies; he is succeeded by his son, Stephen III.

July 15   Ladislas II is crowned as king of Hungary by opponents of King Stephen III. Ladislas is Stephen's uncle and disputed his right to the throne.

1162

- Charles VII, nephew of the former king Sverker I, succeeds as king of Sweden.
- King Haakon II of Norway is defeated and murdered by the jarl (earl) Erling, whose son Magnus VI succeeds as king.

January 14   King Ladislas II of Hungary dies; he is succeeded by his brother, Stephen IV.

February 10   King Baldwin III of Jerusalem dies; he is succeeded by his brother, Amalric (or Amaury) I.

March 3   The Holy Roman Emperor Frederick I Barbarossa makes an alliance against Sicily with the Italian cities of Pisa and Genoa.

March 26   The Italian city of Milan, having surrendered to the Holy Roman Emperor Frederick I Barbarossa, is sacked on his orders and its defenses are razed.

May 5   Pope Alexander III, at Montpellier in France, renews his excommunication of the Holy Roman Emperor Frederick I Barbarossa.

July 6   The Germans and Danes crusading against the pagan Wends, from Germany, east of the Elbe river, defeat them at Demmin.

August 8   Raymond Berengar IV, Count of Barcelona, dies; he is succeeded by his son, Alfonso II.

September 23   Pope Alexander III meets King Louis VII of France and King Henry II of England at Coucy-sur-Loire, France, and is recognized by them as pope.

1163

- Representatives of Aragonese towns attend the Cortes ("courts") of Aragon.
- Shirkuh, the general of Nur-ad-Din, Zangid emir of Aleppo, Syria, leads a Syrian invasion of Egypt.

April 11   With the death of his rival Stephen IV, King Stephen III of Hungary regains full control of his kingdom.

May 5   Abd-al-Mu'min, the Mahdi (Muslim leader) and Almohad ruler of Muslim Spain and northwest Africa, dies; he is succeeded as emir by his son Yūsuf abu Ya'qub.

October 1   Thomas à Becket, archbishop of Canterbury, refuses King Henry II of England's demand for the punishment of clergy to be handed over to secular courts. This is the start of the ongoing conflict between the two men, with Becket vigorously championing the rights of the church against the monarchy.

October 10   The Holy Roman Emperor Frederick I

Barbarossa withdraws from Lombardy, northern Italy, believing he has reestablished imperial authority there.

1164

- King Malcolm IV of Scotland defeats Norse and Gaelic rebels led by Somerled of the Isles, who is killed, at Renfrew, Scotland.
- Pope Alexander III confirms the Order of Knights of Calatrava, founded by Cistercian monks in 1158 to fight against the Muslims in Spain.

January 1   King Henry II of England defines the relations of the church and the monarchy in England in the Constitutions of Clarendon.

April 22   Guido of Crema is (uncanonically) elected as Pope Paschal III in succession to the late antipope Victor IV. The Holy Roman Emperor Frederick I Barbarossa gives him protection, but German prelates who had recognized Victor as pope refuse to accept Paschal.

August 10   Nur-ad-Din, the Zengid ruler of Syria, defeats and captures Prince Bohemond III of Antioch at Artah; he is subsequently ransomed.

October 8   Thomas à Becket, archbishop of Canterbury, is condemned for his contempt of King Henry II of England by the Council of Northampton.

November 2   Thomas à Becket, archbishop of Canterbury, begins his exile from England in France.

1165

- King Henry II of England's invasion of Gwynedd, Wales, is blocked by the Welsh near Corwen. After indecisive maneuvering Henry is forced to retreat to Chester, England, by bad weather and a shortage of supplies.

May 5   The Holy Roman Emperor Frederick I Barbarossa exacts an oath from the German clergy, at Würzburg, that they will not recognize Alexander III as pope.

November 23   Pope Alexander III, returning from exile in France, enters Rome and is established in the Lateran by Sicilian forces.

December 9   King Malcolm IV the Maiden of Scotland dies; he is succeeded by his brother, William I the Lion.

1166

- Alfonso VIII is acclaimed as king of Castile and thereafter subdues a rebellion.
- Grand Prince Bolesław IV of Poland is defeated by the pagan Prussians (an Indo-European Baltic group related to the Latvians and Lithuanians).
- Hoping to take advantage of the weak position of Pope Alexander III following the death of his supporter King William I of Sicily, the Holy Roman Emperor Frederick I Barbarossa begins his fourth expedition to Italy.

May 7   King William I the Bad of Sicily dies; he is succeeded by his young son, William II, with his widow as regent.

August 1   Dermot MacMurrough, King of Leinster (in Ireland), is banished by his people and High King Rory O'Connor (he had abducted the wife of Tiernan O'Ruark, King of Breifne, in 1153 and set off a bitter struggle). He goes into exile in England and then seeks help at the court of King Henry II of England in Aquitaine, France.

1167

- Bijjala, who has usurped the Indian kingdom of Rashtrakuta, is murdered in revenge for his mutilation of two holy men of the Lingayat sect, which is reviving the Siva cult in the Deccan.

- Dermot MacMurrough, the exiled king of Leinster, returns to Ireland to reclaim his kingdom.
- Grand Prince Rostislav I of Kiev dies; his sons dispute the succession.
- King Alfonso II of Aragon succeeds to the county of Provence on the death of his cousin, Raymond Berengar II.

1167–68   The Lombard League, formed to defend the northern Italian cities against the Holy Roman Emperor Frederick I Barbarossa, builds the city of Alessandria to strengthen its defenses.

March 18   King Amalric I of Jerusalem, fighting as the ally of the Fatimid caliph of Egypt, is defeated at Ashmun by the Syrians.

April 11   King Amalric I of Jerusalem, in alliance with the Fatimid vizier Shawar, defeats the Syrians under the Zengid general Shirkuh and his nephew Saladin near Cairo, Egypt. Both the Syrians and the Franks of Jerusalem subsequently agree to leave Egypt.

May 29   The forces of the Holy Roman Emperor Frederick I Barbarossa defeat the Romans outside Rome.

June 6   The Holy Roman Emperor Frederick I Barbarossa unsuccessfully besieges Ancona, Italy, and makes peace with the city.

June 24   The Holy Roman Frederick I Barbarossa camps outside Rome; he subsequently forces an entry, Pope Alexander III flees to Benevento, and the antipope Paschal III is installed.

August 8   The Holy Roman Emperor Frederick I Barbarossa's crusader army is forced to withdraw from Rome following a severe outbreak of malaria.

1168

- Danish crusaders destroy and plunder the sanctuary of the pagan Wends' chief god Svantovit at Arkona on the Baltic island of Rügen.
- Henry the Lion, Duke of Saxony and Bavaria, marries Matilda, the daughter of King Henry II of England.
- Prince Thoros II of Lesser Armenia (Cilicia) dies; he is succeeded by his son, Roupen II.
- The Toltec Empire of Mexico collapses after its capital at Tula is sacked by invaders.

May 5   An army of Norman knights from Wales arrives in Ireland to support Dermot MacMurrough in his bid to regain his kingdom of Leinster, from which he was banished in 1166.

September 9   Abbot John of Struma is elected as the successor to the antipope Paschal III, as Calixtus III, and recognized as pope by the Holy Roman Emperor Frederick I Barbarossa.

November 4   King Amalric I of Jerusalem invades Egypt and takes the town of Bilbeis, near Cairo, from the Fatimids (Shiite Muslims).

November 13   King Amalric I of Jerusalem camps outside the city of Cairo in Egypt, but withdraws when the Fatimid caliph receives forces in response to his appeal to Nur-ad-Din, the Zengid ruler of Syria.

1169

- Duke Casimir (Kazimierz) of Poland invades Russia as far as the Lublin plateau.
- Kilij Arslan II, Sultan of Rūm, takes the city of Ankara in his conquest of the Danishmend Turks.

- Stephen Nemanja becomes grand zupan of Rascia, Serbia.

January 1   Shirkuh, the general of Nur-ad-Din, Zangid emir of Aleppo, Syria, seizes control of Egypt and becomes the Fatimid caliph al-'Adid's vizier.

January 6   King Louis VII of France and King Henry II of England meet at Montmirail, France, to make peace.

March 8   Prince Andrey Bogolyubsky of Suzdal seizes and sacks Kiev; now the most powerful Russian prince, he assumes the title of great prince and establishes his capital at Vladimir (after which his principality subsequently takes its name).

March 23   Salah-ad-Din (Saladin) succeeds his uncle Shirkuh as vizier of the Fatimid caliph of Egypt, in the service of Nur-ad-Din, Zangid emir of Aleppo, Syria.

December 13   King Amalric I of Jerusalem and his Byzantine allies abandon a siege of the city of Damietta, Egypt.

SCIENCE, TECHNOLOGY, AND MEDICINE

Health and Medicine

1160

- The Muslim scholar ibn-Rushd (Averroës) writes his great medical encyclopedia *Kitāb al-Kullīyāt fī-al-Tibb/ Generalities of Medicine*.

1161

- The Italian physician Matthaeus Platearius of Salerno writes *Circa instans*, a popular treatise on simples and drugs. He also writes a commentary on the earlier pharmacopeia, the *Antidotarum/Book of Antidotes* of the French physician Nicholas Provost of Tours.
- The Seljuk sultan Kilij Arslan II builds two baths at Kavza; the Seljuks also developed spas and created a hospital service.

1163

- At the council of Tours in France, the Catholic Church issues an edict against the mutilation of dead bodies. Although primarily aimed at the stripping of crusaders' bones for transport back to Europe, it also affects medical research.

Science

1165

- Abraham ibn-Daud, a Jewish astronomer and philosopher from Toledo, Spain, translates various Arabic scientific works into Latin, including the influential *Secretum secretorum/The Secret of Secrets*, falsely attributed to Aristotle.
- The Spanish Muslim physician al-Ghāfiqi writes *Kitāb al-Adwiyah al-Mufradah* on simples. He also writes an ophthalmology, including illustrations of the instruments of the time.

ARTS AND IDEAS

Architecture

1160

- The Romanesque towers of Tournai Cathedral in Flanders are completed.

1160–1205 The Gothic cathedral at Laon, France, is constructed. It is the first to have a polygonal apse.

1162

- The Iplikci Mosque is built at Konya in central Persia.

c. 1162–c. 1350 The cathedral at Poitiers, France, is constructed.

1163

c. 1163 A wooden stave church is built at Borgund in Norway.

- The early Gothic choir of St. Germain-des-Prés, Paris, France, is consecrated.

1163–1220 The Notre Dame Cathedral in Paris, France, is constructed.

1165

- Construction begins on the Church of Nerez near Skopje, Serbia, which is to include Byzantine frescoes.

1167

April 27 The Lombard League of northern Italian cities begins the reconstruction of Milan, which was sacked by the Holy Roman Emperor Frederick I Barbarossa in 1162.

1168

- The architect Mateo takes charge of work on the cathedral at Santiago de Compostela, Spain.

Arts

1163

- The Bobrinskoy Bucket, an outstanding piece of inlaid metalwork of the Seljuk period, is made at Herat (in modern Afghanistan). Its creators are the caster Mohammad ibn-al-Wahid and the inlayer Ma'sud ibn-Ahmad.

Literature and Language

1160

c. 1160 Benoît de Ste. Maure writes "Roman de Troie"/ "Tale of Troy," a long poem about the Trojan wars in which the story of Troilus and Cressida makes its first appearance.

- Byzantine poet Theodorus Prodromus writes his *Rhodanthe and Dosicles*, a verse romance based on classical models.

1165

- Marie de France, a French poet living in England, writes *Lais/Lays*, verse narratives of Celtic and other folk legends.

Theater and Dance

1160

- Jean Bodel's *Le Jeu de St Nicholas/The Play of St. Nicholas*, the oldest extant miracle play in French literature, is performed at Arras, France.

BIRTHS & DEATHS

1160

August 21 Peter Lombard, bishop of Paris, author of *Four Books of Sentences*, the main theological work during the Middle Ages, dies in Paris (c. 60).

1163

- Abd al-Mu'min (ibn Ali), Berber caliph of the Almohad dynasty 1130–63, who conquered the North African Maghreb from the Almoravids and brought all the Berbers under one rule, dies in Rabat (in modern Morocco).

1164

April 20 The antipope Victor IV (Ottaviano di Monticelli) dies.

May 15 Héloïse, abbess, wife of Peter Abelard, dies in Paraclete Abbey, near Nogent-sur-Seine, France (c. 66).

1165

- Henry VI, German king 1169–97 and Holy Roman Emperor 1191–97, born in Nijmegen, in the modern Netherlands (–1197).

August 21 Philip II (Philip Augustus), King of France 1179–1223, who reconquered French territories lost previously to England, born in Paris (–1223).

December 9 Malcolm IV the Maiden, King of Scotland 1153–65, grandson of David I and brother of William I the Lion, who ceded Northumberland and Cumbria to England, dies (c. 24).

1166

- Abd al-Qadir al-Jīlānī, Muslim ascetic, dies.

1167

- Abraham ben Meir ibn Ezra, Spanish Hebrew scholar best remembered for his biblical commentaries, dies.

- Genghis Khan (original name Temüjin), great Mongol military leader who established the Mongol Empire, born at Deligun Bulduk, on the River Onon (–1227).

September 10 Empress Matilda (or Maud), daughter of Henry I of England, consort of Emperor Henry V, thereafter claimant to the English throne, dies near Rouen, France (c. 65).

December 24 John I ("John Lackland"), King of England 1199–1216, son of Henry II and Eleanor of Aquitaine, brother of Richard I, born in Oxford, England (–1216).

1168

September 9 The antipope Paschal III (Guido of Crema) dies.

Thought and Scholarship

1161
- Chinese historian Chêng Ch'iao writes his *T'ung chih*, an objective and scientific history of China.

1162
- Al-Māzini writes *Tuhfat al-Albāb wa Nukhbat al-a'jāb/ Gift to the Heart and Choice of Wonders*, a world geography which describes peoples, spirits, creatures, and fossils.
- Henry Aristippus translates Plato's *Phaedo* and *Meno*.

1166
- Bulgarus, one of the "four doctors" of Bologna, Italy, writes his "De regulis juris"/"On the Procedures of the Law," a treatise on Roman law.
- St. Ailred of Rievaulx writes his *Speculum caritatis/ Mirror of Charity*, a treatise on friendship.

SOCIETY

Education

1160
- *c.* 1160   The University of Paris is founded in France. It is to become a leading center of theology and scholasticism.

- Peter of Piacenza introduces the study of law from Bologna, Italy, to the emerging University of Montpellier in France.

Religion

1162
- The council of Montpellier in France condemns temporal lords who refuse to exercise their power against heretics.
- June 3   Thomas à Becket, Chancellor to King Henry II of England, is consecrated as archbishop of Canterbury.

1167
- A council of Cathari meets near Toulouse, France. The Cathari are members of a Christian sect who believe that the material world is evil and only the spiritual world is good.

***c.* 1168**
- Jewish philosopher Moses Maimonides completes his commentary on the Mishna, *Kitab al-Siraj* (precepts forming part of the Talmud).

1170–1179

POLITICS, GOVERNMENT, AND ECONOMICS

Business and Economics

1179
- Richard FitzNigel writes his *Dialogus de Scaccario*, a description of the English Exchequer.

Politics and Government

1170
- Qutb-ad-Din of Mosul dies; his brother, Nur-ad-Din, the Zengid ruler of Syria, settles a succession dispute.

- The Korean palace guards massacre civil officials and enthrone a puppet king; a period of civil war follows.
- June 14   King Henry II of England's son, Henry, is crowned as joint king.
- July 22   King Henry II of England and Thomas à Becket, archbishop of Canterbury, are reconciled at Fréteval, France.
- August 25   The English soldier Robert FitzStephen, Earl of Pembroke (known as "Strongbow"), in alliance with Dermot MacMurrough, King of Leinster, takes Waterford. Pembroke had been given permission to invade Ireland by King Henry II in a bid to help MacMurrough regain his throne.
- September 21   The English soldier Robert FitzStephen, Earl of Pembroke ("Strongbow") captures the Irish city of Dublin and is awarded the right to rule Ireland.
- November 27   The Russian principality of Novgorod defeats an attempted take-over by Great Prince Andrey Bogolyubsky of Vladimir–Suzdal.
- December 29   Thomas à Becket, archbishop of Canterbury, is murdered in his cathedral by four knights acting on an

angry outburst by King Henry II of England, expressing his wish to be rid of "this turbulent priest." His tomb becomes one of the most important of all medieval pilgrimage sites.

1171

- Nur-ad-Din, the Zengid ruler of Syria, seizes Mosul and Nisibis.
- The Almohad emir Yūsuf abu Ya'qub is now the supreme Muslim ruler in Spain.

March 12 In an attempt to end Venetian dominance of trade in the Byzantine Empire, the emperor Manuel I Comnenus orders the arrest of all Venetians in the empire and the confiscation of their goods; Venice retaliates by attacking Dalmatia and the islands of Chios and Lesbos.

May 5 The English soldier Robert FitzStephen, Earl of Pembroke ("Strongbow") succeeds Dermot MacMurrough as king of Leinster.

September 13 The last Fatimid (Shiite Muslim) caliph of Egypt, al-Adid, dies. Egypt nominally becomes subject to the caliph of Baghdad but in practice is annexed to the Zangid emirate under the rule of Saladin, the vizier of Nur-ad-Din, Zengid ruler of Syria.

October 16 King Henry II of England lands at Dublin, Ireland, to assert his sovereignty over the Irish lands conquered by the English soldier Robert FitzStephen, Earl of Pembroke ("Strongbow").

1172

- The Byzantine emperor Manuel I Comnenus captures Stephen Nemanja, Grand Zupan of Rascia, in his subjugation of Serbians and Venetians in Dalmatia.
- Turan-Shah, the brother of Saladin, the Muslim Zangid vizier in Egypt, invades Makkura, a Christian kingdom in the Sudan.

May 21 Papal legates at Avranches, France, grant King Henry II of England absolution for the murder of Thomas à Becket, archbishop of Canterbury.

1173

- King Vladislav II of Bohemia abdicates in favor of his son, Frederick. There follows a period of civil war, with 10 changes of ruler in 24 years, in which royal officials become established as feudal magnates; there is a simultaneous increase in German influence and settlement in Bohemia.

January 1 King Henry II of England receives the homage of the Count of Toulouse.

March 3 King Stephen III of Hungary dies; Béla III succeeds him.

March 21 The "young king" Henry and his brothers Richard, Geoffrey, and John rebel against their father, King Henry II of England, with the help and encouragement of King Louis VII of France.

October 30 Grand Prince Bolesław IV of Poland dies; he is succeeded by his brother, Mieszko III the Old of Greater Poland.

1174

- Great Prince Andrey Bogolyubsky of Vladimir–Suzdal is murdered; he is succeeded by his brother Michael.
- Kilij Arslan II, Seljuk Sultan of Rūm, begins the conquest of the Danishmend Turks of eastern Asia Minor (modern Turkey).

- Turan-Shah, the brother of Saladin, the Muslim Zangid vizier in Egypt, conquers the Yemen.

May 15 Nur-ad-Din, the Zengid ruler of Syria, dies. His empire disintegrates as his heir, Ismail, is young; Saladin, Nur-ad-Din's vizier in Egypt, declares his independence, founding the Ayyubid dynasty.

July 11 King Amalric I of Jerusalem dies; he is succeeded by his son, Baldwin IV.

July 13 King William I the Lion of Scotland is captured while invading Northumberland; King Henry II of England has now suppressed his sons' rebellion in England.

August 14 King Henry II of England makes peace with King Louis VII of France at Montlouis, France, following the defeat of his sons' rebellion, which Louis had supported.

September 30 King Henry II of England makes peace with his sons and issues an amnesty for their supporters.

October 29 In his fifth Italian expedition, the Holy Roman Emperor Frederick I Barbarossa begins the siege of Alessandria; he buys Tuscany and Spoleto from Welf VI, Marquis of Tuscany and Duke of Spoleto.

November 26 Saladin, aspiring to take over the late Nur-ad-Din's Zangid empire, takes possession of the Syrian city of Damascus.

December 12 By the Treaty of Falaise, King Henry II of England releases King William I the Lion of Scotland on obtaining his recognition of Henry's feudal supremacy over Scotland.

1175

- By the Treaty of Windsor, Rory O'Connor, High King of Ireland recognizes King Henry II of England's conquests in the east of Ireland but is permitted to retain dominion over the territories not under Anglo-Norman occupation on payment of tribute.

April 13 The Holy Roman Emperor Frederick I Barbarossa abandons the siege of Alessandria, Italy.

April 16 In the Armistice of Montebello, the Lombard League of northern Italy submits to the Holy Roman Emperor Frederick I Barbarossa.

May 5 The caliph of Baghdad recognizes Saladin as sultan of Egypt and Syria.

1176

- Turan-Shah, the brother of Saladin, Sultan of Egypt and Syria, conquers southern Arabia.

April 22 Saladin, Sultan of Egypt and Syria, defeats Sayf-ad-Din of Mosul.

May 29 After Henry the Lion, Duke of Saxony and Bavaria, refuses to send reinforcements, the Holy Roman Emperor Frederick I Barbarossa is decisively defeated by the Lombard League, at Legnano, Italy.

September 17 The Byzantine emperor Manuel I Comnenus invades the sultanate of Rūm but his army is trapped and destroyed by Sultan Kilij Arslan II at Myriocephalum.

October 10 By the Treaty of Anagni, the Holy Roman Emperor Frederick I Barbarossa recognizes Alexander III as the legitimate pope, so ending the schism between the empire and the papacy.

1177

- Grand Prince Mieszko III the Old of Poland is deposed; he is succeeded by his brother Casimir (Kazimierz) II the Just, who

- enforces his suzerainty over Silesia and the city of Kraków.
- King Alfonso VIII of Castile takes the city of Cuenca from the Muslims.
- King Henry II of England arbitrates in a dispute between the kings of Castile and Navarre.
- King Jaya Indravarman IV of Champa sacks Angkor, capital of the Khmer Empire. Tribhuvanadityavarman, who had usurped the Khmer throne, is killed, and Jayavarman, son of Dharanindravarman II, assumes leadership of Khmer resistance to Champa domination.
- Michael Bogolyubsky is succeeded as Great Prince of Vladimir–Suzdal by his brother Vsevolod III.
- Sverre becomes joint king of Norway with Magnus VI.

May 5 King Henry II of England makes his youngest son, John, lord of Ireland.

July 23 In the Treaty of Venice, the Holy Roman Emperor Frederick I Barbarossa makes a truce with the Lombard League of northern Italy and Sicily.

November 25 The invasion by Saladin, Sultan of Egypt and Syria, of the kingdom of Jerusalem is defeated by King Baldwin IV at Montgisard.

1178

- Malatya, the last stronghold of the Danishmend dynasty, falls to Kilij Arslan II, Sultan of Rūm.

July 30 The Holy Roman Emperor Frederick I Barbarossa is crowned as king of Burgundy, at Arles, Burgundy (in modern France).

August 29 Left isolated by the Treaty of Anagni between the Holy Roman Emperor Frederick I Barbarossa and Pope Alexander III, the antipope Calixtus III resigns.

November 11 In a diet (legislative assembly) at Speyer, the Saxons make a formal complaint to the Holy Roman Emperor Frederick I Barbarossa about the oppressive rule of Henry the Lion, Duke of Saxony and Bavaria, who is summoned to answer.

1179

- A naval expedition sent by Yūsuf abu Ya'qub, the Almohad emir of northwest Africa and Muslim Spain, fails to take the Portuguese city of Lisbon.
- King Alfonso VIII of Castile and King Alfonso II of Aragon conclude a treaty defining the boundary between their future conquests within Spain from the Muslims.
- Pope Alexander III recognizes his vassal Alfonso I as king of Portugal.
- The Portuguese crusading Order of Knights of Avís is founded by this date.
- The Toltec city of Chichén Itzá on the Yucatán peninsula of Central America, built entirely on alignments with the rising and setting of the sun and Venus, is sacked and burned by the Mayapán king Hunac Ceel.

June 10 Saladin, Sultan of Egypt and Syria, defeats King Baldwin V of Jerusalem on the River Litani.

June 24 Henry the Lion, Duke of Saxony and Bavaria, is put under the ban of the Holy Roman Empire for failing to appear before Emperor Frederick I Barbarossa to answer charges of oppressive rule in Saxony.

September 9 An antipope, Innocent III, is elected by a schismatic group of cardinals.

November 1 Philip Augustus is crowned as Philip II and associated with his father Louis VII as joint king of France.

SCIENCE, TECHNOLOGY, AND MEDICINE

Health and Medicine

1173

- The earliest authenticated references to an influenza epidemic in Europe are recorded.
- The Spanish-born Jewish physician Moses ben Maimōn (Maimonides) arrives in Cairo, Egypt, where he will become physician to Saladin, the sultan of Egypt, and write his famous medical and philosophical works.

Math

1175

- Arabic numerals are introduced into Europe with Gerard of Cremona's translation of the Egyptian astronomer Ptolemy's astronomical work the *Almagest*.

Science

1175

- The Italian scholar Gerard of Cremona makes a Latin translation from Arabic of Ptolemy's astronomical work the *Almagest*, having learned Arabic especially for the task. It becomes the work's most popular translation of the Middle Ages.

1178

- Monks at Canterbury, England, report seeing fire issue from one of the horns of the new moon. It is the only authenticated record of a lunar meteor impact.
- The Chinese scholar Han Ch'an-chih writes the treatise *Chü lu* on oranges, which describes 27 different varieties.
- The English astronomer Roger of Hereford compiles and publishes astronomical tables to support his treatise on planetary motions.

1179

- The German abbess Hildegard von Bingen writes *Physica/Physics*, a closely observed encyclopedia of natural history, including the earliest known reference to hopped beer.

Technology

1174

- Benedictine monks at Engelberg (in modern Switzerland) develop woodblocks to print illuminated capitals in their manuscripts.

1175

- A water-powered stamp mill for manufacturing wrought metal objects is built at the town of Leoben, in the Styria region of Austria.

1176

- Construction begins on London Bridge, the main crossing over the River Thames in London, England. The bridge has 19 arches, with access controlled by a drawbridge, and buildings overhanging the river on either side of the road.

Transportation

1179–1209

- The "Naviglio Grande" canal in Lombardy, Italy, is constructed. It is built to provide irrigation for the area and to transport building materials for Milan Cathedral.

ARTS AND IDEAS

Architecture

1172

- The Almohads (a group of puritanical Muslims) build a congregational mosque in Seville, Spain. The minaret known as Giralda Tower is later incorporated into the cathedral there.

1174

- The choir of Canterbury Cathedral, England, is destroyed by fire. Its reconstruction by the French mason William of Sens marks the beginnings of English Gothic style.

1176

- Construction begins on Saladin's citadel in Cairo, Egypt.

1178–1208

- The abbey church at Fossanova, near Rome, is constructed.

1179

- William the Englishman succeeds the French William of Sens as mason in charge at Canterbury Cathedral, England, and continues the development of the English Gothic style and the use of Purbeck marble.

Literature and Language

1170

c. 1170 "Richeut," an early extant example of a *fabliau* (fable), is written in French.

c. 1170 French poet Chrétien de Troyes writes *Erec et Enide/Eric and Enid*, a poetic romance about courtly love.

- Etienne de Fougères writes "Le Livre des Manières"/ "The Book of Manners," a poem on morality and the rewards and punishments of the afterlife. It is one of the earliest didactic French poems.
- Heinrich von Veldeke writes his "Servatius," a poem about the patron saint of Maastricht, in a Dutch-German dialect.

1173

- Spanish Jew Benjamin ben Jonah of Tudela writes *Masse'oth Rabbi Binyamin*. This is a Hebrew narrative of his travels to Constantinople and India, and his return journey through Egypt.

1174

- The wandering scholar Garnier de Point-Ste.-Maxence completes *La Vie de St. Thomas Becket/The Life of St. Thomas Becket*, a poem in Alexandrines.

c. 1175

- Ibn-Tufayl writes *Hayy ibn-Yaqzan/The Living One*, a philosophical romance about a man on an uninhabited island, which is probably a model for the book *Robinson Crusoe*.

c. 1176

- French poet Chrétien de Troyes writes "Cligès," an Arthurian romance.

c. 1178

- French poet Chrétien of Troyes writes his Arthurian romances *Yvain* and *Lancelot*.

Music

c. 1170

- The *Magnus Liber/Great Book*, a collection of two-voiced polyphonic music, comes to light. Its compilation is accredited to Master Leoninus, who is thought to have been attached to Notre Dame in Paris, France.

Thought and Scholarship

1170

- Anglo-Norman poet Thomas of Brittany writes a narrative poem on the legend of Tristan and Iseult, the earliest extant text on this theme.

c. 1171

- Helmold writes a chronicle of the Christian missions to the Slavs to 1171.

SOCIETY

Everyday Life

1176

- The first known *eisteddfod*, a session of bardic poetry and music, is held at Cardigan Castle in Wales. The tradition dates back to the 7th century at least.

Religion

1170

- Peter Valdes, a merchant from Lyon, France, forms a Christian movement called the Waldenses, or the "Poor Men of Lyons." He preaches against the worldliness of the clergy and opposes the dualism of the Cathari.

1174

July 12   King Henry II of England does penance at Canterbury for Archbishop Thomas à Becket's murder in 1170.

1175

- The Japanese Buddhist Amida cult becomes a separate sect called Pure Land Buddhism. It is founded by the priest Honen, who specifies that the chanting of the name Amida Buddha is the only practice necessary to reach the pure land (paradise).

1179

March 5–19   The third Lateran Council, held by Pope Alexander III, restricts the election of the pope to the college of cardinals, condemns heretics and their protectors and defenders, and refuses Christian burial to men killed in tournaments.

BIRTHS & DEATHS

1170

c. 1170   St. Dominic, founder of the Dominican order of friars, born in Caleruega, Castile, Spain (–1221).

c. 1170   Wolfram, German poet, author of "Parzival," born (–c. 1220).

- Alexander of Hales, influential theologian and philosopher, born in Hales, Gloucestershire, England (–1245).
- Hemacandra, Jain sage and author who established Jainism in Gujarat India, dies.
- Valdemar II, Danish king 1202–41, who expanded the Danish Empire to include Estonia, and reformed the legal code, born in Denmark (–1241).

November 18   Albert I the Bear, the first elector of Brandenburg, dies.

November 23   King Owain the Great of Gwynedd, ruler of Wales 1137–70, dies (c. 63).

December 29   St. Thomas à Becket, Chancellor of England 1155–62 and archbishop of Canterbury 1162–70, is murdered by knights of the court of King Henry II (52).

1172

- Baldwin I, first Latin emperor of Constantinople 1204–05, born (–1205).

1173

- Shinran, Japanese Buddhist philosopher who founded Jodo Shinshu, the largest school of Buddhism in Japan, born near Kyoto, Japan (–1263).

1175

November 20   St. Edmund of Abingdon (Edmund Rich), scholar and archbishop of Canterbury 1234–40, born in Abingdon, England (–1240).

1176

April 20   Richard de Clare, 2nd Earl of Pembroke (and Striguil), who initiated the conquest of Ireland with his invasion of the island in 1170, dies in Dublin, Ireland (c. 46).

1178

- Dominicus Gundissalinus, archdeacon of Segovia, a major translator from Arabic, is active.

1179

- Snorri Sturluson, Icelandic poet, and writer of sagas, born in Iceland (–1241).

September 17   Hildegard von Bingen, German Benedictine abbess, philosopher, mystic, and musician, dies in Rupertsberg, near Bingen, Germany (c. 81).

1180–1189

POLITICS, GOVERNMENT, AND ECONOMICS

Business and Economics

1180

- The Flemish city of Bruges is now the principal international market center of northern Europe.

1188

- Saladin, Sultan of Egypt and Syria sends Chinese porcelain to Damascus: though it has been produced in China from the 9th century, this is the first reference to its export to the Middle East.

Human Rights

1189–90

- Pogroms against the Jews throughout England culminate in a massacre of 150 Jews at York, England.

Politics and Government

1180

- At the congress of Łęczyca, Grand Prince Casimir (Kazimierz) II of Poland persuades the prelates and nobles present to make his title hereditary.
- Minamoto Yoritomo begins his revolt (known as the Gempeii War) against the Taira samurai clan which, in effect, rules Japan. At the start of his rebellion, Minamoto Yoritomo sets up the Board of Retainers to direct his "feudal" organization.
- Serbia becomes independent of the Byzantine Empire under Stephen Nemanja, Grand Zupan of Rascia.
- The Byzantine emperor Manuel I Comnenus makes *pronoia* (grants of land held subject to military service) heritable; thus they come to resemble Western feudal tenures. They are also evidence of the decay of imperial authority following the defeat at Manzikert in 1176.

January 1 The antipope Innocent III is deposed after being betrayed and captured by one of his supporters.

April 4 Philip II, joint king of France with his father Louis VII, marries Isabel of Hainault, niece of Philip of Flanders and heiress to Artois.

June 28 Philip II, joint king of France with his father Louis VII, and King Henry II of England confer at Gisors, France.

June 29 Sayf-ad-Din of Mosul dies; he is succeeded by his brother Izz-ad-Din.

September 16 In a diet (legislative assembly) at Altenburg, the Holy Roman Emperor Frederick I Barbarossa partitions the duchy of Bavaria, confiscated from Henry the Lion; Otto of Wittelsbach is created duke but Styria is detached as another duchy.

September 18 King Louis VII of France dies; his son Philip II is now sole king.

September 24 The Byzantine emperor Manuel I Comnenus dies; he is succeeded by his son, Alexius II, with his widow, Mary of Antioch, acting as regent.

1181

- Jayavarman VII is crowned as king of the Khmer Empire following his expulsion of the Chams.
- King Béla III of Hungary seizes Dalmatia and parts of Croatia and Sirmium from the Byzantine Empire.
- King Philip II of France confirms the franchises of Bourges: this is the earliest known confirmation by a king of France of the detailed franchises of a town.
- The Holy Roman Emperor Frederick I Barbarossa, supported by King Valdemar I of Denmark, completes his dispossession of Henry the Lion when the port of Lübeck, founded by Henry, surrenders to Frederick; Henry submits and is banished (to the court of his father-in-law King Henry II of England) for three years, retaining only Brunswick.
- The Pomeranian princes of Stettin (modern Szczecin, Poland) become vassals of the Holy Roman Empire; thus western Pomerania, where Germans have settled, leaves the Polish sphere of influence.

1181–1183 King Henry II of England's sons, Henry, John, Richard and Geoffrey, again rebel against him, assisted and encouraged by King Philip II of France.

September 1 Cardinal Ubald of Ostia is elected as Pope Lucius III following the death of Pope Alexander III.

December 4 Ismail, Emir of Aleppo, Syria, dies; he is succeeded by his cousin Izz-ad-Din of Mosul, who thus reunites the Zangid lands.

1182

- The former prince of Antioch, now lord of Oultrejordain, Reynald of Châtillon, launches a piratical expedition on the Red Sea which plunders Muslim pilgrims and merchant shipping.
- The Holy Roman Emperor Frederick I Barbarossa intervenes in the succession dispute among the Přemysl rulers of Bohemia, taking the opportunity to make the Bohemian province of Moravia a margravate subject only to the empire.

May 12 King Valdemar I the Great of Denmark dies; he is succeeded by his son Cnut IV who refuses to do homage to the Holy Roman Emperor Frederick I Barbarossa.

July 7 Saladin, Sultan of Egypt and Syria, and King Baldwin IV of Jerusalem fight indecisively at Belvoir, south of the Sea of Galilee.

September 9 Andronicus I Comnenus, nephew of the former emperor John II Comnenus, usurps the throne of the Byzantine Empire, murdering the current emperor Alexius II, his mother, and her advisers.

October 10 Saladin, Sultan of Egypt and Syria, takes the towns of Edessa and Nisibis from the Zangid emirate.

1183

- Rory O'Connor, the High King of Ireland, is deposed by his son Conchobar who renews Irish resistance to the Anglo-Norman invaders.
- The Taira samurai clan flees from the Japanese imperial capital Kyoto before the advance of Minamoto Yoshinka.

June 12 Following the death of the "young king" Henry, the first rebellion of King Henry II of England's sons collapses.

June 18 Saladin, Sultan of Egypt and Syria, takes the Syrian city of Aleppo from the Zangids.

June 25 By the Treaty of Constance, the Holy Roman Emperor Frederick I Barbarossa makes peace with the Lombard League of northern Italy, granting its cities self-government in return for an oath of allegiance.

August 24 Saladin, Sultan of Egypt and Syria, makes the city of Damascus in Syria his capital.

1184

- King George III of Georgia dies; he is succeeded by his daughter Thamar.
- Minamoto Yoshitsune, brother of Minamoto Yoritomo, defeats and kills his cousin and rival Yoshinaka.
- The island of Cyprus revolts against Byzantine rule.

May 5 Yūsuf abu Ya'qub, the Almohad emir of northwest Africa and Muslim Spain, invades Portugal.

June 15 King Magnus VI of Norway is defeated and killed by his coruler King Sverre who now rules alone.

September 10 Yūsuf abu Ya'qub, the Almohad emir of northwest Africa and Muslim Spain, dies, thus ending his attack on Portugal; he is succeeded by his son Abu-Yūsuf Ya'qub.

October 29 Henry VI, the son of the Holy Roman Emperor Frederick I Barbarossa, is betrothed to Constance, the presumptive heiress to the kingdom of Sicily.

1185

- King Philip II of France suppresses the office of chancellor to avoid the danger of influential offices being held by magnates.
- The Bulgarian brothers Theodore and Asen, from the ruling line of the Second Bulgarian Empire, begin an anti-Byzantine revolt.

February 11   The Holy Roman Emperor Frederick I Barbarossa grants a charter of liberties to the Italian city of Milan and makes an alliance against Pope Lucius III.

March 3   King Baldwin IV of Jerusalem dies; he is succeeded by his young nephew, Baldwin V.

April 4   Prince John, the youngest son of King Henry II of England, recently made Lord of Ireland, begins his unsuccessful expedition to Ireland.

April 25   At the naval battle of Dan-no-ura the Japanese Minamoto clan finally destroys the Taira samurai clan. Minamoto Yoritomo, adopting the title Sei-i-tai Shogun ("barbarian-suppressing generalissimo"), becomes the effective ruler of Japan, making his capital at Kamakura (near Tokyo). Rule by the shoguns (military rulers) continues in Japan until 1868.

June 6   King William I of Sicily takes the island of Corfu and the port of Durazzo in his invasion of the Byzantine Empire.

July 7   By the Treaty of Boves with Count Philip of Flanders, King Philip II of France acquires Amiens and other lands and titles in northeast France, thus doubling the extent of the royal domain.

August 8   The Normans of Sicily sack the Byzantine port of Thessaloníki.

September 9   Henry the Lion, the dispossessed Duke of Saxony and Bavaria, returns to Germany from his exile in England and tries to regain his influence in Saxony.

September 12   The Byzantine emperor Andronicus I Comnenus is killed in a riot in Constantinople; he is succeeded by his cousin, Isaac II Angelus, who defeats the Normans at Mosinopolis and expels them.

November 25   Humbert Crivelli, archbishop of Milan, is elected as Pope Urban III following the death of Pope Lucius III.

December 6   Alfonso I, the first king of Portugal, dies; he is succeeded by his son, Sancho I.

1186

- Mohammad, Sultan of Ghur (modern Afghanistan) destroys the Ghaznavid emirate and occupies its capital, Lahore.
- Pope Urban III encourages Archbishop Philip of Cologne to revolt against the Holy Roman Emperor Frederick I Barbarossa in the summer, who therefore returns from Italy to Germany, while his son King Henry VI of Germany suppresses revolts in Romagna and the Campania, Italy.
- The Bulgarian brothers Theodore and Asen, from the ruling line of the Second Bulgarian Empire, liberate Bulgaria from Byzantine rule in the autumn while their allies the Cumans ravage Thrace.
- The Italian city of Milan is first known to be governed by an elected *rector*.

January 27   Henry VI, son of the Holy Roman Emperor Frederick I Barbarossa, marries Constance, the presumptive heiress to the kingdom of Sicily; he is crowned as king of Burgundy, Germany, and Italy, and entitled "Caesar."

August 8   King Baldwin V of Jerusalem dies; he is succeeded by his mother, Sibylla, who crowns her husband Guy of Lusignan as king of Jerusalem.

December 12   An assembly of German prelates at Gelnhausen declare their support for the Holy Roman Emperor Frederick I Barbarossa in his dispute with Pope Urban III over the archbishopric of Trier.

1187

- King Philip II of France makes an alliance with the Holy Roman Emperor Frederick I Barbarossa to free himself for an (indecisive) campaign against King Henry II of England.
- The Byzantine emperor Isaac II Angelus makes a truce with the Bulgarian brothers Theodore and Asen, from the ruling line of the Second Bulgarian Empire, recognizing Bulgarian independence de facto; Theodore (now named Peter) is crowned as czar, although Asen actually rules.
- The Saracen ruler Saladin institutes the policy of doctors' neutrality, ordering his surgeons to treat the wounded of both sides in battles with the crusaders, and allowing physicians from both sides to move freely between the two camps.

July 3   The army of the kingdom of Jerusalem, advancing to raise the siege of Tiberias, is trapped and destroyed by Saladin, Sultan of Egypt and Syria, at the Horns of Hattin; King Guy of Jerusalem is captured and Reynald of Châtillon beheaded. The kingdom of Jerusalem is left virtually defenseless as Saladin takes the Franks' castles one by one.

October 3   Saladin, Sultan of Egypt and Syria, takes Jerusalem after a short siege.

November 11   Conrad, Marquis of Montferrat, one of the leaders of the First Crusade, repulses an attack by Saladin, Sultan of Egypt and Syria, on the city of Tyre.

December 17   Pope Gregory VIII dies, shortly after proclaiming the Third Crusade to liberate Jerusalem from the Muslims. Two days later, Paul Scolari is elected as Pope Clement III.

1188

- Kilij Arslan II, Sultan of Rūm, abdicates because of his advanced age, dividing his kingdom among his 11 sons; the succession is disputed.
- King Alfonso IX holds the first Cortes (parliament) of León, known to have been attended by representatives of towns as well as prelates and nobles.

January 1   King Henry II of England and King Philip II of France, meeting at Gisors, France, to discuss a truce, are persuaded to make peace and go on crusade; they impose "Saladin tithes" to finance their expeditions.

January 21   King Ferdinand II of León dies; he is succeeded by his son, Alfonso IX.

March 27   The Holy Roman Emperor Frederick I Barbarossa takes the Cross (agrees to go on crusade); by his order Henry the Lion, the dispossessed Duke of Saxony and Bavaria, goes back into exile.

July 7   Saladin, Sultan of Egypt and Syria, releases King Guy of Jerusalem.

November 11   King Henry II of England, his son Richard the Lion-Hearted, and King Philip II of France meet at

Bonmoulins, France; Richard does homage to Philip, thus breaking with Henry.

1189

- Hamburg becomes an imperial free city.
- The Byzantine emperor Isaac II Angelus defeats Stephen Nemanja of Rascia and forces him to cede his recent conquests.
- The Japanese shogun (military ruler) Minamoto Yoritomo destroys the Fujiwara samurai clan of Kiraizumi and so completes his subjection of Japan.

April 3 In the Peace of Strasbourg, Pope Clement III and the Holy Roman Emperor Frederick I Barbarossa resolve their differences over the appointment to the archbishopric of Trier in the Rhineland Palatinate. Both the papal and imperial candidates are dropped and a new election is held.

May 5 The Holy Roman Emperor Frederick I Barbarossa departs for Palestine from Regensburg, Bavaria, on the Third Crusade.

July 3 King Philip II of France, supporting a rebellion by Richard the Lion-Hearted against his father, King Henry II of England, takes the French town of Tours from Henry. The next day, Henry, now dying, capitulates to Philip and his own son Richard the Lion-Hearted at Colombières, France.

July 7 King Sancho I of Portugal takes the towns of Alvor and Silves in the Algarve from Abu-Yūsuf Ya'qub, the Almohad emir of northwest Africa and Muslim Spain, with the aid of English crusaders bound for Palestine.

September 3 Richard I the Lion-Hearted is crowned as king of England; this date becomes the limit of legal memory (from 1290).

October 4 Reinforced by crusaders from Europe, the Franks under King Guy of Jerusalem defeat an attempt by Saladin, Sultan of Egypt and Syria, to raise the siege of Acre (present-day Akko, Israel).

October 10 With the Holy Roman Emperor Frederick I Barbarossa absent on crusade, Henry the Lion, the dispossessed Duke of Saxony and Bavaria, returns to Germany and recovers much of Saxony and Holstein.

November 18 King William II of Sicily dies without issue; his bastard cousin Tancred, Count of Lecce, seizes the throne.

December 12 Having raised money by the sale of offices and privileges, King Richard I the Lion-Hearted leaves England to join the Third Crusade, leaving William de Mandeville, Earl of Essex, and Hugh Puiset, bishop of Durham, in charge of England as justiciars (vice regents in the king's absence).

SCIENCE, TECHNOLOGY, AND MEDICINE

Health and Medicine

1184

- The Armenian physician Mekhitur of Her writes the medical treatise *Consolation in Cases of Fever*.

Technology

1180

- A windmill with vertical sails (not a horizontal post mill) is recorded for the first time in western Europe, at St.-Sauveur-le-Vicomte, Normandy.
- Glazed windows are recorded in use in private English houses. There is no native glass industry, so panels are imported by wealthy landowners.

1189

- The first paper mill in Christian Europe is established at Hérault in France, though parchment remains by far the most popular writing material of the time.

Transportation

1180

- A movable lock gate is installed at the Flemish North Sea port of Damme, linking the Bruges–Sluis canal to the estuary of the River Zwijn.
- The earliest European reference to a sternpost rudder is recorded. The increasing use of sails means that rudders are needed for steering, and oar-powered boats with steering oars become redundant.

1187

- The English scholar Alexander Neckham reports that mariners have a device (clearly a compass) that enables them to navigate "even when the Polar Star is hidden by clouds."

1188

- The bridge across the River Rhône at Avignon, France, the "Pont St. Benezet," is completed.

ARTS AND IDEAS

Architecture

1185

- Construction begins on the third abbey church of Pontigny, France, and the rebuilding of the choir of the abbey church at Vézelay, France.

1188

- A mosque is built at Rabat, in the Almohad Emirate (in modern Morocco), with the intention of making it the largest in the Muslim world.
- Construction begins on Wells Cathedral in Wells, England.
- The mausoleum of Kilij Arslan II is built at Konya, Persia.

Literature and Language

c. **1180**

- Eilhart von Oberg writes *Tristrant*, the first German version of the legend.

- Walter of Chatillon writes his *Alexandreis*, an epic poem in Latin about Alexander the Great.

1182
- Ibn-Munqidh writes *Kitāb al-i'tibār/Learning by Example*, his autobiography of a soldier–poet which includes large sections on hunting, hawking, and fishing.

1185
- Spanish Muslim ibn-Jubayr writes *Rahlat al-Kinānī*, an account of his pilgrimage to Mecca in the period 1183–85, which contains valuable information about the transport of the time.

c. **1187**
- *Slovo o polku Igoreve/The Campaign of Igor*, an anonymous prose poem in epic form, is written about the campaign of Igor of Novgorod–Seversk against the Cumans. This marks the beginning of Russian literature.

c. **1188**
- Persian poet Ilyās ibn-Yūsuf Nizāmī completes his cycle of five poems known as *Khamseh/The Quintuplet*.

c. **1189**
- Heinrich von Veldeke completes his High German poem *Eneit* based on Virgil's *Aeneid*. It marks the beginnings of the *roman d'antiquité* in Germany.

Thought and Scholarship

c. **1180**
- André le Chapelain (Andreas Capellanus), chaplain to King Louis VII of France, writes *De arte honeste amandi/The Honest Art of Love*, a treatise based on Ovid (the Roman poet) that summarizes courtly love.

1183
- John Cinnamos writes a chronicle of the Byzantine emperors John and Manuel Comnenus in the period 1118–76, a continuation of the *Alexiad* written by Anna Comnena.

1184
- Hung Kua writes *Li Shih*, a collection of inscriptions of the Han period in China (206 BC–AD 220) with facsimiles.
- William of Tyre writes his *Historia rerum in partibus transmarinis gestarum/History of Deeds in Overseas Regions*, a history of the Latin kings of Jerusalem in the period 1095–1184.

c. **1186**
- Giraldus Cambrensis (Gerald of Wales) writes *Expugnatio Hibernica/The Campaign in Ireland*, an account of King Henry II of England's conquest of Ireland in the period 1169–85.

1187
- The chronicles of Svend Aagesön, the first known Danish historian, are recorded. They relate the history of the kings of Denmark in the period 300–1187.

1188
c. 1188 *De legibus et consuetudinibus Regni Anglia/On the Laws and Customs of the Kingdom of England*, a Latin treatise on English common law, is written. The first reasoned account of legal procedure, it is probably written by Ranulf Glanville or his nephew Hubert Walter.
- Giraldus Cambrensis (Gerald of Wales) begins his *Itinerarium Cambriae/Journey Through Wales*, a description of Wales.

SOCIETY

Education

1180
- Josce of London founds the first college of the emerging University of Paris, France, the Collège des Dix-huit.

BIRTHS & DEATHS

1181
- St. Francis of Assisi, founder of the Franciscan monastic orders and church reformer, principal patron saint of Italy, born in Assisi (–1226).
- March 22 Ibn al-Farid, celebrated Arab Sufi poet, whose best-known works include the "Khamriyah"/"Wine Ode," born in Cairo, Egypt (–1235).
- August 30 Alexander III (original name Rolando Bandinelli), pope 1159–81, a vigorous defender of papal authority against the Holy Roman Emperor Frederick I Barbarossa and King Henry II of England, dies in Rome, Italy (*c.* 76).

1182
- Franciscus Accursius (Francesco Accorso), Italian jurist responsible for the renovation of Roman law and author of the *Glossa ordinaria/*

General Gloss (1220–50), born in Bagnolo, Tuscany, Italy (–1260).
- May 12 Valdemar I, King of Denmark 1157–82, who defeated the Wends (Slavs) and established the Valdemar dynasty, dies in Denmark (51).

1185
- Ogedai, Mongol ruler 1229–47 who greatly expanded the Mongol Empire, born in Mongolia (–1241).
- November 24 Pope Lucius III (Waldo Allucingoli) dies.

1186
- King Parakramabahu I of Ceylon, leader of successful naval expeditions against Burma (modern Myanmar) and India, dies.

1187
- Gerard of Cremona, Italian scholar and translator of classical Greek

and Arabic texts into Latin, dies in Toledo, Spain (*c.* 73).
- September 5 Louis VIII the Lion, King of France 1223–26 who aided the English barons against King John of England, born in Paris, France (–1226).

1188
- Blanche of Castile, regent of France 1226–34 and 1248–52, wife of Louis VIII and mother of Louis IX, who unified many of the French territories, born in Palencia, Castile (–1252).

1189
- July 6 Henry II, King of England 1154–89, father of Richard I and John, dies near Tours, France (*c.* 56).
- November 18 William II, last Norman king of Sicily, dies in Palermo, Sicily (*c.* 35).

1185

- The University of Oxford, England, is now well established.

Religion

1180

- The Hall of the Great Buddha at Nara, Japan, is destroyed by fire.

1181

- Cardinal Henry of Albano directs fighting against Albigensian (Cathar) heretics in southern France.

1184

- Danish missionaries begin the conversion of the Livs of Latvia.

October   Pope Lucius and the Holy Roman Emperor Frederick I Barbarossa hold the council of Verona, which organizes proceedings against heretics. Both the Waldensians (the "Poor Men of Lyons") and the

Cathari are condemned. However, they fail to resolve their differences over Tuscany.

1186

May 17   Pope Urban III causes a break with the Holy Roman Emperor Frederick I Barbarossa by consecrating the papal candidate for the archbishopric of Trier despite having sworn earlier that he would not do this.

1187

- Albert of Morra is elected as Pope Gregory VIII following the death of Pope Urban III.

Sports

1180

- King Sancho VI of Navarre writes *Los paramientos de la caza/The Regulations for the Chase*, a treatise on falconry.

1190–1199

POLITICS, GOVERNMENT, AND ECONOMICS

Business and Economics

1194

May 12   Having raised money by the sale of charters and a new tax called the Carucage (based on the Danegeld), King Richard I the Lion-Hearted leaves England to reestablish his authority in his French lands.

Politics and Government

1190

- Ballāla II, the Hoysala king, completes the destruction of the Chalukya kingdom in southern India.
- The Bulgarians defeat the Byzantine emperor Isaac II Angelus's attempt to subjugate them.
- The Byzantine emperor Isaac II Angelus defeats Stephen Nemanja of Rascia on the River Morava; Stephen is able, however, to retain his lands, including his former principality of Zeta.
- The Christian military order of the Knights of the Cross (later known as the Teutonic Knights) is founded at

Acre, Palestine (modern Akko, Israel) to crusade against the pagan Slavs and Balts.

February 2   By the Treaty of Adrianople, the Byzantine emperor Isaac II Angelus permits the Holy Roman Emperor Frederick I Barbarossa and his German crusaders to cross into Anatolia (modern Turkey).

May 5   Bernard, Count of Anhalt, defeats Henry the Lion, the dispossessed Duke of Saxony and Bavaria, at Segeberg.

May 18   The Holy Roman Emperor Frederick I Barbarossa and the German crusaders fight their way into Konya, the capital of the sultanate of Rūm.

June 10   The Holy Roman Emperor Frederick I Barbarossa is drowned in the River Saleph (now Göksu) in Lesser Armenia (Cilicia). His son Frederick of Swabia takes command of the crusade but the Germans are demoralized by the death of the emperor and the army begins to break up.

June 21   The remains of the German crusading contingent arrive in Antioch.

July 4   King Philip II of France and King Richard I the Lion-Hearted of England meet at Vézelay, France, and set off on the Third Crusade.

October 4   King Richard I the Lion-Hearted of England's troops in Messina, Sicily, seize control of the town; while here, Richard appoints his chancellor, William Longchamp, bishop of Ely, as justiciar (vice regent in the king's absence) in England.

1191

- Abu-Yūsuf Ya'qub, the Almohad emir of northwest Africa and Muslim Spain, recovers the town of Silves from Portugal, restoring the River Tagus as the Muslim frontier.
- Henry the Lion, the dispossessed Duke of Saxony and Bavaria, is defeated at Boizenburg by Adolf, Count of Holstein, and loses the town of Lübeck.

March 1   King Henry VI of Germany grants a charter of liberties to the Italian town of Pisa in return for the services of its fleet.

March 3   King Philip II of France releases King Richard I the Lion-Hearted of England from his betrothal to his sister Alice at Messina, Sicily.

March 30   Cardinal Hyacinth Bobo is elected as Pope Celestine III following the death of Pope Clement III.

April 4   King Henry VI of Germany takes the town of Tusculum for the Romans, who massacre its inhabitants and raze it to the ground.

April 15   Pope Celestine III crowns Henry VI as Holy Roman Emperor following the death of his father Frederick I Barbarossa on October 10, 1190. Henry then begins his conquest of his wife's kingdom of Sicily, held by Tancred, Count of Lecce.

April 20   King Philip II of France arrives before the Palestinian port of Acre (present-day Akko, Israel).

May 8–June 5   King Richard I the Lion-Hearted of England conquers Cyprus from its Byzantine ruler, Isaac II Angelus. While there, at Limassol, he marries Berengaria of Navarre (May 12).

July 12   Four days after the arrival of King Richard I the Lion-Hearted of England, the crusaders take the Muslim-held port of Acre (present-day Akko, Israel); it becomes the capital of the kingdom of Jerusalem.

July 28   A dispute in England between John, Count of Mortain, and William Longchamp, the justiciar (vice regent in King Richard I's absence), ends with their reconciliation.

August 3   Claiming to be in ill health, King Philip II of France sails for home from Palestine.

August 8   Empress Constance is captured in a revolt in Salerno, Italy, while the Holy Roman Emperor Henry VI is forced by fever in his army to raise the siege of Naples and return to Germany.

September 7   King Richard I the Lion-Hearted of England leads the crusaders to victory over Saladin, Sultan of Egypt and Syria, at Arsuf, Palestine.

October 5   At a council held in Reading, England, Walter of Coutances, archbishop of Rouen, replaces William Longchamp who has proved unable to maintain order in England as justiciar (vice regent during the absence of King Richard I on crusade).

1192

- At the second Battle of Tarain, near Delhi in India, Sultan Mohammad of Ghur (modern Afghanistan) defeats a confederation of Rajput princes and goes on to conquer northern India.
- Empress Constance, wife of the Holy Roman Emperor Henry VI, escapes from Salerno, Italy, where she was captured during a revolt.
- With King Richard I the Lion-Hearted absent on crusade, his brother John claims to be king of England.

January 1   King Richard I the Lion-Hearted of England camps at Beit-Nuba, 19 km/12 mi from Jerusalem, but realizing that the crusaders lack the resources to hold the city, even if they can capture it, he retires to Ascalon which he refortifies.

March 3   King Philip II of France takes possession of the county of Péronne, which formerly belonged to the Count of Flanders who has recently died on crusade.

April 5   Guy of Lusignan is deposed as king of Jerusalem, receiving Cyprus from King Richard I the Lion-Hearted of England in compensation; Conrad, Marquis of Montferrat, is elected in his place.

April 28   Conrad, Marquis of Montferrat and King of Jerusalem, is murdered by Assassins (members of a militant offshoot of the Islamic Ismaili sect) sent by Rashid ad-Din Sinan, the "Old Man of the Mountain;" Henry of Champagne is elected as king of Jerusalem at Acre (present-day Akko, Israel).

May 23   King Richard I the Lion-Hearted of England takes Daron, thus completing the recovery of the Palestinian coast from Saladin, Sultan of Egypt and Syria.

June 6   King Richard I the Lion-Hearted of England camps within sight of the city of Jerusalem, but again withdraws.

June 21   Orio Malipiero, Doge of Venice, dies; he is succeeded by Enrico Dandolo.

June 23   By the Concordat of Gravina, Pope Celestine III recognizes Tancred, Count of Lecce, as king of Sicily in an attempt to prevent a union between the Holy Roman Empire and the kingdom of Sicily that would leave the papal lands surrounded.

July 30   Saladin, Sultan of Egypt and Syria, takes the Palestinian town of Jaffa but is expelled by King Richard I the Lion-Hearted of England the next day.

August 5   King Richard I the Lion-Hearted of England defeats Saladin, Sultan of Egypt and Syria, outside the Palestinian town of Jaffa.

September 2   King Richard I the Lion-Hearted of England negotiates a three-year truce and access to Jerusalem for Christian pilgrims with Saladin, Sultan of Egypt and Syria, thereby ending the Third Crusade.

September 9   The Holy Roman Emperor Henry VI's relations with the papacy deteriorate when he rejects Albert of Brabant, Pope Celestine III's candidate for the vacant bishopric of Liège.

October 9   King Richard I the Lion-Hearted of England sails from Palestine for home, at the end of the Third Crusade.

November 24   The Holy Roman Emperor Henry VI condones the murder by German knights of Bishop Albert of Liège, the papal appointee rejected by Henry in September.

December 11   On his return journey to England from the Third Crusade, King Richard I the Lion-Hearted is captured by Leopold V, Duke of Austria, whom he humiliated at Acre in Palestine.

1193

- Přemysl Ottokar I is deposed as Duke of Bohemia and succeeded by Henry Břatislav, bishop of Prague.

January 1   By the Treaty of Vercelli, the Holy Roman Emperor Henry VI secures the support of the towns of Lombardy, northern Italy.

January 1   The Indian city of Delhi is taken by Aybak, viceroy of Mohammad, Sultan of Ghur (modern Afghanistan), and becomes the Muslim capital in India.

February 14   Leopold V, Duke of Austria, surrenders King Richard I the Lion-Hearted of England to the Holy Roman Emperor Henry VI for ransom; he uses the money to build towns and fortresses and establish the Wiener pfennig.

March 3   Saladin, Sultan of Egypt and Syria, dies; he is succeeded by his sons al-Aziz in Egypt and al-Afdal in Syria.

June 29   By the Treaty of Worms, the Holy Roman Emperor Henry VI agrees to release King Richard I the Lion-Hearted of England, on payment of 150,000 marks ransom and on Richard becoming his vassal.

July 9   By the Treaty of Mantes, King Richard I the Lion-Hearted of England's envoys recognize the conquest of the town of Gisors and the Vexin area of Normandy by King Philip II of France.

August 8   King Philip II of France, building an anti-English alliance, marries, as his second wife, Ingeborg, sister of King Cnut IV of Denmark.

October 10   King Leo II of Lesser Armenia (Cilicia) captures Prince Bohemond III of Antioch and compels him to recognize his suzerainty; Bohemond's subjects refuse to comply.

1194

- Mohammad, Sultan of Ghur (modern Afghanistan), conquers the kingdom of Kanauj, in northern India.
- Tekish, Shah of Khwarizm, defeats Tughril, the Seljuk sultan, and incorporates his dominions into his shahdom.

February 3   Following payment of the first instalment of the ransom, King Richard I the Lion-Hearted of England is released by the Holy Roman Emperor Henry VI in Mainz, in the Rhineland Palatinate, Germany; as he returns to England, he builds up an anti-French coalition in the Rhineland and Low Countries. His brother, the self-proclaimed King John of England, flees to the French court on hearing of his release.

February 20   Tancred, Count of Lecce and King of Sicily, dies; he is succeeded by his son William III, a young child incapable of organizing resistance to the Holy Roman Emperor Henry VI.

March 12   King Richard I the Lion-Hearted arrives back in England.

March 20   The Holy Roman Emperor Henry VI makes territorial concessions in Saxony to win peace with Henry the Lion, the dispossessed Duke of Saxony and Bavaria.

March 28   King Richard I the Lion-Hearted of England captures Nottingham Castle, the last castle held by the supporters of the self-proclaimed King John of England, his brother.

April 17   Richard I the Lion-Hearted is crowned king of England for the second time.

May 4   Civil war follows the death of Grand Prince Casimir (Kazimierz) II the Just of Poland; he is succeeded by his son, Leszek I.

May 5   Guy of Lusignan, ruler of Cyprus and former king of Jerusalem, dies; he is succeeded by his brother Amalric.

June 27   King Sancho VI the Wise of Navarre dies; he is succeeded by his son, Sancho VII.

July 4   King Richard I the Lion-Hearted of England routs King Philip II of France at Fréteval, France.

November 20   Having subdued southern Italy, the Holy Roman Emperor Henry VI enters Palermo, completing his conquest of the kingdom of Sicily.

December 25   The Holy Roman Emperor Henry VI is crowned as king of Sicily.

1195

April 2   The Holy Roman Emperor Henry VI has a crusade proclaimed at Bari, Italy; he dies before it can take place.

April 8   The Byzantine emperor Isaac II Angelus is deposed by his brother, Alexius III.

1196

- Asen I of Bulgaria is murdered; his brother the czar Theodore, until now a figurehead, takes control.
- Ch'oe Ch'ung-hon, a Korean general, massacres his rivals, takes control of the kingdom, and restores its unity; his family, the Ch'oe, retain power until 1258.
- King Béla III of Hungary dies; he is succeeded by his son Imre I.
- Mohammad, Sultan of Ghur (modern Afghanistan), conquers the Hindu kingdoms of Gwalior and Gujarat in India.
- Stephen Nemanja, Grand Zupan of Rascia, abdicates, having founded a Serbian state independent of the Byzantine Empire; he is succeeded by his son Stephen.

January 1   King Richard I the Lion-Hearted of England and King Philip II of France make peace by the Treaty of Louviers, in France.

April 4   In a diet (legislative assembly) at Würzburg, the Holy Roman Emperor Henry VI proposes to make the imperial title hereditary.

April 25   King Alfonso II of Aragon dies; he is succeeded by his son, Pedro II.

June 6   Although his marriage to Ingeborg of Denmark has not been annulled, King Philip II of France marries Agnes, daughter of the Duke of Meran (in Bavaria).

July 7   Al-Adil, the brother of the late Saladin, Sultan of Egypt and Syria, gains control of Egypt and much of Syria, styling himself sultan.

July 7   King Philip II of France renews the war with King Richard I the Lion-Hearted of England by seizing the town of Aumâle in Normandy.

July 18   Berber forces sent by Abu-Yūsuf Ya'qub, the Almohad emir of northwest Africa and Muslim Spain, inflict a crushing defeat on King Alfonso VIII of Castile at Alarcos (west of Ciudad Real); Ya'qub now assumes the title Al-Mansur (Spanish Almanzor, "the Victorious").

November 17   Pope Celestine III rejects the Holy Roman Emperor Henry VI's proposal to make the imperial title hereditary.

December 25   The Holy Roman Emperor Henry VI's young son Frederick II is elected "king of the Romans" (king of Germany).

1197

- Henry Břatislav, Duke of Bohemia, who conquered Moravia, dies. He is succeeded by Vladislav Henry, who soon abdicates in favor of Přemysl Ottokar I (deposed in 1193); his recognition as duke ends a period of frequent civil war and strong imperial influence in ducal elections.

- Mohammad, Sultan of Ghur (modern Afghanistan), conquers the Hindu kingdom of Anhilwara, in India.
- The Holy Roman Emperor Henry VI recognizes Amalric as king of Cyprus.
- Czar Theodore of Bulgaria is murdered; he is succeeded by his brother, Kalojan.

1198

- Přemysl Ottokar I is crowned as king of Bohemia, at Mainz, in return for his support of Philip of Swabia; with the establishment of the kingdom of Bohemia (formerly a duchy) its succession ceases to be a regular cause of dispute and civil war.

January 1　King Amalric of Cyprus is crowned as King Amalric II of Jerusalem.

January 1　Leo II is crowned as king of Lesser Armenia (Cilicia) with the assent of Pope Celestine III, the late Holy Roman Emperor Henry VI, and the Byzantine emperor Alexius III Angelus.

January 8　Lotario di Segni is elected as Pope Innocent III following the death of Pope Celestine III.

February 2　German crusaders besieging Toron flee on the approach of an Egyptian army.

March 6　Philip Hohenstaufen, Duke of Swabia, is elected "king of the Romans" (king of Germany).

May 17　The deceased Holy Roman Emperor Henry VI's son Frederick, aged three, is crowned as king of Sicily.

July 7　Otto IV, a member of the Welf dynasty and son of Henry the Lion, is crowned as "king of the Romans" (king of Germany) after he captures the city of Cologne; civil war breaks out in Germany between him and the Hohenstaufen party of Philip, Duke of Swabia, who has already been elected "king of the Romans."

August 15　Pope Innocent III proclaims the Fourth Crusade to recover Jerusalem from the Muslims and offers an indulgence to those who fight the Albigensians (Cathars: members of a heretical Christian sect) in southern France.

September 9　King Richard I the Lion-Hearted of England routs King Philip II of France at Gisors, France, and recovers the Vexin area of Normandy.

November 11　The young King Frederick of Sicily becomes the ward of Pope Innocent III, who takes possession of Spoleto and the Marches for the papacy.

1199

- Abu-Yūsuf Ya'qub, the Almohad emir of northwest Africa and Muslim Spain, dies; he is succeeded by his son, Mohammad al-Nasir.
- Llywelyn ap Iorwerth the Great, Prince of Gwynedd, north Wales, seizes the strategically important border castle at Mold.
- Minamoto Yoritomo, the first shogun (military ruler) of Japan, dies; his followers retain control of the government but fight for supremacy.
- The Russian principality of Novgorod grants privileges to German traders established in a trading factory there, so ending an embargo begun by the Germans in 1189 in retaliation for restrictions on their operations in Russia.

1199–1202　The Scots recover Ross, Caithness, and Sutherland from the Norse earldom of Orkney.

January 13　King Richard I the Lion-Hearted of England and King Philip II of France meet on the River Seine near Andeli to make a treaty of truce: Philip concedes Richard's recent gains.

April 6　King Richard I the Lion-Hearted of England dies of a wound received at the siege of the castle of Chalus in France.

May 27　John, the younger brother of the late king Richard I the Lion-Hearted, is crowned as king of England.

SCIENCE, TECHNOLOGY, AND MEDICINE

Agriculture

1191

- Tea seeds are planted in Japan by the Buddhist priest Eisai, who returned from a visit to China.

Health and Medicine

1193

- The Italian physician and scholar Burgundo of Pisa translates Galen's medical works from Greek into Latin, thus reintroducing much of Galen's thinking into western Europe.

1195

- The physician Roger of Salerno, a teacher at the medical school there, writes *Practica chirurgiae/Surgical Practice*. This is the earliest European textbook on surgery.

Technology

1190

- Coal is mined for use in iron forges at Liège, Flanders, apparently the first application for which the mineral was used. Coal mining also begins in France at around this time.

1193

- Indigo and brazilwood are imported to England from India for use in the dyeing industry.

1197

- Iron objects are manufactured with the aid of water-powered mills at Soŕs, Denmark, by this time.

ARTS AND IDEAS

Architecture

1190

- The west front of Laon Cathedral, France, continues the Gothic style of the west façades initiated at St.-Denis in Paris, France.

1193

1193–99 Jami' or Quwwat al-Islām mosque is built at Delhi, India, and becomes the first great Indian mosque.

June 10 Chartres Cathedral, France, burns down save for the west front. Its reconstruction heralds the birth of the High Gothic style of architecture.

1194

- The domed taho-to (stupa) of the Ishiyama temple at Otsu, Japan is built.

1197

- Château Gaillard in France is built by King Richard I the Lion-Hearted of England and includes the earliest known European machicolation, a parapet supported on corbels having openings through which missiles can be dropped.

1199–1236

- The Qutb-Minār Mosque is built in Old Delhi, India.

Literature and Language

c. 1190

- *Girart de Roussillon*, a Provençal *chanson de geste* ("song of exploits"), is written.
- Hugoccio, bishop of Ferrara and leading canonist, writes *Summa*, the most thorough commentary on Gratian's *Decretum/Decree*.

c. 1195

- Hartmann von Aue writes *Der Arme Heinrich/Poor Henry*, a moral epic poem written in Middle High German.

Thought and Scholarship

1191

- Jewish philosopher Moses Maimonides completes his major work, *Dalālat al-Hā'irīn/A Guide for the Perplexed*, an attempt at a rational philosophy of Judaism aimed at reconciling Jewish theology and Muslim Aristotelianism.

BIRTHS & DEATHS

1190

c. 1190 Vincent of Beauvais, French priest, theologian, and encyclopedist, author of *Speculum maius/Great Mirror*, an 80-volume encyclopedia and the largest for 500 years, born in Beauvais, France (–1264).

- Saigyō, Japanese Buddhist poet, a master of the *tanka* verse form, whose poetry reflected his love of nature, dies.

June 10 Frederick I Barbarossa, German king and Holy Roman Emperor 1152–90, dies in Armenia during the Third Crusade (*c.* 67).

1191

- Al-Suhrawardi, Islamic theologian who tried to reconcile mysticism with philosophy, dies.

March 30 Pope Clement III (Paolo Scolari) dies.

1193

- Fan Ch'êng-ta, Chinese scholar whose works include *Kuei hai yü hêng chih* on the geography and natural history of southern China, and *Fan ts'un chii p'u*, which describes 35 varieties of chrysanthemum, dies.

- Rashid ad-Din Sinan, the "Old Man of the Mountain," ruler of the Syrian branch of the Assassins from 1162, dies.

March 4 Saladin, Sultan of Egypt, Syria, Yemen, and Palestine 1171–93, who successfully captured Jerusalem from the Franks during the Third Crusade, dies in Damascus (*c.* 56).

1194

July 16 St. Clare of Assisi, abbess who founded the Poor Clares, born in Assisi, Duchy of Spoleto (–1253).

December 26 Frederick II, King of Sicily 1197–1250, king of Germany 1212–50, and Holy Roman Emperor 1220–50, King of Jerusalem 1229–43, grandson of Frederick I Barbarossa, born in Jesi, Ancona, Italy (–1250).

1195

c. 1195 Bernart de Ventadour, Provençal *troubadour* and writer of *chansons d'amour* ("songs of love"), dies.

August 6 Henry III the Lion, Duke of Saxony 1142–80 and Bavaria (as Henry XII) 1156–80, vigorous supporter of the Holy Roman Emperor Frederick I Barbarossa, and founder of the city of Munich, dies in Brunswick, Saxony (*c.* 66).

August 15 St. Anthony of Padua, Franciscan monk, doctor of the church and patron of the poor, born in Lisbon (–1231).

1196

- Béla III, King of Hungary 1173–96, under whom Hungary became a leading central European power, dies.

1197

September 10 Henry of Champagne, King of Jerusalem, dies.

September 28 Henry VI, German king 1169–97 and Holy Roman Emperor 1191–97, dies in Messina, Italy (*c.* 32).

1198

- Abu'l-Walīd ibn-Rushd (Averroës) of Córdoba, influential Muslim philosopher, who wrote important commentaries on the works of Aristotle and Plato, dies in Marrakesh, Morocco (*c.* 72).

- Roderic O'Connor, King of Connaught, last king of Ireland, who failed to repulse the English, dies near Lough Corrib, County Galway, Ireland.

January 8 Pope Celestine III (Giacinto Boboni-Ursini) dies.

August 24 Alexander II, King of Scotland 1214–49, born in Haddington, East Lothian, Scotland (–1249).

1199

April 6 Richard I ("Richard the Lion-Hearted"), King of England 1189–99, who gained popularity through his bravery during the Third Crusade, dies in Châlus, Duchy of Aquitaine (41).

1192

- Chand Bardāī writes *Chand Raīsā*, an epic poem in Hindi about Prithvī Rāj, the last Hindu ruler of Delhi, India, who died in 1192.

1195

c. 1195   Graindor de Douay writes *Chanson d'Antioche/ Song of Antioch*, a verse romance of the First Crusade.

- Nakayama Tadachika writes *Mizu-kagami/The Water Mirror*, a Japanese history spanning the period 660 BC–AD 850.

c. 1196

- Ambroise d'Evreux writes *L'Estoire de la Guerre Sainte/ The History of the Holy War*, a verse narrative of the Third Crusade, which includes the adventures of King Richard I the Lion-Hearted of England.
- Ephraim of Bonn writes his *Emek habacha*, an account of the persecution of Jews in Germany, France, and England during the period 1146–96.

SOCIETY

Everyday Life

1191

- The supposed remains of the legendary King Arthur of the Britons are discovered by monks at Glastonbury, England.

1193

- Licensed prostitution starts in Japan.

Religion

1190

- A reformed Buddhism is introduced into Burma (modern Myanmar) from Ceylon (modern Sri Lanka).

1191

- The priest Eisai introduces the Rinzai sect of Zen Buddhism into Japan from China.

1192–1333

- During this period the tea ceremony develops in Japan as a very important ritual as part of Zen Buddhist spiritual practice.

1195

May 5   Pope Celestine III annuls a sentence by the French bishops dissolving the marriage of King Philip II of France and Ingeborg of Denmark.

1198

- The Juggernaut Pagoda is completed at Orissa, India.
- The series of papal registers, which record popes' correspondence, dates from now.

1199

- A Ghurid army destroys the Buddhist university at Nalanda in Bihar; Buddhism is virtually extinguished in India as a result.
- Pope Innocent III taxes the church to fund the proposed Fourth Crusade, the first direct papal taxation of the church.

Sports

c. 1190

- English clerk William FitzStephen, clerk to Thomas à Becket, describes the sporting life of London, England, in the preface to his *Vita Sancti Thomae/Life of St. Thomas*. Running, jumping, and throwing contests are held at Smithfield on holidays. On Shrove Tuesday the schoolboys of the city of London are permitted to watch cockfighting. At Easter the water quintain, a form of tilting on boats, is staged on the River Thames. In the winter bear- and bull-baiting and boar-fighting events are staged. He also describes horse racing at Smithfield. The races are run between two or three jockeys in the form of matches to prove the quality of a horse as a prerequisite for a sale.

1200–1204

POLITICS, GOVERNMENT, AND ECONOMICS

Business and Economics

c. 1200

- The city-state of Kilwa Kisiwani (in Tanzania) issues the first coinage in sub-Saharan Africa.

Colonization

c. 1200

- The Aztecs migrate into the Valley of Mexico from the north.

Politics and Government

1200

c. 1200   The South American Chimú people of Chan Chan begin to conquer the coast of Peru.

c. 1200–*c.* 1230   Manco Capac founds the Inca state in the Cuzco Valley, Peru.

January 13   Pope Innocent III lays an interdict on France because King Philip II refuses to take back Ingeborg of Denmark as his wife.

May 22   By the Treaty of Le Goulet, King Philip II of France recognizes King John as King Richard I the Lion-Hearted of England's heir in all his French possessions: Brittany is to be held by Arthur (the son of John's illegitimate half brother Geoffrey) as John's vassal. John cedes the Vexin area and the town of Evreux, both in Normandy, to Philip.

August 30   King John of England marries Isabella, the heiress of the Count of Angoulême in France, thereby alienating her fiancé Hugh of Lusignan.

September 7   The papal interdict is lifted from France following King Philip II's separation from Agnes, daughter of the Duke of Meran (in Bavaria).

1201

- Albert, bishop of Livonia, founds Riga as a commercial center and military base for the conversion of the Livs (Latvians); to further his aims he founds the Sword Brothers, a crusading order.
- Mieszko III, former grand prince of Poland who was deposed in 1177, recovers the Grand Principality of Poland, deposing Leszek I.

April 4   By a treaty negotiated by the doge Enrico Dandolo, Venice agrees to transport the Fourth Crusade to Egypt for 85,000 marks. In addition, the Venetians offer 50 war galleys to support the crusade in return for half of its conquests.

June 8   By the Diploma of Neuss, King Otto IV cedes imperial authority in Italy to the papacy. In return, Pope Innocent III agrees to recognize Otto as "king of the Romans" (king of Germany) instead of his rival Philip Hohenstaufen, Duke of Swabia.

July 7   Pope Innocent III formally recognizes Otto IV as "king of the Romans" (king of Germany).

December 11   Pope Innocent III appeals to King Philip II of France to intervene in Languedoc, southern France, against the Albigensian (Cathar) heretics.

1202

- Grand Prince Mieszko III the Old of Poland and ruler of Kraków dies; his title dies with him. Leszek I (deposed by Mieszko in 1201) is restored as Duke of Kraków; he revives the plan to make Kraków a sovereign hereditary principality.
- Pope Innocent III excommunicates King Alfonso IX of León and puts his kingdom under an interdict for allying himself with the Muslim Almohads against the Christian kingdom of Castile.
- With the fall of Kalinjar, Mohammad, Sultan of Ghur (modern Afghanistan), completes his conquest of northern India; other Muslims, under Ikhtiyar-ad-Din, seize Bengal.

March 9   King Sverre of Norway, who has introduced a feudal administration under sheriffs, dies. He is succeeded by his son, Haakon III.

April 30   King Philip II of France declares that King John of England has forfeited his French lands because he fails to appear in Philip's court to answer the charges brought against him by Hugh of Lusignan, Count of La Marche, whose fiancée, Isabella of Angoulême, John has married. John's vassals, tired of his arbitrary rule, revolt against him.

August 1   King John of England defeats and captures Arthur, Duke of Brittany; Hugh of Lusignan, Count of La Marche; and other rebels at Mirabeau, near Poitiers, France.

November 12   King Cnut IV the Pious of Denmark dies; he is succeeded by his brother, Valdemar II the Victorious.

November 15   The crusaders take the Adriatic port of Zadar (Italian Zara) from the king of Hungary for Venice in lieu of payment for their transport to Egypt, which Venice cannot pay. Here the crusaders meet Alexius IV Angelus, son of the deposed Byzantine emperor Isaac II Angelus, who promises them troops and money for the Fourth Crusade if they will help his father regain the Byzantine throne.

1203

- King Otto IV of Germany recognizes Přemysl Ottokar I as king of Bohemia in return for Ottokar's support against his rival Philip, Duke of Swabia.
- Mohammad, Sultan of Ghur (modern Afghanistan), dies; he is succeeded by his brother Shihab-ad-Din Mohammad.
- Sumanguru of the Susu kingdom of Kaniaga sacks Koumbi, the capital of the kingdom of Ghana.
- The Khmer emperor Jayavarman VII conquers and annexes the kingdom of Champa (corresponding roughly to modern southern Vietnam).

April 3 King John of England (probably) murders Arthur, Duke of Brittany; in consequence, John's French vassals mostly desert him so that King Philip II of France easily overruns the Loire Valley.

July 17 Carrying out their part of the arrangement made the previous November with Alexius IV Angelus, son of the deposed Byzantine emperor Isaac II Angelus, the crusaders force an entry into Constantinople; the Byzantine emperor Alexius III Angelus flees and Isaac is restored.

August 1 At the crusaders' insistence, Alexius IV Angelus, the son of the restored Byzantine emperor Isaac II Angelus, is crowned as coemperor.

1204

- Kay-Khusraw I succeeds as sultan of Rūm, which has been disputed since 1188.
- King Imre I of Hungary dies; he is succeeded by his son, Ladislas III.
- Pope Innocent III grants a charter to the Sword Brothers, the military order founded by Bishop Albert of Livonia to assist in the conversion of the Livs.
- The Latins defeat Michael Angelus, the independent Byzantine ruler of Epirus, at Koundoura in Messenia, after which they conquer the Morea (the Peloponnesian area of Greece).

January 1 An anti-Latin mob in Constantinople murders the Byzantine emperor Isaac II Angelus and proclaims Nicholas Canabus as emperor.

January 1 King Haakon III of Norway dies; he is succeeded by his nephew Gottorm.

February 8 The co-Byzantine emperor Alexius IV Angelus dies in an uprising of the citizens of Constantinople, angered at his inability to fulfill his pledge to the crusaders who had helped install him on the throne. Nicholas Canabus, proclaimed emperor by the anti-Latins, is imprisoned; Alexius V Ducas Murtzuphlus, son-in-law of the deposed Alexius III and leader of the anti-Latin forces in Constantinople, assumes the Byzantine throne.

March 8 King Philip II of France takes Château Gaillard, a key fortress protecting King John of England's duchy of Normandy.

April 12 Realizing that the Byzantine promise of help for their crusade is not going to be kept, the crusaders take the Byzantine capital Constantinople by storm and sack it for three days. The emperor Alexius V Ducas Murtzuphlus flees, as does Constantine XI Lascaris after being offered the throne by Byzantine nobles during the attack.

May 5 Alexius Comnenus, grandson of the former Byzantine emperor Andronicus I Comnenus, seizes the Black Sea port of Trebizond (modern Trabzon, Turkey) and establishes an independent Byzantine state.

May 16 Baldwin, Count of Flanders, is crowned as Latin emperor of Constantinople.

June 24 With the fall of the Norman capital Rouen, King Philip II's conquest of Normandy is complete; of his French possessions King John of England retains only Gascony and the Channel Islands (originally part of the duchy of Normandy).

August 8 King Gottorm of Norway dies; he is succeeded by Inge II.

September 9 Sultan al-Adil of Egypt and King Amalric II of Jerusalem make a treaty of peace for six years.

October 10 The Latin emperor Baldwin of Constantinople, the Venetians, and the crusaders partition the Byzantine Empire by treaty. Continuing Byzantine resistance, however, means that many of the crusaders are unable to take possession of their territories.

November 8 Kalojan is crowned as king of Bulgaria (styling himself czar) by a papal legate, following his agreement with Pope Innocent III to reject Orthodox Christianity and accept the Roman church.

November 11 King Pedro II of Aragon swears fealty to Pope Innocent III in Rome, and thus his kingdom becomes a papal fief.

December 12 Theodore Lascaris, the brother of Constantine XI, is defeated by the Latin emperor Baldwin of Constantinople near Poimanenon.

SCIENCE, TECHNOLOGY, AND MEDICINE

Agriculture

1200

- The Spanish Muslim agriculturist ibn-al-'Awwam writes his treatise *Kitāb al-Filāhah*, which describes 585 plants and the many techniques for their cultivation, animal husbandry, and other subjects.

1203

- Many agricultural areas in France have to switch to more profitable ventures when grain is imported from the Baltic region. Farmers adapt by keeping livestock and manufacturing wine.

Health and Medicine

1204

- Jewish philosopher Moses ben Maimōn (Maimonides), physician to Saladin, writes his *Aphorisms of Medicine*, a series of thoughts on the conduct and ethics of the medical profession.

Math

1202

- Italian mathematician Fibonacci writes *Liber abaci/The Book of the Abacus*, which introduces the famous sequence of numbers now called the Fibonacci sequence.

Science

1200

- Alfred of Sareshel (or Shareshill; also known as Alfredus Anglicus) translates the work of the 11th-century Arab physician Avicenna (ibn-Sina). The work is on the subject of geology and alchemy and is called *De mineralibus/On Minerals.*

1204

- The Muslim astronomer Al-Bitrūji (Alpetragius) writes *Kitāb al-Hay'ah*, which discusses the Aristotelian system of the universe.

Technology

c. **1200**

- By this period, the Aztec and Maya peoples of Central America are manufacturing and using rubber, for example to make balls for use in games and sports.
- Chimneys come into common use, greatly increasing the efficiency and comfort of open fires by drawing the smoke up and away. Previously it escaped through a hole in the roof.

Transportation

1201

- The St. Gotthard Pass is opened through the Swiss Alps, connecting the Uri and Ticino regions and establishing a major overland commercial route between Italy and northern Europe.

ARTS AND IDEAS

Architecture

1200

- *c.* 1200 The Great Enclosure is constructed at Zimbabwe in southern Africa.
- Construction begins on the cathedrals of Bourges and Soissons, France, and the towers of Notre Dame in Paris, France.
- 1200–02 The Arhaī-Din-ka Jhomprā Mosque is constructed at Ajmēr in India.

1202–1304

- The Cloth Hall at Ypres, in Flanders (now part of Belgium), one of the finest Gothic secular buildings of the late Middle Ages, is built. It is destroyed in 1915.

Arts

c. **1203**

- The Japanese sculptor Unkei carves the giant, wooden *Ni-o/Two Kings* (guardians of the Buddhist faith) at the gateway of the Todai temple at Nara, Japan.

Literature and Language

c. **1200**

- *Das Nibelungenlied/The Song of the Nibelungen*, a folk epic in Old High German combining factual and mythological elements, is written. It later forms the basis for the 19th-century German composer Richard Wagner's operatic cycle *Der Ring des Nibelungen/The Ring of the Nibelungen.*
- Béroul writes his poem *Tristan* in Norman French, one of the finest early tellings of the myth.
- Kamban writes *Rāmāyana*, the outstanding epic poem in Tamil literature, which had its golden age under the Chola empire of southern India in the period 850–1200.

BIRTHS & DEATHS

1200

- St. Albertus Magnus of Cologne ("Doctor Universalis"), Dominican bishop and Aristotelian philosopher, teacher of St. Thomas Aquinas, born in Lauingen an der Donau, Swabia, Germany (–1280).
- November 16 St. Hugh of Avalon, French-born English Carthusian monk, bishop of Lincoln, dies in London, England (*c.* 60).

1201

- Joachim of Fiore (Gioacchino da Fiore), Italian theologian and mystic, dies in Fiore, Italy (*c.* 70).
- Roger of Hoveden (or Howden), writer of *Chronica majora/Greater Chronicle*, a Latin chronicle in two parts telling the history of England in the period 732–1201, dies.
- October 9 Robert de Sorbon, French theologian who founded the University of the Sorbonne, born in Sorbon, near Rethels, France (–1274).

1204

April 1 Eleanor of Aquitaine, Queen Consort first of King Louis VII of France, then of King Henry II of England, mother of King Richard I the Lion-Hearted and King John of England, and one of the most influential women in 12th-century Europe, dies in Fontevrault, Anjou, France (*c.* 82).

December 13 Moses ben Maimōn (or Maimonides), celebrated Jewish philosopher, jurist, and physician, dies in Egypt (69).

- Shota Rustaveli writes *The Man in the Panther's Skin*, the Georgian national epic poem.
- The *Five Icelandic Sagas*: *Njal's Saga/The Saga of Burnt Njal*; the *Laxdaela/Laxdale's Saga*; the *Eyrbyggja*, *Egla/Egil's Saga*; and *Grettis Saga/The Saga of Grettir the Strong* (legends and stories either about the deeds of the hero, or about events connected with a region) are compiled.
- Tsutsumi Chunagon compiles *Monogatari/Tales*, a collection of Japanese stories by various authors.

1202
- Jean Bodel writes "Congé/Holiday," a poem of farewell to friends on being stricken with leprosy.

Thought and Scholarship

1202
- Italian mystic Joachim of Fiore dies. In his major writings he developed the idea that history unfolds in three spiritual ages, those of the Father, the Son, and the Holy Spirit.
- Jocelyn of Brakelond writes a *Chronicle* of the Abbey of Bury St. Edmunds, England, including some English history for the period 1173–1202.

SOCIETY

Education

1200
- King Philip II's charter to the University of Paris, France, provides the first documentary recognition of its corporate existence.

1203
- The University of Siena, Italy, is founded.

1205–1209

POLITICS, GOVERNMENT, AND ECONOMICS

Business and Economics

1208
- Pope Innocent III taxes the church in France to fund the Albigensian Crusade, and approves the rule of the Society of Poor Catholics, which consists of former heretics from southern France.

Politics and Government

1205
- Azzo VI, Marquess of Este, is recognized as lord of Ferrara.
- Ikhtiyar-ad-Din, the Muslim governor of Bengal, India, fails in an attempt to invade Assam (or, possibly, Tibet).
- King Amalric of Cyprus dies; he is succeeded by his son Hugh.
- King Ladislas III of Hungary is deposed and succeeded by his uncle, Andrew II.

January 1   King John of England organizes defenses against an expected French invasion of England.

January 6   Philip, Duke of Swabia, is crowned as "king of the Romans" (king of Germany).

January 16   Pope Innocent III urges King Philip II of France to organize a crusade against the Albigensian (Cathar) heretics in Languedoc, southern France. Philip, preoccupied with his struggle with King John of England, declines.

March 3   The English barons refuse to fight for King John of England in France.

April 1   King Amalric II of Jerusalem dies; his widow Isabella rules in her own right until her death later in the year, when she is succeeded by her daughter Maria.

April 14   Czar Kalojan of Bulgaria defeats, captures, and executes the Latin emperor Baldwin of Constantinople at Adrianople (modern Edirne, Turkey).

June 1   Enrico Dandolo, Doge of Venice, dies; he is succeeded by Pietro Ziano.

1206
- Having unified most of the Mongol peoples under his leadership, the Mongol conqueror Temüjin adopts the title Genghis (or Chingis) Khan ("Universal Khan") at the *quriltai* (Mongol assembly) in the spring, founding the Mongol Empire. He later promulgates the Great Yasa (imperial law code) for the Mongols.

March 15   Mohammad, Sultan of Ghur (modern Afghanistan), is murdered by Aybak, his viceroy in India, who assumes the title of sultan of Delhi, founding the Mu'izz dynasty (sometimes known as the "Slave dynasty").

June 6   King John of England begins a campaign in western

Mongol Conquests (1206–1402)

1206–47

1206
- Having unified most of the Mongol peoples under his leadership, the Mongol conqueror Temüjin adopts the title Genghis (or Chingis) Khan ("Universal Khan") at the *quriltai* (Mongol assembly) in the spring, founding the Mongol Empire.
- The Mongol leader Genghis Khan promulgates the Great Yasa (imperial law code) for the Mongols.

1208
- At the Battle of the Irtysh, Genghis Khan defeats Gushluk, leader of the Naiman tribe, completing his unification of the Mongol peoples.

1211
- Genghis Khan destroys the Kara-Khitai Empire in east Turkestan and invades the Jin Empire for the first time.

1215
- The Mongols capture and sack Beijing, the former capital of the Jin Empire (the Jin have recently moved their capital to Kaifeng to escape Mongol attacks); its population is massacred.

1219
- Genghis Khan invades the Khwarizmian shahdom (Transoxiana and Persia) after the governor of the border city of Otrar executes Mongol merchants (in 1218).

1220
- Ray (or Rhages), the center of the Persian ceramics industry, is destroyed by the Mongols.
- February 2   Genghis Khan takes the city of Bukhara in the shahdom of Khwarizm; it is depopulated and destroyed.

1222
- May 31   A Mongol army defeats the Russian princes and the Cumans, a pagan nomadic tribe, on the Kalka, near the Sea of Azov.
- June 6   The Mongols take the city of Herat and massacre its population, completing their conquest of the Khwarizm shahdom (modern Iran, Afghanistan, and part of Central Asia).

1226
- Genghis Khan conquers the Tangut state of Xixia (now in northwest China), destroying the Tangut army in a battle on the frozen Huang He River (or Yellow River).

1231
- The Mongols begin their campaigns to conquer Korea.

1233
- The Mongols under Subedai take Kaifeng, the Jin capital: by the intervention of Yeh-lü, a Khitan prince in Mongol service, the population is spared the usual massacre.

1234
- Jin resistance to the Mongol invasions is finally crushed.

1235
- The Mongols invade the Chinese Song Empire for the first time, in retaliation for a Song attempt to seize Kaifeng, the capital of the former Jin Empire.

1236
- A Mongol army led by Batu, a grandson of Genghis Khan, conquers the Volga Bulgars.
- The kingdom of Georgia is conquered by the Mongols and reduced to tributary status.

1237
- December 21   Batu's army destroys the Russian city and principality of Riazan; invading in midwinter, the Mongols use frozen rivers as highways to make rapid progress in Russia.

1238
- February 8   Batu takes the Russian town of Vladimir, and then destroys Moscow and other central Russian cities, massacring their inhabitants.

1240
- The Mongols invade Tibet and sack the monastery of Ra-sgreng.
- December 6   The Mongol leader Batu takes and sacks the Russian principality of Kiev, then ravages the principality of Galicia, also called Red Ruthenia.

1241
- April 9   After sacking Kraków, a Mongol army led by Khaidu defeats the Poles, Silesians, and Teutonic Knights at Legnica in Poland. Grand Prince Henry II the Pious of Poland is killed. The Mongols next ravage Silesia and, when repulsed by the Bohemians, go through Moravia into Hungary.
- April 11   The main Mongol army, under Batu, defeats the Hungarians at Mohi on the River Sajo: they ravage the Danube plain, but are repulsed at Grobnok by the Croatians. A crusade is proclaimed against them in Germany.
- December 22   Lahore is taken and destroyed by the Mongols.
- December 25   Batu captures and destroys Pest on the River Danube, Hungary's largest city.

1242
- Batu withdraws the Mongol army from central Europe in the spring in order to return to the Mongol capital, Karakorum, to elect the late Great Khan Ogedai's successor: a four-year interregnum follows. Batu now organizes the Mongol territories in Russia as a semiautonomous state, known as The Khanate of the Golden Horde (supposedly named for the color of the khan's tent).

1245
- Prince Daniel of Galicia, the dominant prince in eastern central Europe, does homage to the Mongol leader Batu.
- The Mongols take Multan, in the Punjab, India.

1247
- Tibet becomes subject to Mongol rule: the Great Khan Guyuk invests his brother Koden as Sa-skya lama with authority over Tibet.

1250–93

1253
- Hūlāgū, a grandson of Genghis Khan and younger brother of Great Khan Mongka, begins his conquest of the Islamic empire. His army is larger than that of Genghis Khan and contains contingents from all the Mongol princes.
- The Mongol leader Kublai Khan conquers the kingdom of Nanchao in Yunnan, south China. Its Thai people migrate to Thailand. He also attacks Dai Viet (modern northern Vietnam, also known as Annam).

1256

December 19   A Mongol army under Hūlāgū, recently appointed ilkhan of Persia, besieges the stronghold of the Assassins (militant branch of the Islamic Ismaili sect) at Alamūt in the Elburz Mountains. Their grand master, Rukn-ad-Dīn Kūrshāh, surrenders and is put to death. The Mongols now annihilate the Assassins in Persia.

1257

- The Mongols sack the city of Hanoi but Tran Thai-tong forces them to leave Dai Viet (modern northern Vietnam).

December 12   The Mongols raid the Punjab, India.

1258

- The Mongols under Kublai Khan invade China.

February 10   The Mongols take and destroy Baghdad, the capital of the revived Abbasid caliphate in Mesopotamia.

February 20   The last Abbasid caliph (Islamic ruler of Persia) al-Musta'sim and his family are put to death on the Mongol leader Hūlāgū's orders.

1259

September 11   The Mongols, under Hūlāgū, invade Syria.

1260

March 1   The city of Damascus surrenders to the Mongols, who now occupy all Syria, extinguishing the Ayyubid Sultanate. The Mongol leader Hūlāgū is soon forced to withdraw most of his forces because of a succession dispute.

1261

- The Mongol leader Kublai Khan establishes his supremacy as great khan. He continues the conquest of China, where Beijing is rebuilt as his winter capital.

1274

- A fleet sent by Kublai Khan, the Mongol emperor of China, to conquer Japan is repulsed at Hakata Bay and subsequently destroyed by a storm.

1276

- Kublai Khan takes Hangzhou, the Song dynasty capital, after a failed attempt by the empress dowager to achieve an accommodation with the Mongols.

1279

- Kublai Khan completes the Mongol conquest of China with a naval victory near Macao. The southern Chinese Song dynasty is extinguished and Khan become the Chinese Emperor.

1280

October 20   The Mongols under Abāqa, Ilkhan of Persia, sack the city of Aleppo in Syria.

1281

- A typhoon wrecks Kublai Khan's invasion fleet as it attempts to land in Japan. The grateful Japanese name it *kamikaze* (divine wind).

August 15   A second fleet sent by Kublai Khan to conquer Japan is destroyed by a typhoon in Hakata Bay.

1282

- The Mongols ravage the Polish kingdom of Halich (Halicz), destroying its political importance, and go on into Poland proper.

1286

- Kublai Khan's army invading Dai Viet (modern northern Vietnam) is defeated. He therefore abandons his preparations for the conquest of Japan.

1287

- The army of Kublai Khan, the Mongol emperor of China, is repelled during its attempted invasion of Dai Viet (modern northern Vietnam), but then invades Burma (now Myanmar) and destroys the kingdom of Pagan. The fall of Pagan allows the emergence of several principalities of the Thais, who have recently been moving southward into Burma and Cambodia, while Burma itself is divided into three states.

1292

- Kublai Khan, the Mongol emperor of China, sends a fleet to conquer Java in southeast Asia.

1293

- The expedition sent to Java by Kublai Khan, the Mongol emperor of China, is repulsed.
- The Mongols, under Nogay, Khan of the "Nogay Horde" (between the Dnieper and Danube rivers), invade Serbia. King Stephen Uroš becomes his vassal.

1300–44

1300

- The Shans in Burma defeat a punitive Mongol expedition from China, following Burmese rebellion after the death of Quibilai in 1294.

1303

- The Mongols unsuccessfully besiege Delhi, India.

1306

- A Mongol invasion of India, to avenge the defeat of 'Ali Beg, is defeated on the River Indus.

1307

- Temür Öljeitü, the great khan, dies. He is succeeded by his nephew Haishan. Mongol rule in China now declines into dissension and civil war.

1308

- The Ilkhanid sultan of Persia, Uljāytū, invades Syria and reaches Jerusalem.

1324

- Andrew and Leo, princes of Ruthenia, are killed in a battle with Mongols.

1344

- King Casimir (Kazimiera) III of Poland defeats a Mongol force on the River Vistula.
- King Ludwig I of Hungary expels a Mongol force from Transylvania.

1356–1402

1356

- Janibeg, Khan of the "Golden Horde" takes Azerbaijan from the Ilkhan.

1360

- Timur Leng (Tamerlane), the great khan, begins his conquest of Transoxiana (modern Uzbekistan), the region in which he was born, with the seizure of Kesh, near Samarkand, from Ilyas Khoja, the governor of the region for the khanate of Kashgar.

1367

- Tamerlane becomes the effective ruler of the Asiatic Mongols as grand amir to a series of puppet great khans.

Mongol Conquests (1206–1402) *continued*

1380

September 8 Dmitry III of Moscow, Russia, Grand Duke of Vladimir, leads the Russians to victory over the "Golden Horde" at Kulikovo Pole, on the upper River Don, Russia. The supremacy of Moscow in Russia is thus confirmed.

1382

- Hung-wu, Ming emperor of China, completes the conquest of China and finally expels the Mongols.
- Tamerlane, grand amir of the Mongols, conquers Khorasan.

August 26 Tokhtamysh, Khan of the "Golden Horde," sacks Moscow, Russia, and then withdraws after having restored his suzerainty over Russia.

1385

- Tamerlane partially conquers Azerbaijan from the Ilkhanate.

1387

- Tokhtamysh invades Transoxiana but fails to take Bukhara. Tamerlane retaliates by ravaging Khwarizm.

November 11 Tamerlane destroys Isfahan, Persia.

1389

- Tokhtamysh campaigns inconclusively against Tamerlane in central Asia.

1391

June 18 Tamerlane defeats Tokhtamysh on the River Kondurcha, but does not pursue him west of the River Volga.

1392

- Tamerlane takes the city of Baghdad, Mesopotamia, from the Persian Ilkhanate.

1393

- Tamerlane campaigns against the "Golden Horde" in Russia, reaching Moscow. He also completes his conquest of Persia and Mesopotamia, extinguishing the last independent Mongol dynasties.

1398

September 9 Tamerlane invades the Punjab, India.

December 18 Tamerlane sacks the city of Delhi, India.

1399

January–March Tamerlane continues his massacres and ravages in India, causing a famine.

1400

- Tamerlane defeats the Mameluke Egyptians at Aleppo and Damascus and sacks the cities of Syria.

1401

March 24 Tamerlane sacks the city of Damascus, Syria.

July 9 Tamerlane destroys the Persian city of Baghdad to punish its revolt.

1402

July 28 Tamerlane defeats the Ottoman Turks near Ankara in the Ottoman Empire. Bāyezīd I, Sultan of the Ottoman Turks, is captured. Tamerlane then takes the city of Bursa.

France, exploiting a revolt against King Philip II by the barons of Poitou.

July 27 Philip, Duke of Swabia, elected "king of the Romans" (king of Germany) in 1205, defeats his rival king, Otto IV, at Wassenburg.

August 8 Czar Kalojan of Bulgaria destroys the city of Adrianople (modern Edirne, Turkey).

August 20 Following the execution in captivity of the emperor Baldwin, his brother, Henry of Flanders, is crowned as Latin emperor of Constantinople; his daughter, Joanna, succeeds to the county of Flanders.

October 26 King John of England and King Philip II of France make a truce, for two years, at Thouars, France.

1207

- Han T'o-chou, the Chinese Southern Song emperor, is killed by the Jin when attempting to reconquer northern China.
- Marco Sanudo, a Venetian, begins to rule as Duke of the Archipelago (the Aegean islands he has seized, with his capital on Naxos).
- Pope Innocent III confirms Přemysl Ottokar I as king of Bohemia and summons an assembly of representatives of towns in the Papal States.
- Venice takes possession of the island of Corfu, formerly part of the Byzantine Empire.

January 1 Philip, Duke of Swabia and "king of the Romans" (king of Germany), takes the city of Cologne, so achieving a dominant position in Germany; his rival king, Otto IV, flees through Denmark to England.

September 9 Boniface, Marquis of Montferrat and King of Thessaloníki, is killed in an ambush by Bulgars.

October 8 Czar Kalojan of Bulgaria dies; he is succeeded by his nephew Boril.

November 17 Pope Innocent III again urges King Philip II of France to organize a crusade against the Albigensian (Cathar) heretics in Languedoc, southern France.

1208

- At the Battle of the Irtysh, the Mongol leader Genghis Khan defeats Gushluk, leader of the Naiman tribe, completing his unification of the Mongol peoples.
- Llywelyn ap Iorwerth the Great, Prince of Gwynedd (north Wales), seizes Powys.
- Mohammad al-Nasir, the Almohad emir of northwest Africa and Muslim Spain, destroys the last Almoravid strongholds in North Africa.

January 14 A papal legate sent to convert the Albigensian (Cathar) heretics of Languedoc, southern France, is murdered by a vassal of Raymond V, the Count of Toulouse. Pope Innocent III declares a crusade against the heretics, the "Albigensian Crusade."

March 23 Because King John of England refuses to accept Stephen Langton, the papal choice, as archbishop of Canterbury, Pope Innocent III places England under an interdict.

April 4 Theodore I Lascaris is crowned as Byzantine emperor in Nicaea.

June 21 Shortly after Pope Innocent III has recognized him as "king of the Romans" and agreed to crown him Holy Roman Emperor, Philip, Duke of Swabia, is murdered by Otto of Wittelsbach, Count Palatine of Bavaria, over a personal grudge.

July 31 An army from the Latin Empire of Constantinople defeats Czar Boril of Bulgaria.

November 11 Otto IV is unanimously elected "king of the Romans" (king of Germany).

November 17 Pope Innocent III appeals directly to the nobility in northern France to join the crusade against the Albigensian (Cathar) heretics in Languedoc, southern France.

1209

- Queen Thamar of Georgia takes Kars in a victorious campaign against the Turks.
- The French nobleman Geoffrey of Villehardouin assumes the title of prince of Achaea, founding another feudal Latin dynasty in the Morea (that is, the Peloponnese in Greece, known as "Romania" in the West).
- The Uighur Turks of Turfan surrender to the Mongol leader Genghis Khan.

June 17 Raymond VI, Count of Toulouse, submits to the papal legate and is absolved from excommunication incurred by his sympathy for the Albigensian (Cathar) heresy prevailing among his subjects in southern France.

July 22 The southern French town of Béziers is sacked by the Albigensian crusaders, as they take up arms against the Albigensian (Cathar) heresy.

August 2 King John of England, after invading Scotland, makes a treaty of peace with King William II the Lion.

August 15 The southern French town of Carcassonne is taken by the Albigensian crusaders; the Norman crusader Simon IV de Montfort is then elected leader and expropriates land from the Albigensian (Cathar) heretics and their supporters, becoming lord of Béziers and Carcassonne.

October 4 Pope Innocent III crowns Otto IV as Holy Roman Emperor.

October 10 The Welsh princes do homage to King John of England.

November 4 King John of England's continued refusal to accept Stephen Langton, the Pope's choice, as archbishop of Canterbury leads to his excommunication by Pope Innocent III.

SCIENCE, TECHNOLOGY, AND MEDICINE

Agriculture

1206

- Fujiwara Nagatsune, a Japanese courtier, writes the first known work on landscape gardening.

ARTS AND IDEAS

Architecture

1205

- Following the completion of the original Gothic cathedral of Laon, France, its apse is demolished and work begins on the extension of the choir and the west façade.
- The Seljuk Turks, rebuilding the citadel in the recently captured town of Kayseri, Anatolia, found the Çifte Medrese hospital.

1207

- The cathedral in Magdeburg, Germany, burns down. Archbishop Albrecht orders that the new cathedral should be built in the Gothic style.

1208

- The choir of Lincoln Cathedral, England (designed by Geoffrey de Noyer), is completed, but is replaced in 1256.

1209

- King Philip II of France completes the walls of the city of Paris, the French capital.

Literature and Language

c. 1205

- Japanese poet Teika compiles *Shin kokinshu*, an anthology of Japanese poetry including his own work and that of his family.

c. 1206

- Monk and former *jongleur* ("minstrel"), Guiot of Provins, writes his "Bible," a satirical French poem in which various professions are criticized.

BIRTHS & DEATHS

1205

- Baldwin I, first Latin emperor of Constantinople 1204–05, is executed by the Bulgars at Adrianople (c. 33).

1207

- St. Elizabeth of Hungary, Hungarian princess famed for her devotion to the poor, born, probably in Pressburg, Hungary (now Bratislava, Slovak Republic) (–1231).

October 1 Henry III, King of England 1216–72, son of King John, born in Winchester, Hampshire, England (–1272).

1209

- Nezami, Persian poet, who wrote the poem "Haft paykar," dies.

January 6 Richard, Earl of Cornwall, King of the Romans 1256–71, born in Winchester, Hampshire, England (–1272).

Thought and Scholarship

1205

- Yüan Shu writes *T'ung-chien chi-shih pen-mo/ Narratives from Beginning to End from the Comprehensive Mirror*, another version of Su-ma Kuang's history of China of 1086.

1206

- Byzantine historian and theologian Nicetas Acominatos writes a history of Constantinople in the period 1180–1206.

c. 1207

- Geoffroi de Villehardouin writes *De la Conquête de Constantinople/On the Conquest of Constantinople*, an account of the preparations and events of the Fourth Crusade in the period 1198–1207, in which he took part.

c. 1208

- Saxo Grammaticus writes *Gesta Danorum/The Deeds of the Danes*, a history of the legendary kings of Denmark. Based on folklore and poems, it contains the story of Amleth (Hamlet).

SOCIETY

Education

1208

- A group of physicians and students leave the medical school of Bologna University, Italy, and establish a new institution at Montpellier in France.

1209

- Following riots between university scholars and townspeople in Oxford, England, a group of English academics leave and move to the small town of Cambridge, England, where they establish a new university.

Religion

1205

- Bishop Diego of Osma, assisted by St. Dominic, begins his mission to the Albigensians (or Cathari) of Languedoc in southern France.
- Pope Innocent III issues his *Vergentis in senium*, which decrees that heretics and their heirs are to be deprived of all property and goods.
- Hubert Walter, archbishop of Canterbury and chancellor of England, dies; the monks of Canterbury elect Reginald, their subprior, to succeed him. However, on King John of England's insistence, John Grey, bishop of Norwich, is elected, on December 11.

1206

March 3   Pope Innocent III rejects John Grey's election to the archbishopric of Canterbury in England. On December 12, the monks of Canterbury in Rome, under Pope Innocent III's influence, elect Cardinal Stephen Langton as archbishop of Canterbury, England.

1207

- Japanese authorities begin the persecution of the Pure Land Buddhist Sect (founded in 1175). The leader of the sect, Honen, and his chief disciple, Shinran, are both banned from the major Buddhist shrines.

1209

February 24   St. Francis of Assisi's vocation, to live in complete poverty and to preach, is revealed to him.

1210–1214

POLITICS, GOVERNMENT, AND ECONOMICS

Politics and Government

1210

- In the spring, the Byzantine emperor of Nicaea, Theodore I Lascaris, defeats and kills Kay-Khusraw I, Sultan of Rūm, who, with the support of the Latins, was attempting to restore Alexius III Angelus as Byzantine emperor.
- King Valdemar II of Denmark conquers Danzig (modern Gdańsk, Poland) and east Pomerania.
- The grand master Herman of Salza obtains papal privileges for the Teutonic Order (a German Christian military order) of crusading knights.
- The most ancient known Burmese law code dates from the reign of Jayasura II.

June–August King John of England makes an expedition to Ireland, enforcing his authority there.

July 17 King Sverker II of Sweden is defeated, killed, and succeeded by Eric X Cnutson, the first Swedish king to be anointed at his coronation.

October 3 John of Brienne marries Maria of Jerusalem and is crowned as king of Jerusalem at Acre (present-day Akko, Israel).

November 11 Aybak, Sultan of Delhi, India, dies; his dominions begin to disintegrate.

November 11 The Holy Roman Emperor Otto IV, having agreed not to, opens a campaign to conquer the Italian duchy of Apulia and is therefore excommunicated by Pope Innocent III. Thus freed from their vows of obedience to Otto, his subjects in Germany rebel against him.

1211

- Iltutmish, the son-in-law of the late sultan Aybak, becomes sultan of Delhi, India. He suppresses Hindu rebellions against Muslim rule.
- The Mongol leader Genghis Khan destroys the Kara-Khitai Empire in east Turkestan and invades the Jin Empire for the first time.

March 27 King Sancho I of Portugal dies; he is succeeded by his son, Alfonso II.

March 30 Pope Innocent III again excommunicates the Holy Roman Emperor Otto IV, who has returned to Germany to defeat the rebellion against him there.

May 5 King John of England makes war on Llywelyn ap Iorwerth the Great, Prince of Gwynedd (north Wales).

September 9 In a diet (legislative assembly) at Nuremberg, Bavaria, those German princes in revolt against the Holy Roman Emperor Otto IV offer the crown to Frederick II, Duke of Hohenstaufen, King of Sicily.

October 15 Henry of Flanders, Latin emperor of Constantinople, defeats Theodore I Lascaris, the Byzantine emperor of Nicaea, on the River Rhyndacus, near Brusa, and takes the city of Pergamum.

1212

- A survey of military tenures in England ordered by King John is completed.
- Juri II succeeds Vsevolod III as great prince of Vladimir–Suzdal.
- Queen Thamar the Great of Georgia dies; she is succeeded by her son, George IV.
- The Venetians occupy the island of Crete.

January 1 Joanna, Countess of Flanders, marries Prince Ferrand of Portugal.

July 7 Frederick II, Duke of Hohenstaufen, King of Sicily, enters Germany.

July 16 The Spanish kings Alfonso VIII of Castile, Sancho VII of Navarre, and Pedro II of Aragon and a few crusaders win a decisive victory over the Almohads at Las Navas de Tolosa. Muslim power in Spain is permanently broken.

September 9 King John of England abandons his preparations for a campaign against Llywelyn ap Iorwerth the Great, Prince of Gwynedd, leading a Welsh rebellion, because of a baronial plot to murder him.

September 26 In a Golden Bull, Frederick II, Duke of Hohenstaufen, King of Sicily, confirms Přemysl Ottokar I as king of Bohemia and generally recognizes Bohemia as a largely autonomous fief of the Holy Roman Empire.

November 19 By the Treaty of Toul, Frederick II, Duke of Hohenstaufen, King of Sicily, and King Philip II of France make an alliance against King John of England and the Holy Roman Emperor Otto IV.

December 9 Frederick II, Duke of Hohenstaufen, King of Sicily, is crowned as "king of the Romans" (king of Germany).

1213

- King Alfonso VIII of Castile defeats an invasion by the Muslim Almohads at Febragaen.

April 8 King Philip II of France formally accepts Pope Innocent III's mandate to conquer England.

April 19–29 Pope Innocent III proclaims the Fifth Crusade and stops granting indulgences for the Albigensian Crusade against the Albigensian (Cathar) heretics of southern France.

May 13 King John of England accepts Pope Innocent III's terms for ending the interdict placed on England, to avoid severe political consequences, and receives Stephen Langton as archbishop of Canterbury; he also resigns his kingdom to the Pope and receives it again as a papal fief, promising to pay tribute.

May 30   King John of England's fleet destroys that of the French, massed for the invasion of England, at Damme, near Bruges, west Flanders.

June 3   King John of England makes a truce with Llywelyn ap Iorwerth the Great, Prince of Gwynedd (north Wales).

June 6   By the death of his sister-in-law, King Philip II of France adds St. Quentin, Valois, and the remainder of Vermandois to the royal desmesne lands.

July 12   By the Golden Bull of Eger, Frederick II, King of the Romans (king of Germany), recognizes the papacy's territorial claims in Italy and renounces imperial control over the church in Germany.

September 12   The Norman crusader Simon IV de Montfort and the Albigensian crusaders defeat Raymond VI, Count of Toulouse, and kill his ally King Pedro II of Aragon at Muret. Pedro's heir in Aragon is his young son, James I, and civil war follows there.

September 28   Magyar nobles murder Queen Gertrude of Hungary.

October 13   King John of England's allies in the Low Countries defeat Henry, Duke of Brabant, an ally of King Philip II of France, at Steppes, near St. Trond.

November 15   Knights representing the shires are called, for the first known time, to a council held in Oxford by King John of England.

1214

- Ala-ad-Din Mohammad, Shah of Khwarizm, takes Ghazni; he has now conquered most of Persia and Transoxiana.
- Frederick II, King of the Romans (king of Germany), invests the Wittelsbachs with the Rhine Palatinate.

February 15   King John of England begins a campaign in western France to recover his lost lands.

May 5   By the Treaty of Metz, Frederick II, King of the Romans (king of Germany), recognizes King Valdemar II of Denmark's conquests in northern Germany and the Baltic.

July 27   King John of England's allies, the Holy Roman Emperor Otto IV and the Flemings, are decisively defeated by King Philip II of France at Bouvines, Flanders. By capturing the counts of Flanders and Boulogne, Philip establishes French control there; John is forced to abandon his campaign to recover his French lands; and Otto's cause in the Holy Roman Empire suffers a fatal blow.

September 18   King John of England makes a truce with King Philip II of France at Chinon, France, then returns to England.

October 10   King Alfonso VIII of Castile dies; he is succeeded by his son, Henry I, a minor; civil war follows.

October 15   King John arrives back in England from France to face growing baronial discontent with his demands for money to fund his unsuccessful campaigns.

December 4   King William II the Lion of Scotland dies; he is succeeded by his son, Alexander II.

December 12   Theodore I Lascaris, the Byzantine emperor of Nicaea, and Henry of Flanders, the Latin emperor of Constantinople, make a demarcation treaty in Anatolia (modern Turkey) which defines the borders of the Latin Empire and Nicaea.

December 25   Mohammad al-Nasir, the Almohad emir, dies; he is succeeded by his son, Yūsuf II.

SCIENCE, TECHNOLOGY, AND MEDICINE

Agriculture

1212

- Tofu (unfermented soybean curd) is introduced into Japan from China.

Health and Medicine

1210

- The English physician Alfred of Sareshel (or Shareshill; also known as Alfredus Anglicus) writes an Aristotelian medical treatise *De motu cordis/The Movement of the Heart.*

1214

- The Italian physician Marus of the medical school at Salerno, Italy, writes *Anatomia Mauri/Anatomy of a Moor,* one of the earliest Latin texts on anatomy.

Science

1212

- The English abbot Gervase of Tilbury compiles his encyclopedic collection of natural lore *Otia Imperialia* for the Holy Roman Emperor Otto IV.

BIRTHS & DEATHS

c. 1213
- Sa'di, Persian poet, a leading figure in Persian literature, born in Shīrāz, Persia (–1291).

1214
April 25   Louis IX (St. Louis), King of France 1226–70, who led the Seventh Crusade 1248–50, born in Poissy, France (–1270).

December 4   William I, King of Scotland 1165–1214, who succeeded in obtaining independence from England, dies in Stirling, Stirlingshire (81).

ARTS AND IDEAS

Architecture

1210

- Construction begins on the cathedral at Reims, France. The architects are to be Jean d'Orbais, Gaucher of Reims, Jean le Loup, and Bernard of Soissons, in succession.

1211

- Construction begins on the cathedral at Toulouse, France.
- Nevers Cathedral, France, burns down, and its reconstruction is started.

Literature and Language

c. **1210**

- Gottfried von Strassburg writes his unfinished epic poem *Tristan und Isolde/Tristan and Isolde* in Middle High German.

1212

- Japanese writer Kamo No Nagaakira completes his *Hojoki*, an essay on Buddhist philosophy noted for its style.
- Wolfram von Eschenbach writes his *Parzival*, an epic poem in Middle High German on the theme of the Grail.

c. **1214**

- Robert de Borron writes *Joseph d'Arimathie/Joseph of Arimathea*, the first of his three Grail romances.

Thought and Scholarship

1210

- *c.* 1210   Gervase of Canterbury, England, completes his *Gesta regum/The Deeds of the King*, a chronicle of England from Brutus to 1210.
- The study of certain of the Greek philosopher Aristotle's works is forbidden at the University of Paris, France, because they are seen as a possible threat to Christian teaching. The same year his *Metaphysics* is translated into Latin.

1213

- Nicetas Chroniates writes a history of the Byzantine Empire for the period 1118–1206 in his *De Statuis/On Statuary*, which lists works of art destroyed in Constantinople by the crusaders.

SOCIETY

Education

1212

- King Alfonso VIII of Castile establishes the first Spanish university at Palencia; it survives until about 1250.

1214

- The earliest constitution of Oxford University, England, is issued.

Religion

1210

- Pope Innocent III unexpectedly sanctions St. Francis of Assisi's new order, the Friars Minor.

1212

- Kamo Chomei writes *Hojo-ki/Annals of Ten Feet Square*, the story of his life as a hermit following his ordination as a Buddhist priest.
- Nicholas, a boy from the Rhineland, Germany, launches the "Children's Crusade" in Cologne, Germany. Thousands of children from France and the Rhineland set out for the Holy Land in the hope of overcoming the Muslims through their faith. Many are sold into slavery, and the rest die on the journey.

1215-1219

POLITICS, GOVERNMENT, AND ECONOMICS

Business and Economics

1216

- The coal trade of Newcastle upon Tyne, England, is now established.

Human Rights

1215

- A document of King Alfonso IX indicates that the emancipation of Christian serfs has begun in the Spanish kingdom of León.

Politics and Government

1215

- Magha, an adventurer from southern India, becomes king of Polonnaruwa, the dominant center of Ceylon (present-day Sri Lanka).
- Michael Angelus, the independent Byzantine ruler of Epirus, is murdered; he is succeeded by his half brother Theodore.
- The Mongol leader Genghis Khan captures and sacks Beijing, the former capital of the Jin Empire (the Jin have recently moved their capital to Kaifeng to escape Mongol attacks); its population is massacred.

January 6 At a conference in London, England, the English barons demand that King John of England restore their "ancient and accustomed liberties."

January 8 The Norman crusader Simon IV de Montfort is elected lord of Languedoc in a council at Montpellier, southern France.

April 4 King Philip II of France's son Louis musters his troops at Lyon on the way to join the Albigensian Crusade against the Albigensian (Cathar) heretics of southern France.

May 17 Having renounced their allegiance to King John of England, an alliance of rebel barons takes possession of the capital, London.

June 15–17 King John of England and his opponents, the barons, meet at Runnymede (now in Surrey) on the River Thames, England, to agree on terms for peace.

Three days of negotiations result in the Magna Carta (Great Charter) in which the king agrees to various curtailments of his powers and concedes "liberties" to different classes of his subjects.

July 7 Pope Innocent III excommunicates King John of England's opponents. Stephen Langton, archbishop of Canterbury, refuses to promulgate the excommunications.

July 25 Frederick II of Hohenstaufen, having secured general recognition, is again crowned as "king of the Romans" (king of Germany).

September Stephen Langton, the English archbishop of Canterbury, is suspended from office for refusing to promulgate Pope Innocent III's excommunications of King John of England's opponents.

September 9 King John of England receives Pope Innocent III's bull annulling the Magna Carta, which he declares illegal and unjust.

October 13 King John of England resumes the civil war at home by laying siege to Rochester Castle in Kent, held by William de Albini, one of the baronial signatories of the Magna Carta.

November 11–30 Pope Innocent III legislates at the Fourth Lateran Council in Rome for the organization and financing of the Fifth Crusade, for the suppression of heresy, and for the regulation of religious orders, and orders that Jews and Muslims living in Christian lands must wear distinctive clothing. The Norman crusader and lord of Languedoc, Simon IV de Montfort, is confirmed in his lands in southern France.

1216

c. 1216 John I succeeds Eric X as king of Sweden following his death.

- King Leo II of Lesser Armenia (Cilicia) takes the principality of Antioch from Bohemond IV, appointing his nephew Raymond-Roupen as prince.
- King Maravarman Sundara of the Pandyas of southern India drives the Chola king, Kulottunga III, into (temporary) exile; the second Pandya Empire is now founded.
- King Ottokar I of Bohemia has his eldest son, Wenceslas, crowned as king, so establishing the principle of primogeniture in his kingdom.

January 14–23 King John of England harries southern Scotland in retaliation for an invasion in support of the baronial rebellion against him.

May 21 King Philip II of France's son Louis lands in England in response to the invitation of King John's opponents to become king of England.

June 11 Henry of Flanders, the Latin emperor of Constantinople, dies; he is succeeded by Peter de Courtenay, husband of Yolanta of Flanders.

July 16 Pope Innocent III dies of fever at Perugia, Italy,

while trying to encourage Genoa and Pisa to cooperate in the interests of his planned Fifth Crusade.

July 18   Cencio Savelli is elected Pope Honorius III.

October 28   King John of England's son, Henry III, a minor, is crowned king of England at Gloucester. William the Marshal, Earl of Pembroke, is appointed his guardian.

November 12   King Henry III of England's council reissues the Magna Carta.

December 12   The last Ly dynasty emperor of Dai Viet (modern northern Vietnam, also known as Annam) dies without male heirs; his son-in-law Tran Thai-tong is proclaimed as emperor.

1217

- Bishop Albert of Livonia defeats the pagan Estonians at Fellin.
- Haakon IV succeeds Inge II as king of Norway.
- King James I of Aragon succeeds to the French county of Roussillon.
- Stephen Nemanja, Grand Zupan of Rascia, is crowned as king of Serbia with the assent of Pope Honorius III.
- Theodore Angelus, the despot of Epirus, captures the Latin emperor Peter de Courtenay, whose wife Yolanta then acts as regent in Constantinople.

May 20   William the Marshal, leading the loyalists for King Henry III of England, defeats the French dauphin Louis and the rebels who invited him to become king at Lincoln, England.

June 20   King Henry I of Castile dies; he is succeeded by his sister Berenguela, the divorced wife of King Alfonso IX of León.

August 23   The French fleet bringing reinforcements to the dauphin Louis in England is destroyed by the English off Sandwich, Kent.

August 31   Queen Berenguela of Castile abdicates in favor of her son, Ferdinand III.

September 12   By the Treaty of Kingston, the English rebels make peace with King Henry III of England and the French dauphin Louis is paid to leave England.

September 25   King Alfonso II of Portugal defeats the Muslims at Alcazar do Sal.

November 12   The first contingents of the Fifth Crusade (among them, briefly, King Andrew II of Hungary) take and sack Baisan in Palestine.

1218

- A meeting is held of the first Cortes (parliament) of Catalonia known to have been attended by representatives of towns.
- Denmark adopts the first national flag, the Danneborg or "Danish Cloth."
- John Asen II, the son of Asen I, deposes and succeeds Boril as czar of Bulgaria.
- Pope Honorius III announces a new Albigensian crusade (against the Cathar heretics of southern France).

1218–1219   King Valdemar II of Denmark invades Estonia and builds a castle at Revel.

January 10   King Hugh I of Cyprus dies; he is succeeded by his son, Henry I.

February 18   Berthold V, the last Duke of Zähringen, dies; the duchy is partitioned and its rectorate of Burgundy reverts to the Holy Roman Empire.

March 3   King Henry III of England makes peace with Llywelyn ap Iorwerth the Great, Prince of Gwynedd (north Wales), at Worcester, England.

May 5   Frederick II, King of the Romans, makes Bern an imperial free city.

May 29   The main contingent of the Fifth Crusade lands outside Damietta at the mouth of the River Nile, Egypt.

June 25   The Norman crusader and lord of Languedoc, Simon IV de Montfort, is killed besieging Toulouse, France, after Count Raymond VI is restored by a revolt.

August 25   The crusaders of the Fifth Crusade capture a defensive tower on the River Nile outside Damietta, Egypt.

August 31   The Ayyubid sultan al-Adil dies; he is succeeded by his sons, al-Kamil in Egypt and al-Mu'azzam in Damascus, Syria.

September 9   The Fifth Crusade receives further reinforcements at the siege of Damietta (Dimyat) at the Nile Delta, Egypt, and the papal legate Cardinal Pelagius arrives as their leader.

1219

- Minamoto Sanetomo, the shogun (military ruler) of Japan, is murdered by the Hojo. Hojo Yoshitoki, leader of the Hojo, assumes power as regent: the shogunate becomes an honorific title. The Hojo family retains power until 1333.
- Pope Honorius III bans the teaching of Roman law in the University of Paris, France.
- Raymond, the son of Raymond VI, Count of Toulouse, defeats the Albigensian crusaders led by Amauri de Montfort at Basiège, in the spring.
- The Koreans, in alliance with the Mongols, invade the Jin Empire.
- The Mongol leader Genghis Khan invades the Khwarizmian shahdom (Transoxiana and Persia) after the governor of the border city of Otrar executes Mongol merchants (in 1218).

May 2   Leo II, the first king of Lesser Armenia (Cilicia), dies; he is succeeded by his young daughter Isabella.

November 5   The Fifth Crusade takes Damietta; the Egyptian garrison, ravaged by disease and starvation, offers little resistance.

SCIENCE, TECHNOLOGY, AND MEDICINE

Agriculture

1217

- A severe famine causes starvation and thousands of deaths across central and eastern Europe.

Health and Medicine

1215

- St. Thomas's Hospital is founded in London, England, on a site next to London Bridge.

Science

1217

- The English scholar Alexander Neckham writes *De natura rerum*. This is a scientific encyclopedia written in clear and simple Latin, which includes an early description of the compass.
- The Scottish astrologer and reputed magician Michael Scot makes a Latin translation of Alpetragius's Arabic *Kitāb al-Hay'ah* of 1204. The work reintroduces many ideas of Aristotelian astronomy into Europe.

ARTS AND IDEAS

Architecture

1218

- Construction begins on the Abbey of San Galgano, near Siena, Italy.
- Jayavarman VII of the Khmer Empire rebuilds and walls the city of Angkor Thom (in modern Cambodia), the temple of Bayon being the greatest of his buildings.

1219

- Construction begins on the south porch of Chartres Cathedral, France, which is to have a tympanum portraying a Gothic representation of the Last Judgment.
- Ferguniye and Alaeddin Mosques are built in Konya, in the Seljuk Sultanate of Rūm (in modern Turkey). The architect of the second is Mohammed ibn-Kaulan of Damascus.

Thought and Scholarship

c. **1215**

- Tancred of Bologna writes his *Ordo Judiciarius/Judicial Order*, a work which becomes the standard text on procedure in canon law.

c. **1216**

- Henri de Valenciennes writes his *Histoire de L'Empereur Henri/The History of Emperor Henry*, a chronicle of the war fought by Henri, second Latin emperor of the East, against the Bulgarians.

SOCIETY

Religion

1215

- A synod of the Polish church swears to accept clerical celibacy.
- St. Clare becomes the abbess of a Franciscan order of women called Poor Clares or Minoresses in Assisi, Italy.

1216

December 22   Honorius III recognizes St. Dominic's Order of Friars Preacher (Dominicans).

1219

August 8   St. Francis preaches to the sultan and to the crusaders in Egypt. Missions of his friars are sent to France, Germany, Hungary, and Spain.

BIRTHS & DEATHS

1215
- Kublai Khan, Mongol general, grandson of Genghis Khan, conqueror of China, and first emperor of the Yüan dynasty, born (–1294).

1216
October 19   John I ("John Lackland"), King of England 1199–1216, son of Henry II and Eleanor of Aquitaine, brother of Richard I, dies in Newark, Nottinghamshire, England (48).

1218
May 1   Rudolph I, German king (1273–91), first of the Habsburg dynasty, born in Limburg-im-Breisgau, Germany (–1291).

May 19   The former Holy Roman Emperor Otto IV dies.

1219
May 14   William the Marshal, the guardian of King Henry III and regent of England, dies.

1220–1224

POLITICS, GOVERNMENT, AND ECONOMICS

Business and Economics

1223

May 20 Pope Honorius III taxes the church in France for the Albigensian Crusade (against the Albigensian or Cathar heretics of Languedoc, southern France).

Politics and Government

1220

- Confirming an order of the archbishop of Braga in 1219, Pope Honorius III excommunicates King Alfonso II of Portugal for challenging the church's title to various estates and lays an interdict on Portugal.
- Jaya Parameshvaravarman II becomes king of Champa (corresponding roughly to modern southern Vietnam) on the withdrawal of the Khmers (of modern Cambodia). He begins a long and indecisive war with Dai Viet (modern northern Vietnam, also known as Annam).
- Ray (or Rhages), the center of the Persian ceramics industry, is destroyed by the Mongols.
- The ousted Bohemond IV recovers the principality of Antioch from Raymond-Roupen, who was installed by his uncle King Leo II of Lesser Armenia in 1216.

February 2 The Mongol leader Genghis Khan takes the city of Bukhara in the shahdom of Khwarizm; it is depopulated and destroyed.

April 26 By his charter of privileges granted at Frankfurt, Frederick II grants sovereign rights to German prelates in order to secure the election of his son, Henry, as "king of the Romans" (king of Germany).

May 17 King Henry III of England is crowned for a second time in Westminster Abbey, London, England.

November 22 Pope Honorius III crowns Frederick II of Germany as Holy Roman Emperor.

December 12 The shah of Khwarizm, Ala-ad-Din, dies on an island in the Caspian Sea where he has fled from the Mongol leader Genghis Khan, who has captured his capital Samarkand and conquered Transoxiana; he is succeeded by his son, Jalal-ad-Din.

1221

- Hunac Ceel, founder of the Cocom dynasty, conquers Chichén Itzá and overthrows its Toltec ruler.

- The Japanese regent Hojo Yoshitoki defeats a bid for power by the cloistered emperor, Go-Toba, in the Jokyu War. The emperor is exiled and his supporters beheaded.

February 2 King George IV of Georgia is defeated by the Mongols at Khunani, near the capital Tbilisi (modern Tbilisi, Georgia).

March 25 Robert de Courtenay is crowned as Latin emperor of Constantinople, his father Peter having died in captivity in Epirus.

August 8 The army of the Fifth Crusade, advancing into Egypt from Damietta, is trapped by the Nile floods and the Egyptian army; the leader of the crusade, Cardinal Pelagius, is forced to accept Sultan al-Kamil of Egypt's terms for withdrawal, including the surrender of Damietta.

September 8 The evacuation of Damietta, Egypt, marks the end—and the complete failure—of the Fifth Crusade.

November 24 The shah of the central Asian province of Khwarizm, Jalal-ad-Din, defeats the Mongols under Kutikonian at Parvan (near modern Kabul, Afghanistan). The Mongol leader Genghis Khan quickly avenges the defeat, destroying Jalal-ad-Din's army at Bamian (in modern Afghanistan); Jalal-ad-Din flees to India with the Mongols in pursuit. After defeating Jalal-ad-Din again on the River Indus, Genghis Khan withdraws his forces to avoid war with the Sultanate of Delhi.

1222

- A new dynasty based at Singhasari achieves dominance over Java.
- King Alexander II of Scotland conquers the Norse settlements in Argyll, Scotland.
- King Andrew II of Hungary grants his Golden Bull, which protects the rights of the lesser nobility against the magnates and limits the powers of the crown, granting the right to disobey unlawful commands. All subsequent Hungarian kings have to swear to observe these concessions.
- King John I of Sweden dies and is succeeded by Eric XI, son of the former king Eric X.
- King Ottokar I of Bohemia grants ecclesiastical and, later, secular lords sole jurisdiction over their tenants.
- Theodore I Lascaris, the Byzantine emperor of Nicaea, dies; he is succeeded by John III Ducas Vatatzes.

May 31 A Mongol army defeats the Russian princes and the Cumans, a pagan nomadic tribe, on the Kalka, near the Sea of Azov.

June 6 The Mongol leader Genghis Khan takes the city of Herat and massacres its population, completing his conquest of the Khwarizm shahdom (modern Iran, Afghanistan, and part of Central Asia).

August 8 Raymond VI, the Count of Toulouse, dies; his son, Raymond VII, inherits his claims.

1223

- King George IV of Georgia dies; he is succeeded by his sister Rusadan.
- The late Philip II's son, Louis VIII, is crowned king of France; he is the first Capetian king not to have been crowned in his father's lifetime.

March 25 Alfonso II the Fat, the excommunicated king of Portugal, dies; he is succeeded by his son, Sancho II.

April 4 Pope Honorius III declares that King Henry III of England is of age to rule in his own right, but Henry's personal rule does not begin until 1227.

1224

- Bishop Albert of Livonia takes the town of Yuriev from the Russians and Estonians.
- King Andrew II of Hungary grants judicial autonomy to German settlers in Transylvania.
- The Almohad emir Yūsuf II dies; the disintegration of his Muslim empire in northwest Africa and Spain accelerates.
- Theodore Ducas, the despot of Epirus, conquers the Latin kingdom of Thessaloníki and is crowned as Byzantine emperor of Thessaloníki.

January–April King Henry III of England recovers control of royal castles that have been held by various barons since the civil war of King John's reign.

February 2 Amauri de Montfort cedes the conquests made by the Albigensian Crusade in Toulouse to King Louis VIII of France.

May 5 King Louis VIII of France declares war on King Henry III of England; he then overruns Poitou and most of Gascony north of the River Garonne.

August 14 With the capture of Bedford Castle, King Henry III of England suppresses the revolt of Fawkes de Breauté.

SCIENCE, TECHNOLOGY, AND MEDICINE

Health and Medicine

1220

- The earliest statutes of the medical school of Montpellier University, France, date from this year.

1222

- The French poet and Salerno-trained physician Pierre Giles of Corbeil writes a series of medical treatises in verse, including *De urinis/On Seeds* and *De pulsibus/On Pulses*. They become popular as *aides-mémoires* for physicians.

1224

- An Arabic translation is made of *De materia medica/On Medical Matters*, written by the 1st-century Greek surgeon Dioscorides. It describes the medicinal and dietary properties of over 600 plants.

Science

1224

- Arab geographer Yāqūt writes a geographical dictionary of the Muslim world called *Mu'jam al-Buldān*.

Technology

1220

- The English-born poet John of Garland, writing in Paris, France, refers to a brace and possibly a wood-plane, devices unknown in Europe since classical times.

1224

- A glassblowers' guild is established in Venice, Italy, indicating that the glass industry is established there by this time.

ARTS AND IDEAS

Architecture

1220

- Construction begins on the cathedral at Salisbury, England, with Nicholas of Ely as architect.
- Construction begins on the cathedral at Amiens, France. The architects are Robert de Luzarches and Thomas de Cormont in succession.
- Notre Dame Cathedral in Paris, France, is completed according to the plan of 1163.

1220–45 King Henry II of England lays the foundation stone of the new Lady Chapel at Westminster Abbey in London, England, thus beginning the new abbey church.

1221

- Construction begins on the choir of Burgos Cathedral in Spain (in the French Gothic style), Toul Cathedral, France, St. Martin, Ypres, Flanders, and the Dominican church in Bologna, Italy, as a shrine for St. Dominic.

1223

- Alaeddin Mosque, Nigde, is built.
- The mosque of the sultan Iltutmish is built in Badaun.

Literature and Language

c. 1220

- *Aucassin and Nicolette*, an anonymous French *chantfable*, is written in a combination of prose and verse.
- Renaud de Beaujeu writes *Guinglain, ou, Le Bel Inconnu/Guinglan, or The Beautiful Unknown*, a metrical romance belonging to the Arthurian cycle.
- The war story *Heike monogatari/Tales of the Heike* is written. It is considered the finest example of this new Japanese literary genre.

c. 1222

- Snorri Sturluson writes *The Prose Edda* (or "Younger" *Edda*), an instruction manual on the different meters employed by the early Icelandic poets (who are known as *skalds*).

1224

- Chinese scholar Li Chih-ch'ang writes *Hsi yu chi*, a description of the travels of Chiu Ch'ang-ch'un from Beijing, China, to Persia.

Thought and Scholarship

1220

- Buddhist monk Jien completes *Gukanshō/Jottings of a Fool*, the first critical and analytical work of Japanese history.
- Michael Scot, a Scottish scholar at the court of Frederick II the Holy Roman Emperor at Palermo, Sicily, translates Abu'l-Walīd ibn-Rushd (Averroës) of Córdoba's commentaries on Aristotle of 1198 from Arabic into Latin.

SOCIETY

Education

1220

- King Alfonso IX of León founds the University of Salamanca.

1222

- Padua University is established in Italy.

1224

June 5 The Holy Roman Emperor Frederick II founds Naples University, in the southern Italian kingdom of Sicily.

Everyday Life

1220

- Giraffes are brought to Europe and put on public display for the first time, to general amazement.

Religion

1220

May 5 St. Francis resigns the government of his order.
May 22 The first general chapter of the Dominican Order rejects the ownership of property and makes a constitution that embodies the principle of representing its provinces in general chapters.

1221

August 8 Dominican friars arrive in England.

1223

November 29 Honorius III confirms the final form of rules for the Friars Minor.

1224

August 8 St. Francis receives *stigmata* (the wounds of Christ) upon his person.
September 10 Franciscan friars arrive in England.

BIRTHS & DEATHS

1220

c. 1220 Wolfram, German poet, author of "Parzival," dies (*c.* 50).
- Roger Bacon ("Doctor Mirabilis"), English Franciscan philosopher and early experimental scientist, born in Ilchester, Somerset or Bisley, Gloucestershire, England (–1292).
March Charles of Anjou, King Charles I of Naples and Sicily, first of the Angevin dynasty in Italy and creator of an extensive but short-lived Mediterranean empire, born (–1285).

1221

- St. Bonaventure, eminent theologian, minister general of the Franciscan order, and bishop of Albano, whose works include *Itinerarium mentis in Deum/Journey of the Mind to God* (1259), born in Bagnoregio, Tuscany, Italy (–1274).
August 6 St. Dominic, founder of the Dominican order of friars, dies in Bologna, Italy (*c.* 51).
November 23 Alfonso X the Wise, King of Castile and León 1252–84, born in Burgos, Castile (–1284).

1223

July 14 Philip II, King of France 1179–1223, who reconquered French territories lost previously to England, dies in Nantes, France (57).

1224

- Andrew, bishop of Prague, exiled by King Ottokar I of Bohemia for claiming clerical immunity from secular jurisdiction and taxation, dies in Rome.
- St. Thomas Aquinas ("Doctor Angelicus"), Italian Dominican theologian, outstanding medieval scholasticist, author of *Summa theologiae/Summary of Theology* and *Summa contra gentiles/The Main Argument Against the Gentiles*, born in Roccasecca, near Aquino, Sicily (–1274).

1225–1229

POLITICS, GOVERNMENT, AND ECONOMICS

Human Rights

1229

November 11 The Inquisition is established in Toulouse, France, by the Roman Catholic Church, the Dominicans, against the Albigensians (a branch of the Cathars, Christian dualist heretics, in southern France).

Politics and Government

1225

- Jalal-ad-Din, the shah of the central Asian province of Khwarizm, reestablishes control of Persia, then invades Georgia and sacks the capital Tbilisi after defeating the Georgians at Garnhi.
- John III Ducas Vatatzes, the Byzantine emperor of Nicaea, defeats the Latins supporting a rebellion by the sons of the former emperor Theodore I Lascaris, at Poimanenon.
- King Ferdinand III of Castile takes the town of Andújar in his first campaign against the Muslims.
- The Koreans refuse to pay tribute to the Mongols and murder a Mongol emissary.
- Tran Thai-tong becomes sole emperor of Dai Viet (modern northern Vietnam, also known as Annam), founding the Tran dynasty.

February 11 King Henry III of England reissues the Magna Carta and the Charter of the Forests, which give the barons certain rights, in return for the grant by the barons of a general tax to pay for an expedition to Gascony under his brother Richard, Earl of Cornwall (in 1227), to defend it against King Louis VIII of France.

February 15 Pope Honorius III condemns Raymond VII, Count of Toulouse, as a heretic for refusing to purge the Albigensians (Cathars) in his country.

November 7 Archbishop Engelbert of Cologne, the Holy Roman Emperor Frederick II's vice regent in Germany, is murdered.

November 9 The Holy Roman Emperor Frederick II marries Queen Isabel (also known as Yolanda), the daughter of John of Brienne, King of Jerusalem. Frederick forces John to abdicate and assumes the title king of Jerusalem himself.

1226

- Lübeck in Germany becomes an imperial free city.
- The Italian nobleman Ezzelin III da Romano wins control of Verona and is named as its *podestà* (literally "power," the highest judicial and military authority).
- The Mongol leader Genghis Khan conquers the Tangut state of Xixia (now in northwest China), destroying the Tangut army in a battle on the frozen Huang He River (or Yellow River).
- The Polish prince Konrad of Masovia grants the town of Chełmno to the German Order of the Teutonic Knights as a base for their conquest and conversion of the Prussians.

January 30 King Louis VIII of France assumes direction of the Albigensian crusaders' campaigns against Raymond VII, Count of Toulouse.

March 6 A second Lombard League is formed by the northern Italian cities of Milan, Bologna, Brescia, Mantua, Bergamo, Turin, Vicenza, Padua, and others to oppose the Holy Roman Emperor Frederick II.

April 5 By the Treaty of Melun, King Louis VIII of France releases Ferrand, Count of Flanders (imprisoned since his capture by the former king Philip II at Bouvines in 1214), on receiving his admission of French suzerainty.

November 8 King Louis VIII of France dies; he is succeeded by his young son, Louis IX, with his widow, Blanche of Castile, acting as regent.

November 27 The first league of Rhenish towns, directed against the archbishop of Mainz, Germany, is suppressed by the Holy Roman Emperor Frederick II.

1227

- Bishop Albert of Livonia defeats the Osilians and begins their conversion to Christianity.
- King James I of Aragon ends the civil war in his kingdom by a convention with his nobles.

1227–29 Prince Jaroslav of Novgorod campaigns in the area of modern Finland against the Swedes.

January 8 King Henry III of England declares himself to be of full age to rule in his own right.

March 16 By the Treaty of Vendôme, Blanche of Castile, the regent of France, ends a revolt by the Count of Brittany and others.

March 19 Ugolino dei Conti is elected as Pope Gregory IX.

July 22 King Valdemar II of Denmark is defeated at Bornhöved by the allies of Henry, Count of Schwerin, losing the town of Lübeck and other conquests in northern Germany. German colonization toward the east now resumes.

August 24 The Mongol leader Genghis Khan dies; his army numbers about 129,000 at his death. He is succeeded as great khan by his son Ogedai. A subordinate khanate is created for Ogedai's brother Chaghadai in Turkestan.

September 15   The Almohad leader Abu-al-Ala Idris (al-Ma'mun) declares himself the ruler of Muslim Spain.

September 29   Pope Gregory IX excommunicates the Holy Roman Emperor Frederick II for his failure to fulfill his promise to go on crusade (Frederick has claimed to be too ill).

November 11   Al-Mu'azzam, the Ayyubid sultan of Damascus, Syria, dies; al-Kamil, the Ayyubid sultan of Egypt, then seizes Jerusalem.

November 11   Leszek I, Duke of Kraków and Little Poland, is murdered by Świętopełk, the independent ruler of Pomerania; he is succeeded by his son, Bolesław V.

1228

- King James I of Aragon begins the conquest of the Balearic Islands.
- King Stephen of Serbia dies. He is succeeded by his sons Radoslav and Vladislav.
- Robert de Courtenay, the Latin emperor of Constantinople, dies; he is succeeded by his son, Baldwin II, with John of Brienne (ex-king of Jerusalem) as regent and entitled emperor.

June 28   The Holy Roman Emperor Frederick II sails for Palestine on the Sixth Crusade. Pope Gregory IX renews his sentence of excommunication, this time because excommunicates cannot go on crusade.

July 21   The Holy Roman Emperor Frederick II arrives at Limassol and forces the barons and the regents of the child-king Henry to recognize him as lord of Cyprus.

September 9   King Henry III of England relieves the siege of Montgomery by Llywelyn ap Iorwerth the Great, Prince of Gwynedd (north Wales).

1229

- King Alfonso IX of León takes the Spanish city of Badajoz from the Muslims.
- King Ferdinand III of Castile sends an army to Africa to restore his ally al-Ma'mun as emir of the Almohads; the latter permits Castilians to settle in Marrakesh.
- King Valdemar II of Denmark surrenders Holstein, Mecklenburg, and Pomerania in his treaty of peace with Henry, Count of Schwerin.
- Pietro Ziano, Doge of Venice, dies; he is succeeded by Jacopo Tiepolo.
- The first treaty is made between German merchants and the prince of Smolensk.
- The invading Shan tribe of Ahom (in the north of modern Burma) founds the kingdom of Assam, India.

February 8   Iltutmish is recognized as sultan of Delhi, India, by the caliph of Baghdad.

February 18   The Holy Roman Emperor Frederick II negotiates the return of Jerusalem to Christian control with al-Kamil, the sultan of Egypt; the Sixth Crusade thus ends without any fighting.

March 18   The Holy Roman Emperor Frederick II crowns himself as king of Jerusalem, in Jerusalem.

April 11   The Treaty of Paris ends the Albigensian Crusade against the Albigensian (Cathar) heretics of Languedoc, southern France; Count Raymond VII of Toulouse submits to King Louis IX of France, ceding the duchy of Narbonne.

June 6   The Ayyubid prince Al-Ashraf Musa takes Damascus, Syria; as he recognizes the supremacy of his brother al-Kamil Muhammad, Sultan of Egypt, the Ayyubid (Saladin's) sultanate is now reunited.

June 10   The Holy Roman Emperor Frederick II returns to Italy and defeats papal troops, led by John of Brienne, Latin regent of Constantinople, attempting to conquer Sicily as a crusade.

July 29   Mohammad ibn-Hud, who has seized Murcia and Granada, defeats the Almohad emir al-Ma'mun near Turifa.

December 31   King James I of Aragon takes Palma, the capital of the Balearic island of Majorca.

SCIENCE, TECHNOLOGY, AND MEDICINE

Math

1225

- Italian mathematician Fibonacci writes *Liber quadratorum/The Book of the Square*, the first major Western advance in arithmetic since the work of Diophantus a thousand years earlier.

Technology

1225

- Muslim settlers in southern Spain begin to manufacture cotton in Europe for the first time. The new fabric rapidly grows in popularity and spreads to the Christian nations.
- The Muslim engineer and astronomer Qaisar ibn-Abī-al-Qasīm makes an elaborate celestial globe for keeping time and for calculating the movements of the heavens.

1226

- The Norman immigrant glassworker Lawrence Vitronius begins manufacturing glass in England for the first time.

ARTS AND IDEAS

Architecture

1225

- The Carolingian choir of Beauvais Cathedral, France, burns down. Work begins on rebuilding it in 1235.
- Visby Cathedral in Gotland, Sweden, is dedicated after being rebuilt.

1227

- The foundation stone of Toledo Cathedral, Spain, is laid. It is to be built in "the French style" with Martin and Petrus Petri its architects in succession.

1228

- The old cathedral at Troyes, France, is destroyed in a storm. The new cathedral is already under construction.

1228–39 The church and convent of St. Francesco in Assisi, Italy, is constructed.

Literature and Language

1225

c. 1225 "King Horn," the earliest English verse romance, is written.

- St. Francis of Assisi writes his "Il cantico di Frate Sole"/ "Canticle of Brother Sun," a hymn of praise to God written in Italian.
- The *Cycle de la Croisade/Cycle of the Crusade* is recorded. It consists of "Chanson d'Antioche"/"Song of Antioch" and "Conquête de Jérusalem"/"Conquest of Jerusalem" (both by Graindor de Douay), which with "Le Chevalier au Cygne"/"The Knight of the Swan," "Roman de Godefroi Bouillon"/"The Story of Godefroi Bouillon" and "Elioxe," form a group of poems on the theme of the crusades.

1229

- Yāqūt writes *Mu'jam al-Udaba'*, a biographical dictionary of learned men.

Thought and Scholarship

c. 1225

- Eike von Repkow writes his *Sachsenspiegel/Mirror of Saxony*, a Latin treatise on Saxon laws and the oldest example of German legal writing.
- Snorri Sturluson writes his *Heimskringla*, a two part history of the kings of Norway to 1077.
- The "Petition of Daniil the Prisoner" is written. It is an aphoristic epistle addressed to a prince, advising the prince to rule harshly.

SOCIETY

Education

1229

- The University of Angers is founded in France.

Religion

1227

- Dogen introduces the Soto sect of Zen Buddhism from China into Japan.

BIRTHS & DEATHS

1226

October 3 St. Francis of Assisi, founder of the Franciscan monastic orders and church reformer, principal patron saint of Italy, dies in Assisi, Italy (*c.* 44).

November 8 Louis VIII the Lion, King of France 1223–26, who aided the English barons against King John of England, dies in Montpensier, France (39).

1227

March 18 Pope Honorius III dies.

August 18 Genghis Khan (original name Temüjin), great Mongol military leader who established the Mongol empire, dies (*c.* 72).

1228

April 25 Conrad IV, King of the Romans 1237–51, and King of Sicily 1251–54, born in Andria, Italy (–1254).

July 9 Stephen Langton, archbishop of Canterbury 1207–28, who supported the baronial opposition to King John, leading to the signing of the Magna Carta, dies in Slindon, Sussex, England.

1229

- Bishop Albert of Livonia dies.

1230–1234

POLITICS, GOVERNMENT, AND ECONOMICS

Human Rights

1231

April 4   Pope Gregory IX sets up the Holy Office (Inquisition), a permanent tribunal for investigating the various heresies proliferating in France and Germany.

Politics and Government

1230

- Herman of Salza, the grand master of the Teutonic Knights (a German Christian military order of crusading knights), takes possession of the town of Chełmno in Poland, granted to them by Prince Konrad of Masovia; the Knights now begin their conquest of Prussia.
- King Přemesyl Ottokar I of Bohemia dies; he is succeeded by his son, Wenceslas I.
- The local Moorish prince Mohammad ibn-Yūsuf ibn Nasr seizes power in Granada, southern Spain, from the defunct Almohad empire, founding the Nasrid dynasty.

April 4   John Asen II, Czar of Bulgaria, defeats and captures Theodore Angelus, the despot of Epirus, at Klokotinitza; the Bulgarian Empire now extends from the Black Sea to the River Danube, the Adriatic Sea, and Thessaly.

May 3   King Henry III of England arrives in Brittany as the ally of Peter of Dreux (Mauclerc), who is regent for his son, Count John of Brittany.

July 23   By the Treaty of Ceprano, the Holy Roman Emperor Frederick II makes concessions to the church in Sicily and agrees to respect the borders of the Papal States; in return Pope Gregory IX lifts his sentence of excommunication.

August 10   Kay-Qubadh, Sultan of Rūm, defeats Jalal-ad-Din, Shah of Khwarizm, at Erzinjan and then occupies Erzurum.

September 23   King Alfonso IX of León dies; he is succeeded by his son, Ferdinand III of Castile, who thus finally unites the two kingdoms.

October 10   King Henry III returns to England after his expedition to Brittany and Bordeaux.

1231

- Michael II, son of the former despot Michael Angelus, establishes himself as despot of Epirus.

- The Holy Roman Emperor Frederick II promulgates his *Liber Augustalis* for the kingdom of Sicily, the first medieval code of laws based on Roman jurisprudence. He also introduces the *augustales*, the first gold coinage in western Europe since late Roman times.
- The Mongols begin their campaigns to conquer Korea.

May 5   Henry, King of the Romans (king of Germany, son of the Holy Roman Emperor Frederick II), concedes the "constitution in favor of the German princes," granting them territorial sovereignty.

May 26   Henry, King of the Romans (king of Germany), removes the Swiss canton of Uri from the Habsburgs in order to secure control of the St. Gothard Pass through the Swiss Alps.

July 5   King Henry III of England and King Louis IX of France make a truce, for three years.

August 15   Jalal-ad-Din, Shah of Khwarizm, is murdered while fleeing a new Mongol invasion. Kay-Qubadh, Sultan of Rūm, now occupies Ahlat and Queen Rusudan of Georgia reoccupies the Georgian capital Tbilisi; the Mongols conquer the rest of his shahdom.

September 16   Ludwig I, Duke of Bavaria, is murdered. He is succeeded by his son Otto.

December 12   Llywelyn ap Iorwerth the Great, Prince of Gwynedd, north Wales, sacks Montgomery, Radnor, Brecon, Caerleon, and Cardigan, English-held castles in Wales, in the summer, but King Henry III of England's counterattack is indecisive and ends with a truce.

December 25   In a diet (legislative assembly) in Ravenna, Italy, the Holy Roman Emperor Frederick II (ineffectively) legislates against the formation of municipal corporations in Germany.

1232

- John Asen II, Czar of Bulgaria, breaks off relations with the papacy.
- The *Joei shikimoku*, a codification of the Minamoto family law regulating the Japanese warrior class, is drawn up by the Administrative Board, the central organ of the shogun (military ruler) feudal government of Japan.
- The Chinese Song Empire sends troops with siege warfare skills to help the Mongols in an attack on the Jin capital Kaifeng.
- The Holy Roman Emperor Frederick II confirms the "constitution in favor of the German princes" issued by his son Henry, granting them territorial sovereignty.
- The Holy Roman Emperor Frederick II holds an assembly in Sicily attended by representatives of towns.
- The Korean king Ch'oe-u moves his capital to the island of Kangwhado to escape Mongol invasions.
- The Muslims of the Balearic island of Minorca surrender to King James I of Aragon.

- There is an outbreak of public disorder in Abbeville, France; there are similar disturbances, due to conflict between artisans and richer citizens, in other western European towns in the 13th century.

May 2   Richard Filangieri, the Holy Roman Emperor Frederick II's legate in Palestine, defeats, at Casal Imbert (near Tyre), the forces of John of Ibelin, Lord of Beirut, leader of those barons of Outremer (crusader kingdoms established in the Middle East) who oppose Frederick's claim to royal authority there.

June 15   John of Ibelin, Lord of Beirut, defeats the Holy Roman Emperor Frederick II's legate Richard Filangieri at Agridi, Cyprus.

July 29   King Henry III of England dismisses the justiciar Hubert de Burgh, Earl of Essex, and begins the centralization of royal finances under Peter des Rivaux.

October 16   The Almohad emir al-Ma'mun dies; he is succeeded by his son abd-al-Wahid in Morocco, but Mohammad ibn-Yūsuf of Granada proclaims himself king in Spain.

1233

- The Mongols under Subedai take Kaifeng, the Jin capital: by the intervention of Yeh-lü, a Khitan prince in Mongol service, the population is spared the usual massacre.

April 4   With the surrender of the Cypriot port of Kyrenia to John of Ibelin, Lord of Beirut, the Holy Roman Emperor Frederick II's forces are expelled from Cyprus and Henry of Lusignan is restored as king.

July 30   Conrad of Marburg, the ruthless Papal Inquisitor of Germany, is murdered after accusing the Count of Mayn of heresy.

August 8   Richard the Marshal, Earl of Pembroke, in alliance with Llywelyn ap Iorwerth the Great, Prince of Gwynedd (north Wales), begins a revolt against King Henry III of England.

November 25   Richard the Marshal, Earl of Pembroke, defeats King Henry III of England's forces near Monmouth, Wales.

1234

- Jin resistance to the Mongol invasions is finally crushed.
- Pope Gregory IX proclaims a crusade against the city of Rome after a revolt there has forced him into flight.
- Prince Henry I of Wrocław (Lower Silesia) becomes grand prince of Poland.

April 1   Richard the Marshal, the rebel Earl of Pembroke, is fatally wounded by supporters of King Henry III of England in Ireland. He dies on April 16.

April 7   Sancho VII the Strong, the last Spanish king of Navarre, dies; his subjects elect his adopted heir, Theobald IV, Count of Champagne, as king.

April 25   King Louis IX of France attains his majority and begins his personal rule; the regent, his mother Blanche of Castile, retains considerable influence, however.

May 5   King Henry III of England dismisses his unpopular treasurer Peter des Rivaux and is reconciled with the magnates, during the outcry following the murder of Richard the Marshal, Earl of Pembroke, in Ireland.

May 5   King Louis IX of France marries Margaret of Provence, daughter of Raymond Berengar IV of Provence.

SCIENCE, TECHNOLOGY, AND MEDICINE

Agriculture

1231

- A serious famine hits Japan, the first of several to occur in the coming decades.

Health and Medicine

1230

- Crusaders return from the Holy Land to Europe with leprosy, where it is to become a major problem in the following century. It is poorly understood, and inspires fear and superstition everywhere.

1231

- The Holy Roman Emperor Frederick II orders that medical teachers and practitioners should be examined by the University of Salerno.
- The scholarly German king Frederick II reestablishes the medical faculty at the University of Salerno, Italy, under the direction of the physician Nicolaus Praepositus. Frederick also encourages the introduction of human dissection.

Science

1230

- The Chinese scholar Chia Ssu-tao writes the treatise *Ts'u chih ching* on the subject of crickets, which are kept in small cages by the Chinese nobility because of the chirping sounds they make.

Technology

1230

- *c.* 1230   Iron production becomes an important industry in the Westphalia and Swabia regions of western Germany, and in Hungary.
- An early Muslim literary reference indicates that the magnetic compass is now in use throughout the Arab world.

1233

- Coal is mined at the English town of Newcastle and rapidly becomes popular as a fuel, although some complain about the pollution.

ARTS AND IDEAS

Architecture

1230

- Construction begins on the cathedral at Siena, Italy.

1231

- The mausoleum of "Sultan Gharī" (Nasir-ad-Din Mahmud, son of Iltutmish) is built in Delhi, India.
- The upper part of Abbot Suger's choir in St.-Denis, Paris, France, is removed. The architect Pierre de Montereau oversees its reconstruction and takes the opportunity to place the first windows in a triforium (the arcade above the arches of the choir). The Carolingian nave is subsequently replaced.

1232

- Mustansiriyah Mosque is built in Baghdad, Persia.

Arts

1232

- Shuja ibn-Hanfar of Mosul, Mesopotamia, makes a brass ewer inlaid with silver, a fine example of Muslim inlaid metalwork, which reaches its highest standard in the mid-13th century.

Literature and Language

c. 1230

- The long era of *Minnesingers* (German court lyric poets and singers who wrote love lyrics of a formal style and aristocratic beauty) ends. Among the most eminent names were Wolfram von Eschenbach who died in 1220, and Walter von der Vogelweide who may have died in this year.

Thought and Scholarship

1232

- French-born Jewish scholar Samuel ben Tibbon makes Hebrew translations of the works of the great Hebrew philosopher and physician Maimonides, which were written in Arabic.

c. 1233

- Hugolinus of Bologna, Italy, writes his *Summa digestorum* on Roman law.

SOCIETY

Education

1230

- The jurist university is founded at Montpellier, France, in addition to its ancient law school.

1231

- Pope Gregory IX's Bull *Parens Scientiarum* gives privileges to the University of Paris, France, exempting it from control by the local bishop.

1233

- Pope Gregory IX confirms the establishment of the University of Toulouse, France, and grants privileges to the scholars.

1234

- The Abbasid caliph al-Mustansir founds al-Mustansiriyah University in Baghdad.

Religion

1231

- Pope Gregory IX exempts the Friars Preacher and Friars Minor from episcopal jurisdiction.

1232

- Elias is elected the first minister–general of the Friars Minor.

1234

- The decretals (papal edicts) of Pope Gregory IX, known as "Extra," are added to the body of canon law.

BIRTHS & DEATHS

1230

- Azzo of Bologna, whose *Summa codicis et institutionum/Summary of the Legal Code and Institutions*, a summary of Roman law, is highly influential throughout the Middle Ages, dies.
- The Persian mystical poet Attār, writer of the poem *Manteq ot-teyr/ The Conference of the Birds*, an allegory about the quest for union with God, dies.

1231

June 13 St. Anthony of Padua, Franciscan monk, doctor of the church and patron of the poor, dies in Arcella, Verona (36).

November 3 William of Auxerre, French philosopher and theologian who was the first European author to write about free will, dies in Rome (*c.* 81).

November 17 St. Elizabeth of Hungary, Hungarian princess famed for her devotion to the poor, dies in Marburg, Germany (*c.* 24).

1232

- Ramón Llull (or Raymond Lully), Catalan mystic and poet, born in Majorca (–1316).

1233

- Ibn-al-Athir, Arab historian, writer of *Kitāb al-Kāmil fi-al-Ta'rīkh/The Complete Book of Chronicles*, which

abridges al-Tabari's work of 923 and continues Arab history to 1231, dies.

March 2 Władysław I, King of Poland 1320–33, who united several Polish provinces into a kingdom, dies in Poland (*c.* 73).

1234

April 16 Richard the Marshal, the rebel Earl of Pembroke, dies, having been fatally wounded by supporters of King Henry III of England.

1235–1239

POLITICS, GOVERNMENT, AND ECONOMICS

Business and Economics

1236

- The provision of paper currency begins during the late Song dynasty in China.

Politics and Government

1235

- John Asen II, Czar of Bulgaria, makes a marriage alliance with John III Ducas Vatatzes, the Byzantine emperor of Nicaea, against the Latins ruling Constantinople, but their combined attack fails.
- King Wenceslas I of Bohemia grants privileges to the (present-day) "Old Town" of Prague to encourage its settlement by Germans.
- Robert le Bougre is appointed Inquisitor of France.
- Sundiata, a Mandingo chief from the minor state of Kangaba, rebels against Sumanguru of Kaniaga, the dominant ruler in the west African Sahel, and defeats him at the Battle of Kirina (in southwest Mali). Sundiata compels Sumanguru's subjects to recognize his overlordship, so founding the empire of Mali.
- The Mongols invade the Chinese Song Empire for the first time, in retaliation for a Song attempt to seize Kaifeng, the capital of the former Jin Empire.
- With the capture of Ibiza, King James I of Aragon completes his conquest of the Balearic Islands.

March 7 King Andrew II of Hungary dies; he is succeeded by his son, Béla IV.

July 7 In a diet (legislative assembly) in Worms, Henry is deposed as king of the Romans (king of Germany) following his revolt against his father, the Holy Roman Emperor Frederick II.

July 15 The Holy Roman Emperor Frederick II marries his third wife, Isabella, the sister of King Henry III of England.

1236

- A Mongol army led by Batu, a grandson of the Mongol leader Genghis Khan, conquers the Volga Bulgars.
- Alexander, son of Great Prince Jaroslav II of Vladimir–Suzdal, is elected prince of Novgorod.
- Ezzelin da Romano, *podestà* of Verona, becomes *podestà* of Vicenza, Italy.

- The death of John of Ibelin, the powerful and influential lord of Beirut, leads to a worsening of the anarchy among the lords of Outremer, crusader kingdoms established in the Middle East.
- The kingdom of Georgia is conquered by the Mongols and reduced to tributary status.
- The Teutonic Knights (a German Christian military order of crusading knights) complete their conquest of the Pomeranians of west Prussia.

January 1 The Statute of Merton (the first declaration on points of law known by the name "statute") is made after deliberation by King Henry III of England and the barons.

January 14 King Henry III of England marries Eleanor of Provence; his reception and patronage of her relatives in England arouses discontent.

April 29 Iltutmish, Sultan of Delhi, India, dies; he is succeeded, briefly, by Firuz I, then by his daughter Radiyya.

June 29 King Ferdinand III of Castile and León takes Córdoba, the capital of a minor Muslim kingdom in Spain.

July 7 In a diet (legislative assembly) in Piacenza, Italy, the Holy Roman Emperor Frederick II announces his intention of restoring imperial authority in Italy. Pope Gregory IX replies by claiming the supreme temporal dominion of the papacy in Italy under the "Donation of Constantine" (an 8th-century forgery, purporting to show that the Roman Emperor Constantine granted control of all of Italy to Pope Sylvester I and the papacy in the 4th century).

November 11 The Holy Roman Emperor Frederick II burns the Italian city of Vicenza, then returns to Germany.

1237

- Kay-Qubadh, Sultan of Rūm, is murdered; after a family blood bath he is succeeded by his son, Kay-Khusraw II.
- King James I of Aragon conquers the Spanish kingdom of Murcia from the Muslims.
- Pope Gregory IX confirms the union of the Sword Brothers of Livonia to the Teutonic Knights (a German Christian military order of crusading knights).
- The examination system for civil service recruitment is abandoned in the former Jin Empire of north China, now under Mongol rule.

January 1 King Henry III again confirms the Charters (the Magna Carta and the Charter of the Forest) and appoints three baronial councillors in return for the grant of a tax.

January 1 The Holy Roman Emperor Frederick II confers the status of imperial free city on Vienna.

February 2 Ezzelin da Romano, Lord of Vicenza, takes Padua and, later, Treviso.

February 2 The Holy Roman Emperor Frederick II's son

Conrad IV is elected "king of the Romans" (king of Germany).

September 25   By the Treaty of York with King Henry III of England, King Alexander II of Scotland renounces Scottish claims to Northumberland, Cumberland, and Westmorland; the Anglo-Scottish border is now defined by mutual agreement.

November 27   The Holy Roman Emperor Frederick II defeats the Lombard League of northern Italy at Cortenuova, Italy, but by insisting on unconditional surrender, he merely stimulates further resistance.

December 21   The Mongol army of Batu, the grandson of Genghis Khan, destroys the Russian city and principality of Riazan; invading in midwinter, the Mongols use frozen rivers as highways to make rapid progress in Russia.

1238

- Grand Prince Henry I of Poland dies; he is succeeded by his son, Henry II.
- Khus Bang Klang (assuming the title Sri Inthrathit) becomes king of Sukhodaya, the first Siamese (now Thai) state to free itself from the Khmer Empire.
- The Holy Roman Emperor Frederick II makes his son Enzio king of Sardinia.

January 7   Simon IV de Montfort, Earl of Leicester and son of the Norman crusader Simon de Montfort, marries Eleanor, the sister of King Henry III of England.

February 8   The Mongol leader Batu takes the Russian town of Vladimir, and then destroys Moscow and other central Russian cities, massacring their inhabitants.

March 4   Juri (Yury) II, Great Prince of Vladimir–Suzdal, is defeated and killed by the Mongols under Batu on the Sita, near Yaroslavl (which is subsequently sacked). The spring thaw begins shortly afterwards, making the terrain impassable and halting the Mongol advance on Novgorod. Batu then withdraws to the Don basin.

March 8   Al-Kamil, Sultan of Egypt and Damascus, Syria, dies; civil war over the succession breaks out among the Ayyubid family.

August 3   The Holy Roman Emperor Frederick II begins the siege of Brescia, Italy.

September 9   King James I of Aragon takes Valencia from the Moors.

October 9   The Holy Roman Emperor Frederick II abandons the siege of Brescia, Italy.

1239

- Great Prince Jaroslav II of Vladimir–Suzdal begins the payment of tribute to the Mongols; the other Russian princes soon follow suit.
- Jacopo Tiepolo, the doge of Venice, introduces the maritime statutes to regulate shipping.
- King Béla IV of Hungary permits the Cumans, a pagan nomadic tribe in flight from the Mongols, to settle between the River Danube and the Theiss.
- The first notice of the king of France holding a parlement (law court) dates from this year.

March 20   Pope Gregory IX excommunicates the Holy Roman Emperor Frederick II for infringing the church's rights in Italy. In Germany, only Bavaria and Bohemia rebel in consequence.

June 6   The Holy Roman Emperor Frederick II invades Romagna and Tuscany, Italy.

September 1   A new crusade, led by King Theobald of

Navarre and Richard, Earl of Cornwall (King Henry III of England's brother), arrives at the Palestinian port of Acre (present-day Akko, Israel).

October 10   After six weeks, the Holy Roman Emperor Frederick II abandons his siege of the Italian city of Milan.

November 13   King Theobald of Navarre's crusading army is defeated by the Egyptians at Gaza; subsequent negotiations, however, result in modest territorial gains for the kingdom of Jerusalem.

December 7   An-Nasir, Prince of Kerak, expels the Latin garrison from its citadel in Jerusalem and destroys the city's fortifications before withdrawing.

SCIENCE, TECHNOLOGY, AND MEDICINE

Health and Medicine

1236

- The Dominican friar and physician Theodoric of Lucca uses opiates to anesthetize patients before surgery, while teaching in the medical school at Bologna, Italy.

1237

- The Chinese physician Ch'en Tzu-ming writes the treatise *Fu-jên ta-ch'uan liang-fang* on the causes and treatments of "women's diseases."

Science

1235

- French scholar Thomas de Chantimpré writes his popular encyclopedia of natural history *De natura rerum/On the Nature of Things*.

ARTS AND IDEAS

Architecture

1235

- Construction begins on the Church of St. Elizabeth in Marburg, Germany, and Liebfrauenkirche in Trier, Germany.
- The French engineer Villard de Honnecourt produces an architectural sketchbook, including plans of water-driven machinery such as sawmills, and a screw jack for lifting loads. It becomes a standard manual for engineers and architects.

1236

- The nave and transepts of the cathedral at Amiens, France, are completed.

1237–38

- Huand Hatun founds a mosque, including her mausoleum, a *medrese* (college), and a bath at Kayseri in the Seljuk Sultanate of Rūm (modern Turkey).

Literature and Language

c. **1235**

- Gonzalo de Berceo, the first Spanish poet known by name, writes three devotional poems to local saints.

c. **1237**

- Guillaume de Lorris writes the first 4,000 lines of the *Le Roman de la rose/The Romance of the Rose*, an allegory of courtly love and the most famous narrative poem of the Middle Ages.

Thought and Scholarship

c. **1237**

- Roger of Wendover, a monk from St. Albans, England, writes his *Flores historiarum/The Flowers of History*, a chronicle of world history from the creation to 1237, employing several different sources.
- The chronicle *Sächsische Weltchronik/Saxon Chronology of the World*, a world history in Middle Low German, is recorded.

SOCIETY

Education

1238

- Scholars migrating from Oxford set up universities in Salisbury and Northampton, England.

Religion

c. **1235**

- Scholastic philosopher William of Auvergne produces *Magisterium divinale/Religious Instructions*, a theological encyclopedia that opposes superstition and displays an appreciation of psychology.
- Franciscan Friars arrive in Wrocław, Poland.

1237

- Pope Gregory IX introduces statutes for the reform of the Benedictine order.

1238

- Following the failure of the crusades, some Carmelite friars begin to migrate from Palestine to Sicily and southern France. The order subsequently spreads throughout Europe.

1239

- Pope Gregory IX deposes Elias from the general–ministership of the Friars Minor, following protests over his despotic rule.

Sports

1238

- The earliest reference is made to the Palio horse race in Siena, Italy. Similar horse races are held in other Italian cities, usually on important holy days, but it is only in Siena that the tradition survives through to modern times.

BIRTHS & DEATHS

1235

January 23 Ibn al-Farid, celebrated Arab Sufi poet, whose best-known works include the "Khamriyah"/ "Wine Ode," dies in Cairo, Egypt (*c.* 53).

1236

February 7 King Mohammad ibn-Hud of Murcia and Granada is murdered.

1237

c. 1237 Boniface VIII, Italian pope 1294–1303, who published *Liber Sextus/Book Six*, and whose authority was constantly challenged by the emerging European monarchies, born in Anagni, Papal States (–1303).

1239

- Edward I Longshanks, King of England 1272–1307, son of Henry III, who subdued Wales, born in Westminster, London (–1307).

March 20 Herman of Salza, Grand Master of the Teutonic Knights (German Christian military order of crusading knights), dies.

1240–1244

POLITICS, GOVERNMENT, AND ECONOMICS

Colonization

1241

- German immigrants flood into Poland to settle land depopulated by the Mongol invasion.

Politics and Government

1240

- King Sundiata of Mali destroys Koumbi, the capital of Ghana, and incorporates its remaining lands into his empire.
- King Valdemar II of Denmark publishes a collection of Cimbric laws.
- The Mongols invade Tibet and sack the monastery of Ra-sgreng.

February 22 The Holy Roman Emperor Frederick II reaches the outskirts of Rome, but withdraws to Sicily when Pope Gregory IX rouses the Romans to resist. Gregory, ineffectively, orders a crusade against Frederick in Germany.

April 11 Llywelyn ap Iorwerth the Great, Prince of Gwynedd (north Wales), dies; he is succeeded by his son Dafydd ap Llywelyn.

April 22 Radiyya, Sultana of Delhi, India, is deposed in favor of her brother Mu'izz-ad-Din Bahram.

July 15 Prince Alexander of Novgorod defeats the Swedes on the River Neva in modern Estonia; his victory earns him the title *Nevsky* ("of the Neva").

August 15 The Holy Roman Emperor Frederick II takes Ravenna.

September 9 King Theobald of Navarre leaves Palestine, ending his crusade.

September 9 Raymond Trencavel, a sympathizer with the Albigensian (Cathar) heretics of Languedoc, southern France, leads a revolt by the city of Toulouse.

October 10 Radiyya, the deposed sultana of Delhi, India, is murdered.

December 6 The Mongol leader Batu takes and sacks the Russian principality of Kiev, then ravages the principality of Galicia, also called Red Ruthenia.

December 20 The Holy Roman Emperor Frederick II recognizes the inhabitants of the three Swiss Forest Cantons of Schwyz, Uri, and Unterwalden as freemen immediately subject to the empire.

1241

- Kay-Khusraw II, Sultan of Rūm, suppresses a revolt inspired by the popular preacher Baba Ishaq.
- King Henry III of England leads an expedition into Wales to enforce the submission of Prince Dafydd of Gwynedd.
- King Louis IX of France founds Aigues-Mortes, France, as a base for crusading: it is the first French royal port on the Mediterranean coast.
- The German towns of Hamburg and Lübeck form a peace-keeping league (which has been regarded as the origin of the Hanseatic League).
- The Muslim king of Murcia becomes the vassal of King Ferdinand III of Castile and León.

March 28 King Valdemar II the Victorious of Denmark dies; he is succeeded by his son, Eric IV.

April 4 The Holy Roman Emperor Frederick II takes the papal territories of Faenza and Benevento, Italy.

April 9 After sacking Kraków, a Mongol army led by Khaidu defeats the Poles, Silesians, and Teutonic Knights at Legnica in Poland. Grand Prince Henry II the Pious of Poland is killed. The Mongols next ravage Silesia and, when repulsed by the Bohemians, they go through Moravia into Hungary.

April 11 The main Mongol army, under Batu, defeats the Hungarians at Mohi on the River Sajo: they ravage the Danube plain, but are repulsed at Grobnok by the Croatians. A crusade is proclaimed against them in Germany.

May 3 The Pisan fleet, acting in alliance with the Holy Roman Emperor Frederick II, captures the French prelates traveling to a general council in Rome in Genoese ships in a naval battle off the island of Elba, west Italy.

June 6 John Asen II, Czar of Bulgaria, dies; he is succeeded by his infant son, Koloman I.

September 10 Archbishop Siegfried of Mainz, the Holy Roman Emperor Frederick II's vice regent in Germany, leads a revolt against him.

October 25 Goffredo Castiglione is elected Pope Celestine IV.

November 10 Pope Celestine IV dies after a reign of two weeks; the cardinals have dispersed, and there is a vacancy while the Holy Roman Emperor Frederick II attempts to influence the next election.

December 22 Lahore is taken and destroyed by the Mongols.

December 25 The Mongol leader Batu captures and destroys Pest on the River Danube, Hungary's largest city.

1242

- Batu withdraws the Mongol army from central Europe in the spring in order to return to the Mongol capital, Karakorum, to elect the late Great Khan Ogedai's successor: a four-year interregnum follows. Batu now organizes the Mongol territories in Russia as a semiautonomous state, known as The Khanate of the Golden Horde (supposedly named for the color of the khan's tent).
- Jacopo Tiepolo, the doge of Venice, introduces the civil statutes regulating civil and economic affairs.
- King Béla IV of Hungary defeats Frederick, Duke of Austria, on the River Leitha in a war to recover lands that he ceded to Frederick in return for refuge from the Mongol invasion.
- Świętopełk of East Pomerania organizes a revolt by the Prussians against the Teutonic Knights (the German Christian military order of crusading knights).

February 2 A council of barons refuses to grant King Henry III of England a tax on the grounds that he has failed to account for his expenditure of money raised by earlier taxes.

April 5 Alexander Nevsky, Prince of Novgorod, defeats the Teutonic Knights (the German Christian military order of knights) on the frozen Lake Peipus.

May 5 Raymond VII, Count of Toulouse, and the Lusignans, in Poitou, revolt against King Louis IX of France; King Henry III of England supports the Lusignans.

May 15 Sultan Bahram of Delhi, India, is murdered by his soldiers, who elect his nephew Alaad-Din Ma'sud to succeed him.

July 21 King Henry III of England retreats to Saintes after he is defeated by King Louis IX of France at Taillebourg, France. Louis suppresses the revolt of Raymond VII, Count of Toulouse, and the Lusignans.

1243

- Bolesław V is established as grand prince of Poland at Kraków by the other Polish princes.
- King Narasimhavarman of Orissa, India, defeats the Muslim governor of Bengal at his capital Lakhnaur.
- Stephen Uroš I, son of the former king Stephen Nemanja, succeeds as king of Serbia.

January 1 Raymond VII, Count of Toulouse, submits to King Louis IX of France by the Treaty of Lorris.

April 7 King Louis IX of France and King Henry III of England make a truce in the Treaty of Bordeaux: Henry loses all of his possessions north of the River Gironde except for the island of Oléron.

June 25 Sinibaldo dei Fieschi is elected as Pope Innocent IV.

June 26 The Mongols defeat Kay-Khusraw II, Sultan of Rūm, and his Byzantine allies at Köse Dagh, near Erzinjan; he becomes their tributary, as does Queen Rusadan of Georgia.

1244

- King Béla IV of Hungary gives the citizens of Pest, whose city was destroyed by the Mongols in 1241, the right to settle in the royal castle of Buda, on the opposite bank of the River Danube, and grants a city charter.
- King Ferdinand III of Castile and León and King James I of Aragon ratify, at Almizra, the treaty of 1179 defining their frontier in newly conquered Muslim lands.

March 31 The Holy Roman Emperor Frederick II negotiates a treaty with Pope Innocent IV which will lift his excommunication in return for his evacuation of occupied papal lands; however, the treaty is not ratified because it does not settle the question of imperial rights in Lombardy, northern Italy.

April 16 Jajnagar, Raja of Jaipur, in Orissa, India, defeats the Muslim governor of Bengal on the River Mahanadi.

August 23 Jerusalem is captured and sacked by Khwarizmian exiles employed by the sultan Ayyub of Egypt in his war against Damascus, Syria; the Christians are expelled, this time for good.

October 17 The Egyptians defeat the Christian army of Outremer, the crusader kingdoms established in the Middle East, and its Muslim allies of Damascus, Syria, at Harbiyah (or La Forbie), near Gaza.

November 11 A council of prelates and barons refuses to grant King Henry III of England a tax and puts forward a plan for the reform of his government.

December 2 Pope Innocent IV establishes the papal court at Lyons, France, to escape the influence of the Holy Roman Emperor Frederick II.

SCIENCE, TECHNOLOGY, AND MEDICINE

Health and Medicine

1243

- A plague of black rats invades Europe with the Mongol hordes from the East, coinciding with a severe famine in Germany.

Science

1240

- Bartholomaeus Anglicus the Englishman writes his encyclopedia of natural philosophy *De proprietatibus rerum*/*On the Properties of Things*. He is one of the first encyclopedists to offer objective information without opinion.

1242

- The Hindu physician Narahari Pandita writes a dictionary of *materia medica* known as *Rājanighantu*, which includes an early record of the use of hemp as an intoxicant.

Technology

1240

- The English scholar Friar Roger Bacon reports the existence of a diving apparatus that allows people to walk on the seabed without danger. It is an early form of diving helmet.

Transportation

1242

- The first record of ships traveling in convoy for mutual support and protection dates from this time.

ARTS AND IDEAS

Architecture

1240

- Construction begins on the choir of Tours Cathedral, France.
- Construction begins on Tournai Cathedral, Flanders.

1241

- Reims Cathedral, France, is completed except for the transepts. Construction of the west front begins under the architect Jean le Loup.

1245

- Construction begins on the church of Sainte Chapelle in Paris, France.

Literature and Language

1240

c. 1240 Jacopo da Lentini, poet at the court of the Holy Roman Emperor Frederick II, writes sonnets and other Italian poems on courtly love.

- Der Stricker, author of *Schwanke* (humorous stories), writes *Der Pfaffe Amis/Amis the Priest*, a long poem in Middle High German telling stories of trickery and deception.

SOCIETY

Education

1242

- Sirçali Medrese (college) is built at Konya in Persia.

1244

- A university is established in Rome, Italy.

Everyday Life

1240

- The Mongol empire, by permitting safe travel through Asia, allows the first European contact with China. China also comes into contact with western Asia, receiving the influence of Persian culture and Muslim religion; in turn, Chinese civilization influences central and western Asia.

Religion

c. **1241**

- The Surya Deula temple is built at Konarak, Orissa, India. Dedicated to the sun god and representing his chariot, the temple is the high point of Orissan architecture.

1243

- Jews from Belitz, near modern Berlin, Germany, are burned to death in the earliest known case of a massacre of Jews in Germany, following an alleged desecration of the Host (the bread consecrated in the Christian Eucharist).

1244

- Montségur, the last refuge of heretics in southern France, falls to the Catholics.

BIRTHS & DEATHS

1240

- Ibn-al-Arabī, mystic philosopher whose *al-Fūtūhāt al-Makkīyah* and *Fusūs al-Hikam* give Sufi pantheism its philosophical framework, dies.

November 16 St. Edmund of Abingdon (original name Edmund Rich), scholar and archbishop of Canterbury 1234–40, dies in Soisy, France (*c.* 65).

1241

March 28 Valdemar II, Danish king 1202–41, who expanded the Danish Empire to include Estonia, and reformed the legal code, dies in Denmark (*c.* 71).

August 21 Pope Gregory IX dies.

September 4 Alexander III, King of Scotland 1249–86, born (–1286).

September 22 Snorri Sturleson, Icelandic poet, and writer of sagas, is murdered in Reykjaholt, Iceland (62).

December 11 Ogedai, Mongol ruler 1229–47 who greatly expanded the Mongol Empire, dies in Krakorum, Mongolia (*c.* 56).

1242

- King Henry, son of the Holy Roman Emperor Frederick II, dies.

1245–1249

POLITICS, GOVERNMENT, AND ECONOMICS

Politics and Government

1245

- Pope Innocent IV appoints Alfonso III, Count of Boulogne, as curator of Portugal because of the incompetence of his brother, King Sancho II.
- Prince Daniel of Galicia, the dominant prince in eastern central Europe, does homage to the Mongol leader Batu.
- The Mongols take Multan, in the Punjab, India.

June 26–July 17 Pope Innocent IV holds the General Council in Lyons, France. It legislates for reform, calls for new crusades to liberate Jerusalem, and culminates with Innocent's declaration of the Holy Roman Emperor Frederick II's deposition and invitation to the German nobles to elect a new king.

1246

- Frederick the Valiant, the last Babenberger Duke of Austria, dies. After a long succession struggle, Přemysl Ottokar II, son of King Wenceslas I of Bohemia, is elected in his place.
- Koloman I, Czar of Bulgaria, dies; he is succeeded by his brother Michael Asen, who is forced to recognize conquests made at Bulgaria's expense by John Vatatzes, the Byzantine emperor of Thessaloníki.
- Mohammad, the Muslim king of Granada, cedes the town of Jaén to King Ferdinand III of León and Castile and becomes his vassal.
- The Holy Roman Emperor Frederick II suppresses a revolt in Sicily and deports its last Muslim inhabitants to Lucera, Italy.

January 1 Provence becomes part of France with the marriage of Beatrice, heiress of Count Raymond Berengar IV (who died in 1245), to Charles, Count of Anjou, the brother of King Louis IX of France.

February 25 Prince Dafydd ap Llywelyn of Gwynedd (north Wales) dies; he is succeeded by Llywelyn ap Gruffydd.

May 22 At the instigation of Pope Innocent IV, Henry Raspe, Landgrave of Thuringia, is elected as "king of the Romans" (king of Germany).

June 10 Sultan Mas'ud of Delhi is deposed by "the Forty" (Turkish nobles with effective power in Muslim India) in favor of Nasir-ad-Din Mahmud, a son of the former sultan Iltutmish.

August 8 Guyuk, son of the late Great Khan Ogedai, is elected as great khan of the Mongols; he receives Pope Innocent IV's envoy.

1247

- Guyuk, Great Khan of the Mongols, appoints Prince Alexander Nevsky of Novgorod as prince of Kiev and his brother Andrew as Grand Duke of Vladimir–Suzdal.
- King Louis IX of France initiates the *enquêteurs* (itinerant commissioners to receive complaints of maladministration).
- Tibet becomes subject to Mongol rule: the Great Khan Guyuk invests his brother Koden as Sa-skya lama with authority over Tibet.

June 16 The Italian city of Parma is seized by the Holy Roman Emperor Frederick II's enemies; he therefore breaks off his journey to Lyons, France, to besiege the city.

August 20 King Ferdinand III of Castile and León begins his siege of the Muslim city of Seville in southern Spain.

October 3 William, Count of Holland, is elected "king of the Romans" (king of Germany) by the Welfs (the anti-Hohenstaufen faction) in Germany.

October 15 The Ayyubid (Muslim) Egyptians take the city of Ascalon in the kingdom of Jerusalem.

1248

- King Sancho II of Portugal dies; he is succeeded by his brother, the rector, Alfonso III.
- King Wencelas I of Bohemia's order to join Pope Innocent IV's crusade against the Holy Roman Emperor Frederick II provokes (or at least provides the pretext for) a rebellion by the Bohemian nobles under the king's son Přemysl Ottokar II.
- The Genoese conquer the island of Rhodes from the Byzantine empire of Nicaea.

February 18 The Parmesans defeat the imperial forces in Italy, nearly capturing the Holy Roman Emperor Frederick II.

March 3 Pope Innocent IV sends an embassy of friars to the Mongol court, hoping to convert them and make an alliance against the Muslims.

April 4 The death of Guyuk, Great Khan of the Mongols, is followed by an interregnum which lasts until 1251.

August 26 King Louis IX sails from France on the Seventh Crusade.

December 22 The Muslim city of Seville in southern Spain surrenders to King Ferdinand III of Castile and León.

1249

- Birger, jarl (earl) of Sweden, extends Swedish territories in the south of modern Finland throughout the year.

May 26 The Bolognese defeat and capture the Holy Roman Emperor Frederick II's son, Enzio, King of Sardinia, at La Fossalta.

June 5 Having wintered in Cyprus, King Louis IX of France

continues on the Seventh Crusade, lands in Egypt, and enters Damietta without opposition.

July 8   King Alexander II of Scotland dies. He is succeeded by his son, Alexander III.

July 9   Jacopo Tiepolo, the reforming doge of Venice, dies and is succeeded by Marino Morosini.

September 27   Raymond VII, Count of Toulouse, dies; he is succeeded by his son-in-law Alfonse of Poitiers, the brother of King Louis IX of France, marking the definitive integration of Languedoc into France.

November 23   Sultan Ayyub of Egypt dies; he is succeeded by his son Turan Shah.

SCIENCE, TECHNOLOGY, AND MEDICINE

Health and Medicine

1246
- Bartholomew, the English Franciscan monk and physician, writes a treatise on leprosy, stating his belief that it is contagious and hereditary. This contributes to the fear surrounding the disease.

1247
- The Hospital of St. Mary of Bethlehem in London, England, later the famous institute for the insane known as "Bedlam," is founded by Simon FitzMary.

1248
- Spanish-born Muslim Al-Baytār, "chief of botanists" in Cairo, Egypt, writes *Kitāb al-jāmi/Collection of Simple Drugs*, which lists 1,400 different remedies and is the largest and most popular Arab pharmacopeia.
- The Chinese physician Song Tz'u writes the treatise *Hsi-yüan lu/Instructions to Coroners* on forensic medicine.

Science

1245
- The Chinese scholar and naturalist Ch'ên Jên-yü writes his treatise *Chün p'u* on the subject of mushrooms.

1247
- The Norwegian encyclopedic treatise *Konungs skuggsjá/The King's Mirror*, which combines scientific and

political scholarship, is completed for King Haakon IV Haakonson.

1249
- English monk and scholar Roger Bacon records the use of explosives, and documents a recipe for gunpowder (possibly his own invention). He writes this dangerous information in coded form.

ARTS AND IDEAS

Architecture

1245
c. 1245   The great Alhambra Palace is founded at Granada, Spain, capital of the Nasrid dynasty.
- Construction begins on Westminster Abbey in London, England.

1246
- Construction begins on the Church of Santa Maria Novella in Florence, Italy.

1247
- The Sircali Kumbet mausoleum is built at Kayseri in the Seljuk Sulatanate of Rūm (modern Turkey).

1248
- Construction begins on the cathedral at Clermont-Ferrand, France, under the architect Jean des Champs.
April 30   The Carolingian cathedral at Cologne, Germany, burns down. The foundation stone of the new (and present) cathedral will be laid on August 15 and its construction will be supervised by the architect Gerhard. He is responsible for the design of the west towers, which will not be constructed until the 19th century.

Literature and Language

1245
- French poet and priest Gautier de Metz writes his encyclopedic *L'Image du monde/Image of the World*, which discusses scientific topics, metaphysics, and geography in octosyllabic verse.

1248
- Al-Qiftī writes *Ikhbār al'Ulamā' bi-Akhbar al-Hūkamā'/History of Philosophers*, which includes the biographies of 414 Greek, Syrian, and Islamic physicians, astronomers, and philosophers.

BIRTHS & DEATHS

1245
- Alexander of Hales, influential theologian and philosopher, dies in Paris, France (*c.* 75).
- Arnolfo di Cambio, Italian sculptor and architect, whose works include the design of the Duomo and (probably) the Palazzo Vecchio in Florence, born in Colle di Val d'Elsa, Italy (–*c.* 1302).

1246
September 30   Grand Prince Jaroslav II of Vladimir–Suzdal dies at the Mongol court in Karakorum.

1247
- Rashid ad-Din, Persian historian, the author of *Jami' at-tawarikh*, a universal history, born (–1318).
February 17   Henry Raspe, Landgrave of Thuringia and the German

"antiking" appointed at the instigation of Pope Innocent IV, dies.

1249
c. 1249   Jacques Duèse, pope as John XXII 1316–34, born (–1334).
July 8   Alexander II, King of Scotland 1214–49, dies on Kerrera Island, Argyll, Scotland (50).

Thought and Scholarship

1245

- St. Thomas Aquinas, the greatest of medieval philosophers, studies in Paris, France, under Albertus Magnus.

1248

- Ibn-al-Hajib writes *al-Kafiya*, a great work of Arabic grammar.
- Roderigo Jiménez de Rada writes *Chronica Hispaniae/ Chronicle of Spain*, a world history from the creation to 1243, which presents the first general history of Spain (Muslim as well as Christian).

SOCIETY

Education

1245

- Pope Innocent IV confirms the privileges of the University of Toulouse, France, after the university has declined substantially.

1248

- The University of Piacenza is founded in Italy.

1249

- English monk and scholar Roger Bacon argues for the inclusion of scientific studies in the curriculum of Oxford University, England, which is primarily a religious institution at the time.
- University College, the earliest college of Oxford University, England, is founded.

Everyday Life

1245

- Strikes by employees in the cloth-weaving industry at Douai in Flanders are met with repression by the municipal authorities.

Religion

1245

- Pope Innocent IV makes a declaration permitting the Friars Minor to hold property, which causes the order to divide into its "Conventual" and "Spiritual" branches.
- Pope Innocent IV sends John de Plano Carpinis, a Friar Minor, to the court of the great khan at Karakorum, Mongolia. This embassy leads to the establishment of Christian missions in China, which continue until around 1368.

1247

- Pope Innocent IV confirms the new rule for the Carmelite friars.

1250–1254

POLITICS, GOVERNMENT, AND ECONOMICS

Business and Economics

1252

- The Italian city-republic of Florence begins to coin the gold florin. This becomes universally accepted, and greatly facilitates commercial exchange.
- The merchants of Hamburg and Lübeck, Germany, receive privileges in Flanders for themselves and their German associates.

Politics and Government

1250

c. 1250 The west African rain forest state of Benin is founded.

- King Alfonso III of Portugal cedes the Algarve to Alfonso X, son of King Ferdinand of Castile and León.
- Otto and John of Brandenburg found Frankfurt-an-der-Oder and establish the Neumark in Lubusz and other lands formerly parts of Poland and Pomerania.
- Representatives of towns are called to the Cortes (parliament) of Castile for the first time.
- The Gascons revolt against Simon IV de Montfort, King Henry III of England's lieutenant in Gascony.

c. 1250–*c.* 1270 Mansa Yerelenku seizes power in Mali on the death of his father Sundiata.

February 2 King Eric XI of Sweden dies; he is succeeded by his young nephew, Valdemar I, under the regency of his father Birger, jarl (earl) of Sweden.

February 8   King Louis IX of France, on the Seventh Crusade, defeats the Egyptians barring the route to the capital Cairo at Mansurah.

April 6   King Louis IX of France is defeated and captured by the Egyptians at the Battle of Fariskur, while withdrawing from Mansurah.

May 2   Turan Shah, the last Ayyubid sultan of Egypt, is murdered by his Mameluke (slave) guards, who elect their commander Izz-ad-Din Aybak as regent while Shajar-ad-Durr, the widow of the former sultan Ayyub, is made nominal ruler. After 80 days Aybak marries her and assumes the sultanate, founding the Mameluke dynasty.

May 6   King Louis IX of France surrenders the Egyptian town of Damietta as part of the price for his release; he leaves Egypt for the Palestinian port of Acre (present-day Akko, Israel), where he is accepted as ruler (in practice, not in theory) of Outremer, the crusader kingdoms in the Middle East.

July 9   An-Nasir, the Ayyubid governor of Aleppo, Syria, takes Damascus (formerly held by the murdered Ayyubid sultan of Egypt, Turan Shah).

August 9–10   King Eric IV of Denmark is murdered at Schleswig, probably by his brother Abel who succeeds him.

December 13   The Holy Roman Emperor Frederick II (*Stupor mundi*, "wonder of the world"), dies. His son Conrad IV, King of the Romans (king of Germany), succeeds as king of Sicily and (nominal) king of Jerusalem.

1251

- Jatavarman Sundara Pandya I accedes to the throne of the Indian kingdom of the Pandya dynasty. Under his rule the Pandyas enter into hostilities with the Somesvara.
- Pope Innocent IV sends a crown to Mindovg, Prince of Lithuania, for his coronation, in consequence of Mindovg's (feigned) conversion to Christianity.
- The "Crusade of the Pastoureaux," a popular movement in France that has become directed against the clergy, is suppressed on becoming disorderly.
- War breaks out between King Ottokar II of Bohemia, as Duke of Austria, and King Béla IV of Hungary, for the possession of Styria.

1251–52   Balbars, Sultan of Delhi, India, invades Malwa and defeats the raja of Chander and Narwa.

January 7   The Italian city-republic of Florence admits the exiled anti-imperialist party, the Guelphs. A new constitution is formed led by the *capitano del popolo* ("captain of the people") independent of the nobles.

February 2   Aybak, the Mameluke sultan of Egypt, defeats the invading Ayyubid an-Nasir at Abbasa in northern Egypt.

March 3   There are risings against King Conrad IV of Germany and Sicily in the Italian kingdom of Sicily.

May 5   The English soldier and politician Simon IV de Montfort, Earl of Leicester, suppresses the Gascon rebellion under Gaston de Béarn which occurs in reaction to his perceived rough-shod rule of Gascony.

July 1   Mongka, the eldest son of Tolui, is elected great khan of the Mongols .

July 7   The imperialist party, the Ghibellines, are exiled

from the Italian city-republic of Florence, following the return of the papist Guelphs the year before.

November 11   King Conrad IV of Germany enters Italy from Germany, asserting his claim to the throne of Sicily.

1252

- Alexander Nevsky is appointed Grand Duke of Vladimir following the expulsion of his brother Andrew by the Mongols.
- An ordinance issued by King Alfonso III of Portugal regulates prices and the wages of laborers.
- King Jaya Parmesvaravarman II of Champa (corresponding roughly to modern southern Vietnam) is killed during an invasion from Dai Viet (modern Northern Vietnam, also known as Annam). Both states make peace, bringing 30 years of inconclusive warfare to a close.
- Marino Morosini, doge (chief magistrate) of the Italian republic of Venice, dies. He is succeeded by Ranieri Zeno.
- The *popolo* ("people") of Rome revolt against Pope Innocent IV. They establish a constitution under a *podestà* ("mayor").
- The *Sentenario*, a law code, is issued by King Ferdinand III of Castile and León.
- The Teutonic Knights (a German Christian military order) found Memel (Klaipeda) in Lithuania, where Prince Mindovg of Lithuania has admitted them. They win access to the Baltic coastline, from Memel to Polangen.

March 8   A league of propapal Guelph Lombard cities is ineffectually concluded at Brescia in Lombardy, Italy.

March 25   William, Count of Holland, is again elected as Holy Roman Emperor. Pope Innocent IV directs the Germans to accept him, following the death of the previous papal candidate, Henry Raspe of Thuringia, in 1247.

March 31   Ezzelin da Romano and Oberto Pelavicini, the Italian tyrants of the city-republics of Verona and Cremona respectively, form a league of imperialist Ghibelline Italian cities.

May 30   King Ferdinand III of Castile and León dies and is succeeded by his son Alfonso X.

June 6   King Conrad IV of Germany rejects Pope Innocent IV's proposal for the separation of the Italian kingdom of Sicily from the Holy Roman Empire.

June 29   King Abel of Denmark is defeated and killed by the Frisians. He is succeeded by his brother, Christopher I.

July 7   The Holy Roman Emperor William of Holland holds a diet (legislative assembly) outside Frankfurt when King Conrad IV of Germany, his rival as successor to Frederick IV, is again deprived of the duchy of Swabia.

1253

- 'Phags-pa, nephew of the lama of the monastery of Sa-skya in Tibet, succeeds Sa-skya Pandit as regent with the duty of residing at the Mongol leader Kublai Khan's court and passing orders to officials in Tibet.
- Brian O'Neill, King of Tyrone, attacks the English castle of Magh Cobha at Ballyroney, Ireland.
- Hūlāgū, a grandson of Genghis Khan and younger brother of Great Khan Mongka, begins his conquest of the Islamic Empire. His army is larger than that of

Genghis Khan and contains contingents from all the Mongol princes.

- King Louis IX of France sends the friars William of Rubruck and Bartholomew of Cremona to the court of Mongka, Great Khan of the Mongols, at Karakorum in central Asia to seek his alliance against the Muslims of Syria and Egypt.
- King Wenceslas II of Bohemia dies. He is succeeded by his son Přemysl Ottokar II.
- Świętopełk of East Pomerania and the Teutonic Knights (a German Christian military order) make peace.
- The Mongol leader Kublai Khan conquers the kingdom of Nanchao in Yunnan, south China. Its Thai people migrate to Thailand. He also attacks Dai Viet (modern northern Vietnam, also known as Annam).
- The Mongols conquer Tibet.

April 4   The Ayyubid An-Nasir cedes Palestine to Aybak, the Mameluke sultan of Egypt, in a treaty of peace.

July 8   King Theobald I of Navarre dies. He succeeded by his son Theobald II.

October 10   Donato Brancaleone, the *podestà* ("mayor") of Rome, compels Pope Innocent IV to return to the city.

October 10   King Conrad IV of Germany and Sicily completes his suppression of a Sicilian rebellion with the recovery of the Italian kingdom of Naples.

1254

- An ordinance issued by King Louis IX of France regulates the conduct of *baillis* and *sénéchaux* (his regional governors) in an attempt to prevent corruption.
- King Alfonso III of Portugal holds the first Cortes (national assembly) attended by representatives of Portuguese towns. This is the first assembly at which the commons are represented.
- King Alfonso X of Castile and León publishes the *Fuero Real/Royal Law Code*, a legal code influenced by Roman law. It is intended to supplement the forthcoming legal code called the *Siete Partidas/Seven Games*.
- Llywelyn ap Gruffydd, Lord of Snowdonia, makes himself the sole ruler of Wales.
- The Teutonic Knights (a German Christian military order) found Königsberg (modern Kaliningrad), Russia, in the heart of pagan territory.
- William of Holland, the anti-Holy Roman Emperor, holds a diet (legislative assembly) at Worms, Germany, where German towns are represented for the first time.

March 6   King Henry III of England concludes an agreement with papal envoys whereby his second son, Edmund, is to become king of Sicily, Italy, after its conquest. He is offered the title only after Richard of Cornwall and Charles of Anjou have both refused it.

April 9   Pope Innocent IV once more excommunicates King Conrad IV of Germany as a result of his ongoing conflict with William of Holland, the anti-Holy Roman Emperor.

April 22   By the Treaty of Toledo, peace and an alliance are made between King Henry III of England and King Alfonso X of Castile and León. Alfonso renounces his claims to Gascony.

April 24   King Louis IX of France departs from the port of Acre in the kingdom of Jerusalem (modern Akko, Israel), where civil war soon breaks out among the

barons of Outremer, the crusader kingdoms established in the Middle East.

May 21   Conrad IV, Holy Roman Emperor and King of Sicily and Jerusalem, dies on his way to recover control in Germany. He is succeeded in Sicily by his son, Conrad V (Conradin). His death intensifies the factious dispute over succession within the royal house.

July 13   A group of Rhineland towns form the Rhenish League, a confederation for mutual protection.

September 13   King Hethoum of Armenia is received at the Mongol court and accepted as a vassal by the great khan, Mongka.

October 6   In a meeting at Worms, the Rhenish League (confederation of Rhineland towns) issues an edict for peacekeeping.

October 10   Edward Plantagenet, the son of King Henry III of England, marries Eleanor, the sister of King Alfonso X of Castile and León. This helps seal the peace between Alfonso and Henry and ensures English control of Gascony: Prince Edward is endowed with Gascony and resides there.

October 11   Pope Innocent IV enters the Italian kingdom of Sicily, which he reconquered after the death of Conrad IV, to receive recognition as its sovereign.

November 2   Manfred of Sicily, the illegitimate son of the late Holy Roman Emperor Frederick II, begins an antipapal revolt in the Regno with the seizure of Lucera, southeast Italy, in an attempt to assert the imperial cause in Italy.

November 3   The Byzantine emperor of Nicaea, John III Vatatzes, dies. He is succeeded by his son Theodore II Lascaris. Under his rule the Latin Empire is isolated and the groundwork for the recapture of its capital, Constantinople, is laid.

December 2   Manfred of Sicily, the illegitimate son of the late Holy Roman Emperor Frederick II, defeats the papal army near Foggia, Italy. He thus wins the loyalty of the Puglia region for his imperial cause.

December 12   Rinaldo Conti is elected as Pope Alexander IV.

SCIENCE, TECHNOLOGY, AND MEDICINE

Agriculture

1250

- The English agriculturist Walter of Henley writes *Hosebondrie*, which is one of the earliest European treatises on husbandry, agriculture, and the management of estates.

Health and Medicine

1250

- The caliph of Baghdad Al-Mu'tasem appoints the Spanish-born physician ibn-al-Baytār as general apothecary inspector, charged with ensuring the content and safety of treatments offered by physicians.

1252

- The English physician Richard of Wendover writes his brief and portable medical encyclopedia *Micrologus/ Short Discourse*.
- The Italian surgeon Bruno da Longoburgo writes his manual of surgical techniques *Chirurgia magna/Major Surgery*.
- The Italian veterinarian Giordano Ruffo writes his pioneering treatise *Liber mareschalchiae/The book of Marshalship* on the medical treatment of horses.

Science

1253

- The English scholar Robert Grosseteste, chancellor of Oxford University, writes his manual *Compendium spherae/Compendium of the Sphere* on Aristotelian astronomy and geography.

Technology

1250

- *c.* 1250 Norwegian settlers in Greenland reinvent underfloor central heating, last used by the Romans. They pipe hot water from natural springs under their buildings, and are even able to grow orange trees in special conservatories.
- *c.* 1250 The treadle, a rocking lever operated by the foot, is introduced for driving lathes and other forms of simple machinery.
- The earliest European illustration of a wheelbarrow dates to this time, although the device has been known in China since AD 231.

Transportation

c. **1250**

- The bowsprit is introduced on ships, allowing the mainsail to be extended, and letting the vessel sail closer to the wind.

ARTS AND IDEAS

Architecture

1250

- Construction begins on the towers of Bamberg Cathedral, Germany, the choirs of Coutances and Naumberg Cathedrals (in France and Germany respectively), and the north tower and transepts of Notre Dame in Paris, France (architect Jean de Chelle).

1252

- A bronze statue of the Great Buddha (seated) is erected in the precincts of Kotokuin temple, Kamakura, Japan.

- The choir of Ely Cathedral, England, is consecrated.

Arts

1250

- Sculptures are introduced in Mainz, Naumberg, and Meissen Cathedrals in Germany by "the Master of Naumberg."

Literature and Language

1250

- *c.* 1250 *Carmina Burana*, a collection of satirical poems, lyrics, and other goliardic (ribald) verses intended to be sung, is compiled. It belongs to the convent of Benediktbeurin in Munich, Germany.
- The *Grand Coutumier de Normandie/Great Customary of Normandy*, a major compilation of the legal customs of the French duchy of Normandy, is produced.

1253

- *c.* 1253 Thomas of Celano writes the earliest biography of St. Francis of Assisi.
- *Libro de los engaños e los asayamientos de las mugeres/ The Book of Sindibad*, a collection of Arabic stories, is translated into Spanish at the command of Fadrique, brother of King Alfonso X of Castile.
- The last Sanskrit inscription is written in Champa (modern southern Vietnam), where Indian cultural influences, dating from the 4th century AD, have been destroyed.

Theater and Dance

c. **1250**

- *The Harrowing of Hell*, the earliest extant miracle play in English literature, is recorded. It is based on the apocryphal Gospel of Nicodemus.

Thought and Scholarship

c. **1250**

- Rudolf of Ems writes his *Weltchronik/Chronology of the World*, a world chronicle that details events dating back to the Hebrew kings.
- The popular bestiary of real and mythical beasts *Physiologus/Naturalist* is translated into many vernacular languages. Written in the 2nd century, the book is the most widely circulated after the Bible.

1253

- *c.* 1253 Hostiensis writes his *Summa aurea* or *Summa Hostiensis*, a synthesis of Roman and canon law.
- Robert Grosseteste, bishop of Lincoln, England, establishes philosophical studies at Oxford University and writes his commentaries on the Greek philosopher Aristotle.

SOCIETY

Education

1250

- The Dominicans found the first school of oriental studies at Toledo, Spain.

1253

- Çifte Medrese (college) is built at Erzurum in eastern Persia.
- The "Community of Poor Masters and Scholars" is opened as a theological college at the University of Paris, France. It will later bear the name of its founder Robert de Sorbon, chaplain to King Louis IX of France.

1254

- King Alfonso X of Castile and León establishes a school of Latin and Arabic studies in Seville, Castile, Spain.

Religion

1252

- The papal bull *Ad extirpanda* of Pope Innocent IV orders the use of torture in the examination of heretics.

1253

- Pope Innocent IV forms the *Perigrinantes propter Christum* ("Pilgrims for Christ") of Friars Preacher and Friars Minor, the first European missionary society.
- The Buddhist monk Nichiren, after years studying the various Japanese Buddhist sects, declares that the essence of true Buddhism is only to be found in the *Lotus Sutra* and that all other approaches are false. His doctrine is greeted with anger and disbelief.

1254

- Gerard de Borgo San Donnino publishes *The Introduction to the Everlasting Gospel* written by Joachim of Fiore in 1202.

Sports

c. 1250

- *Bonus socius/The Good Companion*, containing the earliest known handbook on chess, is written by Master Nicholas, perhaps Nicholas de St. Nicholai, in Normandy.
- Holy Roman Emperor Frederick II writes a treatise on falconry, *De arte venandi cum avibus/The Art of Falconry.*

BIRTHS & DEATHS

1250

c. 1250 John de Baliol ("Toom Tabard" or "Empty Garment"), King of Scotland 1292–96 who resigned his kingdom to King Edward I of England, born (–1313).

December 13 Frederick II, King of Sicily 1197–1250, king of Germany 1212–50, and Holy Roman Emperor 1220–50, king of Jerusalem 1229–43, grandson of Frederick I Barbarossa, dies in Castel Fiorentino, Apulia, Italy (55).

1252

November 12 Blanche of Castile, regent of France 1226–34 and 1248–52, wife of Louis VIII and mother of Louis IX, and who unified many of the French territories, dies in Paris, France (64).

1253

August 11 St. Clare of Assisi, abbess who founded the Poor Clares, dies in Assisi, Duchy of Spoleto (59).

October 9 Robert Grosseteste, bishop of Lincoln who introduced medieval Europe to works of Greek and Arab philosophers and scientists, dies in Buckden, Buckinghamshire, England (*c.* 78).

1254

c. 1254 Marco Polo, Venetian explorer who spent 17 years in China and whose *Il milione/The Million* (*Travels of Marco Polo*) has become a classic in geography, born in Venice, Venetian Dalmatia (–1324).

- Chao Meng-fu, celebrated Chinese painter and calligrapher, born in Wu-hsing, Chekiang province, China (–1322).

May 21 Conrad IV, "King of the Romans" (king of Germany) 1237–51, and king of Sicily 1251–54, dies in Lavello, Italy (26).

December 7 Pope Innocent IV dies.

1255–1259

POLITICS, GOVERNMENT, AND ECONOMICS

Politics and Government

1255

- Batu, Khan of the "Golden Horde," dies. He is succeeded by his son Sartak.
- Brian O'Neill, King of Tyrone, Ireland, and Aed O'Connor, son of the king of Connacht, Ireland, make an alliance against the English.
- The coppersmiths of Dinant, Flanders, riot.

April 9   Pope Alexander IV confirms Prince Edmund Plantagenet of England's investiture as king of Sicily.

September 9   The papal troops in the Regno, southern Italy, surrender to the leader of the imperialist cause Manfred of Sicily, the illegitimate son of the late Holy Roman Emperor Frederick II.

November 11   The Romans expel their imperialist *podestà* ("mayor"), Donato Brancaleone, enabling Pope Alexander IV to reside in Rome.

1256

- Sartak, Khan of the "Golden Horde," dies. He is succeeded by Ulagchi.

1256–63   King Alfonso X of Castile and León supervises the compilation of the legal code *Siete Partidas/Seven Games*.

January 28   The Holy Roman Emperor William of Holland dies. This dashes any chance for the unanimous election of a successor to the former emperor Frederick II; both Conrad IV and Conradin (Frederick's son and grandson) disgraced themselves politically making the continuation of the Hohenstaufen dynasty unpopular.

June 19   The papal legate leading the crusade proclaimed against Ezzelin da Romano, the leading supporter of the Holy Roman Emperor in Italy, takes the city of Padua in northern Italy.

September 24   King Louis IX of France's award (*dit*) of Péronne ends a civil war in Flanders. John of Avesnes keeps much of Hainault, though he is forced to offer homage to Charles of Anjou in return.

December 19   A Mongol army under Hūlāgū, recently appointed ilkhan of Persia, besieges the stronghold of the Assassins (militant branch of the Islamic Ismaili sect) at Alamūt in the Elburz Mountains. Their grand master, Rukn-ad-Dīn Kūrshāh, surrenders and is put to death. The Mongols now annihilate the Assassins in Persia.

1257

- King Alfonso X of Castile and León and King Mohammad ibn Nasr of Granada expel the last Almohads (members of a Muslim dynasty of Berbers) from Spain.
- Martino della Torre, Italian leader of the anti-imperialist Guelphs, assumes the government of Milan.
- Pope Alexander IV excommunicates King Alfonso III of Portugal and puts the country under an interdict because the king has repudiated his wife, the Countess of Boulognes, and married Beatrix de Guzman.
- The Mongols sack the city of Hanoi but Tran Thai-tong forces them to leave Dai Viet (modern northern Vietnam).
- The Rhenish League (confederation of Rhineland towns formed in 1254 for their mutual protection) gradually disintegrates.

January 13   Richard, Earl of Cornwall, is elected king of the Romans by three of the College of Seven Electors.

April 1   Four members of the College of Seven Electors elect King Alfonso X of Castile and León as king of the Romans.

April 15   Aybak, the Mameluke sultan of Egypt, is murdered by order of his wife, Shajar-ad-Durr, who is then killed by the women of Aybak's harem. She is succeeded by her son, Nūr-ad-Dīn Ali.

May 5   A revolt in Rome, Italy, restores the imperialist Donato Brancaleone as *podestà* ("mayor"). Pope Alexander IV is forced to leave.

May 17   Richard, Earl of Cornwall, is crowned king of the Romans in Aachen, Germany.

December 12   The Mongols raid the Punjab, India.

1258

- Alexander Nevsky, Grand Duke of Vladimir, suppresses a riot in Novgorod, Russia, protesting against a census of all lands under Mongol control ordered by Mongka, the great khan of the Mongols.
- Brian O'Neill, King of Tyrone, is crowned king of the Gaels of Erin at Caol-Uisce, Ireland.
- Ezzelin da Romano, the leading supporter of the Holy Roman Emperor in Italy, takes the city of Brescia from the Guelphs. He was the object of a Guelph crusade.
- Following the murder of the last Ch'oe dictator, Korean resistance to the Mongols ends. The Koryŏ kings remain as vassals.
- Georgia is partitioned. Its rulers remain vassals of the Mongols.
- King Louis IX of France forbids private warfare. This move is not popular with the nobility.
- Pope Alexander IV lays an interdict on Denmark because of King Christopher's quarrel with the archbishop of Lund.

- The Mongols retreat from the Punjab, India, and return to Khorasan. Under Kublai Khan, they invade China.
- Ulagchi, Khan of the "Golden Horde," dies. He is succeeded by Berke, a Muslim.

January 11   The Mongols under Hūlāgū defeat the Abbasid caliph (Islamic ruler of Persia) al-Muta'sim at Anbar, near the River Tigris, in Persia.

February 10   The Mongols take and destroy Baghdad, the capital of the revived Abbasid caliphate in Mesopotamia.

February 20   The last Abbasid caliph (Islamic ruler of Persia) al-Musta'sim and his family are put to death on the Mongol leader Hūlāgū's orders.

March 3   At an assembly of Welsh princes, Llywelyn ap Gruffydd assumes the title of prince of Wales. He now has possession of Anglesey, Snowdonia, and Powys. He also enters into a defensive alliance with the controlling barons of Scotland.

May 2   King Henry III of England accepts the baronial demand that his government should be reformed by a committee of 24 appointed by himself and the barons. They also demand that he mediate with Pope Alexander IV over the papal debt.

May 11   King Louis IX of France and King James I of Aragon make peace by signing the Treaty of Corbeil. This states that Catalonia belongs to Louis and Languedoc to James.

May 28   King Louis IX of France and King Henry III of England agree to the terms of a peace treaty resolving their differences since Hugh of Lusignan, who had Henry's support, was defeated by Louis.

June 12   The Provisions of Oxford establish baronial control over King Henry III of England's government.

August 8   The emperor of Nicaea, the strongest and most enduring of the independent Greek states, Theodore II Lascaris, dies. He is succeeded by his son, John IV Lascaris. Michael Palaeologus is named as his guardian.

August 10   Manfred of Sicily, the illegitimate son of the late Holy Roman Emperor Frederick II, assumes the crown of Sicily.

December 12   John IV Lascaris and his guardian, Michael VIII Palaeologus, are crowned as Nicaean emperors.

December 12   Pope Alexander IV cancels the grant of the Italian kingdom of Sicily to Prince Edmund Plantagenet of England.

1259

- King Louis IX of France abolishes the judicial duel.
- King Ottokar II of Bohemia occupies Styria when it revolts against King Béla IV of Hungary, after Béla allows his vassals to raid Austria and Styria.
- Poland, Lithuania, and Galicia in central Europe are devastated in punitive raids by Mongols and Russians.
- The crown prince of Korea assumes the throne as King Wonjong. He is controlled by a Mongol resident commissioner, and a close relationship grows between Korea and the Mongols.
- The League of Lübeck, Rostock, and Wismar is formed in Germany.
- The Nicaean emperor John IV Lascaris routs the forces of Michael Ducas of Epirus, a member of a noble Byzantine family, at Pelagonia, Greece.
- With the death of the imperialist *podestà* ("mayor") Donato Brancaleone, Rome returns to papal control.

April 4   Pope Alexander IV recognizes Richard, Earl of Cornwall, as king of the Romans.

May 5   The Italian city of Siena accepts King Manfred of Sicily as its overlord in order to have his protection against Florence.

May 29   King Christopher I of Denmark dies. He is succeeded by his son, Eric V.

August 1   King Henry III of England makes peace with Llywelyn ap Gruffydd, Prince of Wales, at the ford of Montgomery in Wales. This prevents a campaign against the Welsh led by Richard de Clare, one of the lords of the Welsh Marches.

September 11   The Mongols, under Hūlāgū, invade Syria.

September 16   The anti-imperialist Milanese defeat and capture Ezzelin da Romano, the leading supporter of the Holy Roman Emperor in Italy, at Cassano. On October 1, he dies. The leadership of the anti-imperialist Guelphs in Lombardy, north Italy, falls to Uberto Pelavicini.

October 13   The Provisions of Westminster, a plan for legal reforms in England, are enacted by a baronial council.

December 4   King Louis IX of France and King Henry III of England make peace in the Treaty of Paris. Henry renounces Normandy, Maine, Anjou, and other lost Angevin territories in France and does homage for Gascony to Louis, who cedes lands on its eastern borders which cannot be precisely defined.

December 12   Nūr-ad-Dīn 'Ali, Sultan of Egypt, is deposed and succeeded by Sayf-ad-Dīn Qutuz.

SCIENCE, TECHNOLOGY, AND MEDICINE

Health and Medicine

1257

- The Italian physician Aldobrandon of Siena writes his treatise *Le régime du corps/The Bodily Regimen* on the need for good hygiene and diet, which is a new concept in western medicine.

Science

1256

- The Chinese scholar and naturalist Ch'ên Ching-i writes the botanical encyclopedia *Ch'üan-fang pei-tsu*.

1259

- The Persian philosopher At-Tūsī, employed by the Mongol Hūlāgū Khan, founds an observatory at Marāghah, Persia.

ARTS AND IDEAS

Architecture

1256–1320
- Construction begins on the "Angel Choir" of Lincoln Cathedral, England.

1258
- The cathedral at Salisbury, England, is dedicated.

Literature and Language

1255
- German *Minnesinger* (lyric poet) Ulrich von Lichtenstein completes his *Frauendienst/The Service of Women*, a collection of 60 songs within an autobiographical framework.

1258
- Persian poet Sa'di writes *Būstān/The Tree–Garden*, a verse epic listing the principal Muslim virtues.
- The Provisions of Oxford, reforms forced upon King Henry III of England by his barons, is the first known document to be written in recognizable Middle English.

Thought and Scholarship

1255
- *c.* 1255 Henry de Bracton writes his *De legibus et consuetudinibus Angliæ/On the Laws and Customs of England*, the first systematic summary of English law, which cites cases.
- Bonacosa, from Padua, Italy, translates Abu'l-Walīd ibn-Rushd (Averroës) of Córdoba's *Kullīyāt* of 1160, calling it *The Colliget*.

1256
- *c.* 1256 Jacob Anatoli translates the works of Abu'l-Walīd ibn-Rushd (Averroës) of Córdoba, influential Muslim philosopher who wrote important commentaries on the works of Aristotle and Plato, into Hebrew.
- Albertus Magnus writes his *De unitate intellectus contra Averroem/On the Unity of the Intellect, against Averroës*, which argues against the unity of the intellect as proposed by Averroës.

1259
- Matthew Paris completes his *Chronica majora/Greater Chronicle*, a chronicle of the world from the creation, but more particularly of England in the author's lifetime.

SOCIETY

Education

1258
- Following the sack of Baghdad by the Mongols in February, the al-Azhar Mosque in Cairo, Egypt, becomes the chief university for Islam. It specializes predominantly in theology and law.
- The Ince Minareli Medrese (college) is founded at Konya, in the Seljuk Sultanate of Rūm (modern Turkey).

Religion

1256
- *The Introduction to the Everlasting Gospel* by Joachim of Fiore (written in 1202), published in 1254, is condemned as heretical.
- Pope Alexander IV recognizes the Augustinian Friars as a mendicant order (dependent on alms).

December 12 Pope Alexander IV organizes Italian hermits independently following the rule of St. Augustine into a single order, the Augustinian Hermits or Friars.

1258
- Crop failures and widespread famine in Germany and Italy inspire the founders of the flagellant movement, whose members beat themselves in atonement for their sins, hoping to stave off natural disasters.

BIRTHS & DEATHS

1255
- Batu, Mongol ruler, grandson of Genghis Khan, and founder of the Khanate of Kipchak or Golden Horde, dies in Russia.

1258
- Osman I, founder of the Ottoman Turkish state, born (–1324).

1259
August 11 Mongka, Great Khan of the Mongols, dies.

1260–1264

POLITICS, GOVERNMENT, AND ECONOMICS

Business and Economics

1260

- At the direction of the emperor Kublai Khan, paper currency becomes the only legal tender in China.

1262

- As part of an ongoing campaign of monetary stabilization and centralization King Louis IX of France brings municipal finances under royal control.

Politics and Government

1260

c. 1260 Kublai and Ariqboga, brothers of the late great khan Mongka, are both separately elected great khan of the Mongols.
- Brian O'Neil, King of the Gaels of Erin, Ireland, is killed whilst assaulting the earldom of Ulster, by a levy from the town of Downpatrick.
- Ghazan, Ilkhan of Persia, abolishes the *jizya*, the compulsory poll tax for non-Muslims, after the intercession of the Uighur-born Nestorian patriarch Mar Yabalaha III.
- The Mongol leader Kublai Khan gives the Tibetan regent 'Phags-pa the title of Ti-Sri, giving him the status of viceroy of Tibet. He is, however, expected to live at Kublai Khan's court.
March 1 The city of Damascus surrenders to the Mongols, who now occupy all Syria, extinguishing the Ayyubid Sultanate. The Mongol leader Hūlāgū is soon forced to withdraw most of his forces because of a succession dispute.
July 7 The Lithuanians defeat the Teutonic Knights (a German Christian military order) at Durben in Lithuania. This is followed by the revolt of Courland (Kurland) against the knights and the apostasy (rejection of his Christian faith) of Prince Mindovg of Lithuania, who conquers the north Baltic region of Livonia.
July 12 King Ottokar II of Bohemia defeats King Béla IV of Hungary and his Russian, Polish, and Bulgarian allies on the march, at Kroissenbrunn. Béla cedes Styria to Ottokar.

September 3 The Mamelukes of Egypt, led by the Mameluke general Baybars, destroy the remaining Mongol army at 'Ayn Jālūt in Palestine, and then occupy Syria. The Mongol leader Ket-Buqa is killed.
September 4 King Manfred of Sicily's Sienese forces, under Count Jordan, defeat the Florentine Guelphs (anti-imperialists) at Montaperto, Italy. The city submits to a Ghibelline (imperialist) *podestà* ("mayor"), Guido Novello.
October 24 The Mameluke general Baybars murders Qutuz, Sultan of Egypt.

1261

- The Mongol leader Kublai Khan establishes his supremacy as great khan. He continues the conquest of China, where Beijing is rebuilt as his winter capital.
- The Muslim vassal king of Murcia revolts against King Alfonso X of Castile and León.
March 13 By the Treaty of Nymphaeum, the Genoese undertake to assist the Nicaean emperor Michael VIII Palaeologus to recover the city of Constantinople from the Latin Empire in return for trading concessions hitherto enjoyed by the Venetians.
June 12 King Henry III of England publishes Pope Alexander IV's bull absolving him from his oath to observe the Provisions of Westminster (a plan for legal reforms in England) and dismisses the baronial officials.
July 4 The Mameluke general Baybars assumes the sultanate of Egypt.
July 25 The Nicaean emperor Michael VIII Palaeologus recovers the city of Constantinople and is crowned there, deposing his ward and fellow emperor, John IV Lascaris. This marks the end of the Latin Empire of Constantinople.
August 29 Jacques Pantaléon of Troyes, a professor of canon law in Paris before becoming a bishop, then patriarch of Jerusalem, is elected Pope Urban IV. He offers the crown of Sicily to Charles of Anjou, in an attempt to dislodge the German Hohenstaufen family from Italy.

1262

- Baybars, the Mameluke sultan of Egypt, establishes the first of a series of puppet caliphs (Islamic rulers) of the Abbasid dynasty in Cairo, Egypt.
- Ganapati, the Kakatiya ruler in southern India, dies. He is succeeded by his daughter Rudramba (Rudradeva Maharaja).
- King James I of Aragon, son of Pedro III of Aragon (1276–85), creates the kingdom of Majorca for his son James.
- Llewellyn ap Gruffydd, Prince of Wales, begins his attacks on England following the death of Richard of Clare, one of the most powerful lords of the Welsh Marches.

1262–1269 War is waged between the Ilkhan of Persia, Hūlāgū, and Berke, Khan of the "Golden Horde." It is inconclusive but saves Egypt from Mongol attack.

June 6 Pedro, the son and heir of King James I of Aragon, marries Constance, the daughter and heir of King Manfred of Sicily.

August 8 The King of the Romans, Richard of Cornwall, recognizes King Ottokar II of Bohemia as ruler of Austria and Styria.

September 14 King Alfonso X of Castile and León takes the city of Cadiz.

1263

- King Alfonso X of Castile and León takes Cartagena, southeast Spain. He also cedes the Algarve to Dinis, son of King Alfonso III of Portugal.

- Prince Mindovg of Lithuania is murdered. His death assists the Teutonic Knights (a German Christian military order), who now complete their near extermination of the Sambians in the suppression of their rebellion.

- The Venetians defeat the Genoese, the allies of the Nicaean emperor Michael VIII Palaeologus, in a naval battle off Settepozzi, Italy, in their struggle to gain control of trade with the Byzantine Empire.

April 4 The English soldier and politician Simon IV de Montfort, Earl of Leicester, returns to England to lead a new baronial movement against King Henry III of England, having been summoned by Roger Clifford. This is a turning point in the dispute between the king and the barons.

April 4 The Mameluke sultan of Egypt, Baybars, attacks the port of Acre (modern Akko, Israel) in the kingdom of Jerusalem and sacks its suburbs.

July 16 King Henry III of England makes peace with his baronial opponents by accepting their terms, following a number of armed clashes and the rising of the city of London, England, against him. The leader of the barons, Simon de Montfort, Earl of Leicester, and his allies occupy London.

October 3 King Alexander III of Scotland defeats King Haakon IV of Norway, in the Battle of Largs, after King Haakon IV attempts to subjugate the Hebrides off the west coast of Scotland, having already received the submission of Iceland and the colonists in Greenland. Alexander then subdues the Hebrides himself.

November 14 The Russian military leader Alexander Nevsky, Grand Duke of Vladimir, dies. He is succeeded by his brother, Jaroslav III.

December 12 Martino della Torre, tyrant of Milan, dies. He is succeeded by his brother, Filippo. Pope Urban IV had put the city under an interdict for its refusal to accept Otto Visconti as archbishop.

December 15 King Haakon IV of Norway dies in the Shetland Islands, off the north coast of Scotland, where he has enforced an act of union with Norway by its people and those of the Orkney Islands. He is succeeded by his son, Magnus VI the Law-Mender.

1264

- King Manfred of Sicily's domination of Tuscany is completed with the submission of the town of Lucca.

- Kublai Khan, the Mongol emperor of China, transfers his capital from Karakorum to Yanjing.

- Prince Bolesław V of Kraków grants a charter to Jews who, with Germans, are settling in Poland. This charter acts as the model for all subsequent confirmations of Jewish liberties in Poland until the end of the 18th century.

- The Poles inflict a great defeat on the Jadźwingas, a Lithuanian tribe, at Zawichost, Poland.

- The Venetians defeat the Genoese off Trapani, Sicily.

- Walter de Burgos, Lord of Connacht, Ireland, is granted the earldom of Ulster by Edward Plantagenet, son of King Henry III of England. This makes him the most powerful noble in Ireland.

January 23 King Louis IX of France, arbitrating between King Henry III of England and the English barons, pronounces in favor of Henry in the Mise of Amiens, freeing him from any obligations to maintain the Provisions of Westminster (plan for legal reforms) and affirming his customary rights as king. This decision drives the baronial leader Simon de Montfort, Earl of Leicester, and the barons into open war.

April 7 In reaction to the buildup of baronial opposition forces in the area, King Henry III of England captures the town of Northampton, in southern central England, renewing the civil war between the king and the barons.

May 14 After a failed attempt to make peace, the leader of the baronial opposition to the monarchy, Simon IV de Montfort, Earl of Leicester, defeats and captures King Henry III of England at Lewes, England.

June 28 King Henry III of England accepts a "form of government" giving control to the baronial party of Simon IV de Montfort, Earl of Leicester. A provisional administration is established by the earls of Gloucester and Leicester and the bishop of Chester. The king's affairs are to be controlled by a council of nine.

October 21 Guy Foulquoi, the papal legate to England, excommunicates King Henry III of England's opponents.

SCIENCE, TECHNOLOGY, AND MEDICINE

Health and Medicine

1260

- The surgeons of Paris, France, form a guild called the "Collège de St. Cosme"—the origin of the Académie de Chirurgie.

Science

1260

- The English friar and scholar Roger Bacon investigates the laws governing optical phenomena such as refraction and reflection.

1263

- The Hebrew astronomers Jehuda Cohen and Isaac ben Sid of Toledo begin work on compiling the *Alfonsine*

Tables for King Alfonso X of Castile. The tables include accurate calculations of planetary motions.

ARTS AND IDEAS

Architecture

1260
- The cathedral at Burgos, Spain, is dedicated.

1262
- Construction begins on the Romanesque cathedral at Valencia, Spain.
- Johannes Anglicus begins the construction of the choir of St. Urbain in Troyes, France.

Arts

1260
- Sculptor Nicola Pisano carves the pulpit in the baptistry of Pisa Cathedral, Italy. It marks the revival of a form of sculpture clearly based on classical models.

Literature and Language

1262
- Adam de la Halle "Le Bossu" ("the Hunchback") writes the comedy and satire *Le Jeu de la feuillée/The Game of Leaves*, the first French farce.

1264
- Vincent of Beauvais completes his influential *Speculum maius/Great Mirror*, an encyclopedia of universal knowledge and history in three parts.

Thought and Scholarship

1260
- Al-Juwainī, a Persian historian under the Mongols, completes his *Ta'rīkh-i-jahān gushā/History of the World Conqueror*, which includes accounts of Genghis Khan and his successors until 1256.
- Franciscus Accursius (Francesco Accorso), the last great glossator–jurist of Bologna, Italy, writes his *Glossa ordinaria/General Gloss* or *Accursiana*, which becomes a standard work on civil law.

1263
- Pope Urban IV renews the papal prohibition on the study of the Greek philosopher Aristotle at the University of Paris, France.

SOCIETY

Education

1264
January 7 The English bishop Walter de Merton founds Merton College, Oxford University, England.

Religion

1260
c. 1260 Penitential flagellants (people who beat themselves in atonement for their sins, hoping to stave off natural disasters) become a common sight throughout Italy.
- The religious toleration of the Mongols antagonizes the Chinese. Kublai Khan upholds the cult of Confucius, but Islam and Christianity re-enter the country and Buddhism and Taoism are revived.

1262
- Shinran, chief disciple of Honen (leader of the Buddhist Pure Land Sect), founds the Shinsu Sect (True Sect) of Japanese Buddhism.
- The Brethren of the Free Spirit, a group of heretical mystics, first appears in Augsburg, Germany.

c. 1264
- Thomas Aquinas writes the famous hymn *Laude Sion/The Praise of Zion* which summons the church to the adoration of the Eucharist.

BIRTHS & DEATHS

1260
c. 1260 Cecco Angiolieri, Italian writer of a body of caustically humorous songs and sonnets, born (–*c.* 1312).
c. 1260 Clement V, French pope 1305–14, who moved the papal residence to Avignon, born in Bordelais region of France (–1314).
c. 1260 Władysław I, King of Poland 1320–33 who united several Polish provinces into a kingdom, born in Poland (–1233).
- Franciscus Accursius (Francesco Accorso), Italian jurist responsible for the renovation of Roman law and author of the *Glossa ordinaria/General Gloss* (1220–50), dies in Bologna, Italy (*c.* 76).
- Johannes Eckhart ("Meister Eckhart"), Dominican theologian, considered the greatest German speculative mystic, born in Hochheim, Franconia (–*c.* 1328).

1261
- Albertino Mussato, Italian statesman, historian, and poet, born in Padua, Italy (–1329).
May 25 Pope Alexander IV dies.

1263
January 9 Shinran, Japanese Buddhist philosopher who founded Jodo Shinshu, the largest school of Buddhism in Japan, dies in Kyoto, Japan (89).

1264
- Daniel, first king of Halich, dies.
- Vincent of Beauvais, French priest, theologian, and encyclopedist, author of *Speculum maius/Great Mirror*, an 80-volume encyclopedia and the largest for 500 years, dies in Paris, France (*c.* 74).
October 2 Pope Urban IV dies (*c.* 64).

1265–1269

POLITICS, GOVERNMENT, AND ECONOMICS

Business and Economics

1266
- Bakers in England begin to mark their loaves of bread as a quality-control measure.
- King Louis IX of France introduces the *gros tournois* in his reform of the French currency. The *gros tournois* and the *gros parisi* soon triumph over baronial money.

Politics and Government

1265
- The Mameluke Egyptian sultan Baybars takes the cities of Caesarea and Arsuf in the kingdom of Jerusalem.
- January 20 The English parliament held under the leader of the barons Simon de Montfort, Earl of Leicester, is the first to be attended by elected shire knights and burgesses.
- February 2 Filippo della Torre of Milan and Obizzo d'Este of Ferrara form a new Lombard League of anti-imperial cities in northern Italy.
- February 8 Hūlāgū, the Mongol ilkhan of Persia, dies. He is succeeded by his son Abāqa.
- April 4 Pope Clement IV grants the Italian kingdom of Sicily to Charles of Anjou.
- June 28 Pope Clement IV invests Charles of Anjou as king of Sicily and appoints him to lead the crusade against the former king, Manfred of Sicily.
- August 4 King Henry III of England and his son Edward Plantagenet defeat and kill the leader of the baronial party Simon IV de Montfort, Earl of Leicester, at Evesham, England.
- August 8 The leading Guelph (anti-imperialist), Napoleone della Torre, is proclaimed lord of Milan.
- December 12 The remaining supporters of the English baronial leader Simon IV de Montfort, Earl of Leicester, (including his son Simon de Montfort the younger), who have fled to the Isle of Axholme off the coast of northeast England, surrender to King Henry III of England.

1266
- Berke, Khan of the "Golden Horde," dies, bringing to an end his war with the ilkhan of Persia, which began in 1262. He is succeeded by Mangu-Temur.

- King Alfonso X of Castile and León, aided by King James I of Aragon, conquers the kingdom of Murcia, taking it from the Muslims and leaving King Mohammad I of Granada as the last Muslim vassal of Castile.
- The Genoese take and rebuild Kaffa, a central Asian province in the Crimea. This colony controls the caravan trade from Khwarizm, which brings in goods from India.
- February 6 Charles of Anjou defeats and kills Manfred, former king of Sicily, at Benevento, southern Italy. From this point until the death of Robert of Naples in 1343 the Angevin dynasty is the dominant power in Italy.
- February 18 Sultan Mahmud of Delhi, India, dies. He is succeeded by his lieutenant, Balban, although he had designated his father-in-law as his successor.
- March 6 Charles of Anjou and his wife Beatrice are crowned as king and queen of Sicily.
- April 4 John I, comargrave of Brandenburg, Germany, dies. He is succeeded by his three sons.
- June 6 King Henry III of England begins his siege of "the Disinherited" who have gathered in Kenilworth Castle, Warwickshire. They include some who previously submitted to Henry at Axholme in December 1265.
- July 2 By the Treaty of Perth agreed with King Alexander III of Scotland, King Magnus VI of Norway renounces his claims to the Hebrides and the Isle of Man. This ends the last stage of the growth of the monarchy of Scotland.
- July 23 The Mameluke sultan of Egypt, Baybars, wins control of the Galilee region of the kingdom of Jerusalem by taking the Templars' fortress of Safed. Despite assurances, all 2,000 knights (members of the Knights Templar) are executed.
- August 24 A second Mameluke army from Egypt defeats the Armenians near Sarventikar and ravages Lesser Armenia (in modern Turkey).
- October 31 King Henry III of England, in the Dictum of Kenilworth, grants terms to the adherents of the late baronial leader Simon de Montfort, Earl of Leicester. It supplements the Winchester ordinance and defines the ways in which the supporters of De Montfort can reclaim their confiscated estates.
- December 14 The besieged disinherited defenders of Kenilworth Castle, Warwickshire, surrender to King Henry III of England.

1267
- Charles of Anjou, King of Sicily, occupies the Greek island of Corfu.
- King Alfonso X of Castile and León and King Alfonso III of Portugal define their frontier in the Convention of Badajoz. The Algarve is now formally annexed to Portugal.

April 4   Pope Clement IV appoints Charles of Anjou, King of Sicily, as peacemaker in the Italian duchy of Tuscany. A propapal Guelph government is established in the city-republic of Florence.

April 9   Gilbert de Clare, Earl of Gloucester, occupies the English capital London against King Henry III of England.

June 6   The people of Rome revolt against Pope Clement IV.

June 6   Through the mediation of the papal legate Ottobuono Fieschi, King Henry III of England is finally reconciled with his former opponents.

August 8   The Sicilians revolt against their king, Charles of Anjou, in an ongoing conflict with the Hohenstaufens.

September 29   By the Treaty of Montgomery, King Henry III of England recognizes Llywelyn ap Gruffydd as prince of Wales and as his vassal.

November 18   King Henry III of England reenacts the clauses of the Provisions of Westminster in the Statute of Marlborough, safeguarding subtenants against their lords.

1268

- Khaidu, a grandson of Ogodai, revolts and seizes the khanate of Chaghadai (modern Turkestan).
- Kublai Khan, the Mongol emperor of China, sends ambassadors to Japan demanding submission.

1268–69   Balban, Sultan of Delhi, India, leads an expedition into the Salt Range in preparation for reasserting his power over the Punjab.

March 7   The Mameluke sultan of Egypt, Baybars, takes the city of Jaffa in the kingdom of Jerusalem without resistance.

April 4   The Nicaean emperor Michael VIII Palaeologus makes peace with the Venetians and restores their trading privileges, though at the same time keeping a similar treaty with Genoa. This double treaty gives distinct political and trading advantages to the Nicaeans.

April 17   Pope Clement IV appoints Charles of Anjou, King of Sicily, as imperial vicar in Tuscany. He also cedes him the office of senator of Rome.

May 21   The Mameluke sultan of Egypt, Baybars, takes Antioch, Syria (modern Antakya, Turkey), from its crusader occupants, and destroys the city with unprecedented slaughter. The city never recovers.

June 9   Rudolph of Habsburg gains possession of Fribourg and the lordship of Berne.

July 23   Ranieri Zeno, the doge of Venice, dies. He is succeeded by Lorenzo Tiepolo.

August 23   Conrad V (Conradin) of the German royal house of Hohenstaufen invades Italy to recover his father, Conrad IV's, kingdom of Sicily. He is defeated by Charles of Anjou, King of Sicily, at Tagliacozzo, northern Italy.

October 29   Charles of Anjou, King of Sicily, has Conrad V (Conradin) executed, extinguishing the German royal house of Hohenstaufen. Conrad was also nominally king of Jerusalem.

November 29   Pope Clement IV dies. There is a vacancy until September 1271 as Charles of Anjou, King of Sicily, tries to secure the papacy for a nominee of his choice.

1269

- Abāqa, Ilkhan of Persia, and Mangu-Temur, Khan of the "Golden Horde," make peace.
- Jatavarman Sundara, the Pandya ruler who has made himself supreme in southern India and Ceylon (modern Sri Lanka), dies. He is succeeded by Maravarman Kulasekhara, who brings the Pandya dynasty into hostility with the Somesvara.
- King Ottokar II of Bohemia succeeds, by treaty, to the duchy of Carinthia, bordering Italy. Verona and some other Italian cities recognize his overlordship.
- Ya'qūb III takes Marrakesh, Morocco, and finally destroys the Muslim dynasty of the Almohads. He founds the Marinid dynasty, which rules until 1465. A new capital is founded at Fès (or Fez).

1269–1273   The Mongols, under their general Bayan, invading China under the Song dynasty emperors, lay siege to the twin cities of Xiangyang.

April 4   On his fourth and last visit to Germany, the king of the Romans, Richard of Cornwall, holds a diet (legislative assembly) of Rhenish princes at Worms, where a land peace is sworn.

September 24   Hugh III of Cyprus is crowned king of Jerusalem in Acre, Palestine (modern Akko, Israel).

SCIENCE, TECHNOLOGY, AND MEDICINE

Ecology

1268

- A major earthquake devastates Asia Minor, killing 60,000 people in the Silicia region.

Science

1266

- The English friar and scholar Roger Bacon writes his *Opus maius/Great Work*, including discussions of the laws of optics and an outline of the principles of the magnifying glass and glasses for the farsighted.

BIRTHS & DEATHS

1265
- Dante Alighieri, Italian poet, prose writer, moral philosopher, and political theorist, author of *Divina commedia/Divine Comedy*, born in Florence, Italy (–1321).

1266
- Prince Świętopełk of Pomerania dies.

1268
- Philip IV, King of France 1285–1314, born in Fontainebleau, France (–1314).

1269

- The French crusader engineer Petrus Peregrinus of Maricourt writes *Epistola de Magnete/Letters from Magnesia*, which describes his experiments with magnetic lodestones, and his plotting of the magnetic field for the first time. In the work he coins the term "poles."

Transportation

1269

- The first toll roads are introduced in England.

ARTS AND IDEAS

Architecture

1268

- The Kesik Köprü Han, a caravanserai (a large inn providing accommodation for caravans), is built at Kirsehir in the Seljuk sultanate of Rūm (modern Turkey).

1269

- The Mosque of Baybars is built in Cairo, Egypt, under the supervision of the sultan Baybars I himself.

October 13   King Henry III of England's abbey church at Westminster, London, England, is dedicated.

Arts

1265–68

- Sculptor Nicola Pisano collaborates with his son Giovanni on the sculpting of the pulpit in Siena Cathedral, Italy.

Literature and Language

c. **1267**

- Brunetto Latini of Florence writes his *Li livres dou tresor/The Book of Treasure*, an encyclopedia of popular knowledge and morality in French.

Thought and Scholarship

c. **1265**

- Jacobus de Voragine, archbishop of Genoa, compiles his *Legenda aurea/Golden Legend*, a collection of the lives and legends of the saints, which becomes an important source book for pre-Reformation artists.

1266

- *Azuma Kagami/Mirror of the Eastland*, a Japanese chronicle of events for the period 1180–1266, is written in Chinese.

SOCIETY

Education

1268

- Balliol College, Oxford University, England, is founded.

Religion

1265

February 5   Guy Foulquoi, the papal legate to England, is elected as Pope Clement.

1270–1274

POLITICS, GOVERNMENT, AND ECONOMICS

Business and Economics

1270

April 27 An English parliament, including some knights, grants a tax to finance a crusade to the Holy Land by Edward Plantagenet, the son of King Henry III.

1274

- The first national debt is established in Genoa.

Politics and Government

1270

- Balban, Sultan of Delhi, India, confiscates lands granted on quasi-feudal terms when the tenants are unable to perform service in person.
- King Béla IV of Hungary dies. He is succeeded by his son, Stephen V, with whom he had been feuding until his death.
- The Italian cities of Pisa, Siena, Turin, Alessandria, and Brescia submit to the dominion of Charles of Anjou, King of Sicily.
- Yekuno Amlak overthrows the Zagwe dynasty of kings of Ethiopia and founds the Solomonid dynasty (which traces its origin from Solomon and the queen of Sheba). His success shifts the center of Ethiopia south to Amhara and Shoa.

July 1 The French king Louis IX sails from France on the Eighth Crusade to the Holy Land to recover Palestine from the Muslims.

July 7 Charles of Anjou, King of Sicily, finally suppresses the revolt in Sicily.

July 18 King Louis IX of France lands at Carthage, North Africa, having been diverted from his crusade to Palestine by his brother Charles of Anjou, King of Sicily, because the emir of Tunis has not been paying the customary tribute to the king of Sicily. On July 25, he takes the city of Tunis in North Africa, and waits for the arrival of his brother Charles.

August 25 King Louis IX of France dies. He is succeeded by his son, Philip III.

November 1 Charles of Anjou, King of Sicily, now leader of the Eighth Crusade to the Holy Land after the death of King Louis IX of France, makes a peace treaty with the emir of Tunis, intending to direct the crusade fleet toward Constantinople. The emir resumes payment of the tribute formerly paid to the Hohenstaufen kings of Sicily.

November 23 The Eighth Crusade fleet is destroyed by a storm at Trapani, Sicily, preventing Charles of Anjou, King of Sicily and leader of the crusade, from directing it toward Constantinople.

December 5 King Theobald II of Navarre dies. He is succeeded by his brother, Henry I, Count of Champagne.

1271

- King Stephen V of Hungary makes Bulgaria a tributary state.
- Kublai Khan, the Mongol emperor of China, adopts the Chinese dynastic name of Yuan.
- Michael II, Despot of Epirus, Greece, dies. His son, Despot Nicephorus, succeeds to Epirus, but Thessaly is taken over by his illegitimate son, John. Both rulers are linked by marriage to Michael VIII Palaeologus, the Nicaean emperor.
- Ulrich von Dürenholz, King Ottokar II of Bohemia's governor of Styria, captures Carniola and gains control of Friuli, northern Italy.

March 13 Henry of Almain, the son of the king of the Romans, Richard of Cornwall, is murdered in Orvieto, Italy, by Guy, son of the late English baronial leader Simon de Montfort, Earl of Leicester, who is in the service of Charles of Anjou, King of Sicily. He is later excommunicated by Pope Gregory X.

April 8 The Mameluke sultan of Egypt, Baybars, takes the Knights Hospitallers' fortress of Krak des Chevaliers in the crusader county of Tripoli.

May 9 Edward Plantagenet, the son of King Henry III of England, arrives at Acre in the kingdom of Jerusalem (modern Akko, Israel), on crusade.

August 21 Alfonse of Poitiers dies. His nephew, King Philip III of France, thus inherits the counties of Poitou and Toulouse, which are absorbed into the royal domain. Philip presents the comtât Venaissin, east of the River Rhône, to the papacy.

September 1 Tedald Visconti of Piacenza is elected as Pope Gregory X.

1272

- Hojo Masamara, in charge of Japanese defense against the Mongols, orders all Kyushi vassals residing elsewhere to return to their estates in the face of an impending Mongol invasion.
- Jaroslav III, Grand Duke of Vladimir, Russia, dies. His brother, Vasili of Kostroma, is offered the throne by Mangu-Temur, Khan of the "Golden Horde."

May 22 The Mameluke sultan of Egypt, Baybars, makes a

treaty of peace for ten years with the vestigial crusader kingdom of Jerusalem at Acre (modern Akko, Israel).

June 16   At the Mameluke Egyptian sultan Baybars's instigation, an Assassin (member of the militant branch of the Islamic Ismaili sect) attempts to murder Edward Plantagenet, the son of King Henry III of England, at Acre, in the kingdom of Jerusalem (modern Akko, Israel).

August 8   King Stephen V of Hungary dies. He is succeeded by Ladislas IV the Cuman, under whose reign there is an increased level of baronial factionalism.

September 22   Edward Plantagenet, the son of King Henry III of England, departs from the kingdom of Jerusalem to return to England.

November 20   Edward Plantagenet, the son of the late King Henry III, is proclaimed king of England by hereditary right.

December 12   The archbishop of Lyons, which is technically in the Holy Roman Empire, takes an oath of fealty to King Philip III of France.

1273

- King Alfonso X of Castile and León organizes the "Mesta," a corporation of sheep-owners. This is needed as the Christian conquest of Andalusia leads to a great increase in sheep-raising in Castile–León.
- The Genoese defeat Charles of Anjou, King of Sicily.
- The Mongols take the Chinese twin cities of Xiangyang after a five-year siege. This is an important set-back for the Chinese Song dynasty.
- The Nicaean emperor Michael VIII Palaeologus makes peace with Nogay, the Mongol ruler of the Lower Danube. Nogay holds influence with the "Golden Horde," and is able to prevent anti-Nicaean action by the Bulgarians.
- The Teutonic Knights (a German Christian military order) complete their suppression of the rebellion of the previously conquered and converted tribes of west Prussia.

January 21   King Mohammad I of Granada dies. He is succeeded by his son, Mohammad II , who adopts a policy of alliance with Abu Yūsuf of Morocco.

October 1   Rudolf I, King of Germany, is elected Holy Roman Emperor at the instigation of the enemies of King Ottokar II of Bohemia, who is excluded from the election.

1274

- A fleet sent by Kublai Khan, the Mongol emperor of China, to conquer Japan is repulsed at Hakata Bay and subsequently destroyed by a storm.
- Henry III the Fat, King of Navarre and Count of Champagne, dies. He is succeeded by his three-year-old daughter, Joanna I. She is placed by her mother, Blanche of Artois, under the protection of her brother Robert at the French court.
- In a diet (legislative assembly) at Regensburg, King Ottokar II of Bohemia is declared by King Rudolf I of Germany to have forfeited Austria, Styria, and his other recent acquisitions after he refuses to appear before the diet.
- King Edward I of England orders an inquiry into English local government. Its reports are recorded on "the Hundred Rolls."
- The examination system is abandoned in South China.

July 6   With the enemies of the Byzantine Empire united under Charles of Anjou, King of Sicily, at the General Council of Lyons the ambassadors of the Byzantine emperor Michael VIII Palaeologus take an oath accepting the pope's supremacy. Pope Gregory X then causes Charles to make a truce with Michael.

August 19   Edward I is crowned king of England.

September 26   Pope Gregory X recognizes Rudolf, son of Albert IV count of Habsburg, as Holy Roman Emperor.

October 26   Genoa makes an alliance with the imperialists of Lombardy, north Italy, who recognize King Alfonso X of Castile and León as Holy Roman Emperor.

SCIENCE, TECHNOLOGY, AND MEDICINE

Ecology

1273

- Complaints in London, England, about pollution produced from the burning of "seacoal" mined at Newcastle lead to an eventual prohibition on coal burning throughout England.

Exploration

1270

- The chroniclers of St. Louis (King Louis IX of France), while recording the last crusade to the Holy Land, make reference to the use of maps for navigation. This is the earliest record of this in Europe.

Health and Medicine

1270

- Muslim physician ibn-abi Usaybi'ah writes his *Valuable Information on the Classes of Physicians*, which contains biographies of approximately 600 Greek and Arab physicians and is the only source by which many of them are known today.

Science

1271

- The astronomer Robert the Englishman writes *De astrolobio canones/Principles of the Astrolabe*, which provides an early European description of the construction and use of the astrolabe, the instrument used to measure the altitude of stars and planets.

1272

- The *Alfonsine Tables* are completed and published by two Jewish astronomers working for King Alfonso X of Castile. They will be used to calculate planetary positions and eclipses for the next three centuries.

- The Persian astronomer At-Tūsī completes his *Zīj-i Ilkhāni*, begun in 1259, and the most accurate table of planetary motions yet.

1274
- The Polish scholar Witelo Ciołek of Wrocław, Poland, writes the most important medieval European treatise on optics, based on the work of the 11th-century Arab scientist Alhazen.

Technology

1270
- The River Maas in the (modern) Netherlands is dammed, creating a huge area of reclaimed land called the Holland Polder.

1271
- Watermarks begin to be used in high quality paper. The earliest known comprises the letter "F," probably signifying the paper mills at Fabriano, Italy.

1272
- Mechanical twisting mills for the rapid winding of silk are constructed for the first time at Bologna, Italy.
- The manufacture of paper begins at Montefano in Italy, probably introduced from Muslim sources in Sicily or Spain, rather than from the small-scale French industry.

1274
- The English astronomer and astrologer John Bate writes his treatise on the astrolabe, the instrument used to measure the altitude of planets and stars.

ARTS AND IDEAS

Architecture

1270
- Construction begins on the choir of Séez Cathedral, France, and the nave of Minden Cathedral in Germany.

1272
- Construction begins on the choirs of Narbonne and Toulouse Cathedrals, France, both under the supervision of the architect Jean des Champs.

1273
- Construction begins on the choir of Limoges Cathedral, France, under the supervision of architect Jean des Champs.

Literature and Language

1270
- Phagspa devises a new Mongol alphabet for Kublai Khan.
- Poet and composer Adam de la Halle "Le Bossu" ("the Hunchback") writes *Lyrics* and *Congé/Holiday*, a satirical farewell on leaving Arras, France, in 1269 to go into enforced exile.

1274
- Ibn-Khallikān completes the compilation of *Wafayāt al'yān wa-Anbā' al-Zamān*, a biographical dictionary of 865 eminent Muslims.

May 5   Italian poet Dante Alighieri first meets Beatrice Portinari, who is to become his ideal and inspiration.

BIRTHS & DEATHS

1270
c. 1270   Cino da Pistoia (de' Sigibuldi), Italian scholar and writer, dies (–1337).

c. 1270   Nicholas de Lyra (Nicolaus Lyranus), Franciscan theologian and biblical scholar, born in Vielle-Lyre, Normandy (–1349).

c. 1270   William Wallace, Scottish hero who led the first resistance movements to free Scotland from English rule, born near Paisley, Renfrew, Scotland (–1305).

July 23   Pietro Paulo Vergerio, Italian educator who wrote *De ingenuis moribus et liberalibus studii/On the Manners of a Gentleman and Liberal Studies* that formed the basis of liberal education methods in Italy, born in Capodistria, Istria (–1444 or 1445).

August 25   Louis IX (St. Louis), King of France 1226–70, who led the Seventh Crusade 1248–50, dies near Tunis, North Africa (56).

1272
April 2   Richard, Earl of Cornwall, King of the Romans 1256–71, dies at Berkhampstead Castle, Hertfordshire, England (63).

November 16   Henry III, King of England 1216–72, son of King John, dies in London, England (65).

1273
- Jalāl al-Dīn, commonly known as Rūmī, Persian mystic poet whose *Masnavī-i ma'navī*, a Sufi mystical poem in six books, explains the mystic Sufi doctrine through fables and anecdotes, dies.

1274
March 7   St. Thomas Aquinas ("Doctor Angelicus"), Italian Dominican theologian, outstanding medieval scholasticist, author of *Summa theologiae/Summary of Theology* and *Summa contra gentiles/The Main Argument Against the Gentiles*, dies in Fossanova, near Terracina, Italy (*c.* 50).

July 11   Robert I the Bruce, King of Scotland 1306–29, who freed Scotland from English rule, winning a decisive victory at Bannockburn (1314), born (–1329).

July 15   St. Bonaventura, Italian theologian and minister general of the Franciscan order, dies in Lyon (*c.* 57).

August 5   Robert de Sorbon, French theologian who founded the University of the Sorbonne, dies in Paris (72).

Thought and Scholarship

1270

- The book *Etablissements de St.-Louis/Establishments of St.-Louis* is written in France. It is for the most part made up of customs of the provinces of Orléanais, Touraine, and Anjou.

1272

- Spanish mystic and poet Ramón Llull (or Raymond Lully) translates his own *Libre de contemplació en Deu/The Book of the Contemplation of God*, an encyclopedia of practical theology, from Arabic into Catalan.

1274

March 7 St. Thomas Aquinas dies, leaving his great work *Summa theologiae/Summary of Theology* incomplete. A vast compendium of moral and political philosophy, it attempts to reconcile reason, faith, and Aristotelian philosophy with Christian theology.

SOCIETY

Education

1270

- Hojo Sanetoki founds a school and library in Kanazawa, Japan.

1271

- The Gök Madrasa (college) is founded in Sivas, Persia.

Everyday Life

1270

- The population of Hangchow (the Song capital) is estimated to be 391,000 households.

1274

- An exodus of weavers and cloth fullers from Ghent, Flanders, when they fail to improve their terms of employment there, carries textile manufacturing techniques across Europe.

Religion

1273

- Followers of the Persian mystic poet Rūmī establish the Dervish Order of the Mevlevīye.
- The Spanish philosopher and poet Ramón Llull (or Raymond Lully) begins his mission to convert Muslims to Christianity.

1274

May 7 Pope Gregory X opens the General Council of Lyons in France, in the hope of ending the schism with the Greek church. The council recognizes the Dominican, Franciscan, Carmelite, and Austin Friars, and orders the suppression of all smaller mendicant orders.

◆

1275–1279

POLITICS, GOVERNMENT, AND ECONOMICS

Politics and Government

1275

c. 1275 The Yoruba kingdom destroys the kingdom of Nubia.

- *Schwabenspiegel/Mirror of Swabia*, a compilation of Swabian laws, is issued.
- Count Florence V of Holland grants a charter of privileges to the city of Amsterdam.

- Kertanegara, King of the Javanese kingdom of Majapahit, launches an attack on Jambi, the capital of the neighboring kingdom of Jambi.
- King Edward I of England holds his first parliament, attended by lords and elected knights and burgesses. The first Statute of Westminster, among other things, corrects abuses in local government. This is one of several important statutes of Edward I's reign. The parliament also makes the first grant of customs on wool and leather.
- King Waldemar I of Sweden dies. He is succeeded by Magnus I Barn-Lock, his younger brother.
- The Mameluke sultan of Egypt, Baybars, raids Lesser Armenia (Cilicia, in modern Turkey).

August 8 Pope Gregory X persuades King Alfonso X of Castile and León to renounce the title of Holy Roman Emperor.

August 16 Lorenzo Tiepolo, Doge of Venice, dies. He is succeeded by Jacopo Contarino.

September 8   Ya'qūb III of Morocco defeats King Alfonso X of Castile and León near Ecija, in Andalusia, Spain.

October 10   Pope Gregory X obtains German support in northern Italy by an agreement with King Rudolf I of Germany. The influence of Charles of Anjou, King of Sicily, now wanes in the north.

November 10   Charles of Anjou, King of Sicily, is defeated at Roccavione by Thomas, Marquess of Saluzzo, and thus loses control of Piedmont.

1276

- King Magnus VI the Law-Mender establishes a common law in Norway.
- King Philip III of France attempts to intervene in a dispute in Castile over the future successor to King Alfonso X of Castile and León. However, his army is so badly organized that its march breaks down before reaching the Pyrenees.
- Kublai Khan, the Mongol emperor of China, takes Hangzhou, the Song dynasty capital, after a failed attempt by the empress dowager to achieve an accommodation with the Mongols.
- Pope Gregory X sanctions the acquisition by Charles of Anjou, King of Sicily, of the titular kingdom of Jerusalem.
- Stephen Uroš I of Serbia is deposed and succeeded by his son, Stephen Dragutin.
- Vasili, Grand Duke of Vladimir, Russia, dies. The throne is assigned by Mangu-Temur, Khan of the "Golden Horde," to his nephew, Dmitri I, the eldest living son of the former Grand Duke Alexander Nevsky.

January 21   Peter of Tarantaise is elected as Pope Innocent V.

June 14   Shih, the seven-year-old half brother of the captured Chinese Song emperor, is enthroned.

July 11   Ottobuono Fieschi is elected as Pope Adrian V after the death of Pope Innocent V.

July 25   King James I the Conqueror of Aragon dies. He is succeeded by his son, Pedro III.

September 8   Peter Juliani of Portugal is elected as Pope John XXI.

November 16   Pedro III is crowned king of Aragon and renounces Aragon's vassalage to the papacy.

November 25   Following King Rudolf I of Germany's siege of Vienna and a revolt in Bohemia, King Ottokar II of Bohemia, by the Treaty of Vienna, surrenders Austria, Styria, Carinthia, and all his other lands except Bohemia and Moravia, for which he does homage to Rudolf. Rudolf then makes Vienna the capital of his Habsburg lands.

1277

- An army sent by Kublai Khan defeats his cousin Khaidu at Karakorum in central Asia, but he survives this and subsequent attempts to suppress his rebellion.

April 4   The Mameluke Egyptian sultan Baybars invades Anatolia (modern Turkey) and defeats the Mongols at Elbistan. He withdraws on the approach of an army sent by the Persian Ilkhan Abāqa, which restores Mongol control over the sultanate of Rūm.

June 24   King Edward I of England begins his first Welsh campaign following the refusal of Llywelyn ap Gruffydd, Prince of Wales, to do homage.

July 1   Baybars, the Mameluke sultan of Egypt and Syria, dies. He is succeeded by his son Baraka.

November 9   Llywelyn ap Gruffydd, Prince of Wales, submits to King Edward I of England in the Treaty of Conway. He is forced to give up all his claims to the kingship of Wales.

November 25   John Gaetan is elected as Pope Nicholas III.

1278

- Pierre de la Broce, chamberlain of King Louis IX of France and his successor King Philip III, is hanged. He has been a royal favorite, but falls after a conspiracy is aimed at him by Philip's second wife, Mary of Brabant.
- The earliest surviving regulations for procedure in the French Parlement date from this year. The Parlement is now permanently installed in the royal palace, Paris, as the supreme court of law in France.

January 1   Charles of Anjou, King of Sicily, is crowned king of Jerusalem.

January 21   Otto Visconti, a member of a powerful Ghibelline family, defeats the Guelph (anti-imperialist) Napoleone della Torre, Lord of Milan, at Desio and expels him from Milan. The city accepts Otto as its archbishop and lord.

May 1   William de Villehardouin, Prince of Achaea, dies. He is succeeded by Charles of Anjou, King of Sicily. Although apparently threatening the Byzantine Empire, Achaea is exhausted by war and the Byzantine Empire is able to extend its territories as far as Arcadia.

May 5   King Rudolf I of Germany surrenders the imperial claims to lordship over the Romagna, Italy, to Pope Nicholas III.

May 24   Charles of Anjou, King of Sicily, surrenders his vicariate of Tuscany and senatorship of Rome to Pope Nicholas III.

August 28   King Ottokar II of Bohemia is defeated and killed by King Rudolf I of Germany and King Ladislas IV of Hungary at Dürnkrut, on the River Danube near Stillfried. He is succeeded by his seven-year-old son, Wenceslas III, in Bohemia only, where civil war breaks out.

1279

- A Mongol raid into the Punjab, India, is repulsed.
- Balban, Sultan of Delhi, India, crushes a rebellion by Tughril, his governor in Bengal.
- Florence, Lucca, Siena, and other northern Italian cities form a Tuscan Guelph (propapal) League, with a customs union and a joint army.
- In the course of a dispute with John Pecham, archbishop of Canterbury, King Edward I of England forbids grants of land to the church in the Statute of Mortmain. This is the first act of anticlerical legislation in England.
- Kublai Khan completes the Mongol conquest of China with a naval victory near Macao. The southern Chinese Song dynasty is extinguished.
- The Byzantines put John Asen III, a member of the Asen dynasty established in c. 1187, on the Bulgarian throne.
- The Indian Pandya ruler Maravarman Kulasekhara defeats Rajendra III, the last ruler of the Chola dynasty.

January 1   King Alfonso III of Portugal dies. He is succeeded by his son Dinis.

February 14   King Rudolf I of Germany, Holy Roman Emperor, recognizes the superior authority of the papacy and cedes all claims to sovereignty over the Papal States and southern Italy.

March 3   Jacopo Contarino, Doge of Venice, dies. He is succeeded by Giovanni Dandolo.

May 23   By the Treaty of Amiens, King Philip III of France cedes Agenais, on the River Garonne, to King Edward I of England and recognizes his recent occupation of Ponthieu.

August 8   Baraka, Mameluke Sultan of Egypt and Syria, is forced to abdicate in favor of his brother Salāmish. His ward, Qalāwūn, the leader of the coup against him, soon afterwards assumes the sultanate.

November 26   King Alfonso X of Castile and León and King Philip III of France make a truce by the mediation of King Edward I of England.

December 10   Bolesław V the Chaste, Grand Prince of Poland, whose reign has been a period of disintegration, dies. He is succeeded by his nephew Leszek III the Black.

SCIENCE, TECHNOLOGY, AND MEDICINE

Ecology

1275
- An earthquake destroys the town of Glastonbury in the southwest of England.

Health and Medicine

1275
- The Italian surgeon William of Saliceto writes *Cyrurgia/ Surgery*, a work which contains an extensive section on human anatomy, indicating experience from dissections.

1279
- The Muslim translator Faraj ben Sālim produces a Latin version of the medical compendium by the great 10th-century Arab physician al-Rāzi, *Liber Continens*.

Science

1276
- The Chinese astronomer Guo Shou-jing builds a 12 m/40 ft tower gnomon (the stationary arm that projects the shadow on a sundial) at Gao Cheng Zhen, China, with a 36 m/120 ft horizontal stone scale for measuring the length of its shadow at midday. He is thus able to maintain a calendar.

1279
- A catalog of stones and minerals called *Lapidario/On Stones*, written for King Alfonso the Wise of Castile and León, is completed. It also contains an early western illustration of a ship equipped with lateen sails, a feature that enables ships to sail into the wind.
- The earliest surviving version of the Chinese ornithology treatise *Ch'in ching* dates to this time, although the work is possibly much older.

Technology

1277
- Chinese military engineers invent the land mine. Early forms comprise a buried explosive charge with a wheel lock detonator to create a spark, which is triggered by pulling an attached cord from a safe distance.

Transportation

c. **1275**
- The earliest surviving *portolano* (pilot's map), the Italian *Carte Pisano*, dates from this time.

ARTS AND IDEAS

Architecture

1275
- The nave of Strasbourg Cathedral, France, is completed. Construction is to begin on the west façade in 1277.

Arts

1278
- Sculptor Nicola Pisano and his son Giovanni sculpt the fountain in the piazza at Perugia, Italy. It is Nicola's last extant work.

BIRTHS & DEATHS

1275
c. 1275   Giovanni Villani, Italian historian, author of *Storia fiorentine/ History of Florence*, a universal history which focuses on Florence and which is one of the first to include statistics and to be objective, born in Florence (–1348).

1276
- Guido Guinizelli, Italian poet and jurist whose love lyrics are regarded as early examples of the *stil nuovo* (new style) because of their introduction of an ethical dimension into the tradition of courtly love, dies.

January 10   Pope Gregory X dies.
June 22   Pope Innocent V dies.
July 25   King James I of Aragon, possible writer of a chronicle of his reign, *Libre del feyts/Book of Deeds*, dies.
August 18   Pope Adrian V dies.

1277
May 20   Pope John XXI is killed when the ceiling of his palace at Viterbo, Italy, collapses. A leading physician of his age, he has written *Commentaries of Isaac* on diets and medicine, *De anima/On the Soul* on psychology, and *Liber de Oculo/The Book of the Eye*.

Literature and Language

1275

c. 1275   French writer Jean de Meun completes the first part of his narrative poem *Le Roman de la rose/The Romance of the Rose*, a continuation of the poem by Guillaume de Lorris.

- Spanish mystic and poet Raymond Lully writes his work on chivalry, written in Catalan, *Libre del orde de cavayleria/The Book of the Order of Chivalry.*

c. 1276

- Philippe de Beaumanoir writes his *La Manekine/The Mannequin*, a metrical romance about Joie, daughter of the king of Hungary, and her severed hand.

c. 1277

- French writer Jean de Meun completes the second part of *Le Roman de la rose/The Romance of the Rose*, a continuation of the poem by Guillaume de Lorris.

c. 1278

- Philippe de Beaumanoir writes his *Jehan et Blonde/Jehan and Blonde*, a romance.

Thought and Scholarship

1276

- Spanish philosopher and mystic Ramón Llull (or Raymond Lully) founds a college of friars for the study of Arabic at Miramar, France.

SOCIETY

Religion

1275

- The Nestorian patriarch of Baghdad, Persia, creates an archbishopric in Beijing, China. Some Mongols, including Kublai Khan's mother, were Nestorian Christians, believing that Christ was two distinct persons, divine and human.

1277

- English scientist, monk, and scholar Roger Bacon is tried for heresy and imprisoned until 1292.
- Etienne Taupier (bishop of Paris, France) and Robert Kilwardby (archbishop of Canterbury, England) issue an attack against astrology and the general spread of Aristotelian secular science in the universities of Europe.
- The Inquisition in France condemns Siger of Brabant for his Averroëist writings.

1279

- Pope Nicholas III's decree *Exiit qui seminat/A Sower Went out to Sow* attempts to reconcile the division among the Franciscans over whether they should own property.

1280–1284

POLITICS, GOVERNMENT, AND ECONOMICS

Business and Economics

1282

- The north European cities of Lübeck, Riga, and Visby make an alliance for the protection of their trade in the Baltic.

Politics and Government

1280

- John Asen III of Bulgaria is deposed by George I Terter, of Cuman descent, who is elected by the Bulgarian *boyars* as successor to Asen. He rules until 1292.
- King Pedro III of Aragon establishes a protectorate over Tunis, North Africa.
- Mangu-Temur, Khan of the "Golden Horde," dies. He is succeeded by his brother Tuda-Mangu, but Nogay, the Mongol ruler of the Lower Danube, assumes joint rule in Russia as khan of "the Nogay Horde," ruling between the Dnieper and Danube rivers. Tuda-Mangu ravages Vladimir and replaces Dmitri with his brother Andrew as grand duke.
- There are riots by employees in the cloth-weaving industry in Flanders.
- William de la Roche succeeds to the lordship of Athens, Greece, and styles himself duke.

February 10   Margaret II, Countess of Flanders, dies. She is succeeded, through the support of King Philip III of France, by her son, Guy of Dampierre. Flanders thus comes under French influence, as Guy has been challenged by John of Avesnes, who has imperial backing.

May 9   Magnus VI the Law-Mender of Norway dies. He is succeeded by his son, Eric II.

October 20   The Mongols under Abāqa, Ilkhan of Persia, sack the city of Aleppo in Syria.

1281

- King Pedro III of Aragon makes an alliance with Michael VIII Palaeologus, the Byzantine emperor, against Charles of Anjou, King of Sicily.

- Kublai Khan, emperor of China, introduces a system to provide against famine, appointing officials to buy excess grain in years of plenty, and to store it in granaries for later distribution.

February 22   Simon de Brie is elected Pope Martin IV. He appoints Charles of Anjou, King of Sicily, as senator of Rome.

April 10   Pope Martin IV, under the influence of Charles of Anjou, King of Sicily, excommunicates the Byzantines and renounces the union of July 6, 1274.

July 3   By the Treaty of Orvieto, the Venetians undertake to assist Charles of Anjou, King of Sicily, to restore the Latin Empire in Constantinople. Pope Martin IV declares Michael VIII Palaeologus, the Byzantine emperor, deposed.

August 15   A second fleet sent by Kublai Khan, the Mongol emperor of China, to conquer Japan is destroyed by a typhoon in Hakata Bay. The grateful Japanese call it *kamikaze* (divine wind).

October 30   The Mameluke sultan of Egypt, Qalāwūn, defeats the Mongols, Armenians, and Knights Hospitallers (members of an order of Christian chivalry) at Homs, Syria, after a failure by the ilkhan of Persia to persuade Pope Martin IV to order a crusade against the Mamelukes.

1282

- King Eric II of Denmark grants a charter of liberties to the Danish nobles.

- Leszek III, Grand Prince of Poland, avenges a devastating raid by the Jadźwingas, a Lithuanian tribe, with their final destruction.

- Stephen Dragutin appoints his brother Stephen Uroš II joint king and effective ruler of Serbia. Stephen Uroš takes the city of Skopje from the Byzantines.

- The Mongols ravage the Polish kingdom of Halich (Halicz), destroying its political importance, and go on into Poland proper.

- The Priors of the Arts, comprising representatives of the leading guilds, is established as the governing body in Florence.

March 21   David ap Gruffydd, brother of Llywelyn ap Gruffydd, Prince of Wales, begins a widespread Welsh revolt against King Edward I of England by capturing Hawarden Castle. A Welsh "parliament" soon commits the Welsh to war.

March 30   The French garrison in Palermo, Sicily, is massacred by the local inhabitants in the "Sicilian Vespers." The revolt spreads, leading to Charles of Anjou, King of Sicily, losing the island and the people

offering the crown to King Pedro III of Aragon, as Manfred of Sicily's heir.

April 1   Abāqa, Ilkhan of Persia, with his capital at Tabriz, dies. He is succeeded by his brother Tekuder, who announces his conversion to Islam, taking the style "Sultan Ahmad."

April 10   Ahmad, the Muslim finance minister of the Chinese emperor Kublai Khan, is assassinated.

April 25   The Welsh revolt against King Edward I of England collapses with the surrender of Harlech Castle to the English.

June 18   King Pedro III of Aragon, making for Sicily, lands in North Africa, ostensibly on crusade.

August 8   King Edward I of England begins his second Welsh campaign in northwest Wales, the heartland of Llywelyn ap Gruffydd, Prince of Wales.

August 30   King Pedro III of Aragon lands in Sicily, soon taking possession as King Peter I, after being summoned by Sicilian rebels against their king, Charles of Anjou.

November 18   Pope Martin IV declares King Pedro III deprived of the crown of Aragon and proclaims a crusade against him.

December 11   Llywelyn ap Gruffydd, Prince of Wales, is killed while invading Builth. His brother David ap Gruffydd assumes his title.

December 11   The Byzantine emperor Michael VIII Palaeologus dies. He is succeeded by his son, Andronicus II Palaeologus, who immediately renounces the reunion of the Greek church with Rome.

December 27   In a diet (legislative assembly) at Augsburg, King Rudolf I of Germany invests his sons Albert and Rudolf of Habsburg with the duchies of Austria and Styria respectively.

1283

- Grand Duke Andrew flees from Vladimir, Russia, after a rising and Nogay, Khan of "the Nogay Horde" (between the Dnieper and Danube rivers), supports the restoration of Andrew's brother Dmitri as grand duke.

- King Pedro III of Aragon concedes the *Privilegio General* to the Union of Aragon, an association of nobles and municipalities, to appease the Aragonese nobles who are resentful of Pedro's acceptance of the Sicilian crown.

- Mayapán becomes the capital of the Cocom dynasty, rulers of Yucatán.

- Skurdo, the last Prussian leader, flees to Lithuania. The Teutonic Knights (a German Christian military order) have now exterminated or subjugated the Prussians, whose lands are colonized by Germans and Poles.

- The Court of the Consulate of the Sea for commercial affairs is created in Valencia. A compilation of commercial law, the *Libre del consolat de mar/Book of the Consulate of the Sea*, now appears.

1283–1284   Indravarman VI Jaya successfully resists a seaborne Mongol invasion of Champa and Dai Viet (modern Vietnam).

October 3   David ap Gruffydd, prince of Wales, is executed as a traitor against King Edward I of England for the newly defined crime of "raising war against the king" and by the new penalty of hanging, drawing, and quartering.

1284

- King Edward I of England's Statute of Rhuddlan provides English government for the Principality of Wales.
- The Bānu Hilal and Bānu Sulaym Arabs of North Africa receive their first charter of iqtā from their Hafisid rulers. This gives the Arab chiefs the right to levy taxes.

January 1 A revolt in Rome destroys the authority there of Charles of Anjou, King of Sicily.

February 2 King Philip III of France accepts Pope Martin IV's offer of the crown of Aragon. It is granted by Martin to Philip's second son, Charles of Valois.

March 4 King Hugh III of Cyprus and Jerusalem dies. He is succeeded by his son, John I.

April 4 King Alfonso X the Wise of Castile and León dies. A civil war follows.

June 5 The Genoese naval commander Roger Loria defeats the Angevin navy in the Bay of Naples and captures Charles of Salerno, the heir of Charles of Anjou, King of Sicily, who is delivered to King Pedro III of Aragon.

August 6 Pisa is ruined by the destruction of its fleet by the Genoese off the island of Meloria.

August 10 The ilkhan of Persia, Tekuder, is murdered in an anti-Muslim revolt. He is succeeded by his elder brother, Arghūn, who was previously persuaded to stand down to allow Tekuder's accession.

August 16 Philip IV, son of King Philip III of France, marries Joanna I, Queen of Navarre and Countess of Champagne.

SCIENCE, TECHNOLOGY, AND MEDICINE

Health and Medicine

1280

- The scholar Paravicius translates Avenzoar's important and influential work on therapeutics and diet *Book of Simplification*, as *Theisir*.

1284

- A Venetian law apparently refers to the use of glasses, *roidi da ogli*, indicating that the invention is in common use.
- Al-Maristan al-Mansuri Qalāwūn founds a hospital, school, and mosque in Cairo, Egypt.

Science

1281

- The English scholar and astrologer Henry Bate writes his autobiography *Liber servi Dei/The Book of the Servant of God*. He also writes *Speculum divinorum/Mirror of the Divine*, an Aristotelian survey of European science of his time.

1282

- The Italian scholar Ristoro d'Arezzo writes his encyclopedia *Della composizione del mondo/On the Composition of the World*. Written in simple Italian, it discusses the structure of the world and develops some sound geological theories despite its links with astrology.

1283

- Count Burchard, a monk of Mt. Sion, writes *Descriptio terrae sanctae/Description of the Holy Land*. This well-observed account of the Holy Land includes an early description of the Dead Sea.

Technology

1280

- *c.* 1280 The method of silvering, allowing mirrors to be manufactured from glass, is known by this time. English monk John Peckham of Oxford, England, describes such a mirror in his writings.
- A spinning wheel for manufacturing thread from fiber is first mentioned in Europe in the Drapers' Statutes of the German town of Speyer. It is introduced from India via the Middle East.
- Alessandro della Spina and Salvino degli Armati of Florence, Italy, are traditionally credited with the invention of glasses. Their first designs use convex lenses to correct long-sightedness.

Transportation

1283

- By this time, Islamic, French, and Italian seamen are using the magnetic compass as an aid to navigation.

ARTS AND IDEAS

Architecture

1280

- Construction begins on the nave of Exeter Cathedral, England.

1281

- Construction begins on the north transept (the Portail des Libraires) at Rouen Cathedral, France.

1282

- Arnolfo di Cambio, a pupil of Nicola Pisano, designs the tomb of Cardinal de Braye at Orvieto, Italy. It sets the pattern for monumental wall–tombs in Italy.
- Construction begins on Albi Cathedral, France.

1284

- In Siena, Italy, construction begins on the façade of Siena Cathedral, under the supervision of the architect Giovanni Pisano, and the Palazzo Communale.
- The vault of the choir of Beauvais Cathedral, France, collapses, and its reconstruction is started.

Literature and Language

c. 1282

- Adanet le Roi writes *Cléomadès*, a romance about "Le Cheval de Fust," a wooden horse which flies through the air, bringing its riders fantastic adventures.

c. 1283

- Adam de la Halle "Le Bossu" ("the Hunchback") writes *Le Jeu de Robin et de Marion/The Play of Robin and Marion*, a dramatic pastoral with music written by the poet.

1284

- A plague of rats throughout Europe gives rise to the German tale *The Pied Piper of Hamlin*, a story which may have some basis in fact.

Thought and Scholarship

c. 1280

- Philippe de Beaumanoir writes his *Coutumes de Clermont en Beauvaisis/Customs of Clermont in Beauvaisis*, an examination of local legal customs and a major work of jurisprudence.

1283

- c. 1283 Spanish philosopher Ramón Llull (or Raymond Lully) begins his *Blanquerna*, a Utopian novel about Christian reform. It is the first novel written in Catalan.
- Jacob van Maerlant completes his *Spieghel Historiael/Mirror of History*, a Flemish chronicle of world history.

SOCIETY

Education

1284

- Peterhouse, the first college at Cambridge University, England, is founded.

Everyday Life

1280

- The Chinese engineer and astronomer Kuo Shou-ching produces his calendar *Shouh-shih li*, for calculating astronomical events.

Religion

c. 1280

- The Cistercian nun Mechthild of Magdeburg records her mystical visions in *Book of the Flowing Light of the Godhead*.

Sports

1283

- King Alfonso X of Castile and León produces his *Libro de acedrex, dados e tablas/Book of Chess, Dice, and Board Games*.

BIRTHS & DEATHS

1280

c. 1280 Marsilius of Padua, Italian political philosopher, forerunner of the Protestant Reformation whose *Defensor pacis/Defender of Peace* influenced the modern idea of the state, born in Padua, kingdom of Italy (–c. 1343).

August 22 Pope Nicholas III dies.

November 15 St. Albertus Magnus of Cologne ("Doctor Universalis"), Dominican bishop and Aristotelian philosopher, teacher of St. Thomas Aquinas, dies in Cologne, Germany. (c. 80).

1282

December Llywelyn ap Gruffydd, native Welsh prince of Gwynedd and prince of Wales who fought against the English kings Henry III and Edward I, is killed in battle.

1283

- Al-Qazwini, Arab scholar, writer of *Marvels of Created Things and their Singularities* (an illustrated cosmographical encyclopedia) and *Marvels of the Countries* (a geographical encyclopedia), dies.
- Margaret the Maid of Norway, Queen of Scotland 1286–90, daughter of Eric II of Norway and last Scottish monarch descended from Malcolm III Canmore, born (–1290).

October David ap Gruffydd, last native Welsh prince of Gwynedd and last native Welsh claimant to the title prince of Wales, leader of a major rebellion against the English, executed in Shrewsbury, England.

1284

- Simone Martini, leading Italian Gothic painter noted for his frescoes, born in Siena, Italy (–1344).

April 4 Alfonso X the Wise, king of Castile and Léon 1252–84, writer of *Cantigas de Santa María*, poems about the Virgin Mary written in Galician–Portuguese, who arranged translations of Arab works on sciences including astronomy, astrology, and clocks, dies in Seville, Spain (62).

April 25 Edward II of Caernarvon, king of England 1307–27, son of Edward I, born in Caernarvon, Wales (–1327).

1285–1289

POLITICS, GOVERNMENT, AND ECONOMICS

Business and Economics

1285

- Two Chinese pirates, Zhu Qing and Zhang Xuan, are granted lucrative contracts to bring grain from the south of China to the north. They exploit their position and make substantial profits.

1286

- King Philip IV of France introduces the "Gabelle," a royal monopoly for the sale of salt in France.

Colonization

1285

- The Teutonic Knights (a German Christian military order) found Strasbourg, on the River Drewenz, beginning their occupation, colonization, and conversion of Lithuania.

Politics and Government

1285

- King Edward I of England issues the second Statute of Westminster, *De donis conditionalibus*, concerning feudal tenures, and the Statute of Winchester, for the maintenance of public order. The former follows a royal inquiry into tenures of the crown known as "Kirkby's Quest."
- King Yekunno-Amlak of Ethiopia dies. His reign has seen a careful policy of support for the church. He is succeeded by his son Yagba-Siyon.
- Umar Walasma, Sultan of Ifat, annexes the Mahzumite kingdom of Shoa.
- An outbreak of the plague devastates the French army of King Philip III the Bold, forcing them to retreat from their invasion of Aragon.

January 7   Charles of Anjou, King of Sicily, dies. He is succeeded by his son, Charles II (of Salerno).

March 9   The Mongols, invading the Punjab, India, under Tamar-Kahn, kill Mohammad Khan, the heir of Balban, Sultan of Delhi.

April 2   Jacopo Savelli is elected Pope Honorius IV.

May 20   King John I of Cyprus and Jerusalem dies. He is succeeded by his 14-year-old brother, Henry II.

June 27   King Philip III of France invades Aragon on his "crusade" for Pope Martin IV against King Pedro III of Aragon and begins the siege of Gerona.

July 7   Dietrich Holzschuh, who claims to be the Holy Roman Emperor Frederick II, is burned to death by King Rudolf I of Germany, the Holy Roman Emperor, thus suppressing a revolt.

September 7   King Philip III of France takes the town of Gerona in Aragon. He now withdraws from his "crusade" against King Pedro III of Aragon as his army is ravaged by disease.

October 5   King Philip III the Bold of France dies of the plague. He is succeeded by his son, Philip IV the Fair.

October 31   King Magnus Birgersson, called Barn-Lock, of Sweden, whose arbitration King Eric V of Norway is compelled to accept because of a blockade by the league of German towns (Hanseatic League), pronounces in favor of the German towns in their dispute with Norway over trading privileges.

November 2   King Pedro III the Great of Aragon dies. He is succeeded by his sons, Alfonso III in Aragon and James II in Sicily.

1286

- In the writ of *Circumspecte agatis*, King Edward I of England defines the issues triable only in ecclesiastical courts.
- The Chinese emperor Kublai Khan's army invading Dai Viet (modern northern Vietnam) is defeated. He therefore abandons his preparations for the conquest of Japan.
- The Mongols under Nogay, Khan of "the Nogay Horde" (between the Dnieper and Danube rivers), raid Poland and Galicia.

March 19   King Alexander III of Scotland dies. His heir is his granddaughter, Margaret, the daughter of King Eric II of Norway.

November 11   Eric V Clipping, King of Denmark, is murdered. He is succeeded by his son, Eric VI Menved.

1287

- Balban, Sultan of Delhi, India, dies. He is succeeded by his grandson, Kaiqubad.
- King Alfonso III of Aragon confirms the *Privilegio General* granted to the Union of Aragon (nobles and municipalities) in 1283.
- Rabban Sauma, a Nestorian monk of Beijing, China, visits European courts as a Mongol envoy. His travels are recorded.
- The army of Kublai Khan, the Mongol emperor of China, is repelled during its attempted invasion of Dai Viet (modern northern Vietnam), but then invades

Burma (now Myanmar) and destroys the kingdom of Pagan. The fall of Pagan allows the emergence of several principalities of the Thais, who have recently been moving southward into Burma and Cambodia, while Burma itself is divided into three states.

- The Mongols invading the Punjab, India, are massacred near Lahore.
- Tuda-Mangu, Khan of the "Golden Horde," dies. He is succeeded by Tele-Buga.

April 20   The Mamelukes take the Christian port of Lattakieh, in Syria, after an earthquake.

May 31   The Genoese defeat the Venetian fleet off the port of Acre in the kingdom of Jerusalem (modern Akko, Israel), and blockade the coast of Outremer, the Christian kingdom in the Middle East.

June 23   King James of Sicily repulses an Angevin invasion of Sicily and his ally the Genoese admiral Roger Loria defeats the Angevin fleet off Castellammare.

July 15   King Edward I of England and King Alfonso III of Aragon make a treaty of alliance at Oléron, France.

1288

- Leszek III the Black, Grand Prince of Poland, dies without issue. There are several candidates for the succession. The Mongol raids into Poland (since 1282) now cease.

February 2   Jerome of Ascoli is elected Pope Nicholas IV. He soon receives an ambassador from the ilkhan Arghūn of Persia, who has been visiting the European kings to organize a joint crusade against Egypt.

July 7   John I, Duke of Brabant, defeats and captures Archbishop Siegfried of Cologne at Worringen, so winning possession of the duchy of Limburg.

October 27   By the Treaty of Campofranco, brought about through the mediation of King Edward I of England, King Alfonso III of Aragon releases King Charles II of Naples.

December 12   Obizzo II, Marquess of Este, is accepted as lord of Modena.

1289

- King Dinis of Portugal makes a concordat with the papacy that regulates the relations of the crown and clergy.
- Pope Nicholas IV sends the Franciscan Giovanni of Monte Corvino to Persia to attempt to establish an alliance with the ilkhan Arghūn. The same year, Nicholas grants half the papal revenues to the College of Cardinals.

May 29   Pope Nicholas IV crowns Charles II (of Salerno) as king of Sicily.

June 2   Florence defeats Arezzo at Campaldino and so establishes its supremacy in Tuscany.

November 6   King Eric II of Norway and the guardians of Scotland make terms with King Edward I of England in the Treaty of Salisbury for his custody of Margaret of Norway, Queen of Scotland, heir to the late Alexander III of Scotland.

November 11   Giovanni Dandolo, Doge of Venice, dies. He is succeeded by Pietro Gradenigo.

SCIENCE, TECHNOLOGY, AND MEDICINE

Ecology

1287

- A storm causes many deaths by drowning in Holland, when the Zuider Zee engulfs more land and reaches its greatest extent to date.

Health and Medicine

1288

- The Muslim physician ibn-al-Nafis writes a *Commentary on the Canon* on the great medical work *Qanun/Canon of Medicine* by the 11th century Arab Avicenna, which includes a theory of the circulation of the blood.

Science

1287

- The Italian physician Rufinus writes his *Herbal*, a popular book of medicinal herbs and botany.

1288

- The Italian astrologer Bartholomew of Parma writes his treatise *Breviloquium geomantiae* on geomancy (divination through geometry and geographical features).

Technology

1285

- When many Europeans damage their eyesight watching an eclipse of the sun, French astronomer William of St-Cloud uses a camera obscura to project its image onto a board and watch it safely.

1288

- The Jewish astronomer Jacob ben Makir ibn Tibbon writes a Hebrew treatise on the construction and use of an instrument called the quadrant. This is a considerably simpler device than the astrolabe for making astronomical measurements.

1289

- Glasses are available; they are mentioned in Sandro di Popozo's work *Traité de Conduite de la Famille/Treatise on the Running of the Family.*
- The block printing of complete manuscript pages is introduced for the first time in Europe at Ravenna, Italy.

Transportation

1285

- English highroads are widened to make travel easier and to increase visibility, deterring the numerous gangs of robbers and bandits hiding in English woodlands.

1289

- The Chinese Mongol ruler Kublai Khan completes the extension of the Chinese Grand Canal (originally completed around 605), linking Beijing with the Chang Jiang River.

ARTS AND IDEAS

Architecture

1289

- The Ali Şerefeddir Arslanhane Mosque is built in Ankara, in the Seljuk sultanate of Rūm (modern Turkey).

Arts

1285

- The *Rucellai Madonna* is painted as the altarpiece for the Church of Santa Maria Novella in Florence, Italy. Once attributed to Cimabue, it is now thought to be the work of the Sienese painter Duccio.

Literature and Language

c. **1285**

- Italian writer Jacopone da Todi writes *Laudi spirituali/ Hymns of Praise*, the finest examples of Franciscan religious verse.

c. **1286**

- Jewish scholar Moses de León compiles the *Zohar*, which brings together classics of cabalistic (mystical) literature.

- William Durandus compiles his *Rationale divinorum officiorum/Rationale of the Divine Offices*, a compendium of liturgical knowledge, which will be printed for the first time in 1459.

c. **1288**

- Persian poet 'Irāqī writes *Lama'āt/The Book of Light Beams*, a work in poetry and prose inspired by the mystical philosopher Ibn-al-Arabī.

Thought and Scholarship

1285

- Giles of Rome, a pupil of Thomas Aquinas, writes *De regimine principium/The Government of Princes* for his pupil, the future King Philip IV the Fair of France.

1286

- William of Moerbeke translates Aristotle's *Politics* and *Nicomachean Ethics* from Greek.

c. **1287**

- Fra Salimbene of Parma writes *Chronica/Chronicle*, which provides valuable historical material on the early history of the Franciscans.

SOCIETY

Education

1289

- Gloucester Hall (now Worcester College, Oxford University) is founded for Benedictine monks in Oxford, England.

BIRTHS & DEATHS

1285

c. 1285 William of Ockham, English Franciscan philosopher, founder of nominalism, and originator of "Ockham's razor," the principle that entities are not to be multiplied beyond necessity, born in Ockham, Surrey (–1349).

March 28 Pope Martin IV dies.

1286

c. 1286 Odoric of Pordenone, Franciscan friar known for the account of his travels in China, born in Villanova, near Pordenone, Aquilia (–1331).

- Bar Hebraeus, Syrian scholar, writer of *The Butter of Wisdom*, an encyclopedia of philosophy, dies.

- John of Jandun, a leading commentator on Aristotle (via Averroës), born in Jandun, France (–1328).

March 19 Alexander III, King of Scotland 1249–86, dies near Kinghorn, Fife, Scotland (44).

1287

- Konrad von Würzburg, a poet writing in Middle High German, dies. His major works are *Der Schwanenritter/The Swan Knight*, a narrative on the Lohengrin theme, and the epic *Der Trojanische Krieg/ The Trojan War*.

April 3 Pope Honorius IV dies.

1288

- Levi ben Gershom (or Gersonides), French Jewish mathematician, philosopher, Talmudic scholar, and astronomer, born in Bagnols-sur-Cèze, France (–1344).

- Orhan, second ruler of the Ottoman Empire 1324–60, who expanded the domain of the empire into the Balkans, born (–1360).

1289

October 4 Louis X, King of France 1314–16 and King of Navarre 1305–14, born in Paris, France (–1316).

1290–1294

POLITICS, GOVERNMENT, AND ECONOMICS

Politics and Government

1290

- King Edward I issues the third Statutes of Westminster, *Quia emptores*—on the sale of feudal tenures—and *Quo warranto*. These establish the accession of Richard I in 1189 as the limit of legal memory.
- King Przemysław II of Poland cedes Little Poland to King Wenceslas II of Bohemia, who also acquires the city of Kraków.
- The 'Bri-gung monastery in Tibet leads a revolt against Mongol overlordship. It is put down by the Sa-skya and Mongol troops, who raze the rebellious monastery.

June 13 Kaiqubad, the last slave king of Delhi, India, is murdered. He is succeeded by Firuz II, founder of the Khalji dynasty.

July 18 By the Treaty of Brigham, the guardians of Scotland agree to the marriage of Margaret of Norway, heir to the late Alexander III of Scotland, to Edward II, son of King Edward I of England.

July 18 King Edward I of England expels the Jews from England.

July 19 King Ladislas IV of Hungary is murdered by Cumans. He is succeeded by his adopted heir, Andrew III, grandson of Andrew II. King Rudolf I of Germany invests his own son, Albert, as king, while Pope Nicholas IV favors Charles Martel of Anjou, who is crowned by a papal legate.

September Margaret, Queen of Scotland, the Maid of Norway, dies on her way from Norway to Scotland. This throws Scotland into turmoil due to the late King Alexander III of Scotland's lack of an heir.

September 8 William of Montferrat, hitherto dominant in Lombardy, north Italy, is captured and imprisoned in Alessandria, where he dies in February 1292.

November 10 Qalāwūn, the Mameluke sultan of Egypt, dies. He is succeeded by his son, al-Ashraf Khalil.

December 18 Magnus I Barn-Lock, King of Sweden, who has established feudalism, dies. He is succeeded by his son, Birger II.

1291

- Following the fall of the port of Acre in the kingdom of Jerusalem (modern Akko, Israel), the Teutonic Knights (a German Christian military order) move the headquarters of their grand master to Venice, Italy.

- Nogay, Khan of "the Nogay Horde" (between the Dnieper and Danube rivers), deposes and kills Tele-Buga and has Tokhta proclaimed as khan of the "Golden Horde."

February 2 King Philip IV of France and King Alfonso III of Aragon make peace by the Treaty of Tarascon. Alfonso restores the island of Majorca to his uncle, James.

April 6 The Mameluke sultan of Egypt, al-Ashraf Khalīl, begins the siege of the port of Acre in the kingdom of Jerusalem (modern Akko, Israel).

May 10 King Edward I of England holds an assembly of Scottish lords at Norham, England, which accepts his claim for recognition as overlord before he determines the succession to the Scottish throne.

May 18 The Mameluke sultan of Egypt, al-Ashraf Khalīl, takes and destroys the port of Acre in the kingdom of Jerusalem (modern Akko, Israel).

June 18 King Alfonso III of Aragon dies. He bequeaths the kingdom to his brother, James II, provided that the latter cedes Sicily to their brother, Frederick. James, however, retains Sicily.

July 31 With the fall of the city of Beirut to the Egyptian Mamelukes, the Latin presence in Palestine and Outremer, the crusader kingdom, is finally ended.

August 1 The Three Forest Cantons of Schwyz, Uri, and Unterwalden (in modern Switzerland) form a defensive league against the Habsburgs.

October 16 The Swiss cantons of Uri and Schwyz make a short-lived alliance with Zürich.

1292

- Albert of Habsburg defeats the Swiss Confederation but fails to take Zürich.
- King Edward I of England orders judges to provide training for the English legal profession. This is the origin of education for the bar by the Inns of Court.
- Kublai Khan, the Mongol emperor of China, sends a fleet to conquer Java in southeast Asia.
- Mongols invading Muslim India, under the leadership of Abāqa, are repulsed at Sunam.

February 2 William V the Great, Marquess of Montferrat, dies in the iron cage in which he has been kept in Alessandria since September 1290.

May 10 Adolf, Count of Nassau, is elected Holy Roman Emperor and becomes king of Germany.

November 17 King Edward I of England awards the Scottish crown to John de Balliol, son of John de Balliol.

1293

- The expedition sent to Java by Kublai Khan, the Mongol emperor of China, is repulsed.
- The German town of Lübeck and other Baltic towns, with some princes, make an alliance for their mutual protection.

- The Mongols, under Nogay, Khan of the "Nogay Horde" (between the Dnieper and Danube rivers), invade Serbia. King Stephen Uroš becomes Nogay's vassal.
- The Ordinances of Justice are enacted in Florence to prevent disorder due to the strife of the Black and White factions of the propapal Guelph party.
- Tokhta, Khan of the "Golden Horde," ravages Russia, including Vladimir and Moscow, in reestablishing Andrew as grand duke in place of Dmitri I, the vassal of Nogay, Khan of "the Nogay Horde" (between the Dnieper and Danube rivers).
- Torkil Knutson conquers Karelia and founds the port of Vyborg.

May 15   Anglo-Gascon and Norman ships fight off St.-Mahé, Brittany.

July 5   Peter, the hermit of Monte Murrone, is elected Pope Celestine V.

December 13   Pope Celestine V abdicates.

December 13   The Mameluke sultan of Egypt, al-Ashraf Khalīl, is murdered. He is succeeded by his son, an-Nasir.

1294

- Ala-ad-Din, Sultan of Delhi, India, sacks Deogir, the capital of a Hindu kingdom in West Deccan.
- King Philip IV of France imprisons Guy of Dampierre, Count of Flanders, following the betrothal of Guy's daughter to Edward of Caernarvon.
- King Przemysław II of Greater Poland inherits East Pomerania from its last prince, Mszczuj.
- King Wenceslas II of Bohemia summons the Italian legal expert Gozzo of Orvieto to codify Bohemian law.
- King Yagba-Siyon of Ethiopia dies. This is followed by a long period of civil war, resulting in the institution of the royal prison at Mt. Gishen.
- Kublai Khan, Great Khan and Mongol (Yuan) emperor of China, dies. He is succeeded by his grandson, Temür.
- The Genoese defeat the Venetians in a naval battle off Laiazzo, in Cilicia (in modern Turkey), in their struggle to control trade with the Byzantine Empire.
- The Treaty of Tönsberg concludes a dispute between King Eric II of Norway and the Hanse in the latter's favor.

January 1   King Edward I of England responds to his summons, by proxy, to the Paris Parlement to answer for attacks by Anglo-Gascons on French seamen, and agrees to surrender castles in Gascony during an inquiry. The consequent French seizure of Gascony leads to war between the two countries.

June 6   John de Balliol, King of Scotland, is subjected to a baronial committee as a result of Scottish opposition to King Edward I of England's domination.

August 24   In the Treaty of Nuremberg, King Edward I of England and the Holy Roman Emperor Adolf I of Nassau make an alliance against France.

September 30   A revolt breaks out in Wales, under Madog ap Llywelyn, preventing King Edward I of England from invading France.

December 23   Benedict Gaetani is elected Pope Boniface VIII.

SCIENCE, TECHNOLOGY, AND MEDICINE

Agriculture

1294

- The harvest fails in England, leading to widespread famine throughout the country, despite the most efficient farming methods in Europe. Continental Europe also suffers when English grain exports are stopped.

Ecology

1290

- An earthquake in China's Hebei (Hopeh) province kills 100,000 people.

1293

- An earthquake at Kamakura, seat of the Japanese shogunate on the island of Honshu, Japan, devastates the city and kills approximately 30,000 people.

Health and Medicine

1293

- Italian physician Simon of Genoa writes his medical dictionary *Synonyma medicinae/Medical Synonyms* or *Clavis sanationis/Key to Healing*, which introduces many new terms from Arab medicine.

Science

1290

- The French astronomer William of St-Cloud obtains an accurate measurement of the obliquity of the ecliptic (the angle of the sun's apparent path around the sky) at Paris, France.

1292

- The French astronomer William of St-Cloud produces an "almanach" outlining the positions of celestial bodies in the period 1292–1312. He also promotes a new and accurate ecclesiastical calendar based on his work.

1293

- The Danish astronomer Peter Nightingale develops an equatorium, an astronomical model for use in calculating and predicting eclipses.

1294

- The Italian mining engineer Gozzo compiles a mining code *Ius regale montanorum/Royal Law* for the silver mines of Kutná Hora (in the modern Czech Republic), which are now flourishing.

Technology

1291

- The glassblowing industry of Venice, Italy, the only one in Europe capable of manufacturing clear glass, is moved to the island of Murano to prevent fires. Harsh laws are passed to protect the city's monopoly in the trade.

1292

- The Italian astronomer Giovanni Campano invents an improved version of the quadrant for measuring the positions and separations of celestial bodies.

ARTS AND IDEAS

Architecture

1291

- Charing Cross, London, England, and nine other stone crosses known as Eleanor Crosses are raised to mark the stops of the funeral cortege of Queen Eleanor, Spanish wife of King Edward I of England. Their ogee arches mark the beginning of the "curvilinear" style of English Gothic architecture.

1294

- Construction begins on Florence Cathedral (the Duomo) in Italy to designs by Arnolfo di Cambio, who also carves the figures for the façade.

Arts

c. **1290**

- *Santa Trinità Madonna*, attributed to the painter Cimabue, introduces a greater naturalist style into the prevailing Byzantine style of medieval Italy.

1293

- The *Mongol Scroll* is created, providing a pictorial record of the Japanese repulse of the Mongol invasions of 1274 and 1281.

Literature and Language

c. **1290**

- The anonymous German narrative poem *Lohengrin* is written.

c. **1294**

- The first English version of the Tristan legend is recorded. Known as *Sir Tristrem*, it is wrongly traditionally attributed to Thomas of Erceldoune (Thomas the Rhymer).

Thought and Scholarship

c. **1292**

- William Durandus compiles his *Pontificale*, a carefully organized liturgical book of the Western church.

SOCIETY

Education

1290

- King Dinis of Portugal founds a university in Lisbon.

Religion

1294

- The Franciscan Giovanni of Monte Corvino establishes a Catholic mission in Beijing, China.

BIRTHS & DEATHS

1290

September Margaret the Maid of Norway, Queen of Scotland 1286–90, daughter of Eric II of Norway and last Scottish monarch descended from Malcolm III Canmore, dies in the Orkney Islands (*c.* 8).

November 28 Eleanor of Castile, Queen Consort of Edward I, dies in Harby, Nottinghamshire, England (*c.* 44).

1291

July 15 Rudolph I, German king 1273–91, first of the Habsburg dynasty, and Holy Roman Emperor, dies in Speyer, Germany (73).

October 31 Philippe de Vitry, French music theorist and composer, born in Paris, France (–1361).

December 9 Sa'di, Persian poet, a leading figure in Persian literature, dies in Shīrāz, Persia (*c.* 78).

1292

- John VI Cantacuzenus, Byzantine emperor 1341–54, later a monk and historian, born (–1383).
- Roger Bacon, English philosopher who was an exponent of experimental science, dies in Oxford, Oxfordshire, England (*c.* 72).

April 4 Pope Nicholas IV dies.

October 12 Piero Della Francesca, Florentine painter noted for his use of perspective and for his frescoes, dies in Borgo San Sepolcro, Republic of Florence (*c.* 72).

December 8 John Pecham, archbishop of Canterbury 1270–92, dies.

1293

- Philip VI, King of France 1328–50, first in the Valois dynasty, born (–1350).

1294

- Charles IV ("the Fair" or "the Bald"), King of France and (as Charles I) of Navarre 1322–28, born (–1328).
- Kublai Khan, Mongol general, grandson of Genghis Khan, conqueror of China and first emperor of the Yüan dynasty 1294, dies (*c.* 79).

1295–1299

POLITICS, GOVERNMENT, AND ECONOMICS

Business and Economics

1295

- King Philip IV of France begins to debase the French coinage.

1297

- The Japanese shogunate cancels all the debts of its retainers in order to relieve their growing impoverishment—the consequence of high living standards and partible inheritances. The Japanese "feudal" structure is collapsing under these strains.
- January 30 King Edward I of England outlaws the English clergy for their refusal to pay taxes. They surrender and are pardoned.

Politics and Government

1295

- Charles Martel of Anjou, the papal nominee to the Hungarian throne, dies.
- Ghazan, Ilkhan of Persia, adopts Islam as the state religion and, styling himself sultan, declares his independence of the great khan.
- King Edward I of England holds his second parliament attended by knights and burgesses. This is known as the "Model Parliament."
- King Sancho IV of Castile and León dies. He is succeeded by his four-year-old son, Ferdinand IV. Ferdinand's minority offers the Spanish kingdom of Aragon a chance to make territorial gains at the expense of Castile.
- Otto IV, Count of Burgundy, cedes his Franche-Comté, which was previously in the Holy Roman Empire, to France.
- Rama Khamheng, second king of Sukhodaya, conquers the Mekong and Menam valleys in Cambodia and the Malay Peninsula.
- March 5 King Edward I of England's forces defeat the Welsh, under Madog ap Llywelyn, at Maes Moydog, near Montgomery, Wales.
- June 6 Pope Boniface VIII arranges a treaty of peace, at Anagni, Italy, between King Philip IV of France, King Charles II of Sicily, and King James II of Aragon, who cedes Sicily to Charles.

- June 26 King Przemysław II of Greater Poland and Pomerania, who is emerging as the accepted ruler over Poland, is crowned its king, with papal consent.
- July 5 Scotland and France seal a treaty of alliance (the "Auld Alliance").
- July 19 Ala-ad-Din Mohammad is proclaimed as sultan of Delhi, India, following his murder of Firuz II, his uncle.
- July 31 Madog ap Llywelyn and his household submit to the justiciar of North Wales.
- August 9 Otto Visconti, archbishop of Milan, dies. His great-nephew, Matteo, succeeds as ruler of Milan and is imperial vicar in Lombardy, north Italy.
- October Ghazan, Ilkhan of Persia, restores the *jizya*, a poll tax paid by all non-Muslims.

1296

- Mangrai, a Thai leader, founds Chiang Mai, the capital of the new Thai kingdom of Lan Na.
- January 15 The Sicilians elect Frederick II of Aragon as their king.
- January 27 Florence V, Count of Holland, is murdered after renouncing the Anglo-German pact.
- February 8 King Przemysław II of Poland is murdered at the instigation of Otto of Brandenburg. He is succeeded by his son, Władysław Łokietek, as grand prince.
- February 29 Pope Boniface VIII, in his papal bull *Clericis laicos*, forbids kings to tax the clergy.
- March 30 King Edward I of England takes the town of Berwick as he begins his campaign to subdue Scotland.
- April 27 King Edward I of England defeats the Scots at Dunbar, Scotland, in his campaign to subdue the country.
- July 10 John de Balliol, King of Scotland, surrenders to King Edward I of England and abdicates.
- August 8 King Edward I of England returns from Scotland, bringing "the Stone of Destiny," on which Scottish kings are crowned, as a symbol of his conquest of Scotland, from Scone to Westminster Abbey, London, England.
- September 9 Pope Boniface VIII modifies his papal bull of February 29, *Clericis laicos*, with his *Ineffabilis amor*.

1297

- Ala-ad-Din, Sultan of Delhi, India, conquers the Hindu kingdom of Gujarat.
- Pope Boniface VIII organizes a crusade by King Charles II of Naples, King James II of Aragon, and the Genoese, against Frederick II of Sicily; he was actually Frederick II but took the title to reflect his Ghibelline sympathies as a successor to the antipapist Holy Roman Emperor Frederick II.
- Sultan Malik al-Saleh becomes the first Muslim ruler of Samudra, in north Sumatra.

- The first Irish parliament with elected members is held. A series of provisions designed to maintain peace in Ireland is outlined.
- The German bishoprics of Metz and Toul, in the Holy Roman Empire, are subjected to French rule.
- The Venetians sack the Genoese port of Kaffa, in the Crimea, in their struggle to seize control of trade with the Byzantine Empire. The Genoese ravage the Venetian island of Crete and are assisted by the emperor Andronicus II Palaeologus in massacring Venetian merchants in the Byzantine Empire.

February 2 King Edward I of England makes an alliance with Count Guy of Flanders.

February 24 In a parliament held by King Edward I of England in Salisbury, the magnates refuse to serve him in Gascony, France, unless he goes with them. He had instead planned to go to Flanders.

March 3 Sciarra Colunna attacks a convoy of papal treasure.

May 5 The Scottish nationalist William Wallace leads a Scottish rising against King Edward I of England, burning an English castle and attacking one of the king's justiciars.

May 23 Pope Boniface VIII excommunicates the Colunnas and proclaims a crusade against them.

July 31 Under pressure from King Philip IV of France, Pope Boniface VIII renounces the claims made in his papal bull *Clericis laicos* of 1296, forbidding kings to tax the clergy, in the bull *Etsi de statu*.

August 20 Guy of Flanders is defeated by French forces at Furnes.

August 24 King Edward I of England sails to Flanders to lead his allies of the Low Countries against France.

September 11 The Scottish nationalist William Wallace defeats the English forces, under Earl Warrene, at Stirling Bridge, Scotland.

October 7 King Edward I of England makes a truce with France at Vyve-St.-Bavon.

October 10 In Parliament, King Edward I of England's regent reissues the Magna Carta and the Charter of the Forest, with supplementary articles, to allay protests against Edward's administration by the magnates and the city of London.

1298

- Nogay, Mongol Khan of the "Nogay Horde" (operating between the Dnieper and Danube rivers), ravages the Crimea after defeating Tokhta, Khan of the "Golden Horde."
- Pope Boniface VIII's constitution *Cum ex eo* permits absenteeism by beneficed clergy attending universities.

1298–1299 Mohammad Abu Abdullah, a Muslim visionary, makes an abortive attempt to conquer the Christian kingdom of Ethiopia.

January 31 King Edward I of England and King Philip IV of France make a truce at Tournai.

June 23 The German electors depose the Holy Roman Emperor Adolf I of Nassau.

July 2 In a battle near Göllheim (near Worms), Germany, the Holy Roman Emperor Adolf I of Nassau is defeated and killed by Albert of Habsburg.

July 22 King Edward I of England defeats the Scots, under the nationalist William Wallace, at Falkirk, Scotland, but is unable to subdue the country.

July 27 Albert of Habsburg is elected Holy Roman Emperor.

September 8 The Genoese destroy the Venetian navy off the Dalmatian island of Curzola in their struggle to gain control of trade with the Byzantine Empire. As a result, Venice "closes" its Great Council, a council of nobles who deal with administrative and legislative affairs, restricting its membership.

September 9 Pope Boniface VIII's "crusade" against the Colunna family concludes with the surrender of Palestrina, which he razes to the ground. He employs the lands confiscated from the Colunnas to found a state for his nephew, Peter Gaetani.

1299

- King Eric II of Norway dies. He is succeeded by his brother, Haakon V.
- The sultan of Delhi, Ala-ad-Din, repulses a Mongol army outside Delhi, India.
- Tokhta, Khan of the "Golden Horde," defeats and kills Nogay, Khan of the "Nogay Horde" (between the Dnieper and Danube rivers), on the River Kagamlyk. The Mongols in eastern Europe are thus reunited.

April 27 Ghazan, Ilkhan of Persia, defeats Sulamish, his rebellious governor of Rūm, at Eskishehir (in modern Turkey). Sulamish escapes to Cairo, Egypt, but on return to Cilicia is handed over to Ghazan.

May 5 Matteo Visconti negotiates a peace between Genoa and Venice, ending their war (since 1261) to control trade with the Byzantine Empire.

June 27 Pope Boniface VIII upholds Scottish independence in his bull *Scimus fili*.

July 4 The fleets of Genoa and Aragon defeat King Frederick II of Sicily off Cape Orlando, Sicily.

September 5 King Philip IV of France and the Holy Roman Emperor Albert I make an alliance by the Treaty of Strasbourg.

November 10 John I, Count of Holland and Zeeland, dies. His uncle, John of Avesnes, Count of Hainault, seizes the counties despite the opposition of the Holy Roman Emperor Albert I.

November 23 Sultan Ghazan of Persia defeats the Mamelukes of Egypt at Salamia, near Homs, Syria.

SCIENCE, TECHNOLOGY, AND MEDICINE

Agriculture

1297

- Dutch farmers drain land around the delta of the River Vistula and found "Prussian Holland."

Ecology

c. 1297

- The moa, a giant flightless bird of New Zealand, is hunted to extinction by the Maori settlers on North

Island, although it may survive a while longer on South Island.

Health and Medicine

1296

- The Milan-born physician Lanfranchi brings Italian surgery to Paris, France, writing his *Chirurgia magna/ Major Surgery*, which promotes a union of surgery and internal medicine.

Science

1297

- The Italian astrologer Guido Bonatti of Forli writes a guide to electional, or horary astrology called *Liber astrologicum/Book of Astrology*.

Technology

1298

- The earliest English record of the spinning wheel in use for the manufacture of woolen yarn dates to this time.
- The victory of the English king Edward I against the Scots at Falkirk, Scotland, demonstrates the value of the longbow, a cheap but powerful weapon capable of firing arrows in rapid succession.

Transportation

c. 1295

- Venetian shipwrights develop the huge, oar-powered boats known as "great galleys," which are up to 50 meters long. These will allow Venetian merchants to dominate Europe.

ARTS AND IDEAS

Architecture

1298–1329

- The choir of Barcelona Cathedral, Spain, is built.

1299–1301

- The Palazzo Vecchio in Florence, Italy, is built.

Arts

1296

- Master Honoré, one of the first identified French miniaturists, decorates a breviary (a book of psalms, hymns, and prayers), possibly for King Philip IV of France.

1297–1301

- Italian sculptor Giovanni Pisano sculpts the pulpit of Sant' Andrea, Pistoia, Italy.

1299

- The Yuan dynasty Chinese artist Li K'an writes the treatise *Chu pu xiang lu* on bamboo, his favorite artistic subject.

Literature and Language

c. 1295

- Brunetto Latini writes *Tesoro/Treasure*, a didactic allegory in verse, which is the earliest extant example in Italian poetry.

1296

- Wang Ying-lin writes *Yü hai/The Sea of Jade* (an encyclopedia) and *San-tzu ching* (a primer for children on history and philosophy).

Thought and Scholarship

1296

- French scholar William of St-Cloud writes *Kalendarium Regine* for Queen Marie of France, an introduction to the use and importance of calendrical science.

1297

- Chou Ta-kuan writes *Chên la fêng t'u chi*, a description of Cambodian customs observed in his embassy in the period 1296–97.

1298

- Marco Polo writes *Il milione/The Million* (*Travels of Marco Polo*) while in prison. It is the first European account of the geography, economy, civilization, and government of China.

BIRTHS & DEATHS

1295

- *c.* 1295 Alexis, Metropolitan of Russia 1353–78, who was the first member of the Russian church to participate in governing Russia, born in Moscow (–1378).
- Thaddeus Alderotti, founder of the medical school at Bologna, Italy, whose works include the pioneering treatise on hygiene *De conservanda sanitate/On the Preservation of Health*, dies.

1296

- Philippe de Rémi, sire de Beaumanoir, French jurist, who wrote *Coutumes de Beauvaisis/ Customs of Beauvaisis*, an early codification of French law, dies (*c.* 50).
- November 1 Guillaume Durand, bishop of Mende, an influential scholar of canon law and the liturgy, dies in Rome, Italy (*c.* 66).

SOCIETY

Everyday Life

1299
- Italian tarot cards are first mentioned in a manuscript. They are used both for gaming and fortune telling, and the modern pack of playing cards derives from them.

Religion

1297
August 8   Pope Boniface VIII canonizes Louis IX of France.

Sports

1299
- Lawn bowls is played at Southampton, England. It is the oldest bowling green still in use.

1300–1304

POLITICS, GOVERNMENT, AND ECONOMICS

Politics and Government

1300
- A new wave of Turks, known as the "Ottomans" after their founder Osman, are driven westward by the Mongols. They defeat the Byzantines in Bithynia, and occupy western Anatolia. The Byzantine Empire holds on only in Nicaea, Heraclea, and Smyrna.
- King Wenceslas II of Bohemia, in a currency reform, issues the coin the *grosch* of Prague.
- The Milanese expel Matteo I, ruler of Milan, nephew of Ottone Visconti, archbishop of Milan, and permit the Torriani to return. The Visconti are one of the most powerful families in Milan and will later achieve dominance.
- The Shans in Burma defeat a punitive Mongol expedition from China, following Burmese rebellion after the death of Quibilai in 1294.

January 1   The city of Damascus surrenders to Sultan Ghazan, ruler of the Mongol ilkhanate of Persia and Anatolia.

February 2   Pope Boniface VIII proclaims a jubilee in Rome. He also initiates a war against Margaret Aldobrandeschi, Countess Palatine of the Patrimony in Tuscany, the estranged wife of his great-nephew, Loffred Gaetani.

May 5   Guy of Flanders, having been deserted by all his allies, surrenders to King Philip IV of France and is imprisoned. Flanders is placed under French governance, and is adminstered by Jacques de Châtillon, the uncle of the queen.

June 14   Roger Loria, a Sicilian admiral who fights for the Aragonese rulers against the Angerins (house of Anjou) for control of Sicily, wins a second naval victory over Frederick III, King of Sicily.

July 7   Whilst campaigning in Scotland with the feudal levy, King Edward I of England takes Caerlaverock Castle in the southwest. This proves to be the high point of an otherwise unsuccessful campaign.

August 8   The Holy Roman Emperor Albert I abandons his siege of Nijmegen in the war against John of Hainault. This failure is followed by a revolt of the Rhenish princes.

December 12   In a struggle for the throne of Sicily, Frederick III, King of Sicily, defeats Charles of Naples at Falconaria, near Trapani, Sicily.

1301
- Ala-ad-Din, Sultan of Delhi, India, initiates regular taxation and prohibits consumption of wine. His anti-Hindu legislation is a departure from the Muslim tradition of toleration.

January 14   King Andrew III of Hungary, the last of the Árpád dynasty, dies. King Wenceslas II of Bohemia declines the crown, but his son Wenceslas is elected and crowned, taking the Hungarian name of László (Ladislas). Pope Boniface VIII supports the candidature of Charles Robert of Anjou.

February 7   King Edward I of England revives the title prince of Wales and confers it on his son, Edward of Caernarvon (later to become Edward II). This act is popular in Wales.

April 13   Pope Boniface VIII summons the Holy Roman Emperor Albert I, whom he refuses to recognize as such, to answer for the murder of the previous emperor Adolf I of Nassau at Göllheim.

May 5   During a period of internal struggle within the propapal Guelph party, the Black faction is expelled from Florence.

July 7   King Edward I of England begins his sixth campaign in Scotland. It is fought in two parts: the prince of Wales, under the guidance of the Earl of Lincoln, fights the campaign in Galloway, whilst Edward I operates in the southeast of Scotland from a base at Berwick.

July 27 Ghazi Osman, founder of the Ottoman (Turkish) dynasty, defeats Byzantine forces at Baphaeum near Nicaea.

November 1 Charles, Count of Valois, whom Pope Boniface VIII has called into Italy as "Peacemaker," enters Florence. He allows the expelled Black faction of the propapal Guelph party to return.

December 12 In response to King Philip IV of France's proceedings for treason against Bernard Saiset, the papal legate in France, Pope Boniface VIII rebukes the king for misgovernment in his papal bulls *Salvator mundi/Savior of the World* and *Ausculta fili* and announces his trial.

1302

January 27 The Black faction of the propapal Guelph party, which has seized power in Florence, sentences its opponents the Whites (including the poet Dante) to death or exile.

April 8 King Mohammad II of Granada dies. He is succeeded by his son, Mohammad III.

April 10 King Philip IV of France holds the first known meeting of the Estates General (assembly containing representatives of the three estates, aristocracy, clergy, and commons) in Paris, France, to rally national opinion against Pope Boniface VIII.

May 5 Pope Boniface VIII appoints Charles of Valois, the younger brother of King Philip IV of France, captain general of the papal and Neapolitan forces.

May 18 The French garrison is massacred in the "Matins of Bruges," beginning the revolt of the Flemings against French occupation. The whole of Western Flanders is soon up in arms, and the French royal army is sent in to crush the rebels.

July 11 The French army, considered to be the finest fighting force of the time, is destroyed by the Flemish urban militia at Courtrai, Flanders. The Flemings repel the French cavalry, inflicting over a thousand casualties at a cost of only a few hundred casualties to their side.

September 24 Following the destruction of Charles of Valois's army by malaria, a truce between Charles of Naples and Frederick II of Sicily is made by the Treaty of Caltabellotta. Frederick's kingdom is named Trinacria. This ends the war of the "Sicilian Vespers." Frederick's Catalan mercenary troops, now unemployed, form the Grand Company and go to Greece.

November 18 Pope Boniface VIII asserts temporal supremacy over secular princes in the papal bull *Unam Sanctam Ecclesiam/One Holy Church*, as part of his ongoing conflict with King Philip IV of France.

1303

- Andronicus II Palaeologus, the Byzantine emperor, engages the Grand Company (formerly Frederick II of Sicily's Catalan mercenary troops).
- King Edward I of England promulgates the *Carta Mercatoria*, which confirms the rights and privileges of foreign merchants, in return for the payment of additional dues. This is part of his attempt to encourage and control trade as his wars become increasingly costly.
- King Eric VI of Denmark confirms the privileges of the Danish church, ending the dispute begun in 1254.

- The Egyptian Mamelukes defeat the Mongols of the ilkhanate at Marj as-Saffar and recover Damascus for the Mameluke sultan an-Nasir.
- The Mongols unsuccessfully besiege Delhi, India.

March 3 King Philip IV of France publishes *La Grande ordonnance/The Great Order* for "the reform of the kingdom" in response to baronial pressure.

April 4 Pope Boniface VIII demands the submission of King Philip IV of France under pain of excommunication.

April 30 Pope Boniface VIII recognizes Albert I of Habsburg as Holy Roman Emperor.

May 5 King Edward I of England begins his seventh campaign in Scotland. The feudal levy is summoned to Berwick, where a military progress to Elgin commences.

May 20 King Philip IV of France and King Edward I of England make peace in the Treaty of Paris, in which the French duchy of Gascony is restored to Edward for which he must pay fealty to Philip.

June 24 King Philip IV of France calls the European princes to a general council to hear charges against Pope Boniface VIII.

September 7 An Italian force, led by King Philip IV of France's agent Guillaume de Nogaret and Sciarra Colonna, breaks into the papal palace at Anagni, Italy, and arrests Pope Boniface VIII as he is preparing to excommunicate Philip IV.

September 9 King Philip IV of France releases Count Guy of Flanders in an attempt to calm the Flemish uprising, after an unsuccessful French campaign in Flanders.

September 12 Pope Boniface VIII, imprisoned in Anagni, Italy, by an Italian force for King Philip IV of France, is released in a rising by the people of Anagni.

September 24 Pope Boniface VIII, in the papal bull *Super Petri solio*, releases the French from their allegiance to King Philip IV of France; this is one of his final moves against the French king.

October 22 The Italian clergyman Niccolò Boccasini is elected Pope Benedict XI following the death of Pope Boniface VIII.

1304

- A revolt in Hungary causes King Ladislas (Wenceslas) IV of Hungary to return to Bohemia. The Holy Roman Emperor Albert I invades Bohemia but retires on failing to take Kutná Hora. King Wenceslas II of Bohemia is then expelled from Poland and King Władysław restored.
- Osman, leader of the Ottoman Turks, takes Nicaea in Anatolia (modern Turkey). The Grand Company (mercenary troops engaged by Andronicus II Palaeologus, the Byzantine emperor) brings to an end the siege of Philadelphia by the Turks and then plunders Byzantine territory.
- The Genoese seize Chios, a town on the Dardanelles, from the Byzantines.
- The Mongols raiding India are defeated by Ala-ad-Din, Sultan of Delhi.

March 3 Prince Daniel of Moscow, who has extended his state by conquest, dies. He is succeeded by his son, Juri.

March 3 The Scots submit to King Edward I of England in a parliament at St. Andrews, Scotland.

April 26 The warring Florentine propapal Guelph factions, the Blacks and the Whites, are reconciled on the initiative of Pope Benedict XI.

June 10   Extreme members of the Black propapal Guelph faction raise a fire which destroys the center of Florence, restarting factional conflict.

August 18   The French defeat the Flemings, but not decisively, at Mons-en-Pévèle, between Lille and Douai.

SCIENCE, TECHNOLOGY, AND MEDICINE

Agriculture

c. 1300
- Beer made from hops is common in the Low Countries.

Ecology

1304

November 1   Northern Germany suffers a devastating flood on All Saints' Day.

Health and Medicine

1300
- The first major outbreak of leprosy in western Europe peters out as the incidence of the disease declines.

1302
- The physician Bartolomeo de Varignana of Bologna, Italy, a strong supporter of the medical tradition of Galen, gives the first written account of an autopsy examination.

Math

1300
- Chinese mathematician Chu Shih-chieh writes *Szu-yuen Yu-chien/The Precious Mirror of the Four Elements*, containing a number of methods for solving equations.

Science

1300

c. 1300   A European alchemist writing under the name of the 9th-century Arab Al-Jabir (Geber) writes *Summa perfectionis/The Sum of Perfection*, giving details of the manufacture of mineral acids.
- Marc the Greek writes *Liber ignium/The Book of Fire*, in which he describes an everlasting light source made from crushed glow worm paste. He also describes the composition of "Greek fire," a mixture which, when wetted, explodes and may be projected as a weapon, as used in the Byzantine Empire.

1303
- The Italian physician Pietro d'Abano of Padua writes *Conciliator differentiarum philosophorum et praecipe medicinorum/Reconciliation of Philosophical and*

Especially Medical Differences, which attempts to reconcile the Arab and Christian interpretations of Aristotelian science, and particularly medicine.

Technology

1304
- Gunpowder blowpipes, made of bamboo with a copper lining, are in use as weapons in Arabia at this time. They are probably used to fire arrows.

Transportation

1302
- Construction work begins on the Porto Grande, an extension to the harbor at the Italian port of Naples, for Charles II of Anjou.

ARTS AND IDEAS

Architecture

1300
- Construction begins on the Franciscan Church of Santa Croce in Florence, Italy, probably to designs by the Italian sculptor Arnolfo di Cambio.

1303
- The Madrassa (collegiate mosque) of an-Nasir Mohammed in Cairo, Egypt, is completed, parts of which are taken from a crusader church.

Arts

1300
- Frescoes are included in the Church of S. Francesco in Assisi, Italy, based on the life of St. Francis and revealing an unprecedented humanity and realism. Their traditional attribution to Giotto is questioned in modern times.
- Italian sculptor Arnolfo di Cambio carves the bust and tomb of Pope Boniface VIII.

1301
- Italian artist Giovanni Pisano sculpts the pulpit in the Church of Sant' Andrea in Pistoia, Italy.

1302
- Italian artist Cimabue completes his mosaic *St. John* in the apse of Pisa Cathedral.

Literature and Language

c. 1300
- Guido Cavalcanti, a friend of the Italian poet Dante Alighieri, writes "Donna mi prega."
- Italian poet Dante Alighieri completes his *Vità nuova/New Life*, including 25 sonnets, 4 canzoni, and a ballata, with linking prose telling the story of the poet's love for Beatrice (Portinari).
- Persian scholar Al-Kāshāni publishes a treatise on

Persian pottery. It includes a description of the Chinese technique of glazing earthenware (faïence).

- The anonymous *Cursor Mundi/Surveyor of the World*, a long religious poem in the Northern English dialect of Middle English, is written.
- The manuscript *The White Book of Ryydderch*, a compilation of traditional Welsh tales, is written. Based on ancient Celtic myths and influenced by French romances, it forms the first part of a collection of Welsh stories known as the *Mabinogion*.
- The Spanish romance *El caballero Zifar/Zifar the Knight*, based on the Arthurian legend, is written. It is the earliest romance in Spanish literature. It may have been written by the priest Ferrán Martínez.

1303
- English scholar Robert Mannyng completes his *Handlynge Synne*, a long didactic poem of pastoral theology enlivened with colorful anecdotes.

c. **1304**
- Italian writer Dante Alighieri writes the first part of his *De vulgari eloquentia/On the Vulgar Tongue*. Written in Latin, it is a defense of Italian as a medium for serious literature.

Theater and Dance

c. **1300**
- Chinese playwright Guan Han-qing is active. Regarded as China's greatest classical dramatist, his most important works include *Snow in Midsummer*.

Thought and Scholarship

c. **1300**
- German theologian and scientist Dietrich of Freiburg publishes *De intellectu et intelligibili/On the Intellect and the Intelligible*, which tries to reconcile Christianity and classical philosophy.

1302
- French Dominican scholar John of Paris publishes *De potestate regia et papali/The Power of the King and the Power of the Pope*, a defense of French sovereignty against the claims of the papacy.

SOCIETY

Education

1303
- The University of Rome is founded in Italy.

Everyday Life

1300
- *c.* 1300 The popularity of home brewing of ale increases in England. The brewing is usually done by women, and the produce is often sold.
- Arnold de Villanova, a Spanish-born physician and professor at the Montpellier medical school in France, distills brandy for the first time.

Religion

1300
- Pope Boniface VIII announces the first Jubilee Year, a centenary year during which special indulgences are authorized.

c. **1301**
- The German nun St. Gertrude, one of the most important mystics of the Middle Ages, inspires the cult of the Sacred Heart of Jesus.

Sports

c. **1300–1400**
- The game of battledore shuttlecock is played in England. It is a precursor of badminton in which players with rackets or paddles aim to keep a shuttlecock in the air for as long as possible.
- Calcio, a form of football, is played in Florence, Italy. The game is still played in Florence on certain festival days. "Calcio" is also the modern Italian term for football.

BIRTHS & DEATHS

1300
- Richard Rolle of Hampole, English ascetic and hermit, and influential mystic writer, born in Thornton, Yorkshire, England (–1349).
- Taddeo Gaddi, painter, follower of Giotto, whose best-known work is the *Tree of Life* fresco at Santa Croce, born in Florence, Italy (–*c.* 1366).

1301
- Khaidu, Khan of Chaghadai in central Asia, dies.
- –1310 Arnolfo di Cambio, Italian sculptor and architect, whose works include the design of the Duomo and (probably) the Palazzo Vecchio in Florence, dies in Florence, Italy (*c.* 65).

1303
- *c.* 1303 St. Bridget, patron saint of Sweden and founder of the Brigantine Order, born in Sweden (–1373).
- October 11 Boniface VIII, Italian pope 1294–1303, who published *Liber sextus/Book Six*, and whose authority was constantly challenged by the emerging European monarchies, dies in Rome (*c.* 66).

1304
- February 24 Ibn Battūtah, celebrated Arab traveler who undertook journeys totaling 75,000 miles to almost all the Muslim world, as well as Russia, China, and Sumatra, and described his travels in *Rihlah*, born in Tangier, Morocco (–1377).
- July 7 Benedict XI (Niccolò Boccasini), Pope 1303–04, dies in Rome.
- July 20 Petrarch (Petrarca), Italian poet whose work was a major influence on the growth of Renaissance poetry, born in Arezzo, Tuscany (–1374).

1305–1309

POLITICS, GOVERNMENT, AND ECONOMICS

Business and Economics

1306

- Tëmur-Öljeitü, the great khan, permanently restores the *jizya*, the compulsory poll tax for non-Muslims.

Human Rights

1306

- French king Philip IV the Fair expels the Jews from France, confiscating their possessions.

Politics and Government

1305

- Andrew III, Grand Duke of Vladimir, dies. He is succeeded by Michael II, Prince of Tver.
- King Edward I of England's Ordinance of Trailbaston empowers the king to appoint judicial commissions to try the perpetrators of particular outrages. It indicates the decline of public order.
- King Edward I of England introduces measures to standardize certain weights and measures, including the yard and the acre.

March 3 Guy, Count of Flanders, dies and is succeeded by his son, Robert of Béthune.

April 2 Queen Joanna of France and Navarre dies. Her son Louis, later King Louis X of France, succeeds to the kingdom of Navarre.

April 4 Roger de Flor, the captain of the Catalan mercenary Grand Company, is murdered in Constantinople. His followers defeat the imperial troops of Andronicus II Palaeologus, the Byzantine emperor, and plunder Thrace.

June 5 The French clergyman Bertrand de Got is elected as Pope Clement V in Rome.

June 6 In the Treaty of Athis-sur-Orge, King Philip IV of France restores Flanders to Robert of Béthune for the payment of an indemnity.

June 21 King Wenceslas II of Bohemia dies. He is succeeded by his son, Wenceslas III, who makes peace with the Holy Roman Emperor Albert I.

August 4 King Wenceslas III of Bohemia is murdered, ending the Přemyslid dynasty.

August 23 The Scottish nationalist William Wallace is executed in London, England, as a traitor against King Edward I of England, after having been betrayed and captured in Glasgow, Scotland. He is tried in Westminster Hall, London, and promptly hanged and quartered. His head is displayed on London Bridge.

September 9 King Edward I of England enacts an ordinance for the government of Scotland. The country is to be ruled by a governor, a lieutenant, and a chamberlain. There is also to be a separate Scottish parliament.

October 10 The Holy Roman Emperor Albert I compels the Bohemians to elect his son, Rudolf of Habsburg, as their king.

November 14 Clement V is crowned as pope in Lyon, France (technically in the Holy Roman Empire).

1306

- A Mongol invasion of India, to avenge the defeat of Ali Beg, is defeated on the River Indus.

January 1 The Italian cities of Modena and Reggio revolt against Azzo d'Este of Ferrara.

January 10 Robert the Bruce, Earl of Carrick, kills John Comyn, nephew of John de Balliol, his rival as a claimant to the Scottish crown.

March 25 Robert I the Bruce is crowned king of Scotland at Scone.

April 10 Pistoia surrenders, after an 11-month siege, to Florence and Lucca, after which they divide its territories between them.

May 7 The Bolognese revolt against the papacy and expel cardinal Napoleon Orsini, the rector.

June 26 English forces defeat Robert I the Bruce, King of Scotland, at Methven in Scotland, after which his power collapses.

August 11 Robert I the Bruce, King of Scotland, is again defeated by the English, at Dalry, Scotland.

November 11 The Knights Hospitallers (a predominantly French order of Christian chivalry) begin their conquest of the island of Rhodes from the Byzantines with the capture of Philermo.

1307

- Andronicus II Palaeologus, the Byzantine emperor, recognizes the seizure of Anchialus and Mesembria by Theodore Svjatoslav, the Bulgarian czar.
- King Kankas Mansa Muss of Mali seizes the kingdom of Songhai.
- Ramachandra, the Hindu king of Deogir, West Deccan, is compelled to pay tribute to Ala-ad-Din, the sultan of Delhi, India.
- Temür Öljeitü, the great khan, dies. He is succeeded by his nephew Haishan. Mongol rule in China now declines into dissension and civil war.

- The earliest known record of the guillotine dates to this time, when it is used on April 1 to execute Murcod Ballagh at Merton in Ireland.
- The Milanese elect Guido della Torre as *capitano del popolo* ("captain of the people").

January 20   King Edward I of England holds his last parliament in Carlisle, northern England. It criticizes papal exactions.

May 5   Frederick of Meissen defeats the Holy Roman Emperor Albert I at Lucca, Italy.

May 5   Robert I the Bruce, King of Scotland, returns from Ireland and defeats English forces in Ayrshire, Scotland.

July 7   King Edward I of England dies whilst leading an army to Scotland. He is succeeded by his son, Edward II.

August 6   King Edward II of England creates his favorite, Piers Gaveston, Earl of Cornwall.

August 8   King Edward II of England campaigns in Scotland, briefly. On his withdrawal Robert I the Bruce, King of Scotland, reestablishes himself.

August 15   Henry, Duke of Carinthia, is elected king of Bohemia. The Holy Roman Emperor Albert I invades Bohemia.

October 6   Corso Donati, an aristocrat and leader of the Black faction of the propapal Guelph party in Florence, is killed while evading arrest. He had planned a coup to reverse the recent reform of the Florentine constitution, produced as a result of financial depression and popular unrest. Donati's failure and death brings to an end the period of dominance of the ancient noble families in Florence.

October 13   King Philip IV of France orders the wholesale arrest of the Knights Templar (members of a German Christian military order) in France and seizure of their property. The judicial investigation of their alleged crimes follows.

November 7   The legendary Swiss archer William Tell is said to have shot Hermann Gessler, the Austrian governor of Tyrol, on this day.

1308

- King Haakon V of Norway makes an ineffective ordinance resuming feudal grants and abolishing baronial powers.
- Prataparudradeva II, the Hindu king of Telingana, is forced to pay tribute to Ala-ad-Din, Sultan of Delhi, India.
- Robert I the Bruce, King of Scotland, defeats the Comyns of Buchan, takes Aberdeen, conquers Galloway, and begins his raids on northern England.
- The Hungarian nobles acclaim Charles Robert of Anjou as their king.
- The ilkhanid sultan of Persia, Uljāytū, invades Syria and reaches Jerusalem.

January 25   King Edward II of England marries Isabella, the 12-year-old daughter of King Philip IV of France.

January 31   Azzo VIII d'Este, Lord of the Italian city of Ferrara, dies. He bequeaths the succession to his illegitimate son, Folco.

February 25   King Edward II of England is crowned, taking a new form of coronation oath.

April 4   Pope Clement V claims Ferrara as a papal fief and disowns Folco d'Este, Lord of Ferrara.

May 1   The Holy Roman Emperor Albert I is murdered by John, Duke of Swabia.

May 5   King Philip IV the Fair of France holds another meeting of the Estates General (assembly containing representatives of the aristocracy, clergy, and commons) to uphold his proceedings against the Knights Templar (a German Christian military order).

May 18   The magnates force King Edward II of England to banish his favorite, Piers Gaveston, Earl of Cornwall.

July 7   Pope Clement V gives way to King Philip IV of France's demands for the further prosecution of the Knights Templar (a German Christian military order).

August 15   The Byzantine island of Rhodes surrenders to the Knights Hospitallers (a predominantly French order of Latin Christian chivalry). It becomes their headquarters.

November 12   The Teutonic Knights (a German Christian military order), having been admitted to Gdańsk as allies of Władysław Łokietek, Grand Prince of Poland, seize the city and massacre its inhabitants.

November 27   Henry IV, Count of Luxembourg, is elected as Holy Roman Emperor.

1309

- An ordinance issued by King Philip IV the Fair of France names his audit office, which is now becoming a permanent, specialized organ of government, as the *Chambre des Comptes*.
- Guzmán el Bueno takes Gibraltar from the Moors. Valencia is permanently annexed to Aragon.
- The Teutonic Knights (a German Christian military order) complete their seizure of East Pomerania. Their grand master moves his headquarters from Venice to Marienburg.

March 14   King Mohammad III of Granada is deposed and succeeded by his brother Nasr.

March 27   Pope Clement V declares that Venice is no longer a Christian state because it supports Folco d'Este, Lord of Ferrara.

May 8   King Charles II of Naples dies. He is succeeded by his son Robert.

June 3   The Holy Roman Emperor Henry VII recognizes the Swiss Confederation.

July 27   In a parliament in Stamford, England, the magnates accept King Edward II of England's recall of his favorite, Piers Gaveston, Earl of Cornwall, when he grants their petitions for reform.

August 8   Papal forces defeat the Venetians at Tedaldo in the War of the Ferrarese Succession.

SCIENCE, TECHNOLOGY, AND MEDICINE

Agriculture

1307

- The Italian agriculturist Pietro dei Crescenzi of Bologna, Italy, writes his agricultural handbook *Opus ruralium/ Work on Rural Matters*, which describes methods of cultivation, livestock farming, and beekeeping.

Ecology

1306

- Following the prohibition on coal-burning imposed in England in 1273, a resident of London is tried and executed for causing pollution.

Health and Medicine

1305

- The Scottish physician Bernard of Gordon writes his textbook *Lilium medicinae/The Lily of Medicine*, which includes one of the first references to the medical use of glasses.

Science

1307

- The German scholar Dietrich of Freiburg writes his treatise *De iride et radialibus impressionibus/On the Rainbow and Radial Impressions*, on optical effects in meteorology, and particularly the rainbow.

ARTS AND IDEAS

Architecture

1305

- The A'la i-Darwaza gateway in Delhi, India, is built, its style illustrating the growing influence of Persian Muslims in India.

Arts

c. **1305**

- Italian artist Giotto di Bondone completes a series of frescoes in the Arena (Scrovegni) Chapel in Padua illustrating the life of the Virgin and the life of Jesus. Bringing a new realism and drama to painting, this major series of frescoes is seen as marking the beginning of Italian Renaissance art.

- Italian artist Giovanni Pisano sculpts *Madonna and Two Angels* for the Arena (Scrovegni) Chapel in Padua.

Literature and Language

c. **1305**

- Dutch chronicler Melis Stoke completes *Rijmkroniek*, a verse history of the Netherlands from 694 to 1305. It is written in Dutch.

1307

- English Augustinian chronicler, Peter Langtoft, completes his *Chronicle*, a history of England to 1307 written in French verse. An English translation appears in 1338.

- Italian writer Dante Alighieri completes his *Il Convivio/ The Banquet*, a selection of poems and prose commentary on them that forms an introduction to the philosophy of Albertus Magnus and Thomas Aquinas.

Thought and Scholarship

c. **1306**

- French lawyer Pierre Dubois publishes *De recuperatione Terrae Sanctae/The Recovery of the Holy Land*, a political tract on the crusades that defends the rights of the French monarchy against the claims of the papacy and the Holy Roman Emperor.

c. **1308**

- Scottish philosopher Duns Scotus completes his *Ordinatio*, commentaries on the philosophy of the French bishop Peter Lombard.

1309

- French chronicler Jean, Sire de Joinville completes his *Mémoires; ou histoire de chronique du très chrétien roi St. Louis/Memoirs, or the Chronicle of the True Christian King St. Louis*, an eyewitness record, including an account of the private life of the French King Louis IX and his deeds on crusade.

SOCIETY

Education

1306

- The University of Orléans is established in France.

BIRTHS & DEATHS

1305

- Ashikaga Takauji, Japanese soldier and statesman who founded the Ashikaga shogunate, born in Japan (–1358).

August 23 William Wallace, Scottish hero who led the first resistance movements to free Scotland from English rule, is drawn and quartered in London for treason (*c.* 35).

1307

June 17 Edward I Longshanks, King of England 1272–1307, son of Henry III, who subdued Wales, dies in Burgh by Sands, near Carlisle, England (68).

1308

c. 1308 Andrea Orcagna, Florentine painter, sculptor and architect, born (–*c.* 1368).

- Stephan Dušan, King of Serbia 1331–46, "Emperor of the Serbs and Greeks" 1346–55, born (–1355).

- The University of Tours is founded in France.

1308
- King Dinis I of Portugal transfers the University of Lisbon, established in 1290, to Coimbra, the Portuguese capital.
- Perugia University, Italy, is recognized by Pope Clement V.

Religion

1306

February 12 At King Edward I of England's instance, Pope Clement V suspends Robert Winchelsey, archbishop of Canterbury, who then goes into exile.

1307
- Pope Clement V appoints the Italian churchman, John of Monte Corvino, archbishop of Beijing, China.

1309
- Pope Clement V begins his (and the papacy's) residence at Avignon, in the south of France. Known as the Babylonian Captivity, the papacy's stay in Avignon lasts until 1377.

Sports

1306
- Al-Dimyāti writes *Fadl al-Khayl/The Excellence of the Horse*. The Mameluke sultans in Egypt keep studs for breeding racehorses.

1310–1314

POLITICS, GOVERNMENT, AND ECONOMICS

Business and Economics

1312

May 6 The General Council of Vienne, France, which has been discussing the taxation of the clergy, closes.

1314

November 28 King Philip IV of France forbids further collection of the tax voted for the Flemish campaign as it is causing revolts by provincial leagues of lesser nobles and towns.

Politics and Government

1310
- Ala-ad-Din, Sultan of Delhi, sends an army to plunder southernmost India and compels the kings of Dvaravatipura and Madura to pay tribute.
- The Catalan mercenary Grand Company ravages the Byzantine province of Thessaly.
- The city of Lyons is incorporated into the kingdom of France on its occupation by King Philip IV of France's forces, who arrests its archbishop.
- The Hoysala capital Dvarasamudra is burned by Malik Kafur, a general of Ala-ad-Din, Sultan of Delhi, India.

May 16 The English magnates compel King Edward II of England to appoint a commission of reform (the Lords Ordainers), as they believe that he is influenced by evil councillors, namely Piers Gaveston, Earl of Cornwall.

June 15 The Council of Ten is instituted in the city-republic of Venice to administer security details following the failure of the plot of Bajamonte Tiepolo and Mario Querini.

June 15 The papacy and Venice make peace, ending the War of the Ferrarese Succession. Pope Clement V makes Robert of Naples his vicar in Ferrara.

1311
- King Philip IV the Fair of France expels the "Lombards" (Italian bankers) from France, seizing their property.
- Mangrai, first king of Lan Na, dies. The Thai kingdom is now divided until 1325.
- On leaving northern Italy for Rome, the Holy Roman Emperor Henry VII appoints Matteo Visconti as imperial vicar of Milan, and Can Grande della Scala as vicar of Verona, thus legitimizing their despotisms. Florence appoints Robert of Naples as its lord to defend it against Henry.
- The Ordinances establish the Privy Seal Office in England by ordering the Keeper's detachment from King Edward II's Household.

January 6 The German king Henry VII is crowned as king of Lombardy in Milan.

March 15 The Catalan mercenary Grand Company defeats and kills Walter of Brienne, Duke of Athens, on the Cephissus, in Boeotia, Greece; Athens becomes a Catalan duchy.

August 13 Pietro Gradenigo, Doge of Venice, dies. He is succeeded by Marino Giorgio.

August 16 A parliament meets in which King Edward II of England accepts the Ordinances for the reform of his government and banishes his favorite, Piers Gaveston, Earl of Cornwall.

September–November King Edward II of England leads an ineffective campaign in Scotland.

September 9 The Holy Roman Emperor Henry VII takes Brescia and punishes it for rebellion.

October 16 The General Council of Vienne, an ecclesiastical assembly convoked by Pope Clement V under pressure from the French king Philip IV the Fair, opens in Vienne, France. It decides to create chairs in Arabic and Tatar at Paris, Louvain, and Salamanca; to suppresses the religious groups, the Béguins and Beghards; and to abolish the Knights Templars.

1312

- Robert of Flanders concedes the castellanies of Lille, Douai, and Béthune to King Philip IV of France in lieu of the indemnity promised in 1305.
- The Catalan mercenary Grand Company seizes power in the Latin duchies of Athens and Thebes, in Greece, under the authority of the Aragonese king Frederick II of Sicily.
- The Shan leader Thihathura establishes his capital at Pinya, in north Burma (modern Myanmar).
- Tokhta, Khan of the "Golden Horde," dies. He is succeeded by Uzbekh, a Muslim who completes the conversion of the horde to Islam.

April 4 Pope Clement V declares the suppression of the Order of Knights Templar (a German Christian military order).

June 6 Marino Giorgio, Doge of Venice, dies. He is succeeded by Giovanni Soranzo.

June 19 The banished Piers Gaveston, Earl of Cornwall, who has returned to England, is captured and killed by the Earls of Lancaster and Warwick. His death causes a split among King Edward II of England's baronial opponents.

June 29 King Henry VII of Germany is officially crowned as Holy Roman Emperor in Rome, in the Lateran Palace because St. Peter's is held by hostile Romans supported by Robert of Naples.

September 17 King Ferdinand IV of Castile and León dies. He is succeeded by his infant son, Alfonso XI. In the chaos caused by Alfonso's minority, civil war breaks out.

October 31 The Holy Roman Emperor Henry VII abandons his attempt to take the city-republic of Florence by storm.

December 22 King Edward II of England makes peace with the magnates.

1313

- The Scots recover the Isle of Man from the English.
- Tran Anh-tong, Emperor of Dai Viet (modern northern Vietnam), occupies Champa (southern Vietnam) and establishes Che Nang, of the Cham royal dynasty, as puppet ruler.

January 13 A Scottish army under their king Robert I the Bruce expel the English garrison from Perth, Scotland.

April 26 The Holy Roman Emperor Henry VII declares Robert of Naples guilty of treason against the empire.

June 13 Under pressure from King Philip IV of France, Pope Clement V declares Naples to be under papal protection.

August 24 The Holy Roman Emperor Henry VII dies while leading an army against Naples.

November 11 Ludwig of Wittelsbach, Duke of Upper Bavaria, defeats an invasion by Frederick the Handsome, Duke of Austria, at Gammelsdorf.

1314

- Amda Seyon the Great succeeds to the throne of Ethiopia.
- King Philip IV of France holds the fourth Estates General (assembly containing representatives of the aristocracy, clergy, and commons) in Paris, France, and, for the first time, seeks its consent to taxation.
- The Egyptian Mamelukes establish a Muslim as king of Dongola (north Sudan), ending a Monophysite Christian monarchy dating from 543. From this time Arabs fleeing Mameluke rule begin to settle in the Sudan.

February 19 King Nasr of Granada abdicates after a rebellion and is succeeded by his cousin, Ismail I.

March 18 Jacques de Molay, former grand master of the suppressed Knights Templar (German Christian military order), is burned at the stake in Paris, France.

June 14 Uguccione della Faggiuola, despot of Pisa, wins control of Lucca through a rising organized by Castruccio Castracani.

June 23 Robert I the Bruce, King of Scotland, repulses English forces attempting to relieve Stirling Castle in Scotland. The next day, he inflicts a disastrous defeat on King Edward II of England in the Battle of Bannockburn and so completes his expulsion of the English from Scotland.

September 9 King Philip IV of France makes peace with Flanders after a brief campaign.

October 19–20 Frederick the Handsome, Duke of Austria, sometimes called Frederick the Fair, is elected Holy Roman Emperor. The following day Ludwig IV of Bavaria is also elected, and civil war ensues.

November 30 King Philip IV the Fair of France dies. He is succeeded by his son, Louis X.

SCIENCE, TECHNOLOGY, AND MEDICINE

Health and Medicine

1313

- The Spanish physician Berengar of Valencia makes Latin translations of many Arabic medical works for the European audience.

Science

1310

- The English scientist John Maudwith writes treatises on trigonometry and astronomy.

1311

- The Ismaili philosopher Al-Shīrāzī writes *Highest Understanding of the Knowledge of Spheres*.

c. 1313

- The German Grey Friar Berthold der Schwarze is traditionally credited with the independent invention of gunpowder. He is also said to have cast the first bronze cannon.

1314

- The *Mappa mundi/Map of the World* of Hereford Cathedral, England, is compiled. This is a famous symbolic map of the world showing Jerusalem at its center, in accordance with the Bible.

Technology

1313

- The Chinese magistrate Wang Chen writes a history of technology. In order to have it printed, he hires craftsmen to carve 60,000 wooden blocks marked with different characters. He also invents a revolving case on which the type is set.

Transportation

1311

- The Italian cartographer Pietro Vesconte makes the earliest dated *portolano* (pilot's map) showing the Mediterranean and Black Sea. He later compiles some of the first atlases.

ARTS AND IDEAS

Architecture

1310

- The Palazzo delle Signoria (the Town Hall) in Florence, Italy, designed by the Italian artist and architect Arnolfo di Cambio, is completed.
- The Palazzo Pubblico (the Town Hall) in Siena, Italy, is completed.

Arts

1310

c. 1310 Italian artist Giotto di Bondone paints *Madonna and Child Enthroned*.

- Italian artist Giovanni Pisano sculpts the pulpit in Pisa Cathedral, a work showing the influence of French Gothic sculpture.

1311

- Italian artist Duccio de Buoninsegna completes his painting *Maestà* for the high altar of Siena Cathedral. It consists of a huge panel painting depicting the Virgin and Child on one side and 26 scenes of the Passion of Christ on the other. Commissioned to commemorate the failure of a siege of Siena, the work is paraded through the streets when it is finished.

c. 1312

- Italian artist Lorenzo Maitani sculpts *Scenes from Genesis* a relief for the façade of Orvieto Cathedral.

Literature and Language

c. 1310

- The anonymous Spanish prose romance *Amadís de Gaula/Amadis the Gaul* (possibly Portuguese in origin) is written. The best-known version of this story is published by the Spanish writer Garcia Rodríguez de Montalvo in 1508.

1311

c. 1311 The sermons of the Italian churchman Giordano de Rivalto are collected. Noted for the purity and grace of the prose style, they are among the finest Italian prose works of the period.

- Arab scholar Ibn-Manzūr completes his *Lisān al-Arab*, an Arabic dictionary.

c. 1313

- The Arab scholar Abu Haiyan completes his *Kitāb al-idrāk lilisān al-Atrāk*, the earliest extant treatise on Turkish grammar.

c. 1314

- Hayton (Haithon), the ruler of Armenia, records his travels in Asia through his secretary Kirakos Gandzaketsi, the earliest detailed account of geography and culture of Mongolia.

Music

c. 1310

- The anonymous English song "Sumer is Icomen In" is first documented.

1311

- German musician Heinrich of Miessen (Frauenlob) founds a company of *Minnesingers* at Mainz in Germany. The *Minnesingers* ("singers of love") were aristocratic troubadours who flourished during the Middle Ages. They gave way to the *Meistersingers*, who were drawn from the merchant classes. The Mainz group lasts until 1876.

Thought and Scholarship

c. 1312

- English scholar Walter of Guisborough (Hemingburgh) completes his *Cronica/Chronicle*, a history of England from 1066 to 1312.

c. 1313

- Italian writer Dante Alighieri completes his *De monarchia/On Monarchy*, a Latin treatise expressing his view that world government should be based on the Holy Roman Emperor and not the pope.

1314

c. 1314 Indian scholar Candesvara completes his *Nitiratnākara/Jewel-Mine of Politics*, a Hindu treatise on the science of government.

c. 1314 The *Chronicle of Bohemia*, the earliest history of the Czechs, tracing their history from mythological origins to 1314, is completed. Authorship is anonymous, though it was once ascribed to Dalimil of Meziříčí.

- Persian scholar Rashid al-Din completes his *Jāmi altāwarikh/Histories*, a universal history based on Arabic, Persian, Mongol, and Chinese sources. This is one of the first of the great Persian illustrated books.

SOCIETY

Education

1314

- The colleges of Navarre and Montaigu, Paris, France, and Exeter College in Oxford, England, are founded by Walter Stapeldon, bishop of Exeter.

Religion

1310

c. 1310   English scholar Henry Bate completes his *Speculum divinorum et quorundam naturalium/Mirror of the Divine and Natural Worlds*, a theological encyclopedia with scientific digressions.

- The French mystic Marguerite Porete is burned as a witch in Paris, France.

1313

- Pope Clement V publishes his *Clementinae*, additions to the corpus of canon law.

Sports

1314

- A Highland Gathering with throwing and other sporting contests is held at Ceres in Fife, Scotland, to commemorate the Scottish victory over the English at the Battle of Bannockburn in the same year.
- The Lord Mayor of London, England, bans football under pain of imprisonment because of the noise and commotion caused by "hustling over large footballs in the fields of the public."

BIRTHS & DEATHS

1310
April 30   Casimir (Kazimierz) III the Great, King of Poland 1333–70, born in Kujavia, Poland (–1370).

1311
- Arnold of Villanova, a Spanish physician of the Montpellier school and a writer on alchemy and witchcraft, dies. Among his works are the medical manual *Opera medica/Medical Works* and the treatise *Tractatus de vinis/Tract on Wines* on wines and viniculture.

1312
c. 1312   Cecco Angiolieri, Italian writer of a body of caustically humorous songs and sonnets, dies (*c.* 52).
November 13   Edward III ("of Windsor"), King of England 1327–77, son of Edward II, who led England into the Hundred Years' War 1337–1453

against France, born in Windsor, Berkshire, England (–1377).

1313
- Cola di Rienzo, Italian leader who attempted to restore Italy to the greatness and splendor of the Roman Empire, born in Rome, (–1354).
- Giovanni Boccaccio, Italian poet and scholar who, with Petrarch, laid the foundations of Renaissance humanism, author of the *Decameron*, born in Paris, France (–1375).
- Ibn al Khatīb, great Arab writer, prime minister of Granada, Spain, born (–1374).
March 5   David II (David Bruce), King of Scotland 1329–71, son of Robert I the Bruce, who spent a large part of his ineffectual reign in exile or in

prison, born in Dunfermline, Fife, Scotland (–1371).
April   John de Baliol ("Toom Tabard" or "Empty Garment"), King of Scotland 1292–96 who resigned his kingdom to King Edward I of England, dies in Château Gaillard, Normandy, France (*c.* 63).

1314
April 20   Clement V, French pope 1305–14, who moved the papal residence to Avignon, dies in Avignon, France (*c.* 54).
November 29   Philip IV, King of France 1285–1314, dies in Fontainebleau, France (46).

1315–1319

POLITICS, GOVERNMENT, AND ECONOMICS

Business and Economics

1315

- A silk industry begins to develop in France, started by Italian immigrants.

Politics and Government

1315

- Frederick of Trinacria assumes the title of king of Sicily, thus provoking a new war with Naples.
- Godymin succeeds as grand prince of Lithuania and takes Brest Litewski.
- King Louis X of France grants charters to various provincial leagues in order to appease their grievances.
- Otto IV, Count of Burgundy (Franche-Comté), dies. He is succeeded by his daughter, Joanna, the wife of Philip of Poitiers.
- The Bohemian nobles force King John of Bohemia to expel his German advisers and employ Bohemian lords.
- The nobility of Estonia forms the Landtag of Pernau, a constitutional assembly.
- The use of examinations for recruitment to the Chinese civil service is restored.

January 20 King Edward II of England holds a parliament when the barons make him purge his council.

March 17 The Holy Roman Emperor Ludwig IV of Bavaria recognizes the Swiss Confederation by summoning representatives to a diet (legislative assembly).

April 30 Enguerrand de Marigny, finance minister of the late king Philip IV of France, is hanged.

May 25 Edward Bruce, brother of Robert I the Bruce, King of Scotland, invades Ireland, having been offered the high kingship by Donal O'Neill, King of Tyrone.

August 8 King Louis X of France fails in a campaign to conquer Flanders.

August 29 Uguccione della Faggiuola, despot of Pisa, routs the forces of Florence and Naples at Montecatini.

September 10 Edward Bruce, brother of Robert I the Bruce, King of Scotland, defeats English forces under the Earl of Ulster near Connor in Antrim, Ireland.

November 15 The Swiss defeat Duke Leopold of Austria at Morgarten.

1316

- By the Peace of Fexhe, the prince-bishop of Liège (in modern Belgium) concedes control of legislation to his subjects.
- The Valencian Order of Knights of Montesa is formally constituted.
- Uljāytū, Sultan of Persia, dies. He is succeeded by his nephew, Abu Sa'id.

January 2 Ala-ad-Din, Sultan of Delhi, India, dies. He is succeeded by his son, Shihan ad-Din Umar, with Malik Naib.

February 12 King Edward II of England confirms the Ordinances and appoints Thomas, Earl of Lancaster, as his chief councillor.

April 1 Qutb-ad-Din Mubarak succeeds as sultan of Delhi, India, after escaping an attempt by Malik Naib to kill him. He has Naib murdered and Shihan ad-Din 'Umar blinded, and assumes the throne.

May 2 Edward Bruce, brother of Robert I the Bruce, King of Scotland, is crowned as king of Ireland at Dundalk in Ireland.

June 5 King Louis X of France dies. His widow is pregnant and his brother, Philip, Count of Poitiers, becomes regent.

August 7 Following the death of Pope Clement V, the French clergyman Jacques Duèse (D'Euze) is elected Pope John XXII.

August 10 Phelim O'Connor, King of Connacht, is defeated and killed by English forces at Athenry, in Galway, Ireland.

1317

- Pope John XXII publishes his *Extravagantes*, additions to the corpus of canon law.
- Qutb-ad-Din Mubarak, Sultan of Delhi, India, annexes the Hindu kingdom of Deogir.
- Robert of Naples promotes a general peace in Tuscany.
- The despot Uguccione della Faggiuola is expelled from Pisa and Lucca.

January 9 Philip, Count of Poitiers, brother of the late king Louis X, is crowned as King Philip V of France.

February–May Robert I the Bruce, King of Scotland, joins his brother Edward Bruce, King of Ireland, to campaign in Ireland.

March 31 Pope John XXII claims imperial rights in Italy for the papacy.

August 15 The citizens of the Italian city of Ferrara, having massacred the Neapolitan garrison, elect Rinaldo, Obizzo, and Nicolò d'Este as their rulers.

December 12 Eric, Duke of Södermanland, leader of the baronial opposition to the monarchy in Sweden, is captured by King Birger of Sweden, his brother, and presumably murdered. This is followed by a general rebellion.

1318

- George V becomes sole king of a newly unified Georgia.
- Go-Daigo becomes the emperor of Japan.
- Tran Minh-tong, Emperor of Dai Viet (modern northern Vietnam), deposes Che Nang of Champa (southern Vietnam) and appoints Che A-nan as military governor.

February 2   Peace is made between the victorious Can Grande della Scala of Verona and the republic of Padua.

March 27   King Philip V of France makes peace with the Burgundians. This marks the end of the Movement of the Leagues.

April 8   Robert I the Bruce, King of Scotland, takes the northern English town of Berwick.

May 5   Robert I the Bruce, King of Scotland, raids as far as Ripon in England, exacting tribute.

July 7   Padua accepts Giacomo da Carrara as its lord.

July 7   Robert of Naples raises the siege of Genoa by Frederick III, King of Sicily.

July 19   Duke Leopold of Austria makes a truce with the Swiss Forest Cantons.

August 9   In the Treaty of Leake, King Edward II of England confirms the Ordinances, at the instances of Aymer de Valence, Earl of Pembroke, and other magnates. Thomas, Earl of Lancaster, loses his position of influence as chief councilor.

October 14   Edward Bruce, King of Ireland, is defeated and killed by an Anglo-Irish force under John de Bermingham at Faughard, near Dundalk, Ireland.

1319

- King Dinis I of Portugal founds the Portuguese Order of Knights of Christ.
- Michael (Mikhail), Grand Duke of Vladimir, is executed for opposing his deposition by Uzbekh, Khan of the "Golden Horde," the Mongol empire in the west including most of Russia and large parts of western Asia. He is succeeded as grand duke by Yury (Juri) of Moscow.
- The death of King Eric V of Denmark ends his attempts to suppress the trading operations of the Hanse. It forms a settlement in Bergen, Norway, and expels the English and Scots, so gaining a monopoly of trade with Norway.

January 19   Robert of Naples accepts the lordship of Brescia.

May 8   King Haakon V of Norway dies. He is succeeded by his grandson, Magnus VIII, son of Eric of Södermanland.

June 26   King Ismail I of Granada defeats a Castilian invasion.

July 23   Pope John XXII appoints Cardinal Bertrand du Poujet as his papal legate in Italy.

August 8   King Edward II of England lays siege to the Scottish-held town of Berwick in northern England.

September 9   King Magnus VII of Norway is elected as king of Sweden in place of King Birger, who has fled to Denmark.

September 20   A Scottish force led by Sir James Douglas defeats the forces raised by Archbishop Melton of York at Myton, in Swaledale, England, following an attempt to kidnap Queen Isabella from York. King Edward II of England then abandons his siege of the Scottish-held English town of Berwick upon Tweed.

November 1   Uguccione della Faggiuola, the expelled despot of Pisa and Lucca, dies while serving Can Grande della

Scala of Verona at the siege of Padua. The Holy Roman Emperor Frederick of Austria raises the siege.

SCIENCE, TECHNOLOGY, AND MEDICINE

Agriculture

1315

- Crops fail throughout western Europe and famine follows. The British isles are not as badly affected as elsewhere, but the reduced crop and increased demand from abroad send wheat prices soaring.

1316

- Famine in western Europe, brought on by the previous bad harvest, causes heavy mortality and brings population growth to a halt.

Health and Medicine

1315

- The French-trained English physician John of Gaddesden writes *Rosa medicinae/The Rose of Medicine*. He is the model for the "Doctor of Physick" in Chaucer's *Canterbury Tales*, which suggests he used astrology and the four humors in his treatments.

1316

- The Italian physician Mondino de Liuzzi conducts the first properly recorded dissection of a human corpse at Bologna University, Italy. His book *Anatomia* will become the standard work on anatomy for two centuries.

1317

- The physician Matthaeus Sylvaticus writes his *Pandectae*, a dictionary of medicinal herbs.

1318

- Islamic physician and scholar Rashid writes an encyclopedia of Chinese medicine called *Fami 'al-tasanif al-Rashidi*.

Science

1318

March 13   The French astronomer Jean de Murs determines the epoch of the spring equinox using the Spanish *Alfonsine Tables*. He also writes an explanatory treatise responsible for increasing the use of the tables in the rest of Europe.

Technology

1319

- It is suggested that the English army uses cannon against the Scots at the siege of Berwick, although King Edward II of England fails to capture the town.

ARTS AND IDEAS

Architecture

1315
- The Church of the Holy Apostles in Thessaloníki (Salonika), Greece, a noted work of Byzantine architecture, is completed.

1319
- The chapterhouse of Wells Cathedral in England is completed. It introduces the late Gothic practice of using vault ribs for decorative rather than purely structural reasons.

Arts

1315
- Italian artist Simone Martini completes the *Maestà* fresco in the Palazzo Pubblico (the Town Hall) in Siena, Italy, as well as *St. Louis of Toulouse*, painted for Robert of Anjou, King of Naples.

1318
- Italian artist Lippo Memmi paints the fresco *Maestà* for the Palazzo Pubblico (Town Hall) in San Gimignano, Italy.

Literature and Language

c. **1316**
- Arab scholar Abul-Barakāt completes his *Al-sullam al-Kabīr*, a Coptic-Arabic vocabulary.

SOCIETY

Religion

1317
- Pope John XXII, leader of the Catholic Church, issues an edict against the practice of alchemy.

1318
- Members of the "Spirituals," an Italian group of Franciscans who insist on a strict interpretation of the beliefs of St. Francis, are burned at the stake in the persecution of this branch of the Franciscans ordered by Pope John XXII in 1318.
- Pope John XXII creates ten bishops to serve under the archbishop of Sultāniyah (Persia). He also divides the Asian mission fields, assigning Greater Armenia, Persia, and India to the Dominicans, and northern Asia, including China, to the Franciscans.

BIRTHS & DEATHS

1316
- Aegidius Romana (Giles of Rome), archbishop of Bourges, philosopher, and Augustinian theologian, who defended the doctrines of St. Thomas Aquinas, dies in Avignon, France (*c.* 71).
- Ramón Llull (or Raymond Lully), Catalan mystic and poet, dies in Tunis or Majorca (*c.* 82).
- March 2 Robert II, King of the Scots 1371–90, first of the Stewart kings, born (–1390).
- May 14 Charles IV (Charles of Luxembourg, original name Wenceslas), King of Bohemia 1346–78 and Holy Roman Emperor 1355–78, renowned for his learning and diplomatic skills, born in Prague (–1378).

- June 5 Louis X, King of France 1314–16 and King of Navarre 1305–14, dies in Vincennes, France (26).
- November 14 King John I of France, son of the late Louis X, born.
- November 19 King John I of France dies.

1317
- December 24 Jean, Sire de Joinville, author of the famous account of the Seventh Crusade *l'Histoire de St.-Louis/History of St. Louis*, dies in Joinville, France (*c.* 93).

1318
- *c.* 1318 Urban V, Italian pope whose election caused the French cardinals to establish the antipope, born in Naples (–1389).

- Duccio di Buoninsegna, outstanding Italian painter of the Middle Ages, founder of the Sienese school, whose best-known work is the altarpiece of Siena Cathedral, *Maestà* (1311), dies, probably in Siena, Italy (*c.* 63).
- Rashid ad-Din, Persian historian, the author of *Jami' at-tawarikh*, a universal history, dies (*c.* 71).

1319
- April 16 John II the Good, King of France 1350–64, captured by the English at the Battle of Poitiers (1356), born near Le Mans, France (–1364).
- November 13 King Eric VI Menved of Denmark dies without issue.

1320–1324

POLITICS, GOVERNMENT, AND ECONOMICS

Business and Economics

1322

- Abu Bakr ben Mohammad, the sultan of the Islamic city-state of Mogadishu (in modern Somalia), issues the first dated coins in Africa.

Politics and Government

1320

- An ordinance issued by King Philip V of France reorganizes the *Chambre des Comptes* (audit office).
- Castruccio Castracani is elected as captain-general of Lucca for life.
- King John of Bohemia abandons the government of the country to Henry of Lipa and other nobles so that he can pursue a career of knight errantry.

January 20   Władysław Łokietek is crowned as king of Poland.

January 25   Christopher II succeeds his brother, Eric VI, as king of Denmark on promising to accept baronial control.

April 14   Qutb-ad-Din Mubarak, Sultan of Delhi, India, is murdered by his favorite, Khusraw Khan, who assumes the throne.

April 26   The Declaration of Arbroath is signed, in which the earls and barons of Scotland announce to Pope John XXII their rejection of English rule and their loyalty to Robert I the Bruce, King of Scotland, stating that "it is not for glory, riches nor honors that we fight, but for freedom alone."

May 5   By the Treaty of Paris, King Philip V of France makes peace with Robert of Flanders.

September 5   Khusraw, Sultan of Delhi, India, is killed after his defeat by Ghazi Malik, who assumes the throne of Delhi as Ghiyath-ad-Din Tughluq.

October 26   Can Grande, the vicar of Verona, makes peace with Padua, Italy.

1321

- A league of Marcher lords seizes the Welsh estates of Hugh Despenser the elder, when he attempts to enforce the English law of property alienation over them, while pursuing a policy of self-aggrandizement by currying favor with King Edward II of England.

- An embassy is sent from Ethiopia to Egypt to protest against the treatment of the Christian Coptic community there.
- Andronicus III begins his rebellion against his grandfather the Byzantine emperor Andronicus II.
- Stephen Uroš II of Serbia is succeeded by his illegitimate son Stephen Uroš III Dečanski.
- The Muslim ruler Ghias ad-Din Tughluq in India founds a new capital at Delhi (its site, now ruins, stands just outside the modern city).

April 4   The Milanese take the city of Vercelli, Italy.

June 28   Thomas, Earl of Lancaster, assembles a northern parliament at Sherburn-in-Elmet, England, which is attended by the archbishop of York and the bishops of Durham and Carlisle. The parliament pledges to destroy the rising power of the Despenser family.

August 19   King Edward II of England is compelled by a parliament at Westminster, England, to banish Hugh le Despenser and his son Hugh. He also formally pardons Thomas, Earl of Lancaster, and 500 of his adherents for resisting the king and the Despensers.

October 31   King Edward II of England takes Leeds Castle in Kent, England, to punish Lord Badlesmere for supporting the Earl of Lancaster's party.

1322

- Robert of Naples' term of office as protector of Florence, Italy, expires and is not renewed.
- Uzbekh, Khan of the "Golden Horde," deposes Juri and appoints Dmitri of Tver as Grand Duke of Vladimir when Juri fails to deliver the khan's tax receipts.

January 2   King Philip V of France dies and is succeeded by his brother Charles IV.

January 5   The Milanese army takes the city of Cremona, Italy.

February 11   Following his successful campaign in the Welsh Marches, King Edward II of England recalls the Despenser family from exile.

March 16   King Edward II of England defeats Thomas, Earl of Lancaster, at Boroughbridge, England. In the course of the battle the Earl of Hereford is killed, the Earl of Lancaster and his captains surrendering to Edward the following day.

March 22   King Edward II of England executes Thomas, Earl of Lancaster, for treason at his own castle in Pontefract, England.

May 2   King Edward II of England holds a parliament at York, England, which repeals the ordinances.

June 24   Matteo Visconti, ruler of Milan, Italy, dies, and is succeeded by his son Galeazzo.

August 8   Following the expiry of the truce between England and Scotland, King Edward II of England mounts an ineffective campaign in Scotland, which is followed by Scottish raids into Yorkshire, England.

September 9   Robert of Béthune, Count of Flanders, dies. He is succeeded by his eldest son Louis of Nevers.

September 28   King Ludwig IV of Bavaria is aided by King John I of Bohemia in defeating and capturing Frederick of Austria on the River Inn at Mühldorf, on the Austrian border.

October 14   King Robert I of Scotland (Robert the Bruce) defeats the English at Byland; King Edward II of England narrowly avoids capture.

1323

- Che Anang, the Dai Viet viceroy of the kingdom of Champa (modern southern Vietnam), rebels against Dai Viet (modern northern Vietnamese, or Annamese) authority.
- Following the death of the antipope Benedict XIII in Avignon, the Spanish clergyman Gil Sánchez Muñoz is elected Antipope Clement VIII, a position he holds until 1328 at the court in Avignon.
- King Edward II of England makes a truce with King Robert I of Scotland (Robert the Bruce), setting up a committee for the negotiation of a permanent peace treaty.
- King James II of Aragon seizes the Mediterranean island of Sardinia from the control of Pisa, Italy.
- Michael Šišman of Vidin, Bulgaria, founds the last Bulgarian dynasty.
- Sultan Tughluq of Delhi, India, annexes the Hindu kingdom of Telingana, renaming its capital Warangal, Sultāpur. A Mongol invasion of India is repulsed.
- The Zayid dynasty captures the city of San'a from the ruling Rasulid dynasty of Yemen.

February 2   The papal legate Bertrand du Poujet opens his campaign against the Lombard "Ghibellines," the German imperialists, with the capture of Tortona and Monza in Italy.

June 6   Following a revolt in Bruges, Flanders, Louis, Count of Flanders, is captured and deposed in favor of his uncle Robert of Cassel .

June 11   The papal legate Bertrand du Poujet begins the siege of Milan, Italy.

July 28   Milan, Italy, besieged by the forces of the papal legate Bertrand du Poujet, is reinforced by troops sent by King Ludwig IV of Bavaria, and the siege is abandoned.

October 8   As a result of King Ludwig IV of Bavaria's claim of imperial authority in northern Italy, Pope John XXII asserts his right to confirm imperial elections and requires Ludwig to surrender the kingship of the Romans.

1324

- Andrew and Leo, princes of Ruthenia, are killed in a battle with Mongols.
- Dmitri II, Grand Duke of Vladimir, kills Juri of Moscow, Russia, in revenge for the execution of his father. After a delay of a year, Uzbekh, Khan of the "Golden Horde," orders his death.
- King Charles I of Hungary finally defeats the rebellious Hungarian nobles and declares against holding further parliaments.

March 23   Pope John XXII excommunicates King Ludwig IV of Bavaria for his refusal to surrender the kingship of the Romans. On May 22, in the Appeal of Sachsenhausen, King Ludwig denounces Pope John

XXII and denies his claim to temporal authority in Germany.

June 24   King Ludwig IV of Bavaria invests his son Ludwig with the state of Brandenburg.

August 8   King Charles IV of France invades Gascony when the parliament of Paris declares the province confiscated because King Edward II of England's lieutenant has sacked the French fortified town of St.-Sardos.

December 10   Galeazzo Visconti of Milan takes Monza, Italy, previously the headquarters of the papal legate Bertrand du Poujet.

SCIENCE, TECHNOLOGY, AND MEDICINE

Health and Medicine

1320

- The first great French surgeon Henri de Mondeville writes his surgical textbook *Cyrurgia/Surgery*, which although compiled mainly from other sources, contains some new insights.

1323

- The Chinese physician Wên-jên Kuei writes the treatise *Wên-jên Shih tou-chên lun* on the treatment of smallpox.

Science

1320

- The Muslim scientist Al-Fārisī writes *Tanqīh al-Manāzur/Correction of the Optics*, which includes his theory on the origin of the rainbow.

1321

- The Islamic scholar Abul-Fidā' writes *Taqwīm al-Buldān/Table of Countries*, describing the geography of Asia, Africa, and Spain.
- The Italian cartographer Marino Sanudo writes a guide to the East called *Opus Terrae Sanctae/Work of the Holy Land*, which incorporates a Jerusalem-centered world map.

Technology

1320

- The English astronomer Richard of Wallingford constructs a mechanical clock which uses an escapement and falling weights to record the time at St. Alban's Abbey, England.

1323

- The earliest reference to water-driven bellows used in an iron forge, at Briey, France, is recorded.

1324

- Cannon are manufactured from forged iron in the German city of Metz (now in northeast France).

ARTS AND IDEAS

Architecture

1321

- The restoration of the monastery of Christ of Chora (Kariye Camii) in Constantinople is completed; the walls are decorated with mosaics and frescoes that are of the highest quality and among the finest examples of late Byzantine art.

1322

- The choir of Cologne Cathedral in Germany is completed.

1324

- The Rukn-i-Alam—the tomb of the Muslim ruler of the Punjab, Tughluq I—is completed in Multan in northern India.

Arts

1320

- *c.* 1320 The Byzantine frescoes in the church at Gracanica, Serbia, are completed. One of the best-known scenes is *The Dormition of the Virgin*.
- Italian artist Pietro Lorenzetti paints his *Virgin and Child* altarpiece for the Church of Pieve di Santa Maria at Arezzo, Italy.
- The mosaics in the monastery of Chora (now the Kahrieh Djami) in Constantinople are completed.

1324

- Italian artist Paolo Veneziano paints *Coronation of the Virgin*.

Literature and Language

c. 1320

- The anonymous *Guy of Warwick*, a long narrative poem in Middle English, is probably written about this time, as is the English verse romance *Bevis of Hampton*, a translation of a 12th-century Anglo-Norman *chanson de geste* ("song of exploits").

1321

- Italian writer Dante Alighieri completes his *Divina commedia/Divine Comedy*, the greatest poetic work of the Middle Ages, and one of the main forces in the development of the Italian language. It has three sections: *Inferno/Hell*, *Purgatorio/Purgatory*, and *Paradiso/Paradise*. The first printed edition appears in 1472.

Music

c. 1320

- English mathematician and musician Walter of Odington (who may also be known as Walter of Evesham) writes his *De speculatione musicae/Thoughts on Music*, which describes contemporary forms of polyphony, and develops the concept of consonancy.
- French composer Philippe de Vitry publishes *Ars nova/The New Art*, a treatise on the "new style" of music that developed in France and Italy in the 14th century. He also writes *Ars contrapunctus/Art of Counterpoint*.

1323

- An academy for troubadours is founded at Toulouse, France, with prizes for music competitions. It is later called the Académie des Jeux Floraux.

Theater and Dance

c. 1320

- The anonymous *Chester Cycle* of miracle plays is written, in Chester, England.

Thought and Scholarship

1320

- The anonymous political treatise *Modus tenendi parliamentum/The Way to Run Parliament* is written in England in Latin.

1323

- French-born Jewish philosopher Levi ben Gerson (Gersonides) completes his commentaries on the philosopher Abu'l-Walīd ibn-Rushd (Averroës) of Córdoba.

BIRTHS & DEATHS

1320

- Waldemar IV, King of Denmark 1340–75, who regained the Danish throne from German control and unified the country, born in Denmark (–1375).

1321

- Ibn-al-Bannā, Moroccan Muslim scientist, writer of *Summary of the operations of calculation* and a calendar called *Kitāb al-manākh* (hence the word "almanac"), dies.

September 14 Dante Alighieri, Italian poet, prose writer, moral philosopher, and political theorist, author of *Divina commedia/Divine Comedy*, dies in Ravenna, Italy (56).

1322

- Chao Meng-fu, celebrated Chinese painter and calligrapher, dies (*c.* 68).

1324

- Marco Polo, Venetian explorer who spent 17 years in China, and whose *Il milione/The Million* (*Travels of Marco Polo*), has become a classic in geography, dies in Venice (*c.* 70).
- Osman I, founder of the Ottoman Turkish state, dies in Sogut, Ottoman Empire (*c.* 66).

1324

- Italian scholar Dino Compagni completes his *Cronica delle cose occorenti ne' tempi suoi/Chronicle of the Events of My Own Times*, a history of Florence from 1280 to 1312.
- Italian scholar Marsilio of Padua publishes his *Defensor pacis/Defender of the Peace*, a political treatise famous for its subordination of the church to princely authority.

SOCIETY

Education

1321

- The University of Florence is founded in Italy.

1324

- Michaelhouse College is founded at Cambridge University in England. It later forms part of Trinity College, which is founded in 1546.

- Oriel College is established at Oxford University in England.

Everyday Life

1322

- The feudal customs of the Latin principalities of Greece are recorded in *The Assizes of Romania*.

Religion

1323

- Pope John XXII condemns the doctrine of apostolic poverty in his bull *Cum inter nonnullos*, denouncing the "Spiritual" Franciscans as heretics. The "Spirituals," already persecuted, resist, but in time are defeated.

1324

- English philosopher William of Ockham, a Franciscan teaching at Oxford, is called to the papal court at Avignon by Pope John XXII to answer charges of heresy (Ockham supported the "Spiritual" Franciscans). In 1328 he flees to Bavaria and is excommunicated.

1325–1329

POLITICS, GOVERNMENT, AND ECONOMICS

Business and Economics

1329

- Mohammed II, Sultan of Delhi, India, fails in his attempt to introduce a fiduciary currency with brass tokens decreed to have the value of silver.

Colonization

1325

- The Aztecs finally settle on an island in Lake Texcoco and found what is to become the city of Tenochtitlán (Mexico City).

1329

December 12   King Ludwig IV of Bavaria returns to Germany from Italy, ending the final attempt to restore German imperial authority in Italy.

Politics and Government

1325

- Dmitri II, Grand Duke of Vladimir, is executed by Uzbekh, Khan of the "Golden Horde," for the murder of Juri of Moscow. Alexander of Tver is appointed Grand Duke of Vladimir in his place.
- King Władysław I of Poland founds the Polish Order of the White Eagle, a medal awarded for particular patriotism and bravery.
- Mohammed Tughluq, Sultan of Delhi, India, initiates the compilation of registers of the revenues and expenditure of his provincial governors.
- Sen Phu reunites the Thai kingdom of Lan Na (modern Laos).
- The city of Gao, on the Niger in eastern Mali, West Africa, is captured by Ghana.
- The cortes of Castile declares that Alfonso XI of Castile is of age, bringing to an end the anarchy prevailing since 1312.
- The first popular rising demonstrates against the Mongol dynasty in China.

January 7   King Dinis of Portugal dies and is succeeded by his son Alfonso IV.

February 2   Andronicus III is crowned coemperor with his father Andronicus II in order to end the civil war in the Greek Empire.

February 2   Mohammed Tughluq, Sultan of Delhi, India, is murdered and succeeded by his son Mohammed II.

March 9   King Edward II of England sends his wife Isabella of France to negotiate for peace with King Charles IV of France. When in France, she becomes the mistress of Roger Mortimer, exiled lord of Wigmore.

March 13   King Ludwig IV of Bavaria makes a treaty by which he releases Frederick of Austria in return for Frederick renouncing his claim to the kingship of the Romans.

July 8   Ismail I of Granada is murdered and is succeeded by his son Mohammed IV.

November 25   The imperialist "Ghibellines" defeat Bolognese forces at Zapolino, Italy.

December 2   Florence, Italy, elects Charles, Duke of Calabria and son of Robert of Naples, as its lord.

1326

- At the instigation of Pope John XXII, King Władysław I of Poland ravages the mark of Brandenburg.
- For the first time, representatives of Scottish burghs attend a parliament held by King Robert I of Scotland (Robert the Bruce) at Cambuskenneth, Scotland.
- John of Gravina, Prince of Achaea, fails in his attempt to expel Greeks who have established themselves in the Morea, the southern peninsula of Greece.
- King Christopher II of Denmark is expelled from Denmark, not to return until 1330.
- With Mongol support, Che A-nan defeats the kingdom of Dai Viet (modern northern Vietnam) and rules the kingdom of Champa (southern Vietnam) independently.

April 6   Ghāzi Orkhan succeeds his father Osman I as ruler of the Ottoman Turks and takes the Byzantine city of Bursa (in modern Turkey), making it his capital.

June 5   The papal legate Bertrand du Poujet takes Modena, Italy, in pursuance of his crusade against Milan, Italy.

September 24   Isabella of France, wife of King Edward II of England, lands at Orwell in Essex, England, with Roger Mortimer, and soon attracts a considerable following.

September 30   The papal legate Bertrand du Poujet takes Parma, Italy.

October 15   Crowds gather in London, England, in support of Isabella of France, killing the treasurer Bishop Stapeldon of Exeter. King Edward II of England flees to Gloucester, England. On October 26, his son is proclaimed keeper of the realm in the absence of his father.

October 26   Isabella of France enters Bristol, England. Hugh Despenser the elder is taken and executed.

November 16   King Edward II of England and Hugh Despenser the younger are captured at Neath Abbey in Wales. Hugh Despenser the Younger is executed.

1327

- Mohammed becomes sultan of Kanem-Bornu.
- Mohammed bin Tughluq, despotic ruler of Delhi, India, transports the city's entire population 500 miles to his new capital at Dalautabad. A blind man, unable or unwilling to make the journey, is fired from a cannon on the city walls.

January 7   A parliament assembles at Westminster in London, England, and in the "articles of deposition" demands that King Edward II of England be deposed and succeeded by his son.

January 20   King Edward II of England abdicates in favor of his son Edward III.

February 8   The papal legate Bertrand du Poujet takes Bologna, Italy.

March 31   Under the Treaty of Paris, King Charles IV of France and King Edward III of England end the "War of Saint-Sardos" and restore Gascony to English rule.

May 5   King Ludwig IV of Bavaria is crowned king of Lombardy in Milan, Italy.

September 21   The former King Edward II of England is murdered in Berkeley Castle, Gloucestershire, in England.

October 31   King James II the Just of Aragon dies and is succeeded by his son Alfonso IV.

1328

- Amda Seyon, King of Ethiopia, takes Haqq al-Din, Sultan of Ifat, prisoner, and annexes the territories of Ifat and Fataja. Sabr al-Din is appointed governor.
- James Butler is created Earl of Ormond, with jurisdiction over the liberty of Tipperary, Ireland.
- On the orders of Uzbekh, Khan of the "Golden Horde," Alexander II, Grand Duke of Vladimir, is deposed by Ivan, son of Daniel, Prince of Moscow. Alexander of Suzdal is appointed grand duke.
- The German jurist Ruprecht von Freising completes his *Rechtsbuch/Book of Law*, a codification of Bavarian laws.
- The Karaman Turks take Konya in Anatolia, the former capital of Rūm, extending their control as the ilkhanate of Persia disintegrates.

January 7   King Ludwig IV of Bavaria enters Rome, Italy, and is crowned emperor by the "four syndics of the Roman people." Pope John XXII declares a crusade against Ludwig who retaliates by declaring John deposed.

January 8   Francesco Dandolo is elected doge of Venice.

January 24   King Edward III of England marries Philippa, daughter of William I, Count of Hainault and Holland, in an attempt to form an anti-French coalition in the Low Countries (the lowland regions of western Europe along the North Sea).

February 1   Charles IV, last Capetian king of France, dies. Philip of Valois becomes regent for the duration of the pregnancy of the king's widow.

March 17   Under the Treaty of Edinburgh, King Edward III of England makes peace with Scotland, recognizing Robert the Bruce as king of Scotland.

April 1   Philip of Valois is elected King Philip VI of France following the birth of a daughter to the widow of Charles IV.

May 4   The Treaty of Edinburgh is ratified by King Edward III of England in the Treaty of Northampton.

May 22   Having deposed Pope John XXII when the Pope declares a crusade against him, King Ludwig IV of Bavaria elects the Italian clergyman Pietro Rainalducci (Peter of Corvara) as the antipope Nicholas V.

May 24   Andronicus II, coemperor of Byzantium, is forced to abdicate, leaving his grandson Andronicus III as sole Greek emperor.

August 4   King Ludwig IV of Bavaria and Pope Nicholas V leave Rome, Italy.

August 8   Galeazzo Visconti, ruler of Milan, Italy, dies and is succeeded by his son Azzo.

August 23 King Philip VI of France defeats the Flemings at Cassel, Flanders, and restores Louis of Nevers to the position of Count of Flanders.

1329

- Joanna, Countess of Evreux, is crowned queen of Navarre, separating the kingdom of Navarre from France.
- King John I of Bohemia gains possession of the town of Görlitz.
- Mohammed II, Sultan of Delhi, India, punishes the inhabitants of Delhi by ordering their removal to Daulatābād.
- The Byzantine emperor Andronicus III recovers the Aegean island of Chios from the Genoese with assistance from the Ottomans, but is defeated by Orkhān, the Ottoman leader, at Pelekanon.
- The head of the Munster Geraldines, Maurice fitz Thomas, is created Earl of Desmond, with jurisdiction over the liberty of Kerry, Ireland.

June 6 King Edward III of England pays homage for Gascony to King Philip VI of France at Amiens, France.

July 22 Can Grande della Scala of Verona, Italy, dies and is succeeded by Mastino della Scala.

December 24 The Italian city of Brescia in Lombardy accepts King John I of Bohemia as its lord, and he breaks Mastino della Scala's siege.

SCIENCE, TECHNOLOGY, AND MEDICINE

Ecology

1326

- The mineral springs from which the town of Spa (in modern Belgium) derives its name are discovered.

1327

- Most of the city of Munich, Germany, is destroyed by a great fire.

Health and Medicine

1328

- The physician John of Milan writes his important illustrated herbal *Flos medicinae/The Flourishing of Medicine*.

Science

1326

- The English astronomer Richard of Wallingford writes *Canones de instrumento*, which describes the astronomical clock he built at St. Albans, England, in 1320.

- The first illustration of an early cannon appears in an English manuscript by Walter of Milemete. The *pot de fer* consists of a simple cauldron with shrapnel loaded on top of an explosive charge.

1328

- The English scholar Thomas Bradwardine of Oxford writes his *Tractatus proportionum/Treatise on Proportion*, an early investigation of kinematics (the mechanics of moving objects) using algebra.

1329

- The French-born Jewish philosopher Levi ben Gerson (Gersonides) writes his astronomical treatise *Sefer tekunah*.
- The scholar Lu Yu writes a history of the manufacture of ink in China called *Mo shih*.

Technology

1325

- A mechanical astronomical clock is installed at Glastonbury Abbey in the west of England.

1326

- Cannon are in use at the Italian city of Florence by this time.

ARTS AND IDEAS

Arts

c. 1325

- French artist Jean Pucell completes his illuminations for the book the *Belleville Breviary*.
- Italian artist Giotto di Bondone completes a series of frescoes in chapels in the Church of Santa Croce in Florence. In the Bardi chapel he paints scenes from the life of St. Francis, in the Peruzzi chapel scenes from the life of John the Baptist.

1328

- Italian artist Simone Martini paints *Equestrian Portrait of Guidoriccio da Fogliano*, a fresco in the Palazzo Pubblico (the Town Hall) in Siena, and completes his frescoes *Scenes from the Life of Saint Martin* in the Church of San Francesco in Assisi, Italy.

c. 1329

- Chinese scholar T'ung Hou completes his *Hua chien*, a history of Chinese painting from the 3rd century AD.

Thought and Scholarship

c. 1326

- German chronicler Peter of Duisburg completes his *Chronica/Chronicle*, a history of the Prussian and the Teutonic Knights.

1327

- French-born Jewish philosopher Levi ben Gerson (Gersonides) completes his *Milhamot Adonai/Wars of the Lord*, a philosophical defense of Judaism based on Aristotle.
- Italian writer and astrologer Francesco degli Stabili (Cecco d'Ascoli) is put to death for heresy, leaving several literary works, including "Acerba", a long poem reflecting on science and moral philosophy.

1328

- English Dominican chronicler Nicholas Trivet completes his *Annales sex regum Angliae/Annals of Six English Kings*, a history of England from 1136 to 1307.
- German Dominican Heinrich Suso writes *Das Büchlein der ewigen Wahrheit/The Little Book of Eternal Truth*, a classic of German mysticism.

1329

May 31　Italian scholar Albertino Mussato dies, leaving several important works, including *De gestis Italicorum/On the Deeds of the Italians*, a history of Italy up to 1329, and *Eccerinis*, a tragedy in Latin verse.

SOCIETY

Education

1326

- Clare Hall is founded in Cambridge, England.

Religion

1326

- The Russian Metropolitan (the leader of the Russian Orthodox Church) establishes an official residence in Moscow.

1327

- Pope John XXII condemns Italian scholar Marsilio of Padua's *Defensor pacis/Defender of the Peace* published in 1324, a political treatise famous for its subordination of the church to princely authority.

1328

- The Italian scholar Agostino Trionfo (Augustinus Triumphus) publishes *Summa de potestate ecclesiastica/The Power of the Church*, a defense of papal supremacy.

Sports

c. **1328**

- William Twici, King Edward II of England's huntsman, writes a brief treatise on hunting, *Le Art de vénerie/The Art of Hunting*.

BIRTHS & DEATHS

1325

c. 1325　Nicholas Orestes, French Roman Catholic bishop, mathematician, economist, and Aristotelian scholar whose work in mathematics laid the foundations leading to the development of analytical geometry, and whose translations of Aristotle were important in the development of French, born in Allemagne, France (–1382).

- Khusrau Dihlavī (Amīr Abu'l-Hasan), Persian-born Indian writer, dies.

1326

- Hāfiz, acclaimed Persian lyric poet, whose best-known work is the *Dīvān*, born in Shīrāz, Persia (–*c.* 1390).

1327

- Johannes Eckhart ("Meister Eckhart"), Dominican theologian, considered the greatest German speculative mystic, dies in Avignon, France (*c.* 67).

September　Edward II of Caernarvon, King of England 1307–27, son of Edward I, dies in Berkeley, Gloucestershire, England (43).

December 12　Giovanni Soranzo, Doge of Venice, dies.

1328

- John of Jandun, a leading commentator on Aristotle (via Averroës), dies in Todi, Italy (*c.* 42).

February 1　Charles IV ("the Fair" or "the Bald"), King of France and (as Charles I) of Navarre 1322–28, dies in Vincennes, France (*c.* 36).

September 3　Castruccio Castracani, captain-general of Lucca, Italy, dies.

October 21　Hongwu or Hung-wu, Chinese emperor 1368–98, founder of the Ming dynasty, born in Hao-chou, China (–1398).

November 11　Charles of Calabria, Lord of Florence, Italy, dies.

1329

May 31　Albertino Mussato, Italian statesman, historian, and poet, dies in Chióggia, Italy (*c.* 68).

June 7　Robert I the Bruce, King of Scotland 1306–29, who freed Scotland from English rule, winning a decisive victory at Bannockburn (1314), dies in Cardross, Dunbartonshire, Scotland (*c.* 55).

1330–1334

POLITICS, GOVERNMENT, AND ECONOMICS

Politics and Government

1330
- Joanna, widow of King Philip V of France and Countess of Burgundy, marries Eudes IV, Duke of Burgundy.
- King Christopher II of Denmark returns home from exile, but is to be exiled again in 1331.
- The German military and religious order the Teutonic Knights occupies Riga, Latvia.

1330–1364 Gaja Mada is appointed chief minister of Majapahit, (in modern Indonesia).

March 19 Edmund, Earl of Kent and son of King Edward I of England, is executed as a traitor for opposing Isabella of France and Roger Mortimer, Earl of March.

June 14 Pope John XXII declares a crusade against the Grand Company in favor of Walter II, son of Walter de Brienne, Duke of Athens.

June 28 Stephen Uroš III, King of Serbia, defeats and kills Michael Šišman, the Bulgarian czar, near Velbužd, thereby establishing Serbian dominance in Macedonia. Michael Šišman is succeeded in 1331 by John Alexander.

July 25 Nicholas V, the pope elected by King Ludwig IV of Bavaria, resigns.

August 4 Under the Treaty of Hagenau, the Habsburgs recognize King Ludwig IV of Bavaria as king.

October 19 King Edward III of England arrests Roger Mortimer, Earl of March, at Nottingham, England, and declares his intention to rule.

1331
c. 1331 Kanka Mansa Musa, ruler of Mali, sends an embassy to the Marinids in Fez, Morocco.
- The Japanese emperor Go-Daigo, who refused to abdicate according to custom and attempted to rule, is defeated and deposed by the Hojo regency for the shogun (military ruler). He is banished to the island of Oki.

March 2 Orkhān, leader of the Ottoman Turks, takes Nicaea in Anatolia (modern Turkey) from the Byzantine Empire.

September 27 King Władysław I of Poland defeats the Teutonic Knights at Płowce, Poland.

1332
c. 1332 The Islamic state of Ifat in East Africa sends an embassy to Mameluke Egypt, to appeal for aid against Ethiopia.
- Alexander III, Grand Duke of Vladimir, dies and is succeeded by Ivan I Kalita (the Pouch) of Moscow, Russia. With the metropolitan (leader of the Russian Orthodox church) Peter also preferring to reside in Moscow, it becomes the civil and ecclesiastical capital of Christian Russia.
- Amda Seyon I, Negus of Ethiopia, defeats an invading force led by the sultan of Ifat, the leading Muslim ruler in northern Ethiopia.
- Gao, Ghana, falls to the Songhai.
- The "crusade" of Walter of Brienne, Duke of Athens, against the Grand Company, a mercenary group, fails to recover Athens, Greece.

April 8 King Philip VI of France passes the sentence of banishment and forfeiture on Robert of Artois.

July 7 King John I of Bohemia is expelled from Brescia, Italy.

July 15 King Christopher II of Denmark dies in exile. Gerhard, Count of Holstein, continues to rule in the interregnum.

July 25 King Philip VI of France takes the cross in order to embark on a crusade to Palestine planned by Pope John XXII.

August 12 Edward, son of John Balliol, and other "disinherited" Scottish nobles make use of English support to defeat and kill the Earl of Mar, regent of Scotland, at Dupplin Moor.

September 9 Italian rulers found the League of Ferrara to unite against King John I of Bohemia and the papal legate Bertrand du Poujet.

September 24 Edward Balliol is crowned king of Scotland at Scone, Scotland.

November 7 Lucerne, Switzerland, accedes to the Confederation of Swiss Forest Cantons.

November 11 Azzo Visconti, ruler of Milan, takes the northern Italian town of Pavia.

November 25 Charles, son of King John I of Bohemia, defeats the Estensi of Ferrara, Italy, at San Felice, Italy.

December 12 Edward Balliol, King of Scotland, is defeated by the Earl of Moray at Annan, Scotland, and flees to England.

1333
c. 1333 Daud ben al Hasan becomes sultan of Kilwa, East Africa.
- Algeciras is recaptured from Spain by the Marinid dynasty of Morocco.
- Go-Daigo, assisted by the great feudatory Ashikaga Takauji, defeats the Hojo regency and establishes himself as emperor of Japan. The Hojos are

extinguished and the effective Japanese capital is removed from Kamakura and restored to Kyoto.

- Mohammed IV, King of Granada, takes Gibraltar from Castile.
- The Byzantine emperor Andronicus III recovers possession of northern Thessaly in Greece.
- The Japanese emperor Go-Daigo escapes from exile on the island of Oki and returns to Kyoto, in an attempt to reestablish his power.
- William de Burgh, Earl of Ulster and Connaught, is assassinated at Carrickfergus, Ireland, by his cousins. The earldoms revert to his cousins and are converted into de facto independent native principalities.

February 6   Forces led by the papal legate Bertrand du Poujet defeat the Ferrarese and take Consándolo, Italy.

March 2   King Władysław I of Poland dies and is succeeded by Casimir (Kazimierz) III.

April 14   The papal legate Bertrand du Poujet and King John I of Bohemia are defeated at Ferrara, Italy.

May 5   King Edward III of England joins Edward Balliol at the siege of the Scottish border town of Berwick.

June 8   King Edward III of England orders the seizure of the Isle of Man from Scotland. The island is henceforth attached to England.

July 19   King Edward III of England defeats the Scots at Halidon Hill when they attempt to relieve the siege of Berwick, Scotland. Berwick surrenders to Edward the following day.

August 25   Mohammed IV of Granada is murdered and is succeeded by his brother Yūsuf I.

September 26   Andrew of Hungary marries Joanna of Naples.

October 10   Pope John XXII leaves Italy for Bohemia, where he puts Charles IV of Luxembourg in charge of its government.

1334

- Ashikaga Takauji, one of the leading Japanese warlords, imprisons his chief rival Prince Morinaga, the son of the Japanese emperor Go-Daigo.

May 5   The exiled King David II of Scotland arrives in France. King Philip VI of France lodges him in the Château Gaillard, France.

June 12   By the Treaty of Newcastle upon Tyne, Edward Balliol recognizes Edward III as his overlord and cedes Berwick and eight shires of southern Scotland to England.

August 17   Bologna revolts and expels the papal legate Bertrand du Poujet.

September 9   A fresh uprising in Scotland forces Edward Balliol to flee to England.

December 20   The French Benedict monk Jacques Fournier is elected Pope Benedict XII following the death of Pope John XXII.

The Black Death (1333–69)

1333

- The Black Death (a comination of bubonic and pneumonic plagues) appears in China, afflicting a population weakened by starvation. It will be spread in the West by travelers and merchants returning from the Far East to Europe.

1343

- Tatar forces of the khanate of the "Golden Horde" are struck by Black Death while besieging the Genoese trading town of Caffa in the Crimea. Escaping merchants carry the disease across Europe.

1347

- The Black Death appears in Constantinople (modern Istanbul, Turkey), Naples and Genoa in Italy, and the south of France.

1348

- England's harvests fail after a period of protracted bad weather. The shortage of food leaves the population particularly vulnerable to the Black Death.
- French surgeon Guy de Chauliac remains at Auvergne, France, as the Black Death rages around him, and produces one of the first detailed medical descriptions of the disease.
- The Black Death spreads in Italy, and into Spain, central and northern France, and southern England, reducing populations by more than half in some parts.
- The Italian physician Gentile da Foligno, who performed the first anatomical dissections at Padua, writes *Consilium contra pestilentiam/Counsel against Pestilence*, an account of the Black Death.

1349

- The Black Death spreads to northern England, Ireland, and Scandinavia, and to Germany and the Swiss Confederation, where Jews are massacred for their supposed responsibility for the pestilence.

March 26   King Alfonso XI of Castile dies of the Black Death while besieging the Muslims in Gibraltar.

1350

- German naturalist Conrad of Megenburg writes *Das Buch der Natur/The Book of Nature*, a treatise on natural history in which he blames earthquakes for the current epidemic of the Black Death.
- Hebrew physician Moses ben Joshua of Narbonne writes *Orah hayyim/Road of Life*, a treatise on medicine, with an astrological explanation for the Black Death.

1352

- The Black Death spreads eastward across Europe, reaching Moscow, Russia, and returning toward India and China.

1361–62

- The second major outbreak of the Black Death in western Europe occurs.

1369

- Further outbreaks of the Black Death occur in England and France.

SCIENCE, TECHNOLOGY, AND MEDICINE

Agriculture

1333

- The onset of famines, which persist until 1347, and the flooding of the Yellow River combine to ruin the Chinese economy and further weaken the Yüan (Mongol) dynasty.

Ecology

1333

- The River Arno floods at Florence, Italy, sweeping away the main bridge across it. The bridge is rebuilt in 1345 as the Ponte Vecchio.

Exploration

1330

- The traveler Jordanus writes *The Wonders of the East*, describing his journey to India.

Health and Medicine

1333

- The Black Death (a combination of bubonic and pneumonic plagues) appears in China, afflicting a population weakened by starvation. It will be spread in the West by travelers and merchants returning from the Far East to Europe.

Science

1330

- English philosopher William of Occam proposes "Occam's razor," the principle that the simplest explanation is most likely to be true—an idea that will be highly influential when applied to scientific theories.

- Italian alchemist Pietro Buono writes a defense of his craft, *Pretiosa margarita novella/The Precious Pearl*.

Technology

1331

- Italian defenders of the besieged town of Civitate, Italy, repel German forces using firearms—their first deployment in European warfare.
- Weaving is recorded for the first time in England, at York.

ARTS AND IDEAS

Architecture

c. **1330**

- The spire of Salisbury Cathedral in England is completed. At just over 123 m/410 ft it is the highest in England.

1334

- Italian artist Giotto di Bondone is put in charge of the building of Florence Cathedral, and designs the campanile.

Arts

1330

- An anonymous Italian artist sculpts the *Equestrian Statue of Can Grande della Scala*.
- Italian artist Pietro Lorenzetti completes his series of frescoes in the Church of San Francesco in Assisi, Italy.

1333

- Italian artists Simone Martini and Lippo Memmi paint *The Annunciation*.

Literature and Language

1330

- *c.* 1330 *I fioretti di San Francisco/The Little Flowers of St. Francis*, a popular collection of stories and legends

BIRTHS & DEATHS

1330

c. 1330 John Wycliffe, English theologian, philosopher, and church reformer who attacked the doctrine of transubstantiation, born in Yorkshire, England (–1384).

- Peter Parler, German architect whose use of extensive ornamentation and complicated vaults influenced later architecture, born in Swäbisch Gmünd, Württemberg (–1399).

January 13 Frederick the Handsome, Duke of Austria, dies.

June 15 Edward (the Black Prince), heir-apparent to the English throne and successful military commander during the Hundred Years' War, born in Woodstock, Oxfordshire, England (–1376).

1331

January 14 Odoric of Pordenone, Franciscan friar known for the account of his travels in China, dies in Udine (*c.* 47).

February 16 Coluccio Salutati, Florentine chancellor and humanist, born in Stignano, Tuscany (–1406).

1332

c. 1332 Franco Sacchetti, Italian writer, creator of a range of poems and the prose text *Trecento Novelle/Three Hundred Stories*, born (–1400).

May 27 Ibn-Khaldūn, Arab historian whose best-known work is the *Muqaddimah/Introduction to History*, born in Tunis (–1406).

1334

December 4 Pope John XXII dies.

describing the life of St. Francis, is written and widely circulated.

- Italian Franciscan friar Odoric of Pordenone writes his *Description of the East*, recording travels in Persia, India, Sumatra, Java, Borneo, China, and Tibet (1316–30) during which he baptized 20,000 people.
- Spanish writer Juan Ruiz publishes *El libro de buen amor/The Book of Love*, a collection of satires and love lyrics written in Spanish. Ruiz is Spain's first great poet.

c. 1331

- Italian-born Jewish writer Emanuel ben Solomon (Manoello Giudeo) completes his *Mahbaroth*, a miscellany of prose and verse.

c. 1333

- Arabic scholar Hamdallāh Mustaufī completes his *Zafar-nāma/Book of Victory*, an Arabic history of Islam from Mohammad to 1331, written in verse.

Thought and Scholarship

c. 1330

- Catalan chronicler Ramón Muntaner completes his *Chronica/Chronicle*, a Catalan history covering the period 1204 to 1328.

1331

- Persian scholar Abul-Fidā completes his *Mukhtasar Ta'rīkh al-Bashar/Epitome of the History of Mankind*, a universal history from the creation to 1329.
- The *Ching-shih ta-tien/The Great Standard of Administration*, a Chinese official encyclopedia, mainly of Mongol institutions, is published.

c. 1332

- Arabic scholar Ahmād al-Nuwayrī completes the *Nihāyat al-Arab*, a general encyclopedia for Muslim administrators, with a large section on Muslim history.

SOCIETY

Education

1332

- The College of Burgundy is founded in Paris, France.

1334

- North Country masters migrate from Oxford, England, and attempt to establish a university at Stamford.

Everyday Life

1332

- Bitter oranges are introduced into Europe for the first time, through the French port of Nice.

Religion

1331

- Pope John XXII's constitution "Ratio juris" defines the functions of the court of audience of the papal palace. From 1336 it is known as the "Rota."

c. 1332

- French scholar Nicholas of Lyra completes his *Postillae perpetuae in universam super Scripturam/Notes on the Universal Holy Scripture*, an early and influential commentary on biblical texts. It is first printed in 1471.

1334

- The Italian friar Giovanni Valle founds a hermitage near Foligno, in Italy. This community becomes the Friars of the Strict Observance (of the Franciscan Order).

1335–1339

POLITICS, GOVERNMENT, AND ECONOMICS

Business and Economics

1336

September 23   King Edward III of England obtains a large grant of taxes in a parliament at Nottingham, England, on complaining that King Philip VI of France refuses to restore Agenais, France, and is sheltering King David II of Scotland and aiding Scottish resistance.

Politics and Government

1335

- Abu Sa'id, Sultan of Persia, dies and the Mongol ilkhanate of southwest Asia disintegrates.
- Ghar Singh, King of Jailsame, is assassinated by his adopted son Keliar Singh.
- Mohammed II, Sultan of Delhi, India, is prevented by disease from making an expedition to Madura, in the south of India, where his governor, Hasan, has declared himself an independent shah.

February 2   King Edward III of England, having reached Roxburgh, Scotland, abandons a projected Scottish campaign.

April 2   Henry, Duke of Carinthia, dies. King Ludwig IV of Bavaria confers the duchy and southern Tyrol on the Habsburgs, and northern Tyrol on his own sons, despite his promise to King John I of Bohemia that Henry's daughter Margaret "Maultasch," who is married to John's son John Henry, should inherit.

July 7   King Edward III of England begins a campaign in southern Scotland.

November 11   King Edward III of England returns to England. On his departure, Edward Balliol's authority in Scotland soon crumbles.

November 11   King John I of Bohemia, King Charles I of Hungary, and King Casimir (Kazimierz) III of Poland meet in congress at Vyšehrad, near Buda, Hungary. King John I of Bohemia and King Charles I of Hungary decide that the Teutonic Knights should restore Kujavia and Dobrzyń to Poland but retain Pomerania as vassals of King Casimir III of Poland. King Casimir III of Poland recognizes Bohemian overlordship in Silesia, while King John renounces his title to the Polish crown.

1336

c. 1336   The Sammās, a Rajput tribe, oust the ruling Sūmras and assume control of the Sind region of India.

- King Edward III of England shelters Robert of Artois, enemy of King Philip VI of France.
- King John I of Bohemia ravages Austria. Peace is made in which the Habsburgs are left holding Carinthia while Margaret, who is married to King John's son John Henry, is established in Tyrol.
- Mubarak Shah rebels against Mohammed II, Sultan of Delhi, and declares eastern Bengal independent.
- Pope Benedict XII cancels the projected crusade to Palestine. King Philip VI of France brings the fleet which he intended for the crusade into the Channel, threatening England.
- Stephen Uroš III, King of Serbia, is murdered and is succeeded by his son Stephen Uroš IV Dušan.
- Timbuktu is captured by Mali.

1336–37   The Marinids besiege Tlemcen (in modern Algeria), and the local ruler Abu Tashfin and his three sons perish.

January 24   King Alfonso IV of Aragon dies and is succeeded by Pedro IV.

April 18   Harihara I, who led a Hindu revolt against Muslim rule, is crowned in his newly built capital, Vijayanagar, and thus founds the Sangama dynasty of the Vijayanagar empire of southern India.

July   The Japanese emperor Go-Daigo's attempt to restore imperial authority in Japan collapses. Forces of the Ashikaga clan under Ashikaga Takauji defeat those of Go-Daigo. Takauji takes Kyoto and enthrones a new emperor, Komyo.

July 7   King Edward III of England campaigns in the Highlands of Scotland.

August 12   King Edward III of England prohibits the export of wool to Flanders and causes unrest there, enabling pressure to be placed on the Count of Flanders not to allow Flemish ports to be used against England in times of war.

November 11   King Edward III of England makes his last visit to Scotland for the purpose of strengthening Edward Balliol's position.

1337

- Azzo Visconti, ruler of Milan, takes Piacenza, Italy.
- Mansa Musa, ruler of the Mali empire, dies. Under his rule, the empire achieved its greatest range, including Gao and Timbuktu.
- Mastino della Scala of Verona takes Lucca, Italy, his dominion now reaching from the Alps to the Mediterranean.
- Orkhān, leader of the Ottoman Turks, takes Nicomedia (modern Izmit, Turkey) from the Byzantine Empire.

- The Byzantine emperor Andronicus III recovers possession of the principality of Epirus, on the west coast of Albania and Greece.

1337–38   The army sent by Mohammed II, Sultan of Delhi, to conquer Tibet, is destroyed in the Himalayas.

January   Go-Daigo, the deposed emperor of Japan, escapes from Kyoto, the capital, and flees to Yoshino, where he sets up a rival imperial court.

January 25   King Frederick II of Sicily dies and is succeeded by his son Peter II.

April 4   King Edward III of England sends an embassy to the Low Countries to recruit allies against King Philip VI of France.

May 24   King Philip VI of France announces the confiscation of Gascony as a reaction to the "rebellion" of King Edward III of England. Its seizure begins the Hundred Years' War.

July 15   Under the Treaty of Valenciennes King Ludwig IV of Bavaria and King Edward III of England become allies against France.

October 7   King Edward III of England claims the French crown through his mother, Isabella of France, daughter of Philip IV.

December 28   James van Artevelde becomes the accepted leader of the Flemings, who are in revolt against the Count of Flanders because of the hardship caused by the English embargo on the export of wool to Flanders.

1338

- Ashikaga Takauji restores the shogunate, which remains in his family until 1573. Its control of Japan is never complete and feudal anarchy prevails. He also issues the *Kemmu Code* to organize his government, which has its capital at Kyoto, Japan.

June 6   A French fleet sacks Portsmouth, England.

July 16   In the Declaration of Rense, a majority of the German electoral princes assert their unfettered right to elect their king, thus rejecting papal claims to approve or confirm such elections.

July 16   King Edward III of England lands at Antwerp in the Holy Roman Empire (in modern Belgium).

September 5   King Edward III of England meets King Ludwig IV of Bavaria at Koblenz, Germany, who appoints him imperial vicar, west of the River Rhine.

1339

- Alī Shāh rebels against Mohammed II, Sultan of Delhi, and declares western Bengal independent.
- By the second Treaty of Vyšehrad, King Casimir (Kazimierz) III of Poland recognizes his nephew, Ludwig, son of King Charles I of Hungary, as his heir.
- Edward Balliol leaves Scotland, having failed to establish his rule.
- King Casimir (Kazimierz) III of Poland attempts to seize Galicia and Volhynia following the murder of King Yury (Juri) II. He is opposed by the Galicians, who elect Lubart, son of Gedymin of Lithuania, to be king, who is given the protection of Uzbekh, Khan of the "Golden Horde."
- Venice makes its first conquest on the Italian mainland with the seizure of Treviso, Italy.

June 21   The forces of the city of Bern are aided by the Forest Cantons in defeating the forces of Fribourg, at Laupen, in modern Switzerland, and the local nobles who are opposing the dominant position of Bern.

August 16   Azzo Visconti dies and is succeeded by his uncle Luchino as ruler of Milan.

September 15   In the "Process of Warsaw," papal agents conclude their hearing of evidence of the occupation of Polish lands by the Teutonic Knights, who have disregarded the earlier award in favor of Poland.

September 23   Following a popular uprising, Simone Boccanegra is elected first doge of Genoa, Italy.

October 10   King Philip VI of France and King Edward III of England conduct an abortive campaign against one another in Picardy, France.

October 31   Francesco Dandolo, doge of Venice, dies, and is succeeded by Bartolomeo Gradenigo.

SCIENCE, TECHNOLOGY, AND MEDICINE

Agriculture

1336

- The failure of the harvest causes famine in India.

Ecology

1335

- The grain harvest fails in England, leading to widespread hardship.

1337–44

- William Merle of Oxford, England, keeps regular records of the weather.

Health and Medicine

1335

- Italian physician and scientist Guido da Vigevano writes *Tesaurus regis Francie/Treasury of the Kings of France*, prescribing a health regime for those departing on crusades, and, in a section on military science, proposing the use of armored vehicles in warfare.

Math

1335

- The English abbot of St. Albans Richard of Wallingford writes *Quadripartitum de sinibus demonstratis*, the first original Latin treatise on trigonometry.

Science

1335

- English scholar William Heytesbury of Oxford, England, produces the first law of uniform acceleration.

Technology

1335

- The world's first public clock, regularly striking the time in hours, is erected in the town square at San Gottardo, Milan, Italy.

1337

- Thomas Blanket installs weaving looms at Bristol, England.

1338

- The ship's manifest of English king Edward I's ship *Christophe de la Tour* shows that its equipment includes a "handgone"—the first recorded handheld firearm.

1339

- The earliest antipersonnel gun known is made. The *ribauldequin* is constructed from a row of separate smallbore firearms on a rack, each loaded separately, but fired off simultaneously.

ARTS AND IDEAS

Arts

1336

- Italian artist Andrea Pisano completes his bronze doors for the south doorway to the Baptistry in Florence. Two other sets are added in the 15th century.

1338

- Italian artist Taddeo Gaddi completes his frescoes *The Life of the Virgin* in the Baroncelli chapel of the Church of Santa Croce in Florence.

1339

- Italian artist Ambrogio Lorenzetti paints the fresco *The Effects of Good and Bad Government* in the Palazzo Pubblico (the Town Hall), Siena, Italy.

Literature and Language

1335

- An illustrated edition of the *Shāh-nāma/Book of Kings*, the Persian national epic, is produced at Tabriz. This edition is one of classics of Persian bookmaking.

- Japanese writer Yoshida Kenko (Yoshida Kaneyoshi) completes his *Tsurezuregusa*, a collection of essays and reflections.

1338

- *c.* 1338 Italian writer Francesco Petrarch (Petrarca) begins his epic poem *Africa*, written in Latin. It is an account of the career of Scipio Africanus, the Roman general who defeated Hannibal. Petrarch never completes this work, which is first published (posthumously) in 1396.

- *c.* 1338 Italian writer Giovanni Boccaccio writes his poem *Il filostrato/The Love-struck* on the theme of Troilus and Cressida.

- English scholar Robert Mannyng completes his translation into English verse of Peter Langtoft's *Chronicle* of 1307.

Thought and Scholarship

c. 1335

- German chronicler Nikolaus von Jeroschin completes his *Kronike von Pruzinlant/Prussian Chronicle*, a history of northern Germany.

1336

- Italian scholar and writer Cino da Pistoia (de' Sigibuldi) publishes the legal treatise *Lectura in codicem/Readings in Law*, a commentary on part of the Code of Justinian.

1337

- Italian scholar Ferreto de' Ferreti completes his *Historia rerum in Italia gestarum/History of Italy* covering the period 1250 to 1318.

SOCIETY

Education

1337

- King's Hall is founded at Cambridge University, England. It later forms part of Trinity College founded in 1546.

1338

- The University of Pisa is established in Italy.

1339

- The University of Grenoble is founded in France.

BIRTHS & DEATHS

1336

- Timur Leng (Tamerlane), ruthless Turkic leader who conquered Persia, India, and Anatolia, born in Kesh, near Samarkand, Transoxiana (–1405).

1337

- Cino da Pistoia (de' Sigibuldi), Italian scholar and writer, dies (*c.* 67)

January 8 Giotto di Bondone, the leading Italian painter of his age, whose works include the *Navicella* mosaic in St. Peter's, Rome, dies in Florence (*c.* 70).

January 21 Charles V the Wise, King of France 1364–80 who led France to recovery after the first phase of the Hundred Years' War (1337–1453), born in Vincennes, France (–1380).

1338

- Jean d'Outremeuse, French writer, creator of *Le Myreur des histoires/The Mirror of History*, a verse history of the world, and *Geste de Liège/The Story of Liège*, an epic, born (–1399).

Religion

1335

- Pope Benedict XII (a Cistercian monk) draws up a new constitution for the Cistercian Order.
- The Russian monk St. Sergius of Radonezh founds the Holy Trinity Monastery near Moscow, one of the first Russian monasteries not in a town. A leading reformer, he establishes over 40 monasteries.

1336

- Pope Benedict XII draws up new constitutions for the Benedictine and Cluniac Orders.

1337

- A controversy develops between the Greek theologian Gregory Palamas and the Italian monk Barlaam on the subject of the "unknowability of God." Gregory defends the mystic's search for an intense experience of God's presence, a position challenged by the rationalism of Barlaam. The dispute highlights differences between the Eastern and Western churches.

c. 1338

- The German Dominican Johann Tauler becomes a leading figure on the mystical sect the Friends of God, a group of lay people and clergy inspired by the teachings of Johannes Eckhart ("Meister Eckhart").

1339

- Pope Benedict XII draws up a constitution for the Augustinian Canons.
- The Byzantine emperor Andronicus Palaeologus III sends an embassy to Pope Benedict XII to negotiate the reunion of the Eastern and Western churches.

Sports

1338

- *Le Livre du roy modus et de la royne racio/The Book of King Method and Queen Reason*, an influential treatise on hunting (mostly stag hunting), appears in France. It is attributed to the comte de Tancarville, a Norman nobleman.

1340–1344

POLITICS, GOVERNMENT, AND ECONOMICS

Business and Economics

1340

- Italian trader Francesco Balducci Pegolotti publishes *The Merchant's Handbook*, a guide to trade routes to the East.
- Italian writer on economics Francesco Balducci Pegolotti publishes *Prattica della mercatura/The Practice of Marketing*, which contains a treatise on economics as well as a guide to international commerce, giving routes, tables of tariffs, international measures and so forth, including those found in China.
- King Philip VI of France first coins gold angels.

1341

- Muso Kokushi, a Zen monk, builds the Tenryuji monastery at Kyoto from profits of a trading expedition to China. Other monasteries follow suit, participating in the contemporary growth of Japanese overseas trade. This is accompanied by an increased incidence of piracy.

- The French government imposes a tax on consumer goods, the gabelle, to raise money for the Hundred Years' War against England.

Politics and Government

1340

c. 1340   The Hoysala ruler, Vīra Ballāa, extends his authority southwest into Chola territory.

- Al-Nasir, Sultan of Egypt, dies, and is followed by a succession of 12 puppets who are ruled and removed by their amirs.
- Gerhard, Count of Holstein and ruler of Denmark, is murdered. Waldemar IV, son of Christopher II, is made king.
- Mohammed II, Sultan of Delhi, creates a department of agriculture to combat the famine in India.

January 25   King Edward III of England assumes the title of king of France at Ghent, Flanders, and is recognized as such by the Flemings.

April 5   Marinid and Hafsid fleets defeat a Spanish force near Gibraltar.

June 24   The English fleet wins a naval victory over the French at Sluys, Flanders.

September 24   King Edward III of England and King Philip VI of France make a truce at Esplechin when Edward runs out of money to continue the war.

October 30   King Alfonso XI of Castile and King Alfonso IV of Portugal defeat a Muslim invasion from Africa on the River Salado.

December 1   On his return to England, King Edward III of England purges his government and begins the prosecution of the dismissed chancellor John Stratford, archbishop of Canterbury.

1341

c. 1341   Sulama, King of Mali, reestablishes control over the former dominions of Mali.

- Gedymin, Grand Prince of Lithuania, dies, having extended his hold over western Russia and making his capital at Vilnius, Lithuania. He is succeeded by his son, Olgierd.

- Ivan Kalita, Prince of Moscow and Grand Duke of Vladimir, dies, and is succeeded by his son Simeon.

- Mastino della Scala of Verona's empire collapses, leaving only the Italian cities of Verona and Vicenza in his hands.

- Rebellions break out in China against the Yüan dynasty.

- Uzbekh, Khan of the "Golden Horde," dies and is succeeded by his son Tinibeg.

1341–42   An alliance is formed between the Earl of Desmond, local townspeople, and lesser landowners in Ireland, following discontent when Irish administrators are blamed for a financial decline and a policy is introduced whereby their jobs are awarded to the English.

March 15   King Ludwig IV of Bavaria abandons his alliance with King Edward III of England and makes peace with King Philip VI at Vincennes, France.

April 23   A parliament meets and clears John Stratford, archbishop of Canterbury, of the charges made by King Edward III of England. Under pressure, the king makes several concessions, including an assent to the request from the commons to accept baronial councillors.

April 30   John III, Duke of Brittany, dies. The succession is disputed by his half brother, John de Montfort, and his niece, Jeanne de Penthièvre, wife of Charles of Blois. The Parlement of Paris pronounces in favor of Jeanne de Penthièvre.

June 6   King David II returns to Scotland from France when his supporters succeed in expelling the English from Edinburgh, Scotland.

June 15   The Byzantine emperor Andronicus III dies and is succeeded by his son John V. Since John V is only nine years old, John Cantacuzenus is appointed regent.

October 26   John Cantacuzenus, grand domestic of the Greek Empire, proclaims himself emperor. This begins a civil war in which the nobility supports John Cantacuzenus, while the populace back the young John V.

November 11   Charles of Blois captures John de Montfort, and imprisons him in France. John's niece, Jeanne, wife of Charles of Blois, recognizes King Edward III of England as king of France and seeks his assistance to continue the Breton war of succession.

1342

- Janibeg deposes and succeeds his brother Tinibeg as khan of the "Golden Horde."

- King Charles I of Hungary dies and is succeeded by his son Ludwig I.

- The Confraternity of St. Nicholas, a guild of barristers and solicitors practicing in the Parlement of Paris, is founded in France.

- The Hoysala ruler, Vīra Ballāa, is killed at Trichonopoly during campaigns in Madura. He is succeeded by his son, Vīra Virūpāksha Ballāla.

- Weakened by wars against the Delhi sultanate and Madura, the Hoysala kingdom collapses after King Balalla III is defeated by Harihara of Vijayanagar.

January 1   King Edward III of England campaigns ineffectively in southern Scotland.

February 2   Following a rising of the Tyrolese people, King Ludwig IV of Bavaria declares that the marriage of Margaret "Maultasch" and John Henry of Bohemia is void. This leaves her free to marry Ludwig, Margrave of Brandenburg, the king's son.

March 31   On capturing Roxburgh, Scotland, the Scots complete their expulsion of the English from Scotland.

May 7   The French clergyman Pierre Roger is elected Pope Clement VI.

June 6   Walter de Manny leads an English expedition to relieve John de Montfort, who has been holding Hennebont, Brittany, against Charles of Blois.

August 8   Peter II of Sicily dies and is succeeded by his son Louis.

September 8   Walter de Brienne, titular Duke of Athens, who has been employed by Florence in the dispute in northern Italy between Florence and Pisa over the possession of Lucca, is proclaimed signore of Florence in a successful plot by Florence city magnates.

September 30   An English force defeats Charles of Blois at Morlaix, in Brittany. King Edward III of England arrives in Brittany on October 10 and campaigns against the French force supporting Charles.

1343

- King Magnus II cedes the crown of Norway to his son Haakon VI.

- Kitabatatake Chikafusa, a leading supporter of the southern Japanese imperial court, is forced to withdraw from his power base in the northeastern province of Hitachi.

- The Byzantine emperor John VI Cantacuzenus conquers Thrace with Ottoman support.

January 4   Andrea Dandolo is elected doge of Venice, Italy.

January 19   King Edward III of England and King Philip VI of France make a truce under the Treaty of Malestroit.

January 20   King Robert the Wise of Naples, Italy, dies. He is succeeded by his granddaughter Joanna I, wife of Andrew of Hungary.

July 8   The Treaty of Kalisz ends the war between the Teutonic Knights and King Casimir (Kazimierz) III of Poland, who cedes Pomerania.

August 1   Following an insurrection, Walter of Brienne, Duke of Athens, surrenders the lordship of Florence, Italy, thus restoring its commune, a government organized by the people with no single ruler.

1344

- King Casimir (Kazimierz) III of Poland defeats a Mongol force on the River Vistula.

- King Ludwig I of Hungary expels a Mongol force from Transylvania.

- Negotiations take place in Avignon, France, between English and French embassies, and Pope Clement VI pronounces in favor of the rights of King Philip VI as king of France.

March 26 A Spanish force under King Alfonso XI of Castile takes Algeciras, Spain, after a 20-month siege.

March 29 King Pedro IV of Aragon reannexes the Balearic Islands to his kingdom, deposing King James II of Majorca.

October 28 A crusading fleet organized by Pope Clement VI takes the Turkish-held port of Smyrna in Anatolia (modern Izmir, Turkey). The port is held, first by papal forces and then by the Knights Hospitaller, until 1402.

SCIENCE, TECHNOLOGY, AND MEDICINE

Ecology

1340

- William Merle of Oxford, England, writes *De futura aeris intemperie/On the Future Storm*, a treatise on various methods of predicting the weather.

Health and Medicine

1340

- The earliest copy of Muslim scholar Al-Baytar's *Kamil al-Sinā'atayn*, a treatise on veterinary medicine, dates from this period.

1342

- Byzantine physician Joannes Actuarios writes his *Methodus medendi/Method of Healing*, a Galenic medical treatise based on the properties of urine.

1343

- French surgeon Guy de Chauliac publishes his *Inventorius medicinae/Medical Inventions*, outlining new surgical techniques such as putting fractures in slings, and operating on hernias and cataracts.
- Tatar forces of the khanate of the "Golden Horde" are struck by Black Death while besieging the Genoese trading town of Caffa in the Crimea. Escaping merchants carry the disease across Europe.

Math

1343

- Hebrew astronomer Levi ben Gerson (Gersonides) writes *De harmonicis numeris/Concerning the Harmony of Numbers*, a treatise on arithmetic, for the musician Philippe de Vitry.
- Jean de Meurs writes a metrical treatise on mathematics, mechanics, and music, *Quadripartitum numerorum/ Four-fold Division of Numbers*.

Science

1340

- Persian scholar Hamdallāh Mustaufī writes *Delight of the Hearts*, an encyclopedia of cosmography and science.

1342

- The work of the Hebrew astronomer Levi ben Gerson (Gersonides) is translated into Latin as *De sinibus, chordis et arcubus/Concerning Sines, Chords and Arcs*, a treatise on trigonometry introducing the use of the cross-staff for astronomical observations.

BIRTHS & DEATHS

1340

c. 1340 Robert Stewart Albany, regent and virtual ruler of Scotland 1388–1420, born.

March John of Gaunt, Duke of Lancaster, English prince, son of Edward III of England, father of Henry IV of England, born in Ghent, Flanders (–1399).

October Geert Groote (Gerardus Magnus), Dutch priest and teacher, who established the Brethren of the Common Life, born in Deventer, Flanders (–1384).

November 30 Jean de France, Duke of Berry, third son of King John II the Good of France, who as lieutenant for Auvergne, Languedoc, Périgord, and Poitou (1358–) controlled at least one third of French territory, also a major patron of the arts, born in Vincennes, France (–1416).

1341

- Muhammad ad-Damīrī, Muslim theologian and mystic, author of a noted encyclopedia of animals (1371), born in Cairo (–1405).

1342

c. 1342 Geoffrey Chaucer, the principal English writer before Shakespeare, whose best-known work is *The Canterbury Tales*, born (–1400).

- Domenico Cavalca, Italian monk, writer of several works—mainly translations and biographies of saints—written in a colorful vernacular, dies.

January 17 Philip II the Bold, Duke of Burgundy 1363–1404 and virtual ruler of France 1392–1404, born in Pontoise, France (–1404).

April 25 Pope Benedict XII dies.

July 31 William Courtenay, archbishop of Canterbury 1381–96, born near Exeter, Devon, England (–1396).

November 10 Henry Percy, 1st Earl of Northumberland, marshal of England who helped King Henry IV gain the crown and later led a rebellion against him, born (–1408).

December 28 Bartolomeo Gradenigo, doge of Venice, Italy, dies.

1343

c. 1343 Marsilius of Padua, Italian political philosopher, forerunner of the Protestant Reformation whose *Defensor pacis/Defender of Peace* influenced the modern idea of the state, dies in Munich (*c.* 63).

1344

- Levi ben Gerson (Gersonides), French Jewish mathematician, philosopher, Talmudic scholar, and astronomer, dies (*c.* 56).
- Simone Martini, leading Italian Gothic painter noted for his frescoes, dies in Avignon, France (*c.* 60).

Technology

1340

- Iron blast-furnaces are known in the Liège district of the Holy Roman Empire (in modern Belgium), producing cast iron for the first time; at Namur, water power is used to operate a tilt-hammer in an iron mill.

1344

- Italian clockmaker Jacopo di Dondi invents the clock dial.

ARTS AND IDEAS

Architecture

1342

- A lantern (small turret) is built on Ely Cathedral in England to replace the tower which collapsed in 1322. It was designed by master mason John Attegrene.

Arts

1340

c. 1340 The richly illustrated *Luttrell Psalter* is completed, one of the finest examples of 14th-century English illumination.

- Italian artist Pietro Lorenzetti paints *The Madonna Enthroned*.

1342

- Italian artist Pietro Lorenzetti paints *Birth of the Virgin*.
- Italian artist Simone Martini paints *Christ Reproved by His Parents*.

Literature and Language

1340

c. 1340 *The Prick of Conscience*, an anonymous religious poem in a northern dialect of Middle English, is written. It was long attributed to the English mystic Richard Rolle.

c. 1340–*c.* 1370 Welsh writer Dafydd ap Gwilym writes a body of poems—mostly love lyrics and nature poems—which are the highpoint of Welsh medieval literature.

1341

April 8 Italian writer Francesco Petrarch (Petrarca) is crowned as poet laureate on the Capitoline in Rome.

Theater and Dance

c. **1340**

- The *York Cycle* of mystery plays—a set of religious plays performed annually by the citizens of York, England—is written.

SOCIETY

Education

1340

- Queen's College is founded at Oxford University in England.

Religion

1340

- Pope Benedict XII sends the Italian Franciscan friar Giovanni da Marignolli to China as emissary to the Mongol emperor Togon Temur. He returns in 1353 and publishes his account of his travels in 1359.

1344

- Pope Clement VI elevates the bishopric of Prague into an archbishopric, thus detaching Bohemia from the province of Mainz.

December 20 Pope John XXII dies leaving a fortune of 18 million florins, leading to tales that he had discovered the philosopher's stone and turned lead into gold.

1345–1349

POLITICS, GOVERNMENT, AND ECONOMICS

Business and Economics

1345

- The great banking houses of Bardi and Peruzzi, in Florence, Italy, go bankrupt following the failure of King Edward III of England to pay his debts. The proletariat (*populo minuto*) makes its first attempt to win political significance and is defeated. Its leader Ciuto Brandini is hanged.

Politics and Government

1345

- King Ludwig I of Hungary conquers Croatia.
- Mohammed II, Sultan of Delhi vainly besieges local officials of the Deccan, India, who are rebelling against him in the citadel of Daulatābād. Rebellions are occurring simultaneously in Warangal and the state of Gujarat in India.

May 20 John de Montfort, Earl of Richmond, who has escaped from France, pays homage for Brittany to King Edward III of England.

July 24 Riots break out between the weavers and fullers of Ghent, Flanders, leading to the murder of the city's ruler, James van Artevelde, an ally of King Edward III of England.

September 9 King William II of Hainault and IV of Holland dies and is succeeded by his sister Margaret, wife of King Ludwig IV of Bavaria.

September 25 King Stephen Dušan IV of Serbia takes Serres, in Macedonia.

October 21 Henry of Grosmont, Earl of Lancaster, defeats a French force at Auberoche in Gascony, France.

November 18 Andrew of Hungary, King of Naples, Italy, is murdered, supposedly at the instigation of his wife Joanna I of Naples. His brother King Ludwig I of Hungary reacts by making war on Naples.

1346

- Mīrzā revolts against Mohammed II, Sultan of Delhi. He founds the Muslim kingdom of Kashmīr.
- The Genoese recover the Aegean island of Chios.
- The Teutonic Knights annex the Danish provinces of Viro and Harju in Estonia.

April 4 By abandoning imperial claims in Italy, Charles of Bohemia receives the consent of Pope Clement VI to his election as king of the Romans. Pope Clement VI subsequently orders the German electors to choose a king to replace Ludwig I of Hungary.

April 16 King Stephen Dušan IV of Serbia is crowned emperor of the Serbs and Greeks in Skopje, Serbia.

July 11 Charles IV is elected king of the Romans.

July 12 King Edward III of England, seeking to exploit Norman disaffection with King Philip VI of France, lands in northern Normandy at St.-Vaast-la-Hougue, France. On July 26, Edward takes and sacks Caen in Normandy.

August 20 Queen Joanna I of Naples, Italy, marries Louis of Taranto, Italy.

August 26 English king Edward III uses cannon against the French at the battle of Crécy, but the battle is actually won by skilled English archers using longbows.

August 26 King Edward III of England defeats a French force at Crécy, France. Among those killed on the French side are King John I of Bohemia who is succeeded by Charles, and Louis of Nevers, Count of Flanders, who is succeeded by his son Louis de Maële. King Philip VI of France escapes to Amiens, France.

September 4 King Edward III of England begins the siege of Calais, France.

October 4 Henry of Grosmont, Earl of Lancaster, takes Poitiers, France.

October 17 King David II of Scotland invades England and is defeated and captured at Neville's Cross, outside Durham, England. His action helps to relieve the pressure placed on France by King Edward III of England.

1347

- King Casimir (Kazimierz) III of Poland promulgates the Statutes of Wiślica and Piotrków, which form the first legal codes for Little and Greater Poland respectively.
- King Magnus II of Sweden completes his codification of Swedish laws.
- Ramadhipati, ruler of the Siamese (now Thai) principality of U Thong, founds a new capital at Ayutthaya on an island in the River Menam.

February 3 The Byzantine emperor John VI Cantacuzenus enters Constantinople (modern Istanbul, Turkey) and ends the civil war there.

May 20 The "Roman people" award the title of tribune to Cola di Rienzo, together with dictatorial powers.

June 20 Sir Thomas Dagworth defeats and captures Charles of Blois, the French candidate for the duchy of Brittany, at Bégard in Brittany, France.

June 25 A French force is defeated by the English in a naval battle at Le Crotoy on the River Somme, France.

August 3   Hasan, leader of the Muslim rebels in the Deccan, India, is proclaimed Bāhman Shāh and founds the Bāhmanī dynasty of Kulbarga, India.

August 4   Calais in France surrenders to King Edward III of England, who expels its citizens and establishes an English colony.

September 28   King Edward III of England makes a truce with King Philip VI of France.

October 11   King Ludwig IV of Bavaria, King of the Romans, dies. His successor Charles IV has already been crowned and now receives general recognition.

November 20   Cola di Rienzo, tribune of Rome, defeats the Roman nobles. On December 15, he abdicates and flees when the people rise against him.

1348

- King Charles IV of Bohemia, King of the Romans, founds the "new town" of Prague in Bohemia.
- King Edward III of England founds the Order of the Garter.
- The Teutonic Knights defeat the Lithuanian princes Olgierd of Vilnius and Kiejstut of Kovno on the Strawa.

January 24   King Ludwig I of Hungary takes the town of Aversa, Italy, in his invasion of the kingdom of Naples.

April 4   An outbreak of plague compels King Ludwig I of Hungary to hold back his invasion of the kingdom of Naples.

April 7   King Charles IV of Bohemia, King of the Romans, confirms the imperial privileges of Bohemia and unites it with Upper Lusatia, Silesia, and Moravia.

July 21   After defeating the "union" of Valencian nobles at Epila, Spain, King Pedro IV of Aragon abolishes the *Privilegio de la Unión*.

1349

- King Casimir (Kazimierz) III of Poland conquers Galicia.
- Ramadhipati, ruler of Ayutthaya, compels Lu Tai (Dharmaja II) of Sukothai to recognize his supremacy.

January 13   Louis of Flanders takes Ghent, Flanders, and completes his suppression of the revolt of the Flemish weavers.

January 24   Luchino Visconti, Lord of Milan, Italy, dies and is succeeded by his brother Archbishop Giovanni.

March 26   King Alfonso XI of Castile dies of the Black Death while besieging the Muslims in Gibraltar. He is succeeded by his son Pedro I.

May 5   King Philip VI of France buys Montpellier, France, from King James II of Majorca.

October 8   Queen Joanna II of Navarre dies and is succeeded by her son Charles II.

October 25   King James II of Majorca is killed in an attempt to recover Majorca from King Philip VI of France with a fleet provided by Queen Joanna I of Naples, Italy. His son James IV is captured and imprisoned.

SCIENCE, TECHNOLOGY, AND MEDICINE

Ecology

1346

- A major earthquake hits the Byzantine capital Constantinople, causing the eastern arch of the huge St. Sophia Cathedral to collapse.

1348

- England's harvests fail after a period of protracted bad weather. The shortage of food leaves the country particularly vulnerable to the Black Death.

Exploration

1348

- German monk Father Felix Fabri writes *Journey to Sinai*, the story of his pilgrimage to the Holy Land.

1349

- Chinese merchant Wang Ta-yüan writes *Tao-i-chi-lio/Description of the Barbarians of the Isles*, an account of his travels since 1330.
- Italian priest Fra Niccolò da Poggibonsi writes *Libro d'oltramare/Book of Overseas*, a book describing the territories of Outremer—Egypt, the Holy Land, and the East.

Health and Medicine

1345

- Italian physician Guido da Vigevano writes his *Anatomia*, one of the first European investigations into anatomy.

1347

- The Black Death appears in Constantinople (modern Istanbul, Turkey), Naples and Genoa in Italy, and the south of France.

1348

- French surgeon Guy de Chauliac remains at Auvergne, France, as the Black Death rages around him, and produces one of the first detailed medical descriptions of the disease.
- The Black Death spreads in Italy, and into Spain, central and northern France, and southern England, reducing populations by more than half in some parts.
- The Italian physician Gentile da Foligno, who performed the first anatomical dissections at Padua, writes *Consilium contra pestilentiam/Counsel against Pestilence*, an account of the Black Death.

1349

- The Black Death spreads to northern England, Ireland, and Scandinavia, and to Germany and the Swiss Confederation, where Jews are massacred for their supposed responsibility for the pestilence.

Technology

1348

- A mechanical clock at Dover castle, England, is dated to this period, but is possibly of later manufacture. It has a central count wheel allowing it to chime the correct number of hours.

ARTS AND IDEAS

Arts

1347

- Italian artist Bernardo Daddi paints *Madonna and Child Enthroned with Angels* for the altar in the shrine of Orsanmichele in Florence.

Literature and Language

c. 1345

- English churchman Richard de Bury, bishop of Durham and chancellor to Edward III, completes his *Philobiblion/The Love of Books*, a work on books by an avid collector. It is first printed in 1473.

c. 1349

- Swiss Dominican monk Ulrich Boner completes his *Der Edelstein/The Gem*, a German anthology of fables from Aesop and others retold and provided with commentaries. It is first printed in 1461.

Thought and Scholarship

c. 1345

- English philosopher and scientific thinker Walter Burley completes his *De vita et moribus philosophorum/*

On the Lives and Deaths of Philosophers. It is first printed in 1467.
- Siamese (now Thai) Buddhist Lu T'ai completes his *Traibhumikatha/The History of the Three Worlds*, a Buddhist cosmological treatise written in Siamese.

1346

- Italian writer Francesco Petrarch (Petrarca) writes his treatise *De vita solitaria/The Life of Solitude*.

1347

- English chronicler Adam of Murimuth completes his *Continuatio chronicarum/Series of Chronicles*, a continuation of Walter of Guisborough's *Chronicle* of 1312, covering English history from 1312 to 1346.

1348

c. 1348   Arabic scholar Al-Umari completes his *Masālik al-absār/Voyages of the Eyes*, a geographical and historical compilation on Muslim lands and parts of Africa.
- Italian scholar Giovanni Villani completes his *Nuova cronica/New History*, a world history (with a special emphasis on Florence) from 1300. On his death it is continued by others until 1364.

SOCIETY

Education

1346

- Pembroke College is established in Cambridge, England.
- Valladolid University in northwest Spain receives its first papal charter, though it has already existed for about 100 years.

1348

- King Charles IV of Bohemia, King of the Romans, founds Prague University in Bohemia.

BIRTHS & DEATHS

1345

c. 1345   Claus Sluter, Dutch sculptor known especially for his works in the chapel of the Carthusian monastery, Chartreuse de Champmol, in Dijon, born in Haarlem, Holland (–1406).

1347

March 25   St. Catherine of Siena, patron saint of Italy who was instrumental in returning the papacy to Rome from Avignon, born in Siena, Tuscany (–1380).

1348

- Ambrogio Lorenzetti, Italian Gothic painter, brother of Pietro Lorenzetti, whose surviving works include the *Annunciation* (1344), dies in Siena, Italy (*c.* 58).

- Giovanni Villani, Italian historian, author of *Chronica*, a universal history that focuses on Florence and which is one of the first to include statistics and to be objective, dies in Florence (*c.* 73).
- Pietro Lorenzetti, Italian Gothic painter, brother of Ambrogio Lorenzetti, whose surviving works include *Birth of the Virgin* (1342), dies in Siena, Italy (*c.* 68).

1349

- Nicholas de Lyra (Nicolaus Lyranus), Franciscan theologian and biblical scholar, dies in Paris, France (*c.* 79).

April 10   William of Ockham, English Franciscan philosopher, founder of nominalism, and originator of

"Ockham's razor," the principle that entities are not to be multiplied beyond necessity, dies in Munich (*c.* 64).

August 25   Thomas Bradwardine, archbishop of Canterbury 1348–49, theologian, and mathematician, dies in London (*c.* 59).

September 29   Richard Rolle of Hampole, English ascetic and hermit, and influential mystic writer of *Incendium amoris/The Fire of Love* in Latin, and *The Form of Perfect Living* in English, dies in Hampole, Yorkshire, England (*c.* 49).

1349

- Florence University is founded in Italy.

Everyday Life

1347

- Joanna, Countess of Provence and queen of Naples, promulgates regulations for the operation of brothels, in Avignon, France—home of the papacy at the time—in an attempt to regulate prostitution and prevent the spread of venereal disease with regular medical inspections of the prostitutes.

Religion

c. **1346**

- The Swedish religious leader, Bridget of Sweden, founds the Brigittine Order of monks and nuns.

1348

January 15   Queen Joanna I of Naples sells Avignon in France to the papacy, where it is currently in residence.

1350–1354

POLITICS, GOVERNMENT, AND ECONOMICS

Business and Economics

1353

- King Edward III of England transfers the wool staple (the town appointed to be the exclusive wool marketplace) from Bruges, Flanders, to England.

Politics and Government

1350

- Hayam Wuruk becomes king of Majapahit (in modern Indonesia), though the chief minister Gaja Mada remains in effective control.
- John O'Byrne is elected leader of the O'Byrnes, in front of the Royal Justiciar in Ireland, and swears to uphold the peace for two years.
- King Charles IV of Bohemia withdraws his law code *Maiestas Carolina* following opposition by the Bohemian estates.
- Louis of Taranto, King of Naples, Italy, flees to Provence, France, when King Ludwig I of Hungary invades. Ludwig's rule in Naples is ineffective, and he soon withdraws.
- Ramadhipati is crowned the first king of Ayutthaya (in modern Thailand). He promulgates the first recorded legal system in the Thai Kingdoms.
- Tadayoshi Ashikaga, brother of Takauji Ashikaga, the shogun (military ruler) of Japan, shifts his support to the rival southern imperial court.

February 14   King Charles IV of Bohemia, King of the Romans, cedes Brandenburg and Tyrol to the Wittelsbachs under the Treaty of Bautzen.

February 17   Giovanni de Manfredi seizes Faenza in the Papal States, where the Pope's temporal authority is now almost nonexistent.

August 22   King Philip VI of France dies and is succeeded by his son John II.

August 29   King Edward III of England defeats Spanish privateers off Winchelsea on the south coast of England in an action known as "Les Espagnols sur Mer" ("The Spanish at Sea").

October 23   Giovanni Visconti, Lord of Milan, takes possession of Bologna, Italy.

November 18   Robert de Brienne, Constable of France, is executed on charges of treason.

1351

- King Ludwig I of Hungary confirms the Golden Bull of 1222, enshrining the rights of the Hungarian nobility as the permanent law of the constitution.
- Tadayoshi Ashikaga occupies Kyoto, having defeated his brother Takauji Ashikaga, the Japanese shogun (military ruler).
- The Chinese government provokes large-scale revolts by impressing labor to rebuild dykes along the Yellow River, and loses control of much of central China.
- The king of Sunda (in modern Indonesia) and his followers are massacred while fighting their way out of an attempt to trick them into paying tribute to Hayam Wuruk, King of Majapahit.
- The Statute of Provisors in England forbids papal appointments to ecclesiastical benefices.

March 20   Mohammed II, Sultan of Delhi, India, dies, having seen the sultanate disintegrate under his rule. He is succeeded by his cousin Firūz.

March 27   The "Battle of the Thirty" is fought between thirty English champions and the same number of Bretons and others of the Montfort party, in an attempt to end the dispute over the occupancy of the duchy of Brittany. The English party lose.

May 1   Zürich accedes to the Swiss Confederation.

October 17   A Milanese invasion of Florentine territory in Italy is defeated.

December 24   Ludwig I, Margrave of Brandenburg, abdicates in favor of his brothers Ludwig II and Otto V.

1352

- Acamapitzin is elected king of the Aztecs.
- Bern, Glarus, and Zug join the Swiss Confederation.
- Firuz, Sultan of Delhi, founds Firuzābād, near Delhi, India, as his new capital.
- Ilyās Shāh of western Bengal annexes eastern Bengal.
- Tadayoshi Ashikaga, brother of Takauji Ashikaga, the shogun (military ruler) of Japan, dies suddenly. His brother is blamed.

January 14   King Ludwig I of Hungary makes peace with Queen Joanna I of Naples.

February 13   An indecisive naval battle takes place in the Bosporus between the Genoese and the Venetians, Aragonese, and Greeks.

March 2   The Ottoman Turks take Gallipoli from the Byzantine Empire. Originally involved only as allies of the Byzantine emperor John VI Cantacuzenus in his new war with John V of Byzantium, they now remain in Gallipoli (in modern Turkey), making it their base for conquests in Europe.

April 28   Pope Clement VI makes peace with Giovanni Visconti, Lord of Milan, granting him the vicariate of Bologna, Italy.

August 8   The English forces in Brittany defeat the Montfort faction at Mauron, Brittany, ending the dispute over the occupancy of the duchy of Brittany.

December 18   The French clergyman Etienne Aubert is elected Pope Innocent VI and sets aside the "compromise" made by cardinals before his election, which was designed to restrict papal prerogatives.

1353

- Fa Ngum, a Siamese (now Thai) prince who has conquered the Upper Mekong Valley, is proclaimed Chieng Dong Chieng Tong, King of Lan Chang ("the country of a million elephants"), at Luang Prabang (modern Laos).
- Simeon of Moscow, Russia, Grand Duke of Vladimir, dies and is succeeded by his brother Ivan II.
- The Chams of Champa (modern southern Vietnam) attempt to regain the Hué provinces ceded to Dai Viet (northern Vietnam) in 1306.
- The first Statute of Praemunire in England prohibits appeals to foreign courts. It is aimed at preventing the clergy from appealing to the papal court concerning English benefices. A second statute follows in 1368.
- The leaders of the Chinese rebellion against the Yüan dynasty begin to compete for supreme command.

March 31   In the Treaty of Sarzana, Milan makes peace with Florence and its Tuscan allies.

August 29   A Venetian force defeats a fleet from Genoa in a naval battle off La Loiera, near Alghero, Sardinia, and Genoa puts itself under the lordship of Giovanni Visconti, ruler of Milan, Italy.

1354

January 8   King Charles II of Navarre murders Charles d'Espagne, Constable of France, and conspires with King Edward III of England against King John II of France.

February 15   The Italian cities of Florence, Siena, and Perugia form a defensive alliance against Milan, to which Venice accedes.

April 6   English and French embassies meet at Guînes, near Calais, France, to prolong the truce, and agree on preliminary terms for peace which the French subsequently reject.

June 5   Under the Treaty of Montefiascone, the papal legate Cardinal Albornoz receives the submission of Giovanni di Vico, prefect of Rome, who has built a state in the Papal States including the cities of Viterbo and Orvieto.

August 1   Cardinal Albornoz, papal legate in the Papal States, establishes Cola di Rienzo as senator of Rome.

October 1   King Charles IV of Bohemia, King of the Romans, begins an expedition into Italy.

October 5   Giovanni Visconti, archbishop of Milan, Italy, dies. His nephews Bernabò, Galeazzo II, and Matteo II Visconti succeed as lords of Milan.

October 7   Andrea Dandolo, Doge of Venice, dies and is succeeded by Marino Falieri.

October 8   Cola di Rienzo, tribune of Rome, is killed in a popular revolt against his repressive government.

October 19   Yūsuf I of Granada is murdered and is succeeded by his son Mohammed V.

November 4   The Venetian fleet defeats the Genoese at Porto Longo, in the island of Sapienza.

November 11   John VI Cantacuzenus is forced to abdicate, leaving John V as the sole Byzantine emperor.

SCIENCE, TECHNOLOGY, AND MEDICINE

Exploration

1354

- Ibn-Battūtah writes his *Gift to Observers Dealing with the Curiosities of Cities and Wonders of Journeys*, an account of his travels in the Middle and Far East and the interior of Africa between 1325 and 1354, including his exploration of the Sahara.

Health and Medicine

1350

- German naturalist Conrad of Megenburg writes *Das Buch der Natur/The Book of Nature*, a treatise on natural history in which he blames earthquakes for the current epidemic of the Black Death.
- Hebrew physician Moses ben Joshua of Narbonne writes *Orah hayyim/Road of Life*, a treatise on medicine, with an astrological explanation for the Black Death.

1352

- The Black Death spreads eastward across Europe, reaching Moscow, Russia, and returning toward India and China.
- The first known illustration of glasses appears in a portrait of Cardinal Ugone on a fresco at Treviso, northern Italy.

Science

1350

- French astrologer Jean de Linières compiles a catalog of stars.

Technology

1350

- Cannon of cast bronze are in use by this date across Europe.

1351

- A water-powered mill for the manufacture of iron wire is established at Augsburg, Germany.

ARTS AND IDEAS

Architecture

1351

- Work begins on the choir of the Church of the Holy Cross in Schwäbisch-Gmünd, Germany, probably following designs by the German architect Heinrich Parler. An important example of the German Late Gothic style known as *Sondergotik*, the church is also a fine example of the German hall-church (in which the nave and the aisles are the same height).

1352

- The Cathedral of Antwerp in Flanders is completed.

Arts

c. 1350

- Italian artist Francesco Traini paints the frescoes *The Last Judgment* and *The Triumph of Death* in the Camposanto in Pisa, Italy.
- Italian artist Nardo di Cione paints the frescoes *Paradise* and *Hell* in the Strozzi chapel of the Church of Santa Maria Novella in Florence.

Literature and Language

1350

c. 1350 Flemish mystic Jan van Ruysbroeck writes *Die chierheit der gheesteleker brulocht/The Adornment of Spiritual Marriage*, a classic both of Middle Dutch prose and of mystical literature.

- The anonymous *Poema de Alfonso Onceno/The Poem of Alfonso XI* is written. It is a Spanish verse chronicle on the life and deeds of Alfonso XI the Avenger, King of Castile, who died this year.

c. 1351

- Italian writer Francesco Petrarch (Petrarca) begins arranging his many poems so that they form a coherent whole (he constantly revised his works). Many are love poems addressed to Laura, a woman he knew only from a distance, falling into two separate categories: *Rime in vita di Laura/Poems During Laura's Life* and *Rime in morte di Laura/Poems After Laura's Death*.

c. 1352

- Italian writer Francesco Petrarch (Petrarca) completes his *I Trionfi/The Triumphs*, six allegorical poems and writes the patriotic ode "*All' Italia/To Italy*."

1353

- Italian writer Giovanni Boccaccio completes his *Decameron*, a collection of tales supposedly told by ten

---

BIRTHS & DEATHS

1350

- Pierre d'Ailly, French theologian, cardinal, and church reformer, born in Compiègne, France (–1420).
- St. Vincent Ferrer, Spanish friar and celebrated preacher, born in Valencia, Spain (–1419).

August 22 Philip VI, King of France 1328–50, first in the Valois dynasty, dies near Paris, France (c. 57).

1351

c. 1351 Władysław II Jagiełło, Grand Prince of Lithuania 1377–1401, and King of Poland 1386–1401, who united Poland and Lithuania and

founded the Jagiellon dynasty, born (–1434).

October 15 Gian Galeazzo Visconti, Milanese leader who controlled much of northern Italy, born in Milan (–1402).

1352

December 6 Pope Clement VI dies.

1353

- Margaret I, regent of Denmark 1375–97, Norway 1380–89, and Sweden 1388–97, thereafter effective ruler of all three countries through her son Erik VIII, born in Søborg, Denmark (–1412).
- Thomas Arundel, English statesman and archbishop of Canterbury

1396–97 and 1399–1414, who supported the opponents of King Richard II and persecuted the Lollards during the reign of King Henry IV, born (–1414).

April 15 Manuel Chrysoloras, Greek scholar who spread knowledge of Greek literature in the West, born in Constantinople (modern Istanbul, Turkey) (–1415).

1354

October 8 Cola di Rienzo, Italian leader who attempted to restore Italy to the greatness and splendor of the Roman Empire, dies in Rome (c. 41).

young people living in the country to escape the plague in Florence. It is one of the major prose works of early Italian literature.

Music

c. 1350

- French composer and writer Guillaume de Machaut writes his *Messe de Notre Dame/Mass for Our Lady*. Machaut is one of the leading figures in the development of *ars nova*, the "new style" of music that developed in France and Italy in the 14th century.

1351

- English Franciscan Simon Tunsted writes *De quatuor principalibus musicae/The Four Principles of Music*, a practical treatise on music.

Theater and Dance

c. 1350

- Indian scholar Simhabhūpala of Rājakonda writes *Rasārnavasudhākara*, a major treatise on Hindu drama.
- The anonymous secular plays *Abele Spelen/Beautiful Plays* are written in Brabant in Middle Dutch. Dramatizations of scenes from chivalric romances, they are the earliest of their type in European literature.

Thought and Scholarship

1352

- English chronicler Ranulf Higden completes his *Polychronicon*, a Latin prose history of the world from

the creation to 1327. It is translated into English in 1387.
- Indian writer Baranī Ziyā-ud-Dīn completes his *Ta'rīkh-i-Firuz Shahī/The History of FiruzShahī*, the first history of Muslim India.

1354

- Japanese historian Kitabatake Chikafusa completes his *Jinno shotoki/Record of the Legitimate Descent of Divine Emperors*, a Japanese history arguing the legitimacy of the line of Go-Daigo.

SOCIETY

Education

1351

- Perpignan University is established in France.

Religion

1351

- A Byzantine church council endorses the mystical theology of Gregory Palamas.

1353

June 30   Pope Innocent VI appoints Cardinal Gil Albornoz as legate in the Papal States.

1355–1359

POLITICS, GOVERNMENT, AND ECONOMICS

Business and Economics

1356

- The Hanse, a guild of merchants in Germany, places an embargo on trade with Bruges, Flanders, in order to secure privileges there.

Politics and Government

1355

- Charles V, as dauphin of Vienne, France, and Amadeus VI of Savoy define their frontier by treaty.
- King Casimir (Kazimierz) III of Poland completes his subjection of Masovia, northeast Poland, with the submission of Ziemowit III, its last prince.
- King Stephen Dušan IV of Serbia dies when advancing to take Constantinople (modern Istanbul, Turkey) and his Serbian empire collapses.

April 5   King Charles IV of Bohemia, King of the Romans, is crowned Holy Roman Emperor in Rome, then returns immediately to Bohemia.

April 17   Marino Falieri, Doge of Venice, is executed when the Council of Ten (the ruling council of Venice) discovers his conspiracy against the Venetian patricians.

May 1   Genoa and Venice make peace.

June 1   Giovanni Gradenigo is elected doge of Venice.

June 7   In the Treaty of Gubbio, Galeotto Malatesta of Rimini, Italy, captive of the papal legate of the Papal States Cardinal Albornoz, cedes his conquests.

June 24   Cardinal Albornoz, the papal legate in the Papal States, takes Ancona, Italy.

October   King Edward III of England campaigns in Picardy, France, for ten days.

October 17   Louis of Aragon, King of Sicily, dies and is succeeded by his brother Frederick III.

December 2   In a meeting in Paris, France, of the Estates General of northern France, Etienne Marcel, leads a critical opposition.

1356

- Che Yüan-chang, leader of the rebellious Chinese peasants, takes Nanjing, China.

- Duke Wenceslas of Brabant concedes the *Joyeuse Entrée/Joyful Entrance*, a charter of liberties, to his subjects and establishes an assembly of the estates of Brabant.

- In a campaign to enforce order in Bohemia, the Holy Roman Emperor Charles IV authorizes commoners to prosecute their lords in courts of law, where Bohemian is to be the official language.

- Janibeg, Khan of the "Golden Horde," takes Azerbaijan from the ilkhan.

- War breaks out between Hungary and Venice.

January 17   Pope Innocent VI declares a crusade against Francesco Ordelaffi, Lord of the northern Italian towns of Cesena and Forli.

January 20   Edward Balliol abdicates as king of Scotland, selling his claim to King Edward III of England who now invades as far as Edinburgh, Scotland.

June 18   Henry of Grosmont, Earl of Lancaster, lands in Normandy, France, to support rebels against King John II of France.

August 8   Giovanni Gradenigo, Doge of Venice, dies and is succeeded by Giovanni Delfino.

September 19   Edward, Prince of Wales, the Black Prince, son of Edward III of England, raids central France from Gascony, defeating and capturing King John II of France at Maupertuis, near Poitiers, France.

October 17   The Estates General reassemble in Paris, France. Etienne Marcel leads the opposition to the government of the dauphin Charles, now regent of France.

November 14   Simone Boccanegra is reelected doge of Genoa, having led the Genoese in expelling the Milanese from the city.

December 12   In a diet at Metz (modern France), the Holy Roman Emperor Charles IV publishes his Golden Bull; this regulates procedure promulgating the election of kings of the Romans by a college of seven electors, who are conceded regalian rights in their territories, which are to be indivisible.

1357

- Italian jurist Bartolus of Sassoferrato completes his legal treatise *Commentaria in codicem/Commentaries on Justinian's Code*.

- Janibeg, Khan of the "Golden Horde," is murdered and succeeded by his son Berdibeg.

March 10   The dauphin Charles, under pressure from the Estates General, concedes *La Grande Ordonnance* for the reform of French government.

March 23   England and France make a truce under the Treaty of Bordeaux.

April 29   Cardinal Albornoz, the papal legate in the Papal States, promulgates the *Egidian Constitutions*, which remain the laws of the Papal States until the 19th century.

May 12   King Alfonso IV of Portugal dies and is succeeded by Pedro I.

June 21   Cardinal Albornoz, the papal legate in the Papal States, takes Cesena, Italy, in his crusade against Francesco Ordelaffi.

August 23   Androin de la Roche, abbot of Cluny, France, replaces Cardinal Albornoz as legate in the Papal States.

October 3   Under the Treaty of Berwick, King Edward III of England releases King David II of Scotland for a ransom and makes a truce for ten years. However his time in England has set David at odds with the Scottish magnates.

1358

- King Casimir (Kazimierz) III of Poland finally suppresses the separatist confederation of the nobles of Great Poland.

- Pyang-chubrGyal-mtsham, ruler of the Tibetan territory of Phag-mo-gru, seizes power from the Sa-skya, and so achieves almost complete control of Tibet.

- Takauji, the first Ashikaga shogun (military ruler) of Japan, dies. He is succeeded by Yoshiakira Ashikaga.

February 18   Venice cedes Istria and Dalmatia to King Ludwig I of Hungary. The republic of Ragusa in Sicily also submits to him.

February 23   A Parisian mob led by Etienne Marcel compels the French dauphin Charles to confirm *La Grande Ordonnance*.

March 27   The dauphin Charles escapes from Paris, France.

April 4   Nicolò Acciajuoli of Florence, Italy, is installed as lord of Corinth, Greece, and founds a dynasty.

May 28   The Jacquerie, a peasant revolt, breaks out among the Beauvaisis in France.

June 24   The Jacquerie peasant revolt in France is savagely suppressed.

July 31   Etienne Marcel, leader of the Parisian mob, is murdered in a riot in Paris, France.

August 2   The dauphin Charles returns to Paris, France, and regains control.

September 18   Cardinal Albornoz is reappointed legate in the Papal States.

1359

- Amadeus VI of Savoy takes possession of Piedmont, Italy.

- Berdibeg, Khan of the "Golden Horde," is murdered and is succeeded by his brother Kulpa. This initiates the "great troubles," a period of turmoil within the "Horde."

- Ivan II, Grand Duke of Vladimir, Russia, dies and is succeeded by Dmitri III Donski, though with opposition from Dmitri IV.

- Orkhān, the Ottoman ruler, dies, having founded an organized state controlling western Anatolia and Thrace. He is succeeded by his son Murad I.

March 24 In the Treaty of London, King John II of France cedes the lands of the Angevin empire, in sovereignty, to King Edward III of England. The following day, the treaty is rejected by the Estates General of France.

July 4 Francesco Ordelaffi of Forli, Italy, surrenders to Cardinal Albornoz, the legate in the Papal States.

August 23 Mohammed V of Granada is deposed and is succeeded by his brother Ismail II.

December 4 King Edward III of England begins his siege of Reims, France, in a new French campaign.

SCIENCE, TECHNOLOGY, AND MEDICINE

Agriculture

1358

- The Holy Roman Emperor Charles IV orders the establishment of vineyards in Bohemia.

Ecology

1356

- An earthquake destroys the city of Basel, in Germany.

Science

1356

- The influential geography text *The Travels of Sir John Mandeville* appears for the first time. Although wildly inaccurate, it will be a standard work for several centuries.

1359

- French philosopher Jean Buridan writes *Quaestiones octavi libri physicorum/Questions on the Eight Books of Physics*, a commentary on Aristotle's *Physics*, modifying Aristotle's laws of motion and introducing the concept of impetus.

ARTS AND IDEAS

Architecture

1355

c. 1355 The campanile of Florence Cathedral in Italy is finally completed using Giotto di Bondone's design of 1334 with modifications by the architect Talenti.

- Italian architect Francesco Talenti is commissioned to make a wooden model of a proposed design for Florence Cathedral.

1357

- The nave of Gloucester Abbey (now Cathedral) in England is completed. A fine example of the English style of Gothic known as Perpendicular, it is notable for its elegant tracery.
- The synagogue (now the Church of El Transito) in Toledo, Spain, is completed.

Arts

1357

- Italian artist Orcagna (Andrea di Cione) paints the altarpiece *Enthroned Christ with Madonna and Saints (Strozzi Altarpiece)* for the Strozzi chapel in the Church of Santa Maria Novella in Florence, Italy.

1359

- Italian artist Orcagna (Andrea di Cione) sculpts the Tabernacle in the shrine of Orsanmichele in Florence, Italy. A complex, richly decorated work, it has been made to house Bernardo Daddi's *Madonna and Child Enthroned with Angels* (1347).

Literature and Language

1357

- Flemish mystic Jan van Ruysbroeck writes *De Spieghel der ewigher salicheit/The Mirror of Simple Souls*, a classic both of Middle Dutch prose and of spiritual devotion.

1358

- Italian writer Francesco Petrarch (Petrarca) completes his autobiographical dialogue *Secretum meum/My Secret*, an account of his spiritual and intellectual development. He began the text in 1342.

BIRTHS & DEATHS

1355

c. 1355 Bernardo Daddi, Italian painter of the early Renaissance, a pupil of Giotto, dies, possibly in Florence, Italy (*c.* 65).

December 20 Stephan Dušan, King of Serbia 1331–46, "Emperor of the Serbs and Greeks" 1346–55, dies (47).

1357

- Tsong-kha-pa, founder of the dGe-lugs-pa religious order, also known as "the Yellow Hats," the most politically powerful order of its kind in Tibet, born.

1358

- Thinhkaba, who founded a new kingdom in south Burma, dies.

February 2 Bāhman Shāh of Kulbarga, India, dies.

June 7 Ashikaga Takauji, Japanese soldier and statesman who founded the Ashikaga shogunate, dies in Kyoto, Japan (53).

Thought and Scholarship

c. 1355

- Indian scholar Gujarati-Jaina completes his *Parikramanabūlavabodha*, a study of ethics written in Gujarati—an Aryan vernacular of the Bombay area.

1359

- Byzantine scholar and historian Nicephorus Gregoras completes his *Historia*, a major history of Byzantium from 1204 to 1359.
- Italian Franciscan friar Giovanni da Marignolli publishes his *Cronaca di Boemia/A History of Bohemia*, which includes an account of his travels to China, where he was sent by Pope Benedict XII in 1340.

SOCIETY

Religion

1355

- French scholar Jean de Sy completes a partial translation of the Bible into French.

◆

1360–1364

POLITICS, GOVERNMENT, AND ECONOMICS

Business and Economics

1360

July 27 King Waldemar IV of Denmark destroys the Hanseatic center of Visby on the island of Gotland in the Baltic Sea. It never regains its importance as a market for fish.

1362

- The English wool staple (exclusive market place) is established at Calais, France.

Politics and Government

1360

- Firuz Shah, Sultan of Delhi, founds the city of Jaunpur, India, on the site of the city of Zafarābād.
- Italian scholar Giovanni da Legnano publishes *Tractatus de bello/Treatise on War*, important as an early contribution to international law.
- King Waldemar IV of Denmark compels rebellious Danish nobles to make peace and moves to conquer Scania in Sweden.
- Kulpa, Khan of the "Golden Horde," is murdered and is succeeded by Nevruz.
- Timur Leng (Tamerlane), the great khan, begins his conquest of Transoxiana (modern Uzbekistan), the region in which he was born, with the seizure of Kesh,

near Samarkand, from Ilyas Khoja, the governor of the region for the khanate of Kashgar.

1360–74 Mani Diala becomes King Mani Diala II of Mali.

January 11 King Edward III of England abandons the siege of Reims, France, and raids Burgundy.

April 7 King Edward III of England besieges Paris, France, then withdraws to Chartres.

April 17 Cardinal Albornoz, the legate in the Papal States, takes possession of Bologna, Italy.

May 8 King Edward III of England concludes the preliminary terms of a treaty of peace with France at Brétigny, France, later to be confirmed in the Treaty of Calais. It gives Edward full sovereignty of Gascony and other debatable lands, as well as territory in the north of France. In return he renounces his claim to the throne of France.

July 12 Ismail II of Granada is murdered and succeeded by Mohammed VI.

August 31 The Hanse, Norway, Sweden, and the Teutonic Knights make an alliance against Denmark.

September 9 The Milanese abandon their siege of Bologna, Italy, following the arrival of Hungarian troops, allies of the papacy, but the Hungarian force is soon disbanded and the Milanese siege is renewed.

October 24 The Treaty of Calais confirms the terms made between England and France at Brétigny, France.

1361

- Che Bong Nga succeeds as king of Champa (modern southern Vietnam) and begins a series of attacks on Dai Viet (northern Vietnam).
- Giovanni Delfino, Doge of Venice, Italy, dies and is succeeded by Lorenzo Celso.
- Nevruz, Khan of the "Golden Horde," is murdered and succeeded by Khidyr. The "Horde" is now disintegrating, with its court tied up with succession disputes.

- The Bulgarian czar John Alexander dies. His lands are divided between his two sons, but the usurper Duvrotik takes the Dobrudja region (named for him) between the Black Sea and the River Danube.

1361–66   An expedition sets out for Ireland, led by Prince Lionel of Clarence, son of King Edward III of England.

May 5   John Hawkweed begins his career as a condottiere (a soldier in a professional mercenary company) with the White Company in Italy.

June 16   Papal forces defeat the Milanese at Rosillo, so ending the siege of Bologna, Italy.

November 21   Philippe de Rouvres, Duke of Burgundy, France, dies without issue. King John II of France takes possession of the duchy.

1362

- King Ludwig I of Hungary defeats and captures King Strascimir of Bulgaria. He conquers northern Bulgaria, extending his control over the Balkans.
- Margaret "Maultasch" cedes Tyrol to Rudolf IV, Duke of Austria.

April 4   King Pedro I of Castile murders Mohammed VI of Granada and restores Mohammed V to Granada.

April 6   United companies of *routiers*, comprised of disbanded soldiers living by organized brigandage, defeat French royal forces at Brignais, in Burgundy, France.

May 26   Louis of Taranto, King of Naples and second husband of Queen Joanna I of Naples, dies, preventing his return to Sicily following the defeat of rebellious barons on the island.

July 7   King Waldemar IV of Denmark defeats the Hanse off the port of Helsingborg, Denmark, when he cuts off its allies, Norway and Sweden, by arranging the marriage of his daughter Margaret to their heir Haakon.

September 28   Guillaume de Grimoard is elected Pope Urban V.

1363

- Duke Amadeus VI of Savoy acquires the marquisate of Saluzzo, Italy.
- Firuz, Sultan of Delhi, India, regains control of the Sind region of India.
- King Olgierd of Lithuania defeats Mongol forces near the mouth of the River Bug and progresses to the Black Sea.

April 4   King John II of France takes the cross in a crusade proclaimed by Pope Urban V.

September 6   King John II of France grants the duchy of Burgundy, France, to his son Philip the Bold.

September 9   Giovanni de Vico dies, thus removing an obstacle to the papacy's control of its states.

November 26   Pope Urban V dismisses Cardinal Albornoz as legate in the Papal States.

November 30   Albert II is elected king of Sweden when his father Albert, Duke of Mecklenburg, Germany, leads a rebellion which deposes King Magnus II of Sweden.

1364

- Ava, capital city of Upper Burma, is founded by the Siamese (now Thai) prince Thadominbya, who becomes king.
- Crete revolts against Byzantine rule.

January 1   King John II of France returns to captivity in England; when one of the hostages for payment of his ransom escapes he feels honor bound to return.

February 10   Under the Treaty of Brno, the Holy Roman Emperor Charles IV grants Tyrol to Duke Rudolf IV of Austria. Both concede that in the event that the dynasty of either party fail, the other and his heirs would inherit.

March 3   Pope Urban V makes peace with Bernabò Visconti, ruler of Milan, Italy, to the advantage of the latter.

April 8   King John II of France dies and is succeeded by his son Charles V.

September 9   King Casimir (Kazimierz) III of Poland acts as mediator between the Holy Roman Emperor Charles IV and King Ludwig I of Hungary in the congress of Kraków, Poland, and is aided by King Waldemar IV of Denmark and King Peter I of Cyprus. They also consider a proposal to crusade against the Turks.

September 29   The Montfort party defeats and kills Charles of Blois in Brittany, France, and captures Bertrand du Guesclin at Auray, Brittany. His freedom is bought subsequently for 40,000 gold franks.

SCIENCE, TECHNOLOGY, AND MEDICINE

Health and Medicine

1361–62

- The second major outbreak of the Black Death in western Europe occurs.

1363

- French physician Guy de Chauliac writes his *Chirurgia magna/Major Surgery*, a treatise on surgery outlining various new techniques, including the use of narcotics for anesthesia.

Science

1360

- Catalonian monk John of Rupescissa writes *Liber de consideratione quintae essentiae/The Book of Consideration of the Quintessence*, an alchemical treatise proposing the same elixir could be used for eternal youth and ennobling base metals.

1362

- Italian inventor Giovanni de Dondi completes construction of an elaborate astronomical clock.

1364

- French astronomer and bishop Nicole d'Oresme writes *Latitudes of Forms*, an early work on coordinate systems.

Hundred Years' War (1337–1453)

1337–59

1337

May 24 King Philip VI of France announces the confiscation of Gascony as a reaction to the "rebellion" of King Edward III of England. Its seizure begins the Hundred Years' War.

July 15 Under the Treaty of Valenciennes King Ludwig IV of Bavaria and King Edward III of England become allies against France.

October 7 Edward III claims the French crown through his mother, Isabella of France, daughter of Philip IV.

1338

June 6 A French fleet sacks Portsmouth, England.

July 16 Edward III lands at Antwerp in the Holy Roman Empire (in modern Belgium).

1340

June 24 The English fleet wins a naval victory over the French at Sluys, Flanders.

September 24 Edward III and Philip VI make a truce at Esplechin when Edward runs out of money to continue the war.

1345

October 21 Henry of Grosmont, Earl of Lancaster, defeats a French force at Auberoche in Gascony, France.

1346

July 12 Edward III, seeking to exploit Norman disaffection with Philip VI, lands in northern Normandy at St.-Vaast-la-Hougue.

July 26 Edward III takes and sacks Caen in Normandy, France.

August 26 Edward III defeats a French force at Crécy, France. Among those killed on the French side are King John I of Bohemia who is succeeded by Charles , and Louis of Nevers, Count of Flanders, who is succeeded by his son Louis de Maële. King Philip VI of France escapes to Amiens, France.

October 4 Henry of Grosmont, Earl of Lancaster, takes Poitiers, France.

1347

June 25 A French force is defeated by the English in a naval battle at Le Crotoy on the River Somme, France.

August 4 Calais in France surrenders to Edward III, who expels its citizens and establishes an English colony.

September 28 Edward III makes a truce with Philip VI.

1351

March 27 The "Battle of the Thirty" is fought between thirty English champions and the same number of Bretons and others of the Montfort party, in an attempt to end the dispute over the occupancy of the duchy of Brittany. The English party lose.

1352

August 8 The English forces in Brittany defeat the Montfort faction at Mauron, Brittany, ending the dispute over the occupancy of the duchy of Brittany.

1354

April 6 English and French embassies meet at Guînes, near Calais, France, to prolong the truce, and agree on preliminary terms for peace which the French subsequently reject.

1356

September 19 Edward, Prince of Wales, the Black Prince, son of Edward III of England, raids central France from Gascony, defeating and capturing King John II of France at Maupertuis, near Poitiers, France.

1359

March 24 In the Treaty of London, King John II of France cedes the lands of the Angevin empire, in sovereignty, to King Edward III of England.

May 25 The Treaty of London between England and France is rejected by the Estates General of France.

1360–1428

1360

April 7 Edward III besieges Paris, France, then withdraws to Chartres.

May 8 Edward III concludes the preliminary terms of a treaty of peace with France at Brétigny, France, later to be confirmed in the Treaty of Calais. It gives Edward full sovereignty of Gascony and other debatable lands, as well as territory in the north of France. In return he renounces his claim to the throne of France.

1368

December 3 King Charles V of France accepts a judicial appeal from Gascon nobles against their governor, Edward, Prince of Wales, the Black Prince, son of Edward III, thus effectively renewing the war against England.

1370

September 19 Edward, Prince of Wales, sacks Limoges, France, earning himself a reputation for brutality.

1372

June 23 In a naval battle off the coast of La Rochelle, France, King Henry II of Castile, as the ally of France, destroys an English fleet bringing John Hastings, Earl of Pembroke and lieutenant of Edward III, to Gascony, France.

August 7 The French recover Poitiers, France, from English control.

December 12 King Charles V of France completes his conquest of the Atlantic province of Poitou, France.

1374

February 11 The English and French make a truce over Picardy, at Bourbourg, Flanders, and begin considering a settlement.

1375

June 27 English and French embassies confer at Bruges, Flanders, and conclude a general treaty of truce. King Edward III of England now holds only Calais, Brest, Bordeaux, and Bayonne in France.

1377

July 7 The French sack the Isle of Wight, off the south coast of England, and harass the English south coast with the aid of their Castilian allies.

1378

June 6 England takes possession of Cherbourg, France, by treaty with King Charles II of Navarre.

1380

June 10 An English force defeats a Franco-Castilian fleet off the coast of Kinsale, Ireland.

August 8 A French fleet raids up the River Thames and burns Gravesend, England.

1415

August 13 King Henry V of England invades France in a campaign to seize the French throne.

September 22 Henry V takes the northern French town of Harfleur, though his army is hit badly by disease. He opens up the town to English settlers.

October 25 Henry V inflicts a crushing defeat on the French at the Battle of Agincourt.

November 16 Following a successful campaign in France, Henry V returns home.

1416

August 15   A Franco-Genoese fleet, attempting to recover the northern French town of Harfleur from the English, is defeated in the River Seine estuary.

1417

August 1   Henry V lands at Trouville on the north French coast to begin his campaign to conquer Normandy.

September 20   Henry V takes the northern French city of Caen.

1418

July 29   Henry V begins the siege of Rouen, the capital of Normandy, France.

September 29   The northern French port of Cherbourg surrenders to Henry V.

1419

January 19   Rouen surrenders to Henry V, whose conquest of Normandy is thus complete.

December 25   Philip the Good, Duke of Burgundy, allies himself with Henry V against the French dauphin Charles.

1420

May 21   By the Treaty of Troyes, Charles VI recognizes Henry V as Duke of Normandy and his own heir to the French throne.

1422

October 21   King Charles VI of France dies. He is succeeded, in accordance with the 1420 Treaty of Troyes, by King Henry VI of England.

1423

July 31   Anglo-Burgundian forces defeat the French at Cravant, France.

1424

August 17   John, Duke of Bedford, the English regent for the infant king Henry VI in France, defeats Charles VII of France at Verneuil, France.

1425

August 2   The French town of Le Mans surrenders to the English.

1428

October 7   The English begin the siege of Orléans, France.

1429–53

1429

February 12   In the "Battle of the Herrings" at Rouvray, France, the English defeat a French attack on supplies for their forces besieging Orléans.

February 23   The French military leader Joan of Arc arrives in Chinon, France, to meet King Charles VII of France.

April   After a second meeting with Charles VII, The French military leader Joan of Arc is supplied with a horse and armor and sent to join the French army at Orléans.

April 29   Joan of Arc arrives at Orléans and relieves the English siege.

May 8   The English abandon the siege of Orléans; this is the turning point in the Hundred Years' War.

June 18   The French defeat the withdrawing English army under John Talbot at Patay, northwest of Orléans, France. Talbot and several other knights are captured.

1430

May 23   Burgundian troops capture Joan of Arc as she attempts to prevent the fall of the town of Compiègne, France. She is sold to the English for 10,000 livres tournois.

1435

August 5   English, French, and Burgundian embassies open the Congress of Arras in northern France to end the Hundred Years' War, proposed by Philip the Good, Duke of Burgundy. This signals the growing gulf between the English and the Burgundians.

September 21   By the Treaty of Arras, the Duke of Burgundy makes peace with Charles VII of France.

1436

April 13   The French city of Paris is taken from the English for King Charles VII of France, who restores it as his capital.

1437

February 12   Richard, Duke of York, the English lieutenant in France, takes the French town of Pontoise, northwest of Paris.

1439

July 6   English and French embassies meet at the Congress of Calais in France. They fail to make peace as the English will not renounce King Henry VI of England's title to be king of France.

September 13   The English garrison of Meaux, east of Paris, France, surrenders to the French. The English make a truce with the Duke of Burgundy on September 28.

1441

September 19   The French take the town of Pontoise, completing their recovery of the Ile-de-France from the English.

1448

March 16   The English surrender the town of Le Mans in France to the French.

1449

October 29   The English surrender Rouen, the capital of Normandy, France, to King Charles VII of France.

1450

April 15   The French defeat the last English force sent to Normandy, France, at Formigny.

August 12   The English holding the northern French port of Cherbourg surrender. Charles VII's conquest of Normandy is thus completed.

1451

June 12   Bordeaux, France, capital of the duchy of Gascony and a stronghold of the English Plantagenet kings for 300 years, surrenders to French forces commanded by Jean, Count of Dunois, "the bastard of Orléans."

August 20   The port of Bayonne in the southwest of France falls to the French army, completing the French conquest of Gascony.

1452

October 17   An English expeditionary force under John Talbot, Earl of Shrewsbury, lands in Guyenne, France, and a week later is welcomed into the city of Bordeaux when a popular revolt ejects French royal forces.

1453

July 17   A French army led by the gunner Jean Bureau repels a rash assault by an English and Gascon force under John Talbot, Earl of Shrewsbury, on their fortified camp at Castillon, 30 miles east of Bordeaux. Talbot is killed in the rearguard and his forces are decimated.

October 19   The beleaguered port of Bordeaux, France, finally surrenders to the forces of King Charles VII of France, an event which sees the fall of the last English stronghold in Gascony and in France (excepting Calais) and ends the Hundred Years' War.

ARTS AND IDEAS

Architecture

1360
- The Cathedral of Freiburg in Germany is completed.

1363
- The Mosque of Sultan Hassan in Cairo, Egypt, is completed.

1364
- The Palace of the Popes at Avignon, France, is completed.

Arts

c. **1360**
- Italian artist Taddeo Gaddi paints the fresco *The Tree of Life* in the refectory of the Church of Santa Croce in Florence.

Literature and Language

c. **1360**
- English writer William Langland writes his long religious allegory *The Vision of Piers Plowman.* A longer version appears in the 1370s.

1362
- With the Statute of Pleading, (Middle) English becomes the official spoken language of the English court.

c. **1363**
- Muslim scholar Al-Safadi completes his *Kitāb al-Wāfibi-wafayāt,* a compilation of Muslim biographies.

Music

1364
- French composer and writer Guillaume de Machaut writes a Mass for the coronation of Charles V of France.

Thought and Scholarship

1360
- Irish churchman Richard FitzRalph publishes *De pauperie salvatoris/Poverty and Salvation,* a tract that contrasts holy poverty with the dangers of wealth. It influences John Wycliffe (Wyclif). Its theory of political authority is also influential.
- The ruler of Milan, Italy, Galeazzo Visconti, establishes a library in the city.

1362
- German scholar Fritsche Closener completes his *Chronik/Chronicle,* one of the oldest extant chronicles in German. It is continued to 1415 by Jakob Twinger von Königshofen.

SOCIETY

Education

1361
- Pavia University is founded in Italy.

1364
- King Casimir (Kazimierz) III of Poland founds Kraków University in Poland.

Everyday Life

1360
- *Schnapsteufel* ("*Schnaps* fiend" or brandy) is seen to cause problems in Germany because of its high alcohol content. Regulations against its consumption are common.

Religion

1363
March 3   Pope Urban V condemns Bernabò Visconti, Lord of Milan, Italy, for heresy.

BIRTHS & DEATHS

1360
- Orhan, second ruler of the Ottoman Empire 1324–60, who expanded the domain of the empire into the Balkans, dies (*c.* 72).
- May 2   Yung-lo, Chinese Ming emperor who moved the capital of China from Nanjing to Beijing and built the Forbidden City, born in Nanjing, China (–1424).
- June 24   Nuno Álvares Pereira, Portuguese military leader whose defeat of the Castilians in 1385 ensured Portugal's independence, born in Bonjardim, Portugal (–1431).

1361
June 9   Philippe de Vitry, French music theorist and composer, dies in Meaux, France (68).

1362
September 12   Pope Innocent VI dies.

1363
- Simone Boccanegra, the first doge of Genoa, dies.
- December 13   Jean de Gerson (original surname Charlier), French theologian and mystic, born in Gerson, France (–1429).

1364
February 20   Henry Percy ("Harry Hotspur"), English rebel who led an uprising against King Henry IV, born in Bridgnorth, Yorkshire (–1403).
April 8   John II the Good, King of France 1350–64, captured by the English at the Battle of Poitiers (1356), dies in London, England (44).

1365–1369

POLITICS, GOVERNMENT, AND ECONOMICS

Business and Economics

1368

- Dyers in Florence, Italy, strike for higher pay.

Politics and Government

1365

- Lorenzo Celso, Doge of Venice, dies and is succeeded by Marco Cornaro.

March 6   King Charles V of France makes peace with King Charles II of Navarre. On March 12, he recognizes John de Montfort as Duke of Brittany under the Treaty of Guérande and receives his homage.

May 5   Parliament repudiates the subjection of England to the papacy, agreed in May 1213 by King John of England, and annuls the payment of tribute.

June 4   After meeting with Pope Urban V at Avignon, France, the Holy Roman Emperor Charles IV is crowned king of Arles and Vienne at Arles, France. This is to be the last Burgundian coronation.

August 22   In order to rid France of the free companies of *routiers*, King Charles V of France engages Bertrand du Guesclin to enlist them to serve Henry of Trastamare, illegitimate brother of King Pedro I of Castile.

October 10   A crusade led by King Peter I of Cyprus takes Alexandria, in Mameluke Egypt. He departs after sacking the town and massacring its population.

November 22   The Hanse are forced to make an unfavorable peace with King Waldemar IV of Denmark.

1366

- King Casimir (Kazimierz) III of Poland wins possession of Volhynia, a Russian principality in northwest Ukraine.
- Murad, leader of the Ottoman Turks, establishes his capital in Adrianople (in modern Turkey).
- Southern Egypt is ravaged by Keniz and Iffrim Arabs. The king of Nubia is murdered, and the capital of Nubia is moved from Dongola to Du.

March 3   The Irish parliament establishes the Statute of Kilkenny, which prohibits the intermarriage of English and Irish individuals and orders other measures designed to divide the two nationalities.

March 5   Having expelled King Pedro I of Castile from Castile, Henry of Trastamare is crowned king.

August 23   Duke Amadeus VI of Savoy takes Gallipoli in the Ottoman Empire in his crusade against the Ottoman Turks. He then attacks Varna (in modern Bulgaria), in order to rescue his cousin, the Byzantine emperor John V Palaeologus.

1367

- Chu Yüan-chang, having defeated rival rebel leaders, takes Beijing, China, and expels Toghan Temur, the last Yüan (Mongol) emperor. Chu Yüan-chang, under the name Hung-wu, founds the Ming Dynasty, establishing his capital at Nanjing.
- Duke Amadeus VI of Savoy returns from the Byzantine Empire and the Ottoman Turks recover Gallipoli.
- The kings of Kulbarga and Vijayanagar, India, agree to a peace treaty in which they undertake not to slaughter noncombatants in future wars.
- Timur Leng (Tamerlane) becomes the effective ruler of the Asiatic Mongols as grand amir to a series of puppet great khans.

January 18   King Pedro I of Portugal dies and is succeeded by his son Ferdinand I.

January 20   Marco Cornaro, Doge of Venice, dies and is succeeded by Andrea Contarini.

April 3   Edward, Prince of Wales, the Black Prince, son of King Edward III of England, invades Castile on behalf of the usurped King Pedro I and defeats King Henry of Castile, capturing his French ally Bertrand du Guesclin at Nájera, Spain. Illness subsequently forces him to withdraw and new rebellions break out against King Pedro I.

November 19   The Hanse, Sweden, and Mecklenburg form an alliance known as the League of Köln against Denmark and Norway.

1368

- Charles Topia assumes the title of king of Albania on gaining control of the country.
- Following the collapse of the Mongol Yuan dynasty in China, the Sa-skya lamas are no longer appointed and Tibet regains full independence.
- Yoshiakira Ashikaga, the shogun (military ruler) of Japan, dies. He is succeeded by his ten-year-old son, Yoshimitsu, with Hosokawa Yonyaki as regent.

March 7   Rudolf IV, Duke of Austria, cedes Zug, Austria, in a treaty of truce with the Swiss Confederation.

November 1   Blanche, the wife of the Holy Roman Emperor Charles IV, is crowned empress in Rome, during his brief and ineffective expedition into Italy.

December 3   King Charles V of France accepts a judicial appeal from Gascon nobles against their governor, Edward, Prince of Wales, the Black Prince, son of King Edward III of England, thus effectively renewing the war against England.

1369

- Hung-wu, Ming emperor of China, receives tribute missions from Korea, Dai Viet, and Champa.
- Ramadhipati, ruler of Ayutthaya (in modern Thailand), dies and is succeeded by his son Prince Ramuesen, who abdicates in 1370 following disturbances and is succeeded by Boromoraja I. Boromoraja I invades the rival Thai kingdom of Sukothai and captures several towns.
- Timur Leng (Tamerlane), grand amir of the Mongols, gains control of the khanate of Chaghadai, centered in Turkestan and with its capital at Samarkand.
- Venice repulses an invasion by Hungarian forces.

1369–72 China sends three missions to Japan, in an unsuccessful attempt to end Japanese piracy.

January 1 A rebellion rises in Gascony, France, against King Edward III of England.

March 14 Henry of Trastamare defeats his half brother King Pedro I of Castile at Montiel, Spain. On March 23, he kills Pedro and becomes King Henry II in uncontested control of the kingdom. This places the Castilian fleet in the hands of an ally of France.

April 4 King Charles V of France conquers Ponthieu.

April 22 Hugues d'Aubriot founds the Bastille, Paris, France, to protect the castle of King Charles V of France.

May 21 King Charles V of France declares war on England.

June 3 King Edward III of England reassumes the title king of France.

June 19 Philip of Burgundy, France, marries Margaret, daughter and heir of Louis de Maële, Count of Flanders, in a marriage arranged by King Charles V of France to prevent her marriage to an English prince.

September 9 John of Gaunt, Duke of Lancaster, carries out a raid into France from Calais to Harfleur in Normandy.

October 10 The Byzantine emperor John V Palaeologus visits Rome, Italy, on a mission to solicit aid against the Ottoman Turks, and is accepted into the Roman church.

November 30 Under the Treaty of Stralsund, King Waldemar IV of Denmark makes peace on terms favorable to the Hanse and its allies, who have conquered Scania, Sweden.

SCIENCE, TECHNOLOGY, AND MEDICINE

Health and Medicine

1368

- The Chinese scholar Chia Ming writes *Yin-shih-hsii-chih/Elements of Dietics*, explaining how the author lived to the age of 100 by a strictly regulated diet.

1369

- Further outbreaks of the Black Death occur in England and France, as well as other countries.

Technology

1367

- Cannon are used by both sides in the battle of Kauthal between the Muslim forces of Kulbarga and the Hindu empire of Vijayanagar in southern India.

Transportation

1367

- Italian navigator Francesco Pizigano publishes a *portolano* (pilot book) of the Mediterranean and northwest Europe.

ARTS AND IDEAS

Architecture

1365

- The Doges' Palace in Venice is completed. Changes, particularly to the façades, continue during the 15th century.

BIRTHS & DEATHS

1366

c. 1366 Taddeo Gaddi, painter, follower of Giotto, whose best-known work is the *Tree of Life* fresco at Santa Croce, dies (*c.* 66).

April Henry IV, King of England 1399–1413, son of John of Gaunt, born in Bolingbroke Castle, Lincolnshire, England (–1413).

1367

January 6 Richard II, King of England 1377–99, born in Bordeaux, France (–1400).

1368

- Andrea Orcagna, Florentine painter, sculptor, and architect, dies (*c.* 60).

February 15 Sigismund, Holy Roman Emperor 1433–37, King of Hungary 1387–1437, King of Germany 1411–37, King of Bohemia 1419–37, and King of the Lombards 1431–37, last emperor of the Luxembourg dynasty, born, probably in Nuremberg, Germany (–1437).

December 3 Charles VI ("the Well-Beloved" or "the Mad"), King of France 1380–1422, born in Paris (–1422).

1367

- The building of Florence Cathedral in Italy is resumed, following architect Francesco Talenti's model of 1355.

Arts

1368

- Italian artist Andrea da Firenze paints the fresco *Triumph of the Church* in the Church of San Francesco in Assisi, Italy.

Literature and Language

c. 1365

- French composer and writer Guillaume de Machaut completes his poem of courtly love *Voir-dit*, a long work with musical interludes.
- Indonesian poet Prapañcā completes his *Nagarakritāgama*, a long poem in old Javanese that gives a detailed account of Java in the 14th century.

1367

- Italian writer Fazio degli Uberti dies leaving his major work *Dicta mundi (Il dittamondo)/Sayings of the World* unfinished. An allegory inspired by Dante's *Divina commedia/Divine Comedy* of 1321, it contains a wealth of stories and several accounts of travels in Asia and Africa.

1369

- English writer Geoffrey Chaucer writes his allegory "The Boke of the Duchesse," his first important poem.

Thought and Scholarship

1366

- Italian writer Francesco Petrarch (Petrarca) completes his Latin treatise *De remediis utriusque fortunae/ Remedies Against Fortune.*

SOCIETY

Education

1365

- Rudolf IV, Duke of Austria, establishes Vienna University in Austria.

1367

- King Ludwig I of Hungary founds Peć University in Hungary.

Religion

1367

October 16   Pope Urban V restores the papacy to Rome.

c. 1368

- The Bohemian religious reformer Jan Milič of Kremsier writes *Libellus de Antichristo/Tract on the Antichrist* while in prison in Rome for heresy.

1370–1374

POLITICS, GOVERNMENT, AND ECONOMICS

Business and Economics

1370

- The first example of insurance in northern Europe is established at Bruges, Flanders, involving a Genoese trader.

1374

- Hongwu, Ming emperor of China, puts an embargo on Japanese trade as a reaction to piracy.

Politics and Government

1370

- Kumāra Kampana, son of Bukka I of Vijayanagar, India, completes his conquest of the Muslim sultanate of Madura, southern India.
- The *Pfaffenbrief* ("Priests' Charter") establishes a common public law among the members of the Swiss Confederation.

February 17   The Teutonic Knights defeat a Lithuanian force at Rudau.

September   Sir Robert Knollys leads a force raiding northern France.

September 19   Edward, Prince of Wales, the Black Prince, son of King Edward III of England, sacks Limoges, France, earning himself a reputation for brutality.

October 2   King Charles V of France appoints Bertrand du Guesclin constable of France.

October 17 Pietro Gambacorta becomes ruler of Pisa, Italy, ending its period as a republic.

November 5 King Ludwig I of Hungary is elected successor to Casimir (Kazimierz) III, King of Poland.

December 4 Bertrand du Guesclin, Constable of France, defeats Sir John Knollys and his men at Pontvallain, Maine, France, interrupting Sir John's march to Brittany.

December 30 Pierre Roger de Beaufort is elected Pope Gregory XI following the death of Pope Urban V.

1371

- Che Bong Nga, King of Champa, sacks Hanoi, Dai Viet (modern northern Vietnam).
- Japan, the Khmer Empire (modern Cambodia), and Ayutthaya (in modern Thailand) send tribute missions to Hung-wu, Ming emperor of China.
- King Albert II of Sweden is compelled to accept baronial control of his government.
- The Holy Roman Emperor Charles IV promulgates the Westphalian Public Peace.

February 22 King David II of Scotland dies without issue and is succeeded by his cousin Robert II, the first Stuart king.

September 26 Murad, leader of the Ottoman Turks, defeats and kills King Vukašin of Serbia at Črnomen, on the Marica. He conquers Macedonia, while the Byzantine Empire and Bulgaria become Turkish tributaries.

1372

- Pyarich, chief of Toungoo (in Burma), is tricked and killed by Minkyiswasawke, King of the Shans.

March 3 John of Gaunt, Duke of Lancaster, claims the throne of Castile on his standing as the son-in-law of King Pedro I of Castile. King Henry II of Castile besieges Lisbon, Portugal, in order to compel King Ferdinand I of Portugal to abandon his alliance with John of Gaunt.

June 6 Sir Owain ap Thomas, self-styled prince of Wales, takes Guernsey in the Channel Islands for King Charles V of France.

June 23 In a naval battle off the coast of La Rochelle, France, King Henry II of Castile, as the ally of France, destroys an English fleet bringing John Hastings, Earl of Pembroke and lieutenant of King Edward III of England, to Gascony, France.

August 7 The French recover Poitiers, France, from English control.

December 12 King Charles V of France completes his conquest of the Atlantic province of Poitou, France.

1373

- John d'Arckel, prince-bishop of Liège in the Holy Roman Empire (modern Belgium), concedes "the peace of the 22" to his subjects, admitting their representation in his government.
- The Genoese take the port of Famagusta in Cyprus.

March 31 Queen Joanna I of Naples recognizes the independence of Sicily, where Frederick III takes the title king of Trinacria.

April 28 Duke John IV of Brittany flees to England following a pro-French revolt by his subjects, leaving only the town of Brest, Brittany, remaining in English hands.

May 8 The English mercenary Sir John Hawkwood, in papal service, defeats the Milanese at Chiesi, Italy. Duke Amadeus VI of Savoy also ravages Milanese territory.

June 16 Under the Treaty of London, England and Portugal make a perpetual alliance.

August 8 John of Gaunt, Duke of Lancaster, sets off from Calais, France, on an expedition through Champagne and Burgundy, France.

August 8 Under the Treaty of Fürstenwalde, Otto Wittelsbach, son of King Ludwig I of Bavaria, surrenders Brandenburg, Germany, to the Holy Roman Emperor Charles IV, who unites it with Bohemia.

December 12 John of Gaunt, Duke of Lancaster, arrives in Bordeaux, France, at the conclusion of his *chivauchée* through France, which achieves little.

1374

- King Ludwig I of Hungary and Poland grants the first general charter of privileges to the Polish nobility at Kessa.

February 11 The English and French make a truce over Picardy, at Bourbourg, Flanders, and begin considering a settlement.

June 6 Bernabò Visconti, ruler of Milan, Italy, makes peace with Duke Amadeus VI of Savoy and makes a truce with Pope Gregory XI.

SCIENCE, TECHNOLOGY, AND MEDICINE

Health and Medicine

1374

- A committee of public health is established in Venice to inspect vessels entering the republic's ports and exclude those carrying Black Death.
- Muslim physician Ibn-al-Khatīb of Granada in Moorish-occupied Spain produces the treatise *On Plague*.
- The French city of Aix-la-Chapelle is swept by a curious dancing mania, driving people to dance for hours in the streets, until they collapse through exhaustion.

Science

1372

- Al-Damīrī writes *The Lives of Animals*, an encyclopedic bestiary of animals both real and mythical. It is the greatest zoological work in Arabic.

Technology

1370

c. 1370 Exeter Cathedral in England, an example of the English style of Gothic known as Decorated, is completed.

- Henri de Vick installs a mechanical clock in the French king Charles V's Palais Royal, in Paris, France. It is used to regulate the chimes in all churches across the city.
- Steel crossbows are used in European warfare for the first time.

- The earliest iron needles are manufactured at Nuremberg, Germany, with a closed hook on the end; needles with eyes are manufactured in the Netherlands about 1400.

Transportation

1373
- The first modern European canal lock is built in the Netherlands, linking the River Lek onto the Utrecht Canal.

ARTS AND IDEAS

Architecture

c. **1370**
- The Beganpuri Mosque near Delhi, India, is completed.

Arts

c. **1374**
- Italian artist Jacopo di Paolo d'Avanzi paints the fresco *The Liberation of the Companions of St. James* in the Church of Sant'Antonio in Padua, Italy.

Literature and Language

1370
c. 1370 The anonymous Middle English poem *The Pearl*, a religious dream allegory that begins as a elegy for a dead daughter, is written.
c. 1370 The anonymous Scottish poem "The Pistill of Suete Susan" is written.
- Donato Velluti writes *La cronica domestica/The Domestic Chronicle*, an autobiographical work describing the daily life of a rich merchant and his children.

1371
- The French book *Le Livre du chevalier de la Tour-Landry/The Book of the Chevalier of Tour-Landry* is published. A collection of fables and stories, it was written for the instruction of the author's three daughters after the death of their mother.

Thought and Scholarship

1370
- French chronicler Jean le Bel completes his *Chronique/Chronicle*, a history of France, Germany, Flanders, and England from 1326 to 1361. The book is one of the principal sources for the contemporary French historian Jean Froissart.

c. **1374**
- The Japanese novel *Taiheiki*, possibly by the priest Kojima, is completed. It describes the civil wars of the period from 1318 to 1367.

BIRTHS & DEATHS

1370
- Gentile da Fabriano (Niccolo di Giovanni di Massio), leading central Italian painter of his age, whose surviving works include *Adoration of the Magi* (1423), born in Fabriano, Italy (–1427).
- Guarino Veronese, leading Italian humanist and Greek scholar, born in Verona, Italy (–1460).
- Leonardo Bruni, Italian humanist scholar, whose *Historiarum Florentini populi libri XII/Twelve Books of Histories of the Florentine People* (1610) is the first to be based on a critical examination of the sources, born in Arezzo, Italy (–1444).
- November 5 Casimir (Kazimierz) III the Great, King of Poland 1333–70 and last of the Piast dynasty, dies in Kraków, Poland (60).
- December 19 Pope Urban V dies.

1371
- Zheng He or Cheng Ho, Chinese admiral who extended his country's economic influence in southern Asia, born in K'unming, Yunnan Province, China (–1435).
- February 22 David II (David Bruce), King of Scotland 1329–71, son of Robert I the Bruce who spent a large part of his ineffectual reign in exile or in prison, dies in Edinburgh, Scotland (57).
- May 28 John the Fearless, first Valois Duke of Burgundy 1404–19, born in Rouvres, Burgundy, France (–1419).

1373
- July 23 St. Bridget, patron saint of Sweden and founder of the Brigantine Order, dies in Rome, Italy (*c.* 70).

1374
- *c.* 1374 Cardinal Henry Beaufort, bishop of Winchester, born in Château Beaufort, Anjou, France (–1447).
- Conrad von Megenburg, German canon, known for his scientific writings in German and his political writings in Latin, dies in Regensburg (*c.* 65).
- Ibn-al-Khatīb, great Arab writer, prime minister of Granada, executed in Granada, Spain (*c.* 61).
- July 19 Petrarch (Petrarca), Italian poet whose work was a major influence on the growth of Renaissance poetry, dies in Arqua, near Padua, Carrara (70).

SOCIETY

Religion

1370

- As Timur Leng (Tamerlane), the grand amir of the Mongols, extends his empire, Islam becomes dominant in central Asia, and Christian missions to the area are brought to an end.

September 27 Pope Urban V returns to Avignon, France.

c. 1374

- The English mystic Julian of Norwich writes the first version of her *Revelations of Divine Love*, a record of her visions. She writes a second longer version *c.* 1400.

1375–1379

POLITICS, GOVERNMENT, AND ECONOMICS

Business and Economics

1376

August 14 The Hanse obtains favorable terms from King Haakon VI of Norway under the Treaty of Kallundborg.

1379

- The Hanse rejects the demands of English merchants for free trade in Hanse towns and in the Baltic.

Colonization

1377

- The Teutonic Knights found Rhein, one of the last German colonies they establish in "the Wilderness" of southeast Prussia; their policy is to keep this area largely uninhabited.

Politics and Government

1375

- Dmitri III of Moscow, Russia, Grand Duke of Vladimir, establishes his primacy in Russia following the surrender of Michael of Tver.

February 24 King Waldemar IV of Denmark dies. An interregnum follows until 1376.

April 13 Mameluke forces from Syria invade the kingdom of Cilician Armenia and capture its capital Sis; and King Leo VI of Armenia flees to western Europe.

June 27 English and French embassies confer at Bruges, Flanders, and conclude a general treaty of truce. King Edward III of England now holds only Calais, Brest, Bordeaux, and Bayonne in France.

October 10 The city of Florence in Italy organizes a league in the Papal States, causing rebellions against Pope Gregory XI.

1376

- King Boromoraja I of Ayutthaya (in modern Thailand) reduces the king of the rival Thai kingdom of Sukothai to the status of governor.
- The Byzantine emperor John V Palaeologus grants the Aegean island of Tenedos to Venice, while his son Andronicus IV, who claims the imperial throne, grants it to Genoa. This triggers a new war between Venice and Genoa.
- The Navarrese Company, comprising mercenaries formerly employed in the war between France and Navarre, takes Durazzo, Albania, on behalf of Louis of Evreux.

March 19 Bologna in Italy revolts against Pope Gregory XI and declares its independence.

March 31 Pope Gregory XI excommunicates the city of Florence in Italy, thus beginning the "war of the eight saints."

April 24 The "good parliament" meets in England. It is the first to impeach the king's ministers, and the first in which the Commons are known to have elected a speaker, which subsequently becomes normal practice.

May 13 Olaf IV of Norway succeeds as king of Denmark under the regency of his mother Margaret, Queen of Norway and daughter of King Waldemar IV of Denmark.

June 10 Wenceslas, eldest son of the Holy Roman Emperor Charles IV, is elected king of the Romans.

1377

- Hayam Wuruk, Emperor of Majapahit (Java), destroys the last remains of the Hindu empire of Srivijaya (Sumatra).
- Olgierd, Grand Prince of eastern Lithuania and conqueror of Podolia and the area of modern Ukraine

after expelling the Mongols, dies. He is succeeded by his son Jagiełło.

- Tran Due-tong, Emperor of Dai Viet (modern northern Vietnam), is killed in his unsuccessful invasion of the kingdom of Champa (southern Vietnam). Che Bong Nga, King of Champa, subsequently again sacks Hanoi, Dai Viet.

January 27   The "bad parliament" meets in England and reverses the acts of the "good parliament," and grants a poll tax of four shillings on everyone over the age of 14 to fund the continuation of the French wars.

February 3   Robert of Geneva, the papal legate in the war against Florence, Italy, heads a force that takes Cesena, Italy and massacres its inhabitants.

February 19   John of Gaunt, Duke of Lancaster, intervenes in an ecclesiastical court on behalf of John Wycliffe (Wyclif), who is being questioned over his belief in the king's secular authority over the pope, and provokes a riot in London, England.

May 21   Ulm and thirteen other German towns that are members of the Swabian League defeat the forces sent by the Holy Roman Emperor Charles IV to suppress their organization, at Reutlingen, Germany.

June 21   King Edward III of England dies and is succeeded by his grandson Richard II, who begins his rule with a council of regency.

July 7   The French sack the Isle of Wight, off the south coast of England, and harass the English south coast with the aid of their Castilian allies.

July 27   King Frederick III of Trinacria (Sicily) dies and is succeeded by his daughter Maria. King Pedro IV of Aragon subsequently claims the duchies of Athens and Neopatras.

1378

- Dmitri III of Moscow, Grand Duke of Vladimir, defeats a Mongol army on the River Vozha.
- King Tammaraja II of Sukothai submits to Boromoraja I, King of the dominant Thai kingdom of Ayutthaya.

January 1   While visiting Paris, France, the Holy Roman Emperor Charles IV grants the imperial vicariate of the kingdom of Arles, France, to the dauphin Charles, son of King Charles V of France.

April 8   On the death of Pope Gregory XI the Italian churchman Bartolomeo Prignano is elected Pope Urban VI in Rome, a position he holds until 1389. When he refuses to move to Avignon in France (where the papal court has been since 1309) his election is declared void and the Swiss churchman Robert of Geneva is elected Pope (in effect, Antipope) Clement VII in Avignon, a position he holds until 1394. This marks the beginning of the Great Schism, when there are two popes, which lasts until 1417.

June 6   England takes possession of Cherbourg, France, by treaty with King Charles II of Navarre.

July 21   In the "revolt of the Ciompi," led by the cloth workers of the city, the *Popolo minuto*, comprising an alliance of merchants, manufacturers, and artisans headed by Michele di Lando, seizes control of Florence, Italy.

July 28   The Italian city of Florence and the papacy make peace under the Treaty of Tivoli.

August 4   Gian Galeazzo Visconti succeeds his father Galeazzo II as joint ruler of Milan, Italy, with his uncle Bernabò.

August 9   Thirteen French cardinals declare that the election of Pope Urban VI is invalid, claiming it was made under pressure. They believe that the papacy would favor the Italian party over the French.

August 31   Michele di Lando suppresses a second rising by the *Popolo minuto* and establishes a government representing a coalition of the different classes in Florence, Italy.

September 9   An English naval expedition led by John of Gaunt, Duke of Lancaster, fails to take St. Malo, France.

September 20   Dissident cardinals, encouraged by King Charles V of France, elect Robert of Geneva as Pope Clement VII. This means that there are two current popes.

October 10   The Venetians take the Aegean island of Tenedos from the Genoese in the "war of Chioggia."

November 11   The Holy Roman Emperor Charles IV and King Richard II of England announce their recognition of Pope Urban VI rather than Pope Clement VII. Five days later, on November 16, King Charles V of France declares his acceptance of Pope Clement VII.

November 29   The Holy Roman Emperor Charles IV, King of Bohemia, dies and is succeeded by his son Wenceslas. His younger sons Sigismund and John are endowed respectively with the mark of Brandenburg and the newly formed duchy of Görlitz.

1379

- The city of Ghent, Flanders, led by Philip van Artevelde, revolts against Count Louis of Flanders and defeats him.
- The Navarrese Company, having left Durazzo, Albania, following the death of Louis of Evreux, takes Thebes, capital of the duchy of Athens, Greece, on behalf of Nerio Acciajuoli, Lord of Corinth.

March 3   Gian Galeazzo Visconti, ruler of Milan, Italy, takes possession of the town of Asti in northern Italy.

April 28   Alberico da Barbiano, leader of the condottieri Company of St. George serving Pope Urban VI, defeats the Breton force of Pope Clement VII at Marino.

May 29   King Henry II of Castile dies and is succeeded by his son John I.

June 6   King Ludwig I of Hungary and Poland declares for Pope Urban VI, and the Holy Roman Emperor Wenceslas IV, King of Bohemia, persuades the German princes to do likewise.

August 3   Duke John IV recovers Brittany for England when an anti-French rebellion follows the confiscation of the duchy by King Charles V of France.

August 16   The Genoese take Chióggia, Italy, from the Venetians.

SCIENCE, TECHNOLOGY, AND MEDICINE

Exploration

1375

- Abraham Cresques, a Jewish mapmaker of Mallorca, makes the first world map showing Marco Polo's travels, the *Catalan Atlas*, as a gift from Pedro of Aragon to French king Charles V of France.

Health and Medicine

1376

- English physician John Arderne writes *Practica de fistula in ano/Practice Concerning Anal Fistula*, a treatise on his treatment of fistula, for which he charges wealthy patients up to £40.
- On the orders of Al-Abbas al-Rasuli, Sultan of Yemen, *The Desired Book of Peasants on Useful Trees and Aromatic Plants*, a book on herbalism, is produced.

1377

- The Balkan port of Ragusa (modern Dubrovnik) orders that travelers from plague-infected areas should spend 30 days in isolation (*trentina*), the first instance of quarantine.

1378

- German physician Joannes Jacobi writes *Secretarium practicae medicinae/Council of Medical Practice*, a summary of medical treatises, prepared for Charles V of France.

1379

- French scholar Jehan de Brie writes *Le Bon Berger/The Good Shepherd*, a manual for shepherds including early veterinary advice.

Science

1375

- French bishop and astronomer Nicole d'Oresme translates the works of Aristotle for the French king Charles V.

1377

- French astronomer and bishop Nicole d'Oresme writes a commentary on Aristotle's *De caelo/Concerning the Heavens*, suggesting a heliocentric theory of the universe, and even that there might be "more than one universe."

1378

- French alchemist Guillem Sedacer writes his *Sedacina totius alchimiae*.

Technology

c. 1375

- Block printing appears throughout Europe around this time.

1376

- An unknown Venetian inventor creates an exploding cannonball, packed with gunpowder and lit by a separate fuse before launching.

ARTS AND IDEAS

Architecture

1376

- The Civic Hall and Grande Place in Bruges, Flanders, are completed.

Arts

1379

- German artist Master Bertram paints the *Grabow Altarpiece* for the Church of St. Peter in Hamburg, Germany.

Literature and Language

1375

- c. 1375   The *Voiage and Travaile of Sir John Mandeville, Knight*, a collection of travel tales, appears in England. It claims to have been written by a gouty English knight, Sir John Maundeville (Mandeville), though it is likely that Sir John is the creation of the French chronicler and poet Jean d'Outremeuse. The work first appears in a French text dated about 1357. Popular throughout Europe, the book appears many times in English, notably in a 1496 printing.
- c. 1375   The manuscript *The Red Book of Hergest*, a compilation of Welsh tales, is written. Based on ancient Celtic myths and influenced by French romances, it forms the second part of a collection of Welsh stories known as the *Mabinogion*.
- *Hung-wu Chêng-yun*, a Chinese phonetic dictionary ordered by Emperor Hung-wu, is completed.
- Czech scholar Beneš of Weitmil completes his *Vita Caroli/Life of Charles*, a biography of the Holy Roman Emperor Charles IV.
- The anonymous Middle English alliterative poem *Sir Gawain and the Green Knight*, a chivalric romance, is written. The author may also have written *The Pearl* about 1370.

1376

- Scottish writer John Barbour completes *The Bruce*, an epic poem in 20 books on the life and deeds of the Scottish king Robert the Bruce. It is best known for its description of the Battle of Bannockburn in 1314.

1378

- Italian scholar Giovanni da Firenze compiles *Il pecorone*, a collection of tales and short stories taken from old chronicles. This collection contains the story that forms the basis of Shakespeare's *The Merchant of Venice*.

1379

- Italian scholar Benvenuto de'Rambaldi writes *Commentum/Commentary*, the first important study of the Italian writer Dante.

Thought and Scholarship

1377

- French scholar Nicholas Oresme translates into French (from Latin texts) the *Politics* and *Ethics* of the Greek philosopher Aristotle.

SOCIETY

Education

1379

- Pope Clement VII recognizes Erfurt University in Germany.

Everyday Life

1376

June 4   Fourteen German towns form the League of Swabian Towns with the aim of protecting its members

from the threat of mortgages and of safeguarding their commercial interests.

1377

- Taillevent, also known as Guillaume Tirel, supervisor of the royal kitchen in France, writes a book of recipes, *Le Viandier/The Butcher*.
- The population of England is estimated at 2 million; before the Black Death it was between 3.5 and 5 million.

Religion

c. **1375**

- The Dutch mystic Gerhard Groot of Deventer forms the Brethren of the Common Life, a religious society of clergy and lay people, at Windesheim. Its teachings, known as the *Devotio moderna/Modern Devotion*, had an important impact during the 14th and 15th centuries.

1376

- The English religious reformer John Wycliffe (Wyclif) publishes *De civili dominio/On Civil Power*, which claims that secular authorities can remove power from churchmen who have failed in their duties.

1377

- Pope Gregory XI condemns 19 of the propositions in the political writings of the English religious reformer John Wycliffe (Wyclif).

January 17   Pope Gregory XI restores the papacy to Rome, Italy.

BIRTHS & DEATHS

1375

- Waldemar IV, King of Denmark 1340–75, who regained the Danish throne from German control, and unified the country, dies in Schleswig (*c.* 55).

December 21   Giovanni Boccaccio, Italian poet and scholar who, with Petrarch, laid the foundations of Renaissance humanism, author of the *Decameron*, dies in Certaldo, Tuscany, Italy (*c.* 62).

1376

June 8   Edward ("the Black Prince"), heir apparent to the English throne and successful military commander during the Hundred Years' War, dies in Westminster, near London (46).

1377

- Algirdas (Olgierd), Grand Duke of Lithuania 1345–77, who made Lithuania one of the largest European 14th-century states, dies (*c.* 81).
- Filippo Brunelleschi, Florentine architect and engineer, pioneer of

early Renaissance architecture, whose works include the dome of Florence Cathedral (1420–36), born in Florence (–1446).

- Ibn Battūtah, celebrated Arab traveler, who undertook journeys totaling 75,000 miles to almost all the Muslim world, as well as Russia, China, and Sumatra, and described his travels in *Rihlah*, dies in Morocco (*c.* 73).

June 21   Edward III of Windsor, King of England 1327–77, son of Edward II, who led England into the Hundred Years' War against France, dies in Sheen, Surrey, England (64).

1378

c. 1378   John Oldcastle, leader and martyr of the Lollard sect and model for Shakespeare's Falstaff, born in Hertfordshire (–1417).

c. 1378   Lorenzo Ghiberti, early Italian Renaissance sculptor, whose best-known work is the *Gates of Paradise* for Florence Cathedral, born in Pelago, Italy (–1455).

- Alexis, Metropolitan of Russia 1353–78, who was the first member of the Russian church to participate in governing Russia, dies in Moscow (*c.* 83).

- Sir John Fastolf, English career soldier in the Hundred Years' War (1337–1453), who fought at Agincourt (1415) and Verneuil (1424), born in Caister, Norfolk, England (–1459).

- Vittorino da Feltre (Vittore dei Ramboldini), Italian humanist educator, born in Feltre, Italy (–1446).

March 27   Pope Gregory XI dies.

November 29   Charles IV (Charles of Luxembourg, original name Wenceslas), King of Bohemia 1346–78 and Holy Roman Emperor 1355–78, renowned for his learning and diplomatic skills, dies in Prague, Bohemia (62).

December 31   Alfonso Borgia (Calixtus III), Pope 1455–58, born near Játiva, Aragon, Spain (–1458).

1378

- The English religious reformer John Wycliffe (Wyclif) publishes *De potestate papae*/*On Papal Power*, in which he rejects papal authority and proposes a range of church reforms.
- The Italian nun Caterina Benincasa writes her *Dialogo*/*Dialogue*, a treatise on the spiritual life, written in Italian.

1379

- The French theologian Henry of Langenstein publishes *Epistola pacis*/*Letter of Peace*, which advocates a general council to end the Great Schism, which began 1378.

June 20   Pope Clement VII establishes his papacy at Avignon, France.

1380–1384

POLITICS, GOVERNMENT, AND ECONOMICS

Business and Economics

1380

November 5   A parliament meets in England and grants the third poll tax in four years. Unlike the previous poll tax of 1379, it is not graduated, and causes much discontent.

1381

June 17   The League of Rhenish towns, formed on January 20, 1381, allies with the Swabian League, the organization formed to protect commercial interests.

***c.* 1382**

- The French scholar Nicole d'Oresme publishes *De moneta*/*On Money*. One of the earliest European treatises on currency, it greatly influences medieval economic thinking.

March 1   The *maillotins* of Paris, France, riot against the introduction of new taxes. Similar riots occur in southern France.

Politics and Government

1380

c. 1380   The Zayid dynasty of Yemen raids the cities of Aden and Zabid.

- King Haakon VI of Norway dies and is succeeded by his son Olaf IV, King of Denmark. King Albert II of Sweden also claims Norway, and in the war that follows, the "Vitalian Brethren" organization comes into being and is to plunder Baltic shipping for the next 50 years.
- While suppressing a conspiracy, Hung-wu, Ming emperor of China, abolishes the office of prime minister

and the central chancellery, thereby introducing a new system in which Chinese emperors assume personal and autocratic rule.

January 14   A parliament meets and declares King Richard II of England old enough to rule.

June 10   An English force defeats a Franco-Castilian fleet off the coast of Kinsale, Ireland.

June 22   The Venetians recover Chióggia, Italy, compelling the occupying Genoese forces to surrender.

June 29   Queen Joanna I of Naples declares Louis, Duke of Anjou and brother of King Charles V of France, to be her heir.

July 29   An expedition led by Thomas of Woodstock, Earl of Buckingham, leaves Calais, France, to raid Picardy, Champagne, and the Loire Valley.

August 8   A French fleet raids up the River Thames and burns Gravesend, England.

September 8   Dmitri III of Moscow, Russia, Grand Duke of Vladimir, leads the Russians to victory over the "Golden Horde" at Kulikovo Pole, on the upper River Don, Russia. The supremacy of Moscow in Russia is thus confirmed.

September 16   Charles V the Wise, King of France, dies and is succeeded by his son Charles VI.

September 23   The expedition led by Thomas of Woodstock, Earl of Buckingham, reaches Brittany, France.

November 16   In the face of public unrest, the council ruling France for King Charles VI of France abolishes all taxes.

1381

- Grand Prince Jagiełło of Lithuania is deposed by his uncle Kiejstut.
- The French theologian Henry of Langenstein publishes *Concilium pacis*/*Peaceful Conciliation*, which argues the superiority of general councils over the pope.
- Tokhtamysh, vassal of Timur Leng (Tamerlane), the grand amir, ruling part of the "Golden Horde," defeats Mamay, ruling the western part, on the Kalka and thus reunites the "Horde" under his rule.

January 15   Under the Treaty of Vincennes, John de Montfort ends his rebellion and is recognized by King

Charles VI of France as Duke of Brittany. Thomas of Woodstock, Earl of Buckingham, accordingly vacates Brittany, leaving a garrison in Brest, France. A truce of six years is made with France.

May 19   King John I of Castile announces his acceptance of Pope Clement VII.

June 1   Pope Urban VI, who has excommunicated Queen Joanna I of Naples, recognizes her cousin Charles, Duke of Durazzo, as king of Naples.

June 14   During the "peasants' revolt" against the poll tax in England, the rebels (originating mainly from Essex and Kent) occupy London and kill the chancellor Archbishop Sudbury and the treasurer Robert Hales. On the following day, King Richard II of England meets the rebel leader Wat Tyler, who is later killed by the mayor of London, Sir William Walworth. The revolt is subsequently suppressed.

July 26   Charles, Duke of Durazzo, Albania, enters Naples claiming the throne of Naples.

August 8   Venice and Genoa make peace under the Treaty of Turin.

August 29   King Ferdinand I of Portugal, under pressure from England, revokes his acceptance of Pope Clement VII and recognizes Pope Urban VI.

1382

- Hung-wu, Ming emperor of China, completes the conquest of China and finally expels the Mongols.
- Grand Prince Jagiełło recovers control of Lithuania by defeating and murdering his uncle Kiejstut.
- Malik Ahmad conquers the area around Tapti, India, and rules it as an independent prince.
- The Burji line (of Circassian origin) of Mameluke sultans of Egypt is established. Its history is one of intrigue and murder, and boasts a total of 23 sultans.
- Timur Leng (Tamerlane), grand amir of the Mongols, conquers Khorasan.

January 14   King Richard II of England marries Anne of Bohemia in accordance with a treaty of alliance with her brother, the Holy Roman Emperor Wenceslas IV, King of Bohemia.

February 2   The introduction of new taxes causes a riot in Rouen, France, known as "La Harelle."

March 3   Queen Joanna I of Naples surrenders to Charles of Durazzo, Albania, and is imprisoned and executed.

March 15   The *Popolo grasso* recover power in Florence, Italy and establish an oligarchy.

May 3   The weavers of Ghent, Flanders, led by Philip van Artevelde, take Bruges, Flanders, from King Charles VI of France. Other Flemish towns also revolt.

May 30   Pope Clement VII crowns Louis of Anjou as king of Naples.

June 6   King Louis of Naples leads an army into Italy.

June 10   Andrea Contarini, Doge of Venice, dies and is succeeded by Michele Morosini.

August 8   King Ferdinand I of Portugal makes peace with King John I of Castile, who has besieged Lisbon, Portugal. An English expedition is forced to evacuate Portugal.

August 26   Tokhtamysh, Khan of the "Golden Horde," sacks Moscow, Russia, and then withdraws after having restored his suzerainty over Russia.

September 11   Ludwig the Great, King of Hungary and Poland, dies. One of his two daughters, Jadwiga, is

elected king of Poland. The Hungarians elect the elder daughter Mary, who is betrothed to Sigismund of Bohemia, but Charles of Durazzo, Albania, claims the throne as the Angevin male heir and invades.

October 16   Michele Morosini, Doge of Venice, dies and is succeeded by Antonio Vernieri.

November 27   A French army defeats Flemish rebels at Roosebeke, killing the rebel leader Philip van Artevelde.

1383

- Poland and Lithuania unite under the Treaty of Volkovysk. Queen Jadwiga of Poland marries Grand Prince Jagiełło of Lithuania and Lithuania accepts Christianity, so ending the crusades of the Teutonic Knights, whose expansion prompted the union.
- The Crispi dynasty of the duchy of Archipelago in Greece is established.
- The Holy Roman Emperor Wenceslas IV, King of Bohemia, proclaims a public peace in Germany.

January 1   The French army, returning from suppressing the rebellion in Flanders, restores royal control in Paris, France, and reimposes taxes.

March 1   Amadeus VI of Savoy, the Green Count, who made Savoy an important state, dies while campaigning in Italy.

May 5   An English expedition led by Henry Despenser, bishop of Norwich, as a "crusade" on behalf of Pope Urban VI, fails to exploit unrest in Flanders and withdraws.

October 10   King Ferdinand I of Portugal dies, having recognized his son-in-law, King John I of Castile, as his heir.

1384

January 30   Louis de Maële, Count of Flanders, dies and is succeeded by his son-in-law Philip the Bold of Burgundy.

July 26   The Holy Roman Emperor Wenceslas IV, King of Bohemia, arranges an alliance between the town leagues and princes of southwest Germany at Heidelberg, Germany.

September 9   King John I of Castile abandons the siege of Lisbon, Portugal, during his attempt to secure the throne of Portugal.

September 21   Louis I of Anjou, the designated king of Naples, dies at Bari in the south of Italy while attempting to conquer Naples. He is succeeded by his son Louis II.

November 20   The Florentines occupy Arezzo, Italy.

SCIENCE, TECHNOLOGY, AND MEDICINE

Exploration

1383

- French scholar John of Ypres compiles a collection of travelers' tales.

Health and Medicine

1383
- Ships entering Marseille, France, are required to spend 40 days in isolation, *quarantina*, to prevent the spread of plague.

Math

1382
- French astronomer and bishop Nicole d'Oresme's *Le Livre du ciel et du monde/The Book of Heaven and Earth* is published. It is a compilation of treatises on mathematics, mechanics, and related areas.

Science

1383
- French alchemist Nicholas Flamel claims, in his later autobiography *Le Livre des figures hiéroglyphiques/The Book of Hieroglyphic Figures*, to have performed a successful transmutation of base metal into gold.

1384
- English alchemist John Dombleday writes *Stella alchimiae/Star of Alchemy*, a manual of the craft.

Technology

1381
- Printers in Limoges, France, begin to use movable type.

ARTS AND IDEAS

Architecture

1380
- The Cathedral of Siena is completed in Italy. It is one of the finest examples of Italian Gothic.

Arts

1384
- Italian artist Altichiero paints the fresco *The Martyrdom of St. George* in the Oratory of San Giorgio in Padua, Italy.

Literature and Language

c. **1380**
- The anonymous English mystical text *The Cloud of Unknowing* is written.
- The poems of the Kashmiri writer and mystic Lal Ded are collected in *Lallā-vakyāni/Lallā's Wise Sayings*. Her works become an integral part of Kashmiri culture.

c. **1381**
- English writer Geoffrey Chaucer writes *The House of Fame*, a long, unfinished dream-vision poem with an allegorical basis that is now obscure.

BIRTHS & DEATHS

1380
- Thomas à Kempis (original name Thomas Hemerken), theologian to whom the highly influential *De imitatione Christi/On the Imitation of Christ* is attributed, born in Kempen, near Düsseldorf, Germany (–1471).
- February 11 Gian Francesco Poggio Bracciolini, Italian humanist, outstanding scholar of the early Renaissance, responsible for rediscovering several classical manuscripts, born in Terranuova, Tuscany (–1459).
- April 29 St. Catherine of Siena, patron saint of Italy, who was instrumental in returning the papacy to Rome from Avignon, dies in Rome (33).
- September 16 Charles V the Wise, King of France 1364–80, who led France to recovery after the first phase of the Hundred Years' War (1337–1453), dies in Nogent-sur-Marne, France (42).

1381
- January 13 St. Colette, abbess and reformer of the Poor Clares or Clarissines, born in Corbie, France (–1447).
- June 15 Wat Tyler, leader of the "peasants' revolt" in England, is beheaded in London.

1382
- July 11 Nicholas Orestes, French Roman Catholic bishop, mathematician, economist, and Aristotelian scholar whose work in mathematics laid the foundations leading to the development of analytical geometry, and whose translations of Aristotle were important in the development of French, dies in Lisieux, France (*c.* 57).

1383
- June 15 John VI Cantacuzenus, Byzantine emperor 1341–54, later a monk and historian, dies in Mistras (*c.* 91).

1384
- Kan'ami Kitotsugo, Japanese dramatist, writer of many of the classic works of the Japanese Nō drama that established Nō's forms and character, dies.
- August 20 Geert Groote (Gerardus Magnus), Dutch priest and teacher, who established the Brethren of the Common Life, dies in Deventer (43).
- December 31 John Wycliffe, English theologian, philosopher, and church reformer who attacked the doctrine of transubstantiation, dies in Lutterworth, Leicestershire (*c.* 54).

c. **1382**

- English writer Geoffrey Chaucer writes his long poem *The Parlement of Foules* (fowls), a dream-allegory that is possibly a commemoration of the marriage of King Richard II to Anne of Bohemia in 1382.

c. **1383**

- English writer John Gower writes *Vox clamantis/The Voice of One Crying in the Wilderness*, a long poem in Latin about the "peasants' revolt" of 1381.

Thought and Scholarship

1383

- Scottish scholar John Fordun completes his *Scotichronicon/Chronicle of Scotland*, a history of Scotland from Noah to 1383. A continuation appears in 1449.

SOCIETY

Religion

1380

c. 1380 The English mystic Walter Hilton writes the *The Ladder of Perfection*, a devotional treatise written in English.

- The English religious reformer John Wycliffe (Wyclif) begins work on translating the entire Bible into English, completed in 1393.
- The German theologian Conrad of Gelnhausen publishes *Epistola concordiae/Letter of Concord*, which advocates a general council to end the Great Schism, which began in 1378.

1381

- The English religious reformer John Wycliffe (Wyclif) publishes *De Eucharistia/On the Eucharist*, which challenges the church's teachings on the Eucharist.

1382

- An English church council condemns the theological opinions of the English religious reformer John Wycliffe (Wyclif).

1385–1389

POLITICS, GOVERNMENT, AND ECONOMICS

Business and Economics

1388

- The Hanse organization puts an embargo on trade with Flanders and makes a treaty with English merchants permitting their return to Danzig (modern Gdańsk, Poland) and other Prussian towns.

Politics and Government

1385

- A Turkish force takes Sofia, Bulgaria.
- Timur Leng (Tamerlane), the grand amir of the Mongols, partially conquers Azerbaijan from the ilkhanate.

February 21 The Rhenish and Swabian Leagues ally with the Swiss at Constance, Germany.

March 23 The nobles of Siena, Italy, overthrow its democratic government.

April 6 The Portuguese cortes (parliament) elects John, Master of the Order of Avis and illegitimate son of Pedro I, as king of Portugal.

May 6 Gian Galeazzo Visconti seizes his uncle Bernabò Visconti and takes sole control of Milan, Italy.

May 21 Pope Clement VII invests Louis II of Anjou as king of Naples.

July 7 The Scots, with French support, raid Northumberland, England.

August 8 King Richard II of England leads a retaliatory expedition which sacks Edinburgh, Scotland.

August 14 With English support, King John II of Portugal decisively defeats King John of Castile at Aljubarrota, Portugal.

December 18 The Peace of Tournai between Philip the Bold of Burgundy and the weavers of Ghent, Flanders, ends a period of social upheaval in Flanders.

1386

c. 1386 Sudanese Arabs expel the ruling family from the west central African kingdom of Bornu, near Lake Chad (in present-day Nigeria). A cadet line of the family is placed in power.

- King Pedro IV of Aragon declares in favor of Pope Clement VII.
- Murad, ruler of the Ottoman Turks, takes Niš, Serbia, and compels Lazar, Prince of Serbia, to become his tributary.
- Philip of Burgundy forms the "chamber" in Flanders, which forms the basis of the judicial councils of Flanders, Brabant, and Holland.
- Timur Leng (Tamerlane), the grand amir, completes his conquest of Persia and sacks Tbilisi (in modern-day Georgia), where he captures King Bagrat V of Georgia. He is subsequently compelled to withdraw from Azerbaijan after Tokhtamysh, Khan of the "Golden Horde," takes Tabriz.

February 7   Charles III of Durazzo, King of Naples, is murdered in Hungary. He is succeeded by his son Ladislas.

March 4   Grand Prince Jagiełło of Lithuania is crowned King Władysław II of Poland.

May 9   The Treaty of Windsor between King Richard II of England and King John II of Portugal makes a perpetual alliance between England and Portugal.

June 10   Sigismund of Bohemia marries Mary of Hungary, having rescued her from Horwath, ban of Croatia. On becoming king of Hungary, Sigismund cedes Brandenburg to Jošt, Margrave of Moravia.

July 7   John of Gaunt, Duke of Lancaster, lands at Coruña, Spain, to open his campaign to win the crown of Castile.

July 9   The Swiss defeat and kill Duke Leopold III of Austria at Sempach.

October 10   The French council abandons its advanced preparations to invade England.

October 24   King Richard II of England is compelled by the magnates to replace his senior ministers and appoint a commission of reform.

1387

- King Władysław II of Poland receives the homage of the rulers of Moldavia.
- Louis of Anjou, son of Louis I of Naples, takes the kingdom of Naples when King Ladislas of Naples, the antipope, and his mother and regent Margaret flee following a revolt.
- Tokhtamysh, Khan of the "Golden Horde," invades Transoxiana but fails to take Bukhara. Timur Leng (Tamerlane), the grand amir of the Mongols, retaliates by ravaging Khwarizm, central Asia.

January 1   Charles II the Bad, King of Navarre, dies and is succeeded by his son Charles III.

January 5   Pedro IV the Ceremonious, King of Aragon, dies and is succeeded by his son John I.

April 8   Louis, Duke of Touraine and brother of King Charles VI of France, marries Valentina, daughter of Gian Galeazzo Visconti of Milan, Italy. She is to succeed to her father's dominions if he has no son.

May 5   Under the Treaty of Troncoso, King John I of Castile makes a marriage alliance with John of Gaunt, Duke of Lancaster, who has abandoned his campaign in Galicia, Spain.

August 3   King Olaf VI of Denmark and Norway dies. His mother Margaret is elected to continue as regent in both countries for her lifetime.

August 25   King Richard II of England questions judges in Nottingham, England, about his prerogative powers and receives favorable responses, leading him to believe that he is able to repudiate the commission of reform.

October 19   Gian Galeazzo Visconti, ruler of Milan, Italy, takes Verona, Italy. Antonio della Scala, ruler of Verona, flees.

October 22   Vicenza, Italy, surrenders to Gian Galeazzo Visconti, ruler of Milan, Italy.

November 11   Timur Leng (Tamerlane), the grand amir of the Mongols, destroys Isfahan, Persia.

November 17   King Richard II of England accepts the demands of the Duke of Gloucester and Earls of Arundel and Warwick to call a parliament to try the ministers they have impeached. The parliament is called for February 3, 1388 in order to allow Richard time to recover his position or, if necessary, to allow those charged to escape.

December 20   Henry, Earl of Derby, defeats King Richard II of England's supporter Robert de Vere, Earl of Oxford, at Radcot Bridge, Oxfordshire, England. The magnates reputedly consider deposing Richard.

1388

February 3   The "merciless parliament" meets and convicts the courtiers of King Richard II of England, who are accused by the lords appellant. The lords appellant take control of the government.

April 9   A Swiss force defeats Duke Albert III of Austria at Näfels, Switzerland.

May 2   Nerio Acciajuoli of Corinth takes the acropolis of Athens, Greece.

August 5   James, Earl of Douglas, is killed while leading the Scottish army to victory against Henry Percy "Hotspur" at Otterburn ("Chevy Chase"), Northumberland, England. The scale of the defeat leads some magnates to consider an arrangement with France.

August 23   The princes of Swabia and the Franconians led by the Count of Württemberg defeat the Swabian League at Döffingen.

September 20   Firuz, Sultan of Delhi, India, dies and is succeeded by his grandson Tughluq II.

October 28   King Charles VI of France announces his intention to rule, though in practice he is dependent on the old councillors of King Charles V of France, known as *Les Marmousets*.

November 6   Rupert, the elector palatine, defeats the Rhenish League at Worms, Germany.

November 24   Gian Galeazzo Visconti, ruler of Milan, takes Padua, Italy.

1389

- King Władysław II of Poland receives homage from the rulers of Wallachia and Bessarabia.
- Rajasanagara, King of Java, dies and his empire, which extends throughout the whole of modern Indonesia, now collapses.
- Tokhtamysh, Khan of the "Golden Horde," campaigns inconclusively against Timur Leng (Tamerlane), the grand amir of the Mongols, in central Asia.

February 19   Abu-Bakr revolts and deposes Tughluq II, Sultan of Delhi, India.

February 24   King Albert II of Sweden is defeated and captured at Falköping, Sweden. Margaret of Denmark is accepted as ruler of Sweden.

April 1 Under the Treaty of Zürich, Duke Albert III of Austria recognizes the recent Swiss conquests.

May 3 King Richard II of England resumes personal government.

May 5 The Holy Roman Emperor Wenceslas IV, King of Bohemia, promulgates a public peace for southern Germany in order to end the wars between the princes and the towns.

May 19 Dmitri III of Moscow, Russia, Grand Duke of Vladimir, dies and is succeeded by his son Vasily I.

June 15 Murad I, ruler of the Ottoman Turks, is killed in defeating the Serbians at Kosovo and is succeeded by his son Bāyezīd I. King Lazar of Serbia is also killed. In the ensuing disintegration of his dominions Montenegro becomes independent.

November 2 Pietro Tomacelli is elected Pope Boniface IX.

SCIENCE, TECHNOLOGY, AND MEDICINE

Exploration

1385
- Florentine banker Leonardo Frescobaldi writes an account of his journey to the Near East and Egypt in 1384.

Technology

1386
- The Salisbury Cathedral clock, the first powered by twin weighted drives—one for the timekeeper, one for the chimes—is constructed in England. Today it is the oldest working mechanical clock in the world.

1389
- The first German paper mill is founded at Nuremberg by German entrepreneur Nicholas Stromer.

ARTS AND IDEAS

Architecture

1387
- Following his conversion to Christianity in 1386, Jagiełło, the ruler of Lithuania, founds Vilnius Cathedral, the first in Lithuania.
- The Batalha Monastery in Spain, inspired by northern European styles of Gothic, is completed.
- Work begins on Milan Cathedral in Italy. A vast building, combining the Romanesque and Gothic styles, it has a complicated history, with work continuing, on and off, for hundreds of years. Over the years a number of architects work on its design, including Simonde da Orsenigo, Bonino da Campioni, Master Johann of Freiburg, Henrich Parler, and Jean Mignot of Paris.

Literature and Language

c. 1385
- English writer Geoffrey Chaucer writes *Troylus and Cryseyde*, a long narrative poem that retells a story familiar in the Middle Ages of Troilus and Cressida, based during the Trojan war, though his immediate source is *Il filostrato/The Love-Struck*, by the Italian writer Boccaccio.
- English writer Thomas Usk writes *The Testament of Love*, a prose allegory of courtly and divine love. It was once ascribed to Chaucer.

BIRTHS & DEATHS

1385
December 18 Bernabò Visconti, joint ruler of Milan, Italy, is murdered.

1386
c. 1386 Donatello, celebrated Italian Renaissance sculptor, whose major works include *David* and the *Feast of Herod* (1433–35), born in Florence, Italy (–1466).
- St. John of Capistrano (St. Giovanni Da Capistrano), celebrated Franciscan preacher and leader of an army that liberated Belgrade from the Ottoman Turks, born in Capistrano, kingdom of Naples, Italy (–1456).

1387
September 16 Henry V, King of England 1413–22, son of Henry IV, born in Monmouth, Wales (–1422).

1388
- The Italian poet Antonio Pucci, creator of a range of work including the historical *Della guerra di Pisa confortando Lucca/On the War Between Pisa and Lucca* and the tales in verse *Istorie/Stories*, dies.

1389
c. 1389 The Persian writer Hāfiz (Mohammad Shams od-Dīn Hāfiz), creator of a collection of lyric poems that are second only to those of the greatest Persian poet Firdausī, best known through the anthology *Dīvān*, dies in Shīrāz, Persia (*c.* 64).
- Murad I, Ottoman sultan 1360–89, father of Bāyezīd I, whose reign saw rapid expansion in Anatolia and the Balkans, killed at the Battle of Kosovo, in Serbia (*c.* 63).

March 1 St. Antoninus, archbishop of Florence who founded modern moral theology, born in Florence (–1459).

September 27 Cosimo de' Medici the Elder, financier and statesman, born in Florence, Italy (–1464).

October 15 Urban V, Italian pope whose election caused the French cardinals to establish the antipope, dies in Rome (*c.* 71).

- French writer Eustache Deschamps completes his long poem *Le Miroir du mariage/The Mirror of Marriage*, a satire against women.

1387

- English writer Geoffrey Chaucer begins *The Canterbury Tales*. Told by a party of 30 pilgrims traveling from London to Canterbury, it consists of 24 tales, told in verse, which provide a vivid picture of 14th-century England.

1389

- French courtier Philippe de Mézières completes his *Le Songe du vieil pèlerin/The Dream of the Old Pilgrim*, an allegory in which he gives an account of his life and beliefs.

Thought and Scholarship

1385

- *c.* 1385 English writer Geoffrey Chaucer translates *De consolatione philosophiae/On the Consolation of Philosophy*, by the Roman philosopher Boethius, under the title *Boece*.
- Italian chronicler Marchionne di Coppo di Stefano Buonaiuti completes his *Cronaca fiorentina/Florentine Chronicle*, a history of Florence from the creation to 1385.

1387

- *c.* 1387 French Benedictine prior Honoré Bonet writes his tract *L'Arbre de batailles/The Tree of Battles*, on the ethics of war.

- English scholar John de Trevisa translates the *Polychronicon* of the English chronicler Ranulf Higden from Latin into English.

SOCIETY

Education

1385

- A dispute between Bohemian and German personnel at Prague University, Bohemia, results in Bohemian members gaining influence.
- Heidelberg University is founded in Germany.

1388

- Cologne University is established in Germany.

1389

- Buda University is founded in Hungary.

Sports

1386

- Spanish writer Pedro López de Ayala writes *El libro de las aves de caça/Book of Domestic Birds*, a Castilian treatise on falconry.

◆

1390–1394

POLITICS, GOVERNMENT, AND ECONOMICS

Business and Economics

1392

- The Hanse recovers its privileges in Flanders and Novgorod, having placed embargoes on trade with them.

Politics and Government

1390

- France and Genoa send an unsuccessful expedition to Mahdia (in modern Tunisia), in an attempt to extract trading privileges from the local emir.
- February 2 Che Bong Nga, King of Champa (modern southern Vietnam), is assassinated. His conquests in Dai Viet (northern Vietnam) are abandoned by his successor La Khai.
- April 4 Gian Galeazzo Visconti, ruler of Milan, Italy, declares war against the Italian towns of Florence and Bologna.
- April 19 King Robert II of Scotland dies. He is succeeded by his son, Robert III.
- June 19 Francesco Carrara recovers Padua, Italy, from the Milanese.
- October 9 King John I of Castile and León dies. He is

succeeded by his son, Henry III. Civil war soon breaks out.

December 12   Mohammad, the son of Firuz, establishes himself as sultan of Delhi, India, after expelling Abu Bakr.

1391

- Grand Duke Vasily I of Moscow annexes the city of Nizhny-Novgorod.
- Queen Maria of Sicily marries Martin of Aragon, who then becomes king of Sicily.
- Yoshimitsu Ashikaga, the Japanese shogun (military ruler), defeats the Yamana family, which is threatening his regime.

February 16   The Byzantine emperor John V Palaeologus dies. He is succeeded by his son Manuel II.

February 24   King Charles VI of France cancels plans for a French expedition to Rome and Naples in expectation of a personal interview with King Richard II of England, who has threatened to attack France if Charles invades Italy.

June 18   Timur Leng (Tamerlane), the grand amir of the Mongols, defeats Tokhtamysh, Khan of the "Golden Horde," on the River Kondurcha, but does not pursue him west of the River Volga.

July 25   John, Count of Armagnac, who is employed by Florence, is defeated and killed by the Milanese outside Alessandria.

1392

- A period of feudal warfare in Japan, which has been taking place since 1336, ends with the abdication of the southern emperor in favor of the northern emperor in Kyoto, who is still controlled by the Ashikaga shoguns.
- King Mohammad V of Granada dies. He is succeeded by his son, Yūsuf II.
- Timur Leng (Tamerlane), the grand amir of the Mongols, takes the city of Baghdad, Mesopotamia, from the Persian ilkhanate.
- Yi Song-gye, a Korean general, usurps the throne, ending the Koryŏ dynasty and founding the Yi dynasty. He recognizes Chinese supremacy.

January 1   Gian Galeazzo Visconti, ruler of Milan, makes peace with Florence and its allies in Genoa.

April 11   The Italian cities of Florence, Bologna, Padua, Ferrara, and others form the League of Bologna for mutual defense against Gian Galeazzo Visconti, ruler of Milan.

June 13   John IV of Brittany instigates an attempt to murder Oliver de Clisson, Constable of France, with whom he has had a long-running feud.

August 8   King Charles VI of France becomes insane while leading an expedition to Brittany. The Dukes of Burgundy and Berry take control of his government.

October 21   Pietro Gambacorta, ruler of Pisa, is killed in a riot instigated by Jacopo d'Appiano, who succeeds him.

1393

- The Ottoman Turks complete their conquest of Bulgaria.
- Timur Leng (Tamerlane), the grand amir of the Mongols, campaigns against the "Golden Horde" in Russia, reaching Moscow. He also completes his conquest of Persia and Mesopotamia, extinguishing the last independent Mongol dynasties.

January 20   Mohammad Tughluq II, Sultan of Delhi, India, dies. He is succeeded by his son, Sikandar.

March 8   Sikandar, Sultan of Delhi, India, dies and is succeeded by his brother, Mahmud. The kingdom of Delhi is dissolving into feudal anarchy.

March 20   John of Pomuk, vicar general of Prague, is murdered by the Holy Roman Emperor, King Wenceslas IV of Bohemia.

July 10   In the Covenant of Sempach, the Swiss Confederation regulates its military organization.

August 10   King Henry III of Castile begins his personal rule.

1394

- King Yi Song-gye of Korea establishes his capital at Seoul.
- On the death of the antipope Clement VII in Avignon, the Spanish clergyman Pedro de Luna is elected as Antipope Benedict XIII.
- The conquest by Bāyezīd, ruler of the Ottoman Turks, of the Karamans of Rūm is recognized in the grant to him of the title of sultan by the caliph of Egypt.

1394–98   King Omar of the central African kingdom of Kanem abandons Kanem and moves to Kagha.

January 11   King Ladislas of Naples, the antipope, recognizes Nerio Acciajuoli as Duke of Athens, a title that he won from the Catalans.

April 12   The Ottoman Turks take the Greek port of Thessaloníki.

May 5   Malik Sarvar founds the Muslim kingdom of Jaunpur, on the middle Ganges River, India.

May 8   The "League of the Lords" in Bohemia temporarily arrests the Holy Roman Emperor Wenceslas IV, King of Bohemia.

June 7   Anne of Bohemia becomes the queen of King Richard II of England.

October 2   King Richard II of England lands at Waterford, Ireland, at the start of an expedition to Ireland that aims to put down a rebellion in Leinster.

SCIENCE, TECHNOLOGY, AND MEDICINE

Exploration

1390

- The Italian traveler Simone Sigoli writes *Viaggio al Monte Sinai/Journey to Mt. Sinai*, an account of his journey with the Florentine banker Frescobaldi in 1385.

Science

1391

- The English writer Geoffrey Chaucer writes *A Treatise on the Astrolabe* in Middle English.

1394

- Italian astrologer Antonio de Montulmo writes *De iudiciis nativitatium/On Judgments of Births*, an exposition on birth charts.

Technology

1392

- Korean printers are known to have been using movable metal type by this date.

ARTS AND IDEAS

Architecture

1391

- The Court of Lions in the Alhambra in Granada, one of the finest examples of Moorish art in Spain, is completed.

Arts

***c.* 1390**

- The anonymous Czech artist known as the Master of Třeboň (Wittingau) paints *The Resurrection of Christ*.
- The Flemish artist Jacquemart de Hesdin completes his illuminations for the book of prayers *Les Petites Heures de Duc de Berry/The Little Hours of the Duke of Berry*.

1393

- Dutch artist Claus Sluter completes his carvings for the portal of the abbey of Chartreuse de Champmol, in Dijon, France.

***c.* 1394**

- Italian artists Jacobello and Pierpaola dalle Masegne sculpt the *Apostles* for the choir screen of San Marco, Venice.

Literature and Language

***c.* 1390**

- English writer John Gower writes *Confessio amantis/Confessions of a Lover*, a long poem in Middle English, a narrative embodying many stories from classical and later sources.

- French writer Jean d'Arras writes *L'Histoire de Lusignan/The Story of Lusignan* (or *Livre de Mélusine/Book of Mélusine*) for the French nobleman Jean, Duke of Berry. A history of the Duke of Berry's ancestors, it is also a romance on the *Mélusine* (fairy-wife) theme.
- The *Leabhar Bhaile an Mhóta/The Book of Ballymote*, a manuscript of Irish poetry and prose, is compiled.
- Turkish writer Al-Ahmedī writes *Iskandar-namā/The Book of Alexander*, an epic poem describing the exploits of Alexander the Great.

1392

c. 1392   The Russian history *Zadonschchina* is written, possibly by the priest Sofoniya Yyazanets. It is a vivid account of the battle of Kulikovo in 1380, which marked the beginning of the end of Tatar power in Russia. It becomes one of the best-known works of early Russian literature.

- French writer Eustache Deschamps writes *L'Art de dictier*, an influential treatise on poetry.

Theater and Dance

1390

- The *Miracles de Notre-Dame/Miracle Plays of Our Lady*, a collection of 42 French miracle plays by different anonymous authors, is compiled.

SOCIETY

Education

1391

- Ferrara University is founded in Italy.

1392

- The Italian scholar Giovanni Conversini is appointed professor of rhetoric at the University of Padua in Italy.

1393

- Yi Song-gye reinstitutes the examination system for the Korean civil service, based on the Chinese model. Confucianism has official acceptance while Buddhism declines and is partially suppressed.

BIRTHS & DEATHS

1390

April 19   Robert II, King of the Scots 1371–90, first of the Stewart kings, dies in Dundonald, Ayrshire, Scotland (74).

1391

- dGe-dun-grub-pa, first Dalai Lama, born.
- Humphrey Plantagenet, Duke of Gloucester, first major patron of

humanism in England, born (−1447).

1393

November 29   Leo VI, the last king of Armenia, dies in Paris, France.

1394

- James I, King of Scotland 1406–37, son of Robert III, born in Dunfermline, Fife, Scotland (−1437).

March 4   Henry the Navigator, Portuguese prince noted for his sponsorship of voyages of discovery and trade, born in Porto, Portugal (−1460).

September 16   Pope Clement VII dies in Avignon, France.

November 24   Charles of Orléans, French courtly poet, born in Paris, France (−1465).

Everyday Life

1393
- Population registers record 60 million Chinese in 10 million households, and land registers show 129 million acres in use.
- The Ming army consists of 493 guard units (of 5,600 men each) under the ministry of war.

1394
- *Le Ménagier de Paris/The Goodman of Paris*, a handbook of instruction for a wife appears. It is written by an anonymous husband, and focuses on domestic, moral, and ethical matters, and includes instructions on cooking.

Religion

1392
- The Tibetan religious leader Tsong Kapa founds the reformed order of Tibetan Lamas, the S'a-ser ("Yellow Hats").

1393
- The first translation of the Bible into English is completed. The work was begun by the English reformer John Wycliffe (Wyclif) in 1380 and continued on Wycliffe's death in 1384 by Nicholas Hereford.

1394
- The Bohemian preacher Matthias of Janov publishes his tract *De regulis veteris et novi testamenti/On the Rules of the Old and New Testaments*, a study critical of the church.

Sports

1392
- Playing cards are printed with blocks for King Charles VI of France.

1395–1399

POLITICS, GOVERNMENT, AND ECONOMICS

Business and Economics

1398

May 14 A council of the French clergy assembles. It proposes to withhold taxes due to Pope Benedict XIII in Avignon, France, to force him to resign.

Politics and Government

1395
- Grand Duke Vitold of Lithuania seizes the city of Smolensk, Russia.
- Timur Leng (Tamerlane), the grand amir of the Mongols, takes Erzinjan and Sivas in Anatolia.
- Yoshimitsu Ashikaga, the Japanese shogun (military ruler), retires to a monastery and is replaced by his son Yoshimochi Ashikaga; he retains considerable power, however.

February 2 King Charles VI of France holds a council of the French clergy who endorse a proposal that both popes, in Rome, Italy, and Avignon, France, should resign. Pope Benedict XIII in Avignon refuses to comply.

April 15 Timur Leng (Tamerlane), the grand amir of the Mongols, defeats Tokhtamysh, Khan of the "Golden Horde," on the River Terek, Russia.

May 11 King Wenceslas IV of Bohemia sells the title of Duke of Milan to Gian Galeazzo Visconti, ruler of Milan.

May 15 King Richard II of England leaves Dublin, Ireland, for England, having received the submission of the Irish chieftains.

May 17 Queen Mary of Hungary dies. Some Hungarians support the claims of King Ladislas of Naples against her husband, Sigismund.

May 17 The Hungarians and Wallachians defeat the Ottoman Turks at Rovine, but Wallachia becomes tributary to the Turks, who also conquer the Dobrudja area of the Balkans.

May 19 King John I of Aragon dies. He is succeeded by his brother, Martin I.

June 17 Queen Margaret of Denmark and Norway releases King Albert II of Sweden and makes peace with him by the Treaty of Lindholm. Stockholm is given to the Hanse, which mediated between the two, as a guarantee for the peace.

August 26 Timur Leng (Tamerlane), the grand amir of the Mongols, abandons his campaign against Moscow,

Russia, having destroyed the economy of the "Golden Horde."

1396

- King Yūsuf II of Granada is succeeded by his son, Mohammad VII.
- Pedro Bordo de San Superano, commander of the Navarrese Company, usurps the principality of the Morea, Greece.
- The kingdom of Gujarat in India is established by Wajih-ul-Mulk of Didwana.

March 12   A treaty of truce for 28 years is made between France and England. Isabella, the daughter of King Charles VI of France, is betrothed to King Richard II of England.

April 2   John of Jenstein resigns as archbishop of Prague, as the outcome of a dispute between the Holy Roman Emperor Wenceslas IV, King of Bohemia, and the Bohemian clergy, whom he is attempting to subject. At about the same time, Wenceslas, through the mediation of King Sigismund of Hungary, is obliged to allow the lords of Bohemia and Moravia control over his government.

September 25   The Ottoman Turks destroy the crusading army of King Sigismund of Hungary and his western allies at Nicopolis, Bulgaria.

September 29   France and Florence make an alliance to partition the duchy of Milan.

November 4   King Richard II of England marries Isabella, the daughter of King Charles VI of France.

November 27   The French take possession of Genoa, which has surrendered itself to King Charles VI of France in order to put an end to its internal strife.

1397

- *Ta-Ming lii/Laws of the Great Ming* is first published. It is a comprehensive code of Chinese criminal and administrative law.
- An agreement is reached, healing the schism between the rival northern and southern imperial courts in Japan.
- The central African kingdom of Kanem rises in revolt.
- Tokhtamysh is deposed as khan by the "Golden Horde" and elects Timur-Kutlugh to replace him, with Edigey actually ruling. Grand Duke Vitold of Lithuania invades the area now known as Ukraine as Tokhtamysh's ally.

March 3   The forces of Gian Galeazzo Visconti, Duke of Milan, invade Mantuan territory.

June 12   The English garrison evacuates Brest, in the west of Brittany, by treaty with John IV of Brittany.

June 17   Queen Margaret of Denmark and Norway holds an assembly of Scandinavian nobles at Kalmar, Sweden, for the coronation of her grand-nephew, Eric VII of Pomerania, as king of Denmark, Norway, and Sweden—the "Kalmar Union."

August 8   The League of Bologna (comprising the Italian cities of Florence, Bologna, Padua, Ferrara, and others) defeats the Milanese at Governolo.

1398

- Grand Duke Vasily I of Moscow is defeated in an attempt to annex the principality of Novgorod, Russia.
- King Harihara II of the Hindu empire of Vijayanagar in southern India invades the Deccan, but he is repulsed.

January 31   King Richard II of England holds a parliament at Shrewsbury, England, which extends his powers by appointing a commission to continue its work and granting him the wool customs for life.

April 5   The Teutonic Knights take the town of Visby, on the Swedish island of Gotland.

May 5   Pir Mohammad, grandson of Timur Leng (Tamerlane), Grand Amir of the Mongols, takes the city of Multan in the Punjab.

May 11   Gian Galeazzo Visconti, Duke of Milan, makes a truce for ten years with Francesco di Gonzaga of Mantua.

July 28   King Charles VI of France announces his country's withdrawal from obedience to Pope Benedict XIII of Avignon. King Henry III of Castile and León does likewise.

September 9   Jacopo d'Appiano, ruler of Pisa, dies. His son, Gherardo, succeeds with support from Gian Galeazzo Visconti, Duke of Milan.

September 9   Timur Leng (Tamerlane), the grand amir of the Mongols, invades the Punjab, India.

December 18   Timur Leng (Tamerlane), the grand amir of the Mongols, sacks the city of Delhi, India.

1399

- The Byzantine emperor Manuel II begins his journey from Constantinople (modern Istanbul, Turkey) to Venice, Italy; Paris, France; and London, England, to seek Western aid against the Ottoman Turks.

January–March   Timur Leng (Tamerlane), the grand amir of the Mongols, continues his massacres and ravages in India, causing a famine.

February 3   John of Gaunt, Duke of Lancaster, dies. King Richard II of England confiscates his estates and sentences his son, Henry, Duke of Hereford, whom he sees as a potential threat, to exile for life.

February 19   Gian Galeazzo Visconti, Duke of Milan, buys Pisa from its ruler, Gherardo d'Appiano.

April 29   Raja Ahmad of Khandesh, India, dies leaving his kingdom to his sons Nasir and Hassan.

June 1   King Richard II of England lands at Waterford, Ireland, on his second Irish expedition. He made the expedition when he discovered that Henry Bolingbroke, in exile in Ireland, had invaded England.

July 4   Henry, the exiled Duke of Lancaster, lands at Ravenspur, Yorkshire, and raises a rebellion against King Richard II of England, who abandons his Irish expedition.

August 5   The "Golden Horde" defeats Grand Duke Vitold of Lithuania and a Russian army on the River Vorskla.

August 19   King Richard II of England surrenders to Henry, Duke of Lancaster, at Flint, north Wales.

September 6   Siena accepts the lordship of Gian Galeazzo Visconti, Duke of Milan.

September 29   King Richard II of England abdicates and is declared deposed in a quasi-parliamentary assembly. Henry, Duke of Lancaster, claims and receives the crown as Henry IV.

SCIENCE, TECHNOLOGY, AND MEDICINE

Health and Medicine

1398

- Italian physician Pietro de Tossignano writes a textbook of therapeutics and *materia medica* ("medical matters"), and also *Consilium pro peste evitanda/Counsel for the Avoidance of Pestilence*, a treatise on avoiding the Black Death by avoiding contagion and other similar hygienic practices.

Science

1398

- John of Trevisa translates *De proprietustibus rerum/On the Properties of Things*, an encyclopedia (*c.* 1240) of Greek, Arab, and Jewish scientific and medical knowledge by Bartholomew the Englishman from Latin into English.

Technology

1398

- Chinese scholar Shên Chi-sun writes *Mo fa chi yao*, an illustrated treatise on the manufacture of ink.

ARTS AND IDEAS

Architecture

1397

- Prague Cathedral in Bohemia, designed by the French architect Matthias of Arras and the German architect Peter Parler, is completed. Parler's choir is one of the major works of German Late Gothic (known as Sondergotik).

Arts

c. 1395

- Italian artist Giovanni dei Grassi completes the illustrations for the book of prayers *The Visconti Book of Hours*.

c. 1398

- French artist Girard d'Orléans paints *King John the Good of France*, one of the earliest true portraits in Western painting.

1399

- Flemish artist Melchior Broederlam paints *The Annunciation and Visitation* and *The Presentation and the Flight into Egypt*.

Literature and Language

c. 1398

- French Benedictine prior Honoré Bonet writes *L'Apparicion maistre Jehan de Meun/The Appearance of*

BIRTHS & DEATHS

1395

c. 1395 Antonio Pisanello, Italian painter in the international Gothic style and one of the first 15th-century painters to paint from life, born (–1455).

- Jacques Coeur, powerful French merchant and counselor to King Charles VII of France, born in Bourges, France (–1456).

March 13 John Barbour, author of *The Bruce*, the national epic that is considered the first major work of Scottish literature, dies in Aberdeen, Scotland (*c.* 70).

1396

June 5 Giannozzo Manetti, Italian humanist and writer, born (–1459).

July 31 Philip III, Duke of Burgundy 1419–67, who founded the state of Burgundy, born in Dijon, Burgundy (–1467).

July 31 William Courtenay, archbishop of Canterbury 1381–96, dies in Maidstone, Kent, England.

1397

- Paolo Uccello, early Renaissance Florentine painter, noted for his use of perspective, born (–1475).

November 15 Nicholas V, Italian pope 1447–55, who founded the Vatican Library, restored peace to the Papal States and Italy, and started a program of architectural reconstruction in Rome, born in Sarzana, republic of Genoa (–1455).

1398

June 24 Hongwu or Hung-wu, Chinese emperor 1368–98, founder of the Ming dynasty, dies (69).

August 19 Inigo López de Mendoza, Marquess of Santillana, Spanish poet and humanist, born in Carrión de los Condes, Spain (–1458).

1399

c. 1399 Rogier van der Weyden, influential Flemish painter, born in Touraine, France (–1464).

- The French writer Jean d'Outremeuse, creator of *Le Myreur des histoires/The Mirror of History*, a verse history of the world, and *Geste de Liège/The Story of Liège*, an epic, dies (61).

February 3 John of Gaunt, Duke of Lancaster, English prince, son of Edward III of England, father of Henry IV of England, dies in London, England (58).

July 13 Peter Parler, German architect whose use of extensive ornamentation and complicated vaults influenced later architecture, dies in Prague (*c.* 69).

July 17 Jadwiga, the wife of King Władysław Jagiełło of Poland, and "king" of Poland in her own right, dies.

Master Jehan de Meun, an allegory on the evils of his times.

1399

- Italian-born French writer Christine de Pisan writes her long poem *L'Epitre au dieu d'amour/Letter to the God of Love*, in which she defends women against the satire directed at them in earlier medieval romances. The work is translated into English by Thomas Hoccleve in 1402.

Theater and Dance

1398

- The Confrérie de la Passion is founded in Paris, France, to perform religious plays.

Thought and Scholarship

1396

- Italian scholar and humanist Coluccio Salutati writes *De fato et fortuna/On Destiny and Fortune*.

SOCIETY

Education

1395

- The Byzantine scholar Manuel Chrysoloras of Constantinople (modern Istanbul, Turkey) holds the first west European chair of Greek, in Florence, Italy.
- The Nizamiyah and Mustansiriyah colleges in Baghdad, Mesopotamia, merge.

1397

- King Władysław Jagiełło of Poland reestablishes Kraków University, Poland, with a new financial foundation.
- The Italian scholar Gasparino da Barzizza, considered the greatest Latin scholar of his day, is appointed professor of rhetoric at Padua University, Italy.

1398

- Gian Galeazzo Visconti, Duke of Milan, suppresses Pavia University and refounds Piacenza University.

Religion

1396

- Gian Galeazzo Visconti, Duke of Milan, founds the Charterhouse (Carthusian monastery) at Pavia, Italy, to the south of Milan.

1400–1404

POLITICS, GOVERNMENT, AND ECONOMICS

Business and Economics

1400

- The introduction of herring curing enables the Dutch of Brill to rival the Hanseatic merchants' fish trade. The Hanse is also hampered by the migration of herring from the Baltic during the 15th century.

Colonization

c. 1400–50

- The Guan people of Ghana reach the coastal area, where they settle.

Politics and Government

1400

c. 1400 Somni Ma Dogo, ruler of Gao, raids the kingdom of Mali.

- King Henry III of Castile sends a military expedition to North Africa, which takes the Moroccan city of Tetuán.
- Le Quy Ly deposes the last Tran emperor of Dai Viet and becomes emperor with the name Ho Quy. After eight months he abdicates in favor of his son, Ho Han Thuong.
- Timur Leng (Tamerlane), the grand amir of the Mongols, defeats the Mameluke Egyptians at Aleppo and Damascus and sacks the cities of Syria.

- Timur-Kutlugh, Khan of the "Golden Horde," dies. He is succeeded by Shadibeg, with Edigey continuing to rule.

January 21   Perugia in Italy accepts the lordship of Gian Galeazzo Visconti, Duke of Milan, as, soon afterwards, do Assisi, Lucca, and Spoleto.

March 20   King Charles VI of France orders the patrons of French benefices to accept his nominees during the withdrawal of obedience from Pope Benedict XIII of Avignon.

March 21   Gian Galeazzo Visconti, Duke of Milan, makes peace with Venice, thus isolating Florence.

August 21   The Rhenish electors elect Rupert III of the Palatinate as Holy Roman Emperor in place of Wenceslas IV, King of Bohemia, whom they declare deposed.

September 16   Owen Glendower (Owain Glyndwr), Lord of Glydyfrdwy and Cynllaith, revolts following a dispute with Reginald Grey of Ruthin, Lord of Dyfryn Clwyd, a member of the council of King Henry IV of England. His first raids into England are checked by his defeat by local English levies at Welshpool, just inside the Welsh border, on September 24.

October 10   King Henry IV of England campaigns in north Wales. He is attacked by Rhys the Black of Erddreiniog, but he still manages to prevent the Welsh revolt from moving south.

December 1   Michele Steno succeeds Antonio Vernieri as doge of Venice.

1401

- A pact is made between Muzaffar I of Gujarat, Dilava Khan of Malwa, Nasir Khan of Khadesh, and Harihara II of Vijayanagar against Firuz Bāhmanī, King of the Deccan.
- King Wenceslas IV of Bohemia, after being besieged in Prague Castle by the "League of the Lords," accepts a permanent committee of nobles to govern Bohemia with him.

January 18   King Władysław Jagiełło of Poland agrees that his lieutenant governor of Lithuania, Vitold, son of Kiejstut, should be its grand duke, as his vassal, for life.

March 3   Giovanni Bentivoglio proclaims himself lord of Bologna in Italy.

March 24   Timur Leng (Tamerlane), Grand Amir of the Mongols, sacks the city of Damascus, Syria.

July 9   Timur Leng (Tamerlane), Grand Amir of the Mongols, destroys the Persian city of Baghdad to punish its revolt.

August 5   Amadeus VIII, Duke of Savoy, acquires the Génevois.

August 8   King Sigismund of Hungary is released by the Hungarians, who had imprisoned him for a few months.

October 10   King Henry IV of England's second Welsh campaign fails to crush the revolt of the Welsh nationalist leader Owen Glendower.

October 10   The Holy Roman Emperor Rupert III, subsidized by Florence, attempts to take Brescia but is repulsed by the Milanese garrison.

1402

- King Henry III of Castile sends an expedition to conquer the Canary Islands. It fails due to the fierce defense of the islanders.

- King Sigismund of Hungary imprisons his brother King Wenceslas IV of Bohemia.
- The Teutonic Knights seize the Neumark of Brandenburg from King Sigismund of Hungary. The order's lands now extend from the River Oder to the River Narva.

February 2   King Henry III of Castile, on popular demand, resumes the kingdom's obedience to Pope Benedict XIII of Avignon.

May 25   Queen Maria of Sicily dies. Her husband, King Martin, rules alone.

June 22   The Welsh nationalist leader Owen Glendower defeats and captures the Anglo-Norman Edmund Mortimer, Earl of Ulster and March, whose family lands lie on the Welsh border, at Pilleth in Maelienydd, Wales.

June 26   Gian Galeazzo Visconti, Duke of Milan, defeats the forces of Florence and Bologna at Casalecchio.

June 27   Bologna surrenders to Gian Galeazzo Visconti, Duke of Milan, recognizing his lordship. Giovanni Bentivoglio, Lord of Bologna, is murdered.

July 28   Timur Leng (Tamerlane), Grand Amir of the Mongols, defeats the Ottoman Turks near Ankara in the Ottoman Empire. Bāyezīd I, Sultan of the Ottoman Turks, is captured. Timur Leng then takes the city of Bursa.

September 3   Gian Galeazzo Visconti, Duke of Milan, dies. He is succeeded by his son, Giovanni Maria, with a regency. Anarchy breaks out in Lombardy, northern Italy, while the war against Florence ends.

September 9   King Henry IV of England again campaigns, without effect, in Wales.

December 12   Timur Leng (Tamerlane), Grand Amir of the Mongols, expels the Knights Hospitallers (an order of Christian chivalry) from Smyrna in the Ottoman Empire.

1403

- After his imprisonment by his brother, King Sigismund of Hungary, King Wenceslas IV of Bohemia escapes from Vienna, Austria, to Bohemia and regains authority there.
- Tatar Khan usurps his father as sultan of Kashmir, India, and imprisons him at Asawal. He is proclaimed king under the title Nasir-Ud-Din Mohammad Shah.
- The Chinese emperor Yongle sends an official trade mission to Nyang-Yang and other states in the Indian Ocean.
- Yongle, son of Hongwu, the first Ming emperor, usurps the Chinese throne.

January   Antonio I, son of Nerio Acciajuoli, Duke of Athens, takes the Acropolis from the Venetians who are now ruling the duchy of Athens.

March 8   The Ottoman sultan Bāyezīd I dies in captivity, a prisoner of the Mongols. He is succeeded by his sons, Suleiman and Mohammad I.

March 11   Pope Benedict XIII escapes from Avignon, France, where the French have been besieging him.

May 30   France resumes its obedience to Pope Benedict XIII of Avignon.

June 3   Valais accedes to the Swiss Confederation.

July 6   The Welsh nationalist leader Owen Glendower captures Carmarthen Castle, Wales, from the English.

July 21   King Henry IV of England defeats and kills Henry "Hotspur," son of the Earl of Northumberland, at

Shrewsbury, England, so ending his revolt and preventing him from joining forces with the Welsh rebels.

August 5 King Ladislas of Naples, the antipope, is crowned as king of Hungary, but soon withdraws from Hungary.

September 29 King Henry IV of England recovers Carmarthen Castle from the Welsh rebels.

December 12 The Welsh nationalist leader Owen Glendower takes the city of Cardiff, Wales.

1404

- Francesco of Padua seizes Verona and Brescia. He is attacked by Venice, which takes Verona and Vicenza.
- Nasir-Ud-Din Mohammad Shah, Sultan of Kashmir, India, is killed by his regent, Shams Kahn, who becomes king as Sultan Muzaffar.
- Timur Leng (Tamerlane), Grand Amir of the Mongols, leaves Anatolia, having reinstated the Turkish princes and thus dismembered the Ottoman Empire.

April 27 Philip the Bold, Duke of Burgundy, dies. He is succeeded by his son, John the Fearless.

June 14 The Welsh nationalist leader Owen Glendower, having won control of Wales, assumes the title of prince of Wales and holds a parliament.

July 14 The prince of Wales, Owen Glendower, makes an alliance with France.

August 8 King Harihara II, who has consolidated the Hindu empire of Vijayanagar in southern India, dies. He is succeeded by his son, Bukka II.

October 17 Cosmo Migliorato is elected Pope Innocent VII in Rome.

November 25 By the Treaty of Flensburg, Margaret, Regent of Denmark, Norway, and Sweden, makes peace with the Teutonic Knights and Albert II of Mecklenburg, who renounces the Swedish crown.

SCIENCE, TECHNOLOGY, AND MEDICINE

Health and Medicine

1400

- Bethlehem Hospital in London, England, has become a medical institution for the treatment of the mentally ill.

1404

- The Venetian Empire imposes a quarantine in an attempt to avoid the Black Death (a form of bubonic plague). Later in the century, it will make the quarantine period a standard 40 days.

Math

1400

- Indian astronomer and mathematician Madhava of Sangamagramma proves a number of results about infinite sums.

Technology

1400

- Chieftain of the Kano kingdom Kanajeji Sarki arms his troops with chain mail and war horses, leading them to a string of victories and dominance over West Africa.
- Cord-driven lathes come into use in Nuremberg, Germany.
- Wrought iron cannons become widely used in Europe.

1403

- Korean king Htai Tjong has a set of type with 100,000 movable pieces cast in bronze for use in the country's burgeoning printing industry.

1404

- A windmill is used to drive an Archimedean screw in order to raise water and drain marshes in Holland.

ARTS AND IDEAS

Architecture

1400

- The minaret of Suq al-Ghazl in Baghdad, Mesopotamia, is completed.

1402

- The Alcazar Palace in Seville, Spain, is completed.

1404

- The Bibikanum Mosque at Samarkand (now in Uzbekistan) is built.

Arts

c. 1400

- *The Wilton Diptych*, a panel painting showing King Richard II of England facing the Virgin Mary, is painted, probably by a French artist. The estimated dates for this work differ widely, ranging from c. 1380 to c. 1410.
- Italian artist Cennino d'Andrea Cennini writes his *Il libro dell'arte/The Artist's Handbook*, a detailed guide to contemporary techniques of painting and sculpture.

c. 1401–02

- A competition is held to choose the designer for a set of bronze doors to in the Baptistry in Florence, Italy. The contestants, notably artists Filippo Brunelleschi and Lorenzo Ghiberti, sculpt versions of the same scene, *The Sacrifice of Isaac*, as a bronze relief. The competition is won by Ghiberti.

1403

- Dutch artist Claus Sluter completes his carving of the Well of Moses, a fountain for the abbey of Chartreuse de Champmol, in Dijon, France.
- Italian artist Lorenzo Ghiberti begins work on sculpting the bronze doors of the Baptistry in Florence, Italy. The work is completed in 1424.

c. 1404

- German artist Konrad von Soest paints *The Niederwildungen Altarpiece*.

Literature and Language

c. 1400

- French writer Jean II le Maingre (known as "Boucicaut") helps to create and contributes to *Les Cent Ballades/The Hundred Ballads*, a collection of poems written by princes and nobles at the court of Charles VI of France.
- The anonymous Middle English poem "The Cuckoo and the Nightingale" is written.

1403

- c. 1403 Italian writer Federigo Frezzi completes his *Quadriregio/Four Kingdoms*, a didactic narrative describing the progress of man through the four kingdoms—of love, Satan, the vices, and the virtues.
- According to tradition, the vast Chinese encyclopedia *Yung-lo Ta-tien* is completed, compiled by over 2000 scholars. None of the work has survived.

1404

- Italian-born French writer Christine de Pisan writes a biography of Charles V, *Le Livre des faicts et bonnes meurs du sage roi Charles/Book of the Deeds and Good Morals of the Wise King Charles*.

Thought and Scholarship

1400

- c. 1400 Arab scholar Abd-ar-Raḥman ibn Khaldan produces a history of the Arab and Persian peoples that takes into account environmental and geographical factors in historical development.
- c. 1400 English writer John Lydgate writes his political

tract *The Damage and Dystruccyon of Realmes*, warning of the dangers of civil strife. It is one of the first political pamphlets in English.
- c. 1400 French historian Jean Froissart completes his *Chronicles*, a history of Europe from 1307 to 1400, the later years of which often include his own eyewitness accounts. It is the most important account of the Hundred Years' War. From 1400 the work was continued by others, ending in 1467. It is translated into English by John Bourchier, Lord Berners, in 1523–25.
- Italian scholar and humanist Coluccio Salutati writes *De tyranno/On Tyranny*, a defense of monarchy.

SOCIETY

Education

1402

- The Italian scholar Pier Paolo Vergerio publishes *De ingenuis moribus et liberalibus studiis/The Conduct Worthy of Free Men*, the first humanist treatise on education.

1403

- Prague University in Bohemia condemns the beliefs of the English religious reformer John Wycliffe (Wyclif).

1404

- The University of Turin is founded in Italy.

Religion

c. 1400

- The English mystic Julian of Norwich writes the second version of her *Revelations of Divine Love*. She wrote the first version about 1374, a year after she began seeing visions.

Toys and Games (*c.* 400 BC–*c.* AD 1400)

c. 400 BC

- Greek scientist Archytas of Tarentum invents the kite. Kites also appear in China about the same time.

c. 754

- The Chinese board game *Wei'ch'i* is introduced to Japan where it becomes known as *Go*.

969

- The Chinese introduce playing cards. The earliest known pack consists of 56 cards divided into 4 suits of 14 cards each. They are used as paper money as well as for gaming.

c. 1000–1100

- "Tables," or backgammon, is introduced to Europe by the Arabs (or reintroduced, as it is similar in name and appearance to the Roman game *Tabula*). It becomes

extremely popular over the next few centuries. The name "backgammon" is first used in the mid-17th century.

c. 1100

- The board game draughts (checkers) evolves in Europe, possibly in southern France.

c. 1200

- The Aztec and Maya peoples of Central America use rubber to make balls for use in games and sports.

1299

- Italian tarot cards are first mentioned in a manuscript. They are used both for gaming and fortune telling.

c. 1400

- The modern playing card suit signs of spades, hearts, diamonds, and clubs are introduced in France, possibly by the French knight Etienne de Vignolles.

- The English prior John Mirk writes *Instructions for Parish Priests* in verse, and *Manuale sacerdotis/A Handbook for Priests*, a more elaborate and learned work on the same theme written in Latin.

1402

- The Bohemian religious reformer Jan Hus is appointed to the Bethlehem Chapel in Prague, Bohemia.

1404

- The English Parliament passes statutes against alchemy, forbidding the creation of gold and silver for economic reasons.

Sports

c. 1400

- The modern card suit signs of spades, diamonds, hearts, and clubs are introduced in France, possibly by the French knight Etienne de Vignolles.

BIRTHS & DEATHS

1400

- Fra Angelico (Guido di Pietro, also known as Giovanni da Fiesole), great Italian painter, whose best-known works include *The Annunciation* (1430s), born in Vicchio, Italy (–1455).
- Franco Sacchetti, Italian writer, creator of a range of poems and of the prose text *Trecento novelle/Three Hundred Stories*, dies (c. 68).
- Guillaume Dufay, French composer of church music and chansons, born (–1474).
- Theodore Gaza, Byzantine philosopher whose translations of Aristotle were influential in the development of Italian humanism, born (–1475).

February 14 Richard II, deposed king of England 1377–99, dies in suspicious circumstances in Pontefract Castle, Yorkshire, England (32).

October 25 Geoffrey Chaucer, the principal English writer before Shakespeare, whose best-known work is *The Canterbury Tales* (1390s), dies in London, England (c. 58).

1401

- Nicholas of Cusa, cardinal, scholar, scientist, and philosopher, born in Kues, near Trier, Germany (–1464).

July 23 Francesco Sforza, Duke of Milan 1450–66, who was a key figure in 15th-century Italian politics, born in Miniato, Tuscany (–1466).

December 21 Masaccio (Tommaso di Giovanni di Simone Guidi), major Italian painter of the early Renaissance, noted for his frescoes, born in Castel San Giovanni di Altura, Italy (–1428).

1402

- Dionysius the Carthusian (Flemish: Denys van Leeuwen, or de Leeuwis, also called Denys Ryckel, or van Rijkel), influential theologian and mystic, born in Rijkel, Belgium (–1471).

September 3 Gian Galeazzo Visconti, Milanese leader who controlled much of northern Italy, dies in Melegnano, near Milan (50).

1403

February 22 Charles VII ("the Well-Served" or "the Victorious"), King of France 1422–61, who expelled the English from France, born in Paris, France (–1461).

March Bāyezīd I the Thunderbolt, Ottoman sultan 1389–1402, founder of the centralized Ottoman state who defeated the Hungarian–Venetian army at the Battle of Nicopolis (1396), dies in Aksehir, Ottoman Empire (c. 43).

July 21 Henry Percy ("Harry Hotspur"), English rebel who led an uprising against King Henry IV, is killed in battle near Shrewsbury, Shropshire, England (39).

1404

February 14 Leon Battista Alberti, Italian humanist, architect, and initiator of Renaissance art history, born in Genoa, Italy (–1472).

June Murad II, Ottoman sultan 1421–44 and 1446–51, who consolidated Ottoman rule in the Balkans, born in Amasya, Persia (–1451).

October 1 Pope Boniface IX dies in Rome.

1405–1409

POLITICS, GOVERNMENT, AND ECONOMICS

Business and Economics

1407

• St. George's Bank is founded in Genoa, Italy.

Human Rights

1405

• Italian-born French writer Christine de Pisan writes her prose work *Le Livre de la cité des dames/The Book of the City of Women*, in which she defends women against attacks on their intelligence and virtue. She also writes *Le Livre de trois vertus/The Book of Three Virtues*. Attempting to define women's role in society, it asserts their rights to a full education, and, as writers, of their right to be regarded on equal terms with male authors.

Politics and Government

1405

• The Chinese emperor Yongle recognizes the Sumatran prince Paramesvara, the founder of the sultanate of Malacca in southeast Asia, as its king. The flow of Chinese seaborne trade with India and the Middle East through Malacca makes it the greatest trading center in southeast Asia by the 1430s.

February 19 Timur Leng (Tamerlane), the grand amir of the Mongols, dies while leading an expedition to China. His heirs retain only Transoxiana and Khorasan, with his son, Shah Rukh, ruling from Heart. The Mamelukes recover Syria; the dynasty of Black Sheep Turkomans from Azerbaijan establishes a dominion from eastern Anatolia to Baghdad.

March 11 John Talbot defeats Owen Glendower, Prince of Wales, at Grosmont, Monmouthshire, Wales.

May 5 Prince Henry of England defeats Owen Glendower, Prince of Wales, at Usk, Wales.

August 8 Owen Glendower, Prince of Wales, takes Carmarthen from the English with French military assistance.

August 8 The Dukes of Orléans and Burgundy raise armies against each other in France. The Duke of Burgundy enters Paris and assumes control of the French government.

September 9 King Henry IV of England recovers Carmarthen, Wales, from the Welsh in an otherwise ineffective campaign.

September 14 John, archbishop of Mainz, and other princes form the alliance of Marbach against the Holy Roman Emperor Rupert III.

October 16 The warring Dukes of Burgundy and Orléans, France, make a truce.

November 11 Francesco Carrara of Padua surrenders to Venice.

November 12 Mallu Khan, the effective ruler of the diminished Indian kingdom of Delhi, is killed in his defeat by Khizr Khan, the Mongol ruler of the Punjab, near Pak Pattan.

1406

• Hushang murders his father, Dilavar Khan, governor of Malwa, and declares himself its king.

• The Burmese overrun the chiefdom of Mohnya.

• War breaks out between Grand Duke Vitold of Lithuania and Grand Duke Vasili (Vasily) of Moscow.

March 30 James, heir to the throne of Scotland and later James I, is captured by the English at sea while on his way to France.

April 4 King Robert III of Scotland dies. He is succeeded by his son, James I, a captive in England since March 30, 1406; during his captivity his uncle Robert, Duke of Albany, is regent, followed by his cousin Murdoch.

June 18 Pope Innocent VII excommunicates King Ladislas of Naples and declares him deprived of his kingdom.

October 9 Florence annexes Pisa.

October 10 The Duke of Orléans invades Gascony in an unsuccessful campaign against the English.

November 30 Angelo Correr is elected as Pope Gregory XII in Rome.

December 25–26 King Henry III of Castile dies. He is succeeded by his infant son, John II.

1407

• Edigey deposes Shadibeg as khan of the "Golden Horde" and appoints Bulat-Saltan.

• The Chinese emperor Yongle occupies Hanoi and annexes Dai Viet, extinguishing the Ho dynasty. Vietnamese resistance continues despite savage reprisals.

March 3 Francesco di Gonzaga of Mantua dies. He is succeeded by his son, Giovanni Francesco di Gonzaga.

November 1 Pope Benedict XIII of Avignon arrives at Savona, Italy, for a meeting with Pope Gregory XII of Rome, who excuses himself.

November 23 Louis, Duke of Orléans, is murdered at the instigation of John the Fearless, Duke of Burgundy.

1408

- The Chinese emperor Yongle invites Tshong-kha-pa, the founder of the dGe-lugs-pa or "Yellow Hat" monastic order in Tibet, to China. For an unknown reason he refuses to come.

January 28   Pope Gregory XII of Rome reaches Lucca but evades a meeting with the rival pope, Pope Benedict XIII of Avignon, who is at Porto Venere to the north of Lucca.

February 28   John the Fearless, Duke of Burgundy, returns to Paris, France, and defends his murder of Louis, Duke of Orléans.

April 25   The excommunicated King Ladislas of Naples, the antipope, occupies Rome. Pope Gregory XII of Rome therefore breaks off his negotiations with Pope Benedict XIII of Avignon.

May 11   King Mohammad VII of Granada dies. He is succeeded by his brother, Yūsuf III.

May 21   A council of the French church declares its neutrality between the rival popes.

June 29   The cardinals who had abandoned Pope Gregory XII of Rome and Pope Benedict XIII of Avignon meet in Livorno, Italy, and call for a general council of the church to be held in Pisa.

September 9   Grand Duke Vitold of Lithuania and Grand Duke Vasili (Vasily) of Moscow make peace, establishing their frontier along the River Ugra.

September 23   John the Fearless, Duke of Burgundy, defeats the bishop of Liège's rebelling subjects at Othée.

December 23   The Mongol leader Edigey unsuccessfully besieges Moscow, Russia, but restores the "Tatar Yoke."

1409

- The Chinese, under the eunuch Tcheng Hou, temporarily conquer Ceylon. The Sinhalese royal family are sent back to China.

January 1   The Welsh rebels holding Harlech Castle surrender to the English. The rebellion of Owen Glendower, Prince of Wales, has now collapsed.

March 25   The general council called by the cardinals who had abandoned Pope Gregory XII of Rome and Pope Benedict XIII of Avignon has its first session in Pisa, Italy.

June 5   The Council of Pisa declares the deposition of Popes Benedict XIII of Avignon and Gregory XII of Rome. The latter holds a council at Cividale.

June 26   The cardinals meeting in Pisa elect Cardinal Peter Philarges as the Antipope Alexander V.

July 7   Venice reconquers Dalmatia from King Sigismund of Hungary.

July 24   King Martin of Sicily dies. King Martin I of Aragon annexes Sicily.

September 3   The Genoese expel the French garrison from Genoa.

October 10   King Ladislas of Naples, the antipope, is expelled from the Papal States. Pope Alexander V supports Louis II of Anjou in an attempt to recover Naples.

November 21   Pope Benedict XIII of Avignon holds a "general" council in Perpignan, France.

SCIENCE, TECHNOLOGY, AND MEDICINE

Health and Medicine

1406

- Chinese herbalist Chu Hsiao writes *Chiu huang pên ts'ao/Herbal to Relieve Famine*, an illustrated work describing 414 species of plants.

1407

- English physician John Mirfield writes his *Breviarium/ Breviary*, a medical encyclopedia.

Science

1406

- Florentine priest James Angelus translates Ptolemy's *Geographia* into Latin, using a copy brought to Italy from Constantinople (modern Istanbul, Turkey). The reintroduction of the text into western Europe will drive the age of exploration.

Technology

1405

- German engineer Konrad Kyeser of Eichstatt publishes *Bellifortis*, an illustrated manual on military technology; it includes sections on hydraulics, cannon operation, and proposals for lighter-than-air flight.

Transportation

1405

- The Baltic city of Lübeck constructs a canal linking Lake Möllner to the River Elbe.

ARTS AND IDEAS

Arts

1406

- Italian artist Jacopo della Quercia sculpts the tomb of Ilario del Caretto in the cathedral of Lucca, Italy.

c. 1407

- The anonymous French artist known as the Bedford Master completes the illuminations for *Le Livre de la cité des dames/The Book of the City of Women* by the Italian-born French writer Christine de Pisan.

1408

- Italian artist Jacopo della Quercia sculpts *Madonna* for the cathedral in Ferrara, Italy.

- Italian artist Nanni di Banco sculpts *Isaiah* for Florence Cathedral, Italy.

1409

- *c.* 1409 The anonymous French artist known as the Boucicaut Master completes the illuminations for the book of prayers *The Boucicaut Hours*.
- Italian artist Donatello (Donato di Niccolò) sculpts *David*, his first version of this subject.

Literature and Language

1406

- English writer Thomas Hoccleve publishes his autobiographical poem *The Regimen of T. Hoccleve*.

c. 1407

- German scholar Ulman Stromer writes *Püchel von mein Geslechet/The Püchel Family*, a chronicle of his Nuremberg family from 1349 to 1407.

Thought and Scholarship

c. 1405

- Bohemian-born German writer Johann von Tepl writes *Ackermann aus Böhmen/The Farmhand from Bohemia*, a dialogue influenced by Italian humanist models.

c. 1407

- Spanish historian López de Ayala writes *Crónica de los reyes de Castilla/A Chronicle of the Kings of Castile*, an eyewitness account of Spanish history from 1350 to 1394.

SOCIETY

Education

1409

- Leipzig University is founded in Saxony.

Religion

1405

November 12   On his conversion to Islam, King Paramesvara of Malacca takes the name of Megat Iskandar Shah.

1406

- French poet Eustache Deschamps writes *Demonstrations contre sortilèges/Demonstrations against Divination*, a treatise against the practice of necromancy, or attempts to communicate with the dead.

c. 1407

- The French theologian Jean de Gerson publishes his tract *De unitate Ecclesiae/On the Unity of the Church*.

1409

- The first dGe-lugs-pa monastery, dGa'ldan, is founded in Tibet by Tshong-kha-pa. The dGe-lugs-pa, or "Yellow Hat" monastic order, begins to challenge the ruling " Red Hats" for both spiritual and secular power.

Sports

1405

- Timur Leng (Tamerlane), Grand Amir of the Mongols, plays "great chess" (a version of the game with 110 squares and unorthodox rules and pieces) with Alā'ddīn al-Tabrizī, a notable player at his court (on whom the Aladdin in the *Arabian Nights* is based).

BIRTHS & DEATHS

1405
c. 1405   George Chastellain, influential Burgundian chronicler and court poet, born in Aalst, Brabant (–1475).

February 19   Timur Leng (Tamerlane), ruthless Turkic leader who conquered Persia, India, and Anatolia, dies in Otrar, near Chimkent, Transoxiana.

October 18   Pius II (Enea Silvio Piccolomini), Italian pope 1458–64, who attempted to unite Europe against the Turks, born in Corsignano, republic of Siena (–1464).

October 27   Muhammad ad-Damīrī, Muslim theologian and mystic, author of a noted encyclopedia of animals (1371), dies in Cairo (*c.* 61).

1406
c. 1406   Edmund Beaufort, Duke of Somerset, English nobleman whose fight with Richard, Duke of York, led to the War of the Roses, born (–1445).

- Fra Filippo Lippi, Italian Renaissance painter whose major works include *Madonna and Child with Two Angels* (*c.* 1465), born in Florence, Italy (–1469).

January 30   Claus Sluter, Dutch sculptor known especially for his works in the chapel of the Carthusian monastery Chartreuse de Champmol in Dijon, dies in Dijon, Burgundy (*c.* 49).

February 17   Francesco Carrara of Padua is murdered in prison.

March 17   Ibn-Khaldūn, great Arab historian whose best-known work is the *Muqaddimah/Introduction to History*, dies in Cairo, Egypt (73).

May 4   Coluccio Salutati, Florentine chancellor and humanist, dies in Florence (75).

November 6   Pope Innocent VII dies in Rome.

1407
- Lorenzo Valla, Italian humanist, philosopher, and literary scholar, who wrote *De elegantia Latinae linguae/Elegances of the Latin Language*, the first Latin textbook since ancient times, born in Rome (–1457).

1408
- John Gower, English poet in the courtly love tradition, author of works in Latin, English, and French, including the *Confessio amantis/Confessions of a Lover*, dies, probably in London, England (*c.* 78).

January 6   Bernardo Giustiniani, Italian humanist historian, born (–1489).

1410–1414

POLITICS, GOVERNMENT, AND ECONOMICS

Politics and Government

1410

- Algiers is taken by Abu Faris, the Hafsid ruler of Morocco.
- Balat-Saltan, Khan of the "Golden Horde," dies. He is succeeded by Timur-Khan.
- The Chinese emperor Yongle campaigns in Mongolia, securing the neutrality of the western Oirats and defeating the eastern Tatars.

January 1   Henry, Prince of Wales, and his associates take control of King Henry IV of England's government.

May 17   Baldassare Cossa is elected as the antipope John XXIII in Rome following the death of the antipope Alexander V.

May 31   King Martin I of Aragon dies, without heirs. His death leads to civil war.

July 15   In the Great Northern War, King Władysław Jagiełło of Poland and Grand Duke Vitold of Lithuania defeat the Teutonic Knights at Tannenberg (modern-day Grunwald, Poland).

September 20   Following the death of the Holy Roman Emperor Rupert III of Wittelsbach, King Sigismund of Hungary is elected as his successor.

October 1   Jošt, Margrave of Moravia, is elected as Holy Roman Emperor, in competition with King Sigismund of Hungary who has also been elected.

October 10   The Poles again defeat the Teutonic Knights at Koronowo.

November 2   John the Fearless, Duke of Burgundy, and the partisans of his rival, the late Louis, Duke of Orléans, who are known as the "Armagnacs," make a temporary treaty of peace at Bicêtre.

1411

- Timur-Khan, Khan of the "Golden Horde," assumes personal power and defeats the Mongol leader Edigey, but is soon expelled by Jalal-ad-Din, son of the former khan Tokhtamysh, who is supported by Grand Duke Vitold of Lithuania. The disintegration of the "Golden Horde" thus continues.

January 8   Jošt of Moravia, rival Holy Roman Emperor, dies. Brandenburg thus reverts to the Holy Roman Emperor Sigismund of Hungary, who later in the year mortgages it to Frederick of Hohenzollern, Burgrave of Nuremberg, in whose family it thereafter remains.

February 1   By the Treaty of Toruń, the Teutonic Knights make peace with Poland and Lithuania, ceding Samogitia to the latter.

February 17   Suleiman, the Ottoman Turk ruling in Europe, is defeated and killed by his brother Musa.

May 9   Louis II of Anjou defeats King Ladislas of Naples, the antipope, at Roccasecca to the north of Naples, then withdraws to France.

July 21   King Sigismund of Hungary is again, this time unanimously, elected Holy Roman Emperor.

November 8   John the Fearless, Duke of Burgundy, supported by an English contingent, defeats the "Armagnacs," the supporters of his late rival Louis, Duke of Orléans, as they attempt to take Paris at St-Cloud.

December 12   King Henry IV of England resumes control of his government, which has been under the leadership of the prince of Wales and his associates for almost two years.

1412

- Al-Malik al-Adil Mohammad ben Sulaiman becomes the sultan of Kilwa (in present-day Tanzania).
- An expedition by the Holy Roman Emperor Sigismund of Hungary fails to recover Dalmatia from Venice.

1412–13   Massala Island in the Red Sea, claimed by Yemen, is raided by King Tewodros I of Ethiopia.

May 16   Giovanni Visconti, Duke of Milan, is murdered. He is succeeded by his brother Filippo Maria Visconti.

May 18   By the Treaty of Eltham, King Henry IV of England makes an alliance with the "Armagnacs" (supporters of the late Louis, Duke of Orléans) against the duchy of Burgundy, France.

June 15   Pope John XXIII makes peace with King Ladislas of Naples, the antipope.

June 28   A commission ends the succession dispute in Aragon by electing Ferdinand, uncle and regent of King John II of Castile and León, as king.

August 22   The warring Burgundian and "Armagnac" factions (the latter being the supporters of the late Louis, Duke of Orléans) make another treaty of peace at Auxerre, France.

November 27   Margaret, Regent of Denmark, Norway, and Sweden, dies. King Eric VII begins his personal rule.

1413

- The northern Shan state of Hsenwi attacks Ava villages, but is defeated by Minkyiswasawke, King of the Shan.

January 30   An assembly of the Estates General (representatives of the aristocracy, clergy, and commons) for northern France, meeting in Paris, refuses to grant taxation and demands reform of the government.

February 2   Mahmud, the nominal sultan of Delhi, India, dies, so ending the Tughluq dynasty. Dawlat Khan Lodi is elected as his successor.

March 20   King Henry IV of England dies. He is succeeded by his son, Henry V.

April 28   The Bastille castle is taken in the Cabochien riots in Paris, France, in support of John the Fearless, Duke of Burgundy, after he promises political reform and lower taxes.

May 29   Despite the issue of the *Ordonnance Cabochienne* reforming the government, fresh riots break out in Paris, France, and the butchers establish a rule of terror, slaughtering supporters of the "Armagnacs" (supporters of the late Louis, Duke of Orléans, rival of John the Fearless, Duke of Burgundy).

June 7   King Ladislas of Naples, the antipope takes Rome. Pope John XXIII flees to Bologna.

July 7   Mohammad I, the youngest son of the late Ottoman sultan Bāyezīd I, defeats and kills his brother Musa at Jamurlu, Serbia, with support from the Byzantines. He thus reunites the Ottoman dominions.

August 4   The "Armagnacs" (supporters of the late Louis, Duke of Orléans) restore royal authority in Paris, France, with the help of the dauphin Louis, quelling the riots that have been sweeping the city.

September 8   The Parisian rebels are savagely prosecuted and the *Ordonnance Cabochienne*, which ordered political reforms, is withdrawn.

October 2   The Union of Horodlo, a charter issued by King Władysław Jagiełło of Poland and Grand Duke Vitold of Lithuania, reaffirms the unity of the two states but makes the autonomy of Lithuania permanent and cedes new privileges to its nobility.

October 10   Pope John XXIII's envoys accept the Holy Roman Emperor Sigismund of Hungary's demand that a general council of the church should be called.

1414

- King Paramesvara of Malacca dies. He is succeeded by his son, Megat Iskandar Shah.
- The Chinese emperor Yongle invades western Mongolia and defeats the Oirats.
- The Council of Constance, a council of the church convoked by Pope John XXIII in 1413, holds its first session, in Constance, Germany. Its main aim is to find a solution to the Great Schism, which began in 1378. The Council of Constance ends in 1417.
- The Jews are expelled from Spain.
- The northern Shan state of Hsenwi attacks Ava villages for a second time.
- War breaks out again between the Teutonic Knights and Poland and Lithuania.
- Yeshaq becomes king of Ethiopia.

January 7   Tomaso Mocenigo is elected doge of Venice.

January 9   King Henry V of England disperses a treasonable Lollard assembly organized by the English Lollard leader John Oldcastle in St. Giles's Fields, outside London, England.

May 23   King Henry V of England makes a treaty of alliance with John the Fearless, Duke of Burgundy.

May 28   Khizr Khan, the Mongol ruler of the Punjab, India, takes the city of Delhi and establishes the Sayyid dynasty of Delhi. He is initially acting as viceroy for Shah Rukh, successor to the late Timur Leng (Tamerlane), Grand Amir of the Mongols.

May 31   King Henry V of England appoints his first embassy to demand the French throne.

August 6   King Ladislas of Naples dies, thus ending his attempt to conquer the Papal States.

August 8   The "Armagnacs" (supporters of the late Louis, Duke of Orléans) take King Charles VI of France on an expedition against the duchy of Burgundy.

November 5   Pope John XXIII opens the General Council of Constance in Germany, which aims to resolve the issue of the papal succession.

SCIENCE, TECHNOLOGY, AND MEDICINE

Health and Medicine

1411

- Italian physician Nicolò Falcucci writes a series of influential medical books: *Sermones medicales septem/Seven Medical Lectures*, *Liber de medica materia/Book of Medical Matters*, and *Commentaria super aphorismos Hippocratis/Commentary upon Hippocrates' Aphorisms*.

1413

- French alchemist Nicholas Flamel has established 14 new Parisian hospitals and 10 religious establishments, by this date.

1414

- Italian physician Jacopo da Forli writes the influential commentaries on Hippocrates and Galen: *In aphorismos Hippocratis expositiones/Expositions on Hippocrates' Aphorisms* and *Super libros tegni Galeni*.

Science

1410

- Venetian botanist Benedetto Rinio writes his herbal, the *Liber de simplicibus/Book of Simples*.

Technology

1410

- Italian artist Filippo Brunelleschi constructs a clock in which the timekeeper is driven by a weight, rather than a coiled spring.

1411

- The French Duke of Orléans equips his army with 4,000 two-person handguns.

ARTS AND IDEAS

Architecture

1412

- Grand Duke Vitold of Lithuania fortifies the River Dnieper to control its passage to the Black Sea. He employs in his garrisons some Mongol groups calling themselves Cossacks, a name also adopted by Russian Ukrainians of this area.

Arts

c. 1410

- The Flemish artists the Limbourg brothers (Pol, Herman, and Jean) complete the illuminations for the book of prayers *Les Belles Heures du Duc de Berry/The Beautiful Hours of the Duke of Berry*.

1411

c. 1411   Russian artist Andrey Rublev paints *The Old Testament Trinity*, one of the finest Russian works of the period.

1411–13   Italian artist Nanni di Banco sculpts *The Four Crowned Martyrs* for the shrine of Orsanmichele in Florence, Italy.

c. 1413

- Italian artist Donatello (Donato di Niccolò) sculpts *St. Mark* for the chapel of Orsanmichele in Florence, Italy.

Literature and Language

1411

- English writer Thomas Hoccleve publishes his didactic poem *De regimine principum/On the Government of Princes*, a treatise on the duties of a ruler written for Henry, Prince of Wales.

1414

- Arabic scholar Al-Firuzābādī completes his *Al-Qāmūs/The Ocean*, an Arabic dictionary.

Thought and Scholarship

c. 1410

- Scottish chronicler Andrew of Wyntoun completes his *Orygynale Cronikil*, a history of Scotland from the creation to 1406.

1412

- Italian-born French writer Christine de Pisan writes *Le Livre de paix/The Book of Peace*, a treatise on government.

SOCIETY

Education

1412

- Pavia University in Italy, which was suppressed in 1398, is reestablished.

1413

- The University of Aix-en-Provence is founded in France.
- The University of Marseille is established in France.

Religion

1410

- Archbishop Zbyněk of Prague, Bohemia, burns works by the English reformer John Wycliffe (Wyclif) and excommunicates the Bohemian reformer Jan Hus.

BIRTHS & DEATHS

1410

- Jakob I Fugger the Elder, wealthy German merchant, born in Augsburg, Germany (–1469).

May 3   The antipope Alexander V dies.

May 18   The Holy Roman Emperor Rupert III of Wittelsbach dies.

1411

- Juan de Mena, innovative Spanish poet whose best-known poem is "El laberinto de Fortuna/"The Labyrinth of Fortune" (1444), born in Córdoba, Spain (–1456).

September 21   Richard, Duke of York, claimant to the English throne whose attempts to gain it led to the War of the Roses, born (–1460).

1412

January 6   St. Joan of Arc ("the Maid of Orléans"), national heroine of France, who led the French to victory over the English at Orléans (1429) in the Hundred Years' War, born in Domrémy, Bar, France (–1431).

November 27   Margaret I, Regent of Denmark 1375–97, Norway 1380–89, and Sweden 1388–97, thereafter effective ruler of all three countries through her son Erik VIII, dies in Flensburg, now in Germany (c. 59).

1413

March 20   Henry IV, King of England 1399–1413, son of John of Gaunt, dies in London, England (46).

December 26   Michele Steno, Doge of Venice, dies.

1414

- Piero (di Cosimo) de' Medici the Gouty, ruler of Florence 1464–69, son of Cosimo the Elder, born (–1469).

July 21   Sixtus IV (Francesco della Rovere), Italian pope 1471–84, who made the papacy a principality, born in Genoa (–1484).

1413

- A general council of the church held in Rome by Pope John XXIII condemns the works of the English reformer John Wycliffe (Wyclif).
- The Bohemian religious reformer Jan Hus publishes *De Ecclesia/On the Church*, in which he challenges the authority of the pope.

1410

- Edward, Duke of York, translates *The Master of Game*, which is largely an English translation of the French Count Gaston Phoebus' treatise on hunting of 1391, *Le Déduits de chasse/The Pleasures of the Hunt* (or *Le Miroir de Phoebus/The Mirror of Phoebus*).

1415–1419

POLITICS, GOVERNMENT, AND ECONOMICS

Politics and Government

1415

- King Yeshaq of Ethiopia besieges and kills Saad al-Din, the sultan of Ifat.
- The Ottoman sultan Mohammad I recovers the city of Ankara from the Mongols.
- The Swiss take Aargau from the Habsburgs.

February 23 By the Treaty of Arras, John the Fearless, Duke of Burgundy, makes another truce with his French enemies, the "Armagnacs" and King Charles VI.

March 14 King Henry V of England's second embassy to demand the French throne ends its negotiations in Paris, France, with its minimum terms refused.

April 30 The Holy Roman Emperor Sigismund of Hungary confers the Electorate of Brandenburg on Frederick of Hohenzollern.

May 29 The Council of Constance deposes Pope John XXIII from the papacy.

July 4 The representatives of Pope Gregory XII of Rome announce his abdication to the Council of Constance in Germany.

July 6 The Council of Constance issues the decree *Haec sancta/These Holy Things*, which asserts the supremacy of general councils in the church. The Council also condemns the Bohemian reformer John Hus as a heretic and he is burned at the stake in Constance, Germany, a year later.

August 13 King Henry V of England invades France in a campaign to seize the French throne.

August 21 A naval expedition sent by King John I of Portugal takes Ceuta, a strategic port in North Africa, on the Strait of Gibraltar.

September 2 The nobility of Bohemia and Moravia protest against the upcoming execution of the Bohemian religious reformer John Hus, after he has been condemned as a heretic by the Council of Constance in Germany. On September 5, they form an association to oppose the church authorities and prevent the execution.

September 22 In his campaign to seize the French throne, King Henry V of England takes the northern French town of Harfleur, though his army is hit badly by disease. He opens up the town to English settlers.

October 25 King Henry V of England inflicts a crushing defeat on the French at the Battle of Agincourt.

November 16 Following a successful campaign in France, King Henry V of England returns home.

December 13 By the Capitulations of Narbonne, the Holy Roman Emperor Sigismund of Hungary obtains the accession of the kings of Aragon, Castile and León, and Navarre to the Council of Constance in Germany.

1416

c. 1416 The Walasmar dynasty takes the sultanate of Adal (in present-day Somalia) and places its capital at Dakka.

- Sikandar Shah, Sultan of Kashmir, India, dies. He is succeeded by his son, Nur Khan, under the title Ali Shah.
- The Venetians defeat the Ottoman Turks off Gallipoli in the Ottoman Empire.

February 9 The Holy Roman Emperor Sigismund of Hungary raises Count Amadeus VIII, ruler of Savoy, to the title of Duke of Savoy.

March 1 The Holy Roman Emperor Sigismund of Hungary arrives in Paris, France, proposing to mediate between France and England.

April 2 King Ferdinand I of Aragon dies. He is succeeded by his son, Alfonso V.

August 15 A Franco-Genoese fleet, attempting to recover the northern French town of Harfleur from the English, is defeated in the River Seine estuary.

August 15 By the Treaty of Canterbury, the Holy Roman Emperor Sigismund of Hungary makes an alliance with King Henry V of England.

October 6 John the Fearless, Duke of Burgundy, meets King Henry V of England at Calais, northern France.

1417

- Mohammad VIII succeeds Yūsuf III as king of Granada.

April 29 Louis II, Duke of Anjou and former king of Naples, dies. He is succeeded by his son, Louis III.

July 26 The Council of Constance in Germany deposes Pope Benedict XIII of Avignon, France.

August 1 King Henry V of England lands at Trouville on the north French coast to begin his campaign to conquer Normandy.

August 27 Attendolo Sforza, the condottiere employed by Queen Joanna of Naples, expels Braccio da Montone, another condottiere, from Rome.

September 20 King Henry V of England takes the northern French city of Caen.

November 11 The Great Schism (the period 1378–1417 of rival popes in Rome, Italy, and Avignon, France) ends with the election of Pope Martin V at the Council of Constance in Germany.

December 14 The English Lollard leader John Oldcastle is declared a traitor against King Henry V of England and burned as a heretic.

1418

- Arabic scholar Ahmad al-Qalqashandi compiles *Subh al-A'sha*, an encyclopedic manual for Egyptian civil servants.
- Firuz Bāhmanī, King of the Deccan, India, invades the Hindu kingdom of Vijayanagar in southern India, but is defeated and expelled.
- Le Loi, a Dai Viet peasant, organizes national resistance to the Chinese occupation.
- The Canary Islands are ceded to Castile and León.
- The Hanse makes its first legislative act, regulating the alliance and its trading operations. The German port of Lübeck is recognized as its leading member.
- Venice captures Friuli from the Holy Roman Emperor Sigismund of Hungary.

April 22 The Council of Constance is dissolved, having settled the question of papal succession and brought to an end the Great Schism (the period 1378–1417 of rival popes in Rome, Italy, and Avignon, France).

May 29 The army of John the Fearless, Duke of Burgundy, is admitted into Paris, France.

June 12 Members of the "Armagnac" faction (Orléanist supporters), including Bernard VII, Count of Armagnac, are massacred in Paris, France.

July 29 King Henry V of England begins the siege of Rouen, the capital of Normandy, France.

September 29 The northern French port of Cherbourg surrenders to King Henry V of England.

December 11 Amadeus, Duke of Savoy, acquires Piedmont.

December 26 The dauphin Charles proclaims himself regent of France.

1419

- King Devaraya I of the Hindu empire of Vijayanagar, in southern India, decisively defeats Firuz Bāhmanī, Shah of neighboring Kulbarga, at Pangal. Firuz has to abandon his attempts to conquer Vijayanagar.

January 19 Rouen, the capital of Normandy, France, surrenders to King Henry V of England, whose conquest of Normandy is thus complete.

July 22 The Taborite sect of extreme Hussites, opposed to German and papal influence, is formed in Bohemia.

July 30 A crowd of Hussites murders anti-Hussite town councillors of Prague, Bohemia, by defenestration (throwing them out of a window).

August 16 King Wenceslas IV of Bohemia dies. He is succeeded by his brother Sigismund, Holy Roman Emperor and King of Hungary.

September 10 John the Fearless, Duke of Burgundy, is murdered at Montereau during a conference with the French dauphin Charles. He is succeeded by his son, Philip the Good.

October 5 Amadeus, Duke of Savoy, acquires Nice.

December 25 Philip the Good, Duke of Burgundy, allies himself with King Henry V of England against the French dauphin Charles.

SCIENCE, TECHNOLOGY, AND MEDICINE

Agriculture

c. 1416

- Dutch fishermen are the first to employ driftnets in fishing.

Science

1416

- Italian scholar Blasius of Parma writes his *Tractatus de ponderibus/Treatise Concerning Weights*, an essay on statics and hydrostatics.

Technology

1415

- Italian inventor Giovanni de' Fontana writes *Bellicorum instrumentorum liber/Book of Instruments of War*, an illustrated treatise on military technology, including discussion of rockets and torpedoes.

ARTS AND IDEAS

Architecture

1416

- The building of the Cathedral of Gerona in Italy is completed.

1417

- The Cathedral of Ulm in Germany is built.

1419

- Italian artist and architect Filippo Brunelleschi designs the façade of the Ospedale degli Innocenti (Foundling Hospital) in Florence, Italy (completed in 1444). It draws in part on Romanesque and Gothic traditions, though, because of its clarity and symmetry and its use of classical elements such as pilasters and Corinthian

capitals, it is traditionally seen as the first Renaissance building.
- The tower of Strasbourg Cathedral in France is completed.

Arts

c. 1415
- German artist Master Francke paints the *St. Barbara Altarpiece*.
- Italian artist Donatello (Donato di Niccolò) sculpts *St. George*, *St. Luke*, and *St. John the Evangelist* for the façade of Florence Cathedral, Italy.

1416
c. 1416 French artists Jean Malouel and Henri Bellechose paint *The Martyrdom of St. Denis*.
- Italian artist Lorenzo Ghiberti sculpts *St. John the Baptist* for the chapel of Orsanmichele in Florence, Italy.

c. 1418
- The anonymous French artist known as the Rohan Master completes the illuminations for the book of prayers *The Rohan Hours*. Among its best-known images is *A Dying Man Commends His Soul to God*.

1419
c. 1419 Italian artist and architect Filippo Brunelleschi draws "perspective panels," boards on which there are a drawing of a scene and a pinhole to view the scene itself. His device helps to create a mastery of linear perspective that plays a major role in Renaissance art.
- Italian artist Jacopo della Quercia sculpts the *Fonte Gaia*, a fountain in the Piazza del Campo (a public square) in Siena, Italy.
- Lorenzo Ghiberti, the Italian artist, sculpts *St. Stephen* for the chapel of Orsanmichele in Florence, Italy.

Literature and Language

c. 1415
- Byzantine scholar Manuel Chrysoloras of Constantinople (modern Istanbul, Turkey) writes a Greek grammar which becomes one of the standard texts during the Renaissance.

c. 1416
- French writer Alain Chartier writes *Livre des quatres dames/The Book of Four Ladies*, a poem in which four women lament the deaths of their loved ones at the Battle of Agincourt in 1415.

c. 1417
- The anonymous *Gesta Henrici Quinti/The Deeds of Henry V*, a biography of the English king Henry V, is written while he is still on the throne.

1418
- Italian scholar Domenico di Bandino writes his *Fons memorabilium universi/Fountain of Memorable Things*, an encyclopedic treatise on many subjects, including cosmography, astronomy, geography, and history.

Music

1415
- The "Agincourt Song," celebrating the English victory at Agincourt, becomes popular in England. Its tune is later used for the hymn "Deo Gracias"/"Thanks to God ."

Thought and Scholarship

1416
- Italian humanist Poggio Bracciolini rediscovers *De Institutione oratoria/On the Training of an Orator*, by the Roman writer Quintilian, in a monastery in St. Gall, Switzerland. Book hunters such as Poggio are rediscovering a wide range of classical works.

1417
- Chinese emperor Yongle has definitive editions of the Confucian classics published in order to exclude heterodox ideas. The restoration of traditional Confucianism is accompanied by the revival of the associated examination system for the Chinese civil service.

BIRTHS & DEATHS

1415
- Jan Długosz (Latin: Johannes Longinus), Polish diplomat and historian, who wrote the first history of Poland, *Historiae Polonicae* (1455–80), born in Brzeźnica, Poland (–1480).

April 15 Manuel Chrysoloras, Greek scholar who spread knowledge of Greek literature in the West, dies (*c.* 62).

September 21 Frederick III, German king 1440–93, Holy Roman Emperor 1452–93 born in Innsbruck, Austria (–1493).

1416
c. 1416 Owain Glyndwr (Owen Glendower), Welsh leader, self-proclaimed prince of Wales and rebel against English rule, dies (*c.* 62).

March 27 St. Francis of Paolo, Italian monk, founder of the Minim Friars, born in Paola, kingdom of Naples (–1507).

June 15 Jean de France, Duke of Berry, third son of King John II the Good of France, who as lieutenant for Auvergne, Languedoc, Périgord, and Poitou controlled at least one third of French territory, and who was also a major patron of the arts, dies in Paris, France (75).

1417
- Maso degli Albizzi, the effective ruler of Florence, dies.

December 14 John Oldcastle, leader and martyr of the Lollard sect and model for Shakespeare's Falstaff, is executed in London (*c.* 39).

1419
April 5 St. Vincent Ferrer, Spanish friar and celebrated preacher, dies in Vannes, France (*c.* 69).

September 10 John the Fearless, first Valois Duke of Burgundy 1404–19, assassinated in Montereau, France (48).

November 22 John XXIII, Italian antipope 1410–15 who was arrested and deposed after he deserted, dies in Naples.

- English chronicler John Capgrave completes his *Chronicle*, a history of England from the creation to 1417.

SOCIETY

Education

1419
- Prince Henry the Navigator of Portugal sets up the first school of navigation in Europe, at Sagres, Portugal.
- Rostock University is founded in Germany.

Religion

1415
- King Henry V founds a Brigittine house (of nuns and monks) at Twickenham, the last monastic foundation in England.
- The English theologian Thomas Netter of Walden publishes *Doctrinale fidei Ecclesiae Catholicae/ Doctrines of the True Catholic Church*, which attacks the Lollards.

1416
- The French theologian Pierre d'Ailly publishes *Tractatus super reformatione Ecclesiae/Tract on the Reformation of the Church*.

May 30 Condemned as a heretic by the Council of Constance, the Bohemian religious reformer Jerome of Prague is burned at the stake in Constance.

1420–1424

POLITICS, GOVERNMENT, AND ECONOMICS

Politics and Government

1420
- The *Dongchang*, or "Eastern Yard," is founded in Beijing, China. The eunuchs in the emperor's service keep secret files on official personnel there.
- Yongle, Emperor of China, transfers the Chinese capital from Nanjing to Beijing, which is rebuilt.

February 21 The Hussite extremists seize Austi and found the fortress of Tabor, after which their sect is named—the Taborites.

March 1 Pope Martin V declares a crusade against the Hussites.

March 25 In the first battle of the Hussite Wars, the extremist antipapal Taborites, led by John Žiška, defeat the Bohemian Catholics at Sudomer, Bohemia.

May 21 By the Treaty of Troyes, King Charles VI of France recognizes King Henry V of England as Duke of Normandy and his own heir to the French throne.

June Shahi Khan, having defeated his brother Ali Shah, Sultan of Kashmir, India, ascends the throne under the title Zain-ul-Abiain.

June 2 King Henry V of England marries Catherine, daughter of King Charles VI of France.

July 14 In the Hussite Wars, the extremist antipapal

Taborites, led by John Žiška, defeat a crusading army led by the Holy Roman Emperor Sigismund, King of Hungary and Bohemia, on the Vitkow, now Ziška's Hill, outside Prague, Bohemia. The "Four Articles of Prague" defining the principles common to the Hussites are now published.

August 8 Louis III, Duke of Anjou, arrives in the Italian kingdom of Naples following Pope Martin V's proposal that he should be Queen Joanna's heir.

September 9 The Italian kingdom of Naples is occupied by the troops of King Alfonso V of Aragon and Sicily, whom Queen Joanna of Naples adopts as her heir.

November 1 The Hussites again defeat the Holy Roman Emperor Sigismund, King of Hungary and Bohemia, under the Heights of Vyšehrad, near Prague, Bohemia: the first anti-Hussite crusade fails. Four further unsuccessful crusades follow.

December 1 King Henry V of England and King Charles VI of France enter Paris, France.

1421

March 22 The French dauphin Charles's troops defeat the English at Baugé, France, during King Henry V of England's absence in England. His brother Thomas, Duke of Clarence, is killed at Anjou while attacking the French and their Scottish allies.

April 23 Philip the Good, Duke of Burgundy, buys Namur (in present-day Belgium) from its marquis, John III.

May 20 Khizr Khan, the first Mongol ruler of Delhi, India, dies. He is succeeded by his son Mubarak, who styles himself shah.

May 26 The Ottoman sultan Mehmed I dies. He is succeeded by his son, Murad II.

June 1 The estates (representatives of the aristocracy, clergy, and commons) of Bohemia and Moravia, meeting at Čâslav, renounce the Holy Roman Emperor Sigismund as their king and form a government.

June 30   Florence buys Livorno from Genoa.

October 6   King Henry V of England begins the siege of Meaux, to the east of Paris, France.

November 2   In the Hussite Wars, the Bohemians defeat a second invading crusade by German princes at Saaz, Bohemia. This marks the failure of the second anti-Hussite crusade.

1422

- Ahmad Khan Bāhmanī, Shah of the Deccan, India, besieges Kherla and defeats King Hushung of Malwa.
- King Hushung of Malwa, India, attacks Orissa in an attempt to capture elephants to use in his war against Gujarat.
- King Hushung of Malwa, India, dies. He is succeeded by Gahzni Khan, though the administration is left to the new king's cousin Mughis and his son Mahmud Khan.

1422–24   The Chinese emperor Yongle campaigns, inconclusively, against the Tatars.

January 6   John Žiška, leader of the antipapal Taborite Hussites, defeats the Holy Roman Emperor Sigismund at Kutná Hora, Bohemia. On January 10, he again defeats Sigismund, at Německý Brod, Bohemia.

May 10   The French town of Meaux surrenders to King Henry V of England.

May 16   The Bohemians accept Korybut, nephew of King Władysław Jagiełło of Poland, as their king.

June 8   The Ottoman sultan Murad II begins the siege of Constantinople, the capital of the Byzantine Empire (modern Istanbul, Turkey). He abandons it on August 8 when his brother Mustafa rebels.

June 30   Francesco Carmagnola, the condottiere, defeats the Swiss at Arbedo, thus gaining the Val d'Ossola for Filippo Maria Visconti, Duke of Milan.

August 31   King Henry V of England dies. He is succeeded by his infant son, Henry VI, with the lords establishing a council to rule in his minority.

September 22   Ahmad Khan Bāhmanī ascends the throne of the Deccan, India, at Gulbarga, deposing his brother Firuz. He defeats Vijayaraya, King of the Hindu kingdom of Vijayanagar, in a battle on the River Tungabhara and devastates his kingdom.

September 27   By the Treaty of Mielno, the Teutonic Knights (a German Christian military order) end their war with Poland and Lithuania.

October 2   Firuz Bāhmanī, the deposed king of the Deccan, India, dies. He may have been murdered by his brother, Ahmad Khan, the new king.

October 21   King Charles VI of France dies. He is succeeded, in accordance with the 1420 Treaty of Troyes, by King Henry VI of England.

October 30   The dauphin Charles, son of the late king Charles VI of France, assumes the title of king (Charles VII) of France, in defiance of the 1420 Treaty of Troyes by which King Henry VI of England is the successor to the French throne.

1423

- A raid on the Irish midlands by a confederation of Ulster chieftains under the O'Donnells forces the county of Louth to pay protection money, known as "black rent."
- Florence declares war on Milan. Hostilities continue until 1454.

- The Ottoman sultan Murad II destroys Hexamilion and ravages the Morea.
- The port of Thessaloníki (Salonika) is ceded to Venice by the Greeks, who have been unable to defend it from the Ottoman Turks.
- Yoshikazu becomes Japanese shogun (military ruler).

April 15   Tomaso Mocenigo, Doge of Venice, dies. He is succeeded by Francesco Foscari.

April 27   John Žiška, leader of the antipapal Taborite Hussites, defeats the moderates at Hořic, Bohemia, in the first battle of the Bohemian civil war.

May 5   Queen Joanna V of Naples begins operations to expel King Alfonso V of Aragon from Naples and adopts Louis III, Duke of Anjou, as her heir in his place.

July 31   Anglo-Burgundian forces defeat the French at Cravant, France.

1424

- Megat Iskandar Shah of Malacca dies. He is succeeded by Sri Maharajah Mohammad Shah.
- The committee of the Lords of the Articles, a select body to consider the principal business in Scottish parliaments, is founded.
- The sultan of Ifat attacks Jedaya. The brother of the sultan of Jedaya is captured and the town is sacked.

January 3   The condottiere Sforza Attendolo dies. He is succeeded by his son Francesco.

March 28   By the Treaty of Durham, King James I of Scotland is released from captivity in England and makes a truce for seven years with England.

August 17   John, Duke of Bedford, the English regent for the infant king Henry VI in France, defeats the forces of King Charles VII of France at Verneuil, France.

October 11   John Žiška, leader of the antipapal Taborite Hussites, dies. His followers take the name "the Orphans."

October 16   Humphrey, Duke of Gloucester, begins his campaign to conquer the lands of his wife, Jacqueline of Bavaria, Countess of Holland, Zeeland, and Hainault, from Philip the Good, Duke of Burgundy.

SCIENCE, TECHNOLOGY, AND MEDICINE

Ecology

1421

- More than 100,000 people die in over 70 Dutch villages when the Zuider Zee floods.

Health and Medicine

1423

- The Venetian republic sets up its first quarantine station, or *lazaretto* on an island near Venice, Italy. Those suspected of carrying disease are detained for 40 days.

Science

1424

- Mongolian ruler and astronomer Ulugh Beg, Prince of Samarkand, builds a great observatory, including a 40-m/132-ft sextant, which enables extremely accurate measurements to be made, cataloging over 1,000 stars.

Technology

1420

- The earliest known illustration of a European tower mill is made, in France. The tower mill has its sails fixed to a movable cap that can be turned in any direction to catch the wind.
- The German *Feuerwerksbuch/Book of Fireworks*, a manual for the manufacture and use of cannon and gunpowder, is written. Among other inventions, it describes a nitro-explosive and the devastation caused by shrapnel.

1423

- An illustration from a German manuscript of this date shows a hand-mill for making flour, providing the earliest evidence for the use of a crank and connecting rod. A wood-boring apparatus is also shown.

1424

- The earliest illustration of a carpenter's brace appears in a painting of Joseph the carpenter (husband of Mary) at work.

Transportation

1420

- Italian inventor Girolamo de'Fontana invents a velocipede—an early form of mechanical transport.

ARTS AND IDEAS

Architecture

1421

- Work begins on the Church of San Lorenzo in Florence, Italy. The design is by the Italian artist and architect Filippo Brunelleschi, whose aim is to construct the entire church in cubic units—a revolutionary approach that has a profound effect on Italian Renaissance architecture.

Arts

c. **1420**

- Flemish artist brothers Hubert and Jan van Eyck develop the technique of painting using oils as a medium to hold the pigment.

BIRTHS & DEATHS

1420

c. 1420 Piero della Francesca, Florentine painter noted for his use of perspective and for his frescoes, born in Borgo San Sepolcro, republic of Florence (–1492).

- John Morton, English cardinal and archbishop of Canterbury, born in Dorset, England (–1500).
- Robert Stewart Albany, Regent and virtual ruler of Scotland 1388–1420, dies in Stirling Castle, Stirling, Scotland (*c.* 80).
- Sesshu, Japanese artist known for his monochrome ink paintings inspired by Zen-Buddhism, born in Akahama, Japan (–1506).
- Tomás de Torquemada, Spanish Dominican, first grand inquisitor in Spain who ordered about 2,000 people to be tortured and burned at the stake, born in Valladolid, Castile (–1498).

August 9 Pierre d'Ailly, French theologian, cardinal, and church reformer, dies in Avignon, France (*c.* 70).

1421

- Andrea del Castagno (Andrea di Bartolo), influential Italian painter of

the Renaissance, noted for his realistic treatment of figures, whose major works include the fresco *St. Julian* (1454–55), born in San Martino a Corella, near Castagno San Godenzo, Italy (–1457).

- Jean II le Maingre (known as "Boucicaut"), French soldier and marshal of France, famous for his chivalry and skill at arms, who defeated the Ottoman Turks at Gallipoli (1399), and was captured by the English at Agincourt, dies in Yorkshire, England (*c.* 55).
- Vespasiano da Bisticci, biographer of illustrious men of 15th-century Italy, born (–1498).

May 26 Mehmed I, Ottoman sultan 1413–21 who reunified the empire after his father Bāyezīd I's defeat by Timur Leng (Tamerlane) at the Battle of Ankara (1402), dies in Edirne, Persia.

December 6 Henry VI, King of England 1422–61 and 1470–71, son of Henry V, born in Windsor, Berkshire, England (–1471).

1422

c. 1422 William Caxton, the first English printer and influential translator and

publisher, born in Kent, England (–1491).

August 31 Henry V, King of England 1413–22, son of Henry IV, dies in Bois de Vincennes, France (34).

October 21 Charles VI ("the Well-Beloved" or "the Mad"), King of France 1380–1422, dies in Paris, France (53).

1423

March Dick Whittington, English merchant and Lord Mayor of London 1397–99, 1406–07, and 1419–20, dies in London.

July 3 Louis XI, King of France 1461–83, son of Charles VII, who unified the French territories after the Hundred Years' War, born in Bourges, France (–1483).

1424

- Giovanni Sercambi, Italian writer of a history of Lucca, *Chroniche delle cose di Lucca/Chronicle of Matters Relating to Lucca*, and a collection of tales, *Novelle*, dies (77).

August 5 Yung-lo, Chinese Ming emperor who moved the capital of China from Nanjing to Beijing and built the Forbidden City, dies en route to Beijing (64).

1421

- Italian artist Nanni di Banco sculpts *The Assumption of the Virgin* for a portal of Florence Cathedral, Italy.

c. 1422

- Italian artist Pisanello (Antonio Pisano) paints frescoes (now destroyed) in the Doge's Palace in Venice, Italy.

1423

- Italian artist Gentile da Fabriano paints the altarpiece *The Adoration of the Magi*.

1424

- Italian artist Lorenzo Ghiberti completes the sculpting of the 28 relief scenes for the second pair of bronze doors of the Baptistry in Florence, Italy (the first are by Andrea Pisano). The work began in 1403. In 1425 he begins a third set, completed in 1452.

Literature and Language

c. 1420

- English writer John Lydgate completes his historical epic *The Siege of Thebes*.

1421

- English writer John Lydgate completes his epic poem *Troy Book*, written at the request of Henry, Prince of Wales.

1422

- *c.* 1422 Indian writer Banda Nawāz writes *Hidāya nāma*, a treatise on Muslim mysticism. It is one of the earliest examples of Urdu prose.
- The earliest of the surviving Paston letters is written, in England. The letters of a Norfolk family, they provide an invaluable picture of everyday life in the 15th century. The last letters date from 1506.

1423

- King James I of Scotland writes the allegorical poem *The Kingis Quair/The King's Book* while in captivity in England.

Thought and Scholarship

1422

- French writer Alain Chartier writes his prose *Quadrilogue invectif/Four-part Invective*, a dialogue— between France, its nobility, the clergy, and the people—on the disastrous state of the nation.

SOCIETY

Education

1420

- A special school is set up in Beijing, China, for the education of eunuchs as court officials.
- Mongolian ruler and astronomer Ulugh Beg, grandson of Timur Leng (Tamerlane), founds a *madrasa* (institute of higher learning) at Samarkand, specializing in mathematics and astronomy.

Religion

1420

- *c.* 1420 The French theologian Jean de Gerson writes *De consolatione theologiae/The Consolation of Theology*.
- September 30 Pope Martin V enters Rome. The papal residence is restored here following the partial pacification of the Papal States.

1423

- On the death of the antipope Benedict XIII in Avignon, the Spanish clergyman Gil Sánchez Muñoz is elected antipope, a position he holds, in Avignon, until 1429.
- April 23 The General Council called by Pope Martin V opens in Pavia, Italy.
- July 21 The General Council, called by Pope Martin V, is transferred from Pavia to Siena.

1424

- March 7 The General Council called by Pope Martin V is dissolved, in Siena.

1425–1429

POLITICS, GOVERNMENT, AND ECONOMICS

Business and Economics

1427

- Giovanni de' Medici introduces the Catasto, probably the first ever tax based on income, in Florence, Italy.

Politics and Government

1425

- Portugal begins the conquest of the Canary Islands.
- Vasily II succeeds his father, Vasily I, who has died, as Grand Duke of Moscow. His uncle Yury (Juri), Prince of Halich, unsuccessfully attempts to oppose his succession.

April 4 Humphrey, Duke of Gloucester, returns to England, abandoning his wife, Jacqueline of Bavaria, Countess of Holland, Zeeland, and Hainault, to Philip the Good, Duke of Burgundy, in favor of Eleanor Cobham, whom he subsequently marries.

May 25 King James I of Scotland, in his restoration of royal authority, has his regent Murdoch, Duke of Albany, executed.

July 21 The Byzantine emperor Manuel II, who has ruled only Constantinople (modern Istanbul, Turkey) while his brothers have ruled other remaining fragments of the empire in Greece, dies. He is succeeded by his eldest son, John VIII.

August 2 The French town of Le Mans surrenders to the English.

September 8 King Charles III of Navarre dies. He is succeeded by his daughter Blanche, wife of Prince John of Aragon.

October 30 A fracas occurs in London, England, between citizens favoring Humphrey, Duke of Gloucester, and the men of Henry Beaufort, Chancellor of the Duchy of Lancaster, and bishop of Winchester. The dispute has its origin in both money matters and different aims in the French wars.

December 3 Venice and Florence make an alliance against Milan.

1426

- Barsbay, Sultan of Egypt, devastates Cyprus, and makes its king tributary.

- Giovanni Francesco di Gonzaga of Mantua takes Brescia from Milan.
- Vanaratna, the last of the Mongol-backed rulers of Tibet, visits the country.

January 27 King Alfonso V of Aragon joins the league against Milan.

February 2 Venice declares war on Milan.

March 12 Humphrey, Duke of Gloucester, and Henry Beaufort, Chancellor of the Duchy of Lancaster and bishop of Winchester, are formally reconciled in the "Parliament of Bats" in Northampton, England.

March 12 The Bohemians defeat Albert V, Duke of Austria, whom they previously expelled from Moravia, at Zwettl, Austria.

June 16 The Hussites, led by Prokop the Great, destroy a German crusading army at Usti, Bohemia: the third anti-Hussite crusade fails.

1427

- A private war breaks out in Poitou, France, between King Charles VII of France's favorite Georges de la Trémoille and Arthur of Brittany, Count of Richemont, the constable of France.
- Abu Zakaria ben Zayar al Wattasi usurps the throne from the last infant Marinid, as mayor of the place, in Fez, Morocco.
- King Yeshaq of Ethiopia sends an embassy to King Alfonso V of Aragon and to the Duke of Berry in an attempt to form a Christian alliance against Islam.
- A revolt causes the flight of King Mohammad VIII of Granada. He is succeeded by Mohammad IX.

April 17 The Bohemians expel their king, Korybut. This is followed by their first raid into Silesia and Lusatia, Germany.

July 11 King Eric VII of Denmark defeats the Hanse (Hanseatic League) off Copenhagen. The war follows Eric's imposition of dues on ships passing the sound between the islands of Zealand (present-day Sjælland) and Scania.

August 27 A crusading army led by the English cardinal Henry Beaufort flees from Stříbo on the approach of the Bohemians: the fourth anti-Hussite crusade fails.

September 5 The French defeat English forces at Montargis, southeast of Paris, France.

October 11 Venetian forces led by Francesco Carmagnola defeat the Milanese at Maclodio, thus winning the town of Bergamo.

1428

- A large-scale uprising takes place in Japan, aimed against moneylenders. In some areas it is put down by force, elsewhere compromise agreements are reached.
- An act of King James I of Scotland requires the election of representatives of the sheriffdoms to Scottish parliaments.

- The English Parliament rejects Pope Martin V's demand for the repeal of the Statute of Provisors, which attempts to curb papal power in England.
- The Holy Roman Emperor Sigismund leads another unsuccessful campaign against the Ottoman Turks on the Lower Danube, Bulgaria.
- The leader of the Vietnamese resistance to Chinese occupation, Le Loi, having defeated the Chinese, declares himself emperor of Dai Viet (Vietnam) as Le Thaito, establishing the Le dynasty. The Ming recognize him on his admission of Chinese suzerainty.

April 19   By the Peace of Ferrara, Milan cedes Brescia and Bergamo to Venice.

July 3   By the Treaty of Delft, Jacqueline of Bavaria recognizes Philip the Good, Duke of Burgundy, as governor and her heir in Holland, Zeeland, and Hainault.

October 7   The English begin the siege of Orléans, France.

1429

- Ahmad Khan Bāhmanī, King of the Deccan, India, transfers his capital from Gulbarga to Bidar.
- Ahmad of Gujarat recovers the Indian city of Bombay from Shah Ahmad I of Kulbarga.
- King Mohammad IX of Granada is murdered and his predecessor, Mohammad VIII, is restored.
- Yoshinori, the younger brother of Yashikazu, becomes Japanese shogun (military ruler).

1429–30   The Bohemians raid Saxony and Franconia, Germany.

January 10   Philip the Good, Duke of Burgundy, establishes the Order of the Golden Fleece.

February 12   In the "Battle of the Herrings" at Rouvray, France, the English defeat a French attack on supplies for their forces besieging Orléans.

February 23   The French military leader Joan of Arc arrives in Chinon, France, to meet King Charles VII of France.

April   The French military leader Joan of Arc returns to Chinon, France, and after a second meeting with King Charles VII of France is supplied with a horse and armor and sent to join the French army at Orléans.

April 29   The French military leader Joan of Arc arrives at Orléans, France and relieves the English siege.

May 8   Defeated by the new-found confidence and strength of the French under the leadership of Joan of Arc, the English abandon the siege of Orléans, France; this is the turning point in the Hundred Years' War.

June 18   The French defeat the withdrawing English army under John Talbot at Patay, northwest of Orléans, France. Talbot and several other knights are captured.

July 18   Charles VII is crowned as king of France at Reims, seven years after the death of his father, King Charles VI.

SCIENCE, TECHNOLOGY, AND MEDICINE

Health and Medicine

1425

- The Italian physician Ugolini of Montecatini, a spa town noted for its saline springs, writes *De balneorum Italiae/On the Baths of Italy*, an early treatise on the benefits of bathing.

ARTS AND IDEAS

Architecture

1428

- The sacristy of the Church of San Lorenzo in Florence, Italy, designed by the Italian artist and architect Filippo Brunelleschi, is completed. A cube topped by a dome, it is highly original in its emphasis on rigorous order and clarity. Later architects will make changes to

BIRTHS & DEATHS

1425

October   Alesso Baldovinetti, Florentine painter whose best known work is the fresco *The Nativity* (1460–62), born in Florence (–1499).

1427

- Gentile da Fabriano (Niccolò di Giovanni di Massio), leading central Italian painter of his age, whose surviving works include *Adoration of the Magi* (1423), dies in Rome, Italy (*c.* 57).

1428

- Julius Pomponius Laetus, Italian humanist, founder of the Accademia Romana, born in Diano, Italy (–1497).

- Masaccio (Tommaso di Giovanni di Simone Guidi), major Italian painter of the early Renaissance noted for his frescoes, dies in Rome, Italy (26).

May 3   Pedro Gonzalez de Mendoza, influential Spanish diplomat and cardinal, a supporter of Christopher Columbus, born in Guadalajara, Spain (–1495).

November 22   Richard Neville, 1st Earl of Warwick, (the "Kingmaker"), English nobleman who obtained the throne for King Edward IV, and restored deposed King Henry VI to the throne, born (–1471).

1429

February 23   Gentile Bellini, Venetian painter, brother of Giovanni Bellini, best known for his portraiture and scenes of Venice, whose works include *The Recovery of the Holy Cross* (1500), born in Venice, Italy (–1507).

March   Margaret of Anjou, Queen Consort of Henry VI of England, leader of the Lancastrians in the Wars of the Roses (1455–85), born, probably in Pont-à-Mousson, Lorraine, France (–1482).

July 12   Jean de Gerson (original surname Charlier), French theologian and mystic, dies in Lyon, France (65).

Brunelleschi's design for the rest of the church, which is finally completed in 1469.

Arts

1425

c. 1425 Flemish artist Jan van Eyck paints *Madonna in a Church.*

- Italian artist Gentile da Fabriano paints *The Quaratesi Altarpiece.*
- Italian artist Jacopo della Quercia sculpts reliefs for the main portal of the Church of San Petronio in Bologna, Italy.

1426

- Italian artist Donatello (Donato di Niccolò) sculpts *Habbakuk (Lo Zuccone)* for the façade of Florence Cathedral, Italy.
- Italian artist Masaccio (Tommaso di Giovanni di Simone Guidi) paints *Madonna and Child (Pisa Altarpiece).*

***c.* 1427**

- Flemish artist Robert Campin (Master of Flémalle) paints *Virgin and Child Before a Fire Screen.*
- Italian artist Masaccio (Tommaso di Giovanni di Simone Guidi) paints the fresco *The Trinity*, one of the major works of the early Italian Renaissance, in the Church of Santa Maria Novella in Florence, Italy.

1428

c. 1428 Flemish artist Robert Campin (Master of Flémalle) paints *The Mérode Altarpiece.*

c. 1428 Italian artist Masolino da Pinicale paints *The Founding of Santa Maria Maggiore.*

- Italian artists Masaccio (Tommaso di Giovanni di Simone Guidi) and Masolino da Pinicale paint frescoes in the Brancacci Chapel in the Church of Santa Maria del Carmine, Florence, Italy. Masaccio's works there, painted according to the newly discovered principles of linear perspective, and with a solidity and drama not seen since Giotto, are among the most important works of the early Renaissance.

Literature and Language

***c.* 1425**

- French writer Alain Chartier writes his poem *La Belle dame sans merci/The Beautiful Lady without Pity*, one of the best-known medieval lyrics of courtly love.

1428

- French writer Alain Chartier publishes *Traité de l'espérance/Treatise on Hope.*

Music

1429

- Italian-born French writer Christine de Pisan writes her poem "Ditié en l'honneur de Jeanne d'Arc"/"Song in Honor of Joan of Arc," written to celebrate Joan of Arc's recent victories against the English.

SOCIETY

Education

1425

- Leuven University is founded in Flanders (now Belgium).

1429

December 19 Lincoln College is founded at Oxford University in England.

Religion

***c.* 1425**

- German Augustinian monk Thomas à Kempis (Thomas Hemerken) writes *De imitatione Christi/On the Imitation of Christ.* A classic of devotional literature, it is first published in 1473 and will become the most widely read Christian book after the Bible.

1430–1434

POLITICS, GOVERNMENT, AND ECONOMICS

Business and Economics

1432
- Japan restores trade links with China. The volume of trade increases until about 1450.

1433
- The first Japanese trade mission is sent to China.

Politics and Government

1430
c. 1430 King Yeshaq of Ethiopia dies. A succession crisis follows.
- A statute restricts the right to elect shire-knights to English parliaments to those who have freehold lands worth not less than 40 shillings per annum.
- Ahmad Khan, King of the Deccan, India, in a policy of aggression against his northern neighbors, attacks Gujarat.
- Zafar Khan, King of Gujarat, India, defeats the army of the Deccan in battle.
1430–34 Ahmed Badly Walasma takes the throne of the sultanate of Adal (in present-day Somalia), with Yemeni help.
March 29 The Ottoman sultan Murad II captures the Greek port of Thessaloníki (Salonika) from the Venetians.
May 23 Burgundian troops capture the French military leader Joan of Arc as she attempts to prevent the fall of the town of Compiègne, France. She is sold to the English for 10,000 livres tournois.
August 4 Philip the Good, Duke of Burgundy, inherits the duchies of Brabant and Limburg.
October 27 Grand Duke Vitold of Lithuania dies. Svidrigełło, brother of King Władysław Jagiełło of Poland, is elected as his successor.
December 2 Niccolò Piccinino, the condottiere serving Milan, defeats Florentine forces under the Count of Urbino on the River Serchio.

1431
- Jalal-ud-din, ruler of Bengal, India, dies. He is succeeded by Shams-ud-din.
- King John II of Castile defeats the Moors of Granada in the Battle of Higveruela as he attempts to place Yūsuf

IV, grandson of the deposed King Mohammad VIII, on the throne.
- King Paramaraja II of Ayutthaya sacks Angkor, the capital of Cambodia.
March 3 Gabriel Condulmer is elected as Pope Eugenius IV.
May 3 Humphrey, Duke of Gloucester, lieutenant of England in the absence of King Henry VI, crushes a Lollard rising in Abingdon, near Oxford, led by "Jack Sharp."
May 3 Pope Eugenius IV excommunicates and wages war on the Colonna family of Rome and attempts to regain the land grants given to them by his predecessor, Pope Martin V, who belonged to the dynasty.
May 17 Niccolò Piccinino and Francesco Sforza, the Milanese condottieri, defeat the Venetian forces under Francesco Carmagnola at Soncino, east of Milan.
May 23 The Genoese, who are subject to Milan, defeat a Venetian fleet on the River Po.
May 30 After being captured by Burgundian troops and then handed over to English troops, the French military leader Joan of Arc is burned as a heretic in Rouen, France.
July 23 The General Council of Basel, originially called by Pope Martin V, is opened to discuss reforms in the church, to settle the Hussite heresy, and to settle the question of papal supremacy. It is dominated by radical demands from the lower clergy.
August 14 A crusading army led by Cardinal Cesarini flees from Domažlice, Bohemia, on the approach of the Bohemians: the fifth anti-Hussite crusade fails.
August 27 The Genoese fleet, subject to Milan, again defeats the Venetians near Portofino, south of Genoa.
December 16 The nine-year-old King Henry VI of England is crowned as king of France in Paris, France.

1432
- A series of peasant revolts breaks out in Saxony, Silesia, Brandenburg, and the Rhineland, Germany.
- King Eric VII of Denmark, Norway, and Sweden is finally defeated by the Count of Holstein, who claims the duchy of Schleswig.
- Sha Ahmad I of Kulbarga completes his new capital at Bidar, India.
- The Latin principality of Achaea surrenders to Thomas Palaeologus, ruler of the Morea.
- The Ottoman sultan Murad II conquers Albania after the death of John Castriota I, the ruler of central Albania.
May 5 The Venetians execute Francesco Carmagnola, their condottiere (mercenary) captain, after he has dealings with the Milanese, their enemies.
June 24 King Yūsuf IV of Granada is murdered. The

deposed Mohammad VIII is restored. He continues his wars with Castile and León.

August 17   Giovanni Caraccioli, the favorite of Queen Joanna of Naples, is murdered.

September 1   Svidrigełło is deposed as grand duke of Lithuania following his anti-Polish alliance with the Teutonic Knights (a German Christian military order). He is succeeded by his conqueror Sigismund, brother of Grand Duke Vitold, the previous ruler.

1433

- Akil, a Tuareg chief, takes the towns of Timbuktu, Arawa, and Walaka, in Mali.

April 4   Prince Juri of Halich takes Moscow and proclaims himself grand duke. He soon withdraws.

June 6   Georges de la Trémoille, a favorite of King Charles VII of France, is seized by his enemies and compelled to retire from the king's court.

August 14   King John I the Great of Portugal dies. He is succeeded by his son Edward.

September 22   The Holy Roman Emperor Sigismund raises Giovanni Francesco di Gonzaga to the title of Marquess of Mantua.

1434

- The capital of the Khmer nation (modern Cambodia) is transferred to Phnom Penh from Angkor Thom.
- The English suppress risings by the peasants of lower Normandy, France.
- Zara Ya'qub, brother of the late King Yeshaq of Ethiopia, is released from the royal prison at Mt. Gishen and takes the throne of Ethiopia.

February 19   Mubarak, Shah of Delhi, India, is murdered at the instigation of his minister Sarvar al-Malik. His nephew, Mohammad, is elected as his successor.

May 30   In the Battle of Lipany, the Bohemian Catholics and Utraquists (the moderate Hussites) defeat the extremist antipapal Taborite Hussites led by Andrew Prokop, who is killed.

May 31   King Władysław Jagiełło of Poland dies. He is succeeded by his son, Władysław III.

June 4   Pope Eugenius IV flees from Rome to Florence following the establishment of a republican government by the Colonnas of Rome and condottieri employed by Milan.

June 6   Prince Juri of Halich dies when again in possession of Moscow. His son Vasili Kosoy proclaims himself grand duke, but the deposed grand duke Vasili II is restored and has Vasili Kosoy blinded.

August 28   Niccolò Piccinino, the condottiere serving Milan, defeats Venetian and Florentine forces near Imola, northeast of Florence.

October 5   The Florentine banker Cosimo de' Medici returns from exile to Florence, becoming its effective ruler. The oligarchy is overthrown, and his rival the political leader Palla Strozzi is banished.

November 15   Louis III, Duke of Anjou and claimant to the Italian kingdom of Naples, dies. He is succeeded by his brother René I, Count of Provence, Duke of Bar and Lorraine.

SCIENCE, TECHNOLOGY, AND MEDICINE

Health and Medicine

1431

- French-born physican Jean Ganivet of Vienna writes *Amicus medicorum/Directory of Astrology Made Medical*.

Technology

1430

- German military engineer Konrad Kyeser illustrates a double crane that uses an elaborate system of pulleys to multiply its lifting power.
- New metallurgical techniques for making plate iron and steel lead to innovations in military equipment. Metal plate armor becomes standard for European knights, and "Mad Marjorie," a huge 5-m/16-ft cast-iron cannon is constructed.

ARTS AND IDEAS

Architecture

1433

- The tower of St. Stephens Cathedral in Vienna, Austria, is completed.

Arts

c. 1430

- Flemish artist Robert Campin (Master of Flémalle) paints *Portrait of a Woman*.
- Italian artist Donatello (Donato di Niccolò) sculpts his bronze *David*, the first free-standing, life-sized nude of the Renaissance. Suggested dates for this work vary widely from 1430 to 1460.

1431

c. 1431   Flemish artist Jan van Eyck paints *Portrait of Cardinal Niccolò Albergati*.

- Italian artist Paolo Uccello completes several mosaics (now lost) in San Marco, Venice.

1432

- Flemish artists Hubert and Jan van Eyck paint *The Adoration of the Lamb (Ghent Altarpiece)*, a polyptych in the Church of St. Bavo in Ghent, Flanders (now Belgium). Van Eyck paints *Portrait of a Man*, which may be a self-portrait.

c. 1433

- Flemish artist Jan van Eyck paints *Madonna with Chancellor Rolin (Virgin of Autun)*.

- Italian architect and writer on art Leon Battista Alberti writes *De statua/On Sculpture*. Suggested dates for this work vary widely: some authorities date it as late as 1460.

1434

c. 1434 Italian artist Fra Angelico (Guido di Pietro) paints *The Annunciation*, an altarpiece for the Church of San Domenico in Cortona, Italy.
- Flemish artist Jan van Eyck paints *The Arnolfini Marriage*, a double portrait, full of complex symbolism, of the Italian banker Giovanni Arnolfini and his wife Giovanna Cenani on their wedding day.

Literature and Language

c. 1430

- Spanish writer Juan Rodríguez de la Cámara writes *El siervo libre de amor/The Willing Servant of Love*, an autobiographical sentimental romance of courtly love.
- Spanish writer Pedro del Corral writes his *Crónica Sarracina/Saracen Chronicle*, a narrative about the invasion of Spain by the Moors.

1431

- Italian scholar and humanist Lorenzo Valla publishes his treatise *De voluptate/On Pleasure* (it later becomes known as *De vero et falso bono/On the True and False Good*).

Music

1430

- The Vire valley (Val-de-Vire) in Normandy is famous for its satirical folk songs, *Chansons du Vaux-de-Vire*. These are said to be the origin of the later term "vaudeville," light drama with interspersed songs and spoken dialogue.

Theater and Dance

c. 1432

- The French morality play *Mystère du Concile de Bâle/Mystery Play of the Council of Basel* is written.

SOCIETY

Education

1432

- The University of Caen is founded in France.
- The University of Poitiers is established in France.

BIRTHS & DEATHS

1430

c. 1430 Jean d'Ockeghem, Franco-Flemish composer, born in Flanders (–1495).
- Giovanni Bellini, leading Venetian Renaissance painter, brother of Gentile Bellini, whose major works include *Coronation of the Virgin* (1470s) and *Portrait of a Young Man* (1490s), born in Venice (–1516).
- Hans Memling, a leading painter of the Bruges School whose works include *Virgin and Child with Saints and Donors* (*c.* 1475), born in Seligenstadt, near Frankfurt am Main (–1494).
- Selim I, Ottoman sultan 1512–20, who extended the Ottoman empire to Egypt, Syria, and the Hejaz, born in Amasya, Ottoman Empire (–1520).

October 16 James II, King of Scotland 1437–60, son of James I, born in Edinburgh, Scotland (–1460).

1431

- Alexander VI (original name Rodrigo Borgia), pope 1492–1503, notorious for his corruption and worldliness, father of Cesare and Lucretia Borgia, born in Játiva, Aragon, Spain (–1503).
- Andrea Mantegna, Italian painter and engraver of the Renaissance whose major works include *The Triumph of Caesar* (begun *c.* 1486), born near Vicenza, Italy (–1506).
- François Villon, French lyric poet known especially for his poems *Le Petit Testament/The Shorter Testament* and *Le Grand Testament/The Longer Testament*, born in Paris (–*c.* 1466).
- William Elphinstone, Scottish bishop and stateman, who founded Edinburgh University, born in Glasgow, Scotland (–1514).

April 1 Nuno Álvares Pereira, Portuguese military leader whose defeat of the Castilians in 1385 ensured Portugal's independence, dies in Lisbon, Portugal (70).

1432

March 30 Mehmed II the Conqueror, Ottoman sultan 1444–46 and 1451–81, an outstanding military commander, son of Murad II, who captured Constantinople (modern Istanbul, Turkey) in 1453 and expanded the empire in Anatolia and the Balkans, born in Edirne, Persia (–1481).

1433

October 19 Marsilio Ficino, Italian theologian, philosopher, and linguist, translator of Plato and other Greek philosophers, born in Figline, Italy (–1499).

November 10 Charles I the Bold, last great Duke of Burgundy 1467–77, who expanded Burgundy's territories and made them independent of French control, born in Dijon, Burgundy, France (–1477).

1434

June 1 Władysław II Jagiełło, Grand Prince of Lithuania 1377–1401, and King of Poland 1386–1401, who united Poland and Lithuania and founded the Jagiellon dynasty, dies in Gródek, near Lvov, Galicia, Poland (c. 83).

Everyday Life

1430

- New legislation imposed by King James I of Scotland forbids drinking after 9 pm and obliges citizens to dress appropriately according to their social status.

Religion

1431

- The Council of Basel, a general council of the church convoked by Pope Martin V, opens in Basel, Switzerland. Its main concerns are the heresy of the Czech reformer Jan Hus and the authority of the pope. On December 18, Pope Eugenuis IV orders its dissolution, but it refuses to comply and continues to meet until 1449.

1432

May 7   Delegates of the General Council of Basel meet Hussite representatives at Cheb, Bohemia, to discuss Hussite doctrines in relation to the teachings of the Catholic Church.

1433

- Spanish theologian Paul of Burgos writes *Dialogus Pauli et Petri contra Judaeos/The Dialogue of Paul and Peter*

Against the Jews, a defense of Christianity by a Jew who converted to Christianity.

- The German churchman and philosopher Nicholas of Cusa (Nicolaus Cusanus) publishes *Concordantia Catholica/Catholic Concord*, a moderate conciliator's plea for unity and tolerance in the church.

January 4   After their preliminary meeting with representatives of the General Council of Basel at Cheb, Bohemia, in 1432, Hussite delegates arrive in Basel to discuss their doctrines with the council.

November 30   The delegates of the General Council of Basel in Prague, Bohemia, make terms for a settlement with the Bohemian Hussite moderates—the "Compacts of Prague"—which grant some degree of freedom to the Moravians and Bohemians if they swear loyalty to the Holy Roman Emperor Sigismund. However the extremist antipapal Taborites do not agree to this.

December 15   Pope Eugenius IV eventually recognizes the General Council of Basel. He had previously refused to recognize it owing to the conflict between the Pope and the council over the conciliar theory that held that ultimate authority rested with the council and not with the Holy See.

1435–1439

POLITICS, GOVERNMENT, AND ECONOMICS

Business and Economics

1436

- The Hanseatic League suspends trade with Flanders following an anti-German riot in Sluys, Flanders.

1438

- The Hanseatic League raises its embargo on trade with Flanders when the city of Bruges cedes its demands.

Politics and Government

1435

- Engelbrecht, the leader of a popular Swedish revolt against King Eric VII of Denmark, Norway, and

Sweden, holds a parliament at Arboga, Sweden, which elects him regent of Sweden.

February 2   Queen Joanna II of Naples dies. She bequeaths her kingdom to René I, Duke of Anjou.

February 18   Ahmad Khan, King of the Deccan, India, dies. He is succeeded by his son, Ala-ud-din Ahmad.

July 17   By the Treaty of Vordingborg, the Hanseatic League makes peace with King Eric VII of Denmark, Norway, and Sweden, settling trading disputes.

August 5   English, French, and Burgundian embassies open the Congress of Arras in northern France to end the Hundred Years' War, proposed by Philip the Good, Duke of Burgundy. This signals the growing gulf between the English and the Burgundians.

August 5   King Alfonso V of Aragon is defeated and captured by the Genoese in a naval battle off the island of Ponza. He is soon afterwards released, having made a treaty of alliance with Milan, in which his claim to the throne of Naples is recognized.

September 1   Grand Duke Sigismund of Lithuania defeats the Teutonic Knights (a German Christian military order) and Lithuanian rebels under the deposed Grand Duke Svidrigełło, at Wiłkomierz, Lithuania.

September 6   The English embassy abandons its

negotiations for peace with France at Arras in northern France, following a peace treaty made by Philip the Good, Duke of Burgundy, with the French.

September 21 By the Treaty of Arras, Philip the Good, Duke of Burgundy, makes peace with Charles VII of France.

October 28 The French capture the port of Dieppe. The English suppress a subsequent rising by the local peasants.

December 27 Francesco Spinola leads a rebellion in Genoa which recovers the city's independence from Milan.

December 31 By the Peace of Brest, the Teutonic Knights (a German Christian military order) cede Samogitia and Sudauen to Poland.

1436

- The Swedish leader Engelbrecht is murdered. Amund Sigurdsson leads a revolt in Norway. King Eric VII of Denmark, Norway, and Sweden pacifies both countries by his concessions to national, anti-Danish, sentiments.

April 13 The French city of Paris is taken from the English for King Charles VII of France, who restores it as his capital.

May 13 Mahmud Khan is proclaimed king of Malwa, India.

August 2 Philip the Good, Duke of Burgundy, is compelled to abandon his attempt to take the northern French port of Calais from the English.

August 15 King James I of Scotland abandons his attempt to take Roxburgh Castle, Scotland, from the English.

August 23 The Holy Roman Emperor Sigismund enters Prague, Bohemia, having been fully recognized as king of Bohemia following his recognition of the 1433 Compacts of Prague.

October 10 The minority of King Henry VI of England ends and his personal rule begins.

1437

- In an attempt to gain further control of the Strait of Gibraltar, a Portuguese expedition led by Prince Henry the Navigator fails to take the Moroccan port of Tangier. The Moors demand the return of the strategic port of Ceuta and keep King John I of Portugal's brother Pedro hostage.
- Philip the Good, Duke of Burgundy, acquires the duchy of Luxembourg by purchase.
- Pope Eugenius IV, concerned at the loss of papal authority, transfers the Council of Basel (convoked in 1431) from Switzerland to Ferrara in Italy. Defying the Pope, most members of the council stay in Basel. They then seek his excommunication and elect Pope Felix V, who is antipope from 1439 to 1449.

February 12 Richard, Duke of York, the English lieutenant in France, takes the French town of Pontoise, northwest of Paris.

February 21 King James I of Scotland is murdered in Perth by a group of nobles because of his efforts to reform government. He is succeeded by his son, James II.

April 4 A conspiracy against King Charles VII of France by the Dukes Charles I of Bourbon, John II of Alençon, René I of Anjou, John V of Brittany, and Count John IV of Armagnac collapses.

November 11 The Byzantine emperor John VIII leaves Constantinople (modern Istanbul, Turkey) for Rome on a mission to seek assistance against the Ottoman Turks.

December 9 The Holy Roman Emperor Sigismund dies. He is succeeded as king of Hungary by Albert V, Duke of Austria. The Bohemians, however, refuse to accept Albert as their king.

1438

- A baronial rebellion forces King Eric VII of Denmark, Norway, and Sweden to flee from Denmark to the Swedish island of Gotland, where he resorts to piracy. The Swedes also revolt and a diet appoints Charles Knutson as regent.

March 3 The Nicaean emperor John VIII Palaeologus and a Greek delegation arrive to attend the General Council of Ferrara in Italy to obtain support from the West. His attendance leads to the agreement uniting the Eastern and Western churches, rejected by his subjects.

March 18 Albert V, Duke of Austria, is elected Holy Roman Emperor as Albert II.

May 21 Niccolò Piccinino enters Bologna on behalf of Filippo Maria Visconti, Duke of Milan. Following the renewal of war between Milan and Venice, he then invades Venetian territory.

July 7 The Pragmatic Sanction of Bourges is published. It is a declaration by a council of the French church held by King Charles VII of France restricting papal authority in France.

September 9 King Edward of Portugal dies. He is succeeded by his infant son, Alfonso V. The regency is held by the queen mother, Leonor, sister of King Alfonso V of Aragon.

1439

- Devaraya II, king of the Hindu kingdom of Vijayanagar in southern India unsuccessfully attacks the neighboring Bāhmanī shahdom.
- Georgios Gemistos Plethon, a Greek delegate to the Council of Florence, prompts the Florentine ruler Cosimo de' Medici to found the Florentine Academy.
- King Eric VII of Denmark, Norway, and Sweden is deposed from the Danish and Swedish thrones.

January 10 The General Council of Ferrara reassembles in Florence.

July 6 English and French embassies meet at the Congress of Calais in France. They fail to make peace as the English will not renounce King Henry VI of England's title to be king of France, but the English make a truce with Philip the Good, Duke of Burgundy (on September 28).

July 6 The union of the Latin and Greek churches is proclaimed at the Council of Florence. Despite the subscription of the Byzantine emperor John VIII and his delegation to the union, the citizens of Constantinople (modern Istanbul, Turkey) refuse to accept it.

September 13 The English garrison of Meaux, east of Paris, France, surrenders to the French.

October 27 The Holy Roman Emperor Albert II dies. He is succeeded as king of Hungary by King Władysław III of Poland.

November 2 King Charles VII of France publishes a *grande ordonnance* designed to organize and discipline French troops.

November 5 The General Council of Basel elects Amadeus VIII, Duke of Savoy, as the antipope Felix V. He abdicates the duchy in favor of his son.

November 9 The condottiere Francesco Sforza, serving Venice, defeats the Milanese under the condottiere Niccolò Piccinino near Riva.

SCIENCE, TECHNOLOGY, AND MEDICINE

Exploration

1436

- The Chinese scholar Fei Hsin writes *Hsing-cha-sheng-Ian/Description of the Star Raft*, an eyewitness account of the Chinese admiral Cheng Ho's voyages of discovery.

Science

1436

- The Italian cartographer Andreas Bianco prepares his *Cartes hydrographiques/Hydrographic Charts*, which consists of a map of Europe and its surrounding oceans.

1437

- Astronomers of Samarkand make the *Tables of Ulugh Beg* for the city's ruler the Mongol mathematician and astronomer Ulugh Beg; they correct several errors made in the works of Ptolemy.

Transportation

1435

- The first known dredger, the *Scraper*, is built at Middelburg, the Netherlands, to help keep access to the port clear.

1439

- Paddles and sluices alongside the lock gates are used for the first time to control the flow of water at locks on canals around Milan, Italy.

ARTS AND IDEAS

Architecture

1436

- The dome of Florence Cathedral in Italy, designed by the Italian artist and architect Filippo Brunelleschi, is completed. This marks the completion of the cathedral (known as the Duomo and as Santa Maria del Fiore), though it is ten years before the lantern surmounting the dome is added. Work began in 1296 to a design by Arnolfo di Cambio, enlarged by Francesco Talenti in the 1350s.

- Work begins on the Church of Santo Spirito in Florence, Italy, designed by the Italian artist and architect Filippo Brunelleschi. The most fully realized of his designs, it is a central work of the early Renaissance. It is completed late in the century.

1437

- The Casa d'Oro (Palazzo Contarini) in Venice, designed by the Italian architects Giovanni Bon, Bartolomeo Bon, and Matteo Raverti, is completed. It is one of the last Gothic buildings to be built in Venice.
- The Church of Santa Maria degli Angeli in Florence, Italy, designed by the Italian architect Filippo Brunelleschi, is completed. Its design is strongly influenced by the architecture of ancient Rome. It is the first domed and centrally planned church of the Renaissance.

Arts

1435

- *c. 1435* Italian artist Jacopo della Quercia sculpts *The Expulsion of Adam and Eve* for the portal of the Church of San Petronio in Bologna, Italy.
- *c. 1435* Italian artist Pisanello (Antonio Pisano) paints the fresco *St. George and the Princess* in the Church of Sant'Anastasia in Verona, Italy.
- *c. 1435* Swiss artist Konrad Witz paints his *Heilspiegel Altarpiece*.
- Italian architect and writer on art Leon Battista Alberti writes *De pictura/On Painting*, an influential treatise on painting, written in Latin. It contains the first description of linear perspective. The Italian version *Della pittura/On Painting* appears in 1436.

1436

- Flemish artist Jan van Eyck paints *The Virgin with Canon van der Paele*.
- Italian artist Paolo Uccello paints the fresco *Equestrian Portrait of Sir John Hawkwood* in Florence Cathedral, Italy.

1437

- Flemish artist Jan van Eyck draws *St. Barbara*.
- Italian artist Fra Filippo Lippi paints *The Madonna and Child (The Tarquinia Madonna)* and the first two of his *Annunciations*.

1438

- *c. 1438* Flemish artist Rogier van der Weyden paints *The Descent from the Cross*.
- *c. 1438* Italian artist Pisanello (Antonio Pisano) sculpts a medal of Emperor John Palaeologus.
- Italian artist Fra Filippo Lippi paints *Madonna Enthroned with Saints (Barbadori Altarpiece)*.
- Italian artist Lucca della Robbia sculpts the *Cantoria* (a singers' gallery) to go above the south sacristy door in Florence Cathedral, Italy.

1439

- Flemish artist Jan van Eyck paints *Portrait of Margaret van Eyck*.
- Italian artists Domenico Veneziano and Piero della Francesca paint the frescoes *The Life of the Virgin* (now lost) in the Church of Sant'Egidio in Florence.

Literature and Language

1435
- Italian historian and humanist Flavio Biondo publishes *De verbis Romanae locutionis/On the Words of Roman Speech.*

c. **1436**
- English mystic Margery Kempe completes *The Book of Margery Kempe*, the earliest "autobiography" in English literature, which was dictated to a scribe as Kempe was illiterate.

c. **1437**
- The anonymous English poem "The Libel of English Policy" appears. It urges the expansion of English trade and the exploitation of England's sea-power.

Music

1436
- French composer Guillaume Dufay composes the collection of motets *Nuper rosarum flores* to commemorate the completion of the dome of Florence Cathedral, designed by Filippo Brunelleschi. The structure of the music reflects the mathematical ratios Brunelleschi used in designing the dome.

SOCIETY

Education

1438
- Henry Chichele, archbishop of Canterbury, founds All Souls College at Oxford University in England.

1439
- Godshouse is founded in Cambridge, England, as a "teachers' training college."

Religion

1435
- The Italian friar Francesco de Paolo founds the religious order the Minims (Ordo Fratrum Minimorum).
- The Nalandaa monastery is founded in Tibet by Rong-ston sMra-ba'I Seng-ge, one of the most important scholar monks in the country.

1437
July 31 The General Council of Basel summons Pope Eugenius IV to answer its charges of disobedience to its decrees due to his exercising of sole power.

1438
January 5 Pope Eugenius IV opens a General Council in Ferrara, Italy. He has transferred the General Council here from Basel in order to meet with the delegation from the Byzantine emperor, but most of the council members refuse to comply. He thus withdraws his recognition of the council.
January 24 The General Council of Basel decrees the suspension of Pope Eugenius IV from the exercise of papal authority.

1439
June 25 The General Council of Basel declares Pope Eugenius IV deposed from the papacy as a result of the council's antipapal measures.

BIRTHS & DEATHS

1435
- Andrea del Verrocchio, Florentine painter and sculptor who taught Leonardo da Vinci, born in Florence (–1488).
- Zheng He or Cheng Ho, Chinese admiral who extended his country's economic influence in southern Asia, dies in China (*c.* 64).

1436
- Cardinal Francisco Jiménes de Cisnéros, religious reformer, grand inquisitor, and regent of Spain 1506 and 1516–17 born in Torrelaguna, Spain (–1517).
June 6 Regiomontanus (Johann Müller), bishop of Regensburg, German astronomer and mathematician who was responsible for the revival of trigonometry, born in Königsberg, archbishopric of Mainz (–1476).

1437
- Isaac Abrabanel, Jewish statesman, philosopher, and biblical commentator, born in Lisbon, Portugal (–1509).
- Nicholas de Clamanges (original name Nicolas Poillevilain), theologian and humanist, advocate of ecclesiastical reform, dies in Paris, France (*c.* 74).
February 21 James I, King of Scotland 1406–37, son of Robert III, assassinated in Perth, Scotland (*c.* 43).

December 9 Sigismund, Holy Roman Emperor 1433–37, King of Hungary 1387–1437, King of Germany 1411–37, King of Bohemia 1419–37, and King of the Lombards 1431–37, last emperor of the Luxembourg dynasty, dies in Znojmo, Bohemia (69).

1438
- Domenico Veneziano, Italian Renaissance painter, one of the founders of the Florentine school of painting, born (–1461).
- Melozzo da Forli, Italian painter of the Umbrian school noted particularly for his frescoes, born in Forli, near Ravenna, Italy (–1494).

1440–1444

POLITICS, GOVERNMENT, AND ECONOMICS

Politics and Government

1440

- Grand Prince Sigismund of Lithuania is murdered. He is succeeded by Casimir (Kazimierz) IV Jagiellończyk, brother of King Władysław III of Poland.
- Itzcoatl, the fourth Aztec king, dies, having established his primacy in the valley of Mexico. He is succeeded by Montezuma I.
- Pope Eugenius IV declares a crusade against the Ottoman Turks.
- Queen Leonor is deposed from being regent for her son, King Alfonso V of Portugal, in favor of his brother Peter, Duke of Coimbra, because of her Aragonese links.
- The Swiss canton of Uri recovers Leventina from Milan.

February 2   Frederick III Habsburg, Duke of Styria, is elected Holy Roman Emperor.

February 15   King Charles VII of France calls his last meeting of the Estates General (assembly of representatives of the aristocracy, clergy, and commons) of northern France to Bourges, but it is not held because of "the Praguerie." This baronial revolt, headed by the dauphin Louis and the Dukes of Bourbon, Brittany, and Alençon, is defeated in a two-month campaign. Charles hereafter regularly raises taxes without calling for assent from the Estates General.

April 9   Christopher III of Bavaria, nephew of King Eric VII of Sweden and Norway, is elected king of Denmark. Royal authority has now been lost to the nobles.

June 29   Florentine and papal forces defeat Milanese forces under the condottiere Niccolò Piccinino at Anghiari, to the northeast of Arezzo. Florence thus gains Borgo San Sepolcro.

September 20   Frederick I, Elector of Brandenburg, dies. He is succeeded by his son, Frederick II.

November 2   The Swiss canton of Schwyz begins a war against the city of Zürich, which it prevents from seizing from Schwyz the lands of the last Count of Toggenburg.

November 24   The judicial murder of William, Earl of Douglas, by James II's councilors begins a feud between the Scottish crown and the Douglas family.

1441

- A revolt of serfs breaks out in Denmark.
- Frederick II, Elector of Brandenburg, declares a public peace for Germany.

- King Władysław III of Poland and Hungary raises the siege of Belgrade by the Ottoman Turks.
- The Cocom dynasty of Mayapán is overthrown by Ah Xupan and their empire breaks up in civil war.
- The first *tokusei* is issued in Japan, an edict remitting debts. It proves difficult to enforce.
- The Japanese shogun (military ruler) Yoshinori is murdered by his enemy Akamatsu Mitsuzuka.
- The Mayan city of Mayapán, in modern Mexico, is destroyed in a revolt. The New Mayan Empire disintegrates and its cities are abandoned.
- The Peace of Copenhagen ends a commercial war between the Hanse and Flanders.

February 21   Venice annexes Ravenna following a revolt there against the Pope, as secular ruler, assisted by Venetian forces.

April 2   Cardinal Giovanni Vitelleschi, the commander of the papal forces in Ravenna, is murdered.

September 8   King Christopher of Denmark is elected king of Sweden.

September 19   The French take the town of Pontoise, northwest of Paris, completing their recovery of the Ile-de-France from the English.

October 23   An ecclesiastical court in England condemns Eleanor Cobham, wife of Humphrey, Duke of Gloucester, for sorcery in an alleged attempt on the life of King Henry VI of England. This may be seen as a move by Henry Beaufort, the chancellor, against his opponent, Gloucester.

November 20   By the Treaty of Cavriana (published December 10), Milan and Venice make peace through the mediation of Francesco Sforza, the Venetian captain who has married Bianca, daughter and heir of Filippo Maria Visconti, Duke of Milan.

1442

- Frederick II, Elector of Brandenburg, suppresses the civic liberties of his capital, Berlin-Cologne.
- János Hunyadi, Voivode (governor) of Transylvania, defeats the Ottoman Turks invading his lands.
- King Charles VII of France takes the town of Dax in a campaign against the English in Gascony.
- The Norwegians accept King Christopher of Denmark and Sweden as their king, in place of King Eric VII.

June 2   René I, Duke of Anjou, escapes from Naples on its capture by King Alfonso V of Aragon.

June 14   The Swiss city of Zürich allies with Frederick of Austria against the Swiss Confederation.

1443

- A commercial treaty is made between King John II of Castile and the Hanseatic League.
- The Albanian national hero George Castriota, known as Skanderbeg, begins the revolt of Albania against the

Ottoman Turks, having served with them against János Hunyadi, Voivode (governor) of Transylvania.

- The Parlement of Toulouse, temporarily established in 1420, is reorganized as a court of appeal for southwest France. It is thus the first provincial parlement in France.

February 26   King Alfonso V of Aragon enters the Italian kingdom of Naples, where he is recognized as king.

May 16   The General Council of Basel holds its last general session. Disputes lasted until 1449 when the council is finally dissolved.

June 5   Bologna revolts and expels the condottiere Niccolò Piccinino.

August 8   John Beaufort, Duke of Somerset, lands at Cherbourg on the northern French coast in a campaign planned to relieve the English in Gascony.

September 28   Pope Eugenius IV returns to Rome. The General Council is transferred there from Florence, though its later history is not known.

November 10   A crusading army led by János Hunyadi, Voivode (governor) of Transylvania, defeats the Ottoman Turks at Niš, Serbia. He subsequently also takes the city of Sofia.

November 21   Philip the Good, Duke of Burgundy, seizes the city of Luxembourg.

December 12   In the Battle of Zlatica, the Ottoman Turks repulse János Hunyadi, Voivode (governor) of Transylvania, from Thrace.

December 21   John Beaufort, Duke of Somerset, retires to Normandy in northern France after raiding the duchy of Anjou on behalf of England.

1444

- George of Poděbrady becomes leader of the Ultraquists in Bohemia.
- János Hunyadi, Voivode (governor) of Transylvania, defeats the Ottoman Turks on Mt. Kunovica, Serbia.
- Mohammad Shah, ruler of Malacca, dies. He is succeeded by Raja Ibrahim, his youngest son.

May 28   By the Treaty of Tours, King Charles VII of France makes a truce for two years with King Henry VI of England, who becomes engaged to marry Margaret, daughter of René I, Duke of Anjou.

June 12   The Ottoman sultan Murad II makes a truce for ten years at Szeged, Bulgaria, with the crusaders, with the Albanian nationalist Skanderbeg, and with George Barnković, who is restored as despot of Serbia.

August 26   The Swiss are defeated at St. Jakob on the Birs by French freebooters ("écorcheurs") sent by King Charles VII of France to assist Frederick of Austria.

September 9   Cardinal Cesarini absolves King Władysław III of Poland and Hungary, János Hunyadi, Voivode of Transylvania, and other crusaders from their oaths to keep the ten-year truce agreed with the Ottoman sultan Murad II.

September 23   Giovanni Francesco di Gonzaga, Marquess of Mantua, dies. He is succeeded by his son, Federico I.

October 21   By the Treaty of Zofingen, King Charles VII of France makes peace with the Swiss Confederation.

November 10   The Ottoman sultan Murad II destroys the crusading army at Varna, Bulgaria. János Hunyadi, Voivode (governor) of Transylvania, escapes; cardinal Cesarini disappears; and King Władysław III of Poland and Hungary is killed.

SCIENCE, TECHNOLOGY, AND MEDICINE

Technology

1440

- German craftsman Johann Gutenberg of Mainz, Germany, is the first European to develop a method of printing by movable metal type, improving on the current Chinese and Korean methods.

ARTS AND IDEAS

Architecture

c. 1440

- Work begins on the Pazzi Chapel in Florence, Italy, designed by the Italian architect Filippo Brunelleschi. It is completed in the 1460s, with changes made by other architects.

1444

- Work begins on the Medici-Riccardi Palace in Florence, Italy, designed by the Italian architect Michelozzo di Bartolommeo. Influenced by the works of the architect Filippo Brunelleschi, the design marks a new sophistication in Italian palaces.

Arts

1440

c. 1440   German artist Stephan Lochner paints *Madonna of the Rose Bower*.

c. 1440   Italian artist Donatello (Donato di Niccolò) sculpts the *Cantoria* (a singers' gallery) to go above the north sacristy door in Florence Cathedral, Italy.

- Italian artist Fra Angelico (Guido di Pietro) paints *Madonna and Saints (San Marco Altarpiece)*, one of the first of many works at the monastery of San Marco in Florence, Italy.

c. 1441

- Italian artist Pisanello (Antonio Pisano) paints *Portrait of Lionello d'Este*.

1442

- Italian artist Lorenzo Ghiberti completes his bronze reliquary of St. Zenobius for Florence Cathedral in Italy.

1443

- Italian artists Andrea del Castagno (Andrea di Bartolo) and Michele Giambono create the mosaic *Death of the Virgin* in the Mascoli Chapel in St. Mark's Cathedral in Venice.

1444

- Italian artist Pisanello (Antonio Pisano) sculpts a medal of Leonello d'Este.

- Italian artist Sassetta (Stefano di Giovanni) completes his *Sansepolcro Altarpiece*, which consists of scenes from the life of St. Francis of Assisi.
- Swiss artist Konrad Witz paints *The Miraculous Draft of Fishes (Altarpiece of St. Peter's)*.

Literature and Language

1440

c. 1440   Catalan poet Jordi de Sant Jordi completes his *Enuigs*, a personal narrative written in Catalan.

July 2   French writer Charles d'Orléans, who was taken prisoner by the English at the Battle of Agincourt in 1415, is released after 25 years' imprisonment. During his captivity he wrote some of the finest 15th-century short lyrics of courtly love.

1442

- Italian architect and writer on art Leon Battista Alberti publishes *Della tranquilità dell'animo/On Peace of Mind*.

c. 1443

- Italian writer and humanist Enea Silvius Piccolomini (later Pope Pius II) publishes the novel *Historia de duobus amantibus/Story of Two Lovers*.

1444

- Italian scholar and humanist Lorenzo Valla publishes *De elegantia Latinae linguae/Elegances of the Latin Language*. It is first printed in 1471.
- Spanish writer Juan de Mena writes his long poem *El Laberinto de Fortuna/The Labyrinth of Fortune*.

Music

1440

- The clavichord, ancestor of the harpsichord and piano, is shown in a German manuscript. This is the first detailed evidence of its invention though some illustrations from the 1430s also show the instrument.

Theater and Dance

1443

September 1   Japanese dramatist Seami Motokiyo, perhaps the greatest of the No dramatists, dies. He was the son of Kan'ami Kiyotsugo, one of the founding figures of No. Motokiyo wrote nearly half of the classic No repertoire, as well as essays on the theater, including the major work *Kadensho/Book of the Flowery Tradition*.

Thought and Scholarship

1440

c. 1440   Italian scholar and humanist Lorenzo Valla publishes his treatise *De libero arbitrio/On Free Will*.

- German churchman and philosopher Nicholas of Cusa (Nicolaus Cusanus) publishes *De docta ignorantia/On Learned Ignorance*.
- Italian scholar and humanist Lorenzo Valla publishes *De falso credita et ementita Constantini donatione/The Donation of Constantine*, which demonstrates the falsity

BIRTHS & DEATHS

1440

c. 1440   Pedro Arias Dávila, Spanish soldier who founded the first Spanish colonies in the Americas, born in Segovia, Castile (–1531).

- Itzcoátl, Aztec ruler of Tenochtitlán (near modern Mexico City) 1428–40, who formed alliances with the states of Texcoco and Tlacopan to form the nucleus of the Aztec empire, dies.
- Margery Kempe, English mystic, author of one of the earliest English autobiographies, dies in Lynn, Norfolk, England (*c.* 67).

February 22   Ladislas Posthumous, son of the late Holy Roman Emperor Albert II, is born. The Bohemians accept him as their king.

July 9   Jan van Eyck, Flemish painter of portraits and religious subjects, including the *Adoration of the Lamb* (1432), dies in Bruges, Netherlands, now in Belgium.

1442

- King Alexander I the Great of Georgia, who has reunited the kingdom, dies.

- Pierre Cauchon, the pro-English bishop of Beauvais who presided over the trial of Joan d'Arc (1430), dies (*c.* 71).

April 28   Edward IV, King of England 1461–70 and 1471–83, a leading participant in the Wars of the Roses (1455–83), born in Rouen, France (–1483).

1443

- Rodolphus Agricola (original name Roelof Huysman), Dutch humanist, born in Baflo, Groningen, Netherlands (–1485).

February 24   Matthias I Corvinus, King of Hungary 1458–90, born in Koloszvár, Transylvania, now Cluj, Romania (–1490).

April 12   Henry Chichele, archbishop of Canterbury 1414–43, dies (*c.* 80).

May 31   Margaret Beaufort, Countess of Richmond and Derby, patron of learning, and mother of King Henry VII of England, born (–1509).

1444

- Donato Bramante da Urbino, Italian architect who introduced the High Renaissance stye of architecture, born in Monte Asdruvaldo, duchy of Urbino (–1514).

March 9   Leonardo Bruni, Italian humanist scholar, whose *Historiarum Florentini populi libri XII/Twelve Books of Histories of the Florentine People* (1610) is the first to be based on a critical examination of the sources, also writer of *Vita di Dante/A Life of Dante*, dies in Florence (*c.* 74).

c. July 8, 1444   Pietro Paulo Vergerio, Italian educator who wrote *De ingenuis moribus et liberalibus studii/On the Manners of a Gentleman and Liberal Studies*, which formed the basis of liberal education methods in Italy, dies in Budapest, Hungary (*c.* 75).

October 15   Niccolò Piccinino, the condottiere (military commander) in the service of Milan, dies.

of the Donation of Constantine, a document dating from 1236 that claimed to establish the papacy's claim to temporal power. Valla's treatise is an example of the growing sophistication of textual analysis.

- Italian writer and humanist Enea Silvius Piccolomini (later Pope Pius II) publishes *De gestis concilii Basiliensis/History of the Council of Basel*.

1442

- Arabic scholar Al-Maqrīzī completes his *Al-Mawāiz w-al-Itibār fi Dhikr al-Khitat w-al-Āthār/An Account of the New Settlements and Remains*, on the geography, history, and antiquities of Egypt.

1443

- German churchman and philosopher Nicholas of Cusa (Nicolaus Cusanus) publishes *De visio Dei/The Vision of God*.

1444

- French historian Enguerrand de Monstrelet completes his *Chronicle*, a history of France from 1400 to 1444. It is considered a continuation of Froissart's work, which ended in 1400.

SOCIETY

Education

1440

- A school is founded at Eton in England, at the instigation of English king, Henry VI.

1441

- Bordeaux University is established in France.
- King Henry VI of England founds King's College at Cambridge University in England.

Everyday Life

1442

- The arrival of the Rom (gypsies) in Europe at Barcelona is reported.

1443

- Ashikaga Yoshimasa, Shogun (military ruler) of Japan, creates rules for the tea ceremony.

Religion

1440

October 26   Gilles de Rais, a Breton noble who is an alchemist and a black magician, is executed in Nantes after having been convicted of numerous crimes including necromancy, satanism, and infanticide.

1445–1449

POLITICS, GOVERNMENT, AND ECONOMICS

Politics and Government

1445

- By a secret ordinance, King Charles VII of France establishes a regular army of cavalry ("*compagnies de Grande Ordonnance*") which is first employed to clear unoccupied France of the "*écorcheurs*" (freebooters).
- János Hunyadi, Voivode (governor) of Transylvania, is elected regent of Hungary for the infant king, Ladislas V.

- King Mohammad VII of Granada is deposed for the third and final time. He is succeeded by his nephew, Mohammad X, who is in turn expelled and succeeded by Sa'd al-Musta'in.
- King Zara Ya'qub of Ethiopia declares war on Mogadishu and Adal (in present-day Somalia).
- Raja Ibrahim, ruler of Malacca, is murdered by Tun Ali, the cousin of Raja Kassum, his older brother. Raja Kassum assumes the throne, taking the title of sultan.
- The sultan of Adal (in present-day Somalia), Ahmed Badly Walasma, is killed by King Zara Ya'qub of Ethiopia. This turns the tide against the Islamic alliance that is threatening Christian Ethiopia.

April 23   King Henry VI of England marries Margaret of Anjou.

July 7   Grand Duke Vasili II of Moscow is defeated and captured by forces of Ulug-Mahmed, Khan of the "Golden Horde." He is released and confirmed as grand duke. Ulug-Mahmed is subsequently murdered and succeeded by his son Mahmudek.

December 26 King Zara Yakub of Ethiopia defeats an invasion by the sultan of Ifat, near Egubba. The sultanate of Ifat now declines.

1446

- Alam succeeds Mohammad IV as shah of Delhi, India.
- The expelled Mohammad X recovers the Spanish kingdom of Granada.

February 2 Muscovite malcontents led by Dmitri Shemiaka, son of Prince Juri of Halich, seize the city and blind Grand Duke Vasili II of Moscow. He is imprisoned but soon released.

June 12 By the Treaty of Constance, Frederick of Austria makes peace with the Swiss Confederation.

1447

- Shah Rukh, the son and successor of Tamerlane, Grand Amir of the Mongols, dies. This is followed by the dissolution of the Timurid house of Herat: the Turkoman dynasty of the White Sheep now rules Persia, except for Khorasan, from Tabriz.

February 17 Grand Duke Vasili II of Moscow returns to the city following the flight of the rebel leader Dmitri Shemiaka.

February 23 Humphrey, Duke of Gloucester, is arrested. He dies soon afterwards, and it is rumored that he has been murdered.

March 6 Tommaso Parentucelli is elected Pope Nicholas V.

May 2 Grand Prince Casimir (Kazimierz) IV of Lithuania grants a great charter of liberties to the Lithuanian nobility at Vilnius.

June 25 Grand Prince Casimir (Kazimierz) IV Jagiellończyk of Lithuania is crowned as King Casimir IV of Poland. It is now presumed that King Władysław III of Poland and Hungary was killed by the Ottoman Turks at Varna, Bulgaria, in 1444; his body was never recovered leading to tales of apparitions in different parts of Europe and Asia.

August 13 Filippo Maria Visconti, Duke of Milan, dies. The Milanese establish the Ambrosian Republic, but a war of succession follows. Visconti's son-in-law, Francesco Sforza, claiming to be his heir, is opposed by Venice and King Alfonso V of Aragon, who also claims the duchy. Charles, Duke of Orléans, also claims Milan.

1448

February 2 Envoys of Pope Nicholas V conclude the Concordat of Vienna with Frederick III, Elector of Brandenburg, and other German princes. In return for the right to exercise some papal powers in their territories, they abandon the General Council of Basel.

March 16 The English surrender the town of Le Mans in France to the French.

April 28 An ordinance issued by King Charles VII of France establishes regular companies of "Free Archers."

May 5 War breaks out between England and Scotland.

June 20 Karl Knutsson is elected as King Charles VIII of Sweden.

July 7 The surviving members of the General Council of Basel move to Lausanne.

September 1 Count Christian of Oldenburg is elected as king of Denmark–Norway.

September 9 George of Poděbrady, the leader of the

Hussites in Bohemia, occupies the capital city Prague in a bid to seize political power.

September 15 Francesco Sforza defeats the Venetians at Caravaggio, to the east of Milan.

October 17 The Ottoman sultan Murad II defeats János Hunyadi, Voivode (governor) of Transylvania, at the second Battle of Kosovo Polje in Serbia and thus regains control of the Balkans, excluding Albania.

October 19 Francesco Sforza makes an alliance with the Venetians against Milan.

October 31 The Byzantine emperor John VIII dies without issue. He is succeeded by Constantine XI, despot of the Morea.

December 12 The Ottoman sultan Murad II ravages the Morea.

1449

- King Devaraya of the Hindu kingdom of Vijayanagar in southern India dies. He is succeeded by his son Mallikarjuna.

March 24 The English forces sack the town of Fougères in Brittany, France, and so give King Charles VII of France cause to renew the war between the two countries.

April 7 The antipope Felix V abdicates in the General Council of Basel at Lausanne.

April 25 The General Council of Basel dissolves itself due to sporadic and weak attendance, meaning attendees could not make valid decisions.

May 24 King Alfonso V of Portugal defeats a rebellion by his brother Peter, who is killed, at Alfarrobeira, Portugal.

September 1 The Ming dynasty Chinese emperor Zhengtong is defeated and captured while attacking the Oirats of Western Mongolia. They briefly besiege Beijing, but withdraw when the defenders elect a new emperor. Zhengtong is held captive for one year, and his brother, Jingtai, succeeds him as emperor on September 17.

October 21 King Christian I Oldenburg of Denmark is deposed as king of Norway and King Charles VIII of Sweden is elected in his place.

October 29 The English surrender Rouen, the capital of Normandy, France, to King Charles VII of France.

SCIENCE, TECHNOLOGY, AND MEDICINE

Science

1446

- The Italian historian and humanist Flavio Biondo publishes *Roma instaurata/Rome Restored*, a survey of Roman archeology.

Technology

1449

- The first British patent of invention is issued by Henry VI to Flemish-born John of Utznam for his technique for making stained glass for Eton College. Patents rapidly become the recognized way of asserting rights over an invention.

ARTS AND IDEAS

Architecture

1446

- Work begins on the Tempio Malatestiano (a church converted into a memorial to a local lord) in Rimini, Italy. It is designed by the Italian architect and writer on art Leon Battista Alberti. Work ends about 1455, though the project, based on reviving the style and grandeur of Ancient Roman architecture, is not completed.

1447

- The Üç Serefeli Mosque in Edirne, the first centrally planned mosque in the Ottoman Empire, is completed. Built in the Ottoman style, it is noted in particular for its fine minarets.

1449

- After their defeat by Mongol invaders, China's Ming dynasty begins the rebuilding of the Great Wall, reconstructing it 9 m/25 ft high, 4 m/12 ft wide, and with brick facing.

Arts

1445

- *c.* 1445   Flemish artist Dirk Bouts paints *The Infancy Altarpiece.*
- *c.* 1445   French artist Jean Fouquet paints *Portrait of Charles VII of France.*
- *c.* 1445   Italian artist Andrea del Castagno (Andrea di Bartolo) paints the fresco *The Last Supper* in the Convent of Sant'Apollonia in Florence, Italy.
- *c.* 1445   Italian artist Bernardo Rossellino sculpts the tomb of Leonardo Bruni for the Church of Santa Croce in Florence, Italy.
- *c.* 1445   Italian artist Domenico Veneziano paints the *St. Lucy Altarpiece (Madonna and Child with Saints)* and *St. John in the Wilderness.*
- *c.* 1445   Italian artist Pisanello (Antonio Pisano) paints *The Apparition of the Madonna to Saints Anthony Abbot and George.*
- French artist Enguerrand Charonton paints *Coronation of the Virgin.*

c. 1446

- Netherlands artist Petrus Christus paints *Portrait of a Carthusian.*

1447

- Italian artist Fra Filippo Lippi paints *Coronation of the Virgin.*
- Italian artist Paolo Uccello paints the fresco *The Deluge* in the Church of Santa Maria Novella, in Florence, Italy.
- Italian artist Sano di Pietro paints *St. Bernadino Preaching in the Campo.*

BIRTHS & DEATHS

1445

- Josquin des Prés, Renaissance composer of motets, masses, and chansons, born in Condé-sur-l'Escaut (–1521).
- Sandro Botticelli (original name Alessandro di Mariano Filipepi), Florentine painter of the early Renaissance, whose major works include *The Birth of Venus* (*c.* 1485) and *Primavera/Spring* (1477–78), born in Florence (–1510).

March 16   Johannes Geiler von Kayserberg, preacher and theologian, born in Schaffhausen, Switzerland (–1510).

May 22   Edmund Beaufort, Duke of Somerset, English nobleman whose fight with Richard, Duke of York, led to the War of the Roses, is killed at the Battle of St. Albans, Hertfordshire (*c.* 39).

1446

- William Grocyn, scholar and early English humanist, born in Colerne, Wiltshire, England (–1519).

February 2   Vittorino da Feltre (Vittore dei Ramboldini), Italian humanist educator, dies in Mantua, Italy (*c.* 68).

April 15   Filippo Brunelleschi, Florentine architect and engineer, pioneer of early Renaissance architecture, whose works include the dome of Florence Cathedral (1420–36), dies in Florence (*c.* 69).

1447

- Bāyezīd II, sultan of the Ottoman Empire 1481–1512, who consolidated the empire in the Balkans, Asia Minor, and eastern Mediterranean, born in Demotika, Thrace, Ottoman Empire (–1512).
- Philippe de Commynes (or Comines), statesman and chronicler, whose *Mémoires* (1524) are considered one of the finest historical works of his age, born in Comines, Flanders, Belgium (–1511).

February 23   Humphrey Plantagenet, Duke of Gloucester, first major patron of humanism in England, dies in London, England (*c.* 56).

March 6   St. Colette, abbess and reformer of the Poor Clares or Clarissines, dies in Ghent, now in Belgium (66).

1448

January 6   Christopher III of Bavaria, King of Denmark, Norway, and Sweden, dies.

1449

- Aldus Manutius the Elder, leading Italian printer, publisher, and typographer, founder of the Aldine Press, born in Bassiano, Italy (–1515).
- Domenico Ghirlandaio (original name Domenico di Tommaso Bigordi), Italian Renaissance painter, noted for frescoes such as *The Birth of the Virgin* (1486–90), born in Florence, Italy (–1494).

January 1   Lorenzo de' Medici the Magnificent, statesman and ruler of Florence 1453–92, born in Florence, Italy (–1492).

October 21   George Plantagenet, Duke of Clarence, English nobleman who took part in a conspiracy against his brother King Edward IV of England, born in Dublin, Ireland (–1478).

1448

c. 1448 Italian artist Piero della Francesca paints the *Madonna della Misericordia (Madonna of Mercy) Altarpiece.*

- Flemish artist Rogier van der Weyden paints *The Last Judgement Altarpiece.*
- Italian artist Andrea del Castagno (Andrea di Bartolo) completes the fresco series *Famous Men and Women* in the Villa Carducci in Legnaia, near Florence, Italy, and paints *David* on a ceremonial leather shield.

1449

- Flemish artist Petrus Christus paints *St. Eligius as a Goldsmith.*

Literature and Language

1445

- Spanish writer and anthologist Juan Alfonso de Baena compiles *Cancionero*, an important anthology of about 600 Spanish poems from the late 14th and early 15th century.

1446

- King Sejong tries to introduce a simpler 28-character alphabet to replace Chinese ideographs in Korea. It is resisted, but a system combining ideographs with an alphabet will eventually evolve.

Thought and Scholarship

c. 1448

- Russian churchman Evfimi, archbishop of Novgorod, organizes the *Novgorodsko-Sofisky Svod/Novgorod-Sophian Digest*, a compilation of Russian historical annals.

1449

- Italian scholar and humanist Poggio Bracciolini publishes his dialogue *Contra hypocritas/Against Hypocrites.*

SOCIETY

Education

1446

- Margaret of Anjou, Queen of England, establishes Queen's College at Cambridge University, England.

Media and Communication

1449

- The *Journal Bourgeois de Paris*, which records events and everyday life, and personal feelings, is written by an unknown Parisian in France.

Religion

1445

- D'Ge-'dun-grub, nephew of Tshong-kha-pa (the founder of the dGe-lugs-pa or "Yellow Hat" monastic order), founds the monastery of bKra-shis-lhun-po in Tibet, on the edge of the lands ruled by the princes of Rin-Spung, supporters of the rival "Red Hats."

1450–1454

POLITICS, GOVERNMENT, AND ECONOMICS

Business and Economics

1450

- Paper currency is abandoned in China.

1454

- King Casimir (Kazimierz) IV of Poland grants vetoes on legislation and military levies to *sejmiki* (local

assemblies) of the *szlachta*, the very numerous Polish nobility in the Privilegium of Nieszawa, Poland.

- The banking and textile merchant brothers Jakob and Andreas Fugger of Augsburg, Germany, dissolve their partnership.
- Trailok, King of Ayutthaya (in modern Thailand), institutes *Sadki Na* grades which fix the permissible size of land-holdings for any individual on the basis of the number of "dignity marks" they hold. The effect is to establish a new social settlement and abolish landlessness.

October The Hanseatic League expels the city of Münster in Westphalia when exiled patricians and merchants complain of the despotism of its bishop John von Hoja, who has allied himself with populist factions.

Politics and Government

1450

c. 1450   Ijebu is conquered by Ozdua, Crown Prince of the west central African kingdom of Bornu (in present-day Nigeria).

c. 1450   The central African empire of Kanem (in present-day Chad) undergoes a period of reorganization.

- The Mongols return the former Chinese emperor Zhengtong to Beijing. His brother, the current emperor Jingtai, places him under house arrest.

February 26   After being besieged by Francesco Sforza, the Milanese Ambrosian Republic agrees to accept him as its duke.

April 15   The French defeat the last English force sent to Normandy, France, at Formigny.

June 6   Rebellion breaks out in the English counties of Kent and Sussex against members of the royal household, including the sheriff of Kent, William Crowmer, and his father-in-law James Fiennes, Lord Saye and Seal. The uprising is led by the Irish rebel "Jack Cade." The peasants control the English capital, London, from July 3 to July 5. "Jack Cade" is killed on July 12.

July 13   The city of Zürich rejoins the Swiss Confederation.

July 29   King Christian I of Denmark is crowned as king of Norway, having compelled King Charles VIII of Sweden to renounce the Norwegian crown.

August 12   The English holding the northern French port of Cherbourg surrender. King Charles VII of France's conquest of Normandy is thus completed.

August 29   The formal union of Denmark and Norway, under King Christian I, is enacted in Bergen, Norway.

September 9   Richard, Duke of York, fails in an attempt to make King Henry VI of England reconstitute his council.

1451

- Frederick II, elector of Saxony, reaches a territorial settlement with his brother William, ending the Saxon civil war known as the Bruderkrieg ("War of the Brothers").

April 19   Buhlul Khan, Afghan governor of Punjab, deposes and retires the last Sayyid (claiming descent from Mohammed's grandson Husein) sultan of Delhi, Alam Shah, and claims the throne for himself, founding the Lodi dynasty.

June 12   Bordeaux, France, capital of the duchy of Gascony and a stronghold of the English Plantagenet kings for 300 years, surrenders to French forces commanded by Jean, Count of Dunois, "the bastard of Orléans."

August 20   The port of Bayonne in the southwest of France falls to the French army, completing the French conquest of Gascony.

October   Frederick III, the Habsburg Holy Roman Emperor and guardian of Ladislas Posthumous, infant king of Hungary and Bohemia, and son of his cousin and predecessor Albert II, appoints George of Poděbrady, leader of the rival Hussite Utraquist faction, governor of Bohemia.

1452

- The grand prince of Muscovy, Vasili II the Blind, establishes a puppet Mongol khanate at Gorodets (Kasimov) on the River Oka, under Kasim, refugee brother of the Mahmud, Khan of Kazan.

- The Habsburgs abandon their claim to the city of Fribourg, Switzerland, leaving it free to ally itself with the Swiss Confederation, gaining full membership in 1481.

February 22   King James II of Scotland personally stabs and kills the powerful magnate William, Earl of Douglas, having invited the earl to Stirling Castle where he refused to dissolve his alliance with Alexander "the Tiger," Earl Crawford. William's son is obliged to submit to the king in August.

March 1   Richard, Duke of York, ends his campaign through England from Ludlow, Shropshire, to Dartford, Kent, by surrendering to King Henry VI of England. Though many of his estates rise to support his claim to the throne, Richard backs down in the face of Henry's army.

March 19   Pope Nicholas V crowns the Habsburg Frederick III as Holy Roman Emperor in Rome, Italy. Frederick will be the last emperor to be thus crowned.

April 27   The diet (assembly) of Bohemia in Prague, Bohemia, elects the leader of the Hussite Utraquists, George of Poděbrady, as regent for the young king Ladislas Posthumous.

June   Holy Roman Emperor Frederick III returns from Rome to find himself besieged in Wiener Neustadt, Austria, by an army formed of Austrian insurgents, Czech Catholics, and Magyars led by Ullrich von Cilli. They demand that he release his nephew and ward Ladislas Posthumous, the twelve-year-old king of Bohemia and Hungary. In August, Frederick gives up his ward to Ullrich von Cilli, cousin of Ladislas and rival for his guardianship. The Austrians soon eject Ullrich.

September   The city of Tabor, Bohemia, last stronghold and headquarters of the Taborites (the radical social revolutionary wing of the Hussite movement), surrenders to George of Poděbrady, leader of the reformist Utraquist wing and governor of Bohemia.

October 17   An English expeditionary force under John Talbot, Earl of Shrewsbury, lands in Guyenne, France, and a week later is welcomed into the city of Bordeaux, France, when a popular revolt ejects French royal forces.

1453

- Jihan Shah, leader of the Kara Koyunlu (Black Sheep) Uzbekh Turkoman tribal federation (rulers of Iraq), takes the Persian provinces of Fars and Isfahan from the Timurids.

1453–54   The Abbey of St. Gall allies with the Swiss Confederation, to be followed by its town in the following year.

January 6   Frederick III, the Holy Roman Emperor, grants his son Maximilian the title archduke of Austria.

April   Margrave Albert Achilles von Hohenzollern of Ansbach, brother of Frederick II of Brandenburg, accepts the verdict of the Battle of Pillenreuth of 1450 and abandons his territorial claims over the city of Nuremberg, Germany, in return for monetary compensation.

April 7   The Ottoman sultan Mehmed II besieges Constantinople, capital of the Byzantine Empire (modern Istanbul, Turkey), throwing a chain across the Golden Horn (the harbor) to prevent relief arriving by sea.

May 29   Ottoman forces under Sultan Mehmed II storm the

city of Constantinople, capital of the Byzantine Empire (modern Istanbul, Turkey), and the Byzantine emperor Constantine XI is last seen fighting on the walls of the city. Following his demise, the empire falls and the city becomes the Ottoman capital.

June 22 King John II of Castile executes his favorite, the constable of Castile, Alvaro de Luna, when the constable is accused by the queen, Isabella of Portugal, and their son Henry of employing sorcery to win influence over the king.

July 17 A French army led by the gunner Jean Bureau repels a rash assault by an English and Gascon force under John Talbot, Earl of Shrewsbury, on their fortified camp at Castillon, 30 miles east of Bordeaux, France. Talbot is killed in the rearguard and his forces are decimated.

July 23 Philip the Good, Duke of Burgundy, defeats and massacres the rebel forces of the city of Ghent at Gavre.

August King Henry VI of England becomes insane, though the fact is concealed by those associated with the loyalist Lancastrian court faction centered around the queen, Margaret of Anjou, amid fears that it might boost the cause of Richard of York.

October 19 The beleaguered port of Bordeaux, France, finally surrenders to the forces of King Charles VII of France, an event that sees the fall of the last English stronghold in Gascony and in France (excepting Calais) and ends the Hundred Years' War.

October 28 Ladislas Posthumous is crowned king of Bohemia, at the age of 13, in Prague, Bohemia. He retains George of Poděbrady as governor of the kingdom.

1454

- The imperial city of Schaffhausen, Switzerland, allies with the Swiss Confederation against the Habsburgs.

March 6 King Casimir (Kazimierz) IV of Poland proclaims the incorporation of Prussia into Poland when the Prussian Union of Cities (led by Gdańsk) and the gentry renounce allegiance to the Teutonic Order of Knights. The Thirteen Years' War follows between Poland and the Teutonic Order of Knights.

March 27 Unable to ascertain for certain the mental condition of King Henry VI of England, the House of Lords appoints Richard of York "protector and defender" of England during the period of the king's insanity.

April 9 The Peace of Lodi ends 30 years of warfare between the republic of Venice, allied with the kingdom of Naples, Savoy, and Montferrat, and the duchy of Milan, allied with Medici Florence, Genoa, and Este Mantua. It confirms the condottiere (mercenary) Francesco Sforza as Duke of Milan.

September 8 The forces of the Teutonic Order of Knights severely defeat Polish forces under King Casimir (Kazimierz) IV of Poland at Chojnice, Poland, in the first major battle of the Thirteen Years' War.

November 1 The private armies "retained" by the Percy family (Dukes of Northumberland and Earls of Egremont) fight a pitched battle at Stamford Bridge, Yorkshire, England, against forces of the Neville family (including the bishop of Durham, the Earl of Westmoreland, and the Earl of Warwick). This exemplifies the disordered state of England.

December 31 King Henry VI of England recovers his sanity, and the protectorate of Richard, Duke of York, ends. Richard leaves for the north, and the faction led by the Duke of Somerset and the queen regains control.

SCIENCE, TECHNOLOGY, AND MEDICINE

Ecology

c. 1453–57
- A series of natural disasters including blizzards, floods, drought, and earthquakes causes widespread famine and internal migration in China.

Exploration

1451
- Chinese scholar Ma Huan writes *Ying-yai-sheng-lan/ Description of the Coasts of the Ocean*, an eyewitness account of Chinese admiral Cheng Ho's voyages.

Science

1450
c. 1450 German philosopher Cardinal Nicholas de Cusa devises the first hygrometer for measuring air humidity. It consists of a ball of wool, the weight of which changes as it absorbs moisture from the atmosphere.
- Austrian astronomer George Peurbach produces the first printed almanac.
- Italian scientist Leone Alberti devises a vane anemometer and makes the first measurements of wind speeds.

1454
- Austrian astronomer Georg Peurbach completes his *New Theory of the Planets*, supporting the "sphere" model of the universe, and using new observations to improve the measurement of celestial distances.

Technology

c. 1451–56
- German craftsman Johann Gutenberg produces the first printed Bible, in Mainz, Germany, using movable, reusable, metal type. The work is printed in Gothic type, with 42 lines per page; 48 copies of the original printing currently survive.

1454
- Johann Gutenberg produces the first printed calendar, in Mainz, Germany.

Transportation

1450

- The German city of Hamburg installs navigational buoys and beacons to guide ships to and from its sea access at the mouth of the River Elbe.

ARTS AND IDEAS

Architecture

c. **1450**

- Winchester Cathedral in England is completed with the remodeling of the nave in the English style of Gothic known as Perpendicular. It is designed by the architect William of Wynford.

1451

- The House of Jacques Coeur in Bourge, France, is completed. Built for one of France's richest men, it brings together many of the finest aspects of domestic building and crafts of the day.

1452

- The Rumeli Hisar fortress in Istanbul is completed.

1454

- The Old Town Hall in Brussels, Flanders (now Belgium), an ornate Gothic building whose lavishness reflects the wealth of the town, is completed.

Arts

1450

- *c.* 1450 Flemish artist Rogier van der Weyden paints *The Entombment, Madonna with Four Saints*, and the *Braque Triptych*.
- *c.* 1450 French artist Jean Fouquet paints *The Melun Diptych*, and an enamel *Self-Portrait*.
- *c.* 1450 Italian artist Paolo Uccello paints three versions of *The Battles of San Romano*.
- *c.* 1450 Italian artist Piero della Francesca paints *The Baptism of Christ*.
- Italian artist Fra Angelico (Guido di Pietro) completes his series of frescoes in the Chapel of St. Nicholas in the Vatican, Rome. One of the best-known scenes is *St. Lawrence Distributing the Treasures of the Church*.

1451

- Italian artist Piero della Francesca paints the fresco *St. Sigismond and Sigismondo Malatesta* in the Tempio Malatestiano in Rimini, Italy.

1452

- *c.* 1452 Flemish artist Rogier van der Weyden paints *Man with an Arrow*.
- Italian artist Lorenzo Ghiberti completes the sculpting of the ten Old Testament relief scenes for the third set of bronze doors (known as the Gates of Paradise) of the Baptistry in Florence, Italy. The work began in 1425.

1453

- Italian artist Donatello (Donato di Niccolò) sculpts *The Equestrian Monument of Gattamelata*, which stands in the Piazza del Santo in Padua, Italy, and completes the bronze relief *The Miracle of the Irascible Son* for the altar of the Church of Sant'Antonio in Padua, Italy.
- Italian artist Mino da Fiesole sculpts *Portrait Bust of Piero de' Medici*.

1454

- Italian artist Piero della Francesca paints the fresco *The Resurrection* in the Palazzo Communale (the Town Hall) of Borgo San Sepolcro, Italy.

Literature and Language

c. **1450**

- Welsh poet Dafydd ab Edmwnd wins the Eisteddfod poetry competition in Wales. One of the finest poets of his day, he is best known for his love lyrics, written in Welsh.

Theater and Dance

c. **1452**

- French dramatist Arnoul Gréban writes *Mystère de la Passion/Mystery Play of the Passion*, a series of plays, taking four days to perform, representing the Christian story.

Thought and Scholarship

c. **1450**

- English chronicler John Capgrave completes his *Liber de illustribus Henricis/Book of Illustrious Henries*, the lives of 24 famous men (mostly kings and emperors) named Henry.
- Portuguese historian Fernão Lopes completes his *Crônica de D Joân I/Chronicle of the Reign of John I*.

c. **1451**

- The anonymous Korean *Koryŏ sa/History of Korea*, a history of the Koryŏ dynasty, 936–1392, is completed.

SOCIETY

Education

1450

- The Scottish prelate James Kennedy establishes St. Salvator's College, St. Andrews University, Scotland.
- The University of Barcelona is founded in Spain.

1451

- Bishop William Turnbull founds Glasgow University under the remit of a papal bull granted to King James II of Scotland by Pope Nicholas V.

1452

- The dauphin, heir to the French throne and later to be King Louis XI of France, founds Valence University for the bishops of Valence, France, in exchange for their relinquishment of secular authority.

1453

- The University of Istanbul is founded in Istanbul, in the Ottoman Empire.

Everyday Life

1450

- Agnès Sorel becomes the first woman to hold the semiofficial position of mistress of the king of France.

Religion

1450

- *c.* 1450 The Spanish theologian Juan de Torquemada completes his *Summa de ecclesia/The Church*, which defends papal supremacy in spiritual matters.
- King Zara Ya'qub of Ethiopia calls a church council, which brings together the divided Ethiopian Coptic monastic movement.

BIRTHS & DEATHS

1450

c. 1450 Bartholomeu Dias (or Diaz), Portuguese navigator, who led the first European expedition round the Cape of Good Hope (1488), born (–1500).

c. 1450 Hieronymus Bosch (pseudonym of Jerome van Aeken), highly original Dutch painter, associated with complex and fantastic symbolism and allegory, whose major works include *The Temptation of St. Antony* and *The Garden of Earthly Delights*, born in 's-Hertogenbosch, Brabant (–1516).

c. 1450 John Cabot (Italian: Giovanni Caboto) Italian-born navigator and explorer, who discovered and laid claim to parts of North America (June 24, 1497) for the English crown, born, possibly in Genoa (–*c.* 1499).

c. 1450 William Warham, archbishop of Canterbury 1504–32 who was opposed to King Henry VIII's anticlerical policies, born in Malshanger, Hampshire, England (–1532).

- Francia (Francesco di Marco di Giacomo Raibolini), Italian artist of the Renaissance, whose works include *Assumption* (1504), born in Bologna, Italy (–*c.* 1518).
- Francisco de Almeida, soldier, explorer, and first viceroy of Portuguese India, born in Lisbon, Portugal (–1510).

1451

c. 1451 Nicolás de Ovando, first royal governor of the West Indies 1502–09, who established a community in Santo Domingo and instituted the *encomienda* system of forced Indian labor, born in Brozas, Castile (–*c.* 1511).

- Christopher Columbus, navigator and explorer, the first discoverer of the New World to achieve long-term historical impact, born in Genoa, Italy (–1506).

February 3 Murad II, Ottoman sultan 1421–44 and 1446–51, who consolidated Ottoman rule in the Balkans, dies in Edirne, Persia (46).

April 22 Isabella I the Catholic, Queen of Castile 1474–1504 and Aragon 1479–1504, who ruled the two kingdoms jointly with her husband, Ferdinand, from 1479, born in Madrigal de las Altas Torres, Castile (–1504).

1452

- Leonardo da Vinci, Italian painter, sculptor, draftsman, architect, engineer, and scientist, one of the most influential Renaissance humanists, who painted *Mona Lisa*, and *Last Supper*, and whose science was ahead of its time, born in Vinci, republic of Florence (–1519).

March 10 Ferdinand the Catholic, King of Sicily (as Ferdinand II) 1468–1516, Aragon (as Ferdinand II) 1479–1516, Castile (as Ferdinand V and joint sovereign with his wife Isabella I) 1474–1504, and Naples (as Ferdinand III) 1504–16, who united the Spanish kingdoms into one nation and began Spain's period of imperial expansion, born in Sos, Aragon (–1516).

May James III, King of Scotland 1460–88, son of James II, born (–1488).

July 27 Ludovico Sforza ("The Moor"), Duke of Milan 1494–98, and patron of the arts, born in Vigevano, Pavia, duchy of Milan (–1508).

September 21 Girolamo Savonarola, Christian preacher, and leader of Florence 1494–98, who set the city up as a democratic republic, born in Ferrara, duchy of Ferrara (–1498).

October 2 Richard III (Richard Plantagenet), King of England 1483–85, born in Fotheringhay Castle, Northamptonshire, England (–1485).

1453

- Alfonso d'Albuquerque, Portuguese soldier, conqueror of Goa (1510) in India and of Melaka (1511) in the Malay Peninsula, born in Alhandra, Portugal (–1515).

September 1 Gonzalo Fernandez de Córdoba ("El Gran Capitán"), celebrated Spanish military commander, born (–1515).

December 24 John Dunstable, English composer whose range of religious works make him the most important English composer of the early 15th century, dies in London, England (*c.* 63).

1454

March 9 Amerigo Vespucci, Italian-born Spanish explorer who participated in a number of voyages to the New World and after whom North and South America are named, born in Florence (–1512).

July 14 Politian (Angelo Ambrogini Poliziana), Italian poet and humanist philosopher, born in Montepulciano, Tuscany (–1494).

1455–1459

POLITICS, GOVERNMENT, AND ECONOMICS

Business and Economics

1458

- A cattle tax imposed on a largely pastoral populace by the archbishop of Salzburg sparks a peasants' revolt which spreads to Styria, Carinthia, and Carniola.

Colonization

c. 1455–58

- Ca' da Mosto explores the coasts of present-day Senegal, Gambia, Guinea, and Guinea Bissau for Prince Henry the Navigator of Portugal.

Politics and Government

1455

- Frederick II, Elector of Brandenburg, buys the territory of Neumark (east of the River Oder) from the impoverished Teutonic Order of Knights, which is attempting to raise funds to continue the Thirteen Years' War with Poland.
- Frederick II, Elector of Saxony, captures and executes the renegade Saxon baron Kunz von Kaufungen following the abduction of Frederick's sons Albert and Ernest in the celebrated *Prinzraub* ("abduction of the princes").
- Trailok, King of the Theravada Buddhist kingdom of Ayutthaya (in modern Thailand), captures the Muslim Malay entrepôt city of Malacca.

March 2 Pope Nicholas V proclaims and joins the "Italian League" formed by Milan, Venice, and Florence following the Peace of Lodi of 1454, to which the kingdom of Naples soon adheres. The League, which is to last for 25 years, is a pact against internecine (mutually destructive) warfare and foreign invasion, with permanent diplomatic representation between its members.

April 8 The College of Cardinals in Rome, Italy, elects the Spanish compromise candidate, Alfonso de Borgia, as pope, in order to satisfy both the Roman Orsini and Colonna factions. Taking the name Calixtus III, he succeeds Nicholas V, who died a fortnight earlier.

May 22 The Wars of the Roses begin when forces under Richard, Duke of York, and the Neville Earls of Warwick and Salisbury are refused a parley and rapidly defeat the armies of King Henry VI of England in St. Albans, England. The king's commander, the Duke of Somerset, is killed, and the king is wounded and captured.

November 19 Richard, Duke of York, who has held the position of constable of England since killing the previous holder, the Duke of Somerset, at St. Albans, England, is reappointed "protector" of England when King Henry VI of England lapses back into insanity. He appoints Richard Neville, Earl of Warwick, as captain of Calais.

December 15 In the continuation of a protracted feud between the Earl of Devon and Lord Bonville, Lord Bonville is defeated by a cavalry charge in "the fight at Clyst" in Devon, England.

1456

- An Ottoman force conquers the duchy of Athens and its Florentine Acciajuoli rulers, though the Acropolis holds out for a further two years.
- Tun Perak is made bendahara (chief minister) by Muzaffar Shah, Sultan of Malacca, Malaya, and immediately recaptures the capital, expelling the occupying armies of Trailok, King of Ayutthaya (in modern Thailand).

1456–1459 Serious rioting recurs in London, England, against the Flemish and Italian communities there, to be manipulated by both Yorkist (Neville) and Lancastrian (Somerset) parties.

February 25 The protectorate of Richard, Duke of York, again lapses when King Henry VI of England recovers his sanity. His queen, Margaret of Anjou, regains control.

July 22 The captain–general of Hungary, János Hunyadi, defeats Ottoman forces besieging Belgrade, Serbia, forcing them to withdraw. He dies on August 11.

September Having enraged his father by raiding the duchy of Savoy, the dauphin (the future King Louis XI of France) abandons his lands in the Dauphiné when an army commanded by his father Charles VII approaches. He takes refuge in Burgundy.

November 9 The Hungarian Hunyadi faction assassinates Ullrich of Cilli, guardian of Ladislas Posthumous, King of Hungary and Bohemia, in Belgrade. Frederick III the Holy Roman Emperor seizes his lands.

1457

- Aided by the voivod of Wallachia, Vlad III Tepes the Impaler, Stephen IV the Great secures the title voivod of Moldavia.

February A group of military and civil service leaders stage a coup against the ailing Ching Ta'i emperor, the

Wars of the Roses (1455–87)

1455

May 22 The Wars of the Roses begin when forces under Richard, Duke of York, and the Neville Earls of Warwick and Salisbury are refused a parley and rapidly defeat the armies of King Henry VI of England in St. Albans, England. The king's commander, the Duke of Somerset, is killed, and the king is wounded and captured.

November 19 The Duke of York, who has held the position of constable of England since killing the previous holder, the Duke of Somerset, at St. Albans, England, is reappointed "protector" of England when King Henry VI of England lapses back into insanity. He appoints Richard Neville, Earl of Warwick, as captain of Calais.

1456

February 25 The protectorate of Richard, Duke of York, again lapses when Henry VI recovers his sanity. His queen, Margaret of Anjou, regains control.

1459

September 23 Richard Neville leads a Yorkist force to repel the attack of the more numerous royal forces under Lord Audley at Blore Heath, Staffordshire, England.

October 12 The Yorkists, reinforced from Calais, France, by the Earl of Warwick, and headed by the Duke of York and the Earl of Salisbury, break and flee abroad ahead of a royal army led by Henry Beaufort, Duke of Somerset, following a skirmish at Ludford Bridge, Shropshire, England.

November 20 The "parliament of devils" called at Coventry, England, by Henry Beaufort and Queen Margaret attaints (condemns and outlaws) the Yorkist leaders the Duke of York, his son Edward, Earl of March (the future King Edward IV of England), the Earl of Salisbury, and his son the Earl of Warwick as traitors against King Henry VI of England.

1460

February Having assiduously used his Lancastrian kinship to build up his lands in Wales over the last four years, Jasper Tudor besieges and takes Denbigh Castle, Welsh base of the Duke of York.

July 10 Yorkist forces led by the Earl of March (the future King Edward IV of England), and Richard Neville, Earl of Warwick, storm the fortified camp of the Lancastrian royal forces at Northampton, England, capturing Henry VI.

August 3 James II of Scotland dies when a cannon explodes as his army captures Roxburgh Castle in the border country, where he is taking the opportunity provided by the civil war in England to attack English outposts. He is succeeded by his eight-year-old son James III.

December 30 Richard, Duke of York, besieged in Sandal Castle in Yorkshire, England, following grievous Lancastrian attacks throughout his journey to pacify Yorkshire, is killed while breaking the siege in the Battle of Wakefield. His head, along with that of the Earl of Salisbury, is impaled on the city gates of York, England.

1461

February 3 Edward's Yorkist forces defeat and break Lancastrian forces including French, Breton, and Irish troops at Mortimer's Cross, Herefordshire, England. Owen Tudor (Pembroke) is captured and beheaded..

February 17 Queen Margaret's Lancastrian "northern" army outflanks the Earl of Warwick's forces at St. Albans, England, and defeats them, recapturing her husband King Henry VI of England. They are subsequently barred entry to London, England, by its citizens.

March 4 Having been welcomed into London three days previously, Edward of York, Earl of March, is acclaimed King Edward IV by the populace. He pursues the Lancastrian forces of Henry VI northward.

March 29 After storming the crossing of the River Aire at Ferrybridge, England, the previous day, Edward IV's Yorkists obliterate Henry VI's Lancastrians in a blizzard at Towton, Yorkshire, England. Following this "Bloody Palm Sunday" the surviving Lancastrian leaders, including Henry VI, flee to Scotland.

1463

December 25 Edward IV faces renewed Lancastrian resistance in the north of England when there is a rising in Lancashire, while Margaret of Anjou, reinforced by French royal troops, captures the Northumbrian castles of Bamburgh, Alnwick, and Dunstanburgh.

1464

April 25 Edward IV's forces, led north by John Neville, Lord Montague, to meet Scots peace commissioners, defeat a Lancastrian ambush at Hedgeley Moor, Northumberland, England.

May 1 King Edward IV of England secretly marries Elizabeth Woodville, widow of Lord Grey of Ferrers, who was killed fighting the Yorkists. The announcement of the marriage in October halts the Earl of Warwick's negotiations for Edward's betrothal to the sister-in-law of King Louis XI of France.

May 15 John Neville leads Yorkist forces to victory at Hexham in Northumberland, England. The defeated Lancastrian army breaks and many are captured, while their leaders, including Henry Beaufort, Duke of Somerset, are executed.

1465

July The deposed Lancastrian king Henry VI is captured near Clitheroe in Lancashire, England, and held in the Tower of London.

1468

June Jasper Tudor, Earl of Pembroke, returns from France, hoping to relieve the long-besieged Lancastrian castle of Harlech in Wales. He succeeds in capturing Denbigh Castle, Wales, but is then defeated by William, Lord Herbert, and Harlech surrenders shortly after.

1469

July 11   Richard Neville, Earl of Warwick, and George, Duke of Clarence, seal their alliance when the Duke of Clarence marries Neville's daughter Isabel at Sandwich, England. They enter London on July 20 and muster support in questioning the paternity of Edward IV.

July 26   King Edward IV's Welsh and Marcher forces, led by William Herbert, Earl of Pembroke, are stopped and annihilated at Edgecote in Northamptonshire, England, by Sir John Conyer's rebels, who are reinforced by the Earl of Warwick. King Edward IV is captured two days later.

September   The distraction of a Lancastrian rising in County Durham enables King Edward IV to free himself from the custody of the Earl of Warwick at Middleham in Yorkshire, England, and to rally his supporters at Pontefract, Yorkshire.

1470

March 4   Local rebellions in Lincolnshire and Yorkshire (led by Sir John Conyers on March 10) draw Edward IV north from London once again. On routing the Lincolnshire rebels at Empingham at "Loosecoat Field" on March 12, he learns of the implication of the Duke of Clarence and the Earl of Warwick, who flee under fire from Exeter on the south coast of England via piracy to Honfleur in Normandy.

July 24   King Louis XI of France arranges a formal reconciliation between Margaret of Anjou and Richard, Earl of Warwick, both of whom are now in exile following their defeats by King Edward IV of England. Warwick subsequently positively switches allegiance to the Lancastrian Henry VI.

October 6   The Earl of Warwick, in alliance with King Louis XI of France and Margaret of Anjou, eludes the Yorkist–Burgundian blockade of the English Channel and invades England via Plymouth, restoring Henry VI as king "the Readeption." King Edward IV of England flees for Burgundian Holland on October 2 as his support fails.

1471

April 14   Having sailed from Burgundy to land at Ravenspur in Holderness, England, on March 14, Edward IV musters support and enters London capturing Henry VI and annihilating the Lancastrian Neville forces in the fog at Barnet. The Lancastrian leaders, the Earl of Warwick and Lord Montague, die in battle.

May 4   Margaret of Anjou, having arrived from France too late to save the Earl of Warwick, sees her own forces obliterated by Edward IV at Tewkesbury, England. She is captured by the Yorkist victors, and her son Edward, Prince of Wales, her general the Duke of Somerset, and many other Lancastrian lords are killed.

May 21   Richard, Duke of Gloucester, brother of Edward IV, defeats an attack on London by the Lancastrian Lord Fauconberg which is aimed at taking Henry VI from confinement in the Tower of London. Edward has Henry executed, extinguishing the Lancastrian dynasty.

1473

May–November   The zealous Lancastrian John de Vere, Earl of Oxford, captures the fortified tidal island of St. Michael's Mount in Cornwall, England, but is besieged there and eventually captured and imprisoned.

1482

June 10   King Edward IV of England recognizes Alexander of Albany, exiled brother of King James III of Scotland, as king of Scotland and his vassal under the Treaties of Fotheringay.

1483

November 2   King Richard III of England executes Henry Stafford, Duke of Buckingham, when the rebellion plotted by the Duke of Buckingham to enthrone Henry Tudor, Earl of Richmond, founders because Tudor fails to land and the Duke of Buckingham's troops desert.

1485

August 7   Henry Tudor lands in his native Wales at Milford Haven with 1,000 mercenaries supplied by France, to begin his campaign against King Richard III for the English throne.

August 22   The armies of King Richard III of England and Henry Tudor meet at the Battle of Bosworth Field in Leicestershire, England. Richard's onslaught is overwhelmed when the Stanley family desert his cause and lead a flank attack for Henry, and Richard is killed. Henry takes the crown as King Henry VII of England and founds the Tudor dynasty.

1486

January 18   King Henry VII of England marries Elizabeth of York, the daughter of Edward IV, thus hoping to unite Yorkist and Lancastrian claims to the throne in his Tudor dynasty.

1487

June 16   King Henry VII of England defeats the army of the pretender Lambert Simnel, who has marched from a landing in Lancashire to the battle site at East Stoke, near Newark, Nottinghamshire, England. Simnel's major backer, the Earl of Lincoln, is killed in this last battle of the Wars of the Roses.

conspirators forcing the palace gate and enthroning the former Cheng-T'ung emperor Ying-tsung (who was deposed while a captive of the Mongol leader Esen in the period 1449–50). Thus begins the T'ien-Shun reign.

June King Charles VIII of Sweden (Karl Knutson) flees from Sweden when there is a rebellion among the nobles (led by the Oxenstierna and Vasa families) over his extension of royal powers. Christian I of Denmark is recalled as king.

June 6 A Polish force under the command of King Casimir (Kazimierz) IV of Poland takes Malbork (Marienburg) in Prussia, fortress of the grand master of the Teutonic Order of Knights, who consequently transfers his base to Königsberg, Prussia.

August French ships under the command of Pierre de Brézé, seneschal of Normandy, land in Kent, England, and sack the port of Sandwich before being driven off by the English force led by Sir Thomas Kyriell.

October 23 Pope Calixtus III settles the factional discord in the city of Münster, Germany, with the Treaty of Krauenburg. He appoints John von Wittelsbach as a compromise bishop and allows the reformulation of the council with half patrician and half popular representation.

November 23 Ladislas Posthumous, King of Hungary and Bohemia, dies suddenly at the age of 17 in Prague, Bohemia, having fled from Hungary after executing László Hunyadi for the murder of Ullrich von Cilli.

1458

- The leader of the Ak Koyunlu (White Sheep) Uzbekhs, seeking allies against the Ottomans, marries Catherine, daughter of Kalo-Ioannes, Greek emperor of Trabzon in Paphlagonia.

January 24 The Hungarian diet elects Matthias I Corvinus, second son of János Hunyadi, as king of Hungary.

March The Kara Koyunlu (Black Sheep) Uzbekhs, led by Jihan Shah, take Heart, capital of the Timurid ruler Abu Sa'id, in a complex struggle, but lose it again when the latter returns with the Ak Koyunlu (White Sheep) Uzbekhs under Uzun Hasan.

March 2 The Bohemian diet elects the regent (and leader of the Hussite Utraquists) George of Poděbrady as king of Bohemia. He invades Habsburg Austria.

May 11 Genoa, seeking protection from the aggression of King Alfonso V of Naples and Aragon, welcomes John of Anjou, heir of René of Anjou and claimant to the crown of Naples, as its governor, backed by a French army.

May 29 The Yorkist captain of Calais, Richard Neville, Earl of Warwick, defeats and destroys a Castilian fleet in the English Channel.

June 27 King Alfonso V the Magnanimous of Aragon, Naples, and Sicily dies while planning an assault on Genoa, Italy. He leaves his kingdom of Naples to his illegitimate son Ferrante, and his other domains to his brother John II, King of Navarre.

August 19 The humanist scholar and diplomat Enea Silvio Piccolomini (of the Sienese banking family) succeeds Calixtus III as Pope Pius II.

October Louis Wittelsbach, Duke of Bavaria-Landshut, seizes the imperial free city of Donauwörth, Germany, antagonizing Albert Achilles von Hohenzollern, Margrave of Ansbach.

1459

- Ottoman forces take the fortress of Smederova, the last Serbian stronghold, thereby completing their conquest of Serbia.
- Vlad IV Tepes the Impaler, voivod of Wallachia, establishes a frontier fortress against the Ottoman Turks on the Danube plain, effectively founding the city of Bucharest, later capital of Romania.

June 1 Pope Pius II finds himself alone on the opening day of his congress in Mantua, Italy, which he has arranged to organize a crusade against the Ottoman Turks. A few delegates arrive later.

August The baronial nobility of the kingdom of Naples revolt against King Ferrante I of Naples in favor of his rival for the crown, René of Anjou, Count of Provence.

September 23 Richard Neville leads a Yorkist force to repel the attack of the more numerous royal forces under Lord Audley at Blore Heath, Staffordshire, England.

October 12 The Yorkists, reinforced from Calais, France, by Richard Neville, Earl of Warwick, and headed by the Duke of York and the Earl of Salisbury, break and flee abroad ahead of a royal army led by Henry Beaufort, Duke of Somerset, following a skirmish at Ludford Bridge, Shropshire, England.

November 20 The "parliament of devils" called at Coventry, England, by Henry Beaufort, Duke of Somerset, and the queen, Margaret of Anjou, attaints (condemns and outlaws) the Yorkist leaders Richard, Duke of York, his son Edward, Earl of March, the Earl of Salisbury, and his son the Earl of Warwick as traitors against King Henry VI of England.

SCIENCE, TECHNOLOGY, AND MEDICINE

Science

1455

- English king Henry VI commissions a number of alchemists, astrologers, and explorers to find the philosopher's stone.

1457

- Hebrew astronomer Judah Verga of Lisbon writes a description of his invention for determining the sun's meridian.
- Venetian monk and cartographer Fra Mauro produces a new map of the world for Prince Henry the Navigator of Portugal, based on information from voyages the prince has sponsored.

ARTS AND IDEAS

Architecture

c. 1456–57
- Ota Dokan founds the city of Yedo (modern Tokyo) in Japan by building a castle near the mouth of the River Sumida, which strategically controls Kanto Plain.

1458
- The Cathedral of Faenza, in Italy, designed by the Italian architect Giuliano da Maiano, is completed.
- The spires of Burgos Cathedral, Spain, designed in the North European Gothic style by the German-born Spanish architect Juan de Colonia (Cologne), are completed.

1459
- Pope Pius II (Enea Silvio Piccolomini) begins the transformation of his hometown of Corsignano, near Siena, Italy, into a model Renaissance city. The name is changed to Pienza and the Italian architect Rossellino (Bernardo di Matteo Gamberelli) is put in charge. His works there include the Cathedral and the Palazzo Piccolomini.

Arts

1455
- c. 1455   Flemish artist Rogier van der Weyden paints *Francesco d'Este*.
- c. 1455   French artist Jean Fouquet paints *Portrait of Guillaume Jouvenal des Ursins*.
- c. 1455   Italian artist Andrea del Castagno (Andrea di Bartolo) paints frescoes in the Church of Santissima Annunziata in Florence, Italy, among them *The Vision of St. Jerome*.
- c. 1455   Italian artist Desiderio de Setignano sculpts *Portrait Bust of Marietta Strozzi*.
- c. 1455   Italian artist Piero della Francesca completes his cycle of frescoes *The Legend of the True Cross* in the Church of San Francesco in Arezzo, Italy. Among the best-known scenes are *The Discovery of the True Cross* and *The Meeting of Solomon and the Queen of Sheba*.
- Flemish artist Rogier van der Weyden paints *The Nativity (Pierre Bladelin Triptych)*.
- Italian artist Donatello (Donato di Niccolò) completes *Magdalen*, a wooden statue for the Florence Baptistry in Italy.
- December 1   Italian artist Lorenzo Ghiberti dies, leaving his *Commentarii/Commentaries* incomplete. The first autobiography by a Western artist, it provides a wealth of information on 14th-century Florentine art.

1456
- Italian artist Andrea del Castagno (Andrea di Bartolo) paints the fresco *Equestrian Portrait of Niccolò da Tolentino* in Florence Cathedral, Italy.
- Italian artist Donatello (Donato di Niccolò) sculpts *Judith and Holofernes*.

1457
- c. 1457   Flemish artist Rogier van der Weyden paints *Portrait of Charles the Bold*.

- Italian artist Andrea Mantegna completes his frescoes (destroyed in 1944) for the Ovetari Chapel in the Eremetani Church in Padua, Italy. Among the best-known scenes is *St. James Led to Execution*.

1458
- French artist Jean Fouquet completes his illuminations for the book *Les Grandes Chroniques de France/The Great Chronicles of France*, a history of France compiled over two centuries by many authors.

1459
- Italian artist Andrea Mantegna paints the *St. Zeno Altarpiece*.

Literature and Language

1455
- Italian poet and humanist Antonio Beccadelli writes his *De dictis et factis regis Alfonsi/The Words and Deeds of King Alfonso*, an overblown account of the life of Alfonso the Magnanimous, King of Naples and Aragon. It is printed in 1485.

c. 1456
- French writer François Villon writes his long poem *Le Lais/The Legacy* (better known by its later title *Le Petit Testament/The Shorter Testament*). One of the most important French literary works of the 15th century, it describes his need to leave Paris because of an ill-starred love affair (though in fact Villon fled because implicated in robbery). It is first published in 1489.

Thought and Scholarship

1459
- Batista Guarino, humanist professor of rhetoric at the University of Bologna, Italy, writes his *De ordine docendi et studente/On the Regulation of Teaching and Study*, which becomes the textbook for Renaissance classical scholars.

SOCIETY

Education

1457
- The Habsburg archduke Albert VI establishes Freiburg University in the Breisgau in southern Germany.

1458
- William Waynflete, bishop of Winchester, founds Magdalen College at Oxford University, England.

Religion

1456
- English churchman Reginald Pecock publishes *The Repressor of Over Much Blaming of the Clergy*, a

defense of the church against the Lollards, followers of the English reformer John Wycliffe (Wyclif). He also publishes *The Book of Faith*, which denies articles of the Apostle's Creed. The book causes him to be tried for heresy in 1457.

July 7 A French ecclesiastical court rehabilitates Joan of Arc. The verdict of heresy passed on her in 1431 by the English-controlled inquisition is declared to have been irregular.

1457

- The English churchman Reginald Pecock is brought to trial in London, England, for the heretical belief

expressed in *The Book of Faith* (1456). He renounces his opinions and is deprived of the bishopric of Chichester. His books are publicly burned.

Sports

1457

- A statute of the Scottish parliament bans football and golf. The ban is repeated in 1471 and 1491, though probably with little effect. It is the first certain reference to the word "golf."

BIRTHS & DEATHS

1455

- Antonio Pisanello, Italian painter in the international Gothic style and one of the first 15th-century painters to paint from life, dies (60).
- Nicholas V, Italian pope 1447–55, who founded the Vatican Library, restored peace to the papal states and Italy, and started a program of architectural reconstruction in Rome, dies in Rome (*c.* 58).

February Fra Angelico (Guido di Pietro, also known as Giovanni da Fiesole), great Italian painter, whose best-known works include *The Annunciation* (1430s), dies in Rome, Italy (*c.* 60).

February 22 Johann Reuchlin, German humanist and classics scholar known for his *De Rudimentis Hebraicis/On the Fundamentals of Hebrew*, born in Pforzheim, Württemberg (–1522).

December 1 Lorenzo Ghiberti, early Italian Renaissance sculptor, whose best-known work is the *Gates of Paradise* for Florence Cathedral, dies in Florence, Italy (*c.* 77).

1456

- Juan de Mena, innovative Spanish poet whose best-known poem is "El laberinto de Fortuna"/"The Labyrinth of Fortune" (1444), dies in Torrelaguna, Castile, Spain (*c.* 45).

October 23 St. John of Capistrano (St. Giovanni Da Capistrano), celebrated Franciscan preacher and leader of an army that liberated Belgrade from the Ottoman Turks, dies in Villach, Duchy of Carinthia, Austria (*c.* 70).

November 25 Jacques Coeur, powerful French merchant and counselor to King Charles VII of France, dies,

probably on the Aegian island of Chios (*c.* 61).

1457

- Filippino Lippi, Italian Renaissance painter, whose major works include *The Vision of St. Bernard* (1480s), born in Prato, Italy (–1504).

January 28 Henry VII, first Tudor king of England 1485–1509, born in Pembroke Castle, Wales (–1509).

August 1 Lorenzo Valla, Italian humanist, philosopher, and literary scholar, who wrote *De elegantia Latinae linguae/Elegances of the Latin Language*, the first Latin textbook since ancient times, dies in Rome (*c.* 50).

August 19 Andrea del Castagno (real name Andrea di Bartolo), influential Italian Renaissance painter, noted for his realistic treatment of figures, whose major works include the fresco *St. Julian* (1454–55), dies in Florence (*c.* 36).

1458

March 25 Inigo López de Mendoza, Marquess of Santillana, Spanish poet and humanist, dies in Guadalajara, Spain (59).

July 28 Jacopo Sannazaro, Italian poet known for his pastoral romance "Arcadia," born in Naples (–1530).

August 6 Alfonso Borgia, Pope Calixtus III 1455–58, dies in Rome, Italy (79).

1459

- Ausiàs March, one of the greatest Catalan poets, dies (*c.* 62).
- Peter Martyr d'Anghiera, historian of the Spanish explorations and collector of manuscripts, who wrote *De orbe novo/On the New World* (1530), born in Arona, Milan, Italy (–*c.* 1527).

February 1 Conradus Celtis (German: Conrad Pickel), German humanist scholar and Latin lyrical poet, born in Wipfeld, near Würzburg, Germany (–1508).

March 2 Adrian of Utrecht (Pope Adrian VI; original name Adrian Florenszoon Boeyens), the only Dutch pope 1522–23, born in Utrecht (now Netherlands) (–1523).

March 6 Jakob II Fugger the Rich, powerful German merchant and financier, born in Augsburg, Bavaria (–1525).

March 22 Maximilian I, Habsburg archduke of Austria, king of Germany, and Holy Roman Emperor 1493–1519, who greatly increased the Habsburg territories, born in Wiener Neustadt, Austria (–1519).

May 2 St. Antoninus, archbishop of Florence who founded modern moral theology, dies in Florence (70).

October 26 Giannozzo Manetti, Italian humanist and writer, dies (63).

October 30 Gian Francesco Poggio Bracciolini, Italian humanist, outstanding scholar of the early Renaissance, responsible for rediscovering several classical manuscripts, dies in Florence (79).

November 6 Sir John Fastolf, English career soldier in the Hundred Years' War (1337–1453), who fought at Agincourt (1415) and Verneuil (1424), dies in Caister, Norfolk, England (*c.* 81).

1460–1464

POLITICS, GOVERNMENT, AND ECONOMICS

Business and Economics

1460

March 5   Christian of Oldenburg, King of Denmark, succeeds his uncle as Duke of Schleswig and Count of Holstein, and overcomes noble opposition by introducing tax–exemptions and a pledge of perpetual union between the two territories.

1462

October 28   Adolf of Nassau, papal nominee as archbishop and elector, seizes the imperial city of Mainz, Germany, home of Johann Gutenberg's printing process. He institutes an authoritarian regime, expelling hundreds of burghers, and as a result accidentally disperses the nascent printing industry across Europe.

1463

- Philip the Good of Burgundy assembles an Estates General in Bruges, the Netherlands, for all his territories. This move to simplify the raising of taxes consolidates his disparate Burgundian lands.

Colonization

1463

- Ivan III, Grand Duke of Muscovy, annexes the principality of Yaroslavl on the River Volga, northeast of Moscow, Russia.

Politics and Government

1460

- James, illegitimate descendant of the Lusignan royal house, lands in Cyprus with the support of an Egyptian Mameluke fleet and takes the crown as King James II of Cyprus.
- Ottoman forces conquer the Byzantine Greek "despotate" of Morea, the principality that controlled most of the Peloponnese, the south peninsula of Greece.
- The Swiss Confederation, led by the canton of Zürich, seizes the Habsburg county of Thurgau on the Bodensee (Lake Constance).

- The Wittelsbachs of Bavaria and a Hohenzollern-Wettin (Brandenburg-Saxony) coalition under Margrave Albert Achilles von Hohenzollern of Ansbach begin a war over the city of Donauwörth, Germany, which was seized by the Wittelsbachs in October 1458. The war is conducted throughout the duchy of Franconia and along the River Rhine.

February   Having assiduously used his Lancastrian kinship to build up his lands in Wales over the last four years, Jasper Tudor besieges and takes Denbigh Castle, Welsh base of Richard, Duke of York.

June 26   Richard Neville, Earl of Warwick, leaves his captaincy of Calais, France, and lands at Sandwich, England, which was established as a base in the previous month by his son Lord Fauconberg.

July 7   King Ferrante I of Naples leads his forces, including a papal contingent, to decimation in battle at Nola, Italy. His crown is only saved by the procrastination of his opponents, led by John of Anjou.

July 10   Yorkist forces led by Edward, Earl of March (the future King Edward IV of England), and Richard Neville, Earl of Warwick, storm the fortified camp of the Lancastrian royal forces at Northampton, England, capturing King Henry VI of England.

August 3   James II of Scotland dies when a cannon explodes as his army captures Roxburgh Castle in the border country, where he is taking the opportunity provided by the civil war in England to attack English outposts. He is succeeded by his eight-year-old son James III.

October 28   King Henry VI of England accepts Richard, Duke of York, as heir apparent to the English throne and prince of Wales. Richard is proclaimed "protector" on November 8.

December 30   Richard, Duke of York, besieged in Sandal Castle in Yorkshire, England, following grievous Lancastrian attacks throughout his journey to pacify Yorkshire, is killed while breaking the siege in the Battle of Wakefield. His head, along with that of the Earl of Salisbury, is impaled on the city gates of York, England.

1461

February   Barcelona, Catalonia, rebels against King John II of Aragon in favor of his son Carlos of Viana, and forces John to appoint Carlos as lieutenant of Catalonia.

February   The German electors gather at Eger, Bohemia, with George of Poděbrady, King of Bohemia and arbitrator in a war over Donauwörth, Germany, and scheme to depose Frederick III the Holy Roman Emperor and offer his crown to George.

February 3   The Yorkist forces of Edward, Earl of March (the future King Edward IV of England), defeat and break Lancastrian forces including French, Breton, and Irish troops at Mortimer's Cross, Herefordshire,

England. Owen Tudor (Pembroke) is captured and beheaded.

February 17 Queen Margaret's Lancastrian "northern" army outflanks the Earl of Warwick's forces at St. Albans, England, and defeats them, recapturing her husband King Henry VI of England. They are subsequently barred entry to London, England, by its citizens.

March 4 Having been welcomed into London, England, three days previously, Edward of York, Earl of March, is acclaimed King Edward IV by the populace. He pursues the Lancastrian forces of Henry VI northward.

March 29 After storming the crossing of the River Aire at Ferrybridge, England, the previous day, the Yorkist army of King Edward IV of England obliterates the Lancastrian force of Henry VI in a blizzard at Towton, Yorkshire, England. Following this "Bloody Palm Sunday" the surviving Lancastrian leaders, including Henry VI, flee to Scotland.

August Prince Carlos de Viana, son and heir of John II of Aragon, dies suddenly in Barcelona, Spain. Civil war breaks out in Aragon and Navarre against John II, and Catalan Barcelona attempts a republican revolution.

August 10 Ts'ao Chi-hsiang, a leader of the 1457 "forcing the palace gate" coup and commander of the Beijing capital garrisons, is executed for plotting rebellion, thereby eliminating the regime of 1457.

September The Ottoman Empire conquers Trebizond on the Black Sea coast of Anatolia, last remnant of the Byzantine Empire.

November–December Disastrous inflation in Vienna, Austria, sparks a popular revolt against Frederick III the Holy Roman Emperor, who is besieged in the castle by his brother Albert VI of Austria. Frederick is finally rescued by George of Poděbrady of Bohemia, who renegotiates Albert's tenancy of Austria from Frederick.

November 27 Louis XI, having succeeded his father Charles VII as king of France three months previously, temporarily revokes the "pragmatic sanction" of Bourges, allowing him greater control over the French clergy.

1462

- Abu-al-Hasan succeeds Ismail III as king of Granada when the former cedes Gibraltar to the Castilian king, Henry IV.
- An Ottoman force devastates the principality of Wallachia, causing its ruler Vlad IV Tepes the Impaler to flee. He is replaced by a native vassal of the Ottoman Empire.

April King Edward IV of England takes the exceptional step of sitting as judge on the "King's Bench," his commitment to enforcing his rule judicially reemphasized by his subsequent progress around the kingdom hearing trial pleas.

June 11 The Generalitat (parliament) of Catalonia in Barcelona declares King John II and Queen Juana of Aragon to be enemies of Catalonia, and therefore to be expelled from its territory.

September 18 King Ferrante I of Naples, aided by the Albanian general Skanderbeg, defeats John of Anjou near Troia in Apulia, Italy. The rebellion in favor of John's father, René of Provence, soon ends.

1463

- Matthias I Corvinus gains acceptance as king of Hungary when he puts down noble insurgency and defeats the forces of Frederick III the Holy Roman Emperor, who claims the throne of Hungary.
- Mohammed Rumfa becomes king of Kano in Nigeria and immediately begins a program of reform, building, and Islamization.

January 9 The French forces of Louis XI take the city of Perpignan (now in southern France) from Aragon, taking advantage of the Catalan revolt to annex Roussillon and Cerdagne. This move is popularly resisted, but confirmed when John II, King of Aragon and Navarre, cedes the provinces.

August George of Poděbrady, King of Bohemia, successfully negotiates a peace in Franconia at Prague, Bohemia, between the Bavarian Wittelsbachs and Albert Achilles von Hohenzollern of Ansbach, but the war drags on along the River Rhine until November 1463.

October 22 Pope Pius II publishes a bull proclaiming a crusade against the Ottoman Turks, which he will lead personally.

December King Louis XI of France relinquishes his claim to suzerainty over Genoa (governed by the house of Anjou in the person of John of Anjou) to Francesco Sforza, Duke of Milan.

December 3 Frederick III the Holy Roman Emperor recovers rule over all Austria following the death of his brother Albert VI, Archduke of Austria.

December 6 Matthias I Corvinus, King of Hungary, takes Jajce, the former capital of Bosnia, from the Ottoman Turks, and claims suzerainty over Bosnia, Serbia, Moldavia, and Wallachia.

December 25 King Edward IV of England faces renewed Lancastrian resistance in the north of England when there is a rising in Lancashire, while Margaret of Anjou, reinforced by French royal troops, captures the Northumbrian castles of Bamburgh, Alnwick, and Dunstanburgh.

1464

- King James II of Cyprus expels the Genoese from their colony of Famagusta in Cyprus.
- Sonni 'Ali accedes to the rule of Gao, Mali, on the River Niger. Relying on cavalry, he defeats Mossi attacks, conquers the Dogon and Fulani peoples in the Bandiagara Hills to the southwest, and expels the Tuaregs, thus founding the Songhai empire (–1591).

1464–74 Ottoman forces conquer the independent Turkish principality of Karaman in Asia Minor.

February 23 Hsien-Tung succeeds as the Ch'eng-Hua emperor following the death of his father Ying-tsung, and immediately orders military reforms, creating 120,000 elite capital troops and introducing military examinations.

April 25 Yorkist forces of King Edward IV of England, led north by John Neville, Lord Montague, to meet Scottish peace commissioners, defeat a Lancastrian ambush at Hedgeley Moor, Northumberland, England.

May 1 King Edward IV of England secretly marries Elizabeth Woodville, widow of Lord Grey of Ferrers, who was killed fighting the Yorkists. The announcement of the marriage in October halts the Earl of Warwick's negotiations for Edward's betrothal to the sister-in-law of King Louis XI of France.

May 15   John Neville, Lord Montague, leads Yorkist forces to victory at Hexham in Northumberland, England. The defeated Lancastrian army breaks up and many are captured, while their leaders, including Henry Beaufort, Duke of Somerset, are executed.

June 19   An *ordonnance* (decree) of King Louis XI of France creates the *Poste Royale*, which organizes relays of horses on the main roads to serve 230 couriers carrying out the king's business.

August 14   Pope Pius II dies at Ancona, Italy, while awaiting the arrival of the crusading army he had hoped to lead. His successor, the Venetian Marco Barbo, is elected Pope Paul II, and begins his papacy by announcing that previous papal capitulations are not binding.

September 7   Frederick II, elector of Saxony, dies shortly after having married his son Albert to the daughter of the Hussite king of Bohemia, George of Poděbrady.

SCIENCE, TECHNOLOGY, AND MEDICINE

Exploration

1460

- Diego Gomés and Antonio de Noli discover the Cape Verde Islands in the Atlantic Ocean, claiming them for Portugal. Two years later, the first settlers arrive there on São Tiago.

1462

- A Portuguese expedition led by Pedro da Sintra reaches Sierra Leone in West Africa.

1464

- Venetian trader Alvise de Cá da Mosto writes *El libro de la prima navigatione per l'oceano a le terre de Negri della bassa Etiopa/The Book of the First Oceanic Navigation to the Land of the Negros at the Base of Ethiopia* (printed 1507), an account of his voyages to West Africa.

Technology

1461

- The manufacture of gunpowder in England is confined, for safety reasons, to the Tower of London by statute of Parliament.

1462

- Italian clockmaker Bartholomew Manfredi writes to the Marchese di Manta offering to make him a "pocket clock" better than the Duke of Modena's—possibly the earliest reference to a watch.
- The dye-fixing mineral alum is discovered at Tolfa in the Papal States. Pope Pius II claims a lucrative monopoly of its supply in Europe.

1463

- Konrad Sweynheim and Arnold Pannartz install the first printing press in Italy in the Benedictine monastery of Subiaco, Lazio, though it is moved to Rome shortly afterwards.

ARTS AND IDEAS

Architecture

1463

- Numbering of houses is introduced on the Pont Notre-Dame in Paris, France.

1464

- Italian architect Filarete (Antonio Averlino) writes *Trattato d'architettura/Treatise on Architecture*, which sets out plans for an ideal city called Sforzinda.

Arts

1460

c. 1460   Flemish artist Albert van Ouwater paints *The Raising of Lazarus*.

c. 1460   Flemish artist Dirk Bouts paints *The Martyrdom of St. Erasmus*.

c. 1460   Italian artist Andrea Mantegna paints the *The Agony in the Garden* and *St. Sebastian*.

c. 1460   Italian artist Antonio del Pollaiuolo paints *Hercules and the Hydra*.

c. 1460   Italian artist Benozzo Gozzoli paints the fresco *The Adoration of the Magi* in the Chapel of Medici-Riccardi Palace in Florence, Italy.

c. 1460   Italian artist Desiderio da Setignano sculpts the relief *Madonna and Child*.

c. 1460   Italian artist Giovanni Bellini paints *The Agony in the Garden*.

c. 1460   The anonymous French artist, the Master of Avignon, paints *The Avignon Pietà*, one of the most striking French paintings of the period.

- French artist Jean Fouquet completes his illuminations for the book of prayers *The Hours of Etienne Chevalier*.

1462

- Flemish artist Dirk Bouts paints *Portrait of a Young Man*.

Literature and Language

1461

- Albrecht Pfister prints the first two books written in a vernacular language, *Der Edelstein/The Gem* by Ulrich Boner and *Der Ackermann aus Böhmen/The Farmhand from Bohemia* by Johannes von Tepl, in Bamberg, Germany.
- French writer François Villon writes his long poem *Le Grand Testament/The Longer Testament*. One of the most important French literary works of the 15th

century, it gives a graphic account of his life as a outlaw. It is first published in 1489.

1463

- Pope Pius II (Enea Silvio Piccolomini) completes his *Commentarii/Commentaries*, the first autobiography by a pope and one of the finest autobiographies of the Renaissance.

SOCIETY

Education

1460

- Backed by a papal bull of Pope Pius II, Duke Francis II of Brittany founds a university in his capital Nantes, France.
- Pope Pius II establishes a university in the city of Basel, the first in the Swiss lands (though Basel does not join the Swiss Confederation until 1501).

1461

- The University of Rennes is founded in France.

1463

- Cambridge University, England, confers its first degree of Bachelor of Music, on the English singer and composer Henry Abyngdon.

Everyday Life

c. 1460

- Dresses with high, full bodices are in fashion in England.

1463

- A new law in England establishes rules on which materials can be used for clothes according to social rank. Commoners are forbidden to wear imported cloth, fur, or scarlet, and gold and purple are restricted to the aristocracy.

Religion

1460–65

January 18 Pope Pius II (Enea Silvio Piccolomini), in his bull *Execrabilis*, condemns all appeals to general councils.

1461

- The first printer in Strasbourg publishes a bible in the vernacular (German).

BIRTHS & DEATHS

1460

c. 1460 Vasco da Gama, Portuguese navigator who established the sea route from Europe to Asia via the Cape of Good Hope, born (–1524).

- Georges d'Amboise, cardinal and chief minister of the French state under King Louis XII, born in Chaumont-sur-Loire, France (–1510).
- William Dunbar, Scottish poet whose works include *The Goldyn Targe*, born in Scotland (–*c.* 1525).

August 3 James II, King of Scotland 1437–60, son of James I, falls in battle at Roxburgh, Scotland (29).

November 13 Henry the Navigator, Portuguese prince noted for his sponsorship of voyages of discovery and trade, dies in Vila do Infante, near Sagres, Portugal (66).

December 14 Guarino Veronese, leading Italian humanist and Greek scholar, dies in Ferrara, Italy (*c.* 86).

December 30 Richard, Duke of York, claimant to the English throne whose attempts to gain it led to the War of the Roses, is killed near Wakefield, Yorkshire (49).

1461

May 15 Domenico Veneziano, Italian Renaissance painter, one of the founders of the Florentine school of painting, dies in Florence (*c.* 23).

July 22 Charles VII, King of France 1422–61, who drove the English from French soil, dies in Mehun-sur-Yèvre, France (58).

1462

c. 1462 Edmund Dudley, English politician and author of the political allegory *The Tree of Commonwealth* (1509), born (–1510).

June 27 Louis XII, King of France 1498–1515 who fought a series of disastrous Italian wars, born in Blois, France (–1515).

September 16 Pietro Pomponazzi, Italian Aristotelian philosopher, born in Mantua, marquisate of Mantua (–1525).

1463

- François Villon, French lyric poet known especially for his poems *Le Petit Testament/The Shorter Testament* and *Le Grand Testament/The Longer Testament*, dies (*c.* 35).

February 24 Giovanni Pico della Mirandola, Count of Concordia, Italian humanist scholar and Platonist philosopher, born in Mirandola, Italy (–1494).

March St. Catherine of Bologna (original name Caterina Vigri), influential Italian mystic and writer, whose major work is *Le sette arme necessarie alla battaglia spirituale/ The Seven Arms Necessary for the Spiritual Battle* (1438), dies in Bologna, Italy (49).

June 4 Flavio Biondo, humanist historian, whose best-known works include *Italia illustrata/Italy Explained* (1474) and the 32-volume *Historiarum ab inclinatione Romanorum imperii decades/ Decades of History From the Deterioration of the Roman Empire* (1483), dies in Rome (*c.* 71).

1464

June 18 Rogier van der Weyden, influential Flemish painter, dies in Brussels (*c.* 64).

August 1 Cosimo de' Medici the Elder, financier and statesman, dies in Careggi, near Florence, Italy (74).

August 11 Nicholas of Cusa, cardinal, scholar, scientist, and philosopher, dies in Todi, Italy (*c.* 63).

August 14 Pius II (Enea Silvio Piccolomini), Italian pope 1458–64, who attempted to unite Europe against the Turks, dies in Ancona, Papal States (58).

1462

- Pope Pius II declares the Compacta of Jihlava (the agreement of toleration granted to the Hussite Utraquists in 1436) null and void.

Sports

1460–65

- René, Duke of Anjou and Naples, writes his *Livre des tournois/On Tournaments*. He stages spectacular and elaborate tournaments (knightly contests) on his estates, which are partly theatrical in character.

1465–1469

POLITICS, GOVERNMENT, AND ECONOMICS

Business and Economics

1465

- Matthias I Corvinus, King of Hungary, establishes his standing "black army" of 30,000 mercenaries, many of them Hussites, under "Black John" Haugwitz. In order to pay for his army he extracts regular high taxes and abolishes exemptions for the Barony, Cumans, and Saxons.

Politics and Government

1465

- Abd-al-Haqq II, last of the Marinid rulers of Morocco, is murdered and the Wattasids regents claim the throne. A period of fragmentation ensues.

March   Duke Francis II of Brittany, Charles the Bold, heir to Burgundy and Count of Charolais, René, Duke of Anjou, the Duke of Nemours, and Charles, brother of King Louis XI of France, form the League of the Public Weal to resist Louis XI's exertions of royal power.

June 5   A faction of nobles led by Alphonso Carillo, archbishop of Toledo, declares King Henry IV of Castile and León deposed in favor of his infant brother Alfonso in the "farce of Avila." This decision, prompted by wrangling over the legitimacy of Henry's heir Joan "La Beltraneja/child of Beltran," provokes civil war.

July   The deposed Lancastrian king Henry VI is captured near Clitheroe in Lancashire, England, and held in the Tower of London, England.

July 16   Armies of King Louis XI of France and forces led by Charles the Bold, Count of Charolais and heir to

Burgundy, clash and draw a hard-fought battle at Montlhéry, south of Paris, France, in the War of the Public Weal, a baronial and civic revolt. The League of the Public Weal (of Charles the Bold) invests Paris, France.

August   Responding to papal calls to Rome, Italy, to answer charges of heresy, the Hussite king, George of Poděbrady, proposes a conference. This fails and Bohemian Catholic nobles led by Zdenek of Sternberk form a league with the Silesian city of Breslau (modern Wrocław, Poland) at Zielona Góra, Poland.

October 5   King Louis XI of France is forced to make the Peace of Conflans with the League of the Public Weal, the price being the cession of territory on the Somme to Burgundy, and the grant of the duchy of Normandy to his brother Charles, Duke of Berry.

December–January 1466   Ming armies under Han Yung defeat the most serious of several Yao tribal insurgencies led by Hou Ta-kuo in Kwangsi province, China, fighting pitched battles in the *Ta-Teng hsia* ("big rattan gorge") campaign.

1466

- Kapilendra, the first king of the Surya dynasty of Hindu Orissa, dies and is succeeded by his son Hamvira, having campaigned in Vijayanagar, India, as far as the Kaveri and taken the kingdom of Rajahmundry and the Bāhmanī provinces of Bidar and Warangal.

- The Albanian prince Skanderbeg defeats an Ottoman force besieging his stronghold of Croya, north of Tiranë, Albania.

1466–1473   Sonni Ali besieges and eventually takes the trading and scholarly city of Djenné from Tuareg occupiers.

January   King Louis XI of France repossesses the duchy of Normandy after granting it to his brother Charles in the previous year under the Treaty of Conflans. He uses interference from Duke Francis II of Brittany as an excuse.

June   Chinese imperial forces under Chu Yung defeat a rebellion among the refugee peasants of Ching-Hsiang (Hupeh), China, where the leader Liu T'ung has been acclaimed "Prince of Han." Liu T'ung is executed and his followers disperse to the Szechwan province.

July The twelve-year-old King James III of Scotland is seized by Robert, Lord Boyd of Kilmarnock, who becomes governor of Scotland.

August 25 Charles the Bold of Burgundy sacks the city of Dinant, part of the insurgent bishopric of Liège, and expels its famous coppersmiths.

October 19 The Thirteen Years' War between Poland and the Teutonic Order of Knights ends with the Peace of Toruń. The Teutonic Order of Knights cedes the disputed areas of Pomerania and West Prussia to Poland, and becomes a vassal of King Casimir (Kazimierz) IV of Poland.

November–July 1467 At the diet of Nuremberg in Germany, Frederick III the Holy Roman Emperor promotes the discussion of a statutory general peace in Germany to last five years, and puts forward the possibility of crusades against the Ottoman Turks and Hussites.

December 23 Pope Paul II excommunicates George of Poděbrady and declares him deposed as king of Bohemia. He faces continual insurgency for the rest of his reign.

1467

- Stephen the Great, Voivod of Moldavia, defeats and repels a Hungarian invasion.
- The Ak Koyunlu (White Sheep) Uzbek tribal confederacy, led by Uzun Hasan, defeats the rival Kara Koyunlu (Black Sheep) confederacy, killing their leader Jihan Shah in battle.

1467–77 The kingdoms of Jaffna and Kandy in the north and center of modern Sri Lanka respectively, wrest their independence from the kingdom of Kotte following the death of its king Parakramabahu VI and end its control over the entire island.

May Disputes between the Hosokawa and Yamana families over rival candidates for the offices of shogun (military ruler) and *kanrei* spark the Onin War. Bitter street battles break out in the Japanese capital Kyoto, and the shogun Ashikaga Yoshimasa is powerless to stop a slide into general warfare.

October 28 Charles the Bold, having succeeded his father Philip as Duke of Burgundy on June 15, defeats the insurgent citizens of Liège at Brusthelem, and repeals their constitution.

November 1 The western Yamano forces storm the Zen monastery of Shokokuji adjacent to the palace of the shogun (military ruler) in Kyoto, Japan, appearing to be on the brink of victory though the carnage has decimated their forces. The Onin War is stalemated.

1468

- A statute of the imperial city of Augsburg, Germany, condemns to death any citizen found guilty of testifying before an unauthorized court in a measure taken to suppress the secret Vehmic system of justice.
- Chan Chan, capital of the Chimú state of northern Peru, is conquered by Tawantisiyu forces led by Topa Inca Yupanqui, son of Pachacuti Inca Yupanqui.
- Sonni Ali, founder of the Songhai empire, takes Timbuktu, Mali, greatest entrepôt of trans-Saharan trade, from the Tuareg nomads who have controlled it since 1433.
- The Ak Koyunlu (White Sheep) Uzbeks under Uzun Hasan take Baghdad, (in modern Iraq), eliminating the

power of the Kara Koyunlu (Black Sheep) Uzbekhs and going on to defeat Abu Sa'id, Timurid shah of Persia.

- Trailok, King of the Thai state of Ayutthaya, promulgates laws of succession and precedence among the princely and noble classes, and defines the rights and duties of all parties at court.

January 17 Skanderbeg, the Albanian national hero and bulwark against the Ottoman Turks, dies at the port of Lezhë, Albania and is succeeded by his son John Castriota II.

February 4 John Tiptoft, Earl of Worcester and deputy of Ireland for King Edward IV of England, brings his predecessor Thomas, Earl of Desmond, and his lord chancellor, the Earl of Kildare, to parliamentary trial for treason. The Earl of Desmond is executed on February 14 having been found guilty, but the Earl of Kildare is pardoned.

March Richard Neville, Earl of Warwick and captain of Calais, piratically captures four ships of the Hanseatic League and sparks a desultory war.

March 8 The impoverished Christian I of Denmark (and Norway) pledges the Orkney Islands (and in 1469 the Shetland Islands) as security on the dowry of his daughter Margaret, who is to be married to King James III of Scotland.

April 6–14 King Louis XI of France holds the only meeting in his reign of the Estates General, at Tours, France. The Estates accede to his wishes and declare Normandy to be a crown possession in perpetuity.

June Jasper Tudor, Earl of Pembroke, returns from France, hoping to relieve the long-besieged Lancastrian castle of Harlech in Wales. He succeeds in capturing Denbigh Castle, Wales, but is then defeated by William, Lord Herbert, and Harlech surrenders shortly after.

July 3 Alfonso, the Infante of Castile and rival of his brother Henry IV for the throne of Castile, dies. Their sister Isabella, though reluctant, is declared heir in the "Pact of Los Toros de Guisando," and Henry repudiates the claim of his daughter Joan "La Beltraneja."

July 3 Charles the Bold of Burgundy marries Margaret, sister of King Edward IV of England, who thus joins the alliance against King Louis XI of France and guarantees free trade between England and Burgundy. The Earl of Warwick's French sympathies cause a division in his relationship with Edward.

August Armies of the Swiss Confederation, led by the cantonal militia of Bern, besiege the Habsburg fortress of Waldshut on the upper River Rhine in support of the strategic trading city of Mulhouse in Alsace, an ally of the cantons of Bern and Solothurn.

September 10 King Louis XI of France concludes a brief punitive campaign in Brittany in retaliation for its opposition to his repossession of Normandy, and forces a peace treaty on Duke Francis II at Ancenis, thereby neutralizing Brittany in his struggle with Charles the Bold of Burgundy.

October 11 King Louis XI of France, negotiating with Charles the Bold of Burgundy on their common frontier in Péronne on the River Somme, has "forgotten" the insurrection in Liège which he has encouraged. When Charles hears of it, he holds Louis under house arrest. On October 30, Charles compels his captive Louis to witness his storming and sacking of Liège. He then releases Louis on the condition that he exempt Charles'

French fiefs from the jurisdiction of the parlement (parliament).

November   James III of Scotland declares himself of age and holds a parliament which condemns his captors and erstwhile governors, the Boyds, for treason. Alexander Boyd is executed but Lord Robert escapes to England. The election of burgh councils is regularized.

1469

- Ivan III, Grand Duke of Muscovy, conquers the Tatars of Kazan and installs a puppet khan.
- Montezuma I, the fifth Aztec ruler, dies after a long reign in which the Aztecs extended their empire as far as the Gulf of Mexico and traded ever more widely; this expansion is to continue until the Spanish conquest.

May 3   At the instigation of Pope Paul II, Matthias I Corvinus is declared king of Bohemia at Brno, Moravia, by the Czech rebels he supported against King George of Poděbrady in an invasion of Moravia in the previous year.

May 9   Forced to pay an indemnity for peace by the Swiss, Sigismund, Habsburg Count of Tyrol, mortgages Upper Alsace and other lands to Charles the Bold of Burgundy, hoping for military aid against the Swiss and their ally, the imperial city of Mulhouse, France.

June   Rebellion breaks out in the north of England, led by "Robin of Holderness" and "Robin of Redesdale," Warwick's lieutenant Sir John Conyers.

June   The Bohemian estates accept Władysław, son of King Casimir (Kazimierz) IV of Poland, as heir to George of Poděbrady. Silesia, Lusatia, and Moravia (the other lands of the kingdom of Bohemia) have accepted the conquering Matthias I Corvinus of Hungary as king.

July 11   Richard Neville, Earl of Warwick, seals his alliance with George, Duke of Clarence, when the Duke of Clarence marries his daughter Isabel Neville at Sandwich, England. They enter London, England, on the July 20 and muster support in questioning the paternity of King Edward IV of England.

July 26   King Edward IV of England's Welsh and Marcher forces, led by William Herbert, Earl of Pembroke, are stopped and annihilated at Edgecote in Northamptonshire, England, by Sir John Conyer's rebels, who are reinforced by the Earl of Warwick. King Edward IV is captured two days later.

August 23   Alfonso, Duke of Calabria and son of Ferrante of Naples, defeats the papal forces attacking Roberto Malatesta of Rimini. His father has quarreled with Pope Paul II over papal demands for tributary taxes.

September   The distraction of a Lancastrian rising in County Durham enables King Edward IV of England to free himself from the custody of the Earl of Warwick at Middleham in Yorkshire, England, and to rally his supporters at Pontefract, Yorkshire.

October 17   Ferdinand, son and heir of King John II of Aragon, marries Isabella, sister and heir of King Henry IV of Castile.

SCIENCE, TECHNOLOGY, AND MEDICINE

Agriculture

1468

- The Spanish introduce rice into northern Italy.

Exploration

1469

- King Alfonso V of Portugal grants Fernão Gomes a monopoly in trade with Guinea on condition that 100 leagues of its coastline are explored annually.

Science

1469

- Roman historian Pliny's *Historia naturalis/Natural History* is printed for the first time.

Technology

1465

- German printers Konrad Sweynheym and Arnold Pannartz settle at the Benedictine monastery of Subiaco, near Rome and, encouraged by the church, set up the first Italian printing press.

Transportation

1466

- The earliest dated illustration—on the Psalter of King Henry VI—of the ship design known as a carrack, with three masts, combining square and lateen sails, is made. These ships carry vast cargoes, which will allow the great voyages of discovery to be undertaken.

ARTS AND IDEAS

Arts

1465

- *c.* 1465   Dutch artist Nicolas Gerhaert carves *Bust of a Man*, which is thought to be a self-portrait.
- *c.* 1465   Italian artist Alesso Baldovinetti paints *Portrait of a Young Woman*.
- *c.* 1465   Italian artist Antonio da Messina paints *The Virgin Annunciate* and *Portrait of a Man*.
- *c.* 1465   The anonymous French (or perhaps Flemish) artist, the Master of Anjou, paints illuminations for the *Livre de Cuer d'Amour/Book of the Heart Seized by Love*, an

allegorical romance written by René of Anjou, King of Naples, in 1457. Some authorities believe the monarch may also have been the artist.

- Italian artist Paolo Uccello paints *The Hunt*.

1466

- Italian artist Fra Filippo Lippi completes his frescoes on the life of St. John the Baptist in Parto Cathedral. One of the best-known scenes is *The Feast of Herod*.

c. 1467

- Italian artist Andrea Mantegna paints the *Dead Christ*.

1468

- Flemish artist Dirk Bouts paints the *Last Supper Altarpiece*.
- Italian artist Antonio Rossellino sculpts the portrait bust *Matteo Palmieri*.

Literature and Language

1465

- German printers Conrad Schweynheym and Arnold Pannartz introduce the roman typeface when they print

the Donatus grammar, a compendium of Latin grammar written by the Roman grammarian Aelius Donatus, at the Benedictine monastery of Subiaco, near Rome.

1468

- Spanish writer Inigo López de Mendoza completes his long poem *Vita Christi/The Life of Christ*.

Theater and Dance

c. 1465

- The French farce *Maistre Pierre Pathelin/Master Pierre Pathelin* is written, possibly by the French monk Guillaume Alexis.

Thought and Scholarship

1469

- Arabic scholar Ibn-Taghri-Birdi completes his *Al-Nujūm al-Zāhirah fi Muluk Misr w-al-Qāhirah/The Brilliant Stars regarding the Kings of Egypt and Cairo*, history of Egypt from AD 640 to AD 1453.

BIRTHS & DEATHS

1465

c. 1465 Johann Tetzel, German Dominican friar whose preaching of indulgences caused Martin Luther to rebel and begin the Reformation, born in Pirna, Saxony (–1519).

c. 1465 Lodovico de Varthema, Italian traveler who explored the Middle East and Asia, and was the first Christian to make a pilgrimage to Mecca, born in Bologna, (–1517).

- Beatriz Galindo ("La Latina"), Spanish humanist and celebrated classical scholar, professor at the University of Salamanca, founder of schools and hospitals, born, probably in Salamanca, Spain (–1535).
- Hans Holbein the Elder, German painter, father of Hans Holbein the Younger, born in Augsburg, Germany (–1524).

January 4 Charles of Orléans, French courtly poet, dies in Ambroise, France (70).

1466

- Andrea Doria, Genoese statesman, mercenary commander, and celebrated admiral, born in Oneglia, Duchy of Milan, Italy (*c.* 94).
- Montezuma II (or Moctezuma), ninth Aztec emperor 1502–20, born (–1520).

March 8 Francesco Sforza, Duke of Milan 1450–66, who was a key

figure in 15th-century Italian politics, dies in Milan (64).

December 13 Donatello, celebrated Italian Renaissance sculptor, whose major works include *David* and the *Feast of Herod* (1433–35), dies in Florence, Italy (*c.* 80).

1467

c. 1467 Pedro Alvarez Cabral, Portuguese explorer who discovered Brazil, born in Belmonte, Portugal (–1520).

January 26 Guillaume Budé (Budaeus), French scholar who helped to revive classical studies in France, cofounder of the Collège de France in Paris, born in Paris, France (–1540).

June 15 Philip III, Duke of Burgundy 1419–67, who founded the state of Burgundy, dies in Bruges, Burgundy (70).

1468

- Jean Régnier, French writer, who wrote *Le Livre des Fortunes et Adversitez/The Book of Fortune and Misfortune*, a long poem written in prison, dies.
- William Lily, English humanist and classical grammarian, born in Odiham, Hampshire, England (–1522).

February 29 Paul III, Italian pope 1534–49, who called the Council of Trent (1545), and started a reform

movement within the church, born in Canino, Papal States (–1549).

1469

- Fra Filippo Lippi, Italian Renaissance painter, whose major works include *Madonna and Child with Two Angels* (*c.* 1465), dies in Florence, Italy (*c.* 63).
- Jakob I Fugger the Elder, German merchant, dies (*c.* 59).
- Nānak, Indian religious leader, first Guru of the Sikhs, born in Rai Bhoi di Talvandi, near Lahore, India (–1539).
- St. John Fisher (John of Rochester), English humanist, who opposed Henry VIII's break with the Roman Catholic Church, born in Beverley, Yorkshire, England (–1535).

May 3 Niccolò Machiavelli, Italian statesman, writer, and political theorist whose best-known work is *Il principe/The Prince* (1513), born in Florence, Italy (–1527).

October 28 Desiderius Erasmus, humanist, considered the greatest scholar of the northern European Renaissance, born in Rotterdam, Netherlands (–1536).

November 2 Edward V, King of England April–June 1483, born in London, England (–1483).

SOCIETY

Sports

c. 1466

- The Lucerne Shooting Guild, the first shooting club, is formed in Switzerland. In 1472 the first recorded shooting match is held in Zürich, Switzerland.

1467

- Thalhotter's *Fechtbuch/Book of Fencing* is one of several fencing handbooks being produced in Europe.

1470–1474

POLITICS, GOVERNMENT, AND ECONOMICS

Business and Economics

1471

June–July Frederick III the Holy Roman Emperor holds a diet at Regensburg, Germany, which eventually grants a tax to support the defense of the Holy Roman Empire from the Ottoman Turks. He opposes princely plans to repudiate imperial arbitration in their states with a planned general peace, to be reinforced by a salaried imperial court.

1474

- William Cannings of Bristol is recorded as the first English shipowner not himself engaged directly in trade.

Human Rights

1473

March Riots and pogroms against the Jewish spread throughout the cities of Spain during Lent. Communities of *conversos* (Jews converted to Christianity) and *marranos* (*conversos* who maintain their Jewish faith in secret) are also targeted in the city of Córdoba.

Politics and Government

1470

c. 1470 English jurist and political writer John Fortescue writes *De laudibus legum Angliae/In Praise of English Law*, a dialogue between the author and Prince Edward, the son of Henry VI. The first printed edition appears in 1546.

- An alliance between the two states that dominates southern India, the Hindu Vijayanagar empire and the Muslim Bāhmanī sultanate, results in the defeat of Orissa, India, taking much of the Indian Carnatic coast.
- Following famine throughout North China, renewed insurrection breaks out among the refugees of the Ching-Hsiang region (Hupeh). Their leader proclaims himself *T'ai p'ing wang* (prince of the era of great peace).
- Frederick II abdicates as elector of Brandenburg, dispirited by the failure of his claim to Pomerania-Stettin, and is succeeded by his brother Albert III Achilles.

March 4 Local rebellions in Lincolnshire and Yorkshire (led by Sir John Conyers on March 10) draw King Edward IV of England north from London once again. On routing the Lincolnshire rebels at Empingham at "Loosecoat Field" on March 12, he learns of the implication of the Duke of Clarence and the Earl of Warwick, who flee under fire from Exeter on the south coast of England via piracy to Honfleur in Normandy.

May An Ottoman force captures the Aegean island of Negropont (Euboea) from Venice, after beating the Venetian fleet.

May 15 King Charles VIII of Sweden dies; his rule is followed by an interregnum and the regency of Sten Sture.

July 24 King Louis XI of France arranges a formal reconciliation between Margaret of Anjou and Richard, Earl of Warwick, both of whom are now in exile following their defeats by King Edward IV of England. Warwick subsequently positively switches allegiance to the Lancastrian Henry VI.

August Following the defeat and death of Abu Sa'id at the hands of the Ak Koyunlu (White Sheep) Uzbekh Turks, Timurid rule retreats to Khorasan, where Husein

Baiqara seizes Herat, Afghanistan, and is proclaimed sultan of Persia.

October 6 The Earl of Warwick, in alliance with King Louis XI of France and Margaret of Anjou, eludes the Yorkist–Burgundian blockade of the English Channel and invades England via Plymouth, restoring Henry VI as king "the Readeption." King Edward IV of England flees for Burgundian Holland on October 2 as his support fails.

December–April 1471 King Louis XI of France invades Picardy and takes the towns of Amiens, St. Quentin, Péronne, and Picquigny along the River Somme, in a campaign against Charles the Bold of Burgundy.

1471

- An Ottoman force captures the Genoese trading colony of Tana at the mouth of the River Don in southern Russia.

- Insurgent Catalan serfs extract their freedom from King John II of Aragon as he recovers Catalonia from the separatist Generalitat (parliament).

- Le Thanh-tong, Emperor of Dai Viet, starts the annexation of the northern provinces of the Champa kingdom. A 500-kilometer stretch of Annam is conquered and settled southward from Da Nang to Nha Trang.

- Pachacuti Inca Yupanqui, the ninth Inca emperor, abdicates in favor of his son Topa Inca Yupanqui, after seeing his reign transform Tawantisiyu (the Inca state) from being a small principality around Cuzco to the dominant state of the Andes through victories over Chimú and Chacan.

- Stephen the Great, Voivod of Moldavia, launches a campaign to expel the Ottoman forces which have recently occupied Wallachia.

March 22 George of Poděbrady, beleaguered Hussite king of Bohemia, dies in Prague, Bohemia, to be succeeded in May by Ladislas (Władysław), son of King Casimir (Kazimierz) IV of Poland, elected by the Bohemian diet as his successor.

April 14 Having sailed from Burgundy to land at Ravenspur in Holderness, England, on March 14, King Edward IV of England musters support and enters London, England, capturing Henry VI and annihilating the Lancastrian Neville forces in the fog at Barnet. The Lancastrian leaders, the Earl of Warwick and Lord Montague, die in battle.

May 4 Margaret of Anjou, having arrived from France too late to save the Earl of Warwick, sees the obliteration of her own forces by King Edward IV of England at Tewkesbury, England. She is captured by the Yorkist victors, and her son Edward, Prince of Wales, her general the Duke of Somerset, and many other Lancastrian lords are killed.

May 21 Richard, Duke of Gloucester, brother of King Edward IV of England, defeats an attack on London, England, by the Lancastrian Lord Fauconberg which is aimed at taking Henry VI from confinement in the Tower of London. Edward has Henry executed, extinguishing the Lancastrian dynasty.

July 3 After suppressing a revolt by the city of Arezzo, Italy, Lorenzo de' Medici secures control of Florence, Italy, when its *signoria* (guild council) appoints his nominees as the ten *accoppiatori* to hold full powers of government.

August A Portuguese expedition led by John, son of King Alfonso V of Portugal, conquers the cities of Tangier and Arzila on the Moroccan coast, gaining him the epithet "the African."

August The Ottoman Turks launch their first raids into Habsburg territory, devastating Styria, Carinthia, and Carniola, duchies of the Holy Roman Emperor Frederick III.

October 10 Sten Sture, nephew of Charles VIII of Sweden, leads a popular rising and drives back the invasion by King Christian of Denmark at Brunkeberg, outside Stockholm, Sweden. He is elected regent of Sweden.

October 11 Following its defeat by Muscovite forces, the extensive and wealthy republic of Novgorod becomes subject to Ivan III, Grand Duke of Muscovy, and Moscow. The ascendancy in Russia of the principality of Muscovy is established.

October 26 Following the death in July of Pope Paul II, the Genoese Francesco della Rovere is elected Pope Sixtus IV.

1472

- A joint papal–Venetian expedition commanded by Cardinal Oliviero Carafa occupies the Turkish port of Smyrna (Izmir) in Anatolia, but is forced to evacuate following disagreements among the parties.

- Albert III Achilles succeeds where his predecessor and brother Frederick II failed, and imposes his suzerainty on Duke Erik of Pomerania by the Treaty of Prenzlau. Duke Erik cedes lands on the River Oder to Albert.

- Bāhmanī armies under the *wazir* Mahmud Gawan retake the important trading port of Goa, India.

- The Orkney and Shetland Islands of Scotland, which have been held as surety for the dowry of Margaret, daughter of Christian I of Denmark and wife of King James III of Scotland, are annexed when the dowry is not paid.

May 24 Charles of France, Duke of Gascony and brother of King Louis XI of France, dies, enabling Louis to reintegrate the duchy, depriving the rebellious Count of Armagnac of his chief support.

June 27 Charles the Bold of Burgundy revokes the truce he made the previous year with King Louis XI of France and invades French Picardy, besieging the city of Beauvais, France.

October 17 Barcelona, Catalonia, surrenders on compromise terms to King John II of Aragon. The secessionist revolt of Catalonia under its Generalitat (parliament) ends, and Catalonia and Aragon are united when they face King Louis XI of France in Roussillon, France.

November 3 King Louis XI of France makes a truce with Charles the Bold of Burgundy following a summer in which Charles ravaged the provinces of Normandy and the Ile-de-France.

1473

c. 1473 English jurist and political writer John Fortescue writes *De dominio regali et politico/The Governance of England*, one of the earliest constitutional treatises in English. The first printed edition appears in 1714.

- A Ming expedition fails to take the city of Hami (Sinkiang), China, retreating when its Mongol cavalry desert at the prospect of attack from Turfan, China.

- Charles the Bold of Burgundy establishes a standing army by means of the statutes of Thionville. He also forms the Parlement (sovereign court) of Malines as the central court of appeal for Burgundy, depriving his French fiefs of Flanders, Burgundy, Artois, and Picardy of the right to appeal to the Parlement of Paris.
- Stephen the Great, Voivod of Moldavia, defeats the Ottoman forces occupying Wallachia at Râmnicu Sarat.

February 1   King John II of Aragon enters Perpignan, capital of Roussillon, France, following a popular revolt against the French occupation.

February 24   The elector of Brandenburg, Albert III Achilles, ensures the indivisibility and succession by primogeniture of Brandenburg by introducing the law known as *dispositio achillea*.

March 4   John V, Count of Armagnac, dies in a battle with the forces of King Louis XI of France which results in the fall of his capital Lectoure, France.

April   King Edward IV of England empowers the council of his infant son Edward, Prince of Wales, to act as a court (usually at Ludlow, Shropshire, England) for Wales and its Marches.

April 15   In Japan, Yamana Mochitoyo, leader of the usurping "western army" and one of the chief protagonists in the Onin War, dies after having sworn to take his own life if a truce is not called.

May–November   The zealous Lancastrian John de Vere, Earl of Oxford, captures the fortified tidal island of St. Michael's Mount in Cornwall, England, but is besieged there and eventually captured and imprisoned.

June   Charles the Bold of Burgundy takes the duchy of Guelders and the county of Zutphen in the Netherlands from the control of the renegade Duke Arnold.

June 6   In Japan, Hosokawa Katsumoto, leader of the loyalist faction in the Onin War, dies. Following the earlier death of his opponent Yamana Mochitoyo, this ends any prospect of a truce and many residents leave the devastated capital, Kyoto, as Japan descends into feudal chaos.

July–September   In negotiations at the city of Trier, Germany, Charles the Bold of Burgundy requests that Frederick III the Holy Roman Emperor invest him king of Burgundy. The negotiations come close to success, but Frederick, at the last moment, flees by night.

August   Ottoman forces defeat the invading Ak Koyunlu (Black Sheep) Uzbekh tribal federation led by Uzun Hasan, allies of Venice, at Terjan in Armenia.

October 15   Under the Treaty of Nancy, Charles the Bold of Burgundy compels René II, Duke of Upper Lorraine, to allow Burgundian troops passage through Lorraine, which separates the two halves of his lands.

1474

- Ivan III, Grand Duke of Muscovy, annexes the principality of Rostov, northeast of Moscow, Russia.

April   Ming forces construct the present-day "Great Wall" along the border of the Ordos desert in the Shensi province of China in order to hold back persistent Mongol incursions.

April 4   King Louis XI of France engineers the formation of the Union of Constance, a defensive pact against Charles the Bold of Burgundy. Sigismund, Habsburg Count of Tyrol, who agrees to recognize Swiss autonomy in the "perpetual peace," joins with them and the "Basse-Union" of Alsatian towns.

July 1474–June 1475   Charles the Bold of Burgundy spends a year unsuccessfully besieging the small city of Neuss, Germany, in support of the archbishop of Cologne's dispute with his chapter and subjects.

July 25   King Edward IV of England and Charles the Bold of Burgundy formalize an alliance for the partition of France, echoing the nearly successful move of 1420, the Treaty of Troyes, made by their predecessors.

August   A Venetian fleet led by the future doge Pietro Mocenigo raises the year long siege of the city of Scutari (Shkodër), Albania, by an Ottoman force.

September   King Edward IV of England ends six years of desultory naval war against the Hanseatic League with the Peace of Utrecht, and restores the league's trading privileges and English depots (steelyards) at London, Boston, and King's Lynn.

December 12   Henry IV the Impotent, King of Castile, dies and is succeeded by his sister Isabella and her husband Ferdinand V, son and heir of John II of Aragon.

SCIENCE, TECHNOLOGY, AND MEDICINE

Exploration

1472

- Afanasy Nikitin, a merchant from Tver in Russia, writes his *Journey across Three Seas*, describing his travels in India and Persia from 1466.

1474

- Italian explorer Christopher Columbus, using Roman calculations for the radius of the earth, first proposes that a sea route to Cathay could be found by sailing west from Europe.

Health and Medicine

1471

- Italian physician Giovanni Matteo Ferrari's medical text *Practicae pars prima et secunda/The Practice of Medicine, First and Second Parts* is printed.

1472

- Italian physician Giovanni Matteo Ferrari writes his *Useful Repertory of the Precepts of Avicenna*, a commentary on the work of the great 11th-century Arab physician Avicenna.

Math

1474

- German astronomer Regiomontanus publishes his *Ephemerides*, astronomical tables for 1475–1500, and proposes a method for calculating longitude by the measurement of lunar distance.

Science

1472

- Halley's comet passes close to earth, appearing as a brilliant "Great Comet," and inspiring a wave of superstition.
- The *Etymologies* by 7th-century Spanish bishop Isidore of Seville, a compilation of scientific knowledge, is printed for the first time. It contains the first printed map.

1473

- Jewish astronomer Abraham Zacuto of Salamanca begins five years of observations to determine accurately the sun's changing declination from day to day.
- The *Flos naturarum/Flower of Nature* of the alchemist "Geber" (thought to be a Spaniard of the 14th century using the name of 8th-century Arab alchemist Jābir ibn Hayyān) is printed.

1474

- Italian astrologer and astronomer Lorenzo Buonincontro publishes *Commentaria in C Manilii astronomicon/Commentary on the Astonomicon of C. Manilius*, a discussion of 1st-century philosopher Manilius' astrological poetry.

Technology

1470

- The rector and librarian of the college of the Sorbonne in Paris, France, invites three Germans to set up the first French print shop there.

1473

- German printer Andrew Hesz of Nuremberg sets up the first printing press at Buda, Hungary, under the patronage of Hungarian King Matthias I Corvinus.
- The first print shops in the Netherlands are set up in the town of Aalst, by Thierry Martens.

1474

- English printer William Caxton sets up a press in Bruges, Belgium.
- The first Spanish printing press is set up in Valencia.

ARTS AND IDEAS

Architecture

1470

- Three designs by the Italian architect and writer Leon Battista Alberti are realized: the façade of the Rucellai Palace in Florence, Italy (designed in the early 1450s); the Church of Sant' Andrea in Mantua, Italy (marking the culmination of his experiments with classical form); and the façade of the Church of Santa Maria Novella in Florence, Italy (designed in 1456). Though built on to a medieval church, the façade at Santa Maria Novella is

boldly structured on simple ratios (the square and its subdivisions), an approach to architecture that characterizes the early Renaissance in Italy.

1471

- The Fatih Mosque in Istanbul is completed.

Arts

1470

- *c.* 1470 Flemish artist Hans Memling paints *The Fall of Man*.
- *c.* 1470 Flemish artist Petrus Christus paints *Portrait of a Young Woman*.
- *c.* 1470 German artist Martin Schongauer engraves *The Temptation of St. Anthony*.
- *c.* 1470 Italian artist Andrea del Verrocchio paints *The Baptism of Christ*. One of the figures is thought to have been painted by the youthful Leonardo da Vinci, who studied in Verrocchio's studio.
- *c.* 1470 Italian artist Giovanni Bellini paints *Pietà with Mary and John*.
- *c.* 1470 Portuguese artist Nuno Gonçalves paints *St. Vincent Altarpiece*, a work that includes vivid portraits of many of leading figures of Portuguese society, including Henry the Navigator.
- Flemish artist Hugo van der Goes paints *Adam and Eve*.
- Italian artist Sandro Botticelli paints *Fortitude*.

1473

- *c.* 1473 Italian artist Leonardo da Vinci paints *The Annunciation*, thought to be his first independent painting.
- Flemish artist Hans Memling paints his *Last Judgment Triptych*.

1474

- *c.* 1474 Flemish artist Joos Van Ghent paints *The Communion of the Apostles*.
- *c.* 1474 Italian artist Francesco Laurana sculpts the portrait bust *Battista Sforza*.
- *c.* 1474 Italian artist Piero della Francesca paints a double portrait of his patrons, *Battista Sforza and Federigo da Montefeltro*, and completes *Madonna and Child with the Duke of Urbino as Donor* (*Brera Madonna*).
- *c.* 1474 Italian artist Andrea del Verrocchio sculpts the bronze *David*, commissioned by Lorenzo de' Medici.
- Italian artist Andrea Mantegna completes his frescoes in the *Camera degli Sposi/Marriage Room* in the Ducal Palace in Mantua, Italy. It presents a vivid depiction of the life at the Mantua court.

Literature and Language

1470

- Sir Thomas Malory completes *Le Morte d'Arthur/The Death of Arthur*. Based on French originals, it is the first prose account in English of the Arthurian legend. Malory remains a shadowy figure. He is thought to be a Welsh knight who translated the story from French while languishing in prison. The book is published by Caxton in 1485.

1471

- A textbook on Latin style, *De elegantia Latinae linguae/ The Elegancies of the Latin Tongue*, by the Italian humanist scholar Lorenzo Valla (written in 1444), is published. It quickly becomes a standard guide on the writing of good Latin.
- The first Italian translation of the Bible is printed in Venice. It was translated by Niccolò di Malermi from the Latin Vulgate. A revised edition will appear in 1477.

1472

- The *Divina commedia/Divine Comedy* (1310–14) by the Italian poet Dante is first printed at Foligno as *Commedia*.

1473

- *De imitatione Christi/On the Imitation of Christ* attributed to the German mystic Thomas à Kempis (Thomas Hemerken) is first printed in Augsburg. The text had been widely circulated in manuscript for many years before being published. A classic of devotional literature, it will become the most widely read Christian book after the Bible.
- *Gesta Romanorum/Roman Tales* is first printed, in Utrecht, Holland. A collection of illustrative tales, anecdotes, and historical narratives written in Latin, it was begun in about 1330 and gradually expanded to become a rich store of tales from Christian, Jewish, and classical sources. It provided many writers (including Geoffrey Chaucer and John Gower) with material.

- Adam von Rottweil prints the first guide book, *Mirabilia Romae/Marvels of Rome* by Benedict, in Rome.
- Italian humanist Niccolò Perotti publishes his *Rudimenta grammatices/Rudiments of Grammar*, one of the first modern Latin grammars.

1474

- Dutch mystic Hendrik Harphius publishes *Speculum aureum/The Golden Mirror*.

Music

1473

- The earliest known example of printed music, the *Constance Gradual*, is published in Germany.

Thought and Scholarship

c. 1470

- Byzantine historian Michael Cristobulus completes his *Historia*, a history of the Ottoman Empire from 1451 to 1467 which contains a flattering account of Mohammad II.
- Florentine priest Marsilio Ficino completes his translation of Plato from Greek to Latin for the Medici family.

BIRTHS & DEATHS

1470

June 30 Charles VIII, King of France 1483–98, who led the first of a series of French expeditions into Italy, born in Amboise, France (–1498).

1471

- Henry VI, King of England 1422–61 and 1470–71, son of Henry V, is murdered in the Tower of London, England (49).

March 12 Dionysius the Carthusian (Flemish: Denys van Leeuwen, or de Leeuwis, also called Denys Ryckel, or van Rijkel), influential theologian and mystic, dies in Roermond, Netherlands (c. 69).

April 14 Richard Neville, 1st Earl of Warwick, (the "Kingmaker"), English nobleman who obtained the throne for King Edward IV, and restored deposed King Henry VI to the throne, is killed at the Battle of Barnet, Hertfordshire (42).

May 21 Albrecht Dürer, considered to be the greatest German painter and printmaker of the Renaissance, born in Nuremberg, Germany (–1528).

August 8 Thomas à Kempis (original name Thomas Hemerken), theologian to whom the highly

influential *De imitatione Christi/On the Imitation of Christ* is attributed, dies in Agnietenberg, near Zwolle, Netherlands (c. 92).

1472

- Lucas Cranach "the Elder," leading German painter and printmaker, whose best-known works include *Adam and Eve* (1526) and *The Judgment of Paris* (1530), born in Cranach, bishopric of Bamberg, now Kronach, Germany (–1553).
- Wang Yang-ming, Chinese administrator and philosopher who emphasized that the world must be understood from within the mind, born in Yu-yao, Chekiang province, China (–1529).

April 25 Leone Battista Alberti, Italian humanist, architect, and initiator of Renaissance art history, dies in Rome (68).

1473

- Pierre Terrail, seigneur de Bayard, French military commander, renowned for his skill and chivalry, born at Château Bayard, near Pontcharra, France (–1524).

February 19 Nicolaus Copernicus, Polish astronomer, who put forward the theory that the earth revolved

about its axis and around the sun, born in Toruń, Poland (–1543).

March 17 James IV, King of Scotland 1488–1513, son of James III, born (–1513).

1474

- Lorenzo Campeggio, Italian cardinal and humanist, papal nuncio at the courts of Holy Roman Emperor Maximilian and King Henry VIII of England, born (–1539).

August Bartolomé de Las Casas, Spanish historian and Dominican missionary in the New World, who exposed the oppression of the Native Americans in works such as *Historia de las Indias/History of the Indies* (first printed in 1875), born, possibly in Seville, Spain (–1566).

September 8 Lodovico Ariosto, Italian Renaissance poet, whose best known work is *Orlando furioso* (1516), born in Reggio Emilia, duchy of Modena, Italy (–1533).

November 27 Guillaume Dufay, French composer of sacred and secular music, dies in Cambrai, France (c. 74).

1472
- Italian diplomat and military adviser Roberto Valturio publishes his influential *De re militari libri XII/Twelve Books on the Art of War*.

1473
- French humanist Guillaume Fillastre writes *Chronique de l'histoire de France/Chronicle of the History of France*. It is first printed in 1517.

1474
- Flemish poet and chronicler George Châstellain completes his *Grand Chronique/Great Chronicle*, a history of France and Burgundy.
- Italian humanist Il Platina (Bartolommeo Sacchi) completes his *Liber de vita Christi ac omnium pontificum/Book of the Life of Christ and of All Popes*, a history of the papacy.

SOCIETY

Education

1471
- The University of Genoa is founded in Italy.

1472
- Ludwig, Duke of Bavaria-Landshut, founds the University of Bavaria in his newly acquired city of Ingolstadt, Bavaria.
- The University of Munich is founded in Germany.

1473
- Lorenzo the Magnificent de' Medici attempts to integrate the city of Pisa, Italy, more thoroughly by transferring the *studium* (university) of Florence, Italy, there.
- The archbishop of Trier, Germany, founds a university in his capital.

1474
- A university is established at Saragossa (Zaragoza), capital of Aragon, and rapidly becomes famous for its medical faculty.

Everyday Life

1472
- German master Ingold's *Das guildin Spil* is the earliest handbook on card playing.

Religion

1473
- The Buddhist monk Gedun-dub becomes the first Dalai Lama of Tibet.
- The devotional work *Speculum conversionis peccatorum/Mirror of the Conversion of Sinners* by the Dutch mystic Dionysus the Carthusian (Denys van Leeuwen) is published posthumously.

Sports

1470
- An inventory in the accounts of King Louis XI of France includes the first reference to the game of billiards as an indoor table game as opposed to a game played on grass as a form of bowls. The table has a stone surface covered with green cloth with a hole in the middle into which the balls are propelled.

1475–1479

POLITICS, GOVERNMENT, AND ECONOMICS

Human Rights

1478

November   Pope Sixtus IV provides Cardinal Rodrigo Borgia (the future Pope Alexander VI) with a bull ratifying the Spanish Inquisition, which was established under the control of King Ferdinand V and Queen Isabella I at Seville, Castile, in the previous year.

Politics and Government

1475

- An Ottoman force conquers the Crimea. The Genoese trading colony at Khaffa (Feodosiya) falls, and the Tatar (Mongol) Krim Khan becomes an Ottoman vassal.
- Following the death of its president and imperial chancellor Archbishop Adolph of Mainz, the imperial appeal court in Germany (established in 1471) withers, ceasing to function in 1480.
- Stephen the Great, Voivod (governor) of Moldavia, leads his forces to victory over an Ottoman incursion at Vaslui, Moldavia.

February   Portuguese forces under Alfonso V of Portugal draw in a battle at Toro, Castile, failing to enforce his claim (through his wife Joan "La Beltraneja") to the throne of Castile against that of her uncle and aunt, King Ferdinand V and Queen Isabella I.

March 10   French forces reconquer Perpignan, France, for King Louis XI of France, ending a savage war with Aragon for the territories of Roussillon and Cerdagne.

July 4–August 29   King Edward IV of England lands at Calais, France, with a large army. He finds his allies unwilling or unable to campaign, and maneuvers as far as the River Somme, where he bargains with King Louis XI of France. The Treaty of Picquigny specifies a seven-year truce, the freedom and security of merchants, and compensation to Edward of 75,000 crowns, followed by annual payments of 50,000 crowns.

September 13   King Louis XI of France, halting the depredations of his armies in Burgundian Picardy and Artois, makes a nine-year truce at Vervins, France, with Charles the Bold of Burgundy, who has been deprived of his major ally by the signing of the Treaty of Picquigny by Louis and King Edward IV of England.

September 29   King Louis XI of France completes his diplomatic triumph by making peace with Duke Francis II of Brittany, following the truces he has made in the last month with England and Burgundy. Duke Francis promises not to participate in any future coalitions against Louis.

November   Troops under Charles the Bold of Burgundy, having ravaged the duchy of Lorraine throughout the summer in the aftermath of the siege of Neuss, Germany, complete their conquest of the duchy by taking its capital Nancy.

December 19   The Count of St.-Pol, constable of Burgundy, who has attempted to play King Louis XI of France and Charles the Bold of Burgundy against each other in the Somme towns of St. Quentin and Ham, France, is executed as a traitor against Louis.

1476

- King Ferdinand V and Queen Isabella I amalgamate the Castilian police associations known as the *Hermandades* ("brotherhoods") into a single *Santa Hermandad* under royal control, the associations originally having been formed by the citizens of Castilian towns in order to suppress banditry.
- Ottoman forces win a Pyrrhic victory at Valea Alba in Moldavia when they defeat the armies of Stephen the Great of Moldavia but are forced to retreat from his principality. Stephen receives the accolade "the athlete of Christ" from Pope Sixtus IV.
- Sonni Ali, founder of the Songhai empire in Mali, leads the subjugation of the Niger lakes region west of Timbuktu, Mali.
- The Chimú empire is conquered by the Incas.
- The lord of the Canary Islands Diego Garcia de Herrera conquers Ifni on the Sahara coast of Morocco, on behalf of Castile.

March 2   The army of Charles the Bold of Burgundy, facing peace on other fronts, invades Switzerland. The Swiss, led by the canton of Bern, promptly defeat the Burgundian army by Lake Neuchâtel at Grandson, Vaud, Switzerland.

June   Rebellion recurs in the unstable populace of Ching-Hsiang (Hupeh) in China; the area is only pacified with the establishment of a new prefecture, Yün-yang, by the official Yüan Chieh, who brings stability by recognizing squatters' rights to land.

June 22   Following his defeat at the Swiss town of Grandson, Charles the Bold of Burgundy directs a new campaign against Bern, Switzerland, and is heavily and decisively defeated by a Swiss army relieving his siege of Morat, outside Bern. In October René II, Duke of Lorraine, recovers his duchy.

July 15   King James III of Scotland deprives John MacDonald, Lord of the Isles, of the earldom of Ross, his most important possession on the mainland.

December 26   During Christmas celebrations, republican revolutionaries assassinate the despotic Galeazzo Maria Sforza, Duke of Milan, in the hope of sparking an insurrection, but his son Gian Galeazzo succeeds, with his mother Bona of Savoy as regent.

1477

- The Ch'eng-Hua emperor authorizes the establishment of a new political police force known as the "western depot" in Beijing, China, placing it under the control of Wang Chih, the eunuch aide of his old nursemaid and favoured consort, the Lady Wan.
- The joint rulers of Castille Ferdinand V and Isabella I receive approval from Pope Sixtus IV to reestablish the Inquisition in Spain.

January 5   Charles the Bold of Burgundy is killed by a Swiss dominated army in a battle outside Nancy, capital of the duchy of Lorraine, France, which was being besieged by the remnants of his forces. His heir is his daughter Mary, but King Louis XI of France quickly seizes the duchy of Burgundy and Picardy, though he faces stubborn resistance in Artois, France.

April 3   A popular insurrection seizes and executes Guillaume Hugon, Chancellor of Burgundy, in Ghent, Flanders.

June 27   Adolf of Egmond, claimant to the duchy of Guelders in the Netherlands, is killed when his force of artisans from Ghent desert while he is leading them to attack French positions at Tournai near the border of France. The militia of Bruges, Flanders, is routed shortly afterwards.

August 18   Mary, heiress to Burgundy, having received a proposal from King Louis XI of France of his son Charles (the future Charles VIII), marries Maximilian of Austria, son and heir of Frederick III the Holy Roman Emperor, who now leads the defense of the Netherlands against Louis.

December 17   The Yamana family army under the *daimyo* (magnate) Ouchi withdraws from the Japanese capital Kyoto and submits to Shogun Ashikaga Yoshimi. Thus the Onin War finally ends, the succession issues that sparked it having become irrelevant in the ensuing feudal chaos.

1478

- Albert III Achilles, elector of Brandenburg, defeats the invading forces of Matthias I Corvinus, King of Hungary, and the Hanseatic League in a war over territory in Pomerania.
- Bali rebels against the rule of Java while the ascendant Hindu Majapahit Empire there is reeling from Muslim attacks.
- Krujë, last stronghold of the Albanian prince George Castriota, son of Skanderbeg, falls to the Ottoman Turks, who thus complete their conquest of Albania save for a few Venetian outposts.

January 18   Ivan III the Great, Prince of Muscovy, uses the pretext of contact with Lithuania as evidence of rebellion and sacks the merchant city and republic of Novgorod, deporting many boyar (noble) families. He incorporates the republic into Muscovy, now the undisputed suzerain of Russia.

January 24   Mary of Burgundy and her husband Maximilian of Austria end the bitter legacy of her father's war with the Swiss and make peace at Zürich, Switzerland.

February 18   George, Duke of Clarence, incorrigibly troublesome to his brother King Edward IV of England and loyal only to himself, is murdered in the Tower of London, England, following his conviction by Parliament for treason.

April 26   Pope Sixtus IV, resentful of Medici intervention against papal authority in the Romagna region of the Papal States, encourages the "Pazzi Conspiracy," an attempted coup in Florence, Italy. Giuliano de' Medici is murdered while at Mass, but his brother and coruler Lorenzo survives, and the conspirators are hunted and killed by the populace.

June 1   Following the failure of the "Pazzi Conspiracy" and the murder of the conspirator, the archbishop of Pisa, Pope Sixtus IV, excommunicates Lorenzo de' Medici and allies with Naples in a war against Forence, Venice, and Milan.

December 7   Under the Treaty of Olmütz, Matthias I Corvinus, King of Hungary, recognizes Władysław II, son of Casimir (Kazimierz) IV of Poland, as king of Bohemia, in return for the cession of the provinces of Lusatia, Silesia, and Moravia, which he is occupying.

1479

- King James III of Scotland quarrels with and arrests his brothers Alexander, Duke of Albany, and John, Earl of Mar. The latter dies soon after, but Alexander escapes to England.
- Le Thanh-tong, Emperor of Dai Viet, launches a military expedition into the Laotian state of Lan Xang, temporarily occupying the capital, Louangprabang.
- Sikandar Lodi conquers and subjugates the Muslim kingdom of Jaunpur for his father Buhlūl Lodi, thereby ending the Sharqi dynasty.

January 19   John II, King of Aragon, dies and is succeeded by his son Ferdinand II (Ferdinand V of Castile). A union of the two crowns is created through the person of Ferdinand.

January 26   The Ottoman sultan Mehmed II makes peace with Venice, Italy, in the Treaty of Constantinople. Venice surrenders bases in Albania and the Morea, paying an annual fee for the restoration of trading privileges.

May   Dole, capital of the county of Burgundy (Franche-Comté) and always an imperial fief, is stormed by French forces under Charles d'Amboise who devastates the city for King Louis XI of France.

August 7   In the bitter war for possession of Burgundy following the death of Charles the Bold of Burgundy, the army of Maximilian of Austria (who is married to Mary of Burgundy) besieges Théroanne in Artois and defeats the attacking forces of King Louis XI of France, but suffers heavy losses at Guinegate.

September   King Louis XI of France sacks, burns, and depopulates the city of Arras in Artois in retaliation for its persistent loyalty to the Burgundians.

September 4   The Peace of Alcáçovas favors Isabella I, ending the succession struggle in Castile between Alfonso V of Portugal, and Ferdinand V and Isabella I of Castile, and Alfonso tries to abdicate from the throne of Portugal. Under the agreement, the Atlantic islands are apportioned. The Canary Islands go to Castile, while Madeira, the Cape Verdes, and the Azores are retained by Portugal.

September 7   In the War of the Pazzi, Alfonso of Calabria, son of Ferrante of Naples, leads the armies of Siena, Naples, and the papacy to break the Florentine defenses at Poggibonzi, between Florence and Siena, Italy.

September 7   Ludovico Sforza returns to the Milanese court where he swiftly gains effective power during the minority of his nephew Gian Galeazzo. Bona of Savoy, Gian Galeazzo's mother, is ousted as regent in the following year.

SCIENCE, TECHNOLOGY, AND MEDICINE

Health and Medicine

1478

- The *De medicina*/*On Medicine* of the classical physician Galen is produced in print for the first time, giving new currency to his theories.

Science

1475

- German astronomer Regiomontanus publishes *De triangulis planis et sphaericis*/*Concerning Plane and Spherical Triangles*, a book on spherical trigonometry as applied to astronomy.
- German astronomer Regiomontanus travels to Rome to advise on possible revisions of the Roman Catholic ecclesiastical calendar.

1476

- Regiomontanus, the German astronomer, dies at Rome. A letter found after his death refers to parallax caused by motion of the earth—indicating he possibly believed in a heliocentric (sun-centered) universe.

1477

- English alchemist Thomas Norton writes *The Ordinall of Alchimy*, giving the earliest known illustration of a balance in a glass case. He emphasizes that alchemy is a question of transformation, not creation.

1478

- Printer Arnold Buckinck publishes an edition of Ptolemy's *Geographia* at Rome, Italy, complete with copperplate engravings of the maps.

Technology

1475

- Italian inventor Francesco di Giorgio Martini illustrates a machine designed specifically for raising columns into place during construction work.

1476

October   William Caxton sets up the first printing press in England at Westminster.

1478

- Oxford University, England, sets up a printing press, following the example of the College of the Sorbonne in Paris, France.

ARTS AND IDEAS

Architecture

1479

- The Cathedral of the Assumption (Uspenskii Sobor) in the Kremlin is completed. Commissioned by Czar Ivan III, it was designed by the Italian architect Rudolfo Fioravanti, who combined Italian Renaissance and traditional Russian styles.

Arts

1475

c. 1475   French artist Jean Fouquet completes his miniatures for the book *Antiquités Judaïques*, an edition of *Jewish Antiquities* by the 1st-century historian Josephus.

c. 1475   Italian artist Antonio Pollaiuolo paints *The Martyrdom of St. Sebastian* and sculpts the small bronze *Hercules and Antaeus*.

c. 1475   Italian artist Giovanni Bellini paints *Coronation of the Virgin (Pesaro Altarpiece)*.

c. 1475   Italian artist Leonardo da Vinci paints the portrait *Ginevra de'Benci*. One of his early works, it shows the influence of Flemish art, which was then in vogue in Italy.

- Flemish artist Dirk Bouts paints the pair of paintings *Justice of the Emperor Otho*.
- German artist Martin Schongauer paints *Madonna of the Rose Bower*.

c. 1475–c. 1485   Italian artist Sandro Botticelli (Alessandro di Mariano dei Filipepi) paints his *Adoration of the Magi* series. The figures in attendance are thought to include several members of the powerful Medici family and Botticelli himself.

1476

c. 1476   Flemish artist Hugo van der Goes paints *The Portinari Altarpiece*, one of his most important works. It was painted for Tommaso Portinari, an Italian banker working in Bruges for the Medicis. When taken to Florence it was greatly admired by Italian artists.

c. 1476   Italian artist and architect Benedetto da Maiano sculpts the portrait bust *Pietro Mellini*.

- French artist Nicolas Froment paints the *Mary of the Burning Bush Altarpiece*.
- Italian artist Carlo Crivelli paints *The Domidoff Altarpiece*.

c. 1477

- Spanish artist Bartolomé Bermejo paints *St. Michael*.

c. 1478

- Italian artist and architect Francesco di Giorgio sculpts the bronze relief *The Flagellation*.

1479

- Flemish artist Hans Memling completes *The Mystical Marriage of St. Catherine*, a triptych for the Hospital of St. John in Bruges.

Literature and Language

1475

c. 1475 Welsh poet Dafydd Nanmor earns a high reputation for his elegies, love lyrics, and eulogies, written in Welsh.

- Bartolomeo Sacchi, also known as Platina, writes *De honeste voluptate et valetudine/Concerning Honest Pleasure and Well-Being*, the first printed cookbook, in Rome.
- English printer William Caxton prints *The Recuyell of the Histories of Troye*, in Bruges, Belgium. His own translation from the French romance by Raoul le Fèvre, it is the first work to be printed in English.

- Italian humanist scholar and poet Politian (Angelo Ambrogini Poliziano) begins writing his most important poetic work *Le Stanze per la giostra/Stanzas on the Joust*, an unfinished epic.

1476

- Flemish printer Boccard Manson of Bruges publishes an edition of Boccaccio's *De casibus illustrum virorum/On the Fates of Illustrious Men*, illustrated with copperplate engravings.
- Italian writer Salernitano Masuccio (Tommaso Guardati) publishes *Novellino*, a collection of fifty short stories, in Naples, Italy.

1477

- Italian humanist Pier Candido Decembrio publishes his biography *Vita Philippi Mariae ducis Mediolanensis/The Life of Filippo Maria Visconti*.
- The first translation of the Bible into Italian (1471) is republished in an edition revised by the scholar Marine de Veneto, in Venice, Italy.

BIRTHS & DEATHS

1475

c. 1475 Francisco Pizarro, Spanish explorer who conquered the Inca Empire and founded the city of Lima, born in Trujillo, Extremadura, Castile (–1541).

c. 1475 Gavin Douglas, Scottish poet and bishop, who produced the first translation of the *Aeneid* into English, born (–1522).

c. 1475 Thomas Wolsey (Cardinal Wolsey), English cardinal and statesman who dominated King Henry VIII's government 1515–29, born (–1530).

- Cesare Borgia, Duke of Valentinois, natural son of Pope Alexander VI and brother of Lucretia Borgia, who attempted to establish a permanent Borgia state in Italy, notorious for his intrigues, model for Machiavelli's *Il principe/The Prince*, born, probably in Rome (–1507).
- George Chastellain, influential Burgundian chronicler and court poet, dies in Valenciennes, France (*c.* 60 or *c.* 70).
- Theodore Gaza, Byzantine philosopher whose translations of Aristotle were influential in the development of Italian humanism, dies (*c.* 75).
- Vasco Núñez de Balboa, Spanish conquistador, explorer, and first European to discover the Pacific Ocean (September 27, 1513), born in Jerez de los Caballeros or Badajoz, Extremadura, Castile (–1519).

March 6 Michelangelo (di Lodovico Buonarroti Simoni), Italian Renaissance sculptor, painter, and architect, also poet, whose best-known works include the fresco *The Last Judgement* (1534–41) and the sculptures *Pietà* (*c.* 1500) and *David* (1504), born in Caprese, Italy (–1564).

May Dieric Bouts, Dutch painter, whose best-known works include the triptych for the Church of St. Peter in Louvain, dies in Louvain, Brabant, now in Belgium (*c.* 75).

December 10 Paolo Uccello, early Renaissance Florentine painter, noted for his use of perspective, dies in Florence (78).

December 11 Giovanni de' Medici, Pope Leo X 1513–21, noted for his political skill and personal extravagance, born in Milan, Italy (–1521).

1476

July 6 Regiomontanus (Johann Müller), bishop of Regensburg, German astronomer and mathematician who was responsible for the revival of trigonometry, dies in Rome (40).

1477

c. 1477 Giorgione (or Giorgio da Castelfranco, original name Giorgio Barbarelli), influential Italian painter, whose works include *The Tempest* (*c.* 1505) and *Sleeping Venus* (*c.* 1510), born in Castelfranco, Veneto, Italy (–1510).

January 5 Charles the Bold, Duke of Burgundy 1467–77, dies near Nancy, Lorraine (43).

February 7 Thomas More, English humanist and statesman, chancellor of England 1529–32, born (–1535).

July 4 Johannes Turmair (Aventinus), German humanist and historian, whose best known work is *Annales Boiorum/Bavarian Annals* (1517–21), born in Abensberg, Bavaria (–1534).

1478

- Jean Mabuse (original name Jan Gossaert), Flemish painter, whose best-known works include *Danae* (1527), born in Hainault, Belgium (–1532).

February 18 George Plantagenet, Duke of Clarence, English noble who took part in a conspiracy against his brother King Edward IV of England, killed in London, England (28).

July 8 Giangiorgio Trissino, Italian dramatist and literary theorist, born in Vicenza, republic of Venice (–1550).

July 22 Philip I ("Philip the Handsome"), King of Spain 1506, founder of the Habsburg dynasty in Spain, born in Bruges (–1506).

December 6 Baldassare Castiglione, Italian diplomat and courtier, whose *Il cortegiano/The Courtier* was widely influential in Europe, born in Casatico, near Mantua, Italy (–1529).

1479

- Jean Grolier de Servières, French book collector, born in Lyons, France (–1565).

1478

- English antiquarian William Worcestre publishes the first of his *Itineraries*, records of his travels in England.

1479

- Spanish poet Jorge Manrique publishes *Coplas de Jorge Manrique por la muerte de su padre/Stanzas by Jorge Manrique on the Death of His Father*, an elegy that will become a classic of Spanish literature.

Thought and Scholarship

c. **1475**

- Italian poet and humanist Matteo Palmieri writes *Della vita civile/On Civil Life*, a treatise on good citizenship. It is not published until 1529.

1476

- The book *Historarium Florentini populi libri/History of Florence* by the Italian writer Leonardo Bruni of Arezzo (also known as Aretino) is published posthumously.

1478

- Arnold Buckinck produces printed maps, in Rome, Italy. Twenty-seven maps by Conrad Sweynheym appear in Ptolemy's *Cosmographia*.
- The origins of the Oxford University Press can be traced to this date, when the essay "Expositio sancti Ieronimi in simbolum apostolorum" by the bishop of Aquileia is printed in Oxford, England. The press is formally established in 1585.

c. **1479**

- English jurist and political writer John Fortescue writes *De laudibus legum Angliae/In Praise of English Law*. A guide to English law, it is written for Edward, Prince of Wales. It is not published until 1714.

SOCIETY

Education

1475

- Robert Woodlark founds St. Catharine's College at Cambridge University, England. He expressly forbids

the study of law, and students are to confine themselves to the subjects of philosophy and theology.

1477

- Ebehard VI, Count (and from 1495 Duke) of Württemberg, an Italianate reformer, founds Tübingen University in Germany.
- The regent of Sweden, Sten Sture the Elder, establishes the first Scandinavian university at Uppsala, Sweden.
- The University of Mainz is founded in Germany.

1478

- King Christian I of Denmark founds Copenhagen University.

Everyday Life

1475

- Kiva Han, the first ever coffee house, opens in Constantinople (modern Istanbul, Turkey).

Religion

1475

- Pope Sixtus IV permits Dominican convents to own property.

1477

- George Ripley, Canon of Bridlington, Yorkshire, England, dedicates his *The Compound of Alchemy* to English king Edward IV.

Sports

1475

c. 1475   A radically new version of chess, very similar to the game played today, is devised in southern Europe and quickly spreads across the continent and beyond. Among the most important changes are the introduction of castling and the elevation in status of the queen from one of the weakest pieces on the board to the most powerful.

- English printer William Caxton prints *The Game and Playe of the Chesse* by Jacobus de Cessolis, in London, England.

1478

December   A document refers to "cricquet" being played near St.-Omer in Flanders (now northeastern France).

1480–1484

POLITICS, GOVERNMENT, AND ECONOMICS

Business and Economics

1480

- King Louis XI of France founds the silk industry at Lyons, France, with a settlement of Italian weavers.
- The Cortes (parliament) at Toledo, Castile, grants concessions to the Castilian towns against the nobility, rescinding the grant of land and the rights to raise taxes and wage war, and returning them to the crown, thereby raising 30 million maravedis annually. The construction of new castles is forbidden and many existing ones are demolished.

1481

- King Louis XI of France proposes to his assembly of "good towns" at Tours, France, that his newly inherited Provençal port of Marseille, France, become the entrepôt for trade with the East. He proposes a national merchant company to conduct this trade.
- The yield of the *taille*, the depredatory French poll tax levied on commoners, reaches 4,600,000 livres, compared with 1,055,000 livres in 1461 before the accession of King Louis XI of France.

1482

- The Portuguese found the first European trading post in the tropics, building a fort at Elmina (São Jorge de Minha) in modern Ghana.

Human Rights

1480

October   The Spanish Inquisition, having encountered widespread opposition, begins to operate against Muslims, heretics, Jews, and *conversos* (Jewish converts to Christianity) in Seville, the largest city in Castile.

1481

- The first *Auto da fé* (Act of Faith), the pronouncement and enactment of sentences (including burning) on victims of the Spanish Inquisition, is carried out in Seville, Castile. Approximately 300 *conversos* (Jewish converts to Christianity) are burned in the first year.

1482

January–April   Reports of the excesses of the Spanish Inquisition lead Pope Sixtus IV to rescind his bull of 1478, which authorized it. He later reinstates it when he needs King Ferdinand V and Queen Isabella I as allies in Italy.

1483

October 17   The Spanish Inquisition is extended to Aragon, where Tomás de Torquemada is also appointed Grand Inquisitor. Catalonia resists, postponing the arrival of the Inquisition there for four years.

1484

- The Grand Inquisitor of Aragon and Castile, Thomás de Torquemada, issues his "Twenty-eight Articles" for the regulation of the Spanish Inquisition, widening its scope to include the crimes of sorcery, sodomy, polygamy, and blasphemy in addition to its original remit of heresy and apostasy.

Politics and Government

1480

- Ivan III, Grand Duke of Muscovy, dispels the last relics of domination by the Mongol Tatar "Golden Horde" when his armies face down the forces of its khan Akhmet at the "Battle" of the River Ugra, at which the Horde's Lithuanian allies fail to appear.

March 6   Having traveled to Naples, Italy, after receiving overtures of peace, Lorenzo de' Medici reaches agreement with Ferrante, King of Naples, for peace between Naples and Florence, Italy. The papacy, Milan, and Venice accede shortly afterward, ending the War of the Pazzi.

May 23–July 28   An Ottoman fleet assaults the Aegean fortress island of Rhodes, headquarters of the crusading Order of the Knights of St. John of the Hospital, but is repulsed.

July 10   René the Good, Duke of Anjou and Count of Provence dies, having willed his territories, the important county of Provence (never before French), the duchies of Bar and Anjou, and the county of Maine to King Louis XI of France.

August 10   An Ottoman expeditionary force takes the Neapolitan port of Otranto in Puglia, Italy, sending the country into panic.

1481

- Abu-al-Hasan (Muley Hacen), Sultan of Granada, surprises and takes the fortified Castilian town of Zahara, starting the War of Granada, the final phase of the *Reconquista* ("Reconquest").
- The usurping Rin-Spungs princely clan, supporters of the Karma-Pa (Red Hat) Buddhist sect, complete their conquest of Tibet, deposing the Phag-mo-gru rulers and assuming the throne of the *Gong-ma*.

April   The governor of Telingana, Malik Hasan, deceives

the drunken Bāhmanī sultan, Mohammed Shah, into ordering the summary execution of his chief minister Mahmud Gawan. The Bāhmanī empire subsequently fragments.

May 3 The death of the Ottoman sultan Mehmed II leaves the succession in dispute between his sons Djem and Bāyezīd. On May 20, Bāyezīd arrives in Constantinople (modern Istanbul, Turkey) to be proclaimed sultan; his partisans among the janissaries (royal guards) have killed his brother Djem's chief supporter, the unpopular vizier Mehmed Pasha.

June 20 The janissary (royal guard) forces of Bāyezīd II defeat the army of his brother and rival for the Ottoman throne, Djem, at Yenishehir in Bithynia, and Djem flees to Mameluke in Egypt.

July 26 Djem, brother and rival of Bāyezīd II for the Ottoman throne, flees to the Knights Hospitaller of Rhodes, and subsequently flees first to the Pope and then to King Charles VIII of France, dying in exile in 1495.

August 28 Alfonso V the African, King of Portugal, dies before the Cortes (parliament) will ratify his abdication. His son and successor John II calls the Cortes at Evora, Portugal, in November, and requires rigorous homage from the nobility.

August 30 King Casimir (Kazimierz) IV of Poland, Grand Prince of Lithuania, has two Lithuanian princes executed for conspiring against him with Ivan III, Prince of Muscovy.

September Alfonso of Calabria, son of King Ferrante of Naples, receives the surrender of the besieged port of Otranto, Italy, from Ottoman forces who have been abandoned because of the dispute over the Ottoman succession.

December 22 The hermit Nicholas von Flüe arbitrates an agreement between fractious rival pacts of urban and rural cantons at the Swiss diet of Stans. Fribourg and Solothurn are subsequently admitted as cantons in the now strengthened Swiss Confederation.

1482

February 11 The Dominican Tomás de Torquemada is appointed inquisitor-general in Spain. His main task is to investigate those *conversos* (Jews who had converted to Christianity) and Moors who were suspected of secretly practicing their ancestral faith.

February 26 Castilian forces under Ferdinand of Aragon capture the stronghold of Alhama from Muslim Granada. Abu-Abd-Il (Boabdil), governor of Guadix, Granada, is aided by the Abencerrajes family in usurping the throne of Granada from his father Ali Abu-al-Hasan (Muley Hacen) who retreats to Málaga, Spain.

March 27 Mary of Burgundy, heir of Charles the Bold of Burgundy, dies. Her husband Maximilian of Austria competes with the Estates for the regency of their infant son Philip.

May 2 Venice, Italy, anxious to enlarge its territory and strike at Ferrante of Naples, uses a dispute over salt production to declare war on Duke Ercole d'Este of Ferrara, who is Ferrante's son-in-law. Pope Sixtus IV supports Venice, opposing Milan and Florence.

June Kasim Beg, dispossessed prince of Karaman, allies with Djem, brother of Bāyezīd II and claimant to the Ottoman throne, but they fail in their assault on the Ottoman city of Konya.

June 10 King Edward IV of England recognizes Alexander of Albany, exiled brother of King James III of Scotland, as king of Scotland and his vassal under the Treaties of Fotheringay.

July The new "Great Wall" in the province of Shensi in China is instrumental in the defeat of a large Mongol raiding force.

August 1 An English invasion on behalf of Alexander, Duke of Albany, under Richard, Duke of Gloucester, takes Edinburgh, Scotland, having pillaged their way from Berwick on the border between England and Scotland. Meanwhile, a Scottish noble faction led by Archibald "Bell the Cat" Douglas, Earl of Angus, imprisons King James III of Scotland and hangs his "base favorites."

August 21 The army of Roberto Malatesta, the condottiere (mercenary) employed by the papacy and Venice, Italy, storms Alfonso of Calabria's position at Campo Morto in Lazio, Italy. Malatesta dies of malaria shortly afterward.

August 24 Richard, Duke of Gloucester, having received the submission of the Scots at Haddington, Scotland, returns to the border fortress of Berwick, which surrenders and definitively becomes English. King James III of Scotland remains king.

August 30 The communal army of Liège, the Netherlands, led by Guillaume la Marck, defeats and kills the bishop of Liège, Louis de Bourbon, in battle.

September 1 Tatar allies and vassals of Ivan III of Moscow sack the Ukrainian metropolis of Kiev, which is part of Lithuania and hence ruled by King Casimir (Kazimierz) IV of Poland.

October The estates of the county of Flanders and the duchy of Brabant form a defensive league against Archduke Maximilian of Austria.

December 12 Pope Sixtus IV, realizing that his ally, Venice, will be the only beneficiary of continued war, makes peace with the hard-pressed Duke Ercole d'Este of Ferrara.

December 23 By the Treaty of Arras, King Louis XI of France and the Habsburg regent Maximilian agree the partition of the Burgundian lands. Maximilian's daughter Margaret is to marry the dauphin (soon to be Charles VIII), taking as her dowry Artois and the Franche-Comté. Maximilian's infant son Philip is to retain the Netherlands, while the duchy of Burgundy, with Picardy and the Boullonais, will go to France.

1483

- Lhe-Tang Trong, ruler of the Dai Viet kingdom, promulgates a new legal code, the *Code of Hong-duc.*
- Ottoman forces complete the conquest of the Ottoman vassal of Herzegovina.

January 8 Habsburg forces under Archduke Maximilian's captain, Philip von Cleves Ravenstein, defeat the popular La Marck faction in battle at Liège, installing the Burgundian John van Hoorne as bishop of Liège.

February In the War of Ferrara, Pope Sixtus IV joins the alliance between Milan, the kingdom of Naples, Ferrara, and Florence against his erstwhile ally Venice, Italy.

April 9 King Edward IV of England dies and is succeeded by his son Edward V. The Woodville family of Queen Elizabeth pushes for the early coronation of Edward V and the regency that Edward IV has willed to his brother Richard, Duke of Gloucester.

April 23   Castilian forces defeat the army of Granada that is besieging the town of Lucena, Spain, and capture Abu-Abd-Il, Sultan Mohammed XI. His father, the usurped Abu-al-Hasan, retakes the throne of Granada with the aid of the Zegries family.

June 21   King John II of Portugal arrests, tries, and executes Ferdinand II, Duke of Braganza, at Evora, Portugal, for his part in a conspiracy with Castile, thereby eliminating the most powerful magnate in the country in his quest to establish a royal dictatorship.

June 26   Richard, Duke of Gloucester, having queried the legitimacy of his nephew Edward V, deposes him and assumes the crown as Richard III.

August   John II (Hans), having succeeded his father Christian I as king of Norway and Denmark in 1481, is recognized by the Swedish state council as king of Sweden. The regent Sten Sture contrives to postpone the coronation.

August   The "princes in the Tower," Edward V and his brother Richard, disappear. Rumors suggest that they have been murdered by their uncle and guardian, Richard III of England.

August 30   King Louis XI of France dies and is succeeded by his son Charles VIII. His daughter Anne of Beaujeu acts as regent for the sickly youth.

November 2   King Richard III of England executes Henry Stafford, Duke of Buckingham, when the rebellion plotted by the Duke of Buckingham to enthrone Henry Tudor, Earl of Richmond, founders because Henry Tudor fails to land and the Duke of Buckingham's troops desert.

1484

- King Richard III of England empowers his council in Yorkshire to act as a court, forming an antecedent of the Council of the North.

January 5–March 11   Anne of Beaujeu, regent of the young Charles VIII of France, holds an Estates General (excluding Brittany) at Tours, France, which attempts to consolidate its powers over taxation and appointments to the Conseil du Roi.

July 15   An Ottoman force takes the fortress of Kilia at the mouth of the River Danube, going on to conquer the whole Black Sea coast of Moldavia.

August 7   The Treaty of Bagnolo between Venice, Italy, and the coalition of the Italian cities of Florence, Milan, Naples, Ferrara, and the Pope, ends the War of Ferrara when the duchy of Ferrara cedes Rovigo to Venice, but otherwise maintains the status quo.

August 12   Pope Sixtus IV dies, to be succeeded by Battista Cybò, Pope Innocent VIII, who publishes a papal bull against the spread of witchcraft, Summis desiderantes, during his first year in office.

August 28   King John II of Portugal personally slays the Duke of Viseu, his brother-in-law and rival claimant to the throne of Portugal, while repelling an assassination attempt. He subsequently forms a royal bodyguard.

September 21   King James III of Scotland makes a three-year truce with King Richard III of England in the Treaty of Nottingham; the price is the payment of tributes.

October 25   The county of Flanders signs a military alliance with France against Archduke Maximilian of Austria.

SCIENCE, TECHNOLOGY, AND MEDICINE

Exploration

1482

August   Diogo Cão, a navigator who was in the service of King Alfonso V of Portugal, leads his fleet to become the first Europeans to navigate the River Congo of Zaire.

Health and Medicine

1482

- The first printed Latin editions of 12th-century Islamic philospher Averroës' Colliget/General Medicine are available.

Technology

1480

- Italian scholar Leonardo da Vinci sketches a design for an early horizontal turbine, mounted in a chimney, where the force of rising hot air can be transmitted, through a series of cranks and gears, to turn a spit.
- The German Mittelalterliche Hausbuch/Medieval Housebook, a military manual, is published. It includes many new inventions, such as a specially designed lathe for cutting accurate screw threads.

1481

- English printer William Caxton publishes The Myrrour of the Worlde, an English version of Vincent of Beauvais' encyclopedia of 1264. It is the first illustrated book printed in England.

1484

- The English Parliament passes an act restricting foreigners from trading in England, but King Richard III specifically exempts printers from the restrictions.

Transportation

1480

- Italian scholar and inventor Leonardo da Vinci experiments with parachutes.

1484

- A navigational and nautical almanac is completed for John III of Portugal. It uses tables of the sun's changing position to enable latitude to be determined in southern seas where the Pole Star is not visible.

ARTS AND IDEAS

Architecture

1480

- The Tatipara Mosque of Gaur is completed in Bengal, India.

1481

- The Church of the Certoza in Pavia, Italy, designed by the Italian architect Giovanni Antonio Amadeo, is finished.
- Work is completed on the Sistine Chapel, Rome, commissioned by Pope Sixtus IV. Work began in 1472, probably to a design by the Italian architect Baccio Pontelli, and was carried out under the direction of the Italian architect Giovanni di Dolci.

1483

- Japanese shogun (military ruler) Ashikaga Yoshimasa builds a residence, Higashiyamadono, in Kyoto, Japan. It is one of the finest works of Japanese architecture of the period.

Arts

1480

- *c.* 1480 Flemish artist Hieronymus Bosch paints *Christ Mocked.*
- *c.* 1480 Flemish artist known as The Master of the St. Lucy Legend paints *Virgin Among Virgins in a Rose Garden.*
- *c.* 1480 Italian artist Andrea della Robbia sculpts *Adoration.* He is one of the few outstanding artists to work in glazed terracotta.
- *c.* 1480 Italian artist Cosmè Tura paints *Enthroned Madonna and Child with Angels (Roverella Altarpiece).*
- *c.* 1480 Italian artist Giovanni Bellini paints *The Resurrection of Christ.*
- Flemish artist Hans Memling paints *Scenes from the Life of the Virgin.*
- Flemish artist Hugo van der Goes completes his painting *The Trinity Altarpiece.* The work includes panels depicting the Scottish royal family: James III, the queen, and their son, the future James IV.
- Flemish artist Nicholas of Leiden sculpts the tomb of Frederick III in St. Stephen's in Vienna, Austria.
- German artist Erasmus Grasser carves *Moorish Dancer.*
- Italian artist Ercole Roberti paints *Portrait of Ginevra Bentivoglio.*
- Italian artist Ghirlandaio (Domenico Bigordi) paints the fresco *Last Supper* in the monastery of Ognissanti in Florence.

1481

- *c.* 1481 Flemish artist Hugo van der Goes paints *The Death of the Virgin,* his last major work.
- Italian artist Ghirlandaio (Domenico Bigordi) paints the fresco *The Calling of Saints Peter and Andrew* in the Sistine Chapel in Rome.
- Italian artist Leonardo da Vinci begins his painting the *Adoration of the Magi.* His first major work,

introducing a new drama and emotional range to Italian painting, it is left unfinished.

1482

- *c.* 1482 Italian artist Sandro Botticelli (Alessandro di Mariano dei Filipepi) paints *Primavera/Spring,* commissioned by a member of the Medici family. One of his most important and characteristic works, it is a depiction of spring ("primavera") in terms of classic mythology. It may also be an allegory based on the Neoplatonist philosophy of the contemporary scholar Ficino (also a member of the Medici circle).
- Italian artist Perugino (Pietro Vannucci) paints *Christ Handing the Keys to St. Peter,* a fresco in the Sistine Chapel in Rome. Other frescoes he painted in the Vatican have been destroyed.

c. 1483

- German artist Michael Pacher paints *Altarpiece of the Church Fathers.*
- Italian artist Sandro Botticelli (Alessandro di Mariano dei Filipepi) paints *Venus and Mars.*

1484

- *c.* 1484 Italian artist Filippino Lippi paints the fresco *The Judgment and Martyrdom of St. Peter* in the Brancacci Chapel in Florence.
- *c.* 1484 Italian artist Leonardo da Vinci paints the first version of *The Madonna of the Rocks* (Louvre version), and *Lady with an Ermine,* thought to be a portrait of the mistress of his patron Duke Lodovico Sforza.
- *c.* 1484 Italian artist Niccolò dell'Arca sculpts *Lamentation.*
- German artist Albrecht Dürer draws his *Self-Portrait* at the age of 13.

Literature and Language

1482

- Italian poet Luigi Pulci publishes *Morgante maggiore* in Florence and Venice. Written in racy Italian, it is a burlesque epic of chivalry in 28 cantos. Its tone is often satirical and irreverent, and it influences Rabelais.

1483

- English printer William Caxton publishes an English translation of *Legenda aurea/Golden Legend,* a collection of religious stories by the author Jacobus de Voragine.
- Italian poet Matteo Maria Boiardo completes the first two parts of *Orlando innamorato,* a long and unfinished epic of chivalry based on tales of Charlemagne and King Arthur. The work is published in 1495.

Theater and Dance

1480

- Italian humanist scholar and poet Politian (Angelo Ambrogini Poliziano) writes *Favola di Orfeo,* the first pastoral drama in Italian. It is first performed in Mantua, Italy.

Thought and Scholarship

1480

- Dutch humanist scholar and poet Rudolph Agricola (Roelof Huysman) publishes *De inventione dialectica/On Dialectic Invention*, a defense of Renaissance humanism. Agricola's works make a deep impression on Desiderius Erasmus.
- Polish historian Jan Długosz completes his *Historia Polonicae/A History of Poland*. Though not printed until 1614, the work is widely admired for its scholarship.
- René of Anjou, the Duke of Anjou, Lorraine, and the Bar, publishes *Mortifiement de vaine plaisance/ Mortification of Vain Pleasure*, a moral treatise.

1481

- English jurist Thomas Littleton publishes *Tenures*. Written in legal French, it becomes a classic study of landholding. An English translation appears about 1500.

1482

- English printer William Caxton publishes an English version of *Polychronicon*, a world history written by the English Benedictine Ranulf Higden in the mid-14th century. The translation is by the 14th-century English scholar John of Trevisa.

SOCIETY

Everyday Life

c. 1480

- "Courtesy Books" begin to appear, teaching social and dining etiquette to those whose wealth is recently acquired. *The Booke of Curtesye* is published by the English printer Wynkyn de Worde in Westminster, England, in 1492. The best example is *Il cortegiano/The*

BIRTHS & DEATHS

1480

c. 1480 Conn O'Neill, Earl of Tyrone, Irish chieftain leader, first of the O'Neill leaders, born (–1559).

- Ferdinand Magellan, Portuguese navigator and explorer, born in Sabrosa or Porto, Portugal (–1521).
- Lorenzo Lotto, Italian painter of the Renaissance whose best-known works include the *Madonna of the Rosary* (1539), born in Venice (–1556).

April Lucretia Borgia, daughter of Pope Alexander VI and sister of Cesare Borgia, Italian noblewoman, and a central figure in the notorious Borgia family, born in Rome (–1519).

May 19 Jan Długosz (Johannes Longinus), Polish diplomat and historian, who wrote the first history of Poland, *Historia Polonicae/A History of Poland* (1455–80), dies in Kraków, Poland (*c.* 65).

1481

May 3 Mehmed II the Conqueror, Ottoman sultan 1444–46 and 1451–81, son of Murad II, an outstanding military commander who captured Constantinople (modern Istanbul, Turkey) in 1453 and expanded the empire in Anatolia and the Balkans, dies in Hunkârçayiri, near Maltepe, Persia (49).

August 23 Sir Thomas Littleton (or Lyttleton), influential English jurist, dies in Frankley, Worcestershire (*c.* 66).

1482

c. 1482 Stephen Gardiner, English bishop and statesman, Lord Chancellor under Queen Mary I, born in Bury St. Edmunds, Suffolk, England (–1555).

- Hugo van der Goes, outstanding Flemish painter, whose works include the *Portinari Altarpiece* (*c.* 1474–76), dies in Roode Kloster, near Brussels (*c.* 42).

August 25 Margaret of Anjou, Queen Consort of Henry VI of England, a leader of the Lancastrians in the Wars of the Roses (1455–85), dies near Saumur, France (52).

1483

c. 1483 François Rabelais, French humanist and writer, author of *Gargantua* and *Pantagruel*, born in Poitou, France (–1553).

February 15 Bābur (original name Zahīr-ud-Dīn Mohammad), Emperor of India 1526–30, founder of the Mogul dynasty, descendant of Genghis Khan and of Timur Leng (Tamerlane), born in the principality of Fergana, Uzbekistan (–1530).

March 6 Francesco Guicciardini, Italian statesman and historian, known for his *Storia d'Italia/History of Italy*, born in Florence, Italy (–1540).

April 6 Raphael Sanzio, Italian artist of the High Renaissance, born in Urbino, duchy of Urbino (–1520).

April 9 Edward IV, King of England 1461–70 and 1471–83, a leading participant in the Wars of the Roses (1455–83), dies in Westminster, London, England (42).

June Edward V, King of England April–June 1483, deposed and possibly murdered by King Richard III (*c.* 14).

August 30 Louis XI, King of France 1461–83, son of Charles VII who unified the French territories after the Hundred Years' War, dies in Plessis-les-Tours, France (60).

November 10 Martin Luther, great German theologian, preacher, and biblical translator, instigator of the Protestant Reformation, born in Eisleben, Saxony (–1546).

December 3 Nikolaus von Amsdorf, Protestant reformer and major supporter of Martin Luther, born in Torgau, Saxony (–1565).

1484

c. 1484 John Stewart Albany, regent of Scotland 1515–24, and heir to the Scottish throne, born (–1536).

January 1 Ulrich Zwingli, leading Swiss Protestant reformer, born in Wildhaus in the Toggenburg, St. Galen, Swiss Confederation (–1531).

January 17 Georg Spalatin, German humanist and writer who helped establish the early stages of the Protestant Reformation, born in Splat, Bavaria (–1545).

April 23 Julius Caesar Scaliger, French physician and classical scholar, born in Riva, republic of Venice (–1558).

August 12 Sixtus IV (Francesco della Rovere), Italian pope 1471–84, who made the papacy a principality, dies in Rome (70).

Courtier by the Italian diplomat, courier, and writer Baldassare Castiglione (1478–1529).

- In the English court, it is the fashion for men to wear fur-lined garments, short doublets and pointed shoes, and their hair long; women wear tight bodices with low-cut necklines and elaborate head-dresses, often in the shape of butterflies or horns.

Religion

1483

August 2   A bull of Pope Sixtus IV appoints Queen Isabella I's confessor, the harsh Dominican Tomás de Torquemada, as the first Grand Inquisitor of Castile. His implacable paranoid hostility toward Jews and Muslims subsequently directs the actions of the Inquisition.

1485–1491

POLITICS, GOVERNMENT, AND ECONOMICS

Business and Economics

1491

- King Henry VII of England raises money for the troops he has sent to Brittany, and for an invasion of France, by collecting "benevolences." This provokes further insurrection in Yorkshire.

Human Rights

1485

- Resistance to the Spanish Inquisition continues in Aragon, and the inquisitor Pedro de Arbués is killed in Saragossa Cathedral, Aragon.

Politics and Government

1485

- Abu-al-Hasan (Muley Hacen) surrenders the citadel of the Alhambra, Granada, and with it the throne of Granada, to his brother Mohammed XII al-Zaghall. Both oppose the exiled son of Muley Hacen, Mohammed XI (Boabdil), who seeks support from King Ferdinand V and Queen Isabella I.
- Ivan III of Moscow, Russia, annexes the principality of Tver. Its last prince, Mikhail Borisovich, had sought the protection of King Casimir (Kazimierz) IV of Poland against Muscovite hegemony.
- King Ladislav (Władysław) II signs the Treaty of Kutná Hora in Bohemia, which confirms the Compacts of Prague from 1433 and other concessions to Hussite opinion.

- Ottoman forces under Karagöz Pasha seize the Mameluke possessions of Adana and Tarsus in Cilicia, southern Asia Minor. When he is replaced as military commander, he stands aside and allows the Mameluke forces to defeat and capture Hersek-oghlu Ahmed Pasha, *beglerbeg* (provincial governor) of Anatolia.
- The sons of Elector Frederick II of Saxony (who died in 1464) agree a lasting division of the Wettin Saxon territories, such that Albert III receives the western lands and the title of duke, and his brother Frederick the eastern portion and the office of elector.

January 14   The Duke of Orléans (the future Louis XII) and Duke Francis II of Brittany lead a coalition of French magnates in defiance of the regent, Anne of Beaujeu, and supporting the rights of the Estates General. Thus begins *la Guerre Folle* (the "Mad War").

March   Catholic and Hussite nobles reaffirm the Compacta of Jihlava, the grant of toleration of 1436 made by the council of Basel toward the moderate Utraquist wing of the Hussite movement.

May 20   The fortified hill town of Ronda, western bulwark of the kingdom of Granada, falls to the forces of King Ferdinand V and Queen Isabella I.

June 1   The burghers of Vienna, Austria, surrender their city to the besieging army of Matthias I Corvinus, King of Hungary. Frederick III the Holy Roman Emperor loses his capital, as he has already lost much of his territory in the duchies of Austria, Styria, and Carinthia.

July 22   Having isolated and subjugated the county of Flanders, Archduke Maximilian of Austria publicly tears up the charter of liberties and abolishes the militia of Ghent, the largest city in Flanders. The republican leader Jan Coppenhole flees to France.

August 7   Henry Tudor, Earl of Richmond, lands in his native Wales at Milford Haven with 1,000 mercenaries supplied by France, to begin his campaign against King Richard III for the English throne.

August 22   The armies of King Richard III of England and Henry Tudor meet at the Battle of Bosworth Field in Leicestershire, England. Richard's onslaught is overwhelmed when the Stanley family deserts his cause and leads a flank attack for Henry, and Richard is killed. Henry takes the crown as King Henry VII of England and founds the Tudor dynasty.

September 15 During a campaign against the Ottoman and Tatar forces advancing along the Black Sea coast, King Casimir (Kazimierz) IV of Poland receives the homage of the voivod of Moldavia, Stephen III the Great.

September 22 Louis, Duke of Orléans and heir to the French throne, submits to the French regent Anne of Beaujeu, ending the noble rebellion known as *la Guerre Folle* (the "Mad War").

September 30 The city of L'Aquila in Abruzzi, Italy, rebels, signaling a widespread baronial insurrection against King Ferrante of Naples, backed by Pope Innocent VIII.

November The Ikki Buddhist league of peasants of Yamashiro province in Japan launches an uprising against the Hatakeyama armies warring across the province following the Onin War, and demands that the troops withdraw and make restitution.

1486

- Ferdinand II of Aragon (also Ferdinand of Castile) abolishes serfdom in Aragon and confirms the actions of John II of Aragon, replacing feudal services with monetary rents and taxes in the *Sentencia de Guadalupe*.
- Sāluva Narasimha, the militarily successful prince of Chandragirirājya in the disintegrating Vijayanagara Empire, usurps the throne after a succession of intrigues and murders and founds the Sāluva dynasty.
- The Aztecs found and fortify the city of Oaxaca in order to consolidate their conquests on the coast of the Gulf of Mexico.

1486–94 Having expelled rampaging feudal armies, leaders of the insurgent Yamashiro Ikki league (in which the gentry have joined with the peasants) meet at Uji, Japan, to formulate a provisional government for the province.

January 18 King Henry VII of England marries Elizabeth of York, the daughter of Edward IV, thus hoping to unite Yorkist and Lancastrian claims to the throne in his Tudor dynasty.

February 16 The diet at Frankfurt, Germany, elects Maximilian I of Habsburg as king of the Romans, a subsidiary title of the Holy Roman Emperor. His father Frederick III the Holy Roman Emperor relinquishes government to Maximilian, who proclaims a general peace in Germany for ten years.

March 9 A plot by Francis, Viscount Lovell, to ambush King Henry VII of England at Clifton Moor, Yorkshire, fails when the king, forewarned, arrives with a strong retinue and scatters the plotters.

May 1486–November 1487 Archduke Maximilian of Austria campaigns unsuccessfully in France, while the tax burden of his wars and failures leads to widespread revolt against his authority at home.

May 7 Alfonso of Calabria, son of King Ferrante of Naples, defeats papal forces at Montório, Italy.

December Louis, Duke of Orléans, René of Lorraine, and other French nobles ally with Duke Francis II of Brittany, who is reinforced by English and imperial troops in a new league against the French regent Anne of Beaujeu.

1487

- King Henry VII of England's Star Chamber Act establishes a judicial subcommittee of his council to act as a court outside the common law for the prosecution of the perpetrators of riot and rebellion.
- Quito, capital of the Shyris rulers of the Cara state in the northern Andes, falls to the Tawantisiyu armies of Topa Inca Yupanqui.
- The exiled aristocratic merchant Pandolfo Petrucci returns to the city of Siena, Italy, and begins a gradual seizure of power.
- Venetian diplomat Ambrogio Contarini publishes his *Viaggio al Ussum-Cassan, re di Persia/Journey to Uzun Hasan, King of Persia*, describing his embassy to the court of Uzun Hasan in Persia, 1473–77.

May King Ferrante of Naples, Italy, brutally dispossesses and decimates the Neapolitan nobles who had rebelled against him, after defeating their backer Pope Innocent VIII.

May 24 The youth Lambert Simnel, pretending to be Edward IV's nephew the Earl of Warwick (who has been kept imprisoned in the Tower of London, England, by King Henry VII), is crowned in Dublin, Ireland, as "King Edward VI." He is backed by the Yorkists John de la Pole (Earl of Lincoln), Margaret of Burgundy (sister of Edward IV), and 2,000 German mercenaries.

June 16 King Henry VII of England defeats the army of the pretender, Lambert Simnel, who has marched from a landing in Lancashire to the battle site at East Stoke, near Newark, Nottinghamshire, England. Simnel's major backer, the Earl of Lincoln, is killed in this last battle of the Wars of the Roses.

July Maximilian, King of the Romans, calls an assembly at Esslingen, Germany, to form the Swabian League of bishops, knights, princes, and towns against the expansion of the Wittelsbach dukes of Bavaria and the Swiss Confederation.

August 11 Pope Innocent VIII is forced by the Roman populace, nobility, and church hierarchy to make peace with King Ferrante of Naples, whose armies are at the gates of the city.

August 18 Ferdinand of Aragon and Castile, having finally led the Christian Spanish forces to break the resistance of the Muslim forces of Mohammed XII Zagal in battle near Vélez Málaga, Granada, takes the Spanish port of Málaga.

1488

- Trailok, King of the Thai kingdom of Ayutthaya, dies, having consolidated central administration, codified laws, promulgated a new land settlement, and expanded the state into the Malay Peninsula.
- Waldensians (Vaudois) are massacred in the Dauphiné in southeast France, following Pope Innocent VIII's bull decreeing their extermination as heretics. A group of religious reformers dating back to the 12th century, the Waldensians were often persecuted and survived best in the mountainous regions of southwest France and northern Italy, and also in Bohemia, where they formed links with the Hussites.

1488–91 Johann Cicero, Elector of Brandenburg, defeats a rebellion of the cities of the Altmark in the "Beer War" over rights to tolls and excises; he is able to curb their constitutional autonomies.

February 5–May 16 Maximilian, King of the Romans, and his court are taken prisoner while trying to garrison the rebellious city of Bruges in Flanders. They are sent to Ghent, Flanders, as hostages, and Maximilian is forced to proclaim his acquiescence to a peace that guarantees the autonomy of the Netherlands "Union."

June 11 An unknown cleric murders King James III of Scotland, in flight from his defeat by rebellious nobles at Sauchieburn near Stirling, Scotland. He is succeeded by his son James IV, who has sided with the rebels.

July 9 The Safavid Shiite leader Shayk Haydar is killed in battle by the Ak Koyunlu (White Sheep) Uzbekh forces of Ya'qub while leading an expedition against Circassian Christians near Darband.

July 27 The forces of Anne Beaujeu, the French regent and sister of Charles VIII, defeat the rebel league of Duke Francis II of Brittany at St.-Aubin du Cormier and capture Louis, Duke of Orléans (the future Louis XII).

August 17 Ali Pasha leads a strong Ottoman force of janissaries (royal guards) and sipahis (cavalry) to a defeat by a coalition led by the Mameluke leadership near Adana in Turkey.

August 20 Duke Francis II of Brittany is subjugated by the Treaty of Sablé, agreed with the French regent Anne of Beaujeu, and must expel foreign troops and promise that his heir Anne will not marry without royal consent.

September 9 Duke Francis II of Brittany dies and is succeeded by his daughter Anne. The French regent, Anne of Beaujeu, determines to secure the duchy for the crown, but is opposed by the Bretons.

1489

- A statute of King Henry VII of England attempts to halt enclosures, the depopulation of the countryside, and the conversion of arable land into more profitable sheepwalks by its landlords.
- Frederick III the Holy Roman Emperor appoints Franz von Taxis as imperial postmaster. He develops a courier service for official mail through his firm "Thurn und Taxis."

February–August Albert of Saxony, Archduke Maximilian's *Statthalter* in the Netherlands, cajoles and beats the estates of Brabant into submission.

February 14 King Henry VII of England and Maximilian, King of the Romans, form an alliance to assist the Bretons in their efforts to prevent the duchy of Brittany being taken by Anne of Beaujeu, the French regent. They outline their opposition to France in the Treaty of Dordrecht.

March 14 Venice, Italy, buys Cyprus from Catherine Cornaro, Queen of King James II of Cyprus. James II had died in 1473 as the last of the Lusignan dynasty of kings of Cyprus.

April 28 A rioting mob kills Henry Percy, Earl of Northumberland and chief supporter of the Tudor regime, while he is collecting taxes in Yorkshire, England. King Henry VII of England goes north to suppress and punish the insurgents.

June 13 An Anglo-Habsburg force under Henry Lovell, Lord Morley, defeats and massacres Flemish rebels, relieving the rebel siege of Dixmunde.

October 30 Archduke Maximilian of Austria revokes the Peace of Ghent in the Treaty of Montils-lez-Tours, requiring the cities of Flanders to pay an indemnity and

allowing them to reestablish their freedom only through negotiation. Ghent and Bruges remain defiant.

November 25 Mohammed XII Zagal of Granada surrenders to King Ferdinand V and Queen Isabella I of Aragon and Castile when they capture the city of Baza in Granada. Mohammed XI Boabdil resumes the rule of the kingdom of Granada, which has been reduced by the surrender of the cities of Almería and Guadix with Mohammed XII Zagal.

December 14 Archduke Maximilian of Austria attempts a currency revaluation in the counties of Flanders and Holland, further antagonizing the populace and spurring insurrection.

1490

- An Egyptian Mameluke invasion fails to take the Ottoman city of Kayseri in Asia Minor but devastates the province.
- Malik Ahmad Nizam-ul-Malk founds the dynasty of Nizam Shahi and the kingdom of Ahmadnagar, having twice secured his independence from the Bāhmanī sultanate in battle.

March 16 Frederick III the Holy Roman Emperor obtains Tyrol for his son Maximilian through the abdication of its debt-ridden Count Sigismund, thus consolidating the Habsburg lands against the Wittelsbachs of Bavaria.

April 6 Matthias I Corvinus, King of Hungary, dies without an heir. His empire dissolves and the Habsburgs, under Maximilian, King of the Romans, recover his conquests in Austria.

July 11 The Hungarian diet elects the vacillating Władysław II, King of Bohemia, as king of Hungary under the name Ulászló II.

November 29 Bruges capitulates to Archduke Maximilian of Austria's blockade of its port Sluys, the Netherlands.

December 19 Anne of Brittany marries Maximilian by proxy, contravening the Treaty of Sablé of 1488, which dictated that she should acquire French royal consent before marrying.

1491

- Saluva Narasimha, ruler of Vijayanagara, India, dies while besieged by the forces of Orissa in his city of Udayagiri, and is succeeded by Narasa Nayaka acting as regent.
- The popular Yorkist faction in the city of Cork, Ireland, persuades the flamboyant young Fleming Perkin Warbeck to impersonate one of the sons of Edward IV, one of "the princes in the Tower."

January 25 Polish–Lithuanian forces under Jan Olbracht, son of King Casimir (Kazimierz) IV of Poland, decisively defeat the Kazan Tartars at Zasław, Poland, gaining respite from their raids.

November 7 Maximilian, King of the Romans, is unable to pay his mercenaries and abandons his attempt to conquer Hungary. He recognizes Władysław (Ulászló) II as king of Hungary in the Treaty of Bratislava, which also states that the throne is to revert to the Habsburgs if Władysław dies without an heir.

November 25 Mohammed XI Boabdil concludes a treaty that guarantees tolerance of Islam and grants him the Alpujarras, in return for the surrender of Granada to King Ferdinand V and Queen Isabella I of Aragon and Castile, who have besieged the city since March.

December 6 Anne of Brittany, coerced by the victory of the invasion forces of Anne of Beaujeu, regent of France, forsakes Maximilian, King of the Romans, and marries Charles VIII of France, thus incorporating the duchy of Brittany into France. Its autonomy is guaranteed through the Treaty of Laval.

SCIENCE, TECHNOLOGY, AND MEDICINE

Exploration

1488

January   The Portuguese expedition led by Bartolomeu Dias rounds the Cape of Good Hope and enters the Indian Ocean.

1489

- *Pictures and Descriptions of Strange Nations*, a geography based on the travels of Admiral Cheng Ho during his exploration of China 1392–1430, is printed in China.

Health and Medicine

1486

- *Liber Continens/The Comprehensive Work*, a respected manual of medicine by the 10th-century Muslim physician al-Razi, is first printed at Brescia, Lombardy.

1488

- The first *Apotheke* (public dispensing chemist) is opened, in Berlin, Germany.

1489

- The first major typhus epidemic in Europe occurs when Spanish soldiers returning from Cyprus introduce the disease.

Science

1490

- While visiting Milan, Italy, the Italian scholar Leonardo da Vinci begins to keep notebooks detailing his ideas and inventions. He discovers and describes capillarity, the way in which liquids rise up through small-bore tubes.

Technology

1487

- The Genoese army use explosive land mines for the first time, against their Florentine enemies at the siege of Serezanella, Italy.

1489

- The first printing presses in Portugal are set up by Jewish merchants in Faro and Lisbon.

ARTS AND IDEAS

Architecture

1485

c. 1485   The Villa Medici, at Poggio a Caiano (just outside the city), designed by the Italian architect Giuliano da Sangallo, is completed in Florence, Italy.

- The rebuilding of the Church of Santa Maria presso San Satiro, designed by Bramante (Donato di Pascuccio d'Antonio), is completed in Milan, Italy.

1486

c. 1486   *De architectura/On Architecture*, a treatise on architecture written by 1st-century BC Roman architect Marcus Vitruvius Pollio, is printed in Rome, Italy. Versions of the text were known throughout the Middle Ages, but the discovery of a superior manuscript in 1414 renewed interest in classical architecture. This book had a profound effect on the development of Renaissance architecture.

- The Cathedral of Faenza, designed by the Italian architect Giuliano da Maiano, is completed in Italy.

1488

- The Frauenkirche church in Munich, Germany, designed by the German architect Jörg von Ganghofer, is completed.

1489

- The court church of Ivan III, the Annunciation Cathedral (Blagoveshchenski Sobor) in the Moscow Kremlin, is completed in Moscow, Russia.

1490

- The spire of Milan Cathedral, built in the Gothic style, is completed in Italy.

Arts

1485

c. 1485   Italian artist Filippino Lippi paints *The Vision of St. Bernard* and *Virgin and Child with Angels*.

c. 1485   Italian artist Sandro Botticelli (Alessandro di Mariano dei Filipepi) paints *The Birth of Venus*.

c. 1485   Spanish artist Pedro Berruguete paints *St. Eulalia Altarpiece*.

- Italian artist Ghirlandaio (Domenico Bigordi) paints *Adoration of the Shepherds*.

1485–1490   Italian artist Ghirlandaio (Domenico Bigordi) paints frescoes in the Church of Santa Maria Novella in Florence. They include one of his best-known works, *The Birth of the Virgin*.

c. 1486

- Italian artist Andrea Mantegna paints *The Triumph of Caesar*, a series of nine paintings.

1487

- Flemish artist Hans Memling paints the *Diptych of Martin van Nieuwenhove*.
- Italian artist Antonello da Messina paints *St. Sebastian*.

- Italian artist Ghirlandaio (Domenico Bigordi) paints *Old Man with Child*.

1487–1502 Italian artist Filippino Lippi paints a series of frescoes in the Strozzi Chapel in Florence, Italy. One of the best-known is *The Exorcism of the Demon from the Temple of Mars*.

1488

c. 1488 Italian artist Giovanni Bellini paints *The Transfiguration of Christ* and *Enthroned Madonna and Child* (*The Job Altarpiece*).

- Persian miniaturist Kamal al-Din Bihzad illustrates scenes in an edition of the poem *Būstān/The Tree–Garden* by the 13th-century poet Sa'di.

1489

- Flemish artist Hans Memling completes *The Shrine of St. Ursula*, an ornate reliquary box painted with scenes from the life of St. Ursula.

1490

c. 1490 Flemish artist Geertgen Tot Sint Jans paints *St. John in the Wilderness*.

c. 1490 Italian artist Sandro Botticelli (Alessandro di Mariano dei Filipepi) paints *The Annunciation*.

c. 1490 The painting *The Virgin Among Virgins with Saints Barbara, Catherine, Cecilia, and Ursula* is composed by an anonymous Netherlands artist known only by the title of his work.

- Italian artist Luca Signorelli paints *The School of Pan*. A complex allegory based on Greek mythology, it illustrates the growing interest in classical subjects in Renaissance Italy. It is destroyed during World War II.
- Spanish artist Bartolomé Bermejo paints *Pietà of Canon Luis Despla*.

Literature and Language

1485

- English printer William Caxton prints his first edition of *Le Morte d'Arthur/The Death of Arthur*, written by Sir Thomas Malory in 1470.

1486

- French poet Guillaume Alexis (Alecis) publishes "Les Faintises du monde" (a philosophical poem) and "Le Blason de faulses amours"/"The Blazon of False Loves" (a didactic poem).
- French poet Henri Baude publishes *Les Lamentations Bourrien*, a verse satire in the style of Villon, directed against priests.
- Italian poet Jacopo Sannazaro completes *Arcadia*, a pastoral romance in Italian first published in 1504.

1487

- German humanist Konrad Celtis is crowned the first German poet laureate by Emperor Maximilian.

1490

- Catalan writer Joanot Martorell publishes his novel *Tirant lo blanc*. A classic of Catalan literature, it is a tale of knight-errantry based on several European models.
- Scottish poet Robert Henryson publishes his long poem *The Testament of Cresseid*, a sequel to Chaucer's *Troylus and Cryseyde*.

Music

1490–1504

- *The Eton Choirbook (Eton College Manuscript)*, a book of choral music, is completed in England.

Theater and Dance

1488

- Italian poet Bernardo Pulci writes his sacred play *Barlaam e Josafat/Barlaam and Josephat*.

1489

- The religious play *San Giovanni e San Paolo/St. John and St. Paul* by the Italian scholar-prince Lorenzo de' Medici is first performed in his own home in Florence, Italy, with Lorenzo playing one of the parts.

Thought and Scholarship

1486

- Italian philosopher and humanist Giovanni Pico della Mirandola publishes his *Conclusiones*, inviting scholars and philosophers to come to Rome, Italy, to debate the 900 propositions he has drawn up concerning *de omni re scribili* (all things knowable). He also writes *Oratio de hominis dignitate/Oration on the Dignity of Man*. An eloquent expression of humanity's unlimited power of self-development, it becomes a key work in Renaissance thought.
- Swedish historian Erik Olai completes his *Chronica regni Gothorum/Chronicle of the Kingdom of the Goths*, a chronicle of Scandinavian history.
- The *Historiae Croylandensis Continuatio/Continuation of the History of Crowland*, the last English monastic chronicle, is completed in England.

1489

- Italian humanist scholar and poet Politian (Angelo Ambrogini Poliziano) publishes *Miscellanea*, in which he provides commentaries on a selection of Latin and Greek texts.
- Italian philosopher and humanist Giovanni Pico della Mirandola publishes his *Apology* to defend himself against the charge of heresy brought by Pope Innocent VIII in 1487.
- Italian scholar and statesman Bernardo Giustiniani publishes *De origine urbis Venetiarum/The Origins of the City of Venice* in Venice, Italy. It presents Venice as the heir to the social virtues of ancient Romans.

1490

- Greek historian Laonicus Chalcocondylas publishes *Historiarum demonstrationes*, a history of the Byzantine Empire 1298–1463, best known for its account of the struggles between a declining Byzantium and the ever more powerful Ottoman Turks.

1491

c. 1491 English antiquarian John Rous completes his two *Warwick Rolls*, a history of the Earls of Warwick that provides an illustrated history of armor. Rous also wrote *Historia regum Angliae/History of the Kings of England*, a history of England notable for its account of legends and topography.

- German humanist Johannes Trithemius (Tritheim) publishes *Catalogus illustrium virorum Germaniae/The Lives of Illustrious Germans*, containing almost a thousand biographies.

SOCIETY

Religion

1486

- *Malleus maleficarum/The Hammer of Witches*, a book accepting the existence and powers of witches, is published. It is written by two Dominican monks,

BIRTHS & DEATHS

1485

c. 1485   Joachim Patinir, Dutch painter and the first European artist to specialize in landscapes, born in Bouvines, near Dinan, Namur (–1524).

c. 1485   Sebastiano del Piombo, Italian painter, born in Venice (–1547).

- Giovanni da Verrazzano, Italian navigator who was the first European to sight modern-day New York, born in Tuscany, Italy (–1528).

- Hernán Cortés, Spanish conquistador who led the conquest of Mexico, defeating the Aztec Empire (1519–21), born in Medellín, Extremadura, Spain (–1547).

- Hugh Latimer, English Protestant preacher, bishop of Worcester, born in Thurcaston, Leicestershire, England (–1555).

- Thomas Cromwell, Earl of Essex, who, as chief adviser of King Henry VIII of England, was largely responsible for establishing the English Reformation, born in modern-day Putney, London, England (*c.* 55).

August 22   Richard III (Richard Plantagenet), King of England 1483–85, is killed in battle at Bosworth, Leicestershire (32).

October 28   Rodolphus Agricola (original name Roelof Huysman), Dutch humanist, dies in Heidelberg, palatinate, Germany (*c.* 42).

December 16   Catherine of Aragon, first wife of King Henry VIII of England, who ruled as regent 1512–14, mother of Mary I of England, born in Alcala de Henares, Spain (–1536).

1486

c. 1486   Francisco de Vitoria, Spanish theologian who defended the rights of Native Americans against Spanish colonialists, born in Vitoria, Alava, Castile (–1546).

July 16   Andrea del Sarto, Italian painter and draftsman, born in Florence (–1530).

November 13   Johann Eck (original surname: Maier), German Roman Catholic theologian, main opponent of Martin Luther, born in Egg, Swabia, Germany (–1543).

1488

c. 1488   Miles Coverdale, bishop of Exeter, whose English translation of the Bible was the first to be printed, born in York, England (–1569).

- Andrea del Verrocchio, Florentine painter and sculptor who taught Leonardo da Vinci, dies in Venice (*c.* 53).

- Audley of Walden, Lord Chancellor of England 1533–44, who was instrumental in helping King Henry VIII break with the papacy, born in Earls Colne, Essex (–1544).

April 21   Ulrich von Hutten, German knight, humanist, satirist, and supporter of Martin Luther, born near Fulda, Germany (–1523).

June 11   James III, King of Scotland 1460–88, son of James II, killed after Battle of Sauchieburn, near Stirling, Scotland (36).

1489

c. 1489   Titian (Tiziano Vecellio), major Italian Venetian painter, born in Pieve di Cadore, republic of Venice (–1576).

- Kaspar Schwenckfeld, German theologian and preacher, leader of the "Reformation by the Middle Way" movement, and founder of the Schwenckfelder Church that still exists in the United States, born in Ossig, Lower Silesia (–1561).

March 10   Bernardo Giustiniani, Italian humanist historian, dies (81).

July 2   Thomas Cranmer, first Protestant archbishop of Canterbury 1533–56, adviser to Henry VIII and Edward VI of England, who drew up the *Book of Common Prayer*, born in Alsacton, Nottinghamshire, England (–1556).

1490

c. 1490   Ávar Núñez Cabeza de Vaca, Spanish explorer who discovered present-day Texas, explored much of South America, and whose stories of the seven Golden Cities of Cibola led to extensive exploration of southern and southwestern North America, born in Extremadura, Castile (–*c.* 1560).

c. 1490   Adrian Willaert, Flemish composer, who helped establish Venice as a center of music, born in Flanders (–1562).

c. 1490   Ludwig Senfl, German composer, born in the Swiss Confederation (–*c.* 1556).

c. 1490   Sir Thomas Elyot, English administrator and author, whose best-known work is *The Governour* (1531), born (–1546).

April 6   Matthias I Corvinus, King of Hungary 1458–90, dies in Vienna, Austria (47).

1491

- Jacques Cartier, French explorer of the North American Atlantic coast and the St. Lawrence River, born in St.-Malo, Brittany, France (–1557).

- St. Ignatius de Loyola, highly influential Spanish theologian, founder of the Jesuits (1534), born in Loyola, Castile, Spain (–1556).

- William Caxton, the first English printer and influential translator and publisher, dies in London (*c.* 69).

June 28   Henry VIII, King of England 1509–47, who broke with the Roman Catholic Church and had six wives, two of whom he executed and two of whom he divorced, born in Greenwich, near London, England (–1547).

November   Martin Bucer (or Butzer), Protestant reformer and scholar, born in Schlettstadt, Alsace (–1551).

November 8   Teofilo Folengo (original name Girolamo Folengo), Benedictine monk and poet, born in Mantua, Italy (–1544).

Heinrich Krämer and Jakob Spränger, and authorized by Pope Innocent VIII. It becomes infamous for encouraging witch-hunts throughout Europe over the next few centuries.

1487

- During the inauguration of the Aztecs' Great Temple at Tenochtitlán, Mexico, 20,000 people are sacrificed. The temple is aligned so that the equinox sun rises framed in its twin peaks.
- Pope Innocent VIII condemns Giovanni Pico della Mirandola's *Conclusiones* published in 1486, asserting that 13 of the 900 propositions in the work are heretical, and issues an instruction for the reform of monastic orders.

Sports

1486

- The first edition of the *Boke of St Albans*, containing a *Treatyse perteynynge to Hawkynge, Huntynge, Fysshynge, and Coot Armiris*, traditionally believed to have been written about 1400 by Dame Juliana Berners, is published in England. The treatise is essentially a courtesy book on hunting manners and conventions useful to those seeking social advancement.

INDEX

TITLES INDEX